The picture you saw here in Vol. 3 was of my editor, which I used a computer to alter and make him look like Komui. It is not a picture of myself. My editor was at a loss for words. And what you see above is a portrait of Katsura Hoshino drawn by my older sister.

—Katsura Hoshino

Shiga Prefecture native Katsura Hoshino's hit manga series *D.Gray-man* has been serialized in *Weekly Shonen Jump* since 2004. Katsura's first series "Continue" first appeared in *Weekly Shonen Jump* in 2003.

Katsura adores cats.

D.GRAY-MAN
3-in-1 Edition
Volume 2

SHONEN JUMP Manga Omnibus Edition
A compilation of the graphic novel volumes 4–6

STORY AND ART BY
KATSURA HOSHINO

English Adaptation/Lance Caselman
Translation/Toshifumi Yoshida
Touch-up Art & Lettering/Elizabeth Watasin, Kelle Han
Design/Yukiko Whitley (Graphic Novel and 3-in-1 Editions)
Editors/Urian Brown, Gary Leach (Graphic Novel Edition)
Editor/Nancy Thistlethwaite (3-in-1 Edition)

D.GRAY-MAN © 2004 by Katsura Hoshino. All rights reserved.
First published in Japan in 2004 by SHUEISHA Inc., Tokyo. English translation rights arranged by
SHUEISHA Inc.

The stories, characters and incidents mentioned in this publication are entirely fictional.

Printed in the U.S.A.

Published by VIZ Media, LLC
P.O. Box 77010
San Francisco, CA 94107

10 9 8 7 6 5 4 3 2
3-in-1 edition first printing, November 2013
Second printing, December 2015

VIZ
media
www.viz.com

SHONEN
JUMP
ADVANCED
www.shonenjump.com

CHARA

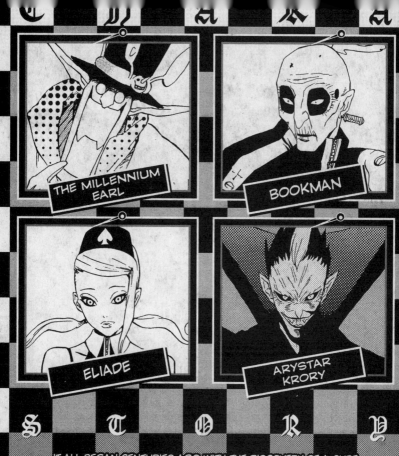

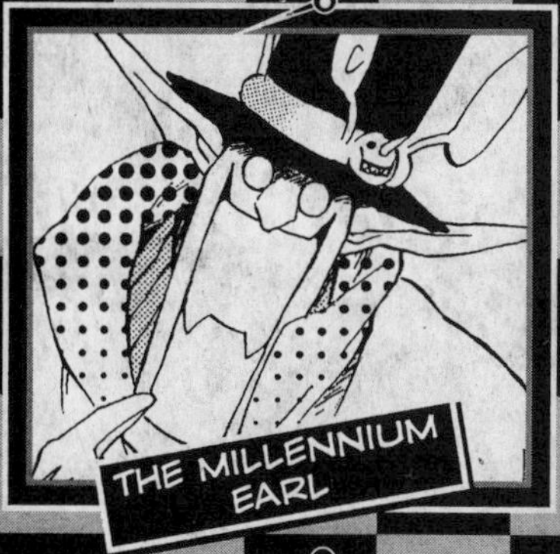
THE MILLENNIUM EARL

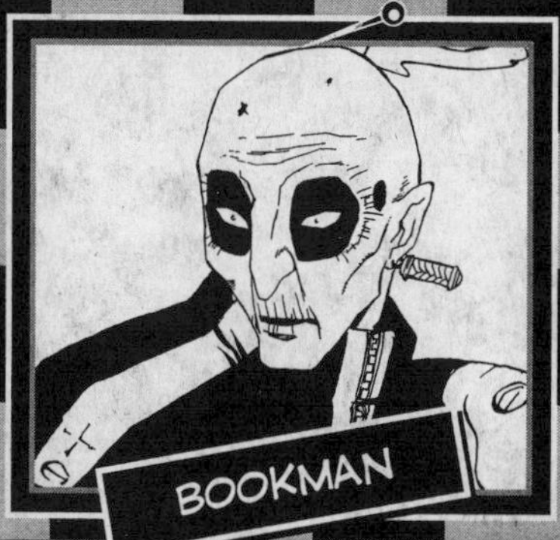
BOOKMAN

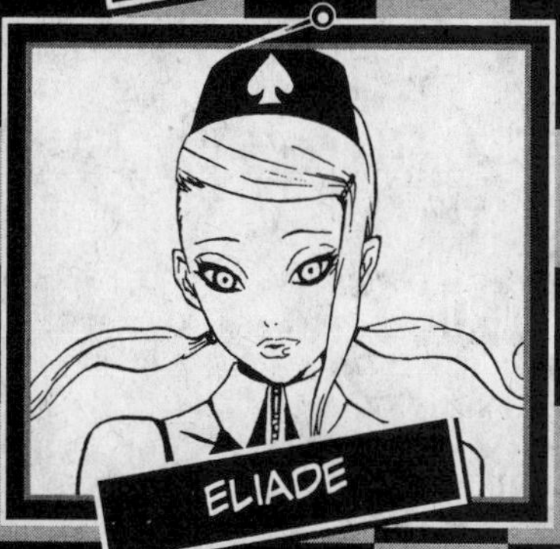
ELIADE

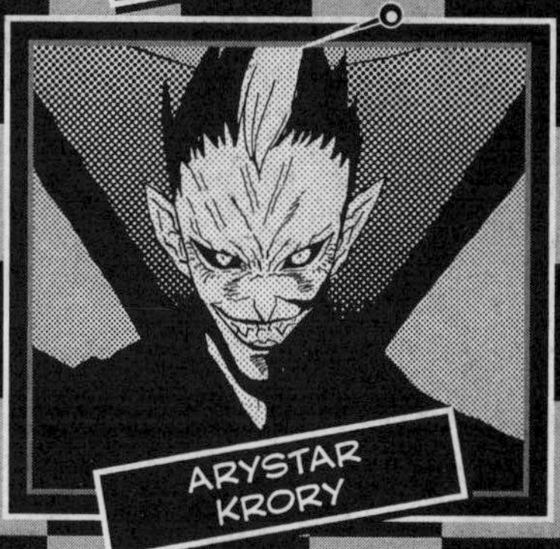
ARYSTAR KRORY

STORY

IT ALL BEGAN CENTURIES AGO WITH THE DISCOVERY OF A CUBE CONTAINING AN APOCALYPTIC PROPHECY FROM AN ANCIENT CIVILIZATION, AND INSTRUCTIONS IN THE USE OF INNOCENCE, A CRYSTALLINE SUBSTANCE OF WONDROUS SUPERNATURAL POWER. THE CREATORS OF THE CUBE CLAIMED TO HAVE DEFEATED AN EVIL KNOWN AS THE MILLENNIUM EARL USING THE INNOCENCE. NEVERTHELESS, THE WORLD WAS DESTROYED BY THE GREAT FLOOD OF THE OLD TESTAMENT. NOW TO AVERT A SECOND END OF THE WORLD, A GROUP OF EXORCISTS WIELDING WEAPONS MADE OF INNOCENCE MUST BATTLE THE MILLENNIUM EARL AND HIS TERRIBLE MINIONS, THE AKUMA.

IN THE MYSTERIOUS REWINDING CITY, WHERE EVERY DAY IS OCTOBER 9, ALLEN MEETS ROAD KAMELOT, A GIRL FROM THE CLAN OF NOAH, HUMAN DISCIPLES OF THE MILLENNIUM EARL. THE BATTLE THAT FOLLOWS LEAVES LENALEE IN A COMA, AND ALLEN'S SPECIAL AKUMA-SEEING EYE BADLY DAMAGED. BUT THERE IS LITTLE TIME TO RECOVER. THE AGENTS OF THE EARL ARE ON THE MOVE, AND ALLEN IS SOON THRUST INTO A STILL DARKER MYSTERY.

D.GRAY-MAN
Vol. 4

CONTENTS

The 27th Night: Slump   7

The 28th Night: Uniform   25

The 29th Night: Crisis of the Generals   43

The 30th Night: Missing in Action   61

The 31st Night: Vampire of the Castle (1)

    - The Mysterious Emissary -   79

The 32nd Night: Vampire of the Castle (2)

    - Exorcist vs. Vampire -   97

The 33rd Night: Vampire of the Castle (3)

    - Krory Castle -   116

The 34th Night: Vampire of the Castle (4)

    - The Hated One -   137

The 35th Night: Vampire of the Castle (5) - Eliade -   157

The 36th Night: Vampire of the Castle (6) - Return -   175

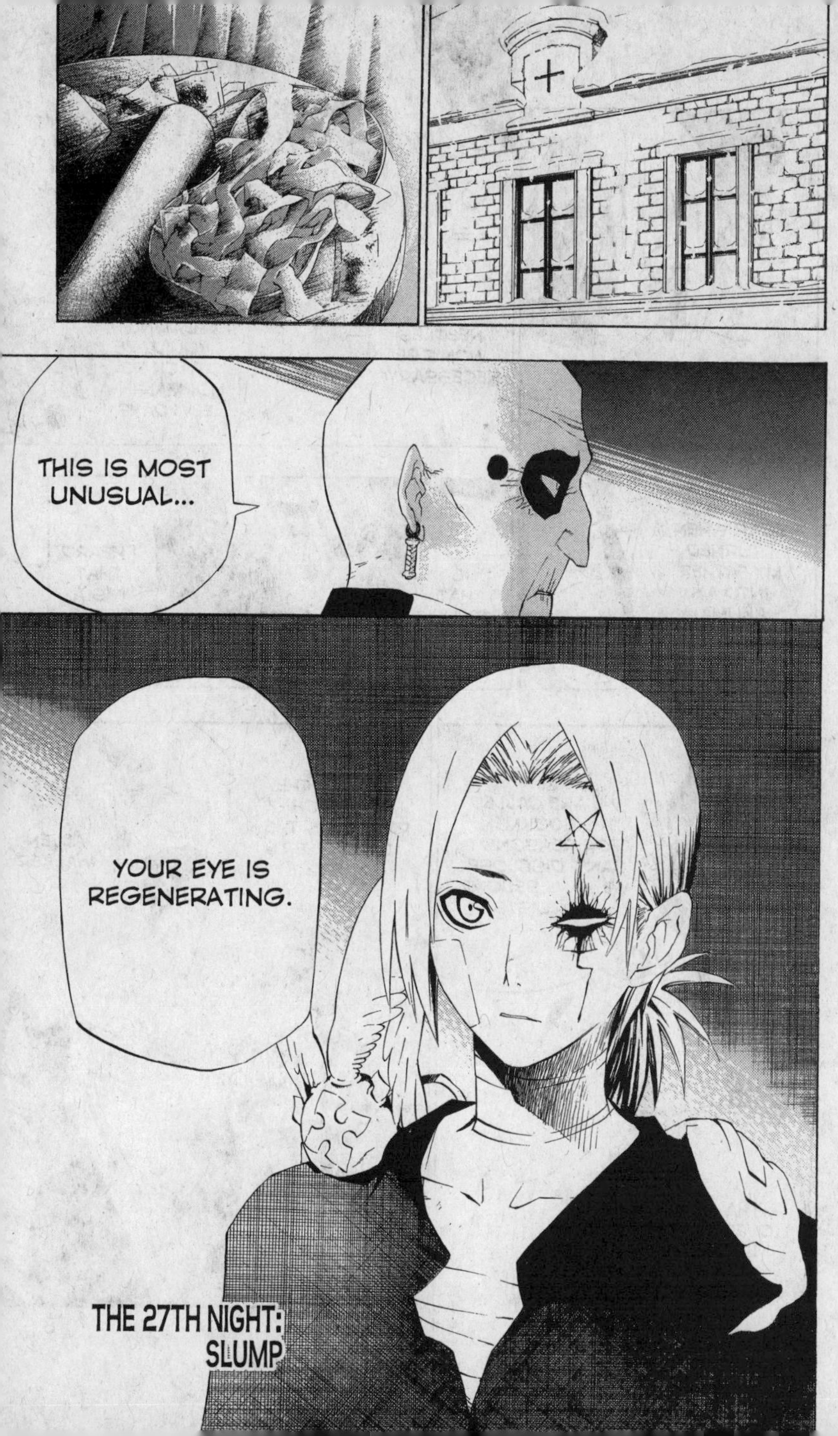
THIS IS MOST UNUSUAL...
YOUR EYE IS REGENERATING.
THE 27TH NIGHT: SLUMP

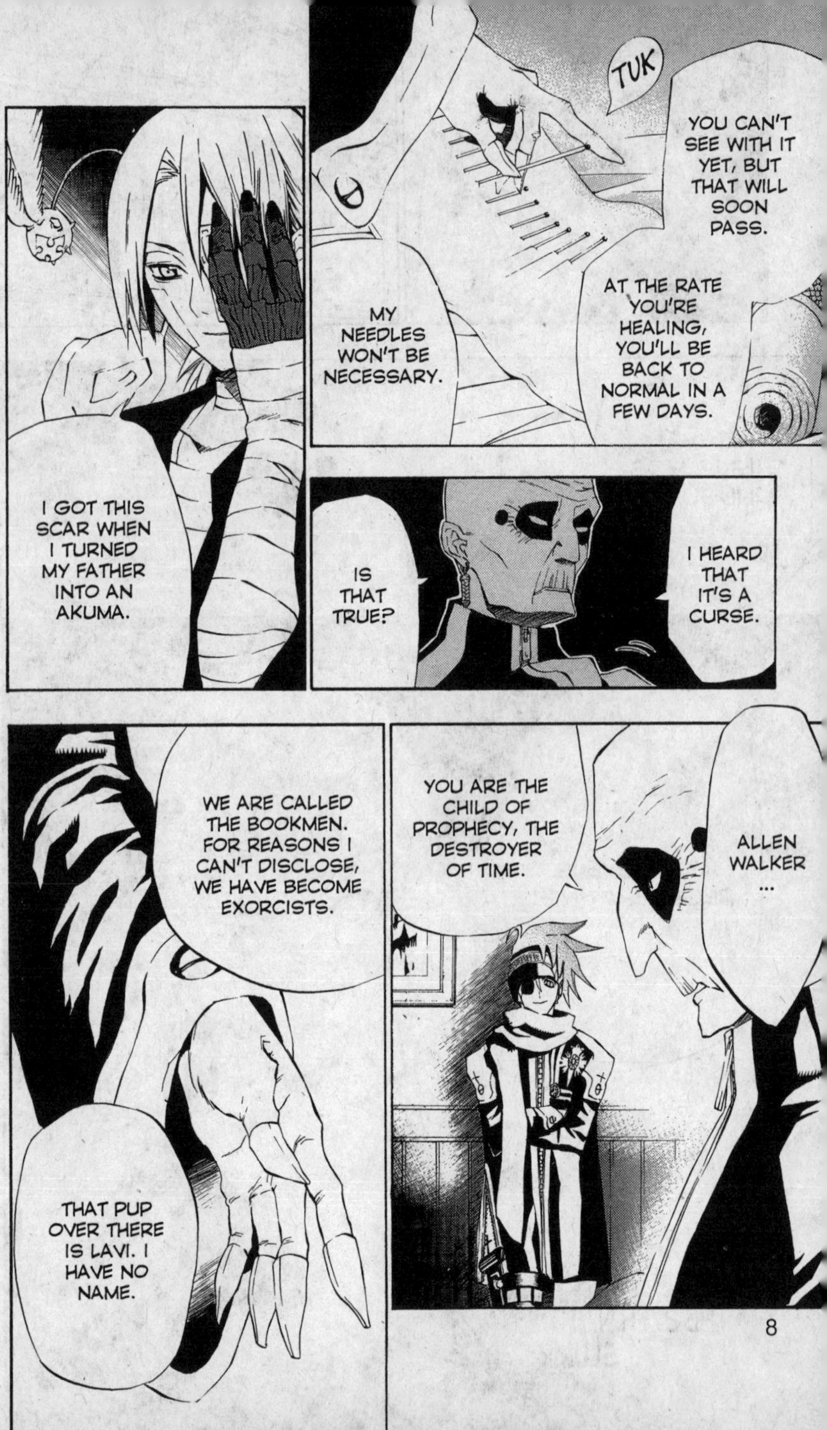
TUK
YOU CAN'T SEE WITH IT YET, BUT THAT WILL SOON PASS.
AT THE RATE YOU'RE HEALING, YOU'LL BE BACK TO NORMAL IN A FEW DAYS.
MY NEEDLES WON'T BE NECESSARY.
I HEARD THAT IT'S A CURSE.
IS THAT TRUE?
I GOT THIS SCAR WHEN I TURNED MY FATHER INTO AN AKUMA.
ALLEN WALKER ...
YOU ARE THE CHILD OF PROPHECY, THE DESTROYER OF TIME.
WE ARE CALLED THE BOOKMEN. FOR REASONS I CAN'T DISCLOSE, WE HAVE BECOME EXORCISTS.
THAT PUP OVER THERE IS LAVI. I HAVE NO NAME.

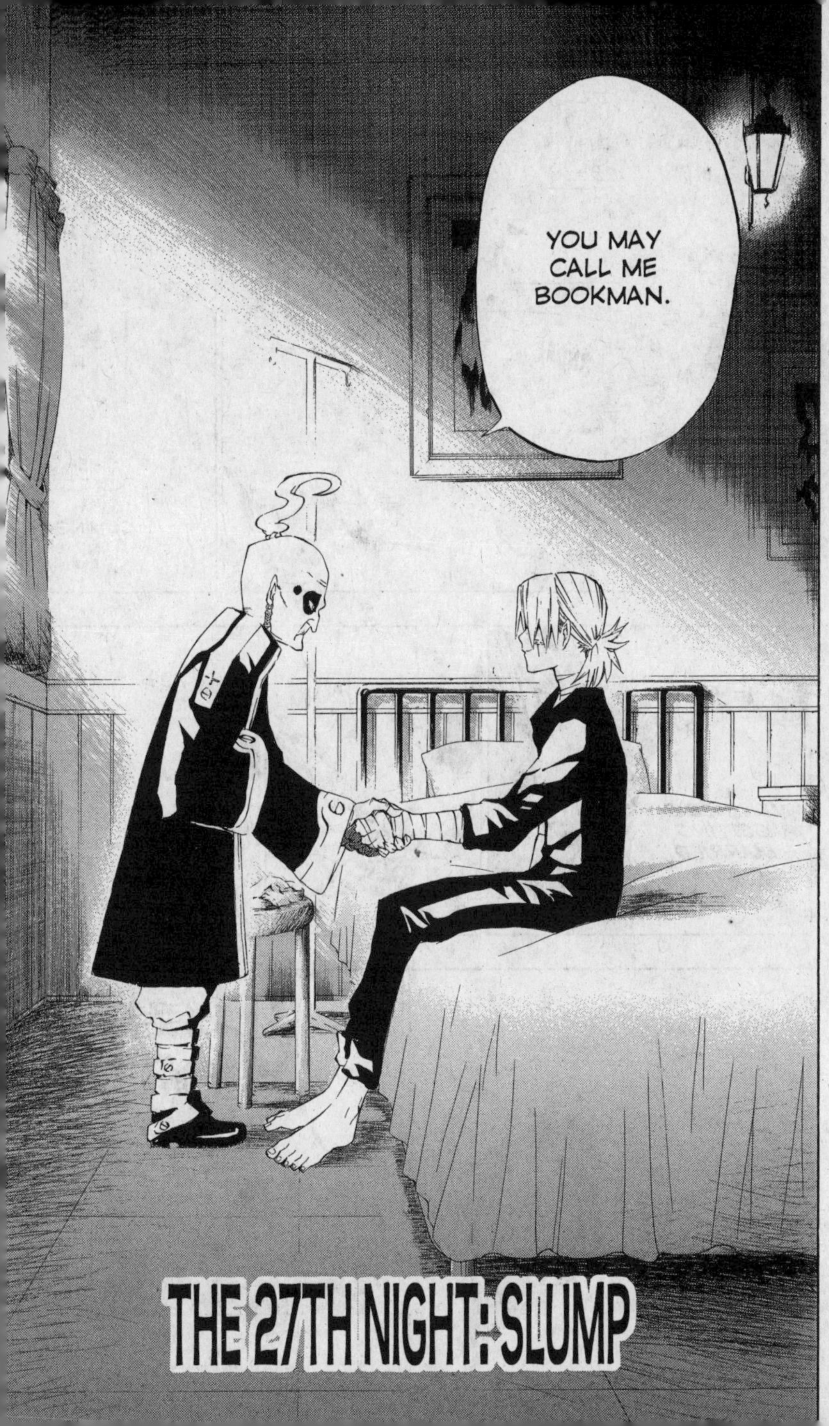
YOU MAY CALL ME BOOKMAN.

THE 27TH NIGHT: SLUMP

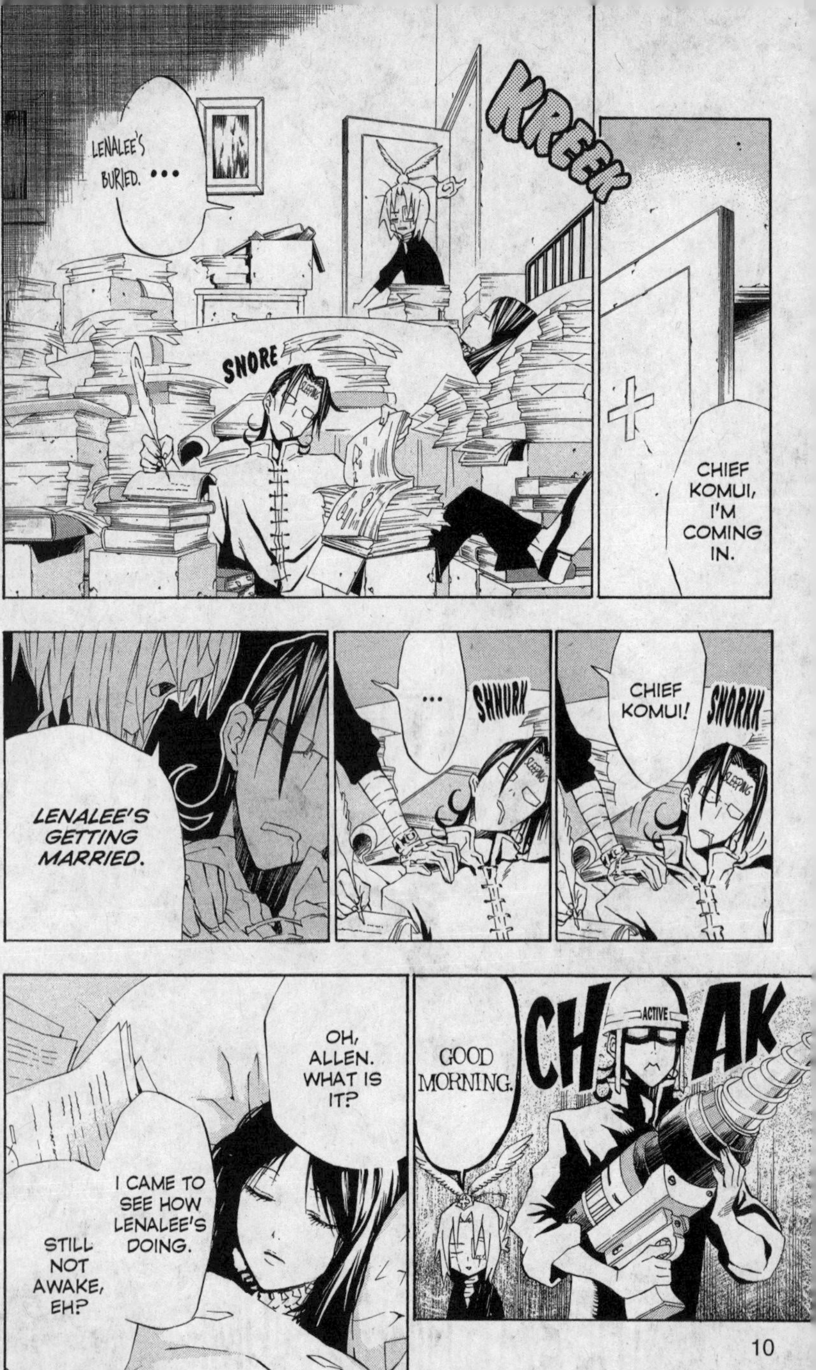
KREEK
CHIEF KOMUI, I'M COMING IN.
LENALEE'S BURIED. ...
SNORE
CHIEF KOMUI!
SNORKK
SLEEPING
...
SHNURK
SLEEPING
LENALEE'S GETTING MARRIED.
CH AK
ACTIVE
GOOD MORNING.
OH, ALLEN. WHAT IS IT?
I CAME TO SEE HOW LENALEE'S DOING.
STILL NOT AWAKE, EH?

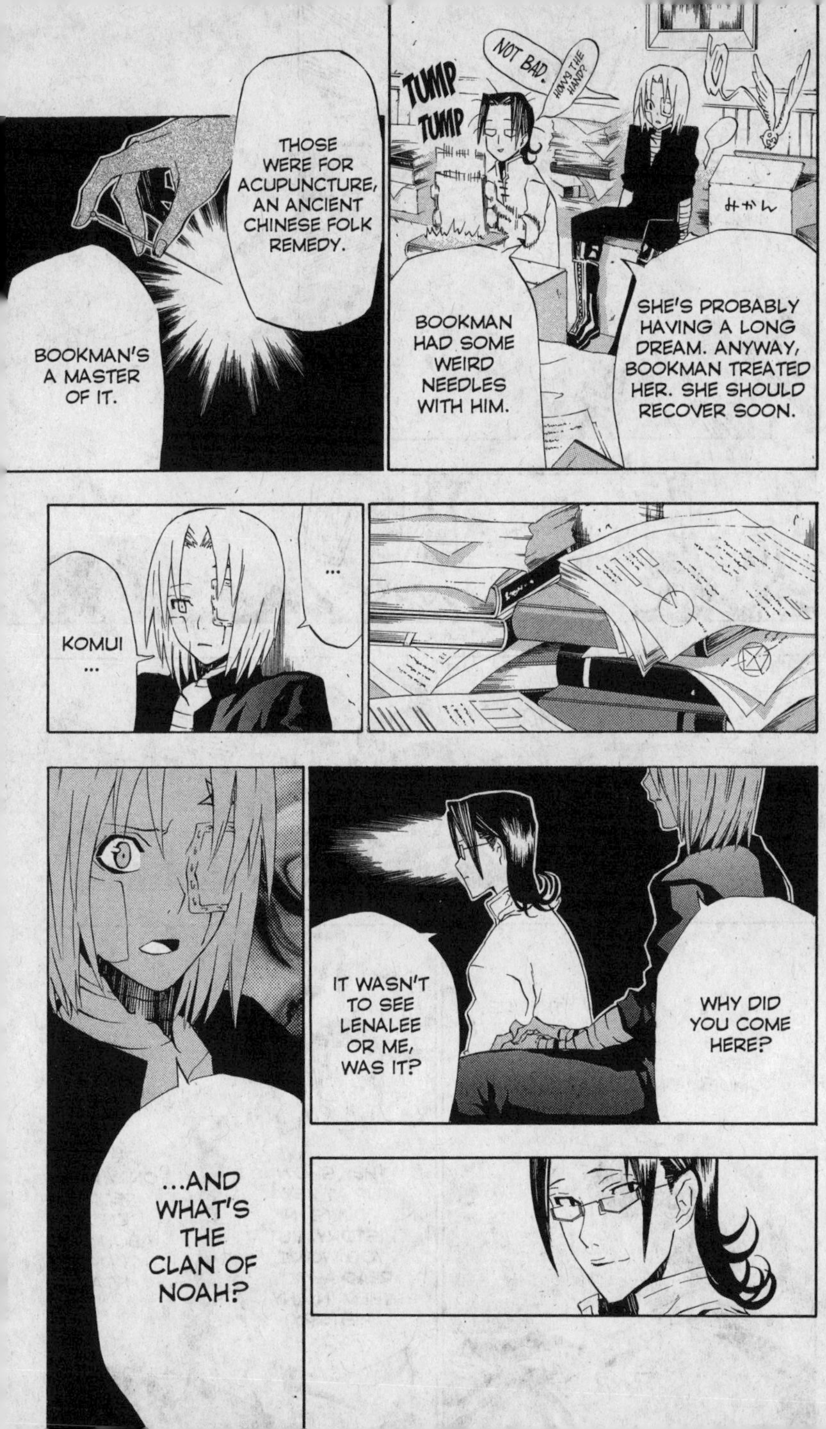
HOW'S THE HAND?
NOT BAD.
TUMP
TUMP
みかん
SHE'S PROBABLY HAVING A LONG DREAM. ANYWAY, BOOKMAN TREATED HER. SHE SHOULD RECOVER SOON.
BOOKMAN HAD SOME WEIRD NEEDLES WITH HIM.
THOSE WERE FOR ACUPUNCTURE, AN ANCIENT CHINESE FOLK REMEDY.
BOOKMAN'S A MASTER OF IT.
...
KOMUI ...
WHY DID YOU COME HERE?
IT WASN'T TO SEE LENALEE OR ME, WAS IT?
...AND WHAT'S THE CLAN OF NOAH?

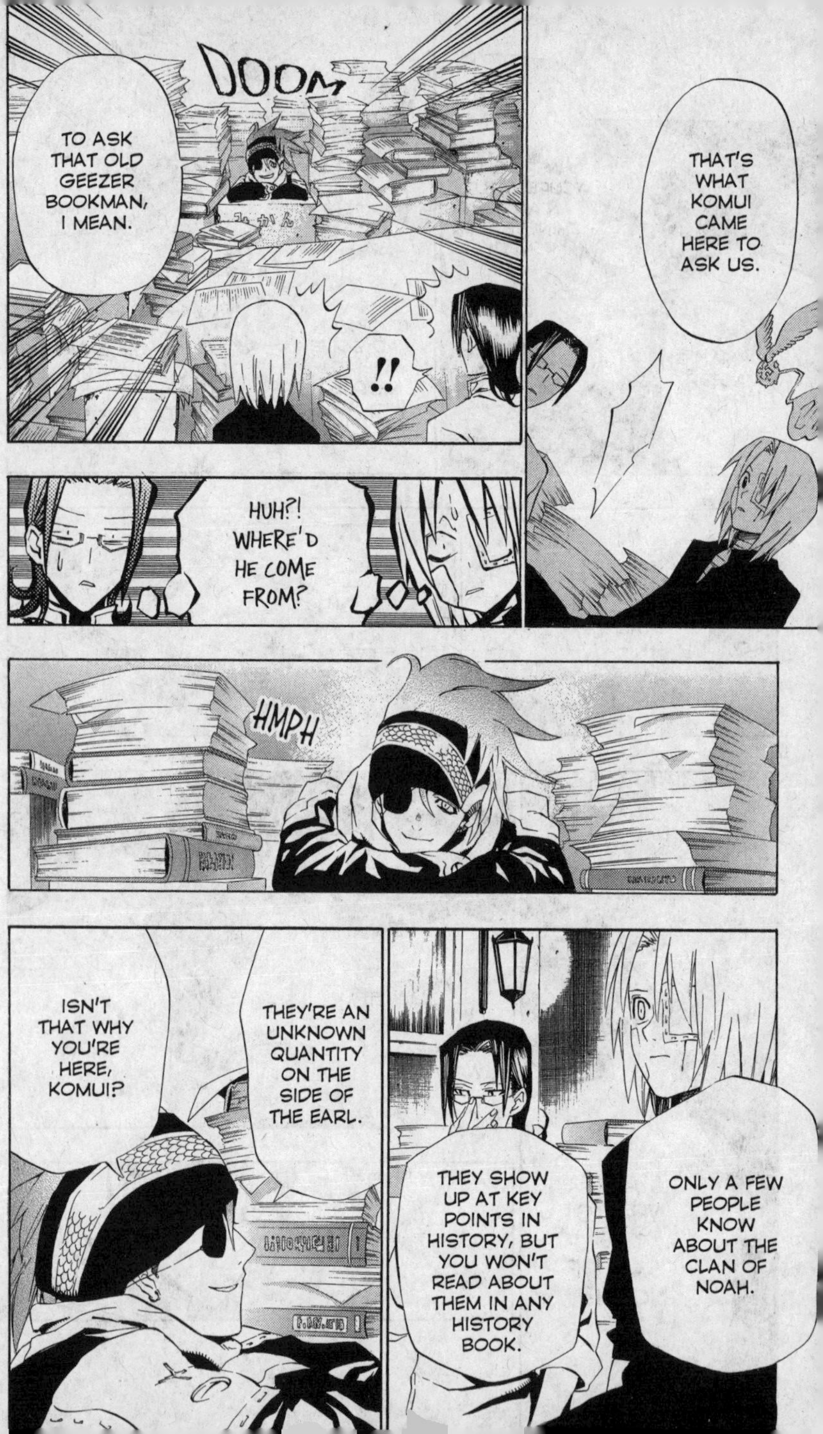
THAT'S WHAT KOMUI CAME HERE TO ASK US.
TO ASK THAT OLD GEEZER BOOKMAN, I MEAN.
DOOM
!!
HUH?! WHERE'D HE COME FROM?
HMPH
ONLY A FEW PEOPLE KNOW ABOUT THE CLAN OF NOAH.
THEY SHOW UP AT KEY POINTS IN HISTORY, BUT YOU WON'T READ ABOUT THEM IN ANY HISTORY BOOK.
THEY'RE AN UNKNOWN QUANTITY ON THE SIDE OF THE EARL.
ISN'T THAT WHY YOU'RE HERE, KOMUI?

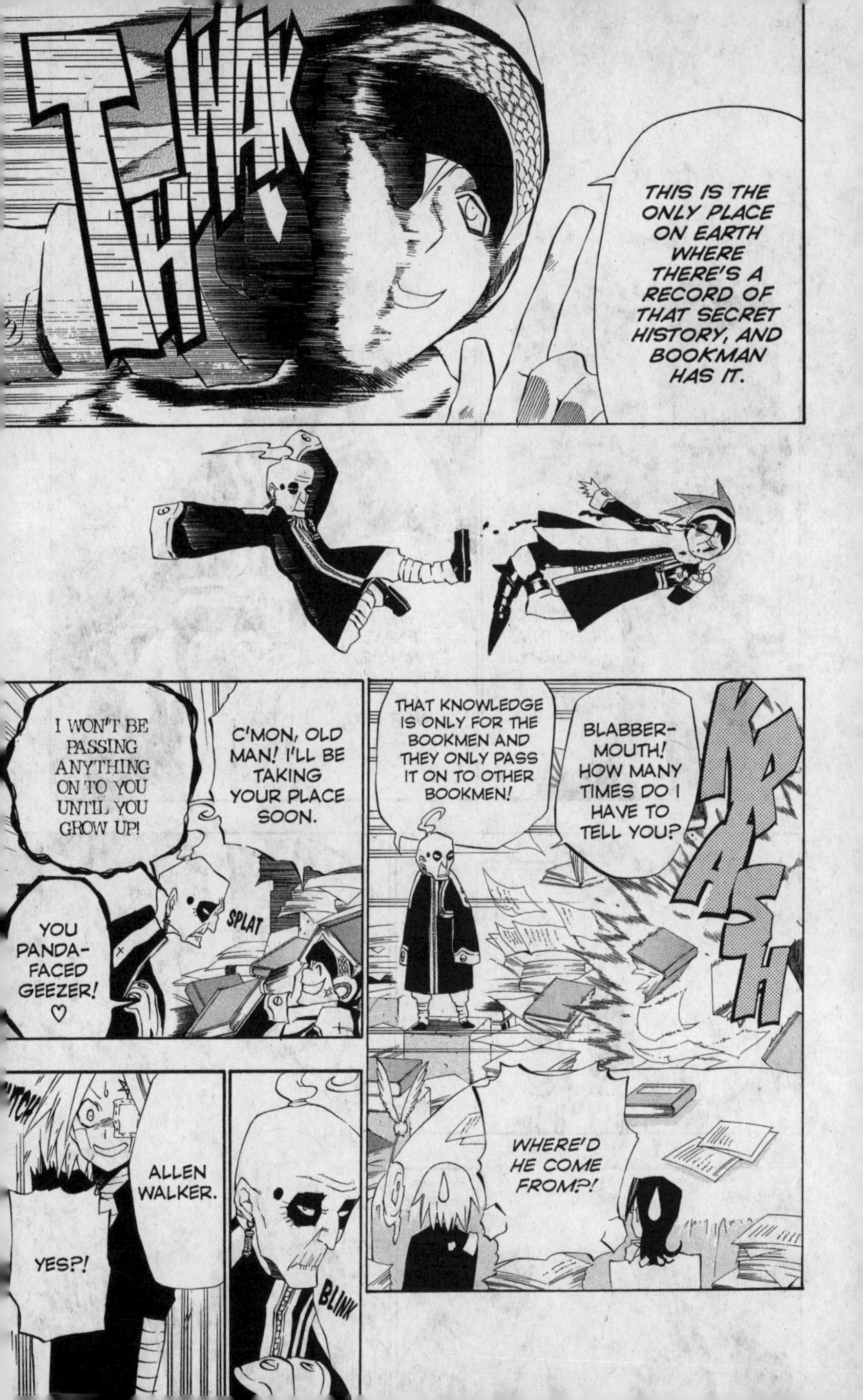
THWAK
THIS IS THE ONLY PLACE ON EARTH WHERE THERE'S A RECORD OF THAT SECRET HISTORY, AND BOOKMAN HAS IT.
KRASH
BLABBER-MOUTH! HOW MANY TIMES DO I HAVE TO TELL YOU?
THAT KNOWLEDGE IS ONLY FOR THE BOOKMEN AND THEY ONLY PASS IT ON TO OTHER BOOKMEN!
C'MON, OLD MAN! I'LL BE TAKING YOUR PLACE SOON.
I WON'T BE PASSING ANYTHING ON TO YOU UNTIL YOU GROW UP!
SPLAT
YOU PANDA-FACED GEEZER! ♡
WHERE'D HE COME FROM?!
ALLEN WALKER.
BLINK
YES?!

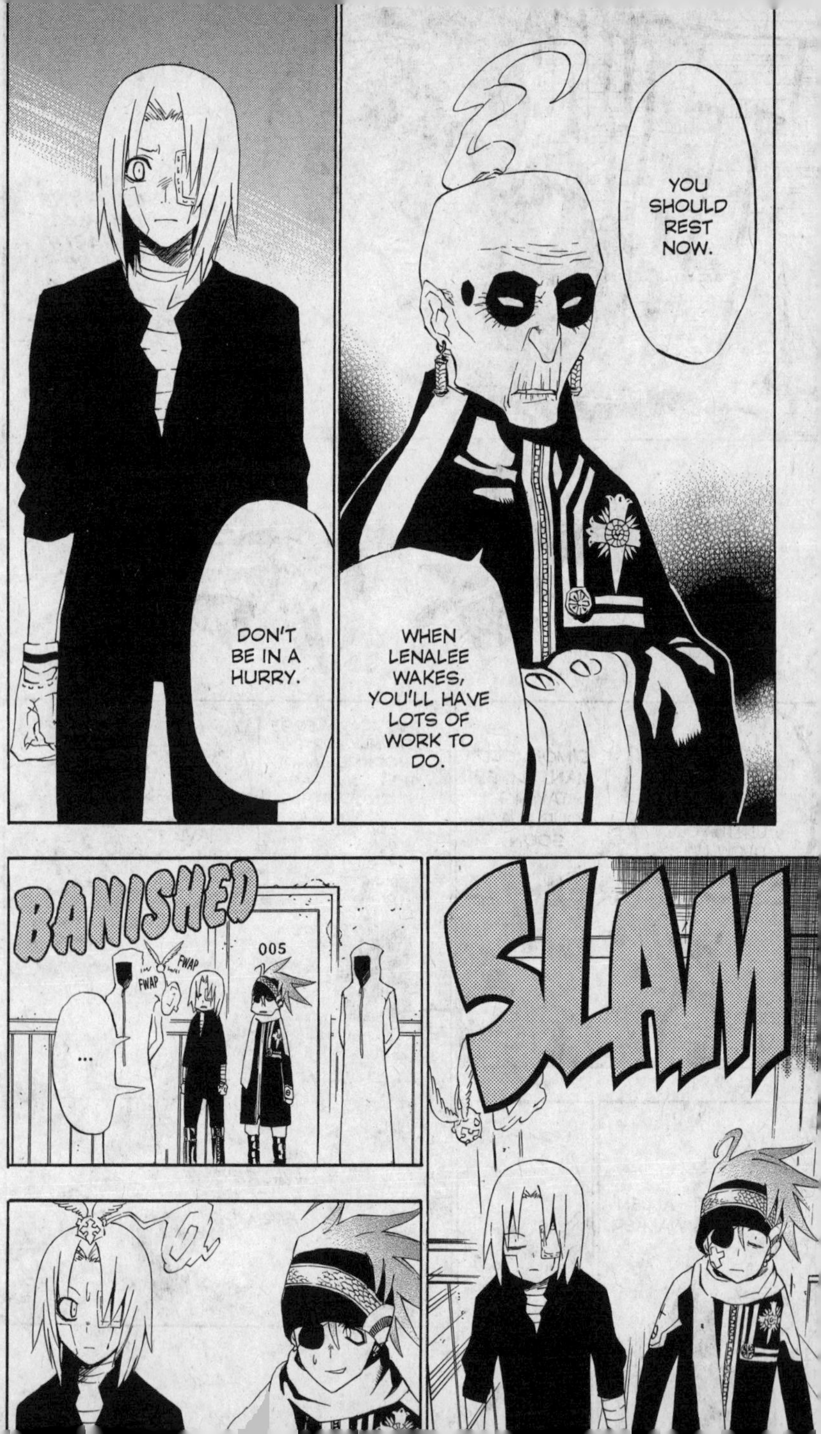
YOU SHOULD REST NOW.
WHEN LENALEE WAKES, YOU'LL HAVE LOTS OF WORK TO DO.
DON'T BE IN A HURRY.
SLAM
BANISHED
FWAP
FWAP
005
...

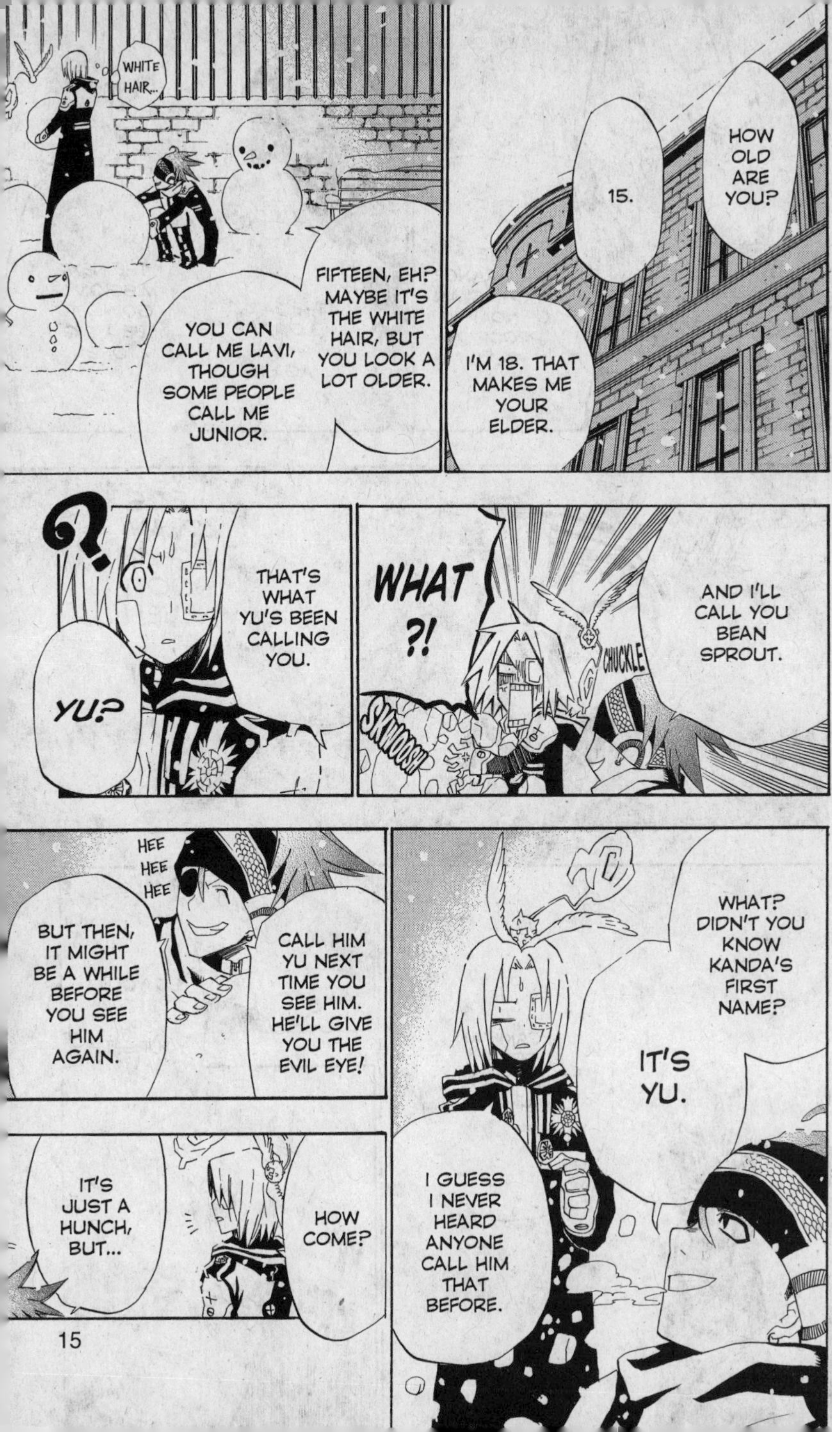
HOW OLD ARE YOU?
15.
I'M 18. THAT MAKES ME YOUR ELDER.
WHITE HAIR...
FIFTEEN, EH? MAYBE IT'S THE WHITE HAIR, BUT YOU LOOK A LOT OLDER.
YOU CAN CALL ME LAVI, THOUGH SOME PEOPLE CALL ME JUNIOR.
AND I'LL CALL YOU BEAN SPROUT.
CHUCKLE
WHAT ?!
SKWOOSH
THAT'S WHAT YU'S BEEN CALLING YOU.
YU?
WHAT? DIDN'T YOU KNOW KANDA'S FIRST NAME?
IT'S YU.
I GUESS I NEVER HEARD ANYONE CALL HIM THAT BEFORE.
HEE HEE HEE
CALL HIM YU NEXT TIME YOU SEE HIM. HE'LL GIVE YOU THE EVIL EYE!
BUT THEN, IT MIGHT BE A WHILE BEFORE YOU SEE HIM AGAIN.
HOW COME?
IT'S JUST A HUNCH, BUT...

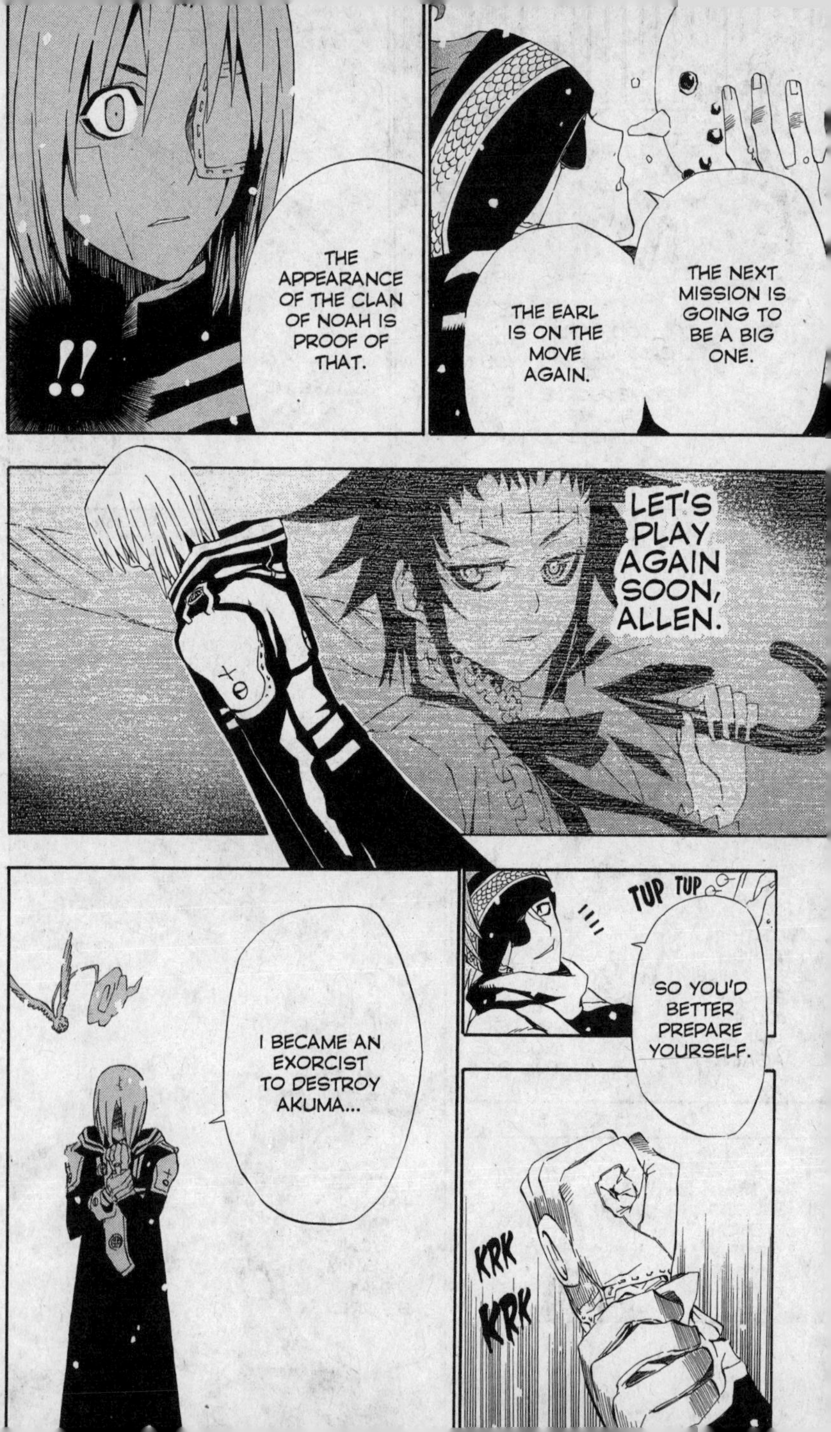
THE NEXT MISSION IS GOING TO BE A BIG ONE.
THE EARL IS ON THE MOVE AGAIN.
THE APPEARANCE OF THE CLAN OF NOAH IS PROOF OF THAT.
!!
LET'S PLAY AGAIN SOON, ALLEN.
TUP TUP
SO YOU'D BETTER PREPARE YOURSELF.
KRK KRK
I BECAME AN EXORCIST TO DESTROY AKUMA...

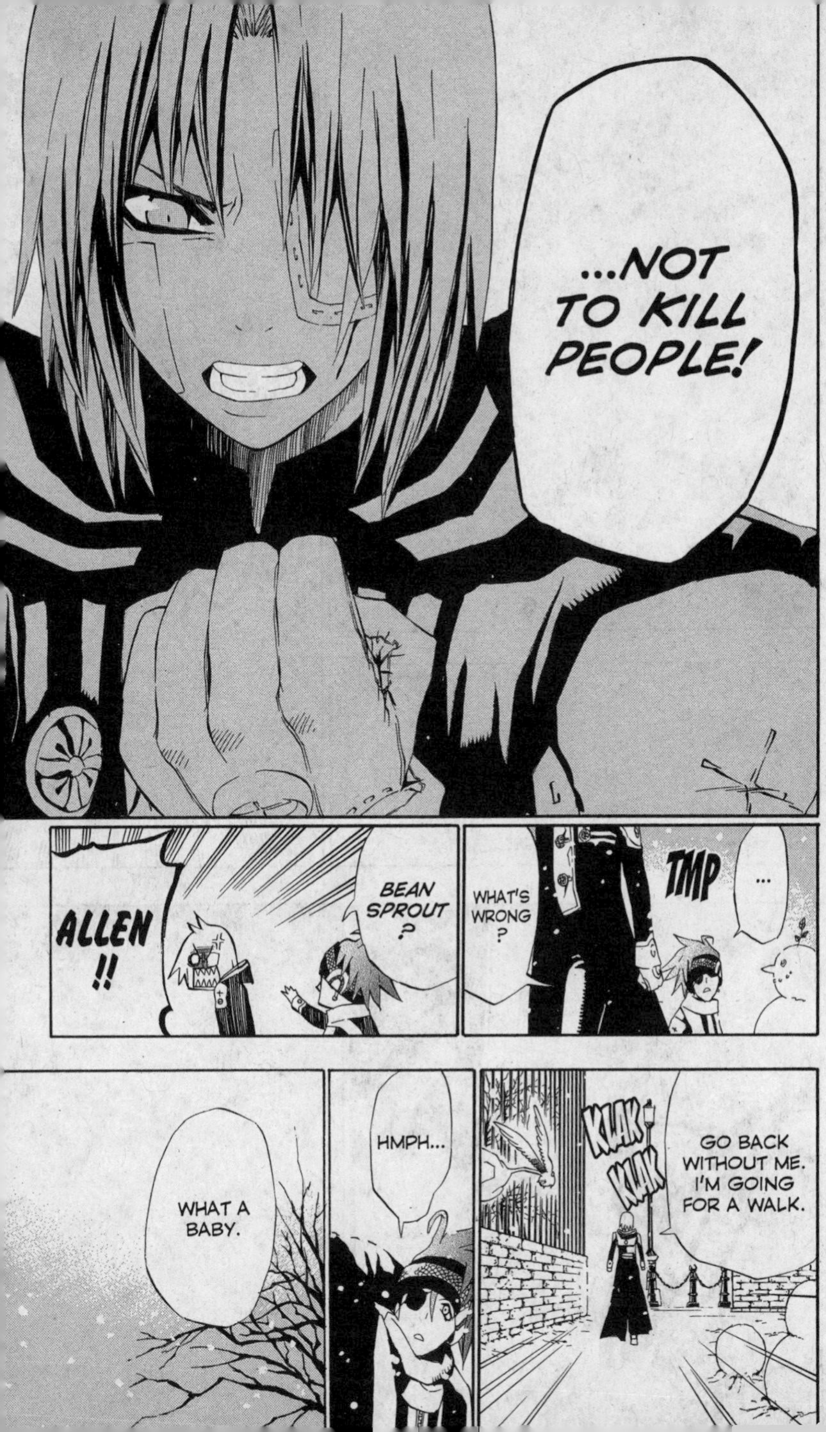
...NOT TO KILL PEOPLE!
...
TMP
WHAT'S WRONG ?
BEAN SPROUT ?
ALLEN !!
GO BACK WITHOUT ME. I'M GOING FOR A WALK.
KLAK KLAK
HMPH...
WHAT A BABY.

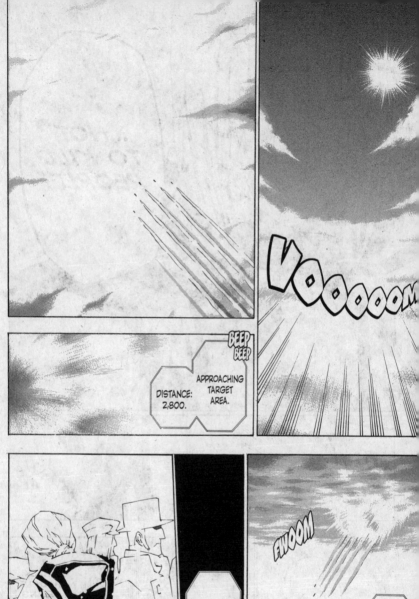

VOOOOOM

BEEP
BEEP

APPROACHING
TARGET
AREA.

DISTANCE:
2,800.

100.

FWOOM

1,000...
5,00...

2,000...
1,500...

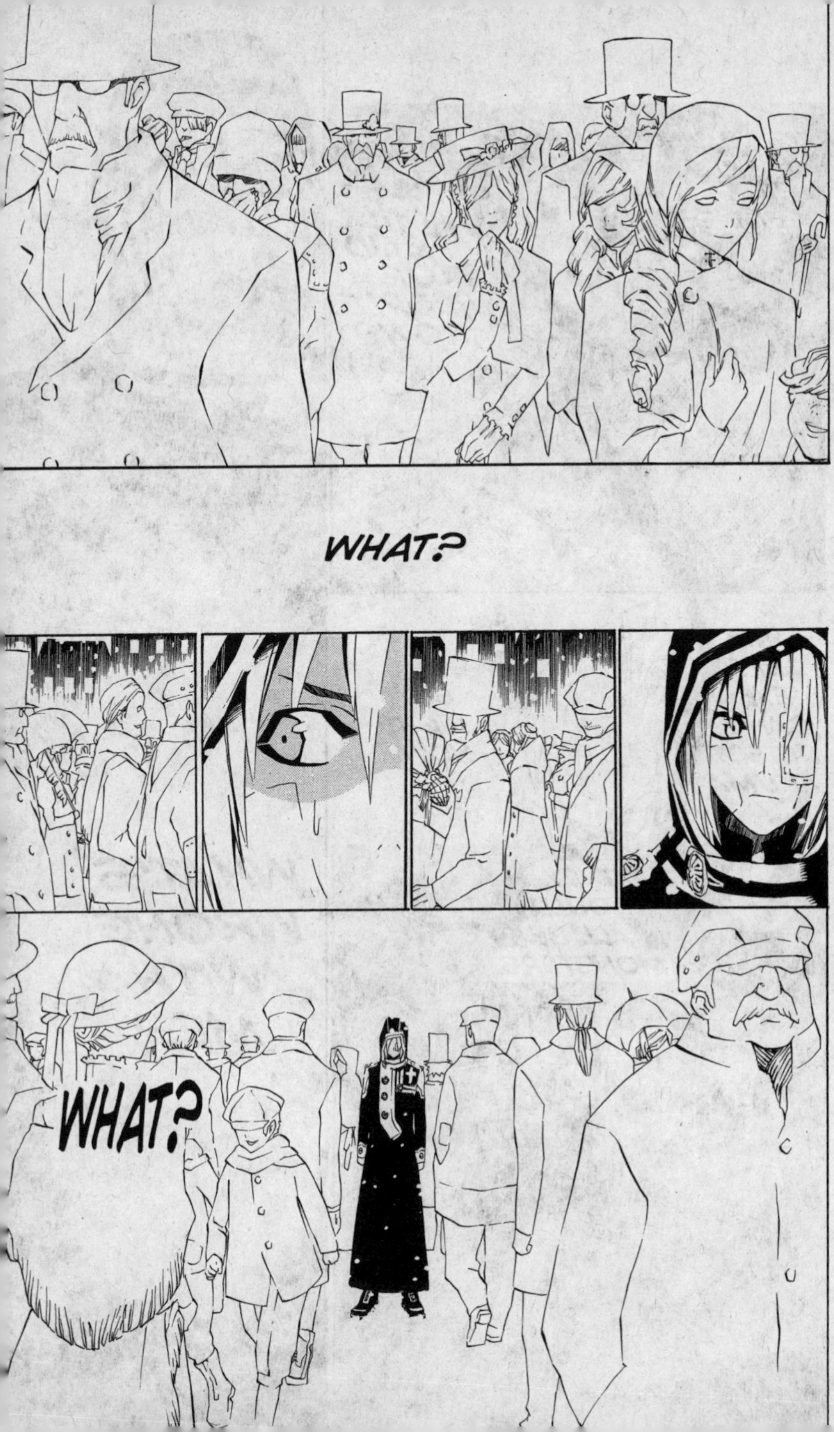
WHAT?
WHAT?

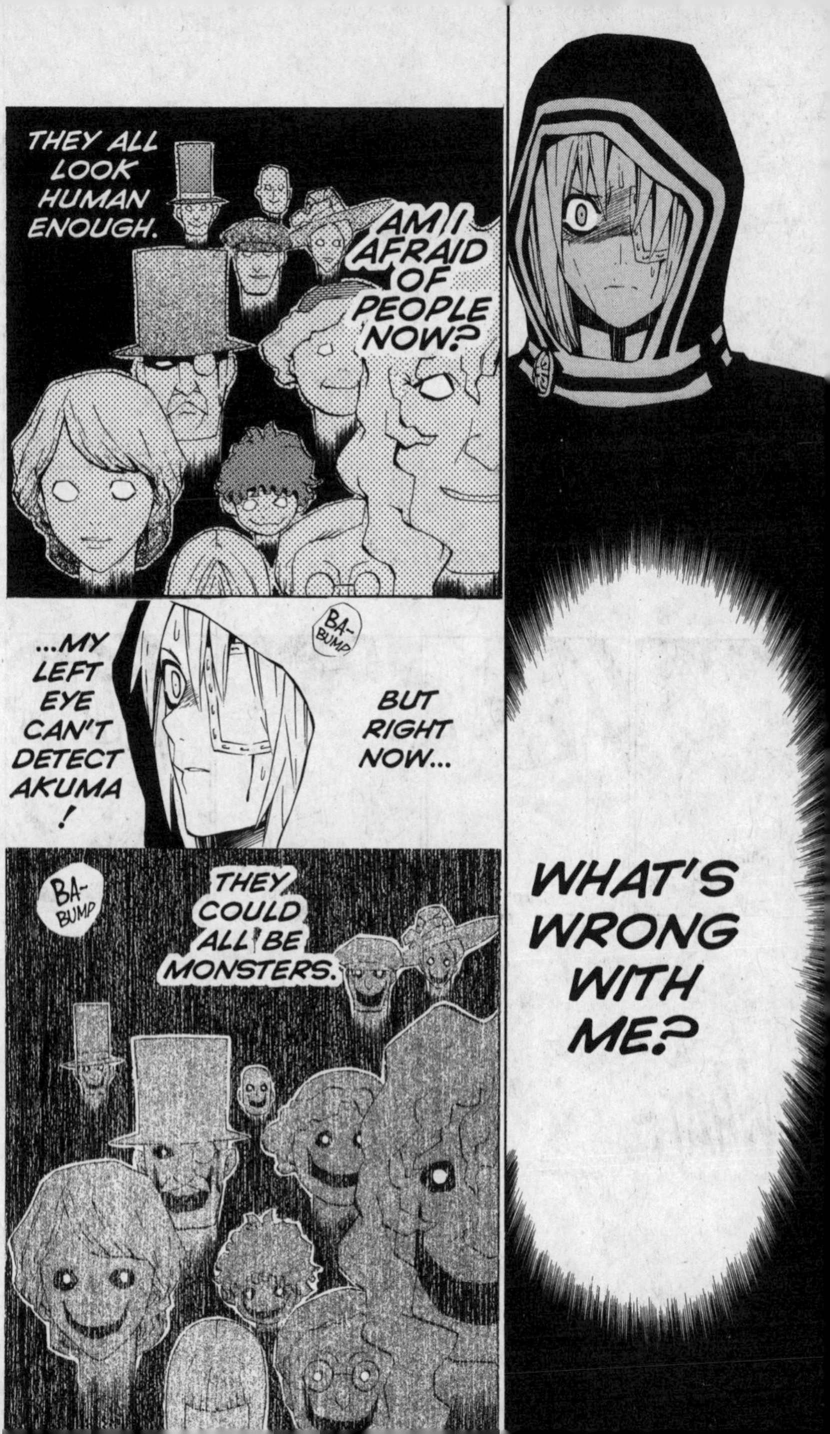
WHAT'S WRONG WITH ME?
THEY ALL LOOK HUMAN ENOUGH.
AM I AFRAID OF PEOPLE NOW?
BA-BUMP
BUT RIGHT NOW...
...MY LEFT EYE CAN'T DETECT AKUMA!
THEY COULD ALL BE MONSTERS.
BA-BUMP

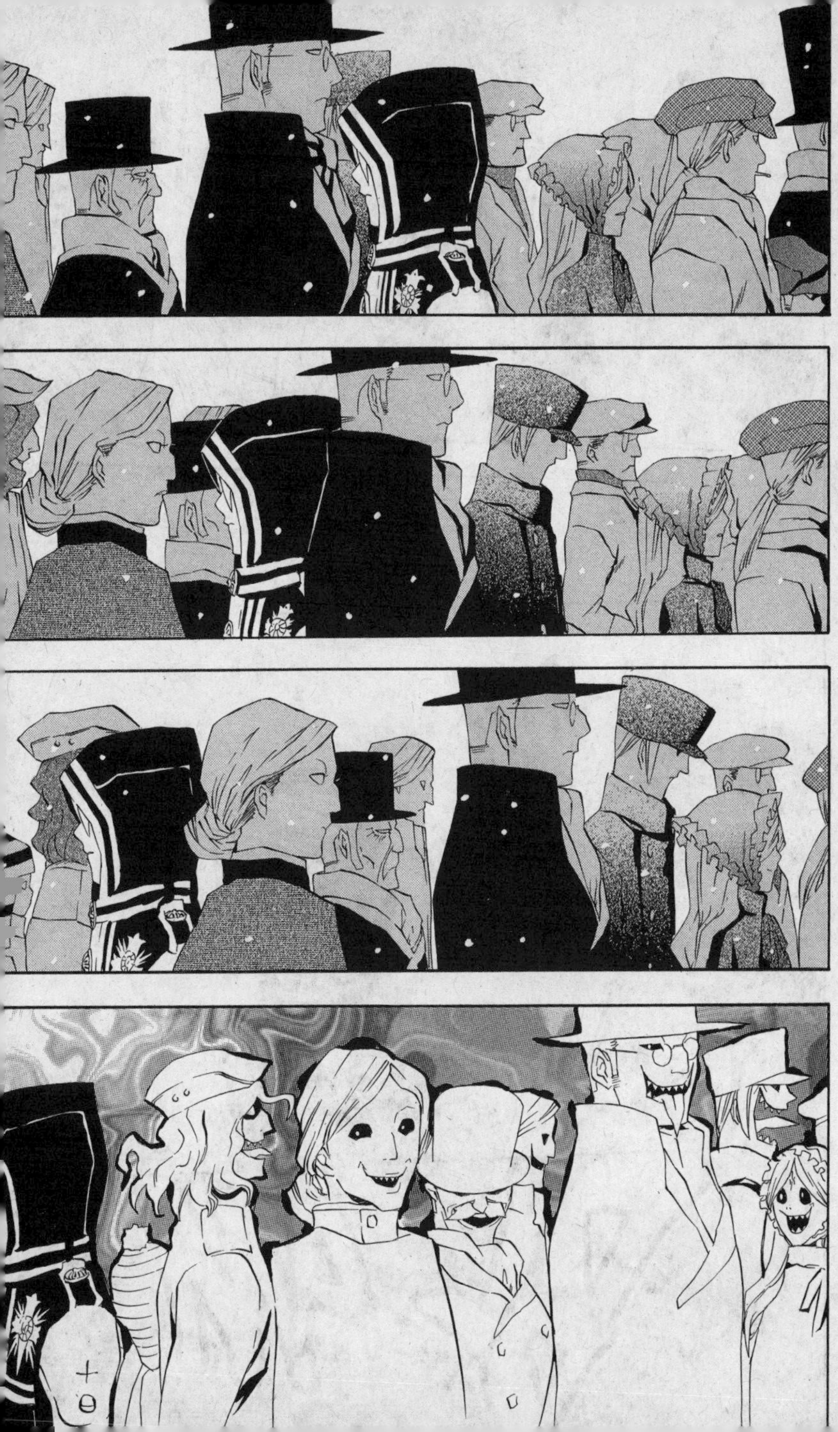

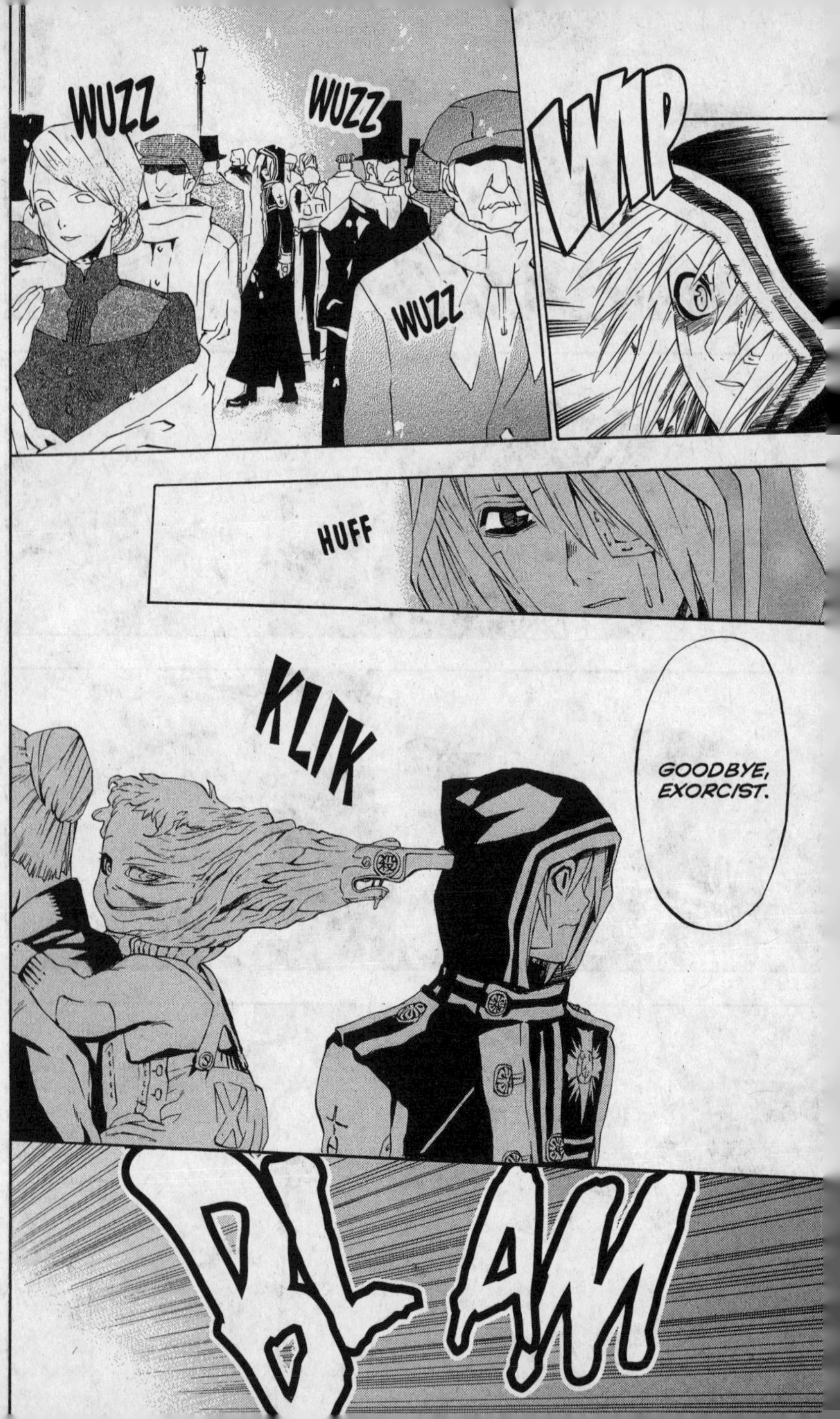
WMP
WUZZ
WUZZ
WUZZ
HUFF
GOODBYE, EXORCIST.
KLIK
BLAM

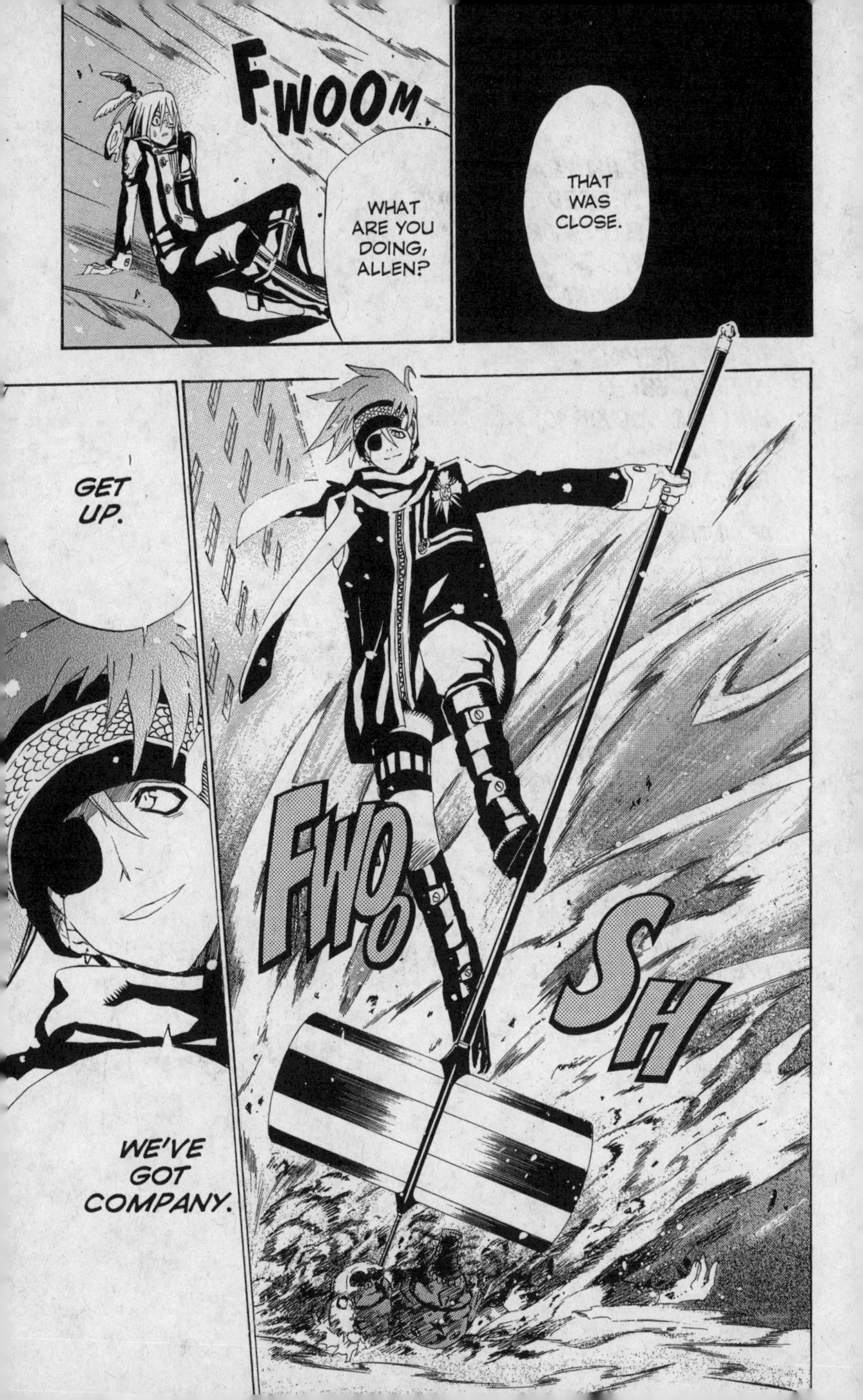
THAT WAS CLOSE.
FWOOM
WHAT ARE YOU DOING, ALLEN?
FWOOSH
GET UP.
WE'VE GOT COMPANY.

LAVI

HE GAVE UP HIS REAL NAME
WHEN HE DECIDED TO BECOME
BOOKMAN'S SUCCESSOR.
RACE MONGREL
NATIONALITY UNKNOWN
AGE 18
HEIGHT 177CM
WEIGHT 68KG
BIRTHDAY AUGUST 10
SIGN LEO
BLOOD TYPE O

ORIGINALLY LAVI WAS
GOING TO BE THE MAIN
CHARACTER OF A SERIES
CALLED BOOK-MAN, WHICH
DIDN'T HAPPEN. BUT I
REALLY LIKED HIM SO I'M
GLAD I FINALLY GOT TO USE
HIM. THE SECRET HISTORY
OF THE WORLD AND THE
ROLE OF THE BOOKMAN ARE
KEY POINTS IN THE STORY
OF D.GRAY-MAN. THE
REASON LAVI WEARS A
PATCH OVER HIS RIGHT
EYE WILL BE REVEALED
EVENTUALLY (IF THE
SERIES LASTS.) PLEASE
BE PATIENT.

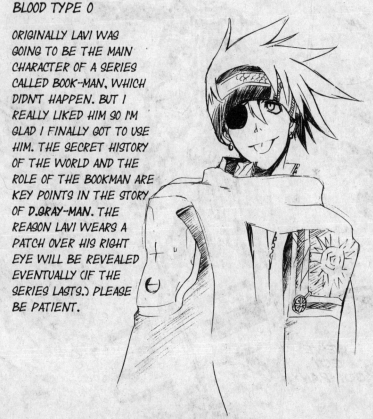

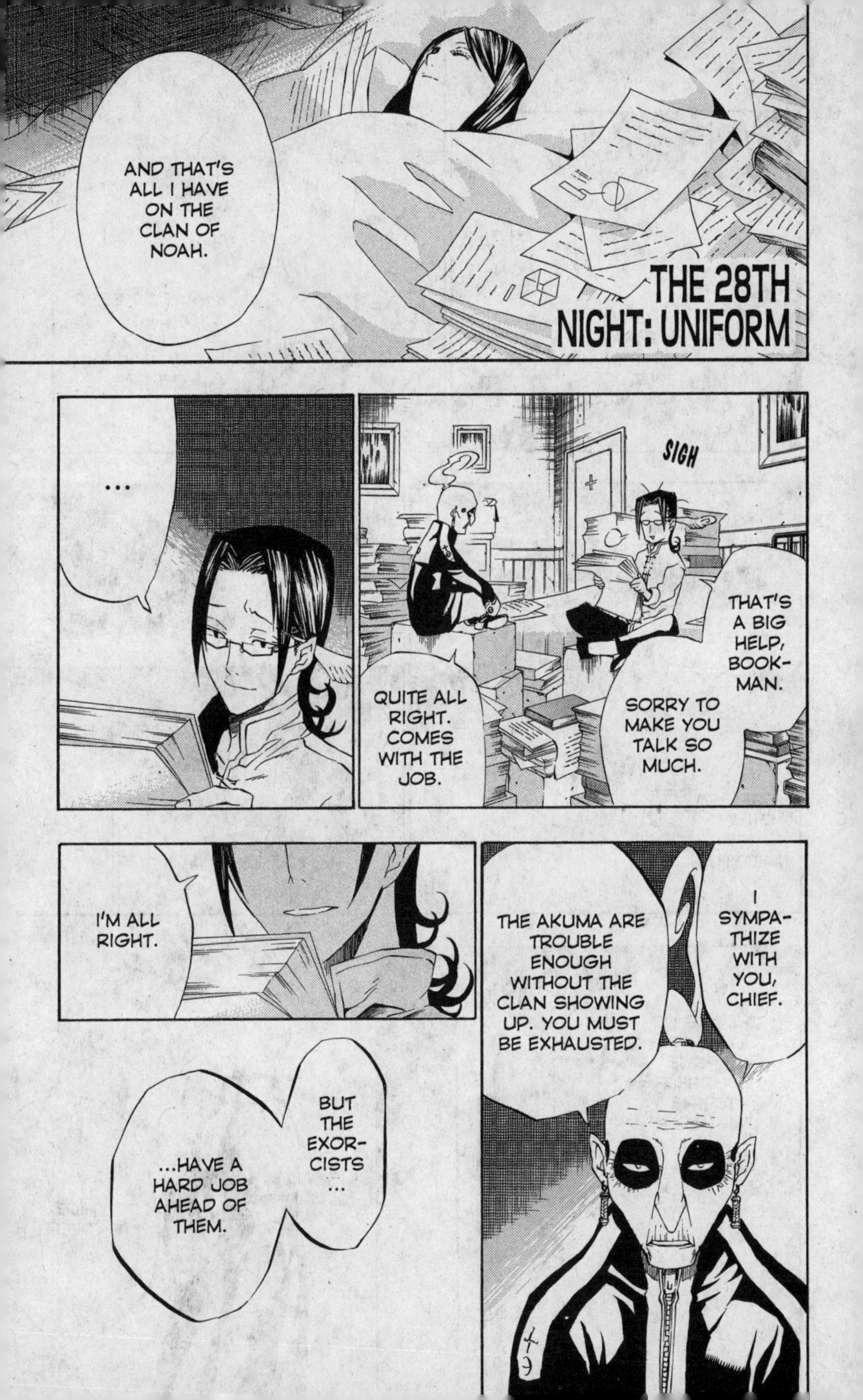
AND THAT'S ALL I HAVE ON THE CLAN OF NOAH.
THE 28TH NIGHT: UNIFORM
SIGH
THAT'S A BIG HELP, BOOK-MAN.
SORRY TO MAKE YOU TALK SO MUCH.
QUITE ALL RIGHT. COMES WITH THE JOB.
...
I SYMPA-THIZE WITH YOU, CHIEF.
THE AKUMA ARE TROUBLE ENOUGH WITHOUT THE CLAN SHOWING UP. YOU MUST BE EXHAUSTED.
I'M ALL RIGHT.
BUT THE EXOR-CISTS ...
...HAVE A HARD JOB AHEAD OF THEM.

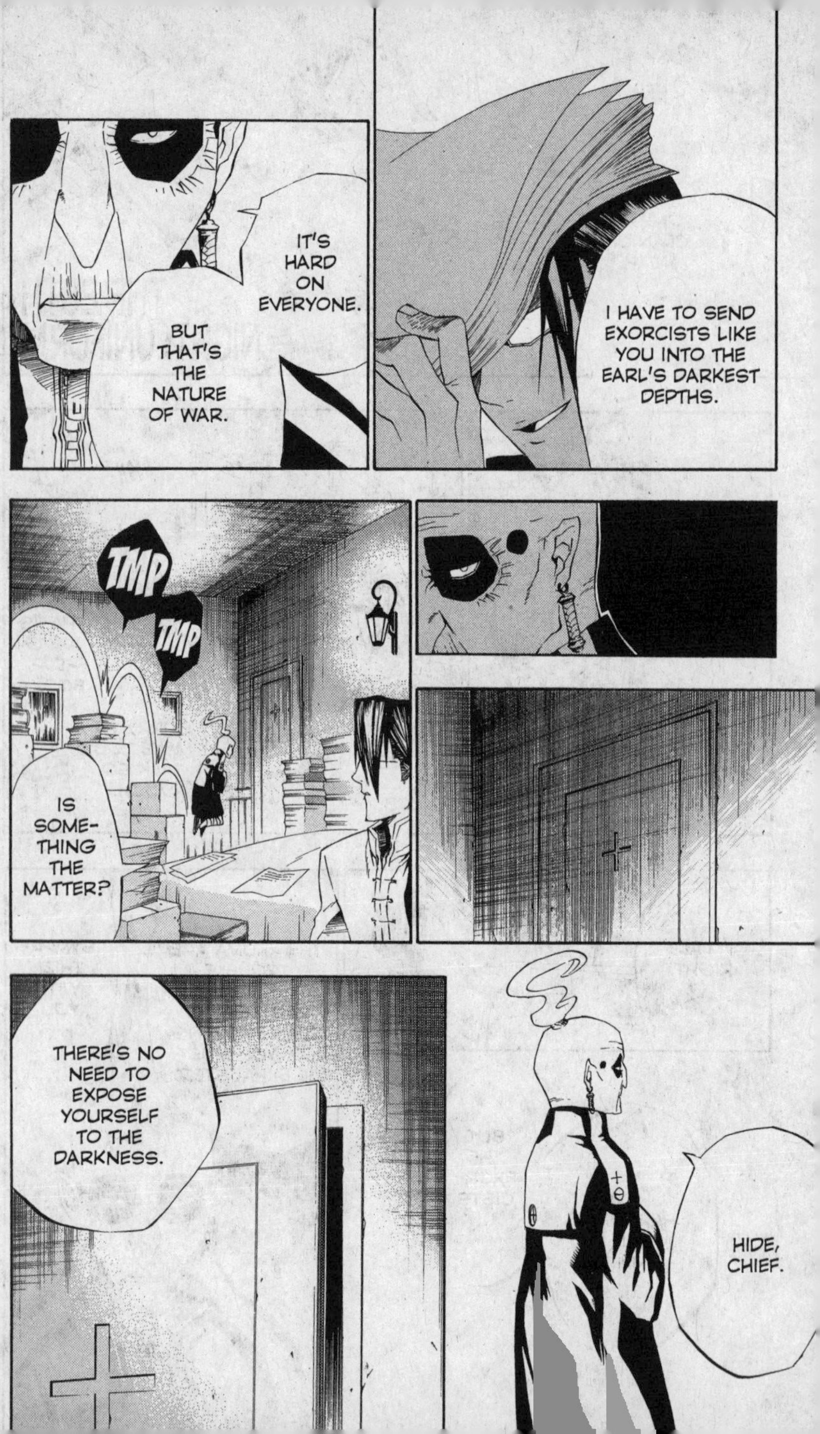
I HAVE TO SEND EXORCISTS LIKE YOU INTO THE EARL'S DARKEST DEPTHS.
IT'S HARD ON EVERYONE.
BUT THAT'S THE NATURE OF WAR.
TMP
TMP
IS SOME-THING THE MATTER?
HIDE, CHIEF.
THERE'S NO NEED TO EXPOSE YOURSELF TO THE DARKNESS.

THE 28TH NIGHT: UNIFORM

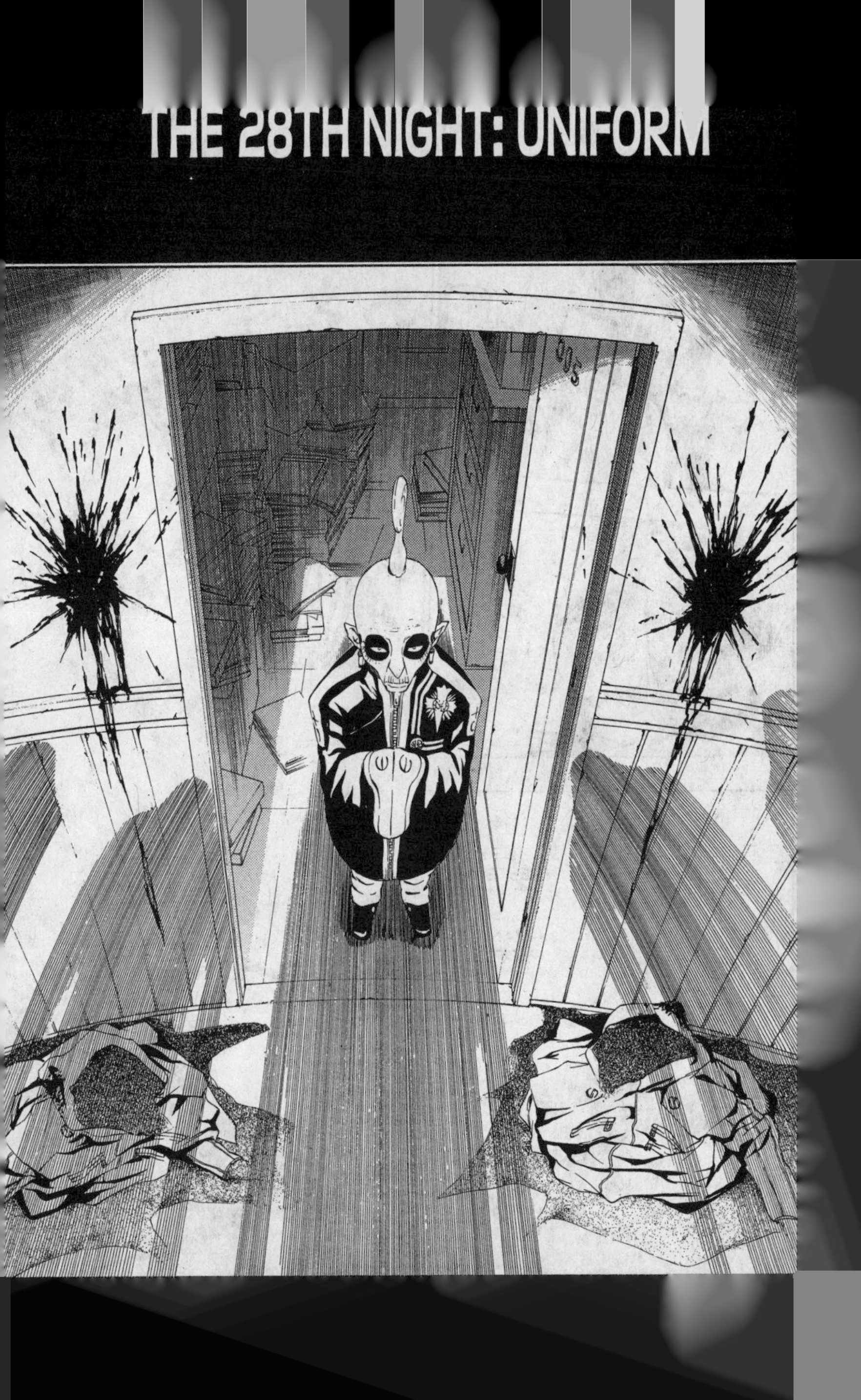

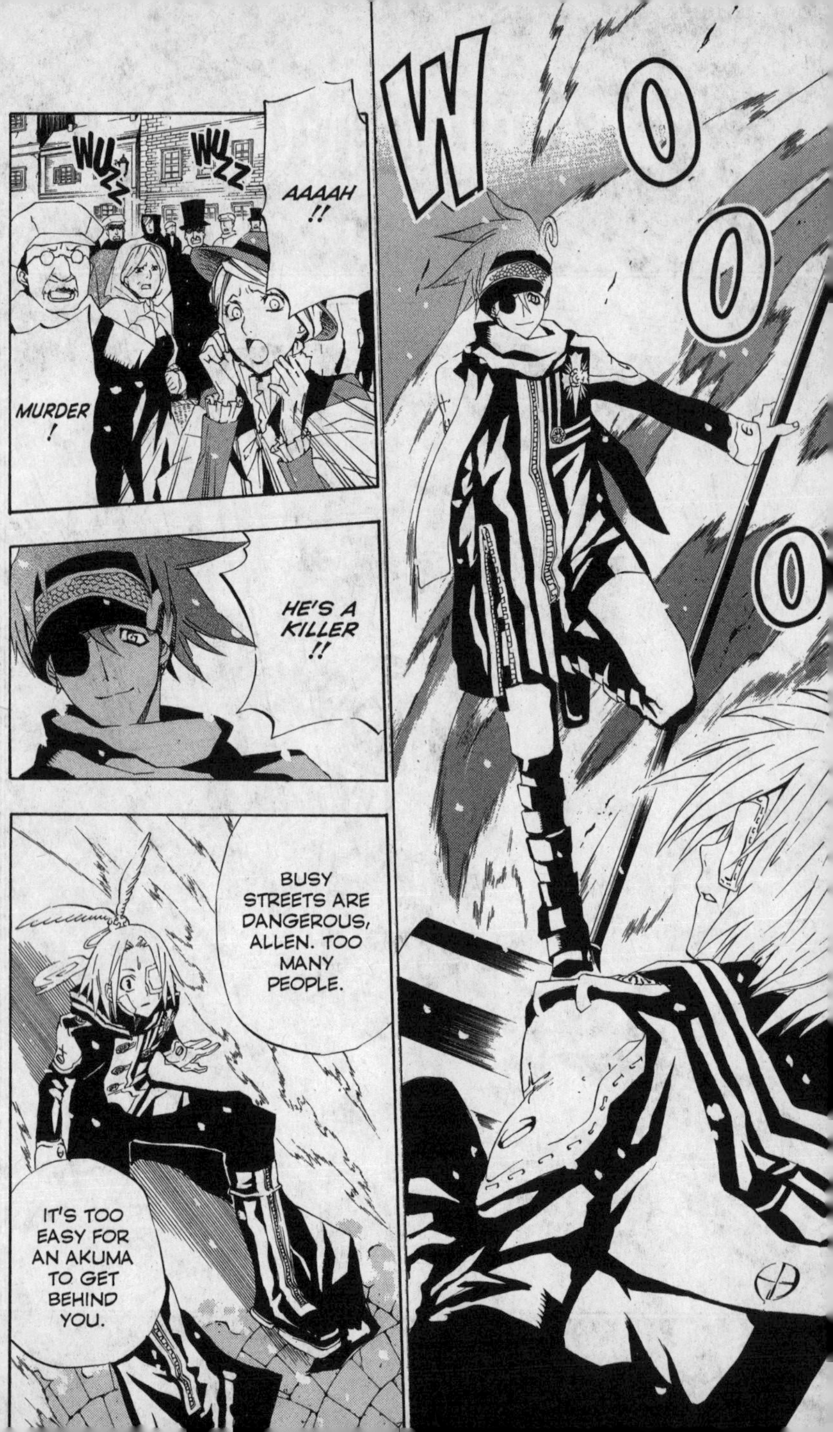
WOOOO
AAAAH!!
WUZZ
WUZZ
MURDER!
HE'S A KILLER!!
BUSY STREETS ARE DANGEROUS, ALLEN. TOO MANY PEOPLE.
IT'S TOO EASY FOR AN AKUMA TO GET BEHIND YOU.

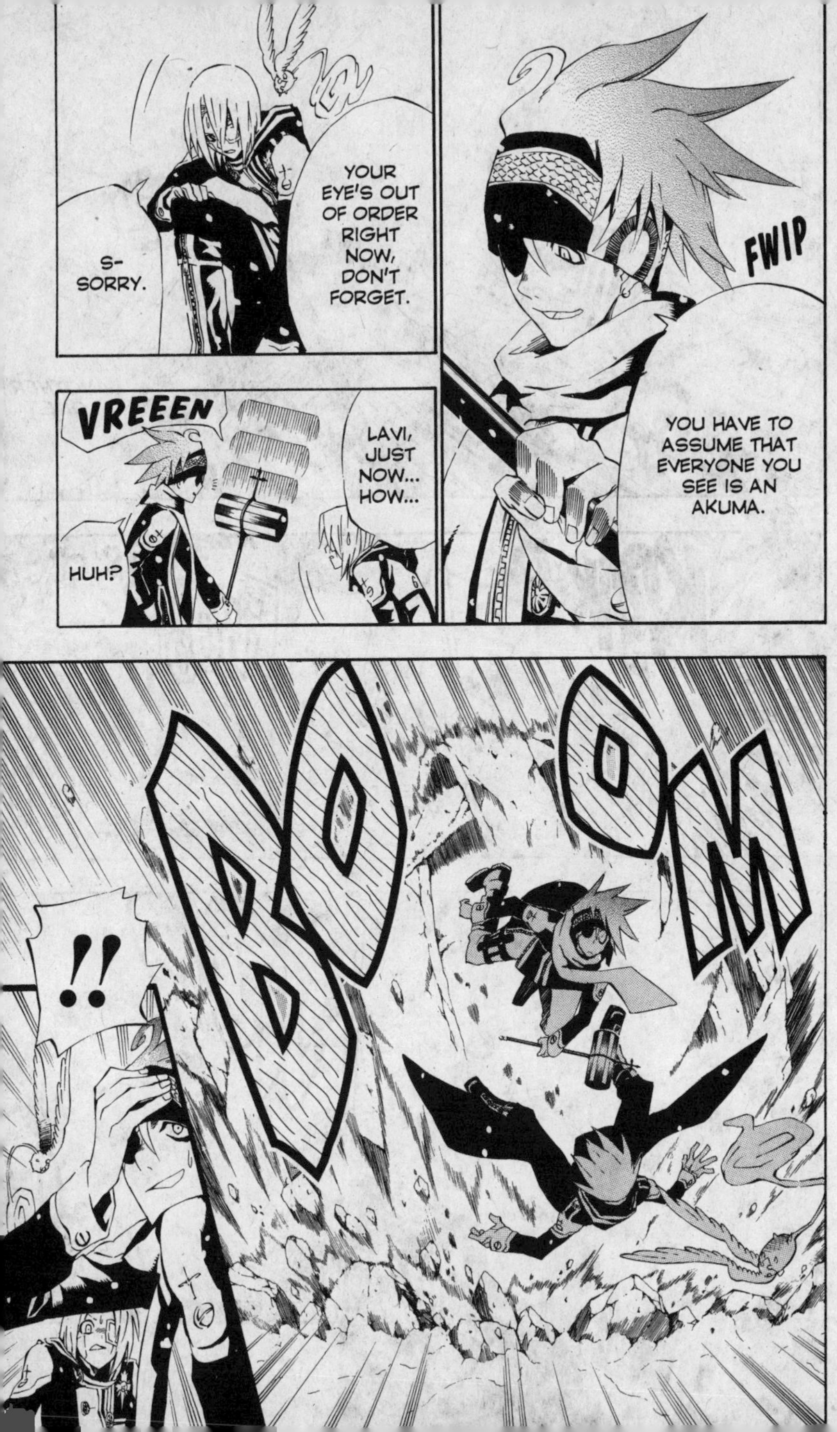
FWIP
YOU HAVE TO ASSUME THAT EVERYONE YOU SEE IS AN AKUMA.
YOUR EYE'S OUT OF ORDER RIGHT NOW, DON'T FORGET.
S-SORRY.
LAVI, JUST NOW... HOW...
VREEEN
HUH?
BOOM
!!

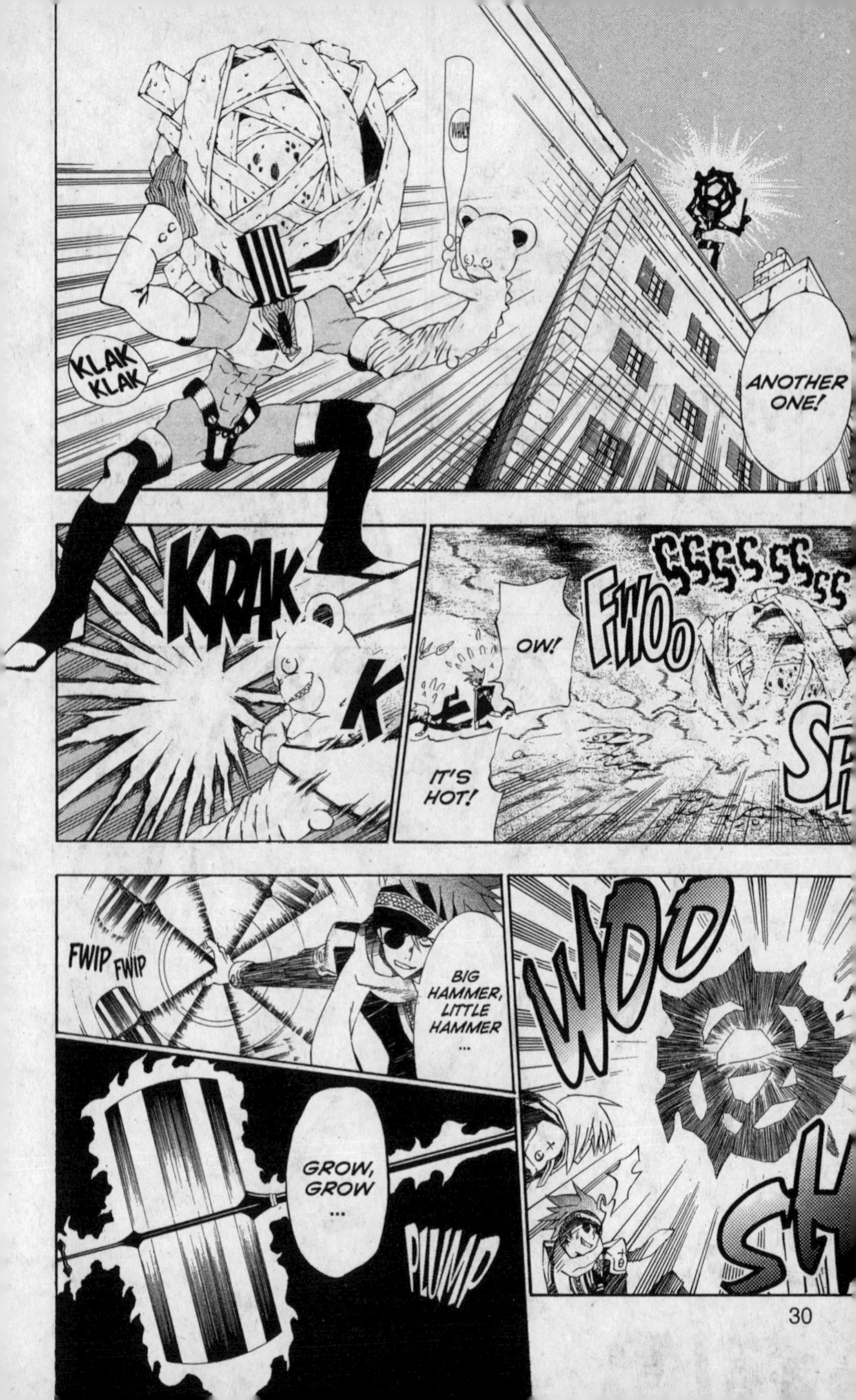
ANOTHER ONE!
KLAK KLAK
WHACK
SSSSSSSS
FWOO
SH
OW!
IT'S HOT!
KRAK
K
WOO
SH
BIG HAMMER, LITTLE HAMMER ...
FWIP FWIP
GROW, GROW ...
PLUMP

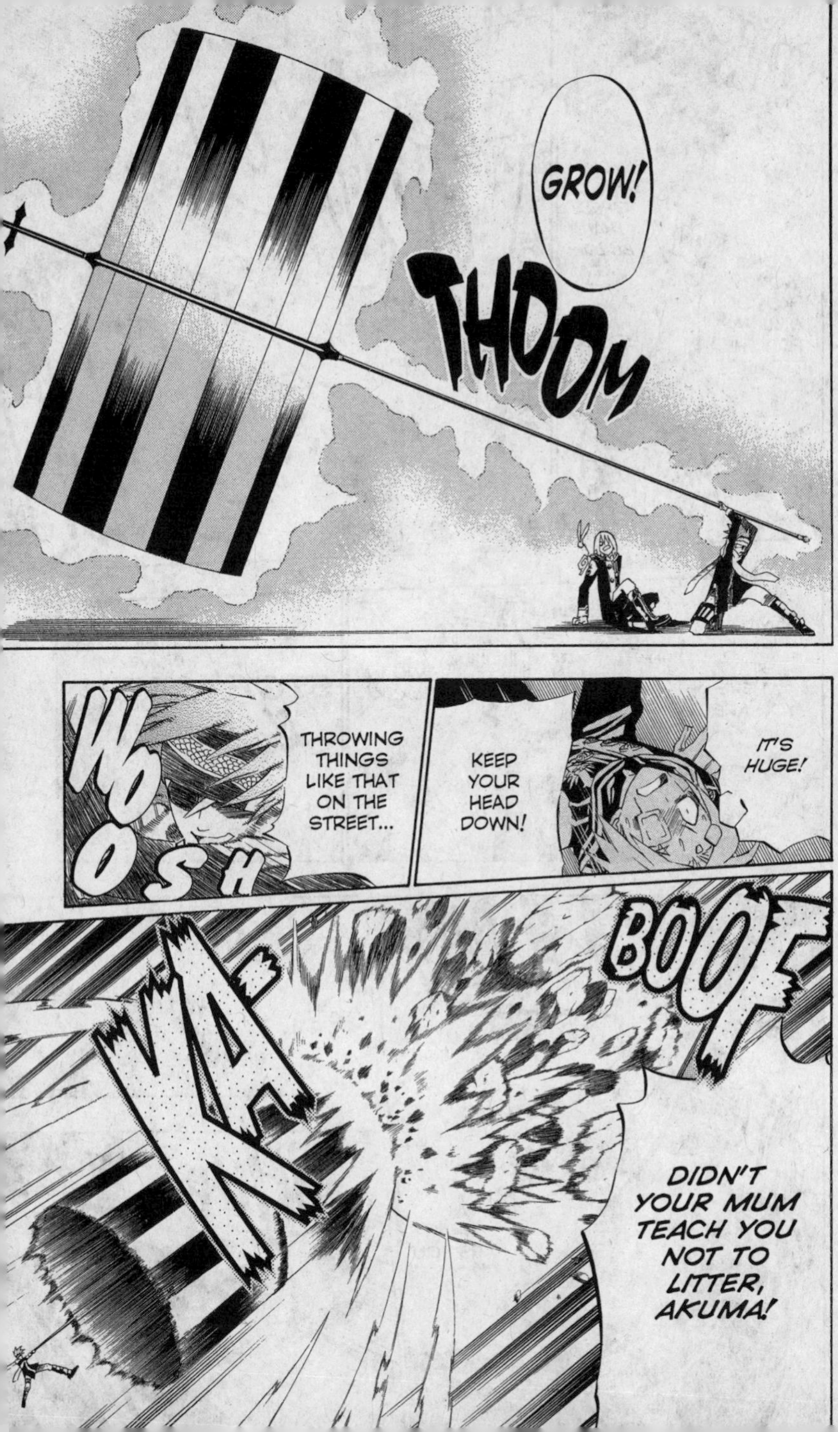

GROW!
THOOM
IT'S HUGE!
KEEP YOUR HEAD DOWN!
THROWING THINGS LIKE THAT ON THE STREET...
WOOSH
BOOF
KA
DIDN'T YOUR MUM TEACH YOU NOT TO LITTER, AKUMA!

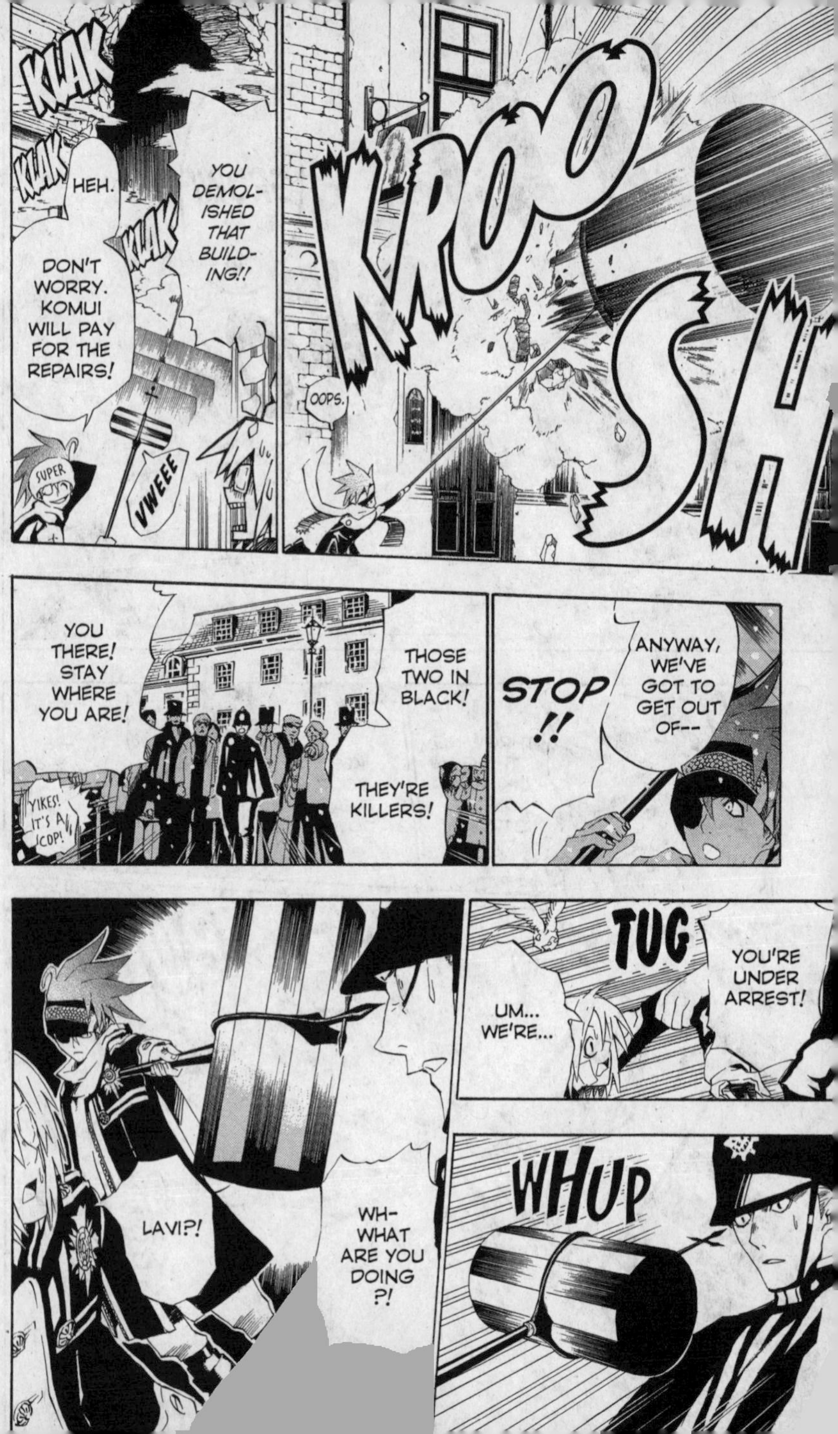

KROOSH
OOPS.
YOU DEMOLISHED THAT BUILDING!!
KLAK
HEH.
KLAK
KLAK
DON'T WORRY. KOMUI WILL PAY FOR THE REPAIRS!
VWEEE
SUPER
ANYWAY, WE'VE GOT TO GET OUT OF--
STOP!!
THOSE TWO IN BLACK!
THEY'RE KILLERS!
YOU THERE! STAY WHERE YOU ARE!
YIKES! IT'S A COP!
TUG
YOU'RE UNDER ARREST!
UM... WE'RE...
WHUP
WH-WHAT ARE YOU DOING?!
LAVI?!

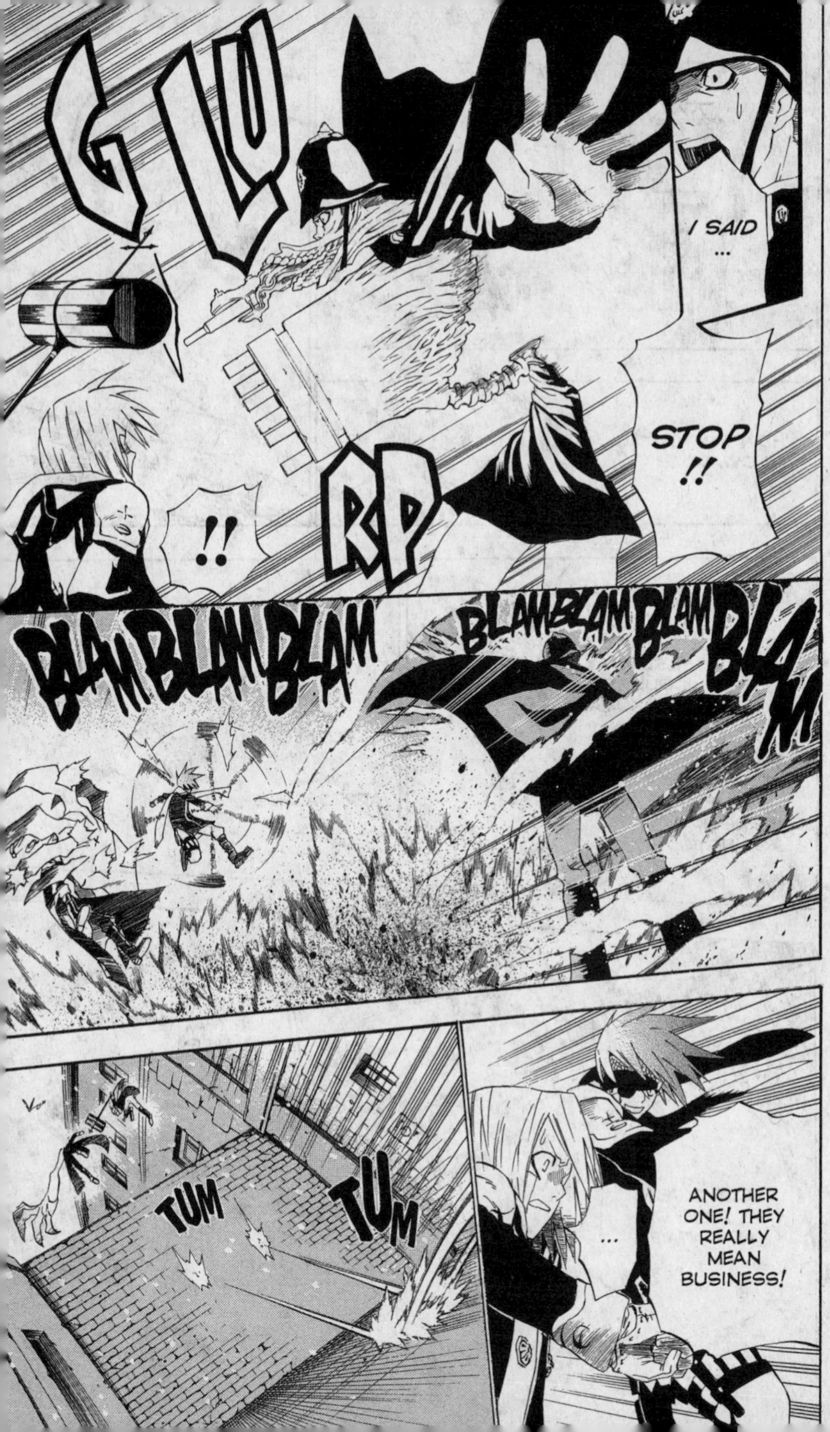
I SAID ...
STOP !!
GLU
RP
!!
BLAMBLAM BLAM BLAM
BLAM BLAM BLAM
ANOTHER ONE! THEY REALLY MEAN BUSINESS!
...
TUM
TUM

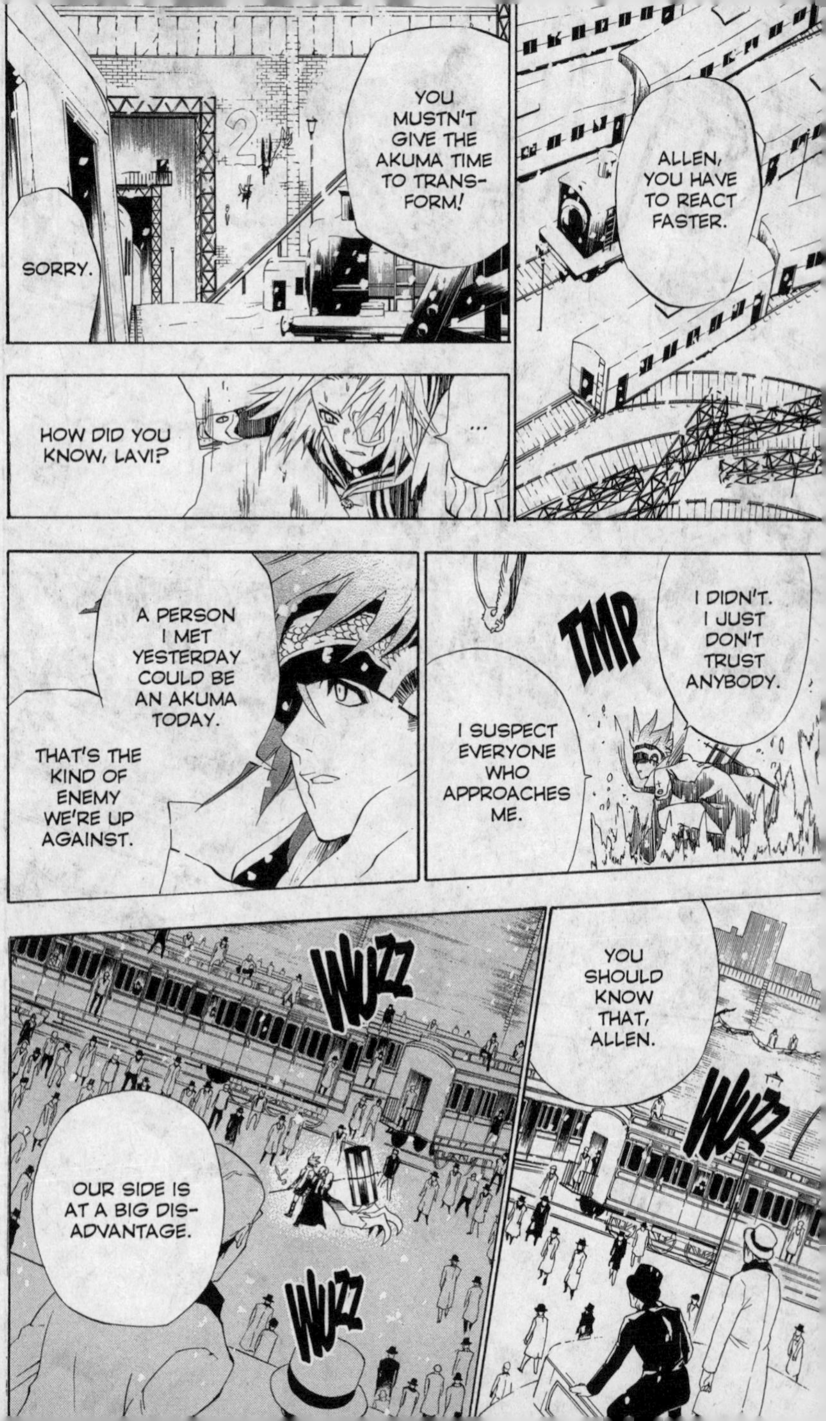
ALLEN, YOU HAVE TO REACT FASTER.
YOU MUSTN'T GIVE THE AKUMA TIME TO TRANS-FORM!
SORRY.
...
HOW DID YOU KNOW, LAVI?
TMP
I DIDN'T. I JUST DON'T TRUST ANYBODY.
I SUSPECT EVERYONE WHO APPROACHES ME.
A PERSON I MET YESTERDAY COULD BE AN AKUMA TODAY.
THAT'S THE KIND OF ENEMY WE'RE UP AGAINST.
YOU SHOULD KNOW THAT, ALLEN.
WUZZ
WUZZ
OUR SIDE IS AT A BIG DIS-ADVANTAGE.
WUZZ

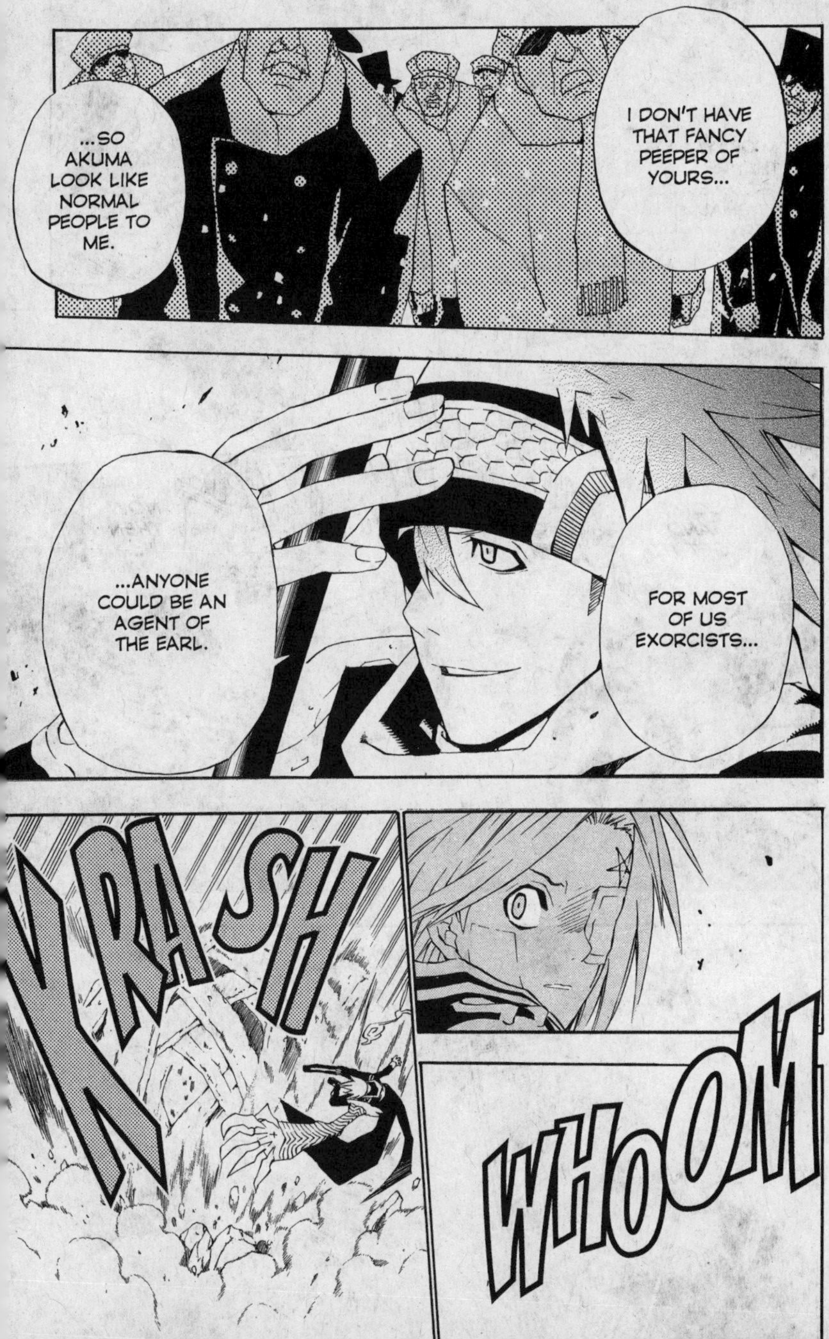
I DON'T HAVE THAT FANCY PEEPER OF YOURS...
...SO AKUMA LOOK LIKE NORMAL PEOPLE TO ME.
FOR MOST OF US EXORCISTS...
...ANYONE COULD BE AN AGENT OF THE EARL.
WHOOM
KRASH

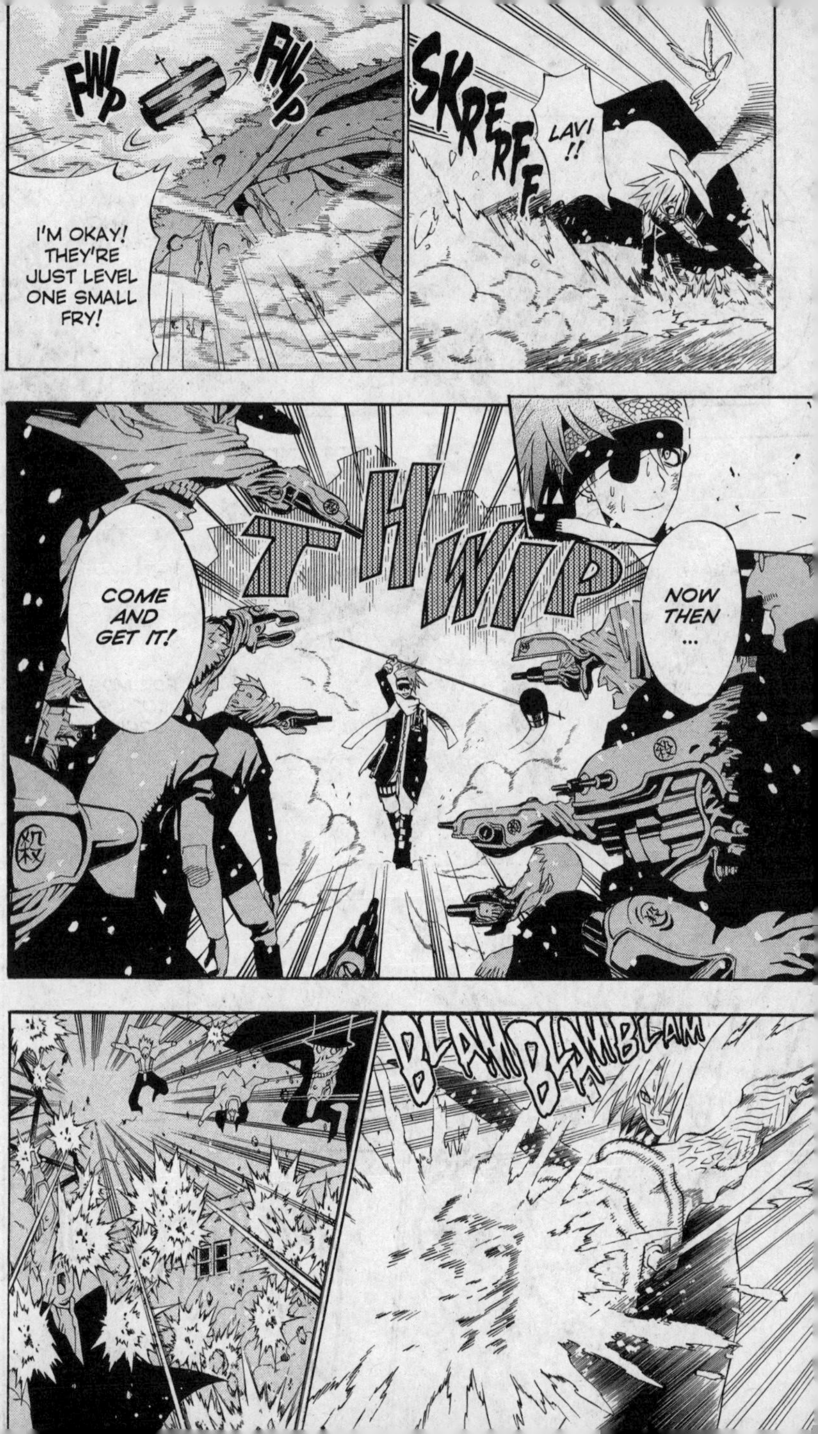
SKREFF
LAVI!!
FWIP
FWIP
I'M OKAY! THEY'RE JUST LEVEL ONE SMALL FRY!
NOW THEN ...
THWIP
COME AND GET IT!
BLAM BLAM BLAM

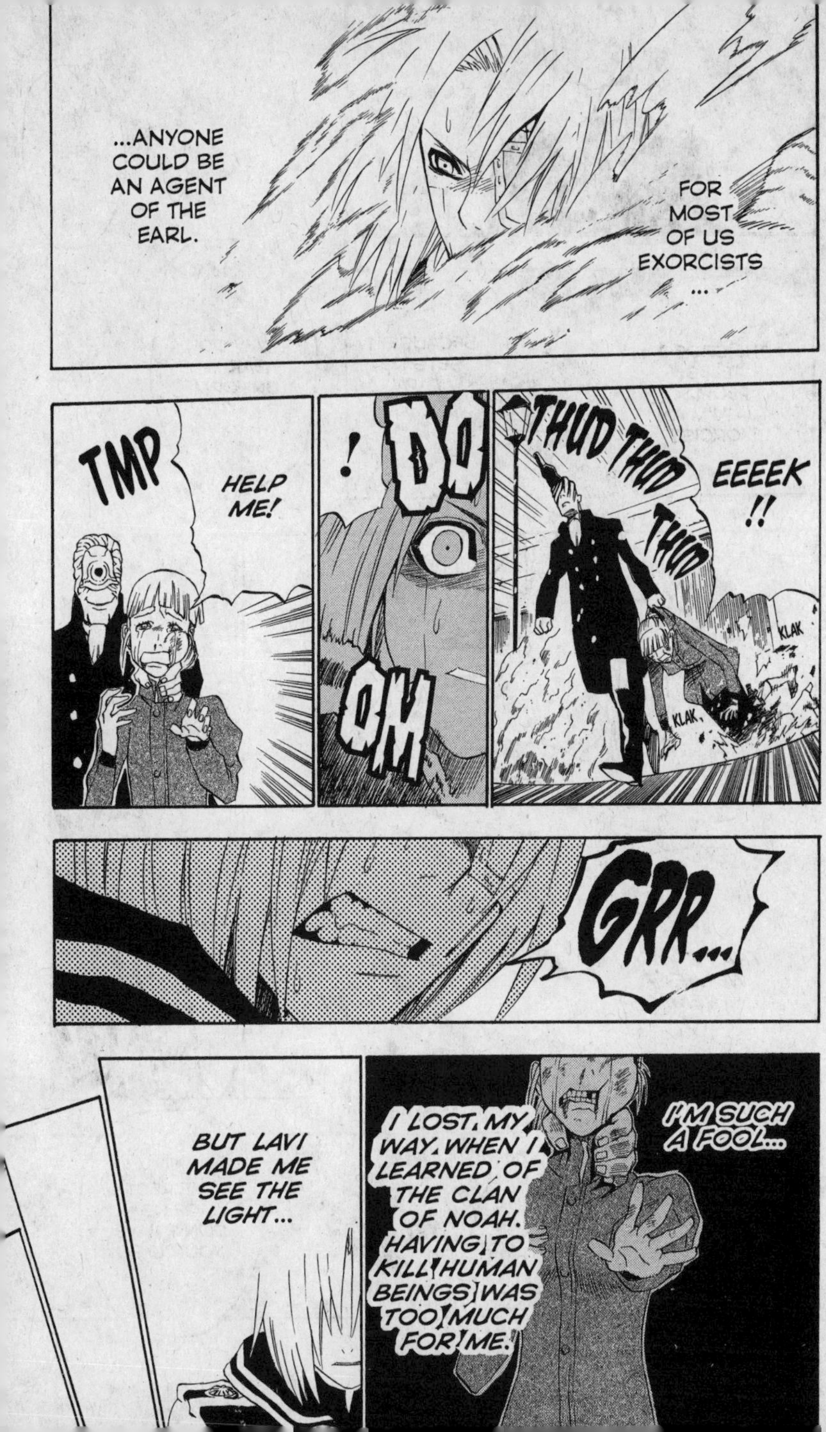
FOR MOST OF US EXORCISTS ...
...ANYONE COULD BE AN AGENT OF THE EARL.
EEEEK!!
THUD THUD THUD
KLAK
KLAK
DOOM
!
HELP ME!
TMP
GRR...
I'M SUCH A FOOL...
I LOST MY WAY WHEN I LEARNED OF THE CLAN OF NOAH. HAVING TO KILL HUMAN BEINGS WAS TOO MUCH FOR ME.
BUT LAVI MADE ME SEE THE LIGHT...

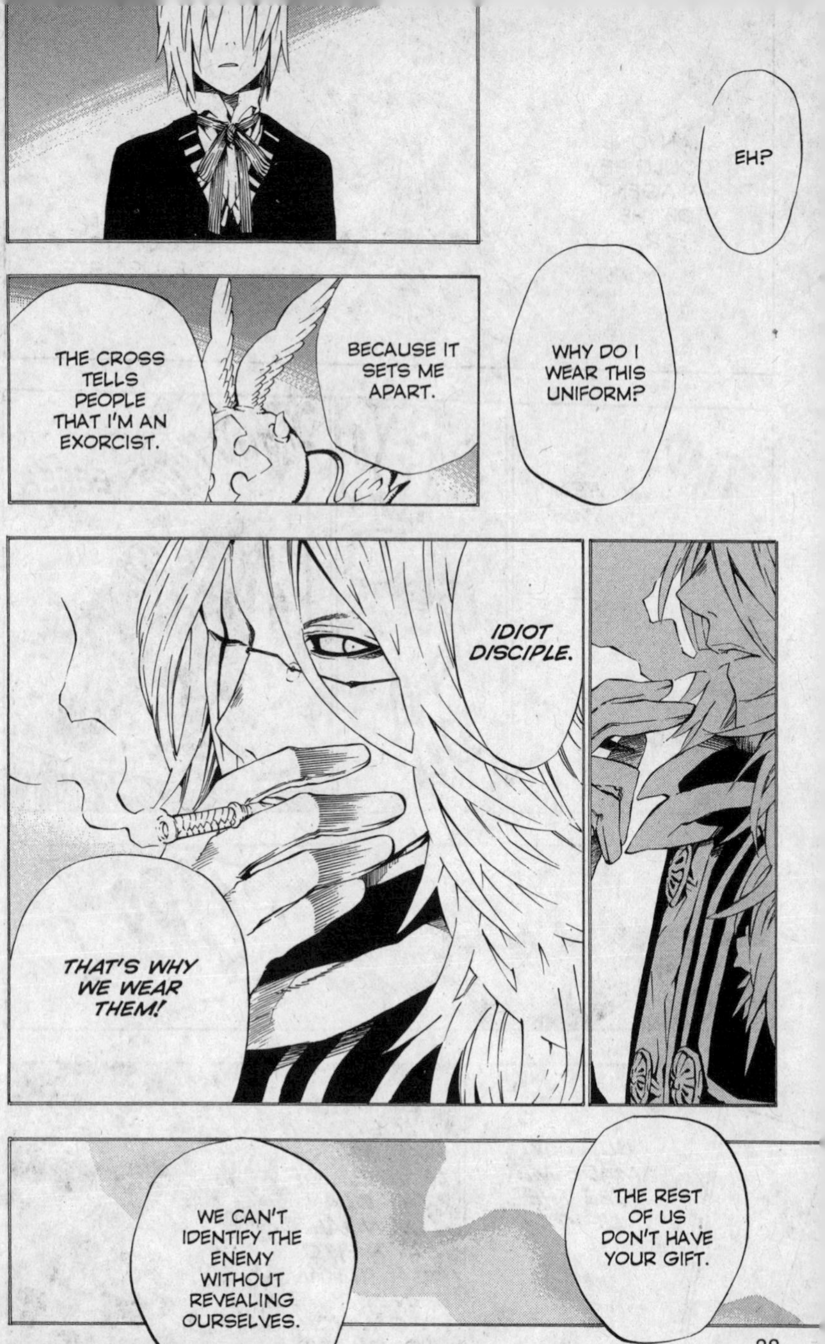
EH?
WHY DO I WEAR THIS UNIFORM?
BECAUSE IT SETS ME APART.
THE CROSS TELLS PEOPLE THAT I'M AN EXORCIST.
IDIOT DISCIPLE.
THAT'S WHY WE WEAR THEM!
THE REST OF US DON'T HAVE YOUR GIFT.
WE CAN'T IDENTIFY THE ENEMY WITHOUT REVEALING OURSELVES.

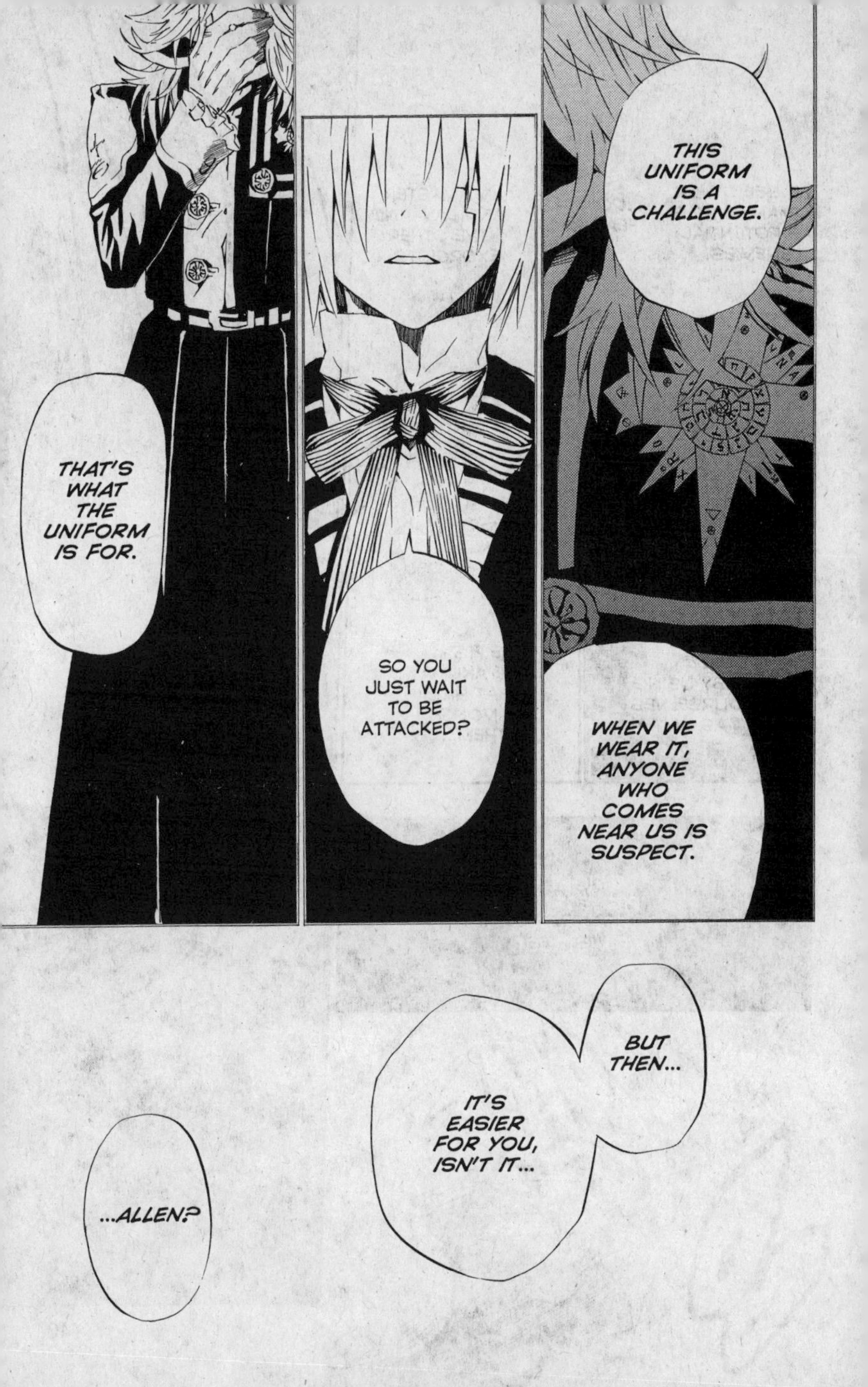
THIS UNIFORM IS A CHALLENGE.
WHEN WE WEAR IT, ANYONE WHO COMES NEAR US IS SUSPECT.
SO YOU JUST WAIT TO BE ATTACKED?
THAT'S WHAT THE UNIFORM IS FOR.
BUT THEN...
IT'S EASIER FOR YOU, ISN'T IT...
...ALLEN?

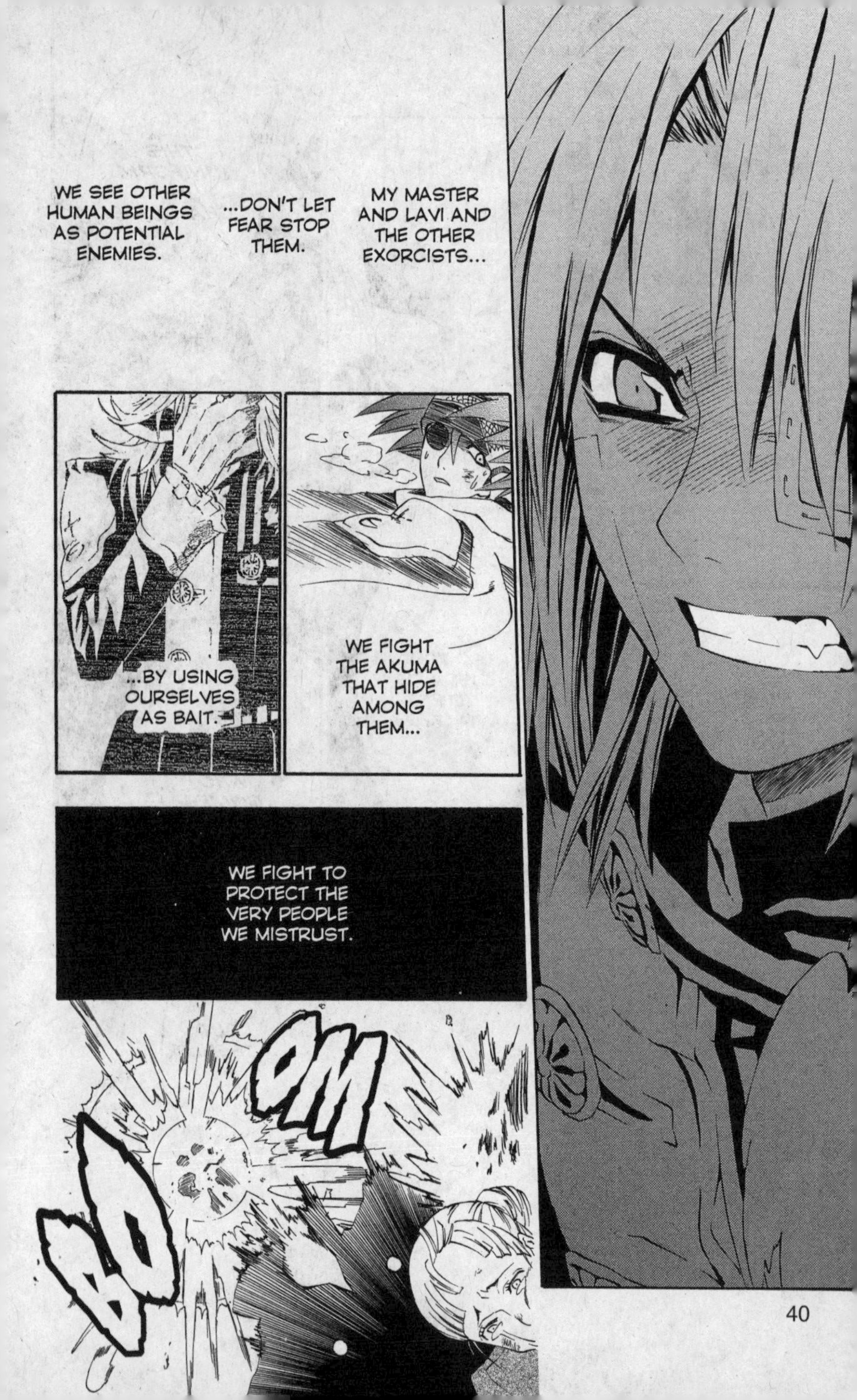
MY MASTER AND LAVI AND THE OTHER EXORCISTS...
...DON'T LET FEAR STOP THEM.
WE SEE OTHER HUMAN BEINGS AS POTENTIAL ENEMIES.
WE FIGHT THE AKUMA THAT HIDE AMONG THEM...
...BY USING OURSELVES AS BAIT.
WE FIGHT TO PROTECT THE VERY PEOPLE WE MISTRUST.
BOOM

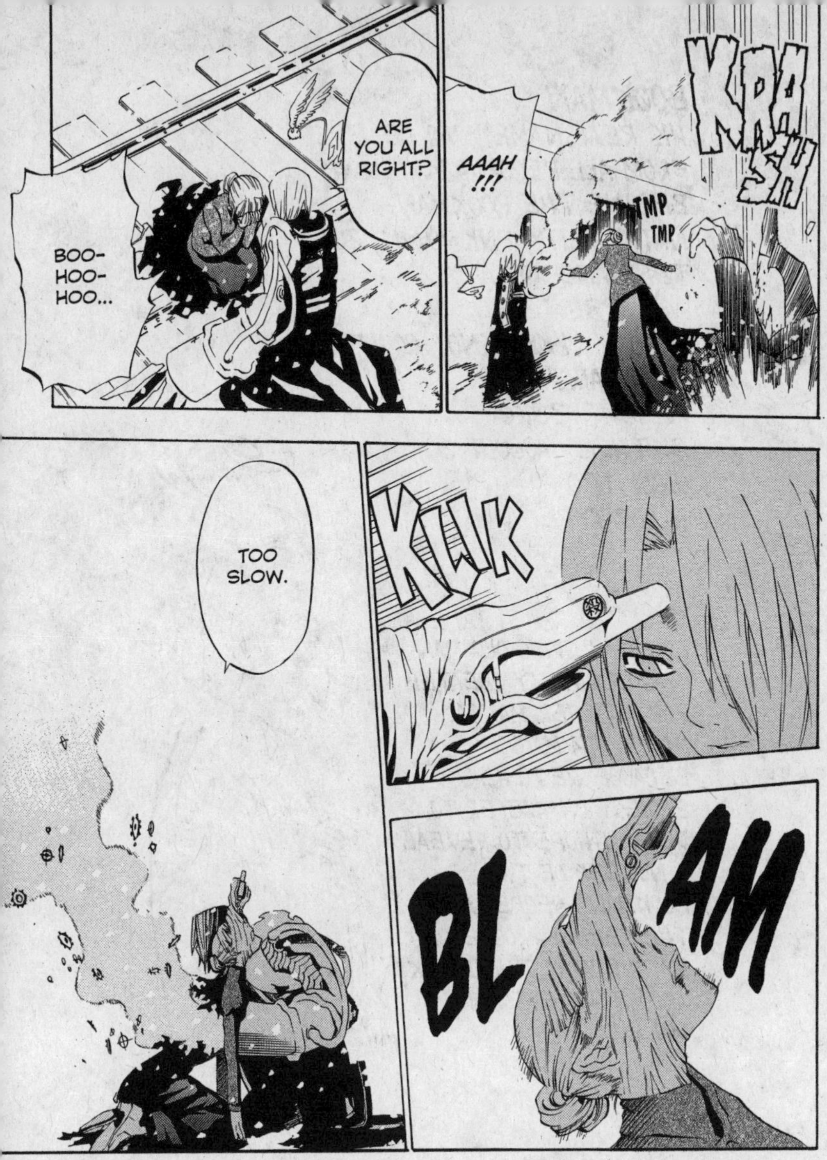
KRASH
AAAH !!!
TMP TMP
ARE YOU ALL RIGHT?
BOO-HOO-HOO...
KLIK
BLAM
TOO SLOW.

I'M GOING TO KEEP FOLLOWING THE PATH.

BUT IF I'M GOING TO WEAR THIS UNIFORM, I'LL HAVE TO BE ON MY GUARD.

BOOKMAN

HIS REAL NAME WAS DELETED FROM ALL RECORDS WHEN HE BECAME THE BOOKMAN.
NATIONALITY UNKNOWN, BUT THE SAME AS LAVI'S.
AGE 88
HEIGHT 140CM (NOT COUNTING THE HAIR)
WEIGHT 38KG
BIRTHDAY AUGUST 5
SIGN LEO
BLOOD TYPE A

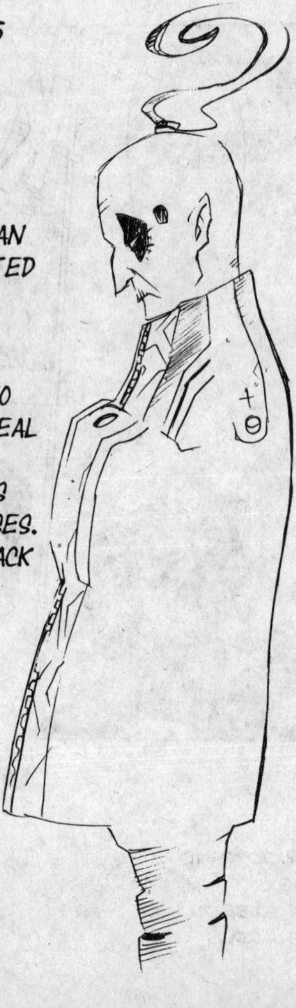

LIKE LAVI, THIS OLD MAN WAS ORIGINALLY CREATED FOR ANOTHER MANGA. I LIKE HIM MAINLY BECAUSE HE'S THE EASIEST CHARACTER TO DRAW. I HOPE TO REVEAL A NUMBER OF THE BOOKMAN'S SECRETS AS THE SERIES PROGRESSES. BY THE WAY, THE BLACK AROUND HIS EYES IS MAKEUP.

THE 29TH NIGHT: CRISIS OF THE GENERALS

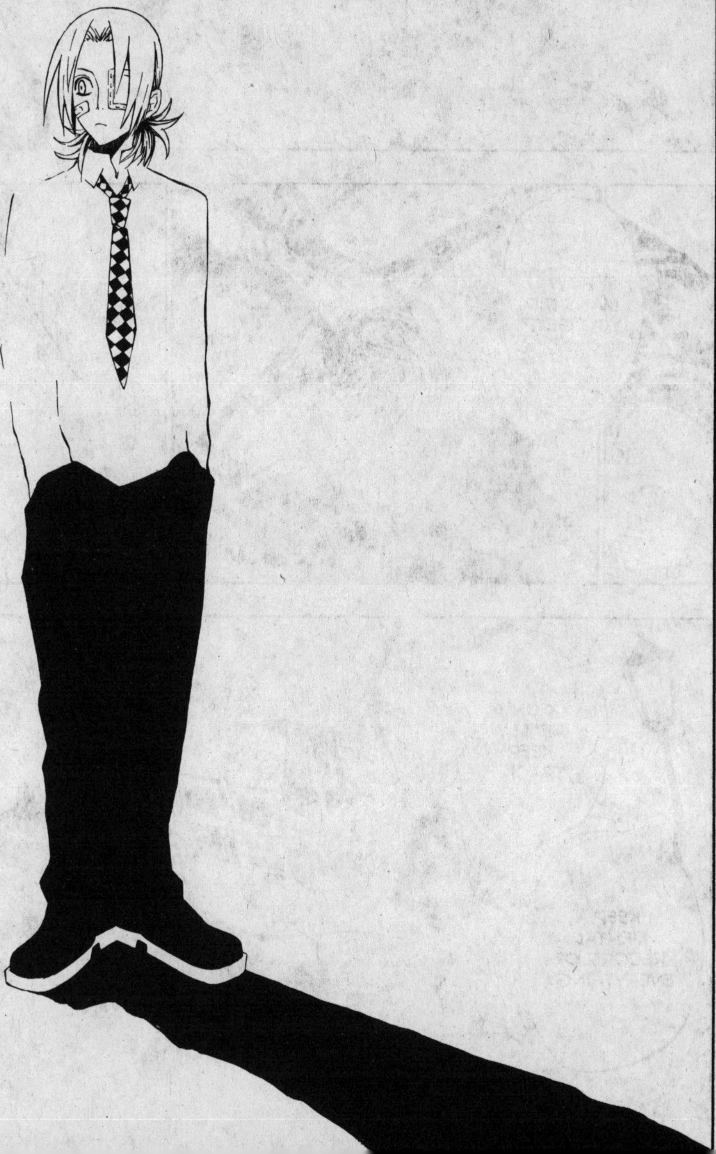

HOW MANY DID YOU GET?

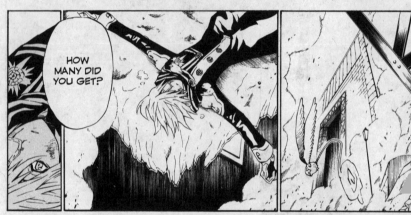

...

I DON'T REALLY KEEP TRACK.

THIRTY OR SO.

I KEEP A MENTAL RECORD OF EVERYTHING.

I GOT 37. I WIN.

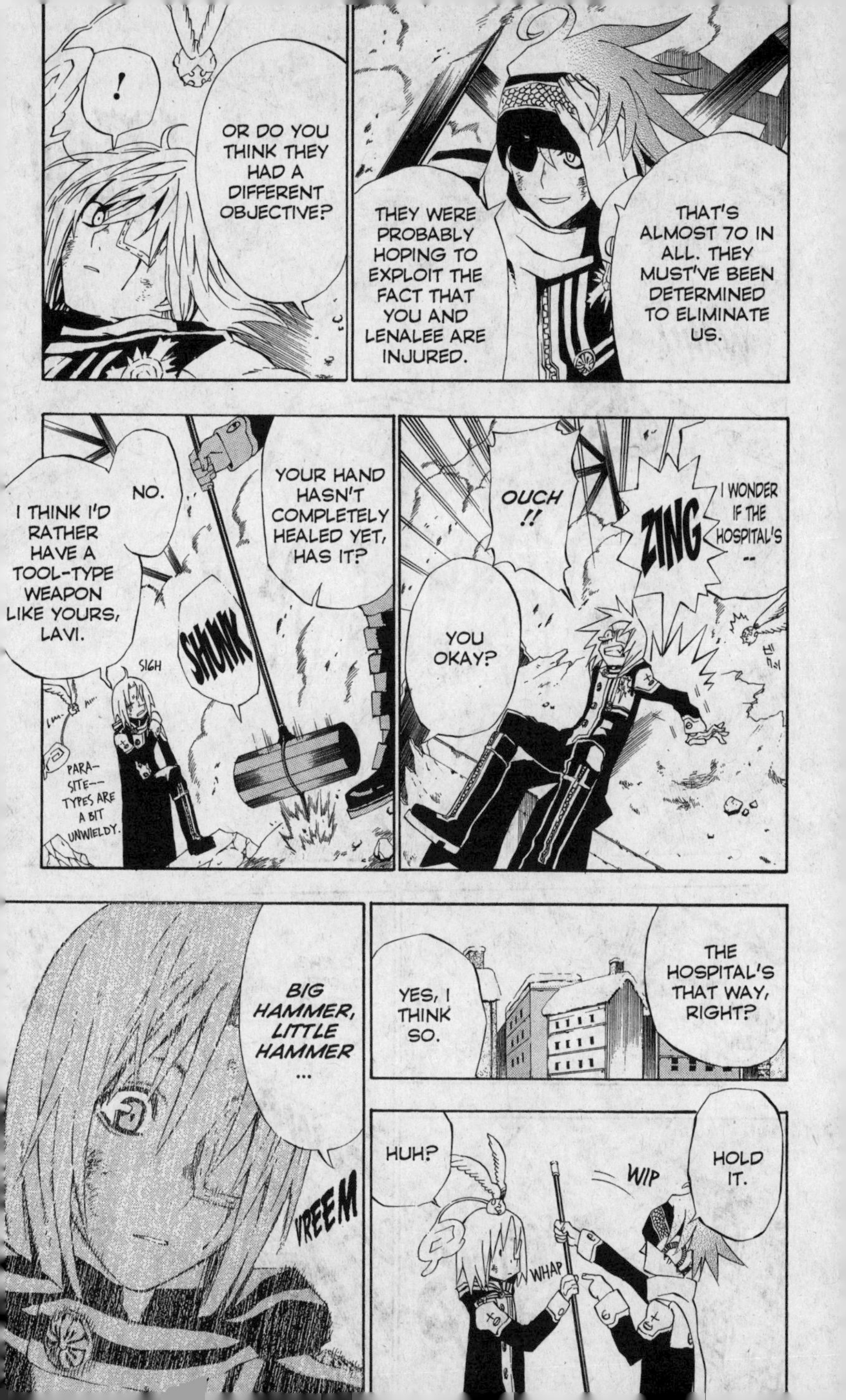
THAT'S ALMOST 70 IN ALL. THEY MUST'VE BEEN DETERMINED TO ELIMINATE US.
THEY WERE PROBABLY HOPING TO EXPLOIT THE FACT THAT YOU AND LENALEE ARE INJURED.
OR DO YOU THINK THEY HAD A DIFFERENT OBJECTIVE?
!
I WONDER IF THE HOSPITAL'S --
ZING
OUCH !!
YOU OKAY?
YOUR HAND HASN'T COMPLETELY HEALED YET, HAS IT?
NO.
I THINK I'D RATHER HAVE A TOOL-TYPE WEAPON LIKE YOURS, LAVI.
SHUNK
SIGH
PARA-SITE--TYPES ARE A BIT UNWIELDY.
THE HOSPITAL'S THAT WAY, RIGHT?
YES, I THINK SO.
HOLD IT.
WIP
HUH?
WHAP
BIG HAMMER, LITTLE HAMMER ...
VREEM

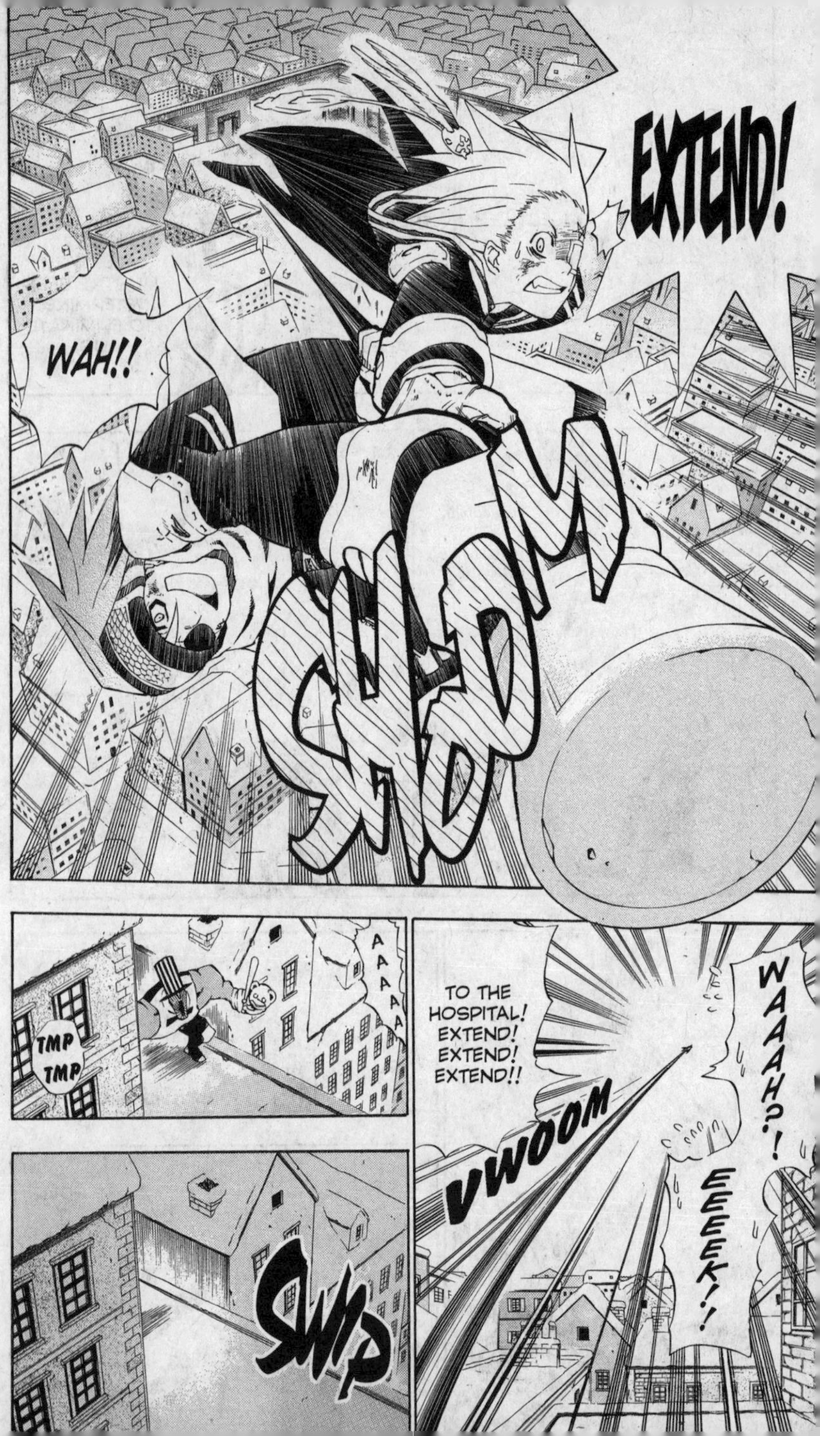
EXTEND!
WAH!!
TO THE HOSPITAL! EXTEND! EXTEND! EXTEND!!
WAAAAH?!
VWOOM
EEEEK!!
AAAAA
TMP TMP

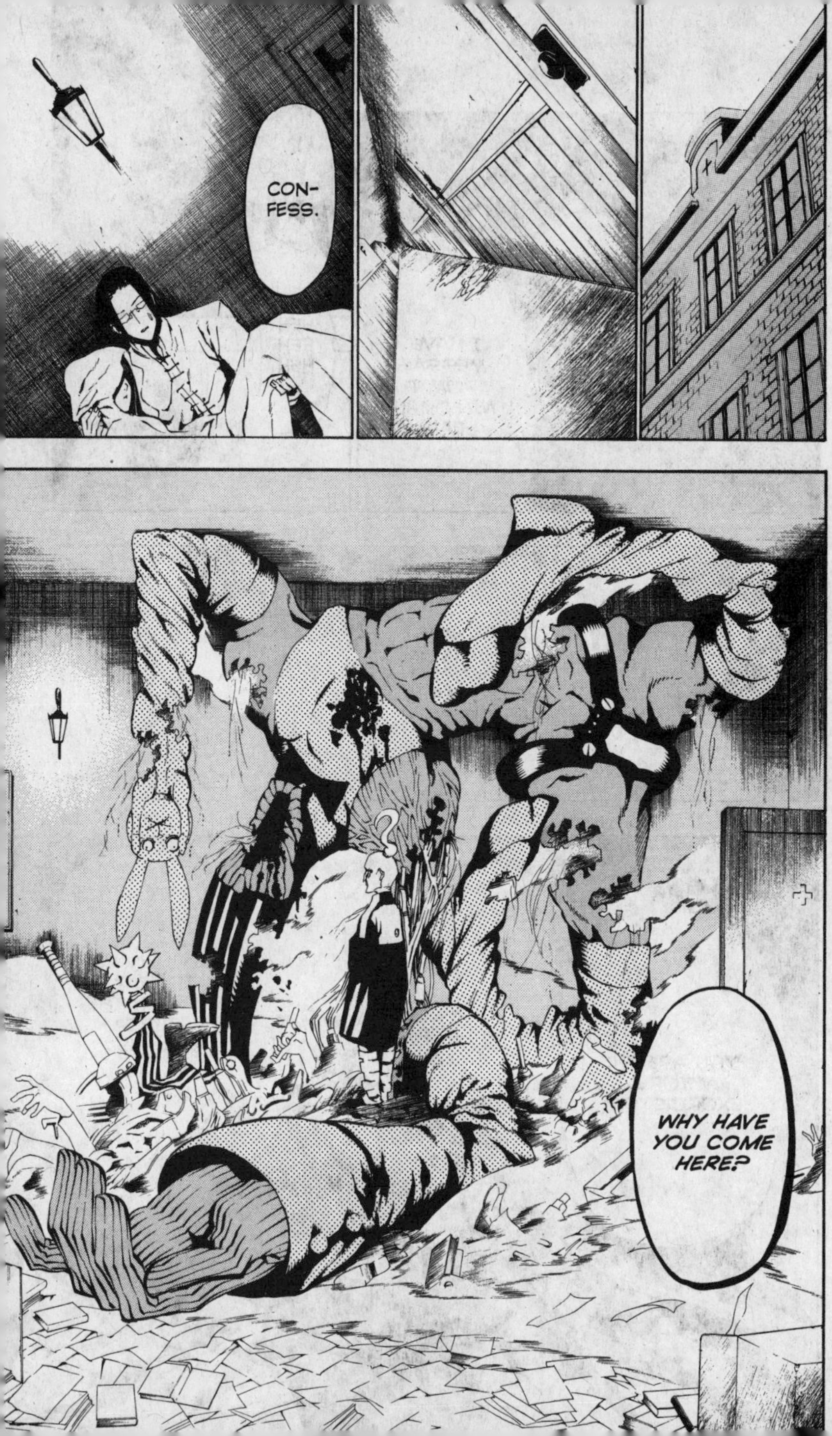
CON-
FESS.
WHY HAVE YOU COME HERE?

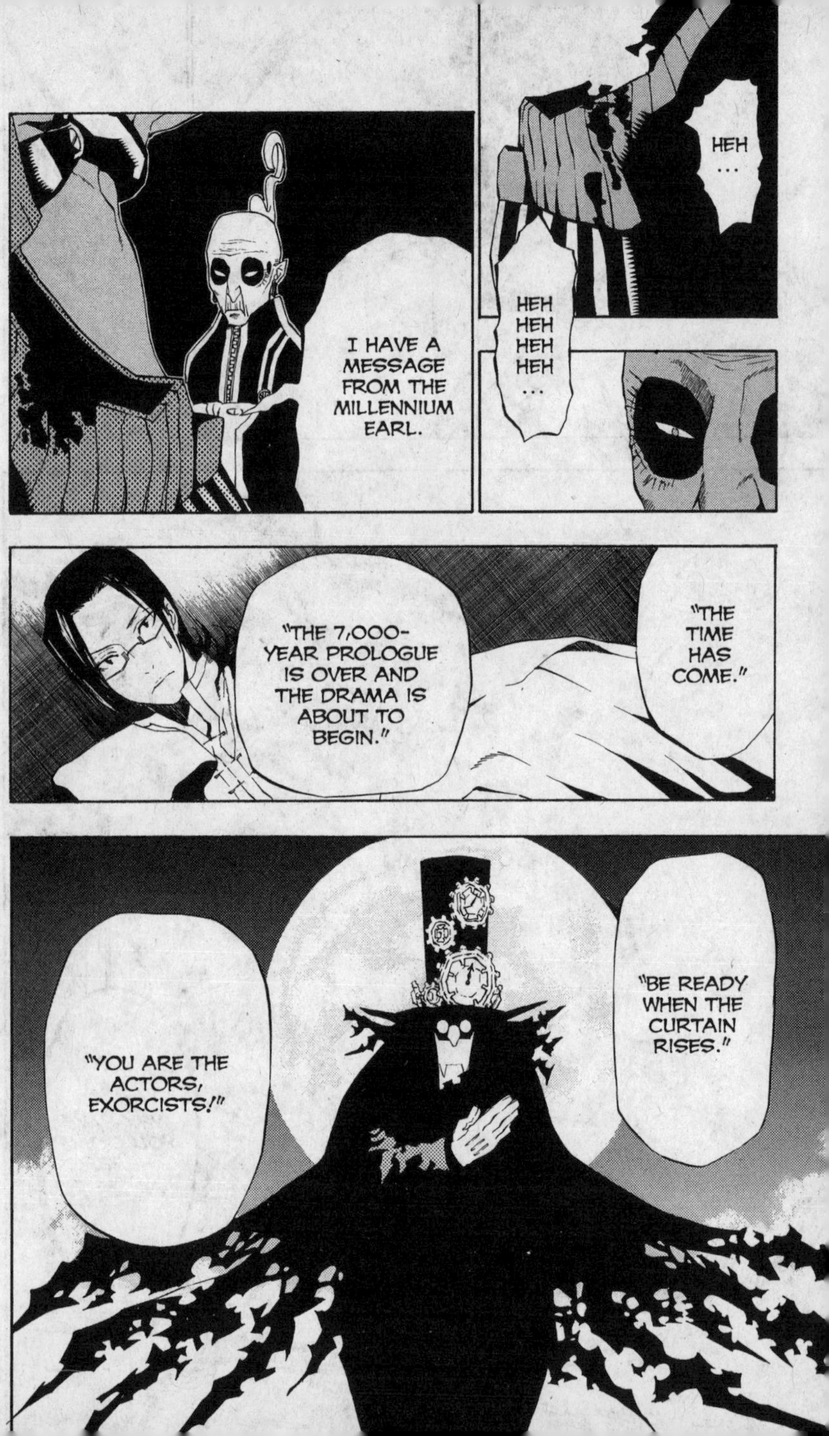
HEH ...
HEH HEH HEH HEH ...
I HAVE A MESSAGE FROM THE MILLENNIUM EARL.
"THE TIME HAS COME."
"THE 7,000-YEAR PROLOGUE IS OVER AND THE DRAMA IS ABOUT TO BEGIN."
"BE READY WHEN THE CURTAIN RISES."
"YOU ARE THE ACTORS, EXORCISTS!"

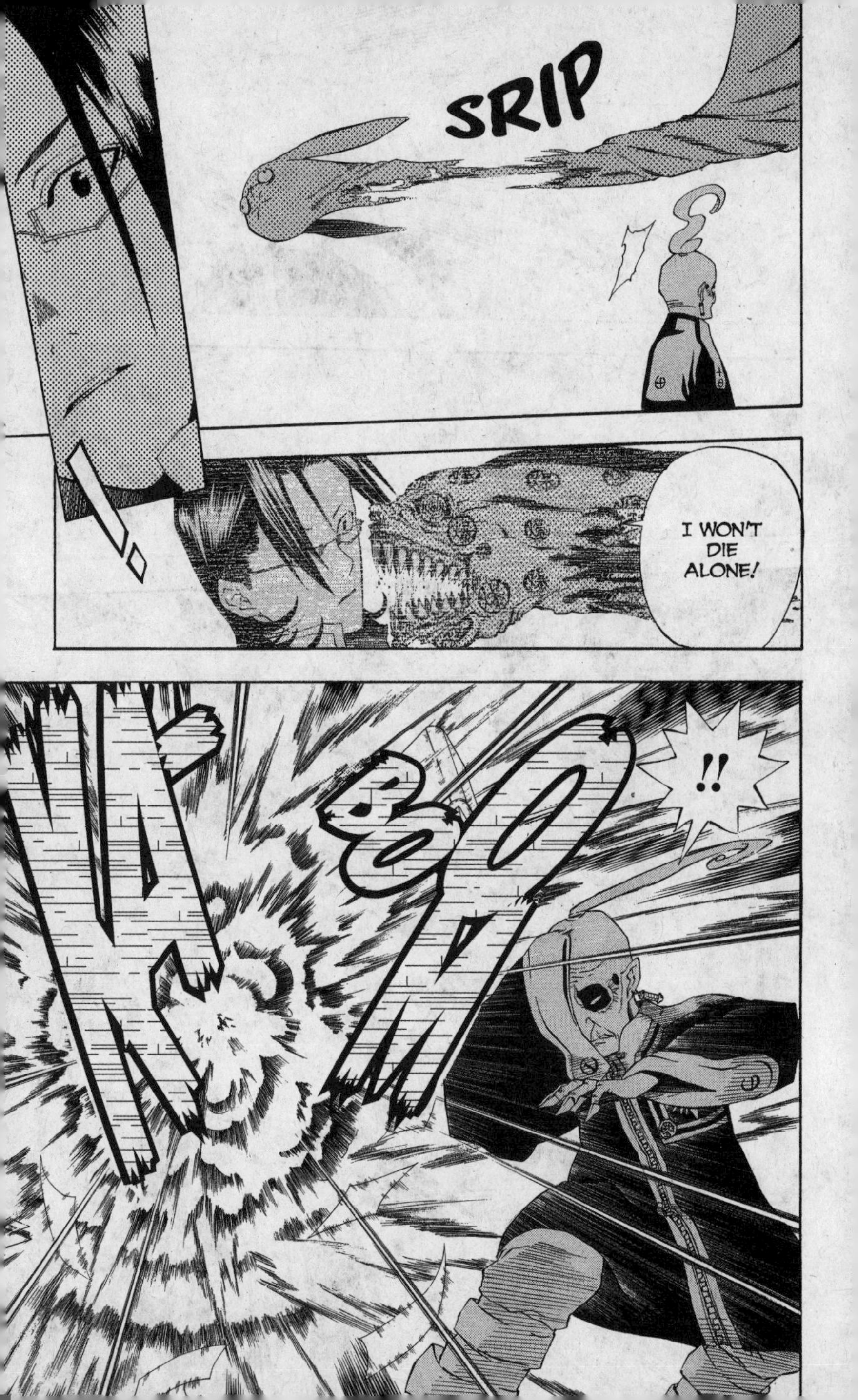
SRIP
I WON'T DIE ALONE!
!!

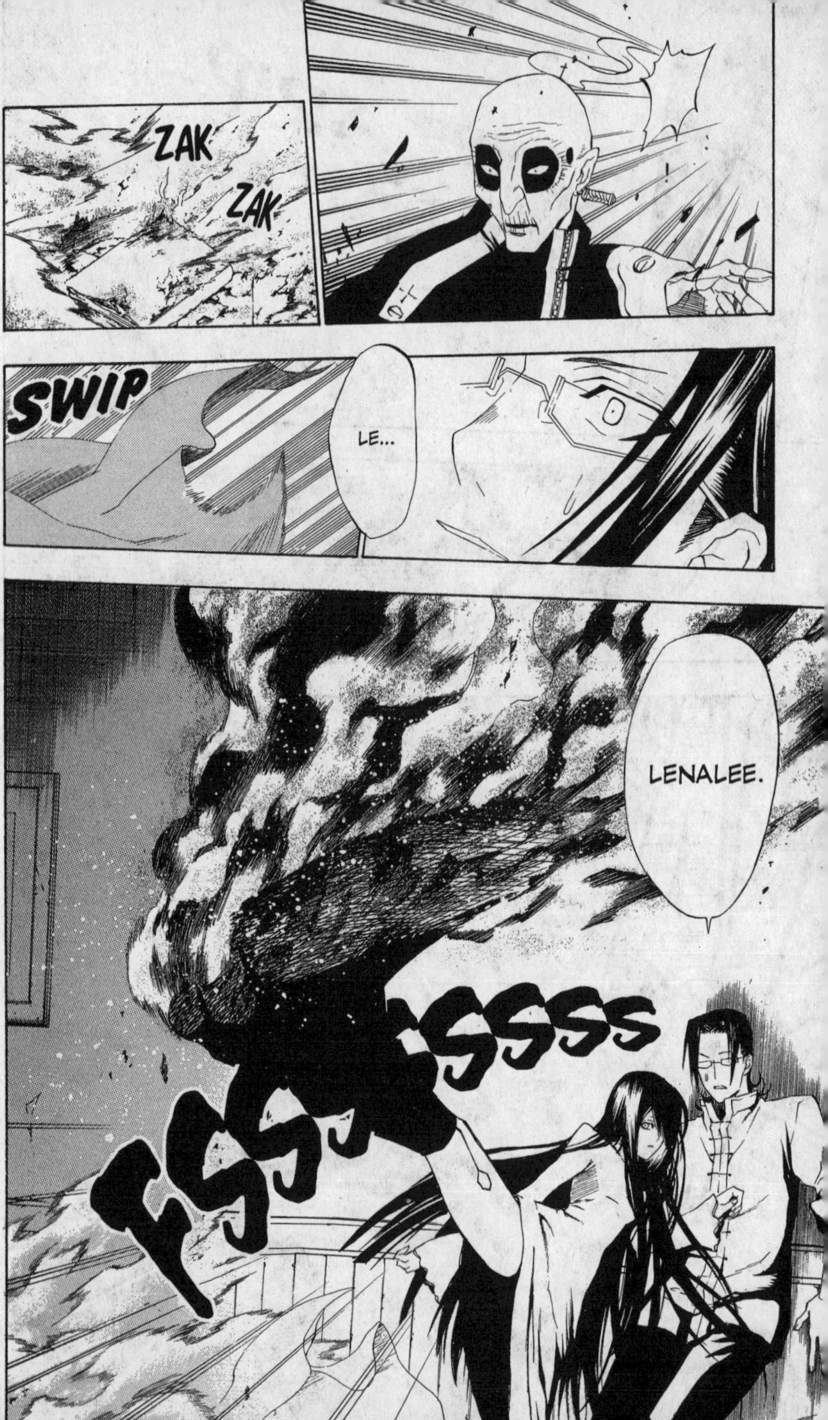
ZAK
ZAK
LE...
SWIP
LENALEE.
FSSSSSSS

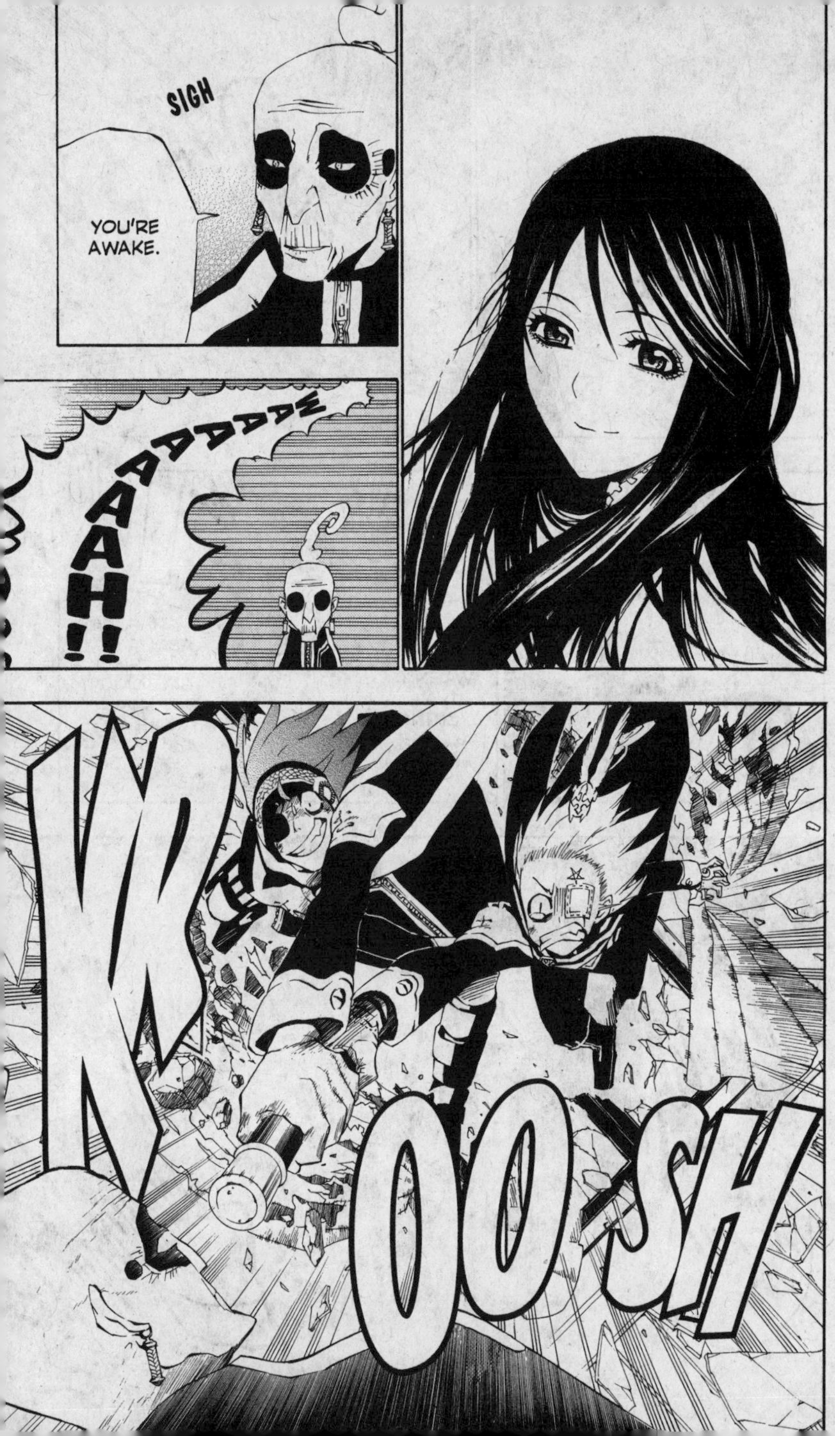
SIGH
YOU'RE AWAKE.
AAAAAAAH!!
KWOOSH

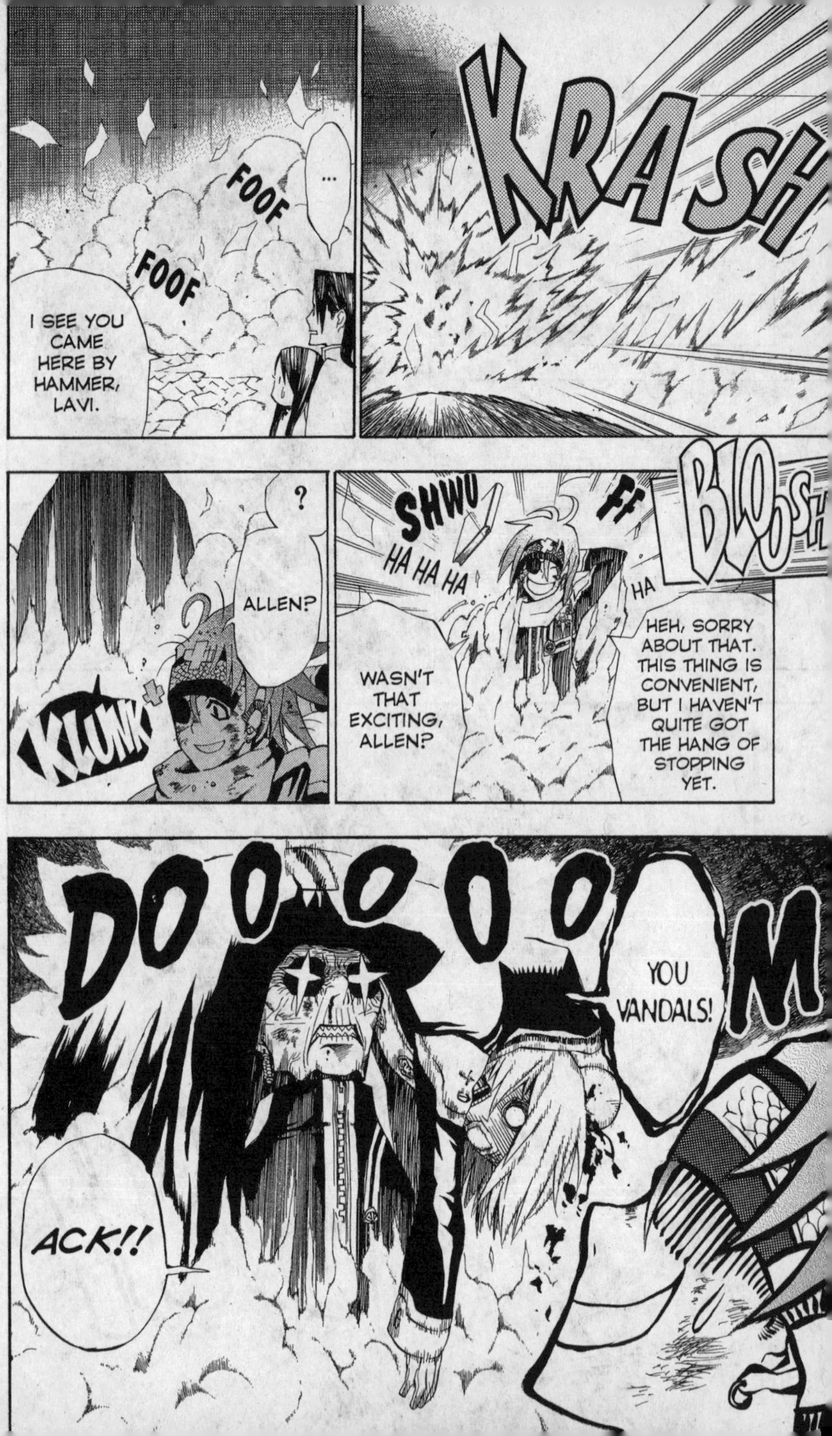
KRASH
...
FOOF
FOOF
I SEE YOU CAME HERE BY HAMMER, LAVI.
BLOOSH
SHWUFF
HA HA HA HA
HEH, SORRY ABOUT THAT. THIS THING IS CONVENIENT, BUT I HAVEN'T QUITE GOT THE HANG OF STOPPING YET.
WASN'T THAT EXCITING, ALLEN?
?
ALLEN?
KLUNK
DOOOOOOM
YOU VANDALS!
ACK!!

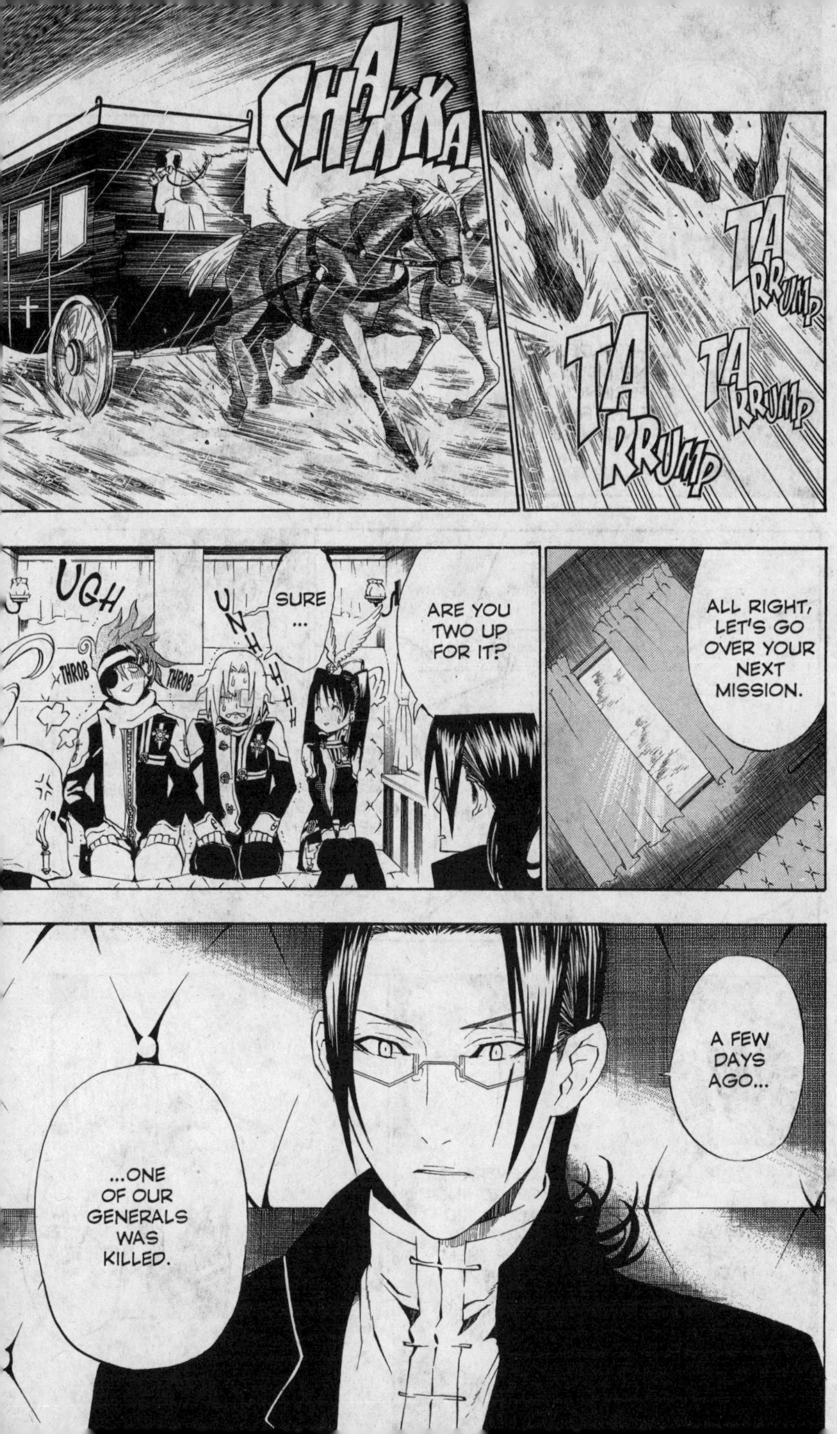
TA RRUMP
TA RRUMP
TA RRUMP
CHAKKA
ALL RIGHT, LET'S GO OVER YOUR NEXT MISSION.
ARE YOU TWO UP FOR IT?
SURE ...
UNHHHHHH
UGH
THROB
THROB
A FEW DAYS AGO...
...ONE OF OUR GENERALS WAS KILLED.

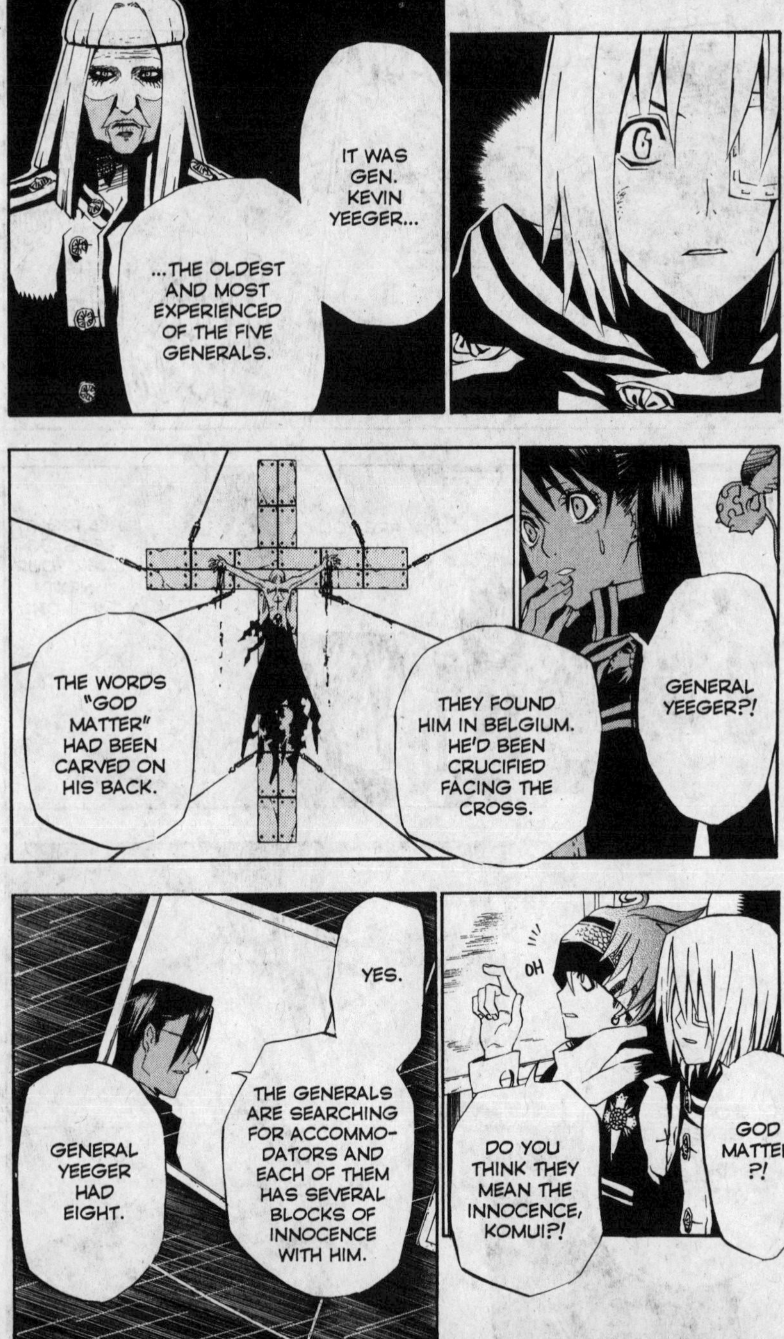
IT WAS GEN. KEVIN YEEGER...
...THE OLDEST AND MOST EXPERIENCED OF THE FIVE GENERALS.
GENERAL YEEGER?!
THEY FOUND HIM IN BELGIUM. HE'D BEEN CRUCIFIED FACING THE CROSS.
THE WORDS "GOD MATTER" HAD BEEN CARVED ON HIS BACK.
GOD MATTER?!
OH
DO YOU THINK THEY MEAN THE INNOCENCE, KOMUI?!
YES.
THE GENERALS ARE SEARCHING FOR ACCOMMODATORS AND EACH OF THEM HAS SEVERAL BLOCKS OF INNOCENCE WITH HIM.
GENERAL YEEGER HAD EIGHT.

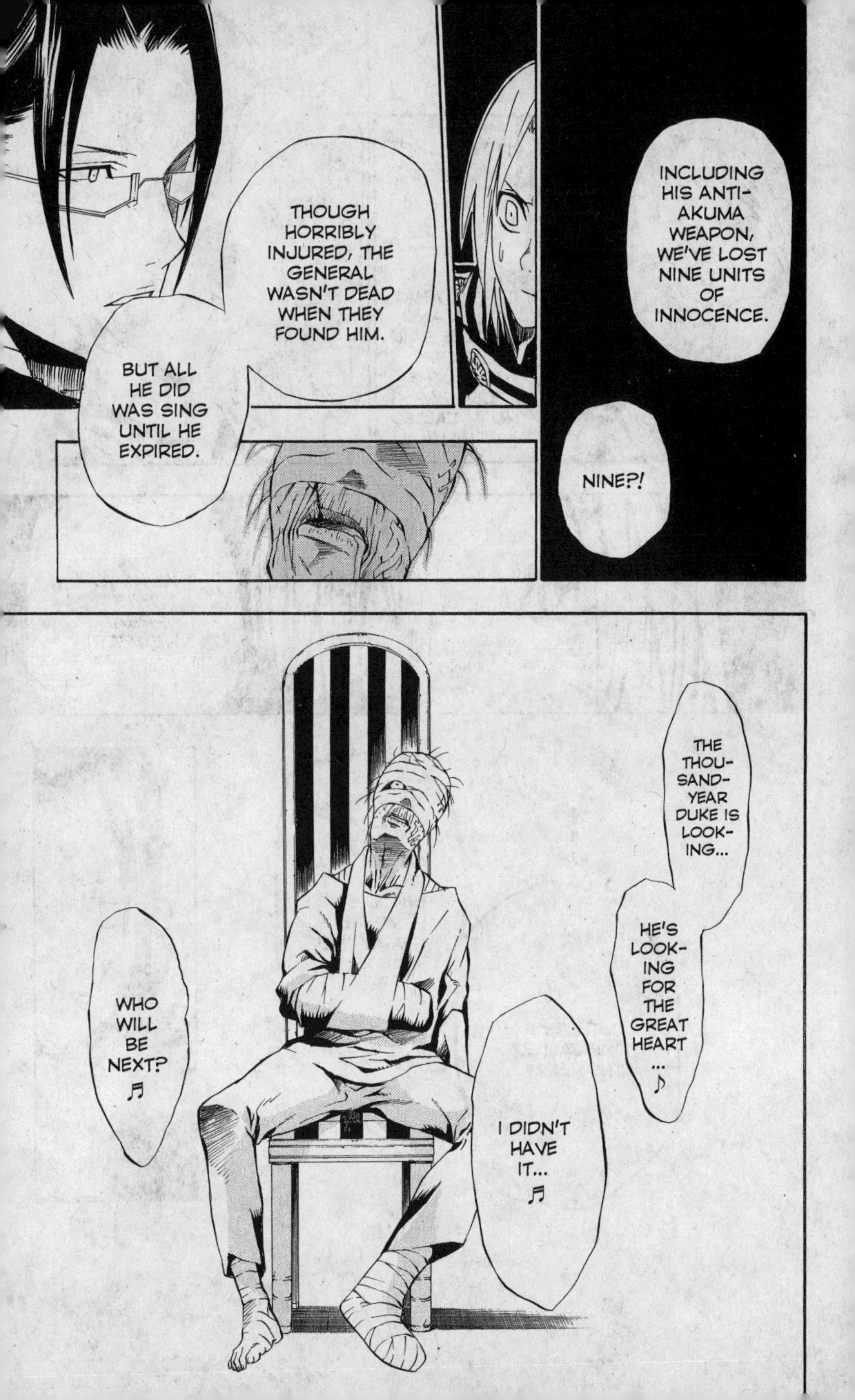
INCLUDING HIS ANTI-AKUMA WEAPON, WE'VE LOST NINE UNITS OF INNOCENCE.
NINE?!
THOUGH HORRIBLY INJURED, THE GENERAL WASN'T DEAD WHEN THEY FOUND HIM.
BUT ALL HE DID WAS SING UNTIL HE EXPIRED.
THE THOUSAND-YEAR DUKE IS LOOKING...
HE'S LOOKING FOR THE GREAT HEART... ♪
I DIDN'T HAVE IT... ♬
WHO WILL BE NEXT? ♬

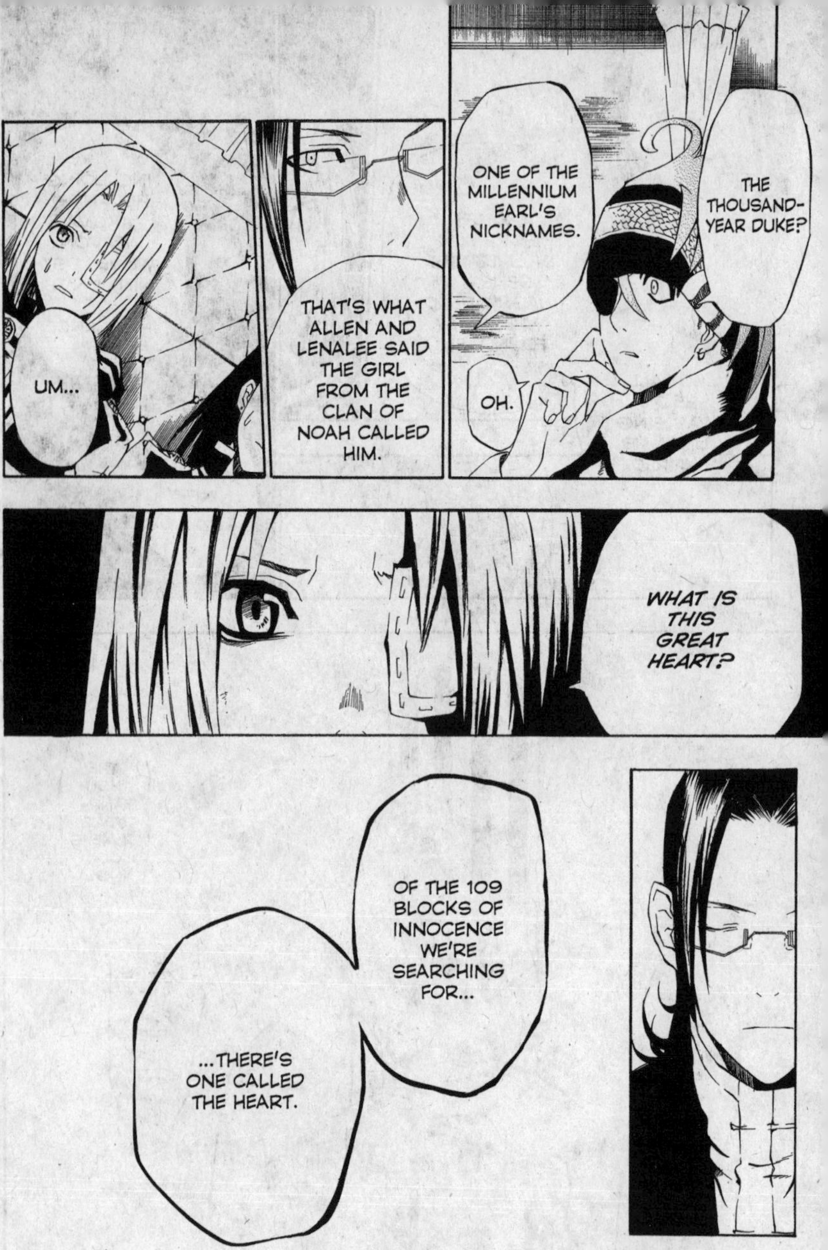
THE THOUSAND-YEAR DUKE?
ONE OF THE MILLENNIUM EARL'S NICKNAMES.
OH.
THAT'S WHAT ALLEN AND LENALEE SAID THE GIRL FROM THE CLAN OF NOAH CALLED HIM.
UM...
WHAT IS THIS GREAT HEART?
OF THE 109 BLOCKS OF INNOCENCE WE'RE SEARCHING FOR...
...THERE'S ONE CALLED THE HEART.

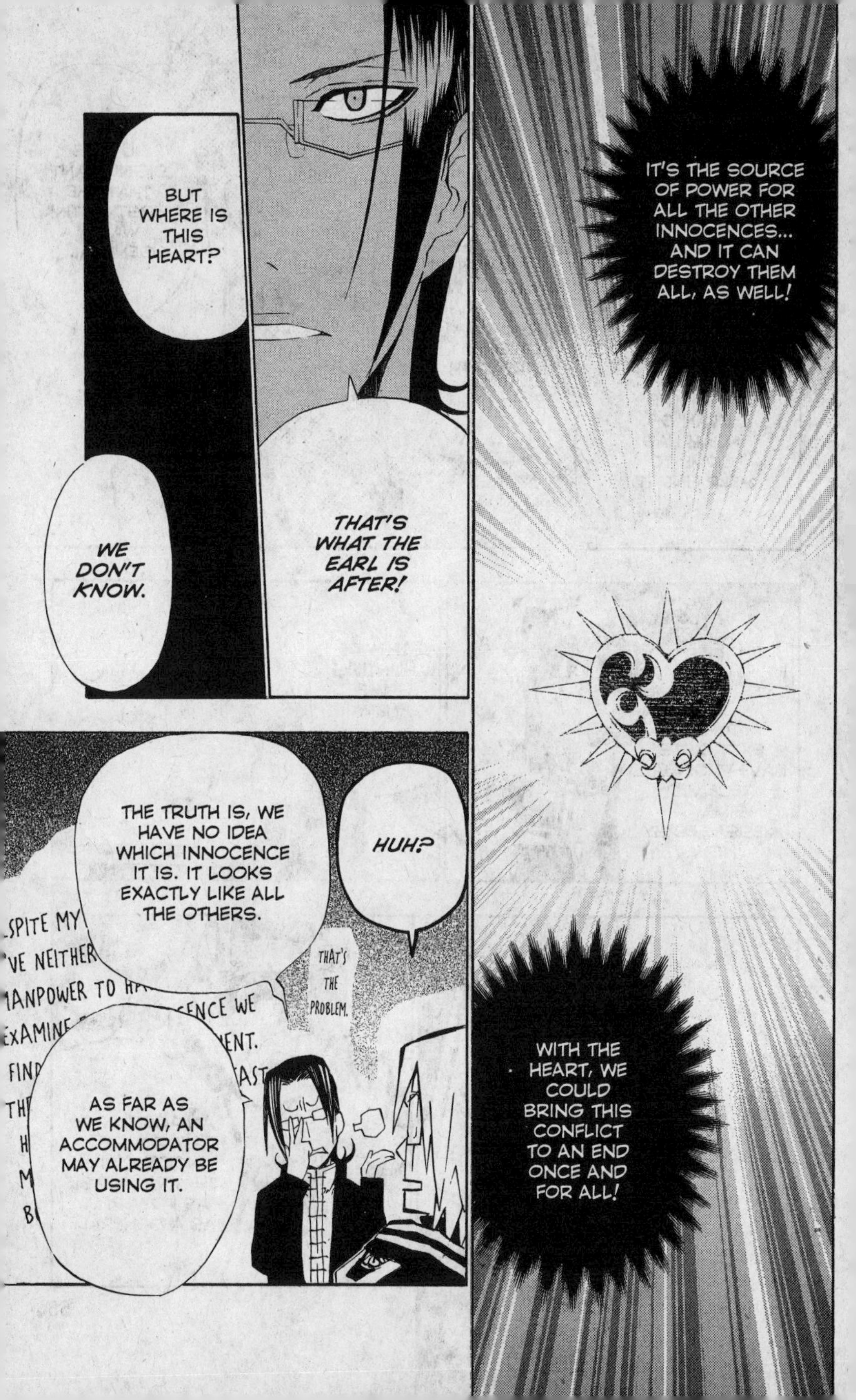
IT'S THE SOURCE OF POWER FOR ALL THE OTHER INNOCENCES... AND IT CAN DESTROY THEM ALL, AS WELL!
WITH THE HEART, WE COULD BRING THIS CONFLICT TO AN END ONCE AND FOR ALL!
THAT'S WHAT THE EARL IS AFTER!
BUT WHERE IS THIS HEART?
WE DON'T KNOW.
HUH?
THE TRUTH IS, WE HAVE NO IDEA WHICH INNOCENCE IT IS. IT LOOKS EXACTLY LIKE ALL THE OTHERS.
THAT'S THE PROBLEM.
AS FAR AS WE KNOW, AN ACCOMMODATOR MAY ALREADY BE USING IT.

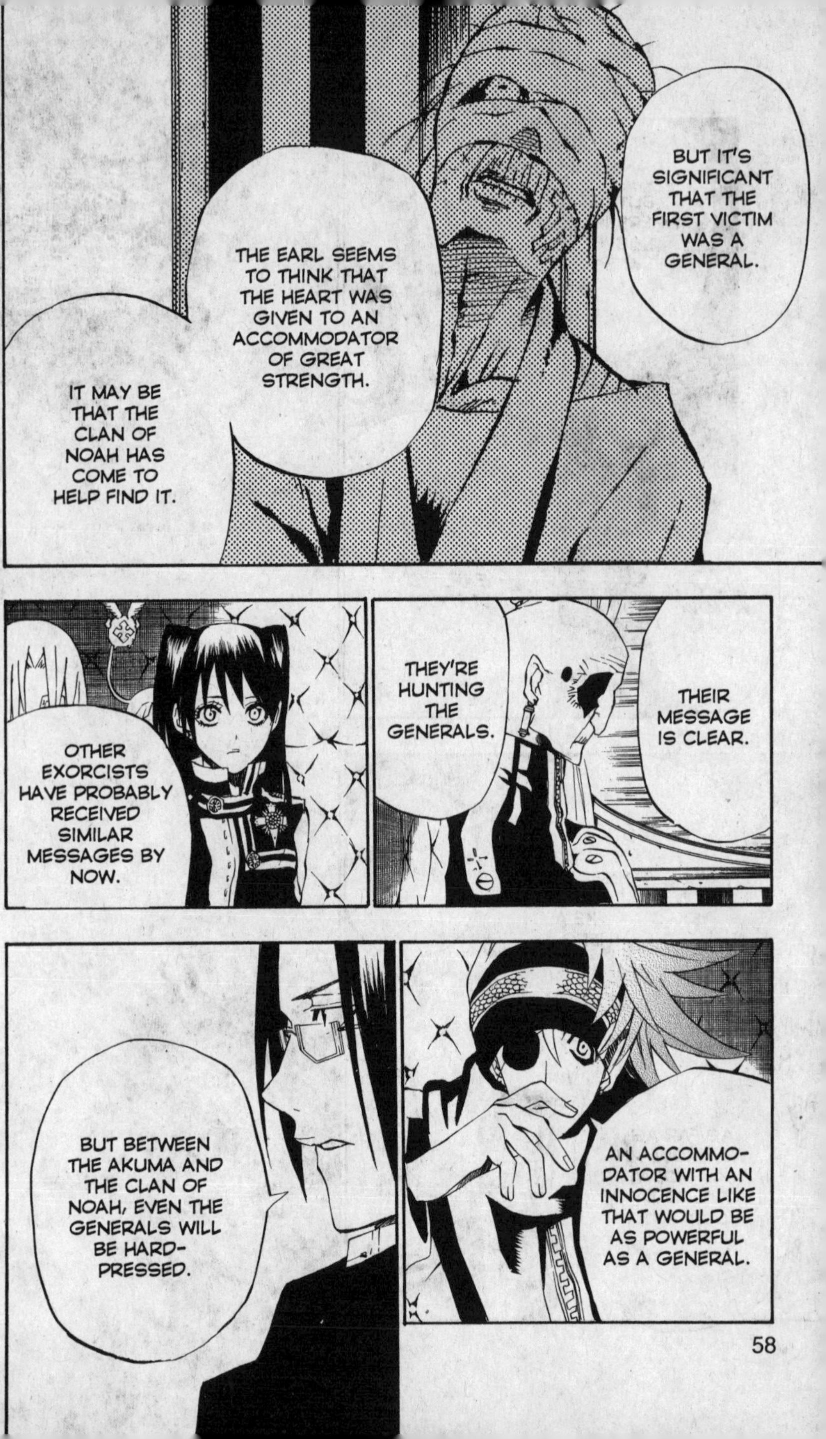
BUT IT'S SIGNIFICANT THAT THE FIRST VICTIM WAS A GENERAL.
THE EARL SEEMS TO THINK THAT THE HEART WAS GIVEN TO AN ACCOMMODATOR OF GREAT STRENGTH.
IT MAY BE THAT THE CLAN OF NOAH HAS COME TO HELP FIND IT.
THEIR MESSAGE IS CLEAR.
THEY'RE HUNTING THE GENERALS.
OTHER EXORCISTS HAVE PROBABLY RECEIVED SIMILAR MESSAGES BY NOW.
AN ACCOMMO-DATOR WITH AN INNOCENCE LIKE THAT WOULD BE AS POWERFUL AS A GENERAL.
BUT BETWEEN THE AKUMA AND THE CLAN OF NOAH, EVEN THE GENERALS WILL BE HARD-PRESSED.

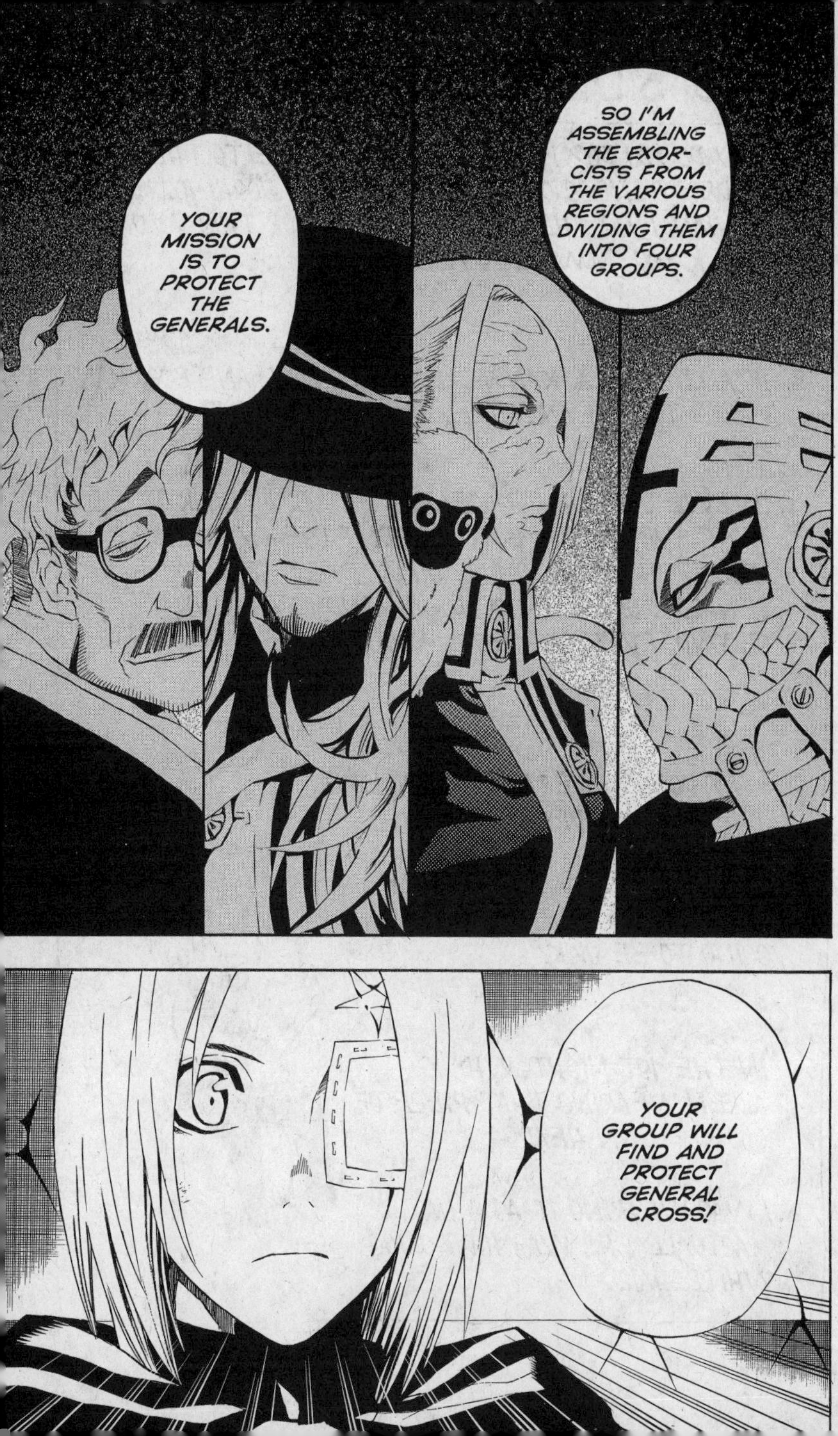
SO I'M ASSEMBLING THE EXOR-CISTS FROM THE VARIOUS REGIONS AND DIVIDING THEM INTO FOUR GROUPS.
YOUR MISSION IS TO PROTECT THE GENERALS.
YOUR GROUP WILL FIND AND PROTECT GENERAL CROSS!

KOMUI'S DISCUSSION ROOM VOL. 1

★ HOW DO YOU DO? I'M ALLEN WALKER. DUE TO THE SUDDEN ILLNESS OF CREATOR KATSURA HOSHINO, I'LL BE HANDLING THE DISCUSSION ROOM FOR THIS VOLUME. THANK YOU. NOW LET'S BEGIN.

Q. IF ALLEN, LALA, KANDA, LENALEE, LAVI, AND BOOKMAN WERE TO ARM-WRESTLE, WHO WOULD WIN?

A. CAN WE USE OUR INNOCENCES? IF SO, I THINK I MIGHT WIN. :) OH, BUT I COULDN'T USE MY FULL STRENGTH AGAINST THE GIRLS, SO EITHER LENALEE OR LALA WOULD WIN AND I'D COME IN SECOND. EVERYONE ELSE WOULD BE BELOW ME. :)

Q. WHY DOES GENERAL CROSS DISLIKE THE BLACK ORDER?

A. I REALLY DON'T WANT TO TALK ABOUT MY MASTER. I THINK I'M GOING TO BE SICK.

Q. IN THE 1ST NIGHT, WHY IS ALLEN WEARING THAT PIECE OF CLOTH ON HIS HEAD?

A. I WAS WEARING IT AS A HAT. (ACTUALLY, HE WAS HIDING HIS WHITE HAIR.)

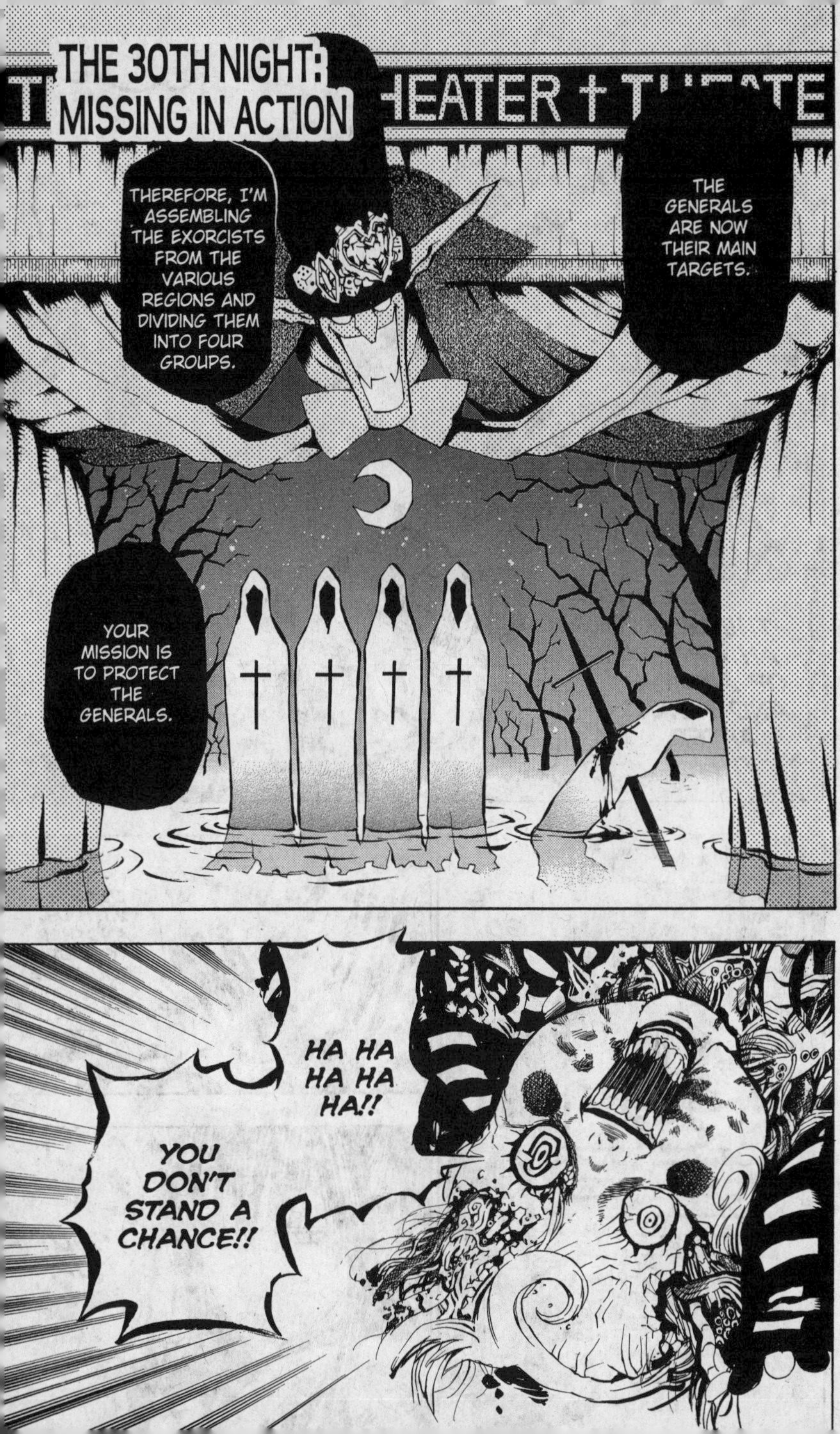
THE 30TH NIGHT: MISSING IN ACTION
HEATER † THEATE
THE GENERALS ARE NOW THEIR MAIN TARGETS.
THEREFORE, I'M ASSEMBLING THE EXORCISTS FROM THE VARIOUS REGIONS AND DIVIDING THEM INTO FOUR GROUPS.
YOUR MISSION IS TO PROTECT THE GENERALS.
HA HA HA HA HA!!
YOU DON'T STAND A CHANCE!!

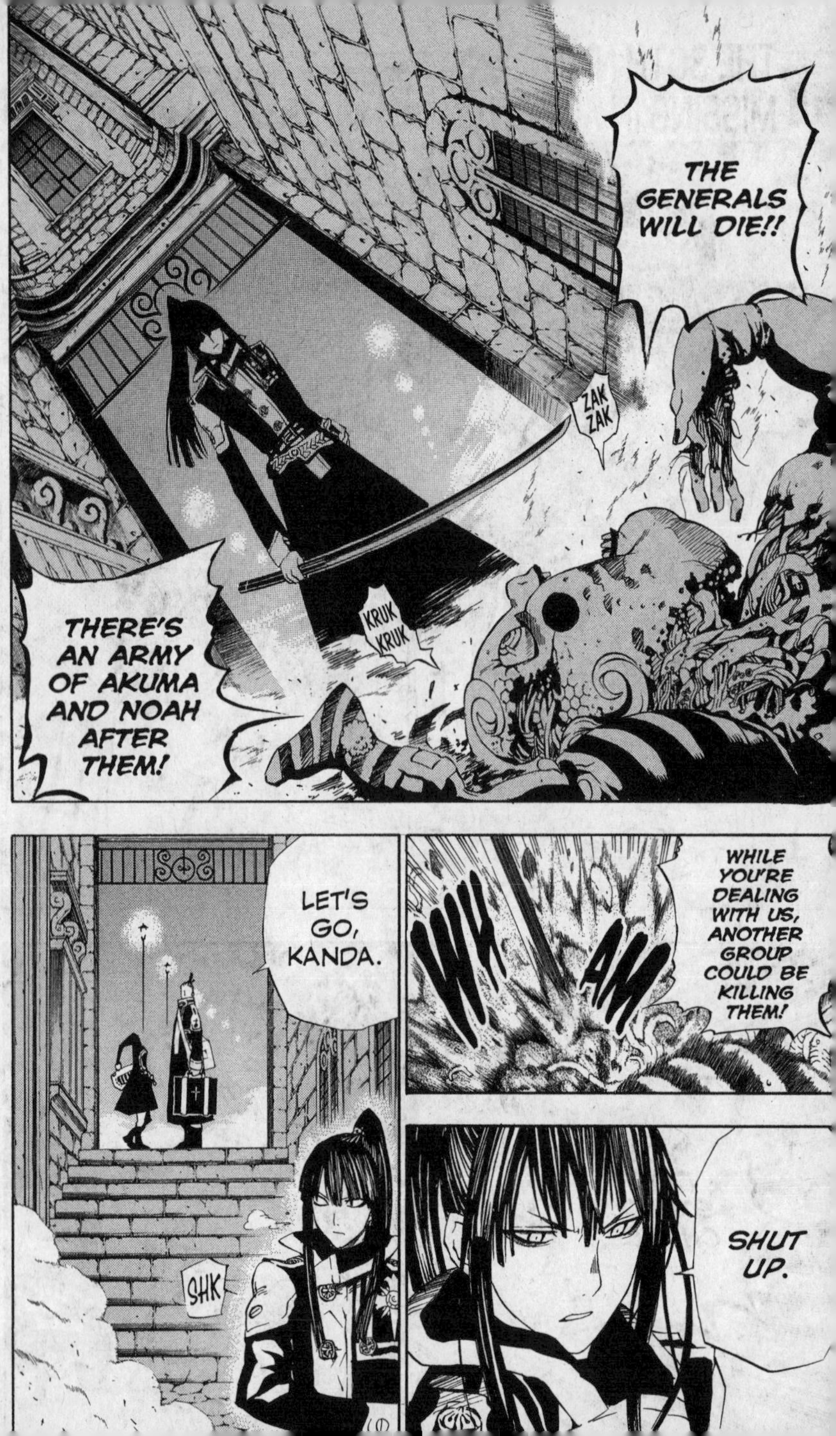
THE GENERALS WILL DIE!!
ZAK ZAK
KRUK KRUK
THERE'S AN ARMY OF AKUMA AND NOAH AFTER THEM!
WHILE YOU'RE DEALING WITH US, ANOTHER GROUP COULD BE KILLING THEM!
WHAM
SHUT UP.
LET'S GO, KANDA.
SHK

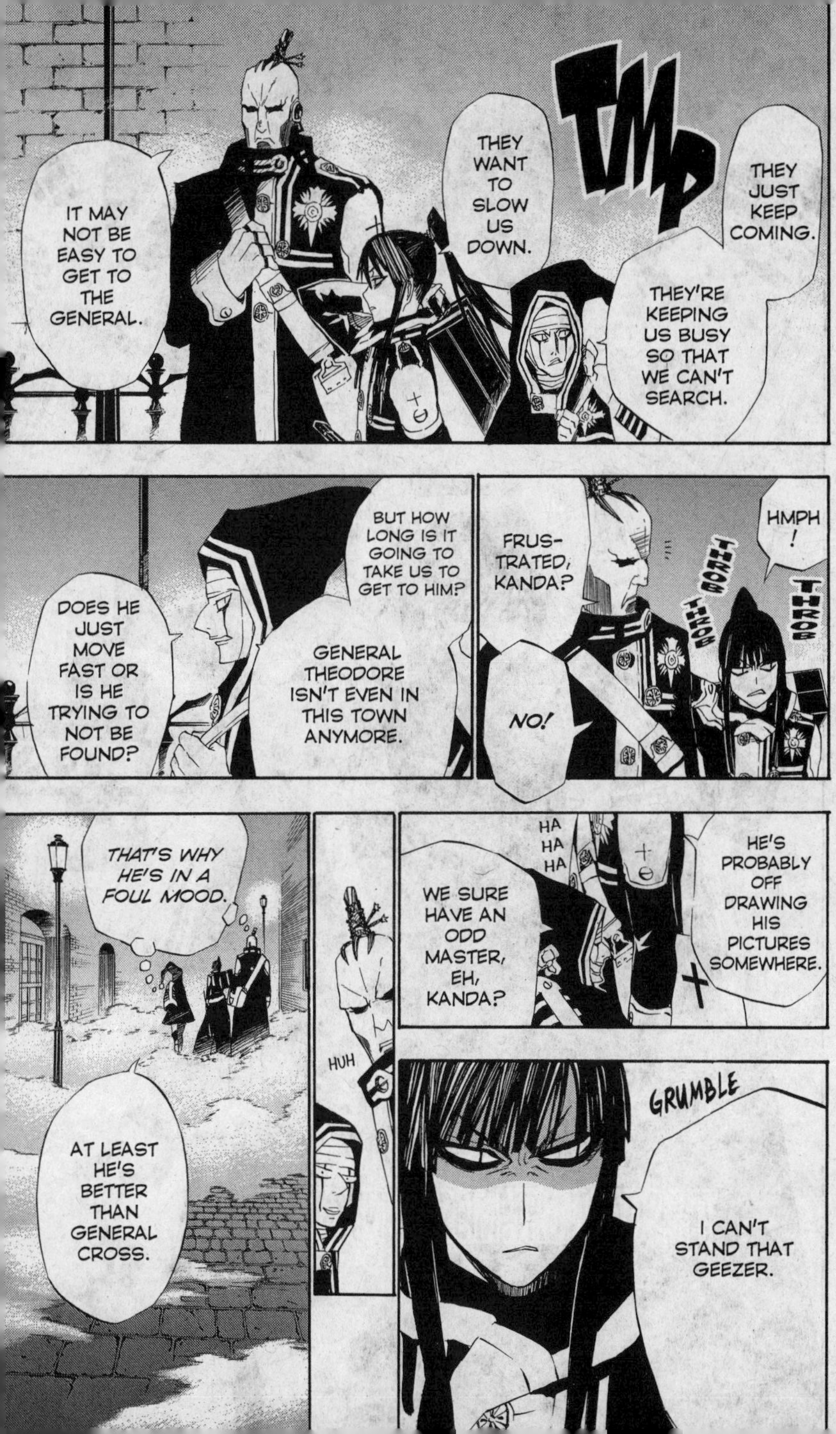
TMP
THEY JUST KEEP COMING.
THEY'RE KEEPING US BUSY SO THAT WE CAN'T SEARCH.
THEY WANT TO SLOW US DOWN.
IT MAY NOT BE EASY TO GET TO THE GENERAL.
HMPH!
THROB THROB THROB
FRUS-TRATED, KANDA?
NO!
BUT HOW LONG IS IT GOING TO TAKE US TO GET TO HIM?
GENERAL THEODORE ISN'T EVEN IN THIS TOWN ANYMORE.
DOES HE JUST MOVE FAST OR IS HE TRYING TO NOT BE FOUND?
HE'S PROBABLY OFF DRAWING HIS PICTURES SOMEWHERE.
HA HA HA
WE SURE HAVE AN ODD MASTER, EH, KANDA?
GRUMBLE
I CAN'T STAND THAT GEEZER.
HUH
THAT'S WHY HE'S IN A FOUL MOOD.
AT LEAST HE'S BETTER THAN GENERAL CROSS.

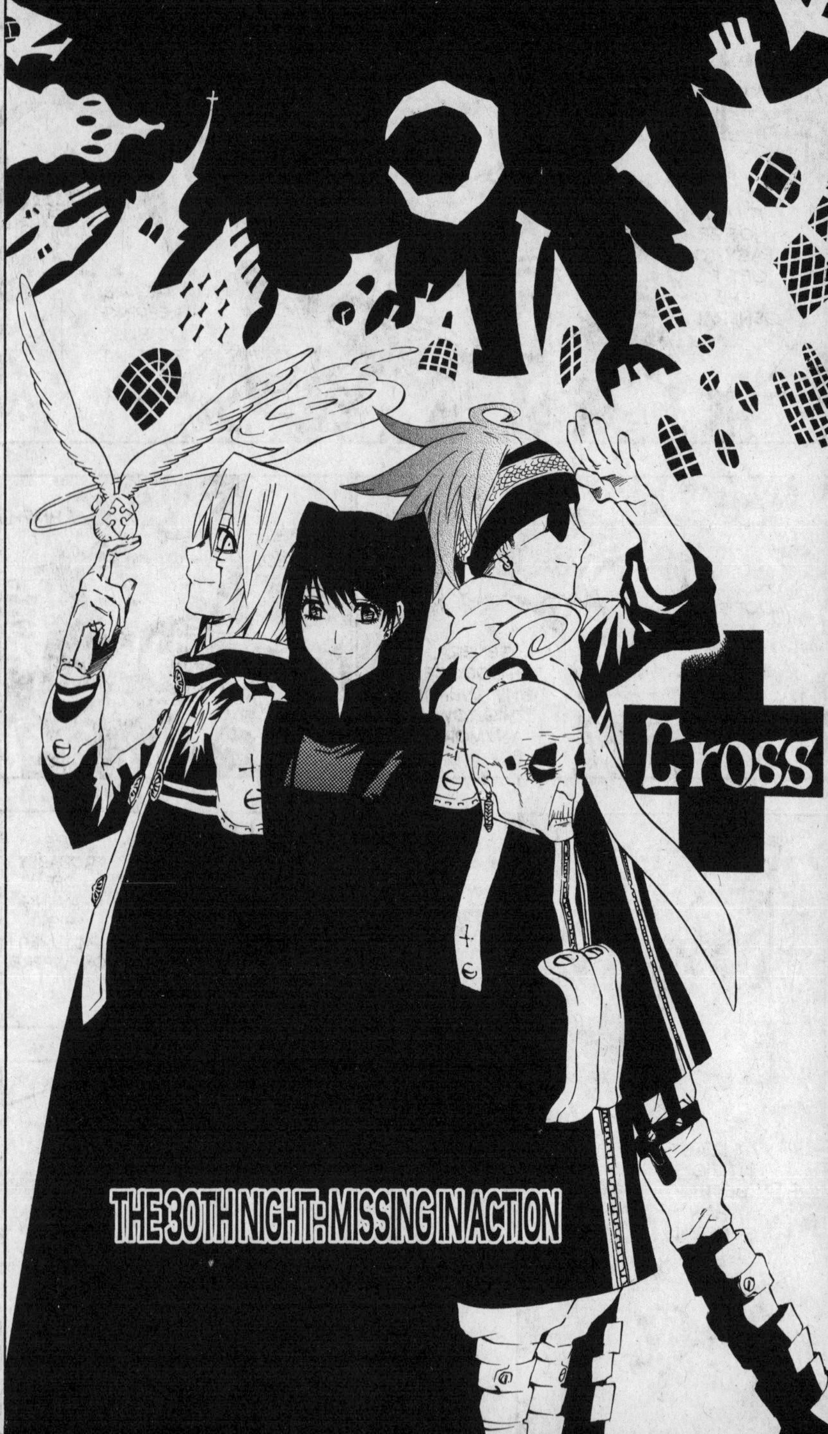
Cross
THE 30TH NIGHT: MISSING IN ACTION

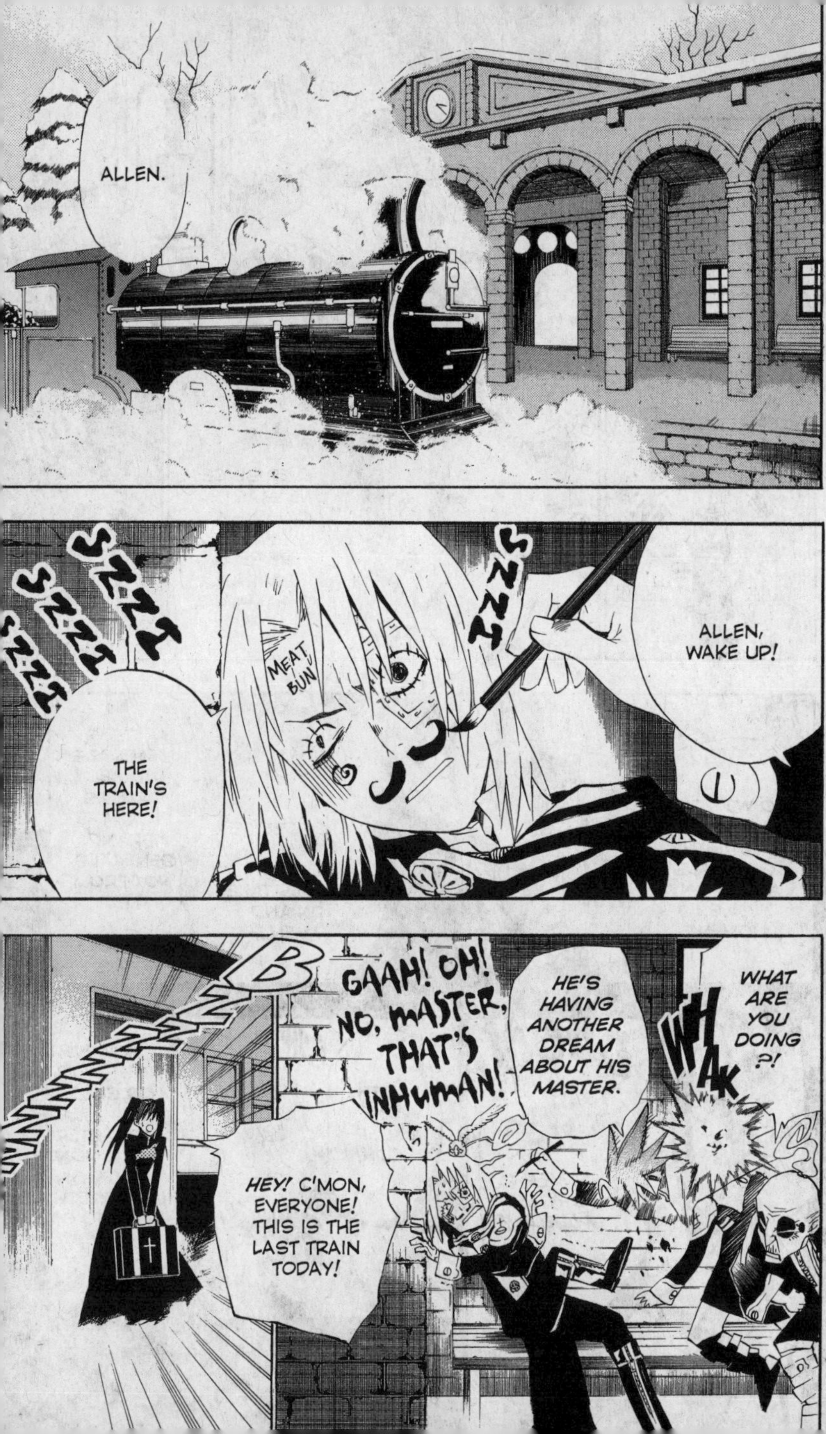
ALLEN.
ALLEN, WAKE UP!
MEAT BUN
THE TRAIN'S HERE!
WHAT ARE YOU DOING?!
WHAK
HE'S HAVING ANOTHER DREAM ABOUT HIS MASTER.
GAAH! OH! NO, MASTER, THAT'S INHUMAN!
HEY! C'MON, EVERYONE! THIS IS THE LAST TRAIN TODAY!

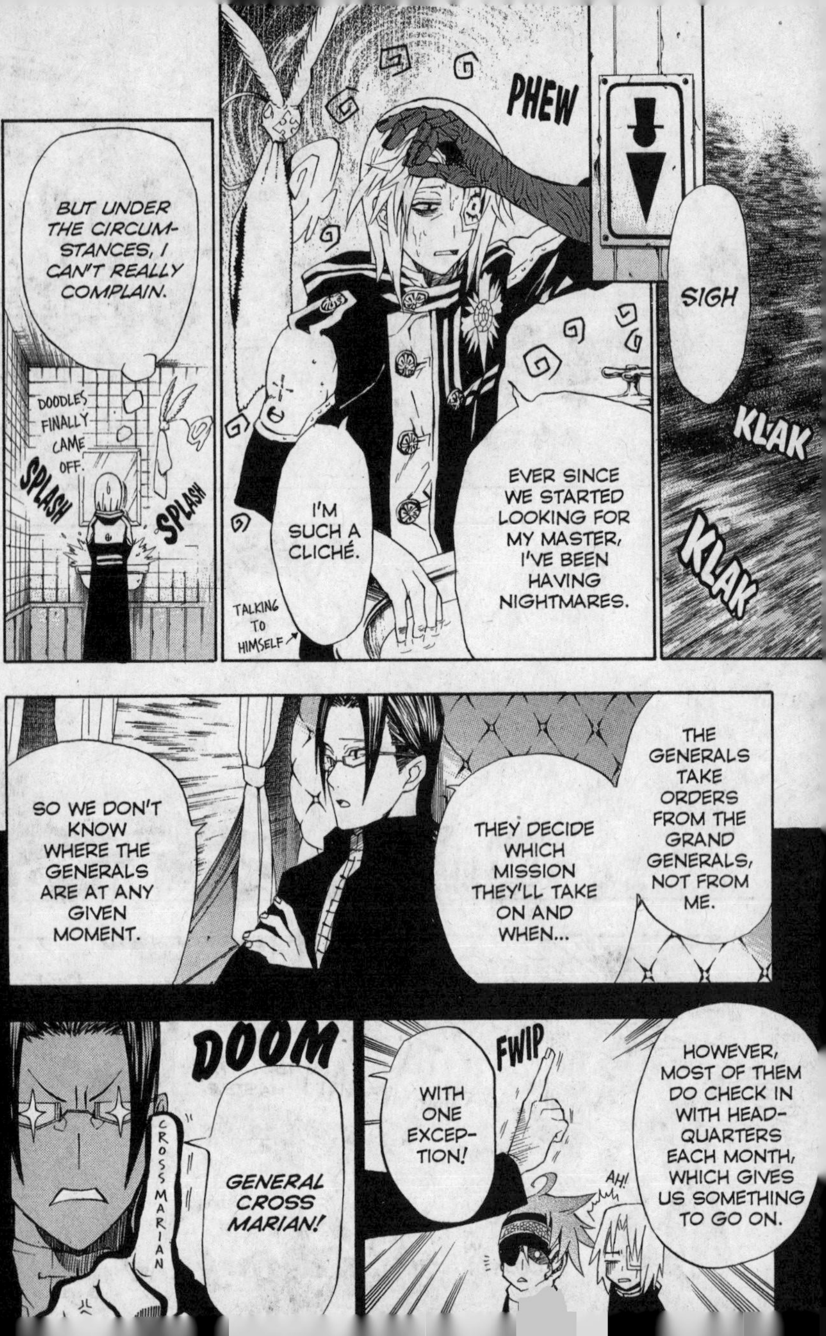
KLAK
KLAK
SIGH
PHEW
EVER SINCE WE STARTED LOOKING FOR MY MASTER, I'VE BEEN HAVING NIGHTMARES.
I'M SUCH A CLICHÉ.
TALKING TO HIMSELF
BUT UNDER THE CIRCUM-STANCES, I CAN'T REALLY COMPLAIN.
DOODLES FINALLY CAME OFF.
SPLASH
SPLASH
THE GENERALS TAKE ORDERS FROM THE GRAND GENERALS, NOT FROM ME.
THEY DECIDE WHICH MISSION THEY'LL TAKE ON AND WHEN...
SO WE DON'T KNOW WHERE THE GENERALS ARE AT ANY GIVEN MOMENT.
HOWEVER, MOST OF THEM DO CHECK IN WITH HEAD-QUARTERS EACH MONTH, WHICH GIVES US SOMETHING TO GO ON.
FWIP
WITH ONE EXCEP-TION!
AH!
DOOM
GENERAL CROSS MARIAN!
CROSS MARIAN

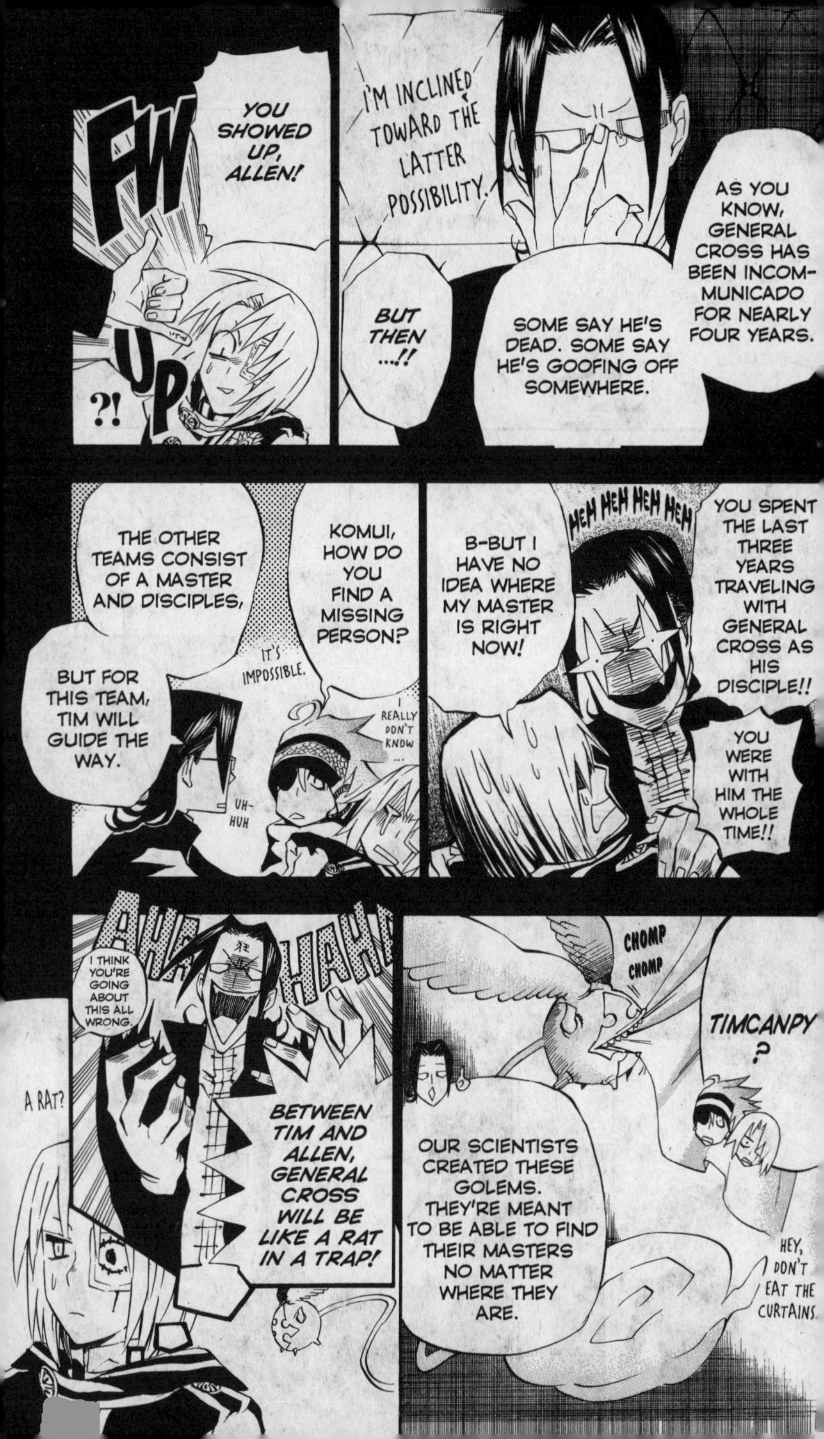
AS YOU KNOW, GENERAL CROSS HAS BEEN INCOMMUNICADO FOR NEARLY FOUR YEARS.
SOME SAY HE'S DEAD. SOME SAY HE'S GOOFING OFF SOMEWHERE.
I'M INCLINED TOWARD THE LATTER POSSIBILITY.
BUT THEN ...!!
YOU SHOWED UP, ALLEN!
FWUP
?!
YOU SPENT THE LAST THREE YEARS TRAVELING WITH GENERAL CROSS AS HIS DISCIPLE!!
HEH HEH HEH HEH HEH
YOU WERE WITH HIM THE WHOLE TIME!!
B-BUT I HAVE NO IDEA WHERE MY MASTER IS RIGHT NOW!
KOMUI, HOW DO YOU FIND A MISSING PERSON?
IT'S IMPOSSIBLE.
I REALLY DON'T KNOW ...
THE OTHER TEAMS CONSIST OF A MASTER AND DISCIPLES,
BUT FOR THIS TEAM, TIM WILL GUIDE THE WAY.
UH-HUH
CHOMP CHOMP
TIMCANPY?
OUR SCIENTISTS CREATED THESE GOLEMS. THEY'RE MEANT TO BE ABLE TO FIND THEIR MASTERS NO MATTER WHERE THEY ARE.
HEY, DON'T EAT THE CURTAINS.
BETWEEN TIM AND ALLEN, GENERAL CROSS WILL BE LIKE A RAT IN A TRAP!
I THINK YOU'RE GOING ABOUT THIS ALL WRONG.
A RAT?

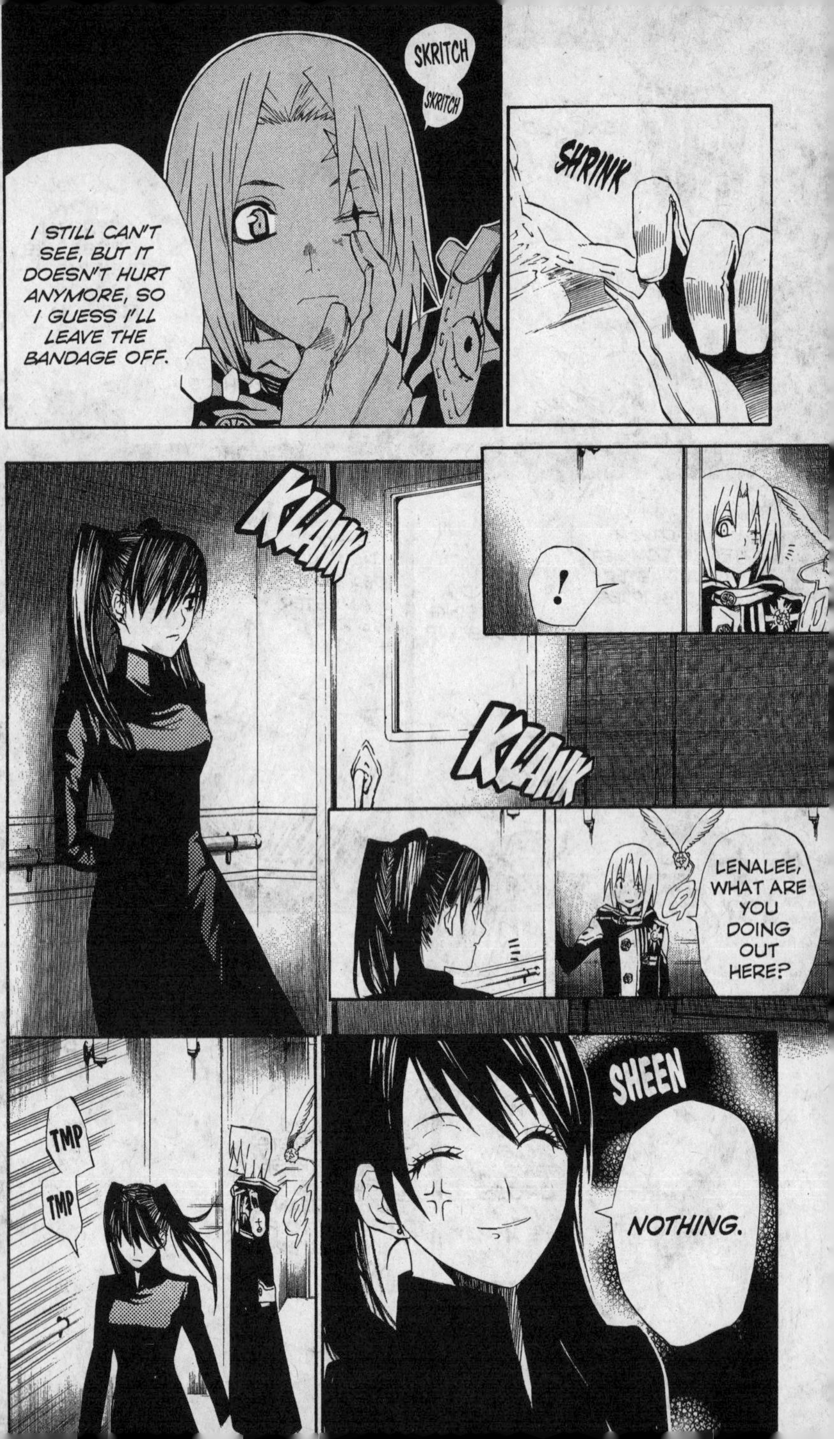
SHRINK
SKRITCH
SKRITCH
I STILL CAN'T SEE, BUT IT DOESN'T HURT ANYMORE, SO I GUESS I'LL LEAVE THE BANDAGE OFF.
!
LENALEE, WHAT ARE YOU DOING OUT HERE?
KLANK
KLANK
SHEEN
NOTHING.
TMP
TMP

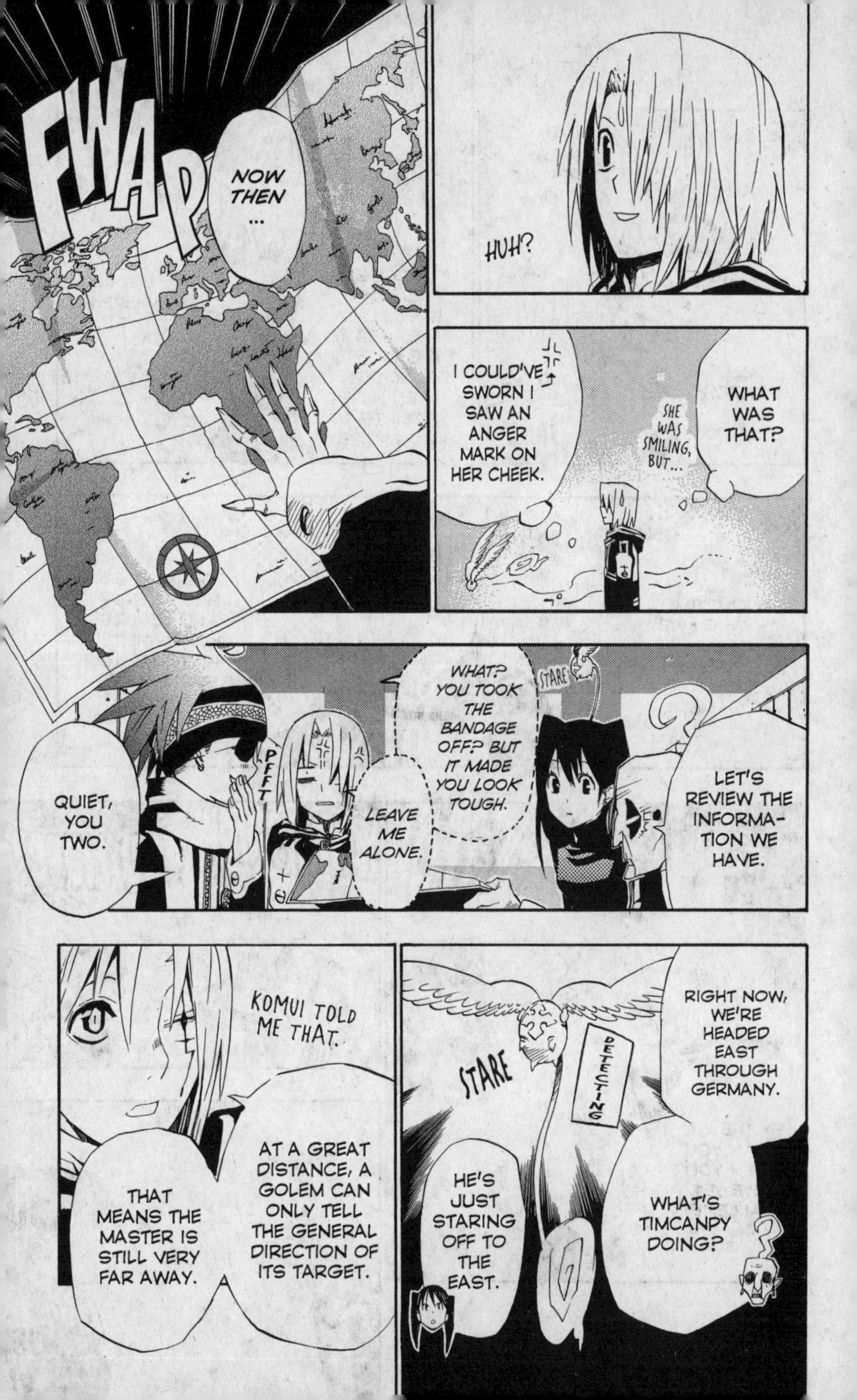
HUH?
WHAT WAS THAT?
SHE WAS SMILING, BUT...
I COULD'VE SWORN I SAW AN ANGER MARK ON HER CHEEK.
FWAP
NOW THEN ...
LET'S REVIEW THE INFORMATION WE HAVE.
STARE
WHAT? YOU TOOK THE BANDAGE OFF? BUT IT MADE YOU LOOK TOUGH.
LEAVE ME ALONE.
PFFT
QUIET, YOU TWO.
RIGHT NOW, WE'RE HEADED EAST THROUGH GERMANY.
DETECTING
STARE
WHAT'S TIMCANPY DOING?
HE'S JUST STARING OFF TO THE EAST.
KOMUI TOLD ME THAT.
AT A GREAT DISTANCE, A GOLEM CAN ONLY TELL THE GENERAL DIRECTION OF ITS TARGET.
THAT MEANS THE MASTER IS STILL VERY FAR AWAY.

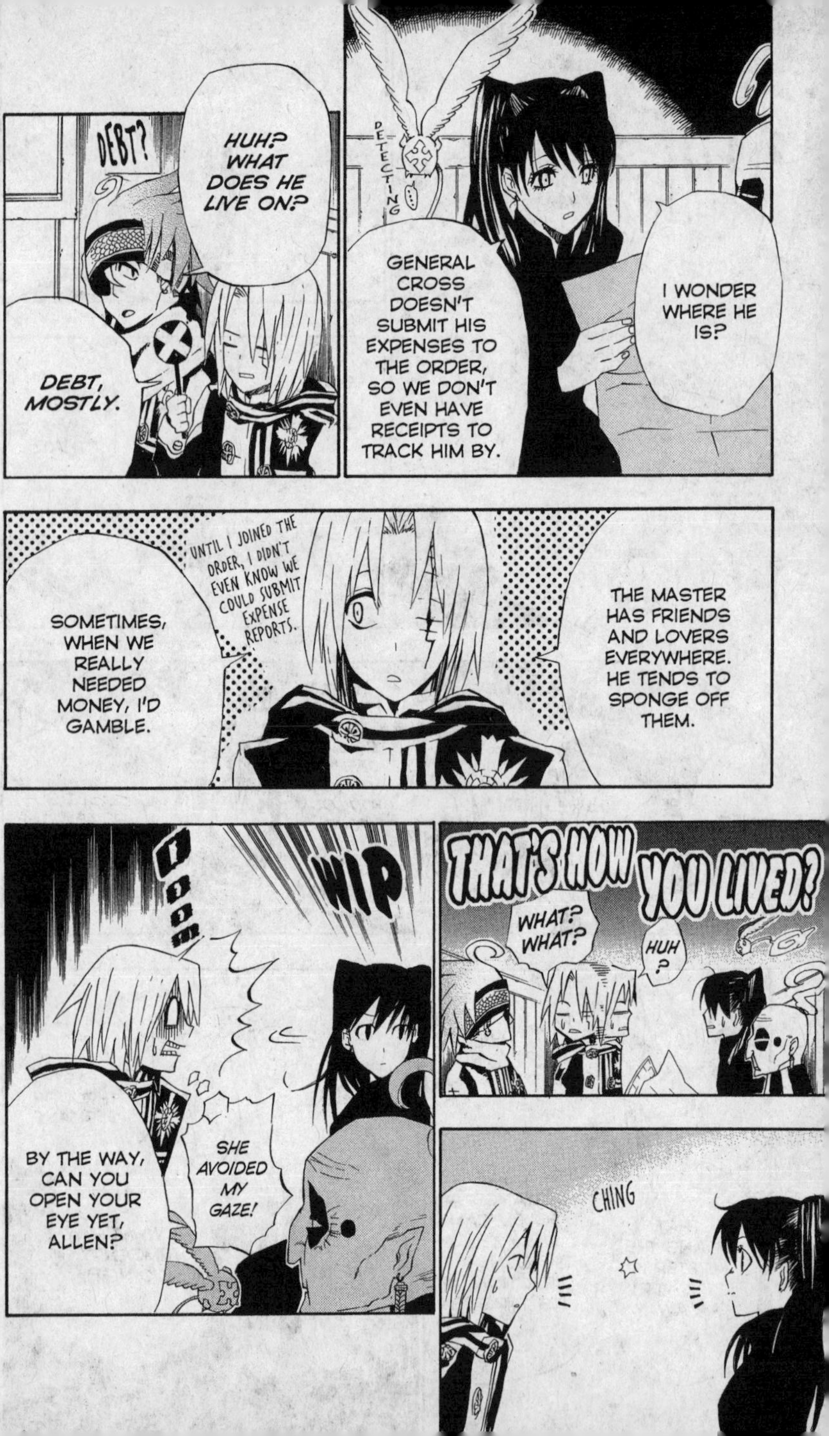
I WONDER WHERE HE IS?
DETECTING
...
GENERAL CROSS DOESN'T SUBMIT HIS EXPENSES TO THE ORDER, SO WE DON'T EVEN HAVE RECEIPTS TO TRACK HIM BY.
HUH? WHAT DOES HE LIVE ON?
DEBT?
DEBT, MOSTLY.
THE MASTER HAS FRIENDS AND LOVERS EVERYWHERE. HE TENDS TO SPONGE OFF THEM.
UNTIL I JOINED THE ORDER, I DIDN'T EVEN KNOW WE COULD SUBMIT EXPENSE REPORTS.
SOMETIMES, WHEN WE REALLY NEEDED MONEY, I'D GAMBLE.
THAT'S HOW YOU LIVED?
HUH?
WHAT? WHAT?
CHING
WHIP
SHE AVOIDED MY GAZE!
BY THE WAY, CAN YOU OPEN YOUR EYE YET, ALLEN?

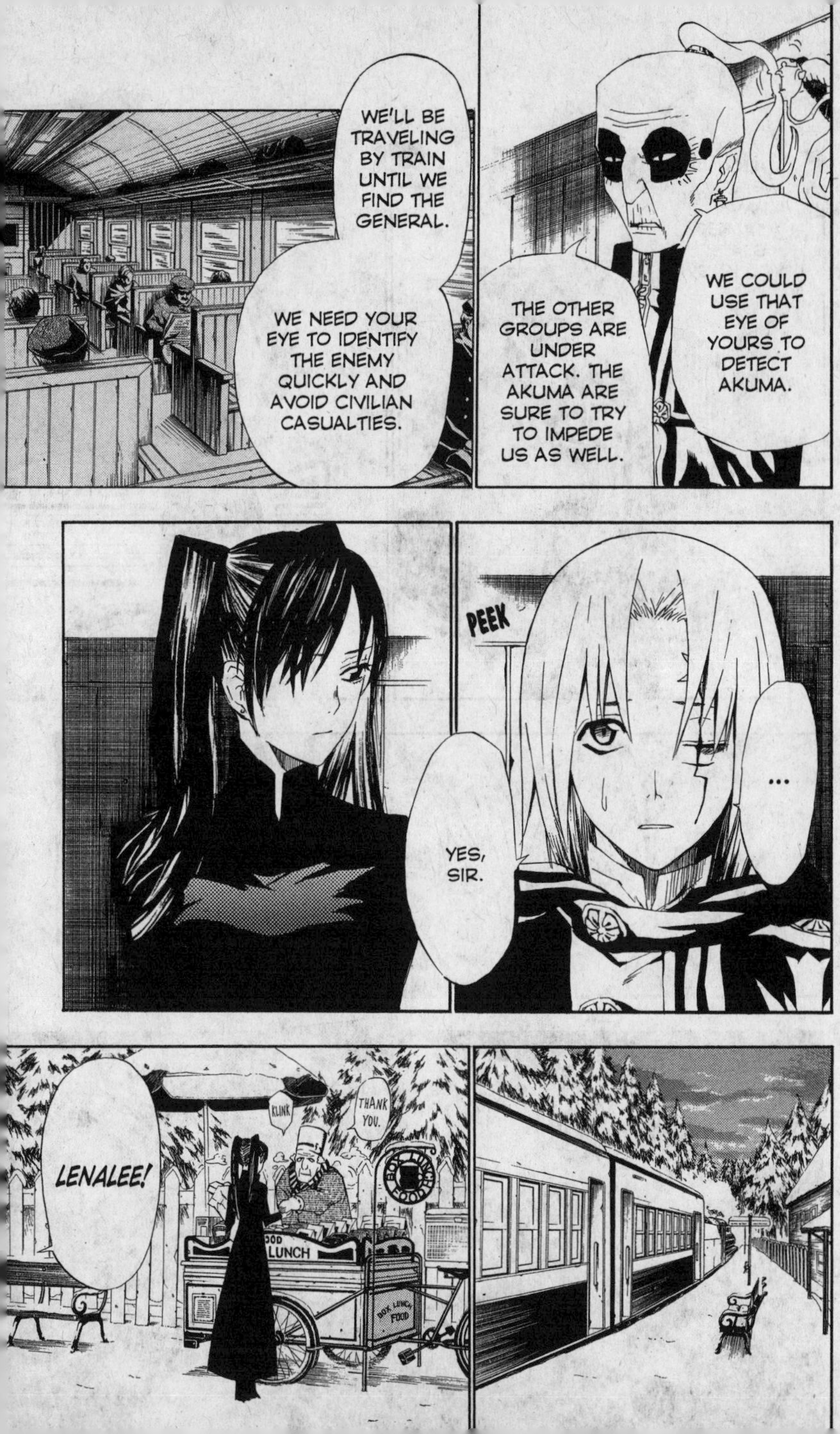
WE COULD USE THAT EYE OF YOURS TO DETECT AKUMA.
THE OTHER GROUPS ARE UNDER ATTACK. THE AKUMA ARE SURE TO TRY TO IMPEDE US AS WELL.
WE'LL BE TRAVELING BY TRAIN UNTIL WE FIND THE GENERAL.
WE NEED YOUR EYE TO IDENTIFY THE ENEMY QUICKLY AND AVOID CIVILIAN CASUALTIES.
PEEK
...
YES, SIR.
THANK YOU.
KLINK
LENALEE!

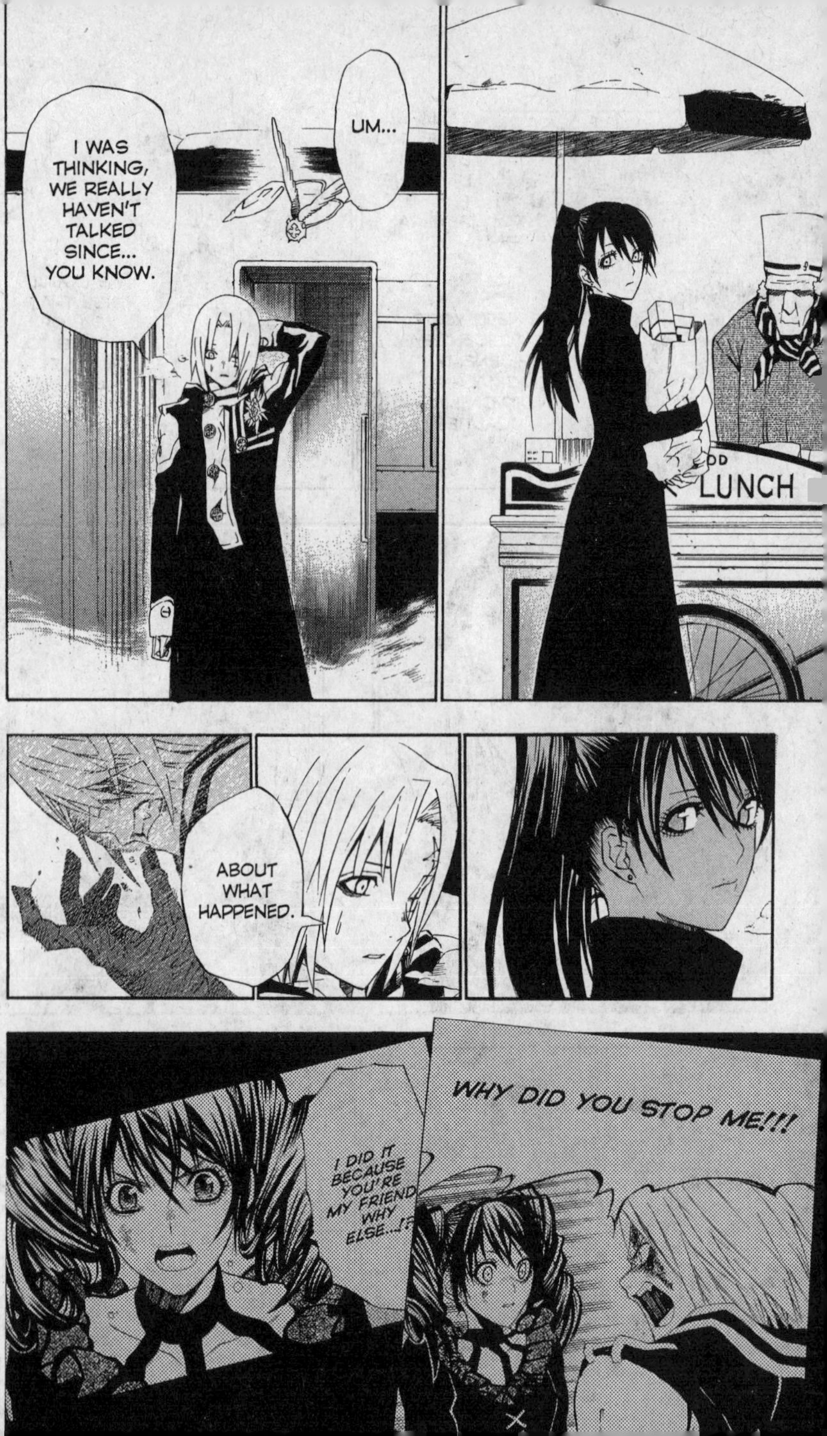
LUNCH
UM...
I WAS THINKING, WE REALLY HAVEN'T TALKED SINCE... YOU KNOW.
ABOUT WHAT HAPPENED.
WHY DID YOU STOP ME!!!
I DID IT BECAUSE YOU'RE MY FRIEND WHY ELSE...!?

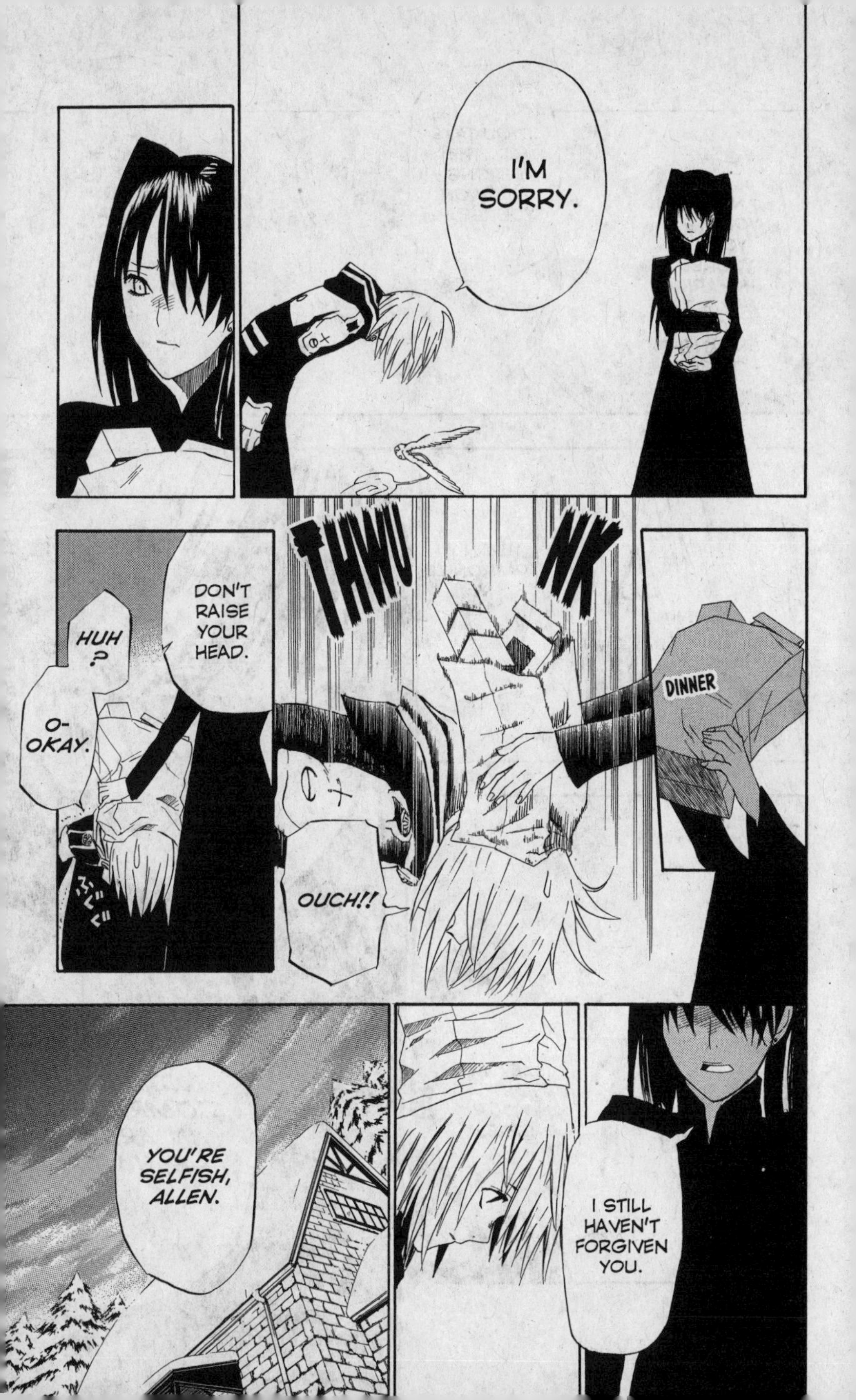
I'M SORRY.
DINNER
THWUNK
OUCH!!
DON'T RAISE YOUR HEAD.
HUH?
O-OKAY.
I STILL HAVEN'T FORGIVEN YOU.
YOU'RE SELFISH, ALLEN.

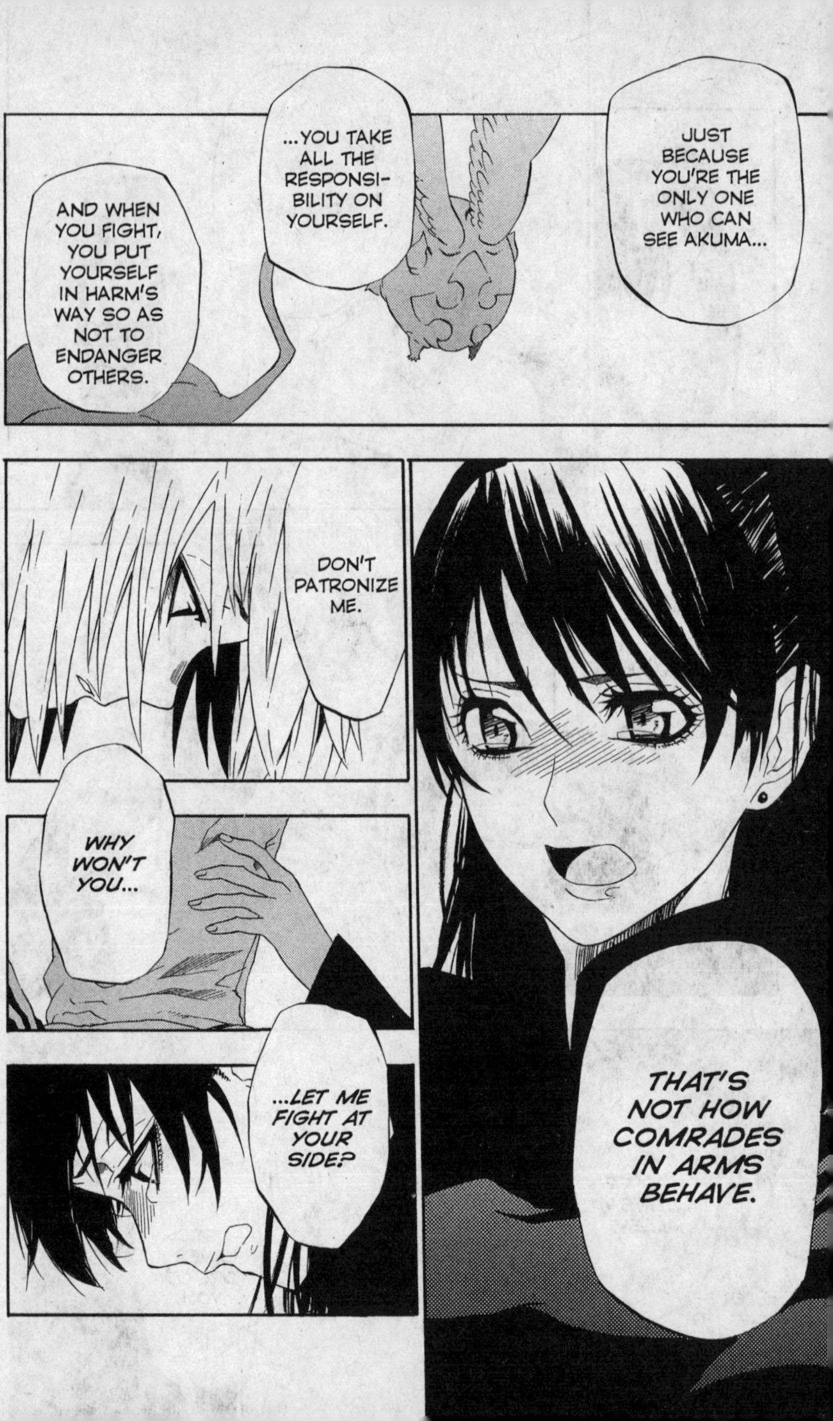
JUST BECAUSE YOU'RE THE ONLY ONE WHO CAN SEE AKUMA...
...YOU TAKE ALL THE RESPONSI-BILITY ON YOURSELF.
AND WHEN YOU FIGHT, YOU PUT YOURSELF IN HARM'S WAY SO AS NOT TO ENDANGER OTHERS.
THAT'S NOT HOW COMRADES IN ARMS BEHAVE.
DON'T PATRONIZE ME.
WHY WON'T YOU...
...LET ME FIGHT AT YOUR SIDE?

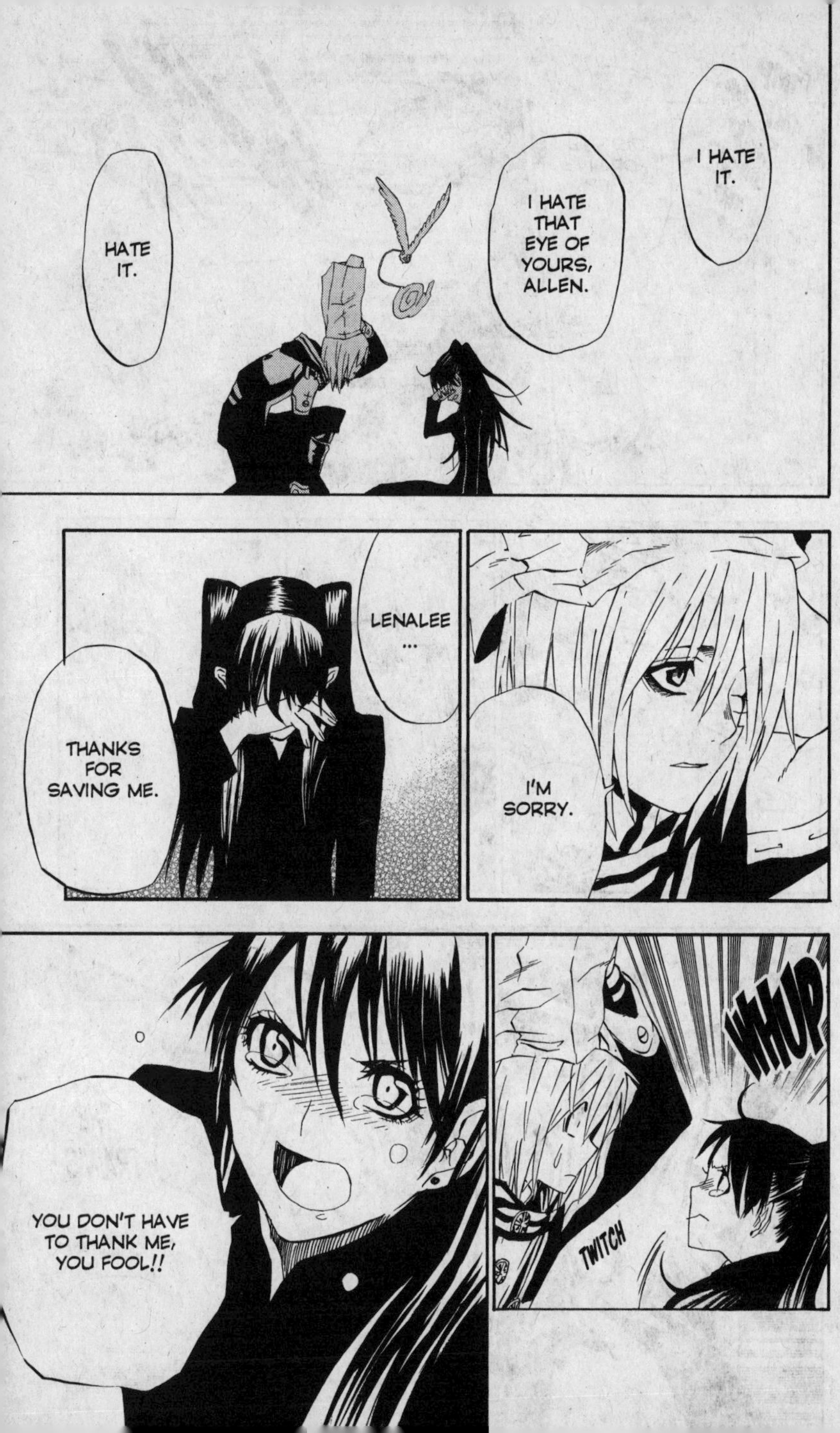
I HATE IT.
I HATE THAT EYE OF YOURS, ALLEN.
HATE IT.
I'M SORRY.
LENALEE ...
THANKS FOR SAVING ME.
WHUP
TWITCH
YOU DON'T HAVE TO THANK ME, YOU FOOL!!

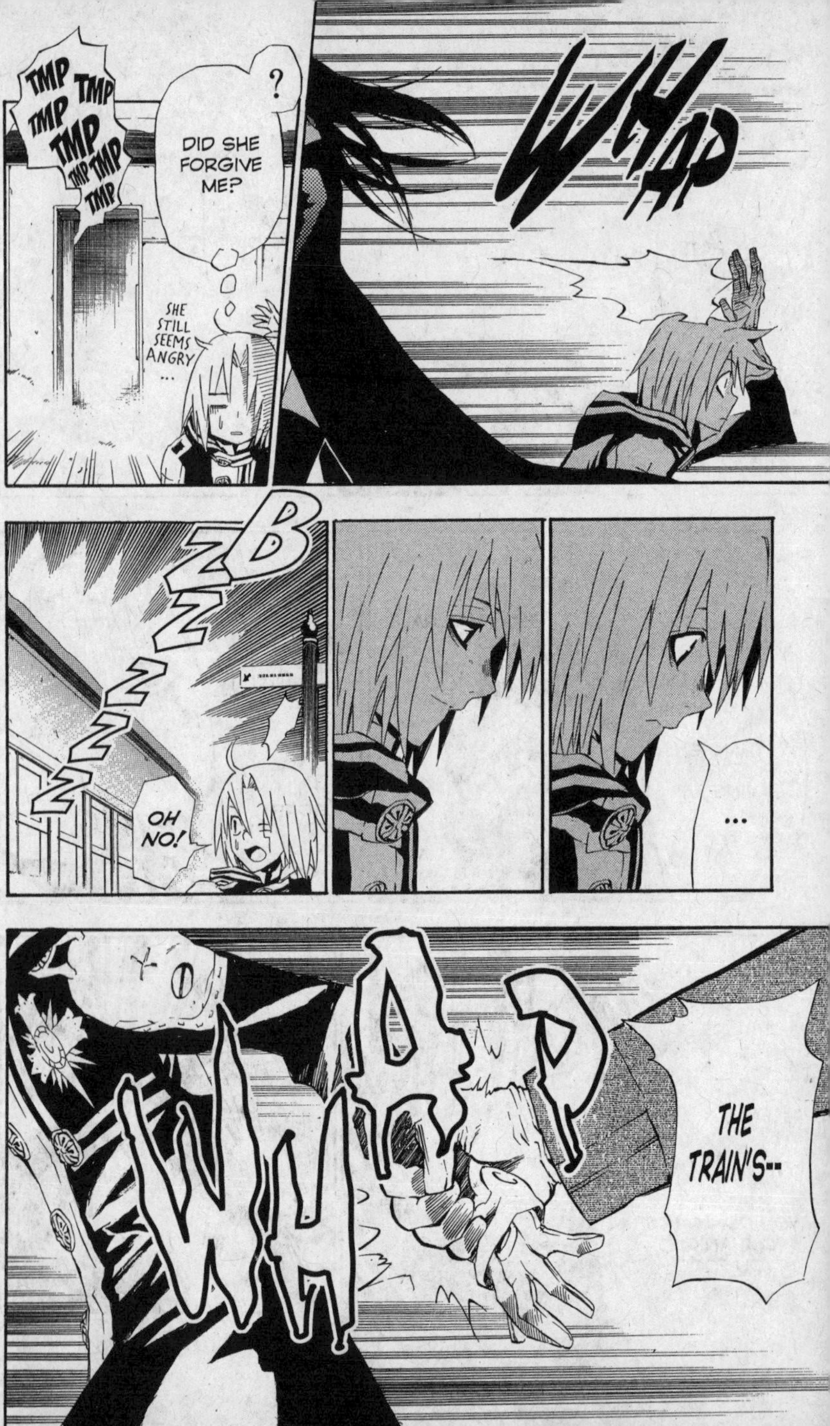
WHAP
?
DID SHE FORGIVE ME?
TMP TMP TMP TMP TMP TMP TMP TMP
SHE STILL SEEMS ANGRY ...
...
ZZZZZB
OH NO!
WHAP
THE TRAIN'S--

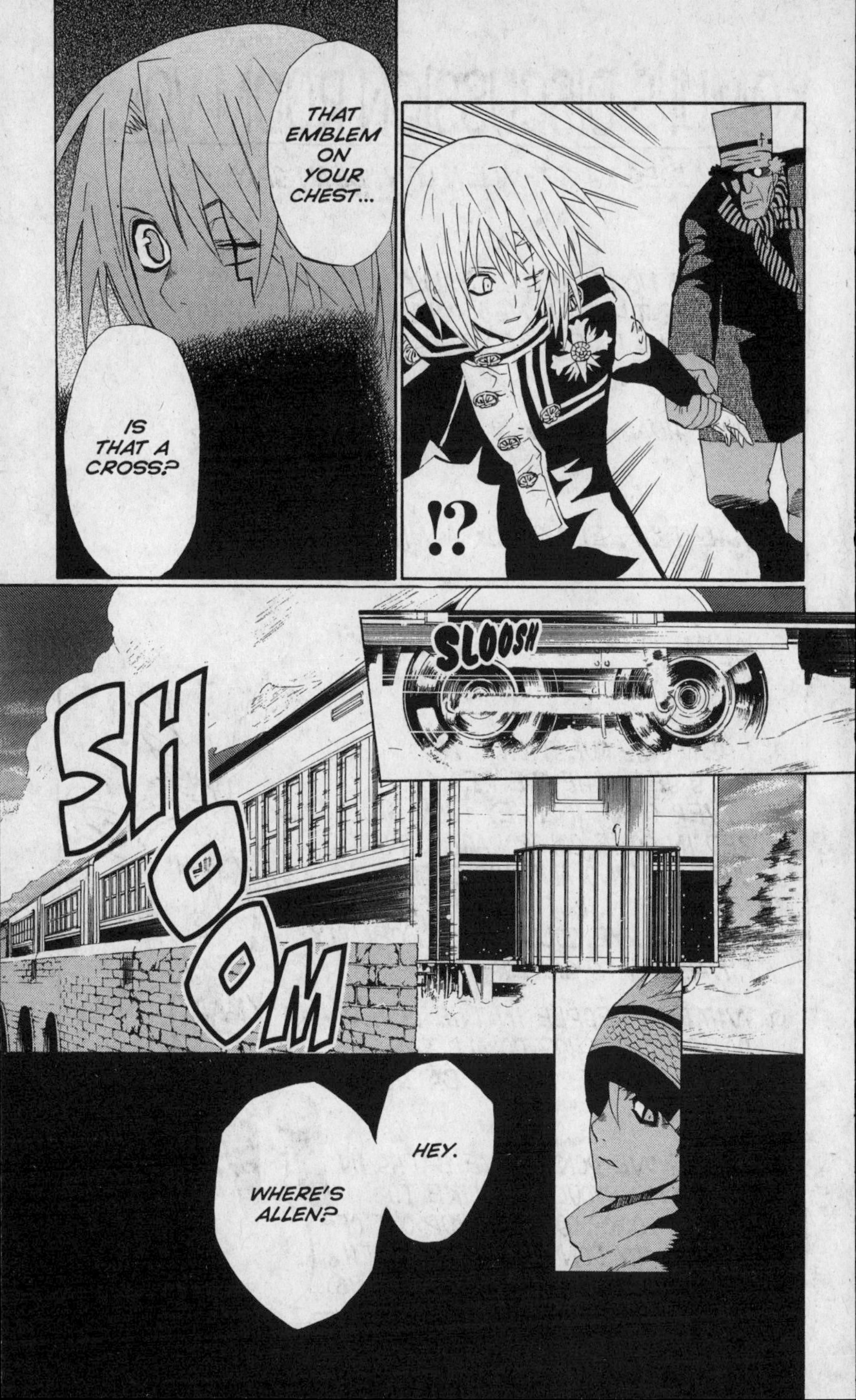
!?
THAT EMBLEM ON YOUR CHEST...
IS THAT A CROSS?
SLOOSH
SHOOM
HEY.
WHERE'S ALLEN?

KOMUI'S DISCUSSION ROOM VOL. 2

Q. WHY DOES KANDA CALL ALLEN "BEAN SPROUT"?

A. I HAVE NO IDEA! IT'S REALLY RUDE, DON'T YOU THINK? THAT DARNED PONYTAIL! WHAT PART OF ME LOOKS LIKE A BEAN SPROUT?! (HMPH!)

Q. JUST HOW DEEPLY IS GENERAL CROSS IN DEBT?

A. UGH? I'M FEELING SICK AGAIN...

Q. WHAT COLOR ARE ALLEN'S EYES REALLY?

A. I GET THIS QUESTION A LOT. WELL, LET'S SEE. THEY'RE REALLY SILVER-GRAY. IF THEY LOOK BLUE OR RED IN SOME COLOR PAGES, THAT'S JUST HOSHINO AND HIS EDITOR HAVING FUN. BUT I HEAR THAT MY OFFICIAL EYE COLOR WAS RECENTLY FINALIZED AS SILVER-GRAY.

Q. WHAT DO PEOPLE IN THE ORDER DO ABOUT BATHS? DO ALL THE LIVING QUARTERS HAVE BATHS?

A. BATHS? WE DON'T HAVE BATHS IN OUR ROOMS. WOULD YOU LIKE TO HAVE A LOOK? (GETTING UP OUT OF CHAIR) WHY DON'T YOU COME WITH ME NOW. LET'S GO! (GO TO PAGE 96)

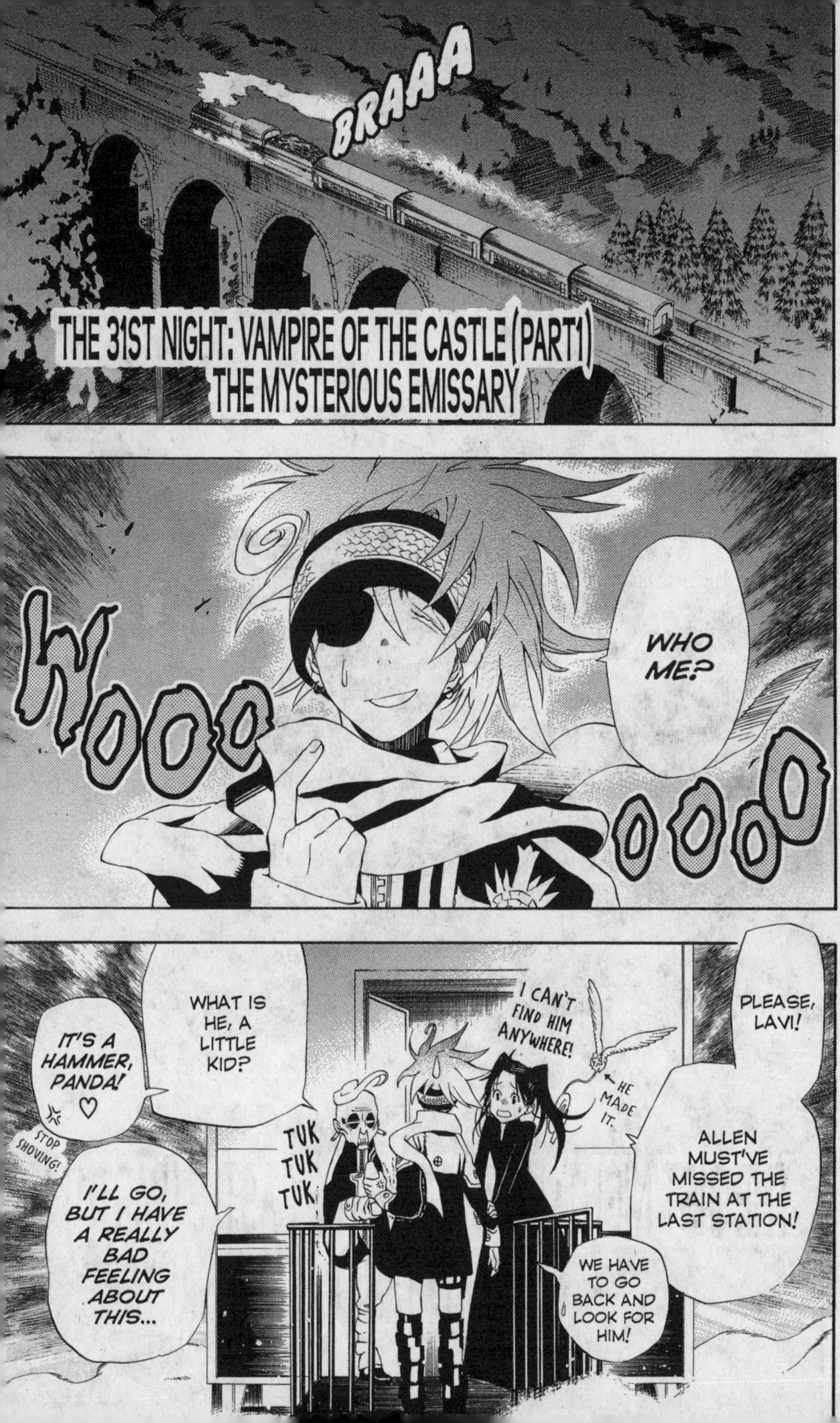
BRAAA
THE 31ST NIGHT: VAMPIRE OF THE CASTLE (PART1)
THE MYSTERIOUS EMISSARY
WHO ME?
WOOOOOOOO
PLEASE, LAVI!
ALLEN MUST'VE MISSED THE TRAIN AT THE LAST STATION!
WE HAVE TO GO BACK AND LOOK FOR HIM!
I CAN'T FIND HIM ANYWHERE!
← HE MADE IT.
WHAT IS HE, A LITTLE KID?
IT'S A HAMMER, PANDA! ♡
STOP SHOVING!
TUK TUK TUK
I'LL GO, BUT I HAVE A REALLY BAD FEELING ABOUT THIS...

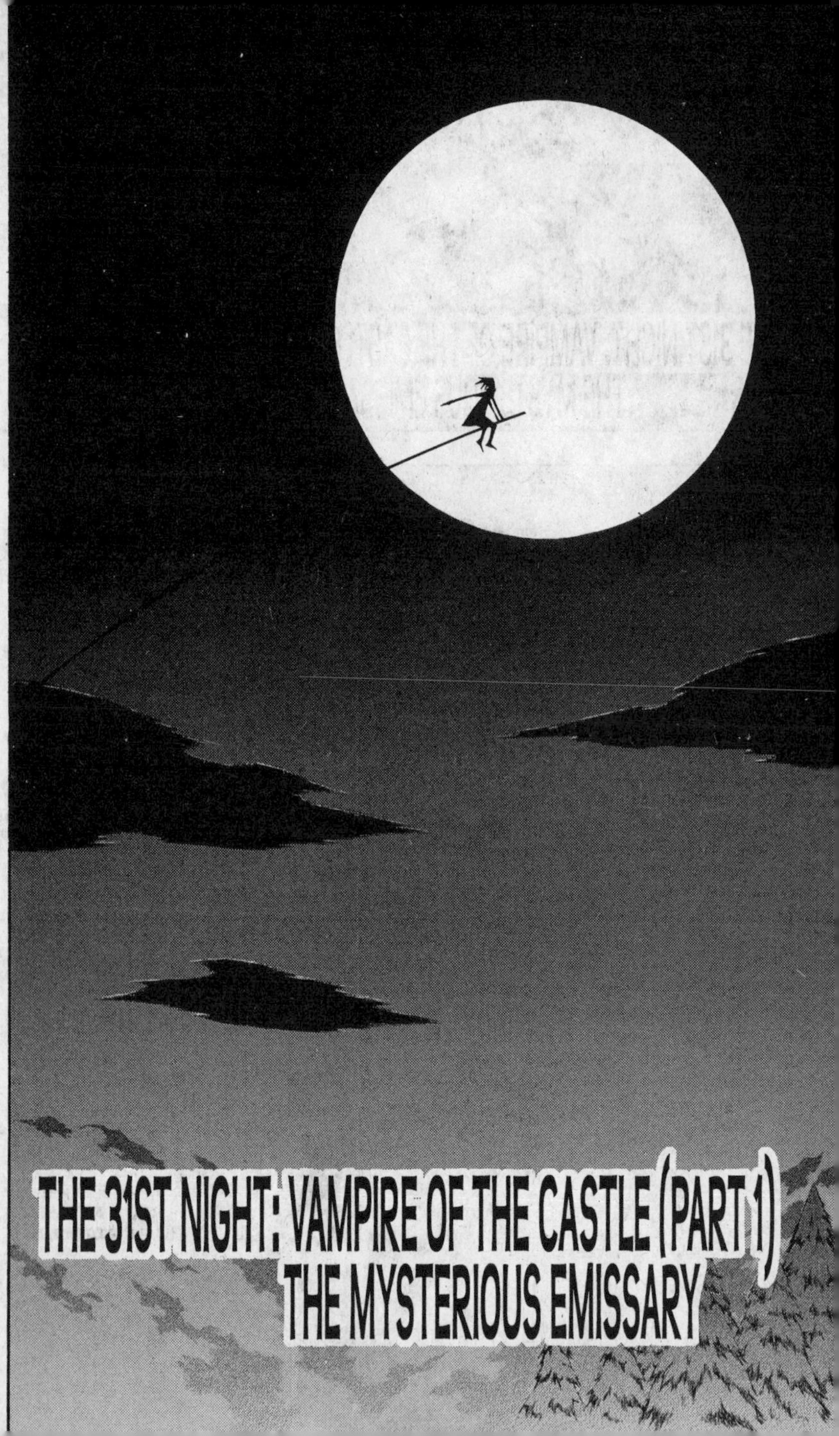
THE 31ST NIGHT: VAMPIRE OF THE CASTLE (PART 1)
THE MYSTERIOUS EMISSARY

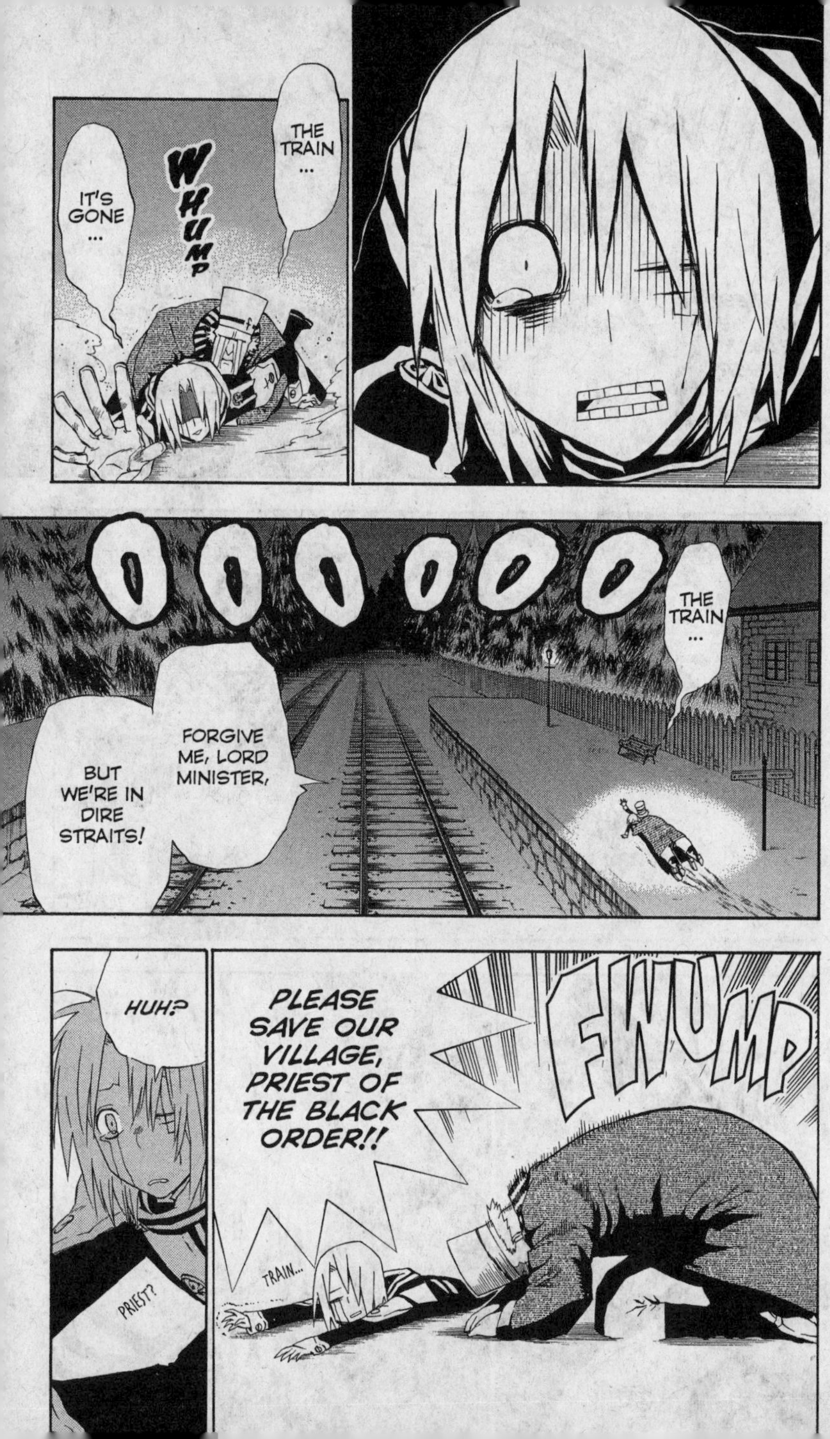
THE TRAIN ...
WHUMP
IT'S GONE ...
THE TRAIN ...
FORGIVE ME, LORD MINISTER,
BUT WE'RE IN DIRE STRAITS!
FWUMP
PLEASE SAVE OUR VILLAGE, PRIEST OF THE BLACK ORDER!!
TRAIN...
HUH?
PRIEST?

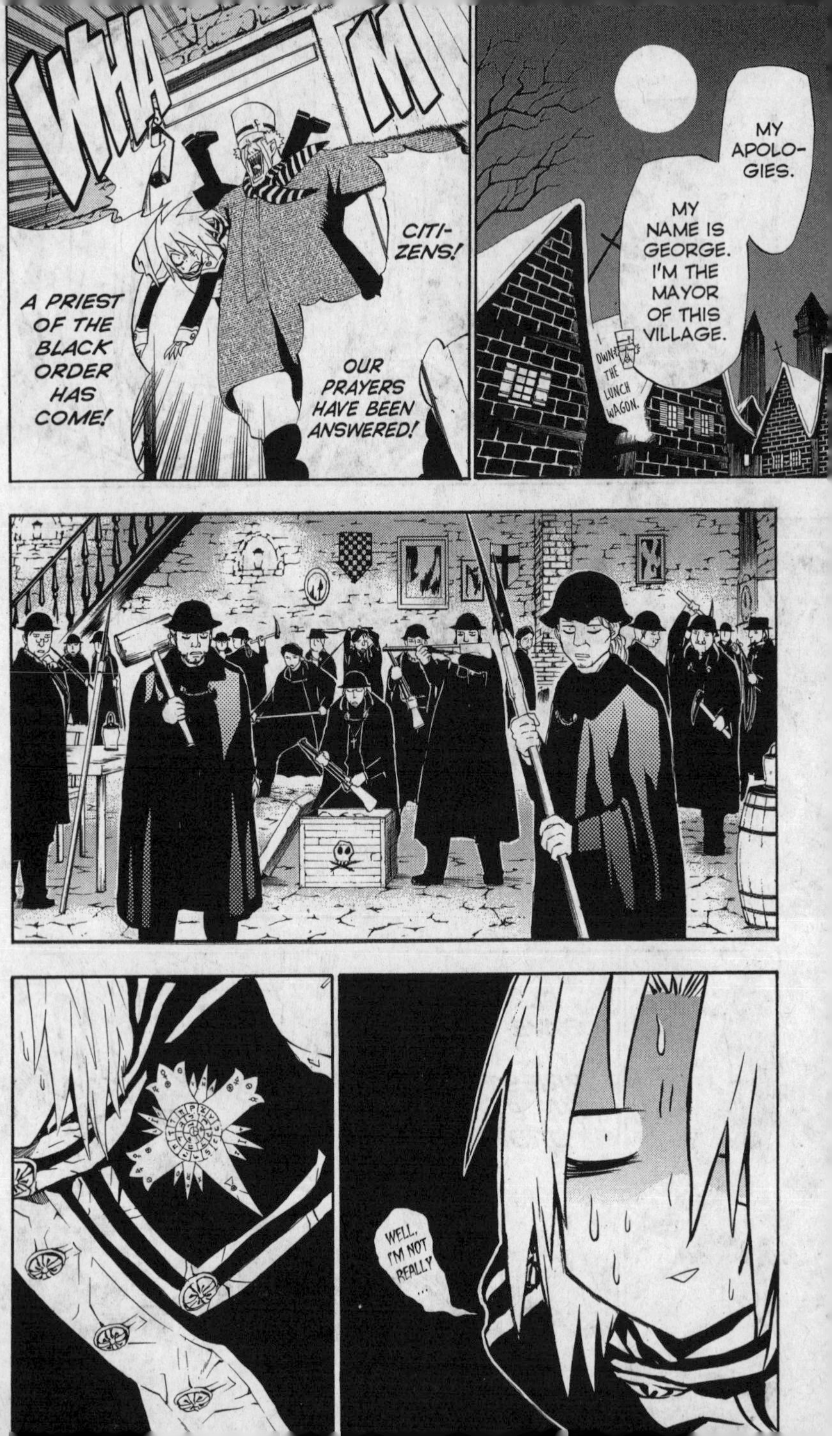
MY APOLOGIES.
MY NAME IS GEORGE. I'M THE MAYOR OF THIS VILLAGE.
I OWN THE LUNCH WAGON.
WHAM
CITIZENS!
OUR PRAYERS HAVE BEEN ANSWERED!
A PRIEST OF THE BLACK ORDER HAS COME!
WELL, I'M NOT REALLY...

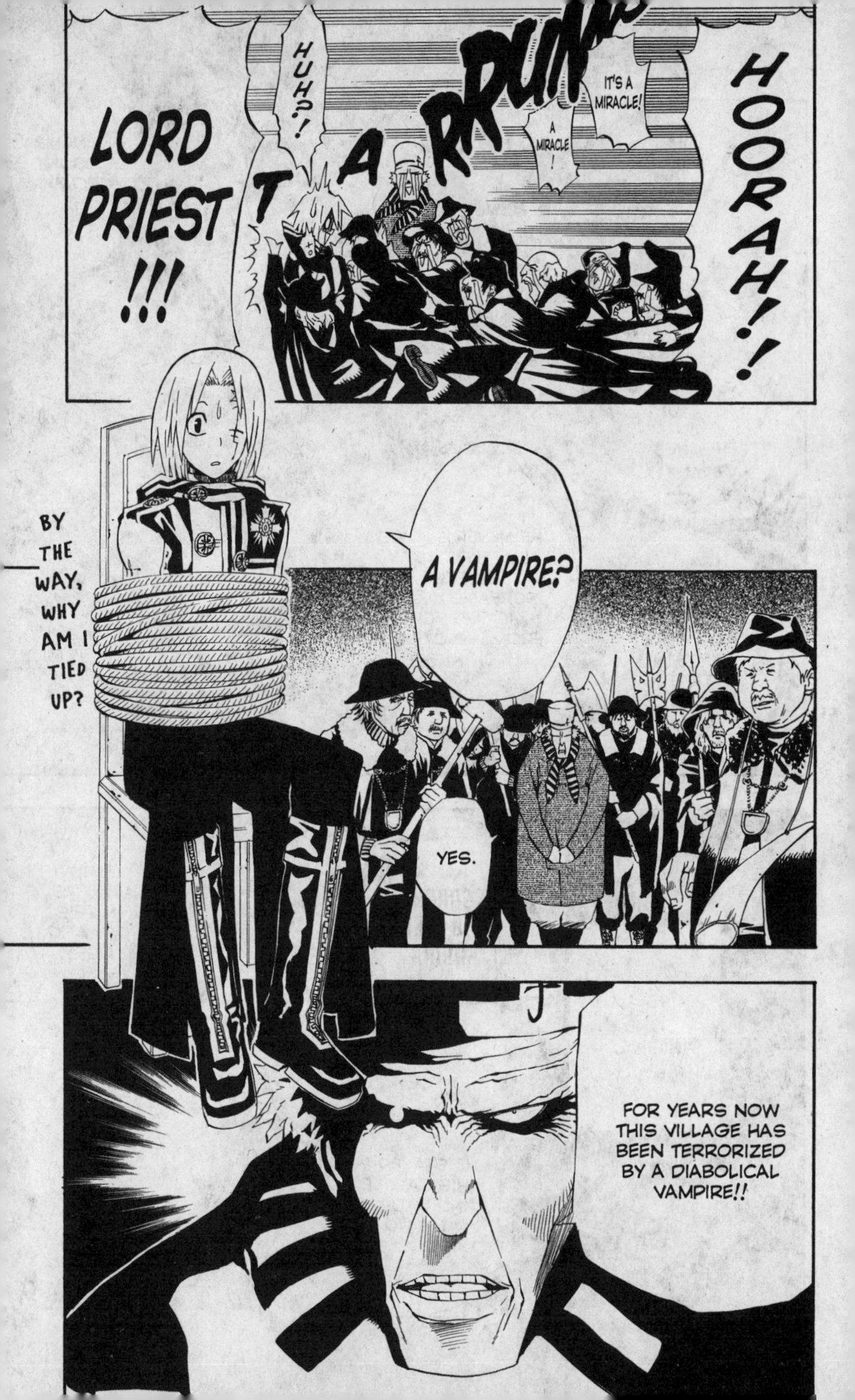

HOORAH!!
IT'S A MIRACLE!
A MIRACLE!
TARRUN
HUH?!
LORD PRIEST!!!
A VAMPIRE?
YES.
BY THE WAY, WHY AM I TIED UP?
FOR YEARS NOW THIS VILLAGE HAS BEEN TERRORIZED BY A DIABOLICAL VAMPIRE!!

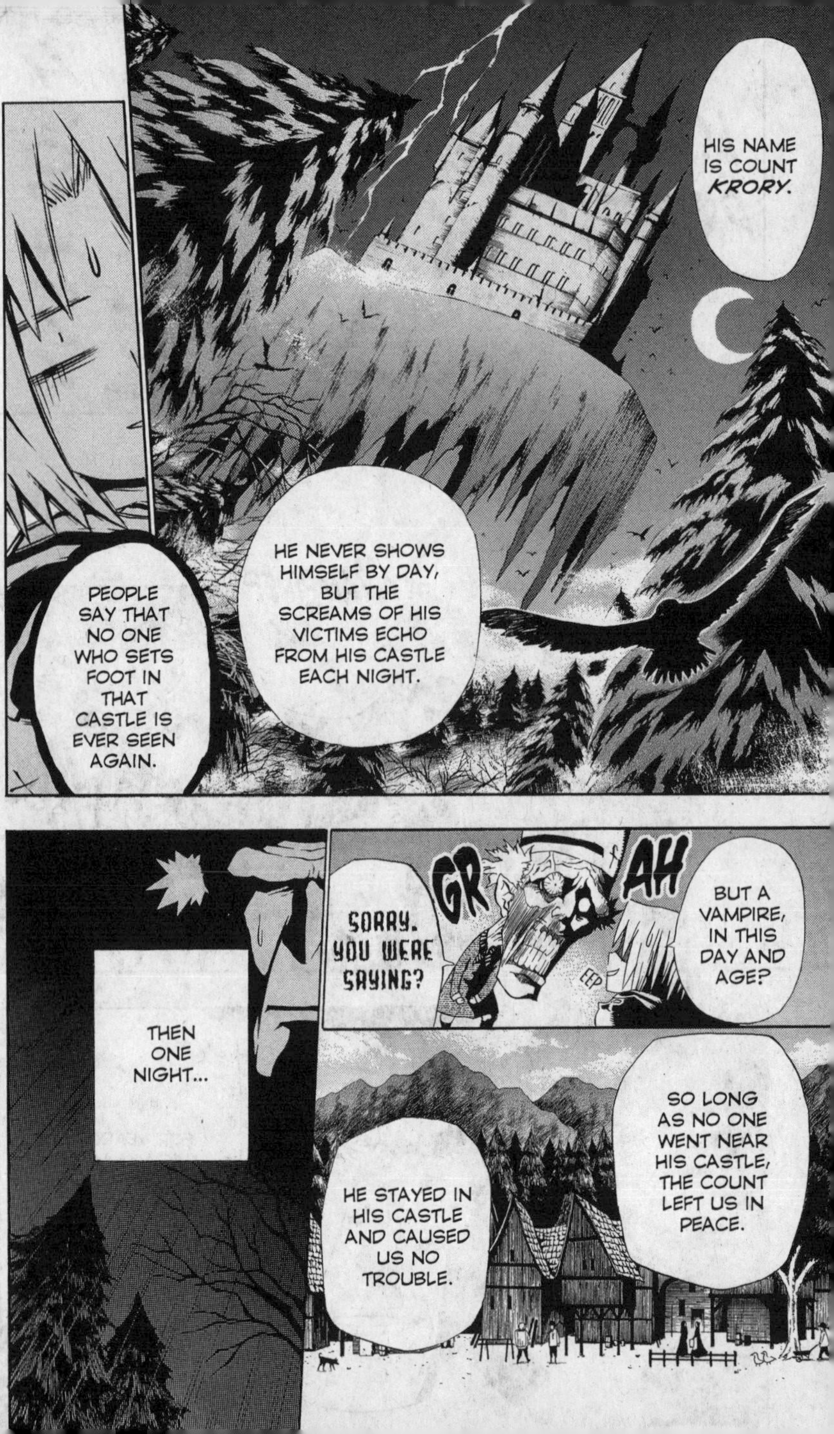
HIS NAME IS COUNT *KRORY*.
HE NEVER SHOWS HIMSELF BY DAY, BUT THE SCREAMS OF HIS VICTIMS ECHO FROM HIS CASTLE EACH NIGHT.
PEOPLE SAY THAT NO ONE WHO SETS FOOT IN THAT CASTLE IS EVER SEEN AGAIN.
BUT A VAMPIRE, IN THIS DAY AND AGE?
GR AH
EEP
SORRY. YOU WERE SAYING?
SO LONG AS NO ONE WENT NEAR HIS CASTLE, THE COUNT LEFT US IN PEACE.
HE STAYED IN HIS CASTLE AND CAUSED US NO TROUBLE.
THEN ONE NIGHT...

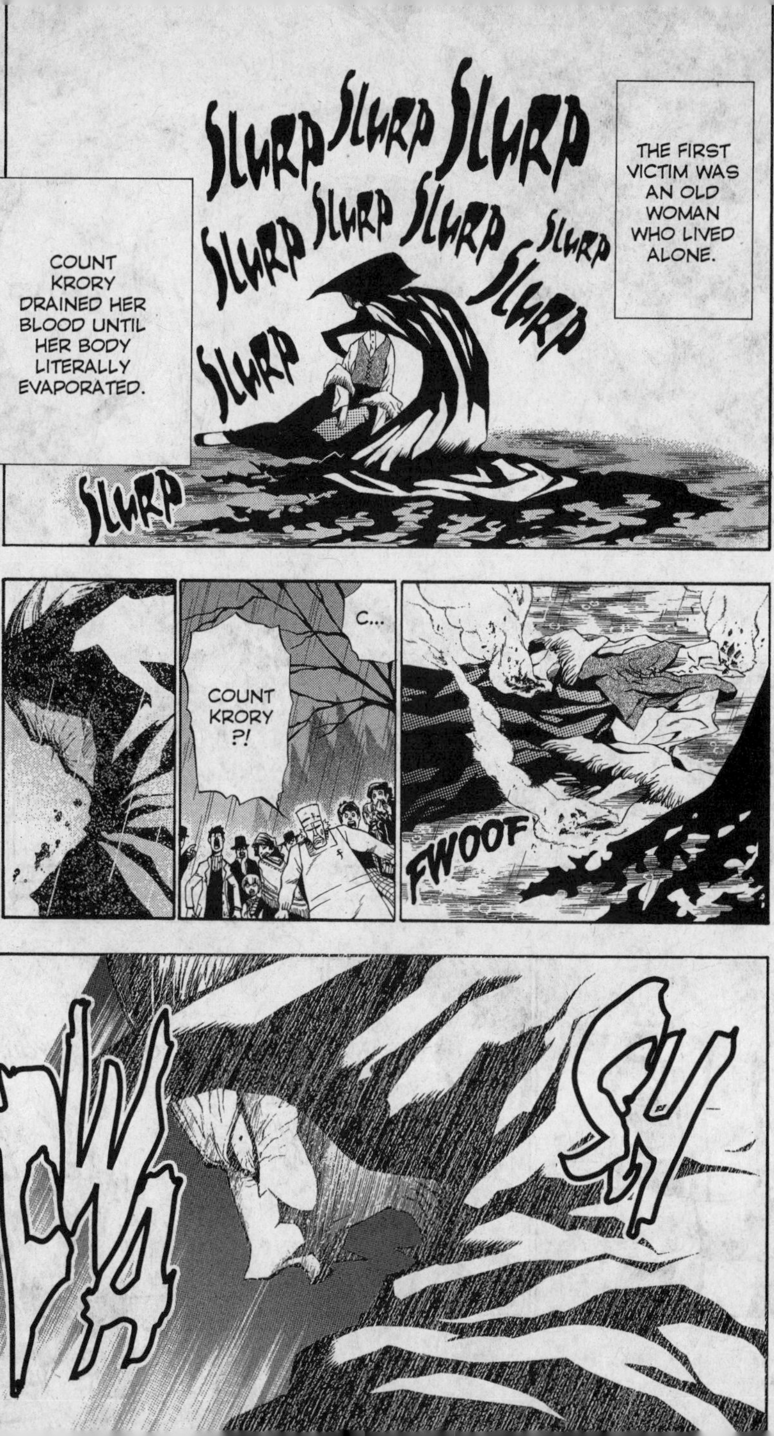
THE FIRST VICTIM WAS AN OLD WOMAN WHO LIVED ALONE.
SLURP SLURP SLURP
SLURP SLURP SLURP SLURP
SLURP SLURP
SLURP
COUNT KRORY DRAINED HER BLOOD UNTIL HER BODY LITERALLY EVAPORATED.
SLURP
FWOOF
C...
COUNT KRORY ?!
?

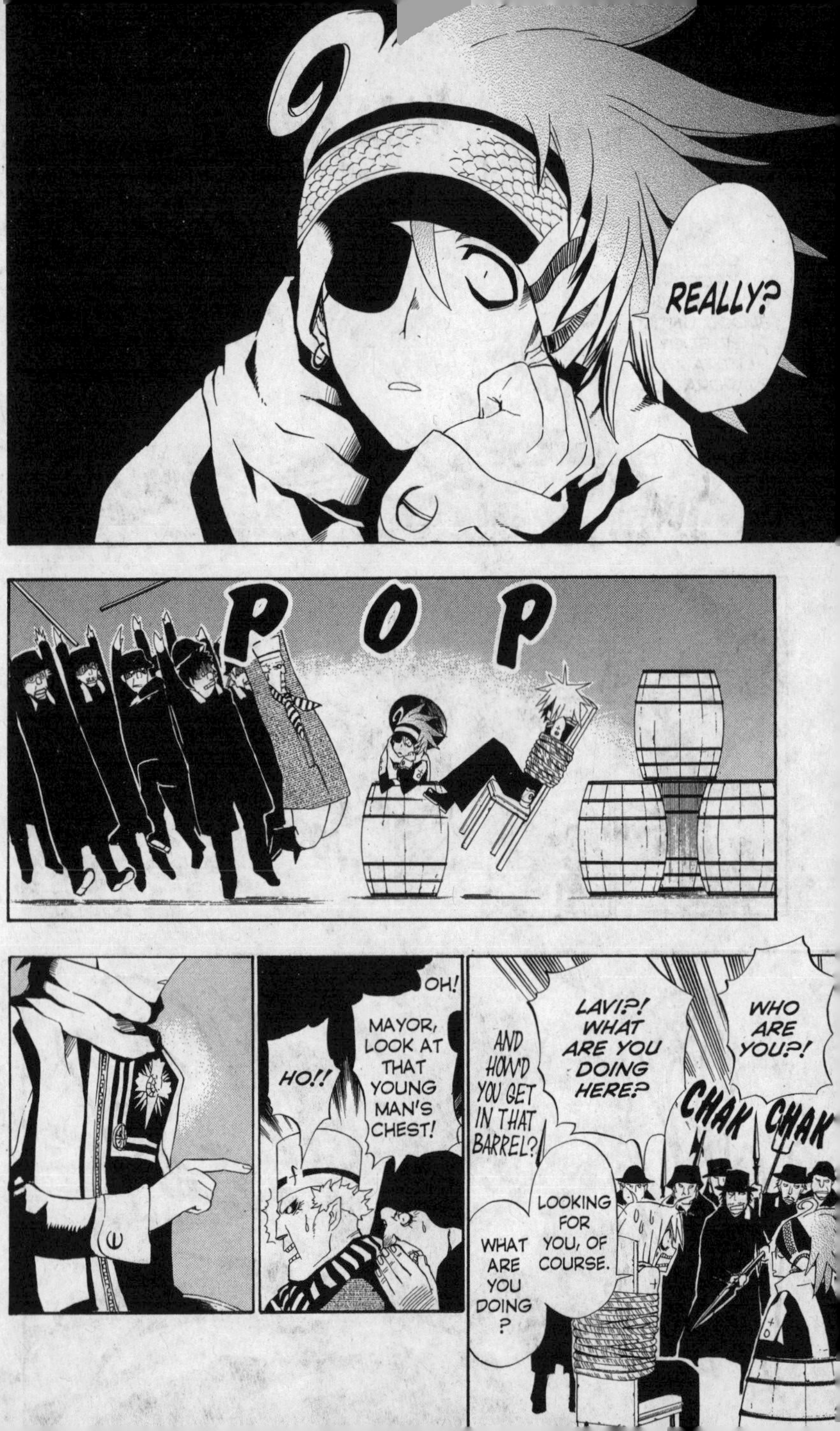
REALLY?
POP
WHO ARE YOU?!
CHAK CHAK
LAVI?! WHAT ARE YOU DOING HERE?
AND HOW'D YOU GET IN THAT BARREL?
LOOKING FOR YOU, OF COURSE.
WHAT ARE YOU DOING?
OH!
MAYOR, LOOK AT THAT YOUNG MAN'S CHEST!
HO!!

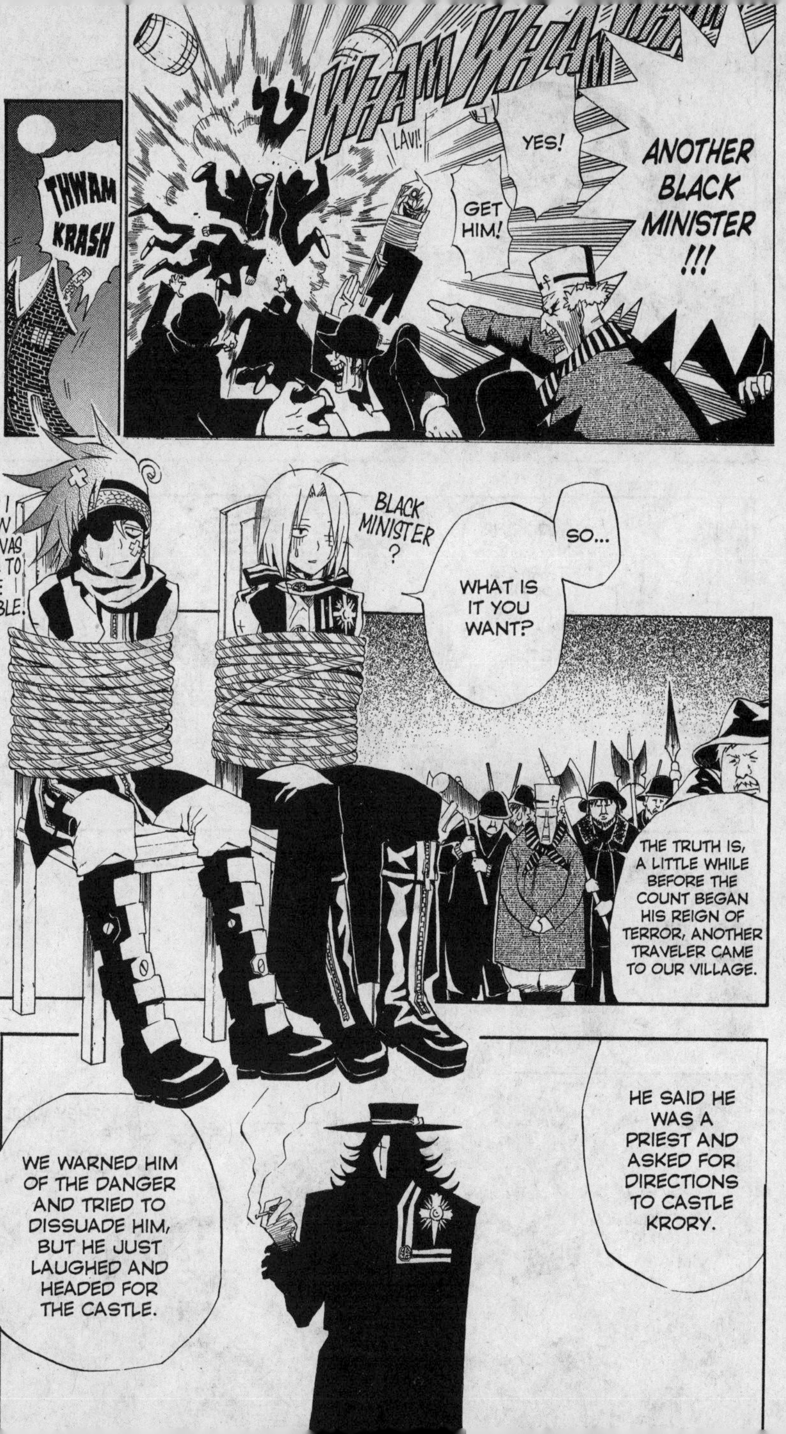
WHAM WHAM
ANOTHER BLACK MINISTER!!!
YES!
GET HIM!
LAVI!
THWAM KRASH
SO...
WHAT IS IT YOU WANT?
BLACK MINISTER?
SEE? I KNEW THIS WAS GOING TO BE TROUBLE.
THE TRUTH IS, A LITTLE WHILE BEFORE THE COUNT BEGAN HIS REIGN OF TERROR, ANOTHER TRAVELER CAME TO OUR VILLAGE.
HE SAID HE WAS A PRIEST AND ASKED FOR DIRECTIONS TO CASTLE KRORY.
WE WARNED HIM OF THE DANGER AND TRIED TO DISSUADE HIM, BUT HE JUST LAUGHED AND HEADED FOR THE CASTLE.

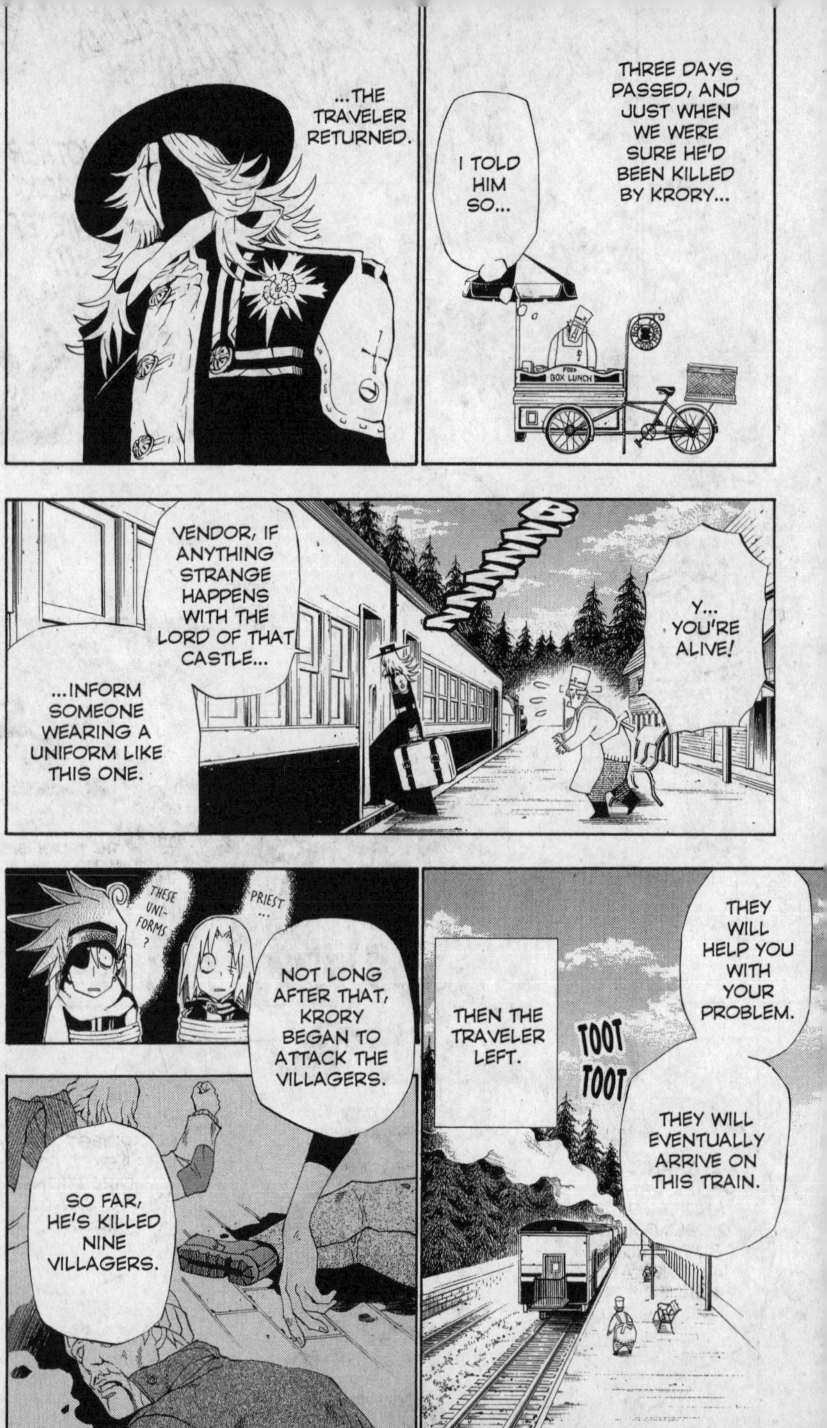
THREE DAYS PASSED, AND JUST WHEN WE WERE SURE HE'D BEEN KILLED BY KRORY...
I TOLD HIM SO...
FOOD
BOX LUNCH
...THE TRAVELER RETURNED.
Y... YOU'RE ALIVE!
VENDOR, IF ANYTHING STRANGE HAPPENS WITH THE LORD OF THAT CASTLE...
...INFORM SOMEONE WEARING A UNIFORM LIKE THIS ONE.
THEY WILL HELP YOU WITH YOUR PROBLEM.
THEY WILL EVENTUALLY ARRIVE ON THIS TRAIN.
TOOT TOOT
THEN THE TRAVELER LEFT.
PRIEST...
THESE UNIFORMS?
NOT LONG AFTER THAT, KRORY BEGAN TO ATTACK THE VILLAGERS.
SO FAR, HE'S KILLED NINE VILLAGERS.

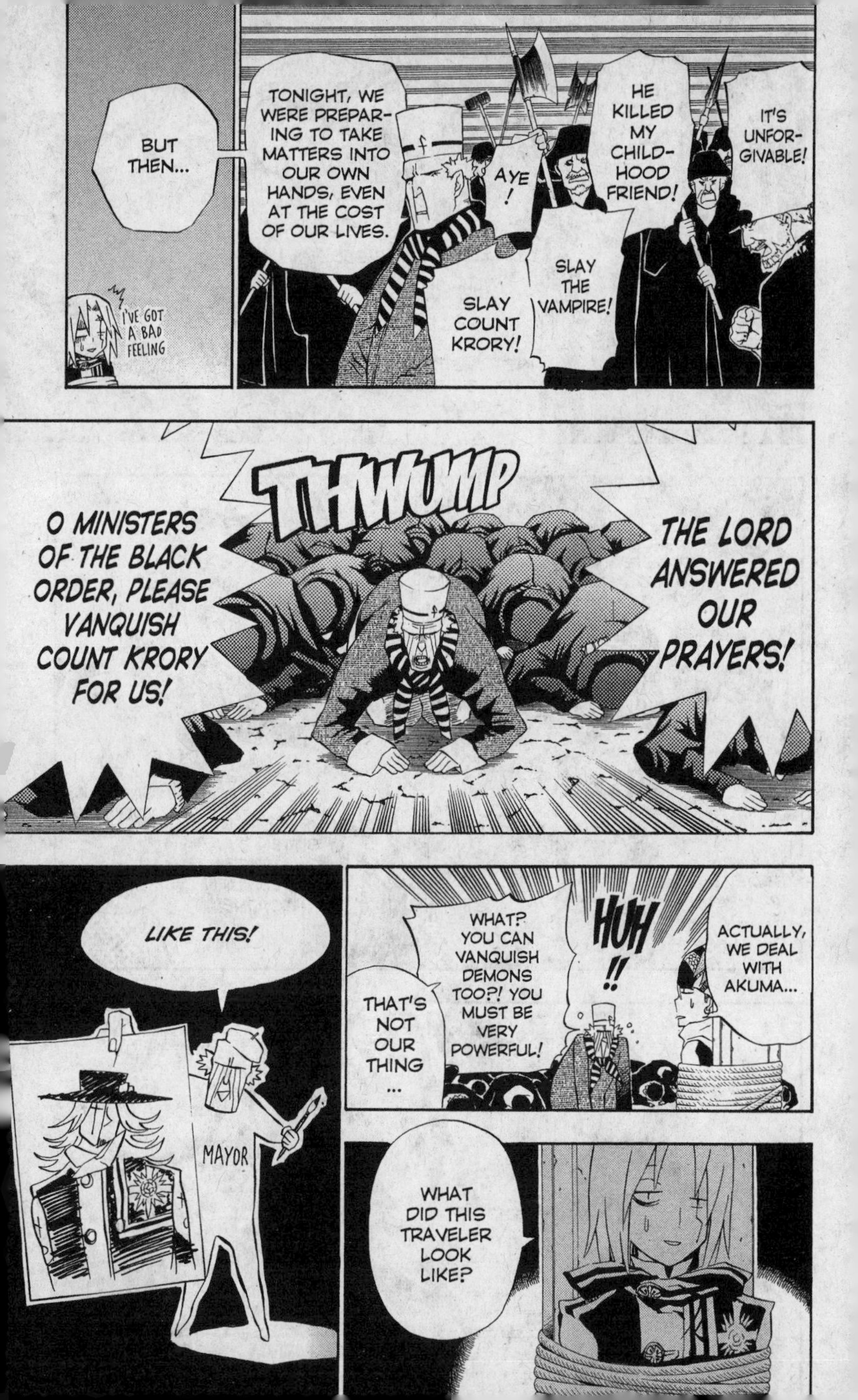
IT'S UNFORGIVABLE!
HE KILLED MY CHILDHOOD FRIEND!
AYE!
TONIGHT, WE WERE PREPARING TO TAKE MATTERS INTO OUR OWN HANDS, EVEN AT THE COST OF OUR LIVES.
SLAY THE VAMPIRE!
SLAY COUNT KRORY!
BUT THEN...
I'VE GOT A BAD FEELING
THWUMP
THE LORD ANSWERED OUR PRAYERS!
O MINISTERS OF THE BLACK ORDER, PLEASE VANQUISH COUNT KRORY FOR US!
ACTUALLY, WE DEAL WITH AKUMA...
HUH!!
WHAT? YOU CAN VANQUISH DEMONS TOO?! YOU MUST BE VERY POWERFUL!
THAT'S NOT OUR THING...
WHAT DID THIS TRAVELER LOOK LIKE?
LIKE THIS!
MAYOR

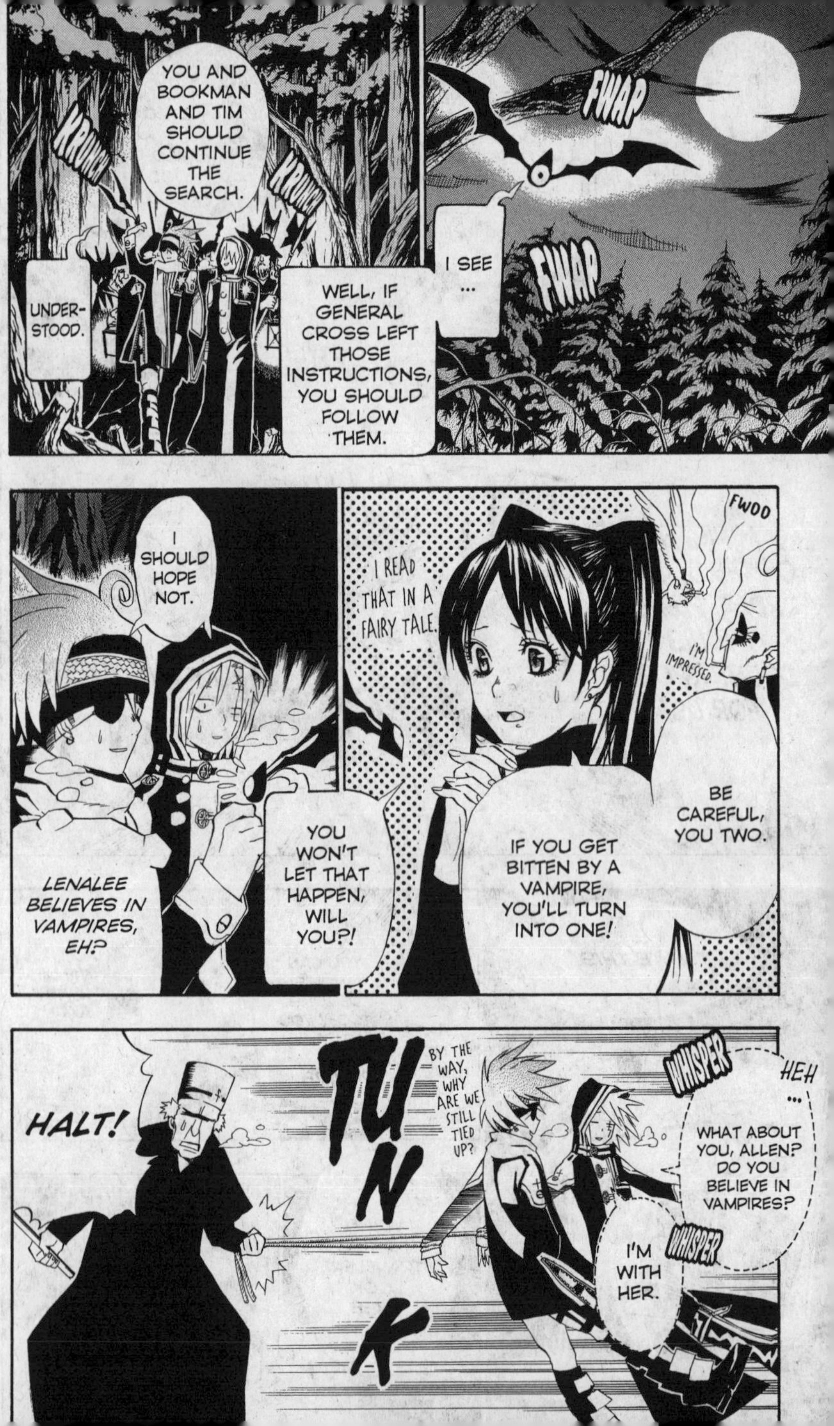
FWAP
I SEE ...
FWAP
WELL, IF GENERAL CROSS LEFT THOSE INSTRUCTIONS, YOU SHOULD FOLLOW THEM.
YOU AND BOOKMAN AND TIM SHOULD CONTINUE THE SEARCH.
KRUNK
KRUNK
UNDER-STOOD.
FWOO
I'M IMPRESSED.
BE CAREFUL, YOU TWO.
IF YOU GET BITTEN BY A VAMPIRE, YOU'LL TURN INTO ONE!
I READ THAT IN A FAIRY TALE.
YOU WON'T LET THAT HAPPEN, WILL YOU?!
I SHOULD HOPE NOT.
LENALEE BELIEVES IN VAMPIRES, EH?
WHISPER
HEH ... WHAT ABOUT YOU, ALLEN? DO YOU BELIEVE IN VAMPIRES?
WHISPER
I'M WITH HER.
BY THE WAY, WHY ARE WE STILL TIED UP?
TUNK
HALT!

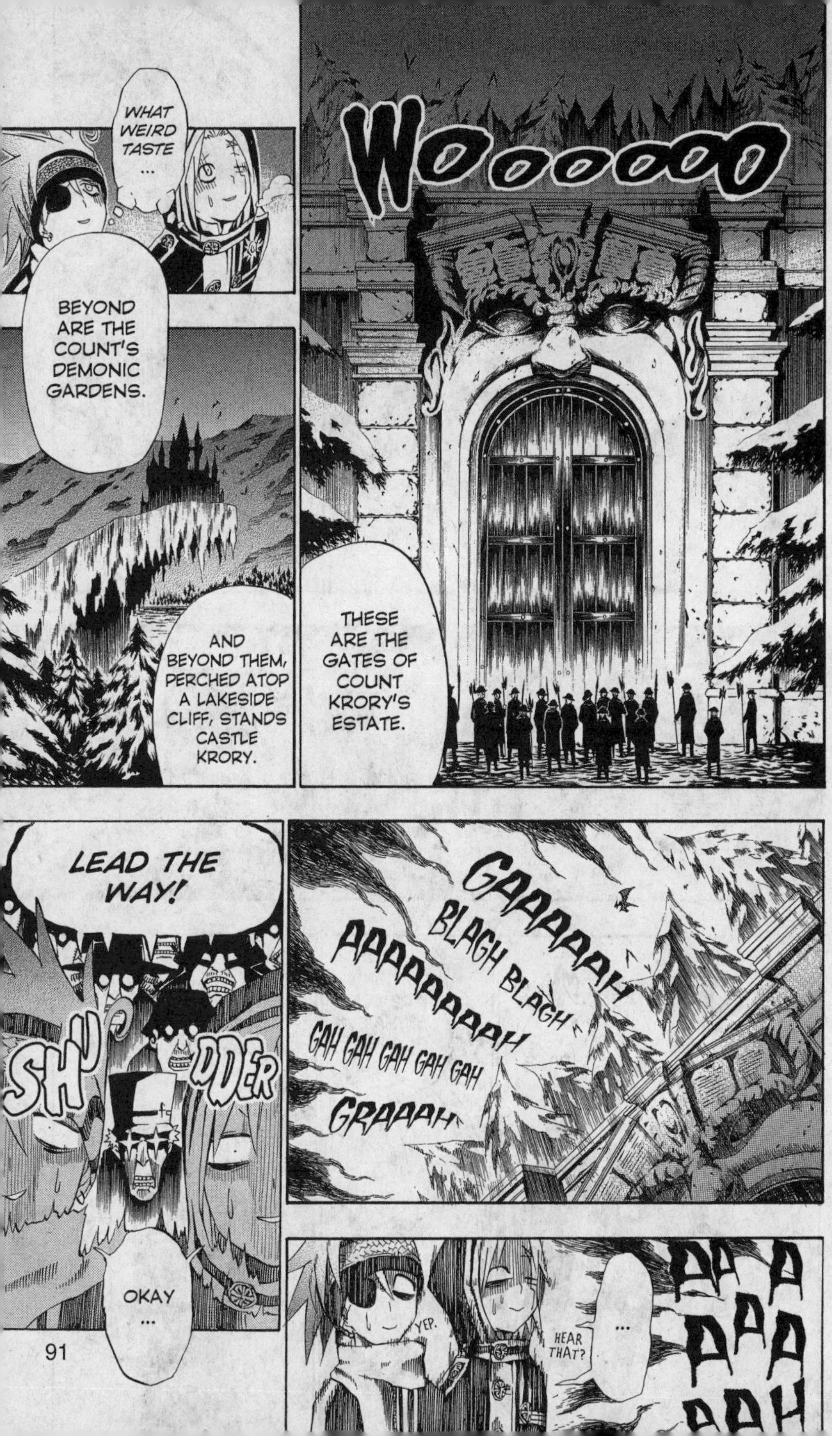

WOOOOOO
THESE ARE THE GATES OF COUNT KRORY'S ESTATE.
WHAT WEIRD TASTE ...
BEYOND ARE THE COUNT'S DEMONIC GARDENS.
AND BEYOND THEM, PERCHED ATOP A LAKESIDE CLIFF, STANDS CASTLE KRORY.
GAAAAAAH
BLAGH BLAGH
AAAAAAAAAH
GAH GAH GAH GAH GAH
GRAAAH
LEAD THE WAY!
SHUDDER
OKAY ...
AAAAAAAAH
...
HEAR THAT?
YEP.

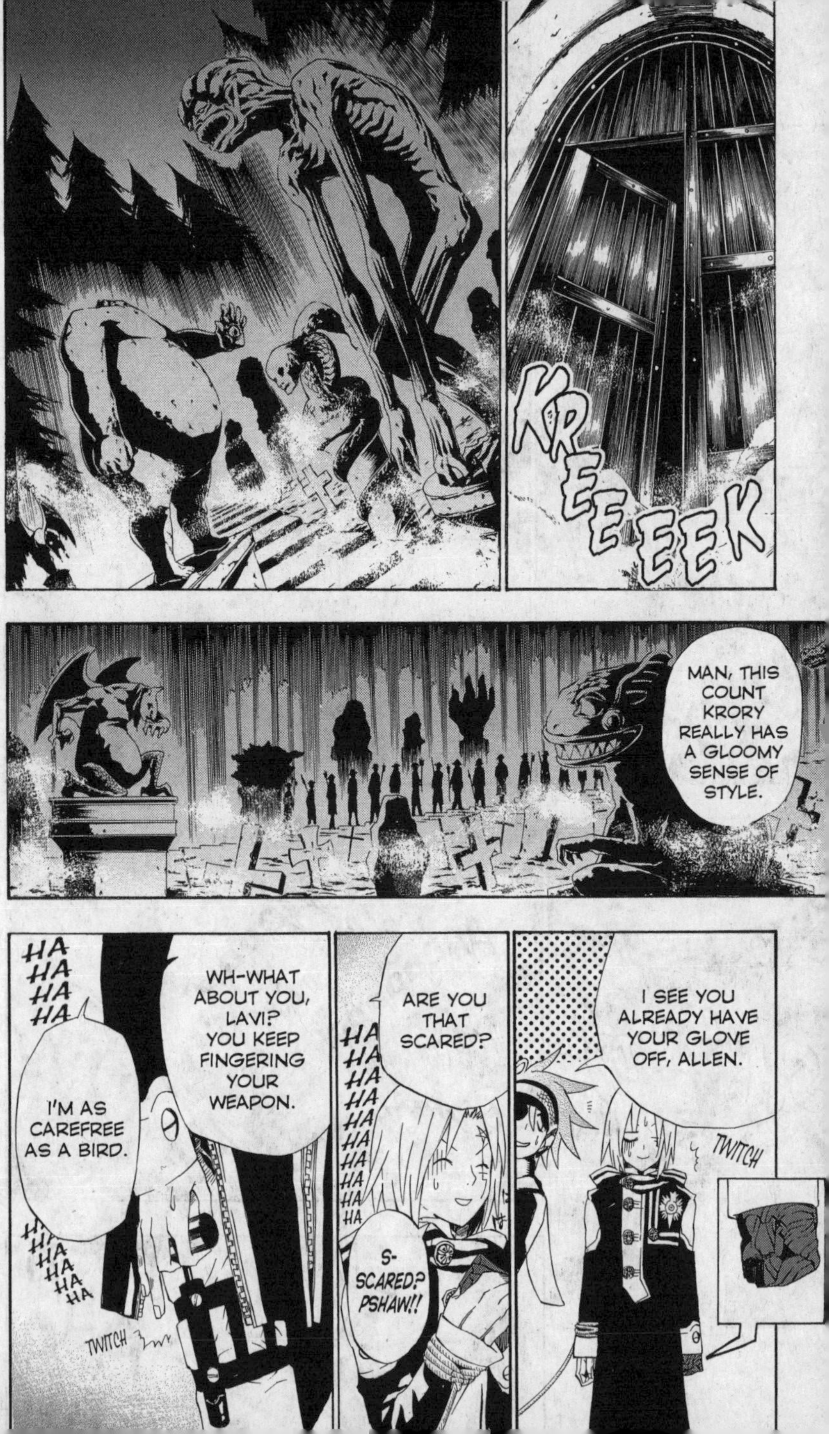
KREEEEEK
MAN, THIS COUNT KRORY REALLY HAS A GLOOMY SENSE OF STYLE.
I SEE YOU ALREADY HAVE YOUR GLOVE OFF, ALLEN.
TWITCH
ARE YOU THAT SCARED?
HA HA HA HA HA HA HA HA HA HA HA HA
S-SCARED? PSHAW!!
WH-WHAT ABOUT YOU, LAVI? YOU KEEP FINGERING YOUR WEAPON.
HA HA HA HA
I'M AS CAREFREE AS A BIRD.
HA HA HA HA HA HA
TWITCH

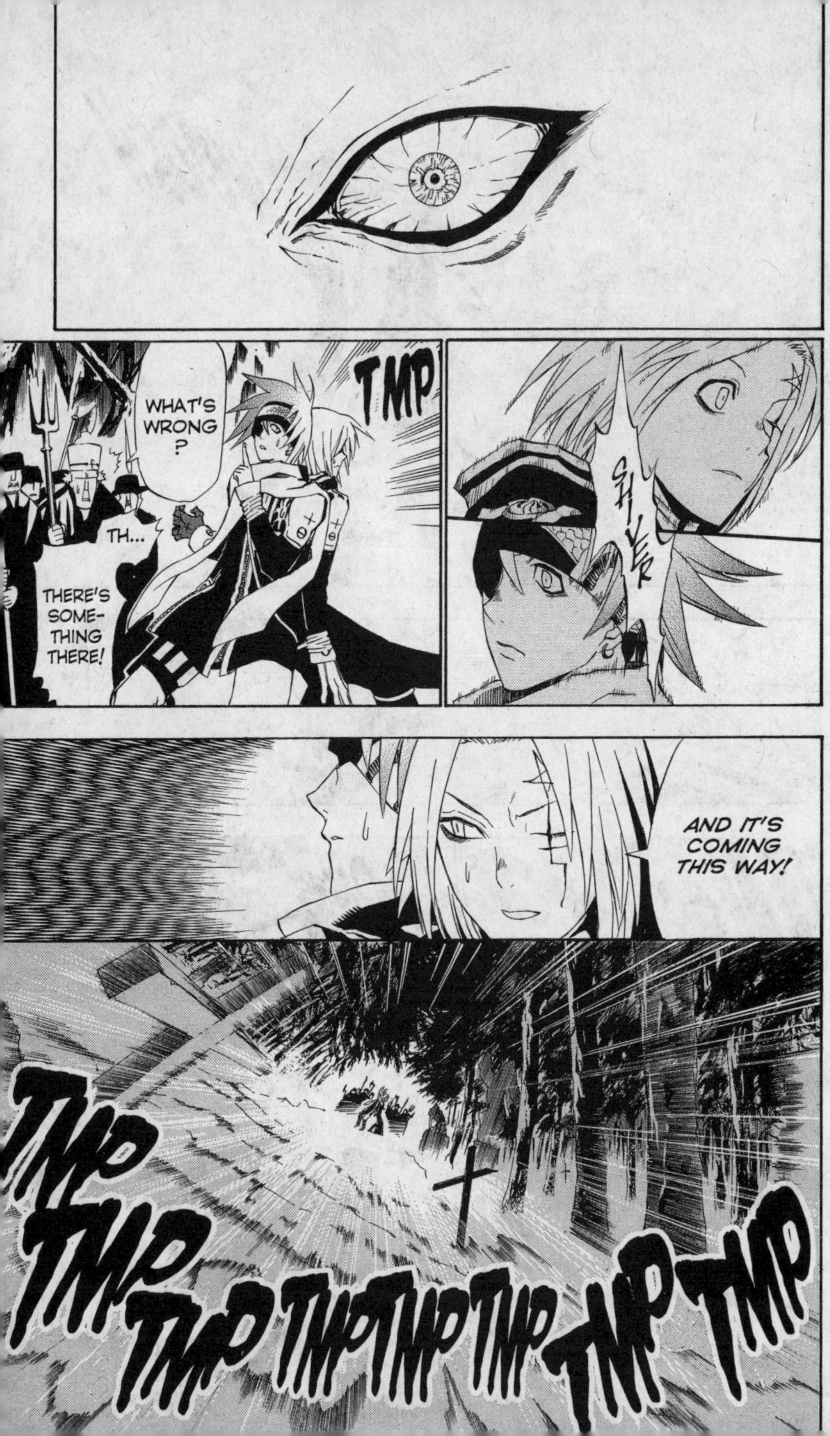
SHIVER
TMP
WHAT'S WRONG?
TH...
THERE'S SOME-THING THERE!
AND IT'S COMING THIS WAY!
TMP TMP TMP TMP TMP TMP TMP TMP

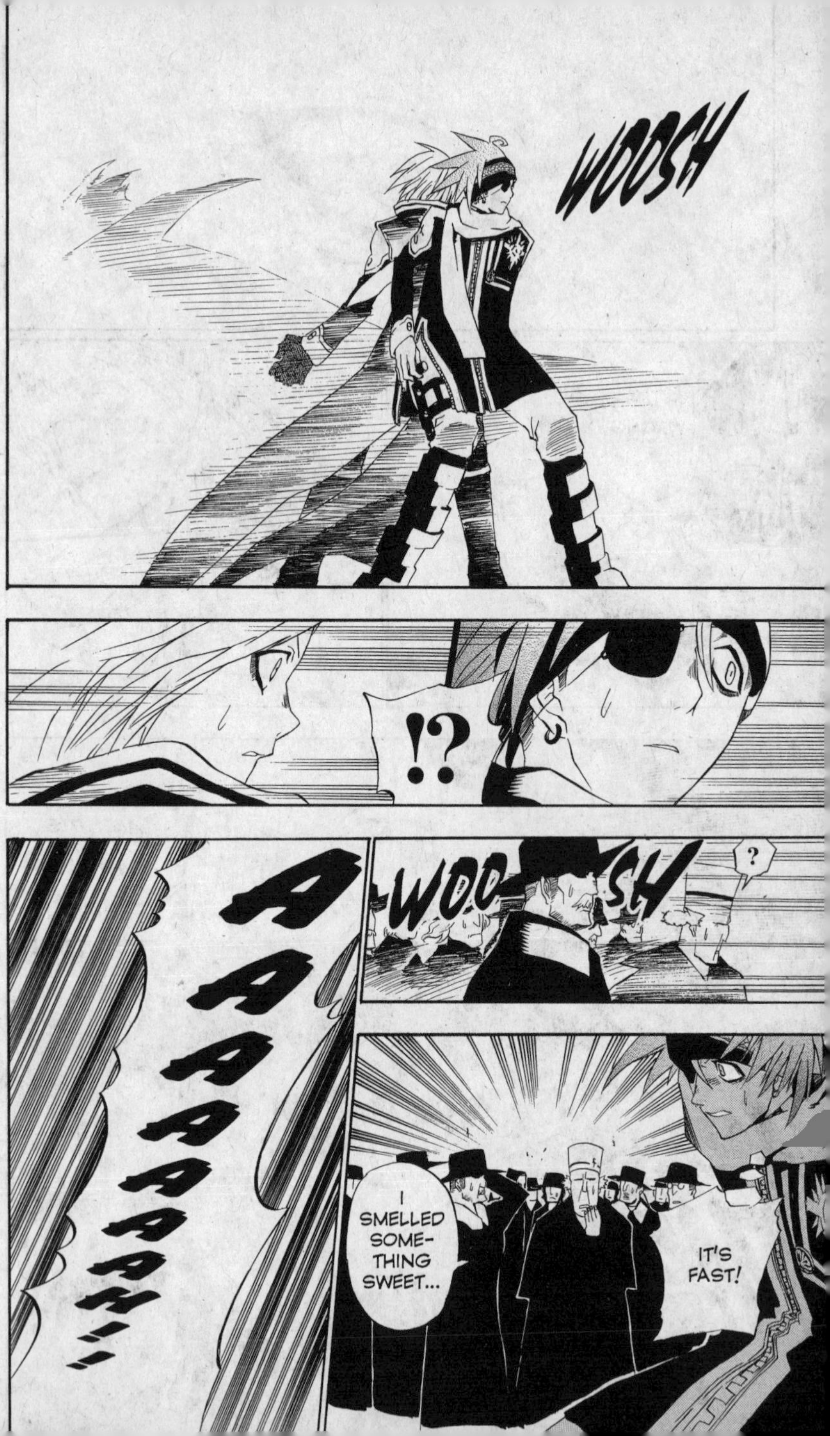
WOOSH
!?
WOOSH
?
IT'S FAST!
I SMELLED SOMETHING SWEET...
AAAAAAAAAAH!!!

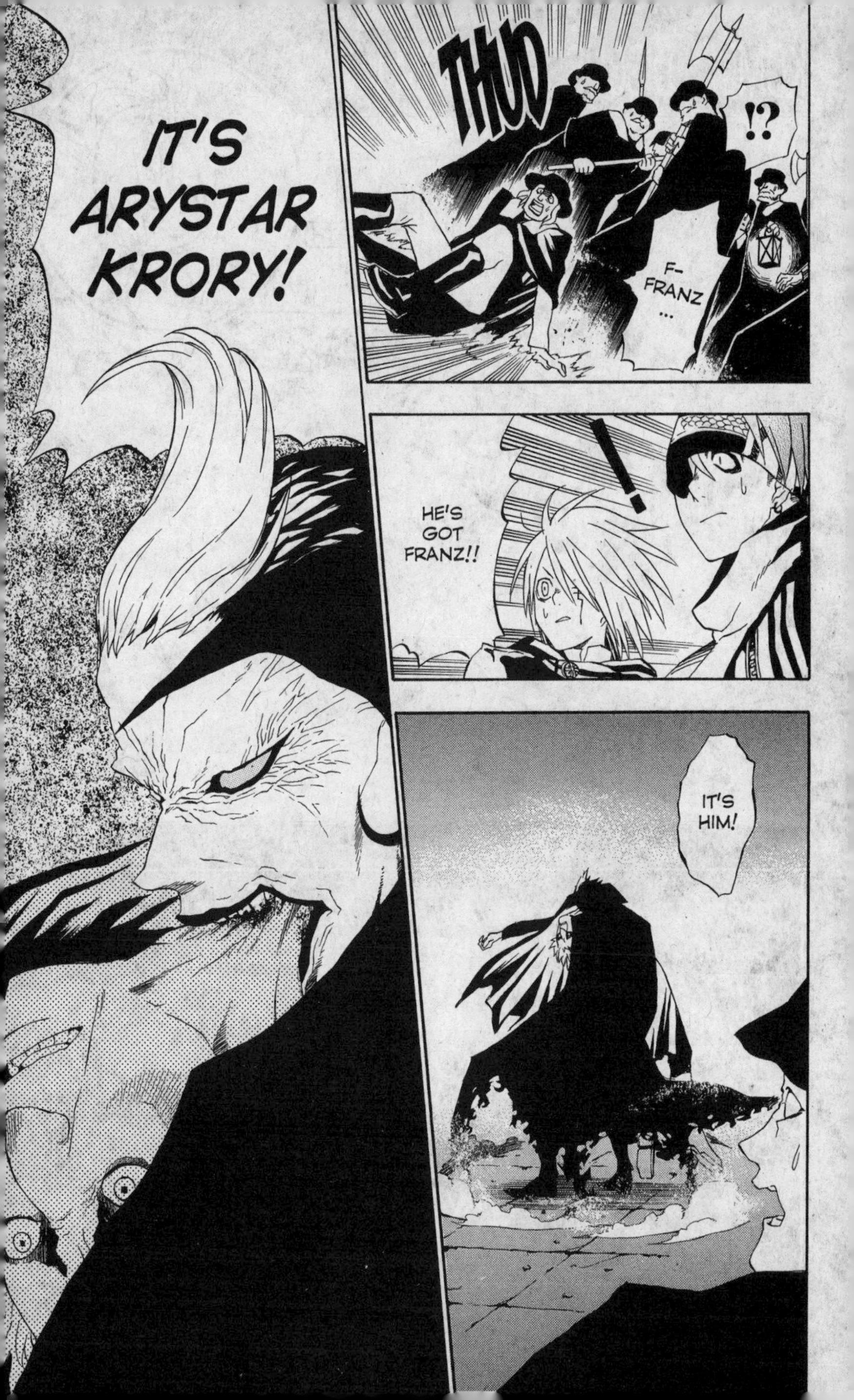
THUD
!?
F-FRANZ...
HE'S GOT FRANZ!!
IT'S HIM!
IT'S ARYSTAR KRORY!

KOMUI'S DISCUSSION ROOM VOL. 3

SORRY TO KEEP YOU WAITING. THESE ARE THE
BATHS OF THE BLACK ORDER. (MEN'S.) AREN'T
THEY AMAZING? FROM WHAT I'VE HEARD, THE
LIVING QUARTERS USED TO BE EQUIPPED WITH
SHOWERS, BUT WHEN KOMUI BECAME THE CHIEF,
THERE WAS A MAJOR RENOVATION AND THESE
BATHS WERE PUT IN. I GUESS PEOPLE FROM THE
THE FAR EAST LIKE TAKING BATHS. THE WATER SEEMS
FINE TODAY, BUT OCCASIONALLY KOMUI ADDS UNKNOWN
SUBSTANCES TO IT, SO ONE HAS TO BE CAREFUL.

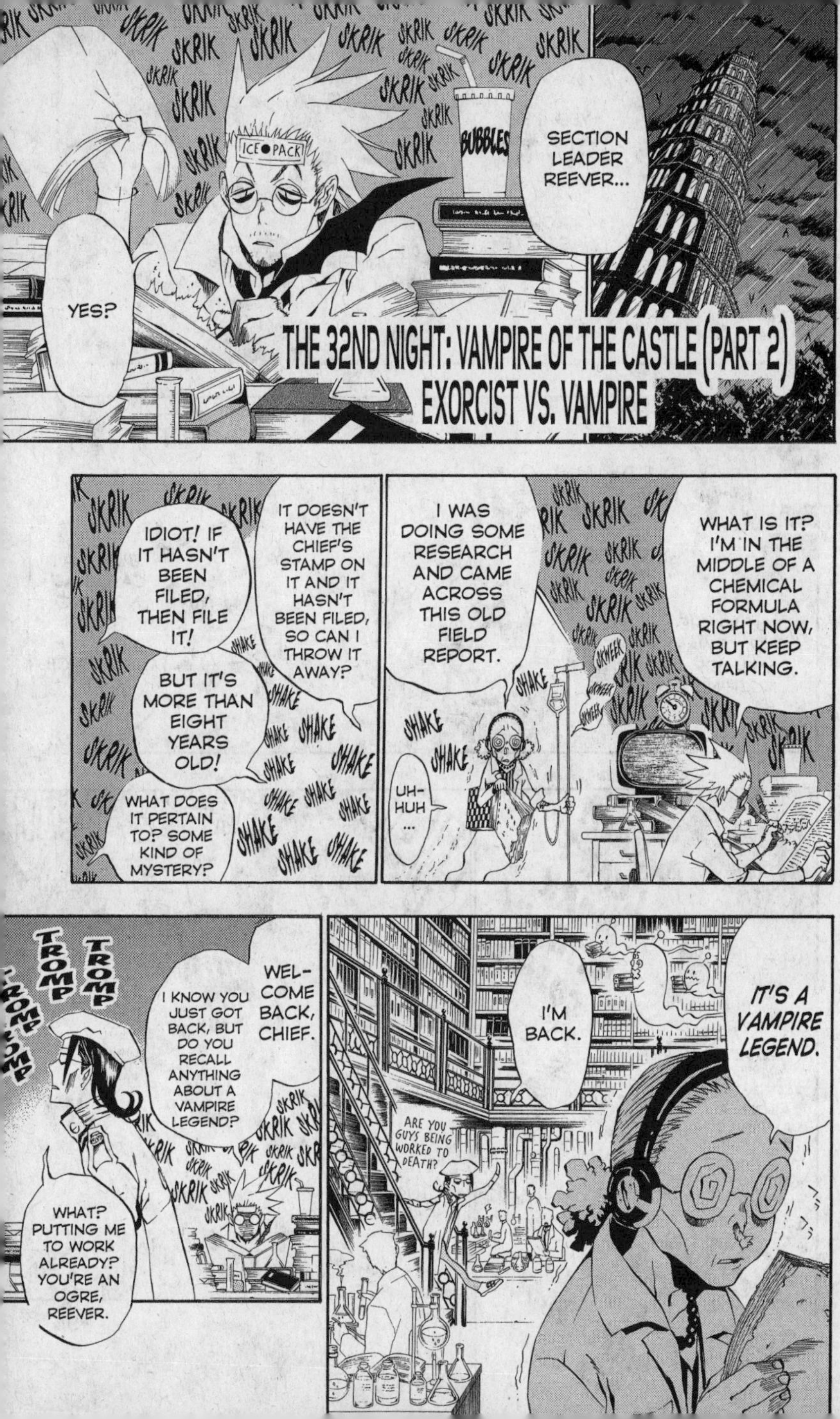
SECTION LEADER REEVER...
SKRIK
ICE PACK
BUBBLES
YES?
THE 32ND NIGHT: VAMPIRE OF THE CASTLE (PART 2)
EXORCIST VS. VAMPIRE
WHAT IS IT? I'M IN THE MIDDLE OF A CHEMICAL FORMULA RIGHT NOW, BUT KEEP TALKING.
I WAS DOING SOME RESEARCH AND CAME ACROSS THIS OLD FIELD REPORT.
SKWEEK
SHAKE
UH-HUH...
IT DOESN'T HAVE THE CHIEF'S STAMP ON IT AND IT HASN'T BEEN FILED, SO CAN I THROW IT AWAY?
IDIOT! IF IT HASN'T BEEN FILED, THEN FILE IT!
BUT IT'S MORE THAN EIGHT YEARS OLD!
WHAT DOES IT PERTAIN TO? SOME KIND OF MYSTERY?
IT'S A VAMPIRE LEGEND.
I'M BACK.
ARE YOU GUYS BEING WORKED TO DEATH?
WEL-COME BACK, CHIEF.
I KNOW YOU JUST GOT BACK, BUT DO YOU RECALL ANYTHING ABOUT A VAMPIRE LEGEND?
TROMP TROMP TROMP TROMP
WHAT? PUTTING ME TO WORK ALREADY? YOU'RE AN OGRE, REEVER.

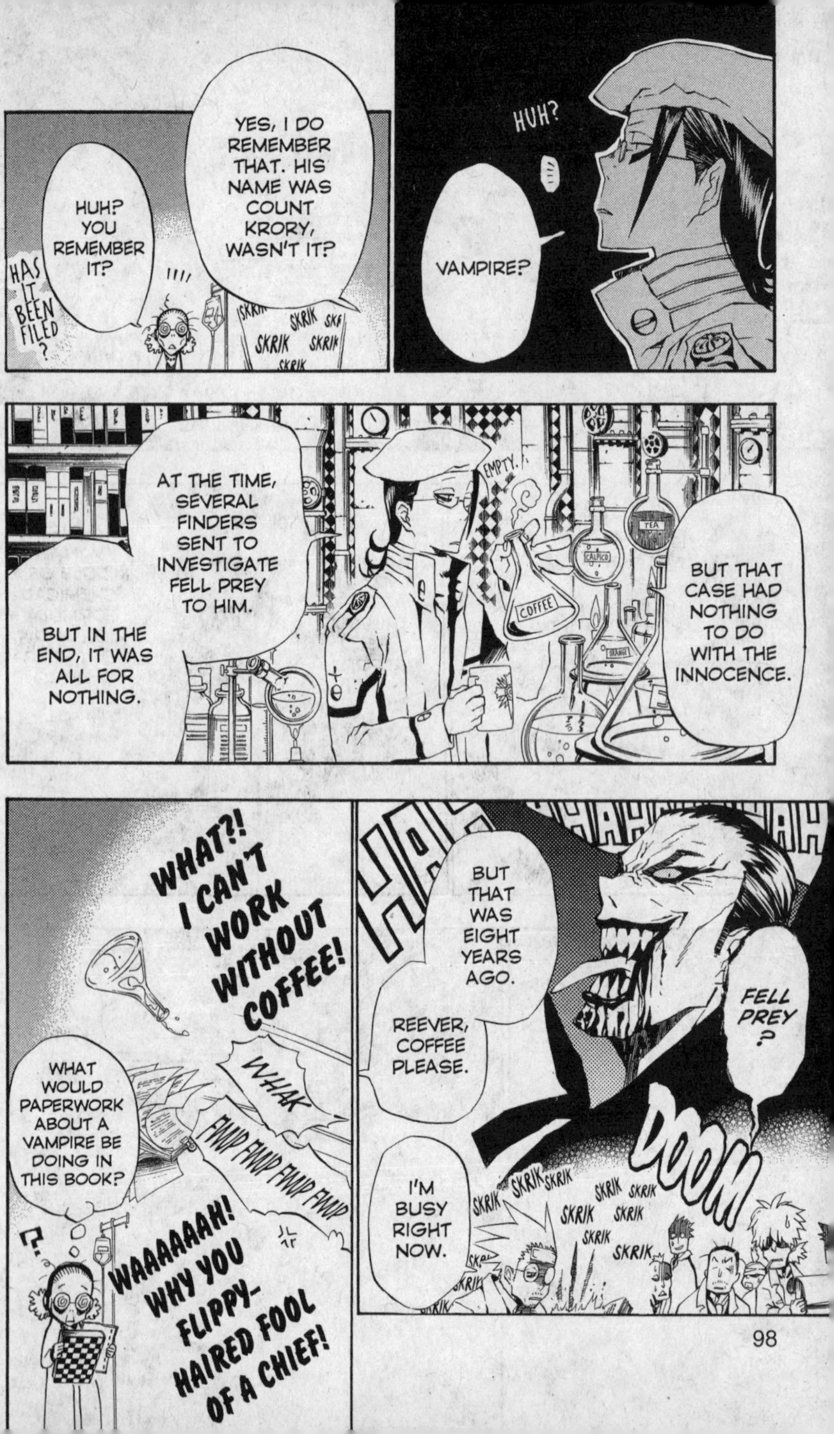
HUH?
...!
VAMPIRE?
YES, I DO REMEMBER THAT. HIS NAME WAS COUNT KRORY, WASN'T IT?
!!!!
HUH? YOU REMEMBER IT?
HAS IT BEEN FILED?
SKRIK SKRIK SKRIK SKRIK SKRIK SKRIK
EMPTY.
AT THE TIME, SEVERAL FINDERS SENT TO INVESTIGATE FELL PREY TO HIM.
BUT IN THE END, IT WAS ALL FOR NOTHING.
BUT THAT CASE HAD NOTHING TO DO WITH THE INNOCENCE.
TEA
CALPICO
COFFEE
ORANGE
BUT THAT WAS EIGHT YEARS AGO.
FELL PREY?
REEVER, COFFEE PLEASE.
DOOM
I'M BUSY RIGHT NOW.
SKRIK SKRIK SKRIK SKRIK SKRIK SKRIK SKRIK SKRIK SKRIK SKRIK
WHAT?! I CAN'T WORK WITHOUT COFFEE!
WHAK
FWUP FWUP FWUP FWUP
WHAT WOULD PAPERWORK ABOUT A VAMPIRE BE DOING IN THIS BOOK?
?
WAAAAAAH! WHY YOU FLIPPY-HAIRED FOOL OF A CHIEF!

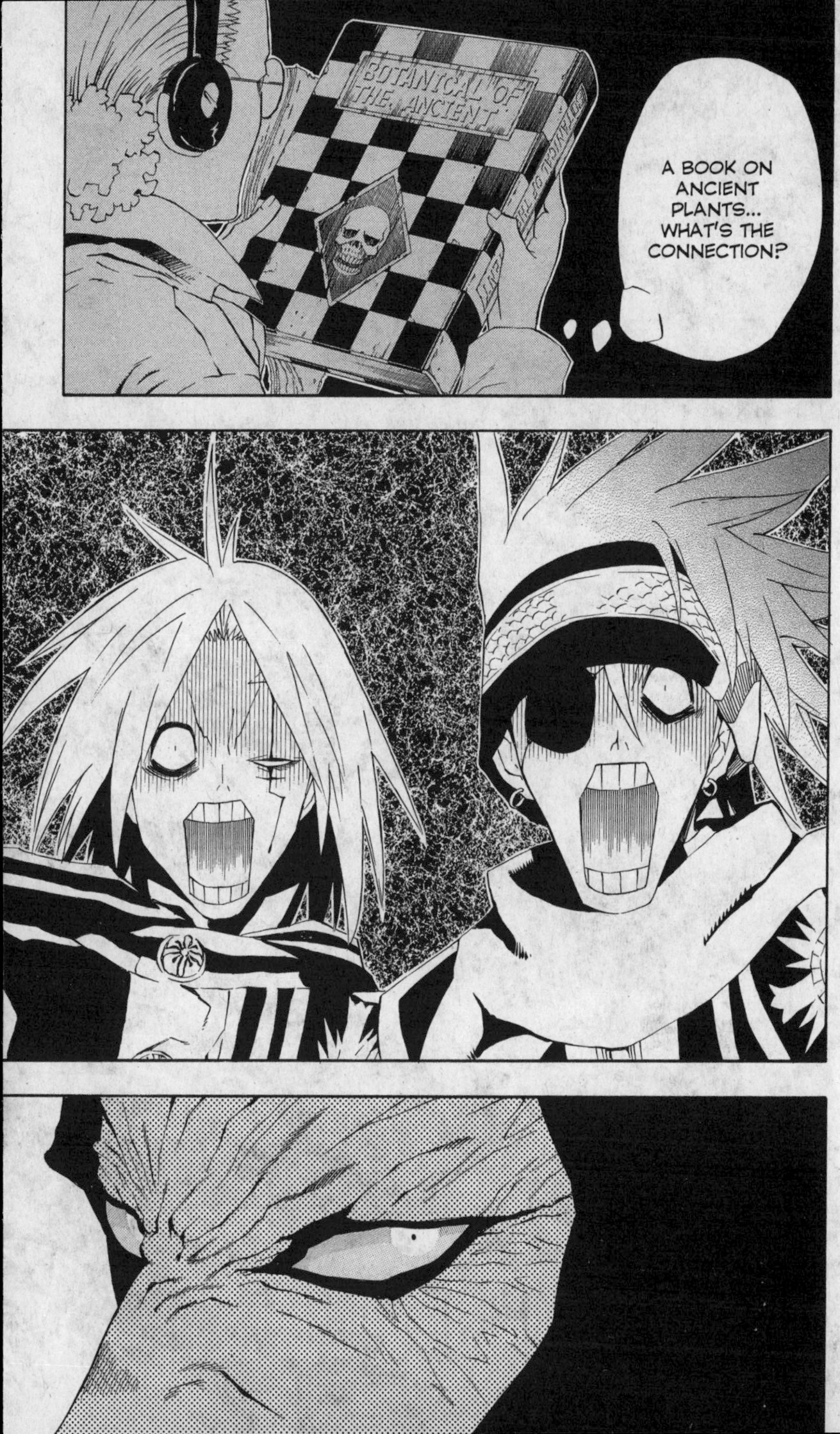
A BOOK ON ANCIENT PLANTS... WHAT'S THE CONNECTION?
BOTANICAL OF THE ANCIENT

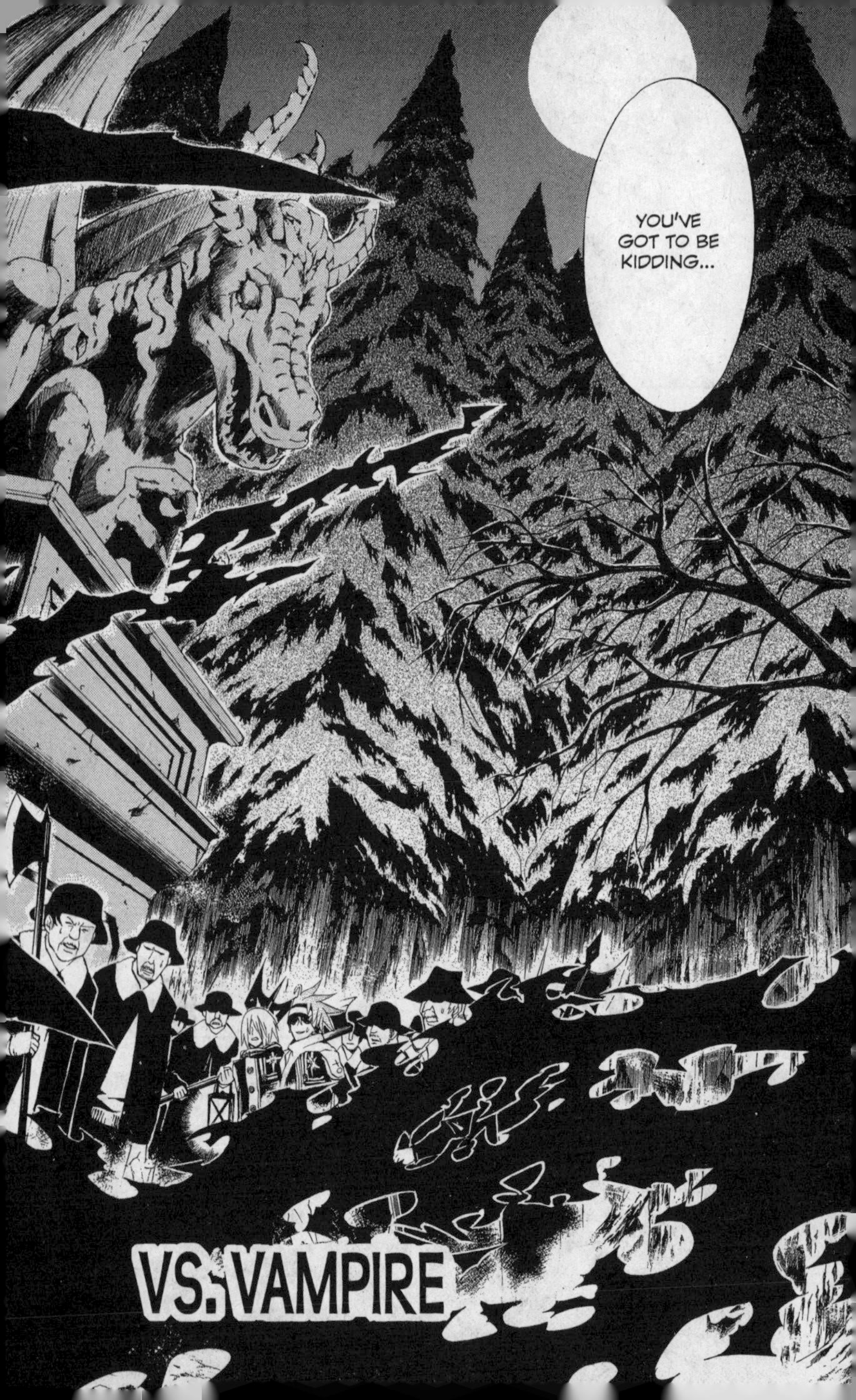
YOU'VE GOT TO BE KIDDING...
VS. VAMPIRE

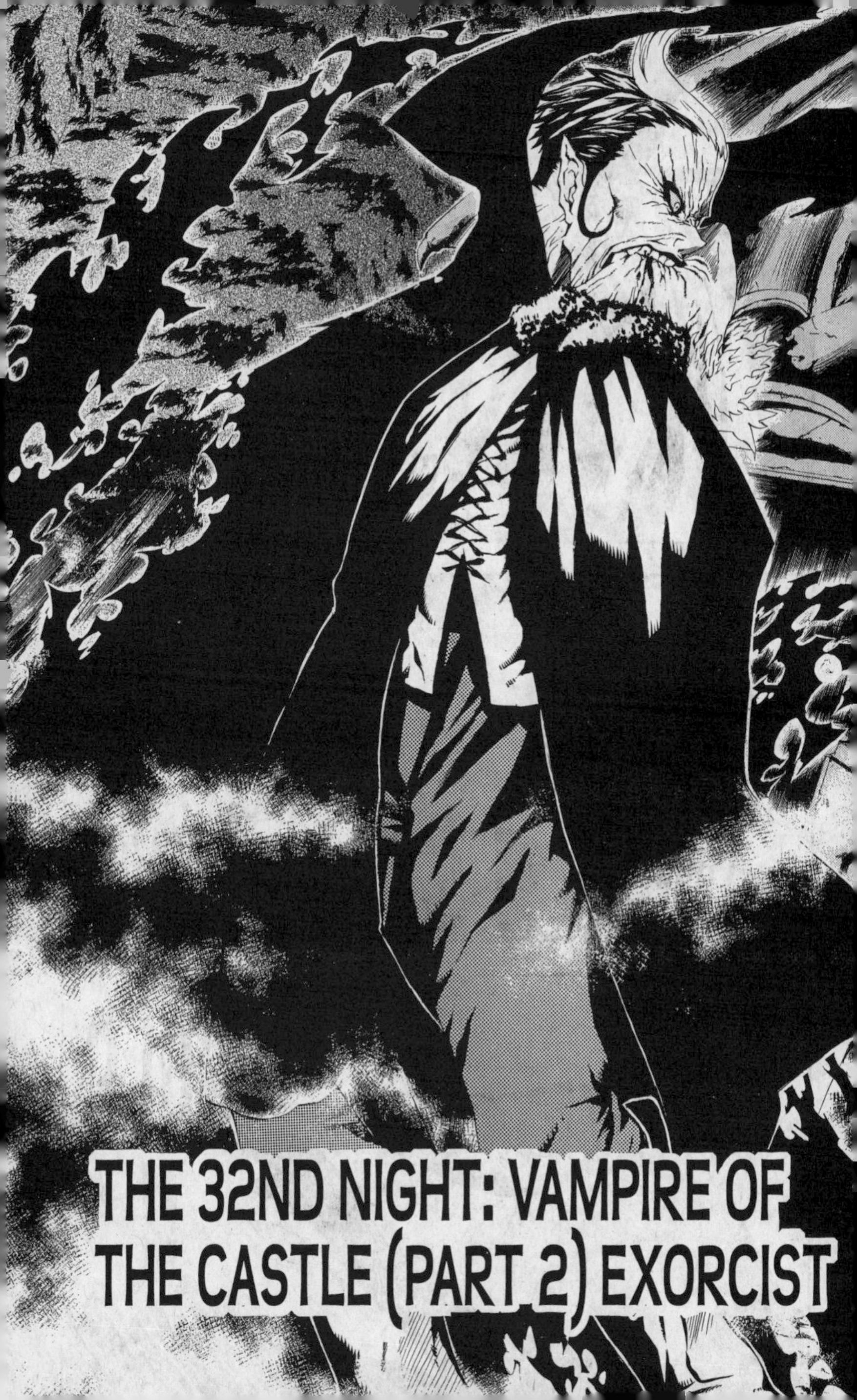
THE 32ND NIGHT: VAMPIRE OF
THE CASTLE (PART 2) EXORCIST

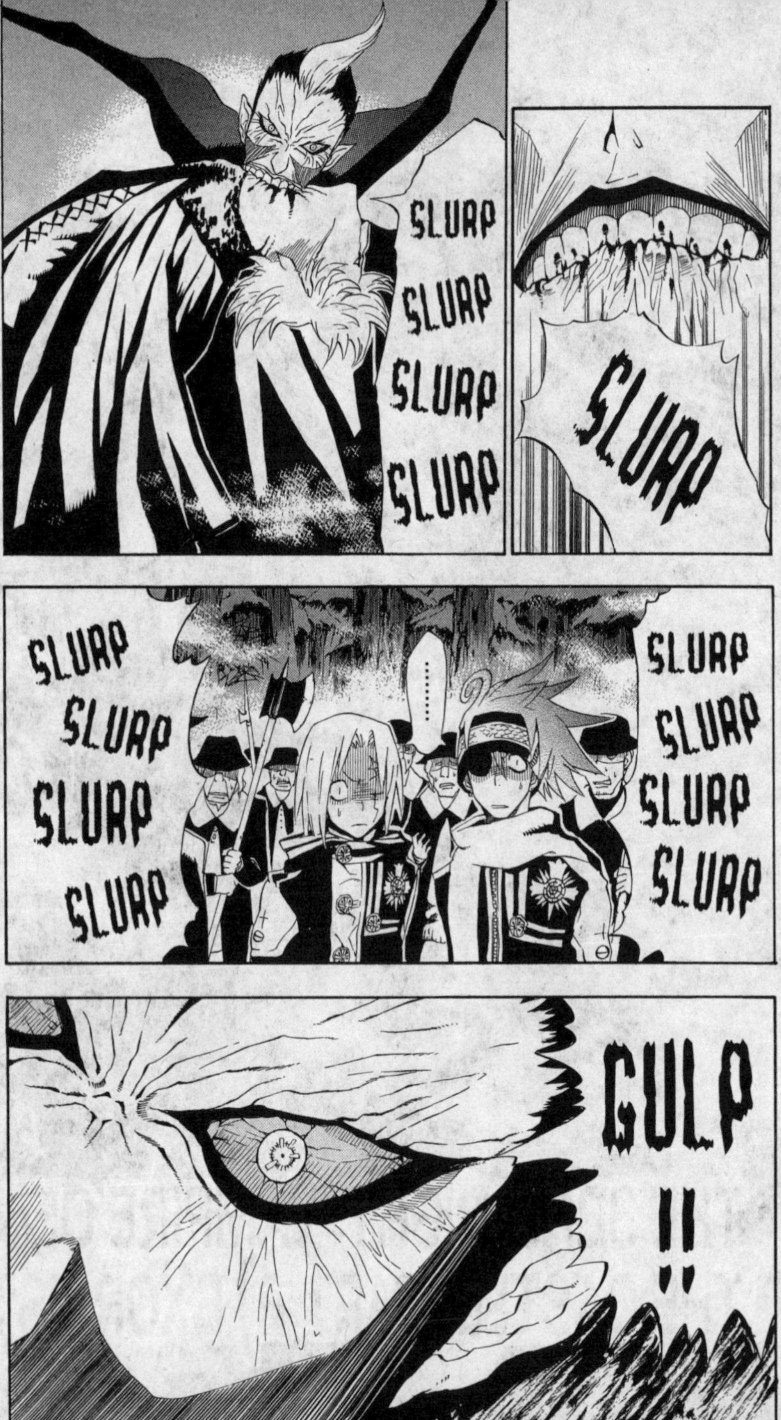
SLURP
SLURP
SLURP
SLURP
SLURP
SLURP
SLURP
SLURP
SLURP
......
SLURP
SLURP
SLURP
SLURP
GULP!!

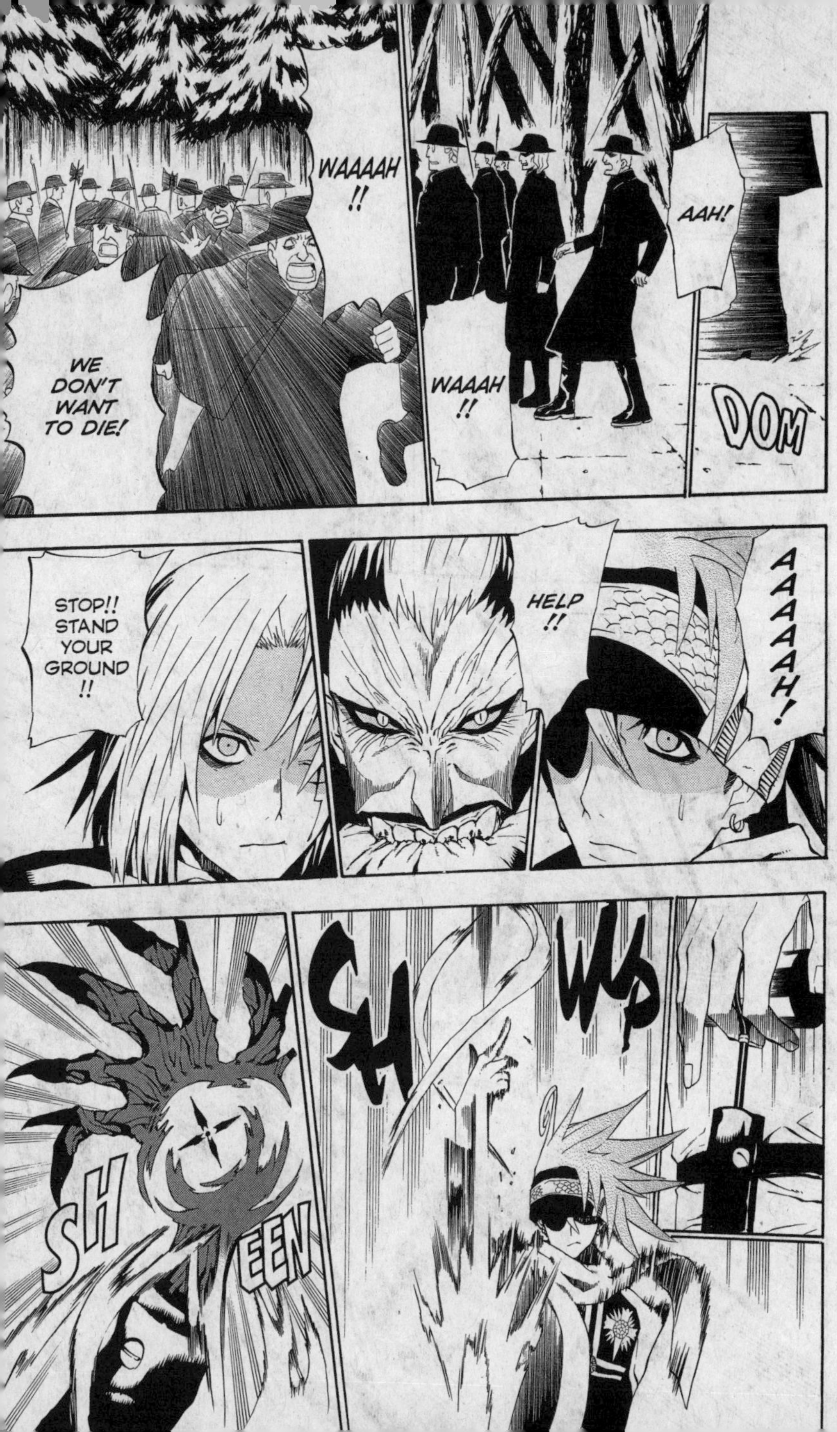
AAH!
DOM
WAAAH!!
WAAAAH!!
WE DON'T WANT TO DIE!
AAAAAAH!
HELP!!
STOP!! STAND YOUR GROUND!!
SHWSH
SHEEN

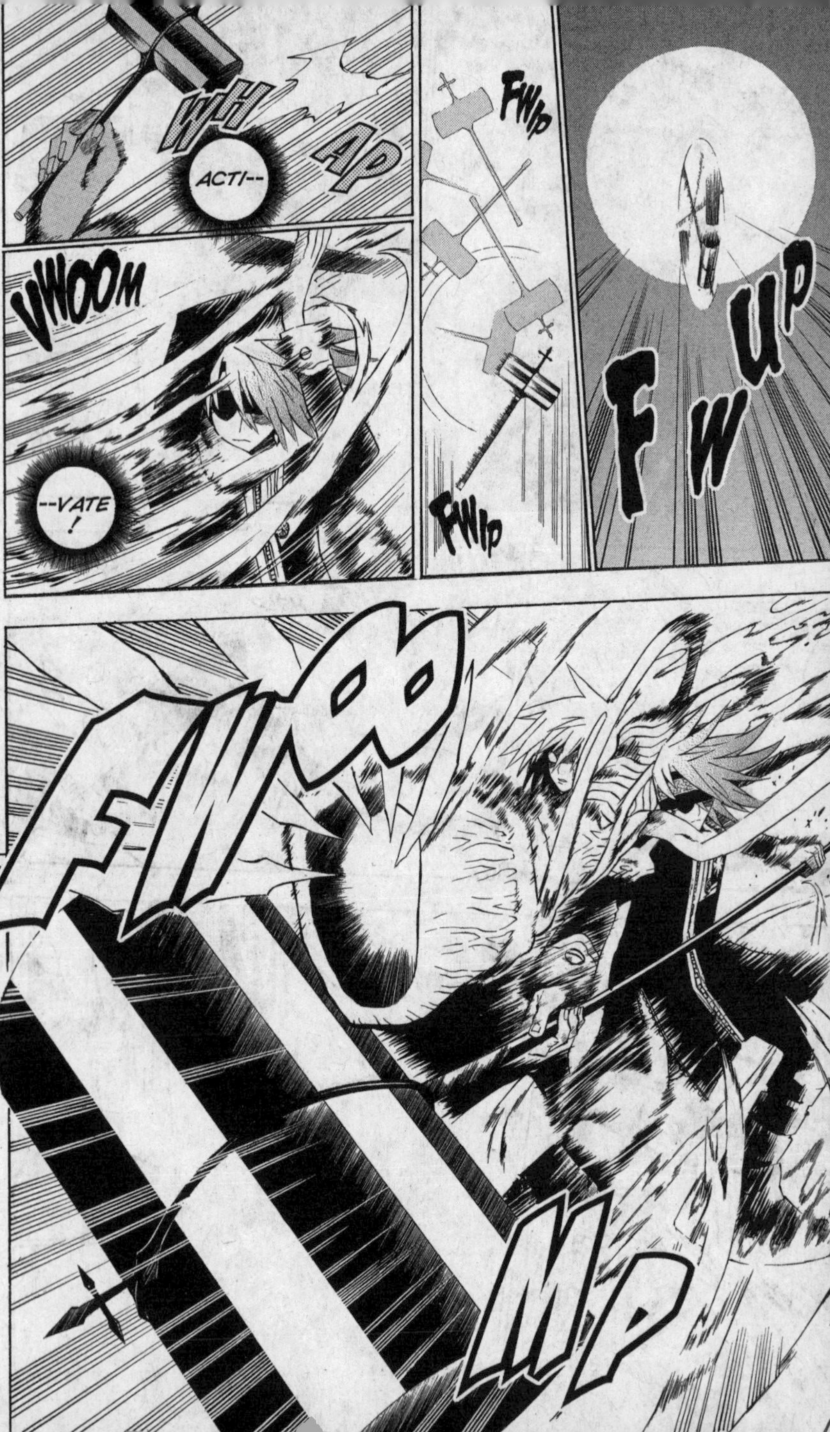
FWUP
FWIP
FWIP
WHAP
ACTI--
VWOOM
--VATE!
FWOMP

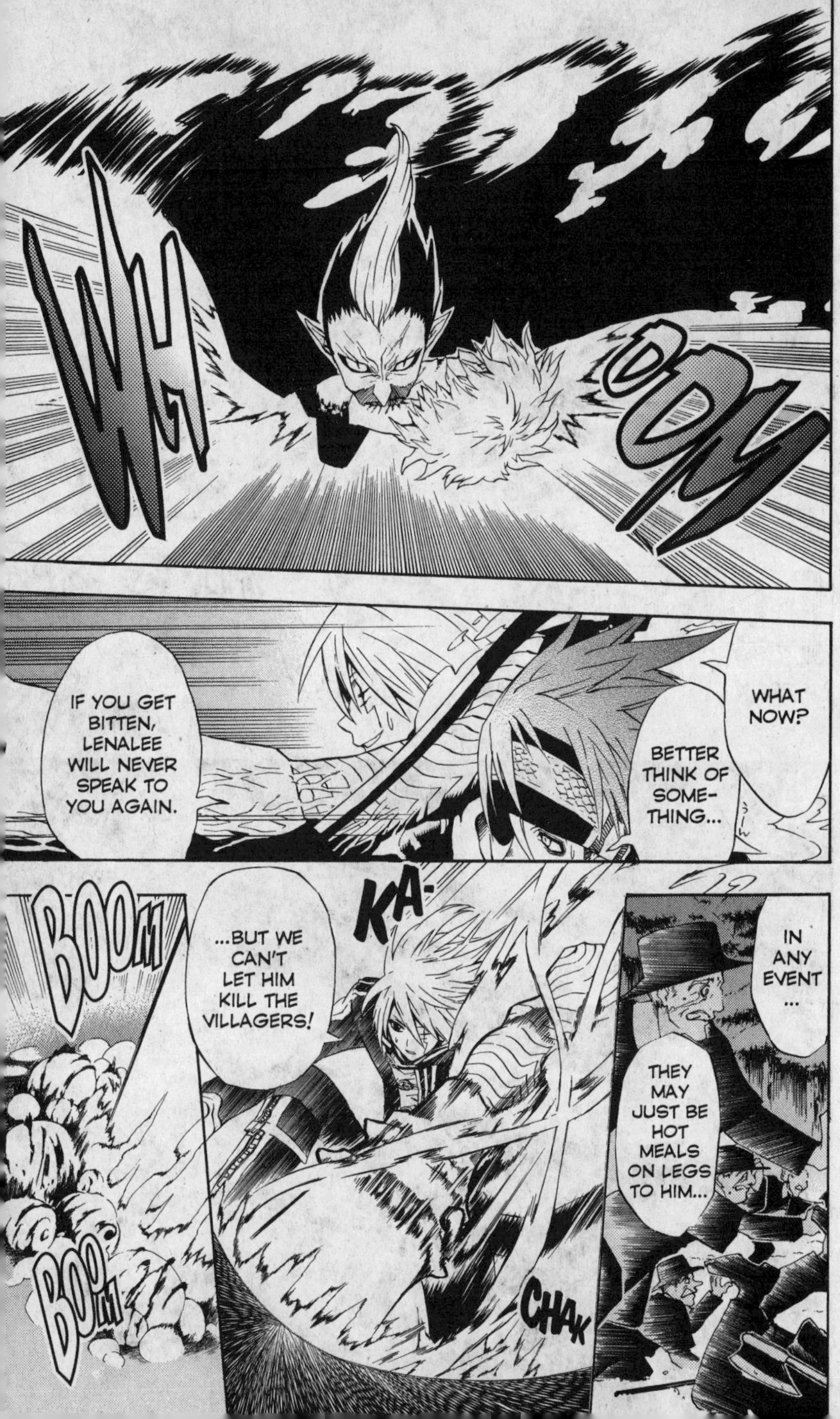
DOM
WH
WHAT NOW?
BETTER THINK OF SOME-THING...
IF YOU GET BITTEN, LENALEE WILL NEVER SPEAK TO YOU AGAIN.
IN ANY EVENT ...
THEY MAY JUST BE HOT MEALS ON LEGS TO HIM...
KA-
...BUT WE CAN'T LET HIM KILL THE VILLAGERS!
CHAK
BOOM
BOOM

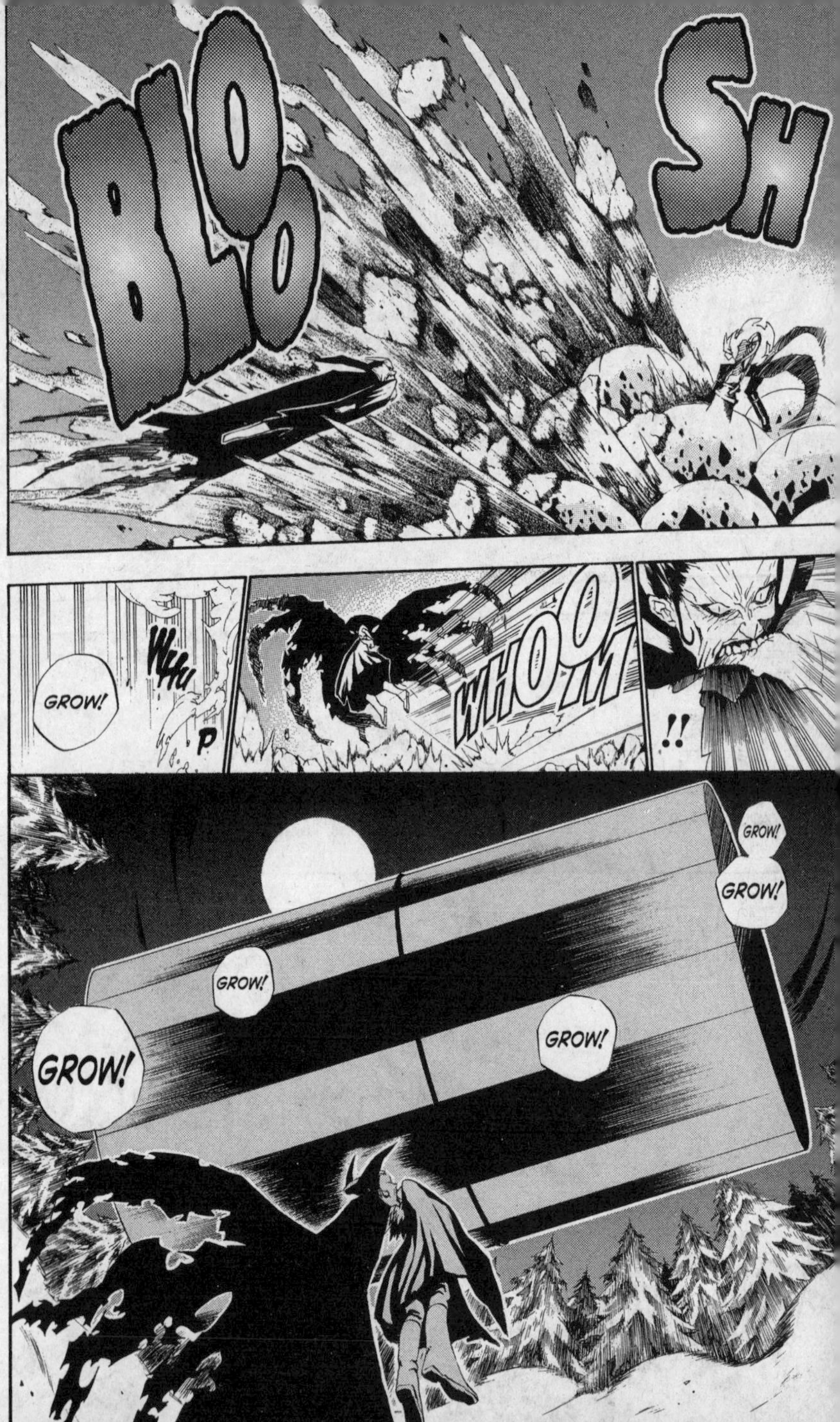
BLOOSH
!!
WHOOM
WHUP
GROW!
GROW!
GROW!
GROW!
GROW!
GROW!
GROW!

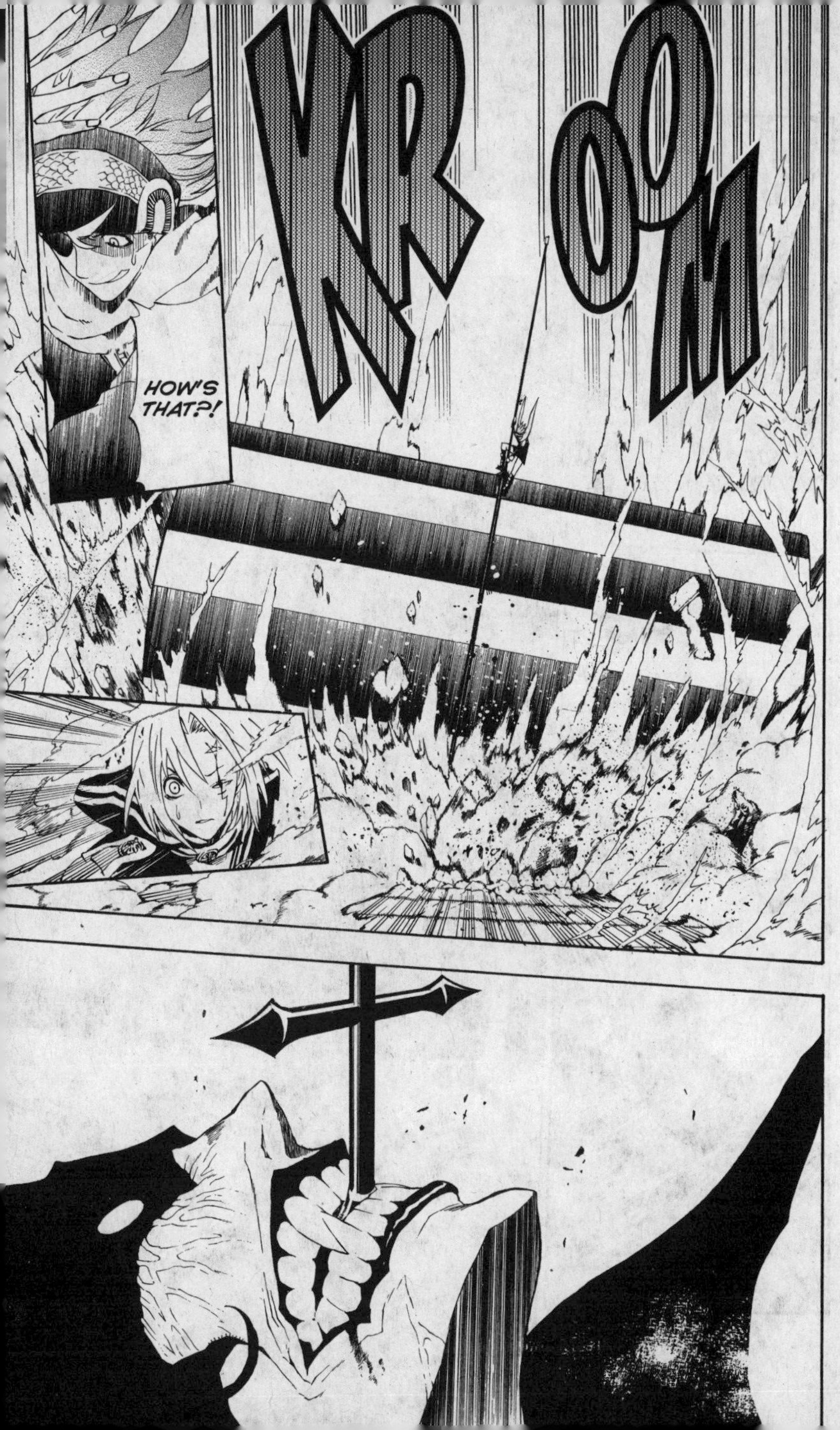
KRBOOOM
HOW'S THAT?!

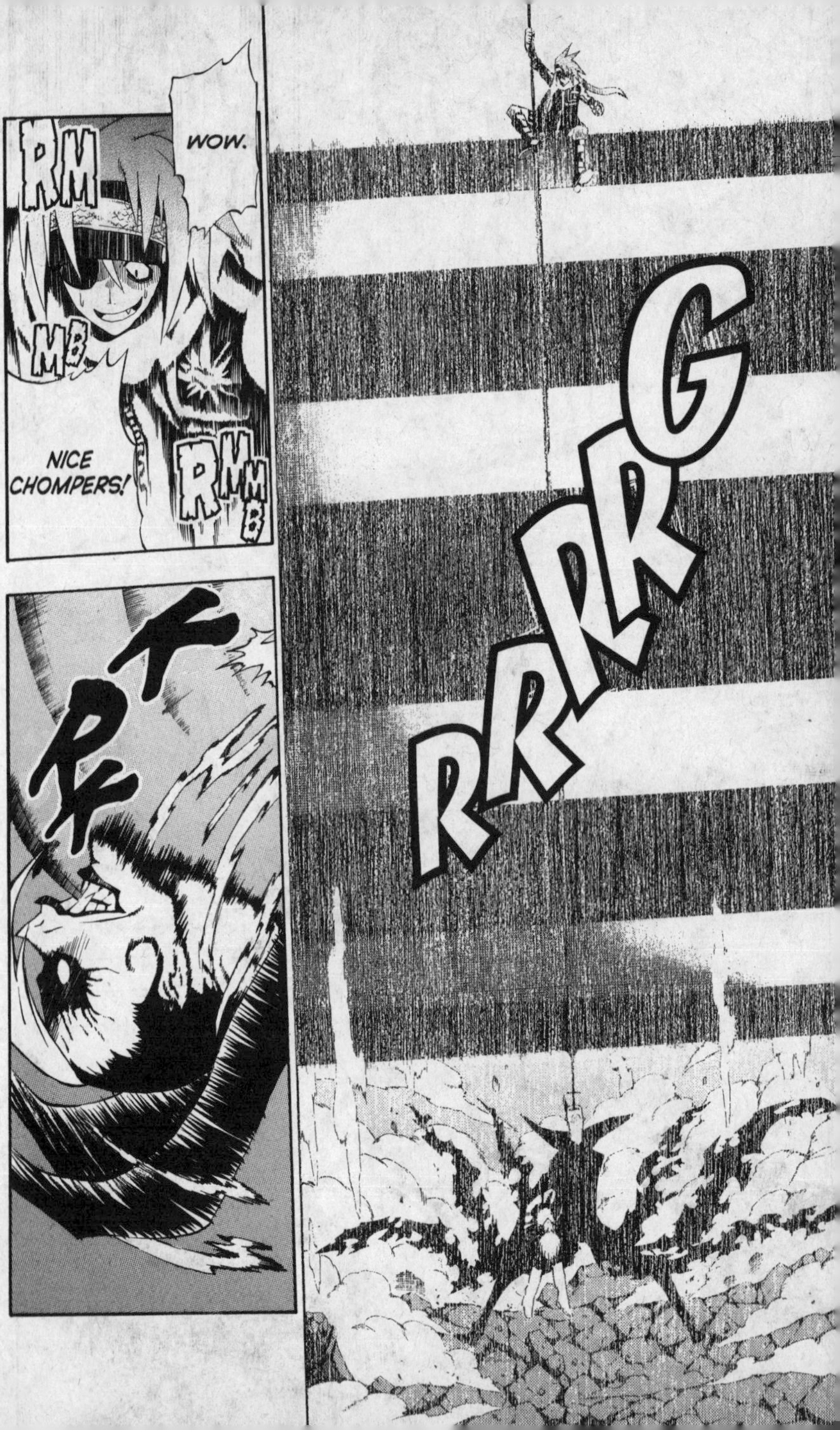
RRRRG
WOW.
RMMB
NICE CHOMPERS!
RMMB

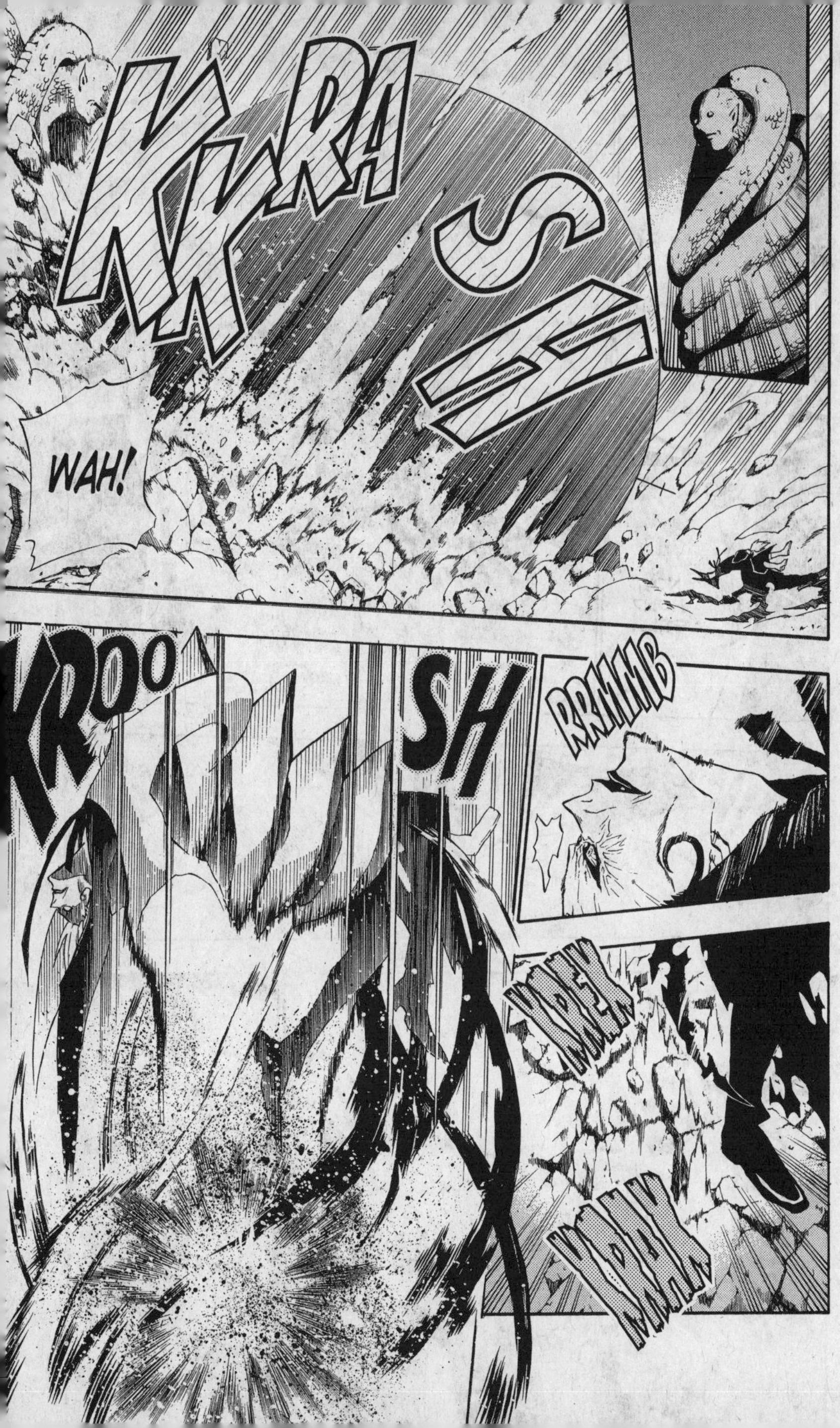
KRASH
WAH!
RRMMB
KROOSH

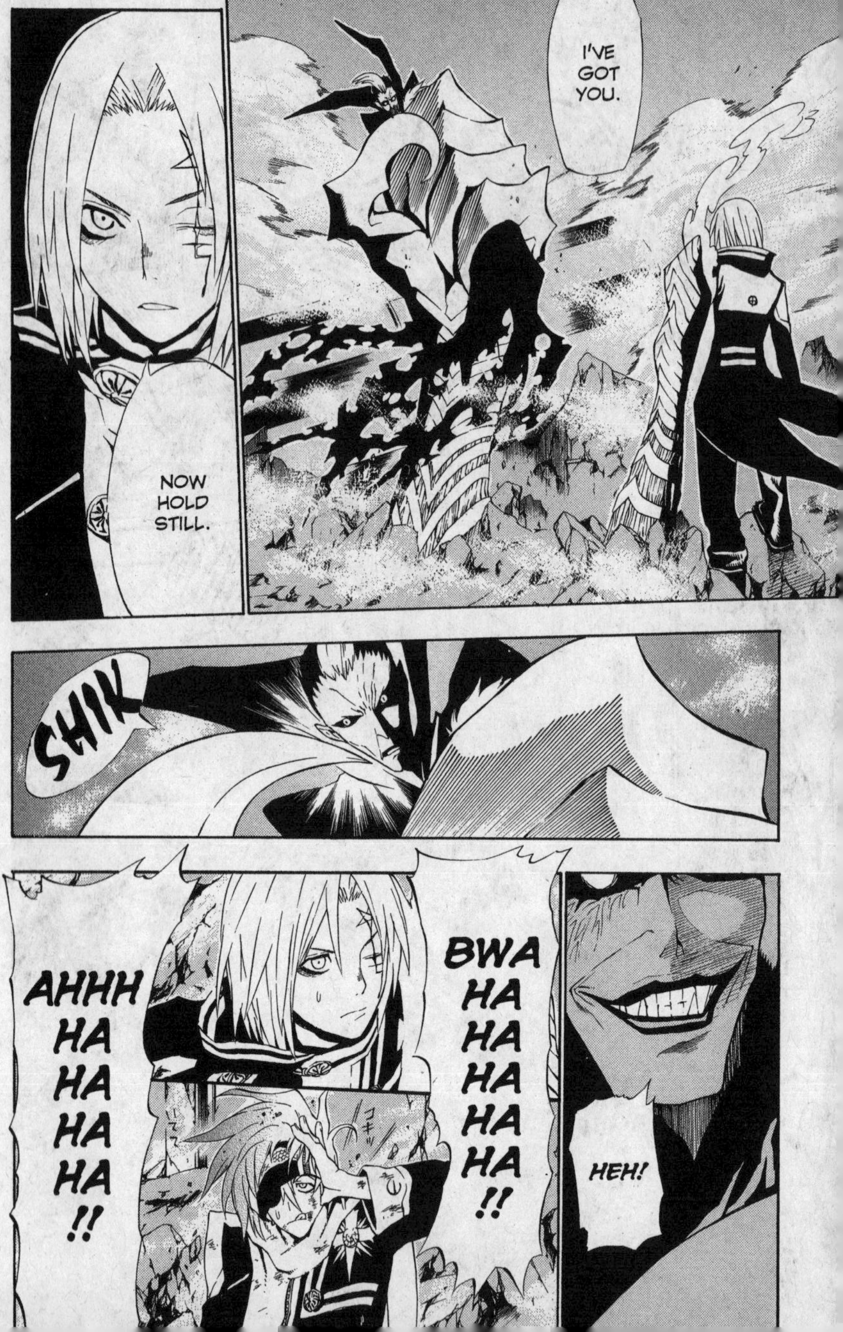
I'VE GOT YOU.
NOW HOLD STILL.
SHIK
HEH!
BWA HA HA HA HA HA HA!!
AHHH HA HA HA HA HA!!

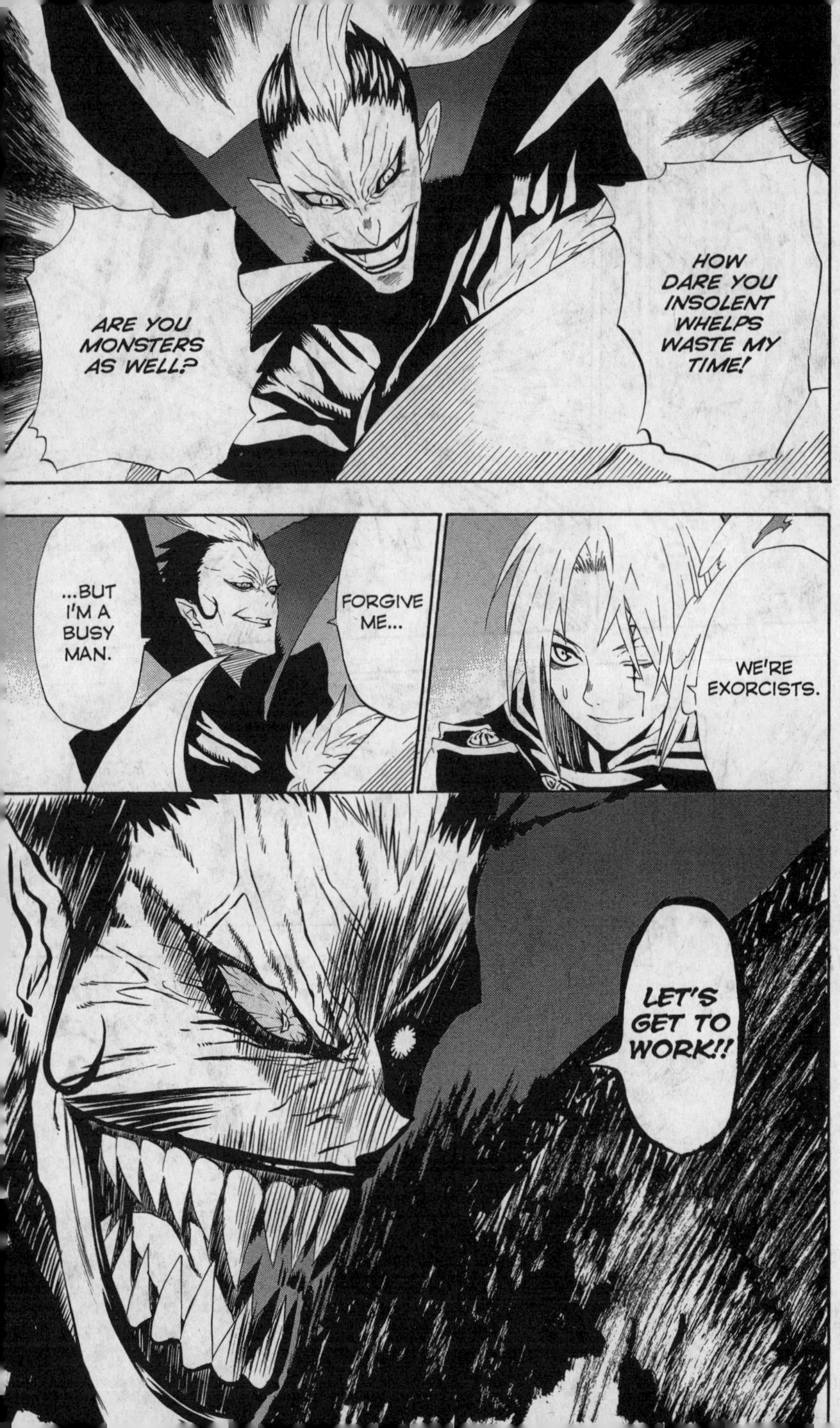
HOW DARE YOU INSOLENT WHELPS WASTE MY TIME!
ARE YOU MONSTERS AS WELL?
WE'RE EXORCISTS.
FORGIVE ME...
...BUT I'M A BUSY MAN.
LET'S GET TO WORK!!

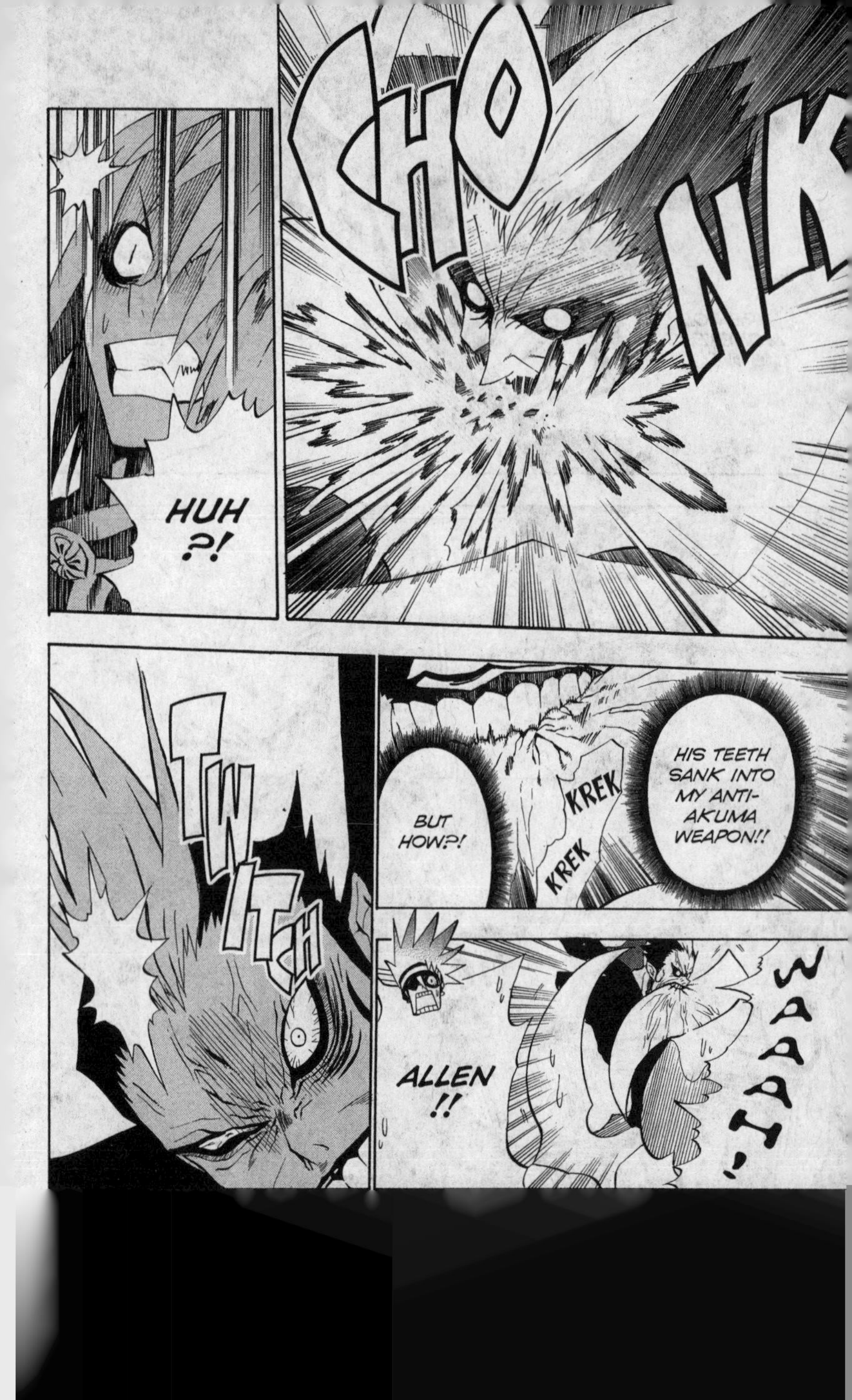
CHONK
HUH?!
HIS TEETH SANK INTO MY ANTI-AKUMA WEAPON!!
KREK
KREK
BUT HOW?!
WAAAH!
ALLEN!!
TWITCH

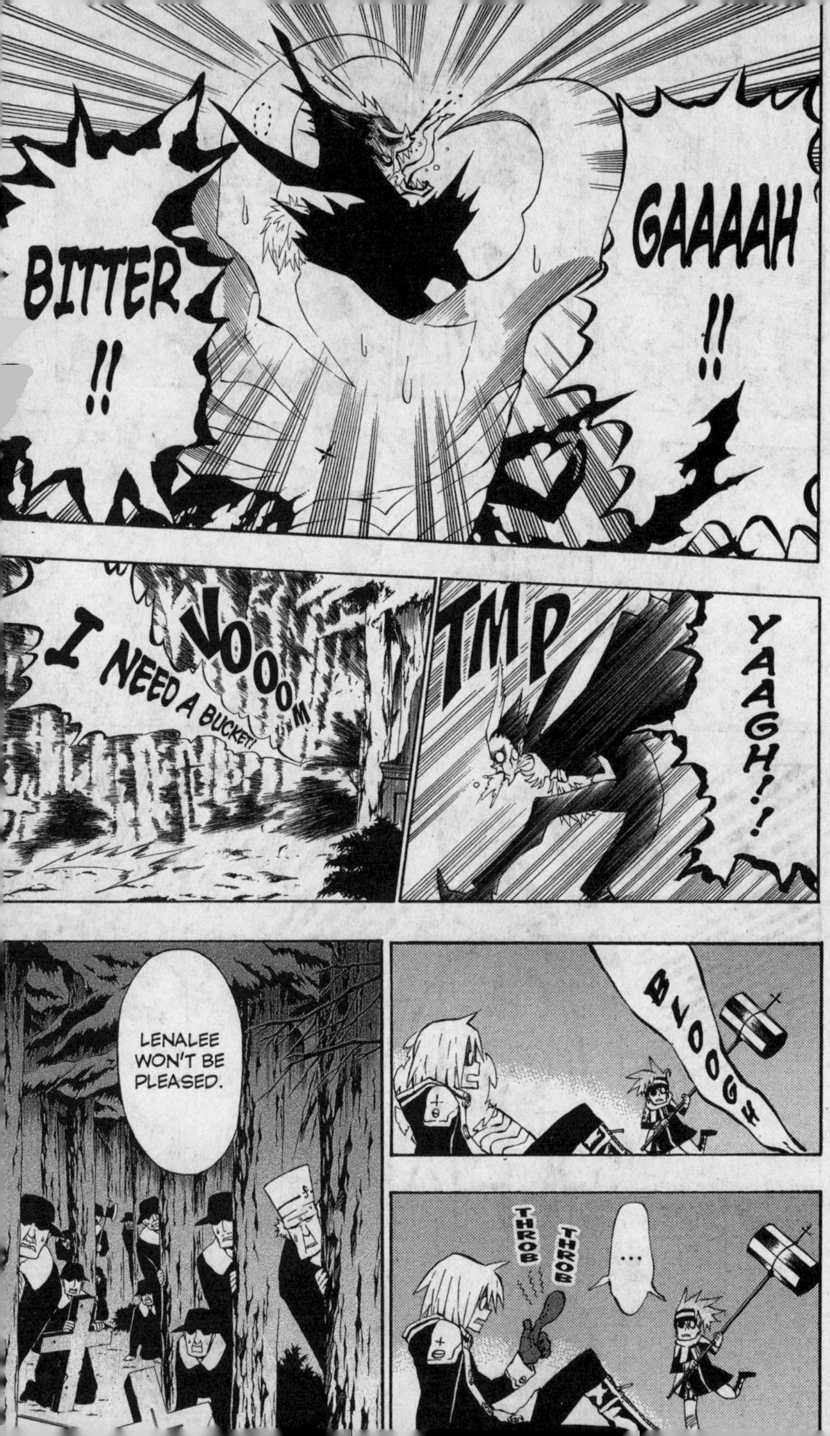
GAAAAH!!
BITTER!!
YAAGH!!!
TMP
VOOOOM
I NEED A BUCKET!!
BLOOOGH
...
THROB THROB
LENALEE WON'T BE PLEASED.

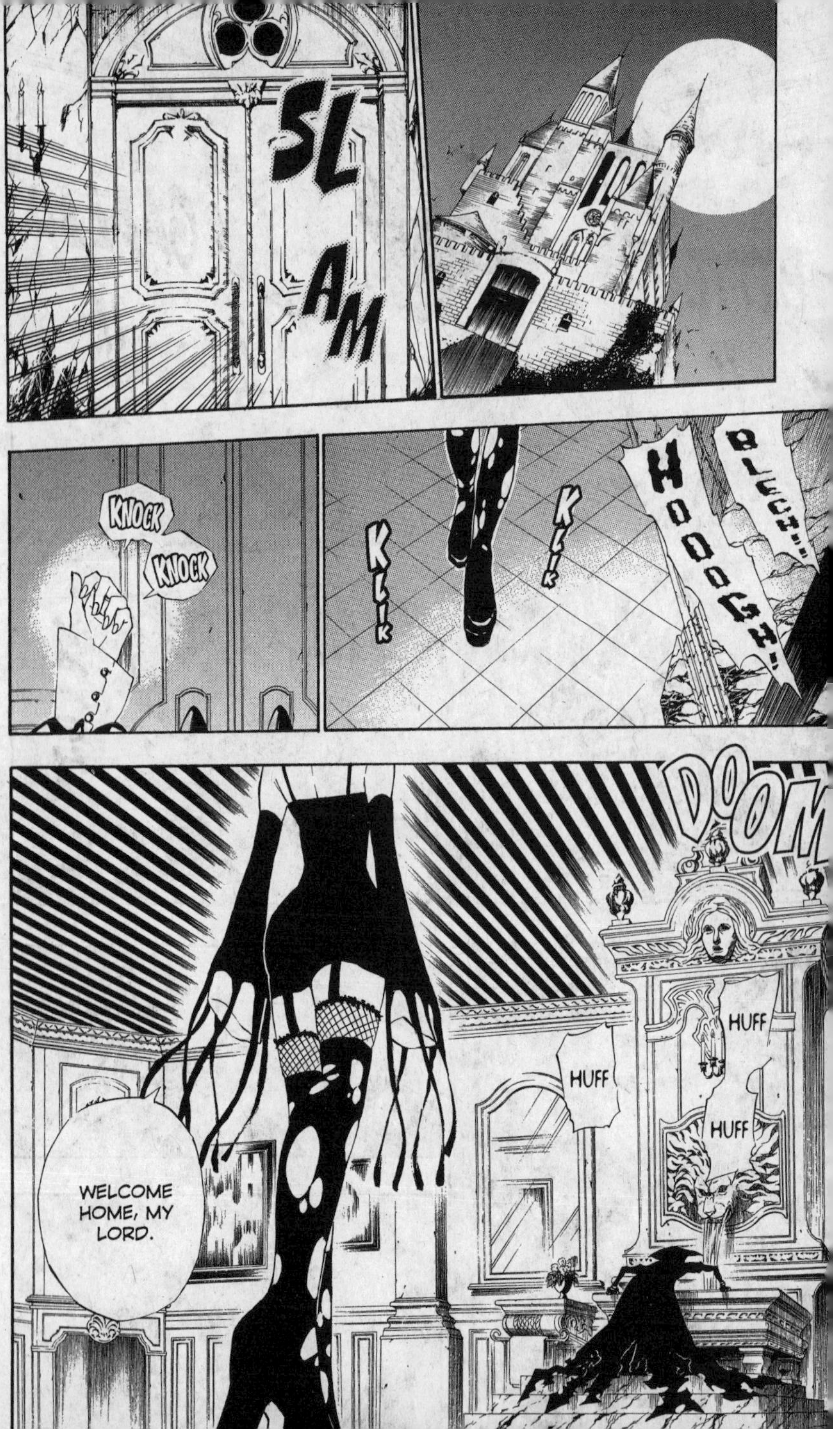
SLAM
BLECH!!!
HOOOGH!!
KLIK
KLIK
KNOCK
KNOCK
DOOM
HUFF
HUFF
HUFF
WELCOME HOME, MY LORD.

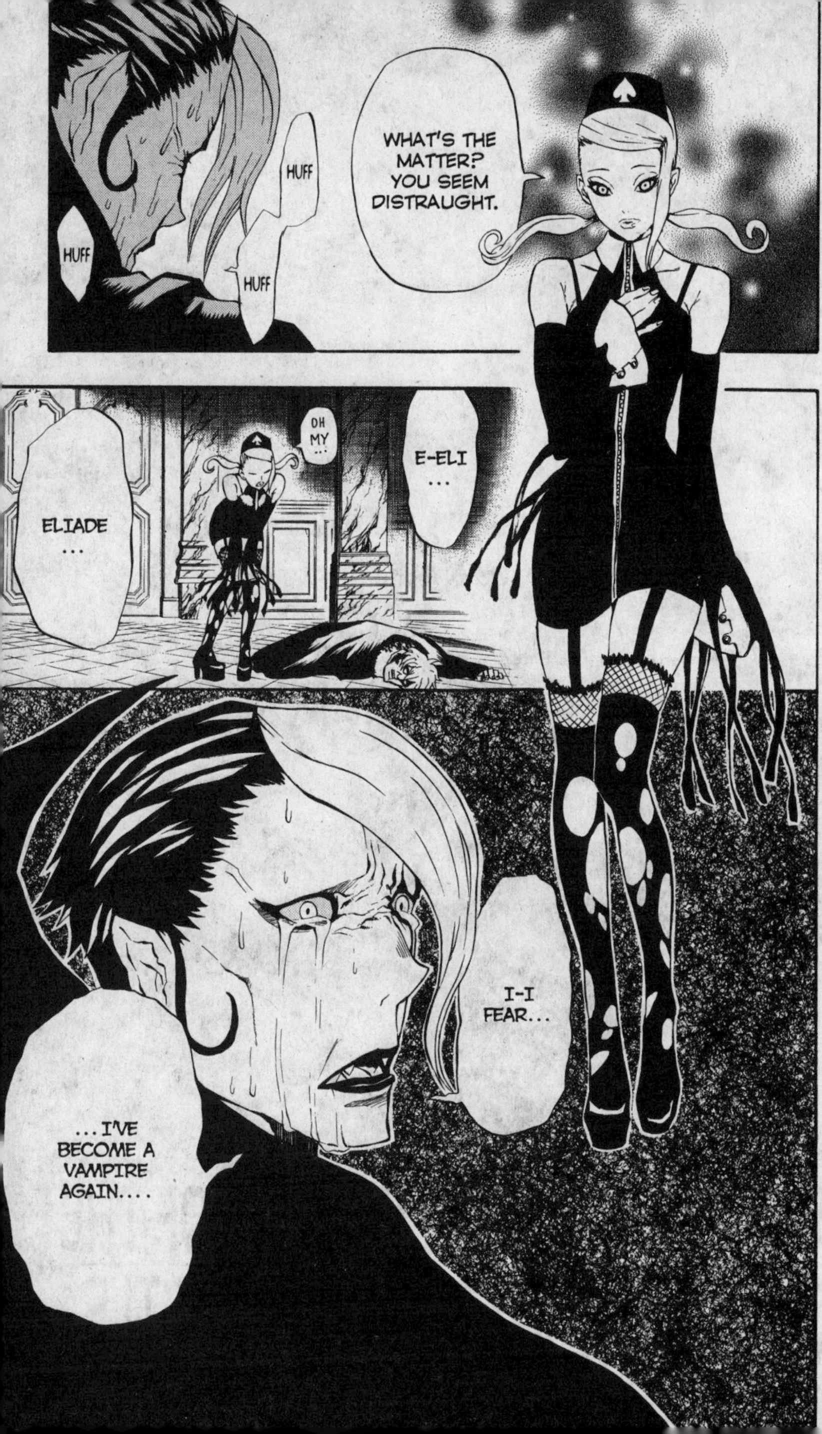
WHAT'S THE MATTER? YOU SEEM DISTRAUGHT.
HUFF
HUFF
HUFF
E-ELI ...
OH MY ...
ELIADE ...
I-I FEAR...
...I'VE BECOME A VAMPIRE AGAIN....

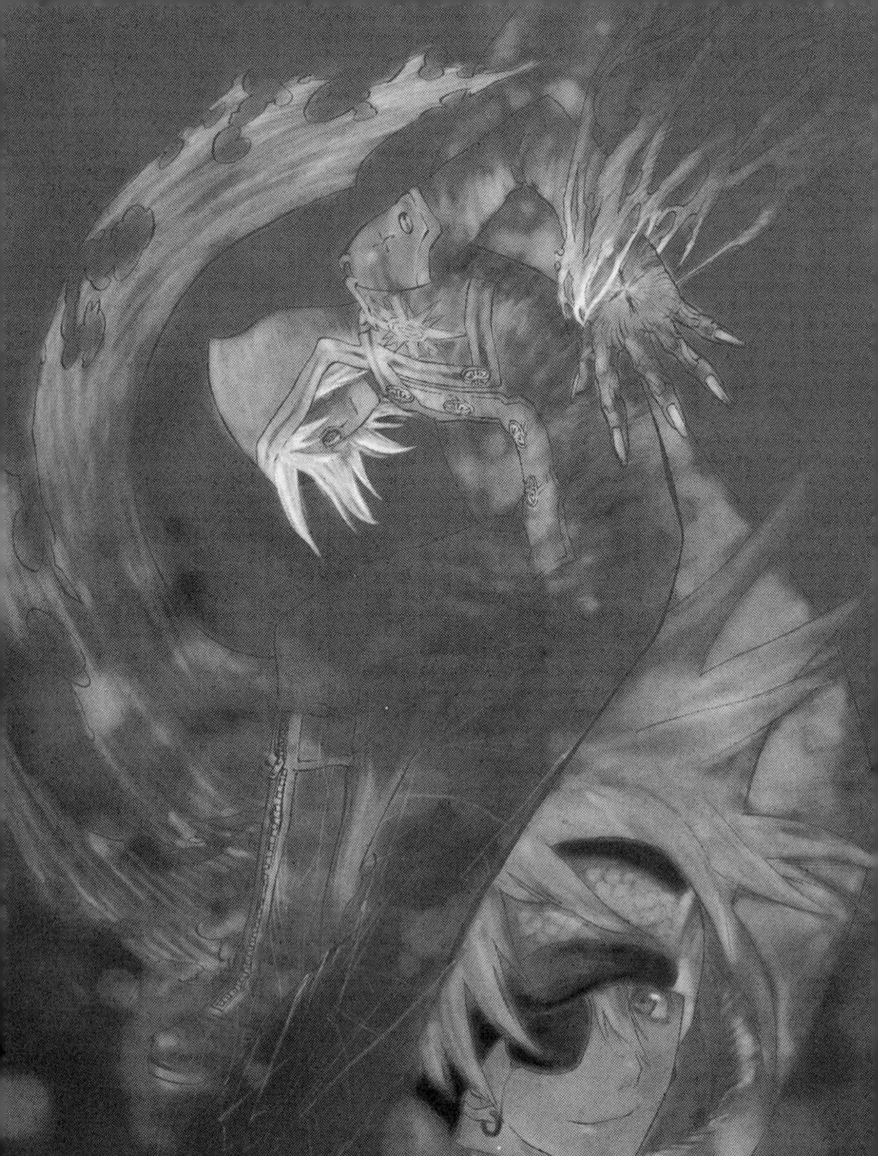

THE 33RD NIGHT: VAMPIRE OF THE CASTLE (PART 3) KRORY CASTLE

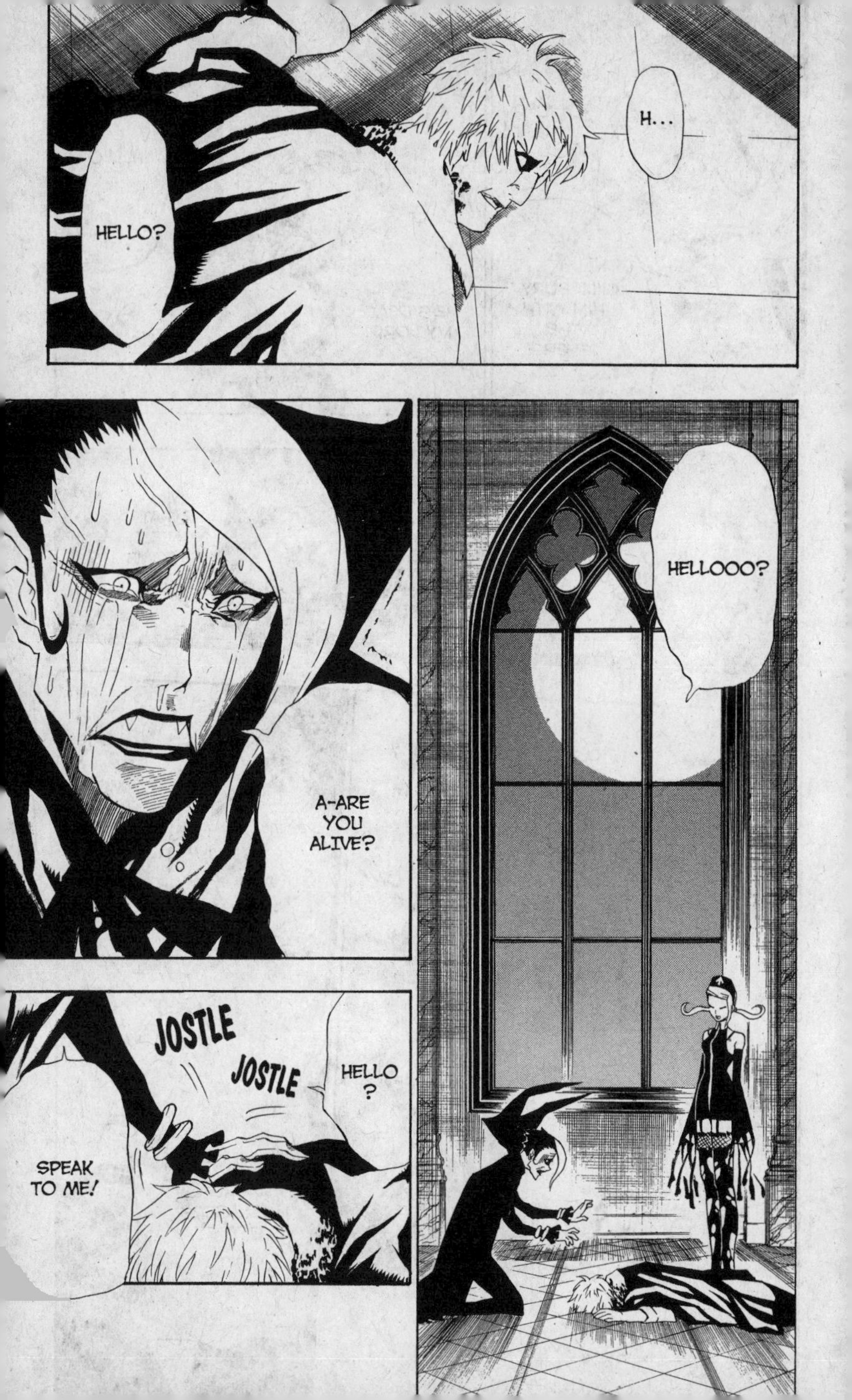
H...
HELLO?
HELLOOO?
A-ARE YOU ALIVE?
HELLO ?
JOSTLE
JOSTLE
SPEAK TO ME!

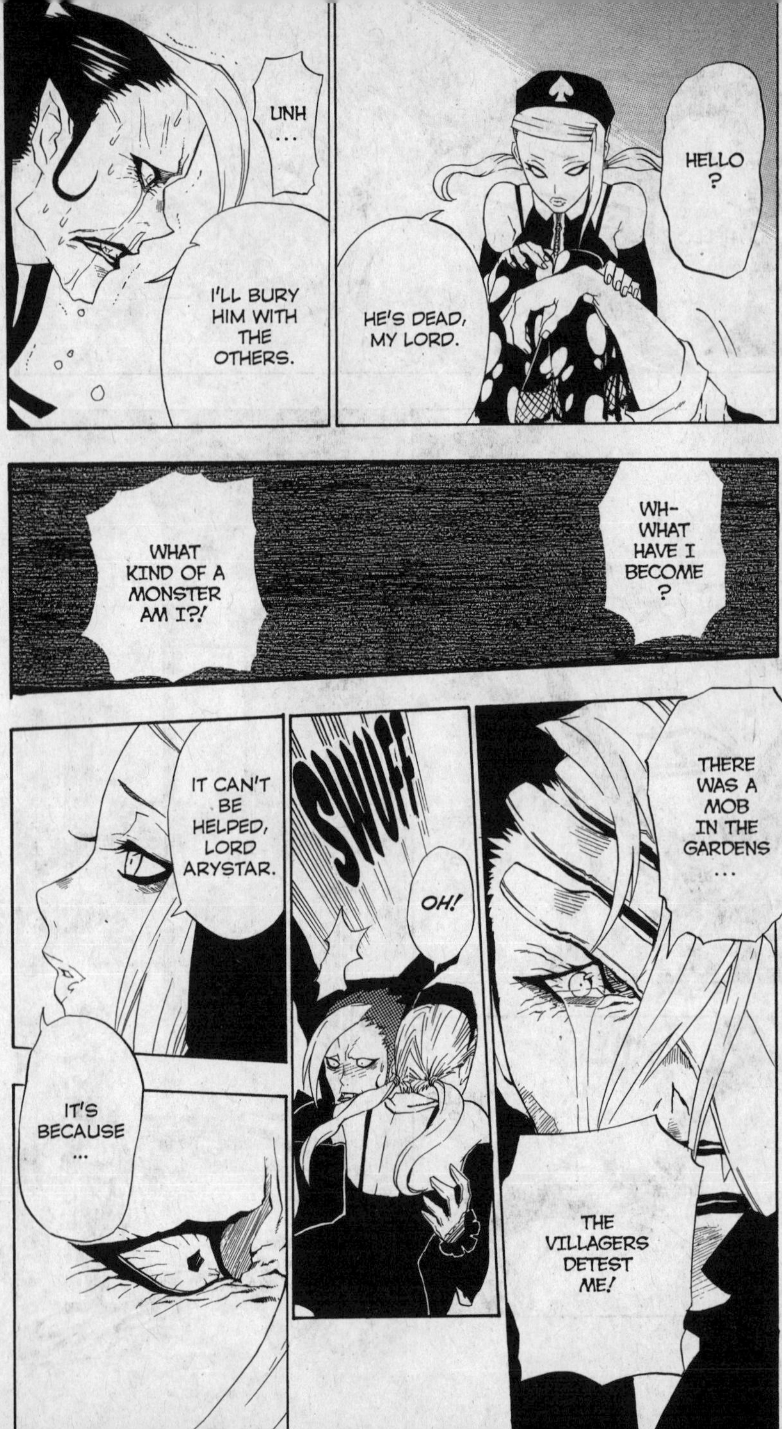
HELLO ?
HE'S DEAD, MY LORD.
UNH ...
I'LL BURY HIM WITH THE OTHERS.
WH- WHAT HAVE I BECOME ?
WHAT KIND OF A MONSTER AM I?!
THERE WAS A MOB IN THE GARDENS ...
THE VILLAGERS DETEST ME!
SWUFF
OH!
IT CAN'T BE HELPED, LORD ARYSTAR.
IT'S BECAUSE ...

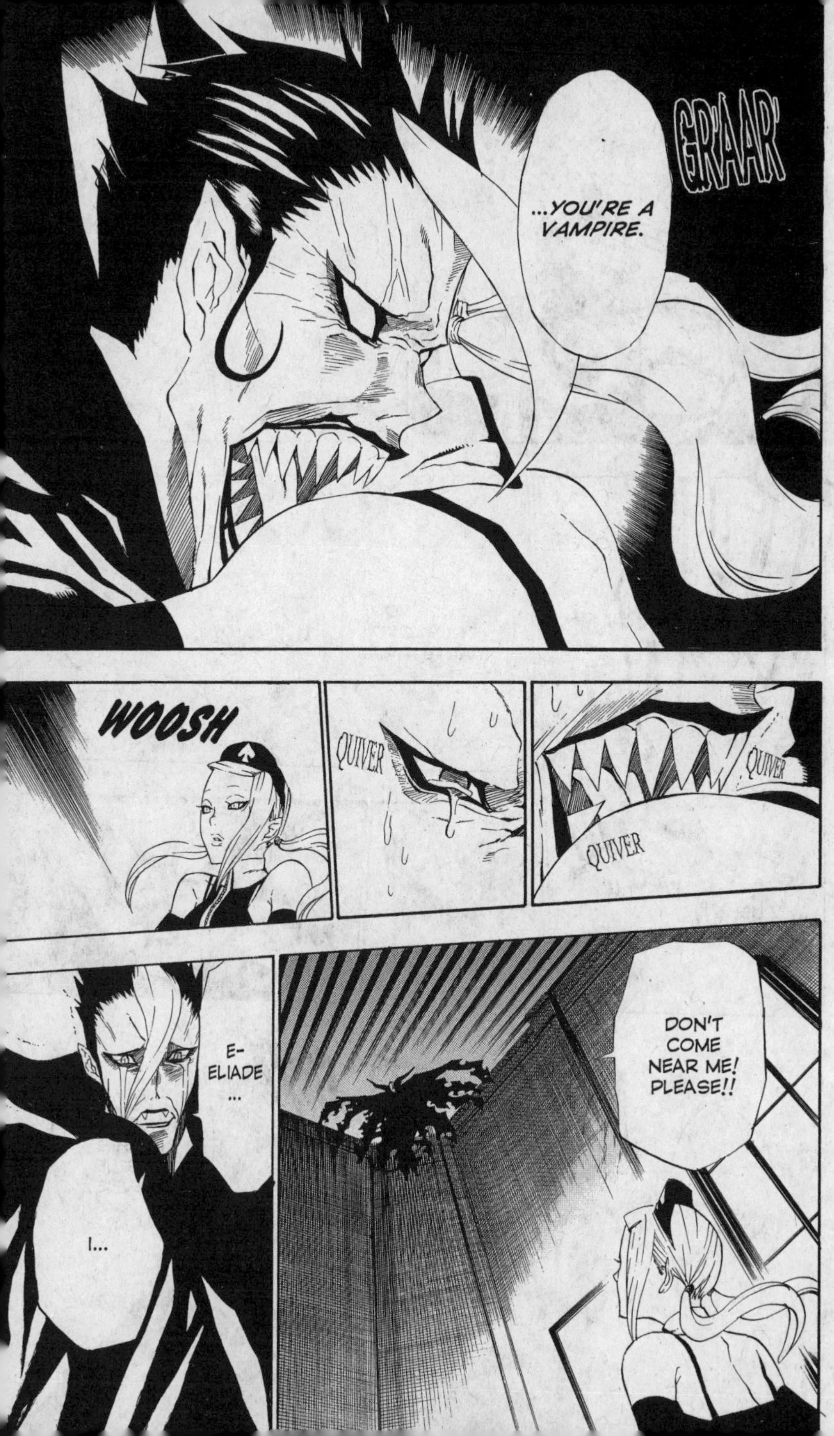
GR'AAR'
...YOU'RE A VAMPIRE.
QUIVER
QUIVER
QUIVER
WOOSH
DON'T COME NEAR ME! PLEASE!!
E-ELIADE...
I...

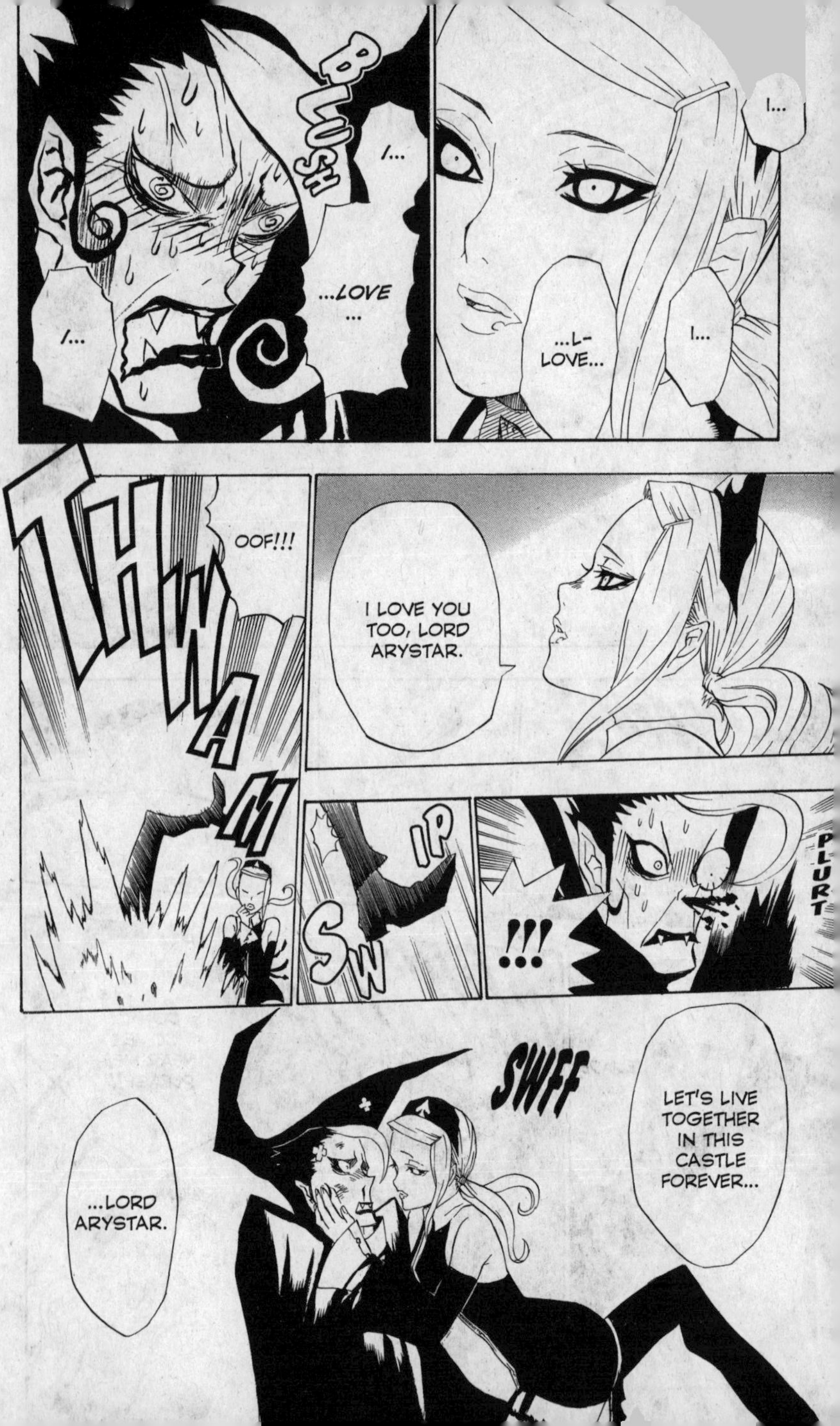

I...
I...
...L-
LOVE...
BLUSH
I...
...LOVE
...
I...
I LOVE YOU TOO, LORD ARYSTAR.
PLURT
!!!
SWIP
THWAMM
OOF!!!
LET'S LIVE TOGETHER IN THIS CASTLE FOREVER...
SWFF
...LORD ARYSTAR.

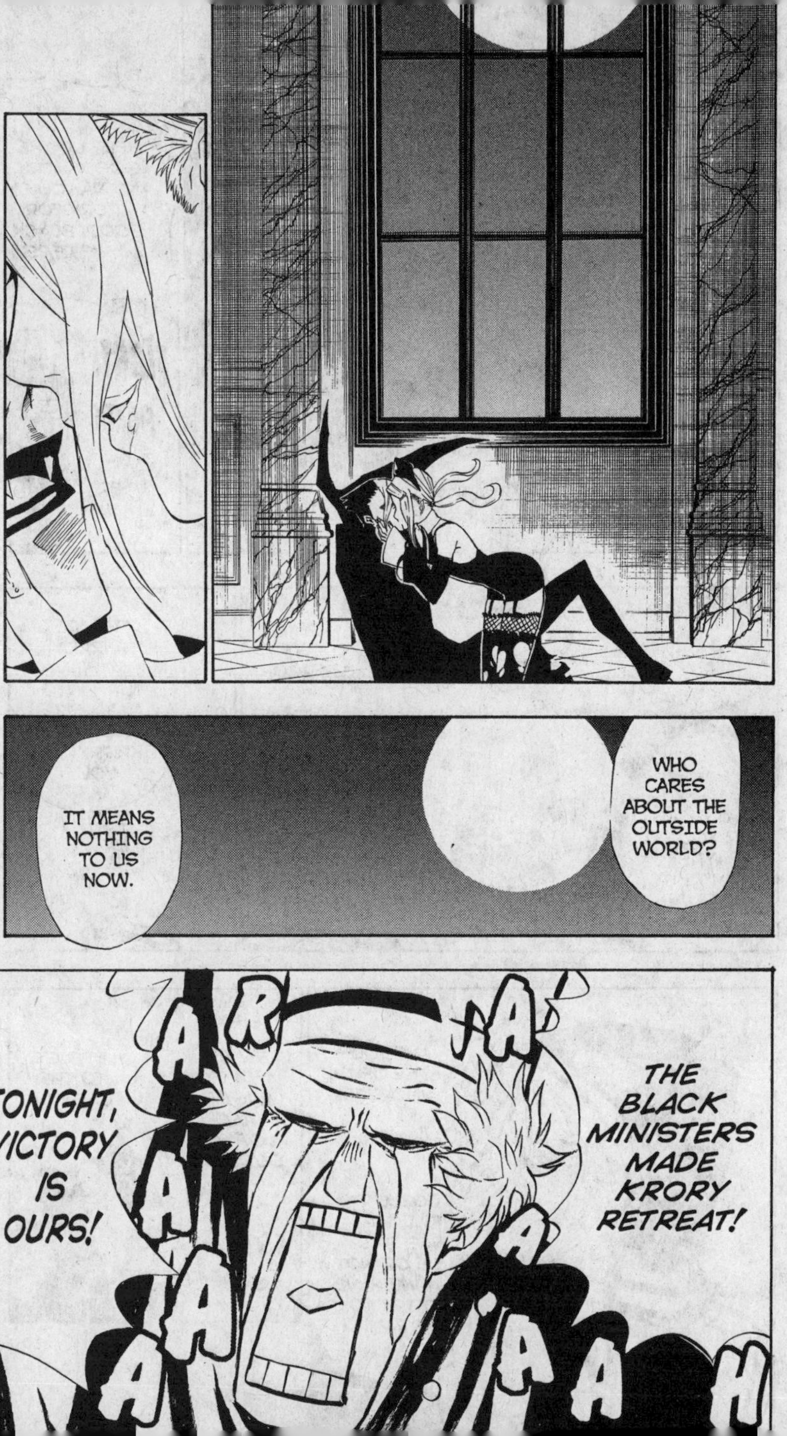
WHO CARES ABOUT THE OUTSIDE WORLD?
IT MEANS NOTHING TO US NOW.
THE BLACK MINISTERS MADE KRORY RETREAT!
TONIGHT, VICTORY IS OURS!

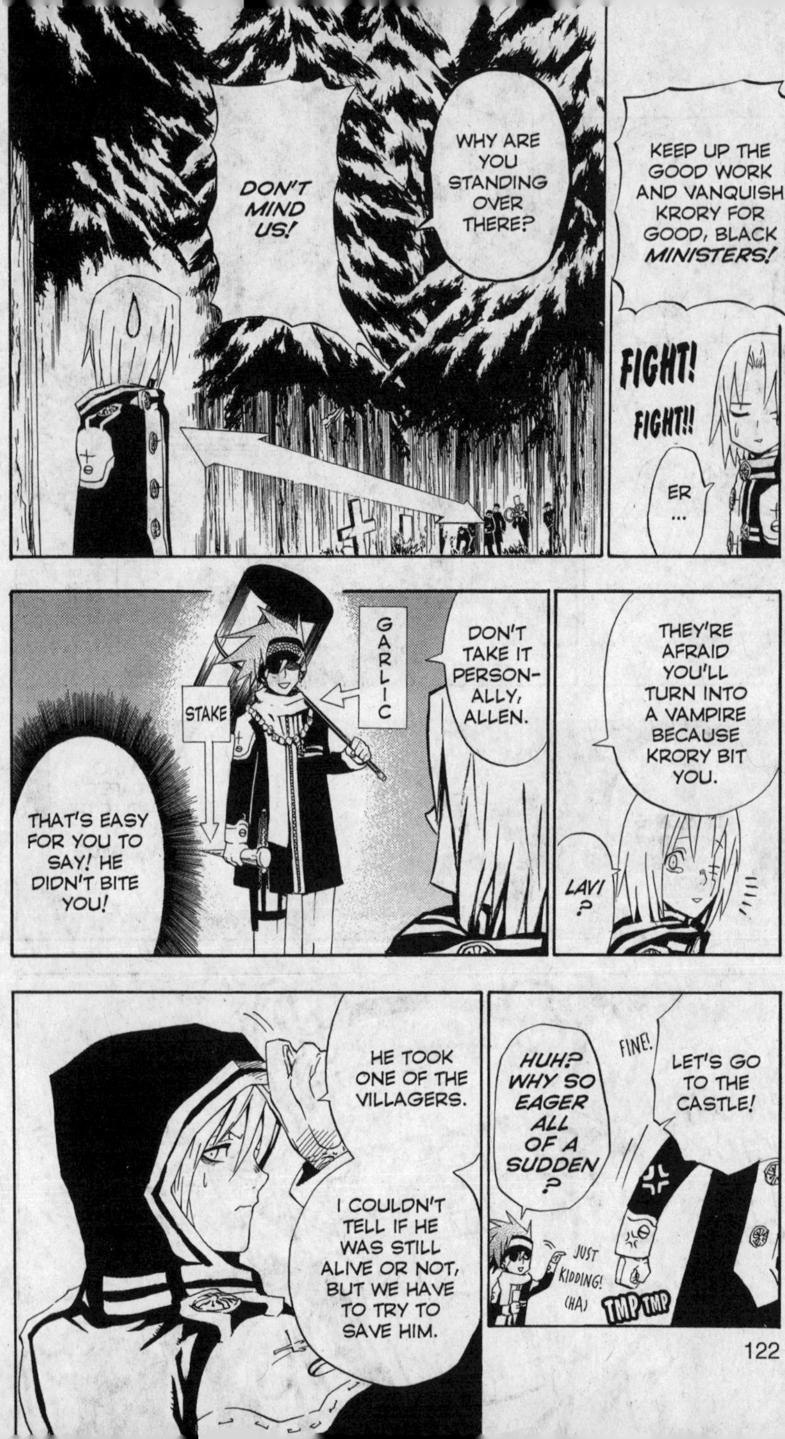
KEEP UP THE GOOD WORK AND VANQUISH KRORY FOR GOOD, BLACK MINISTERS!
FIGHT!
FIGHT!!
ER ...
WHY ARE YOU STANDING OVER THERE?
DON'T MIND US!
THEY'RE AFRAID YOU'LL TURN INTO A VAMPIRE BECAUSE KRORY BIT YOU.
LAVI ?
DON'T TAKE IT PERSON-ALLY, ALLEN.
GARLIC
STAKE
THAT'S EASY FOR YOU TO SAY! HE DIDN'T BITE YOU!
LET'S GO TO THE CASTLE!
FINE!
HUH? WHY SO EAGER ALL OF A SUDDEN ?
JUST KIDDING! (HA)
TMP TMP
HE TOOK ONE OF THE VILLAGERS.
I COULDN'T TELL IF HE WAS STILL ALIVE OR NOT, BUT WE HAVE TO TRY TO SAVE HIM.

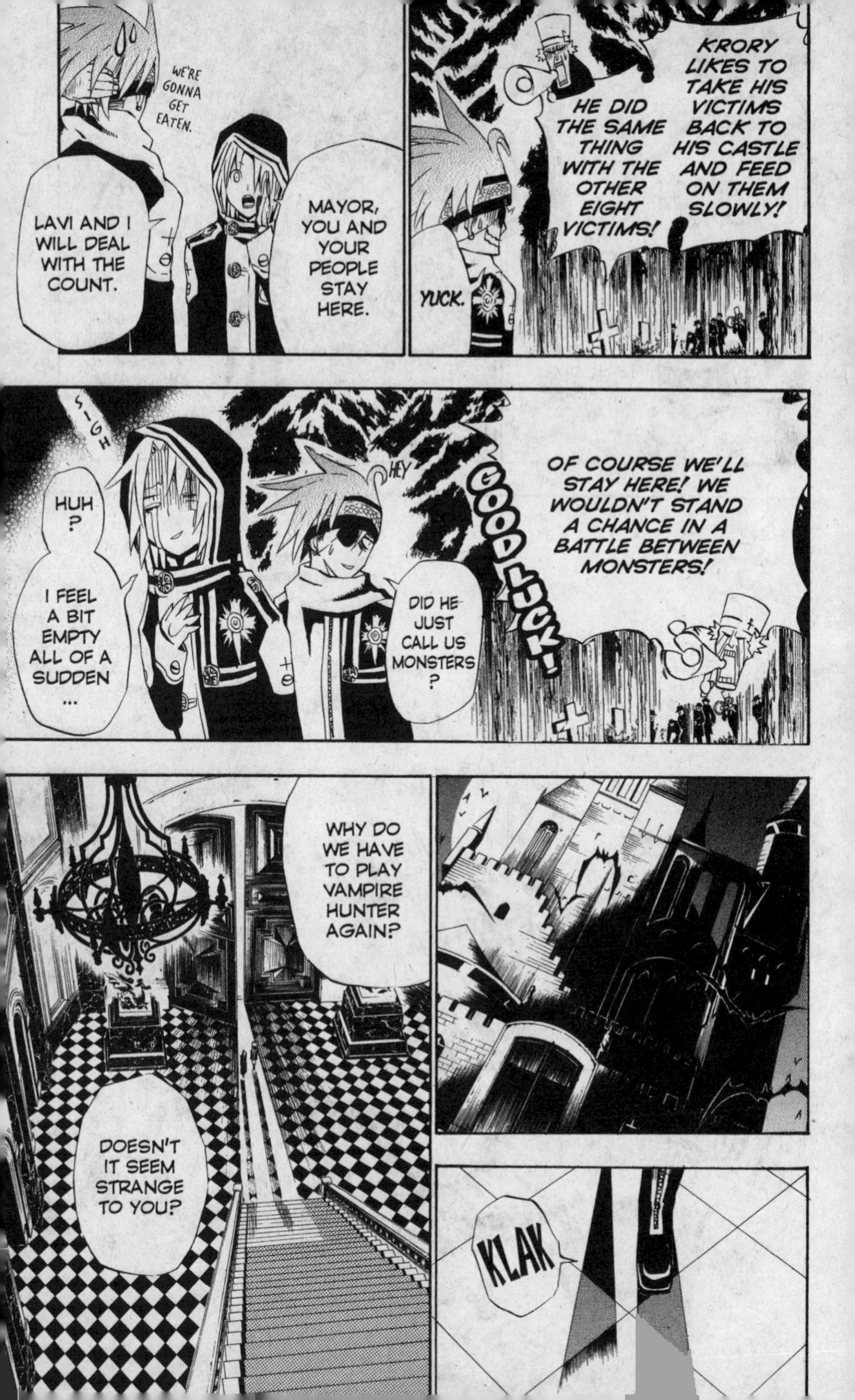

KRORY LIKES TO TAKE HIS VICTIMS BACK TO HIS CASTLE AND FEED ON THEM SLOWLY!
HE DID THE SAME THING WITH THE OTHER EIGHT VICTIMS!
YUCK.
MAYOR, YOU AND YOUR PEOPLE STAY HERE.
WE'RE GONNA GET EATEN.
LAVI AND I WILL DEAL WITH THE COUNT.
OF COURSE WE'LL STAY HERE! WE WOULDN'T STAND A CHANCE IN A BATTLE BETWEEN MONSTERS!
GOOD LUCK!
HEY
DID HE JUST CALL US MONSTERS?
SIGH
HUH?
I FEEL A BIT EMPTY ALL OF A SUDDEN...
KLAK
WHY DO WE HAVE TO PLAY VAMPIRE HUNTER AGAIN?
DOESN'T IT SEEM STRANGE TO YOU?

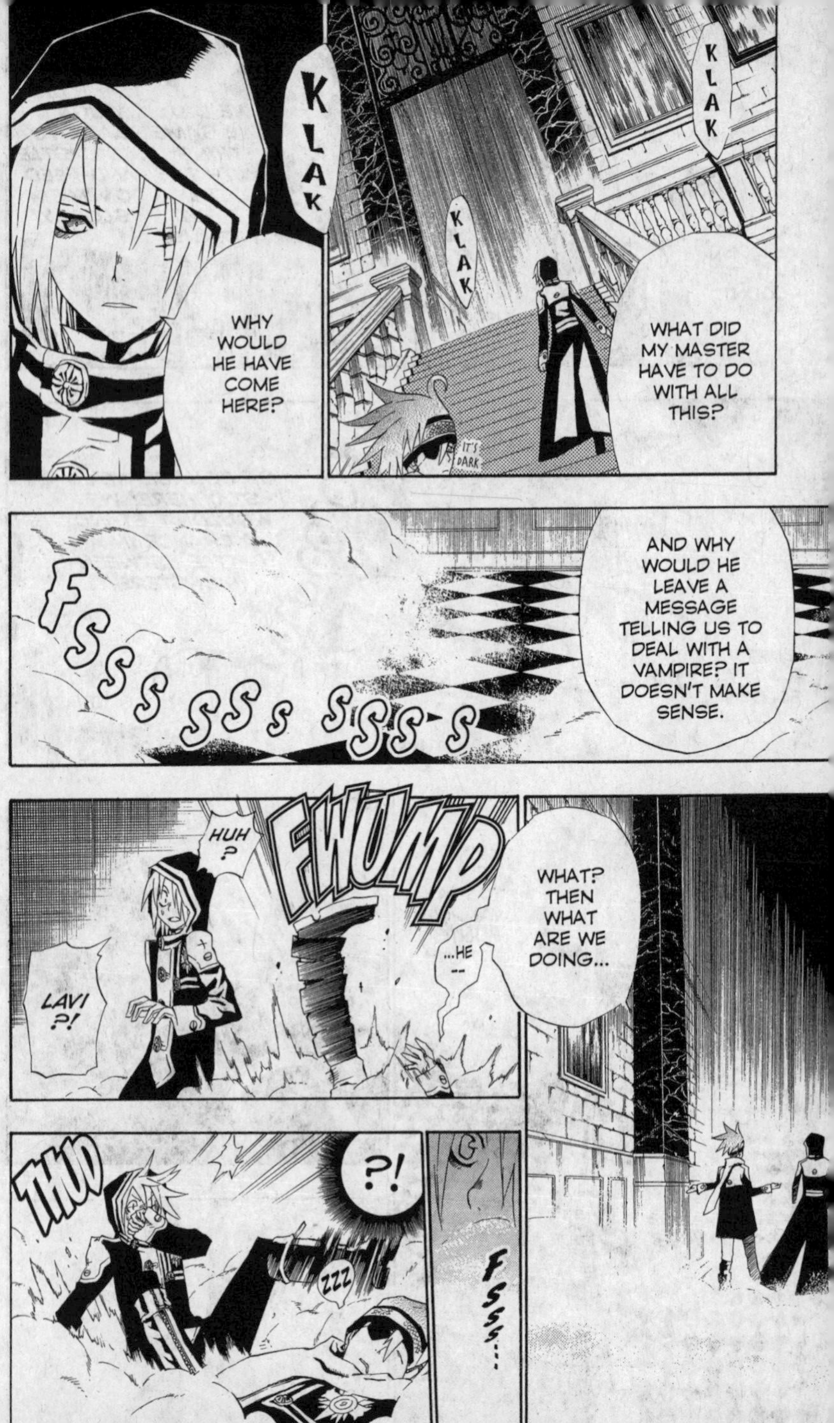
KLAK
KLAK
WHAT DID MY MASTER HAVE TO DO WITH ALL THIS?
IT'S DARK
KLAK
WHY WOULD HE HAVE COME HERE?
AND WHY WOULD HE LEAVE A MESSAGE TELLING US TO DEAL WITH A VAMPIRE? IT DOESN'T MAKE SENSE.
FSSSSSSSSS
WHAT? THEN WHAT ARE WE DOING...
FWUMP
...HE --
HUH?
LAVI?!
FSSS...
?!
ZZZ
THUD

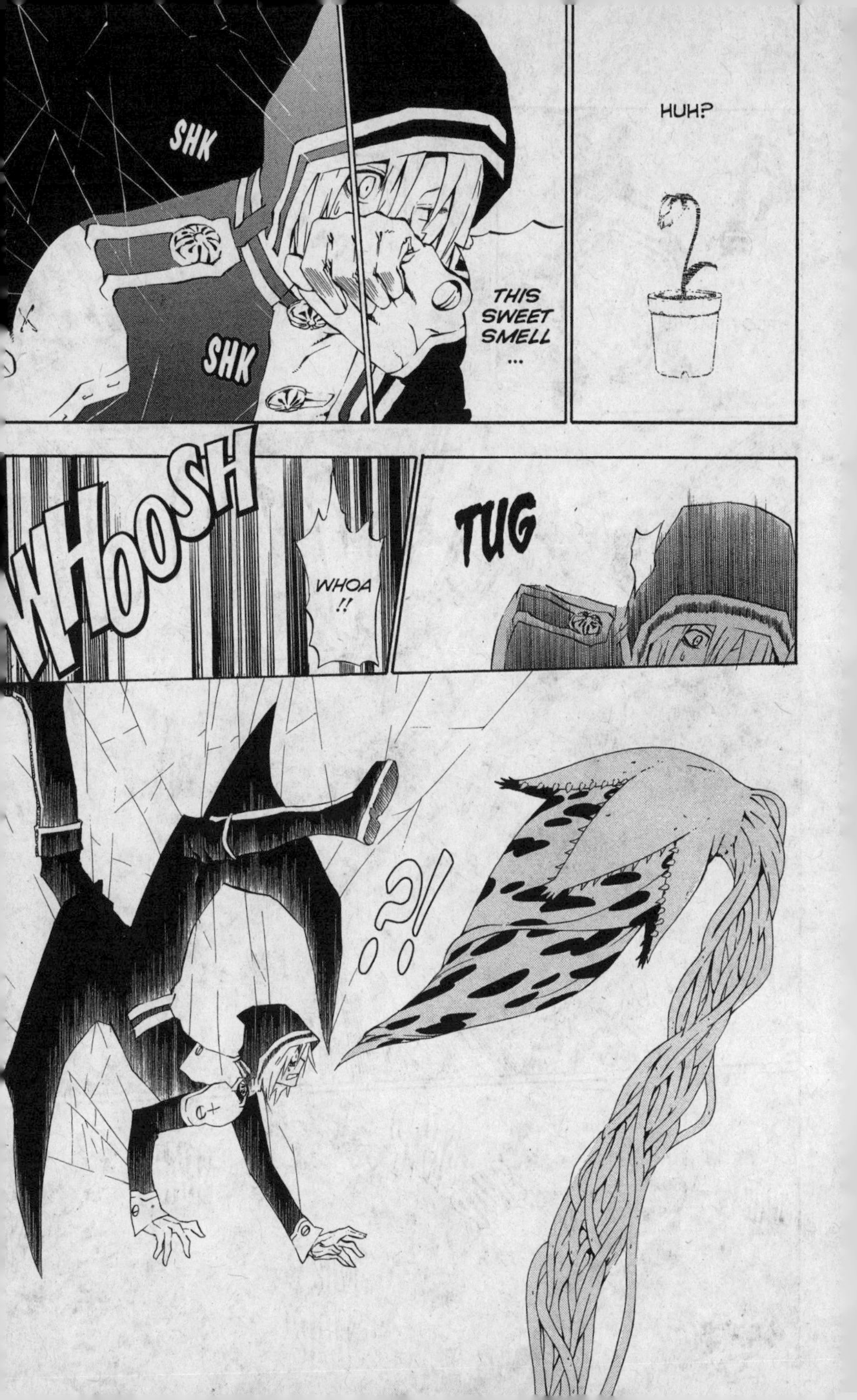
HUH?
SHK
THIS SWEET SMELL ...
SHK
TUG
WHOOSH
WHOA !!
?!

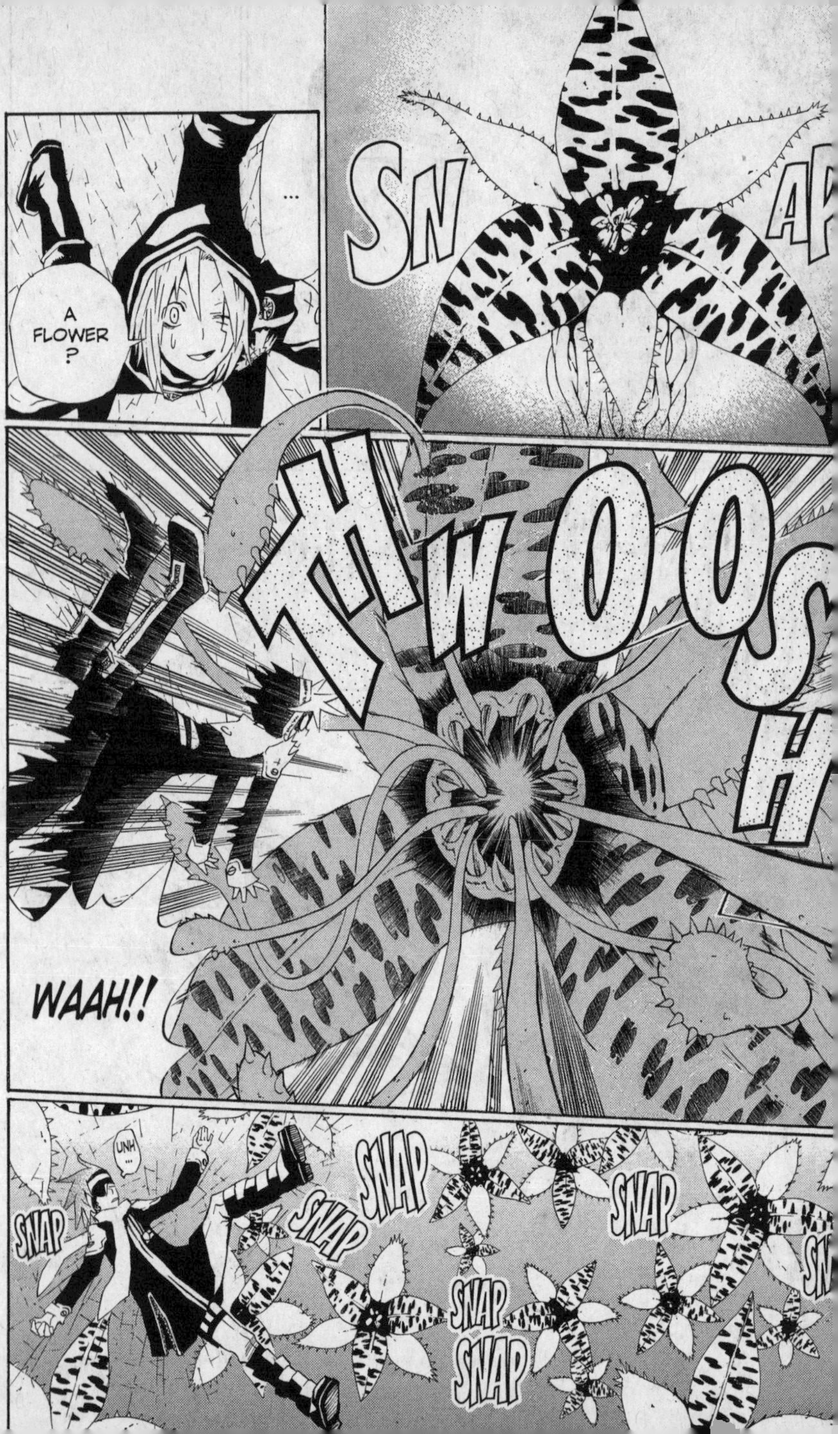

SN
AP
...
A FLOWER ?
THWOOSH
WAAH!!
SNAP
SNAP
SNAP
SNAP
SNAP
SNAP
UNH ...
SNAP

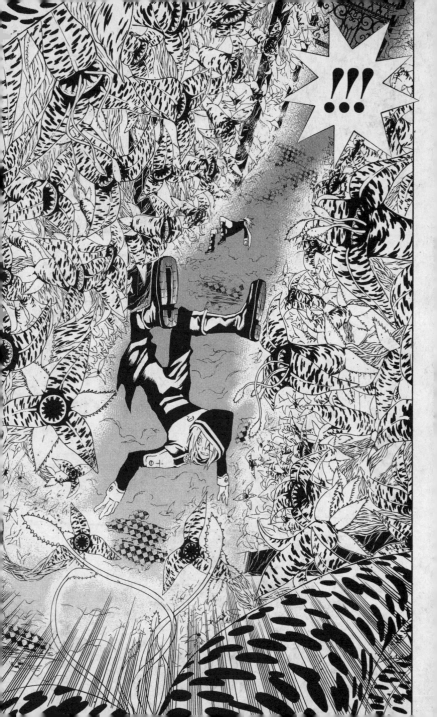

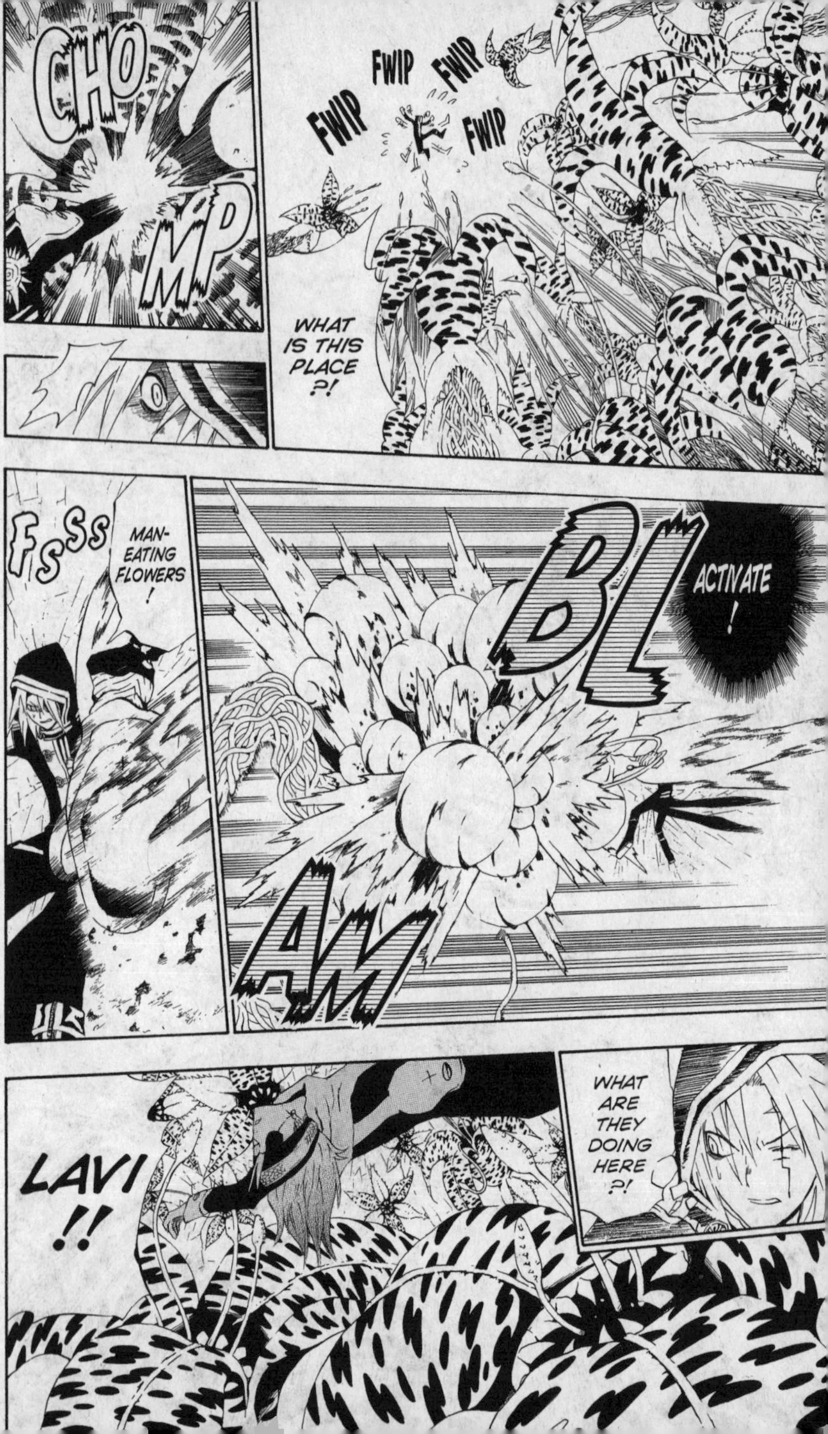
FWIP
FWIP
FWIP
FWIP
WHAT IS THIS PLACE ?!
CHOMP
ACTIVATE !
BLAM
FSSS
MAN-EATING FLOWERS !
WHAT ARE THEY DOING HERE ?!
LAVI !!

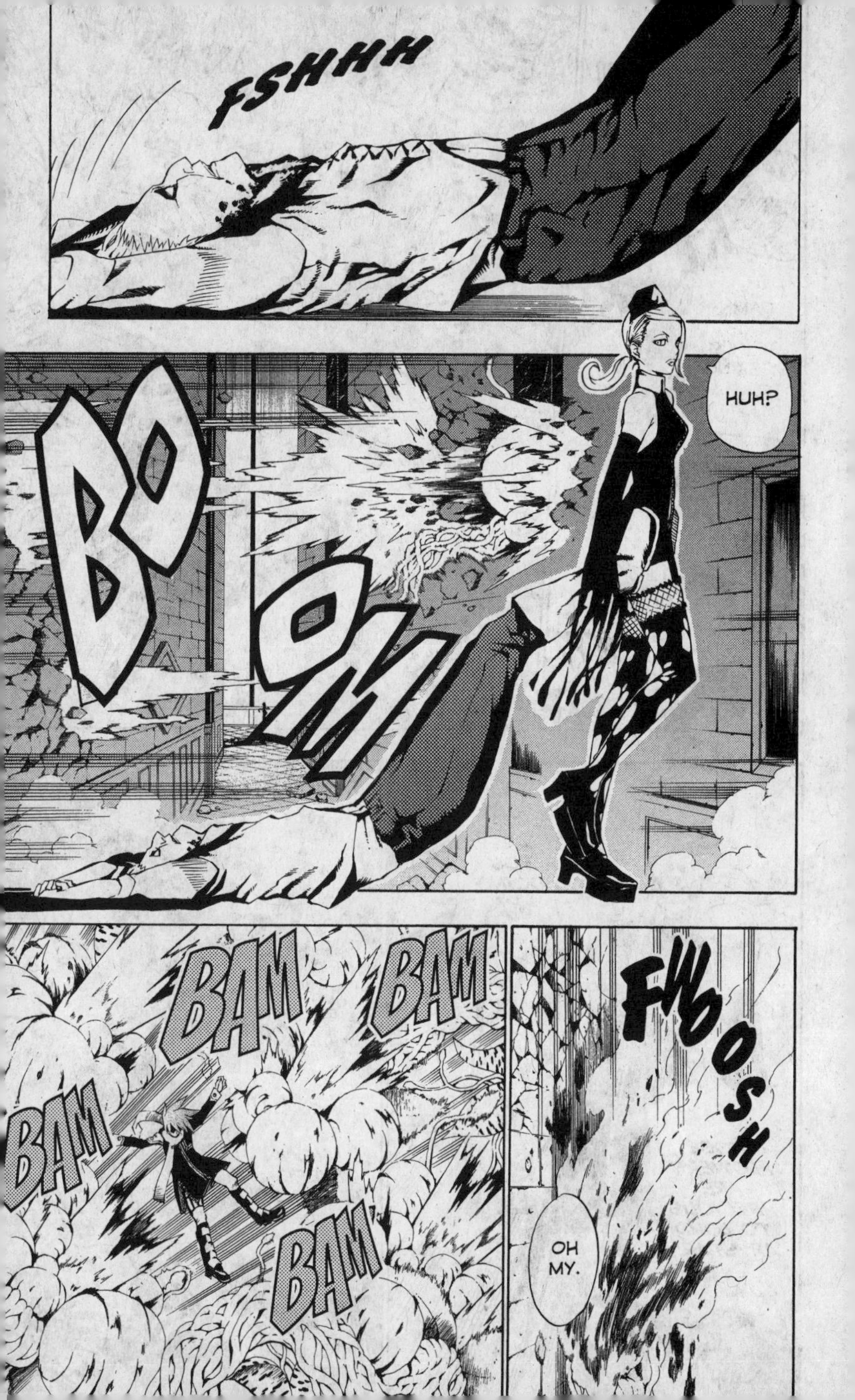
FSHHH
HUH?
BOOM
FWOOSH
OH MY.
BAM
BAM
BAM
BAM

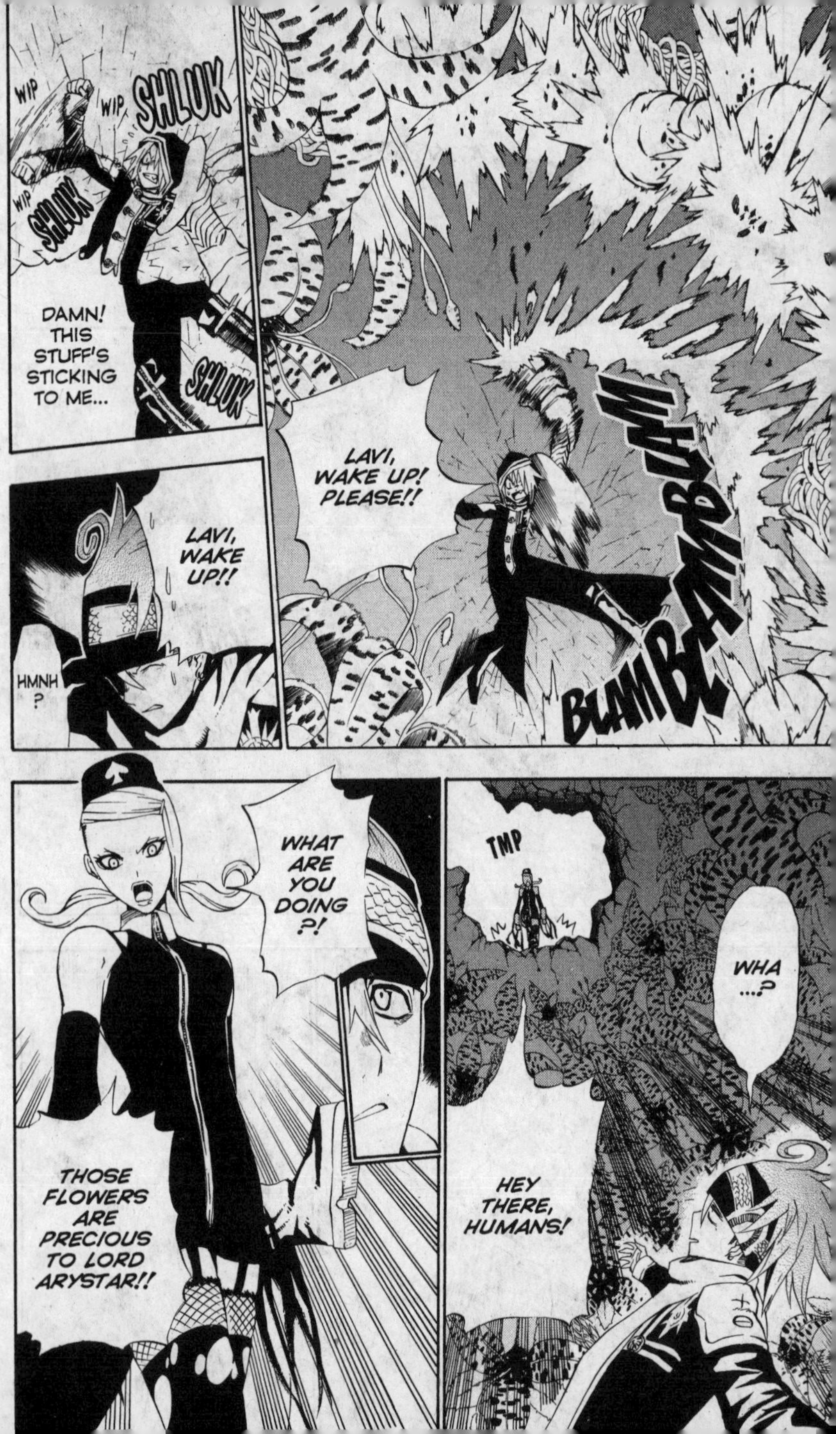
BLAMBLAMBLAM
LAVI, WAKE UP! PLEASE!!
WIP
WIP
SHLUK
WIP
SHLUK
SHLUK
DAMN! THIS STUFF'S STICKING TO ME...
LAVI, WAKE UP!!
HMNH ?
TMP
WHA ...?
HEY THERE, HUMANS!
WHAT ARE YOU DOING ?!
THOSE FLOWERS ARE PRECIOUS TO LORD ARYSTAR!!

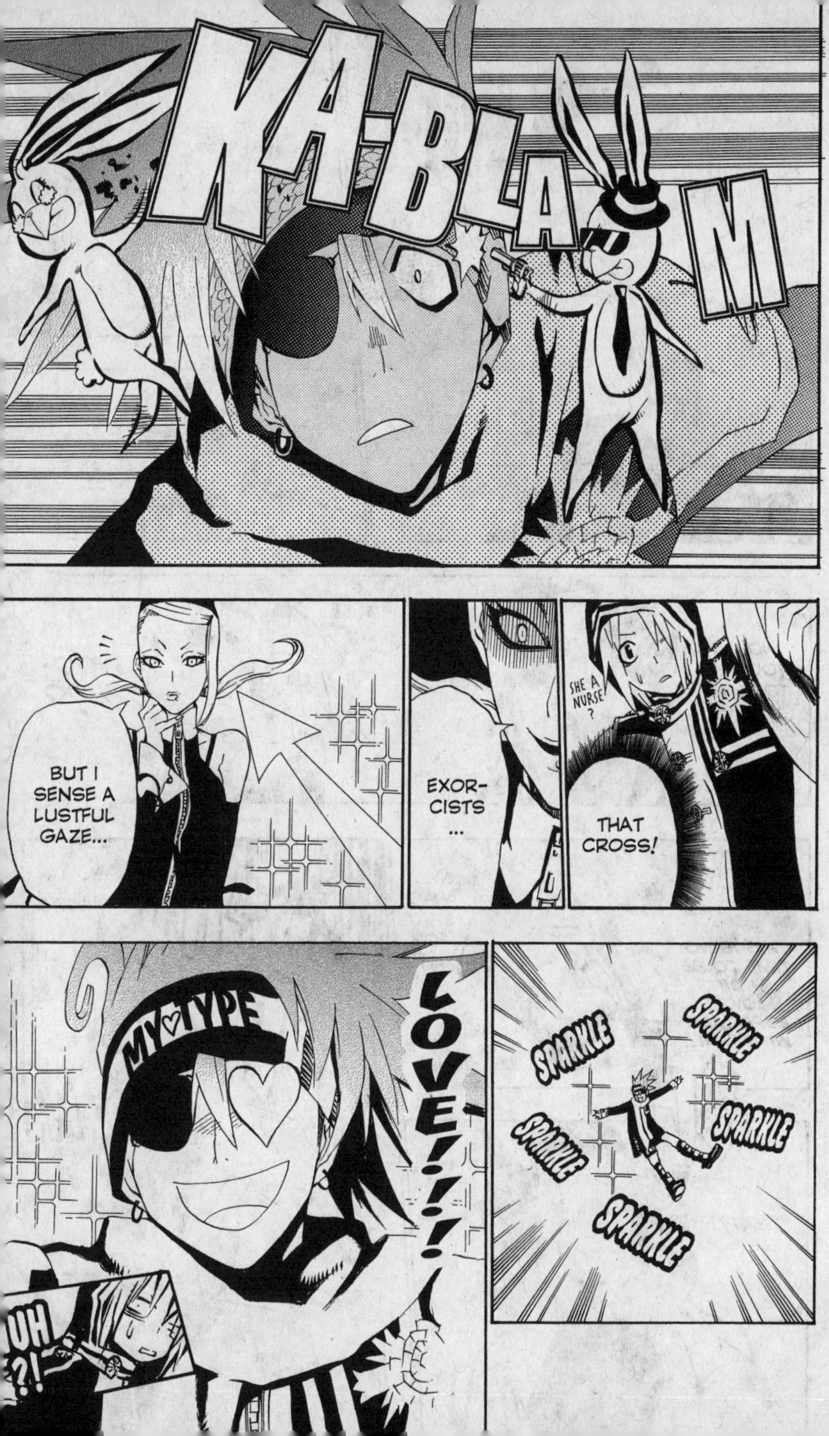
KA-BLAM
SHE A NURSE?
THAT CROSS!
EXOR-CISTS...
BUT I SENSE A LUSTFUL GAZE...
SPARKLE
SPARKLE
SPARKLE
SPARKLE
SPARKLE
MY♥TYPE
LOVE!!!!
UH?!

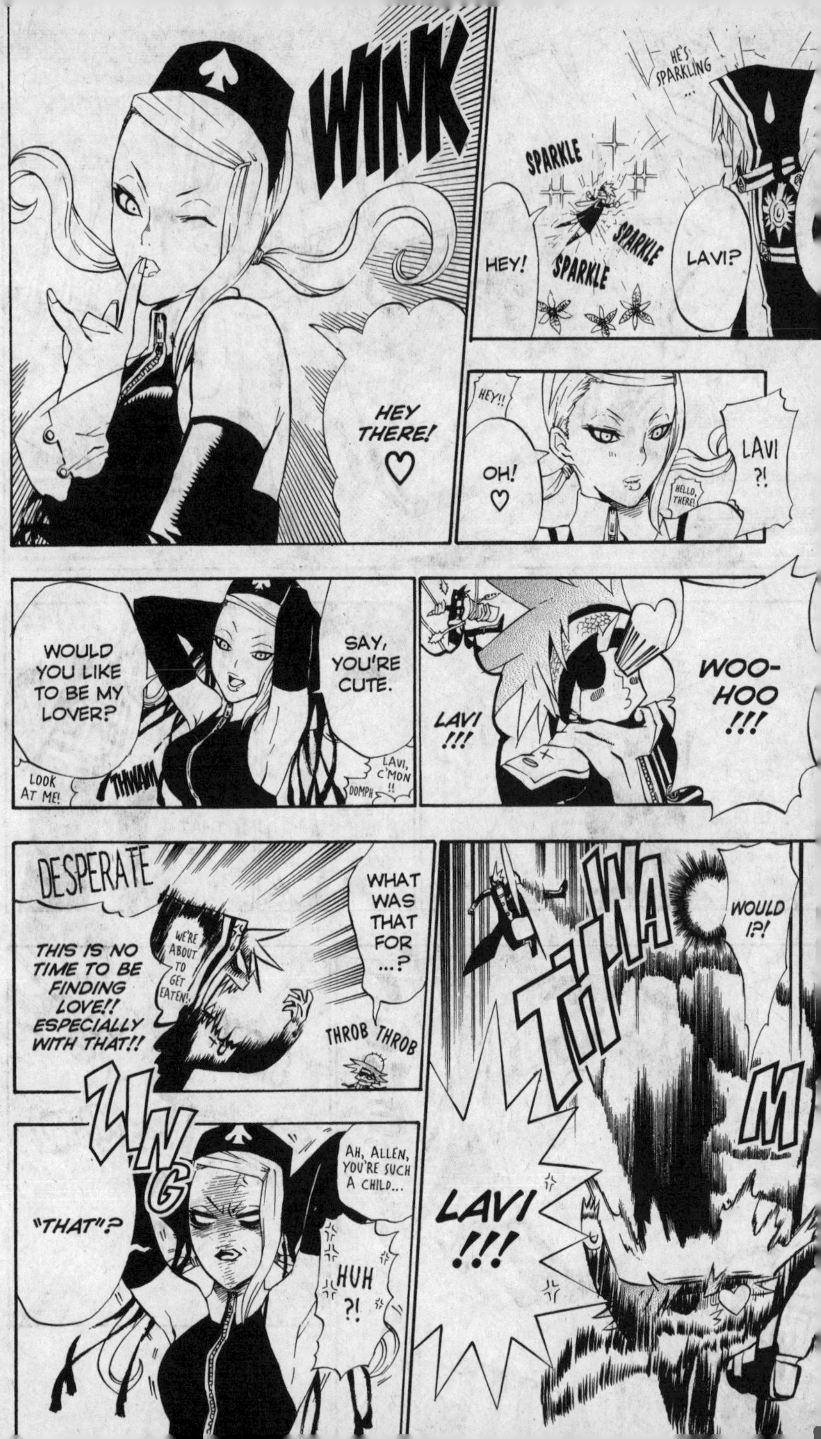
HE'S SPARKLING ...
SPARKLE
LAVI?
HEY!
SPARKLE
SPARKLE
HEY!!
LAVI ?!
HELLO, THERE!
OH! ♡
WINK
HEY THERE! ♡
WOO-HOO !!!
LAVI !!!
SAY, YOU'RE CUTE.
WOULD YOU LIKE TO BE MY LOVER?
LAVI, C'MON !!
OOMPH
THWAM
LOOK AT ME!
THWACM
WOULD I?!
LAVI !!!
WHAT WAS THAT FOR ...?
DESPERATE
WE'RE ABOUT TO GET EATEN!
THIS IS NO TIME TO BE FINDING LOVE!! ESPECIALLY WITH THAT!!
THROB THROB
ZING
AH, ALLEN, YOU'RE SUCH A CHILD...
"THAT"?
HUH ?!

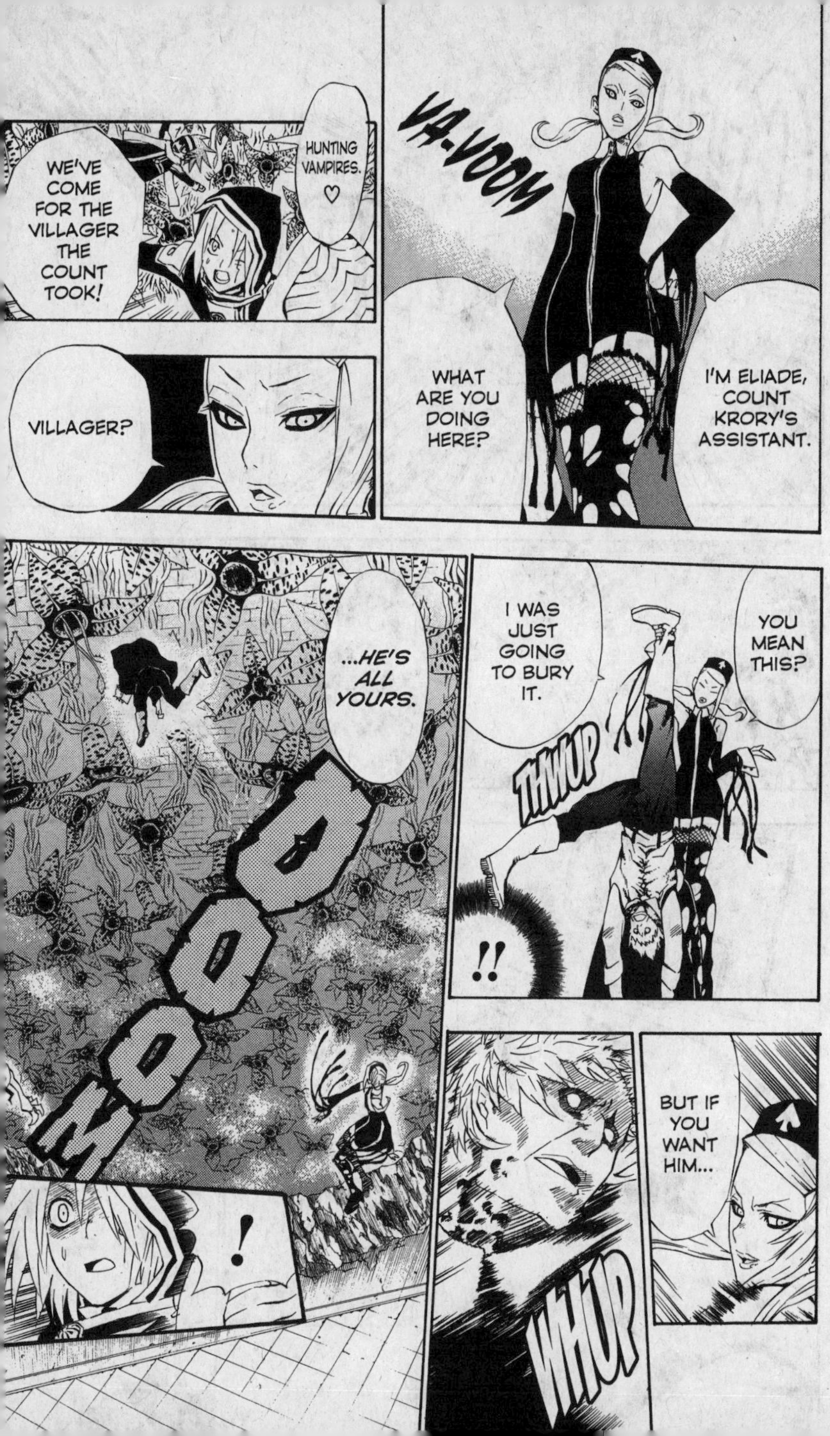
VA-VOOM
I'M ELIADE, COUNT KRORY'S ASSISTANT.
WHAT ARE YOU DOING HERE?
HUNTING VAMPIRES. ♡
WE'VE COME FOR THE VILLAGER THE COUNT TOOK!
VILLAGER?
YOU MEAN THIS?
I WAS JUST GOING TO BURY IT.
THWUP
!!
...HE'S ALL YOURS.
BUT IF YOU WANT HIM...
WHUP
!

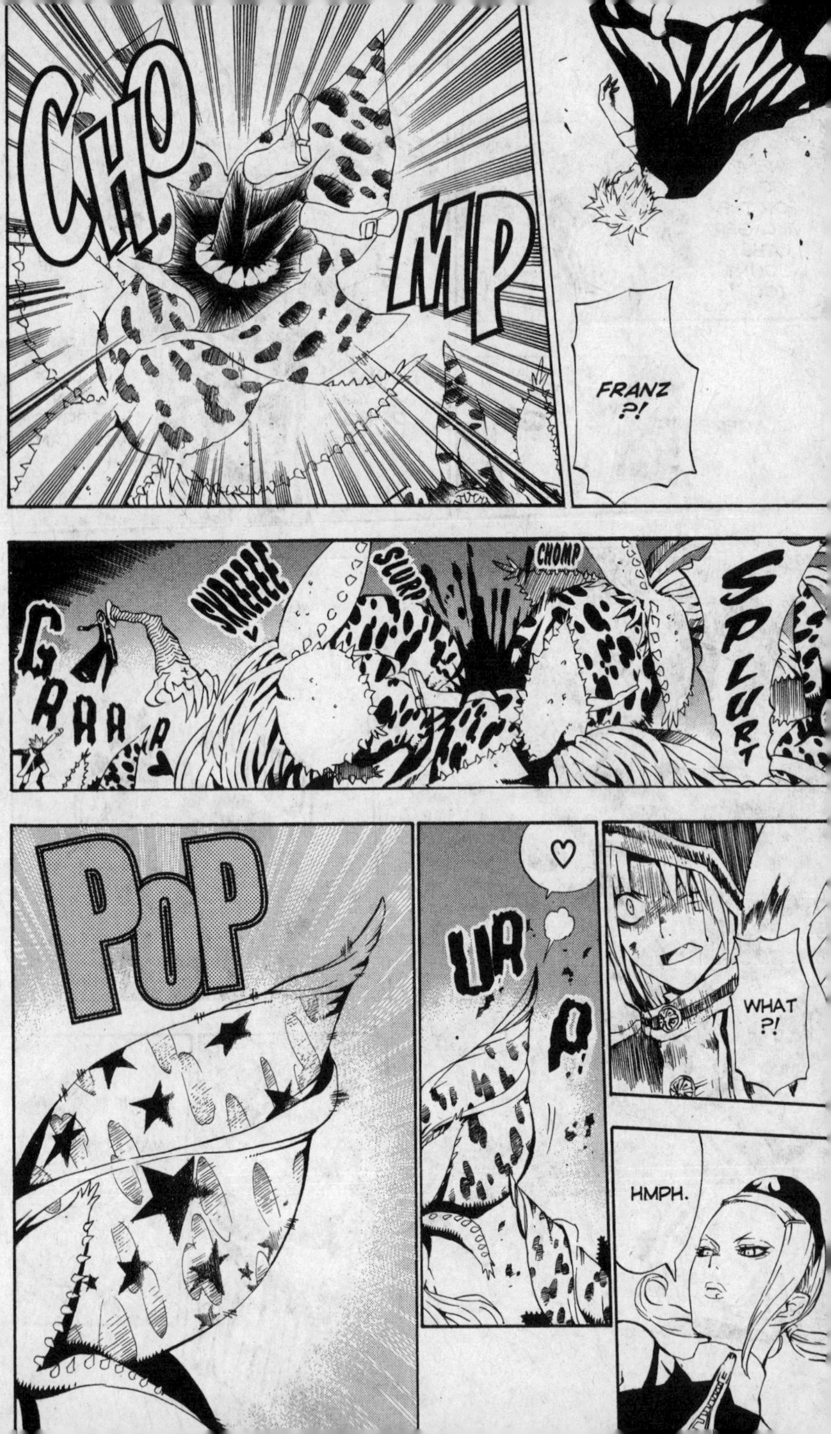
FRANZ ?!
CHOMP
SPLURT
CHOMP
SLURP
SKREEEE
GAAAAA
WHAT ?!
HMPH.
♡
URP
POP

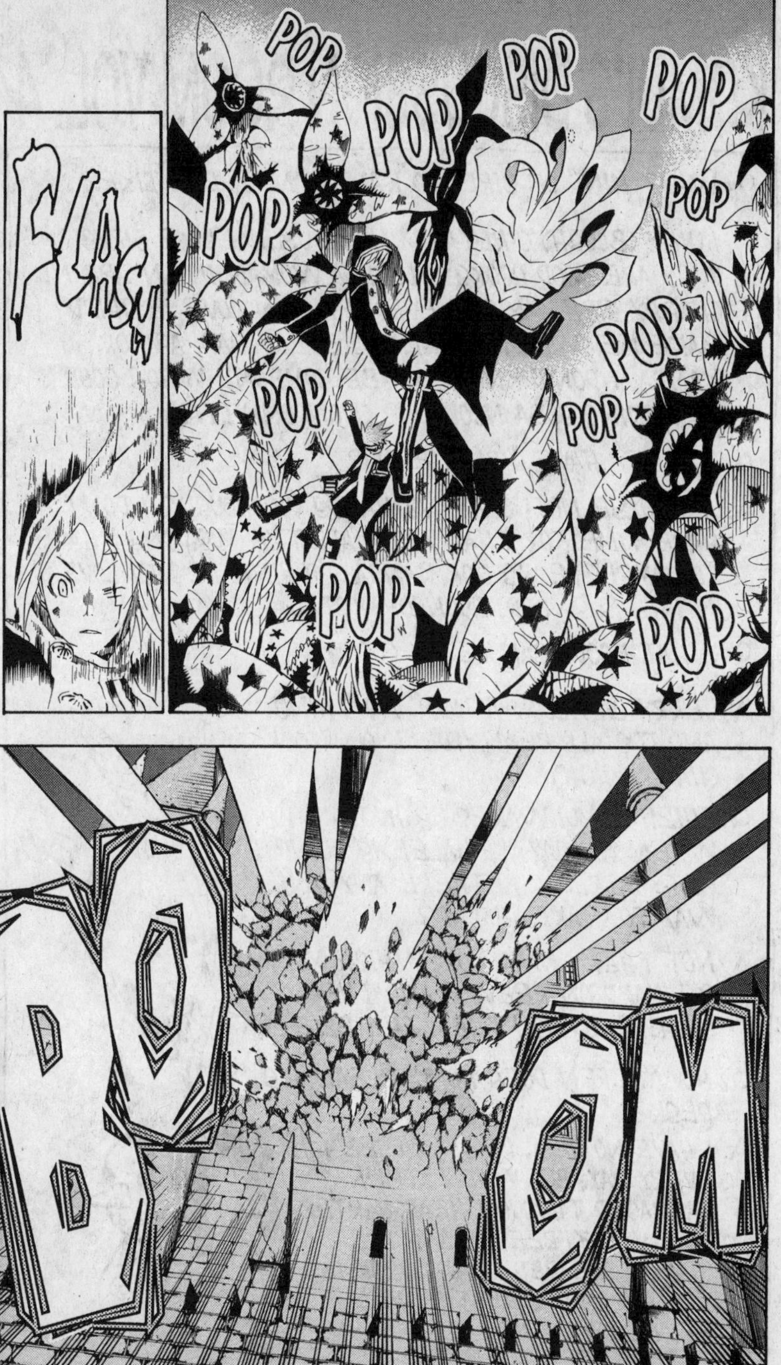
POP
POP
POP
POP
POP
POP
POP
POP
POP
POP
POP
FLASH
BOOM

KOMUI'S DISCUSSION ROOM VOL. 4

Q. WHAT KIND OF GIRLS DO KANDA AND ALLEN LIKE?

A. HUH?! (BLUSH) GIRLS? I DUNNO. UM... I LIKE GIRLS
WHO ARE GOOD COOKS. I LOVE A WOMAN IN AN APRON.
(HAPPY SIGH) I MIGHT EVEN FALL IN LOVE IF SHE'D
MAKE ME SWEET DUMPLINGS EVERY DAY. AS FOR
KANDA, I DON'T KNOW. MAYBE SOMEONE WHO'S GOOD
AT MAKING SOBA NOODLES? (NONCOMMITTAL)

Q. DO THEY HAVE GIRLFRIENDS?

A. OF COURSE NOT! (WAVING HANDS VIGOROUSLY) I DON'T
HAVE TIME FOR THAT WITH ALL THE MISSIONS I HAVE
TO COMPLETE. AS FOR KANDA, I THINK HE'S IN LOVE
WITH HIS SWORD. (NONCOMMITTAL)

Q. WHAT FOODS CAN JERRY COOK?

A. JERRY CAN COOK ALMOST ANYTHING.
AND IT'S ALL REALLY DELICIOUS TOO!
(HAPPY SIGH)

Q. CHIEF KOMUI WAKES UP INSTANTLY
WHEN YOU SAY "LENALEE IS GOING TO
GET MARRIED." IS THERE ANY OTHER
WAY TO WAKE HIM UP?

A. NOT THAT I KNOW OF. WHICH MUST
BE HARD ON REEVER AND THE
OTHERS. I WISH THEM THE BEST.

Q. HOW OFTEN DOES KOMUI CLEAN HIS
DESK?

A. I HAVE NO IDEA. I DON'T GO SEE HIM
EVERY DAY, BUT WHEN KOMLIN
RAMPAGED THROUGH HEADQUARTERS
(SEE VOL. 3) REEVER AND THE
OTHERS CLEARED KOMUI'S DESK IN
THE CLEAN UP. BUT THE VERY
NEXT DAY, IT WAS A MESS AGAIN.

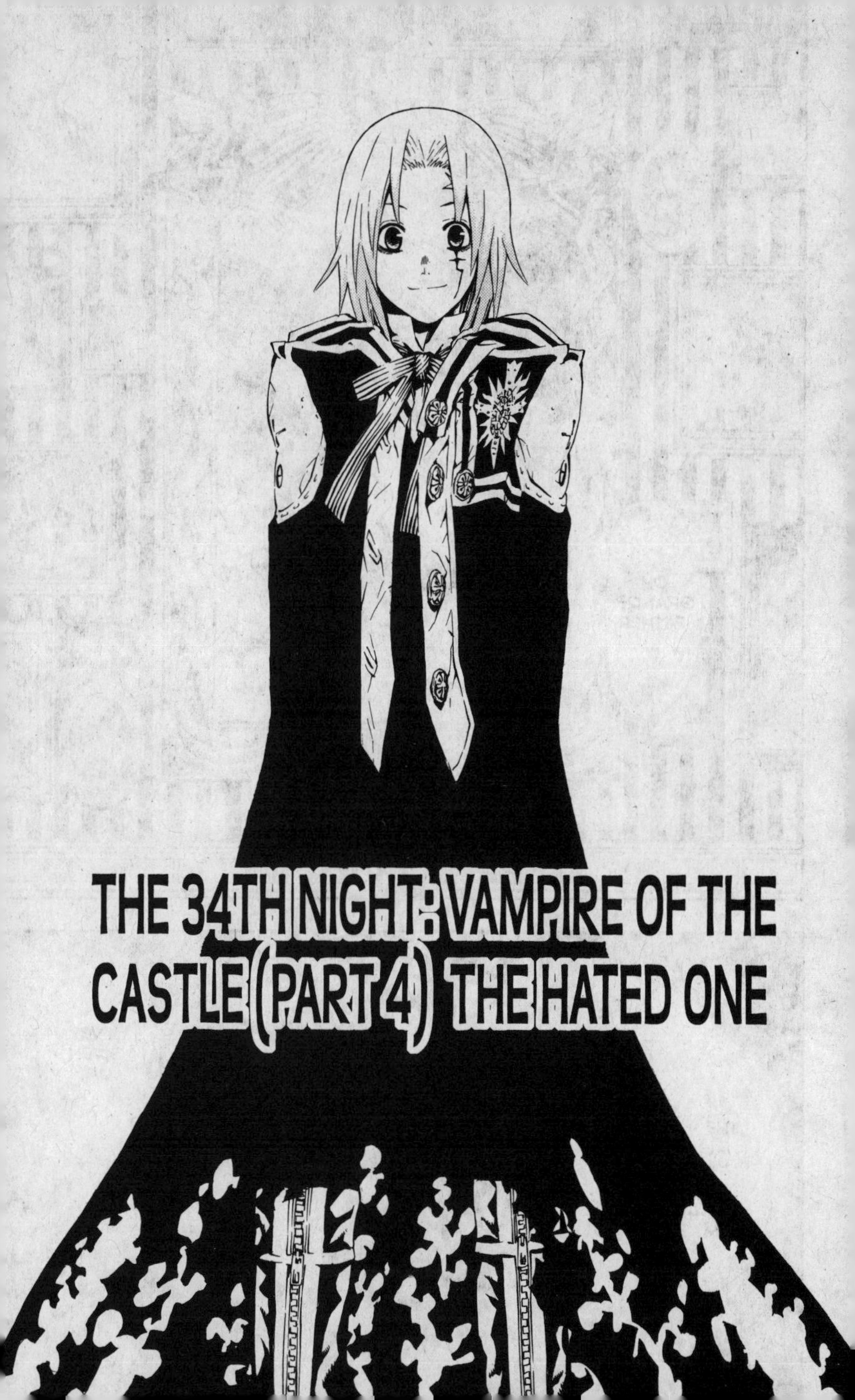
THE 34TH NIGHT: VAMPIRE OF THE
CASTLE (PART 4) THE HATED ONE

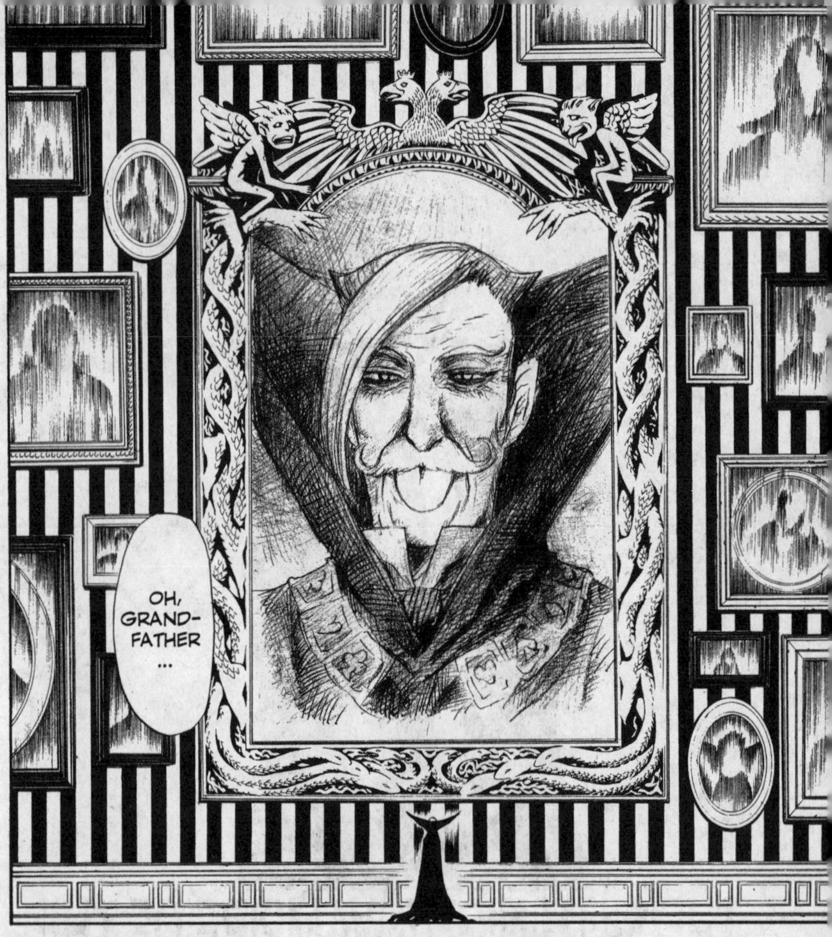
OH, GRAND-FATHER ...

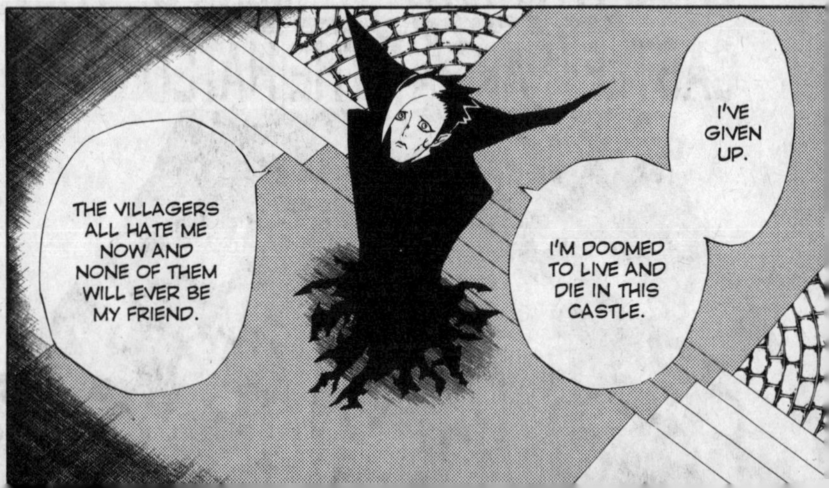
I'VE GIVEN UP.
I'M DOOMED TO LIVE AND DIE IN THIS CASTLE.
THE VILLAGERS ALL HATE ME NOW AND NONE OF THEM WILL EVER BE MY FRIEND.

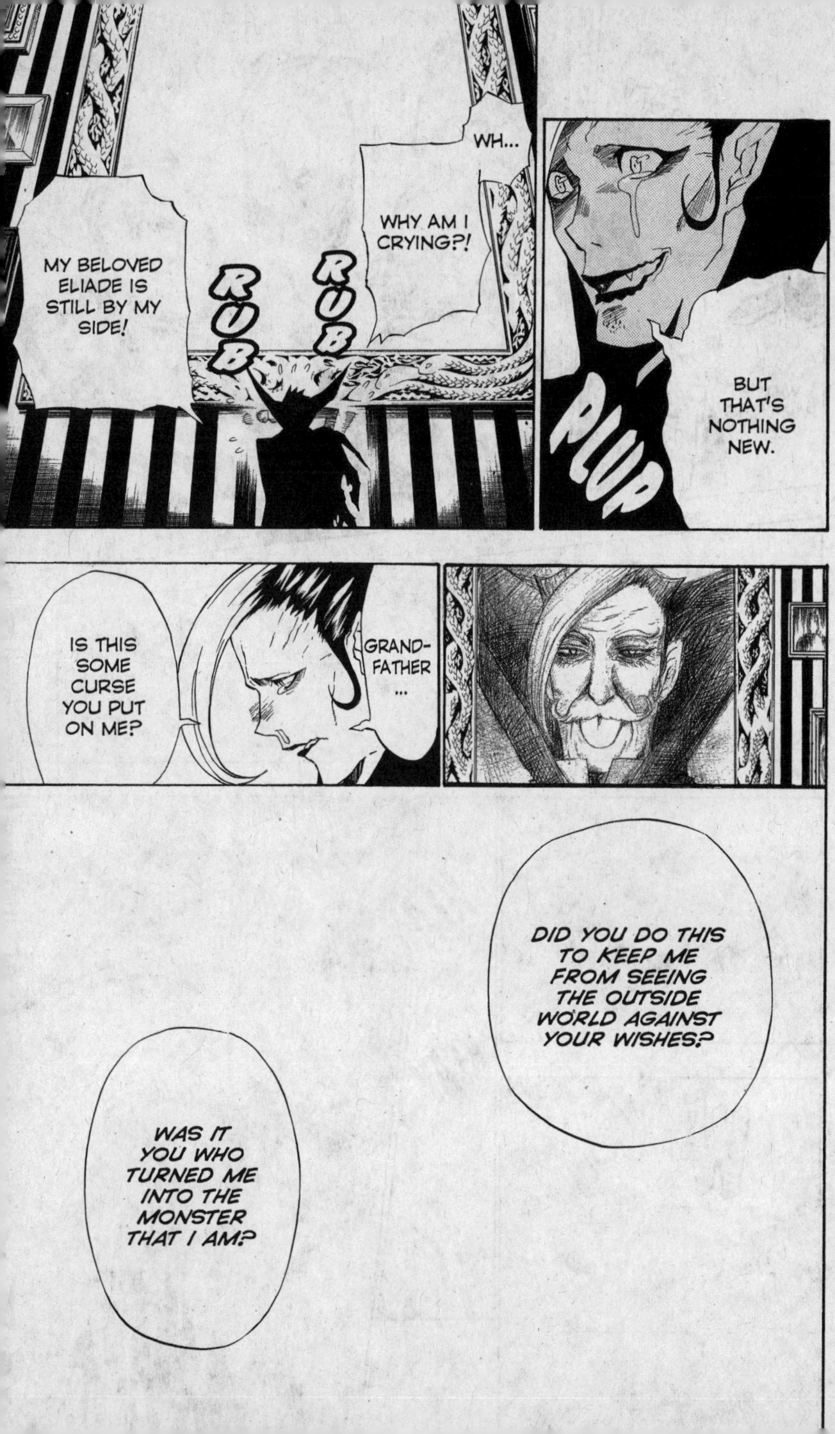
PLUP
BUT THAT'S NOTHING NEW.
WH...
WHY AM I CRYING?!
RUB
RUB
MY BELOVED ELIADE IS STILL BY MY SIDE!
GRAND-FATHER...
IS THIS SOME CURSE YOU PUT ON ME?
DID YOU DO THIS TO KEEP ME FROM SEEING THE OUTSIDE WORLD AGAINST YOUR WISHES?
WAS IT YOU WHO TURNED ME INTO THE MONSTER THAT I AM?

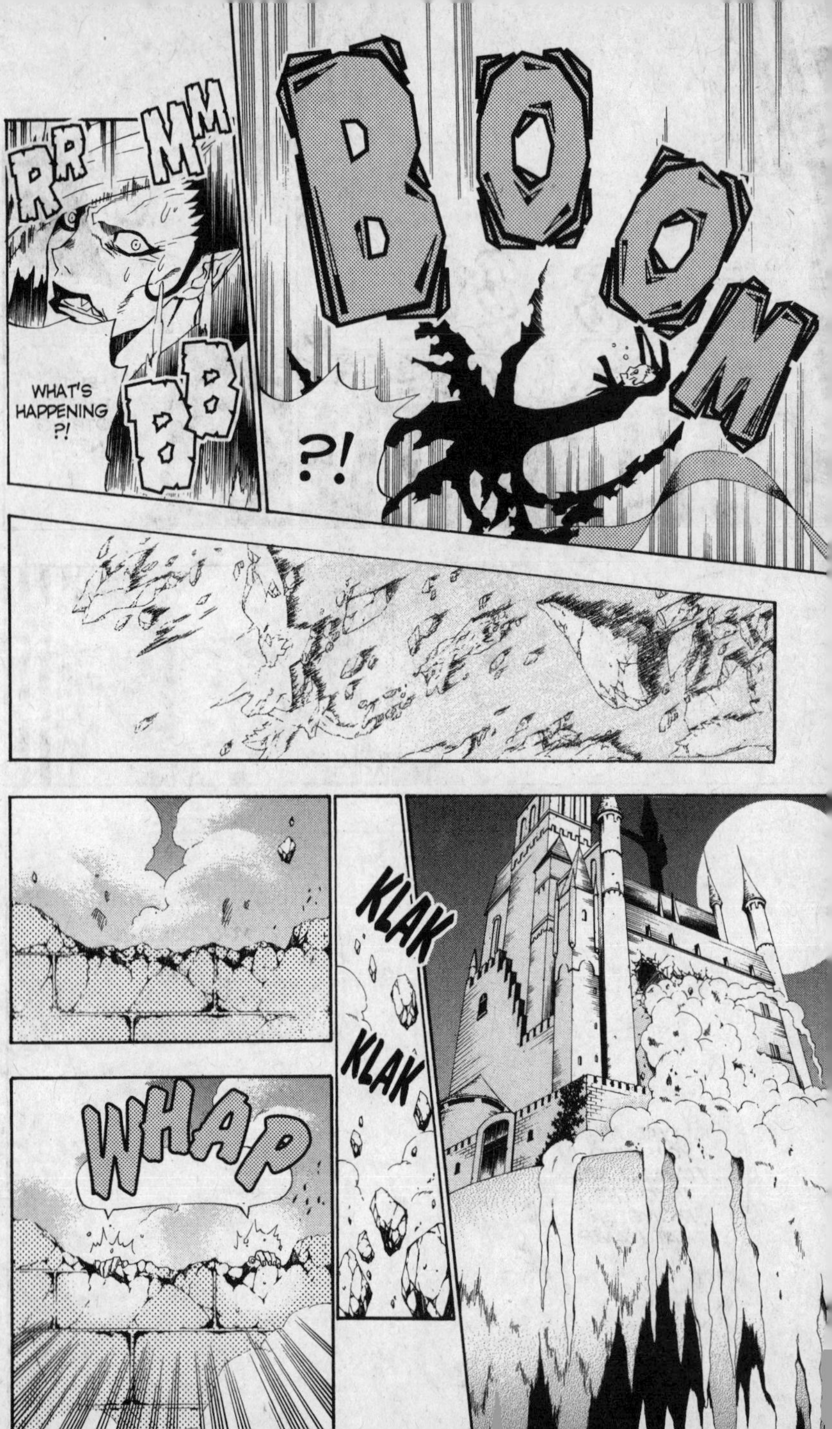
BOOM
?!
RRMM
WHAT'S HAPPENING ?!
BB
KLAK
KLAK
WHAP

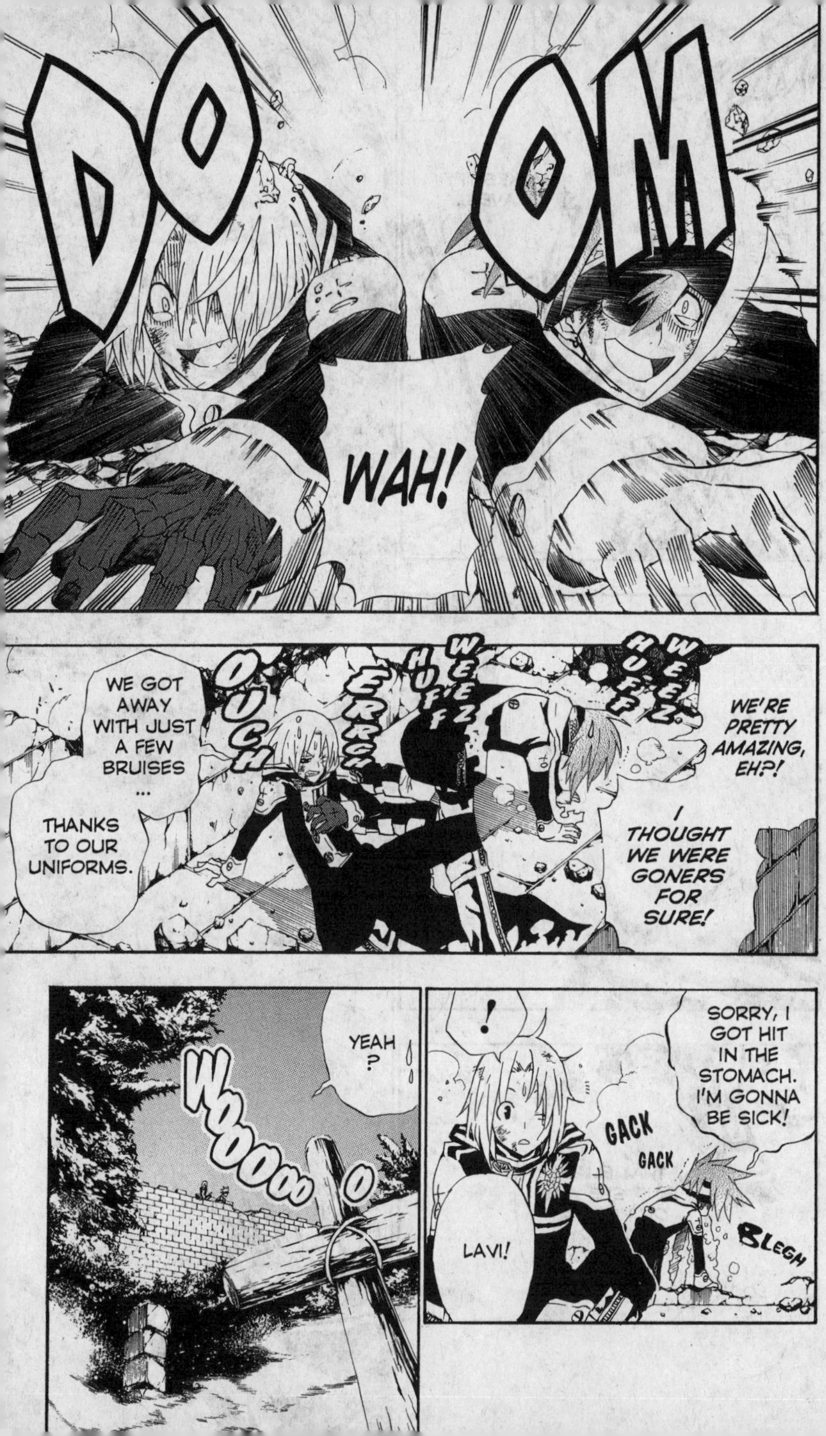
DOOM
WAH!
WE'RE PRETTY AMAZING, EH?!
I THOUGHT WE WERE GONERS FOR SURE!
WEEZ HUFF
WEEZ HUFF
ERRGH
OUCH
WE GOT AWAY WITH JUST A FEW BRUISES ...
THANKS TO OUR UNIFORMS.
!
SORRY, I GOT HIT IN THE STOMACH. I'M GONNA BE SICK!
GACK
GACK
BLEGH
LAVI!
YEAH?
WOOOOOOO

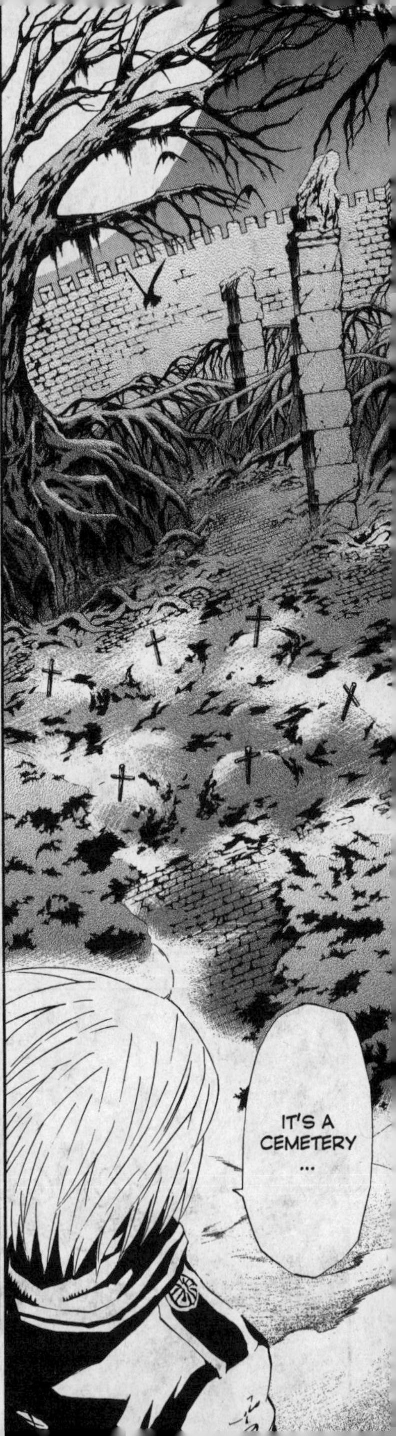
IT'S A CEMETERY ...
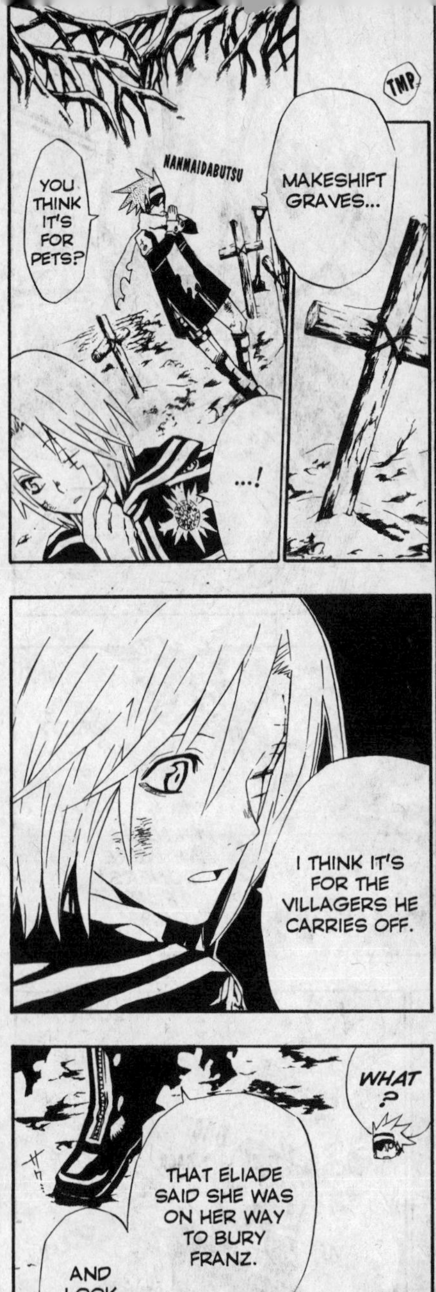
TMP
MAKESHIFT GRAVES...
NANMAIDABUTSU
YOU THINK IT'S FOR PETS?
...!
I THINK IT'S FOR THE VILLAGERS HE CARRIES OFF.
WHAT?
THAT ELIADE SAID SHE WAS ON HER WAY TO BURY FRANZ.
AND LOOK ...

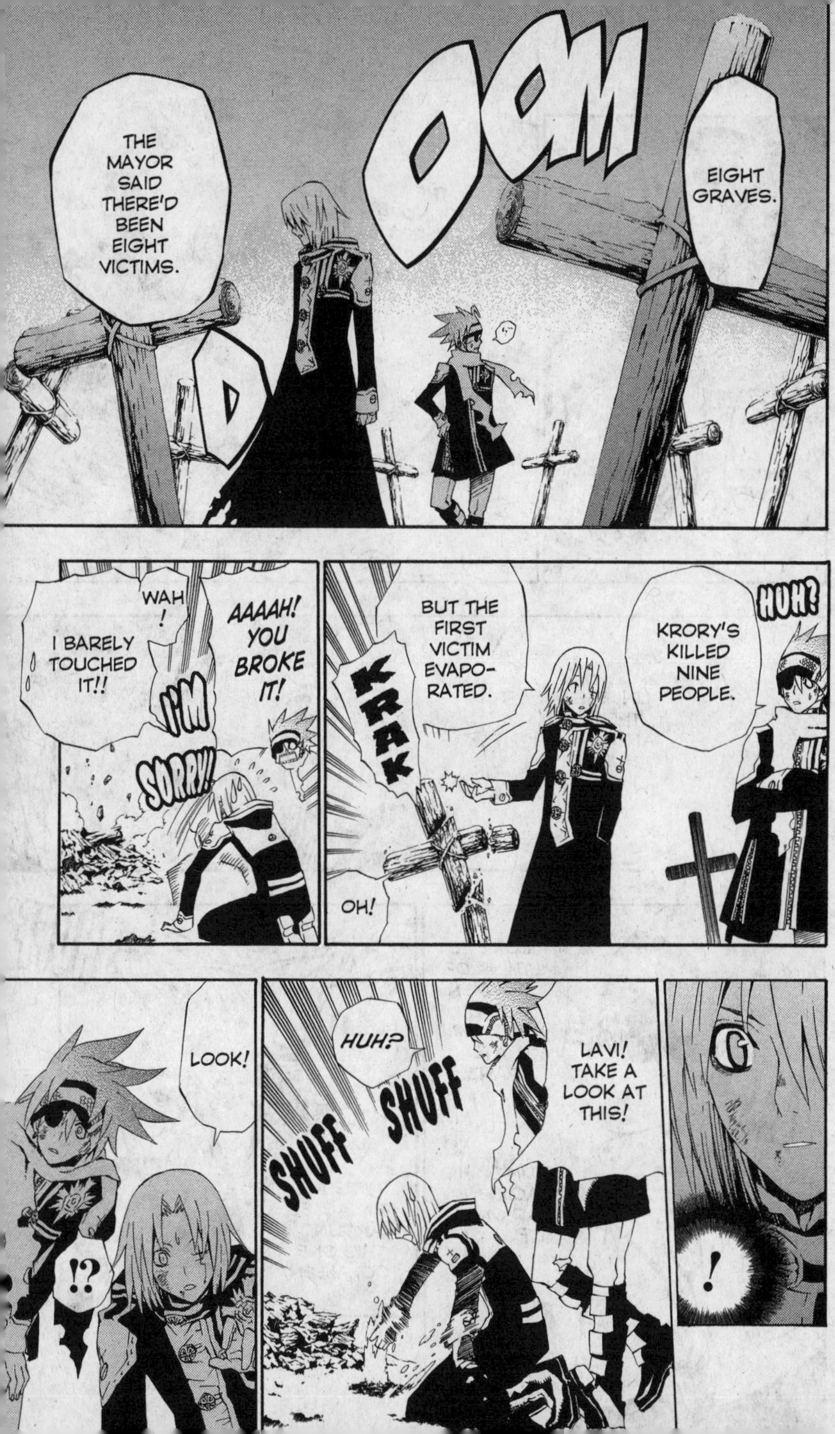
EIGHT GRAVES.
OOM
D
THE MAYOR SAID THERE'D BEEN EIGHT VICTIMS.
HUH?
KRORY'S KILLED NINE PEOPLE.
BUT THE FIRST VICTIM EVAPO-RATED.
KRAK
OH!
AAAAH! YOU BROKE IT!
WAH!
I BARELY TOUCHED IT!!
I'M SORRY!!
!
LAVI! TAKE A LOOK AT THIS!
SHUFF
SHUFF
HUH?
LOOK!
!?

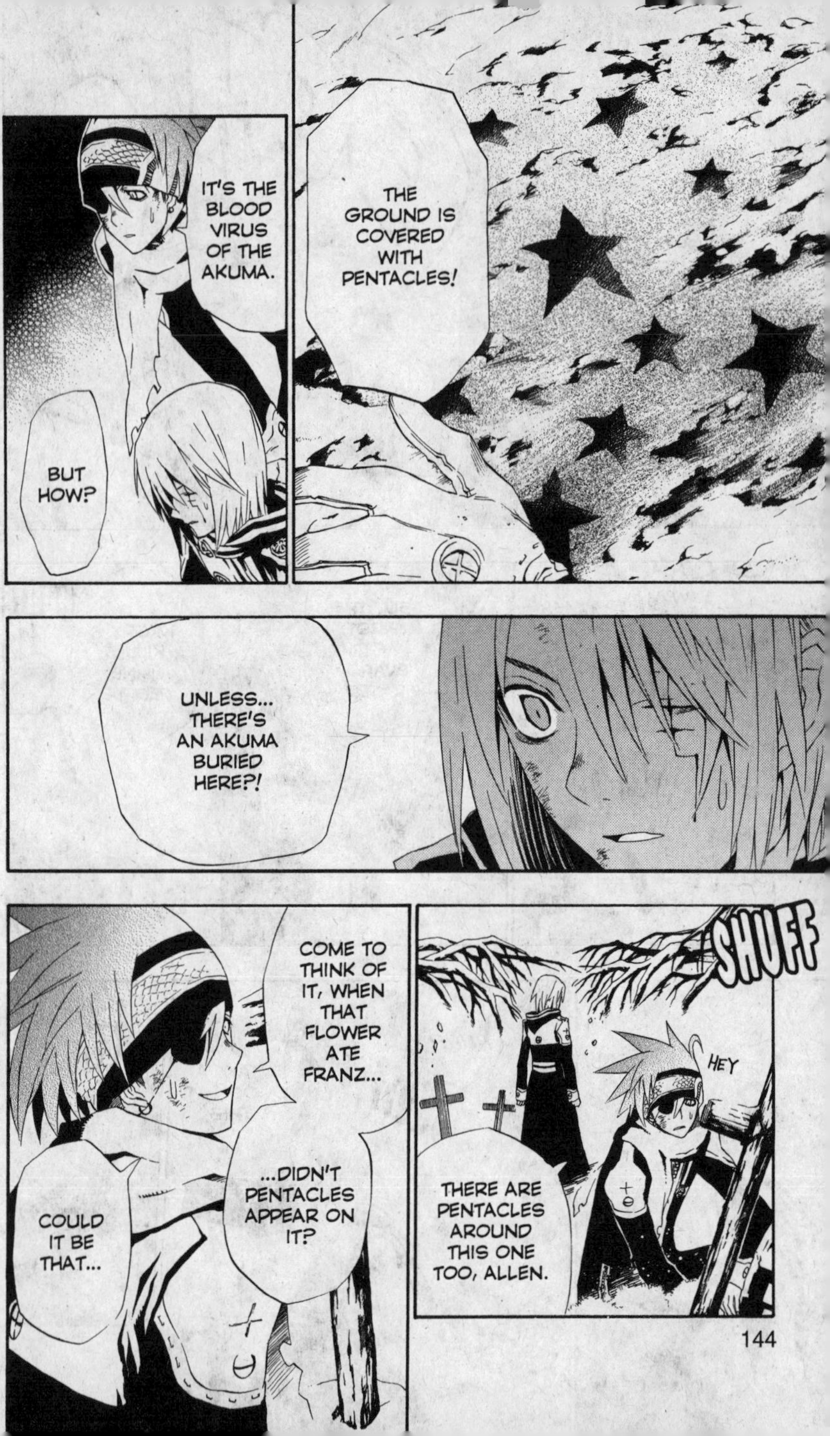

THE GROUND IS COVERED WITH PENTACLES!
IT'S THE BLOOD VIRUS OF THE AKUMA.
BUT HOW?
UNLESS... THERE'S AN AKUMA BURIED HERE?!
SHUFF
HEY
THERE ARE PENTACLES AROUND THIS ONE TOO, ALLEN.
COME TO THINK OF IT, WHEN THAT FLOWER ATE FRANZ...
...DIDN'T PENTACLES APPEAR ON IT?
COULD IT BE THAT...

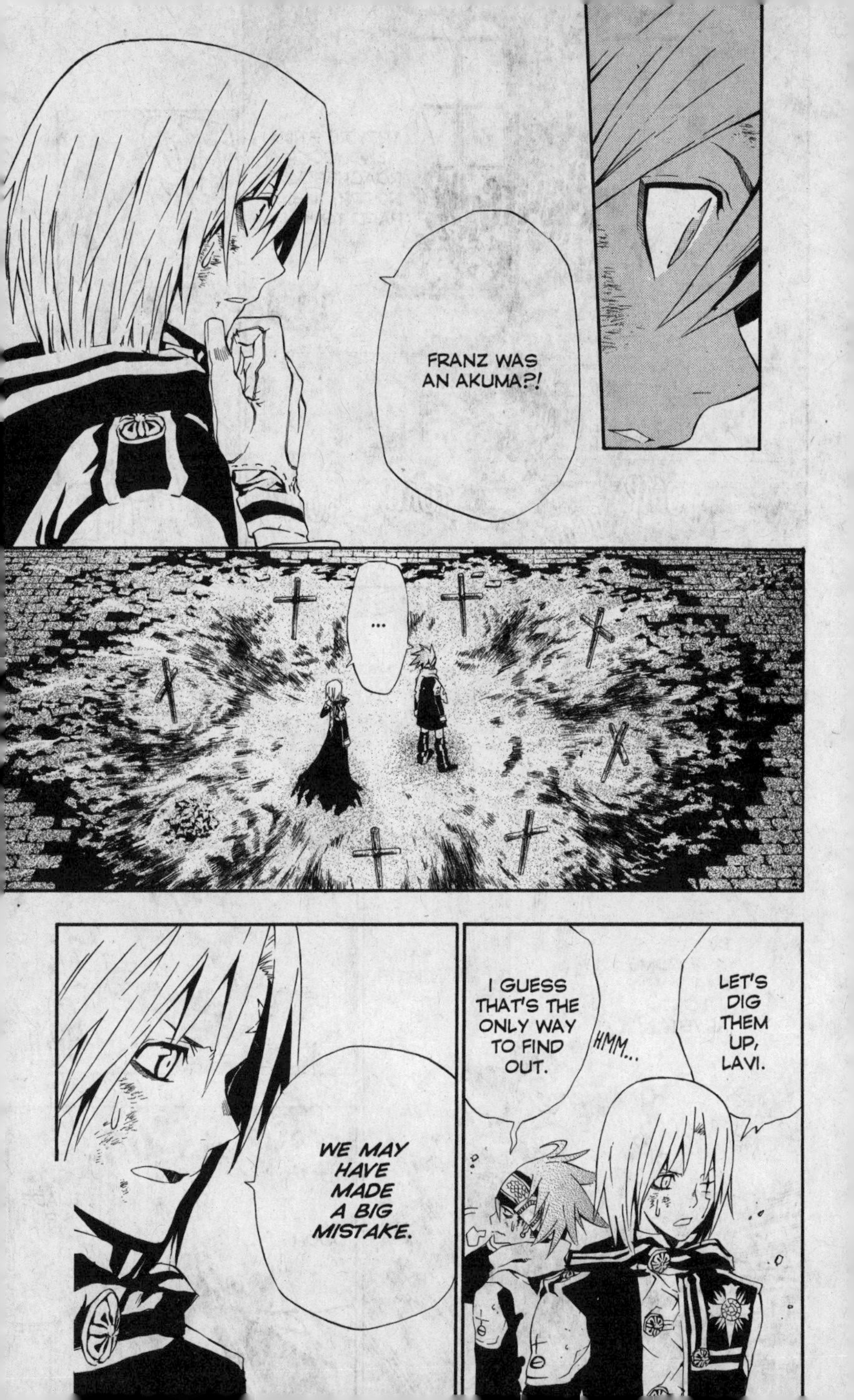
FRANZ WAS AN AKUMA?!
...
LET'S DIG THEM UP, LAVI.
HMM...
I GUESS THAT'S THE ONLY WAY TO FIND OUT.
WE MAY HAVE MADE A BIG MISTAKE.

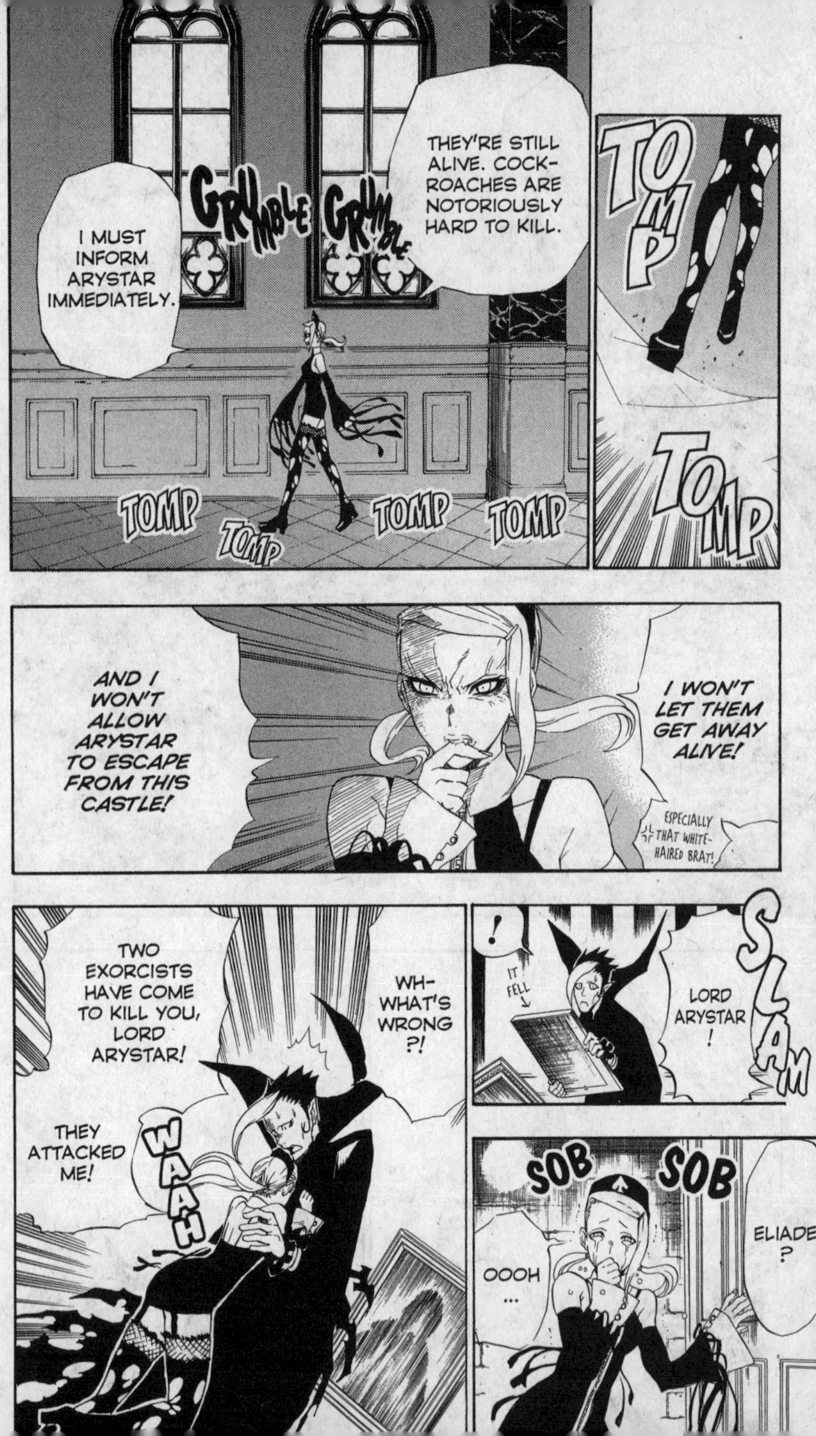
TOMP
TOMP
THEY'RE STILL ALIVE. COCKROACHES ARE NOTORIOUSLY HARD TO KILL.
GRUMBLE GRUMBLE
I MUST INFORM ARYSTAR IMMEDIATELY.
TOMP
TOMP
TOMP
TOMP
I WON'T LET THEM GET AWAY ALIVE!
ESPECIALLY THAT WHITE-HAIRED BRAT!
AND I WON'T ALLOW ARYSTAR TO ESCAPE FROM THIS CASTLE!
SLAM
LORD ARYSTAR!
IT FELL
!
ELIADE?
SOB SOB
OOOH...
WH-WHAT'S WRONG?!
TWO EXORCISTS HAVE COME TO KILL YOU, LORD ARYSTAR!
WAAH
THEY ATTACKED ME!

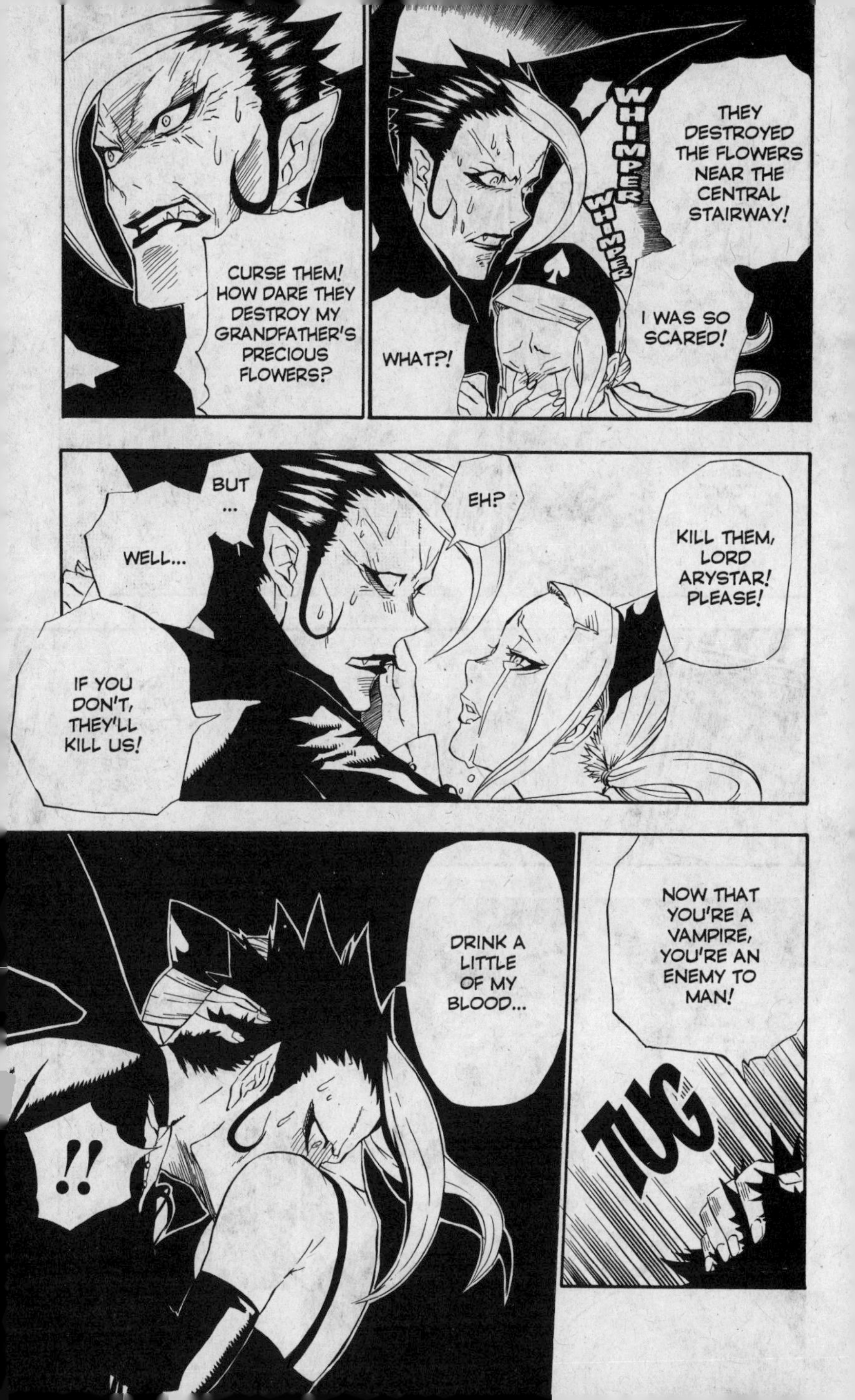
THEY DESTROYED THE FLOWERS NEAR THE CENTRAL STAIRWAY!
WHIMPER WHIMPER
I WAS SO SCARED!
WHAT?!
CURSE THEM! HOW DARE THEY DESTROY MY GRANDFATHER'S PRECIOUS FLOWERS?
KILL THEM, LORD ARYSTAR! PLEASE!
EH?
BUT ...
WELL...
IF YOU DON'T, THEY'LL KILL US!
NOW THAT YOU'RE A VAMPIRE, YOU'RE AN ENEMY TO MAN!
TUG
DRINK A LITTLE OF MY BLOOD...
!!

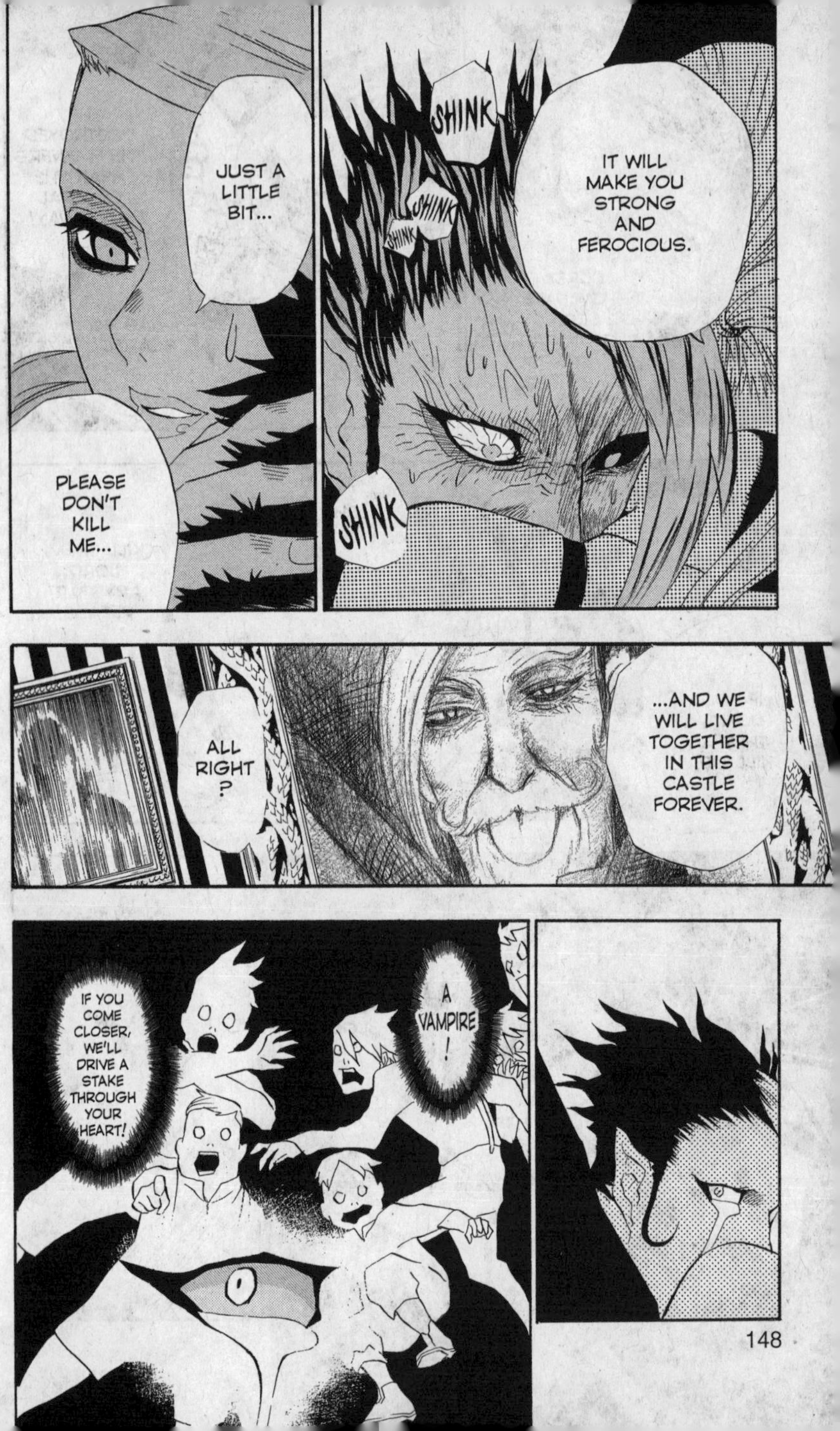
IT WILL MAKE YOU STRONG AND FEROCIOUS.
SHINK
SHINK
SHINK
SHINK
JUST A LITTLE BIT...
PLEASE DON'T KILL ME...
...AND WE WILL LIVE TOGETHER IN THIS CASTLE FOREVER.
ALL RIGHT?
A VAMPIRE!
IF YOU COME CLOSER, WE'LL DRIVE A STAKE THROUGH YOUR HEART!

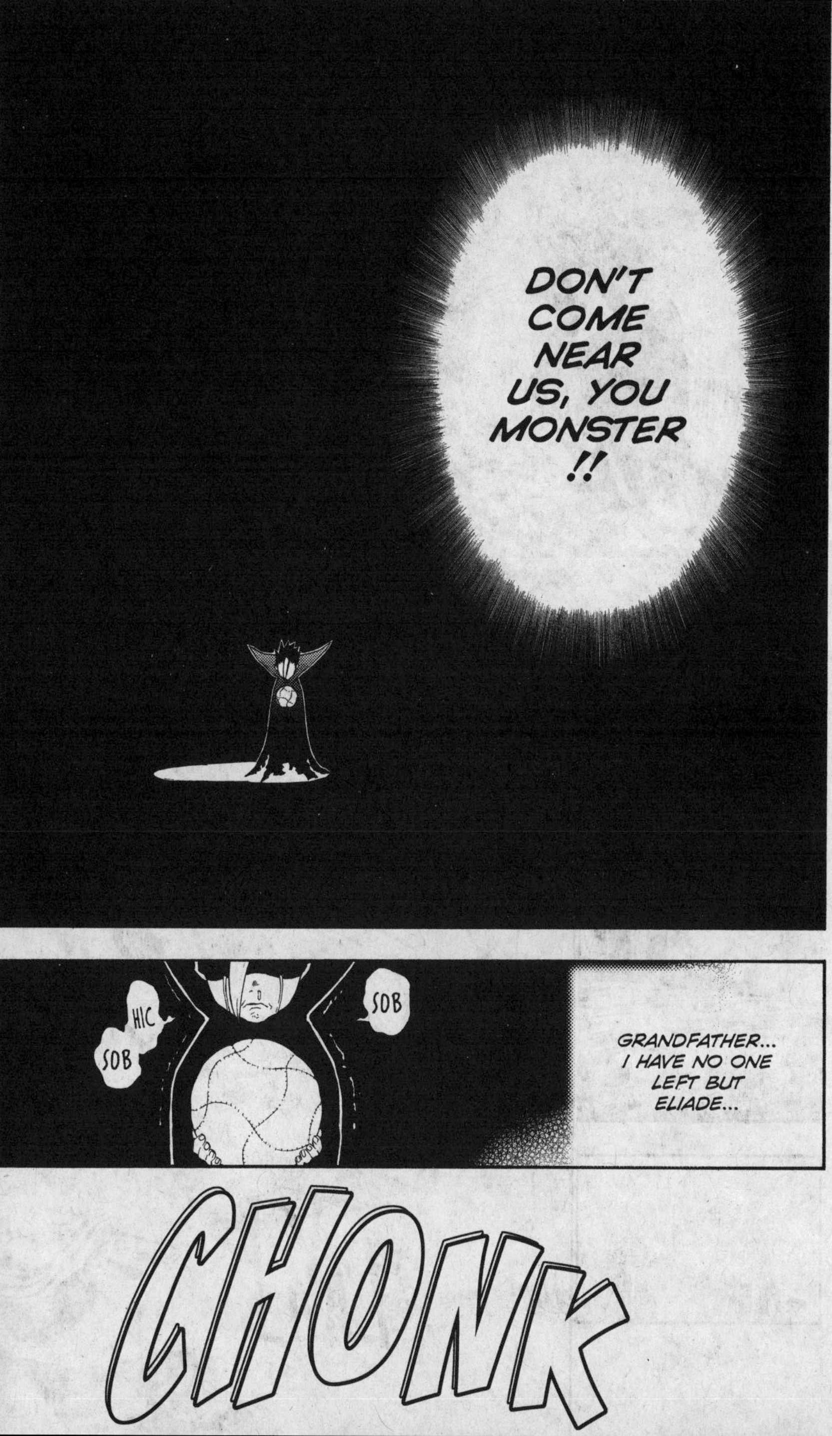
DON'T COME NEAR US, YOU MONSTER !!
GRANDFATHER... I HAVE NO ONE LEFT BUT ELIADE...
SOB
HIC
SOB
CHONK

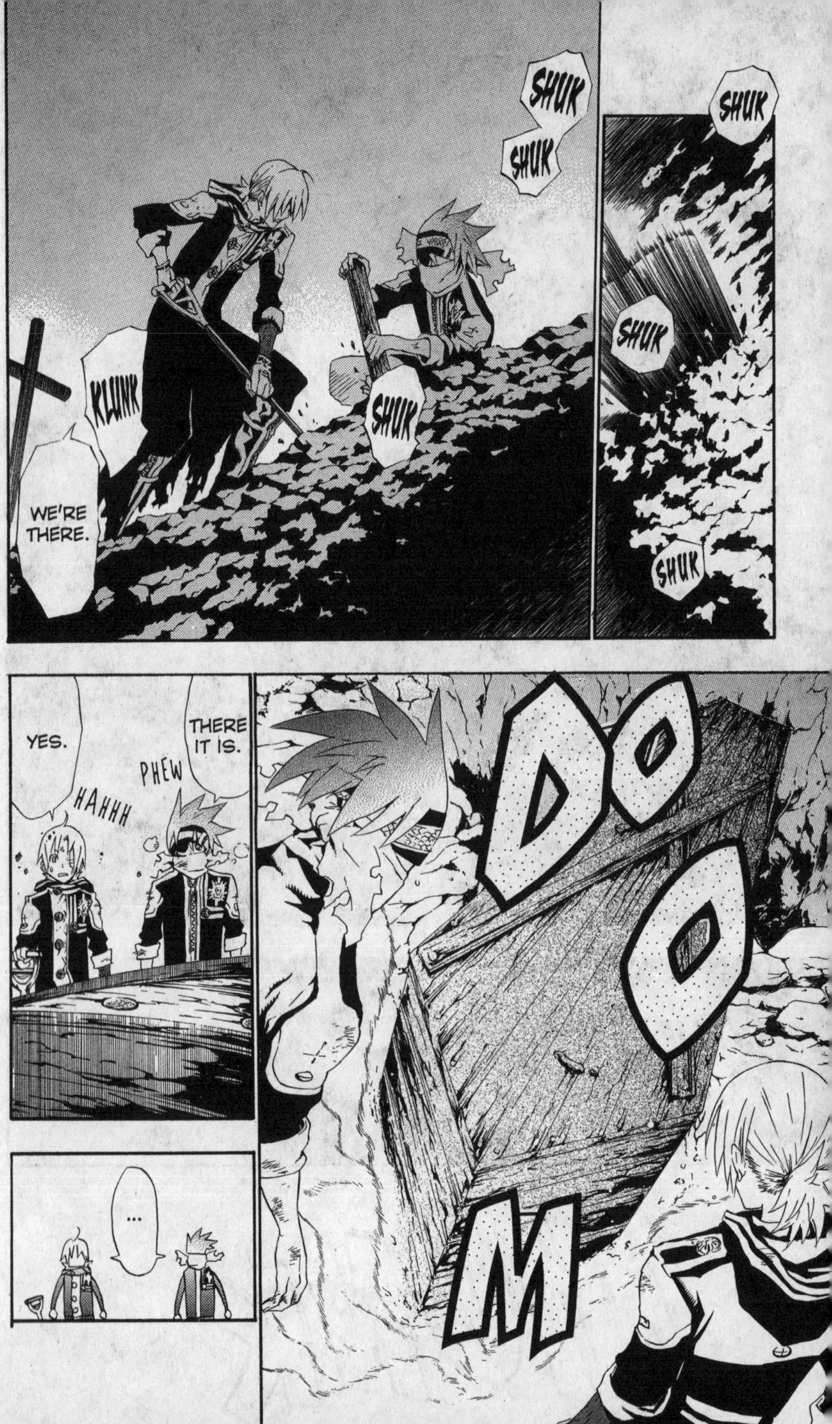
SHUK
SHUK
SHUK
SHUK
SHUK
KLUNK
SHUK
WE'RE THERE.
DOOM
THERE IT IS.
PHEW
YES.
HAHHH
...

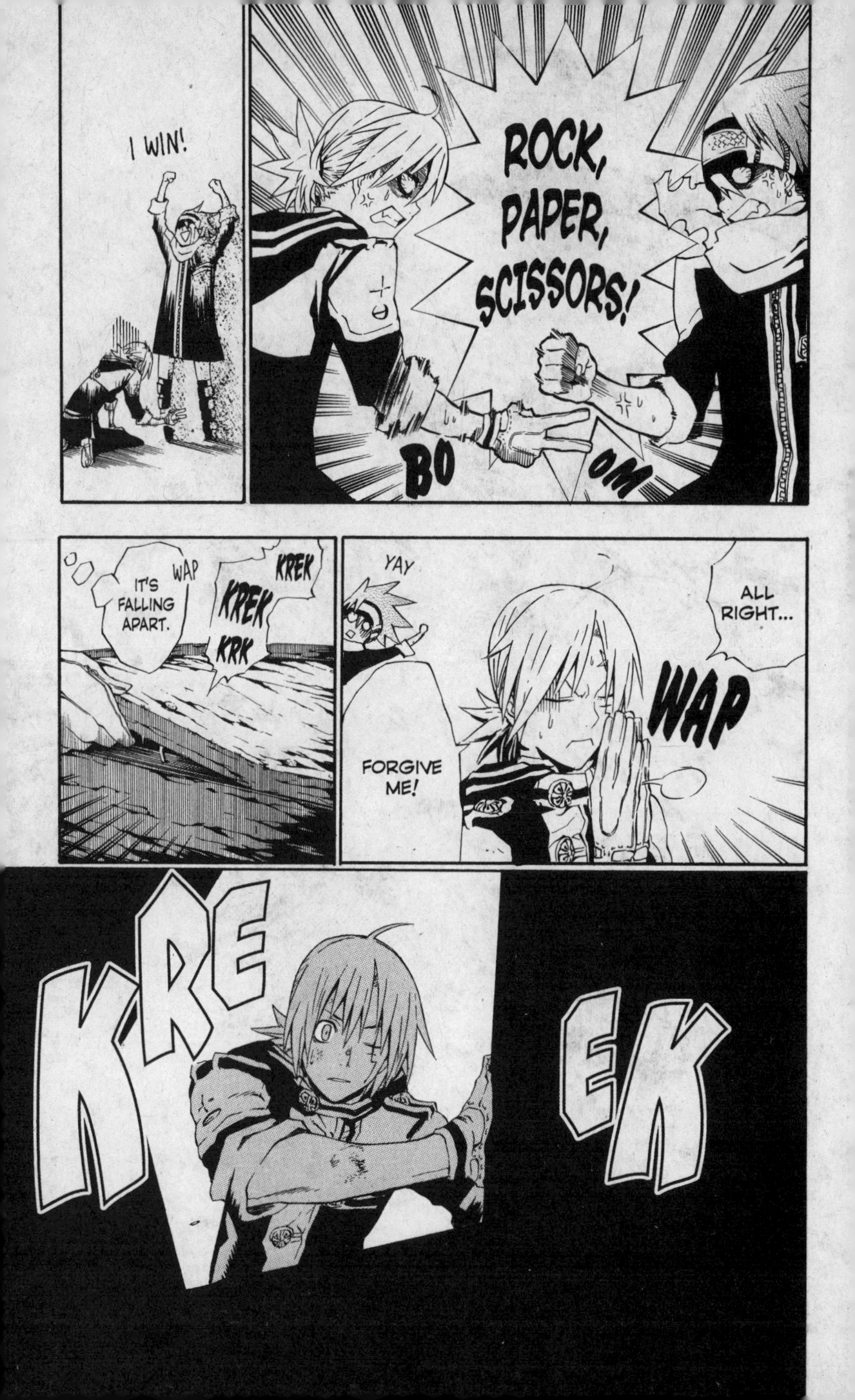
ROCK, PAPER, SCISSORS!
BO
OM
I WIN!
ALL RIGHT...
YAY
WAP
FORGIVE ME!
KREK
WAP
IT'S FALLING APART.
KREK
KRK
KRE
EK

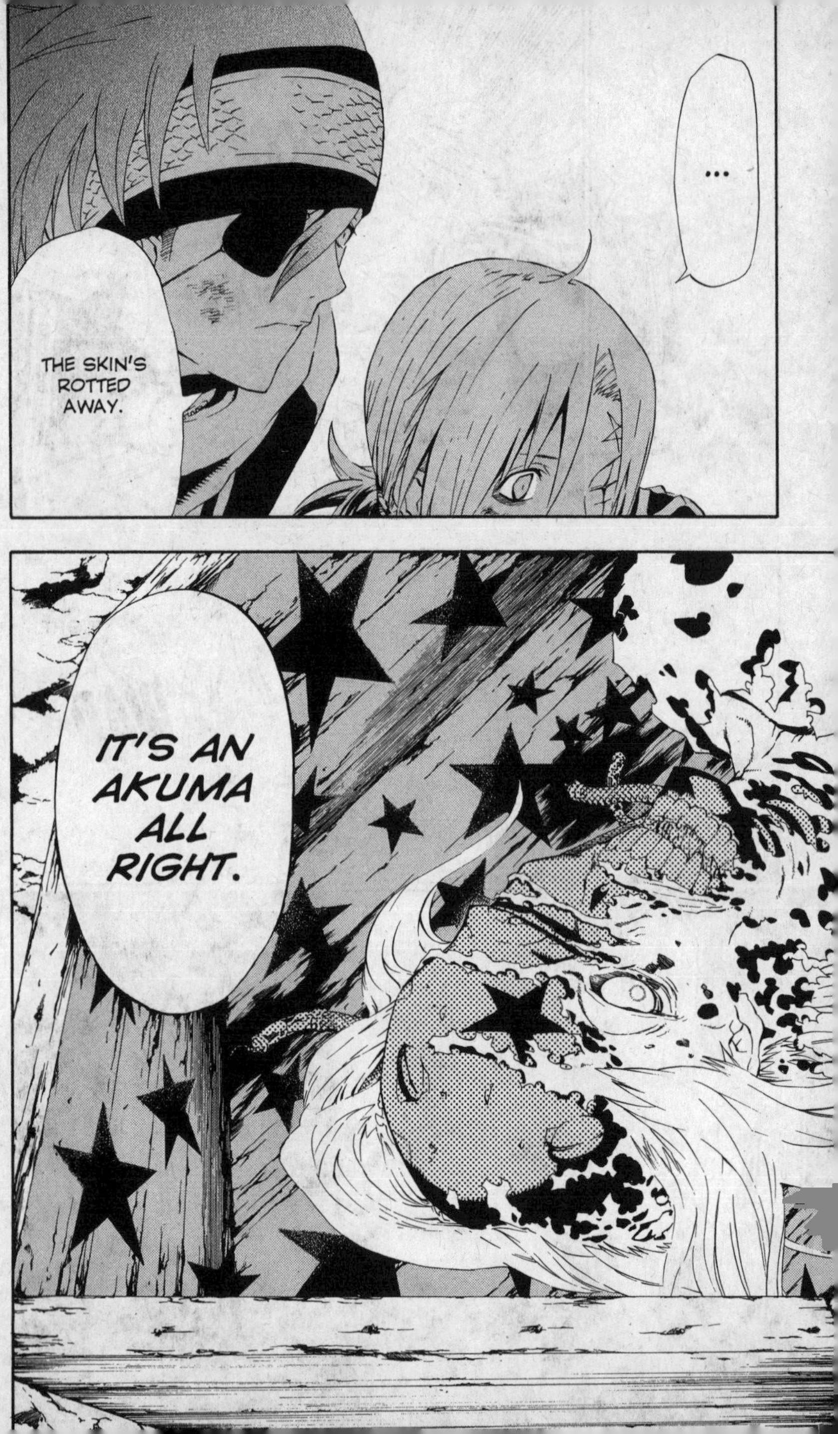
...
THE SKIN'S ROTTED AWAY.
IT'S AN AKUMA ALL RIGHT.

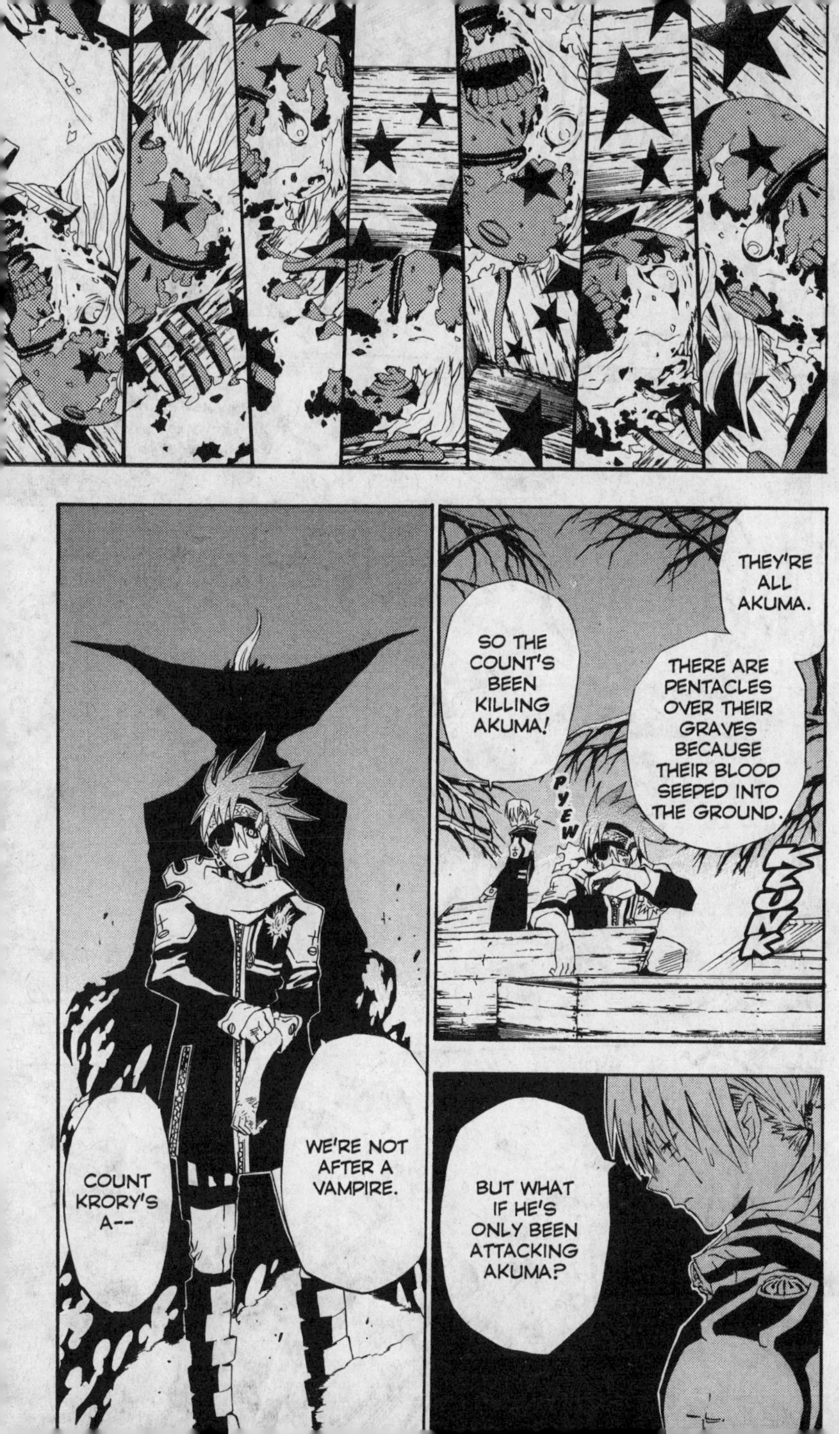
THEY'RE ALL AKUMA.
THERE ARE PENTACLES OVER THEIR GRAVES BECAUSE THEIR BLOOD SEEPED INTO THE GROUND.
SO THE COUNT'S BEEN KILLING AKUMA!
KLUNK
PYEW
BUT WHAT IF HE'S ONLY BEEN ATTACKING AKUMA?
WE'RE NOT AFTER A VAMPIRE.
COUNT KRORY'S A--

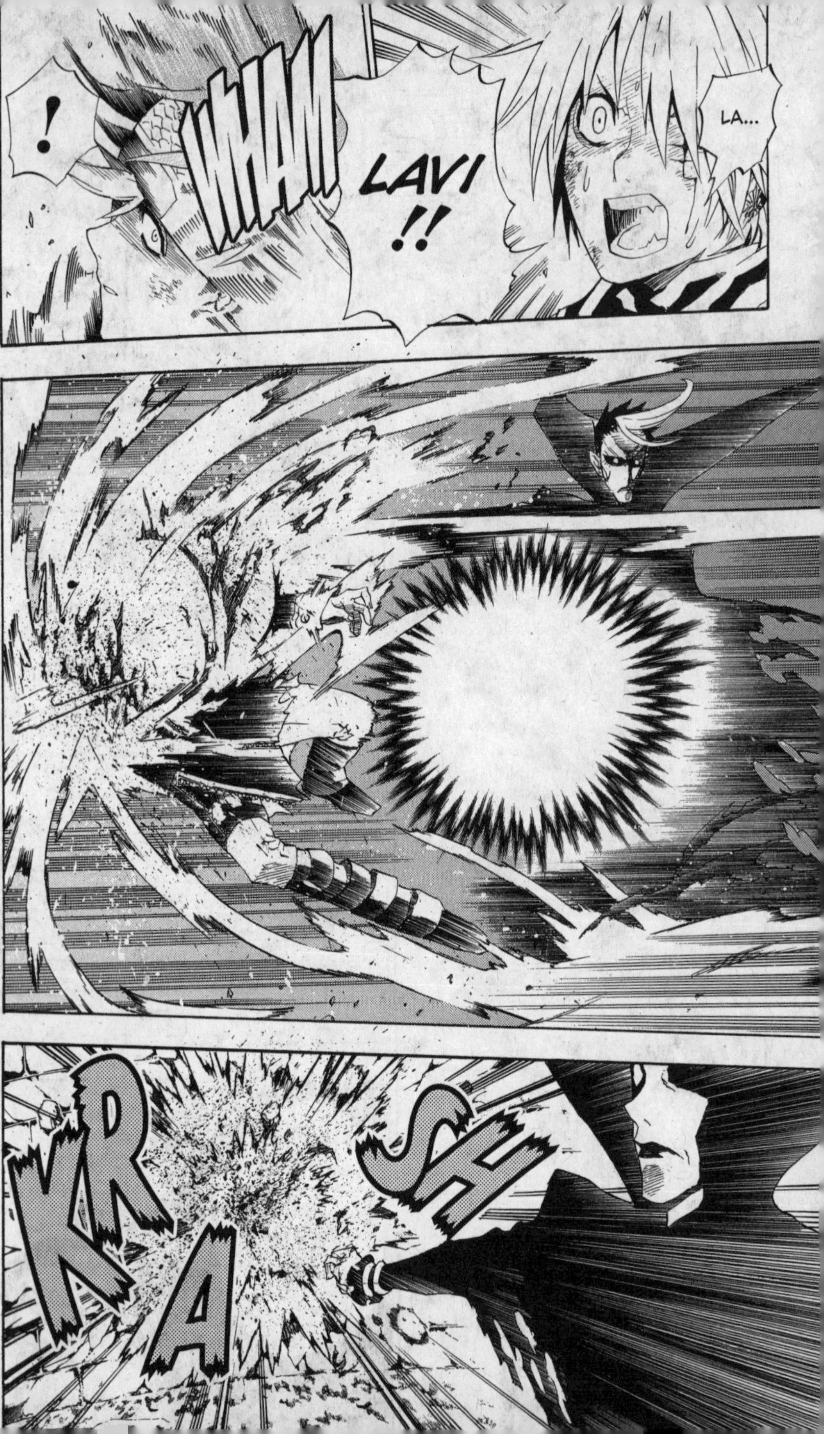
LA...
LAVI !!
WHAM
!
KRASH

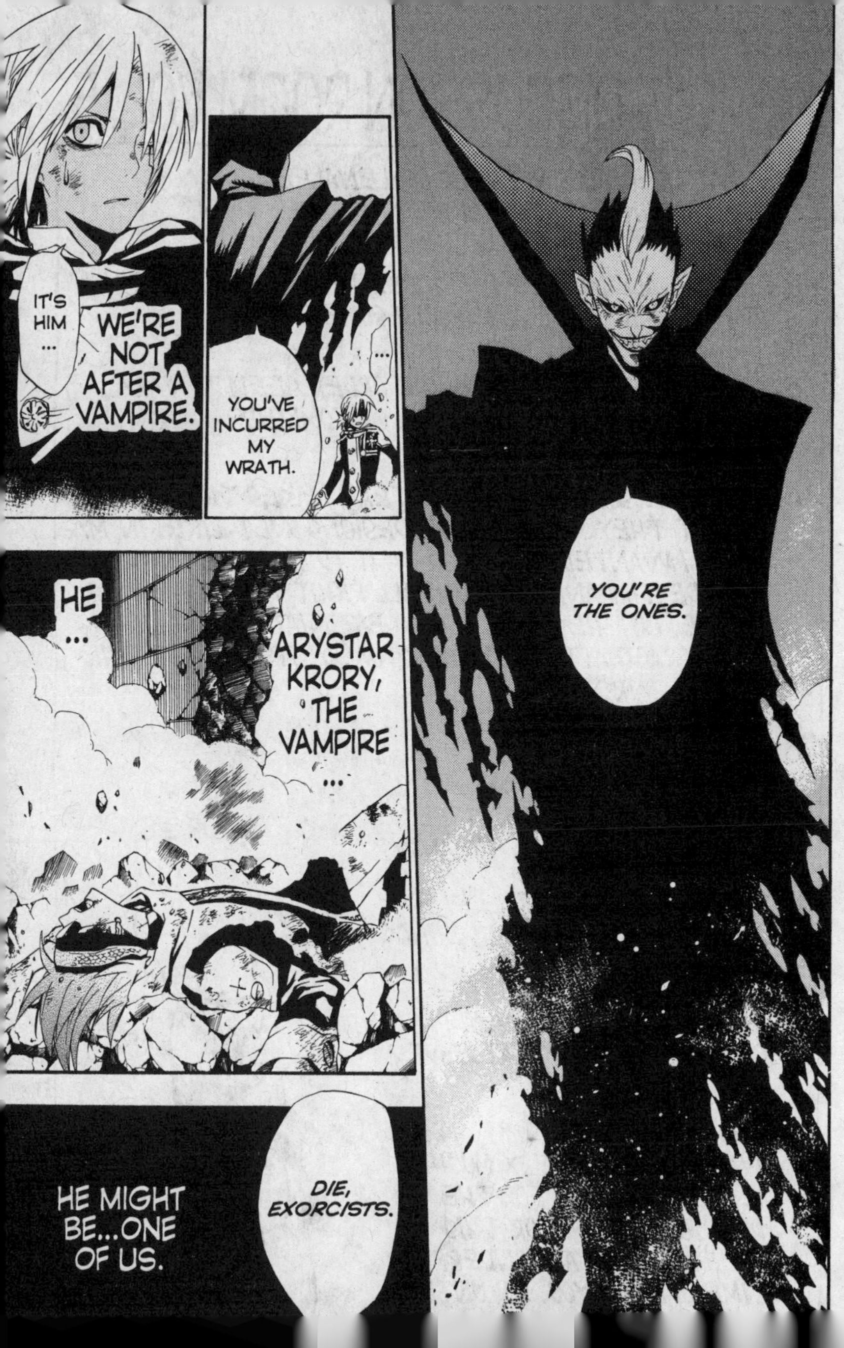
YOU'RE THE ONES.
DIE, EXORCISTS.
...
YOU'VE INCURRED MY WRATH.
IT'S HIM ...
WE'RE NOT AFTER A VAMPIRE.
HE ...
ARYSTAR KRORY, THE VAMPIRE ...
HE MIGHT BE...ONE OF US.

KOMUI'S DISCUSSION ROOM VOL. 5

Q. WHAT DOES ALLEN THINK OF LENALEE'S TANTALIZINGLY SHORT SKIRT?

A. I THINK ALL MEN LIKE MINISKIRTS. BUT I WONDER IF IT DOESN'T GET A BIT COLD SOMETIMES.

Q. THE UNIFORMS OF THE BLACK ORDER SEEM TO VARY CONSIDERABLY. ARE THEY ALL CUSTOMIZED?

A. I SUPPOSE SO. THE SCIENCE TEAM MAKES THEM FOR US, BUT THEY ASK US WHAT DESIGNS WE'D LIKE. IN MY CASE, I WANTED A HOOD SO THAT I'D HAVE SOMEPLACE TO HIDE TIMCANPY. IT WAS ALL RIGHT WHEN HE WAS LITTLE, BUT HE'S GETTING SO BIG THAT HE'S STARTING TO ATTRACT ATTENTION. (*ACTUALLY, IT'S TO HIDE THE WHITE HAIR.)

Q. IN THE AUTHOR'S COMMENTS AT THE BEGINNING OF VOLUME 2, WHAT'S THE NAME OF THE KITTEN THAT'S GOT TIMCANPY?

A. OH, THAT CUTE LITTLE KITTY? (HAPPY SIGH) THAT'S HOSHINO'S BELOVED KORO.

Q. HOW MANY VALENTINE'S DAY CHOCOLATES DID YOU RECEIVE? WHO GOT THE MOST?

A. I GOT THE MOST---115. (SMILES) THANK YOU ALL VERY MUCH. WELL, THAT'S IT FOR THE DISCUSSION ROOM FOR THIS VOLUME. I HAD A WONDERFUL TIME, THANK YOU. SO, UNTIL NEXT TIME.

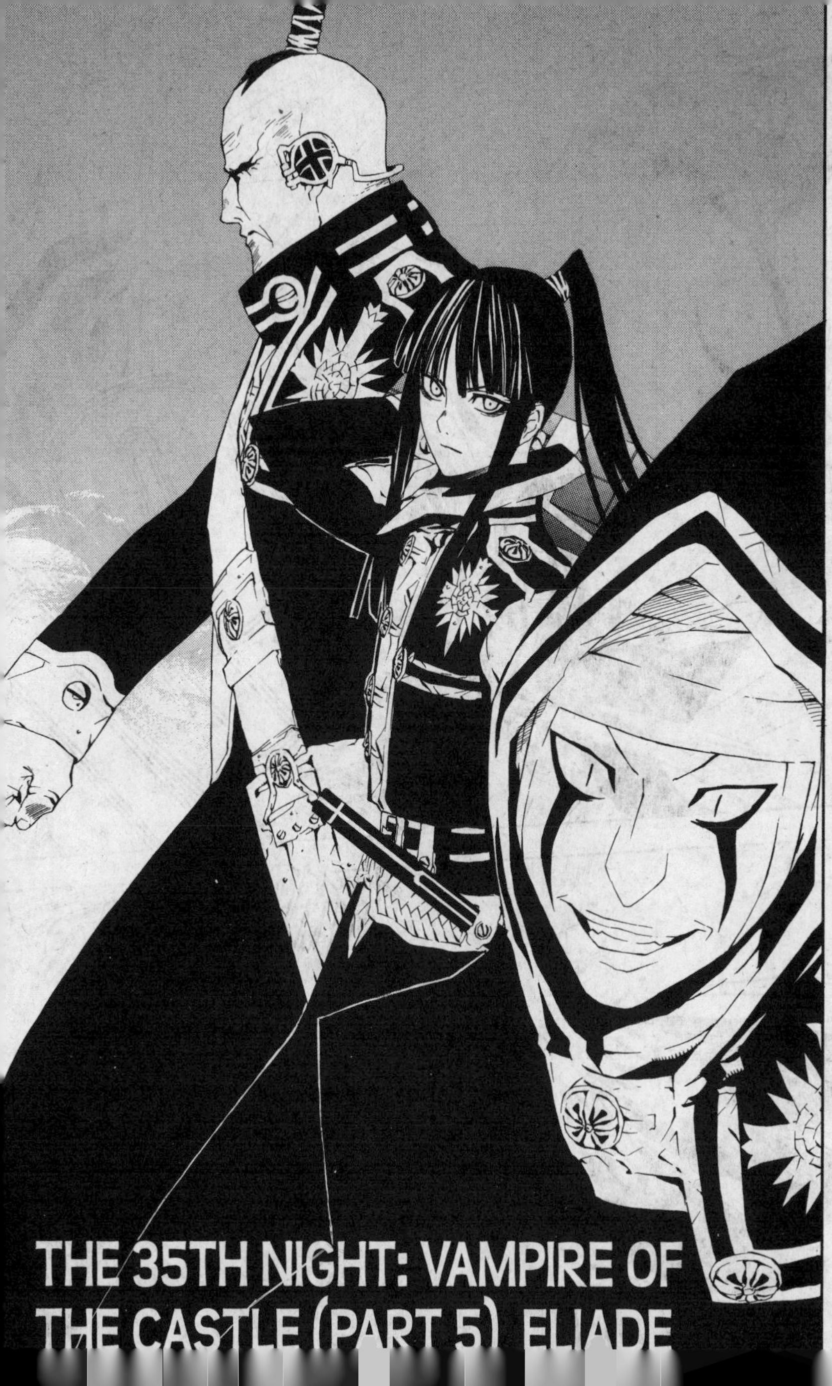
THE 35TH NIGHT: VAMPIRE OF THE CASTLE (PART 5) ELIADE

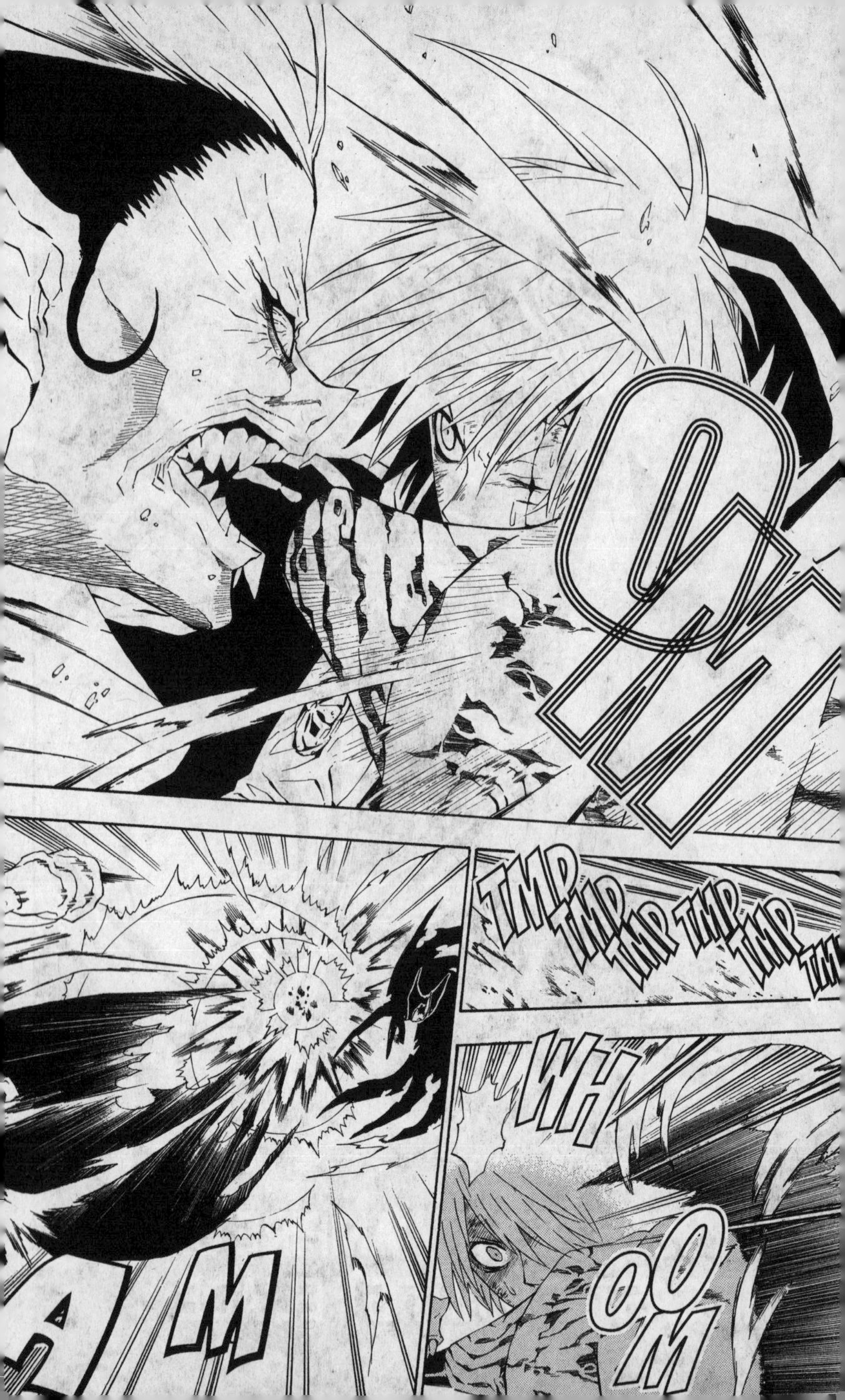
TMP TMP TMP TMP TMP TM
WHOOM

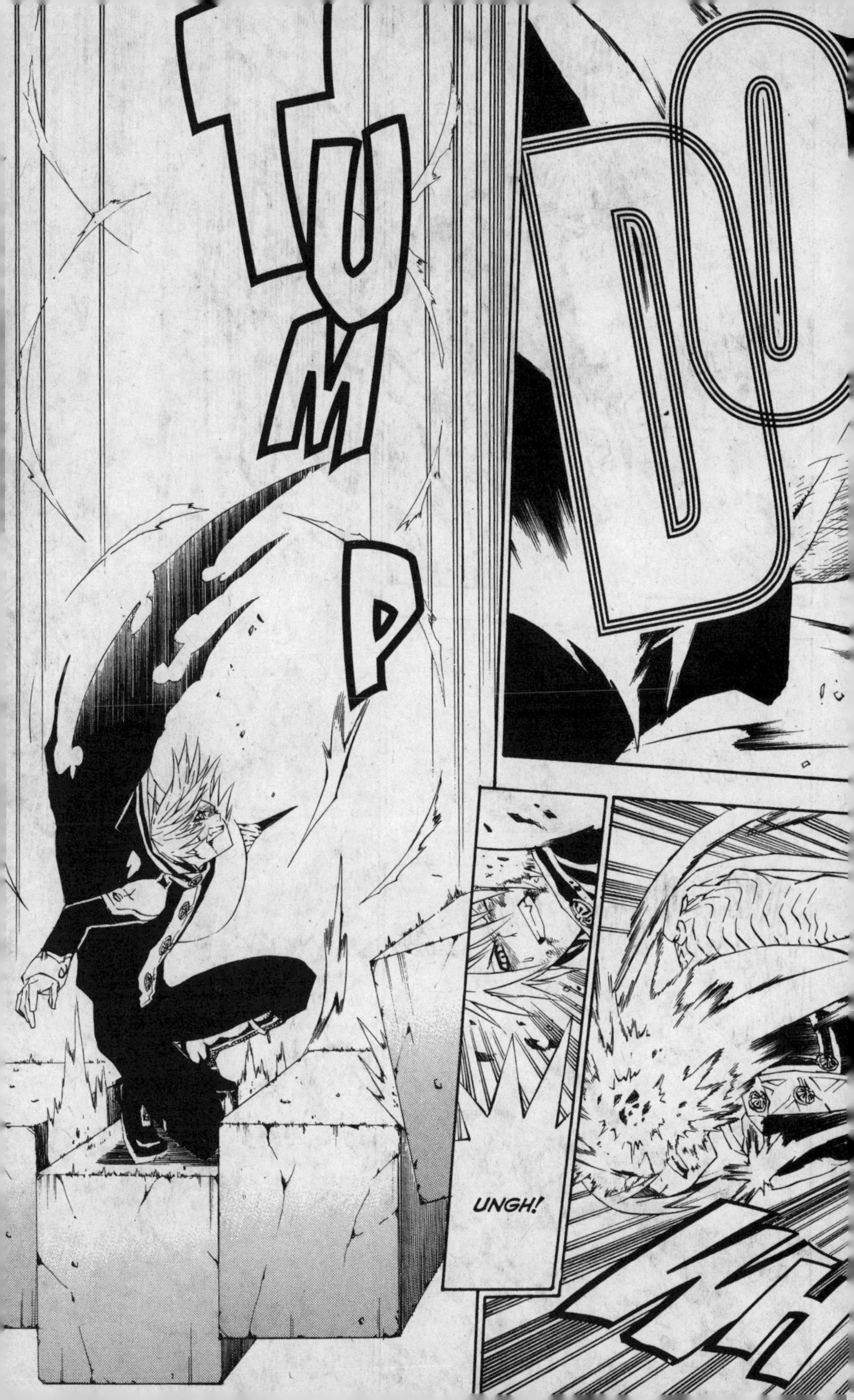
DO
UNGH!
TUMP

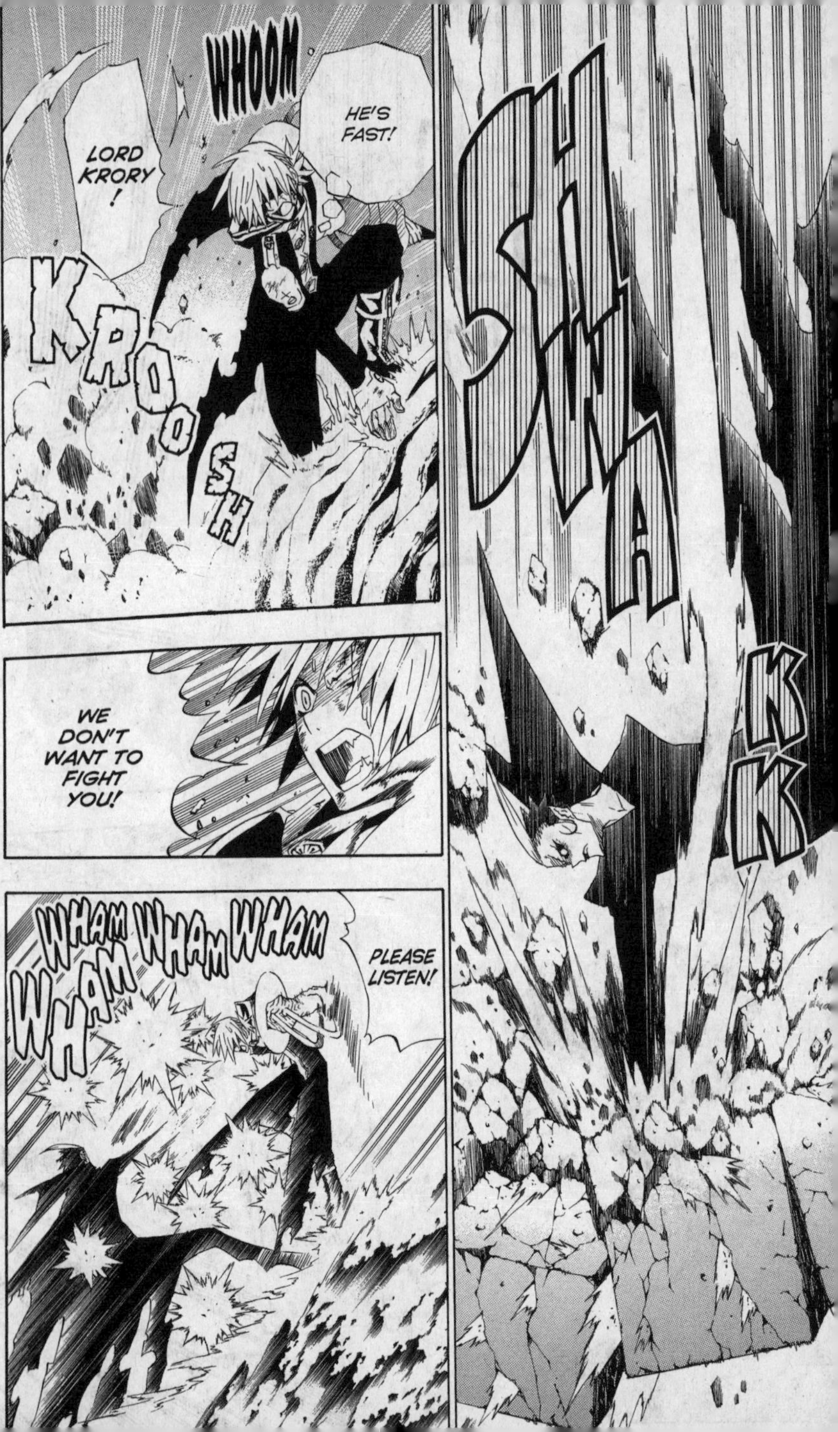
SHNA
KK
WHOOM
HE'S FAST!
LORD KRORY!
KROOSH
WE DON'T WANT TO FIGHT YOU!
PLEASE LISTEN!
WHAM WHAM WHAM WHAM

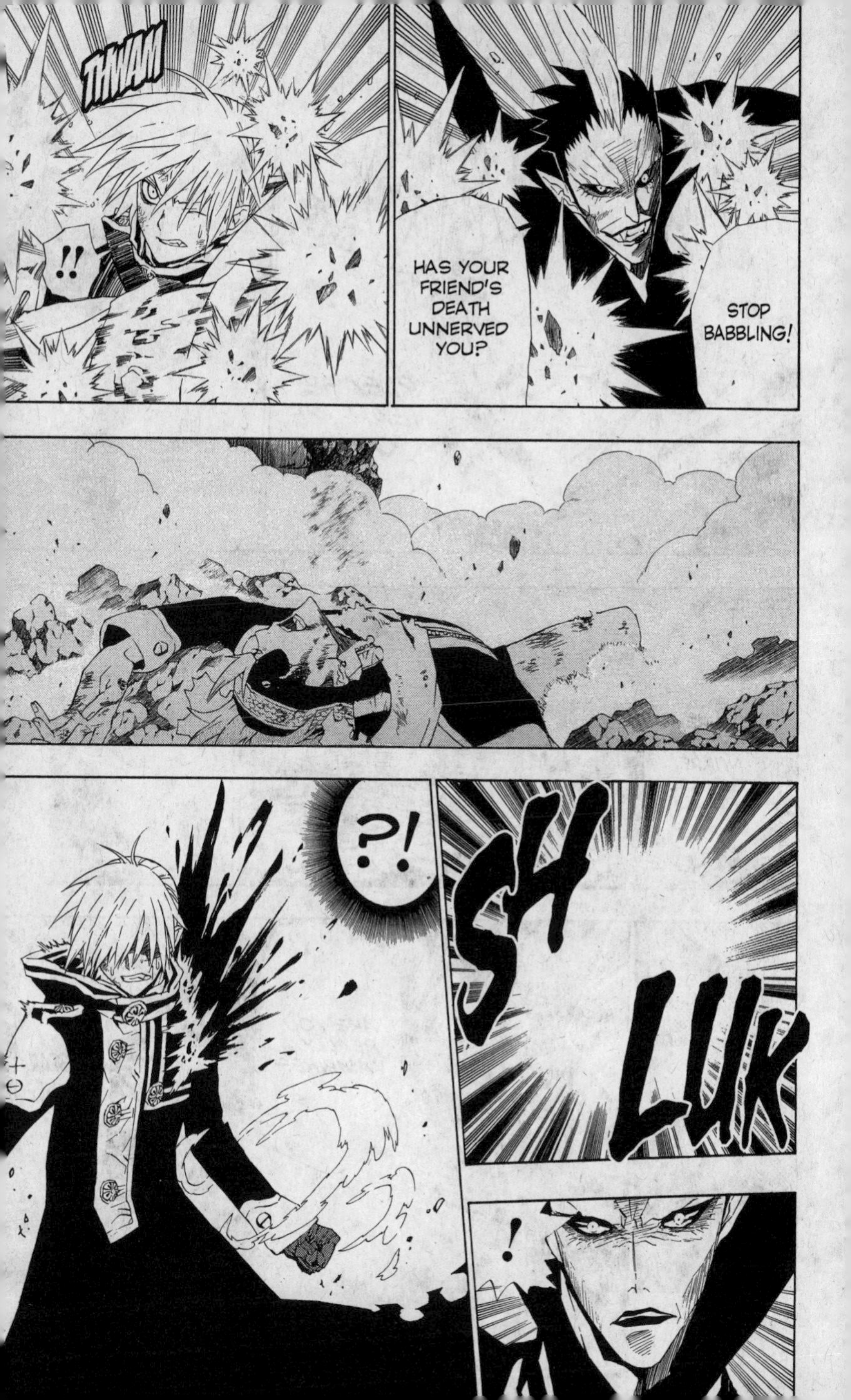
HAS YOUR FRIEND'S DEATH UNNERVED YOU?
STOP BABBLING!
THWAM
!!
SHLUK
!
?!

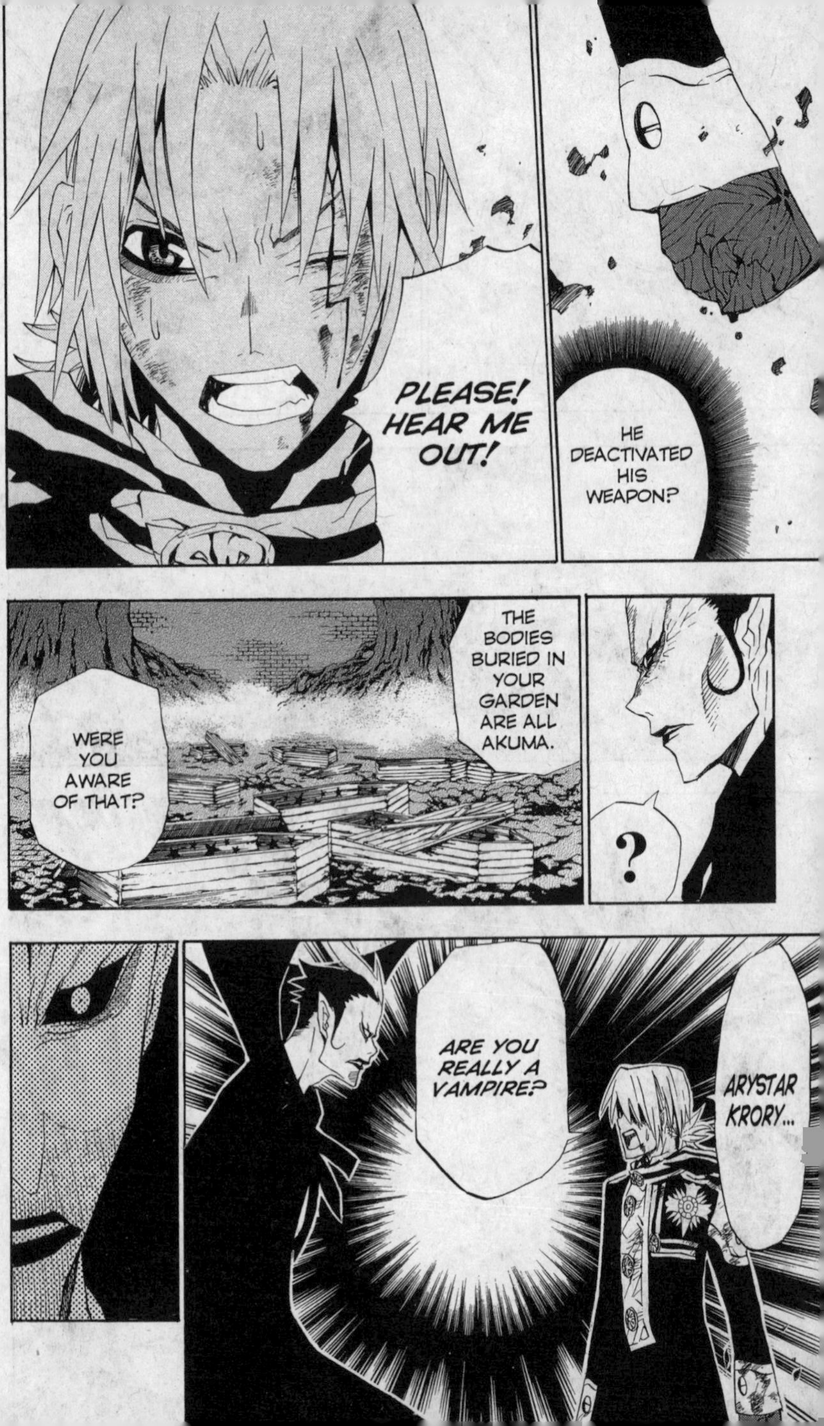
HE DEACTIVATED HIS WEAPON?
PLEASE! HEAR ME OUT!
?
THE BODIES BURIED IN YOUR GARDEN ARE ALL AKUMA.
WERE YOU AWARE OF THAT?
ARYSTAR KRORY...
ARE YOU REALLY A VAMPIRE?

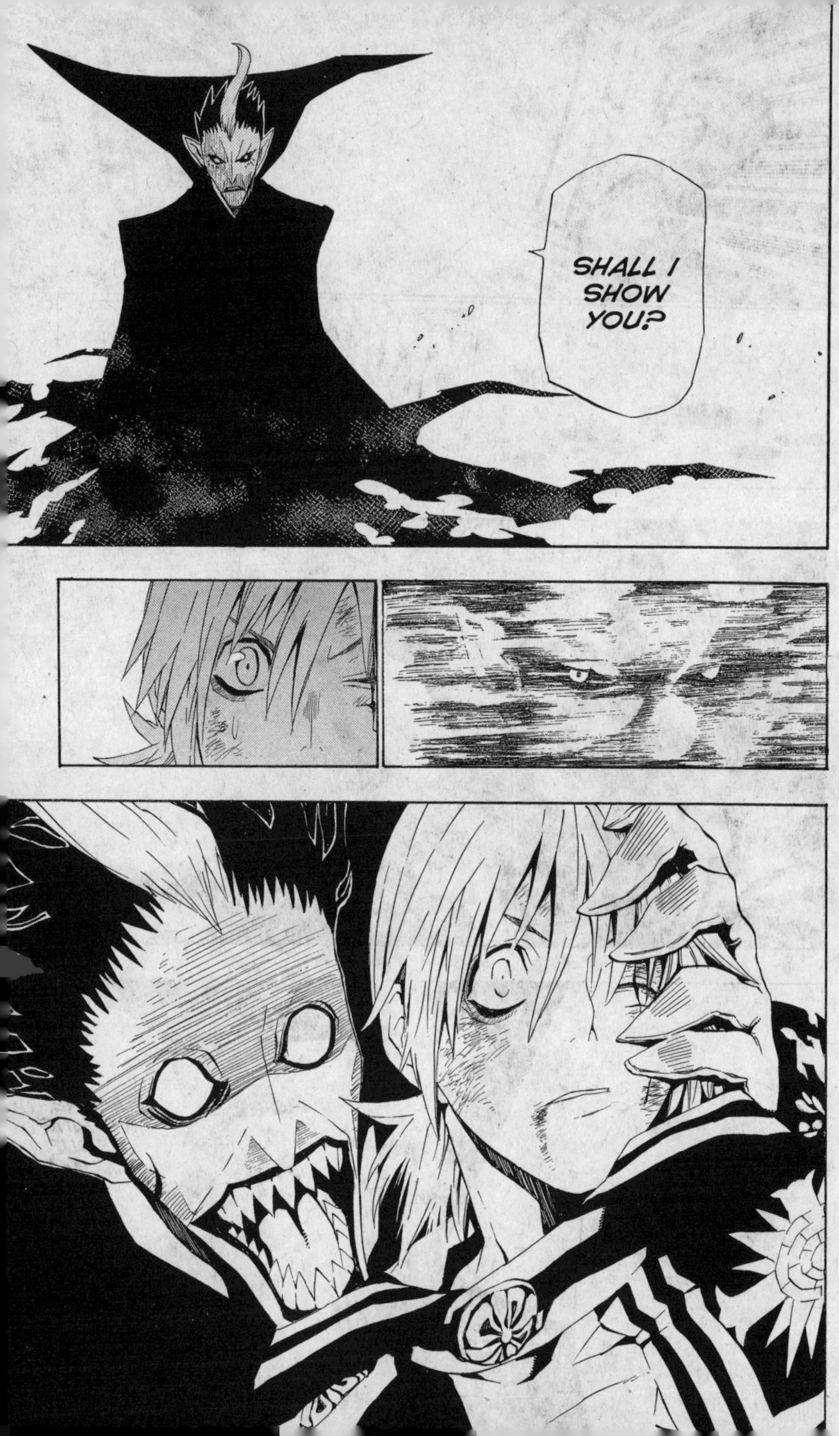
SHALL I SHOW YOU?

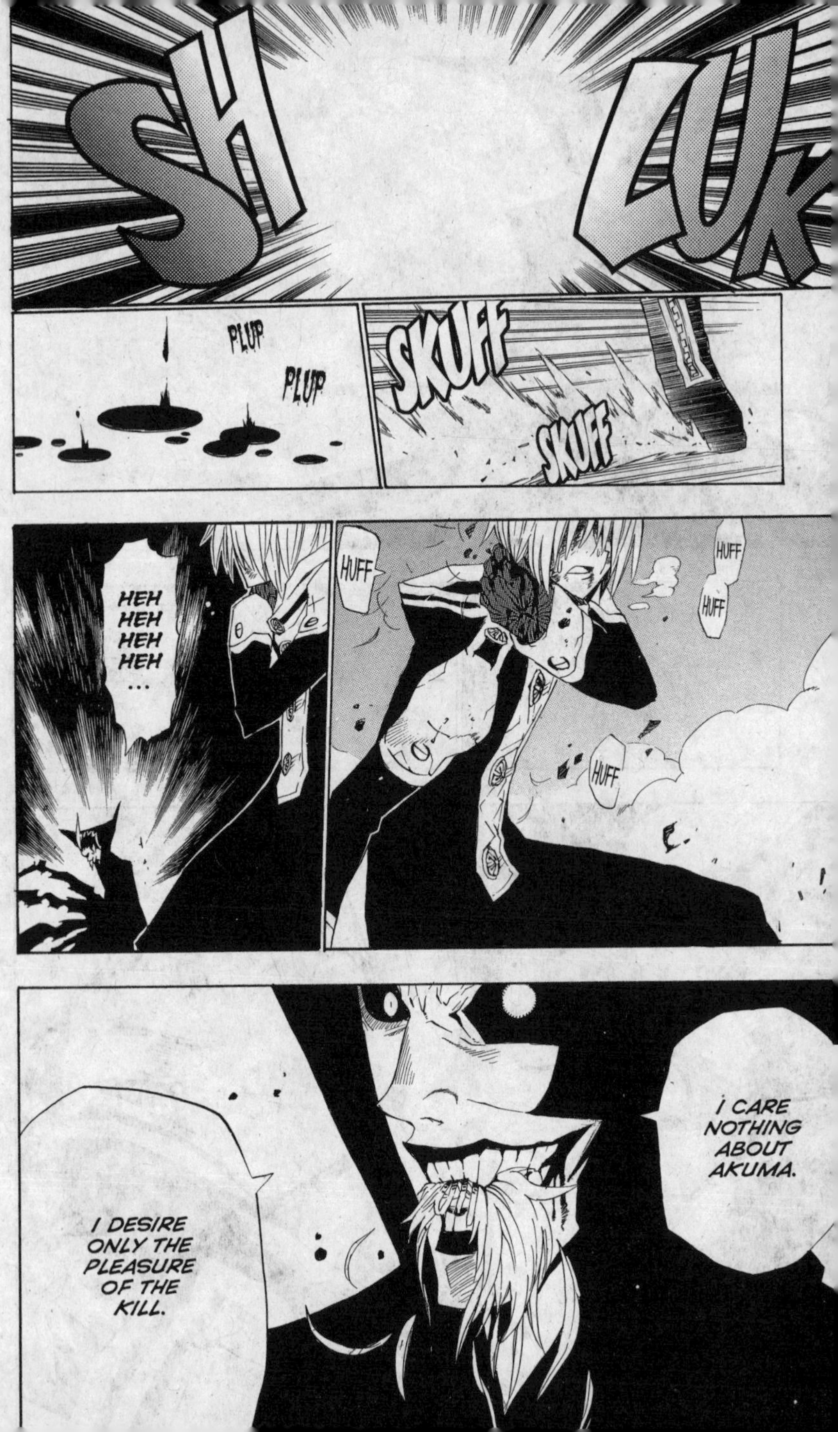
SHLUK
SKUFF
SKUFF
PLUP
PLUP
HUFF
HUFF
HUFF
HUFF
HEH HEH HEH HEH ...
I CARE NOTHING ABOUT AKUMA.
I DESIRE ONLY THE PLEASURE OF THE KILL.

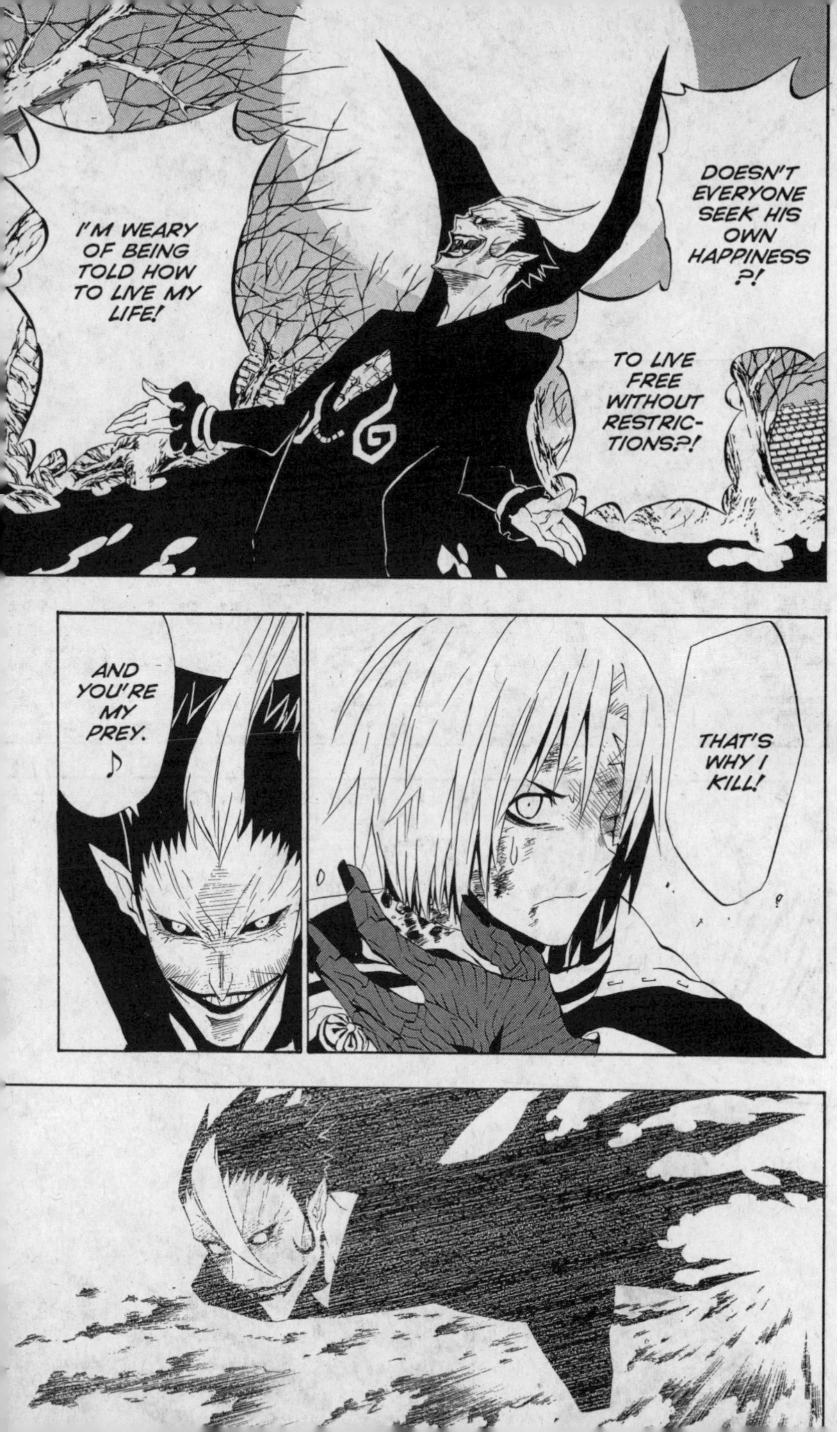
DOESN'T EVERYONE SEEK HIS OWN HAPPINESS?!
TO LIVE FREE WITHOUT RESTRICTIONS?!
I'M WEARY OF BEING TOLD HOW TO LIVE MY LIFE!
THAT'S WHY I KILL!
AND YOU'RE MY PREY. ♪

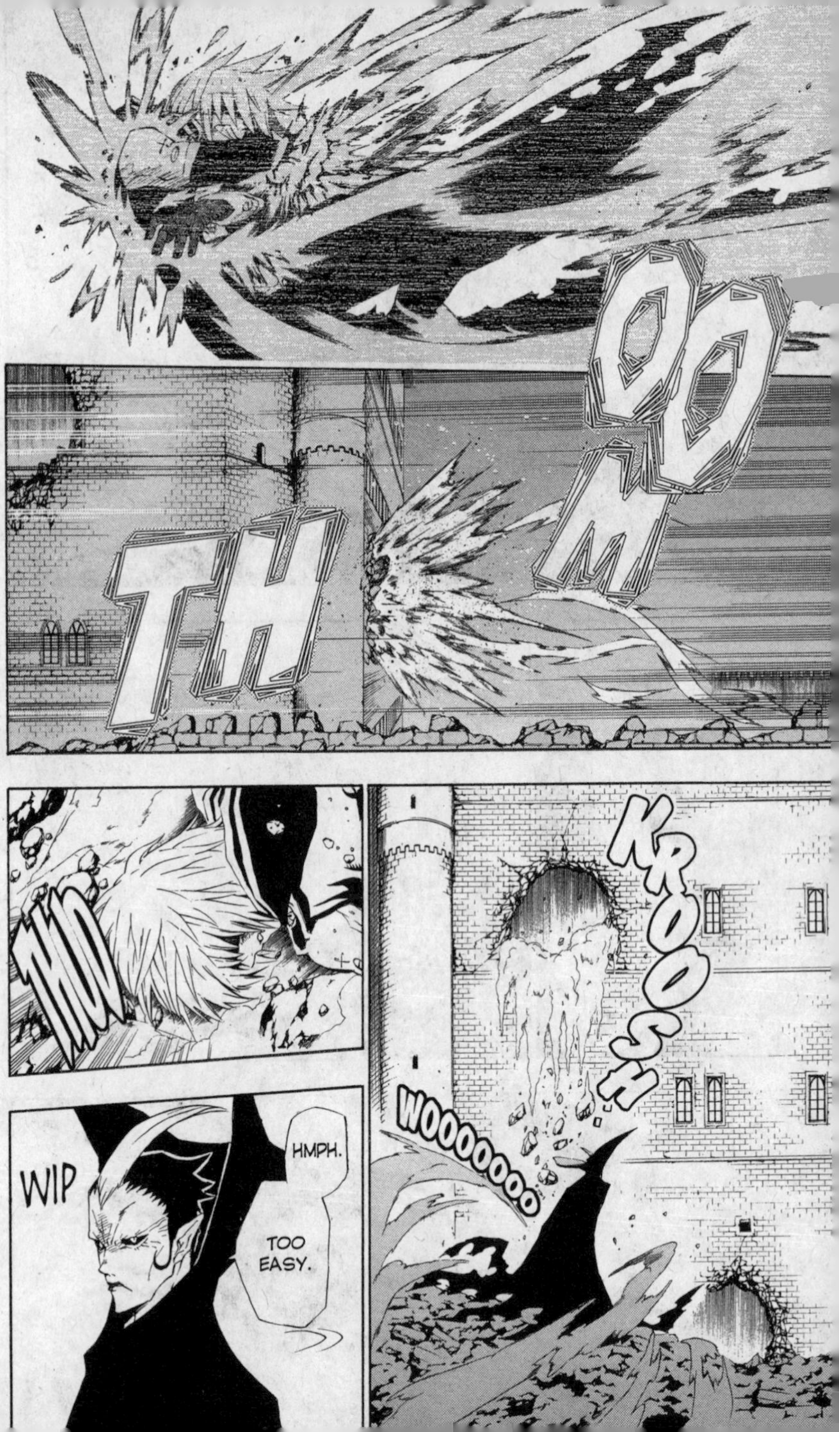
THOOM
KROOSH
WOOOOOOOO
THO
HMPH.
TOO EASY.
WIP

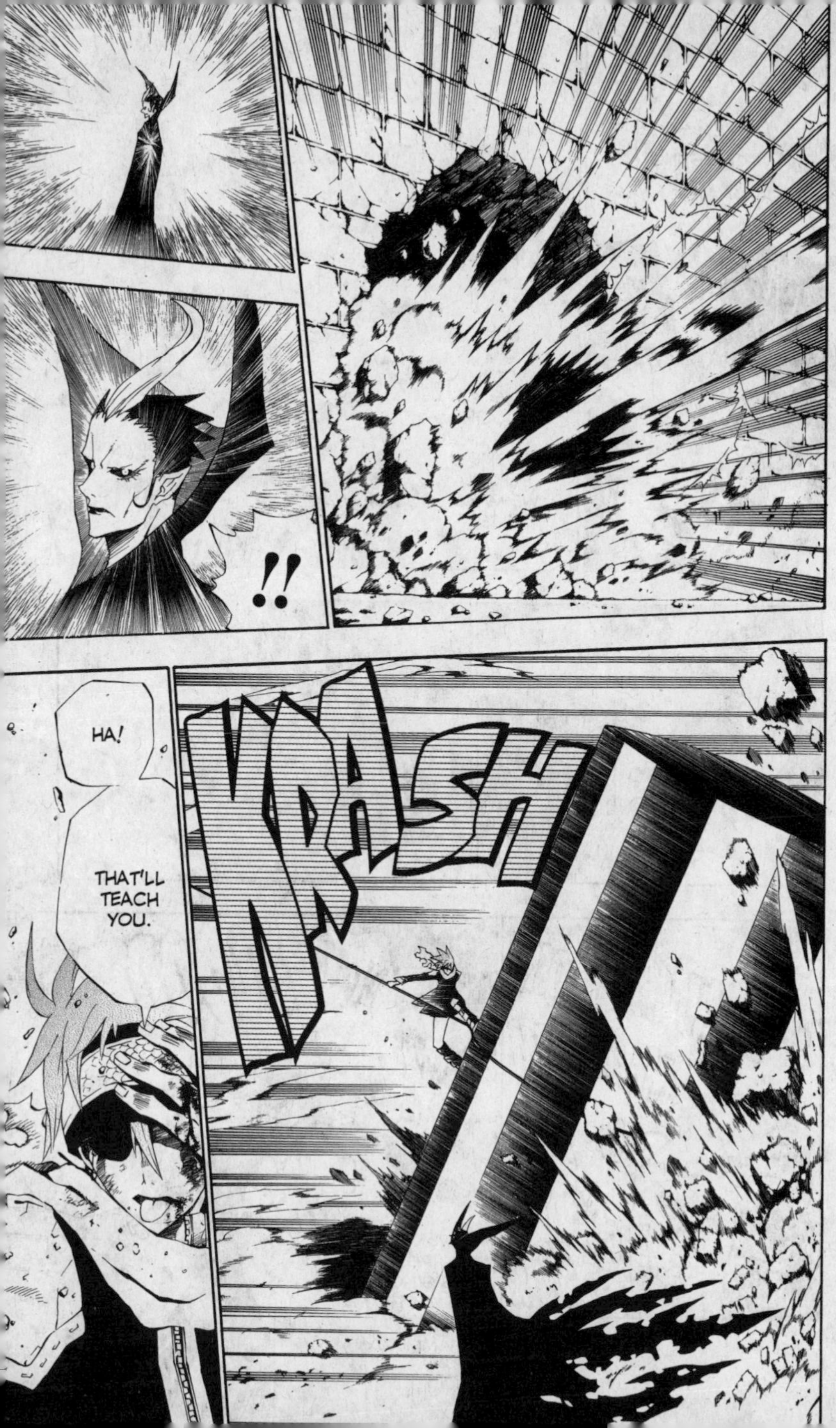
!!
KRASH
HA!
THAT'LL TEACH YOU.

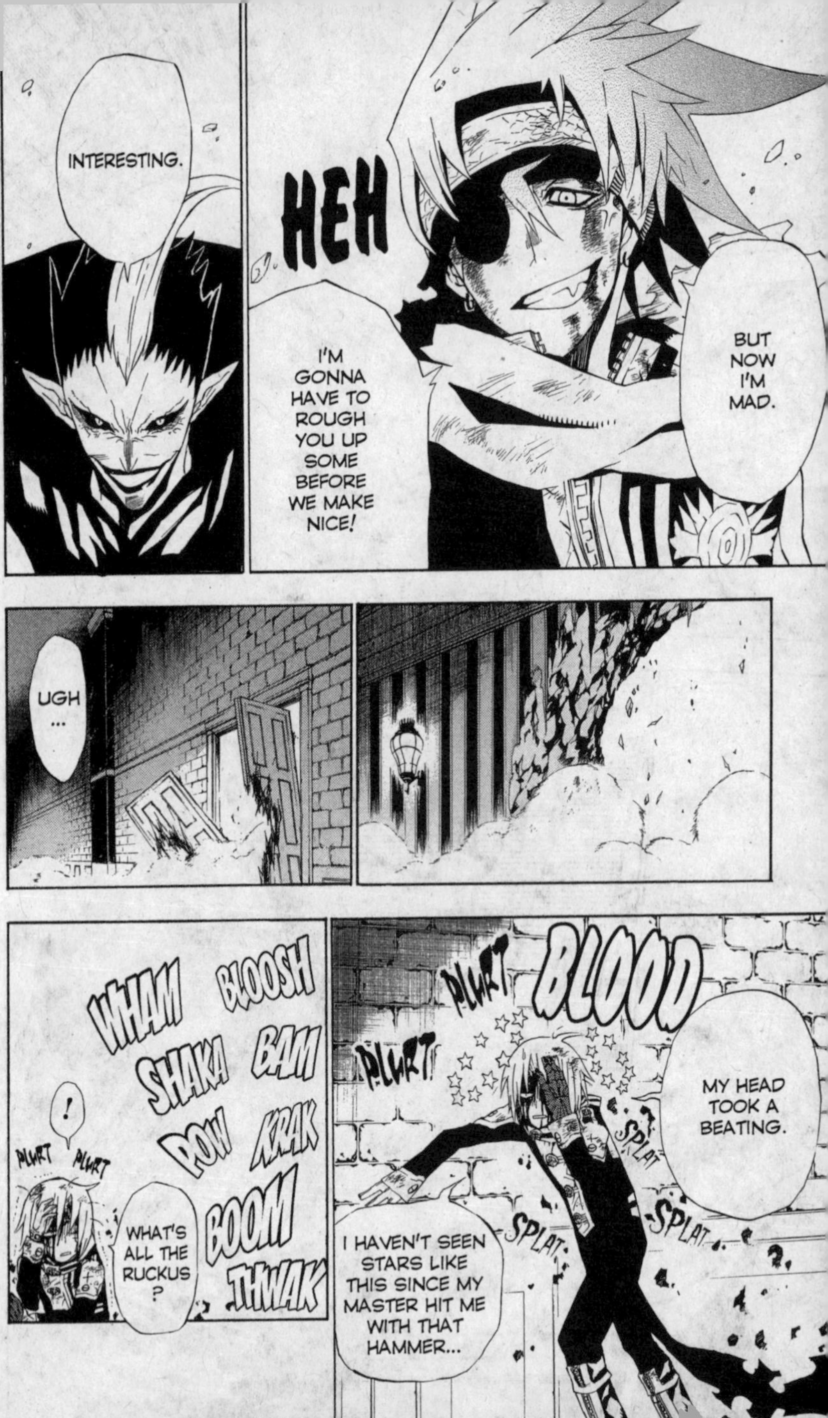
HEH
BUT NOW I'M MAD.
I'M GONNA HAVE TO ROUGH YOU UP SOME BEFORE WE MAKE NICE!
INTERESTING.
UGH...
BLOOD
PLURT
PLURT
MY HEAD TOOK A BEATING.
SPLAT
SPLAT
SPLAT
I HAVEN'T SEEN STARS LIKE THIS SINCE MY MASTER HIT ME WITH THAT HAMMER...
BLOOSH
WHAM
BAM
SHAKA
KRAK
POW
BOOM
THWAK
!
PLURT
PLURT
WHAT'S ALL THE RUCKUS?

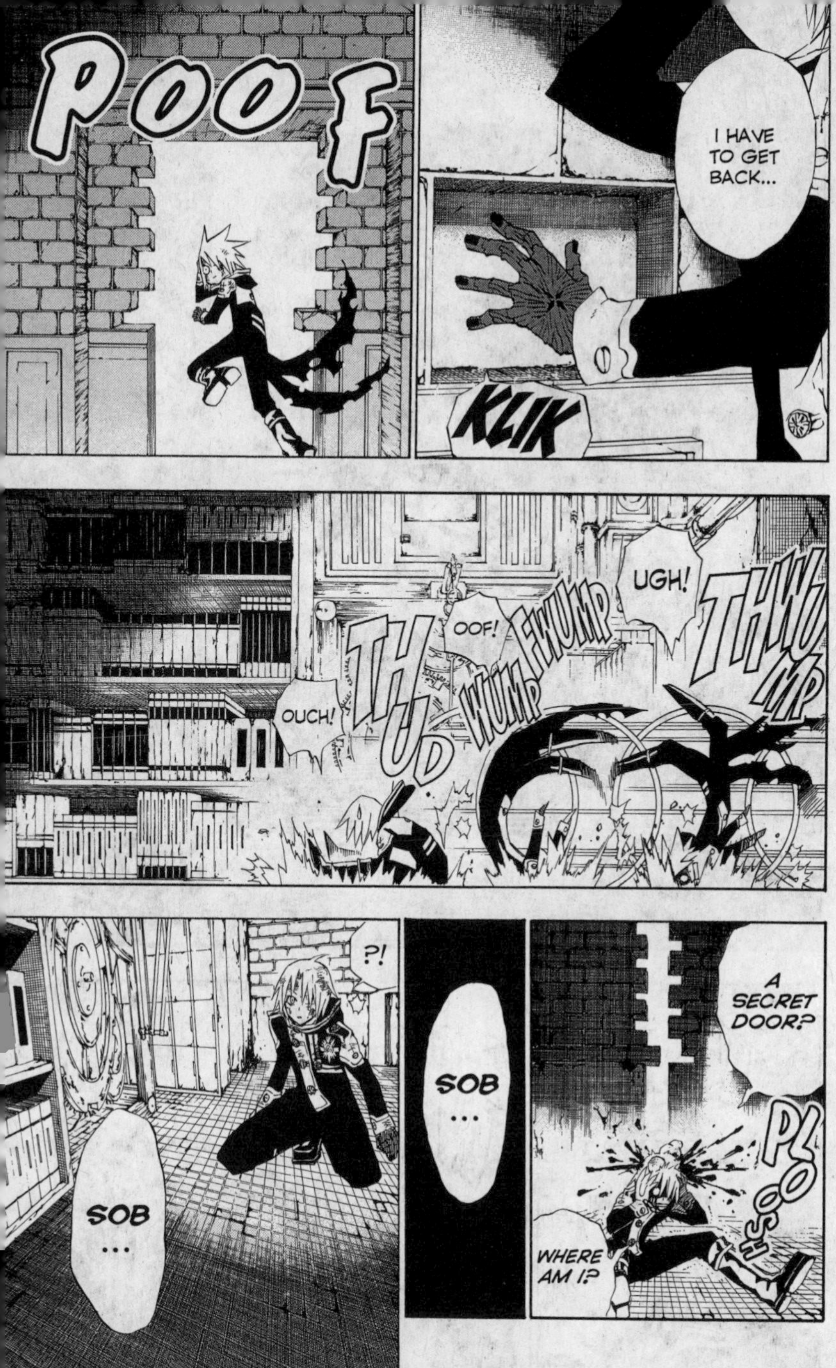
I HAVE TO GET BACK...
KLIK
POOF
THWUMP
UGH!
FWUMP
WUMP
OOF!
THUD
OUCH!
A SECRET DOOR?
PLOOSH
WHERE AM I?
SOB...
?!
SOB...

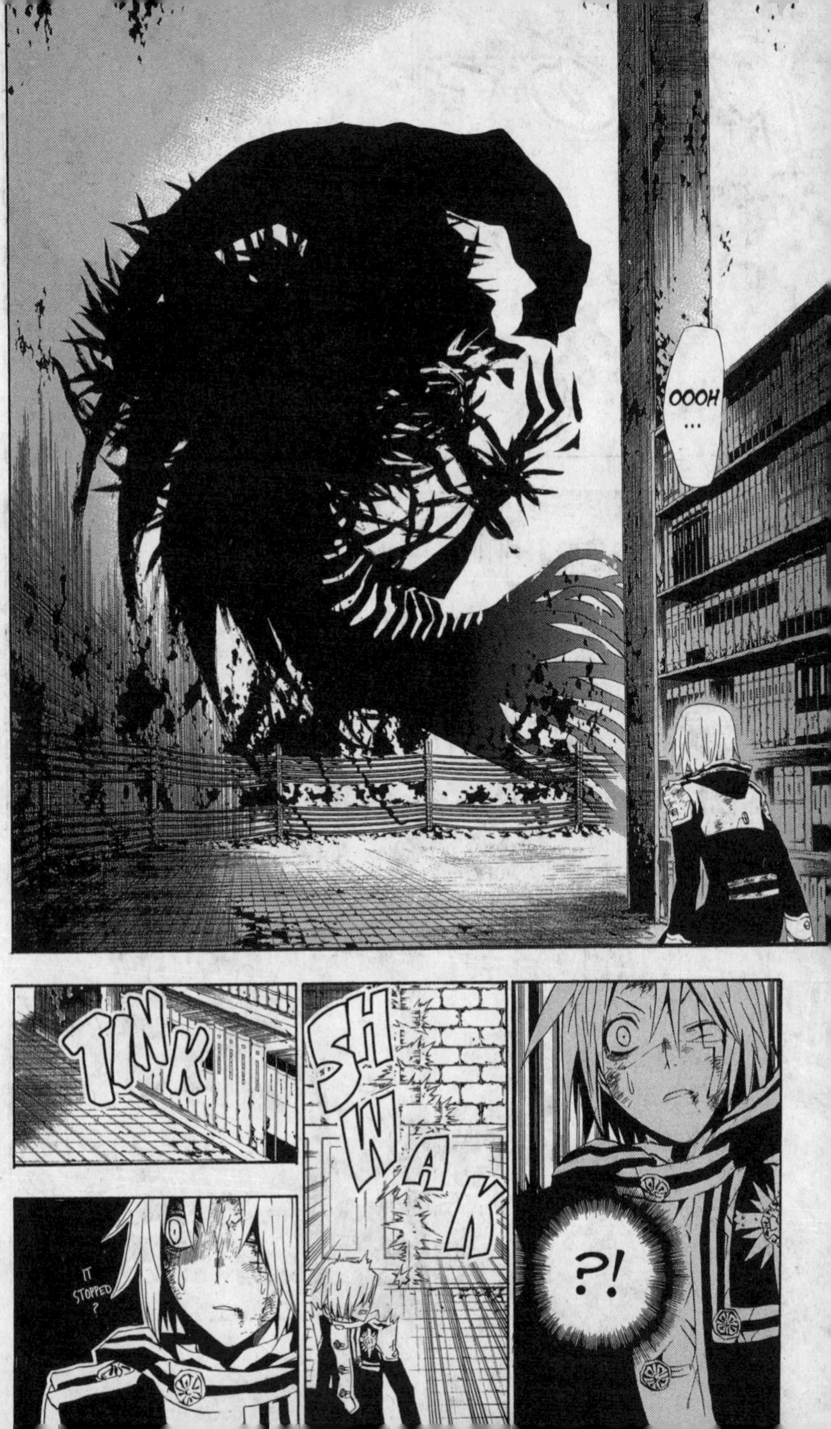
OOOH ...
?!
SHWAK
TINK
IT STOPPED ?

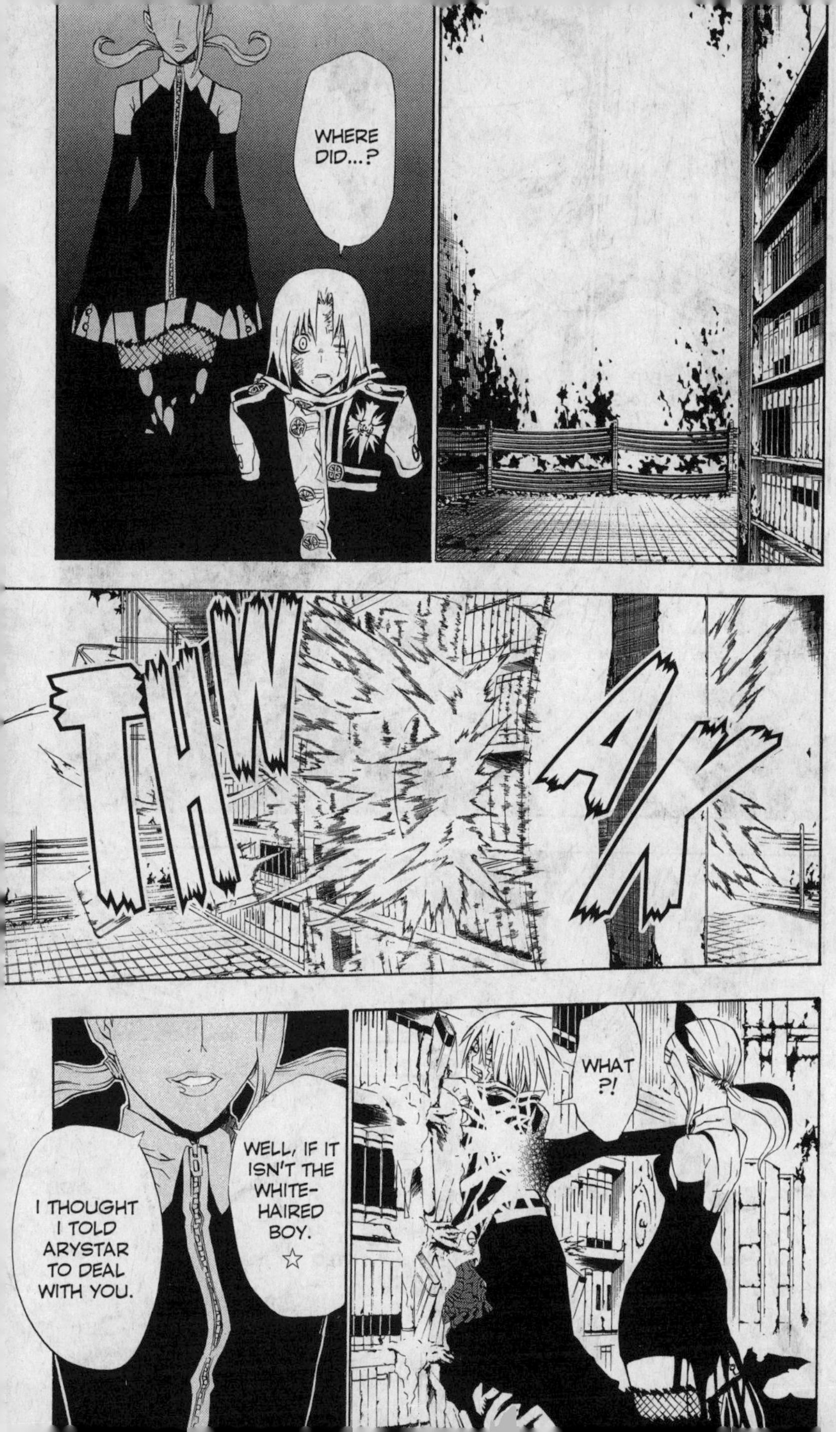
WHERE DID...?
THWAK
WHAT?!
WELL, IF IT ISN'T THE WHITE-HAIRED BOY. ☆
I THOUGHT I TOLD ARYSTAR TO DEAL WITH YOU.

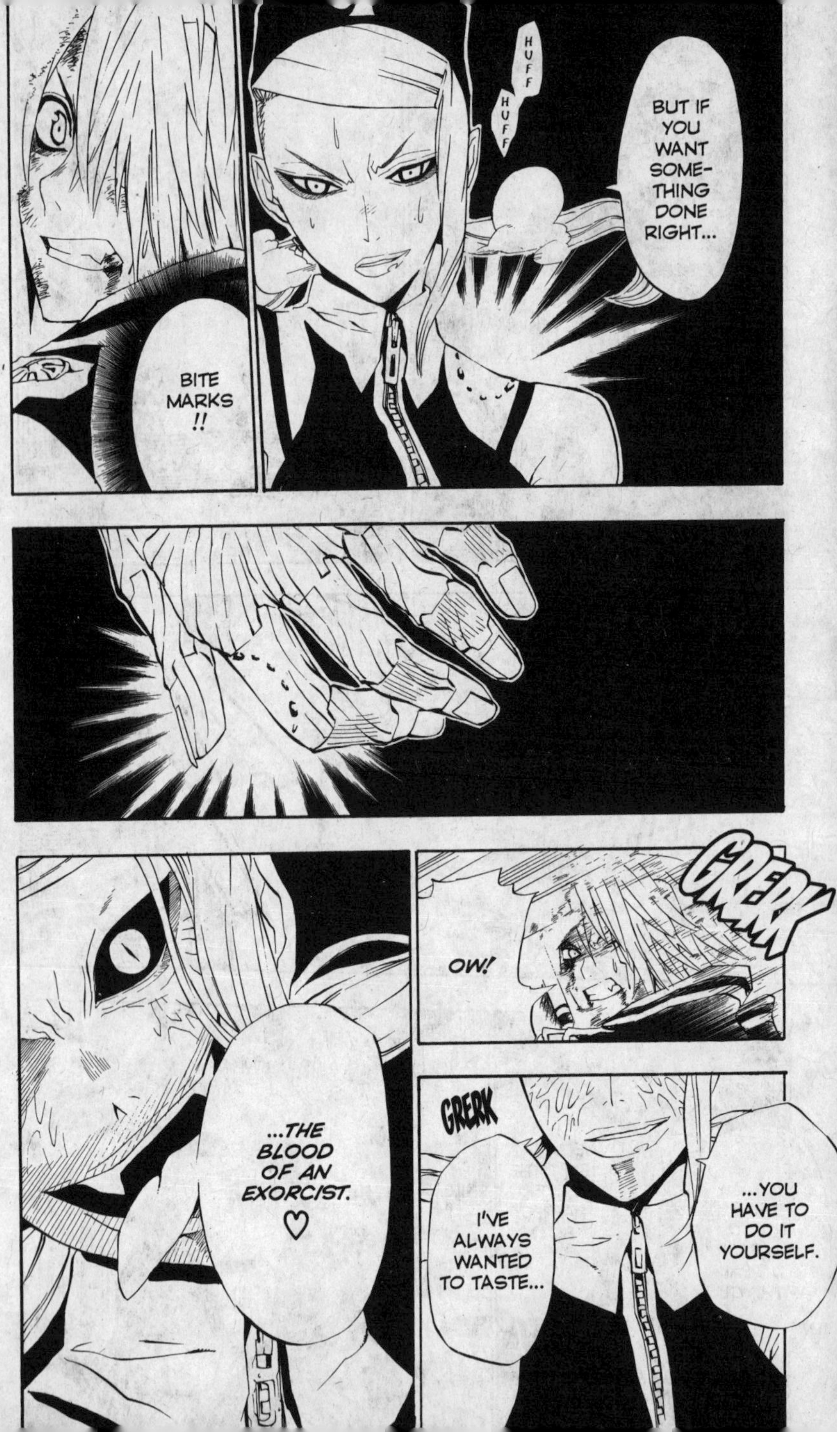
HUFF HUFF
BUT IF YOU WANT SOME-THING DONE RIGHT...
BITE MARKS !!
GRERK
OW!
GRERK
...YOU HAVE TO DO IT YOURSELF.
I'VE ALWAYS WANTED TO TASTE...
...THE BLOOD OF AN EXORCIST. ♡

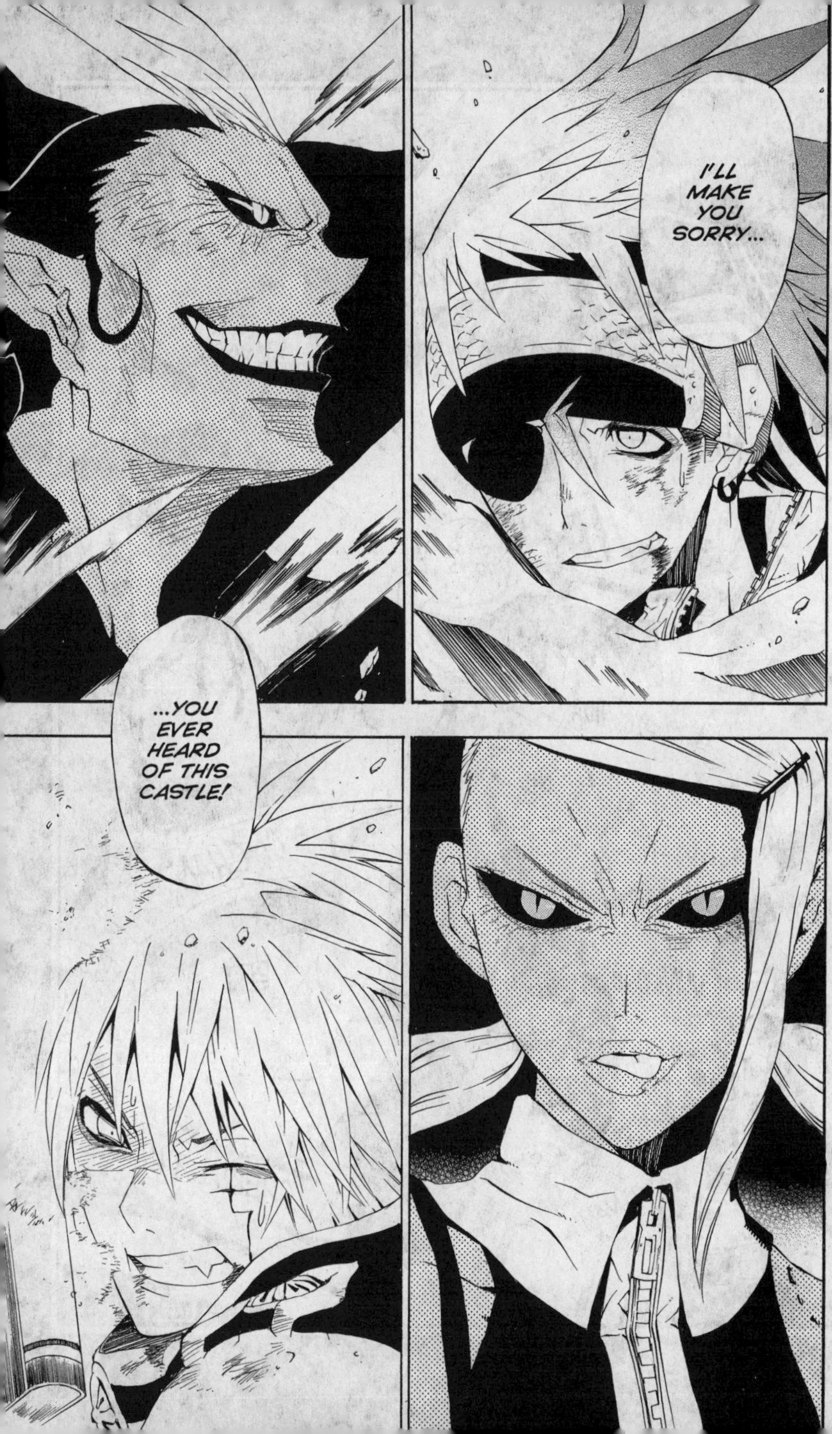
I'LL MAKE YOU SORRY...
...YOU EVER HEARD OF THIS CASTLE!

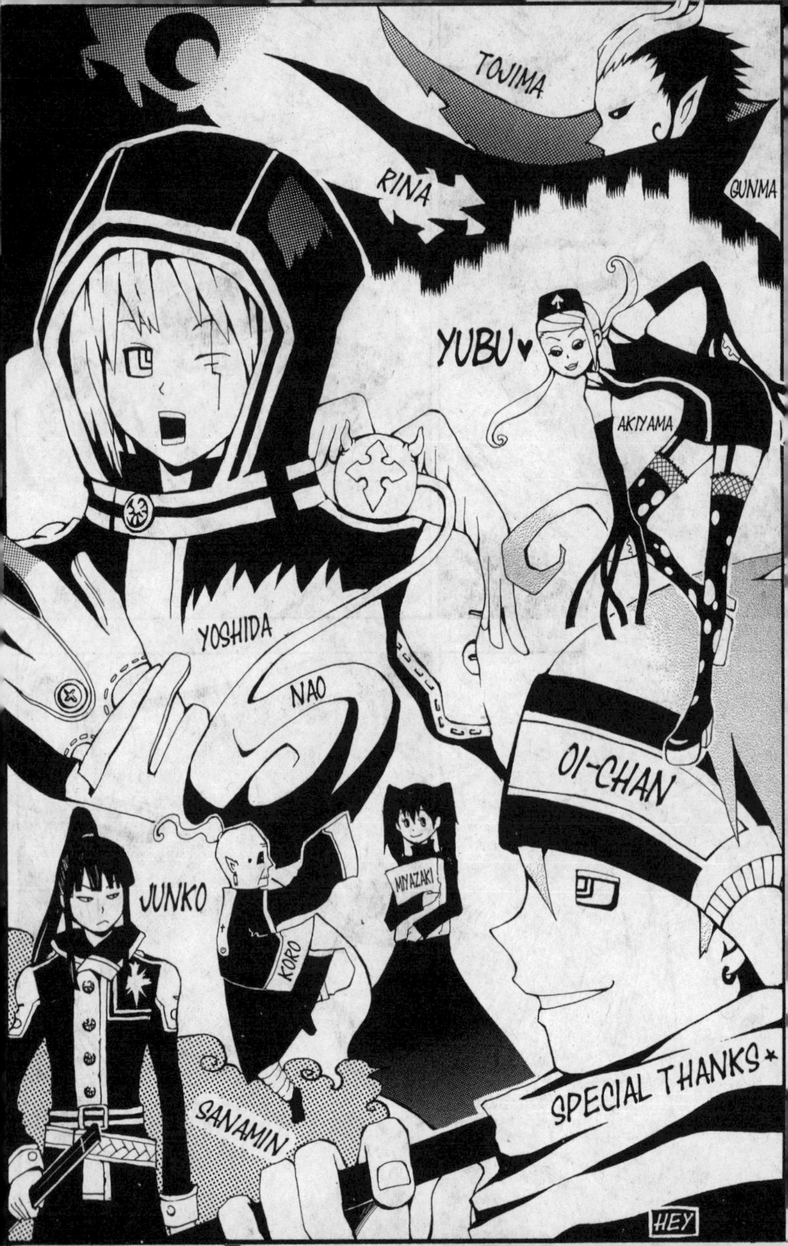
TOJIMA
GUNMA
RINA
YUBU♥
AKIYAMA
YOSHIDA
NAO
OI-CHAN
MIYAZAKI
JUNKO
KORO
SPECIAL THANKS*
SANAMIN
HEY

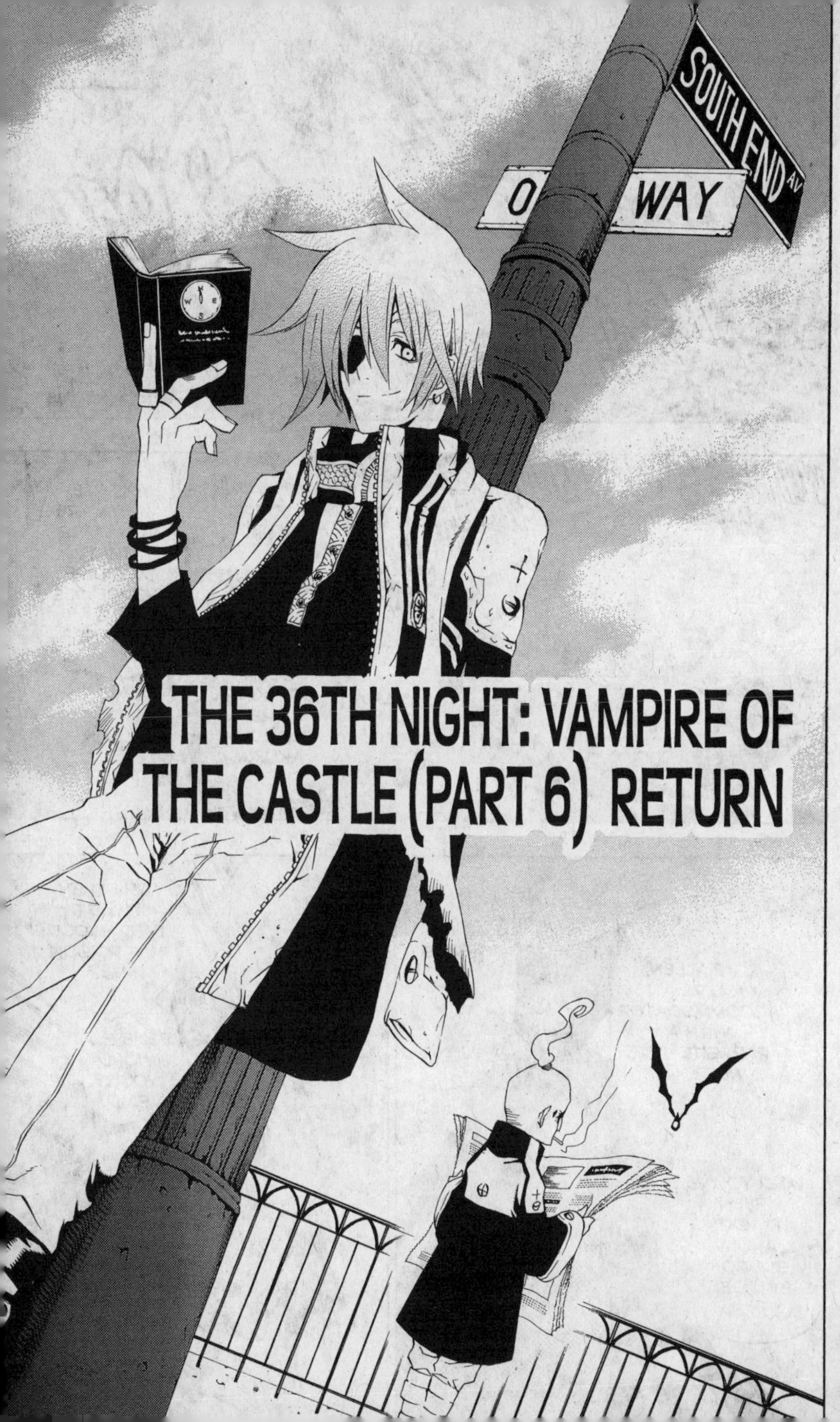
SOUTH END AV
O WAY
THE 36TH NIGHT: VAMPIRE OF THE CASTLE (PART 6) RETURN

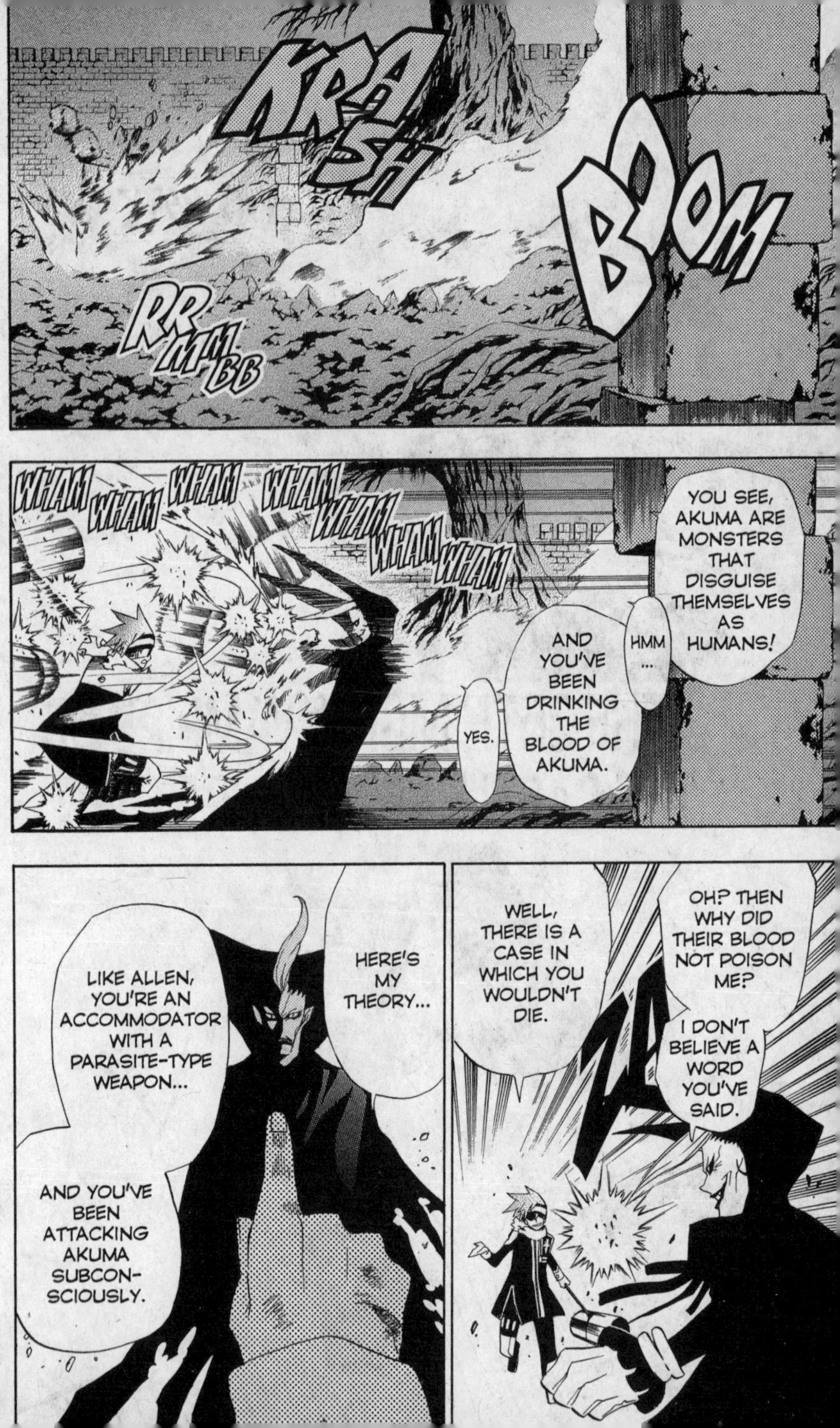
BOOM
KRASH
RRMMBB
YOU SEE, AKUMA ARE MONSTERS THAT DISGUISE THEMSELVES AS HUMANS!
HMM...
AND YOU'VE BEEN DRINKING THE BLOOD OF AKUMA.
YES.
WHAM WHAM WHAM WHAM WHAM WHAM WHAM
OH? THEN WHY DID THEIR BLOOD NOT POISON ME?
WELL, THERE IS A CASE IN WHICH YOU WOULDN'T DIE.
I DON'T BELIEVE A WORD YOU'VE SAID.
HERE'S MY THEORY...
LIKE ALLEN, YOU'RE AN ACCOMMODATOR WITH A PARASITE-TYPE WEAPON...
AND YOU'VE BEEN ATTACKING AKUMA SUBCONSCIOUSLY.

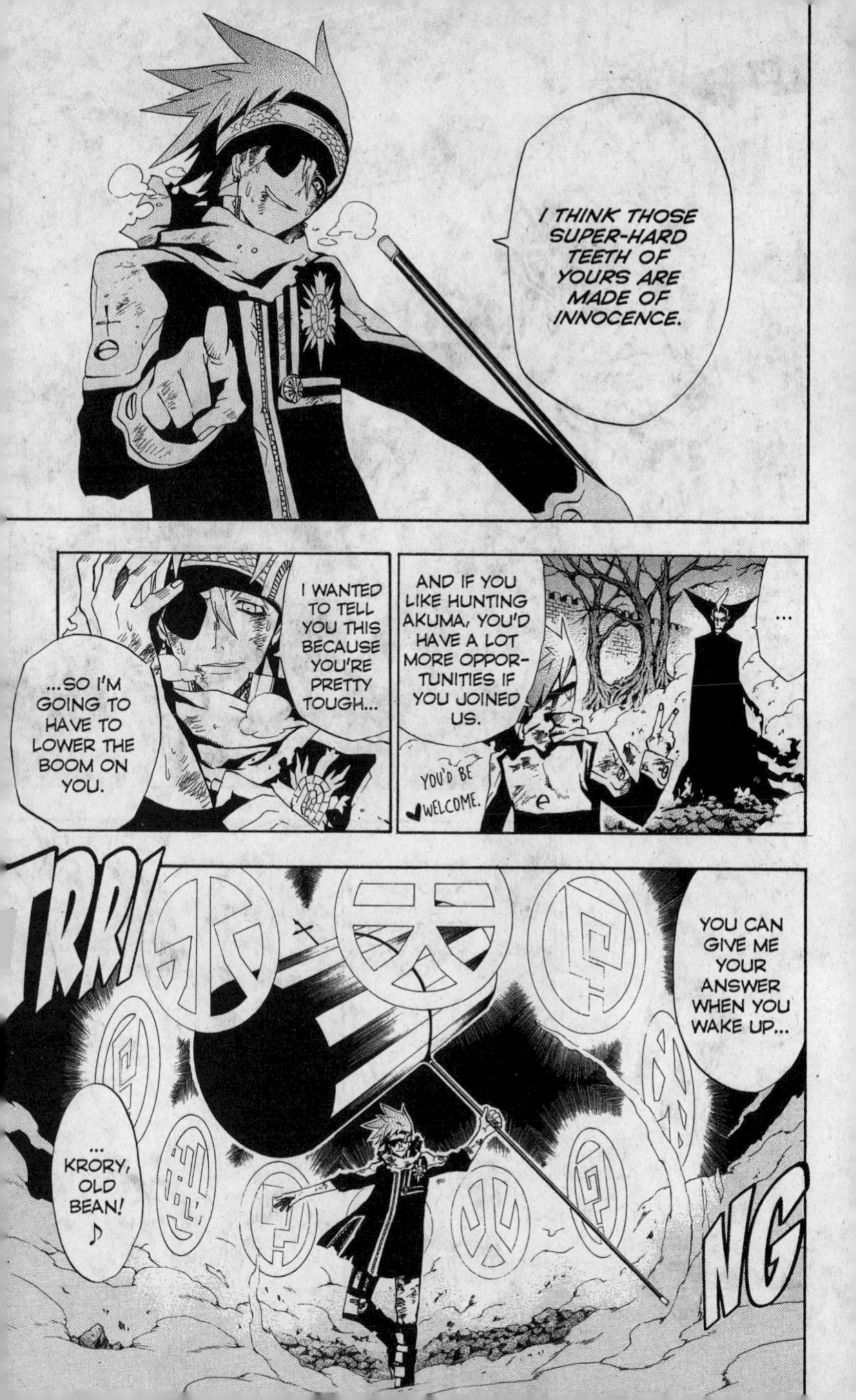
I THINK THOSE SUPER-HARD TEETH OF YOURS ARE MADE OF INNOCENCE.
AND IF YOU LIKE HUNTING AKUMA, YOU'D HAVE A LOT MORE OPPOR-TUNITIES IF YOU JOINED US.
YOU'D BE WELCOME.
...
I WANTED TO TELL YOU THIS BECAUSE YOU'RE PRETTY TOUGH...
...SO I'M GOING TO HAVE TO LOWER THE BOOM ON YOU.
YOU CAN GIVE ME YOUR ANSWER WHEN YOU WAKE UP...
TRRI
NG
... KRORY, OLD BEAN! ♪

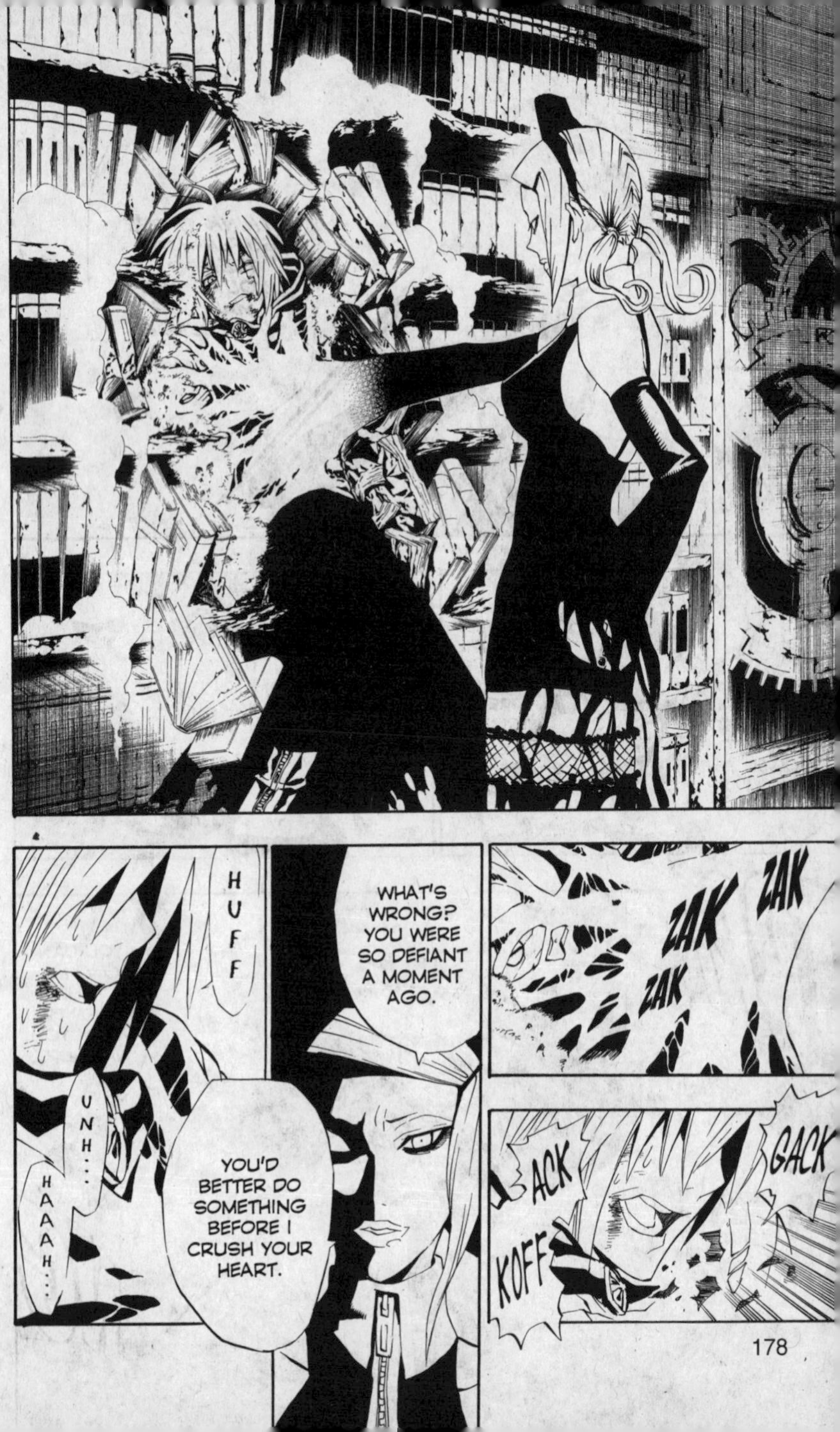
ZAK
ZAK
ZAK
ZAK
GACK
ACK
KOFF
WHAT'S WRONG? YOU WERE SO DEFIANT A MOMENT AGO.
YOU'D BETTER DO SOMETHING BEFORE I CRUSH YOUR HEART.
HUFF
UNH...
HAAAH...

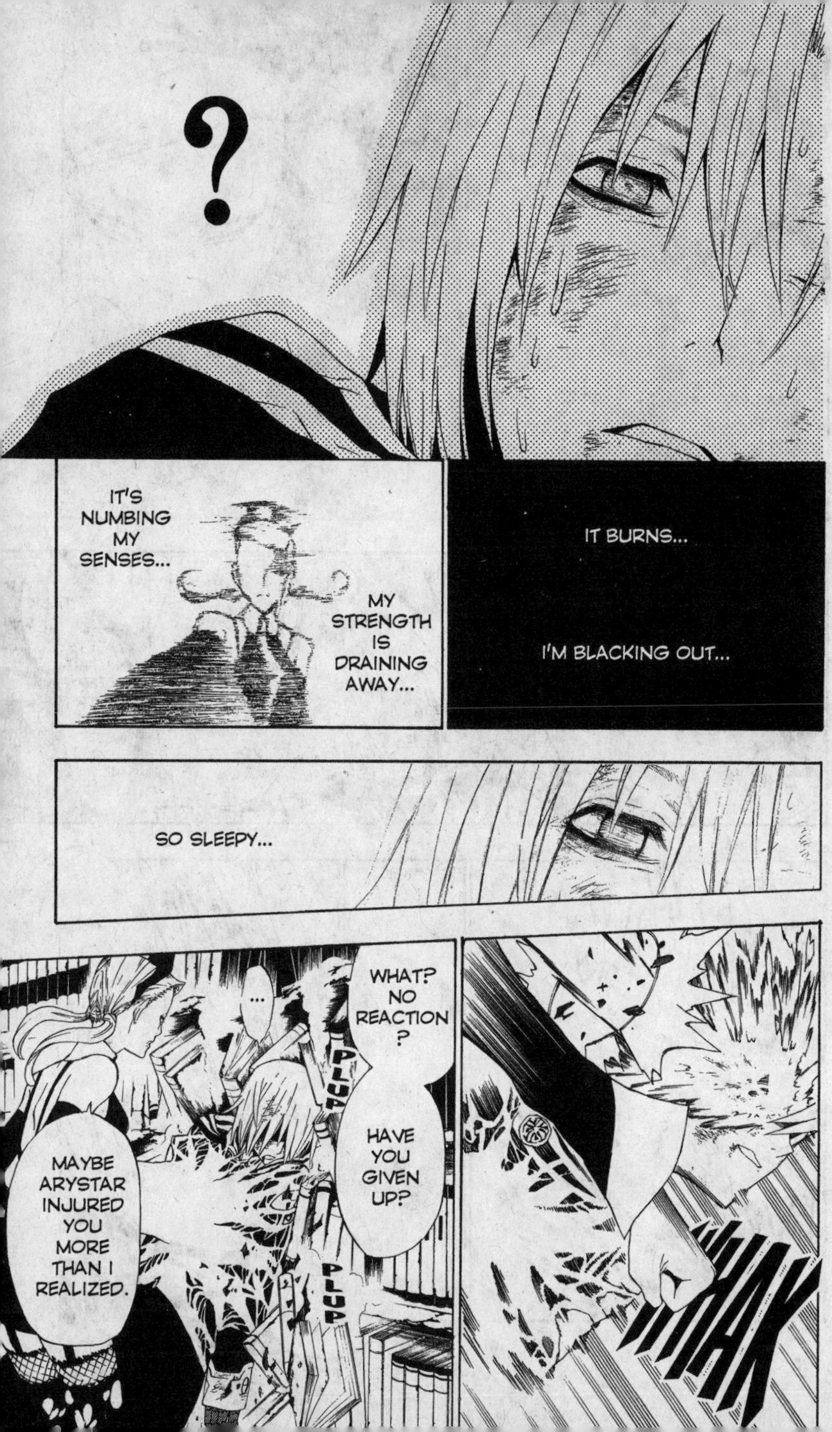
?
IT BURNS...
I'M BLACKING OUT...
IT'S NUMBING MY SENSES...
MY STRENGTH IS DRAINING AWAY...
SO SLEEPY...
WHAT? NO REACTION?
...
PLUP
HAVE YOU GIVEN UP?
MAYBE ARYSTAR INJURED YOU MORE THAN I REALIZED.
PLUP

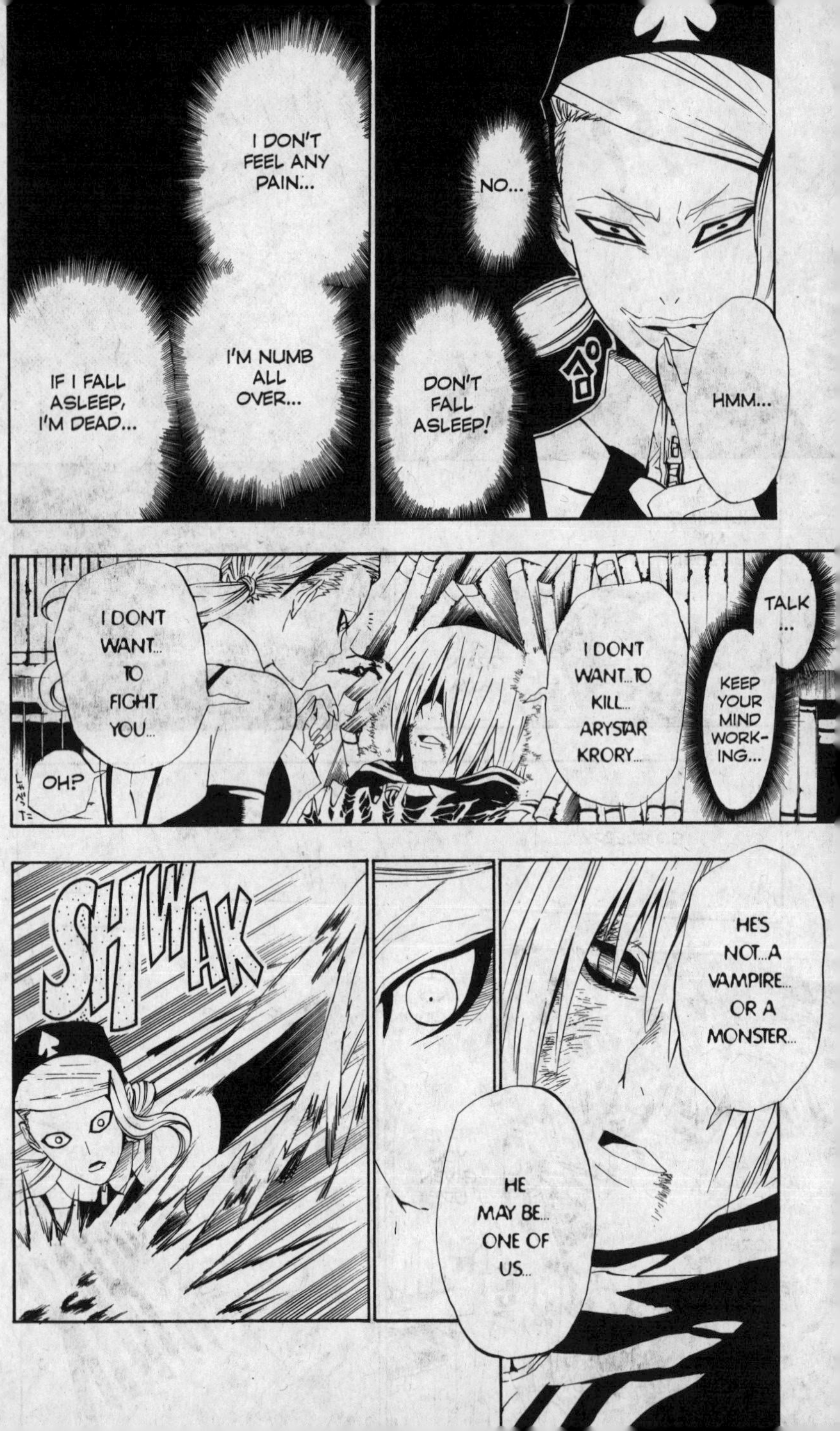
HMM...
NO...
DON'T FALL ASLEEP!
I DON'T FEEL ANY PAIN...
I'M NUMB ALL OVER...
IF I FALL ASLEEP, I'M DEAD...
TALK...
KEEP YOUR MIND WORKING...
I DONT WANT...TO KILL... ARYSTAR KRORY...
I DONT WANT... TO FIGHT YOU...
OH?
HE'S NOT...A VAMPIRE... OR A MONSTER...
HE MAY BE... ONE OF US...
SHWAK

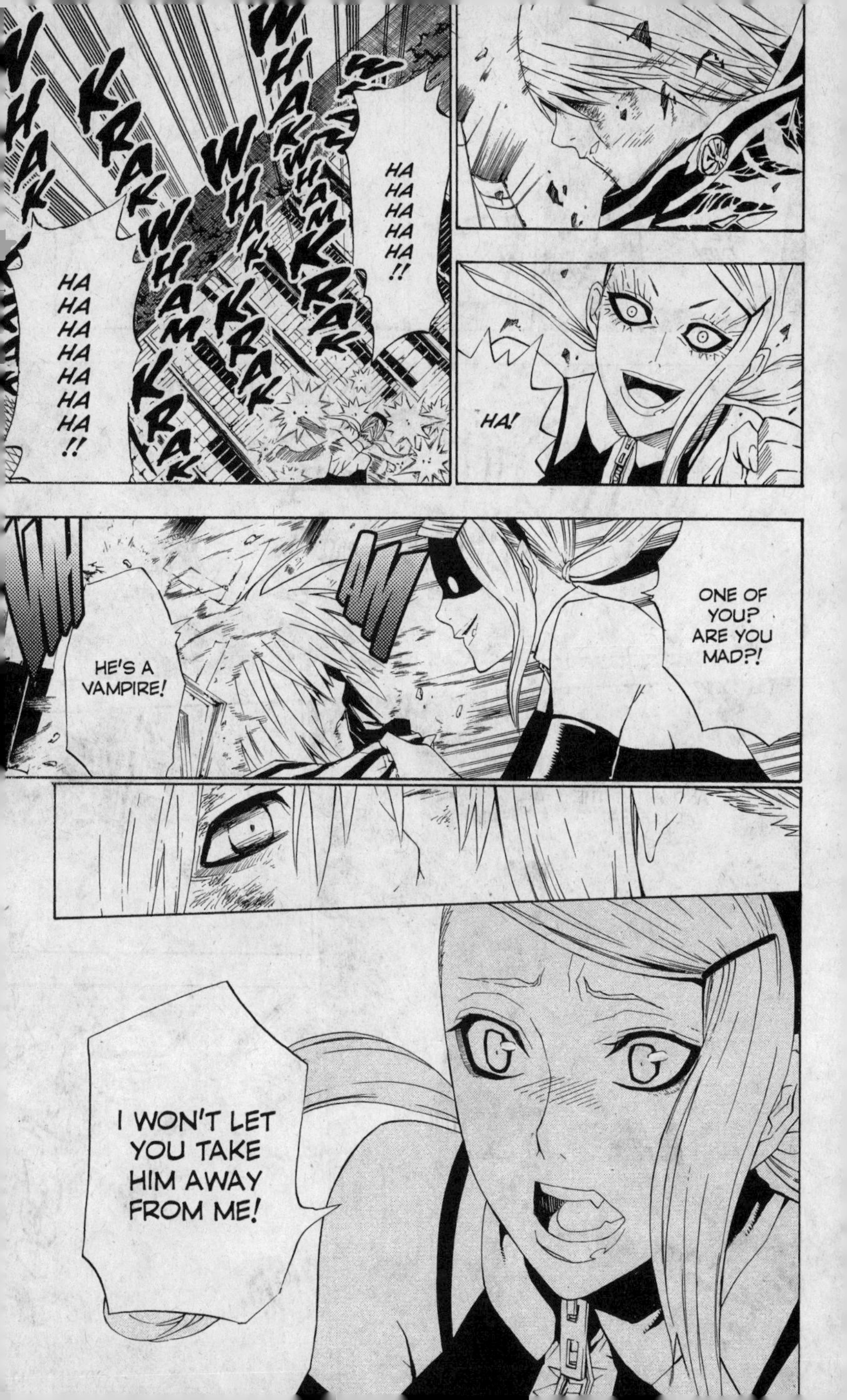
HA!
HA HA HA HA HA!!
WHAM KRAK
WHAK WHAM KRAK
WHAK KRAK
HA HA HA HA HA HA HA!!
ONE OF YOU? ARE YOU MAD?!
HE'S A VAMPIRE!
I WON'T LET YOU TAKE HIM AWAY FROM ME!

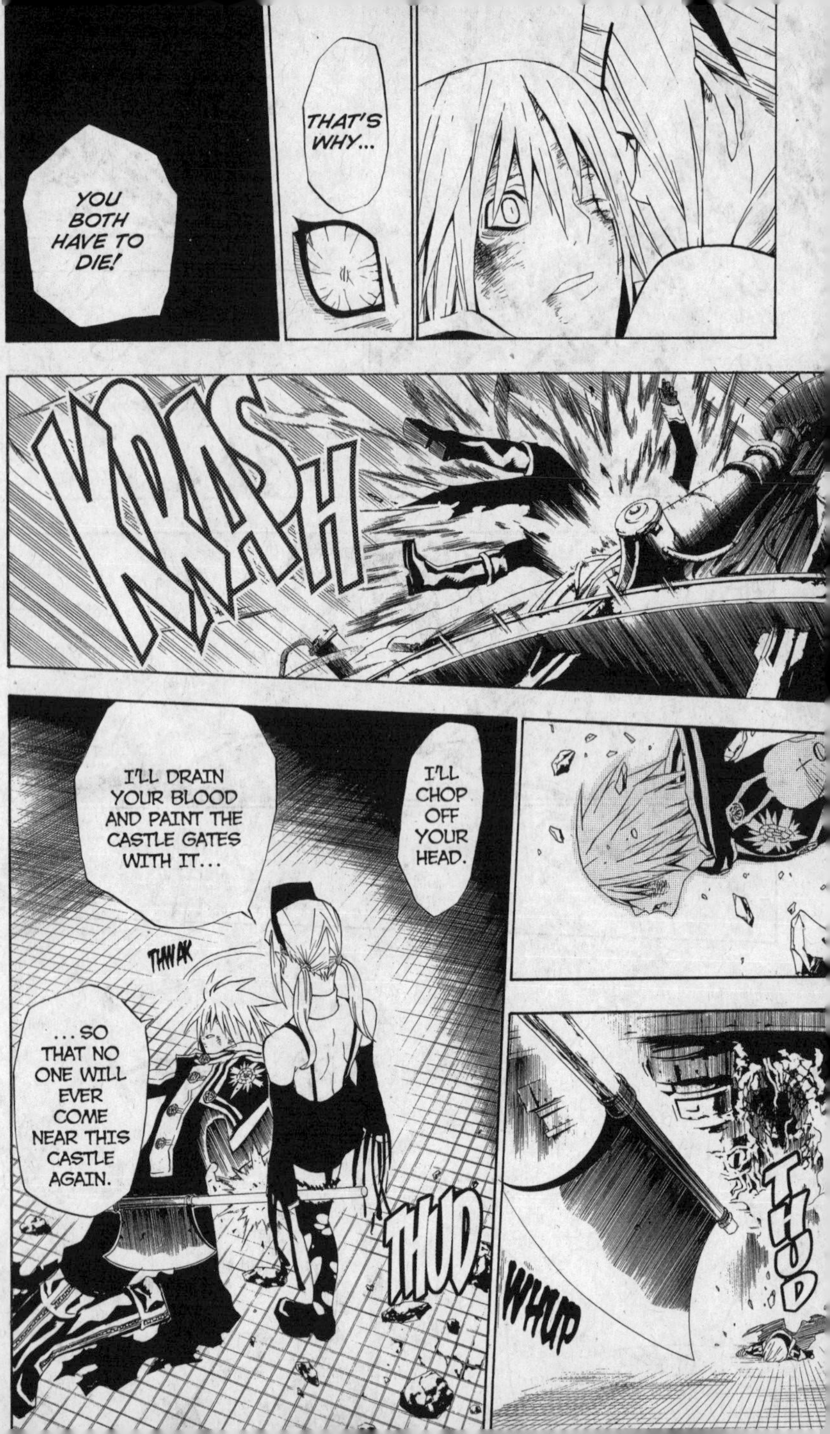
THAT'S WHY...
YOU BOTH HAVE TO DIE!
KRASH
THUD
WHUP
I'LL CHOP OFF YOUR HEAD.
I'LL DRAIN YOUR BLOOD AND PAINT THE CASTLE GATES WITH IT...
THWAK
...SO THAT NO ONE WILL EVER COME NEAR THIS CASTLE AGAIN.
THUD

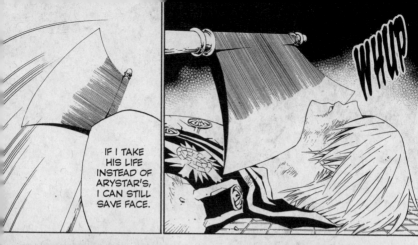

IF I TAKE HIS LIFE INSTEAD OF ARYSTAR'S, I CAN STILL SAVE FACE.

WHUP

WHAK

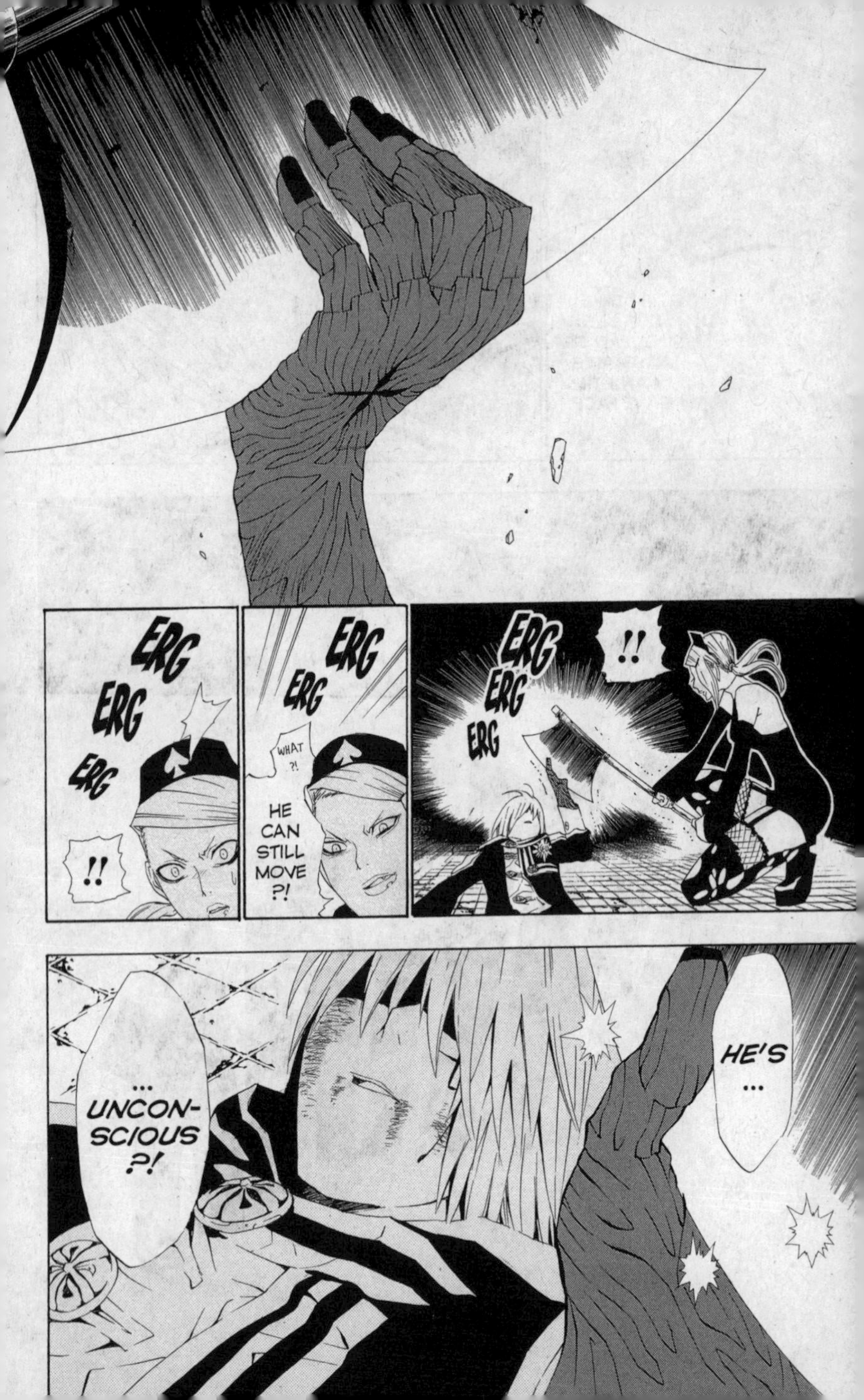
!!
ERG ERG ERG
ERG ERG
WHAT ?!
HE CAN STILL MOVE ?!
ERG ERG ERG
!!
HE'S ...
... UNCONSCIOUS ?!

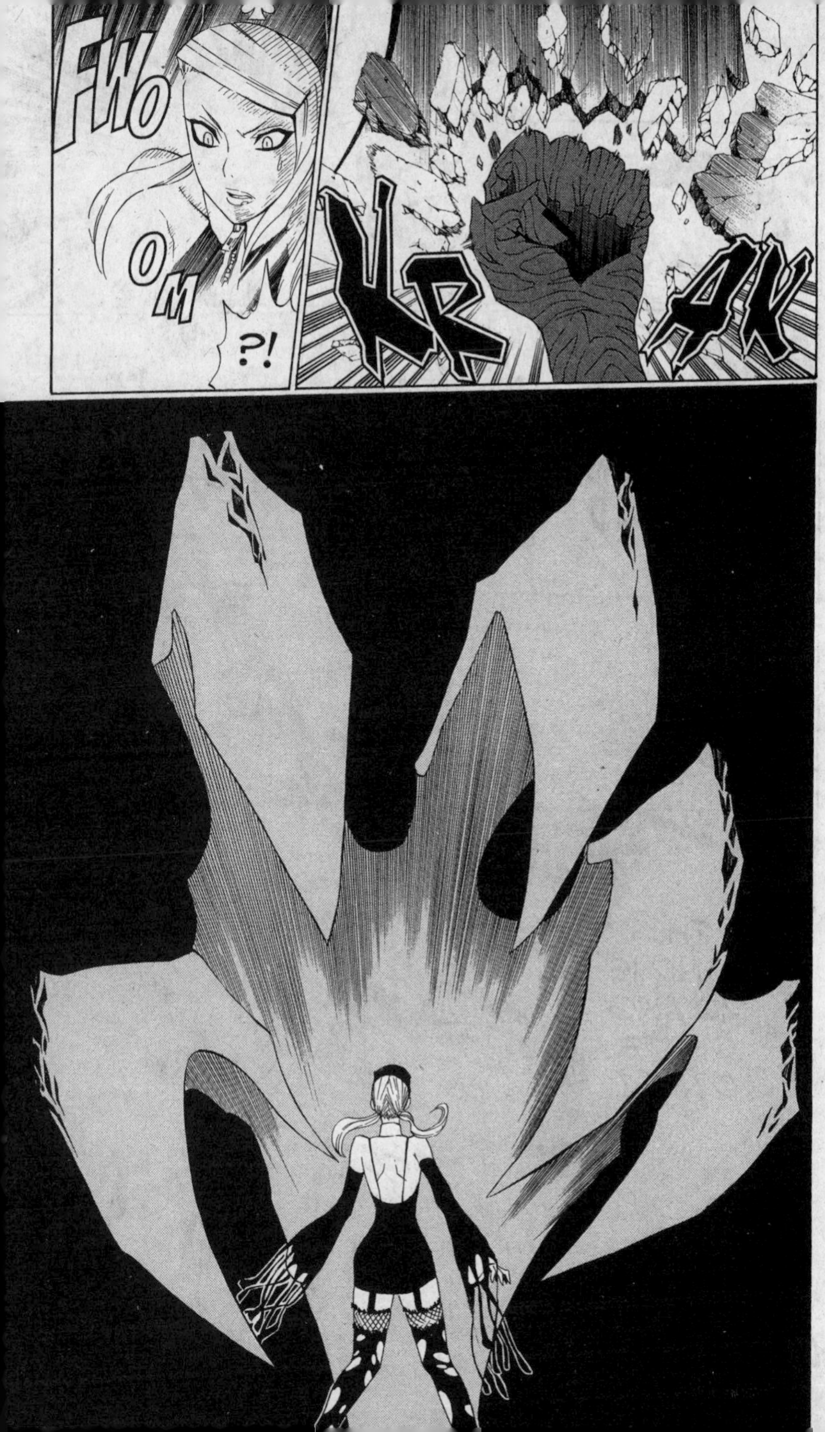
KRAK
FWOOM
?!

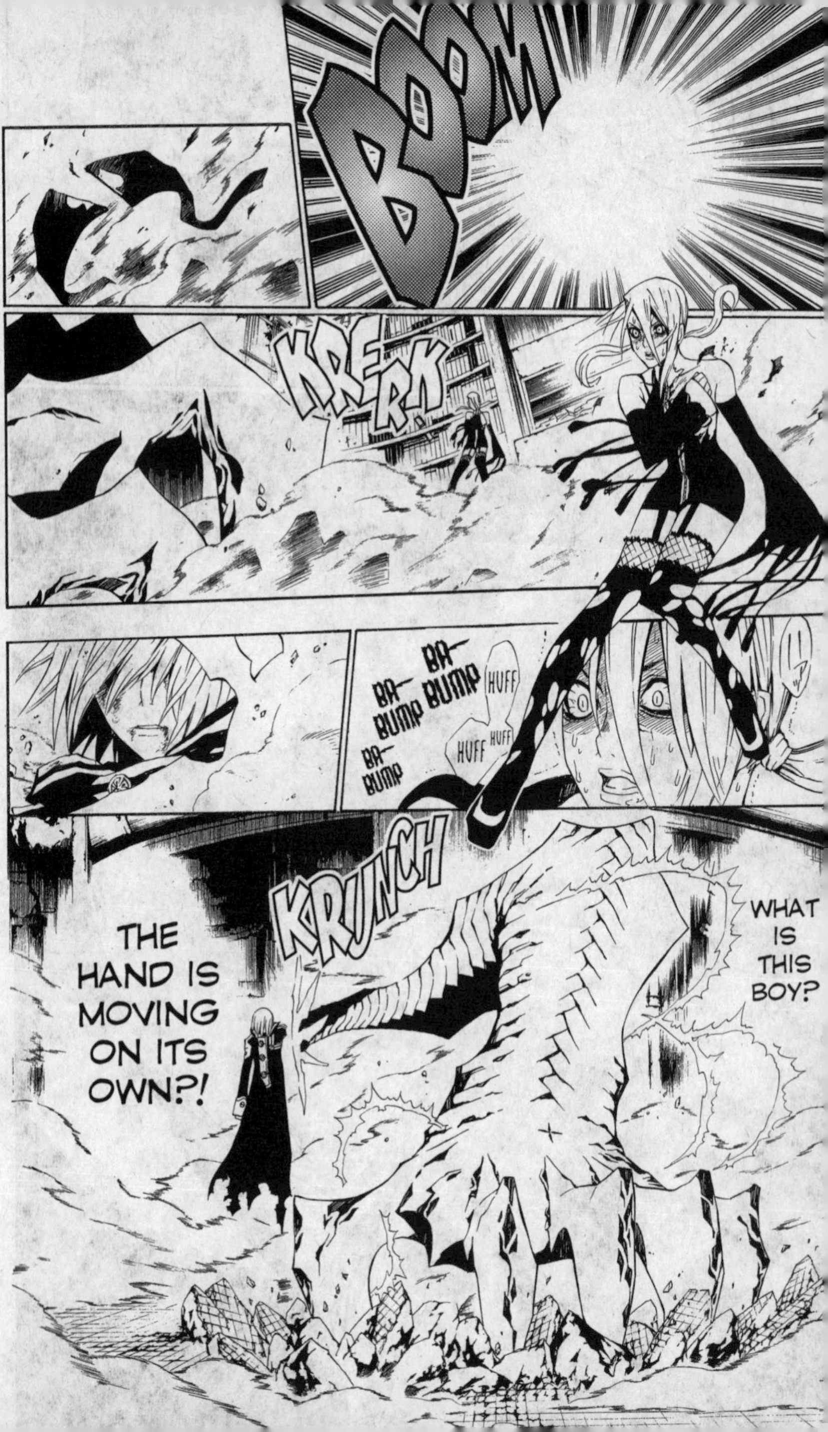
BOOM
KREKK
!!
HUFF
BA-BUMP
BA-BUMP
HUFF HUFF
BA-BUMP
WHAT IS THIS BOY?
KRUNCH
THE HAND IS MOVING ON ITS OWN?!

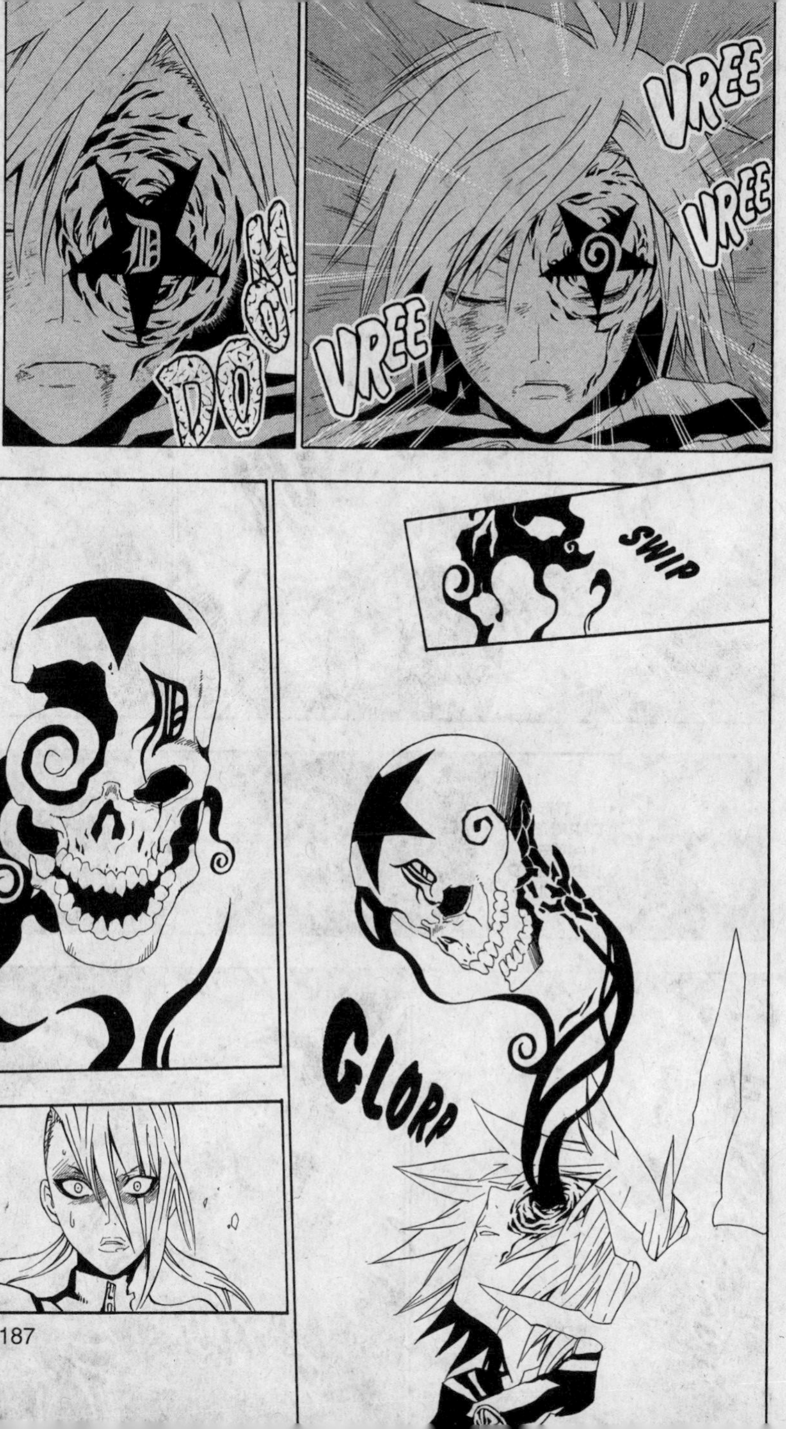
VREE
VREE
VREE
DOOM
SWIP
GLORP

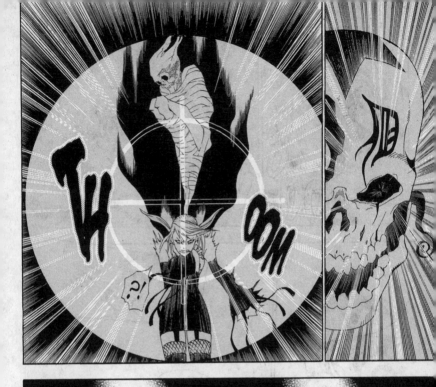

THE DARKNESS HAS RETURNED TO YOU...

I'M BACK, ALLEN.

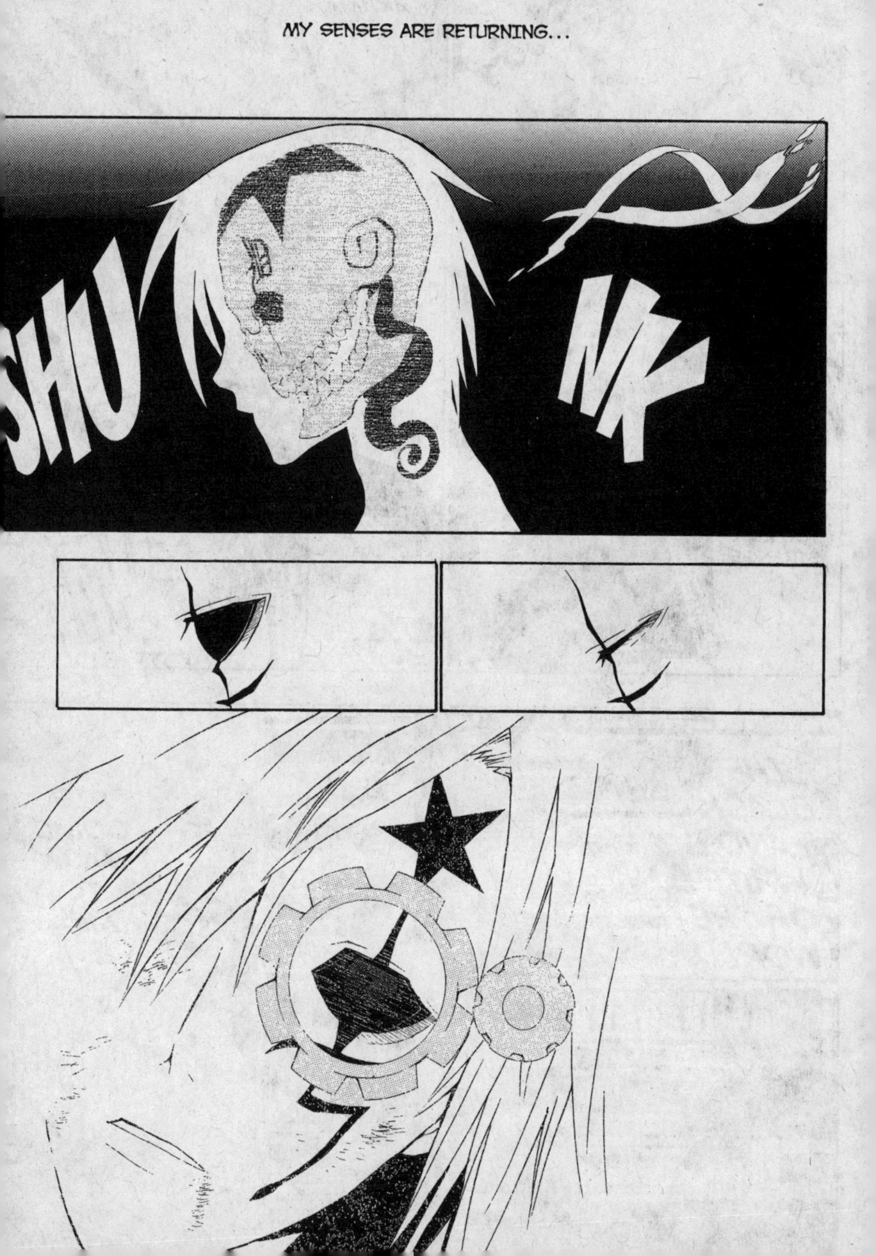
MY SENSES ARE RETURNING...
SHU
NK

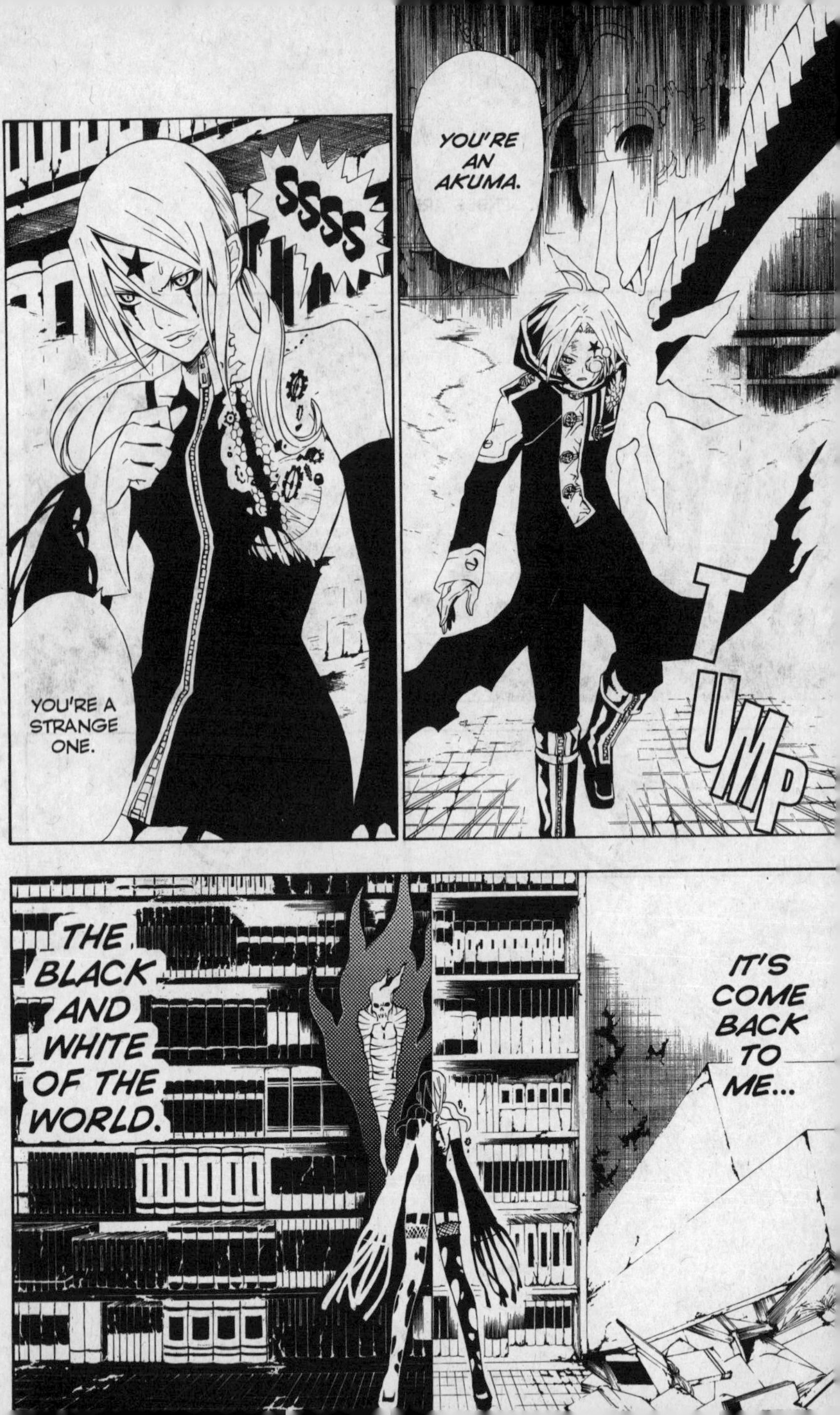
YOU'RE AN AKUMA.
TUMP
SSSS
YOU'RE A STRANGE ONE.
IT'S COME BACK TO ME...
THE BLACK AND WHITE OF THE WORLD.

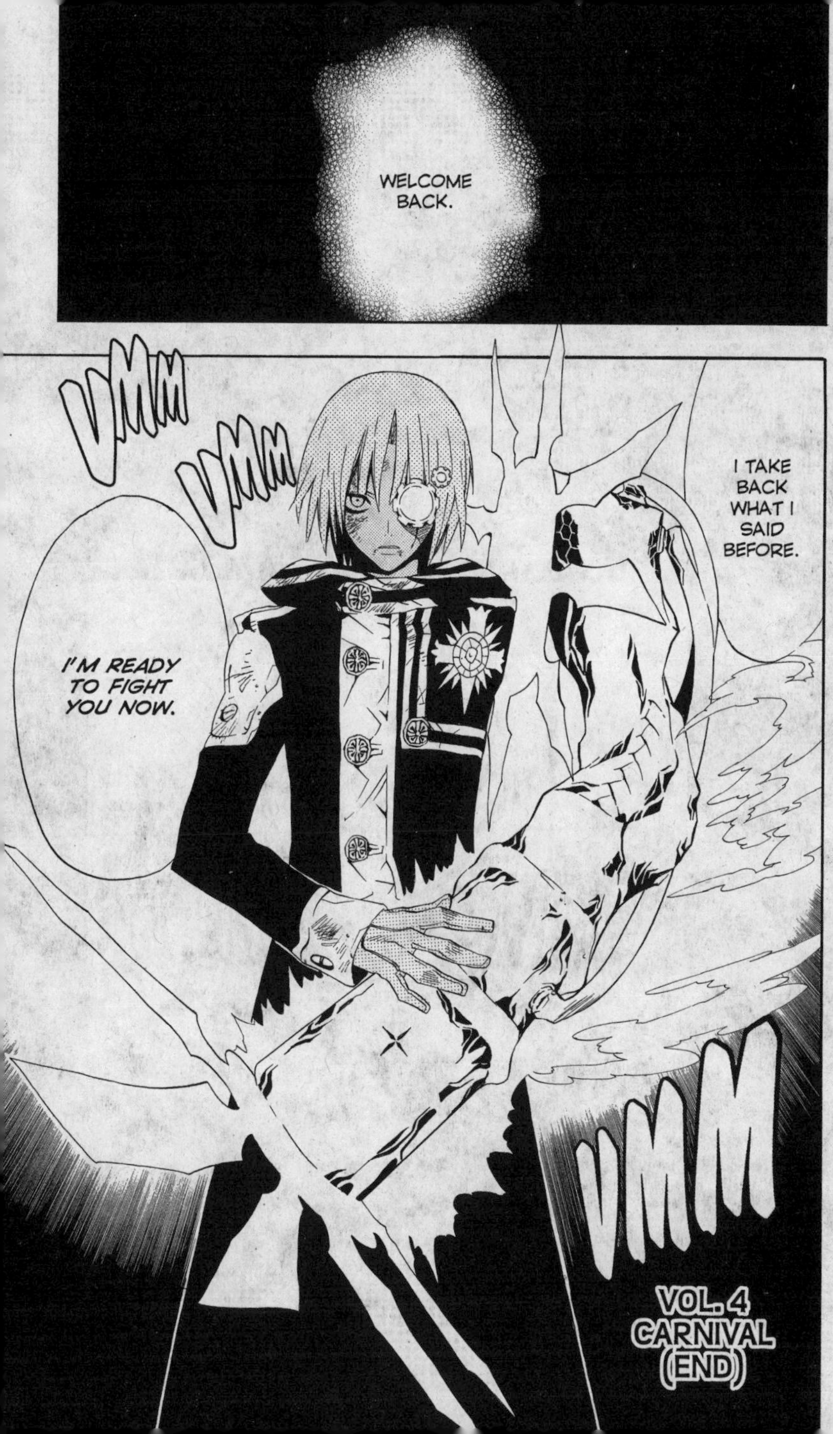
WELCOME BACK.
I TAKE BACK WHAT I SAID BEFORE.
VMM
VMM
I'M READY TO FIGHT YOU NOW.
VMM
VOL. 4 CARNIVAL (END)

IN THE NEXT VOLUME...

The battle rages on against Arystar Krory and Eliade. Allen's eye is now healed and strange truths begin to reveal themselves. Allen's companion Lavi realizes that Arystar might not be a vampire but something else entirely. Plus Allen and Lavi find themselves with an unexpected traveling companion—but who could it be?

Available now!

SHO [redacted] EDITION

STORY & ART BY
Katsura Hoshino

D.Gray-man™

vol. 5

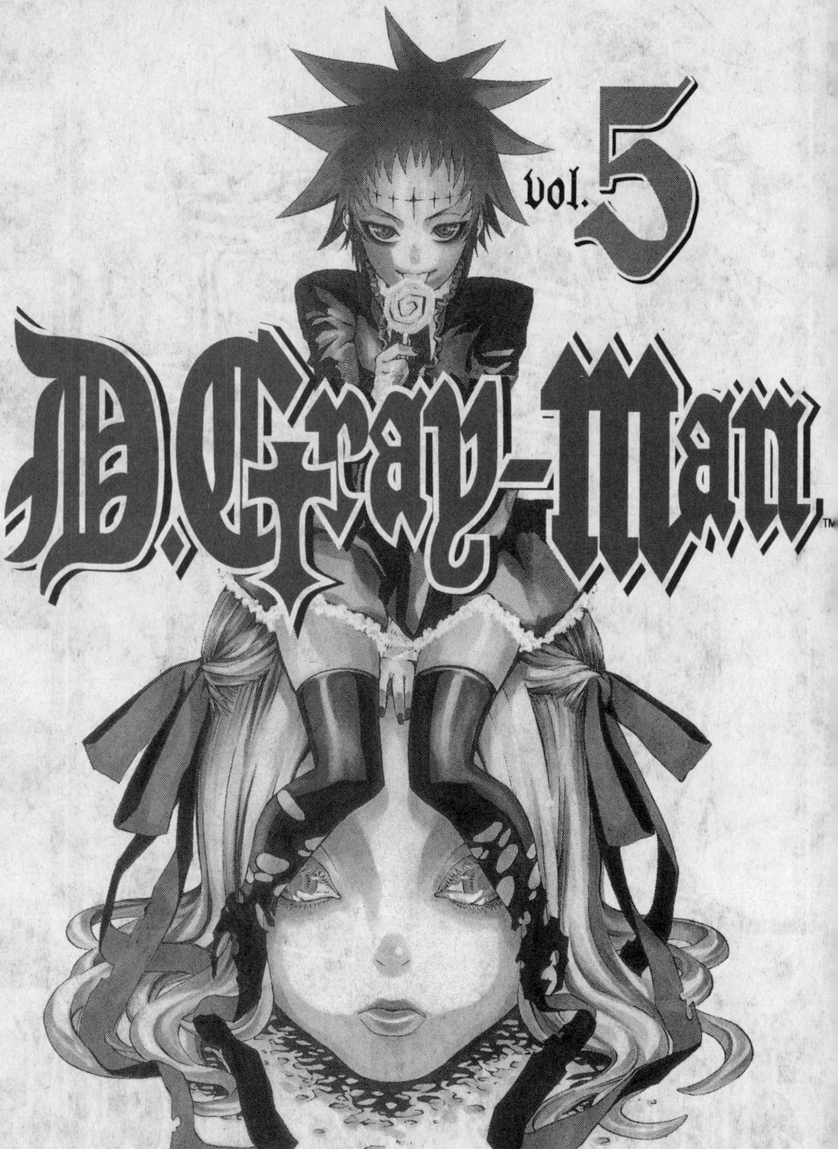

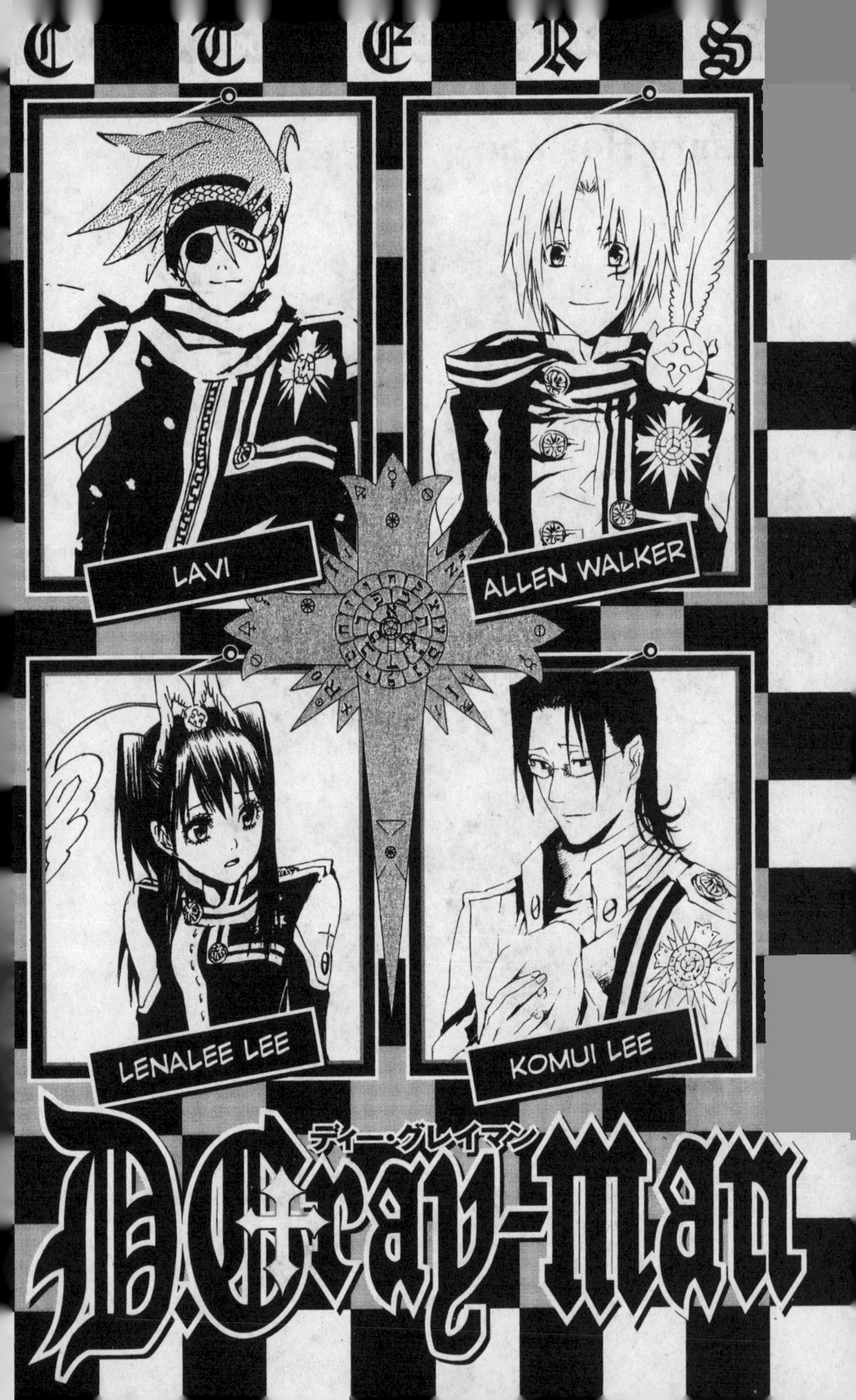
C T E R S
LAVI
ALLEN WALKER
LENALEE LEE
KOMUI LEE
D.Gray-man
ディー・グレイマン

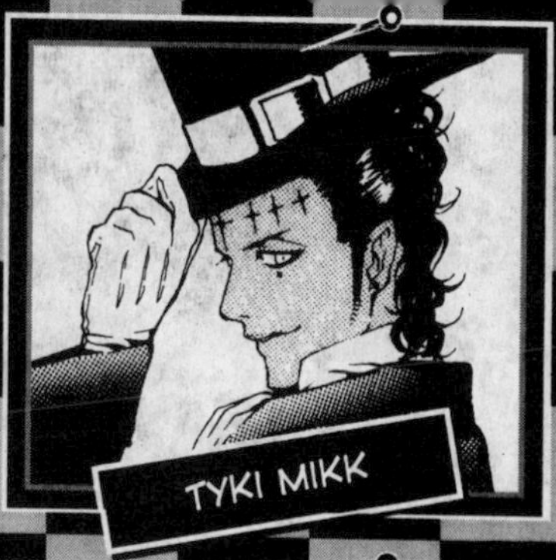
TYKI MIKK

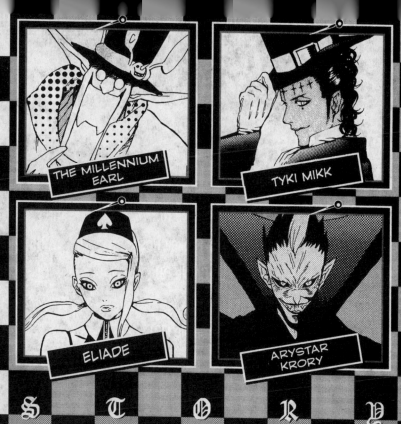

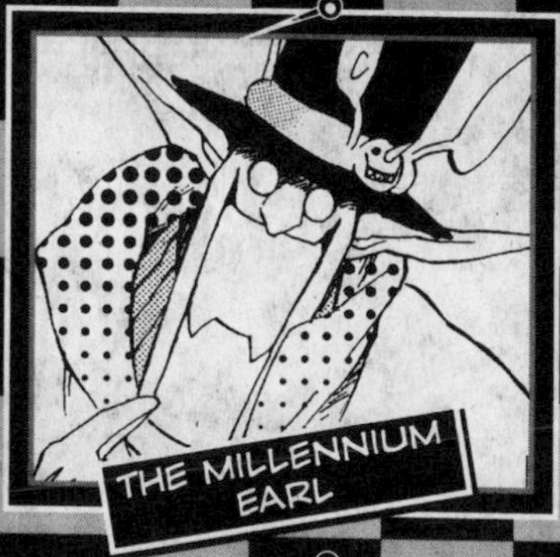
THE MILLENNIUM EARL

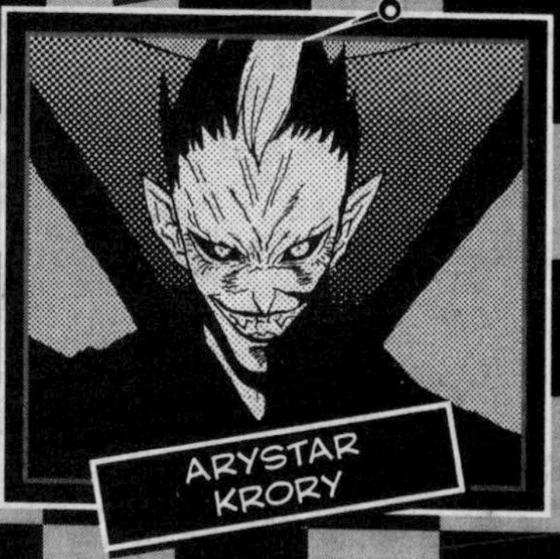
ARYSTAR KRORY

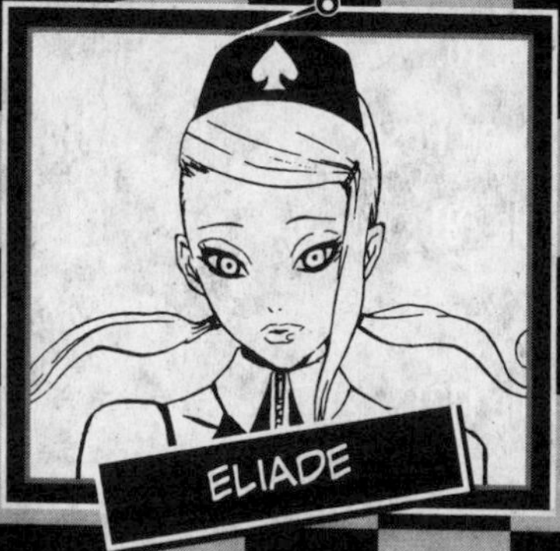
ELIADE

STORY

IT ALL BEGAN CENTURIES AGO WITH THE DISCOVERY OF A CUBE CONTAINING AN APOCALYPTIC PROPHECY FROM AN ANCIENT CIVILIZATION, AND INSTRUCTIONS IN THE USE OF INNOCENCE, A CRYSTALLINE SUBSTANCE OF WONDROUS SUPERNATURAL POWER. THE CREATORS OF THE CUBE CLAIMED TO HAVE DEFEATED AN EVIL KNOWN AS THE MILLENNIUM EARL USING THE INNOCENCE. NEVERTHELESS, THE WORLD WAS DESTROYED BY THE GREAT FLOOD OF THE OLD TESTAMENT. NOW TO AVERT A SECOND END OF THE WORLD, A GROUP OF EXORCISTS WIELDING WEAPONS MADE OF INNOCENCE MUST BATTLE THE MILLENNIUM EARL AND HIS TERRIBLE MINIONS, THE AKUMA.

WITH ONE GENERAL ALREADY DEAD, AND ITS FORCES UNDER CONSTANT ATTACK, THE BLACK ORDER MUST FIND A SPECIAL INNOCENCE CALLED THE "HEART" BEFORE THE MILLENNIUM EARL DOES. ALLEN IS ASSIGNED TO FIND AND PROTECT GENERAL CROSS, BUT FIRST HE MUST DEAL WITH A VERY UNUSUAL VAMPIRE!

D.GRAY-MAN
Vol. 5

CONTENTS

The 37th Night: Vampire of the Castle (7) - Merge -   197

The 38th Night: Vampire of the Castle (8)

      - Broken Hearts, Broken Roses -   215

The 39th Night: Vampire of the Castle (9)

      - Affection -   233

The 40th Night: Vampire of the Castle (10)

      - A Reason -   251

The 41st Night: Omen   269

The 42nd Night: Three Men and a Child   287

The 43rd Night: Laughing Out Loud   305

The 44th Night: Number on the Desktop   323

The 45th Night: Signs   341

The 46th Night: News of Cross Marian   359

THE 37TH NIGHT: VAMPIRE OF THE CASTLE (PART 7) MERGE

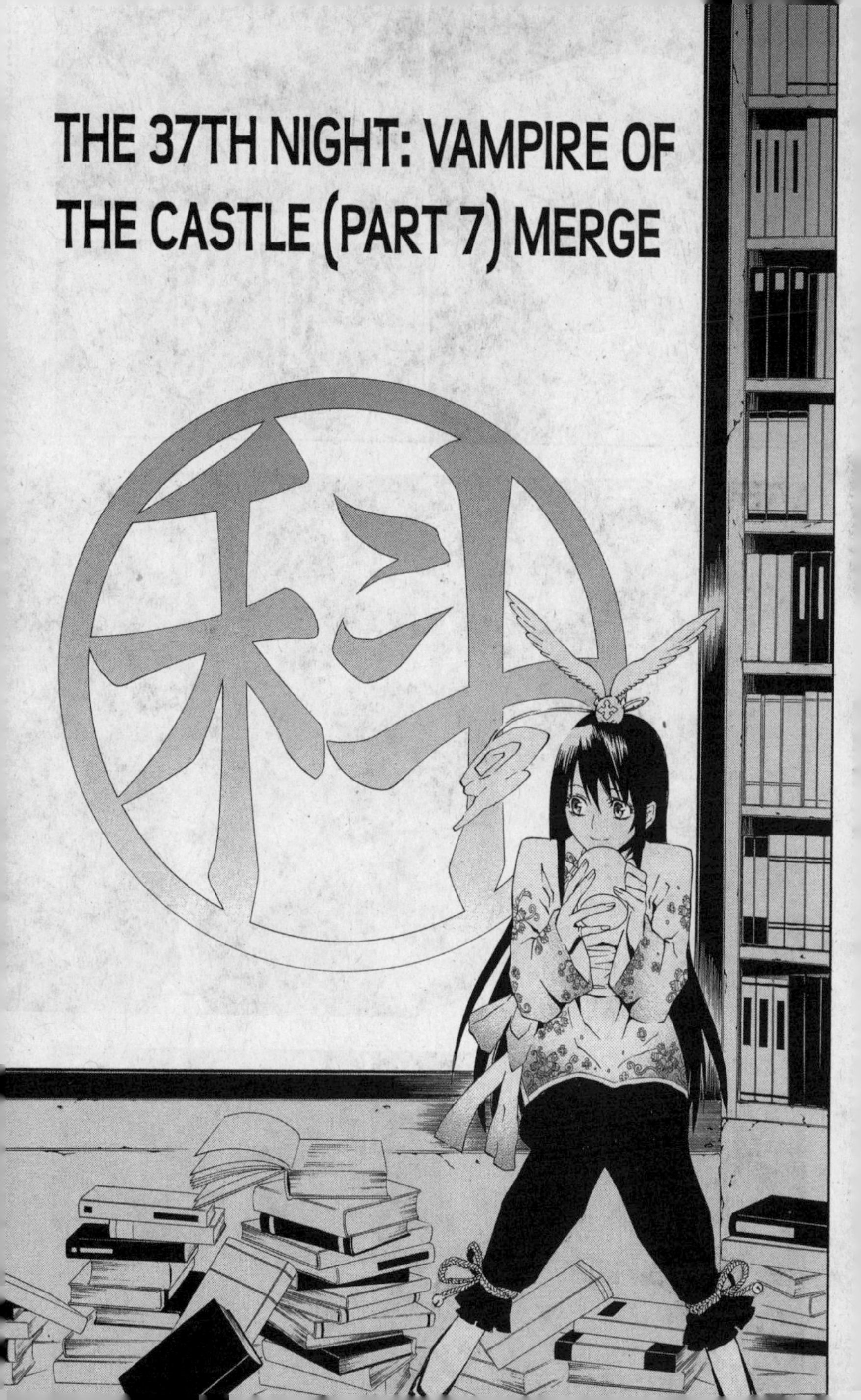

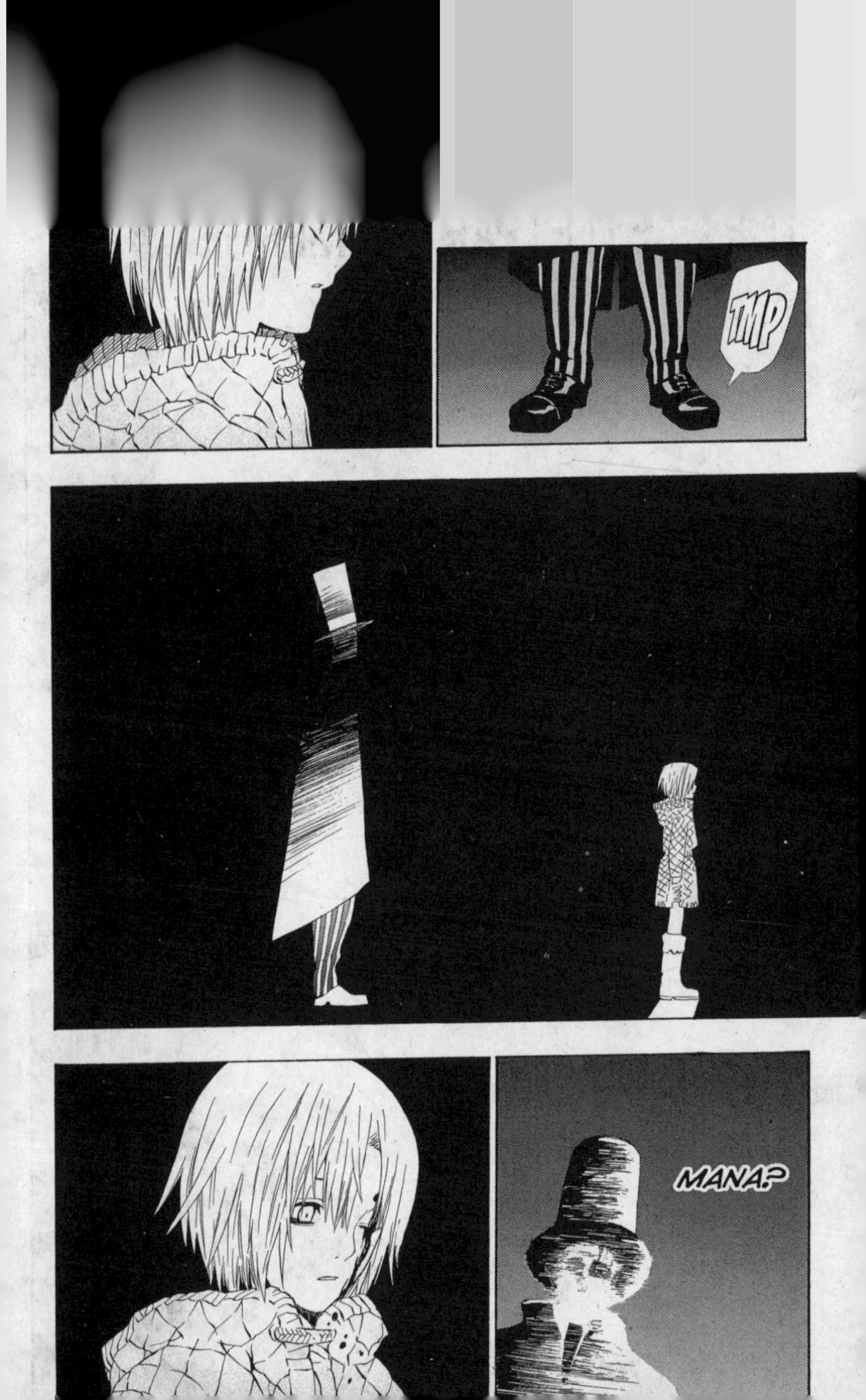
TMP
MANA?

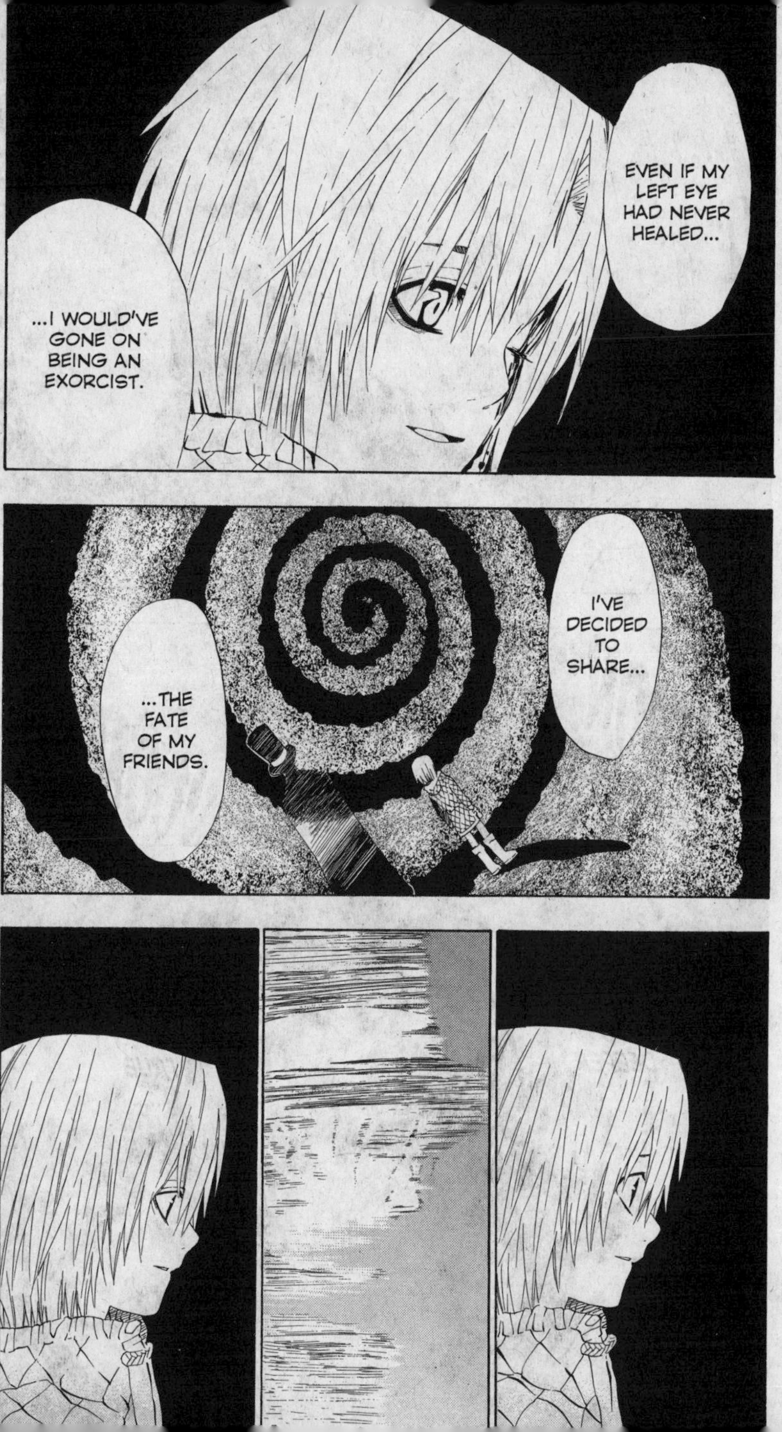
EVEN IF MY LEFT EYE HAD NEVER HEALED...
...I WOULD'VE GONE ON BEING AN EXORCIST.
I'VE DECIDED TO SHARE...
...THE FATE OF MY FRIENDS.

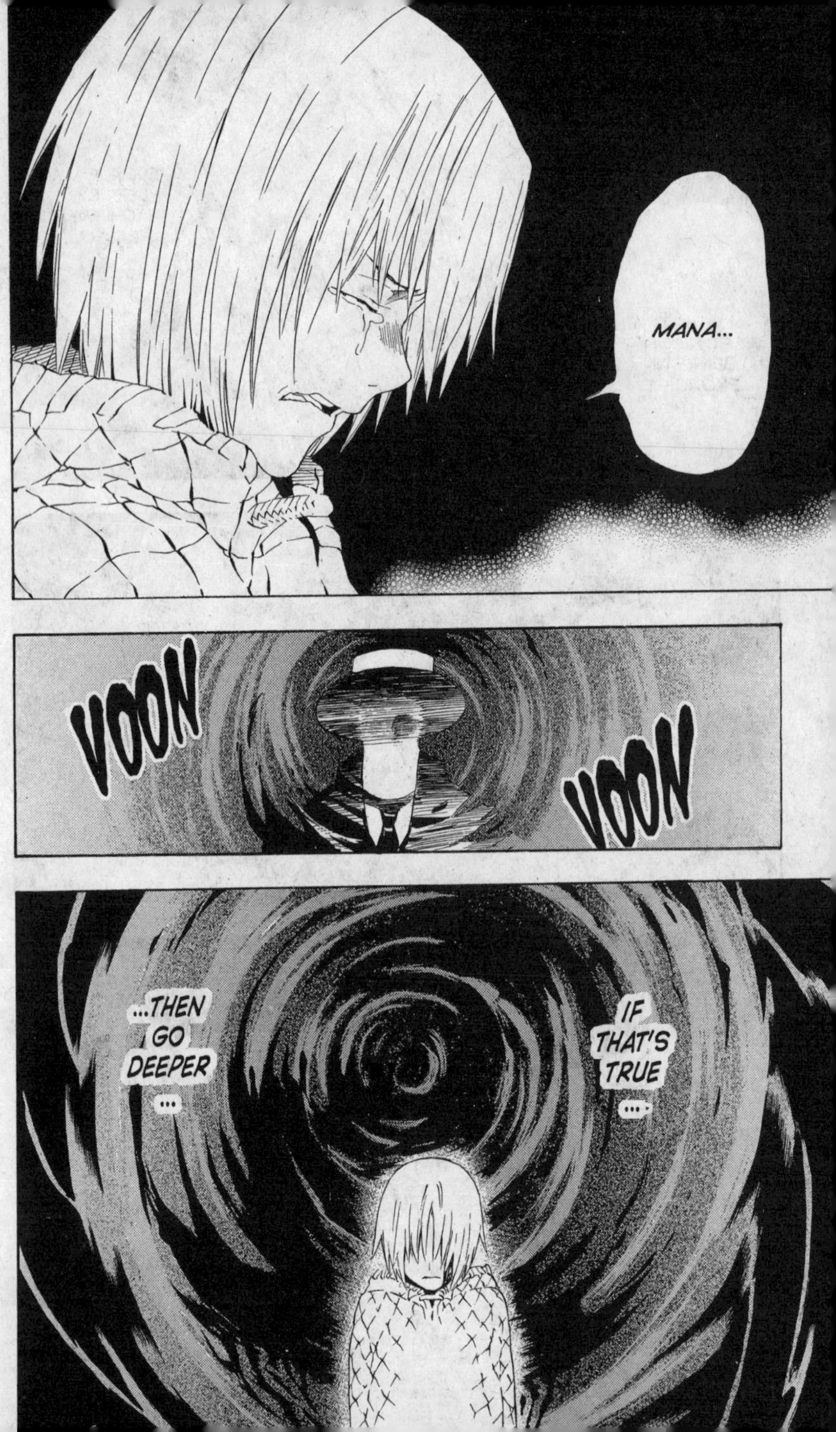
MANA...
VOON
VOON
IF THAT'S TRUE...
...THEN GO DEEPER...

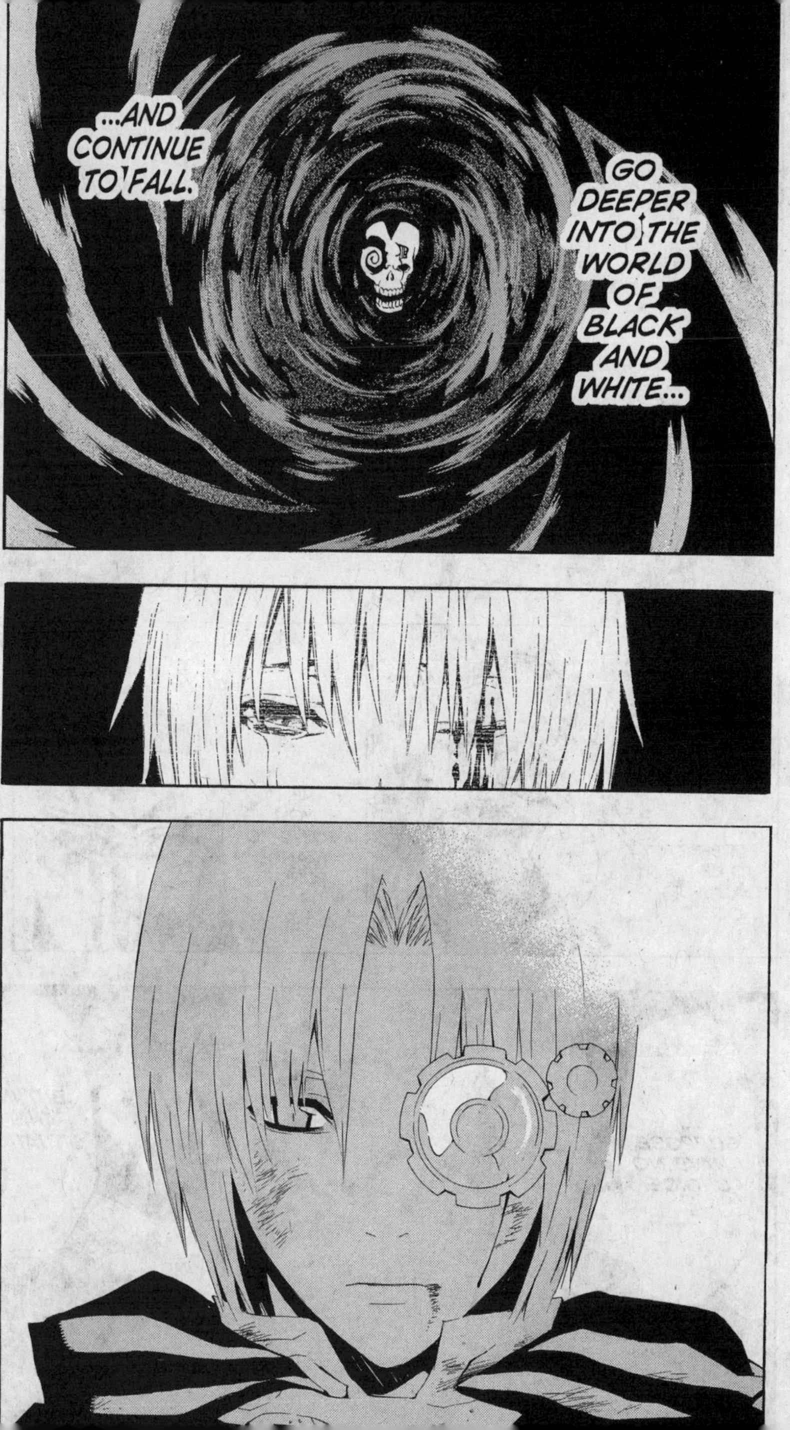
GO DEEPER INTO THE WORLD OF BLACK AND WHITE...
...AND CONTINUE TO FALL.

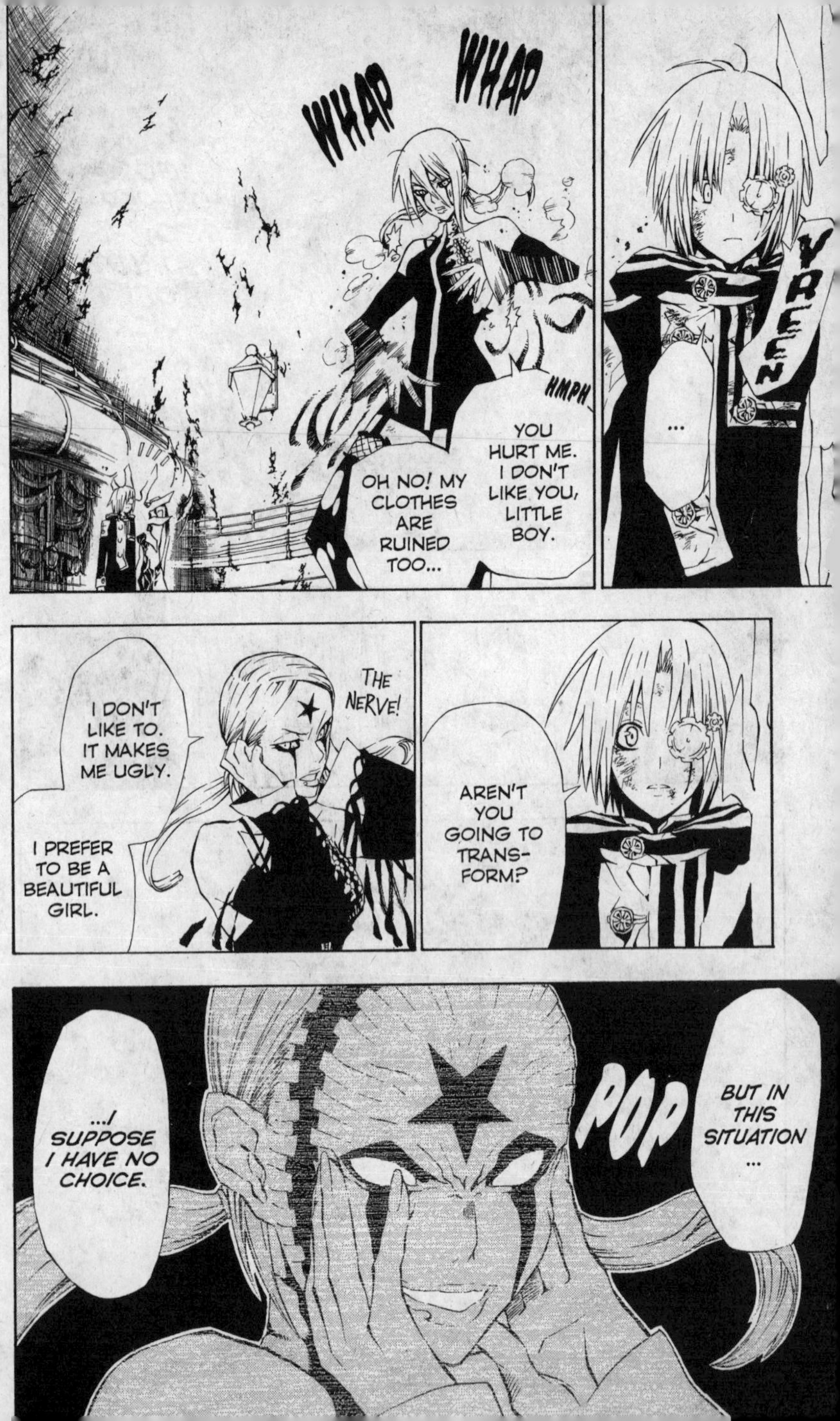
VREEN
...
WHAP
WHAP
HMPH
YOU HURT ME. I DON'T LIKE YOU, LITTLE BOY.
OH NO! MY CLOTHES ARE RUINED TOO...
AREN'T YOU GOING TO TRANS-FORM?
THE NERVE!
I DON'T LIKE TO. IT MAKES ME UGLY.
I PREFER TO BE A BEAUTIFUL GIRL.
BUT IN THIS SITUATION...
POP
...I SUPPOSE I HAVE NO CHOICE.

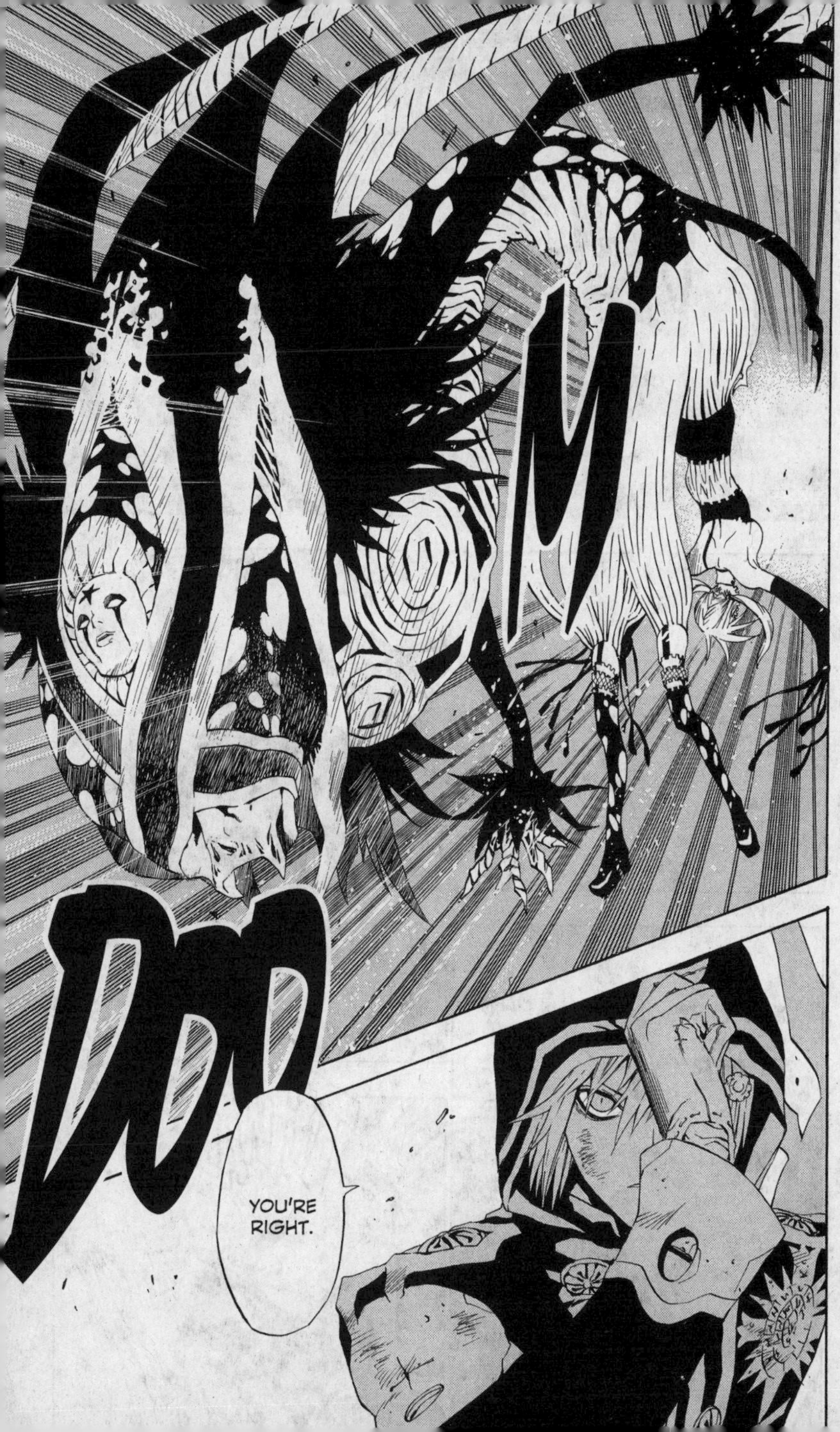
YOU'RE
RIGHT.

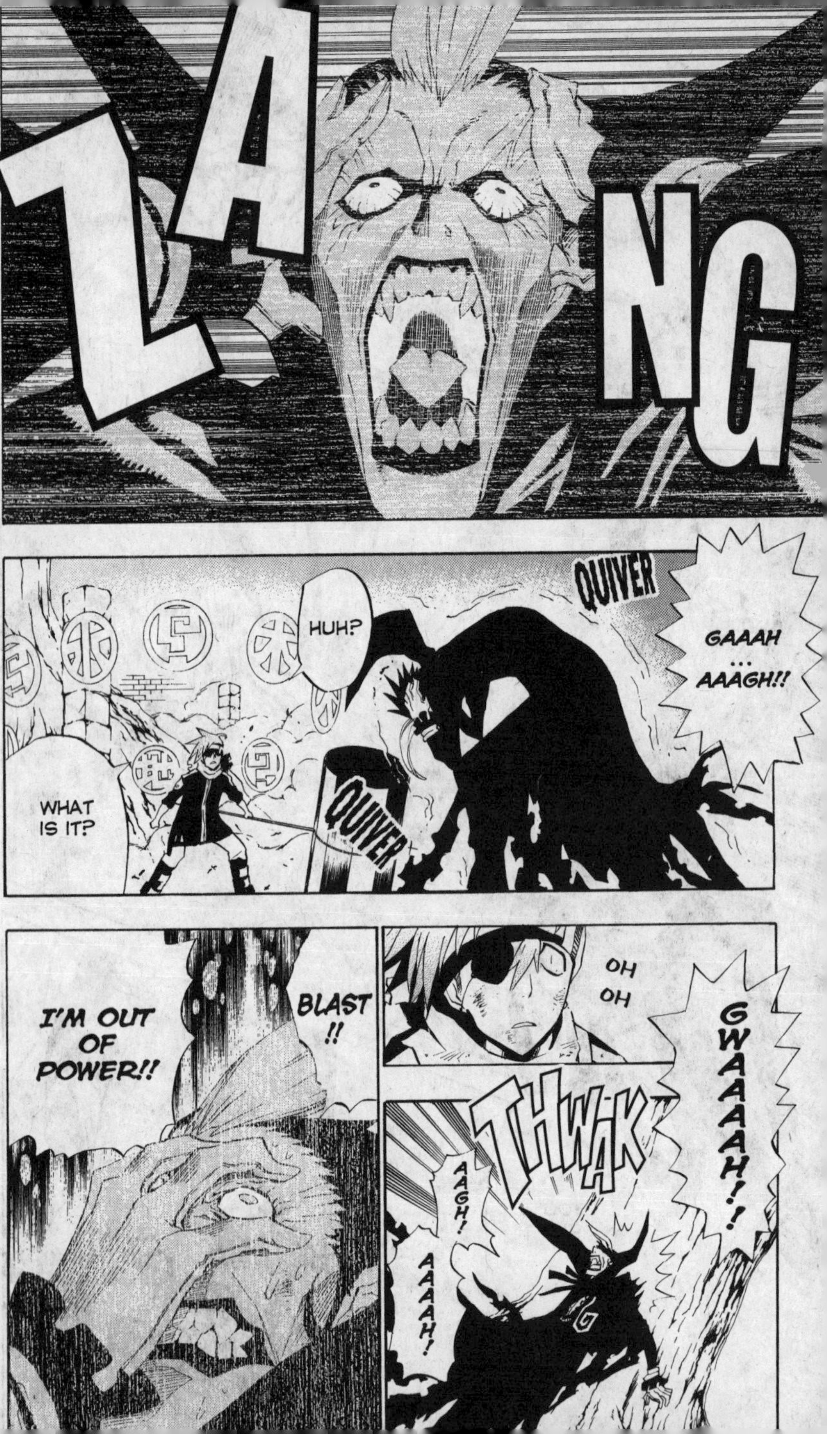

ZLANG
GAAAH ... AAAGH!!
QUIVER
HUH?
QUIVER
WHAT IS IT?
OH OH
GWAAAAAH!!!
THWAK
AAGH!
AAAAAH!
BLAST!!
I'M OUT OF POWER!!

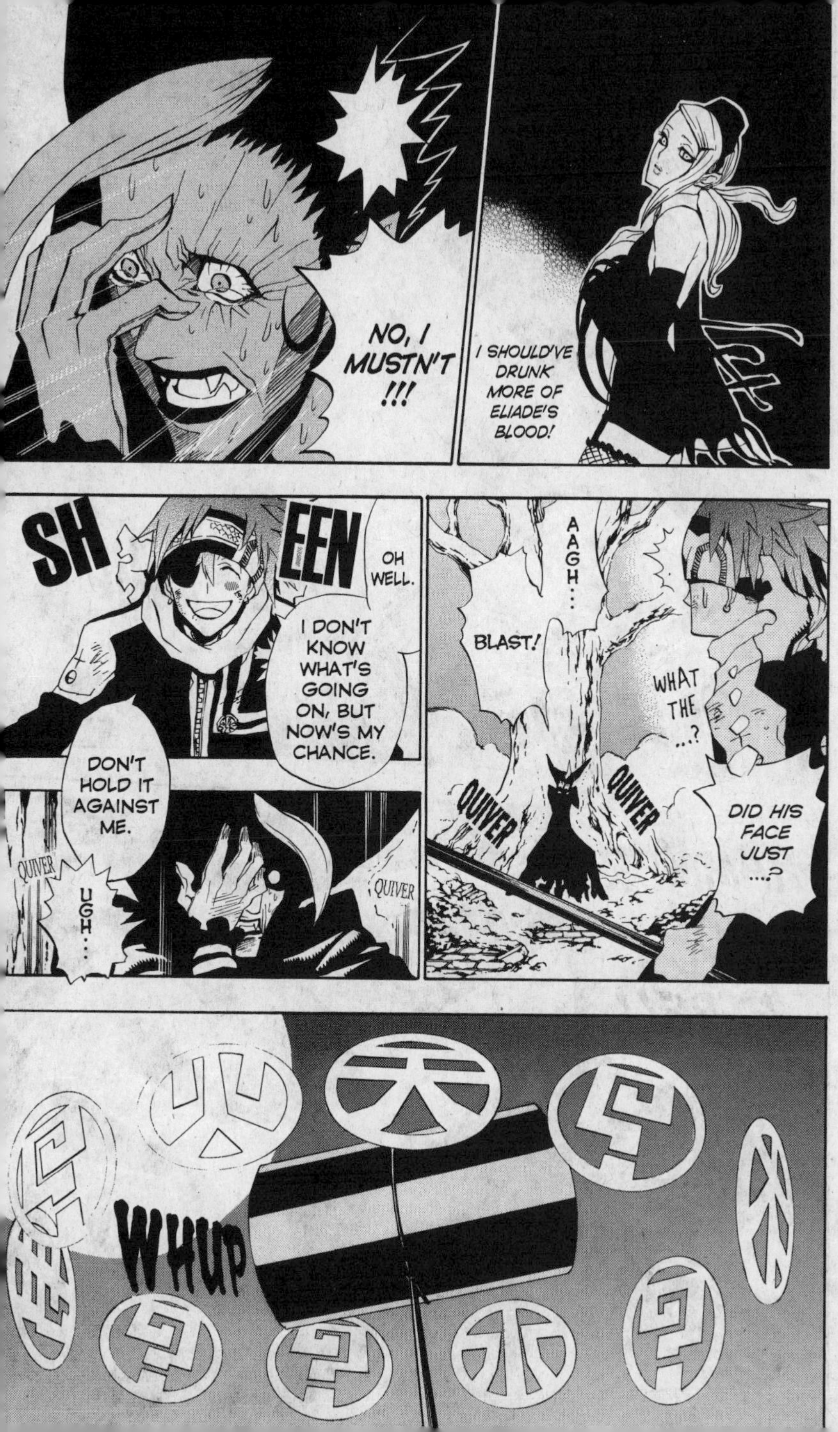
I SHOULD'VE DRUNK MORE OF ELIADE'S BLOOD!
NO, I MUSTN'T !!!
AAGH...
BLAST!
WHAT THE ...?
DID HIS FACE JUST ....?
QUIVER
QUIVER
SH EEN
OH WELL.
I DON'T KNOW WHAT'S GOING ON, BUT NOW'S MY CHANCE.
DON'T HOLD IT AGAINST ME.
QUIVER
QUIVER
UGH...
WHUP

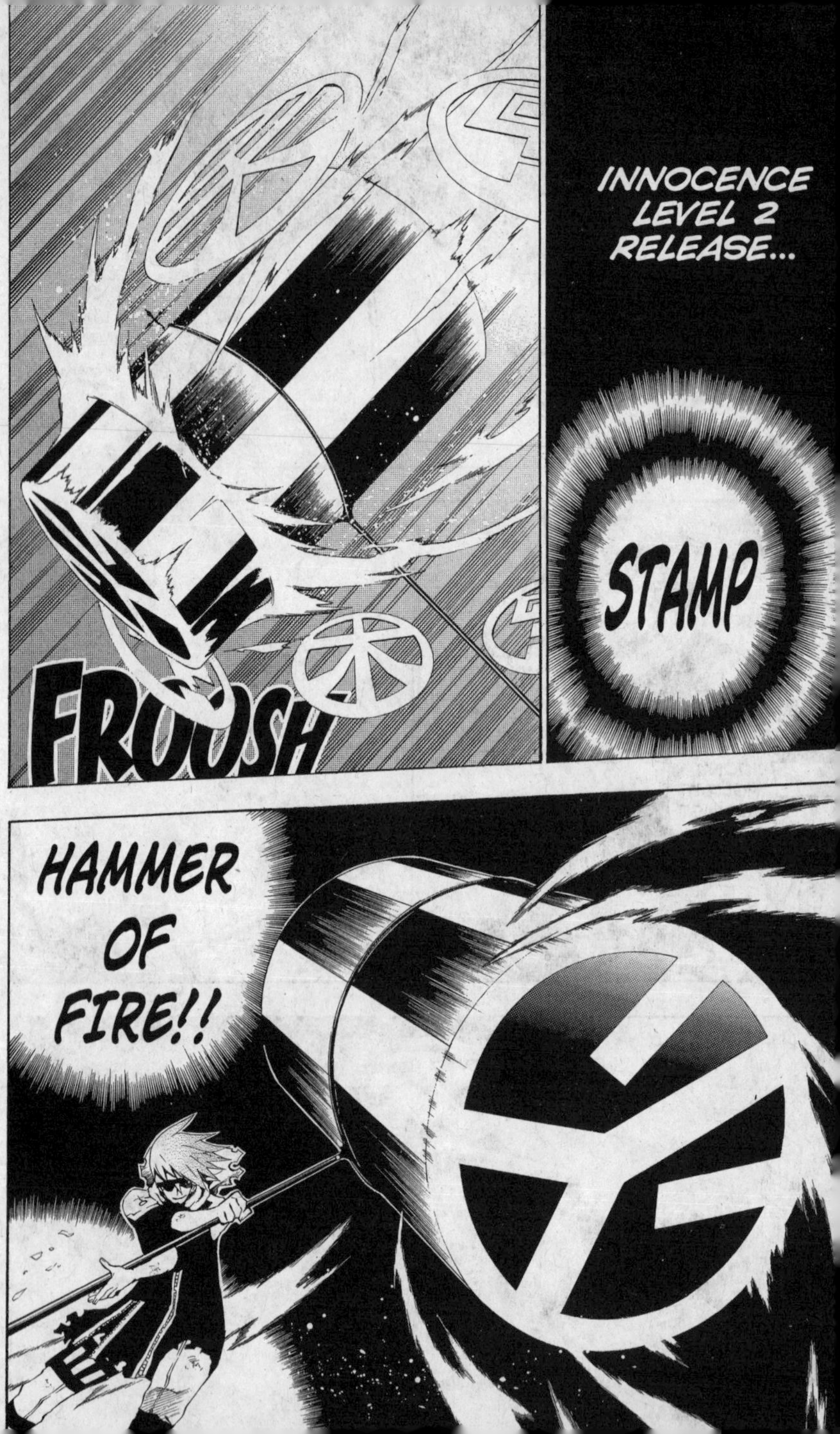
INNOCENCE LEVEL 2 RELEASE...
STAMP
FROOSH
HAMMER OF FIRE!!

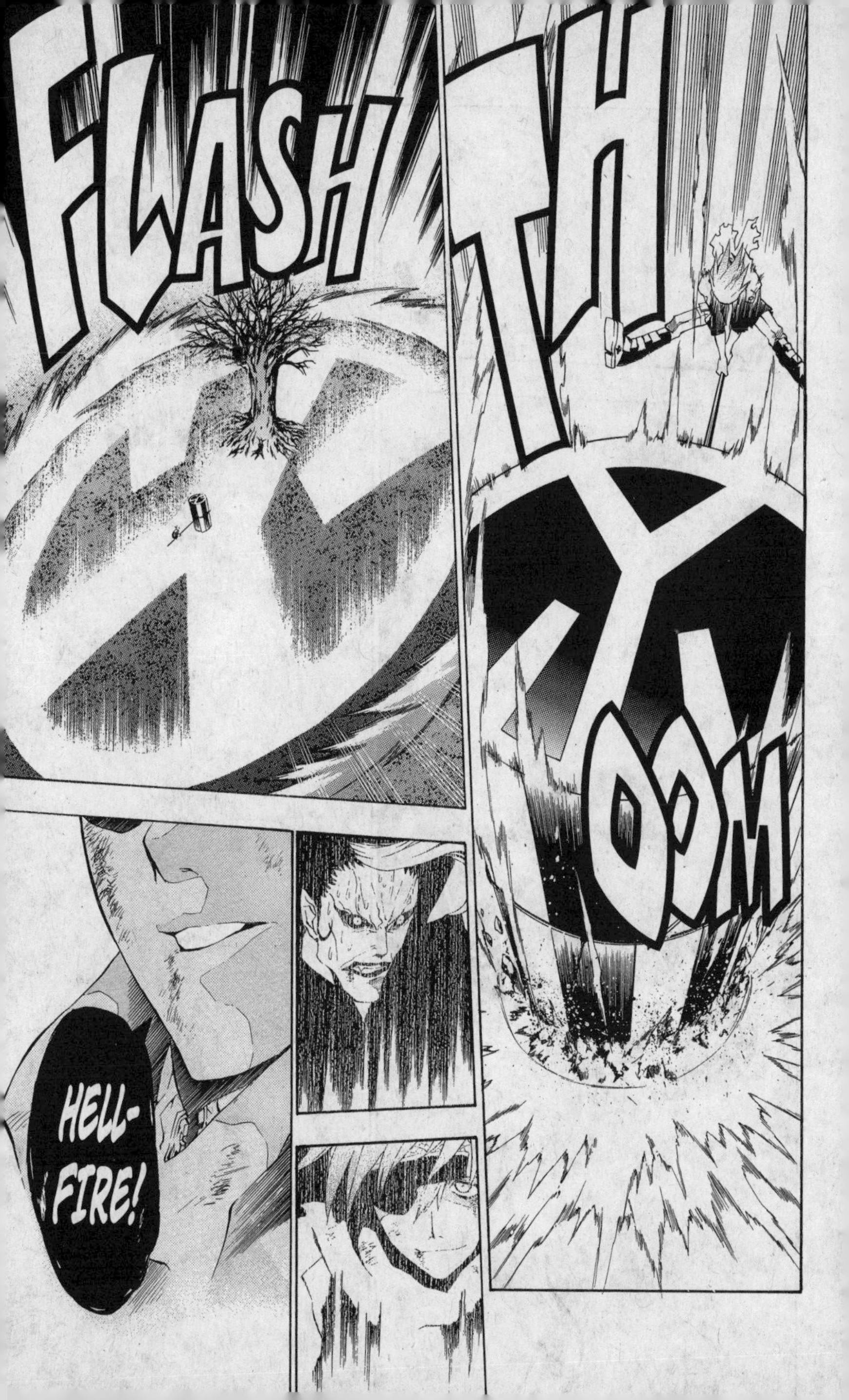
THOOM
FLASH
HELL-FIRE!

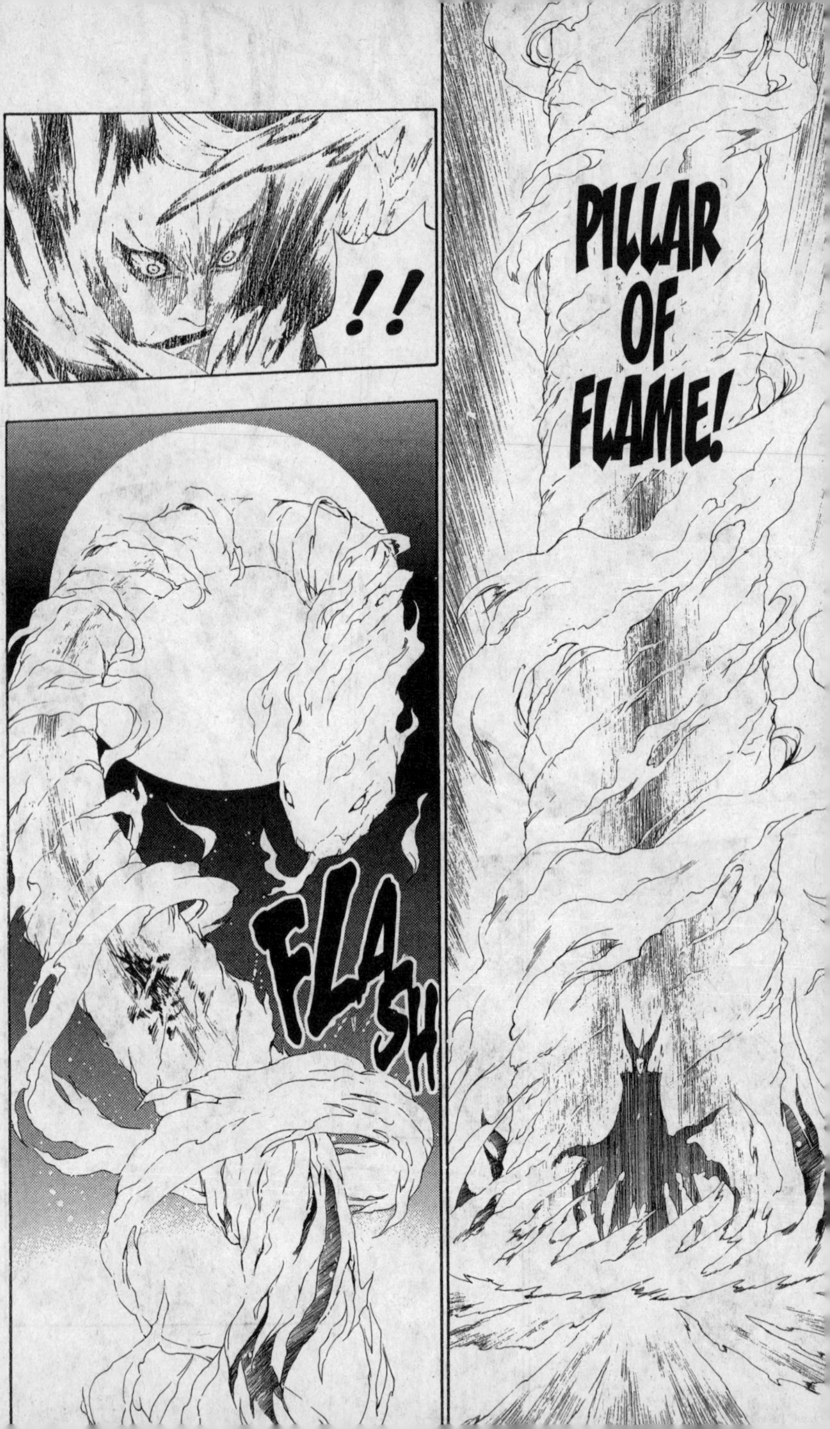
PILLAR OF FLAME!
!!
FLASH

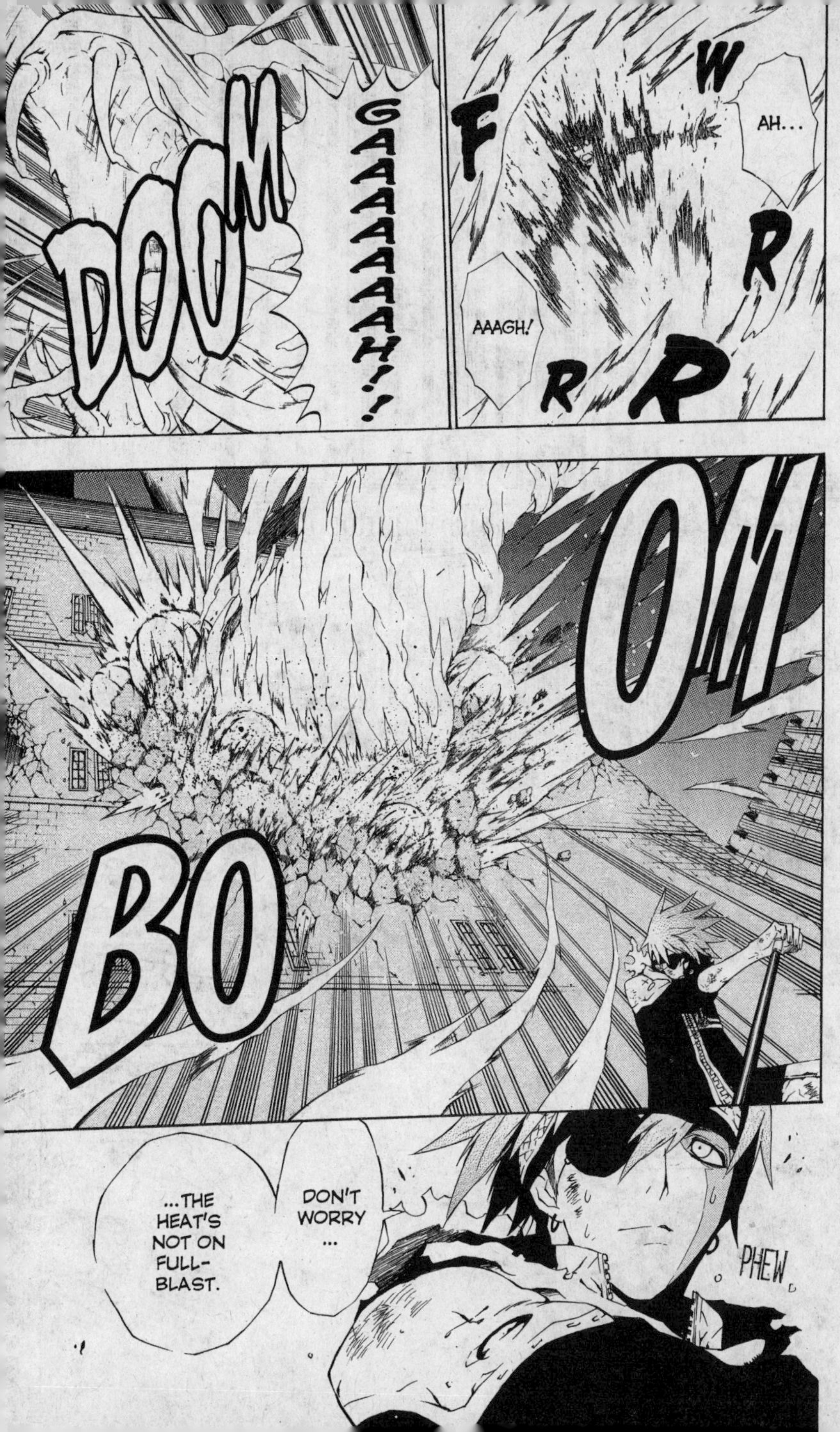
AH...
WRRR
F
AAAGH!
GAAAAAAAH!!
DOOM
OM
BO
DON'T WORRY ...
...THE HEAT'S NOT ON FULL-BLAST.
PHEW

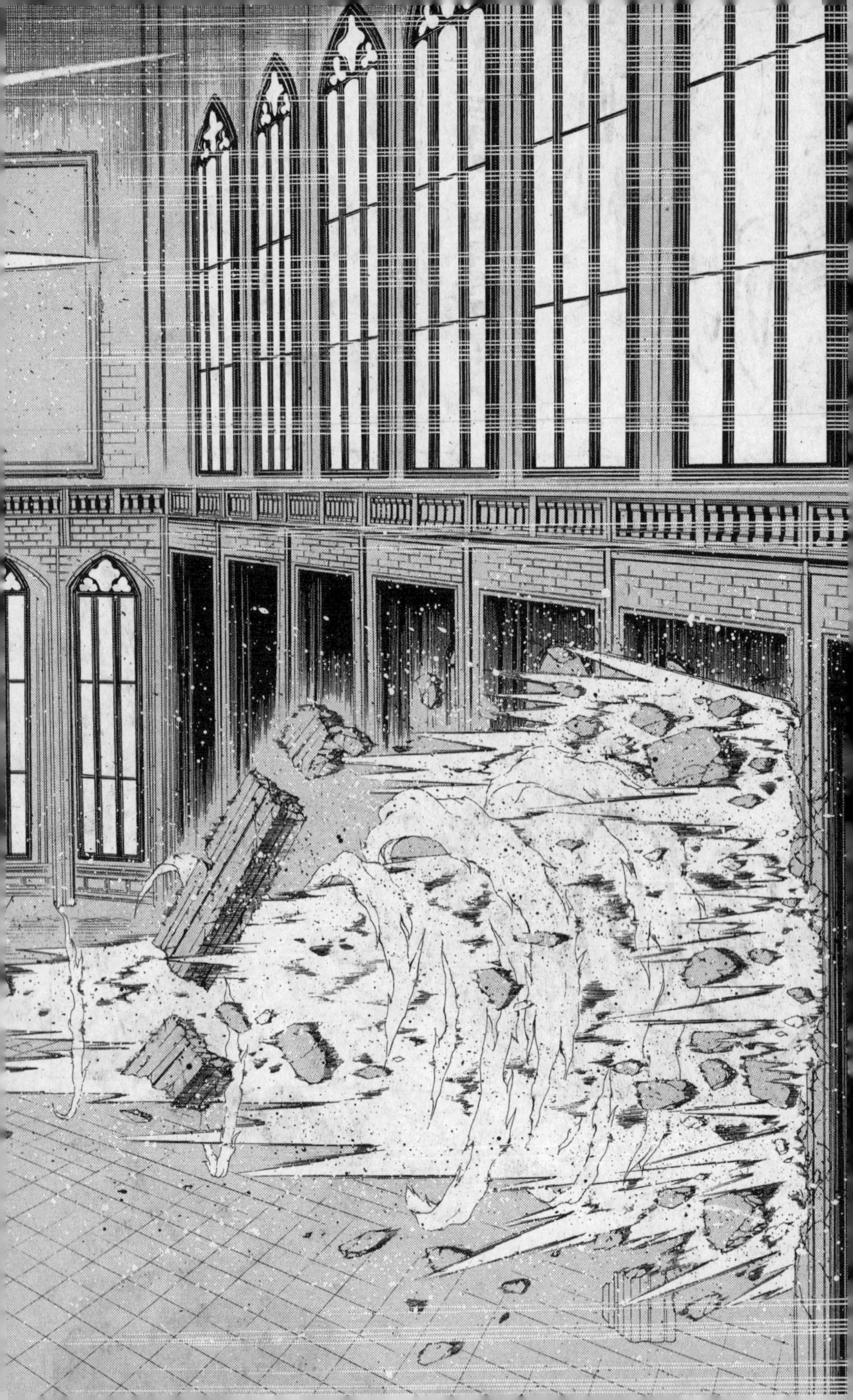

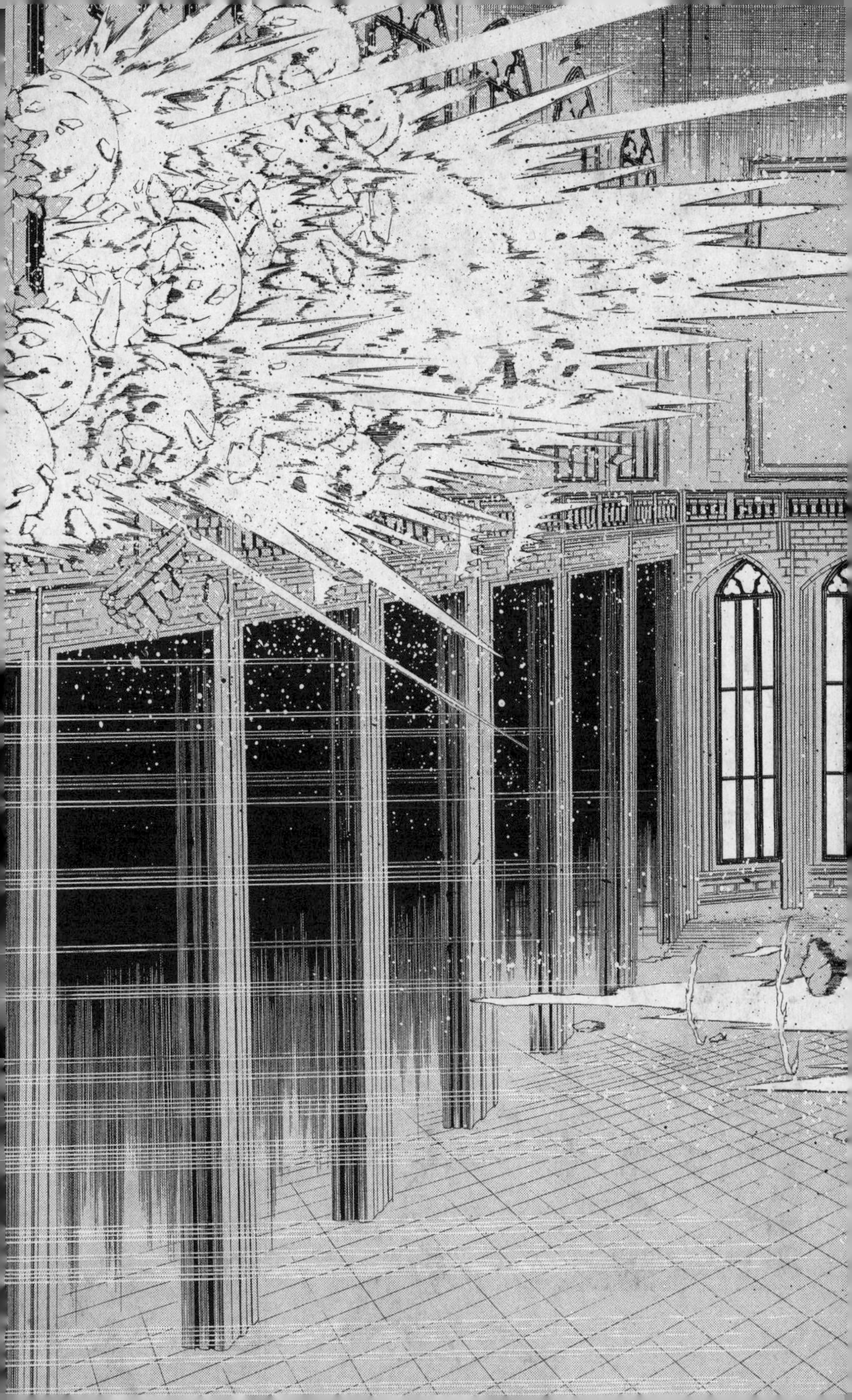

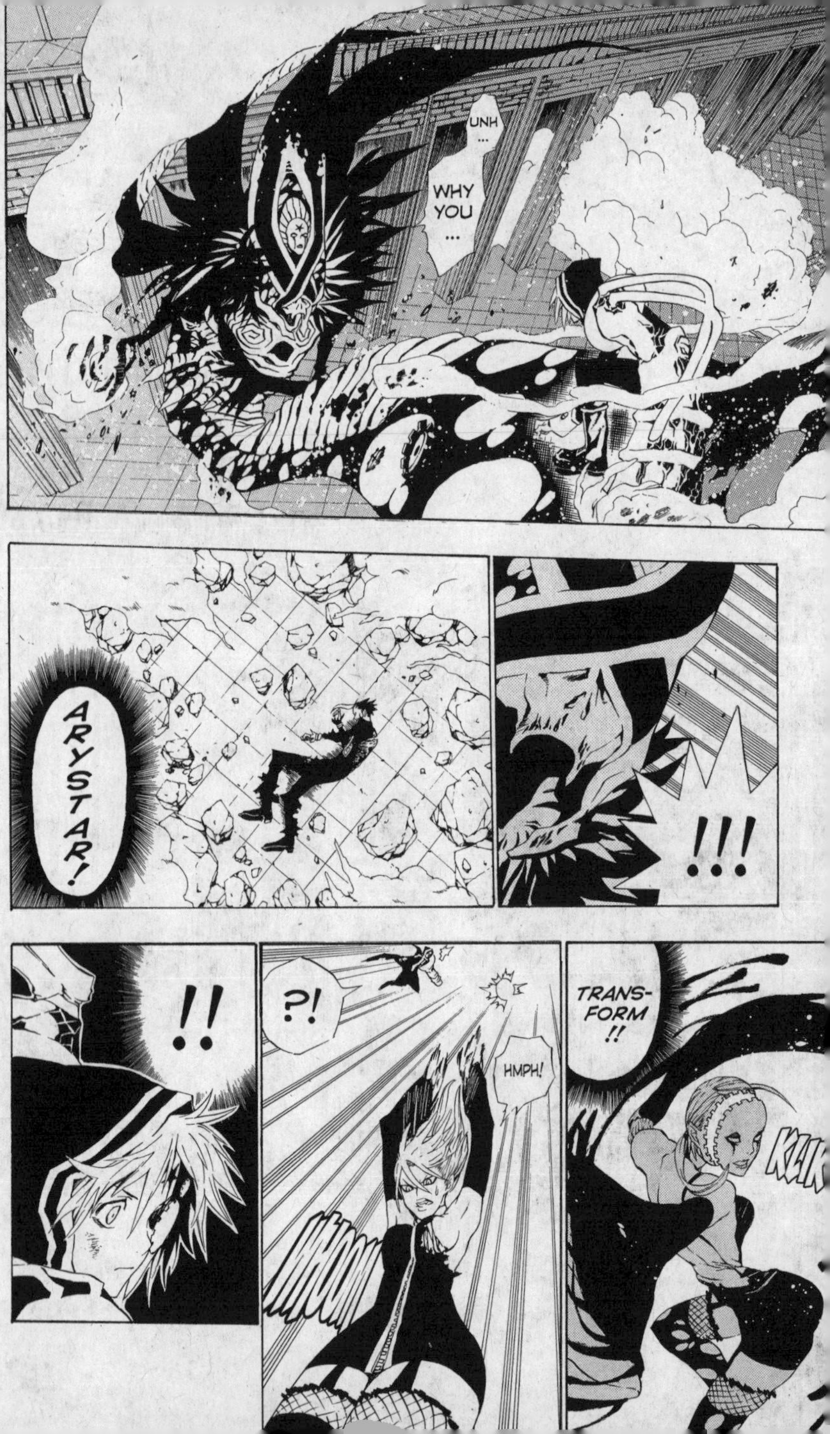
UNH ...
WHY YOU ...
!!!
ARYSTAR!
TRANS-FORM !!
KLIK
HMPH!
?!
!!

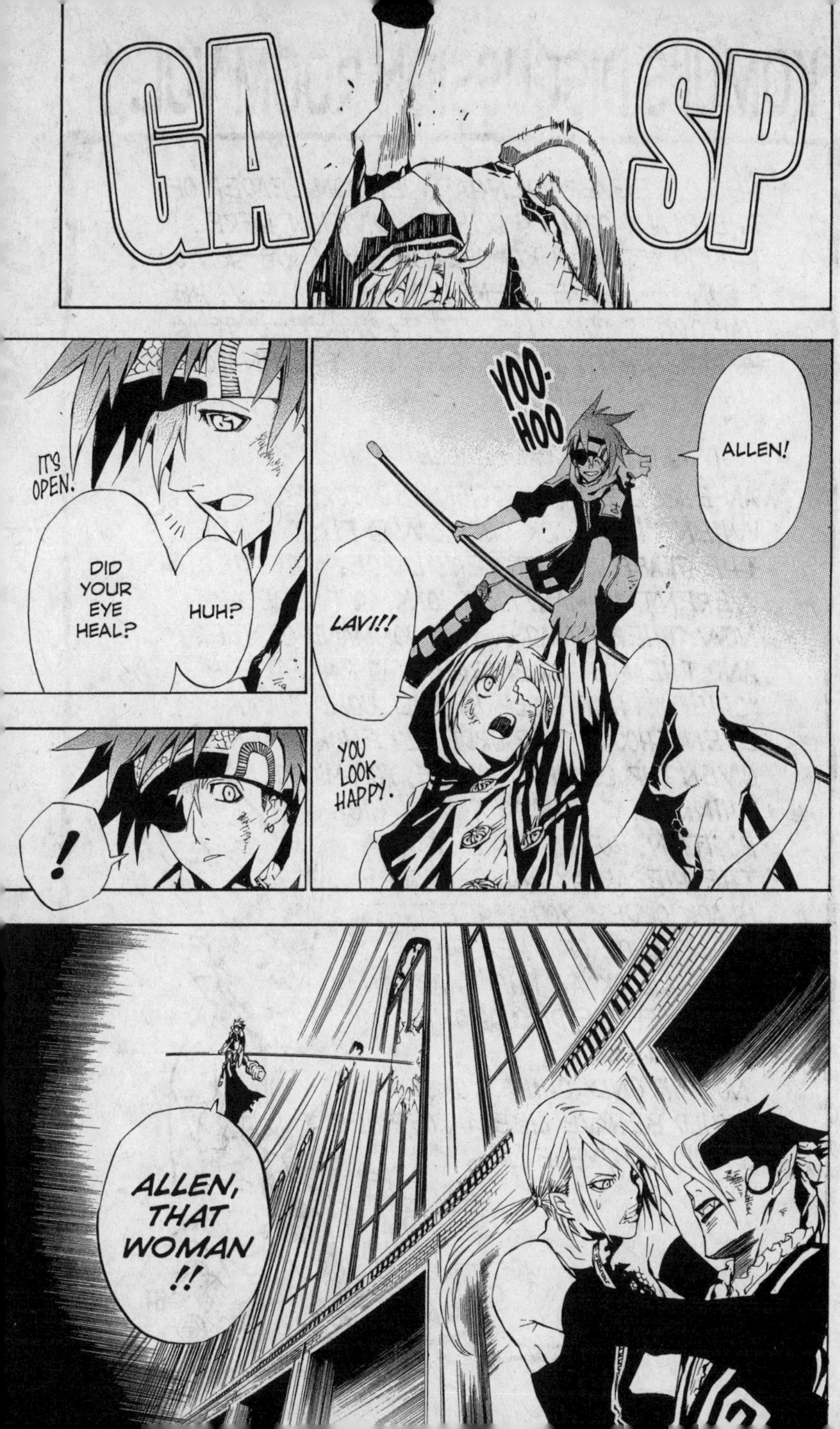
GASP
YOO-HOO
ALLEN!
LAVI!!
YOU LOOK HAPPY.
HUH?
DID YOUR EYE HEAL?
IT'S OPEN!
!
ALLEN, THAT WOMAN!!

KOMUI'S DISCUSSION ROOM VOL. 1

★ HELLO, REEVER WENHAM, SECTION LEADER OF THE BLACK ORDER'S SCIENCE DIVISION HERE. THIS IS ACTUALLY KOMUI'S JOB, ~~BUT THAT SON OF A GUN DUMPED IT ON ME!~~ UNFORTUNATELY, HE HAD OTHER COMMITMENTS, ~~THOUGH I'M JUST AS BUSY AS HE IS,~~ SO THE DUTY HAS FALLEN TO ME. SHALL WE BEGIN?

Q. WHY IS CHIEF KOMUI CALLED "CHIEF"?

A. AN EXCELLENT QUESTION. CENTURIES AGO, WHEN THE BLACK ORDER WAS FIRST FORMED, THE STAFF WASN'T VERY LARGE, AND THERE WEREN'T AS MANY SECTIONS AS THERE ARE NOW. THERE WAS JUST A COMMAND CENTER, AND THE MAN IN CHARGE WAS CALLED THE "CHIEF." THAT TITLE IS STILL USED TODAY, EVEN THOUGH THE ORDER IS ENORMOUS NOW. GIVEN OUR CURRENT CHIEF, YOU MIGHT NOT THINK THAT THIS IS A VERY HIGH POSITION, BUT IF YOU LOOK AT THE HIERARCHY CHART OF THE BLACK ORDER, YOU'LL SEE THE IMPORTANCE OF THE CHIEF.
HAVE A LOOK AT THE CHART IN VOL. 2 OF THE DISCUSSION ROOM!
(SEE PAGE 42!)
NOW IF ONLY CHIEF KOMUI WOULD BEHAVE LIKE AN OFFICER. (MUMBLE MUMBLE...)

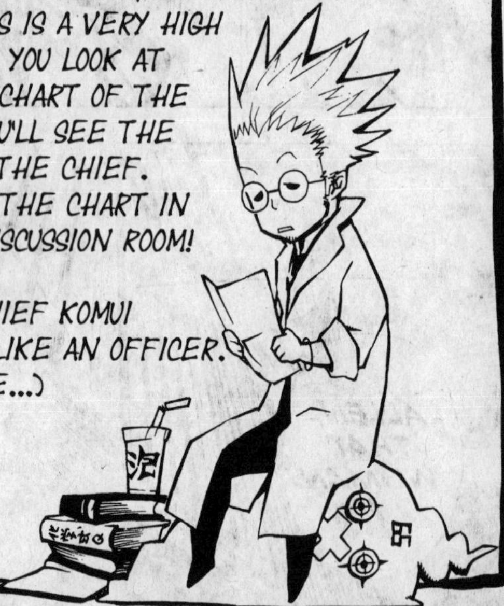

THE 38TH NIGHT: VAMPIRE OF THE CASTLE (PART 8)
BROKEN HEARTS, BROKEN ROSES

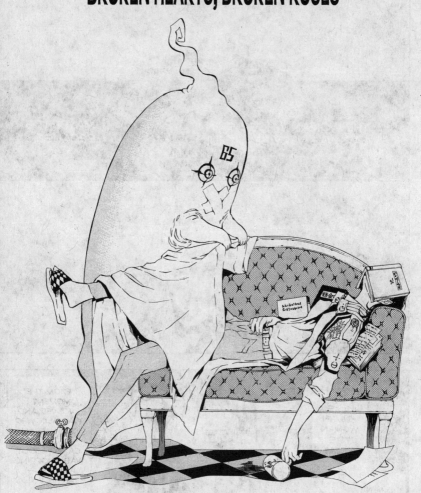

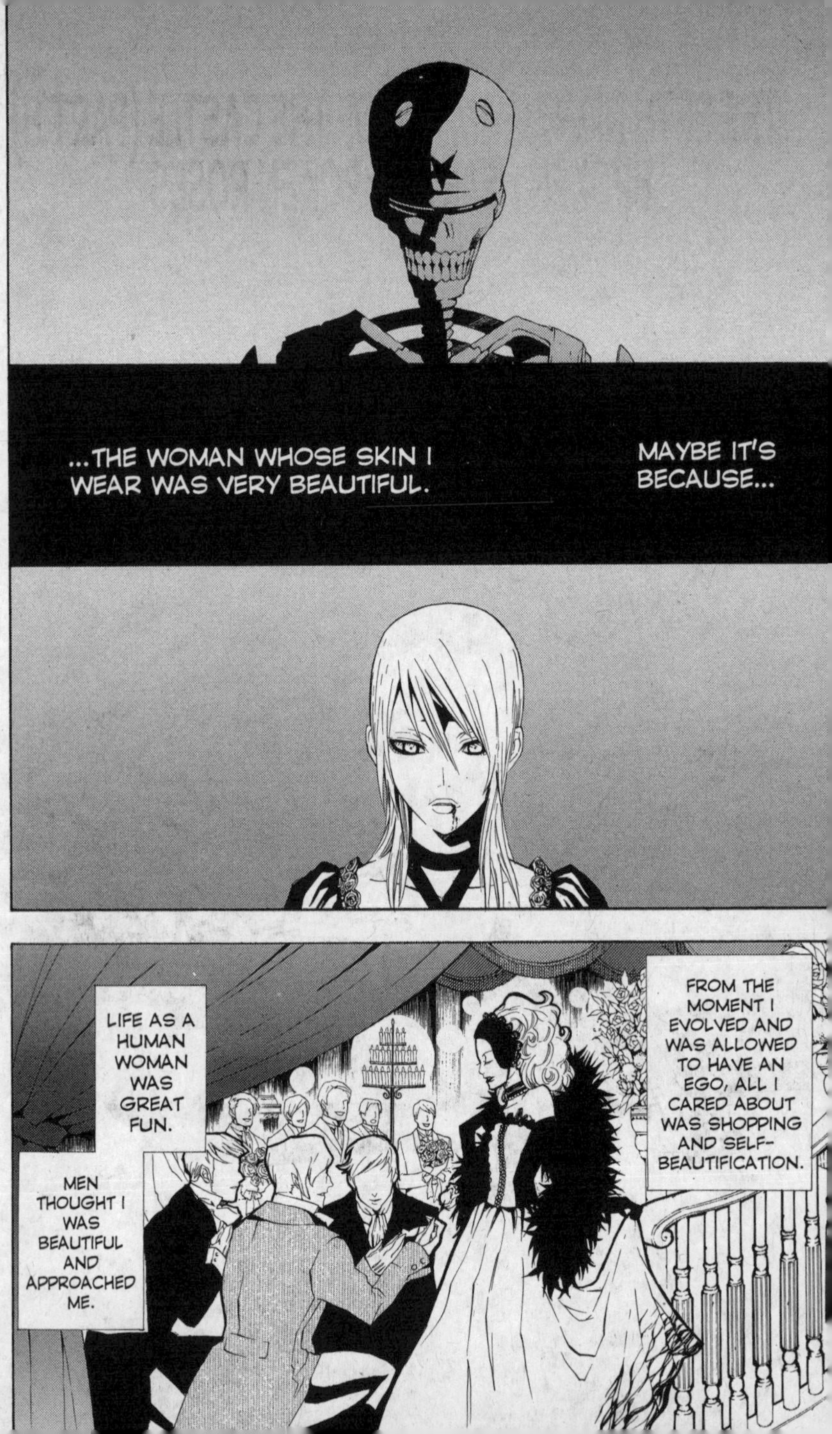
MAYBE IT'S BECAUSE...
...THE WOMAN WHOSE SKIN I WEAR WAS VERY BEAUTIFUL.
FROM THE MOMENT I EVOLVED AND WAS ALLOWED TO HAVE AN EGO, ALL I CARED ABOUT WAS SHOPPING AND SELF-BEAUTIFICATION.
LIFE AS A HUMAN WOMAN WAS GREAT FUN.
MEN THOUGHT I WAS BEAUTIFUL AND APPROACHED ME.

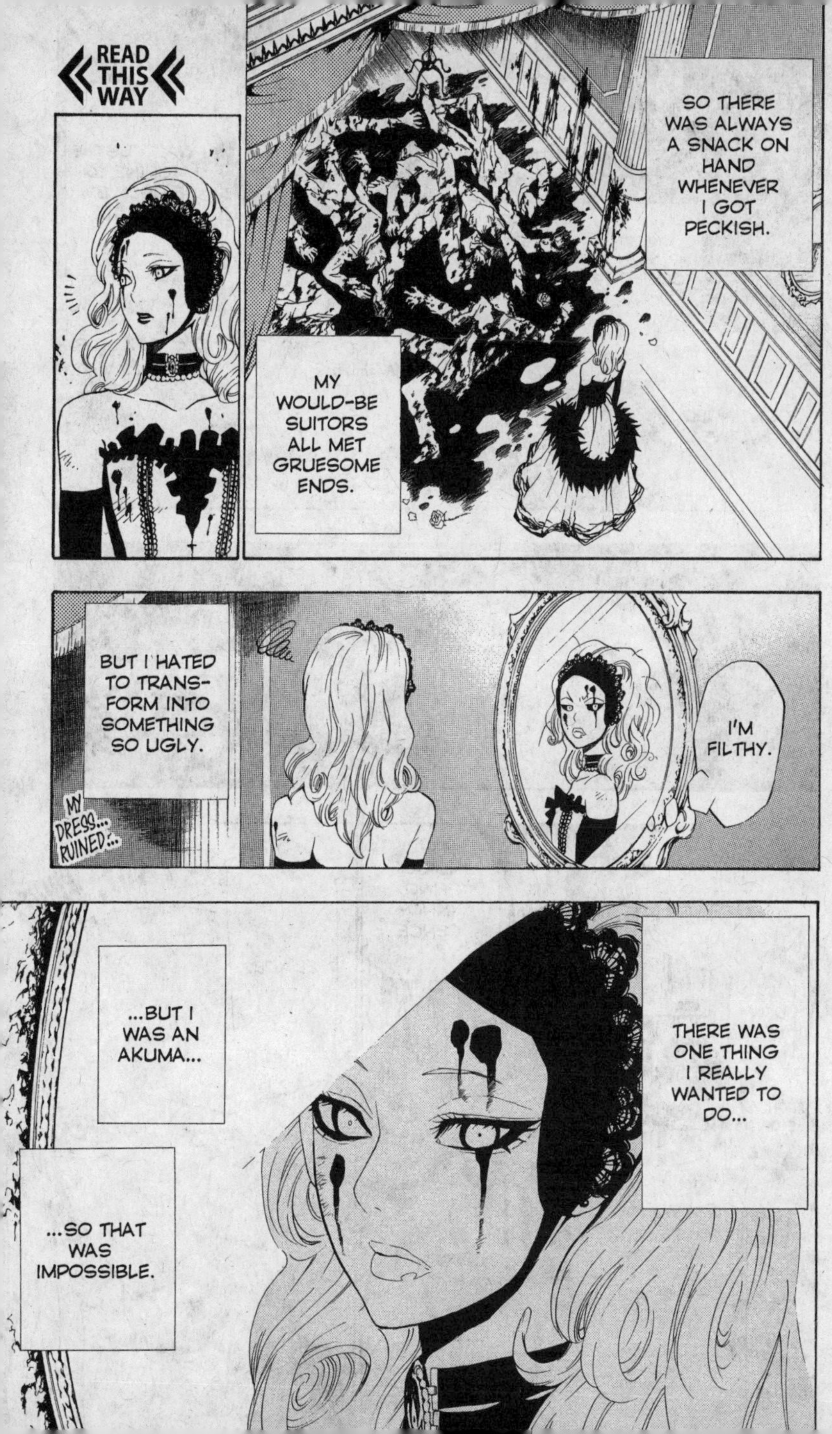
READ THIS WAY
SO THERE WAS ALWAYS A SNACK ON HAND WHENEVER I GOT PECKISH.
MY WOULD-BE SUITORS ALL MET GRUESOME ENDS.
I'M FILTHY.
BUT I HATED TO TRANS-FORM INTO SOMETHING SO UGLY.
MY DRESS... RUINED...
THERE WAS ONE THING I REALLY WANTED TO DO...
...BUT I WAS AN AKUMA...
...SO THAT WAS IMPOSSIBLE.

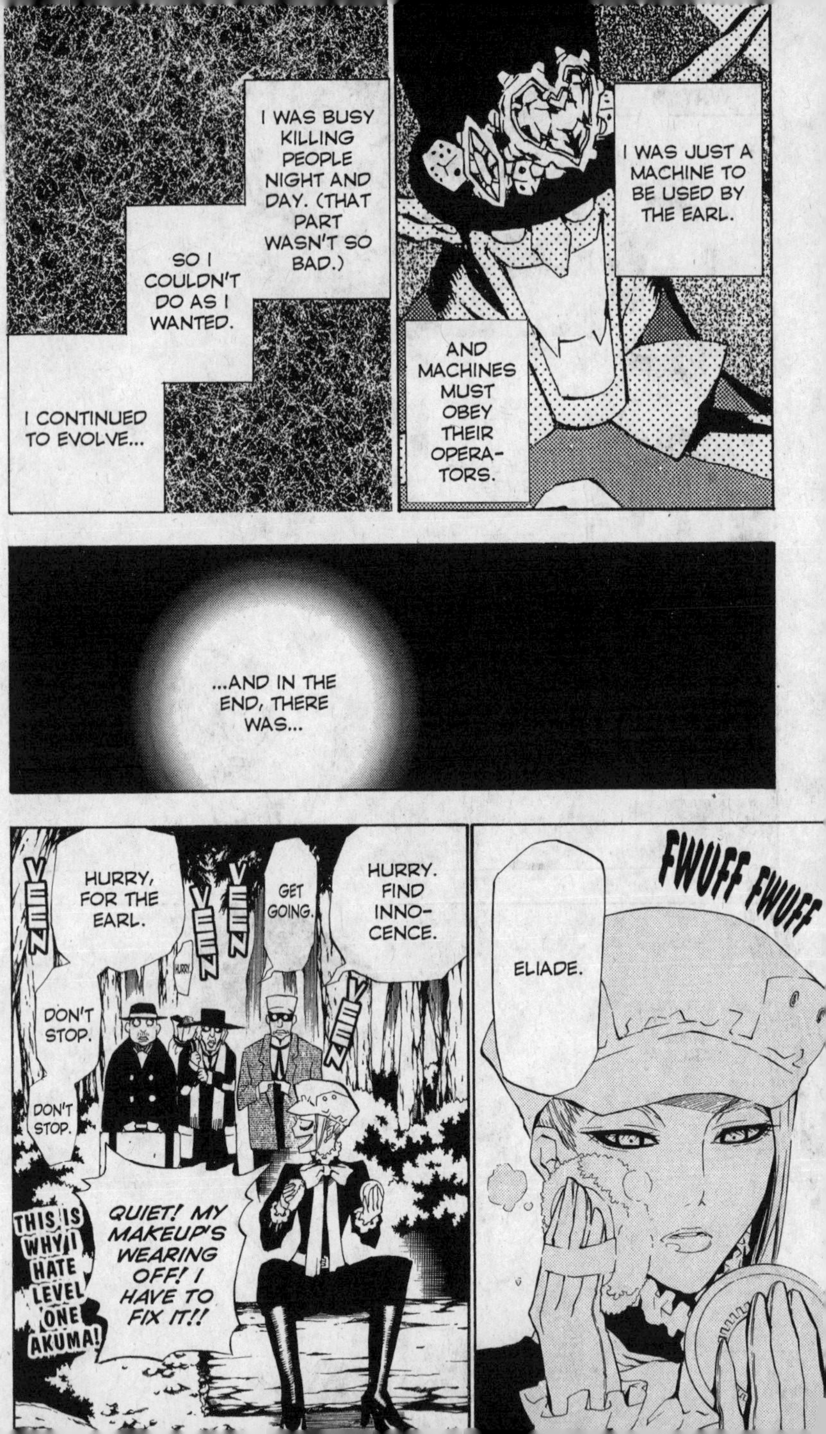
I WAS JUST A MACHINE TO BE USED BY THE EARL.
AND MACHINES MUST OBEY THEIR OPERA-TORS.
I WAS BUSY KILLING PEOPLE NIGHT AND DAY. (THAT PART WASN'T SO BAD.)
SO I COULDN'T DO AS I WANTED.
I CONTINUED TO EVOLVE...
...AND IN THE END, THERE WAS...
FWUFF FWUFF
ELIADE.
HURRY. FIND INNO-CENCE.
GET GOING.
VEEN
VEEN
VEEN
VEEN
HURRY, FOR THE EARL.
HURRY.
DON'T STOP.
DON'T STOP.
QUIET! MY MAKEUP'S WEARING OFF! I HAVE TO FIX IT!!
THIS IS WHY I HATE LEVEL ONE AKUMA!

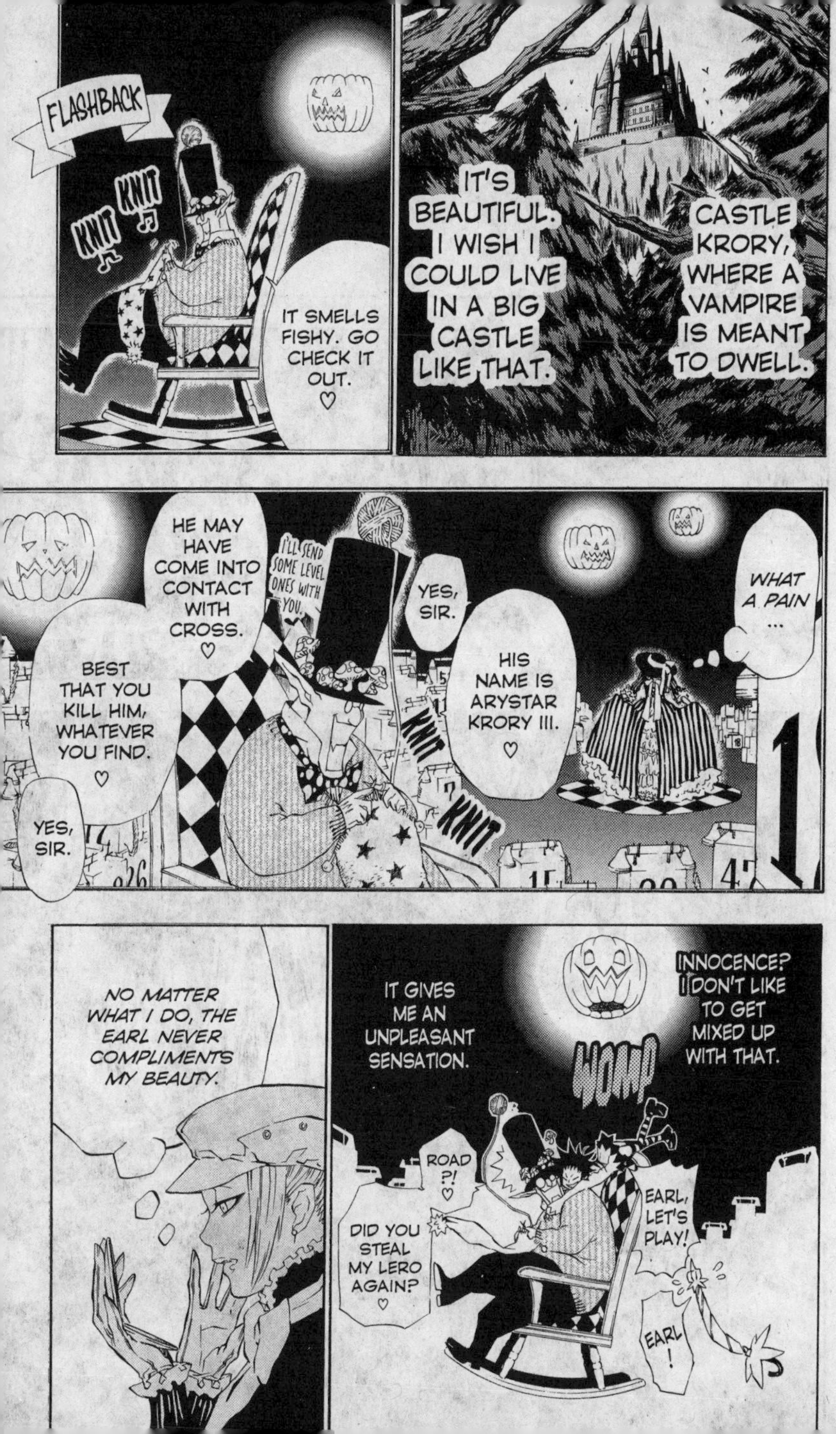
CASTLE KRORY, WHERE A VAMPIRE IS MEANT TO DWELL.
IT'S BEAUTIFUL. I WISH I COULD LIVE IN A BIG CASTLE LIKE THAT.
FLASHBACK
KNIT KNIT
IT SMELLS FISHY. GO CHECK IT OUT. ♡
WHAT A PAIN ...
HIS NAME IS ARYSTAR KRORY III. ♡
YES, SIR.
I'LL SEND SOME LEVEL ONES WITH YOU.
KNIT KNIT
HE MAY HAVE COME INTO CONTACT WITH CROSS. ♡
BEST THAT YOU KILL HIM, WHATEVER YOU FIND. ♡
YES, SIR.
INNOCENCE? I DON'T LIKE TO GET MIXED UP WITH THAT.
IT GIVES ME AN UNPLEASANT SENSATION.
WOMP
EARL, LET'S PLAY!
ROAD?! ♡
DID YOU STEAL MY LERO AGAIN? ♡
EARL!
NO MATTER WHAT I DO, THE EARL NEVER COMPLIMENTS MY BEAUTY.

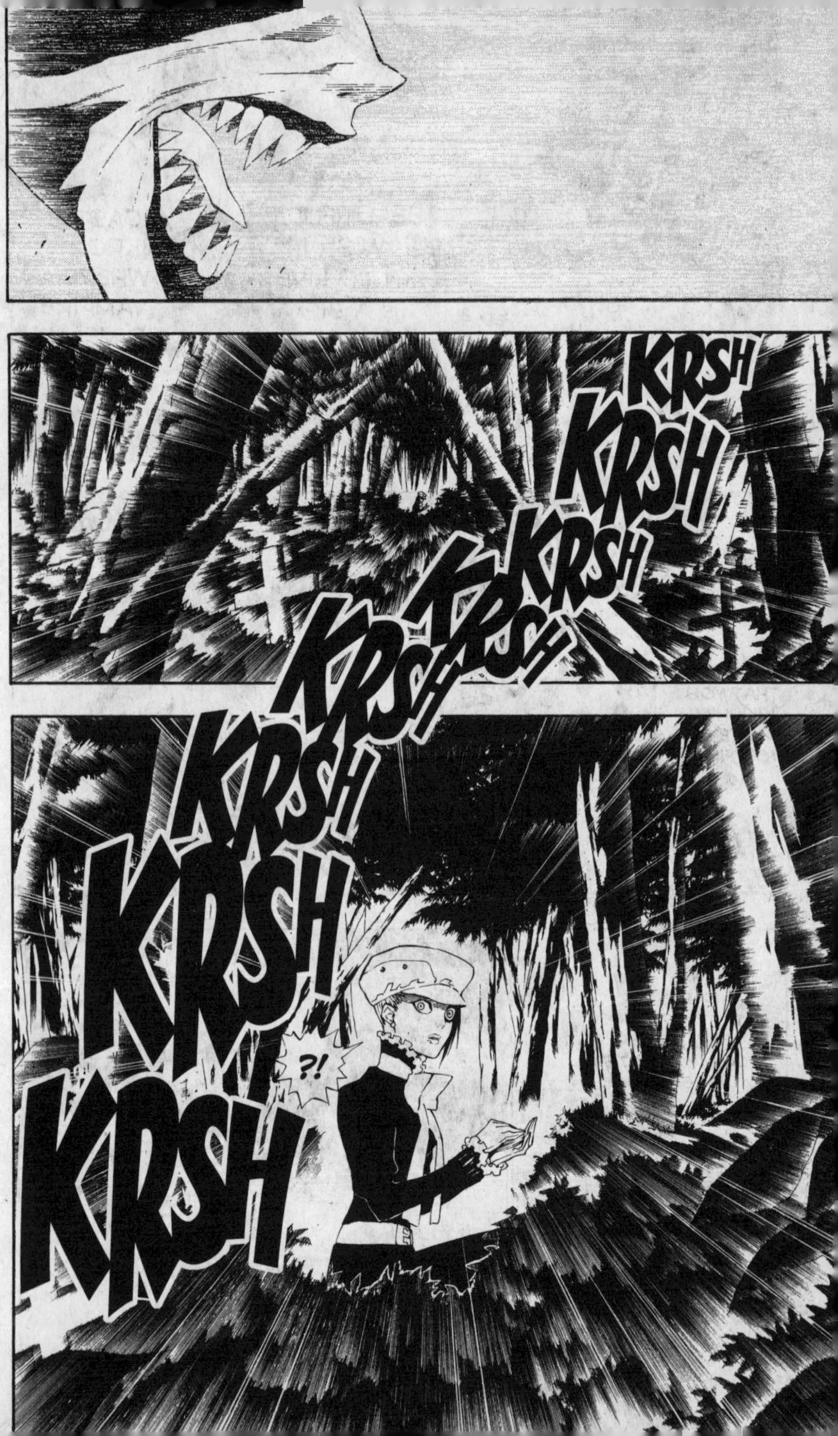

KRSH
KRSH
KRSH
KRSH
KRSH
KRSH
KRSH!
KRSH
?!

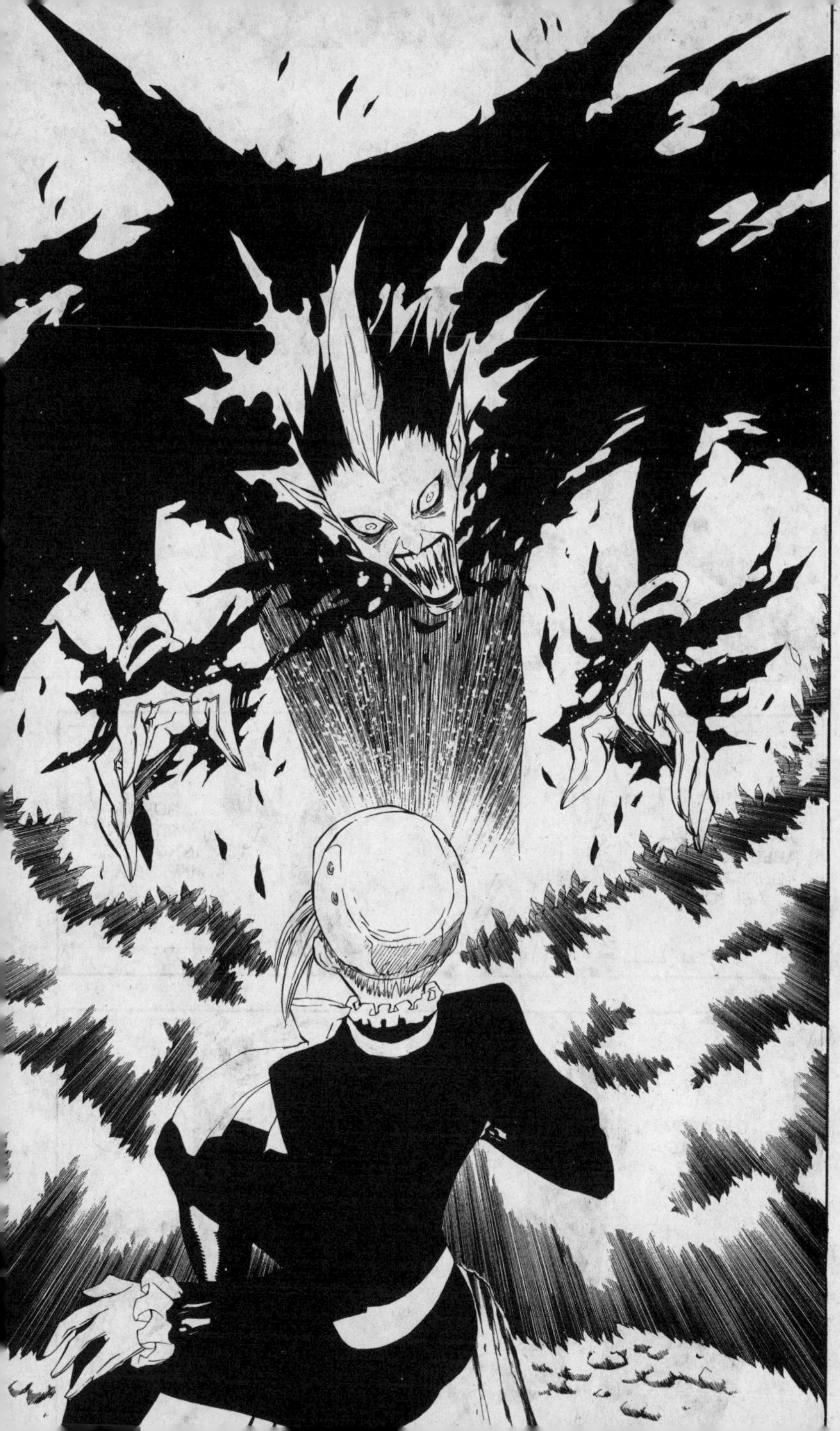

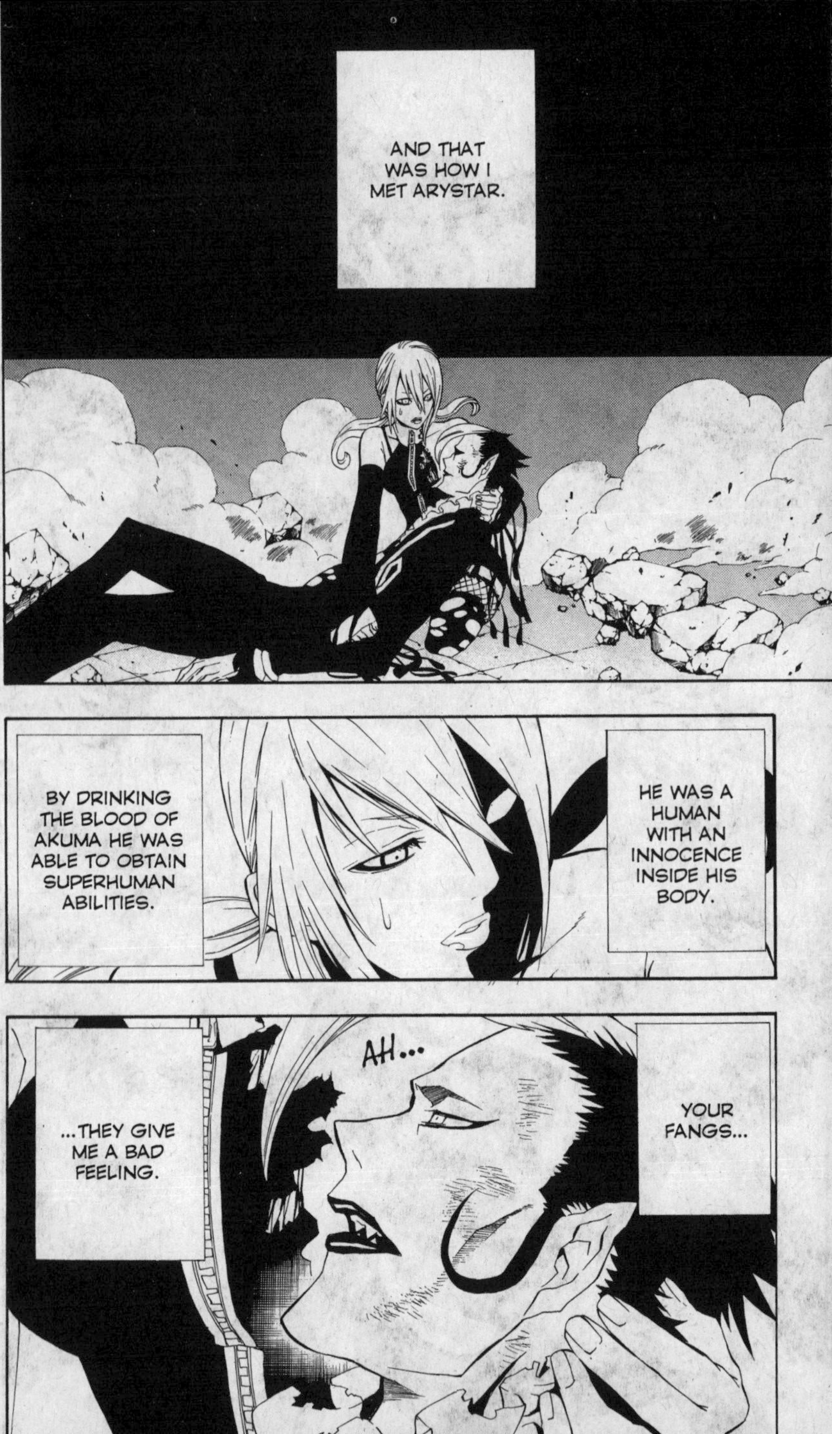
AND THAT WAS HOW I MET ARYSTAR.
HE WAS A HUMAN WITH AN INNOCENCE INSIDE HIS BODY.
BY DRINKING THE BLOOD OF AKUMA HE WAS ABLE TO OBTAIN SUPERHUMAN ABILITIES.
YOUR FANGS...
AH...
...THEY GIVE ME A BAD FEELING.

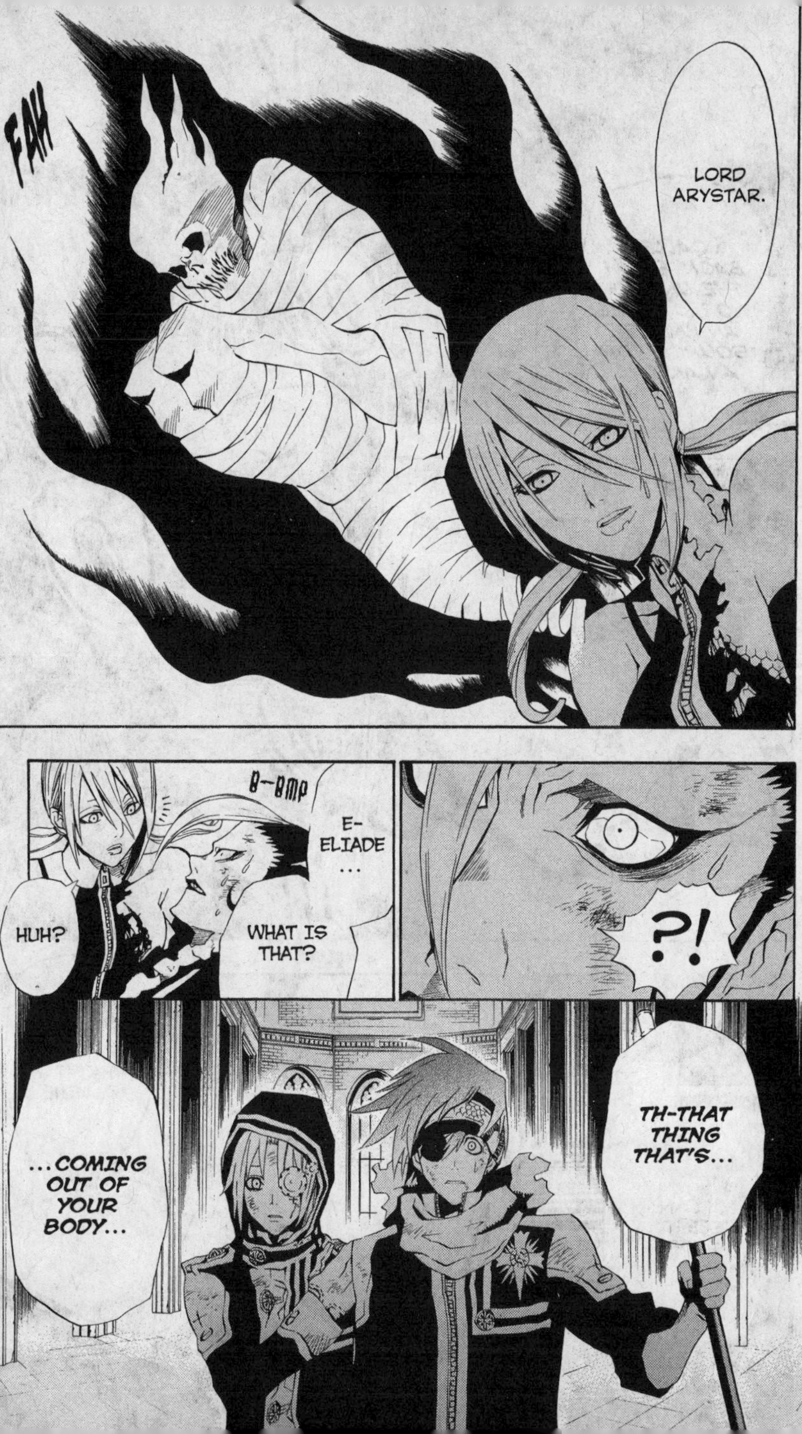
FAH
LORD ARYSTAR.
?!
B-BMP
E-ELIADE...
WHAT IS THAT?
HUH?
TH-THAT THING THAT'S...
...COMING OUT OF YOUR BODY...

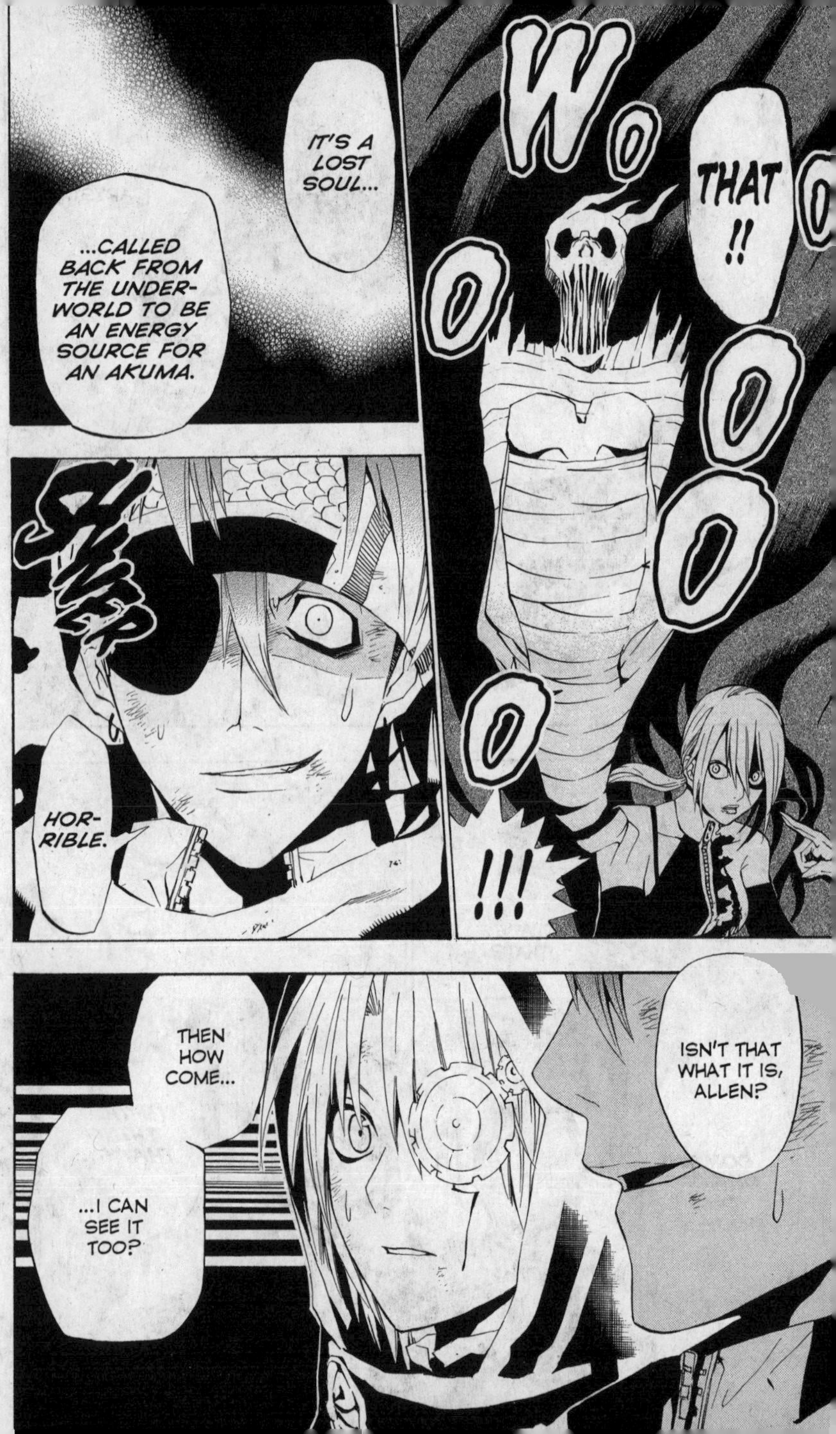
WOOOOOO
THAT!!
!!!
IT'S A LOST SOUL...
...CALLED BACK FROM THE UNDER-WORLD TO BE AN ENERGY SOURCE FOR AN AKUMA.
SHIVER
HOR-RIBLE.
ISN'T THAT WHAT IT IS, ALLEN?
THEN HOW COME...
...I CAN SEE IT TOO?

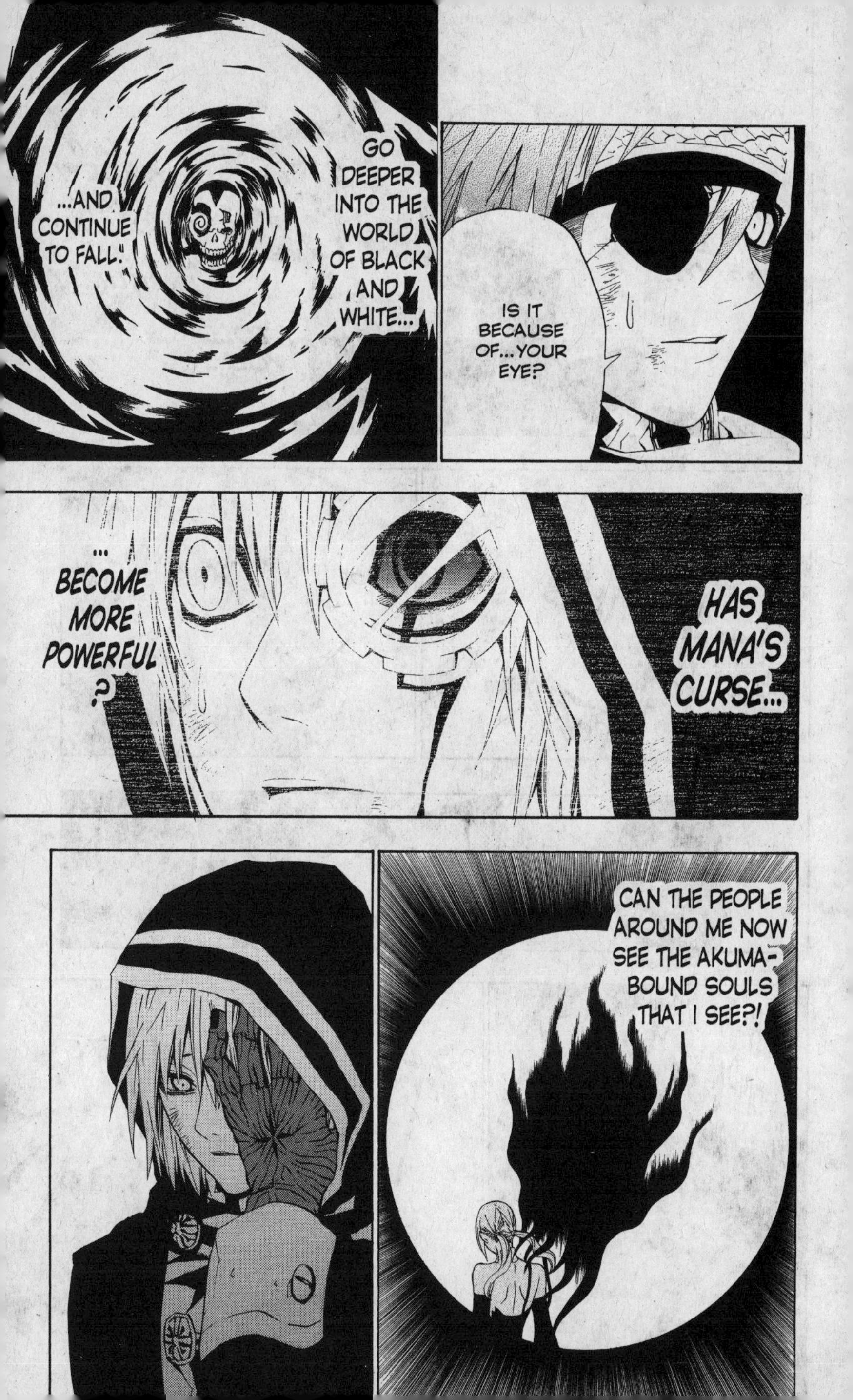
IS IT BECAUSE OF...YOUR EYE?
GO DEEPER INTO THE WORLD OF BLACK AND WHITE...
...AND CONTINUE TO FALL.
HAS MANA'S CURSE...
...BECOME MORE POWERFUL?
CAN THE PEOPLE AROUND ME NOW SEE THE AKUMA-BOUND SOULS THAT I SEE?!

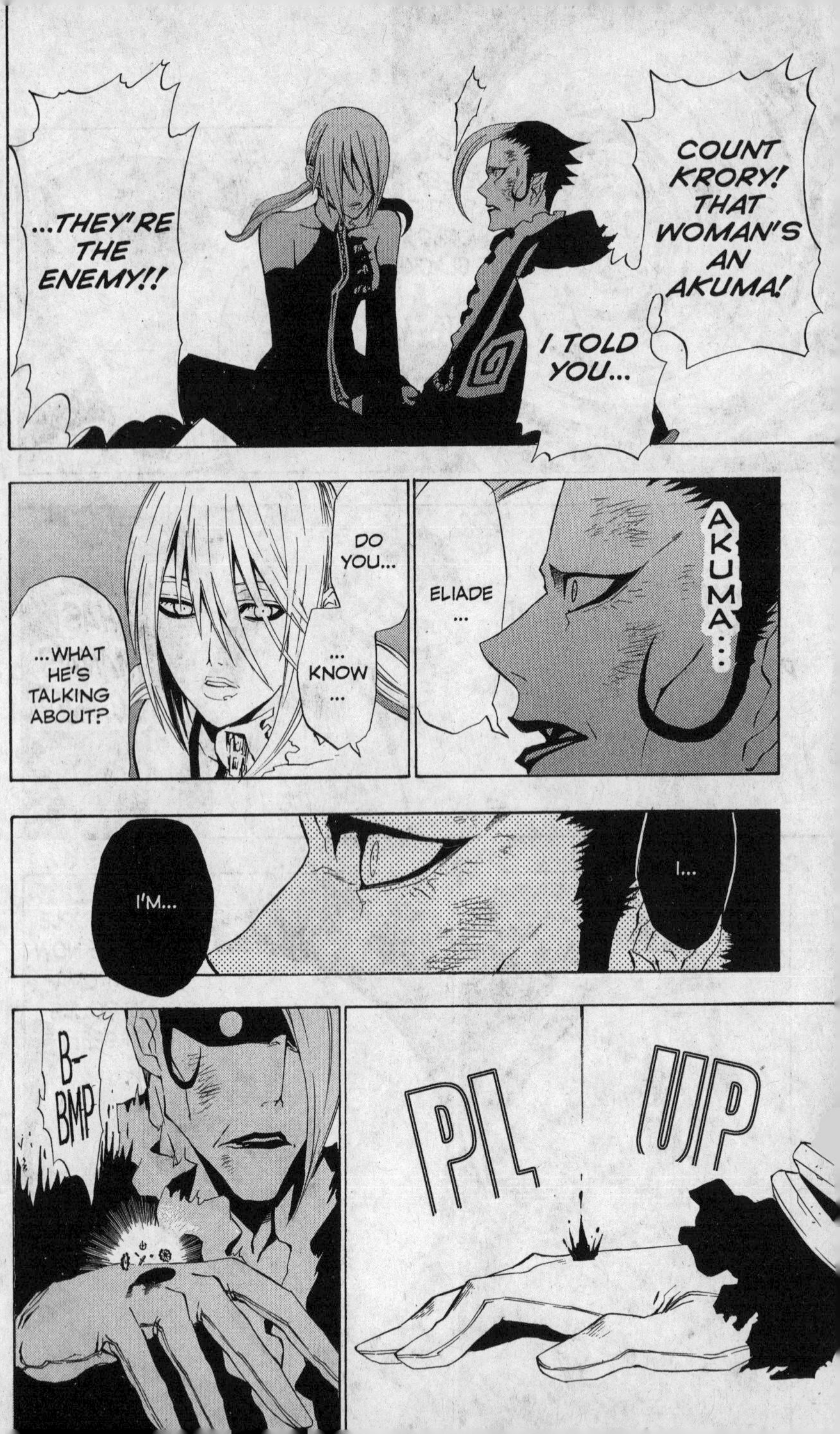
COUNT KRORY! THAT WOMAN'S AN AKUMA!
I TOLD YOU...
...THEY'RE THE ENEMY!!
AKUMA...
ELIADE ...
DO YOU...
... KNOW ...
...WHAT HE'S TALKING ABOUT?
I...
I'M...
PLUP
B-BMP

READ THIS WAY

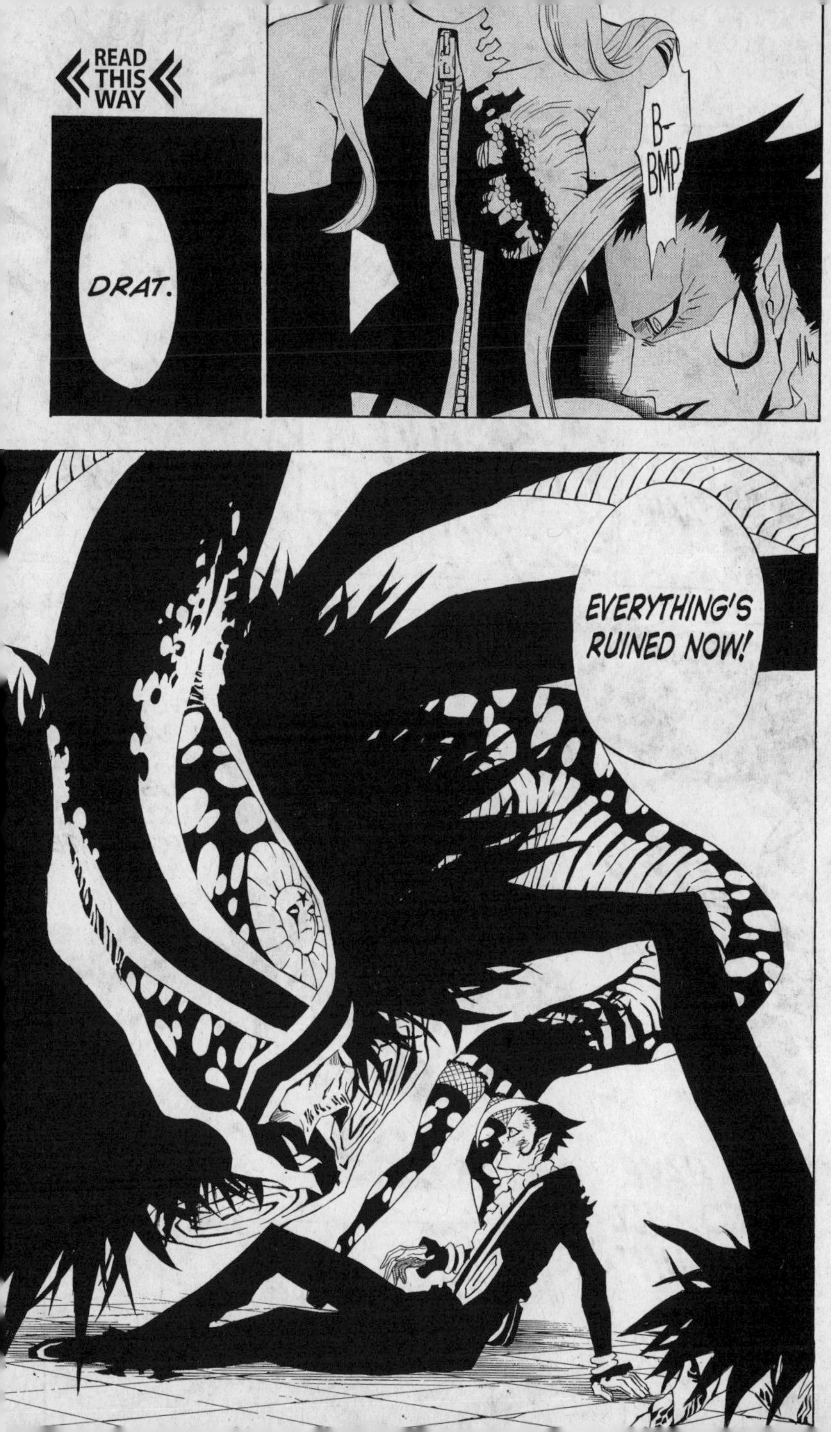
B-BMP
DRAT.
EVERYTHING'S RUINED NOW!

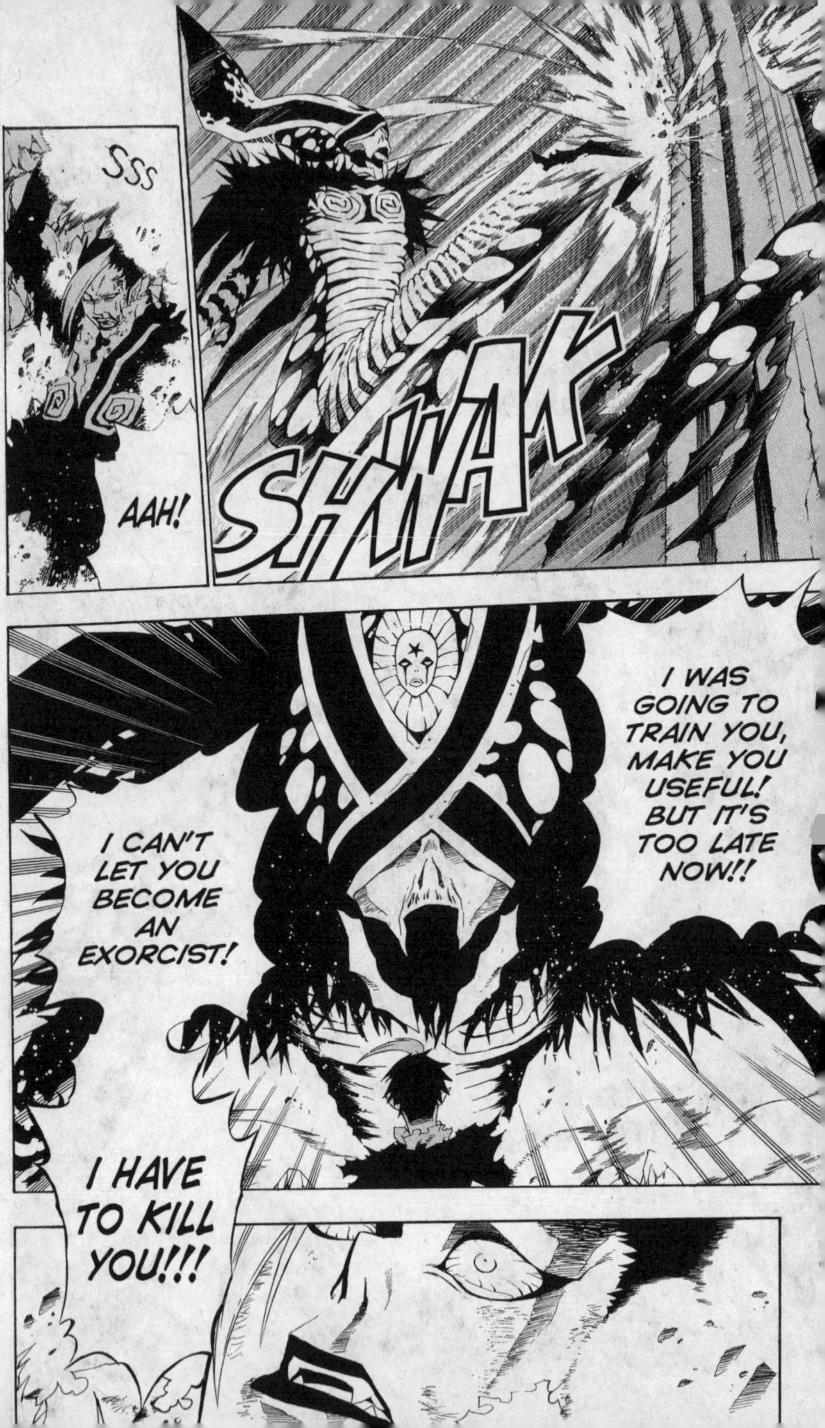
SHWAK
SSS
AAH!
I WAS GOING TO TRAIN YOU, MAKE YOU USEFUL! BUT IT'S TOO LATE NOW!!
I CAN'T LET YOU BECOME AN EXORCIST!
I HAVE TO KILL YOU!!!

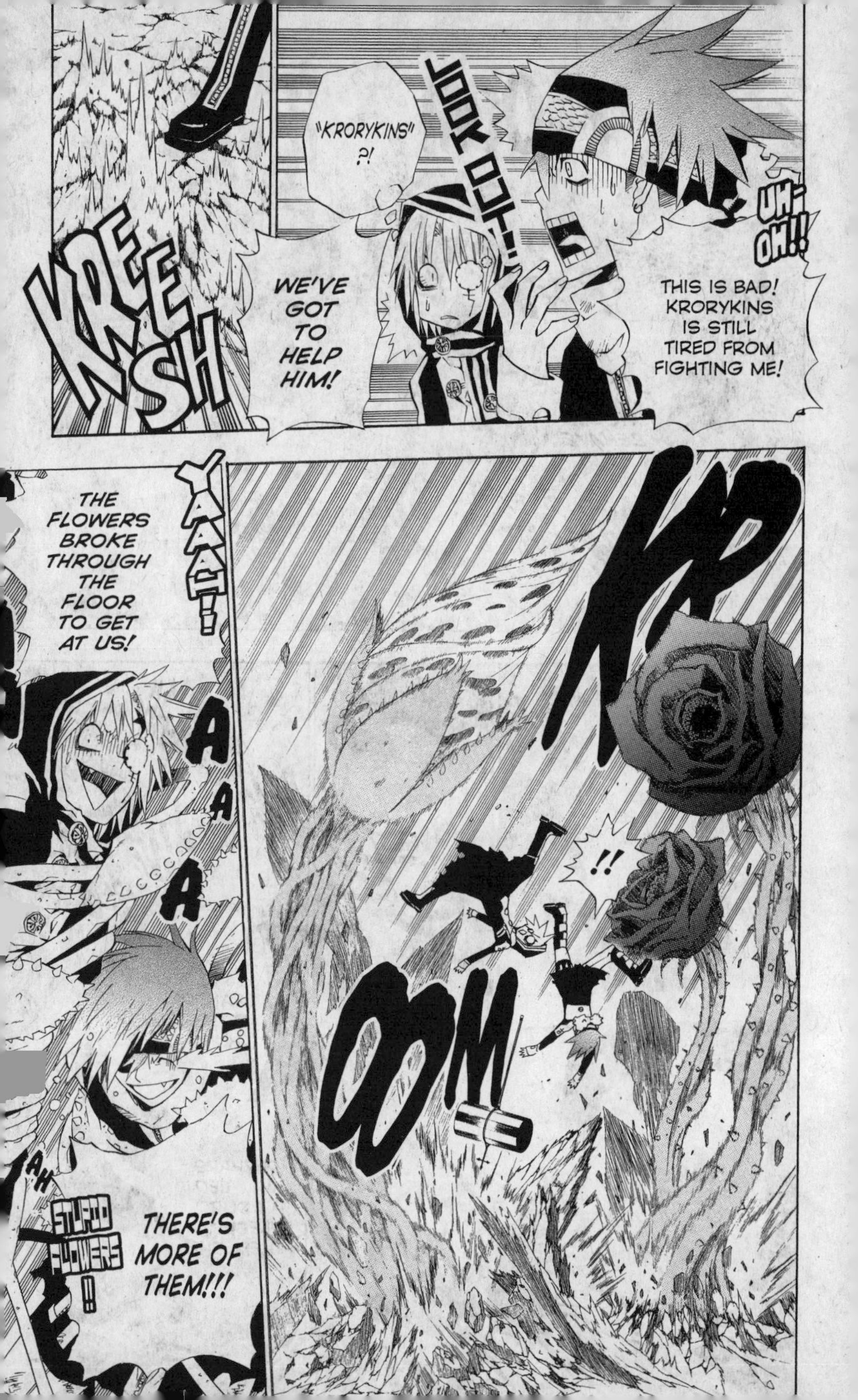
UH-OH!!
THIS IS BAD! KRORYKINS IS STILL TIRED FROM FIGHTING ME!
LOOK OUT!!
"KRORYKINS" ?!
WE'VE GOT TO HELP HIM!
KREESH
KR
!!
OOM
YAAAAAAH!
THE FLOWERS BROKE THROUGH THE FLOOR TO GET AT US!
AH
STUPID FLOWERS!!
THERE'S MORE OF THEM!!!

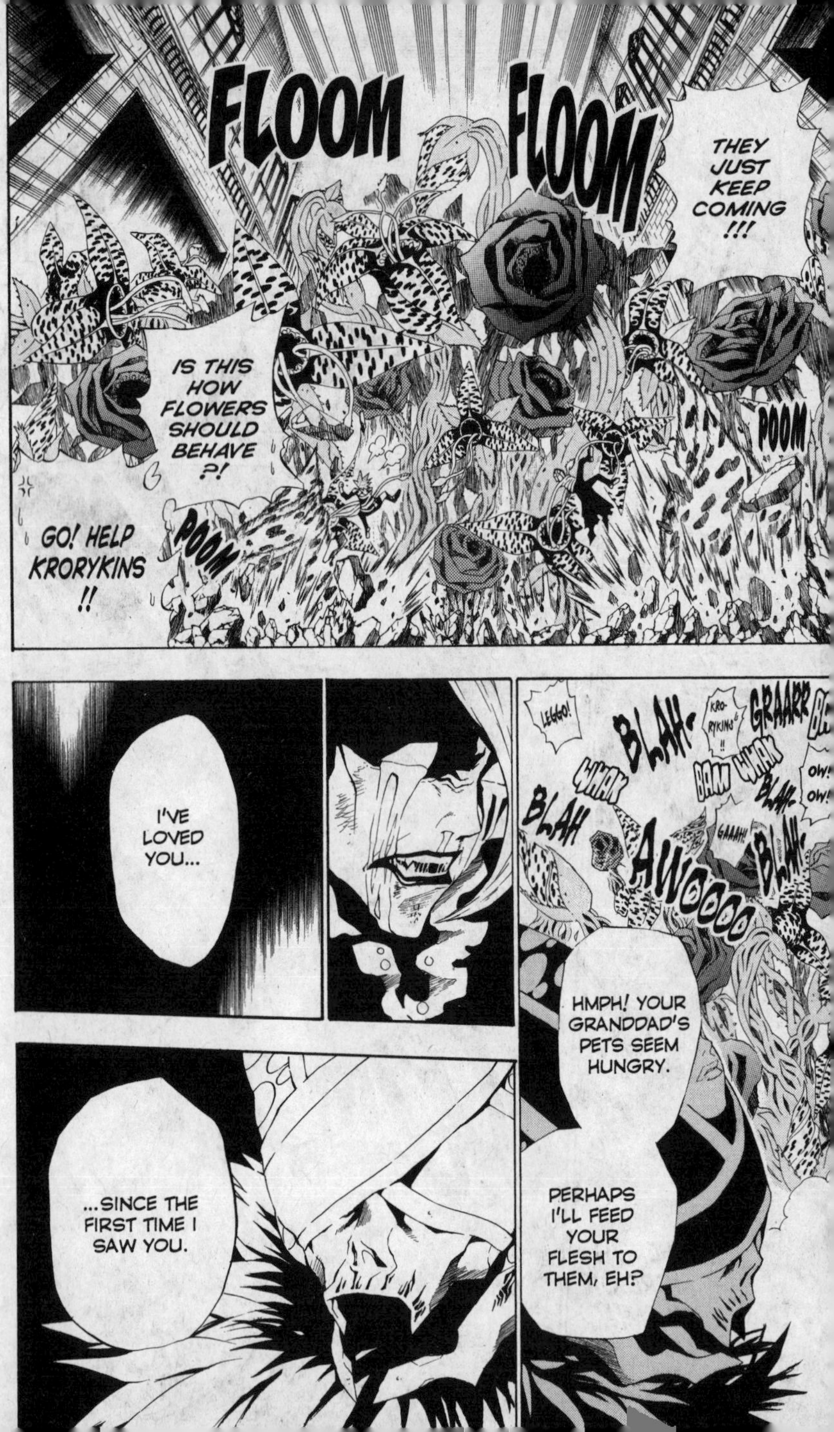
FLOOM
FLOOM
THEY JUST KEEP COMING!!!
POOM
IS THIS HOW FLOWERS SHOULD BEHAVE?!
POOM
GO! HELP KRORYKINS!!
GRAARR
KRORYKINS!!
BLAH
LEGGO!
OW! OW!
WHAK
BAM
BLAH
WHAK
BLAH
GAAAH!
AWOOOO
BLAH
HMPH! YOUR GRANDDAD'S PETS SEEM HUNGRY.
PERHAPS I'LL FEED YOUR FLESH TO THEM, EH?
I'VE LOVED YOU...
...SINCE THE FIRST TIME I SAW YOU.

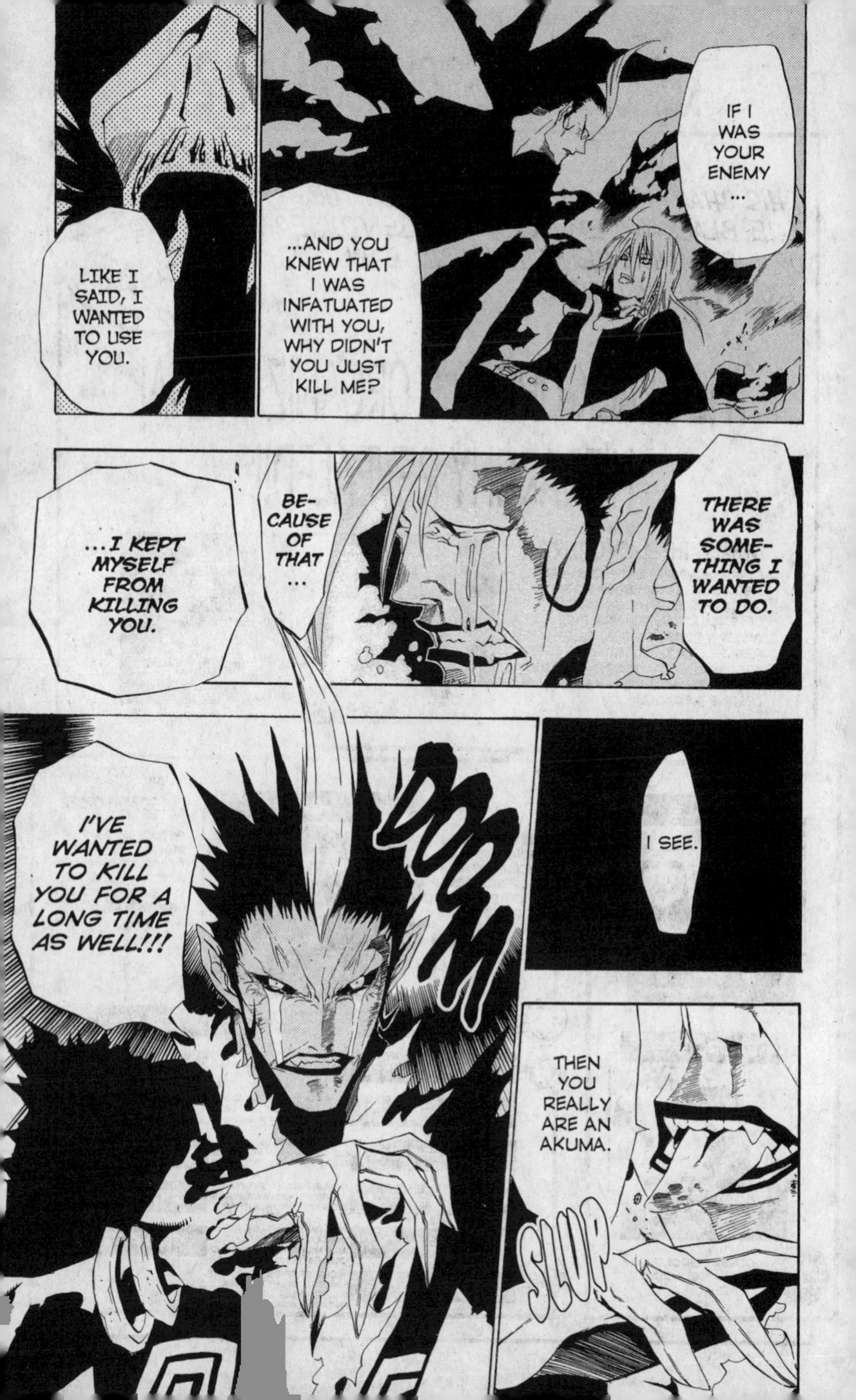
IF I WAS YOUR ENEMY ...
...AND YOU KNEW THAT I WAS INFATUATED WITH YOU, WHY DIDN'T YOU JUST KILL ME?
LIKE I SAID, I WANTED TO USE YOU.
THERE WAS SOMETHING I WANTED TO DO.
BE-CAUSE OF THAT ...
...I KEPT MYSELF FROM KILLING YOU.
I SEE.
THEN YOU REALLY ARE AN AKUMA.
SLUP
I'VE WANTED TO KILL YOU FOR A LONG TIME AS WELL!!!
DOOM

KOMUI'S DISCUSSION ROOM VOL. 2

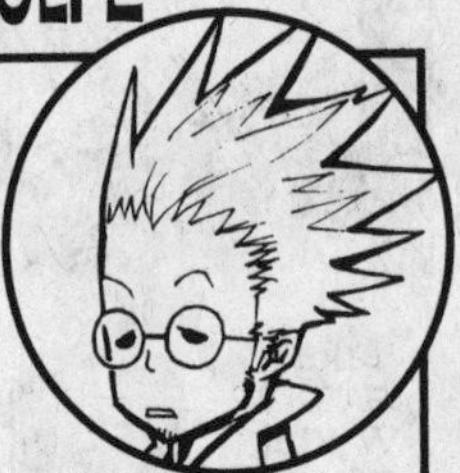

THIS CHART SHOWS THE HIERARCHY OF THE BLACK ORDER. OVER THE CENTURIES OF FIGHTING THE MILLENNIUM EARL, IT'S GROWN VERY LARGE.

THE BLACK ORDER'S ORGANIZATIONAL HIERARCHY REVEALED!!

WHAT IS THE BLACK ORDER?!

CENTURIES AGO, WHEN THE CUBE WAS DISCOVERED IN NORTHERN EUROPE, THE VATICAN FORMED AN ORGANIZATION OF PEOPLE ATTUNED TO INNOCENCE CALLED "ACCOMMODATORS." THESE PEOPLE SCOUR THE WORLD FOR INNOCENCE. WITHIN THE ORGANIZATION ARE AGENTS OF THE VATICAN SENT TO OBSERVE THE ORDER.

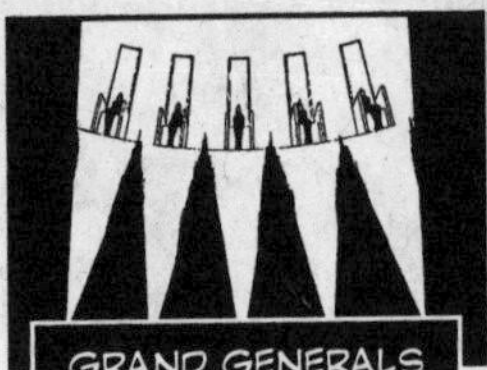

GRAND GENERALS

THEY GIVE THE ORDERS TO THE GENERALS AND OTHER OFFICERS. RUMOR HAS IT THEY HAVE LINKS TO THE VATICAN.

ACTIVE SERVICES

GENERALS

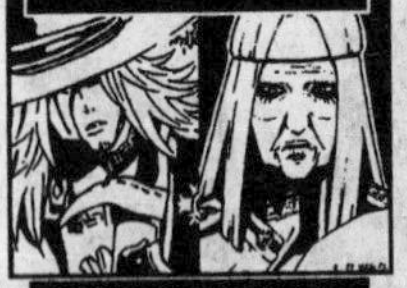

GENERALS RANK HIGHER THAN STANDARD EXORCISTS AND OFTEN GO ON SOLO MISSIONS.

EXORCISTS

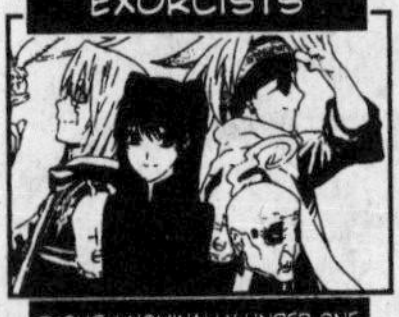

THOUGH NOMINALLY UNDER ONE OF THE GENERALS, DAY-TO-DAY ORDERS COME FROM KOMUI!

SECRET: A COVERT GROUP MAY EXIST IN THE ACTIVE SERVICES...

SUPPORT SERVICES

CHIEF

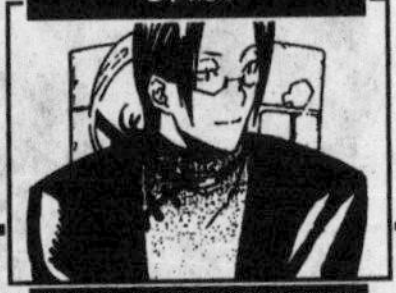

HE IS THE CHIEF OFFICER AND BRAINS OF THE ORDER, AND DIRECTS THE EXORCISTS.

WITHIN THE ORDER

THERE ARE SEVEN DEPARTMENTS WITHIN THE ORDER, EACH LED BY A SECTION CHIEF. MAIN DUTIES ARE OVERSEEING EUROPE AND COORDINATING THE VARIOUS WORLDWIDE BRANCHES.

Section	Duties
SCIENCE SECTION	RESPONSIBLE FOR R&D OF THE INNOCENCE, AND DESIGNING ORDER UNIFORMS.
INTELLIGENCE SECTION	IN CHARGE OF THE FINDERS, WHO GATHER INFORMATION FROM AROUND THE WORLD.
MEDICAL SECTION	RESPONSIBLE FOR THE GENERAL HEALTH AND WELFARE OF BLACK ORDER PERSONNEL
SIGNAL SECTIONS	IN CHARGE OF ALL COMMUNICATIONS BETWEEN EXORCISTS, FINDERS, AND THE ORDER.
SECURITY SECTION	THEY GUARD ALL ENTRY POINTS (GATES, WATERWAYS, ETC.) INTO THE FACILITY.
DIPLOMATIC SECTION	THEY HANDLE AFFAIRS WITH VARIOUS COUNTRIES AND ARRANGE FOR SUPPORT AND COOPERATION.
LOGISTICS SECTIONS	IN CHARGE OF THE DAY-TO-DAY FUNCTIONING OF THE ORDER, INCLUDING MEALS, CLEANING, AND ACCOUNTING.

OUTSIDE THE ORDER

THE BLACK ORDER HAS BRANCHES THROUGHOUT THE WORLD TO SUPPORT THE EXORCISTS WHEREVER THEY MAY GO. EACH BRANCH IS OVERSEEN BY A BRANCH CHIEF.

- ASIA BRANCH
- MIDDLE EAST BRANCH
- AFRICA BRANCH
- NORTH AMERICA BRANCH
- SOUTH AMERICA BRANCH
- OCEANIA BRANCH

THE 39TH NIGHT: VAMPIRE OF THE CASTLE (PART 9) AFFECTION

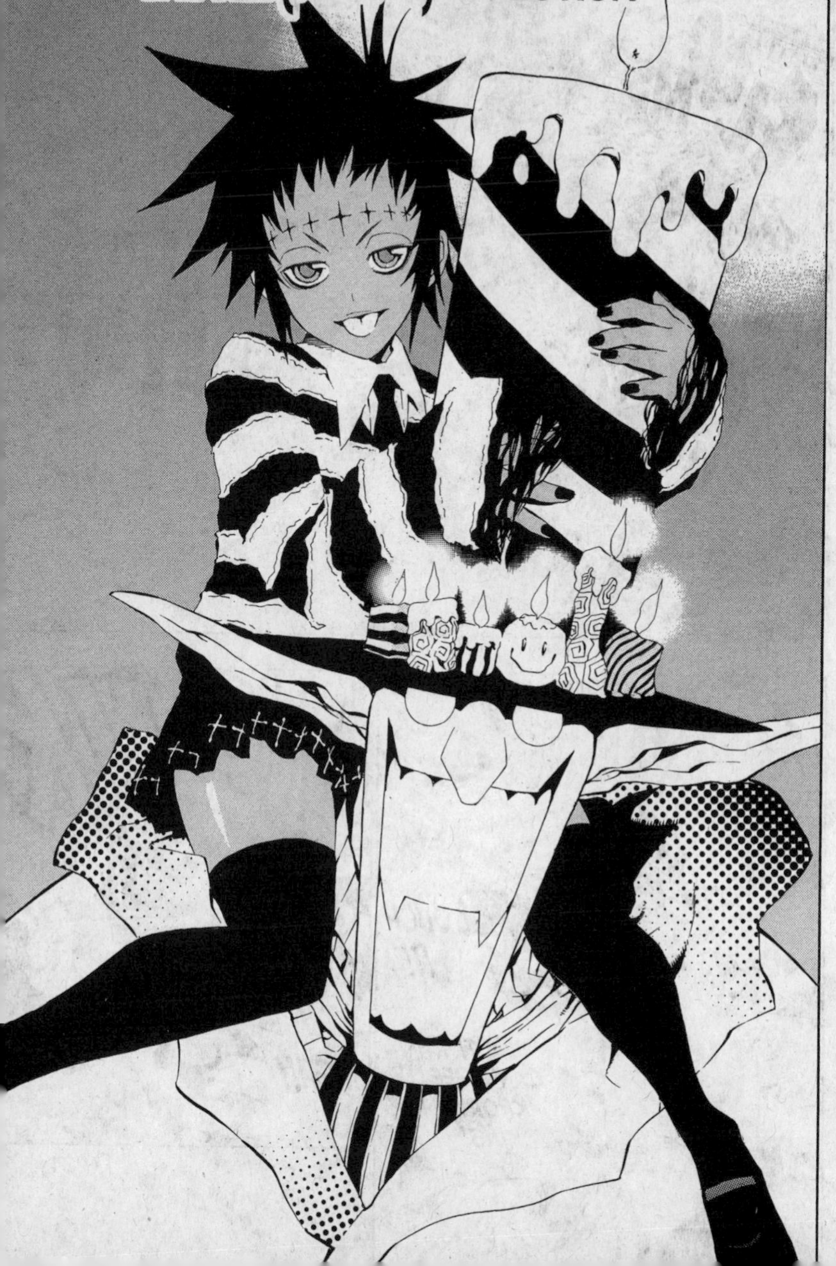

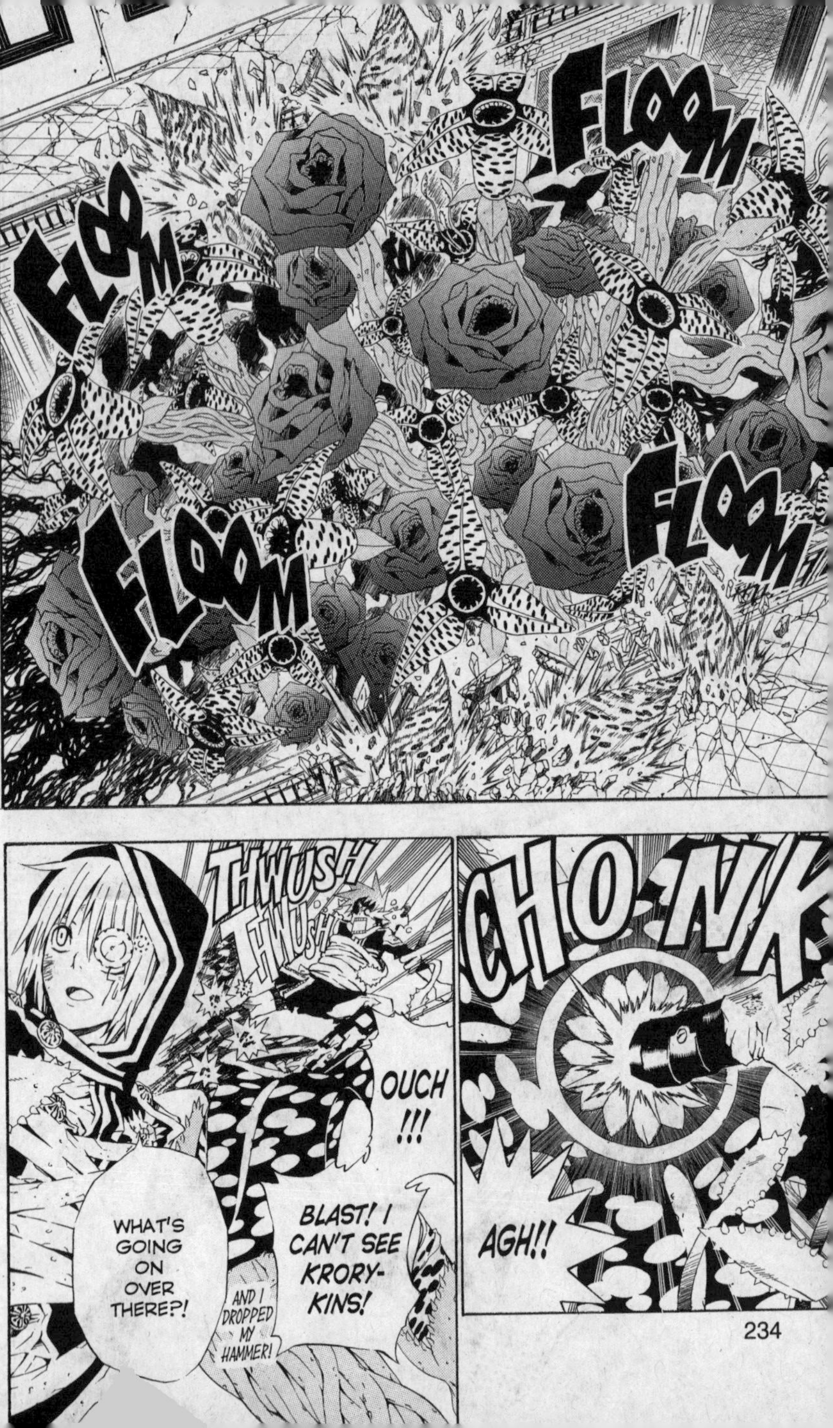
FLOOM
FLOOM
FLOOM
FLOOM
CHONK
AGH!!
THWUSH
THWUSH
OUCH!!!
BLAST! I CAN'T SEE KRORY-KINS!
AND I DROPPED MY HAMMER!
WHAT'S GOING ON OVER THERE?!

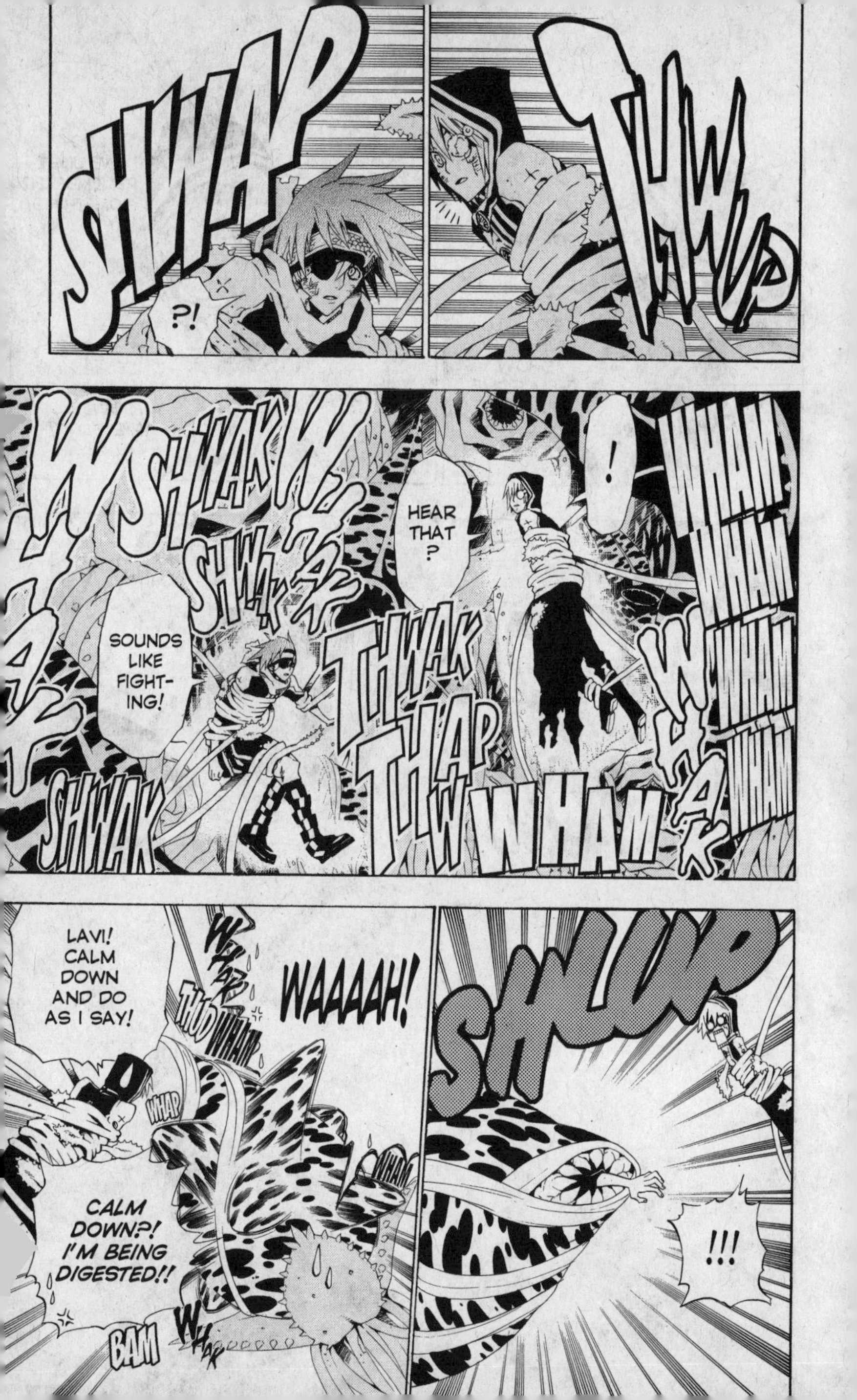
THWUP
SHWAP
?!
WHAM
WHAM
WHAM
WHAM
WHAM
!
HEAR THAT?
WHAK
THWAK
THAP
WHAM
SHWAK
SHWAK
SOUNDS LIKE FIGHT-ING!
SHWAK
SHLUP
!!!
WAAAAH!
LAVI! CALM DOWN AND DO AS I SAY!
THUD
WHAM
WHAP
WHAM
CALM DOWN?! I'M BEING DIGESTED!!
BAM
WHAK

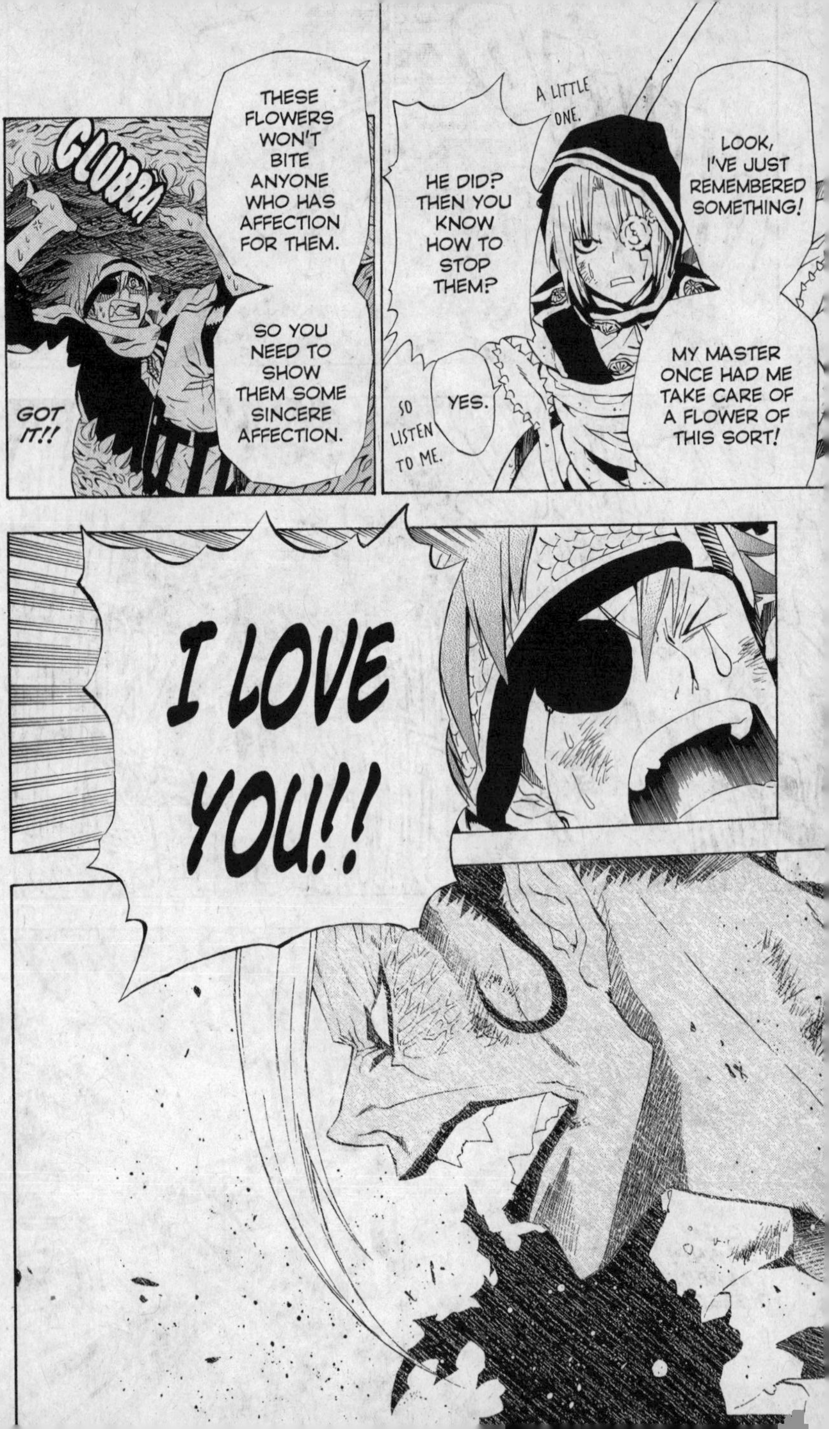
LOOK, I'VE JUST REMEMBERED SOMETHING!
MY MASTER ONCE HAD ME TAKE CARE OF A FLOWER OF THIS SORT!
A LITTLE ONE.
HE DID? THEN YOU KNOW HOW TO STOP THEM?
YES.
SO LISTEN TO ME.
GLUBBA
THESE FLOWERS WON'T BITE ANYONE WHO HAS AFFECTION FOR THEM.
SO YOU NEED TO SHOW THEM SOME SINCERE AFFECTION.
GOT IT!!
I LOVE YOU!!

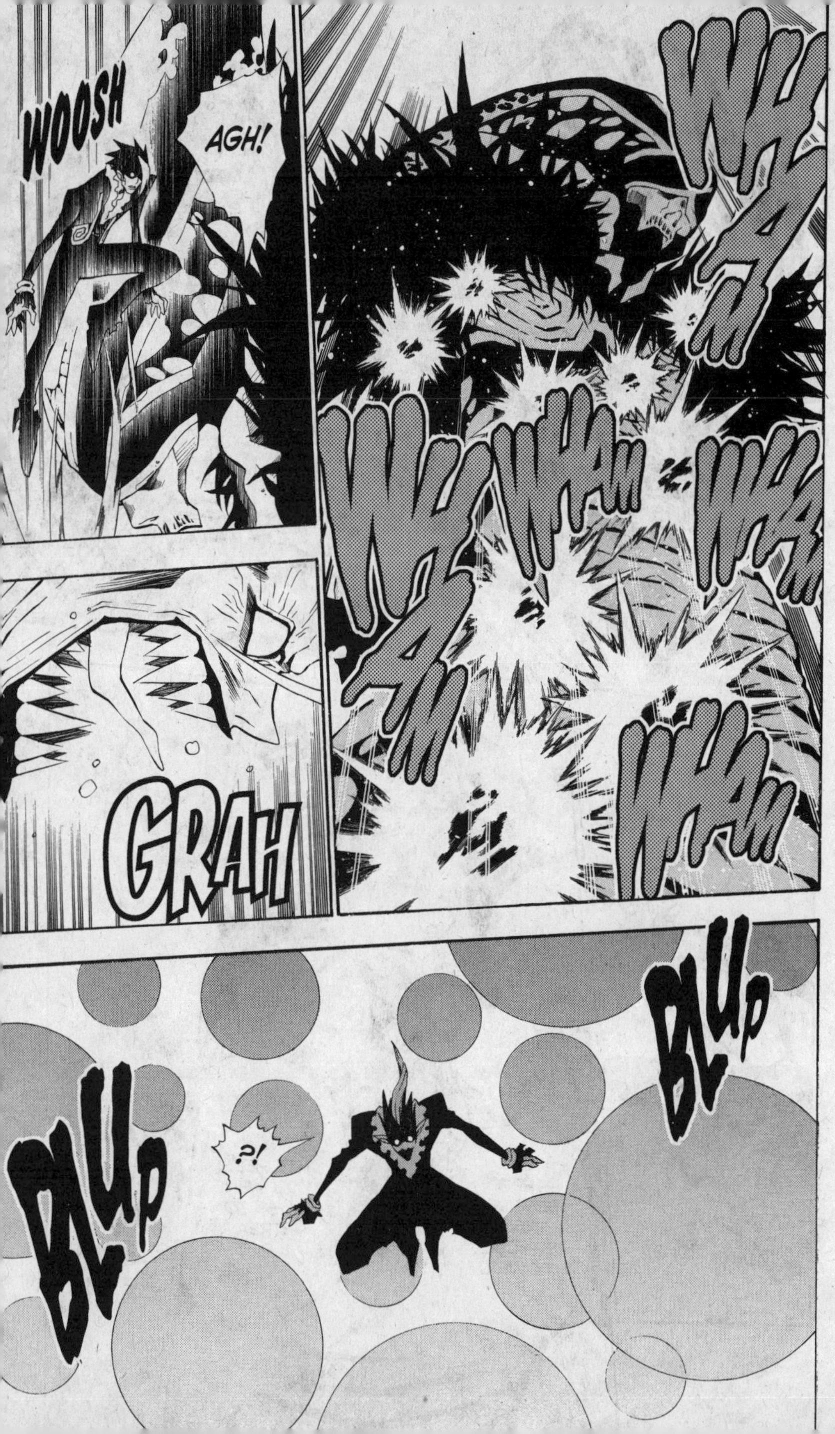
WHAM
WHAM
WHAM
WHAM
WHAM
AGH!
WOOSH
GRAH
BLUP
?!
BLUP

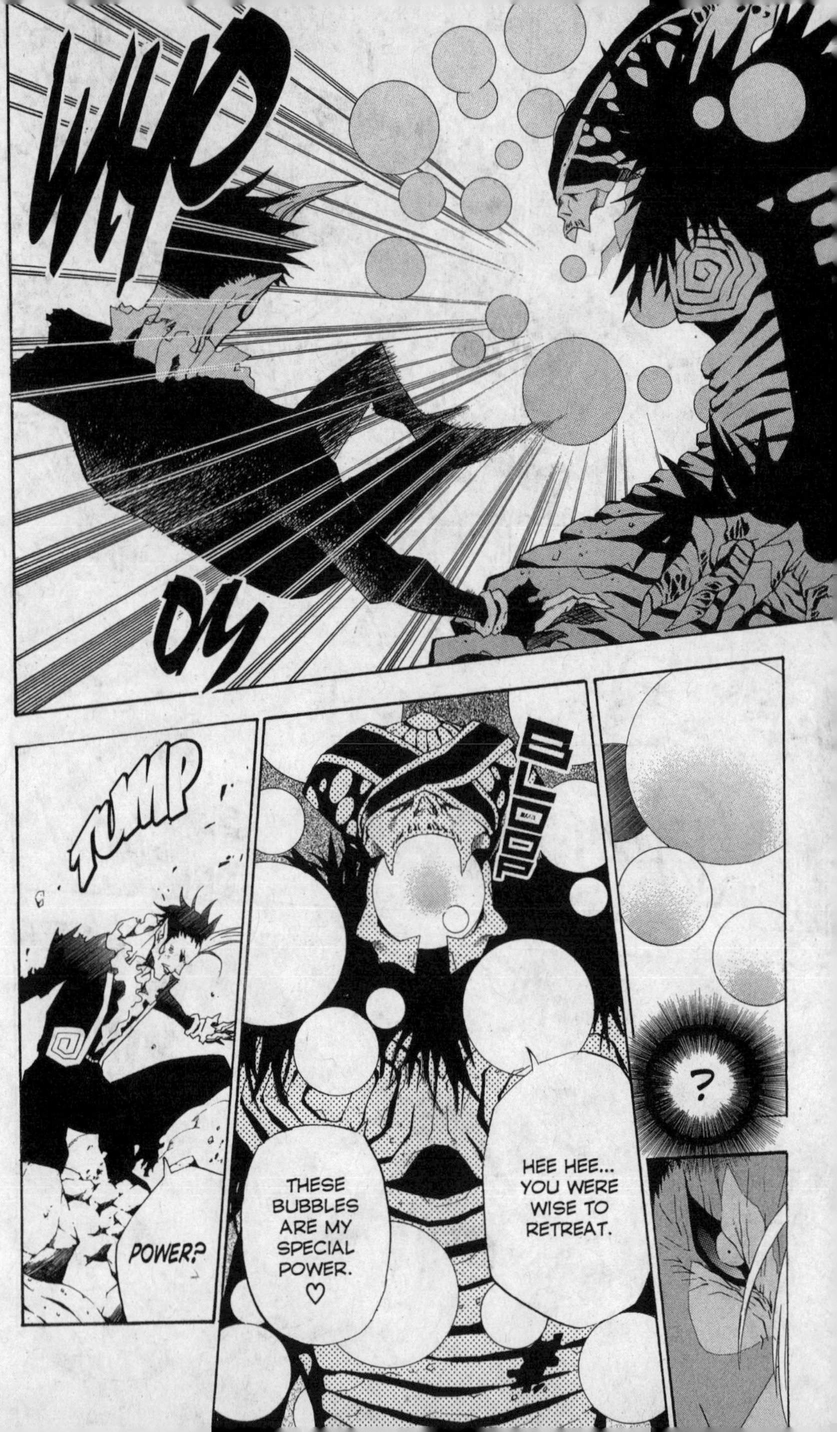
WHP
OY
?
BLOOP
HEE HEE... YOU WERE WISE TO RETREAT.
THESE BUBBLES ARE MY SPECIAL POWER. ♡
TUMP
POWER?

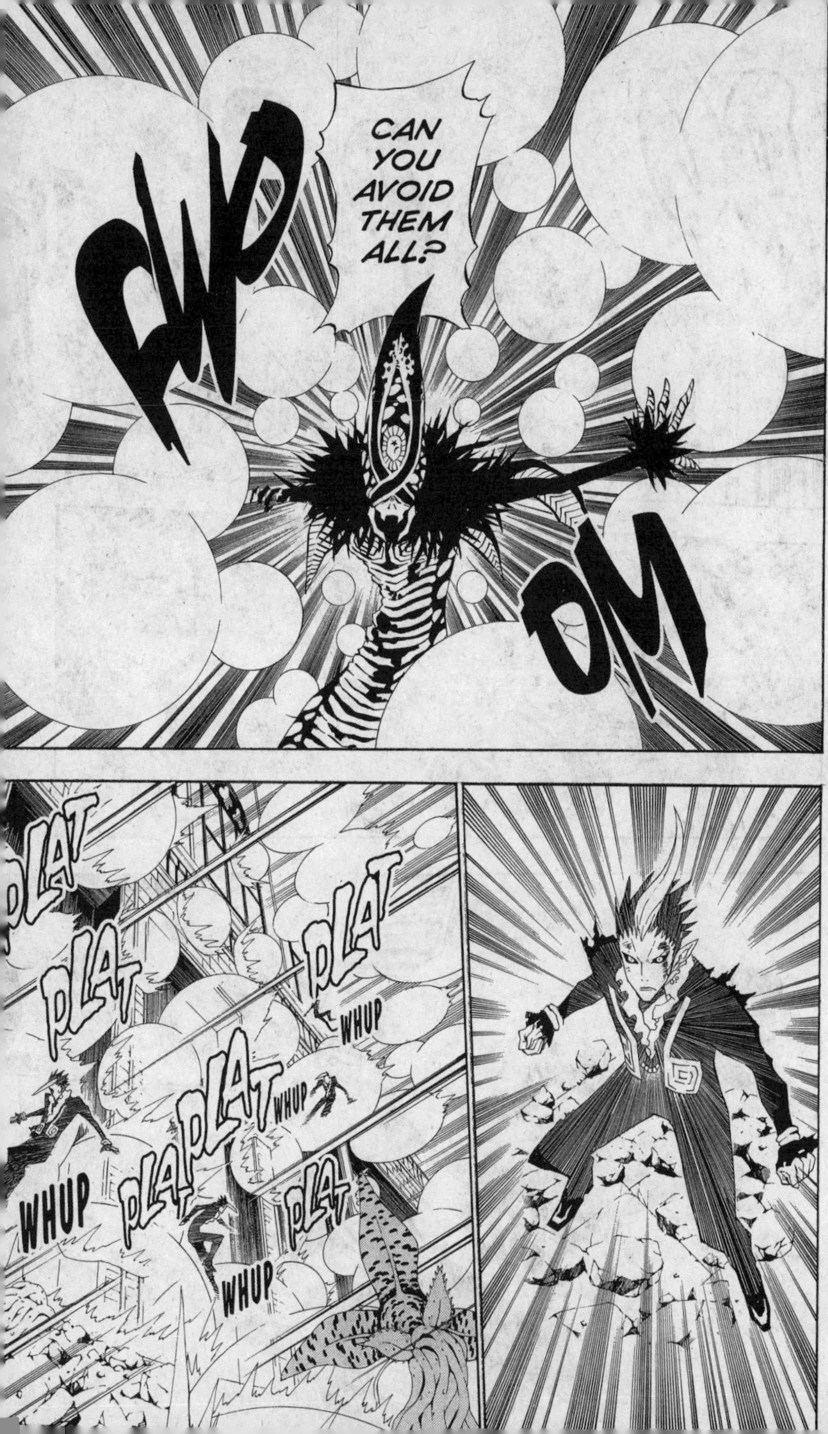
CAN YOU AVOID THEM ALL?
PLAT
PLAT
PLAT
WHUP
PLAPLAT
WHUP
WHUP
PLAT
WHUP

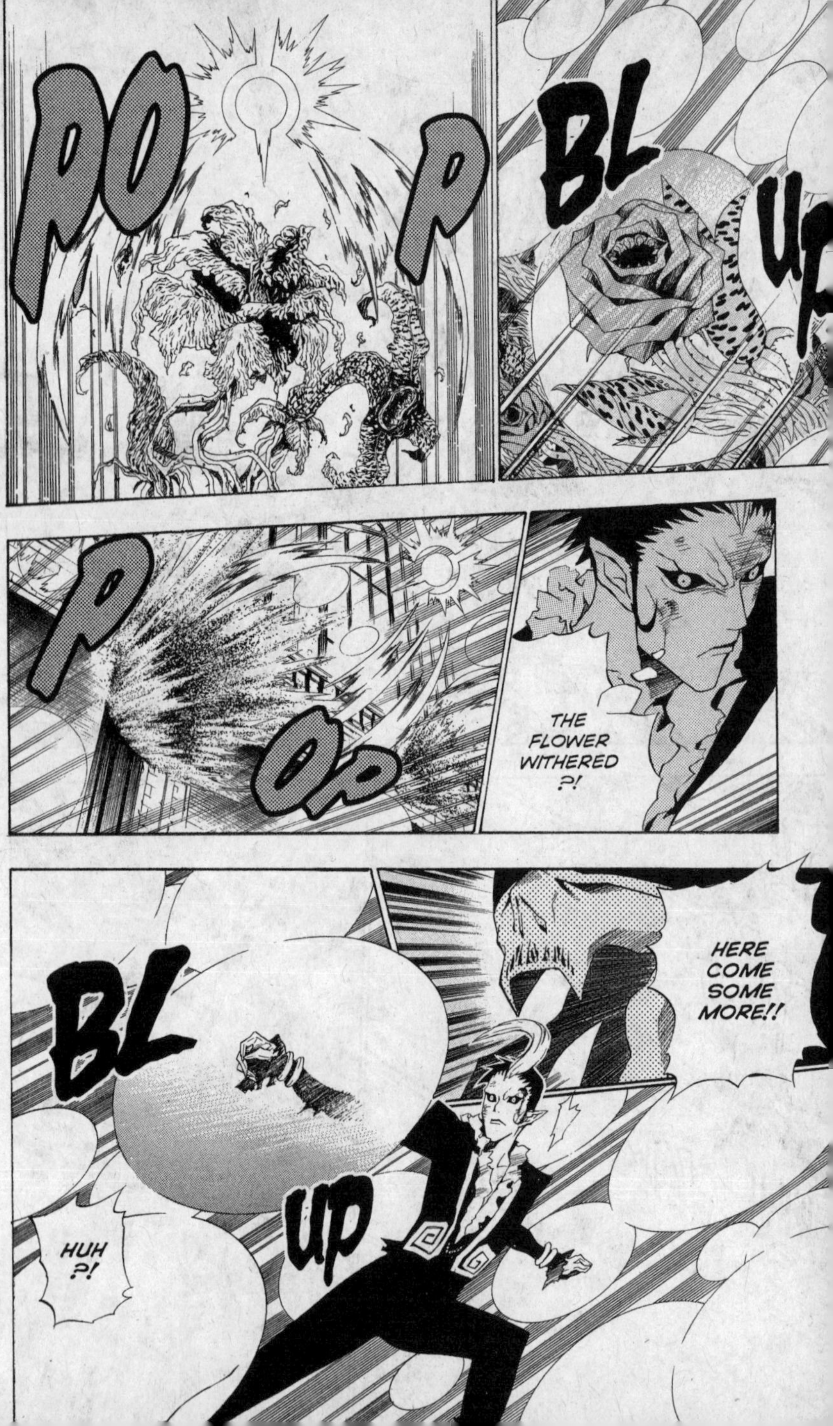
BLUP
POP
THE FLOWER WITHERED?!
POP
HERE COME SOME MORE!!
BLUP
HUH?!

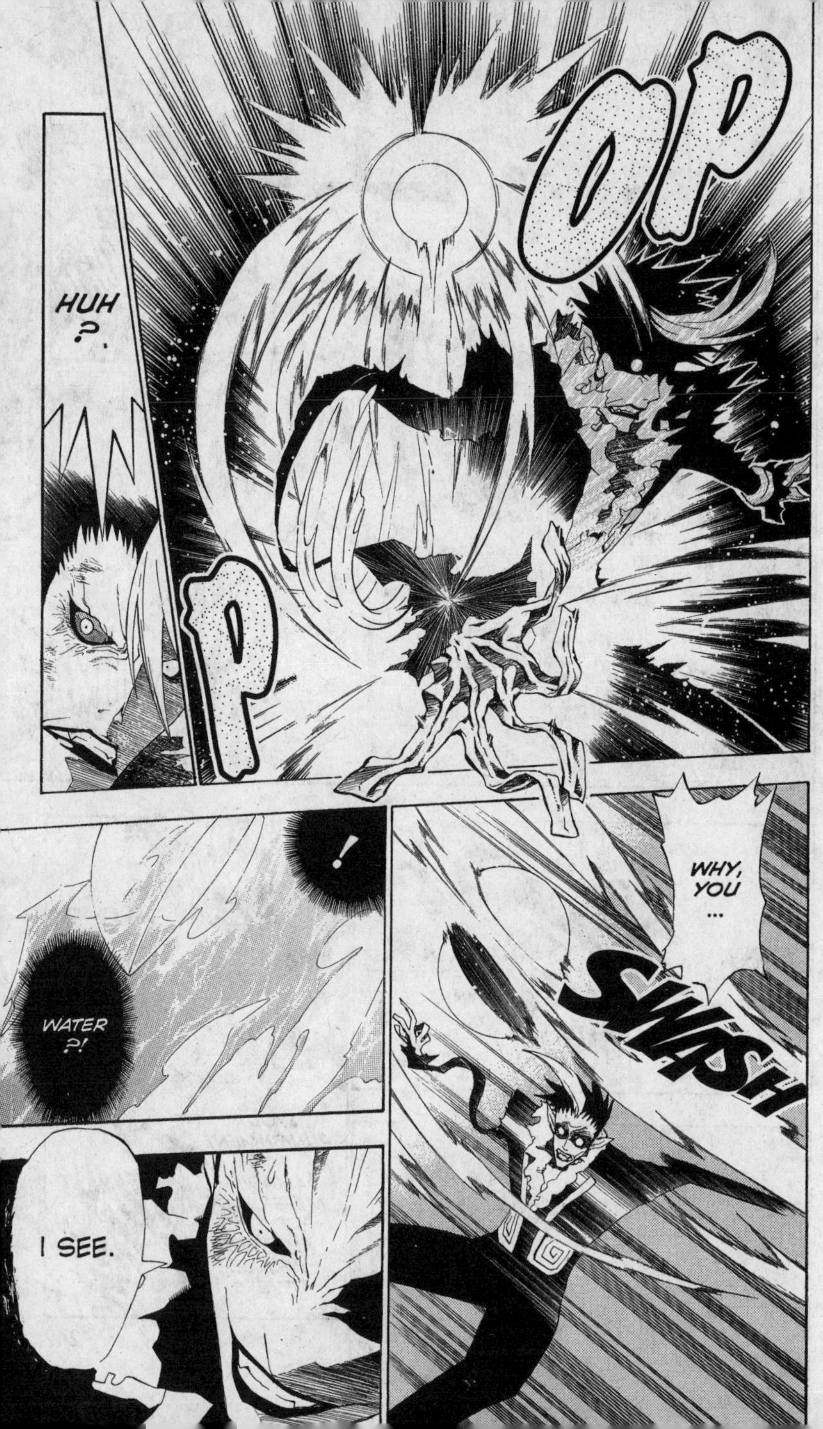
OP
HUH ?.
P
WHY, YOU ...
SWISH
!
WATER ?!
I SEE.

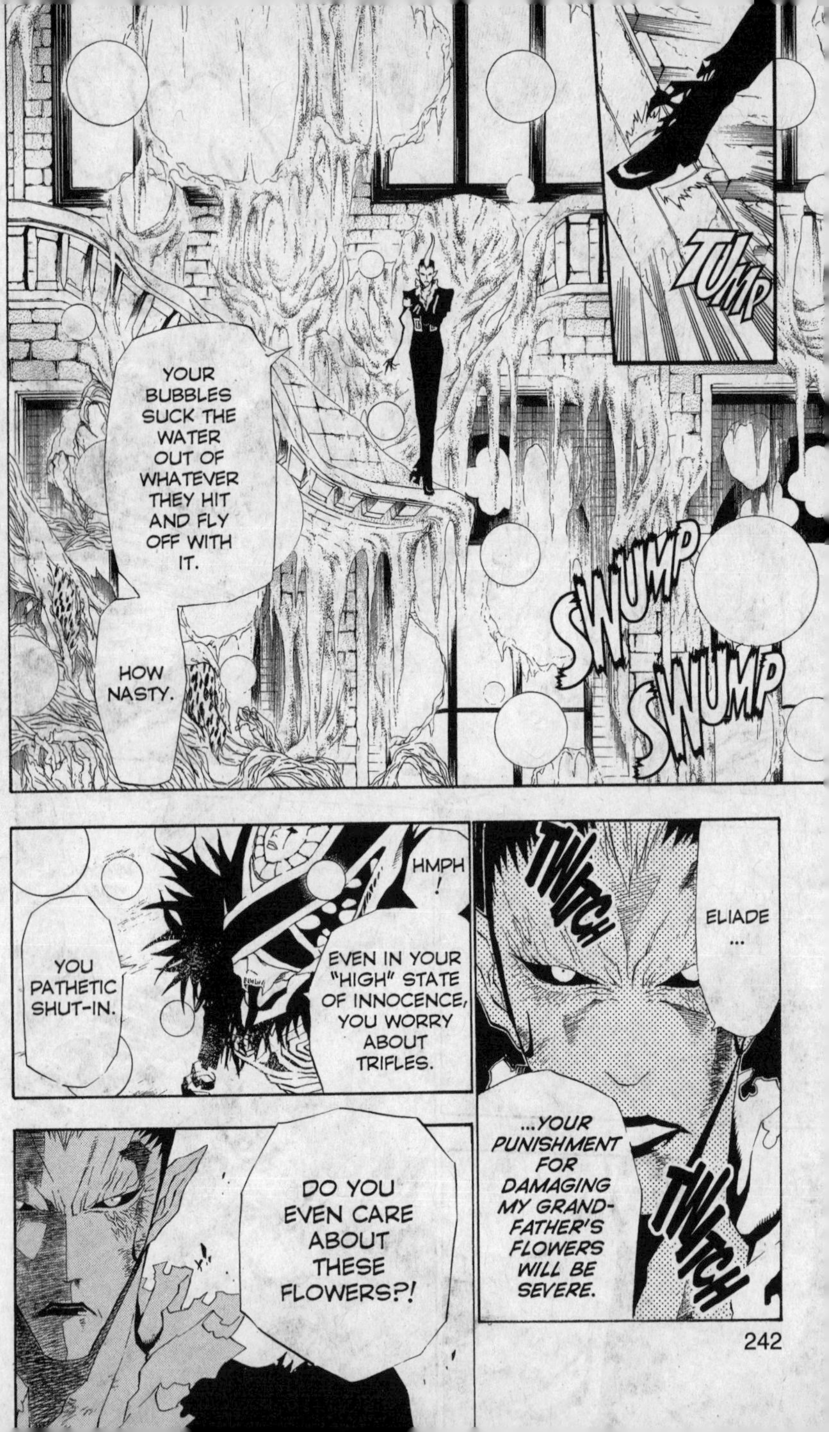
TUMP
SWUMP
SWUMP
YOUR BUBBLES SUCK THE WATER OUT OF WHATEVER THEY HIT AND FLY OFF WITH IT.
HOW NASTY.
TWITCH
ELIADE...
...YOUR PUNISHMENT FOR DAMAGING MY GRAND-FATHER'S FLOWERS WILL BE SEVERE.
TWITCH
HMPH!
EVEN IN YOUR "HIGH" STATE OF INNOCENCE, YOU WORRY ABOUT TRIFLES.
YOU PATHETIC SHUT-IN.
DO YOU EVEN CARE ABOUT THESE FLOWERS?!

READ THIS WAY

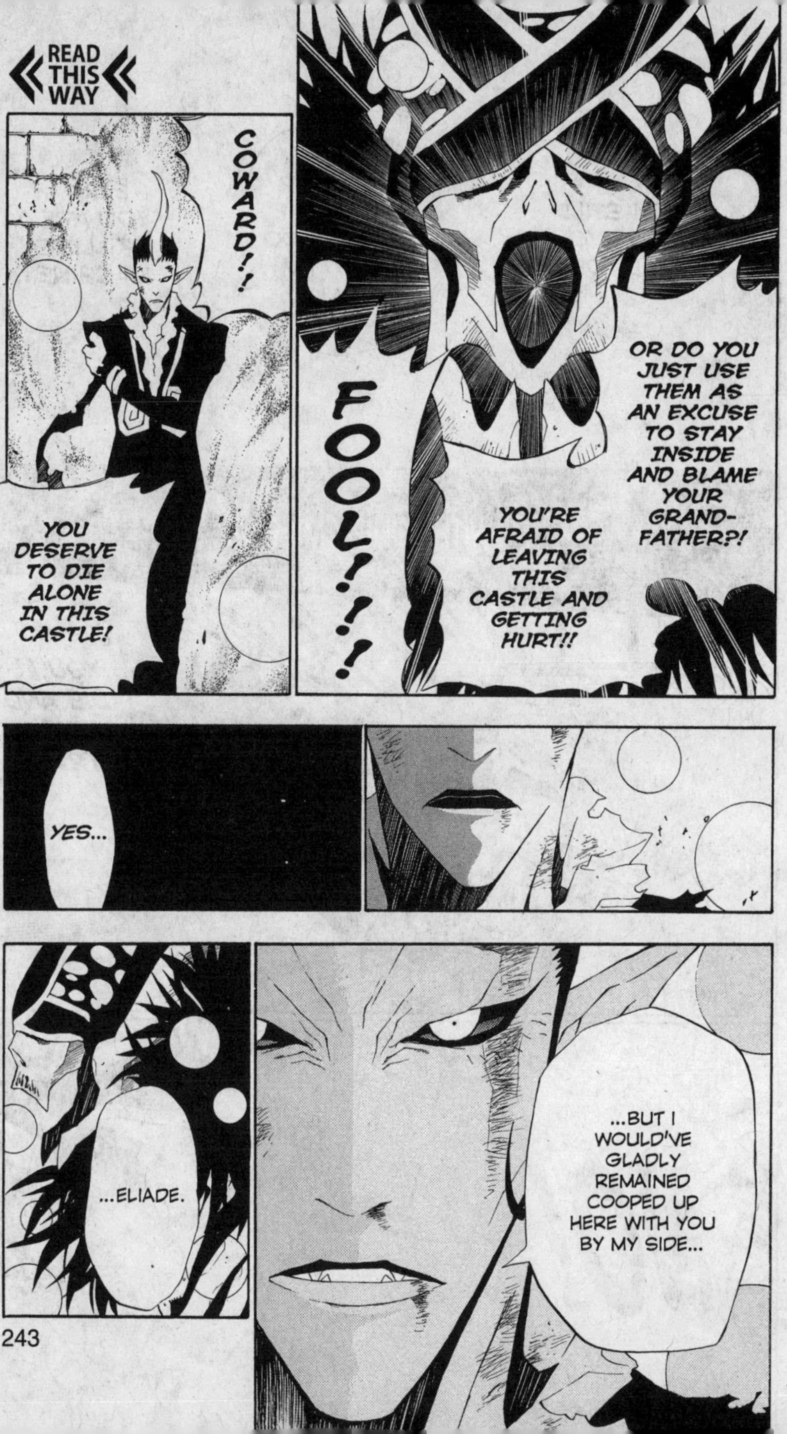
FOOL!!!
YOU'RE AFRAID OF LEAVING THIS CASTLE AND GETTING HURT!!
OR DO YOU JUST USE THEM AS AN EXCUSE TO STAY INSIDE AND BLAME YOUR GRAND-FATHER?!
COWARD!!
YOU DESERVE TO DIE ALONE IN THIS CASTLE!
YES...
...BUT I WOULD'VE GLADLY REMAINED COOPED UP HERE WITH YOU BY MY SIDE...
...ELIADE.

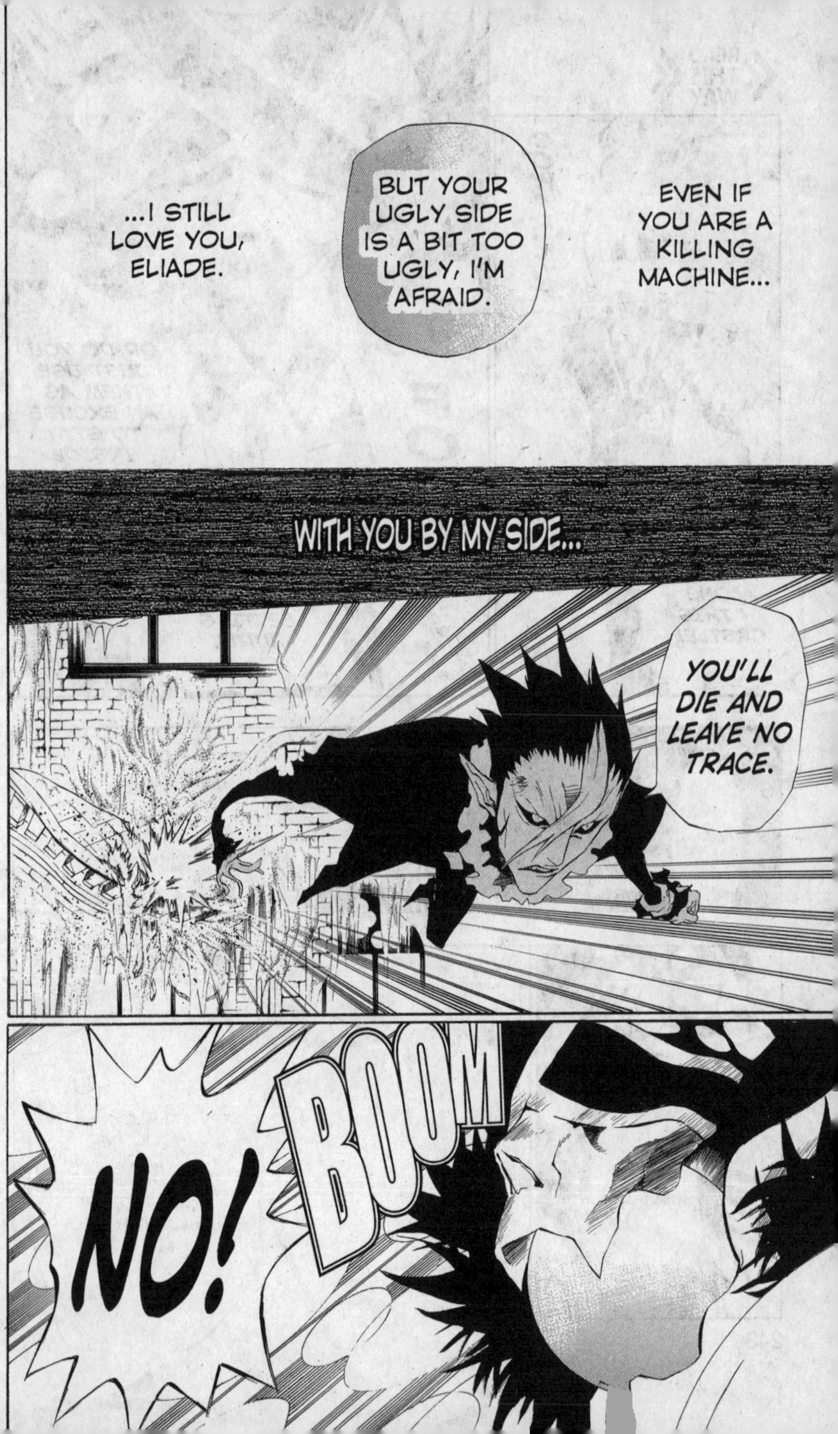
EVEN IF YOU ARE A KILLING MACHINE...
BUT YOUR UGLY SIDE IS A BIT TOO UGLY, I'M AFRAID.
...I STILL LOVE YOU, ELIADE.
WITH YOU BY MY SIDE...
YOU'LL DIE AND LEAVE NO TRACE.
BOOM
NO!

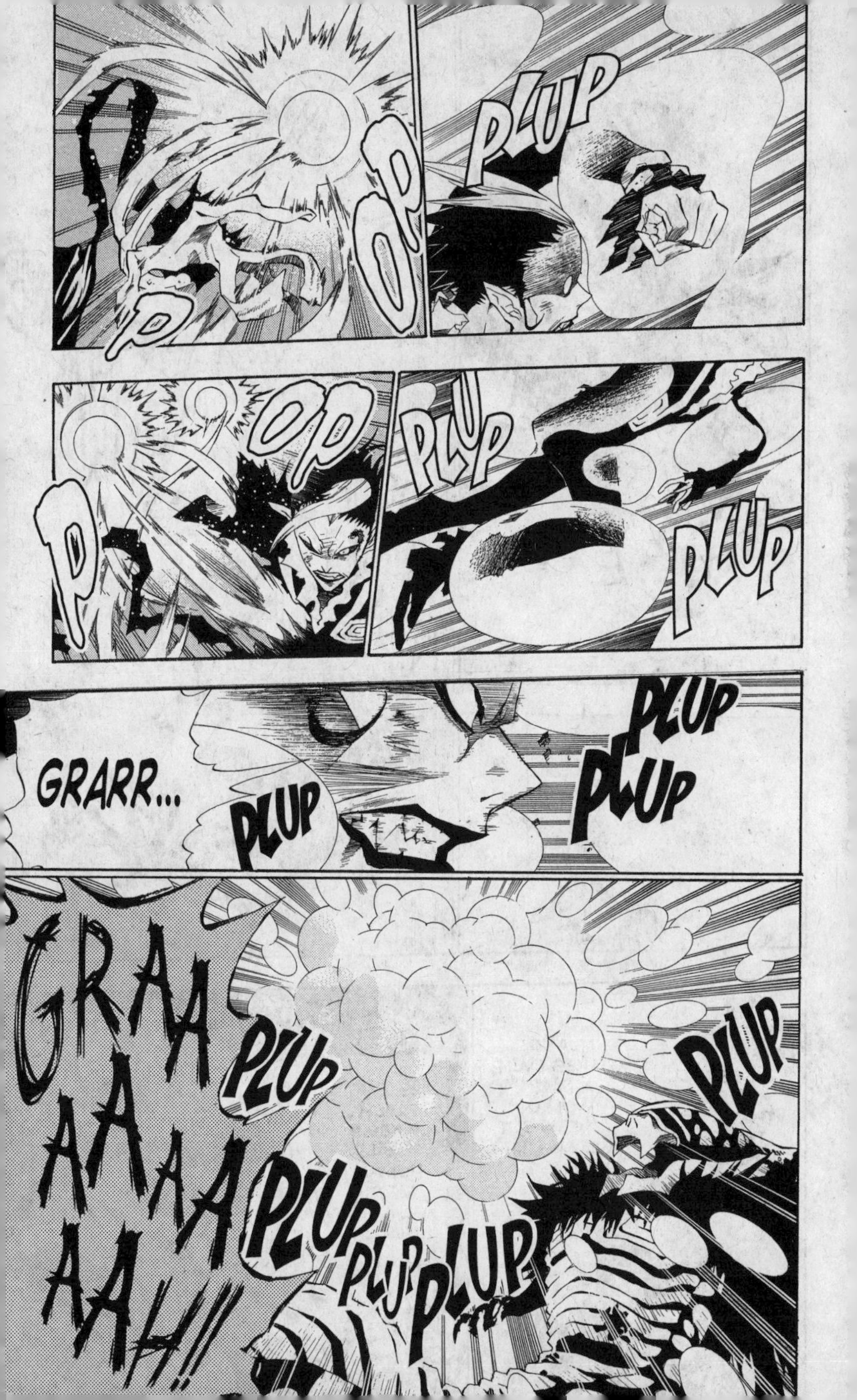
PLUP
POP
PLUP
PLUP
POP
PLUP
PLUP
PLUP
GRARR...
PLUP
PLUP
PLUP PLUP PLUP
GRAAAAAAAAH!!

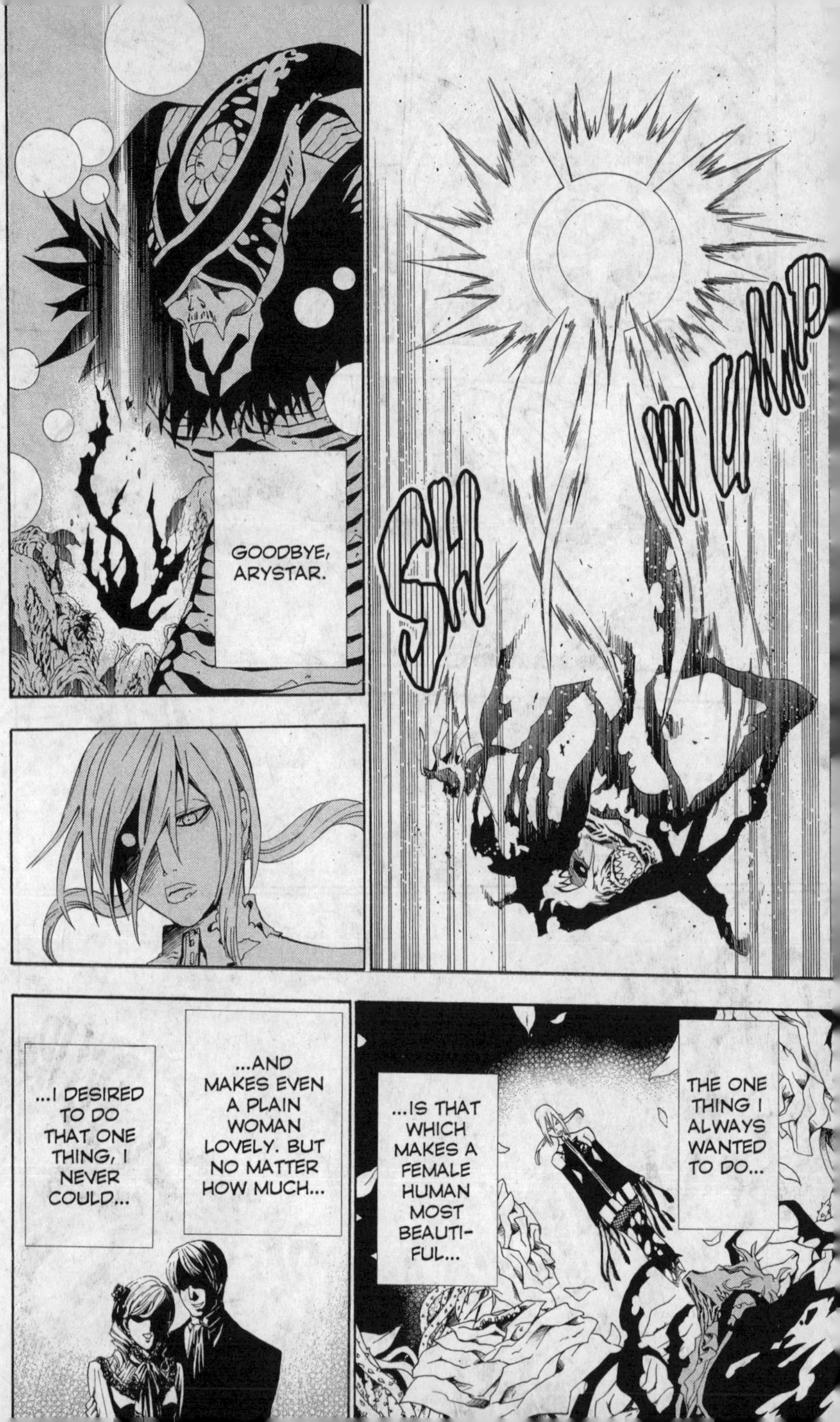
SHTHUMP
GOODBYE, ARYSTAR.
THE ONE THING I ALWAYS WANTED TO DO...
...IS THAT WHICH MAKES A FEMALE HUMAN MOST BEAUTIFUL...
...AND MAKES EVEN A PLAIN WOMAN LOVELY. BUT NO MATTER HOW MUCH...
...I DESIRED TO DO THAT ONE THING, I NEVER COULD...

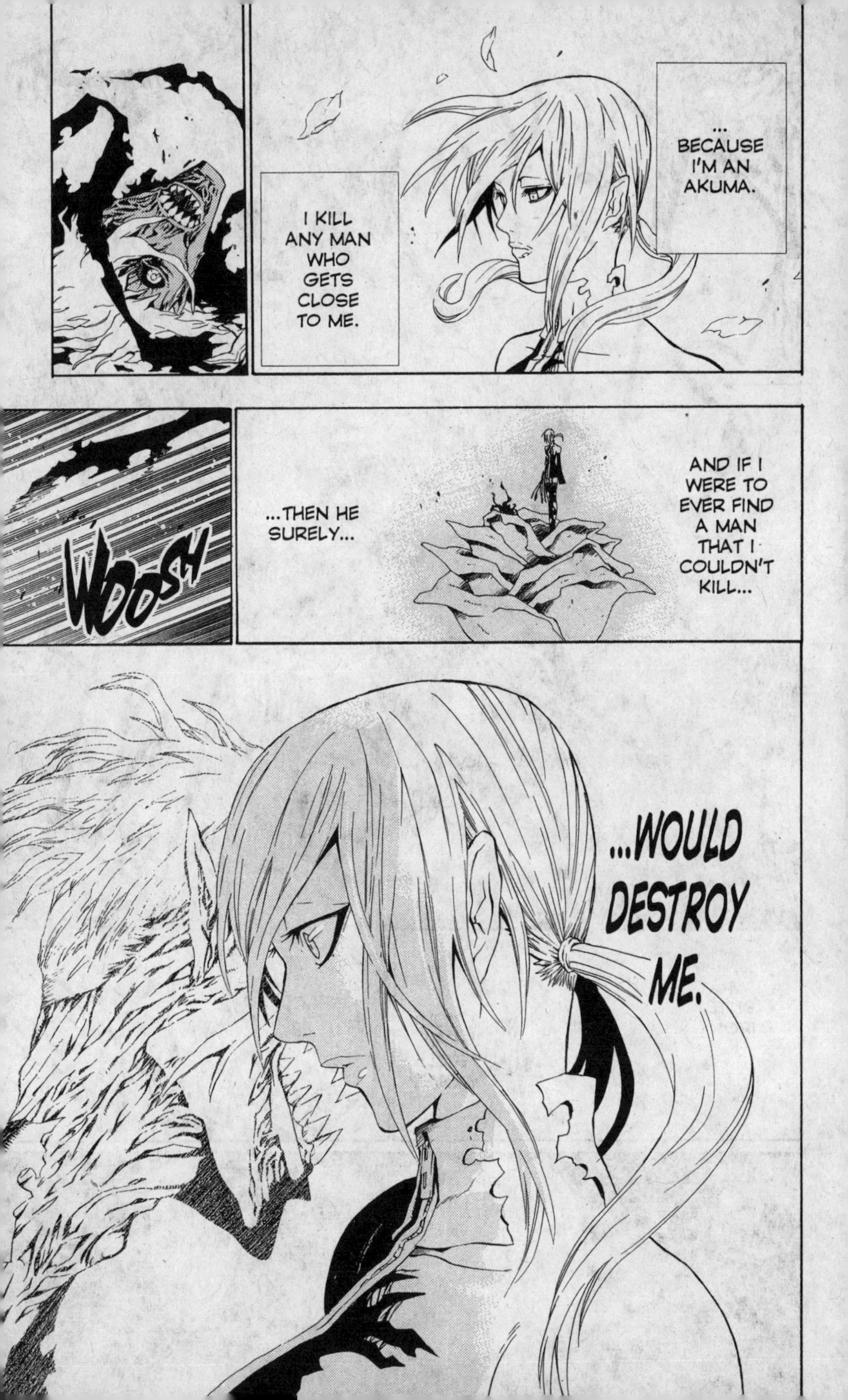
...BECAUSE I'M AN AKUMA.
I KILL ANY MAN WHO GETS CLOSE TO ME.
AND IF I WERE TO EVER FIND A MAN THAT I COULDN'T KILL...
...THEN HE SURELY...
WOOSH
...WOULD DESTROY ME.

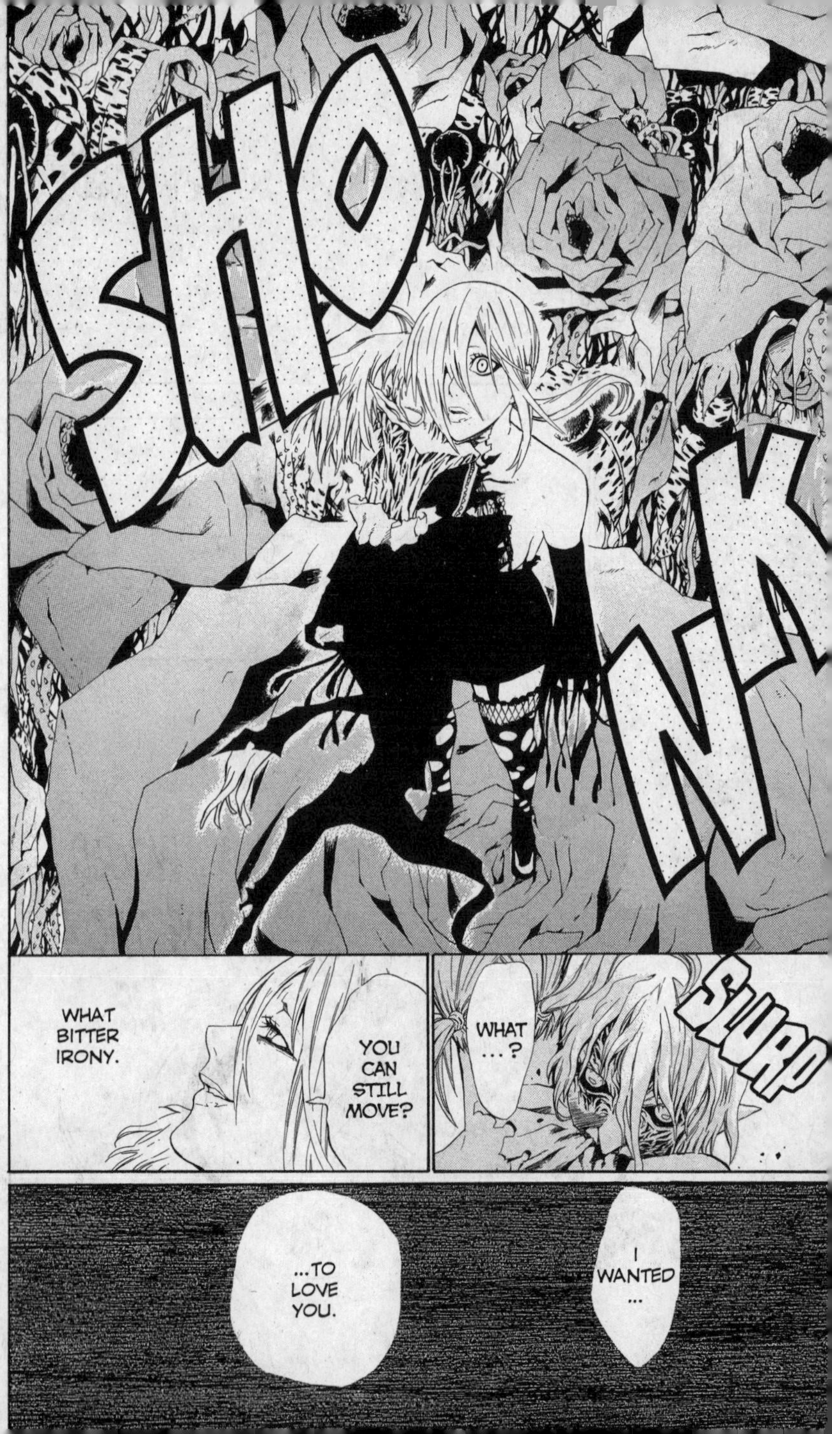
SHONK
SLURP
WHAT ...?
YOU CAN STILL MOVE?
WHAT BITTER IRONY.
I WANTED ...
...TO LOVE YOU.

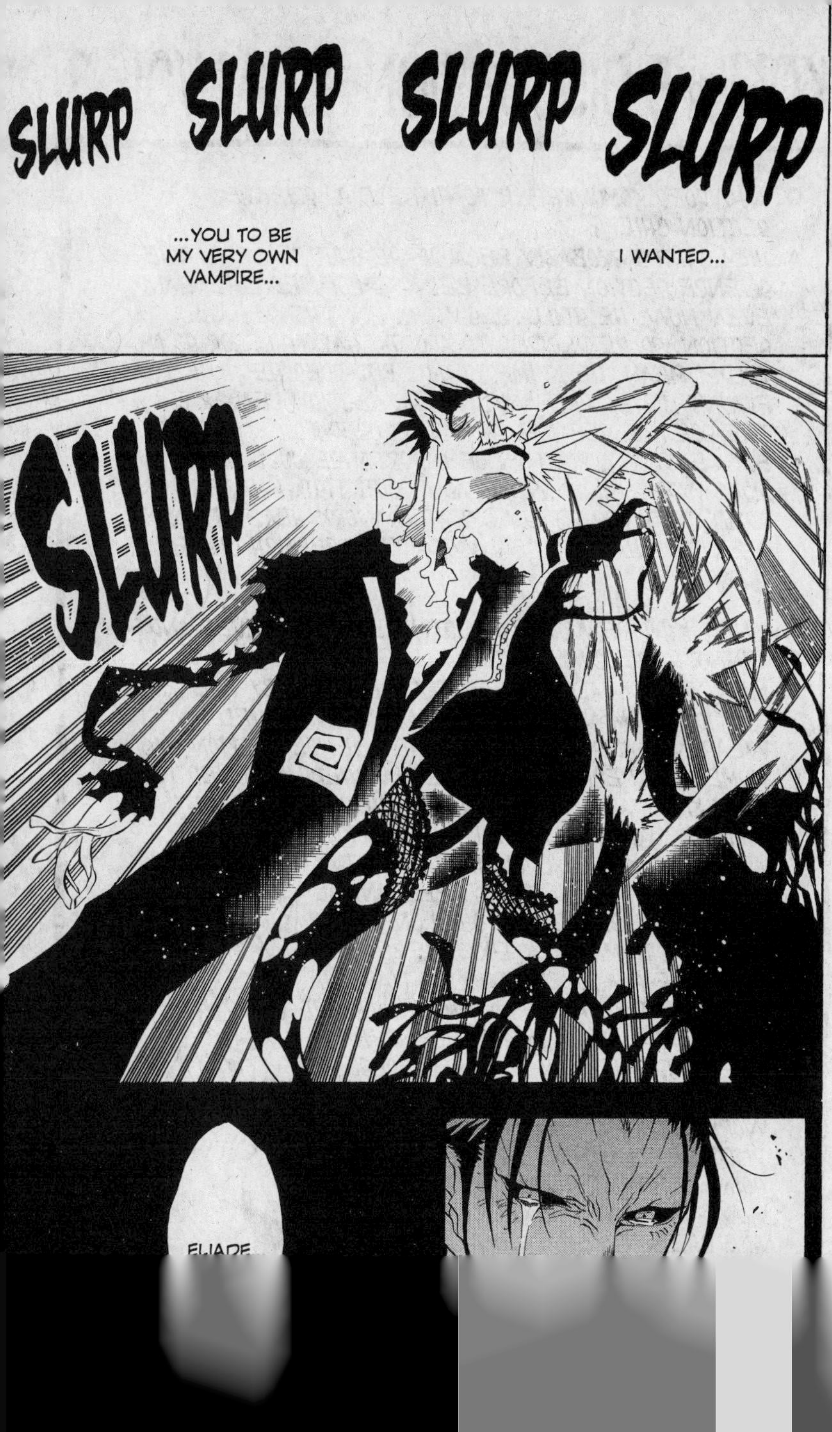
SLURP
SLURP
SLURP
SLURP
I WANTED...
...YOU TO BE MY VERY OWN VAMPIRE...
SLURP
ELIADE

KOMUI'S DISCUSSION ROOM VOL. 3

Q. WHY DOES KOMUI REFER TO HIMSELF AS SCIENCE SECTION CHIEF?

A. HMM...THAT'S PROBABLY BECAUSE HE USED TO BE IN THE SCIENCE SECTION BEFORE BEING APPOINTED CHIEF. AND EVEN NOW, HE STILL DOES WORK FOR THE SCIENCE SECTION, SO HE DECIDED TO ADOPT THAT TITLE...OR SO I'M TOLD. I MEAN, HE IS IMPORTANT, BUT DOES HE HAVE TO FLAUNT IT? BY THE WAY, I'M THE SECTION LEADER OF THE SCIENCE SECTION, SO I'M SUPPOSED TO BE IN CHARGE. BUT GETTING A POSITION OF IMPORTANCE JUST MEANS MORE WORK. (SIGH) WELL, AS A SCIENTIST, I HAVE TO ADMIT THAT IT'S REALLY GREAT TO WORK HERE. IF ONLY WE DIDN'T HAVE TO DEAL WITH THAT SELFISH CHIEF...

Q. WHAT KIND OF WORK DO SECTION LEADER REEVER AND THE OTHERS USUALLY DO?

A. MAINLY WE ANALYZE THE DATA COLLECTED BY THE SURVEY SECTION FROM ALL OVER THE WORLD, AND DEVELOP WEAPONRY AND EQUIPMENT. THE SCIENCE SECTION HAS NUMEROUS SPECIALISTS AND RESEARCHERS ASSIGNED TO VARIOUS DEPARTMENTS. THERE'S PHYSICS, ASTRONOMY, BIOLOGY, ARCHEOLOGY, GEOLOGY, LINGUISTICS, ANTHROPOLOGY, PSYCHOLOGY, CHEMISTRY, MATHEMATICS, MINERALOGY, MECHANICAL ENGINEERING...THE LIST GOES ON AD NAUSEUM. IT MAY LOOK LIKE WE'RE ALL OVER THE PLACE, BUT THE BOTTOM LINE IS THAT WE'RE ALL STRIVING TO FIND OUT ALL WE CAN ABOUT INNOCENCE. EVERY SCIENTIST THAT COMES HERE IS OBSESSED WITH IT. HOWEVER DIFFICULT THE WORKPLACE MAY BE, THE CHANCE TO DISCOVER SOMETHING NEW KEEPS US GOING. (DISTANT STARE) BY THE WAY, MY AREAS OF EXPERTISE ARE CHEMISTRY, MATHEMATICS, AND LINGUISTICS.

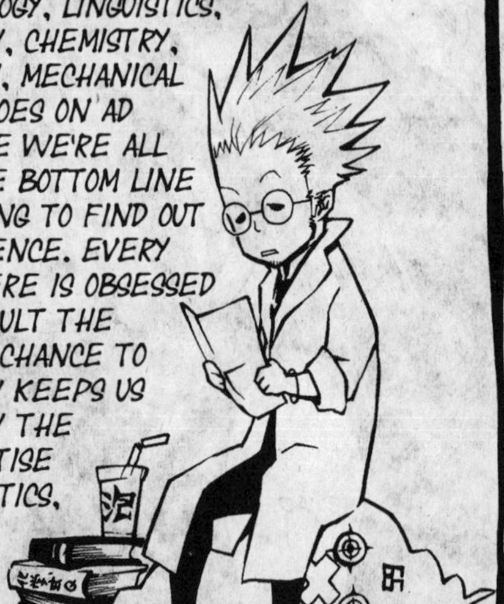

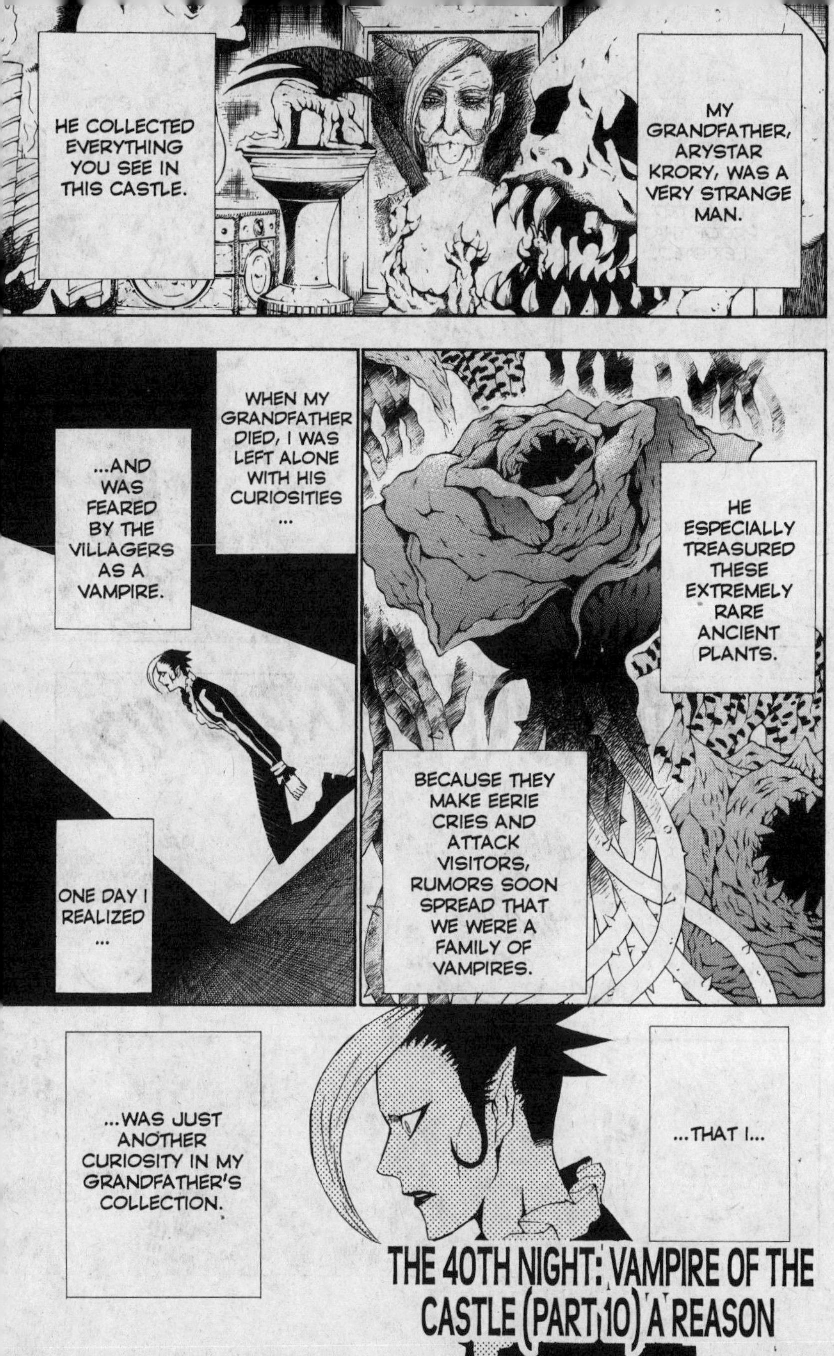
MY GRANDFATHER, ARYSTAR KRORY, WAS A VERY STRANGE MAN.
HE COLLECTED EVERYTHING YOU SEE IN THIS CASTLE.
HE ESPECIALLY TREASURED THESE EXTREMELY RARE ANCIENT PLANTS.
BECAUSE THEY MAKE EERIE CRIES AND ATTACK VISITORS, RUMORS SOON SPREAD THAT WE WERE A FAMILY OF VAMPIRES.
WHEN MY GRANDFATHER DIED, I WAS LEFT ALONE WITH HIS CURIOSITIES ...
...AND WAS FEARED BY THE VILLAGERS AS A VAMPIRE.
ONE DAY I REALIZED ...
...THAT I...
...WAS JUST ANOTHER CURIOSITY IN MY GRANDFATHER'S COLLECTION.
THE 40TH NIGHT: VAMPIRE OF THE CASTLE (PART 10) A REASON

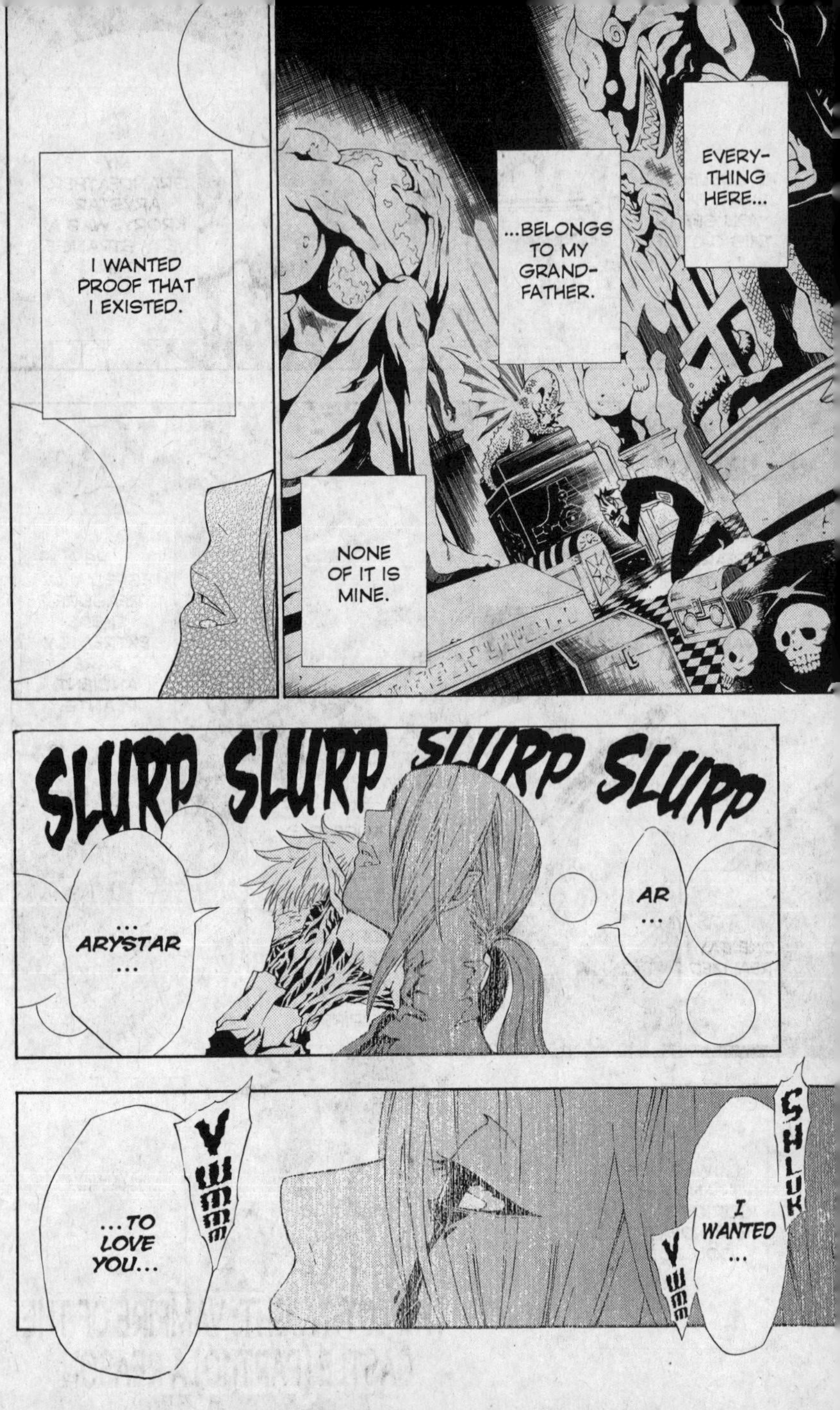
EVERYTHING HERE...
...BELONGS TO MY GRANDFATHER.
NONE OF IT IS MINE.
I WANTED PROOF THAT I EXISTED.
SLURP SLURP SLURP SLURP
AR...
...ARYSTAR...
SHLUK
VUMMM
I WANTED...
VUMMM
...TO LOVE YOU...

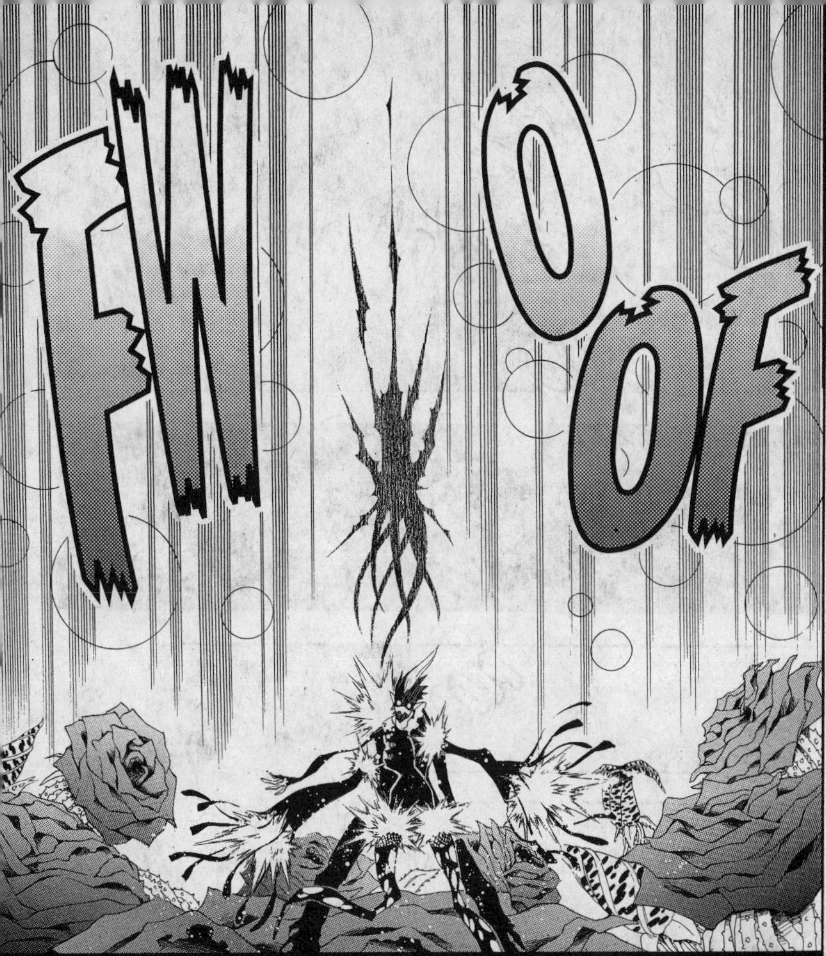
FWOOF

THE 40TH NIGHT: VAMPIRE OF THE CASTLE (PART 10) A REASON

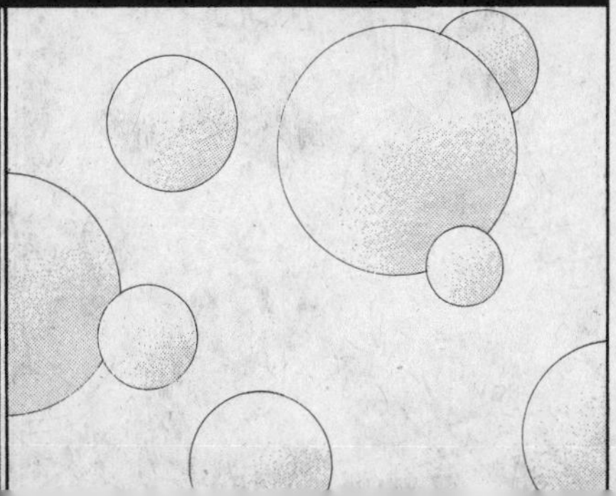

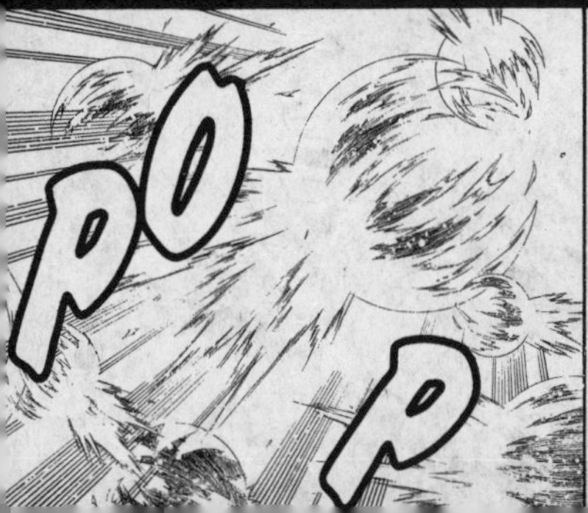
POP

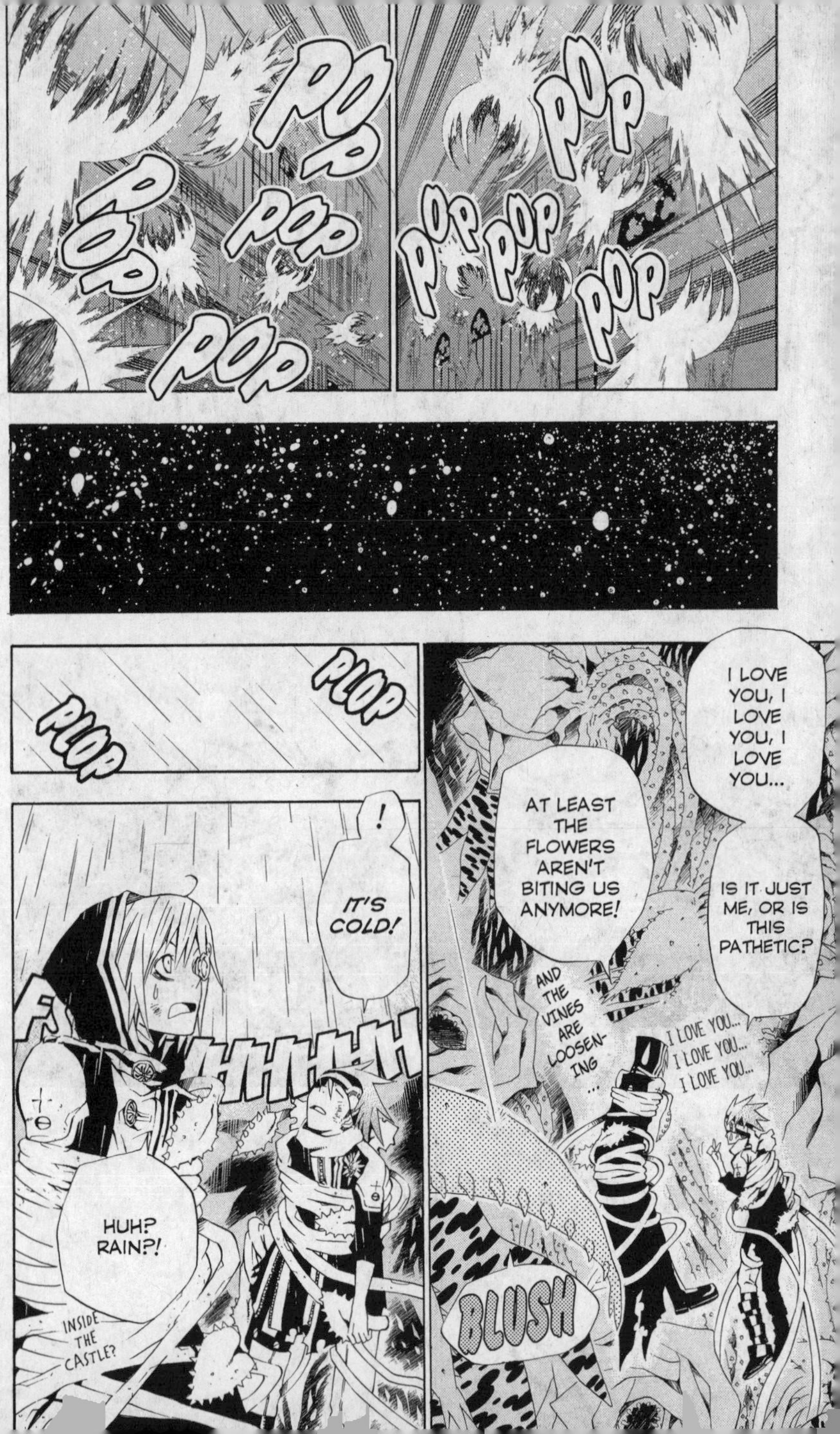
POP
POP
POP
POP
POP
POP
POP
POP
I LOVE YOU, I LOVE YOU, I LOVE YOU...
AT LEAST THE FLOWERS AREN'T BITING US ANYMORE!
IS IT JUST ME, OR IS THIS PATHETIC?
AND THE VINES ARE LOOSENING...
I LOVE YOU... I LOVE YOU... I LOVE YOU...
BLUSH
PLOP
PLOP
!
IT'S COLD!
HUH? RAIN?!
INSIDE THE CASTLE?

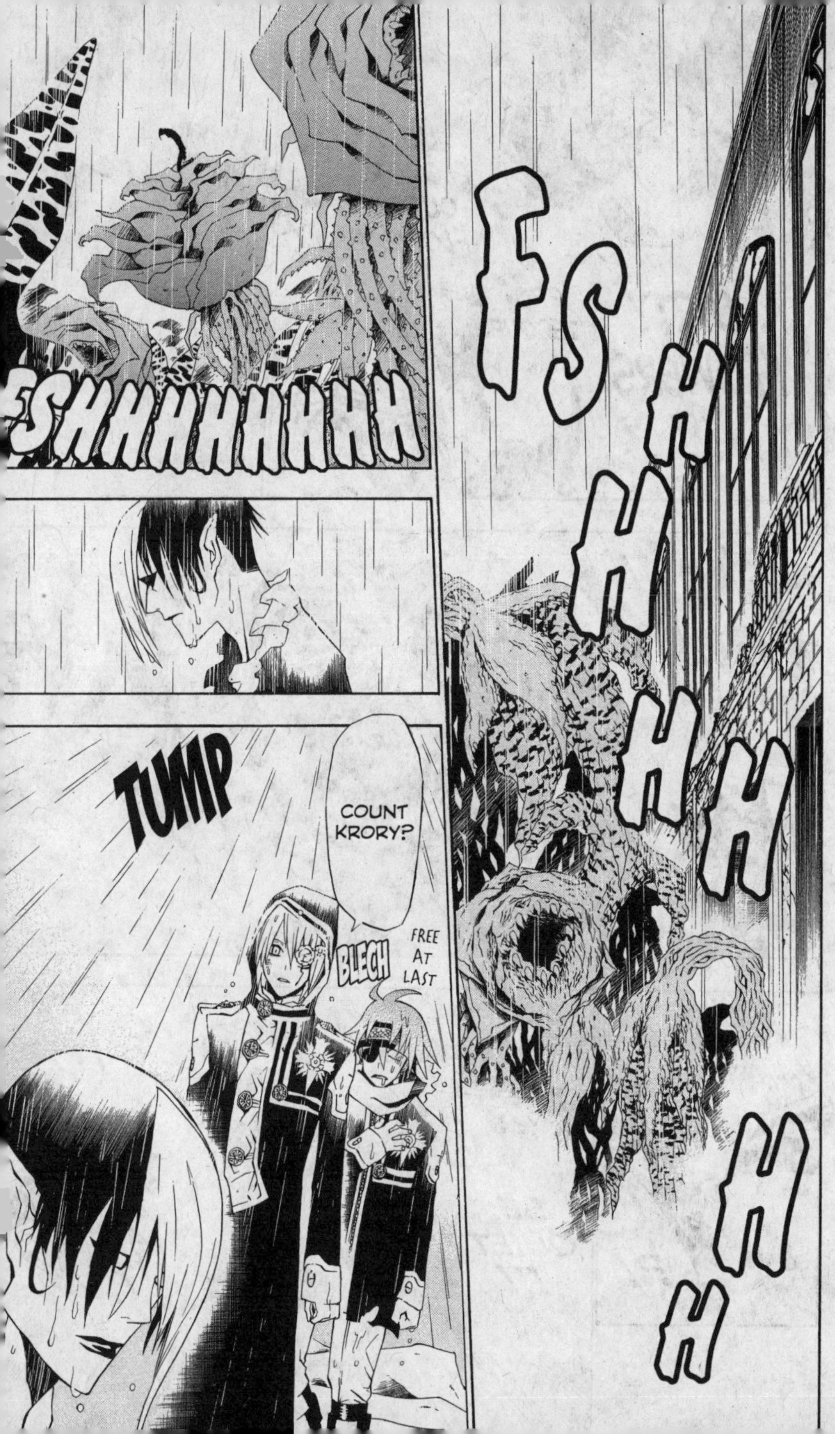
FSHHHHHHHH
FSHHHHHHHHHH
TUMP
COUNT KRORY?
BLECH
FREE AT LAST

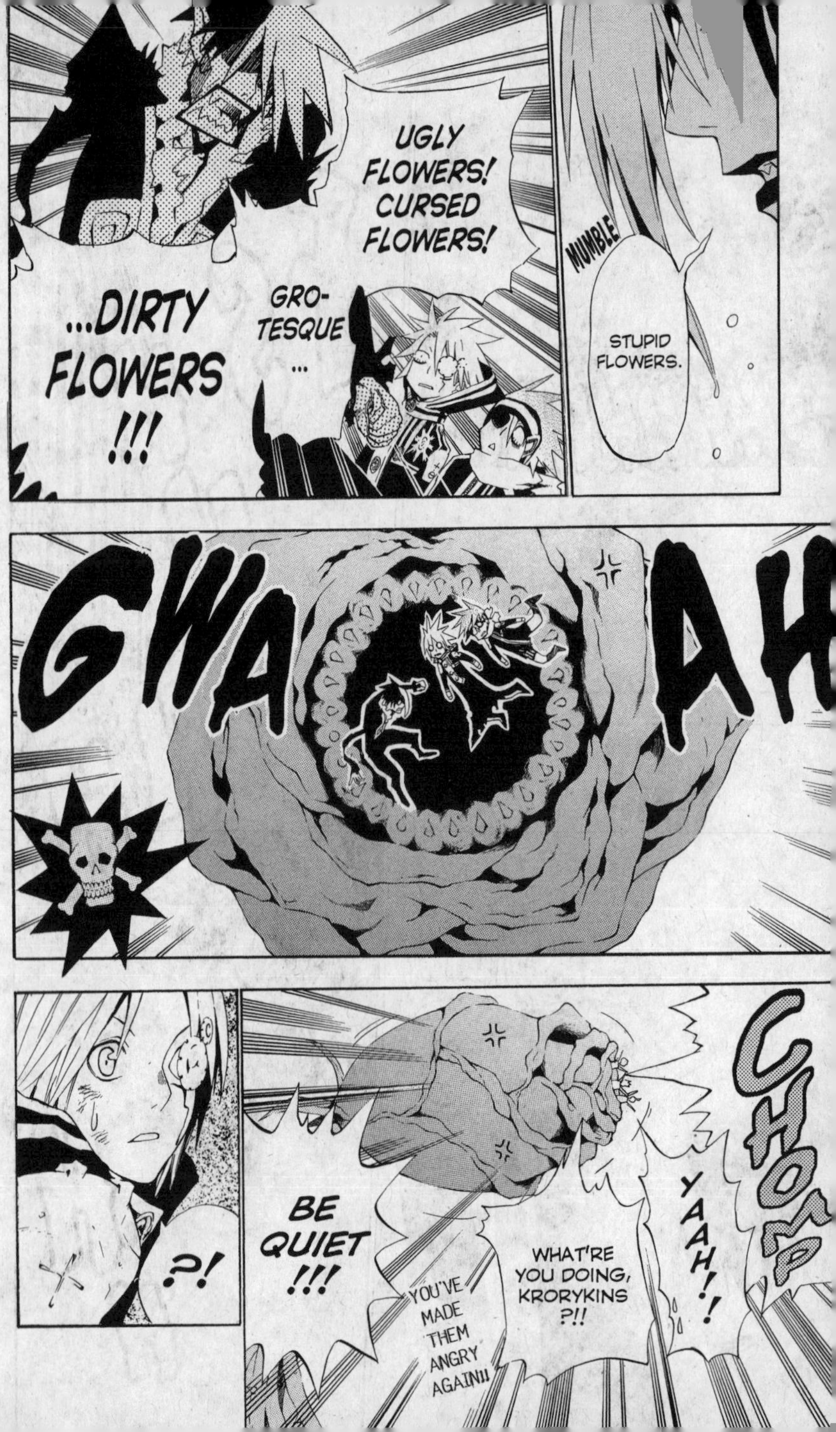
MUMBLE
STUPID FLOWERS.
UGLY FLOWERS! CURSED FLOWERS!
GRO-TESQUE ...
...DIRTY FLOWERS !!!
GWA AH
CHOMP
YAAH!!
WHAT'RE YOU DOING, KRORYKINS ?!!
YOU'VE MADE THEM ANGRY AGAIN!!
BE QUIET !!!
?!

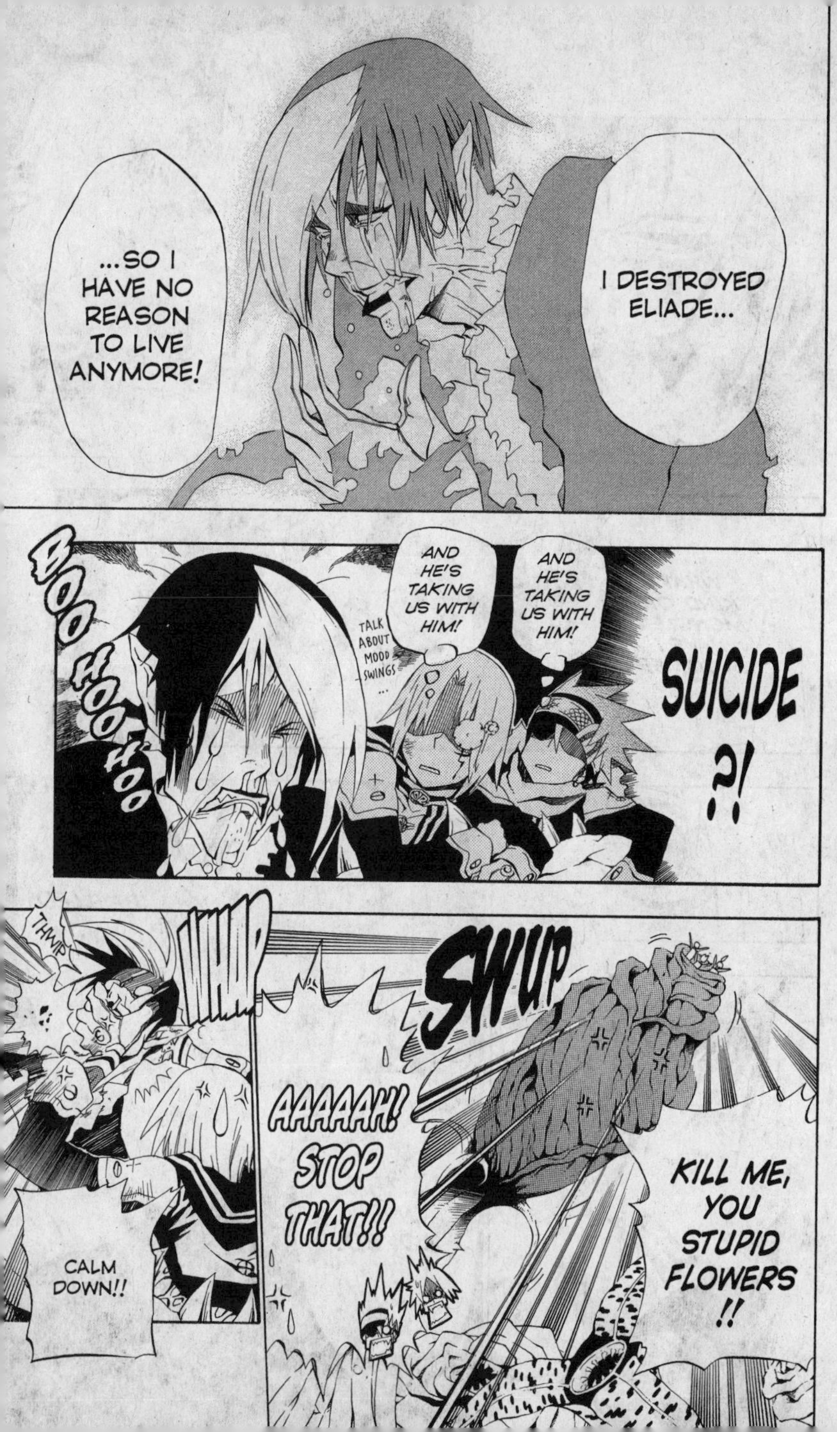
I DESTROYED ELIADE...
...SO I HAVE NO REASON TO LIVE ANYMORE!
SUICIDE ?!
AND HE'S TAKING US WITH HIM!
AND HE'S TAKING US WITH HIM!
TALK ABOUT MOOD SWINGS ...
MOO HOO HOO HOO
KILL ME, YOU STUPID FLOWERS !!
SWUP
AAAAAH! STOP THAT!!
WHAP
THWIP
CALM DOWN!!

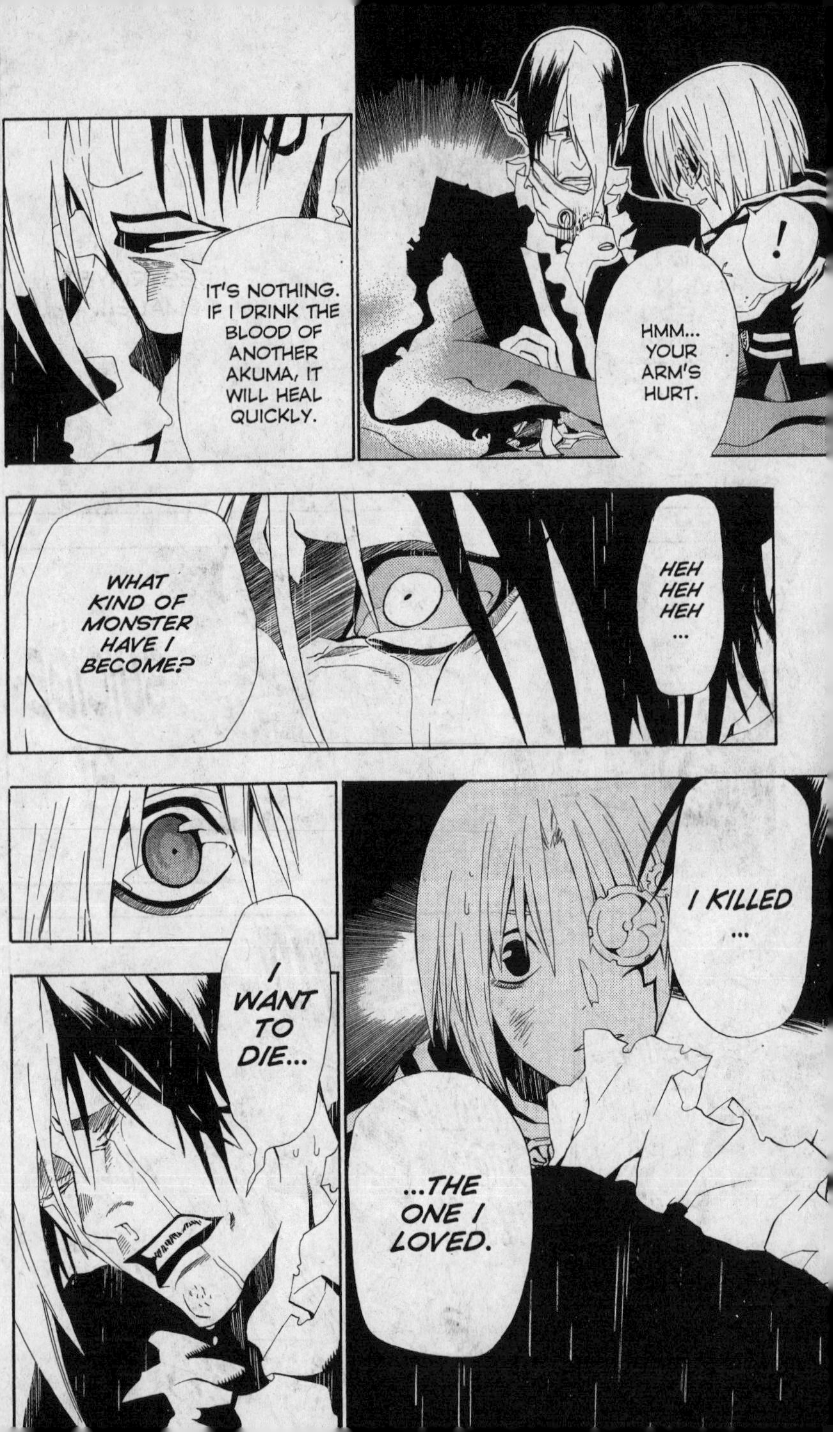
!
HMM... YOUR ARM'S HURT.
IT'S NOTHING. IF I DRINK THE BLOOD OF ANOTHER AKUMA, IT WILL HEAL QUICKLY.
HEH HEH HEH ...
WHAT KIND OF MONSTER HAVE I BECOME?
I KILLED ...
...THE ONE I LOVED.
I WANT TO DIE...

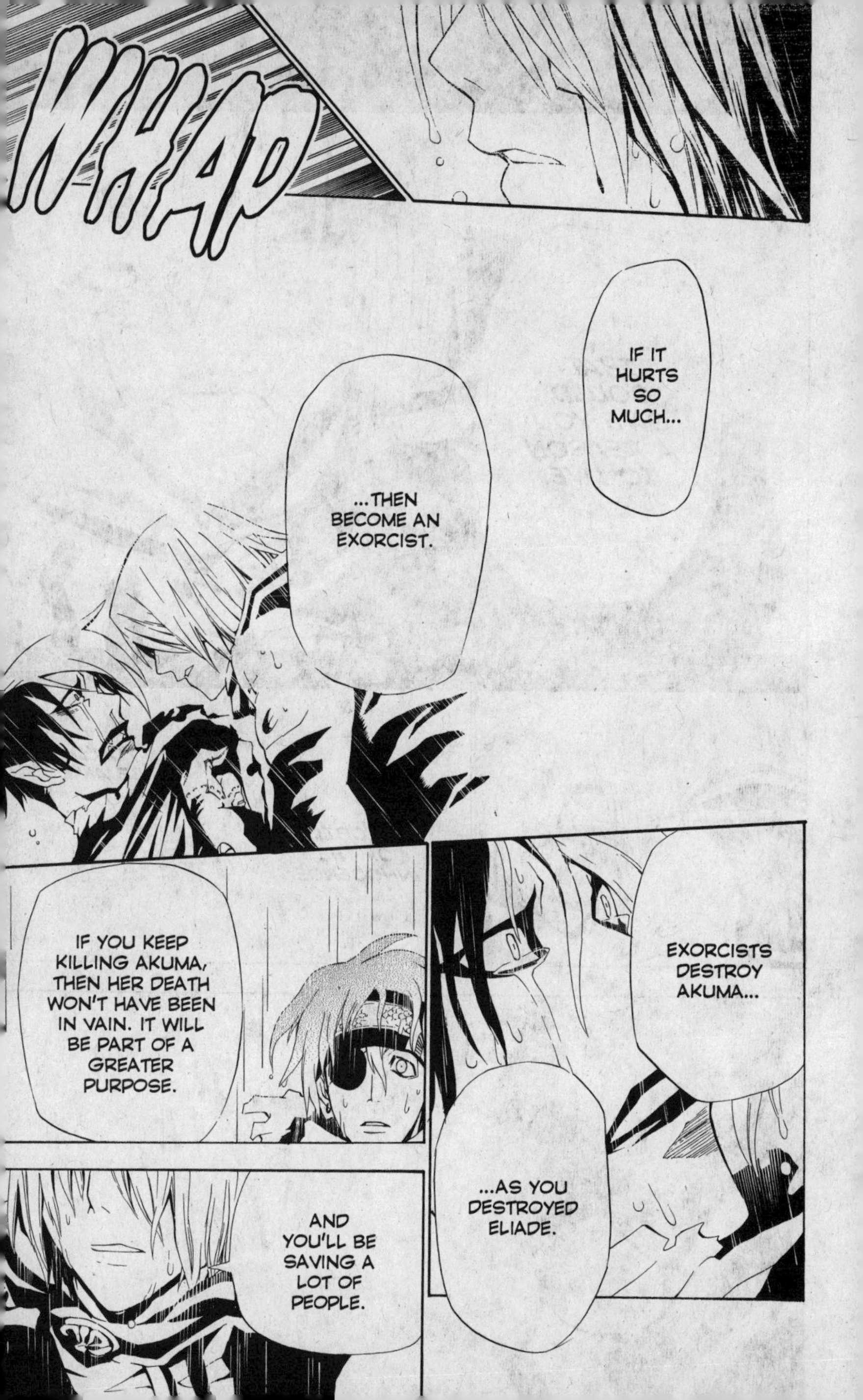
WHAP
IF IT HURTS SO MUCH...
...THEN BECOME AN EXORCIST.
EXORCISTS DESTROY AKUMA...
...AS YOU DESTROYED ELIADE.
IF YOU KEEP KILLING AKUMA, THEN HER DEATH WON'T HAVE BEEN IN VAIN. IT WILL BE PART OF A GREATER PURPOSE.
AND YOU'LL BE SAVING A LOT OF PEOPLE.

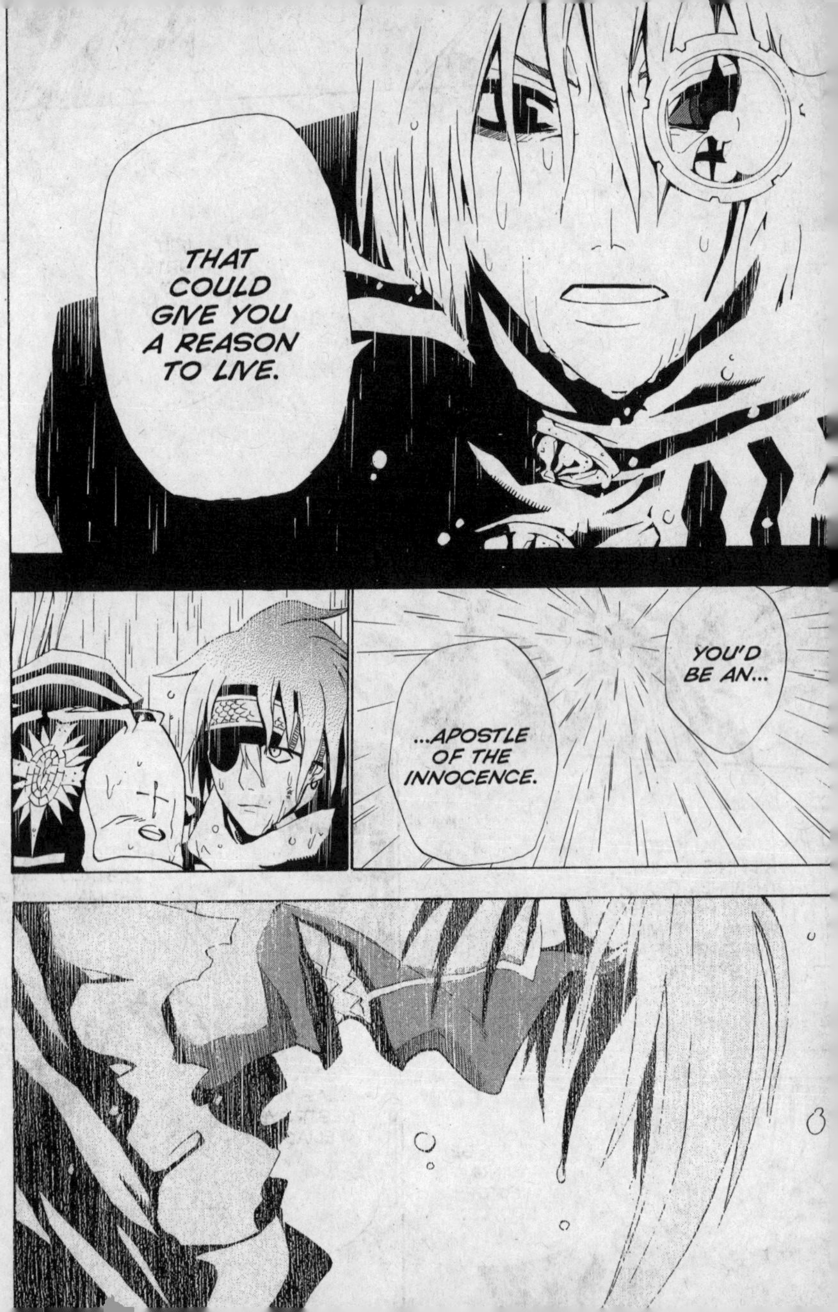
THAT COULD GIVE YOU A REASON TO LIVE.
YOU'D BE AN...
...APOSTLE OF THE INNOCENCE.

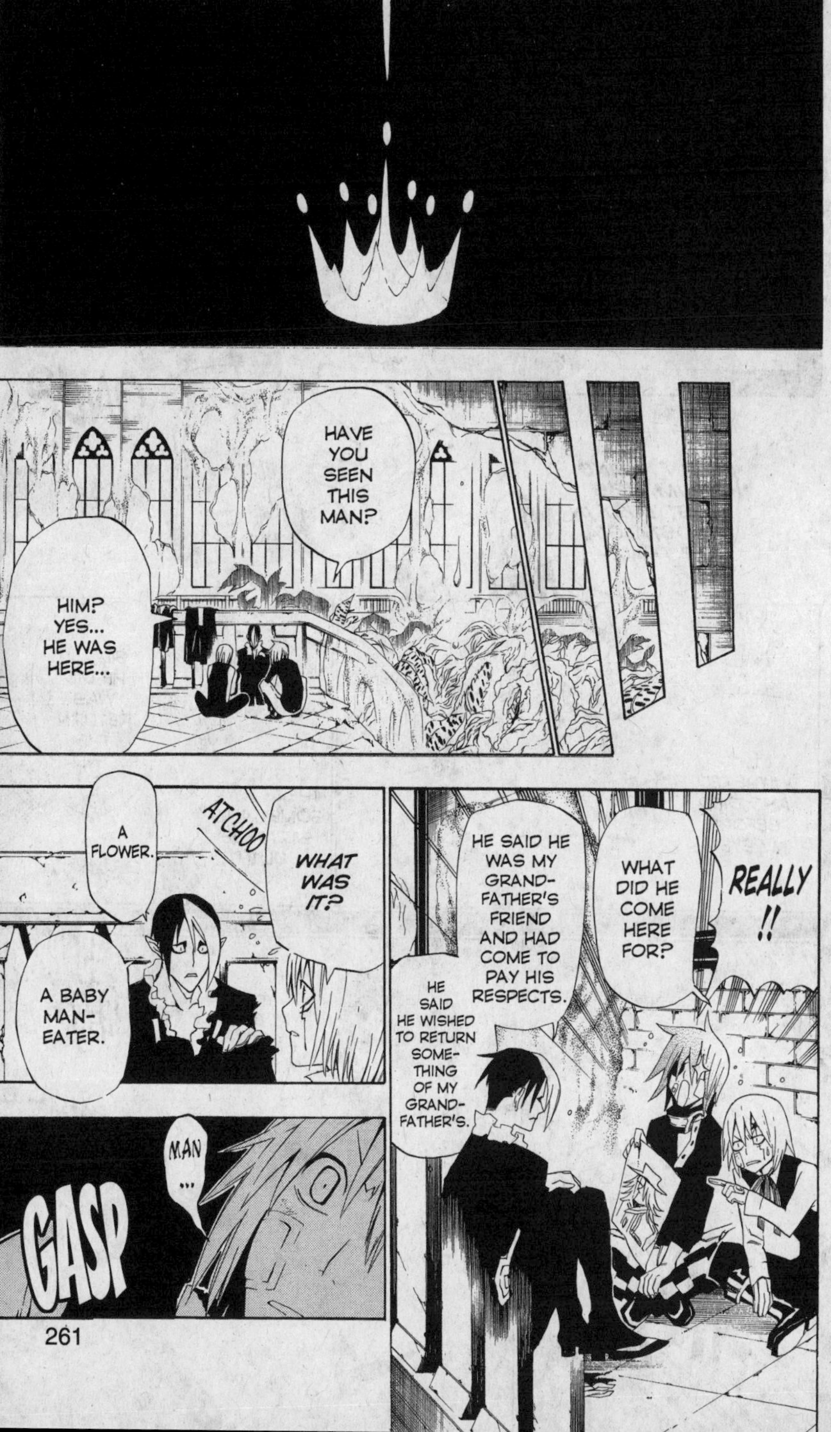
HAVE YOU SEEN THIS MAN?
HIM? YES... HE WAS HERE...
REALLY!!
WHAT DID HE COME HERE FOR?
HE SAID HE WAS MY GRAND-FATHER'S FRIEND AND HAD COME TO PAY HIS RESPECTS.
HE SAID HE WISHED TO RETURN SOME-THING OF MY GRAND-FATHER'S.
WHAT WAS IT?
ATCHOO
A FLOWER.
A BABY MAN-EATER.
MAN ...
GASP

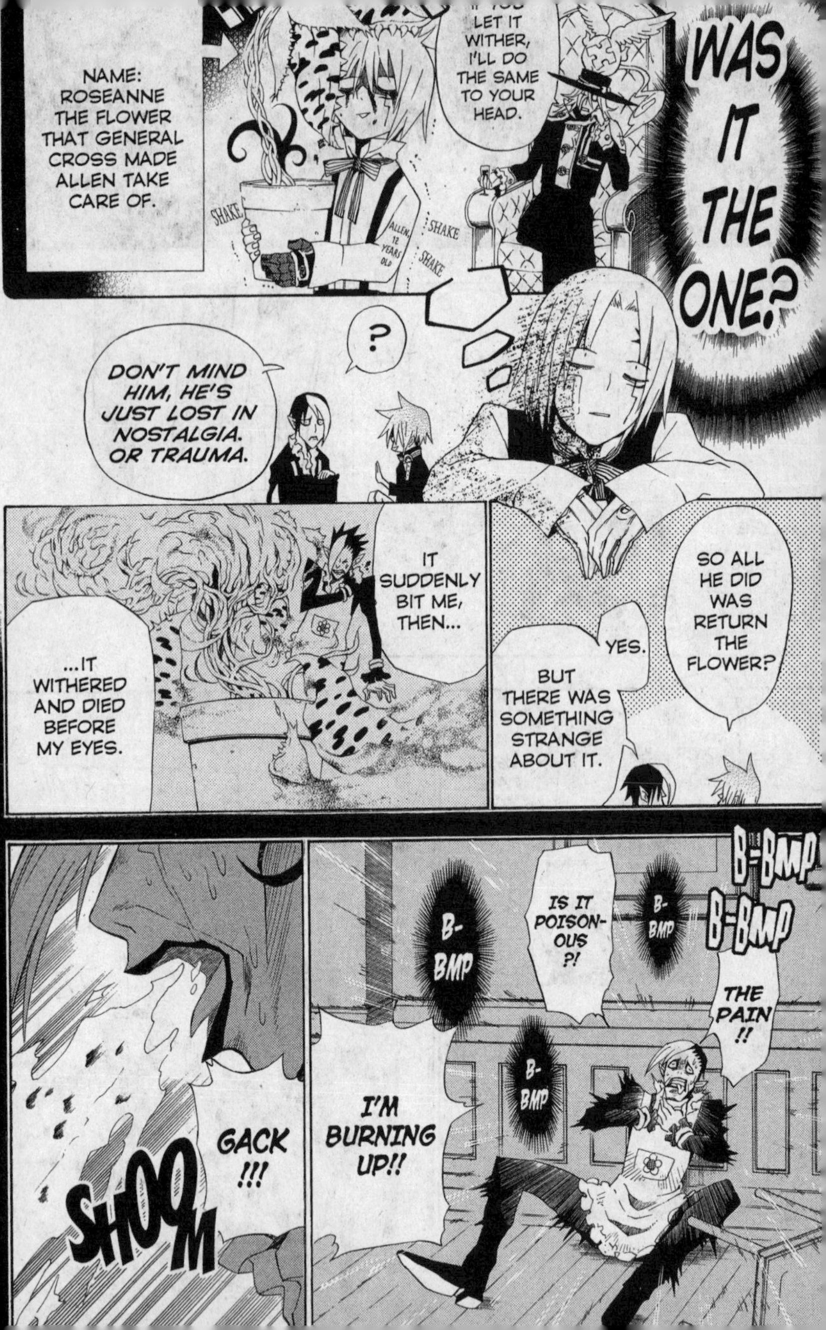
WAS IT THE ONE?
LET IT WITHER, I'LL DO THE SAME TO YOUR HEAD.
NAME: ROSEANNE THE FLOWER THAT GENERAL CROSS MADE ALLEN TAKE CARE OF.
SHAKE
SHAKE
SHAKE
ALLEN, 12 YEARS OLD
?
DON'T MIND HIM, HE'S JUST LOST IN NOSTALGIA. OR TRAUMA.
SO ALL HE DID WAS RETURN THE FLOWER?
YES.
BUT THERE WAS SOMETHING STRANGE ABOUT IT.
IT SUDDENLY BIT ME, THEN...
...IT WITHERED AND DIED BEFORE MY EYES.
B-BMP
B-BMP
THE PAIN!!
B-BMP
IS IT POISON-OUS?!
B-BMP
B-BMP
I'M BURNING UP!!
GACK!!!
SHOOM

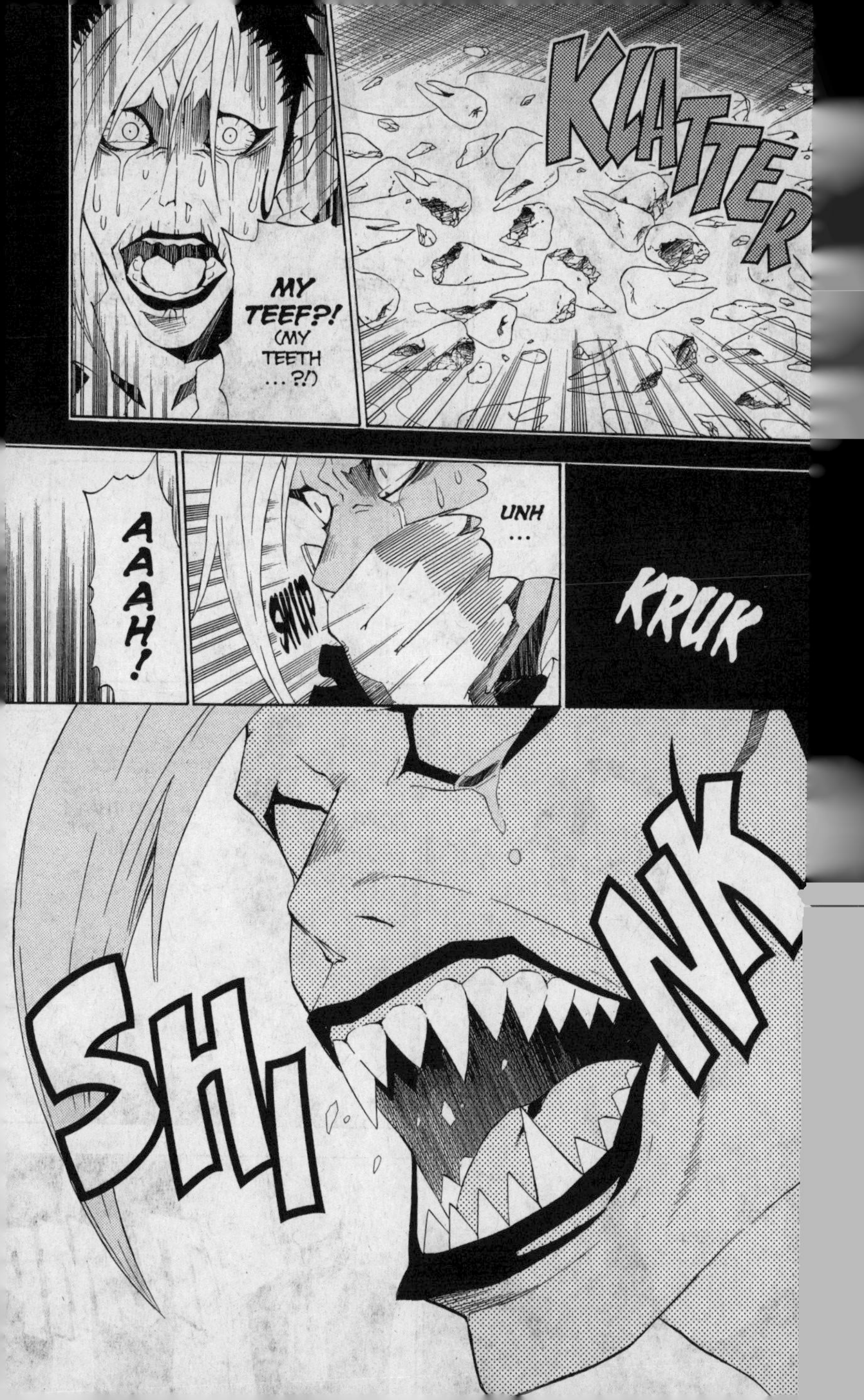
KLATTER
MY TEEF?! (MY TEETH ...?!)
KRUK
UNH ...
SHLUP
AAAAH!
SHINK

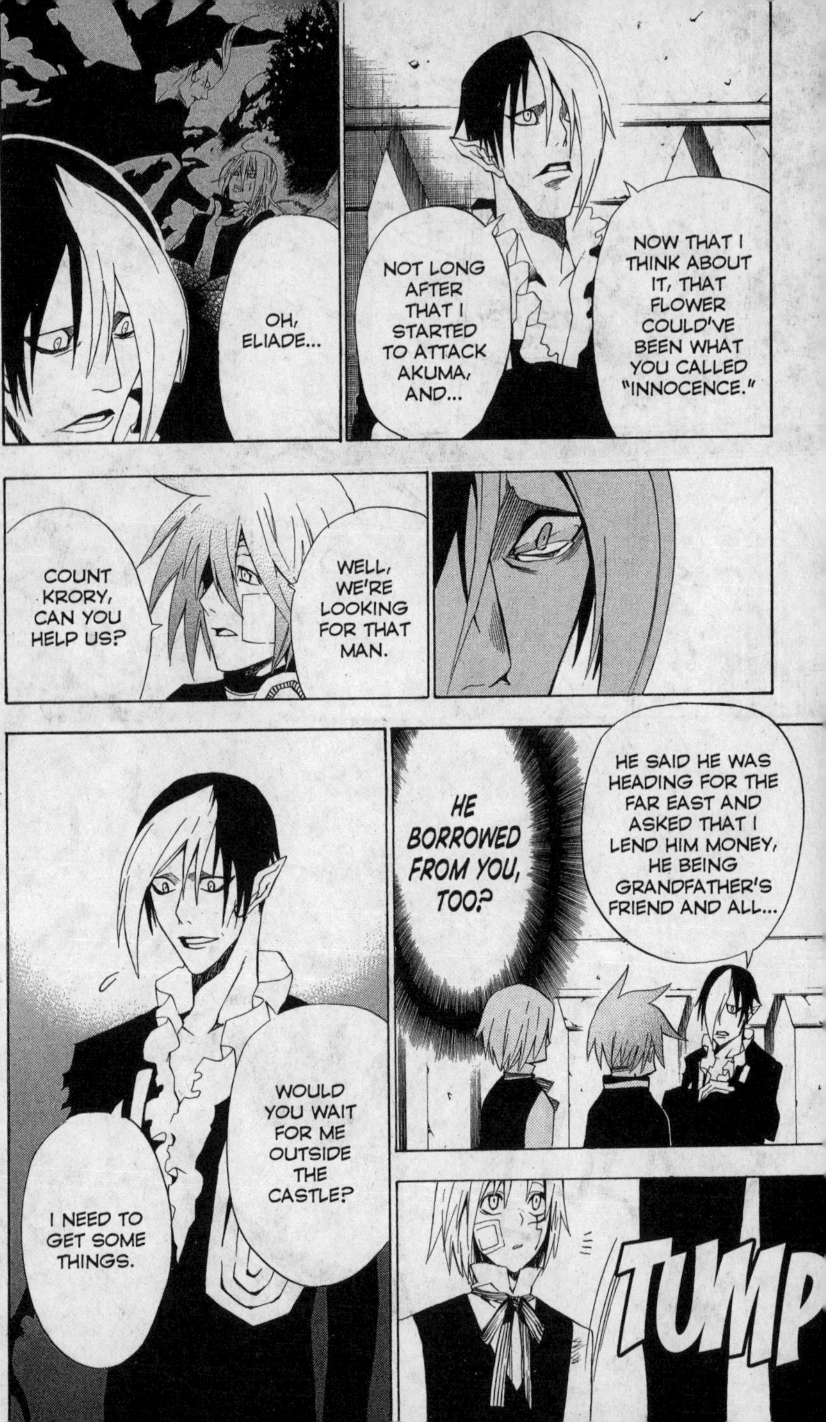
NOW THAT I THINK ABOUT IT, THAT FLOWER COULD'VE BEEN WHAT YOU CALLED "INNOCENCE."
NOT LONG AFTER THAT I STARTED TO ATTACK AKUMA, AND...
OH, ELIADE...
WELL, WE'RE LOOKING FOR THAT MAN.
COUNT KRORY, CAN YOU HELP US?
HE SAID HE WAS HEADING FOR THE FAR EAST AND ASKED THAT I LEND HIM MONEY, HE BEING GRANDFATHER'S FRIEND AND ALL...
HE BORROWED FROM YOU, TOO?
TUMP
WOULD YOU WAIT FOR ME OUTSIDE THE CASTLE?
I NEED TO GET SOME THINGS.

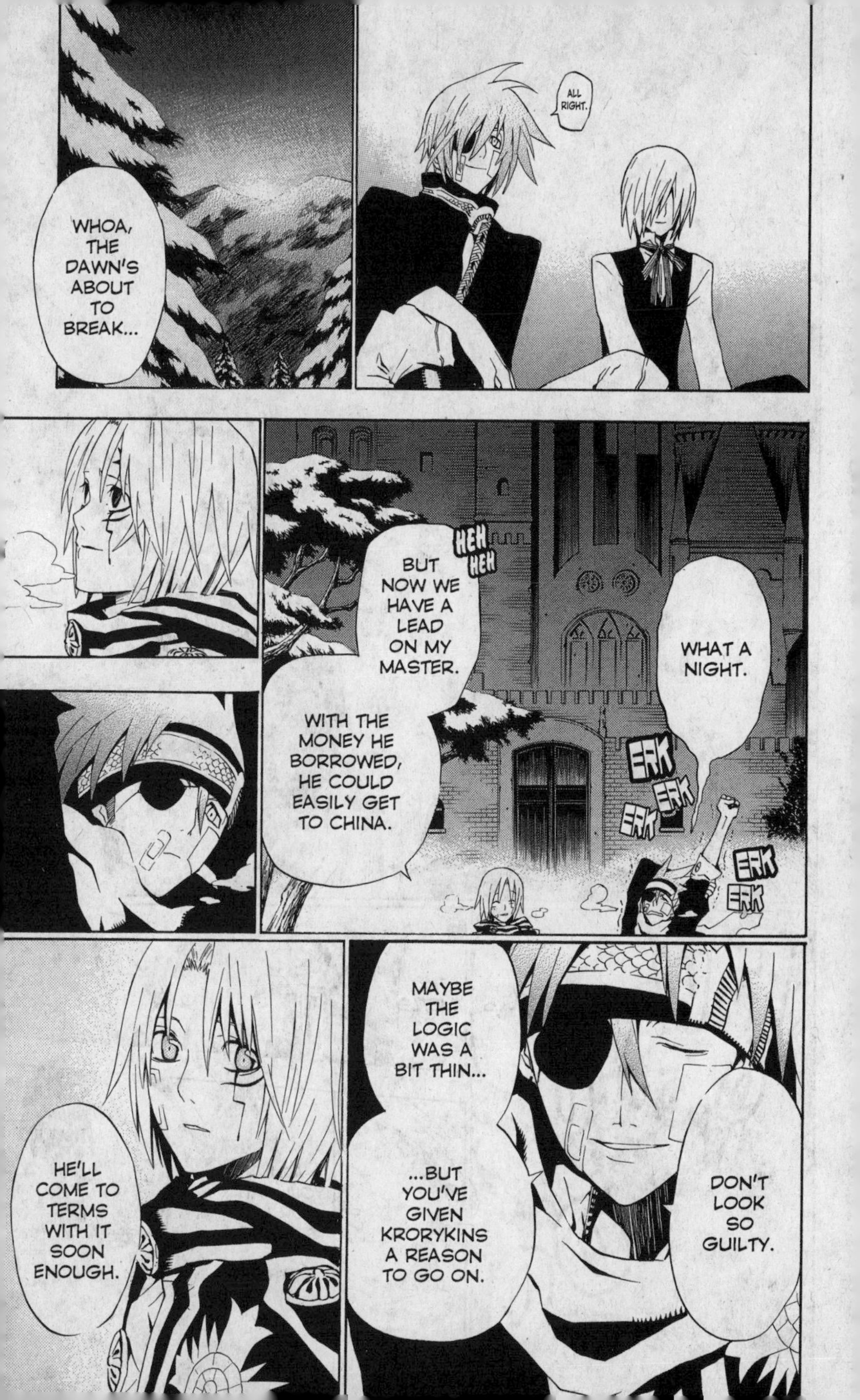
ALL RIGHT.
WHOA, THE DAWN'S ABOUT TO BREAK...
WHAT A NIGHT.
HEH HEH
BUT NOW WE HAVE A LEAD ON MY MASTER.
ERK ERK ERK
ERK ERK
WITH THE MONEY HE BORROWED, HE COULD EASILY GET TO CHINA.
MAYBE THE LOGIC WAS A BIT THIN...
...BUT YOU'VE GIVEN KRORYKINS A REASON TO GO ON.
DON'T LOOK SO GUILTY.
HE'LL COME TO TERMS WITH IT SOON ENOUGH.

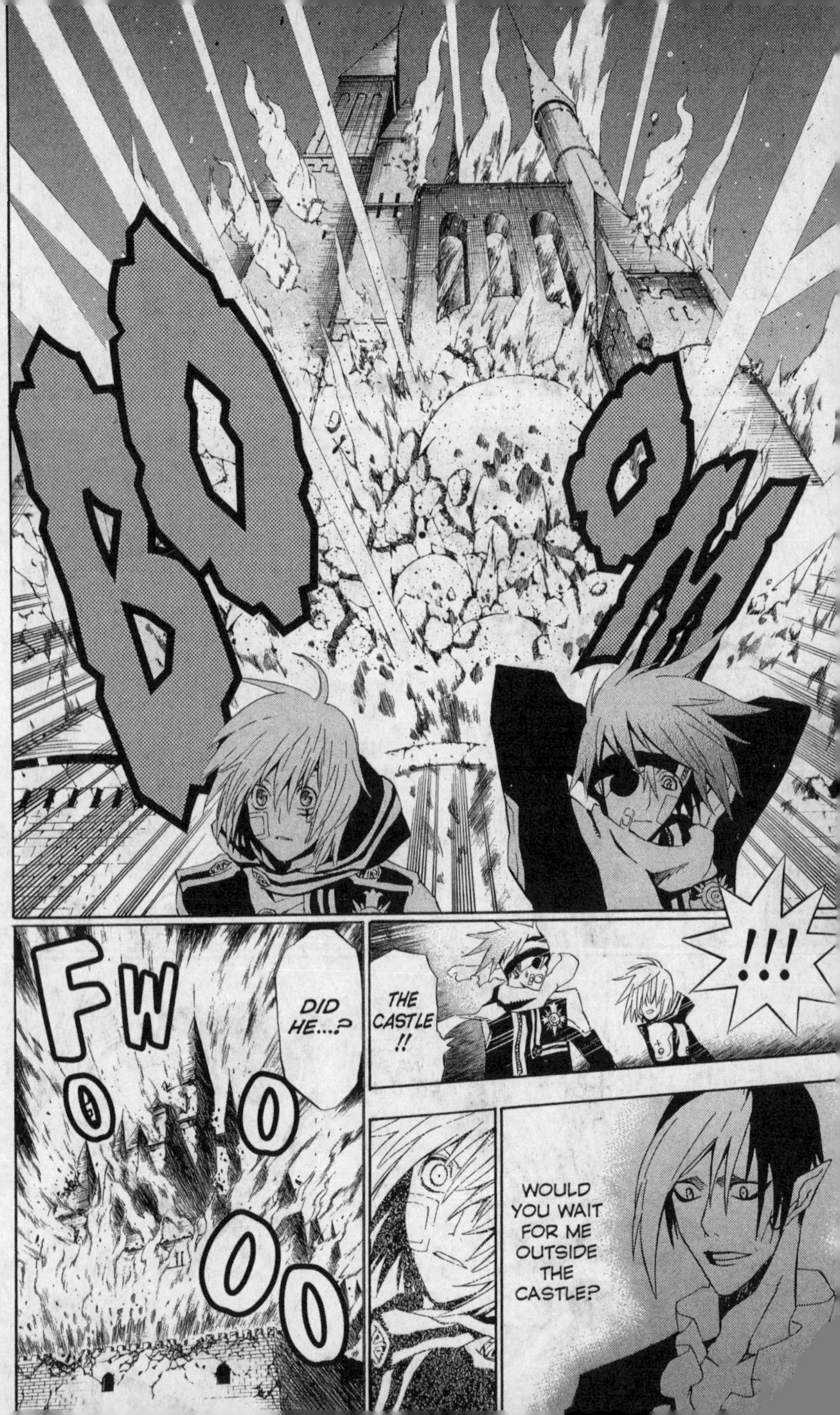
BOOM
!!!
THE CASTLE !!
WOULD YOU WAIT FOR ME OUTSIDE THE CASTLE?
FWOOOOO
DID HE...?

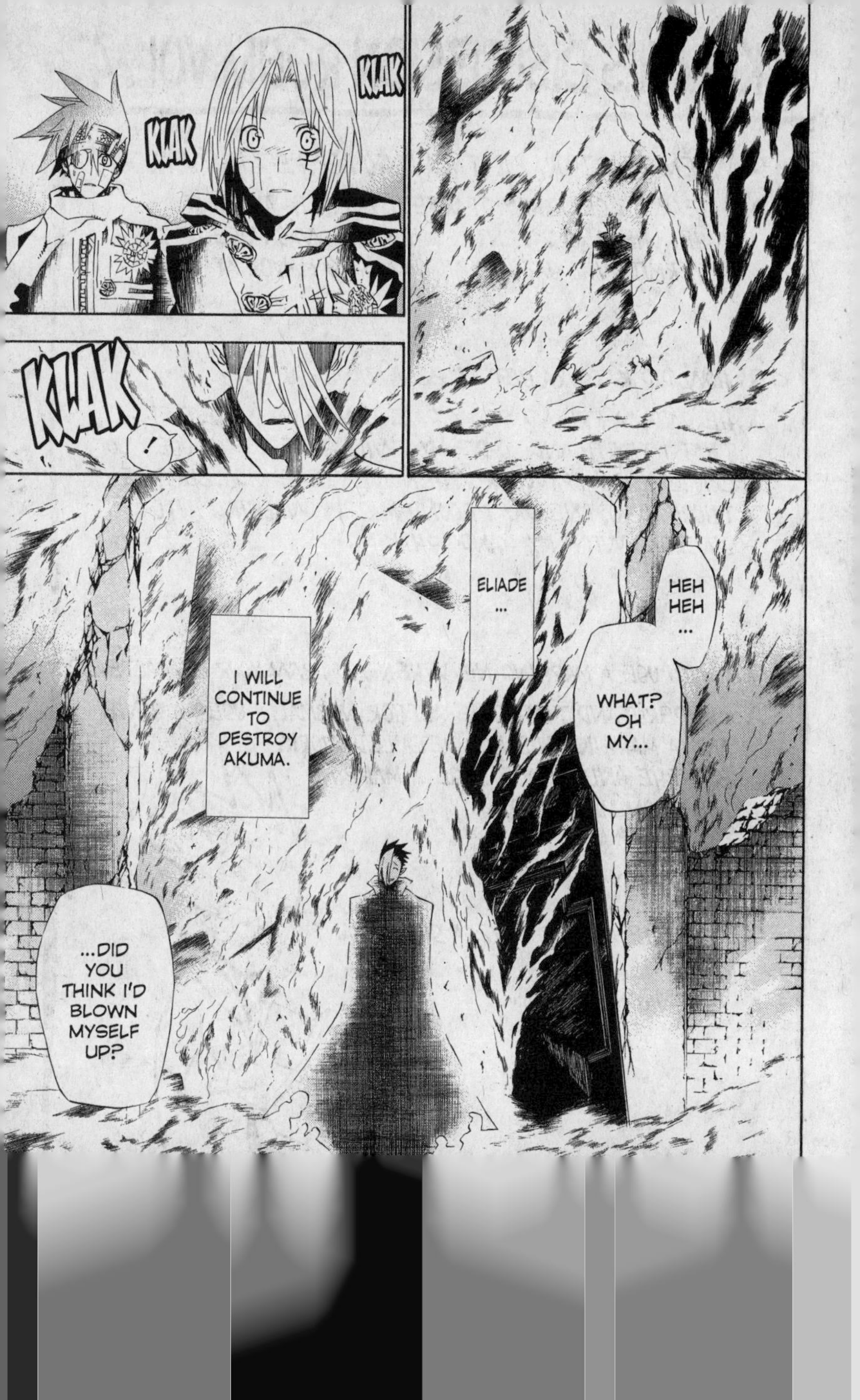
KLAK
KLAK
KLAK
!
HEH HEH ...
WHAT? OH MY...
ELIADE ...
I WILL CONTINUE TO DESTROY AKUMA.
...DID YOU THINK I'D BLOWN MYSELF UP?

KOMUI'S DISCUSSION ROOM VOL. 4

Q. WHEN DID KATSURA FIRST WANT TO BECOME A MANGA ARTIST?

A. I HEAR HE SERIOUSLY STARTED TO THINK ABOUT IT WHEN HE WAS 21. UNTIL THEN, HE WAS MORE OR LESS A HERMIT WHO SAT AROUND DRAWING MANGA AT HOME.

Q. HOW DID KATSURA GET TO BE A MANGA ARTIST?

A. HE SAID, "A FRIEND AT MY PART-TIME JOB SUGGESTED THAT I TRY IT AND SO DID MY TWIN SISTER, WHO USED TO CRITICIZE MY ARTWORK WHEN WE WERE KIDS. BECAUSE OF THOSE TWO, ONE DAY I FOUND MYSELF WALKING INTO SHUEISHA WITH MY HANDS SHAKING."

Q. DO YOU USE A MAPPING NIB WHEN YOU DRAW YOUR CHARACTERS?

A. I UNDERSTAND THAT THE AUTHOR NORMALLY USES A G NIB AND A MAPPING NIB FOR DETAILED WORK. BUT THE ONLY PLACE I USE A MAPPING NIB IS ON MY BEARD.

Q. DOES THE AUTHOR HAVE A SIGNIFICANT OTHER?

A. YES, HIS CAT "KORO."

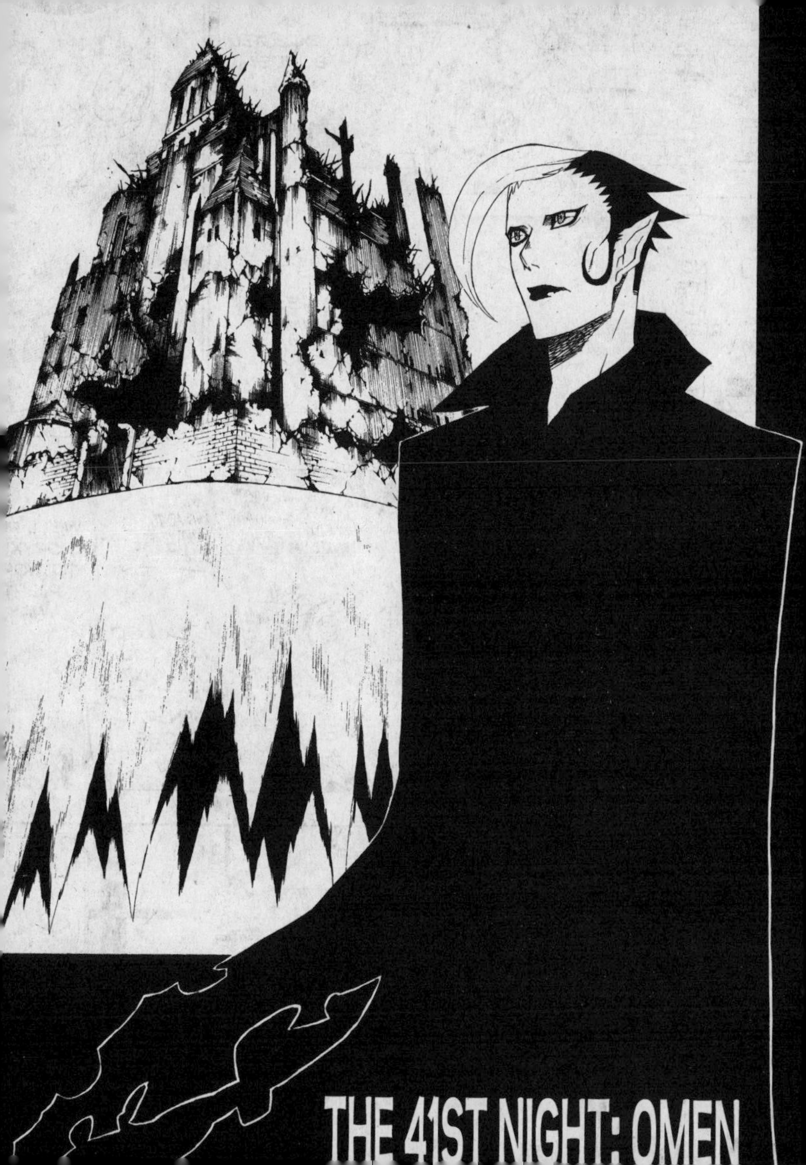
THE 41ST NIGHT: OMEN

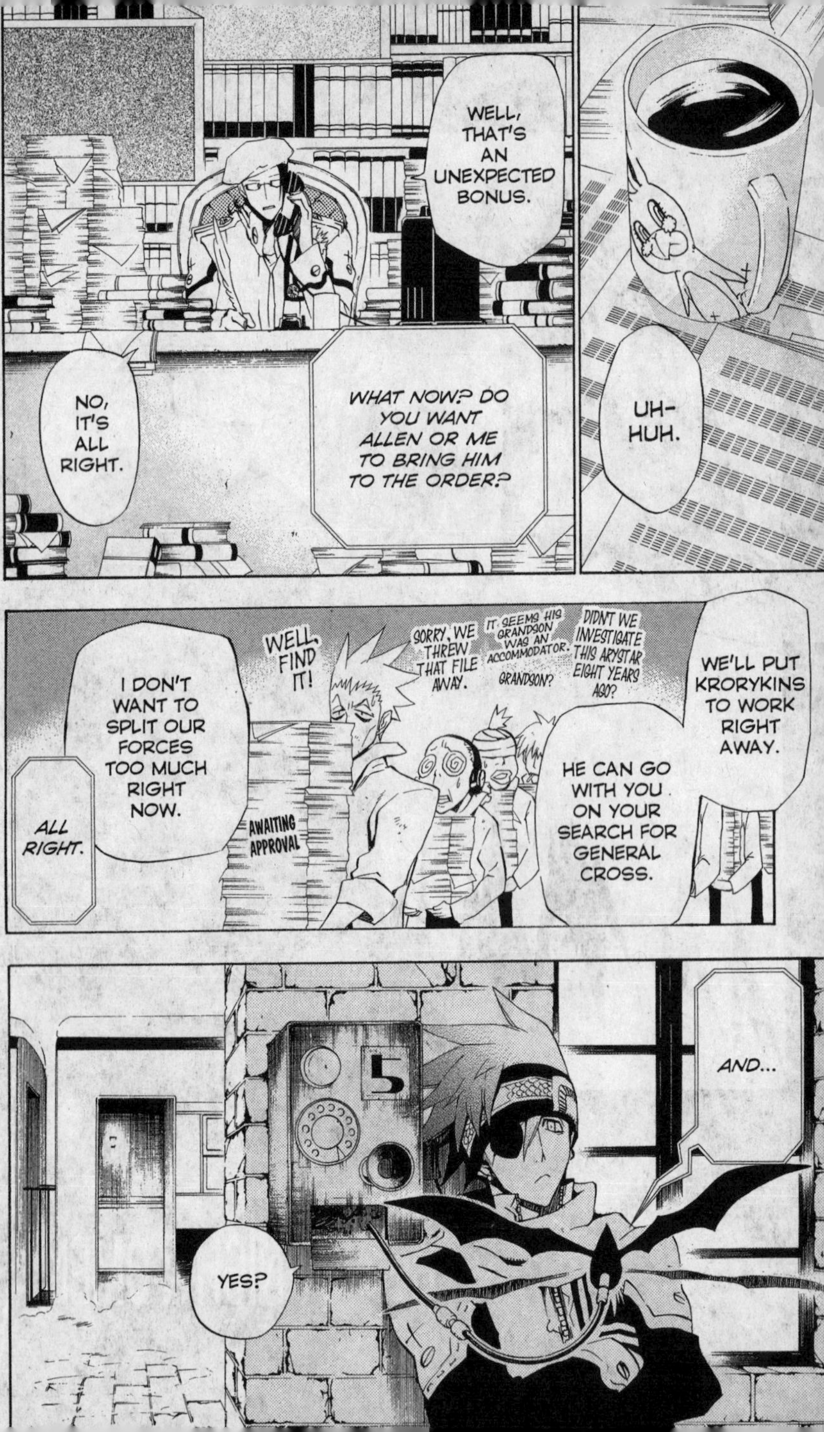
UH-HUH.
WELL, THAT'S AN UNEXPECTED BONUS.
WHAT NOW? DO YOU WANT ALLEN OR ME TO BRING HIM TO THE ORDER?
NO, IT'S ALL RIGHT.
WE'LL PUT KRORYKINS TO WORK RIGHT AWAY.
HE CAN GO WITH YOU ON YOUR SEARCH FOR GENERAL CROSS.
DIDN'T WE INVESTIGATE THIS ARYSTAR EIGHT YEARS AGO?
IT SEEMS HIS GRANDSON WAS AN ACCOMMODATOR.
GRANDSON?
SORRY, WE THREW THAT FILE AWAY.
WELL, FIND IT!
AWAITING APPROVAL
I DON'T WANT TO SPLIT OUR FORCES TOO MUCH RIGHT NOW.
ALL RIGHT.
AND...
YES?

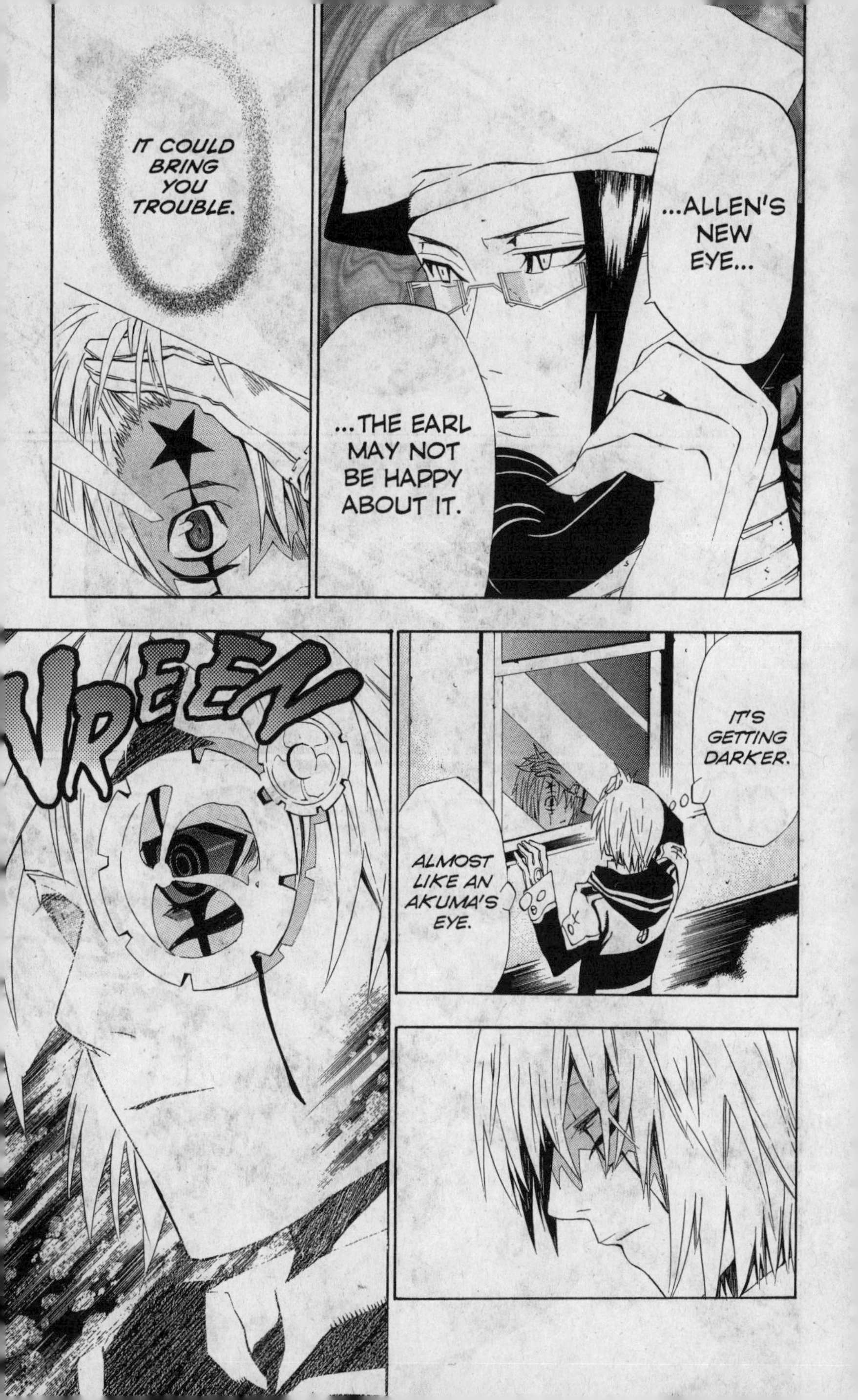
...ALLEN'S NEW EYE...
...THE EARL MAY NOT BE HAPPY ABOUT IT.
IT COULD BRING YOU TROUBLE.
IT'S GETTING DARKER.
ALMOST LIKE AN AKUMA'S EYE.
VREEN

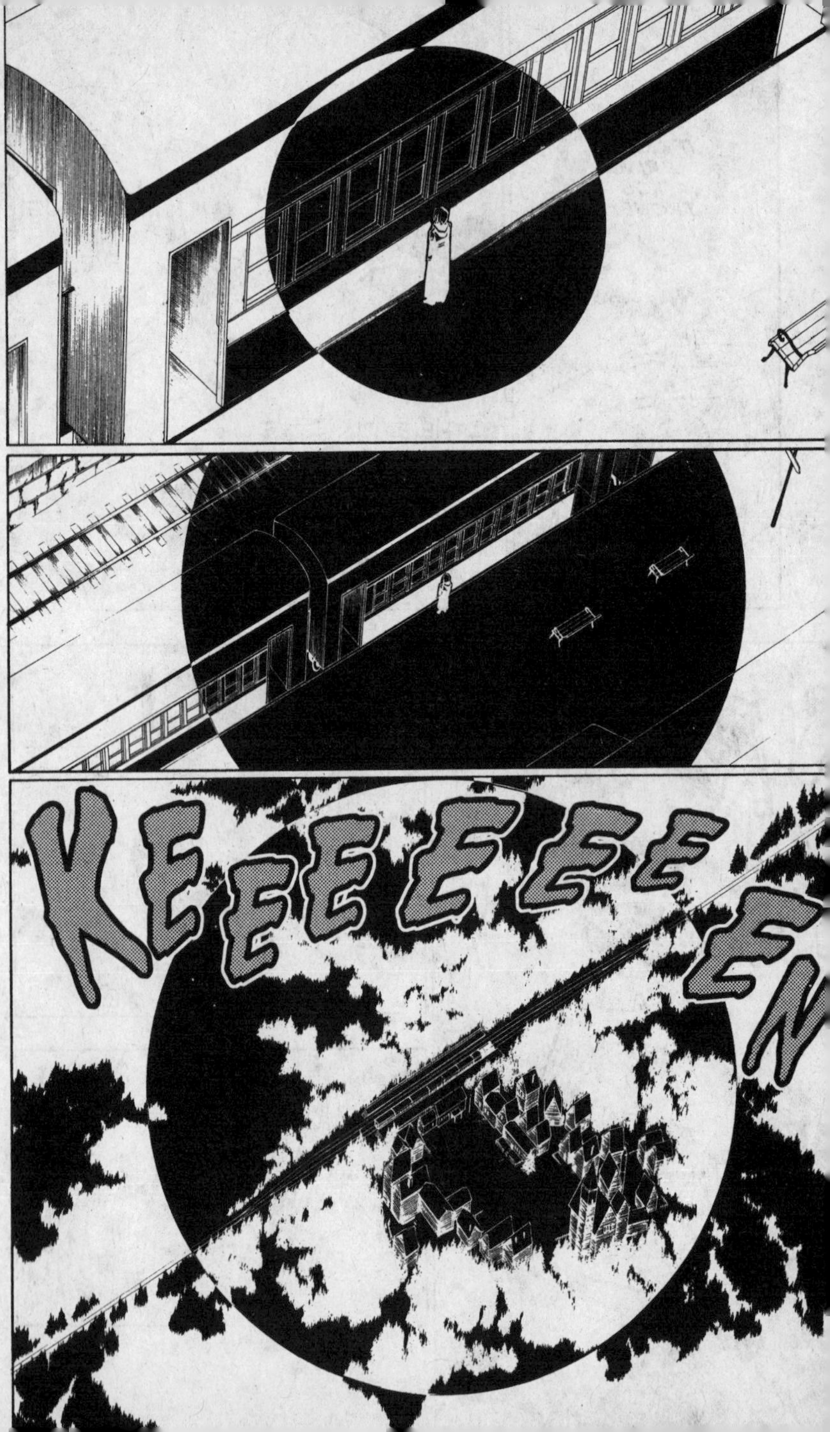
KEEEEEEEN

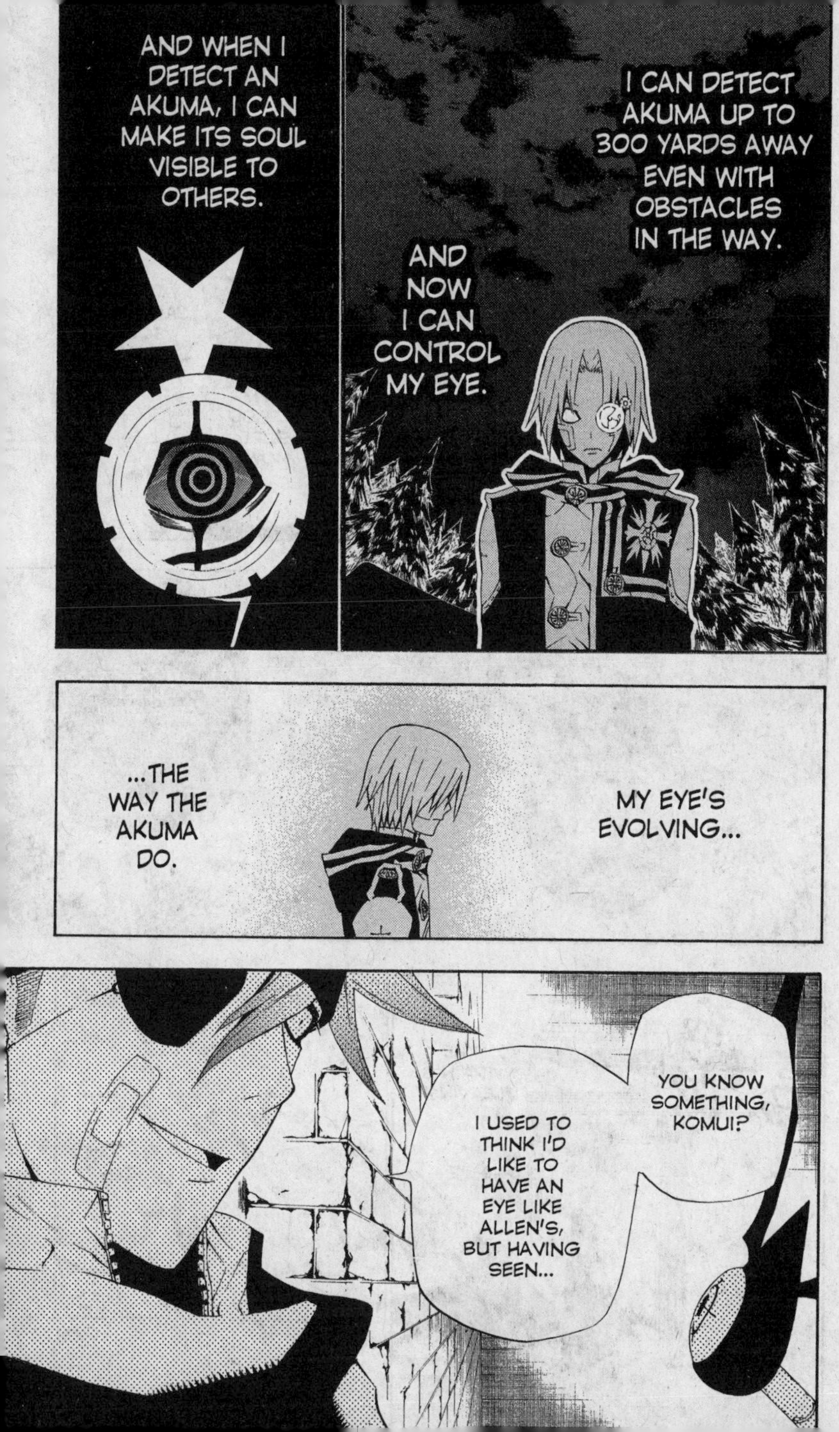
I CAN DETECT AKUMA UP TO 300 YARDS AWAY EVEN WITH OBSTACLES IN THE WAY.
AND NOW I CAN CONTROL MY EYE.
AND WHEN I DETECT AN AKUMA, I CAN MAKE ITS SOUL VISIBLE TO OTHERS.
MY EYE'S EVOLVING...
...THE WAY THE AKUMA DO.
YOU KNOW SOMETHING, KOMUI?
I USED TO THINK I'D LIKE TO HAVE AN EYE LIKE ALLEN'S, BUT HAVING SEEN...

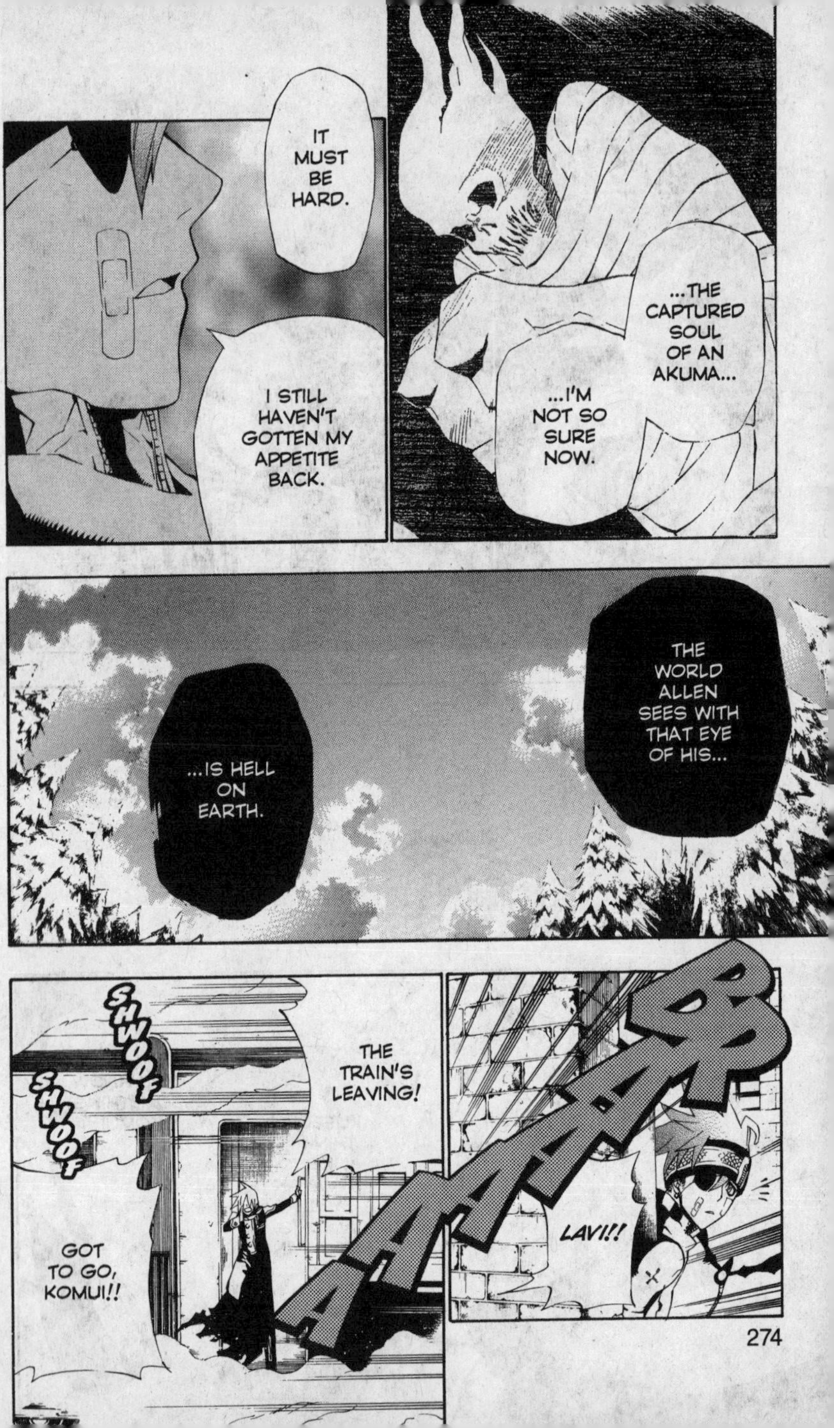
...THE CAPTURED SOUL OF AN AKUMA...
...I'M NOT SO SURE NOW.
IT MUST BE HARD.
I STILL HAVEN'T GOTTEN MY APPETITE BACK.
THE WORLD ALLEN SEES WITH THAT EYE OF HIS...
...IS HELL ON EARTH.
LAVI!!
THE TRAIN'S LEAVING!
SHWOOF
SHWOOF
GOT TO GO, KOMUI!!

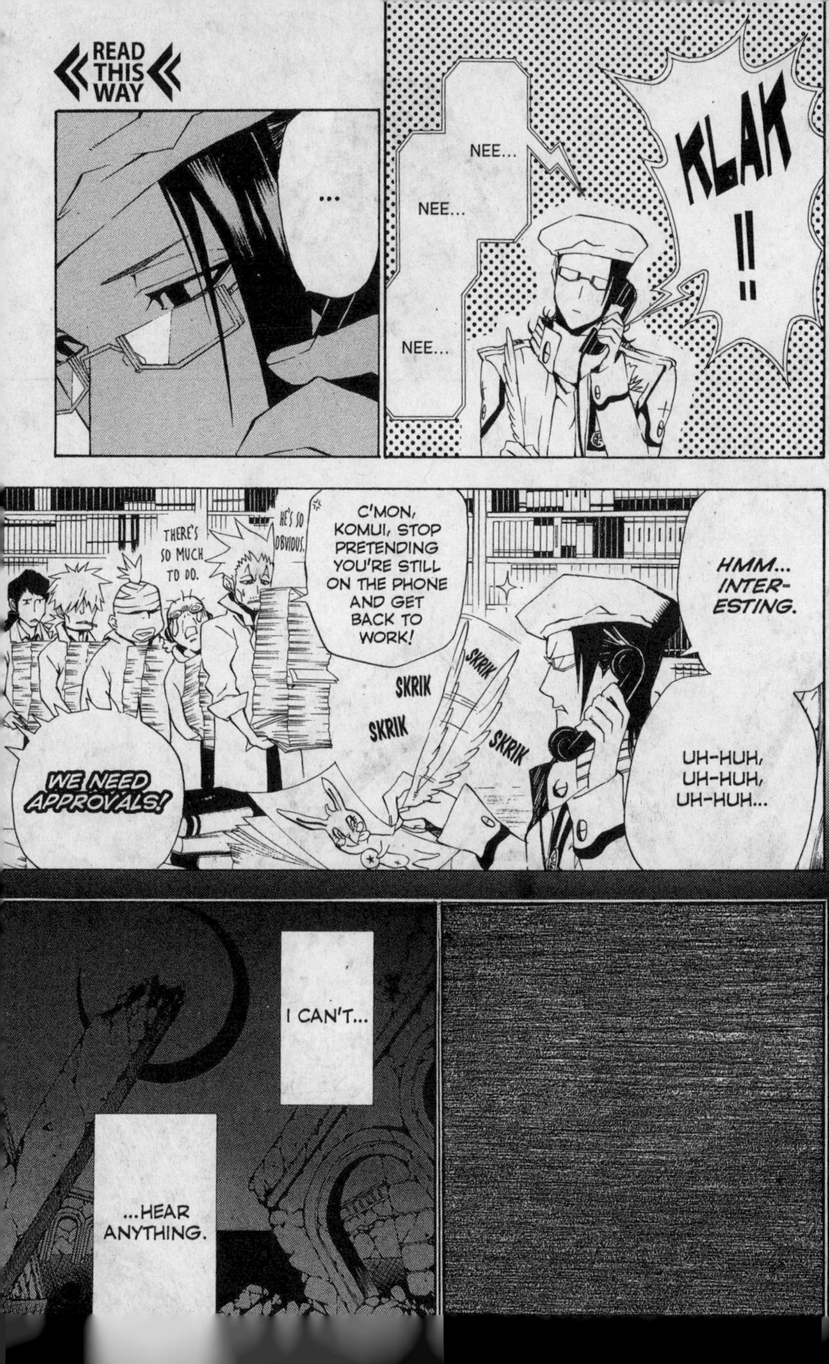
READ THIS WAY
KLAK!!
NEE...
NEE...
NEE...
...
HMM... INTERESTING.
UH-HUH, UH-HUH, UH-HUH...
C'MON, KOMUI, STOP PRETENDING YOU'RE STILL ON THE PHONE AND GET BACK TO WORK!
HE'S SO OBVIOUS.
THERE'S SO MUCH TO DO.
SKRIK
SKRIK
SKRIK
WE NEED APPROVALS!
I CAN'T...
...HEAR ANYTHING.

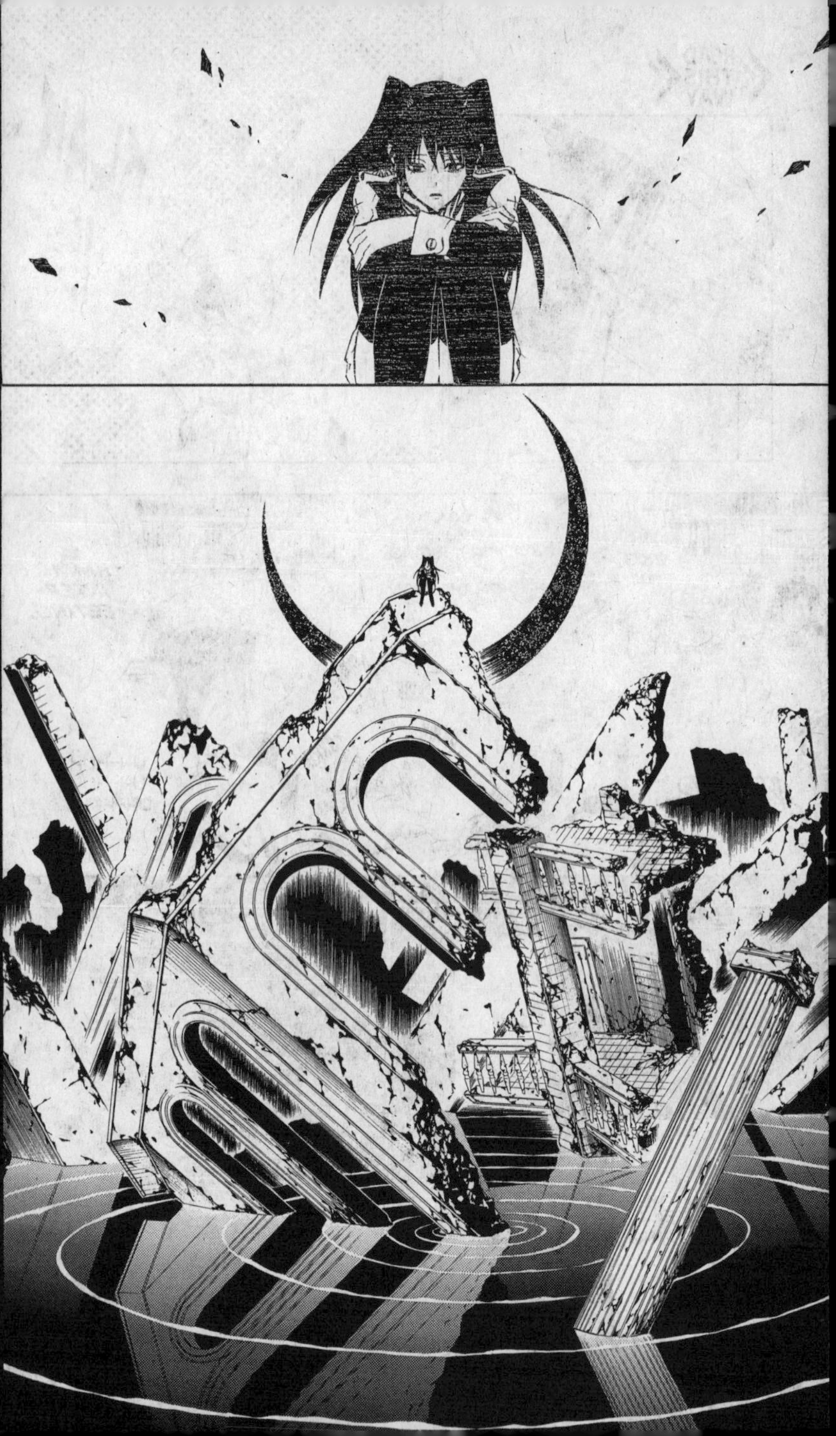

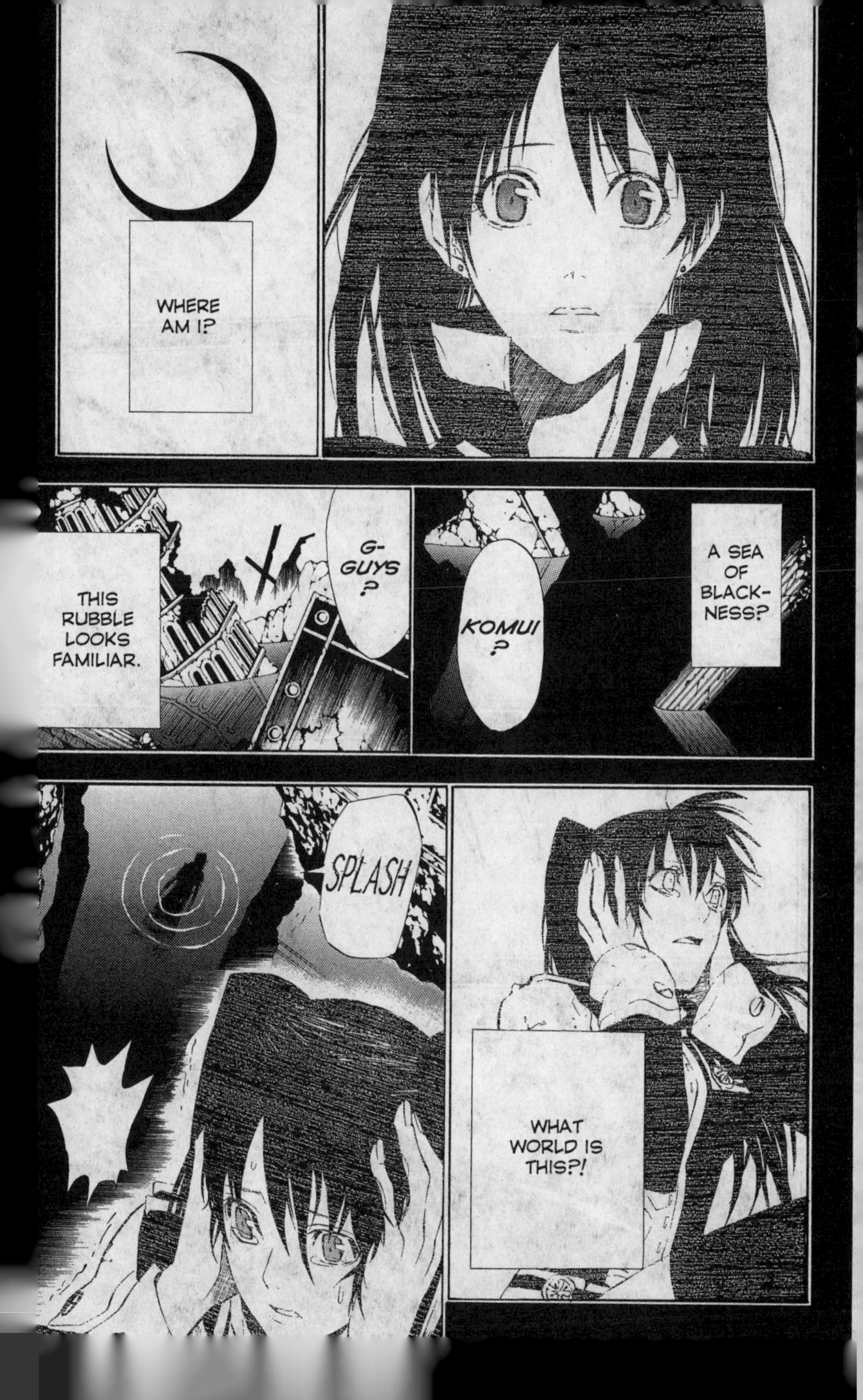
WHERE AM I?
A SEA OF BLACKNESS?
KOMUI?
G-GUYS?
THIS RUBBLE LOOKS FAMILIAR.
WHAT WORLD IS THIS?!
SPLASH

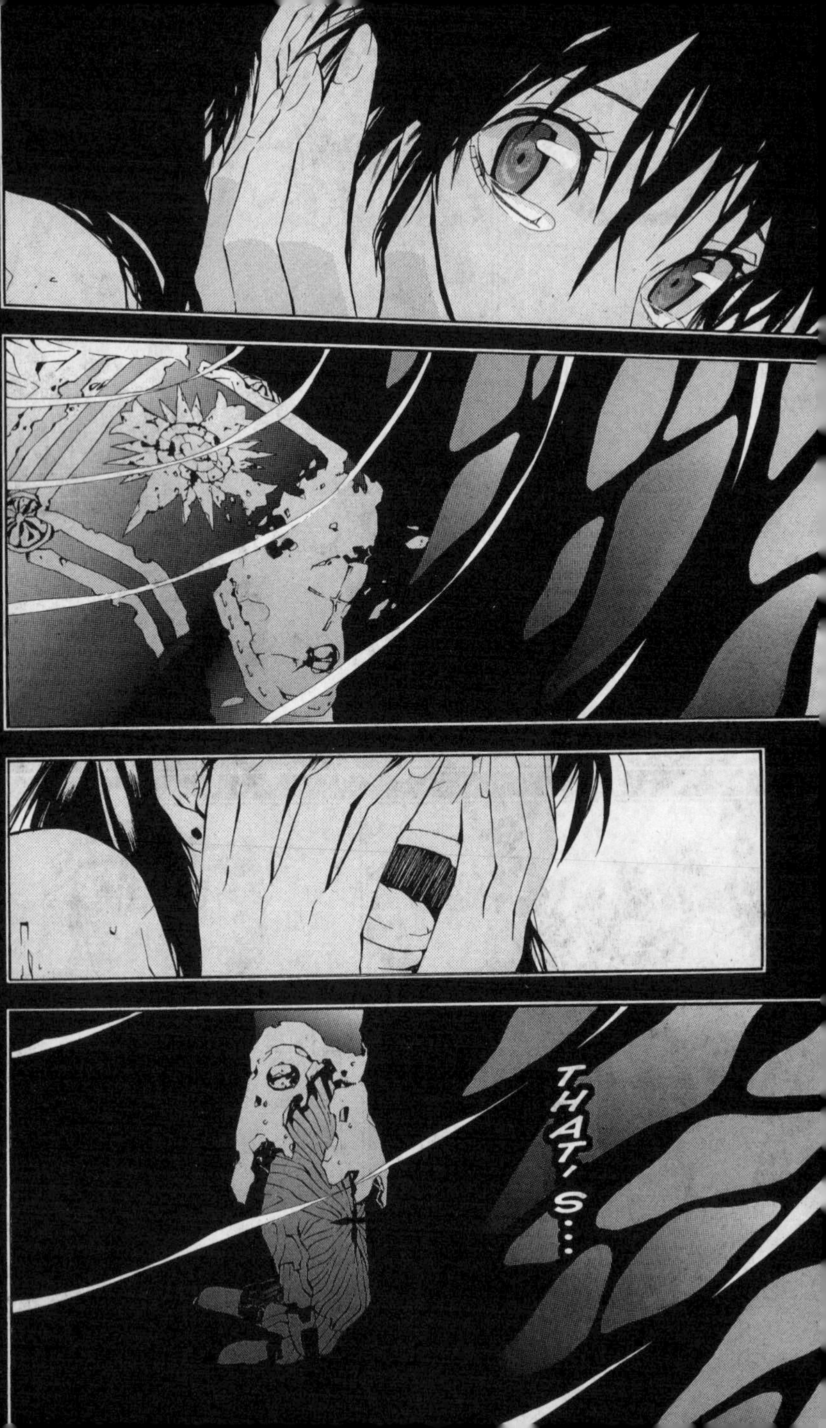
THAT'S...

READ THIS WAY

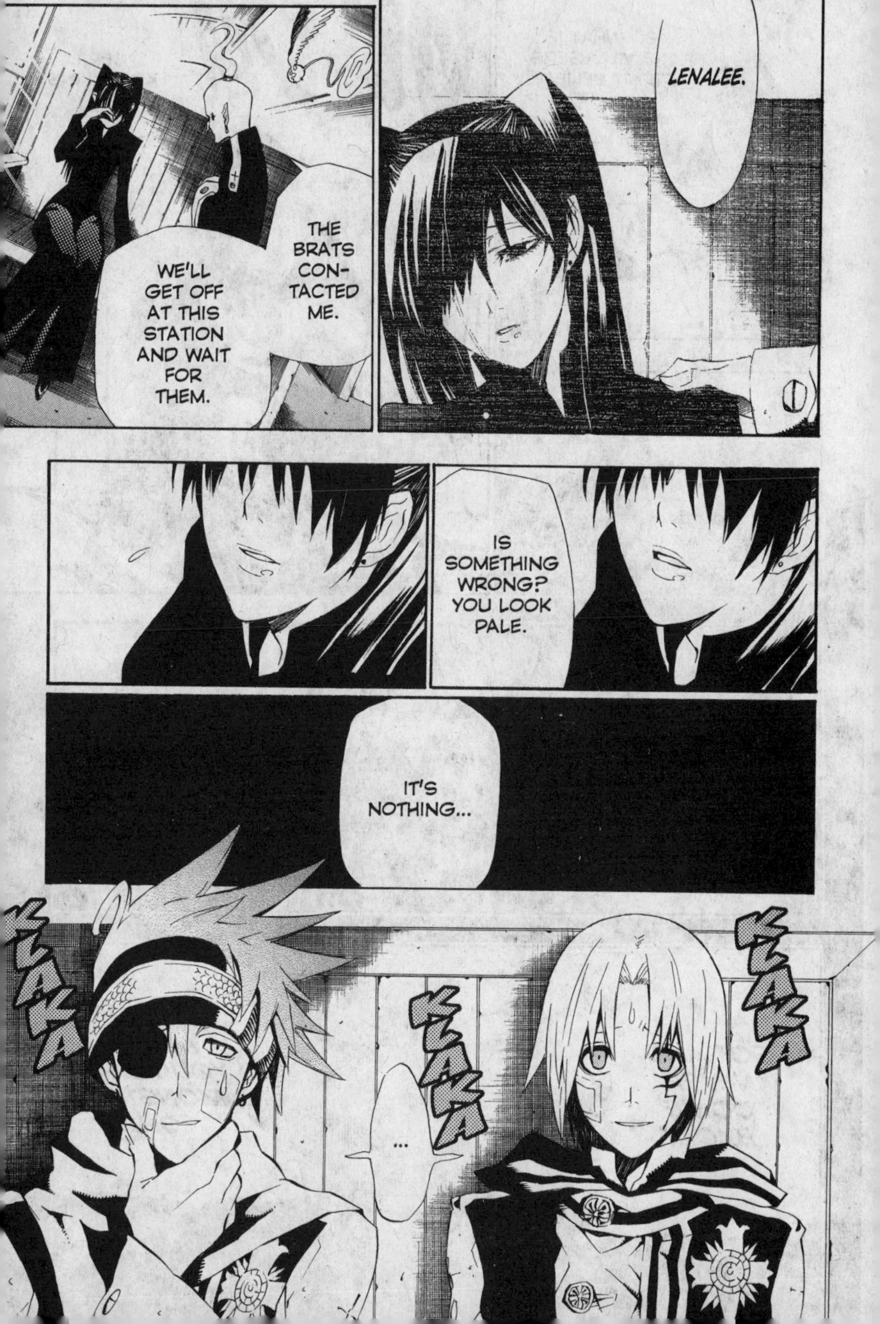

LENALEE.
THE BRATS CON-TACTED ME.
WE'LL GET OFF AT THIS STATION AND WAIT FOR THEM.
IS SOMETHING WRONG? YOU LOOK PALE.
IT'S NOTHING...
KLAKA
KLAKA
...
KLAKA

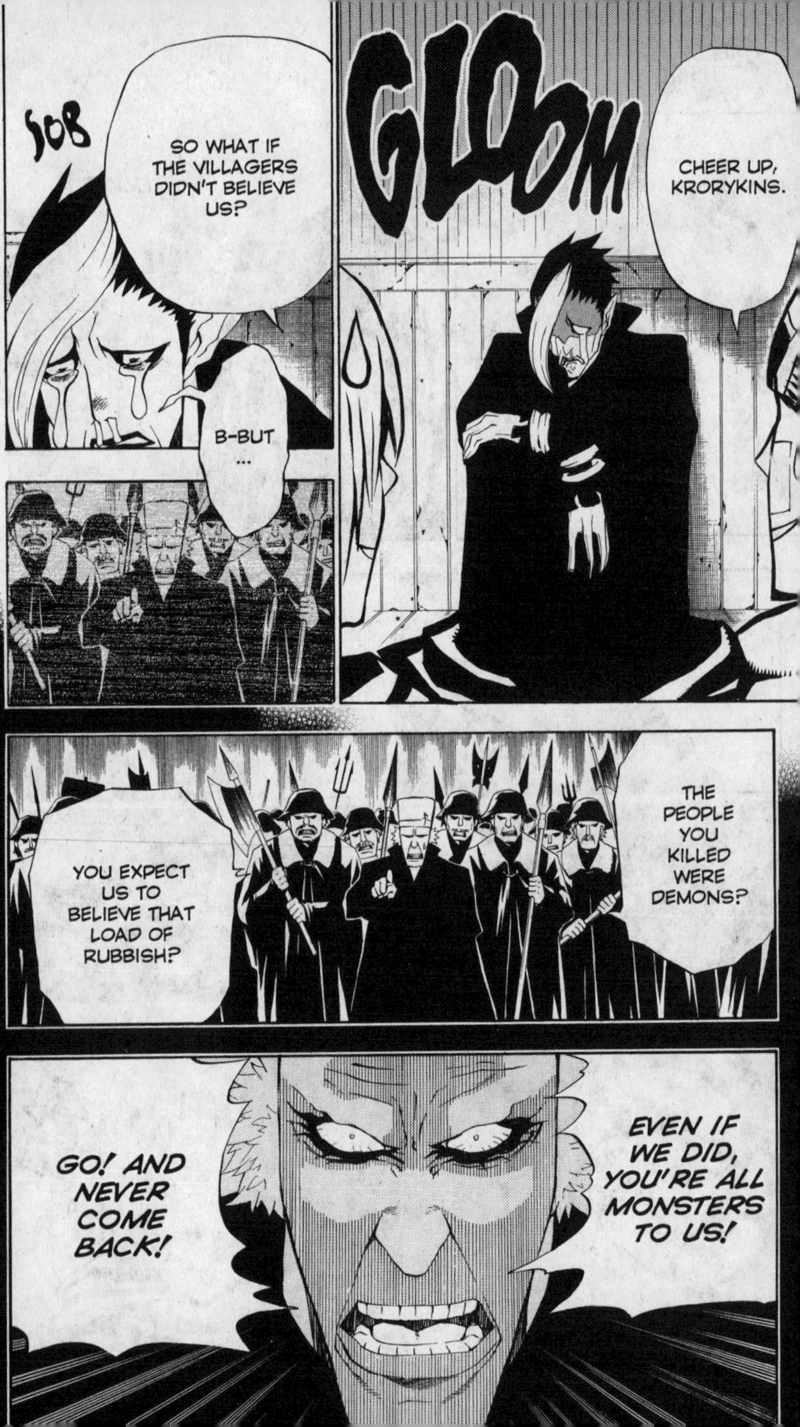
GLOOM
CHEER UP, KRORYKINS.
SO WHAT IF THE VILLAGERS DIDN'T BELIEVE US?
SOB
B-BUT ...
THE PEOPLE YOU KILLED WERE DEMONS?
YOU EXPECT US TO BELIEVE THAT LOAD OF RUBBISH?
EVEN IF WE DID, YOU'RE ALL MONSTERS TO US!
GO! AND NEVER COME BACK!

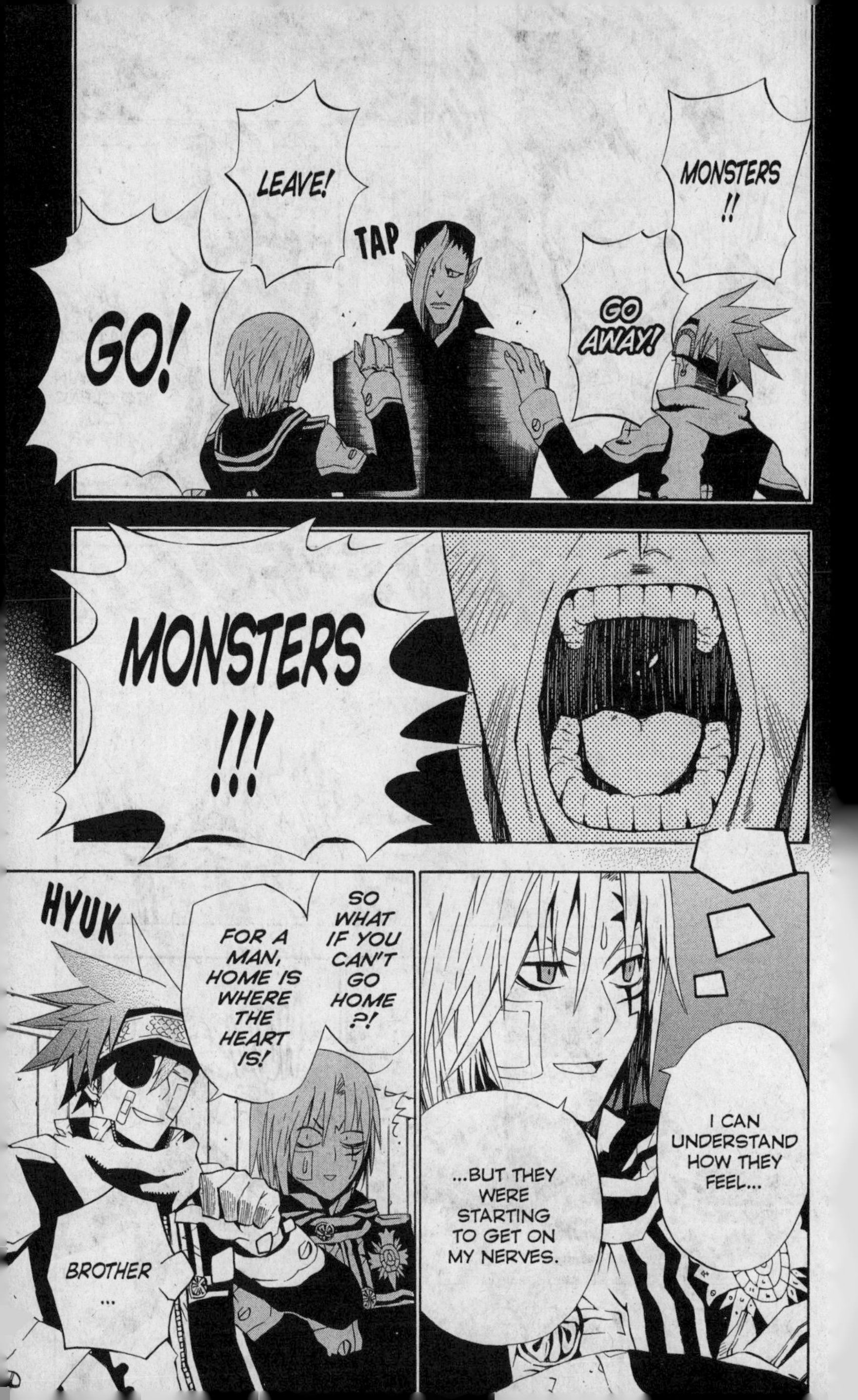
MONSTERS !!
GO AWAY!
TAP
LEAVE!
GO!
MONSTERS !!!
I CAN UNDERSTAND HOW THEY FEEL...
...BUT THEY WERE STARTING TO GET ON MY NERVES.
SO WHAT IF YOU CAN'T GO HOME?!
FOR A MAN, HOME IS WHERE THE HEART IS!
HYUK
BROTHER ...

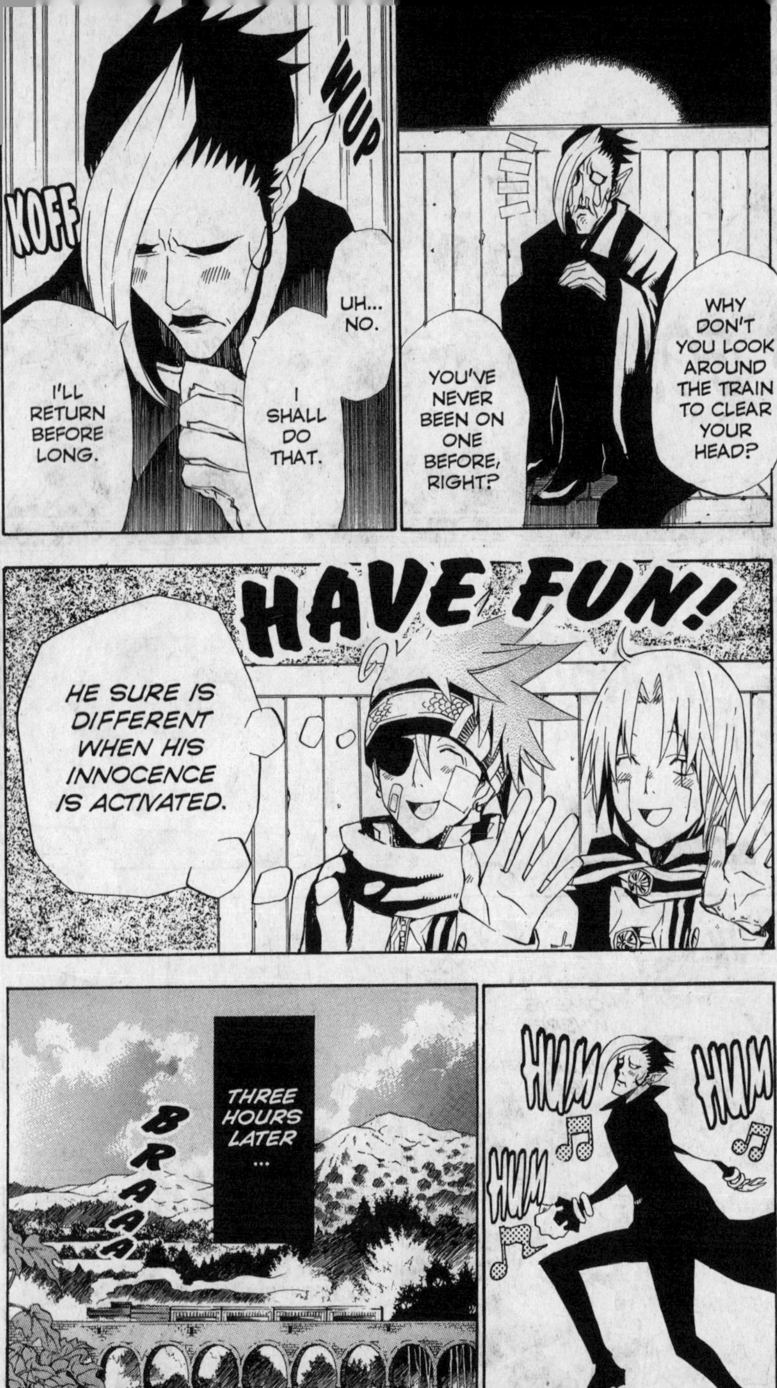
WHY DON'T YOU LOOK AROUND THE TRAIN TO CLEAR YOUR HEAD?
YOU'VE NEVER BEEN ON ONE BEFORE, RIGHT?
WUP
UH... NO.
I SHALL DO THAT.
KOFF
I'LL RETURN BEFORE LONG.
HAVE FUN!
HE SURE IS DIFFERENT WHEN HIS INNOCENCE IS ACTIVATED.
HUM
HUM
HUM
THREE HOURS LATER ...
BRAAAA

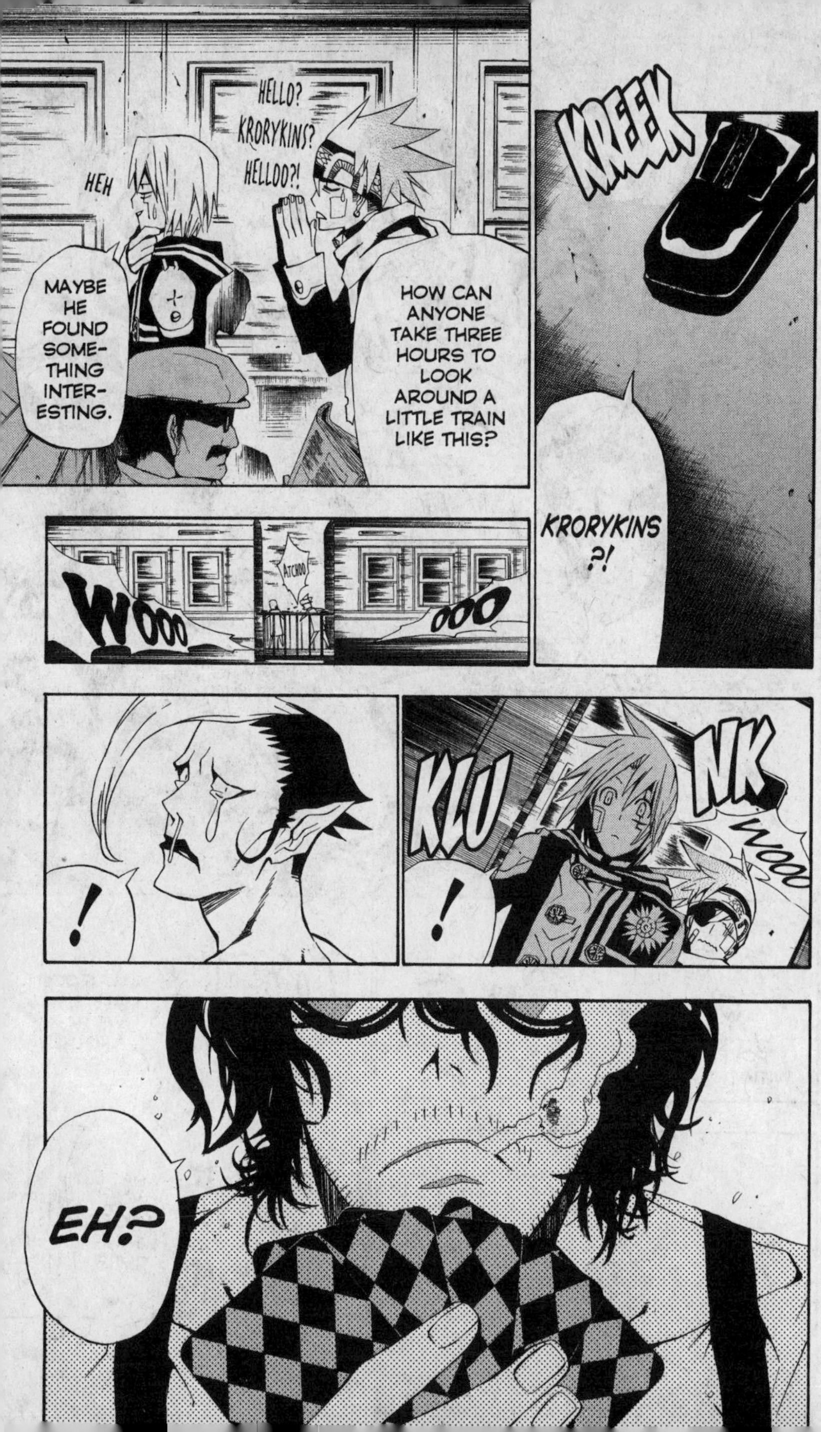
HELLO? KRORYKINS? HELLOO?!
HEH
HOW CAN ANYONE TAKE THREE HOURS TO LOOK AROUND A LITTLE TRAIN LIKE THIS?
MAYBE HE FOUND SOME-THING INTER-ESTING.
WOOO
ATCHOO
OOO
KREEK
KRORYKINS ?!
KLUNK
WOOO
!
!
EH?

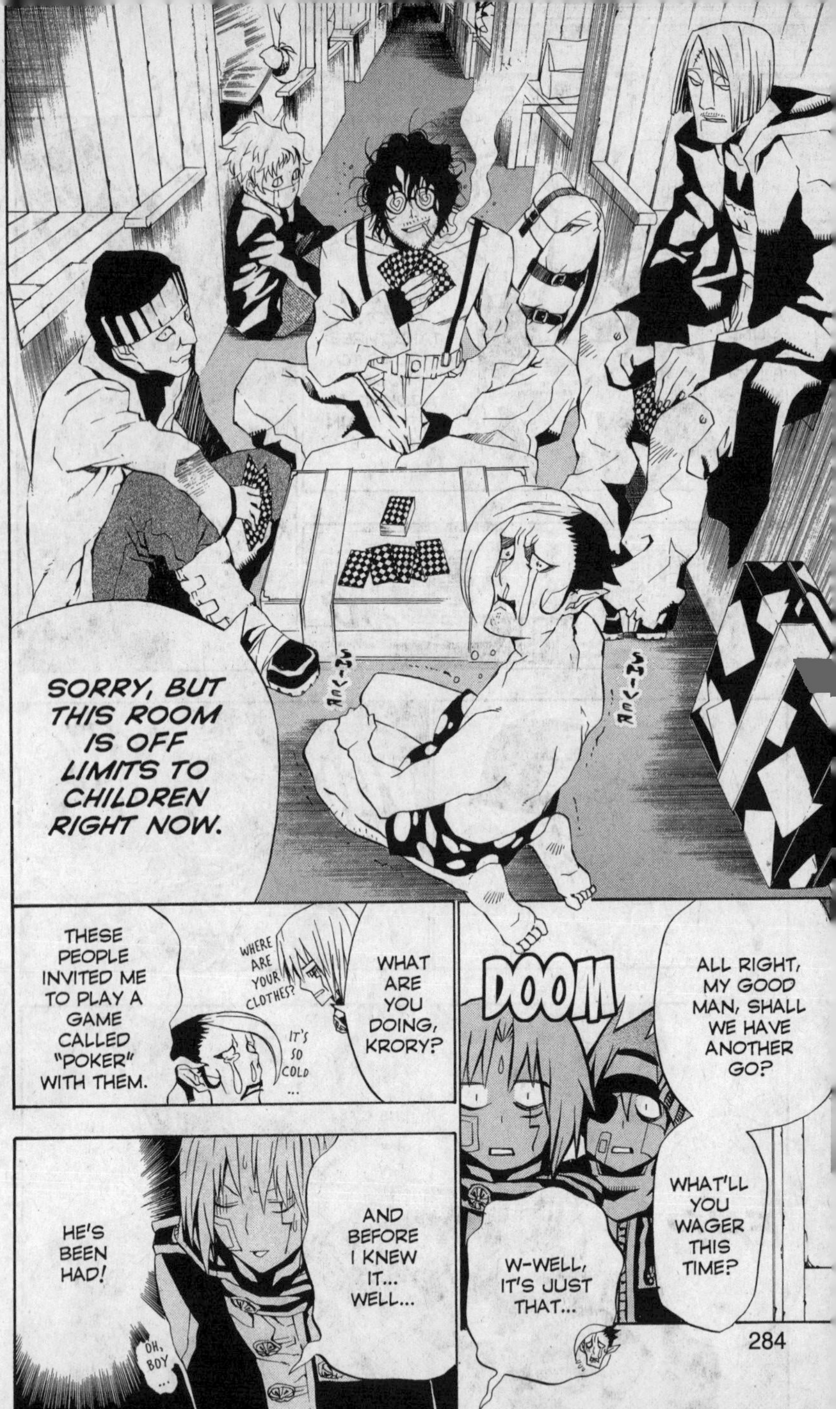
SORRY, BUT THIS ROOM IS OFF LIMITS TO CHILDREN RIGHT NOW.
SHIVER
SHIVER
ALL RIGHT, MY GOOD MAN, SHALL WE HAVE ANOTHER GO?
DOOM
WHAT'LL YOU WAGER THIS TIME?
W-WELL, IT'S JUST THAT...
WHAT ARE YOU DOING, KRORY?
WHERE ARE YOUR CLOTHES?
IT'S SO COLD...
THESE PEOPLE INVITED ME TO PLAY A GAME CALLED "POKER" WITH THEM.
AND BEFORE I KNEW IT... WELL...
HE'S BEEN HAD!
OH, BOY...

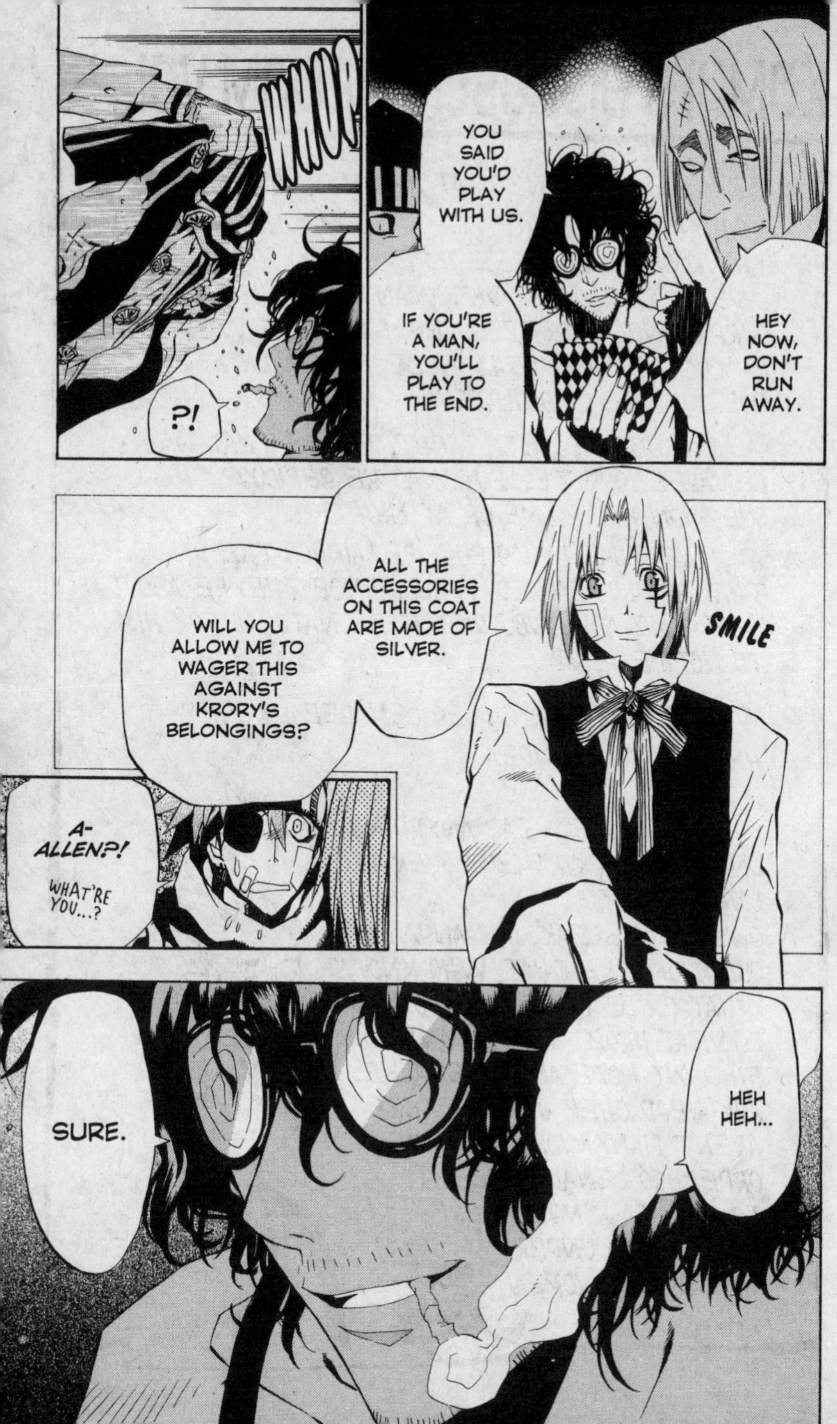
YOU SAID YOU'D PLAY WITH US.
HEY NOW, DON'T RUN AWAY.
IF YOU'RE A MAN, YOU'LL PLAY TO THE END.
WHOP
?!
SMILE
ALL THE ACCESSORIES ON THIS COAT ARE MADE OF SILVER.
WILL YOU ALLOW ME TO WAGER THIS AGAINST KRORY'S BELONGINGS?
A- ALLEN?!
WHAT'RE YOU...?
HEH HEH...
SURE.

KOMUI'S DISCUSSION ROOM VOL. 5

Q. IS THERE ANYTHING THAT ALLEN CAN'T EAT?

A. SOMETHING ALLEN CAN'T EAT, EH? WELL, COME TO THINK OF IT, LENALEE OFFERED HIM SOMETHING SWEET THAT SHE DIDN'T WANT TO FINISH AND, SURPRISINGLY, HE DECLINED. I THINK IT WAS CHOCOLATE CAKE. COULD IT BE THAT ALLEN DOESN'T LIKE CHOCOLATE?

Q. ALLEN, ON THE 18TH NIGHT, THINKS THAT LENALEE IS "CUTE," BUT WAS HE SERIOUS? THIS QUESTION KEEPS ME UP AT NIGHT!

A. AT THAT TIME I WAS BUSY REPAIRING THE DAMAGE THAT KOMLIN CAUSED. WELL, SINCE THEY'RE ABOUT THE SAME AGE, WOULDN'T IT BE NATURAL FOR HIM TO NOTICE HER?

Q. WHAT KIND OF BOYS DOES LENALEE LIKE?

A. HMM...I HAVE NO IDEA.

Q. DOES LENALEE WEAR ANYTHING UNDER HER SKIRT (BUT OVER HER UNDERWEAR)?

A. GIVE ME A BREAK. IF I ANSWER A QUESTION LIKE THAT, WHO KNOWS WHAT CHIEF KOMUI WILL DO TO ME? [SWEAT DROP] IF YOU WANT TO FIND OUT MORE ABOUT LENALEE, ASK HEAD CHEF JERRY. THERE AREN'T MANY WOMEN IN THE ORDER, SO LENALEE SEEMS TO LIKE TALKING TO JERRY BECAUSE HE UNDERSTANDS HOW WOMEN THINK.

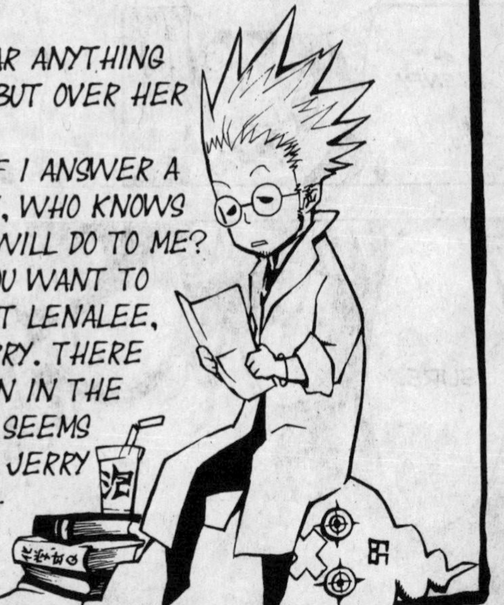
泥

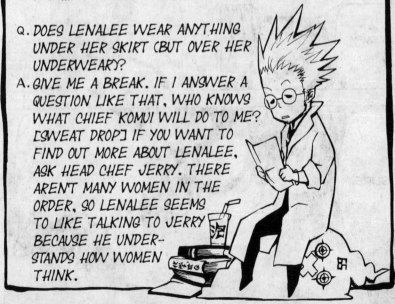

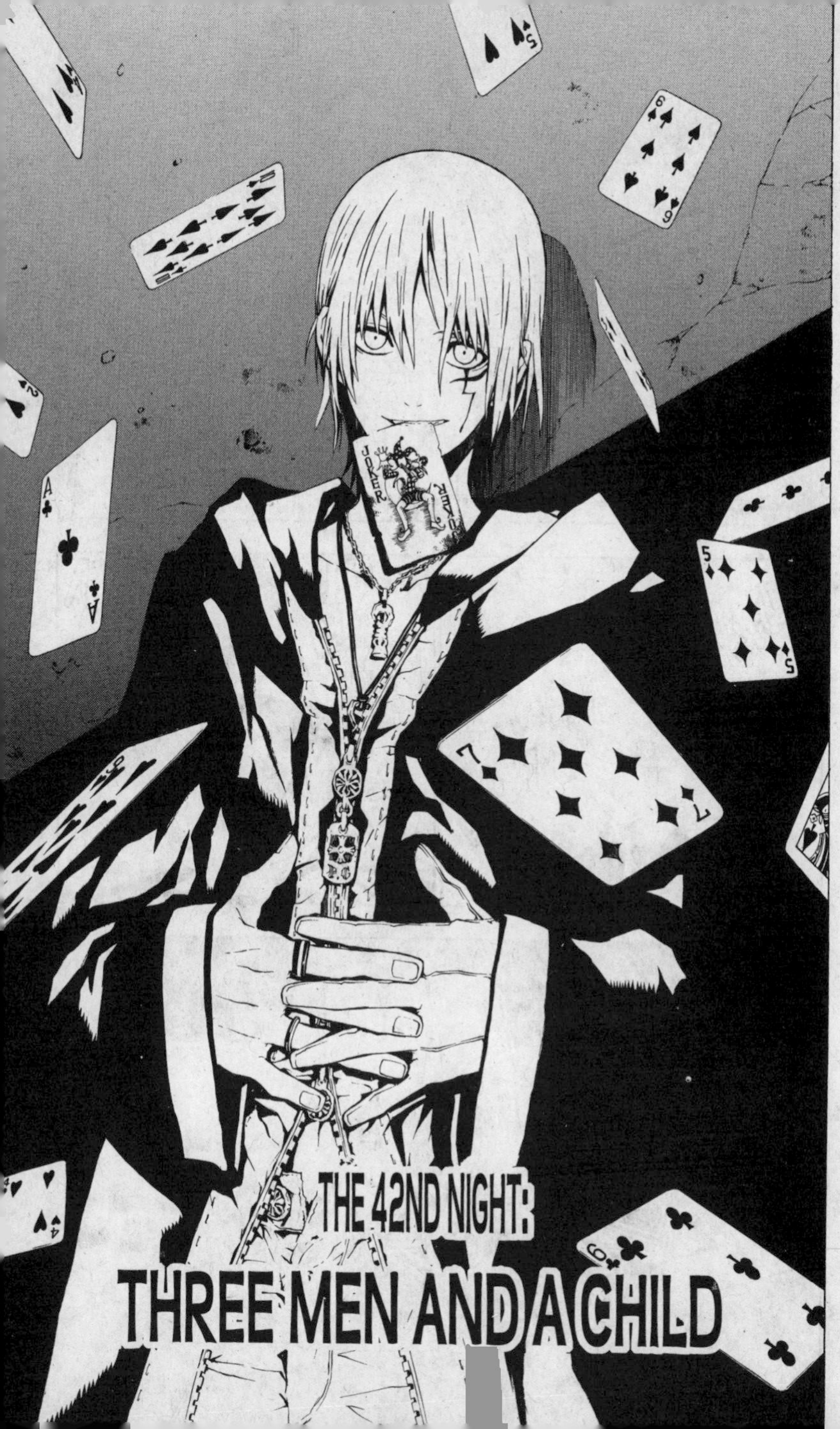
JOKER
THE 42ND NIGHT:
THREE MEN AND A CHILD

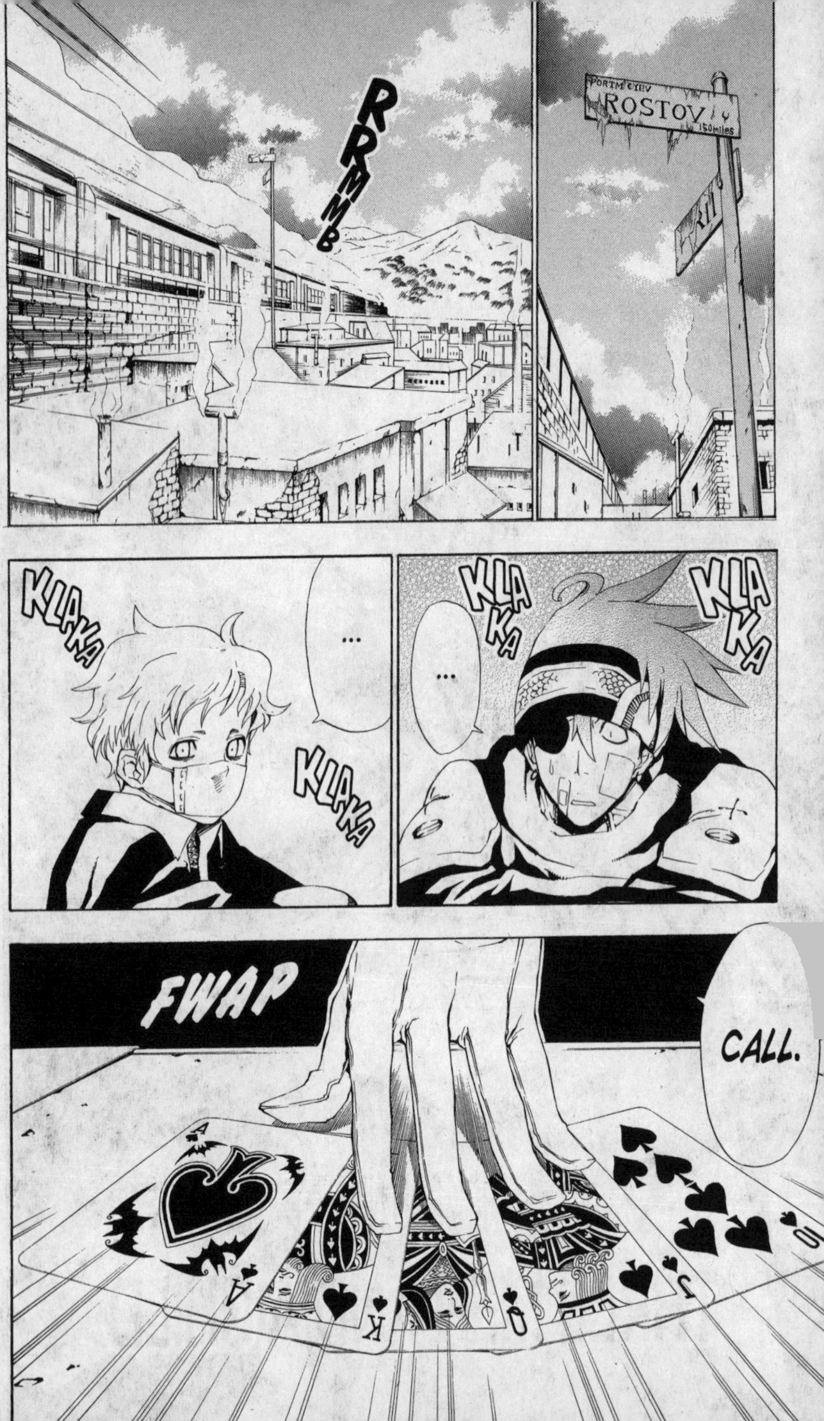
ROSTOV
150 miles
RRMMB
KLA KA
...
KLA KA
KLAKA
...
KLAKA
FWAP
CALL.

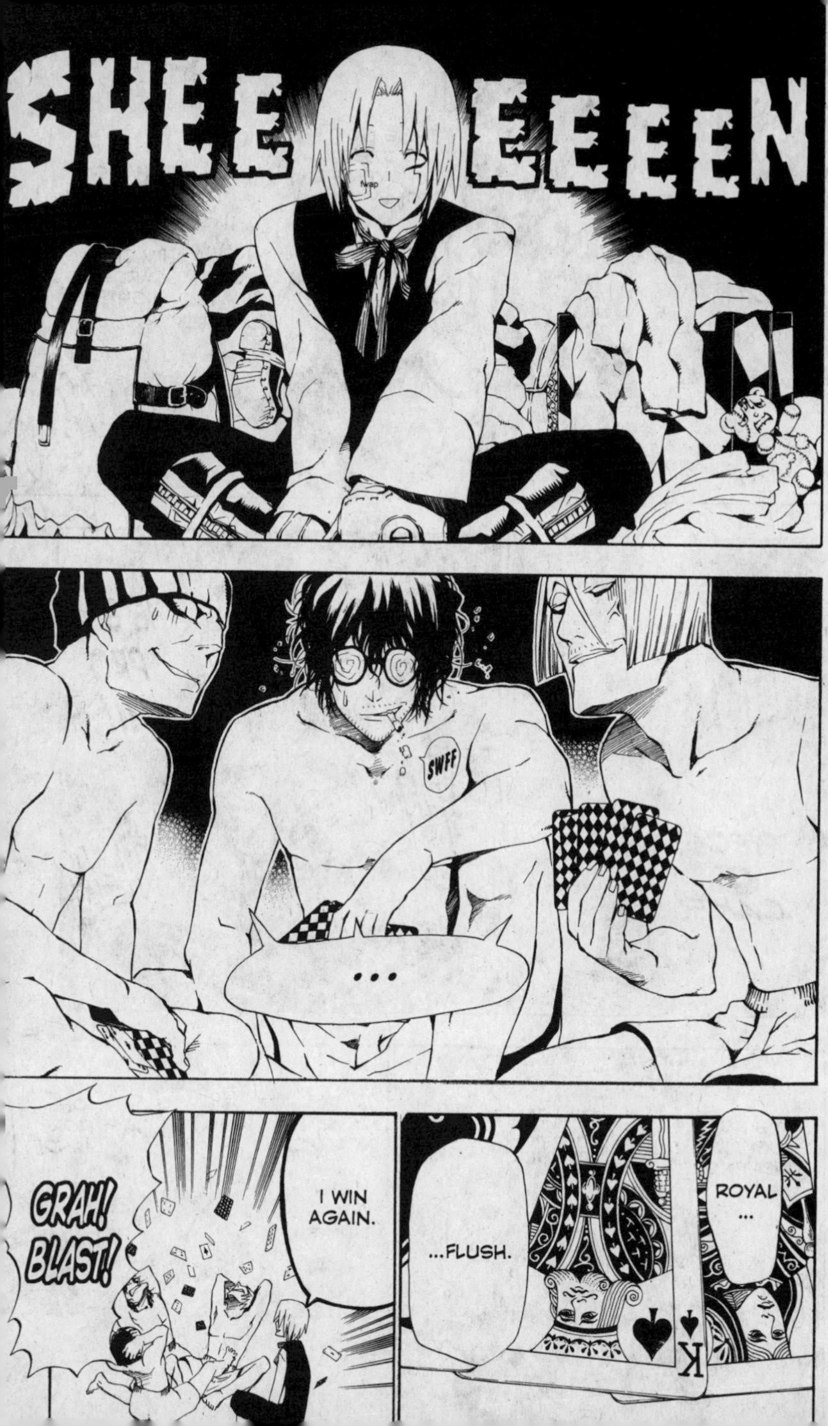
SHEEEEEEN
fwap
SWFF
...
ROYAL ...
...FLUSH.
I WIN AGAIN.
GRAH! BLAST!

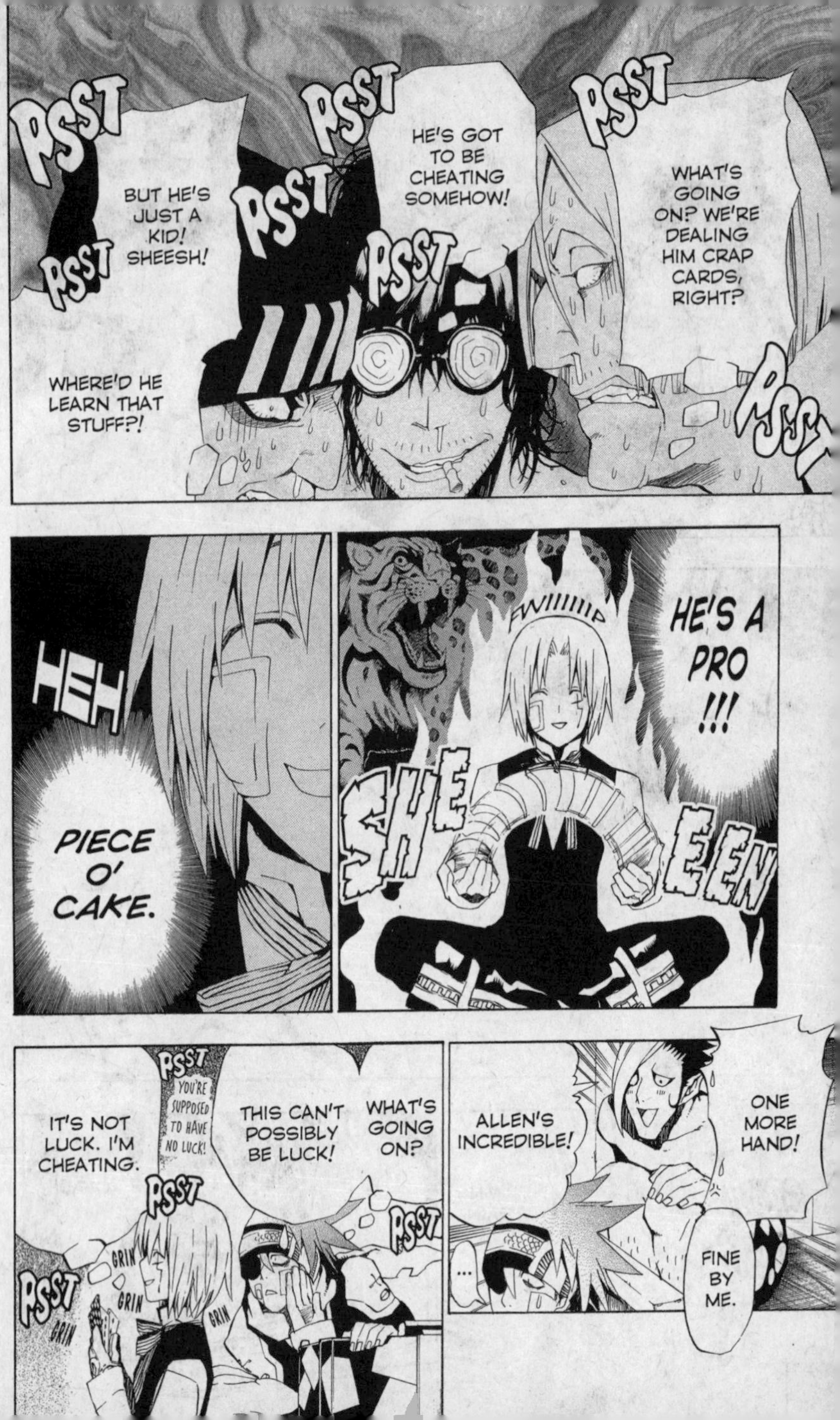
PSST
WHAT'S GOING ON? WE'RE DEALING HIM CRAP CARDS, RIGHT?
PSST
HE'S GOT TO BE CHEATING SOMEHOW!
PSST
PSST
PSST
BUT HE'S JUST A KID! SHEESH!
PSST
WHERE'D HE LEARN THAT STUFF?!
PSST
HE'S A PRO!!!
FWIIIIIP
SHEEEN
HEH
PIECE O' CAKE.
ONE MORE HAND!
ALLEN'S INCREDIBLE!
FINE BY ME.
...
WHAT'S GOING ON?
THIS CAN'T POSSIBLY BE LUCK!
PSST
YOU'RE SUPPOSED TO HAVE NO LUCK!
IT'S NOT LUCK. I'M CHEATING.
PSST
PSST
GRIN
GRIN
GRIN
GRIN
PSST

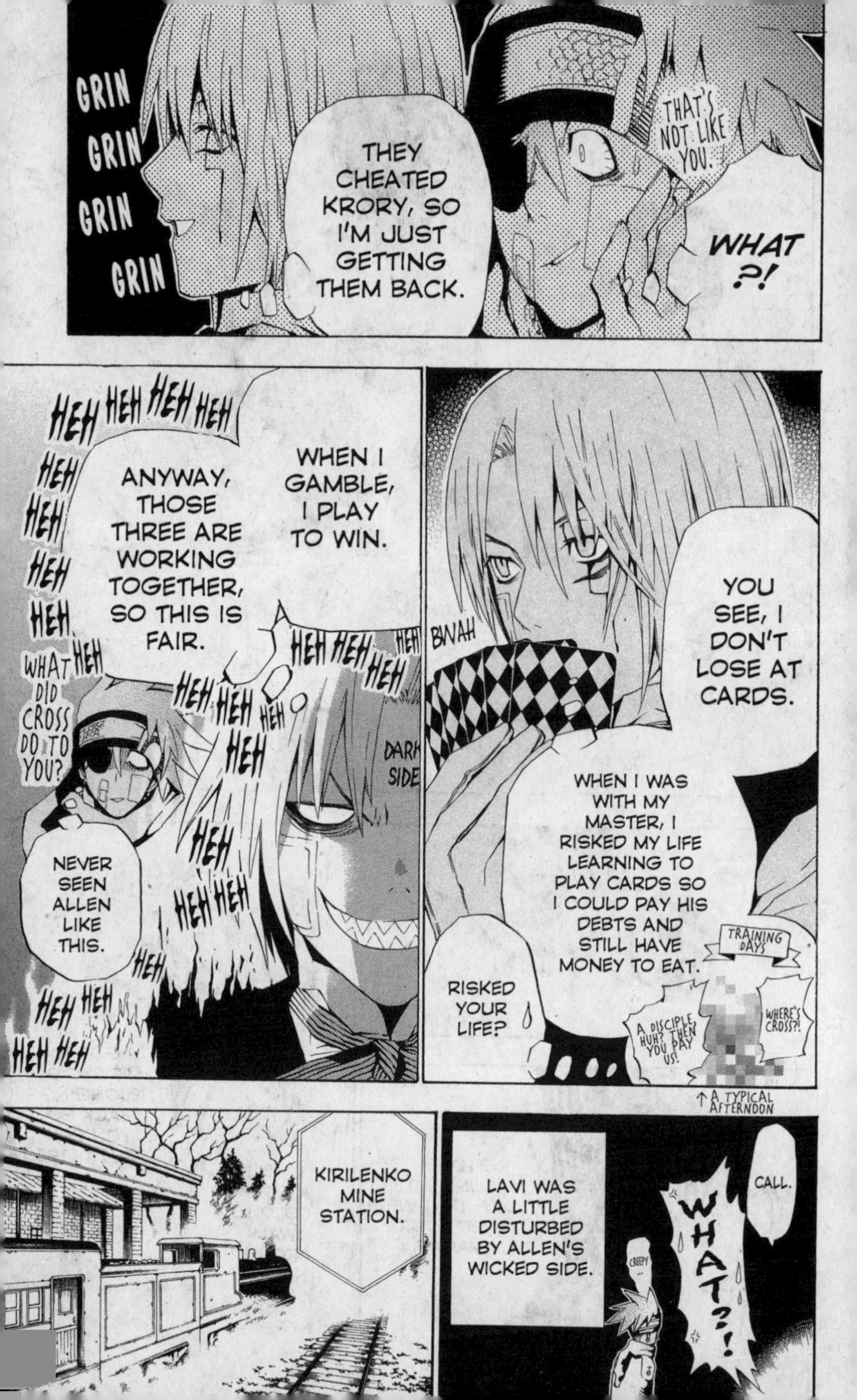
THAT'S NOT LIKE YOU.
WHAT?!
THEY CHEATED KRORY, SO I'M JUST GETTING THEM BACK.
GRIN GRIN GRIN GRIN
YOU SEE, I DON'T LOSE AT CARDS.
BWAH
WHEN I WAS WITH MY MASTER, I RISKED MY LIFE LEARNING TO PLAY CARDS SO I COULD PAY HIS DEBTS AND STILL HAVE MONEY TO EAT.
TRAINING DAYS
WHERE'S CROSS?!
A DISCIPLE, HUH? THEN YOU PAY US!
RISKED YOUR LIFE?
↑A TYPICAL AFTERNOON
WHEN I GAMBLE, I PLAY TO WIN.
HEH HEH HEH HEH
ANYWAY, THOSE THREE ARE WORKING TOGETHER, SO THIS IS FAIR.
HEH HEH HEH HEH HEH HEH HEH HEH HEH HEH HEH HEH HEH HEH
DARK SIDE
WHAT DID CROSS DO TO YOU?
NEVER SEEN ALLEN LIKE THIS.
HEH HEH HEH HEH HEH HEH HEH HEH HEH
CALL.
WHAT?!
WHAT?!
CREEPY...
LAVI WAS A LITTLE DISTURBED BY ALLEN'S WICKED SIDE.
KIRILENKO MINE STATION.

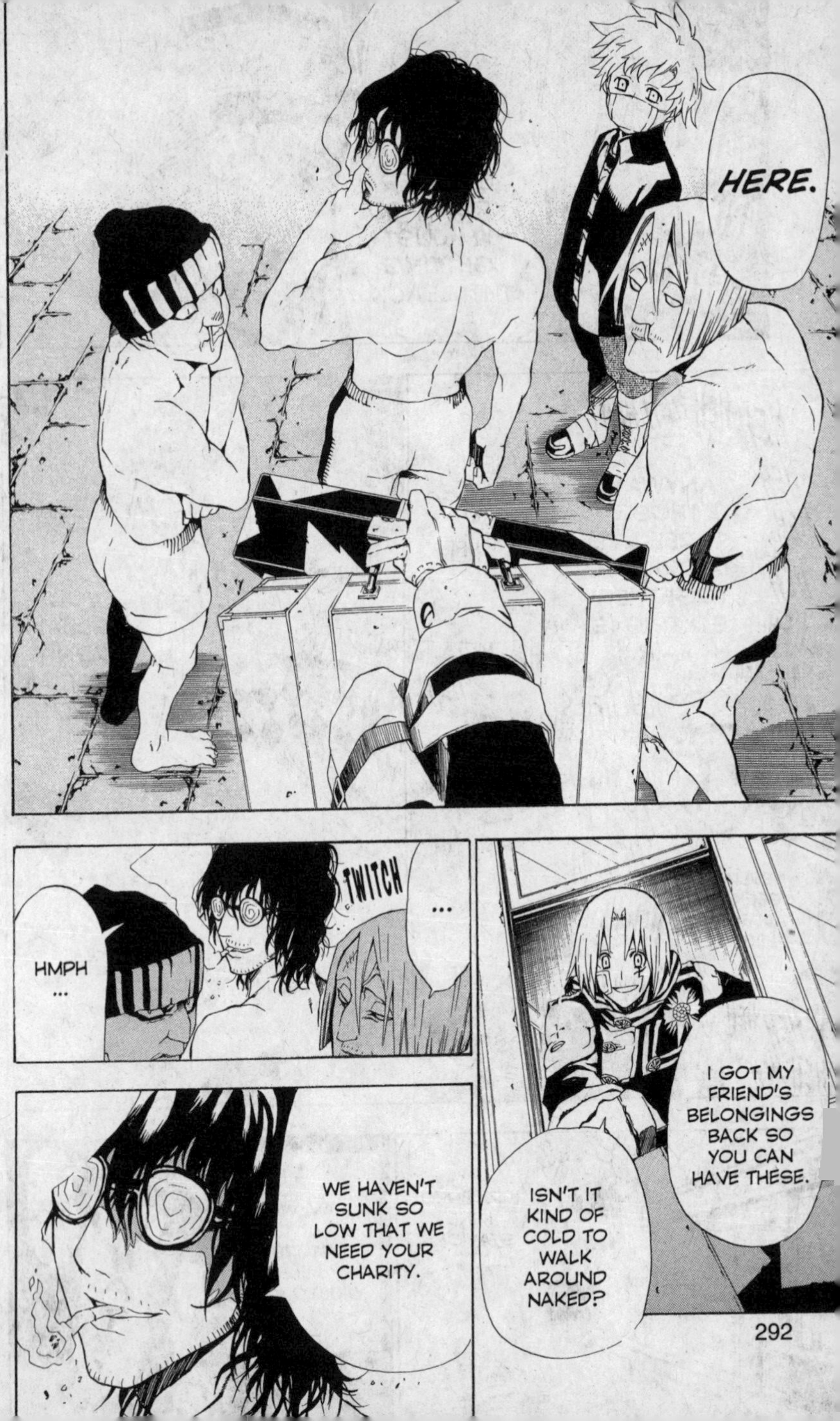
HERE.
I GOT MY FRIEND'S BELONGINGS BACK SO YOU CAN HAVE THESE.
ISN'T IT KIND OF COLD TO WALK AROUND NAKED?
TWITCH
...
HMPH ...
WE HAVEN'T SUNK SO LOW THAT WE NEED YOUR CHARITY.

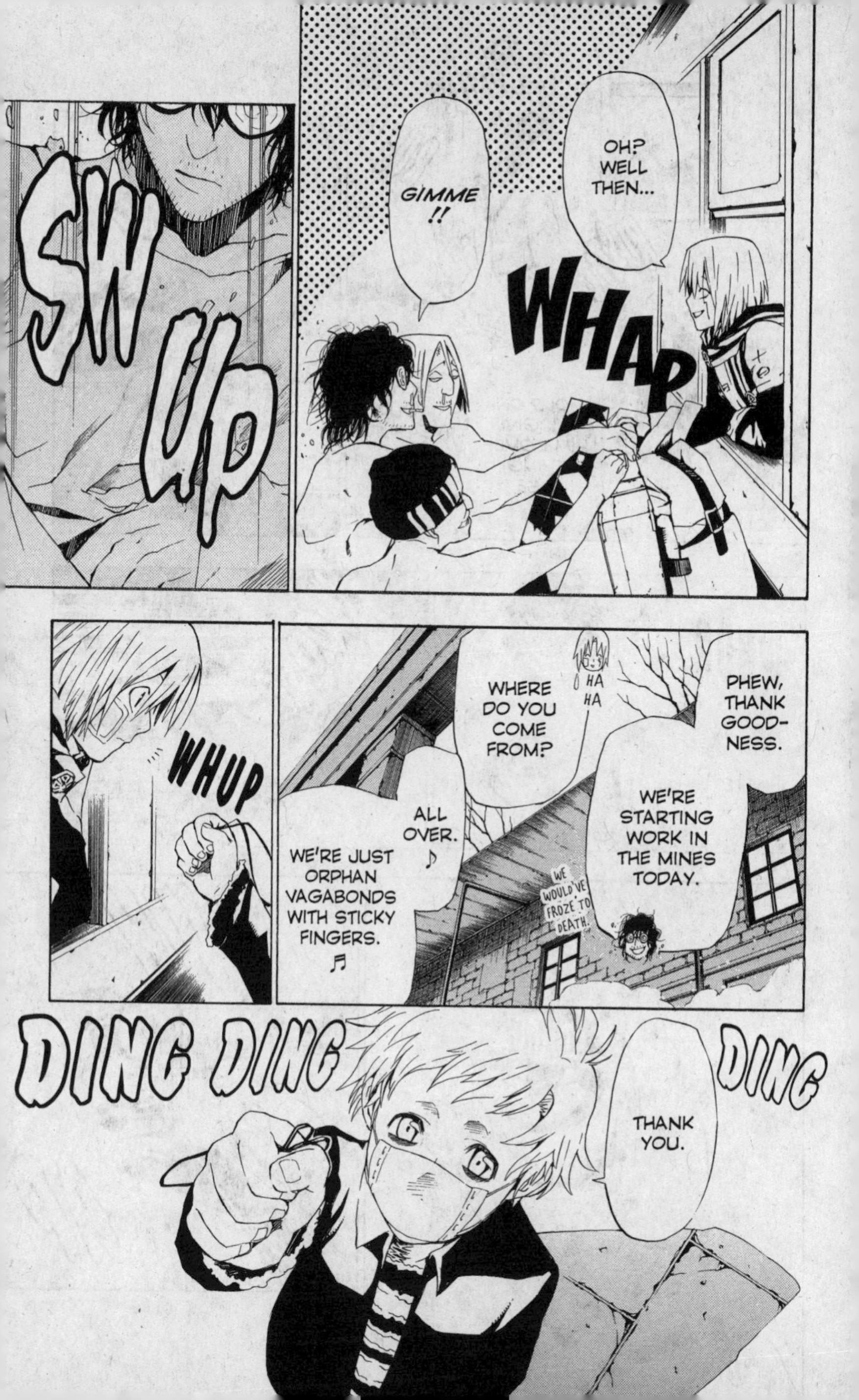
OH? WELL THEN...
WHAP
GIMME !!
SWUP
PHEW, THANK GOOD-NESS.
WHERE DO YOU COME FROM?
HA HA
WE'RE STARTING WORK IN THE MINES TODAY.
WE WOULD'VE FROZE TO DEATH!
ALL OVER. ♪
WE'RE JUST ORPHAN VAGABONDS WITH STICKY FINGERS. ♬
WHUP
DING DING DING
THANK YOU.

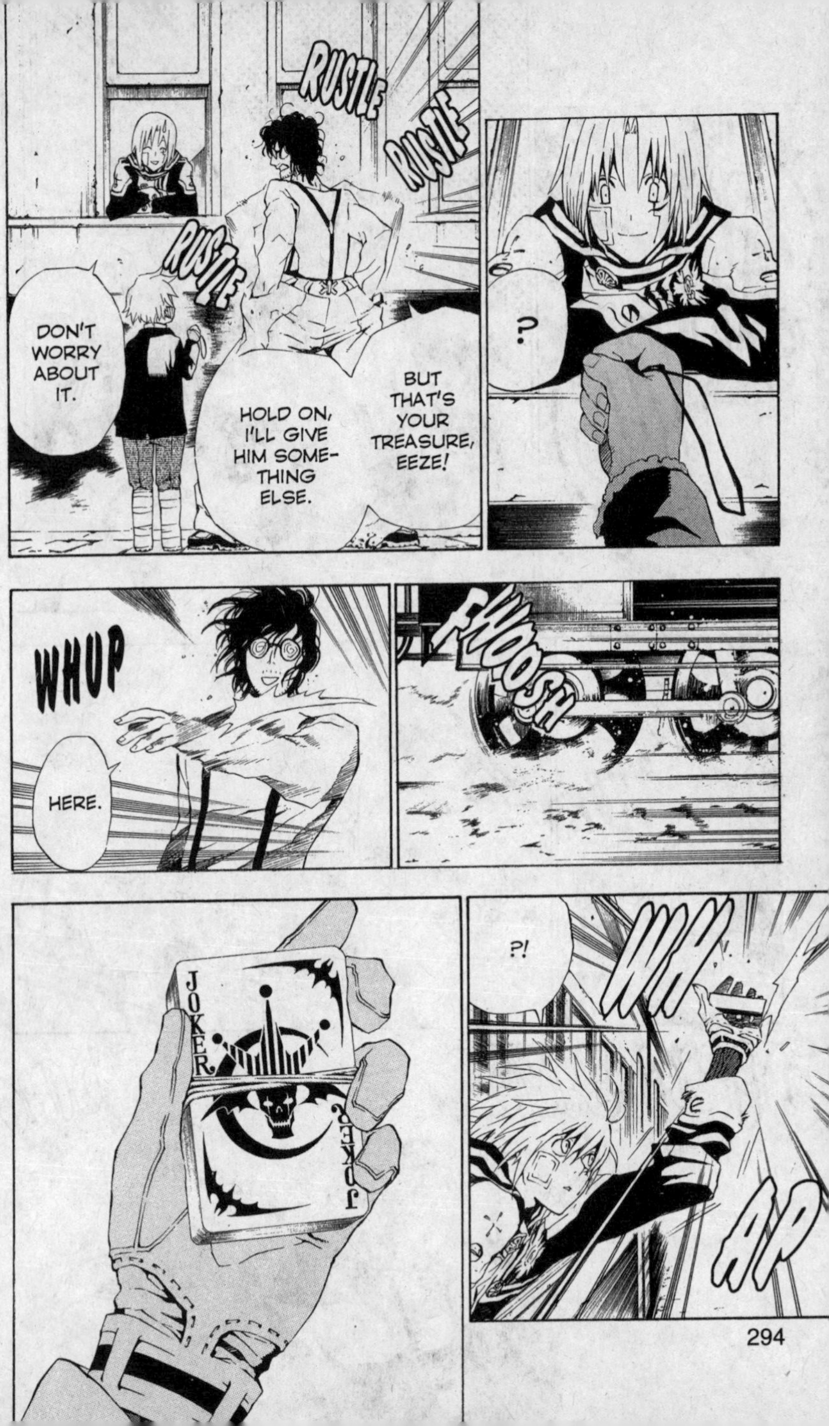
?
RUSTLE
RUSTLE
RUSTLE
BUT THAT'S YOUR TREASURE, EEZE!
HOLD ON, I'LL GIVE HIM SOMETHING ELSE.
DON'T WORRY ABOUT IT.
FWOOSH
WHUP
HERE.
?!
WHAP
JOKER
JOKER

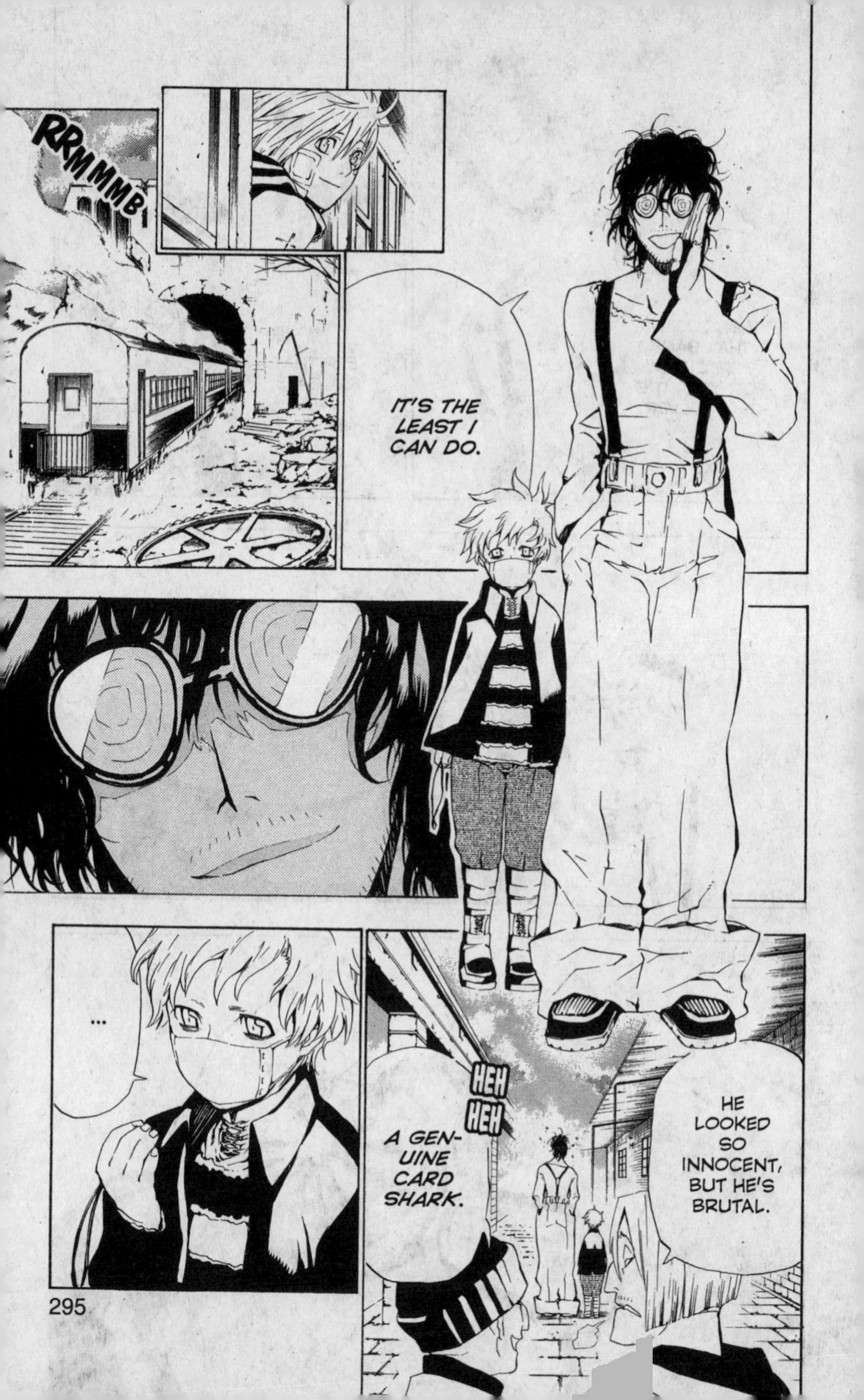

IT'S THE LEAST I CAN DO.
RRMMMB
HE LOOKED SO INNOCENT, BUT HE'S BRUTAL.
HEH HEH
A GEN-UINE CARD SHARK.
...

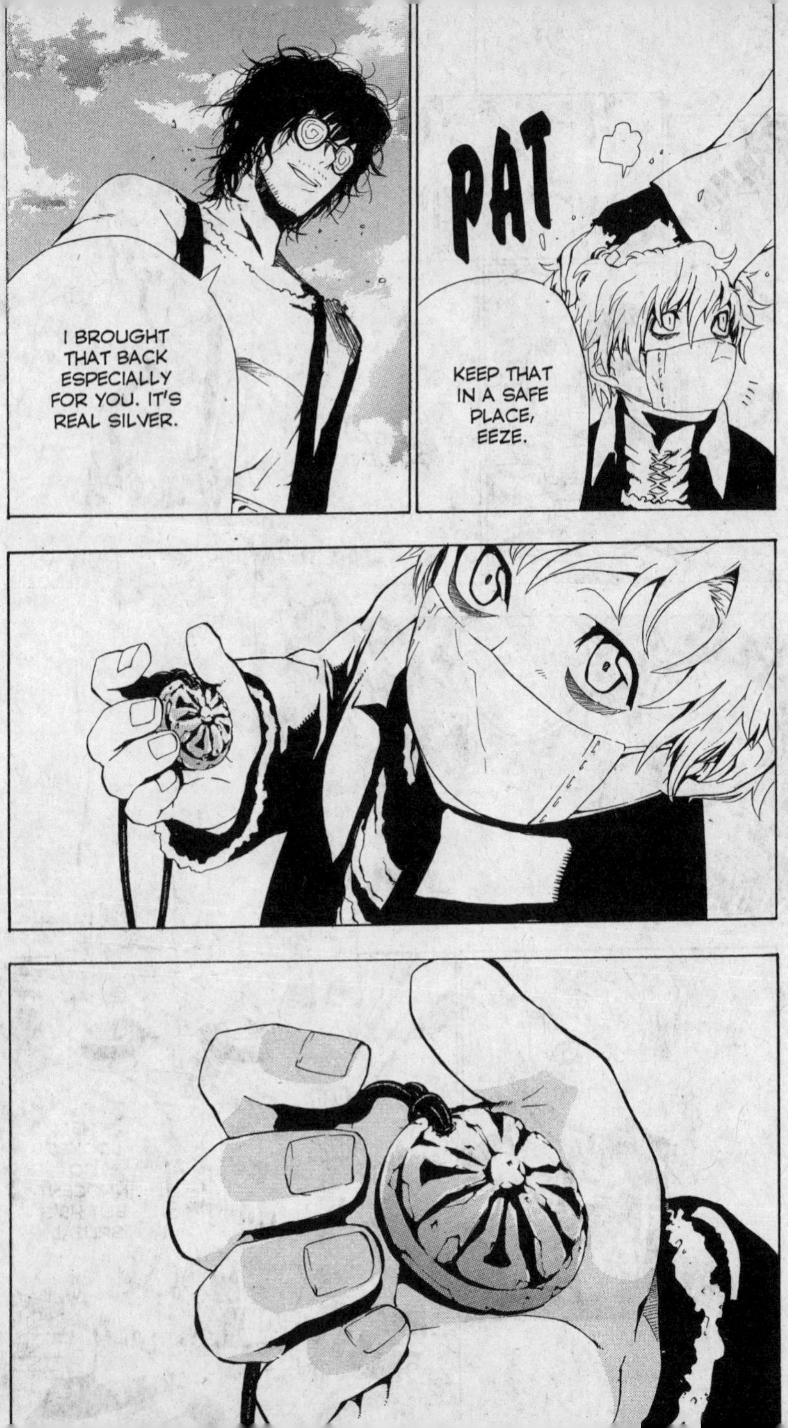
PAT
KEEP THAT IN A SAFE PLACE, EEZE.
I BROUGHT THAT BACK ESPECIALLY FOR YOU. IT'S REAL SILVER.

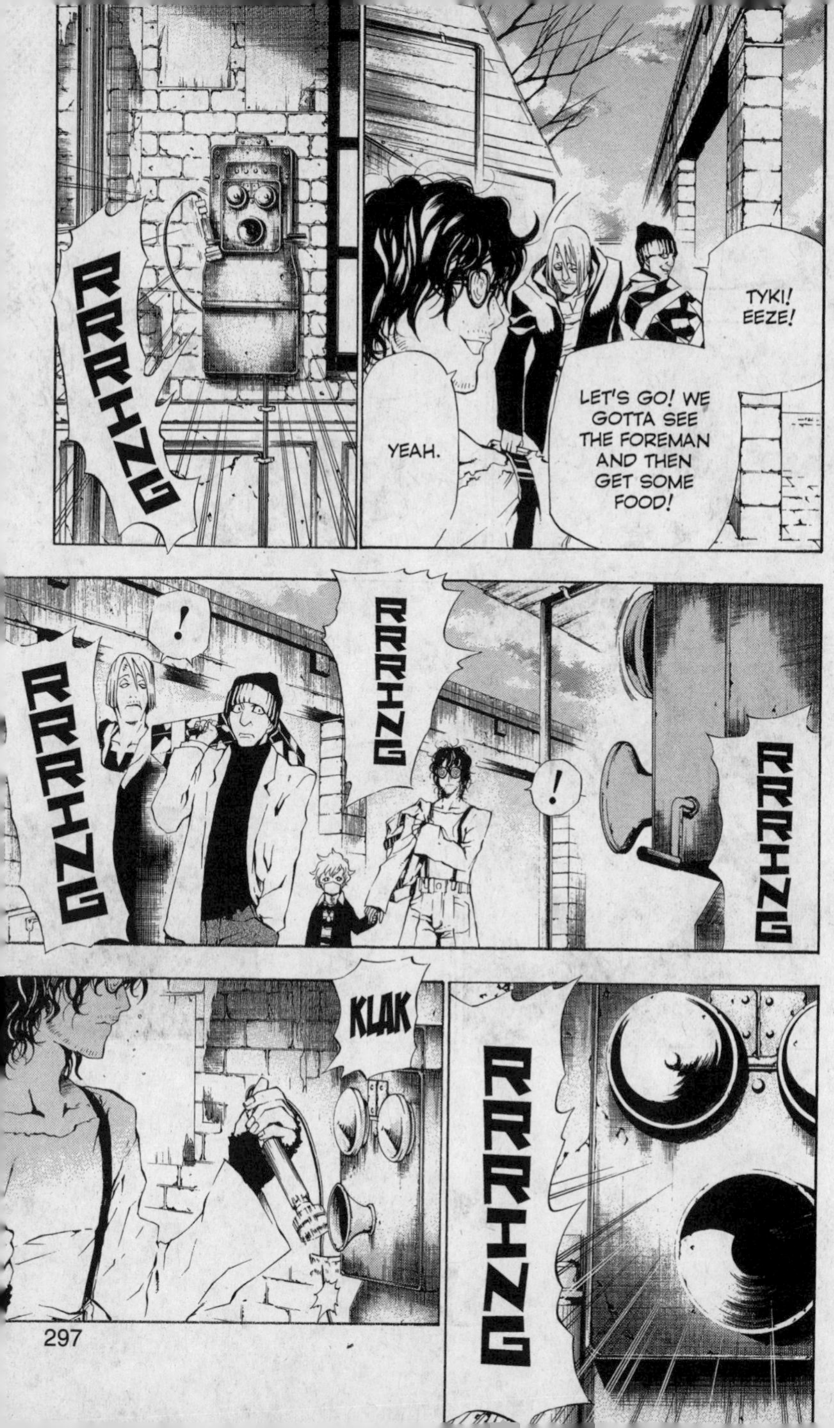
TYKI! EEZE!
LET'S GO! WE GOTTA SEE THE FOREMAN AND THEN GET SOME FOOD!
YEAH.
RRRING
RRRING
!
RRRING
!
RRRING
RRRING
KLAK

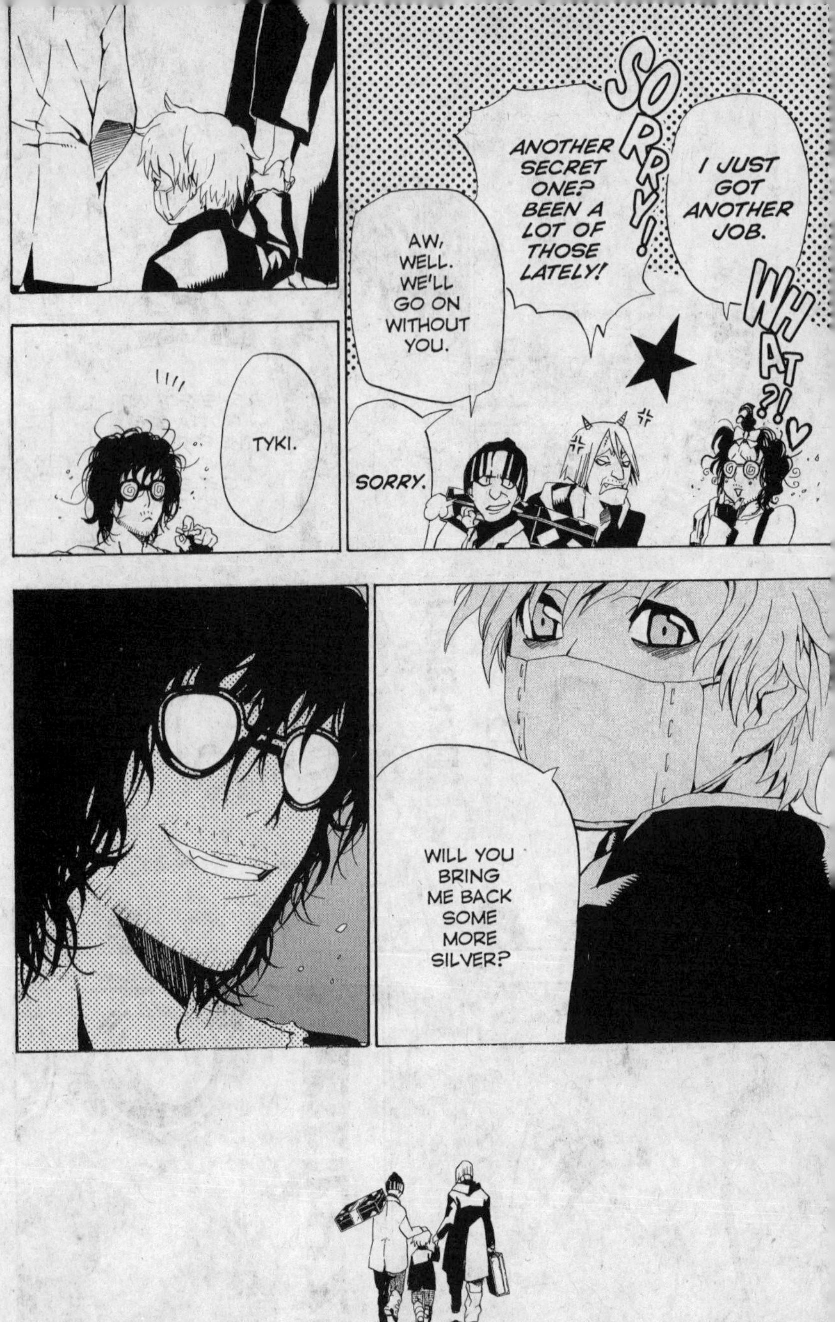
I JUST GOT ANOTHER JOB.
WHAT?!
SORRY!
ANOTHER SECRET ONE? BEEN A LOT OF THOSE LATELY!
AW, WELL. WE'LL GO ON WITHOUT YOU.
SORRY.
TYKI.
WILL YOU BRING ME BACK SOME MORE SILVER?

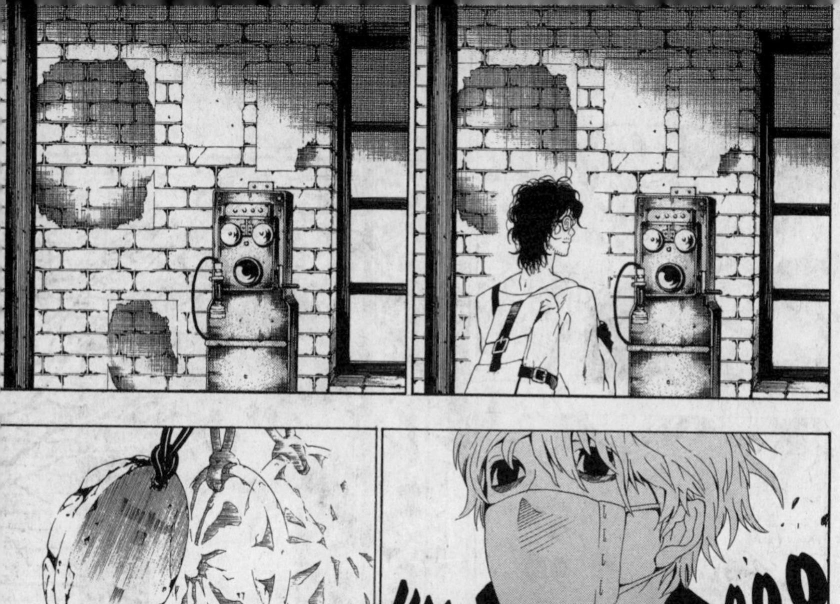
WOO
OOO
Kevin Yeegar

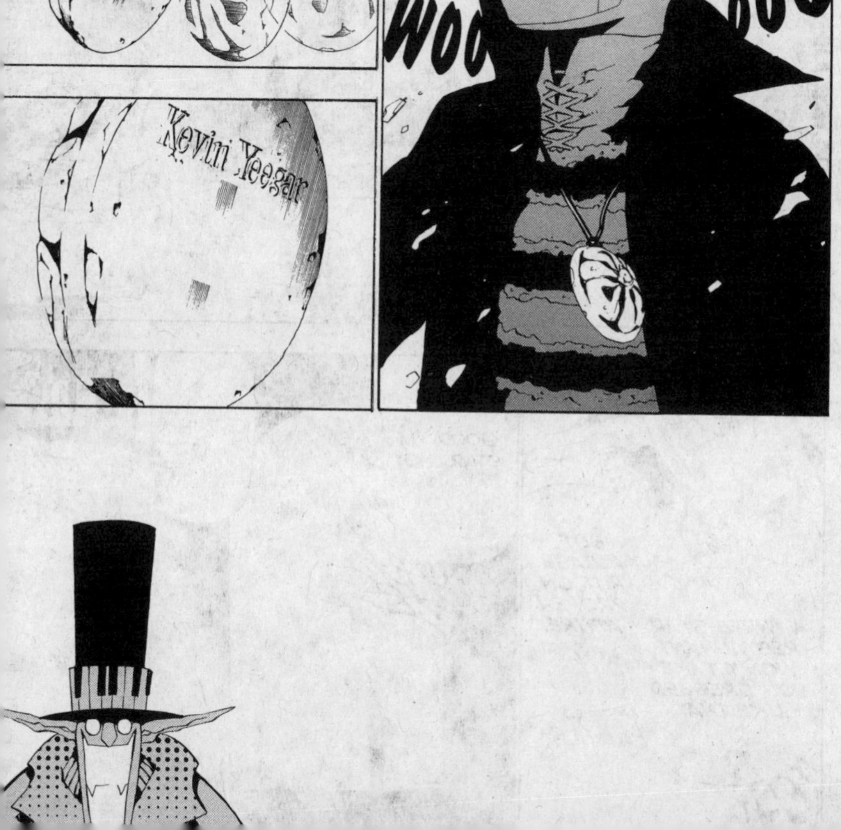

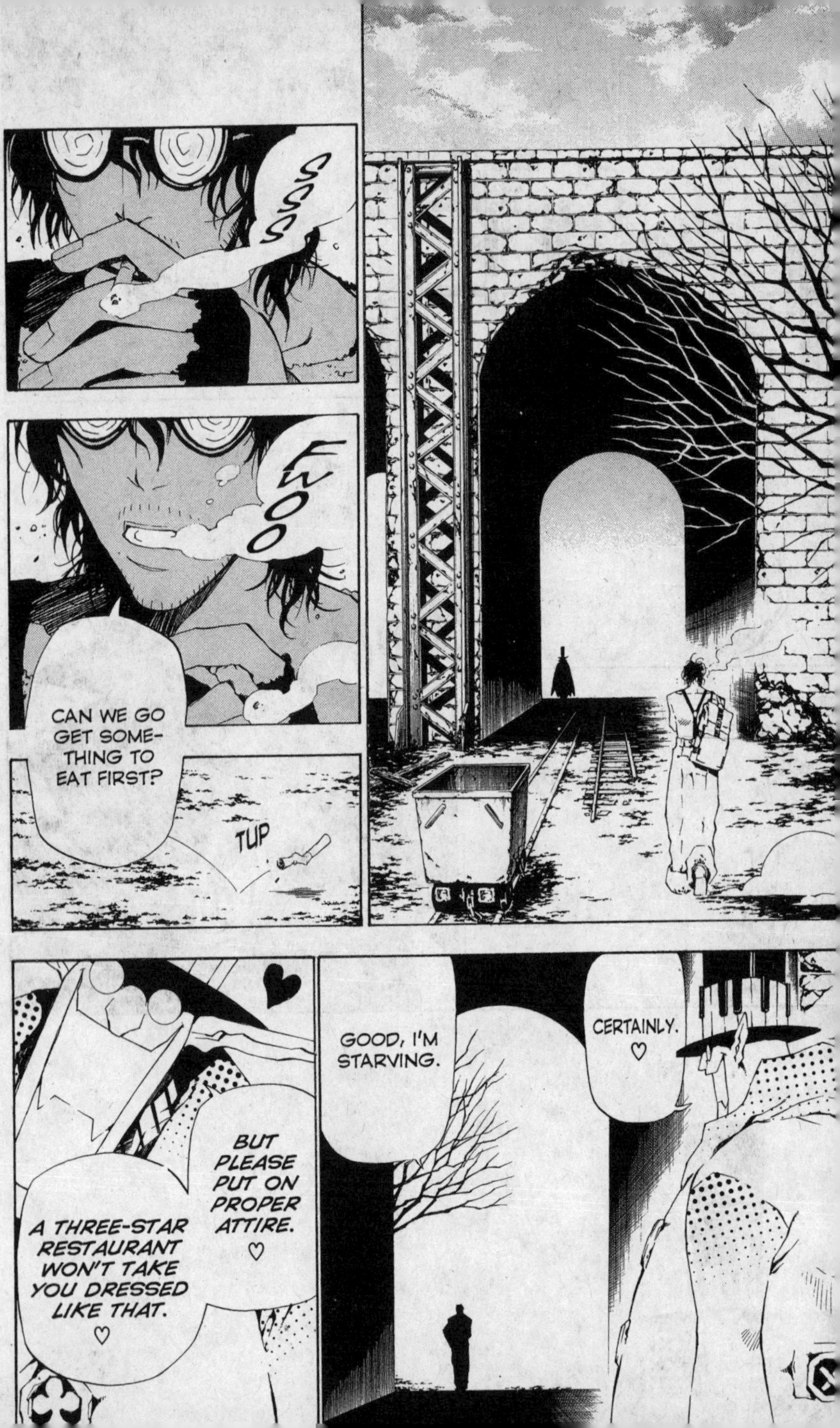
SSSS
FWOOO
CAN WE GO GET SOME-THING TO EAT FIRST?
TUP
CERTAINLY. ♡
GOOD, I'M STARVING.
BUT PLEASE PUT ON PROPER ATTIRE. ♡
A THREE-STAR RESTAURANT WON'T TAKE YOU DRESSED LIKE THAT. ♡

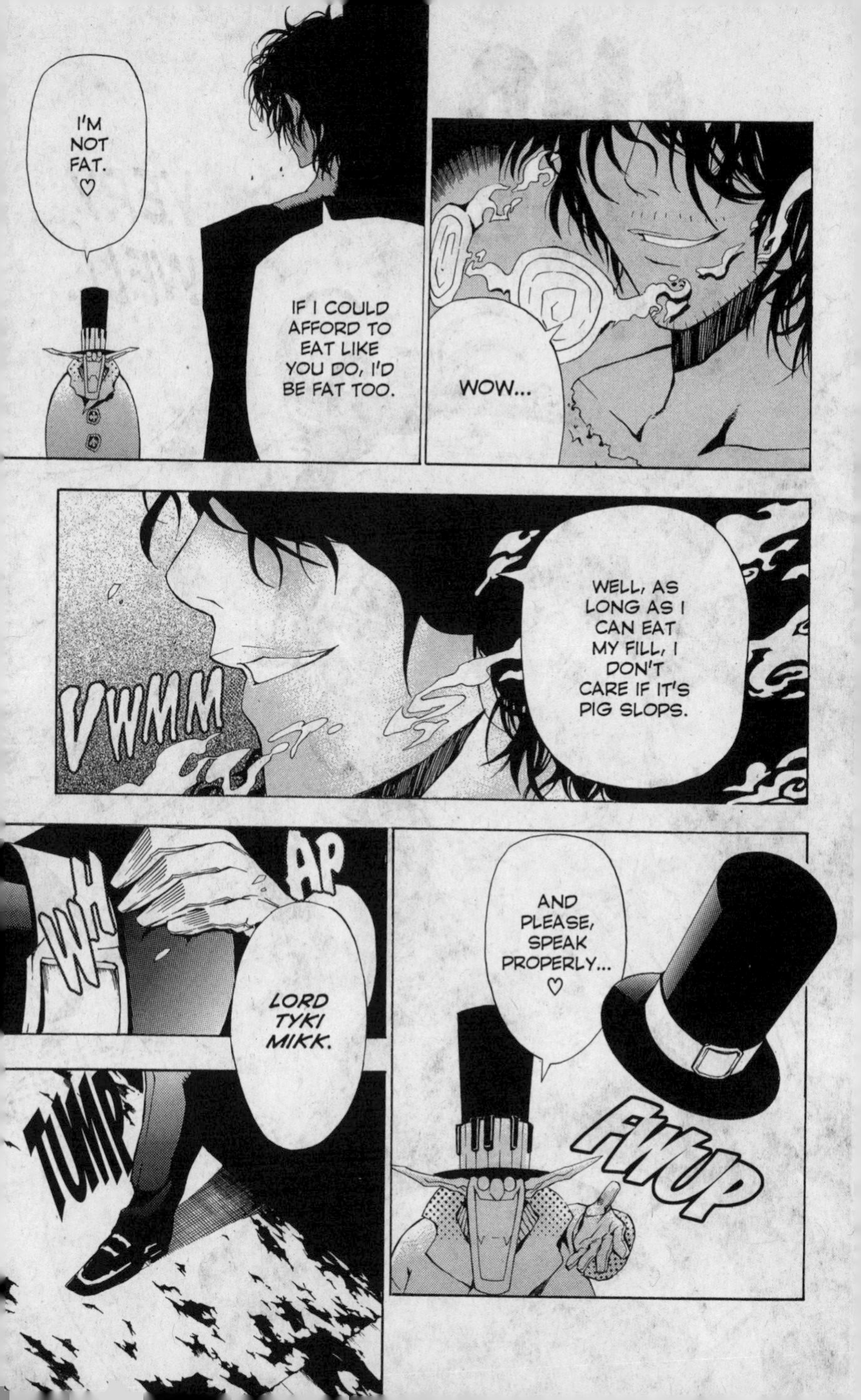
WOW...
IF I COULD AFFORD TO EAT LIKE YOU DO, I'D BE FAT TOO.
I'M NOT FAT. ♡
WELL, AS LONG AS I CAN EAT MY FILL, I DON'T CARE IF IT'S PIG SLOPS.
VWMM
AND PLEASE, SPEAK PROPERLY... ♡
FWUP
AP
WH
LORD TYKI MIKK.
TUMP

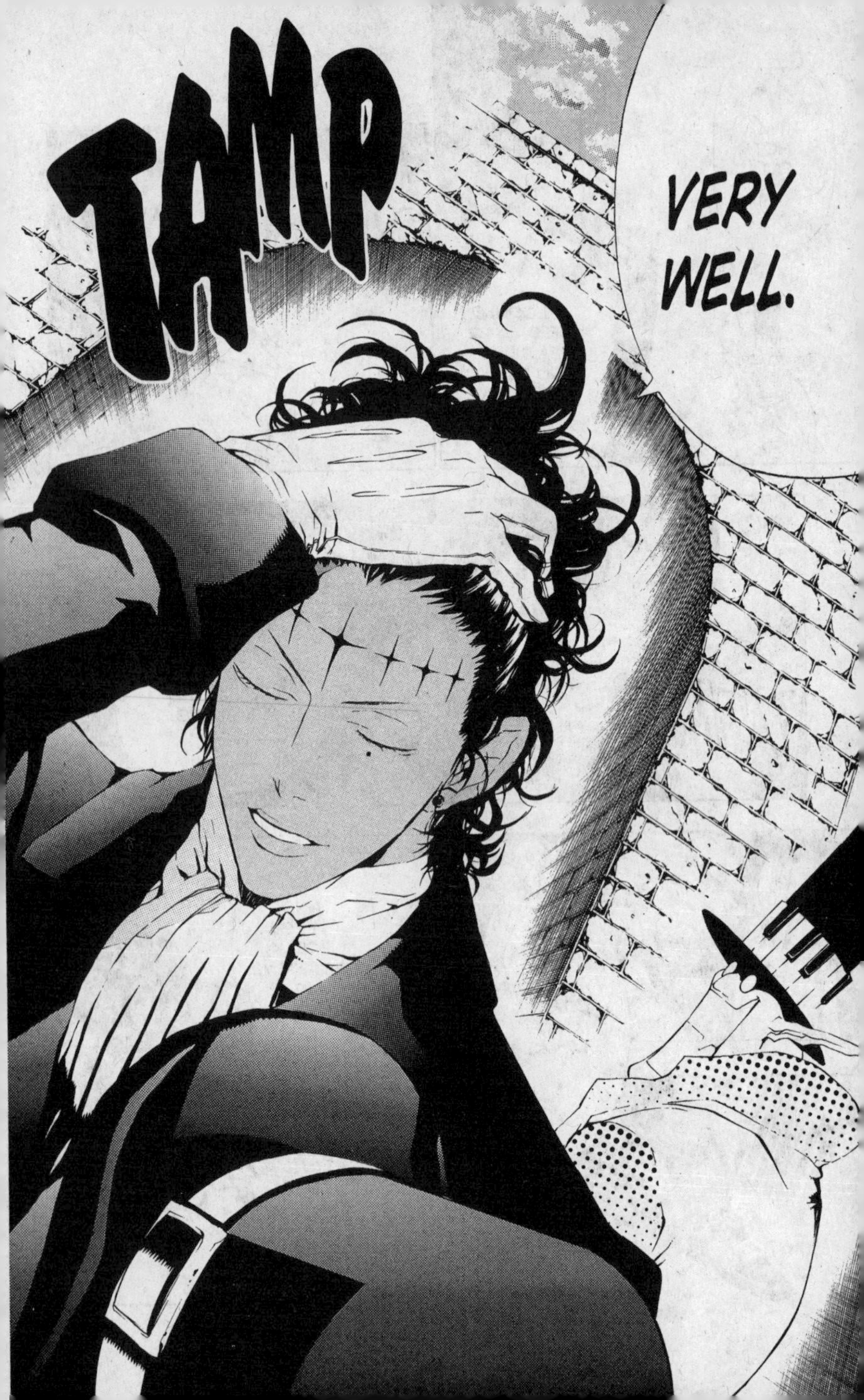
VERY WELL.
TAMP

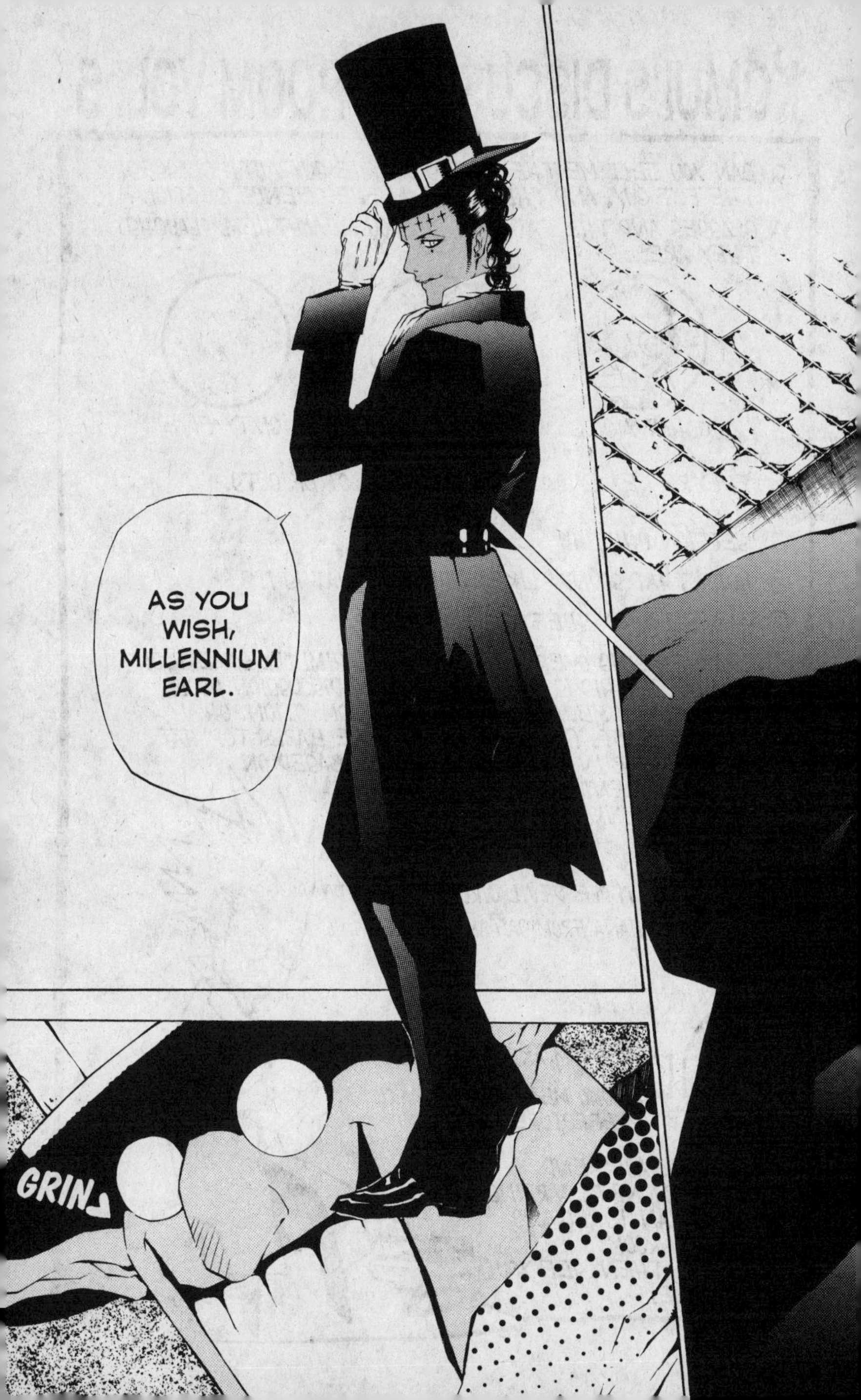
AS YOU WISH, MILLENNIUM EARL.
GRIN

KOMUI'S DISCUSSION ROOM VOL. 6

Q. CAN YOU TELL ME THE NAMES OF THE GUY WITH GLASSES, THE FAT GUY, AND THE GHOST IN THE SCIENCE SECTION?

A. GLASSES AND THE FAT GUY? OH, YOU MEAN THEM. (LAUGHS) THEY ARE...

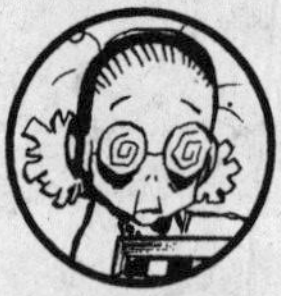

JOHNNY GILL

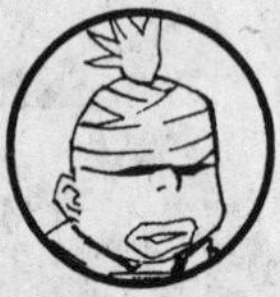

TAP DOP

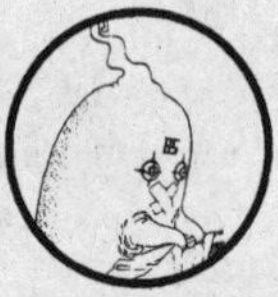

SIXTY-FIVE

THEY'RE REALLY GOOD GUYS WITH A LOT OF GUTS.

"SECTION CHIEF!!!"

Ⓡ HUH? THAT SOUNDS LIKE JOHNNY. WHAT IS IT?

Ⓙ W-WE FOUND CHIEF KOMUI!

(CHAIR FALLING OVER) WHAT?! CATCH HIM! I'LL COME TOO! OH, I GUESS THIS IS THE END OF THE DISCUSSION ROOM FOR THIS VOLUME. SORRY ABOUT THE COMMOTION. OH, I ALMOST FORGOT. THE DESIGNS FOR THE EARL'S TOP HAT THAT APPEAR IN THIS VOLUME WERE BASED ON THE IDEAS SENT IN BY THESE KIDS. THANKS AGAIN!

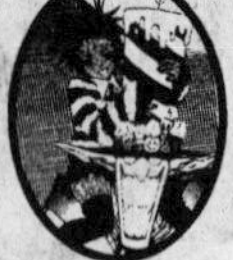

LITTLE DEVIL JIRO OF HOKKAIDO
HANA FROM SAITAMA PREFECTURE

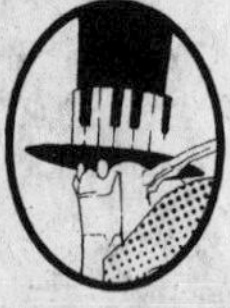

RIO FROM AKITA PREFECTURE
BISUKO MEITO OF MIYAZAKI PREFECTURE

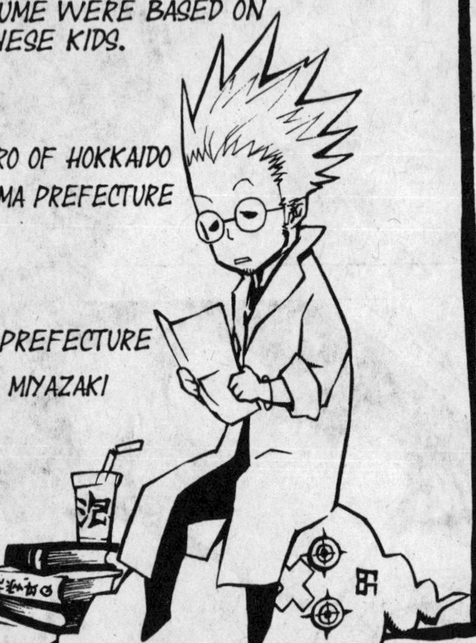

LASTLY, PLEASE SEND YOUR QUESTIONS REGARDING D. GRAY-MAN TO "KOMUI'S DISCUSSION ROOM." ALL RIGHT THEN, SEE YOU NEXT TIME!

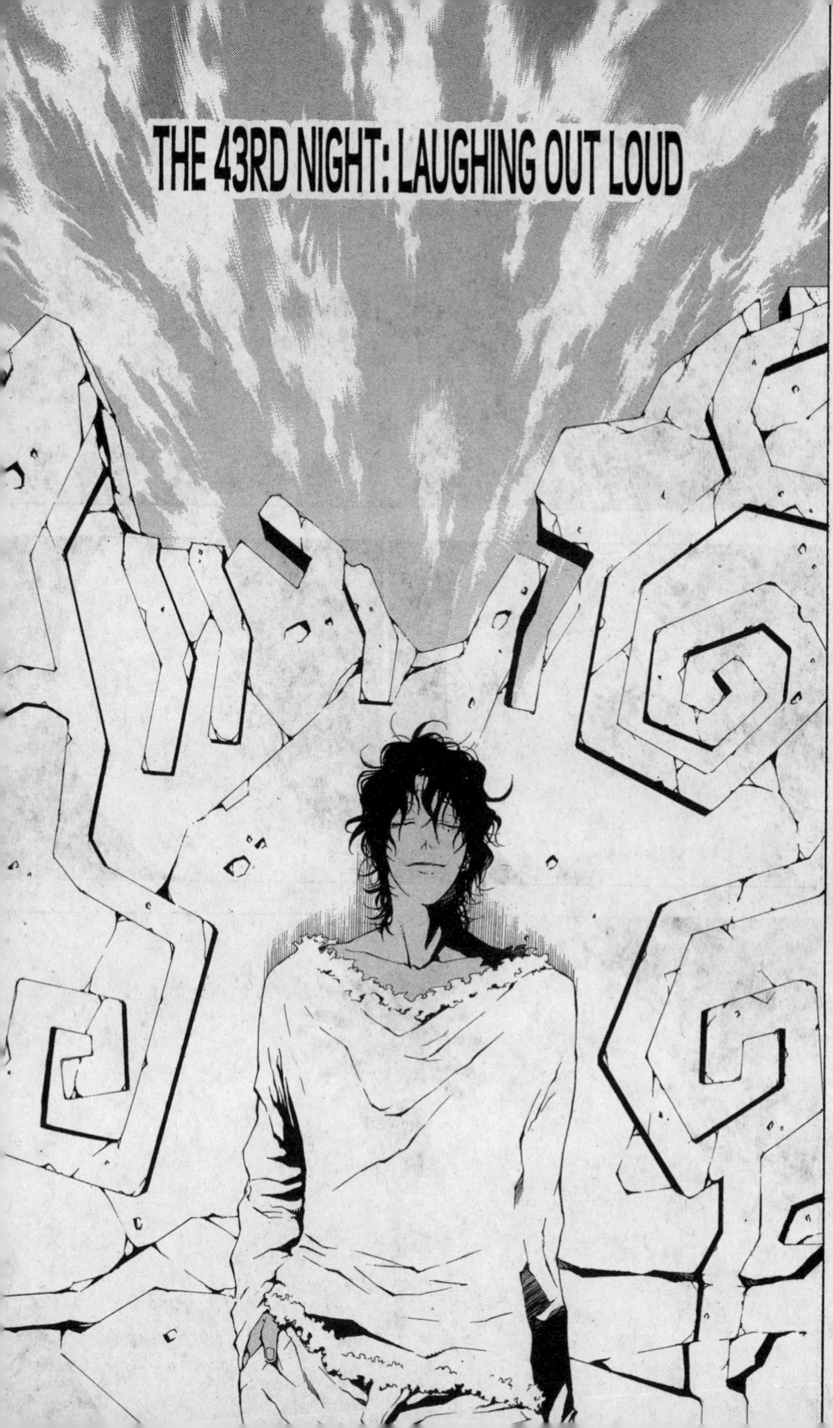
THE 43RD NIGHT: LAUGHING OUT LOUD

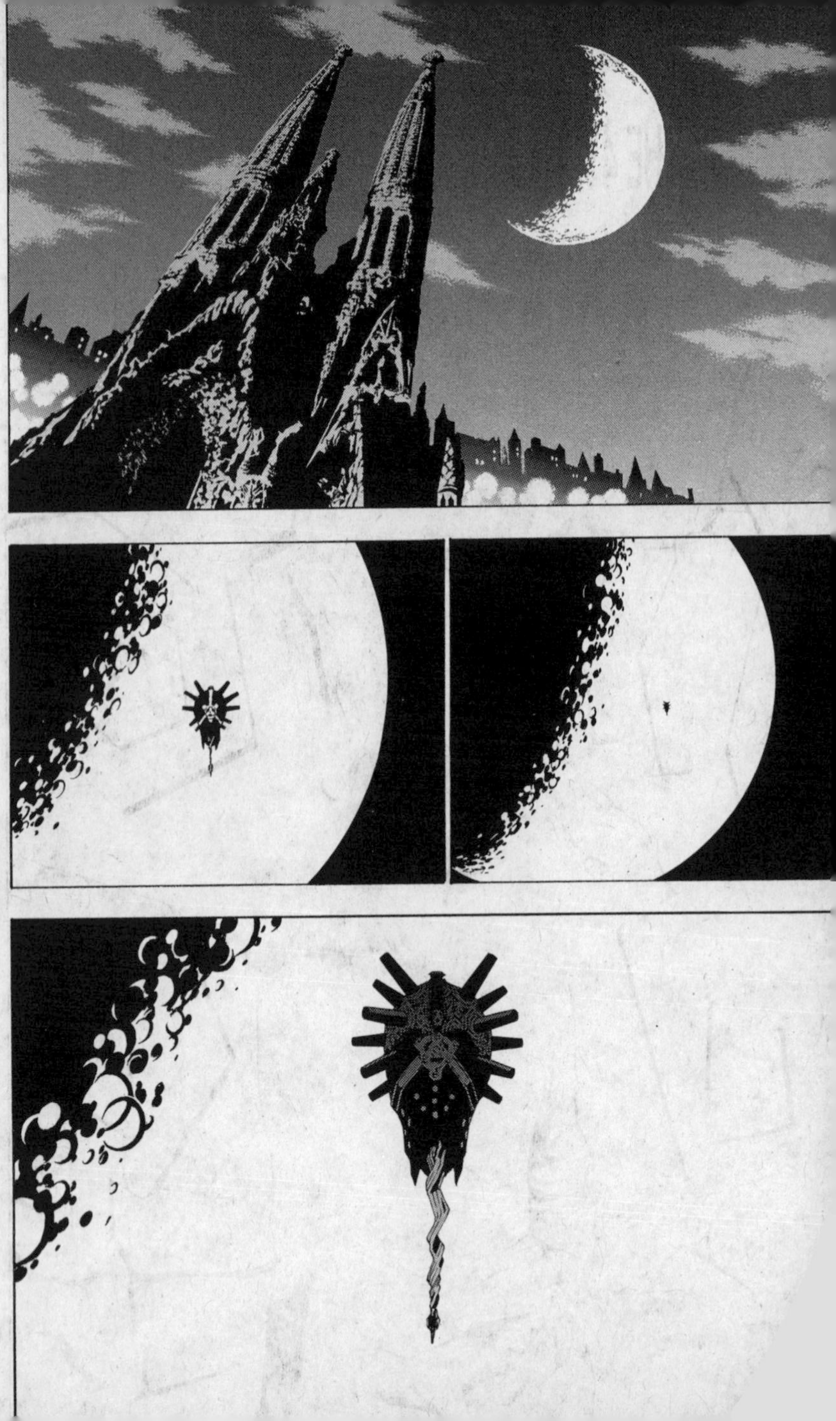

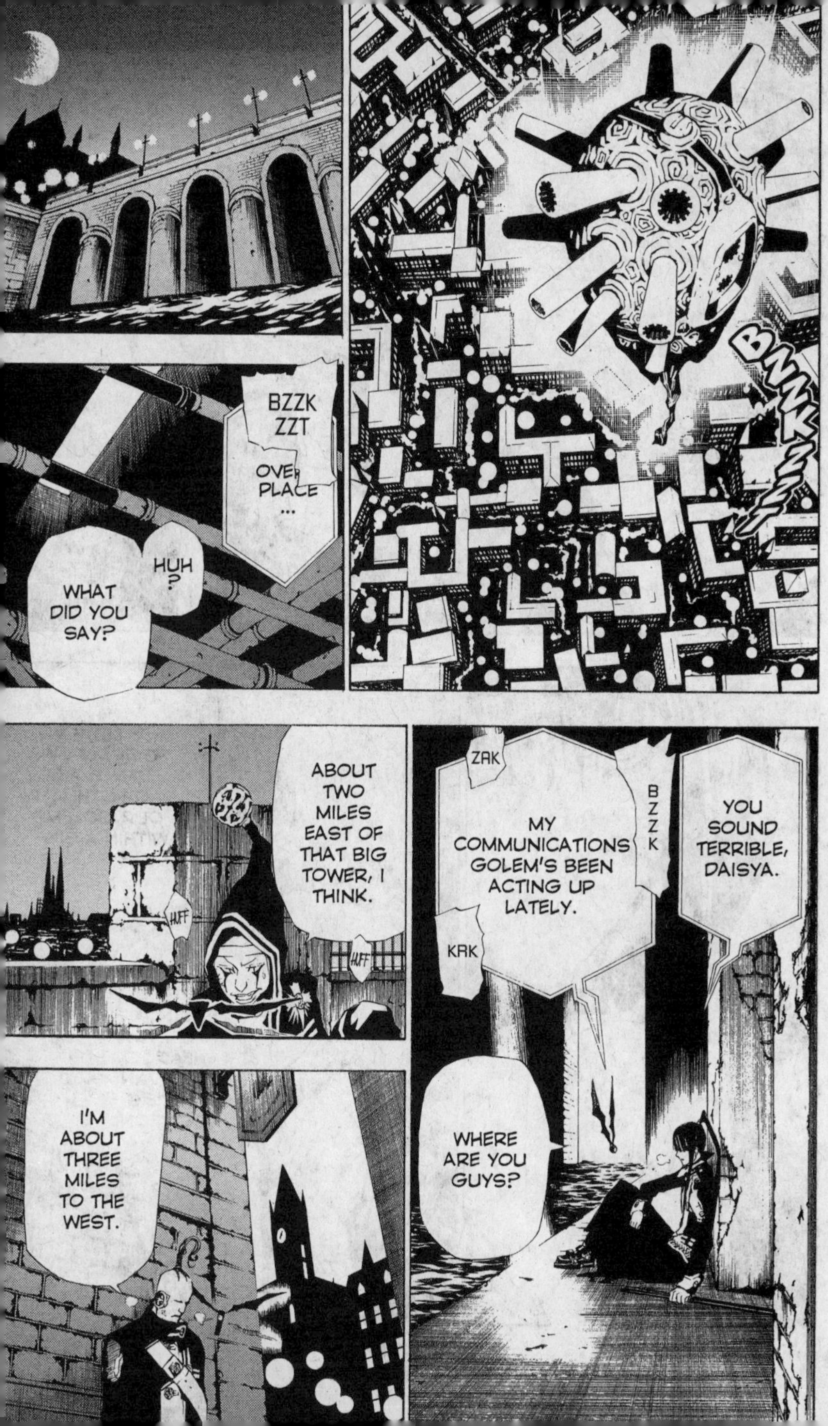
BNNK
BZZK ZZT
OVER PLACE ...
HUH?
WHAT DID YOU SAY?
YOU SOUND TERRIBLE, DAISYA.
BZZK
ZAK
MY COMMUNICATIONS GOLEM'S BEEN ACTING UP LATELY.
KRK
WHERE ARE YOU GUYS?
ABOUT TWO MILES EAST OF THAT BIG TOWER, I THINK.
HUFF
HUFF
I'M ABOUT THREE MILES TO THE WEST.

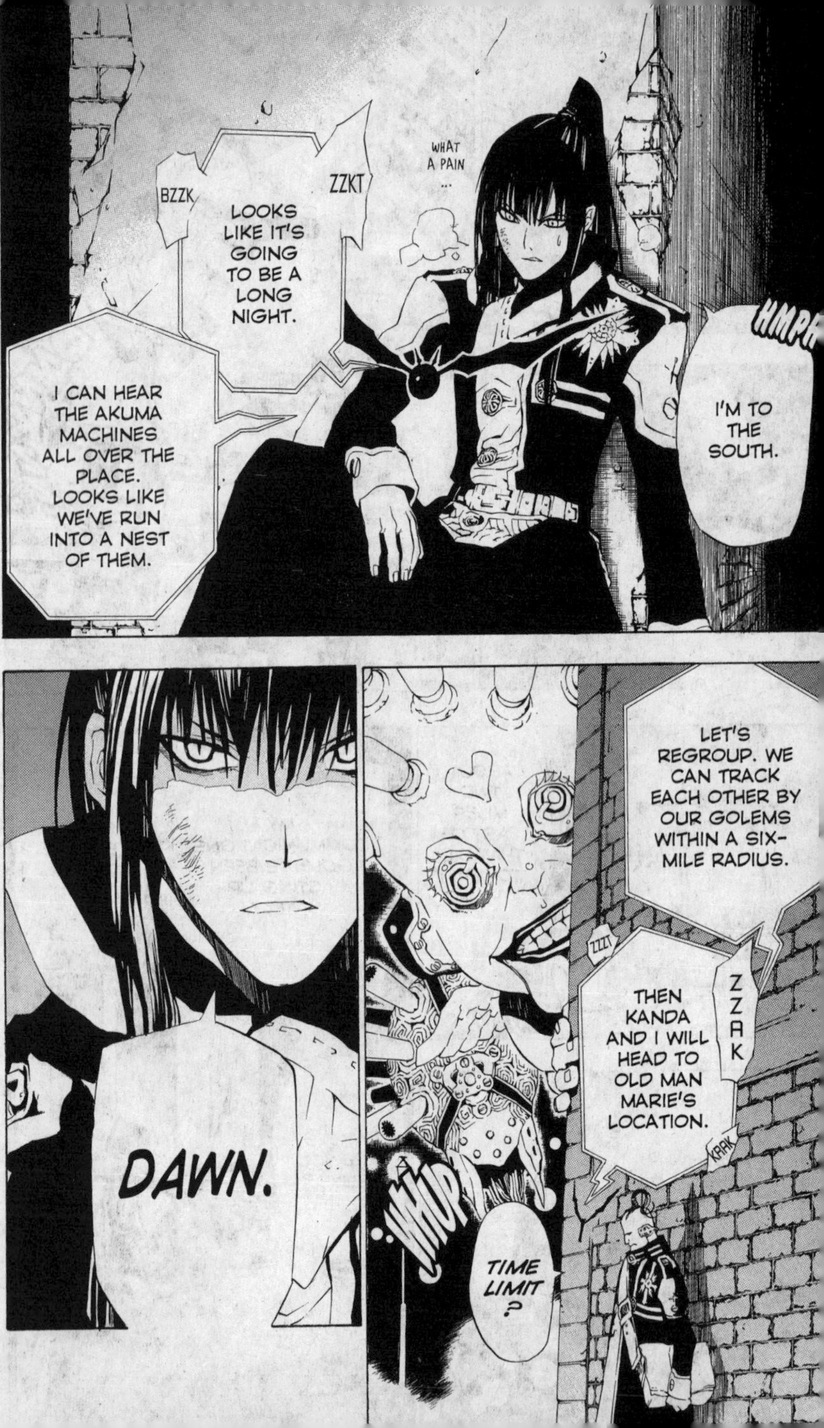
WHAT A PAIN ...
ZZKT
BZZK
LOOKS LIKE IT'S GOING TO BE A LONG NIGHT.
I CAN HEAR THE AKUMA MACHINES ALL OVER THE PLACE. LOOKS LIKE WE'VE RUN INTO A NEST OF THEM.
HMPH
I'M TO THE SOUTH.
LET'S REGROUP. WE CAN TRACK EACH OTHER BY OUR GOLEMS WITHIN A SIX-MILE RADIUS.
ZZZT
ZZAK
THEN KANDA AND I WILL HEAD TO OLD MAN MARIE'S LOCATION.
KRAK
WHUP
TIME LIMIT?
DAWN.

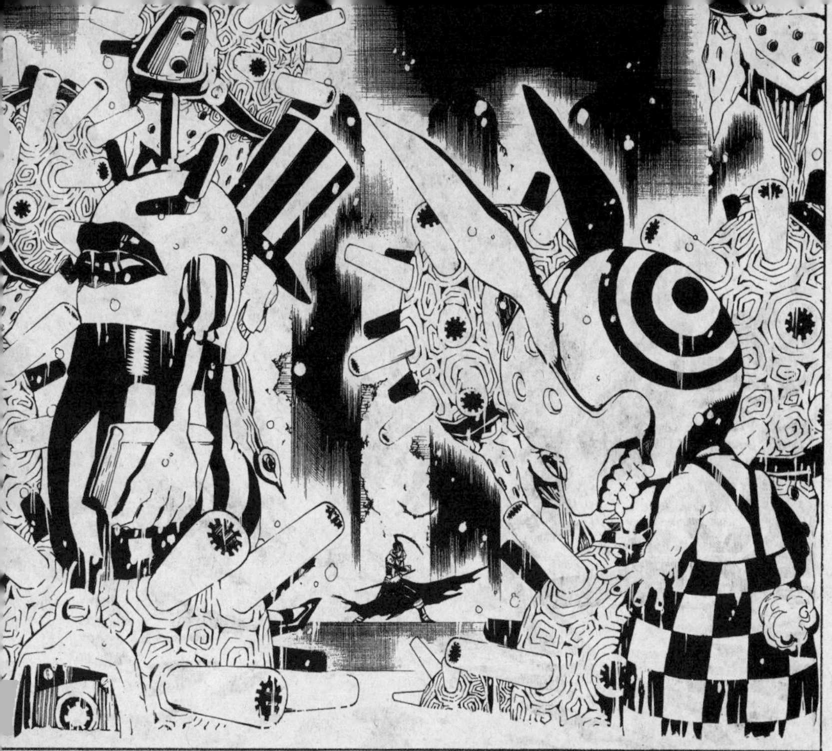

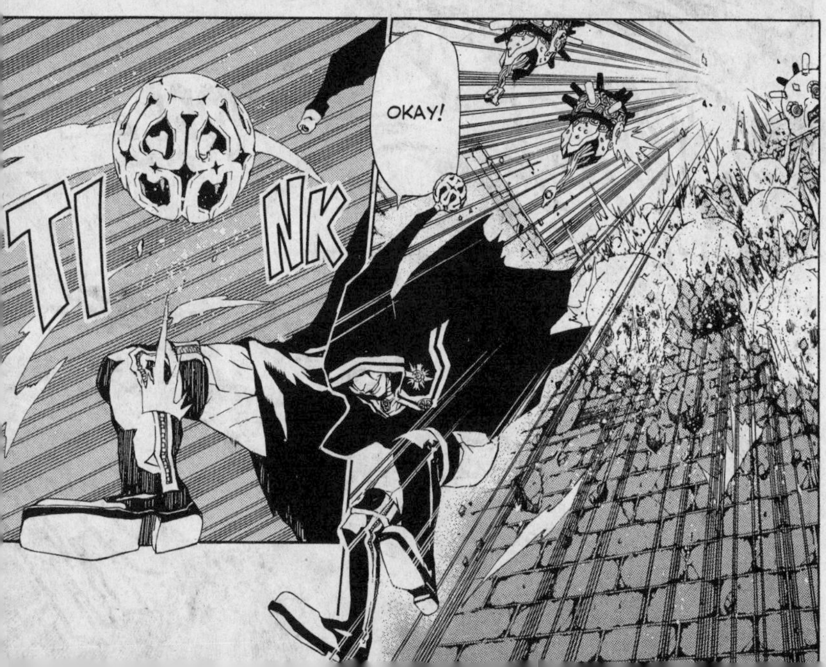
OKAY!
TI NK

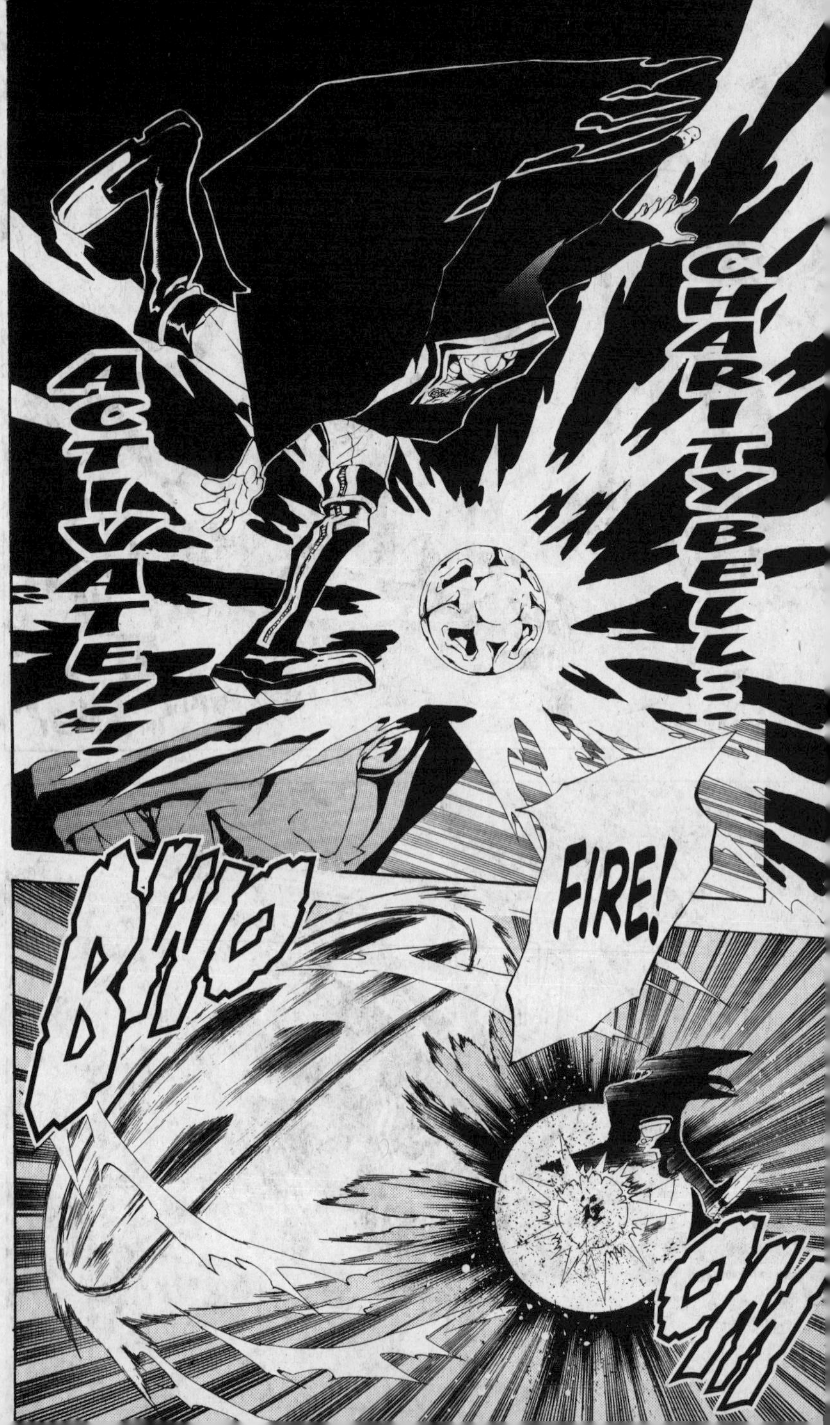
CHARITY BELL...!
ACTIVATE...!
FIRE!
BHO

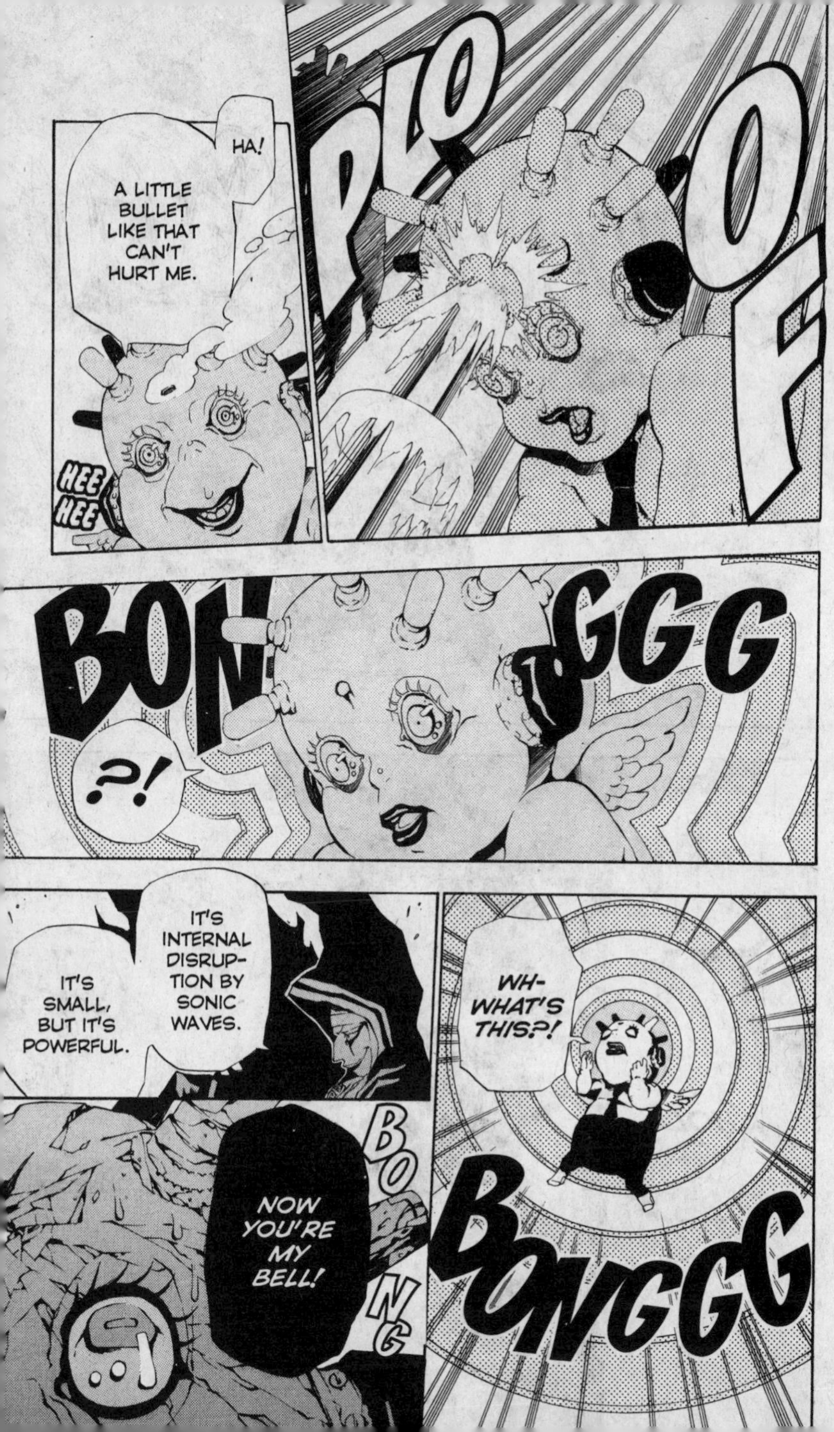
DZOOF
HA!
A LITTLE BULLET LIKE THAT CAN'T HURT ME.
HEE HEE
BONGGGG
?!
WH-WHAT'S THIS?!
BONGGG
IT'S INTERNAL DISRUP-TION BY SONIC WAVES.
IT'S SMALL, BUT IT'S POWERFUL.
BONG
NOW YOU'RE MY BELL!

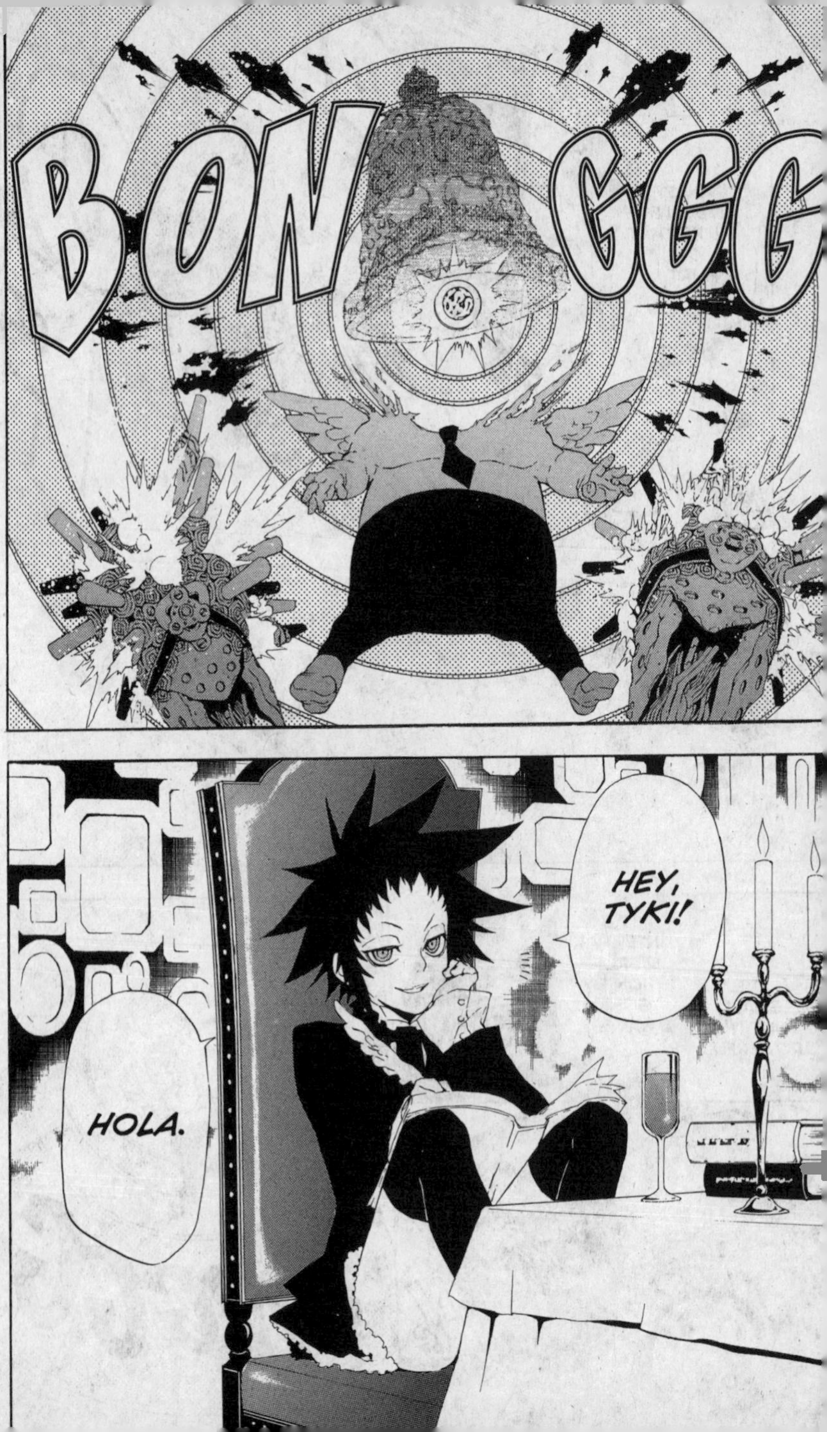
BONGGG
HEY, TYKI!
HOLA.

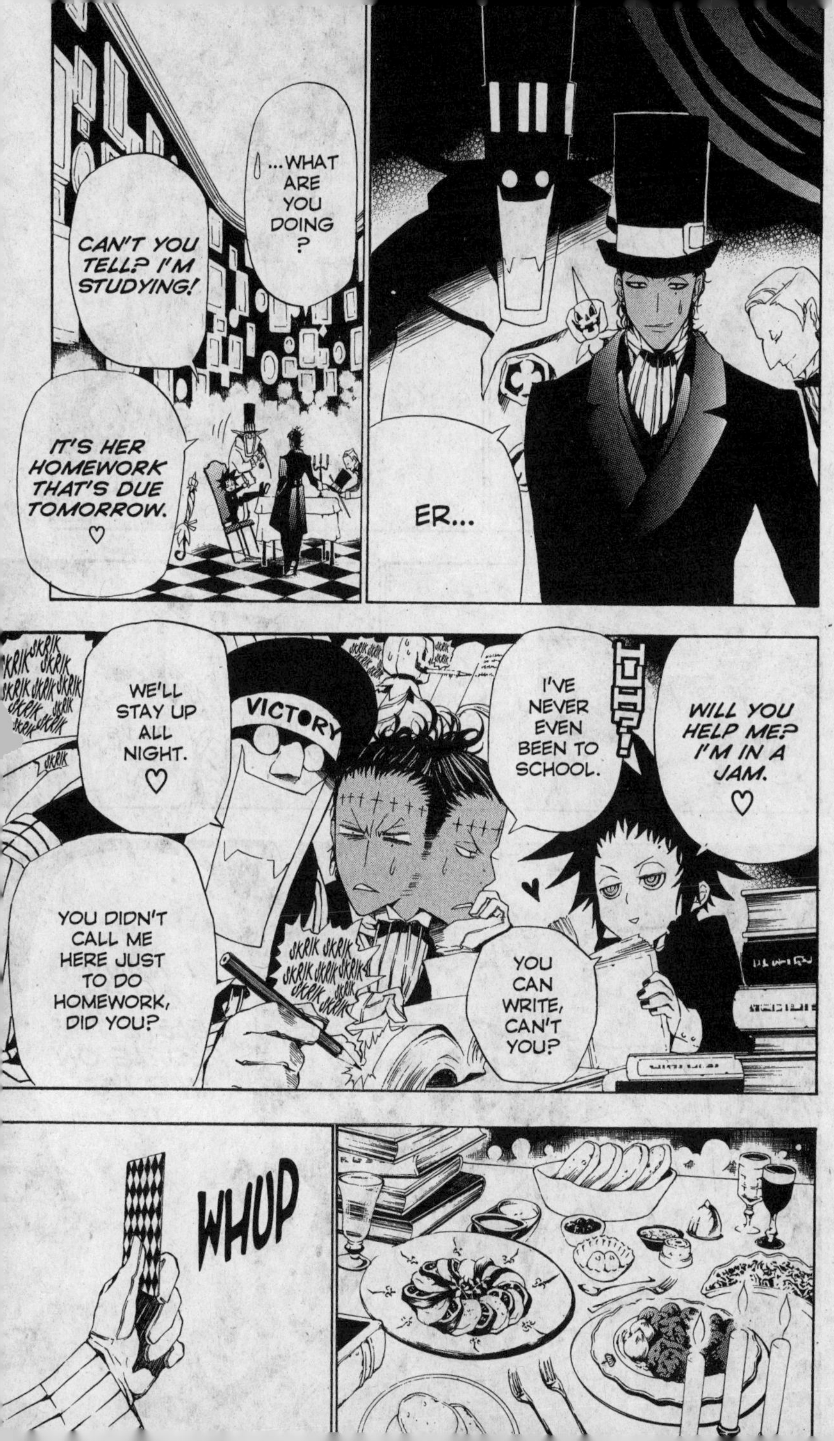
ER...
...WHAT ARE YOU DOING?
CAN'T YOU TELL? I'M STUDYING!
IT'S HER HOMEWORK THAT'S DUE TOMORROW. ♡
WILL YOU HELP ME? I'M IN A JAM. ♡
I'VE NEVER EVEN BEEN TO SCHOOL.
YOU CAN WRITE, CAN'T YOU?
SKRIK SKRIK SKRIK SKRIK
VICTORY
WE'LL STAY UP ALL NIGHT. ♡
SKRIK SKRIK SKRIK SKRIK
YOU DIDN'T CALL ME HERE JUST TO DO HOMEWORK, DID YOU?
WHUP

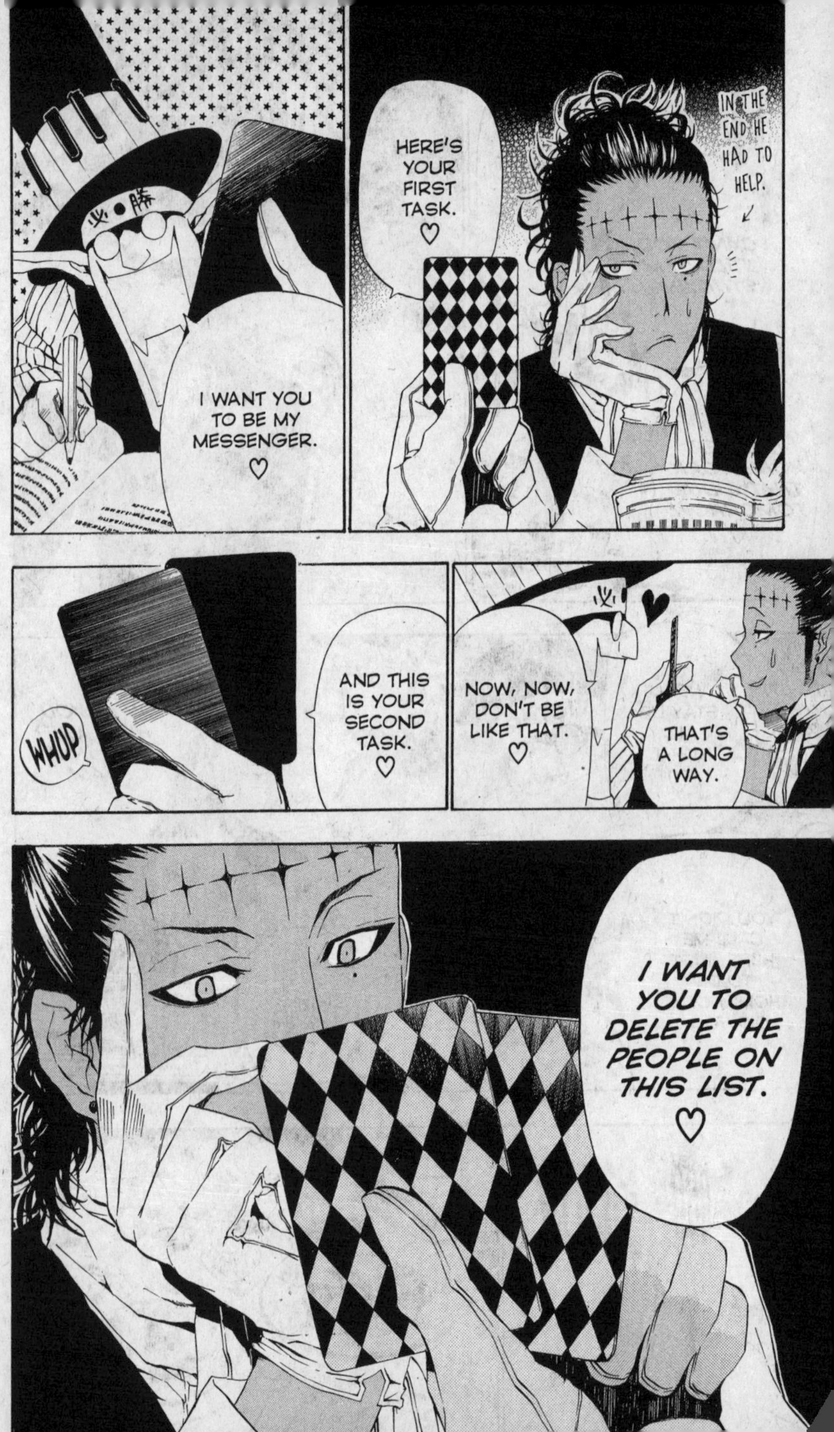
IN THE END HE HAD TO HELP.
HERE'S YOUR FIRST TASK. ♡
I WANT YOU TO BE MY MESSENGER. ♡
THAT'S A LONG WAY.
NOW, NOW, DON'T BE LIKE THAT. ♡
AND THIS IS YOUR SECOND TASK. ♡
WHUP
I WANT YOU TO DELETE THE PEOPLE ON THIS LIST. ♡

READ THIS WAY

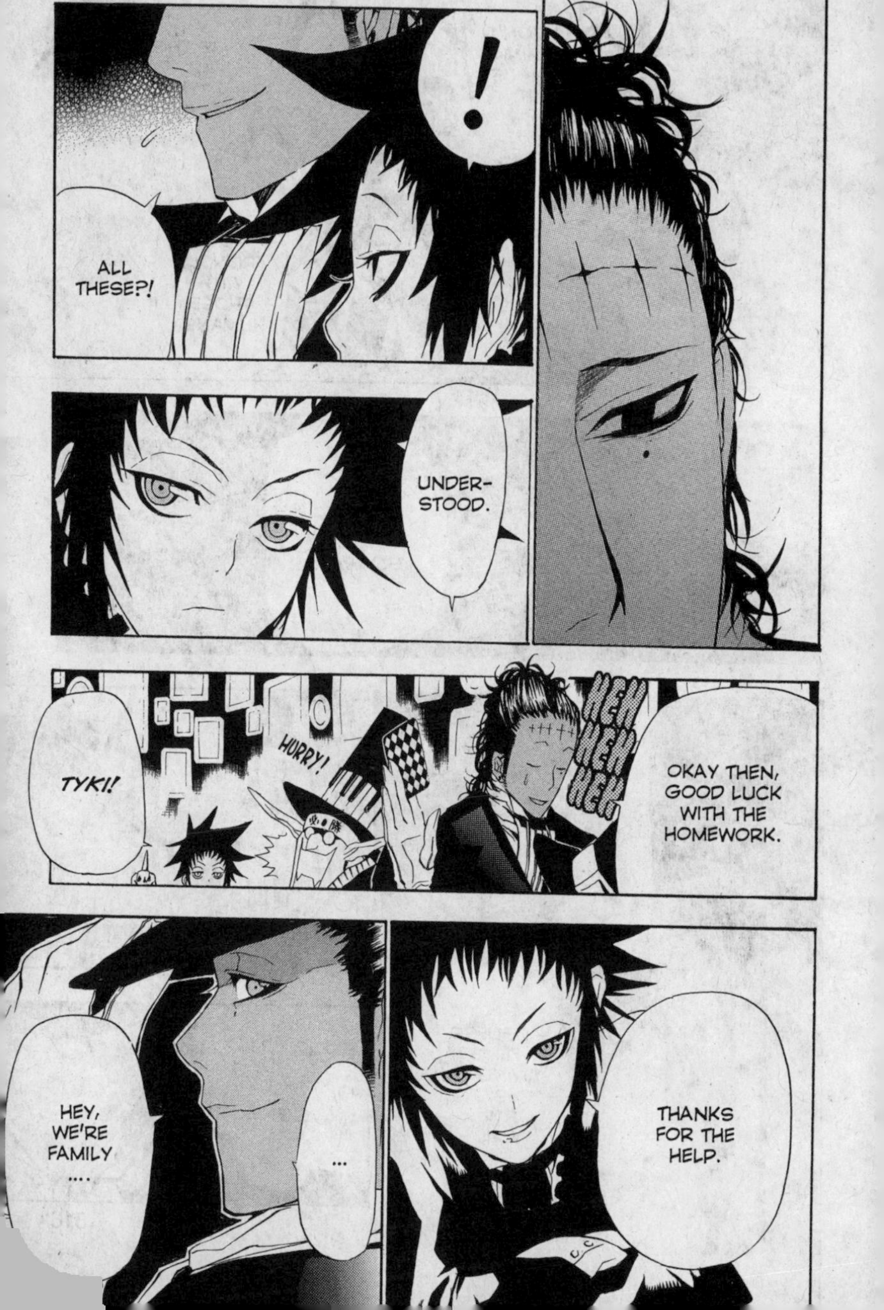
!
ALL THESE?!
UNDER-STOOD.
OKAY THEN, GOOD LUCK WITH THE HOMEWORK.
HEH HEH HEH
HURRY!
TYKI!
THANKS FOR THE HELP.
...
HEY, WE'RE FAMILY ....

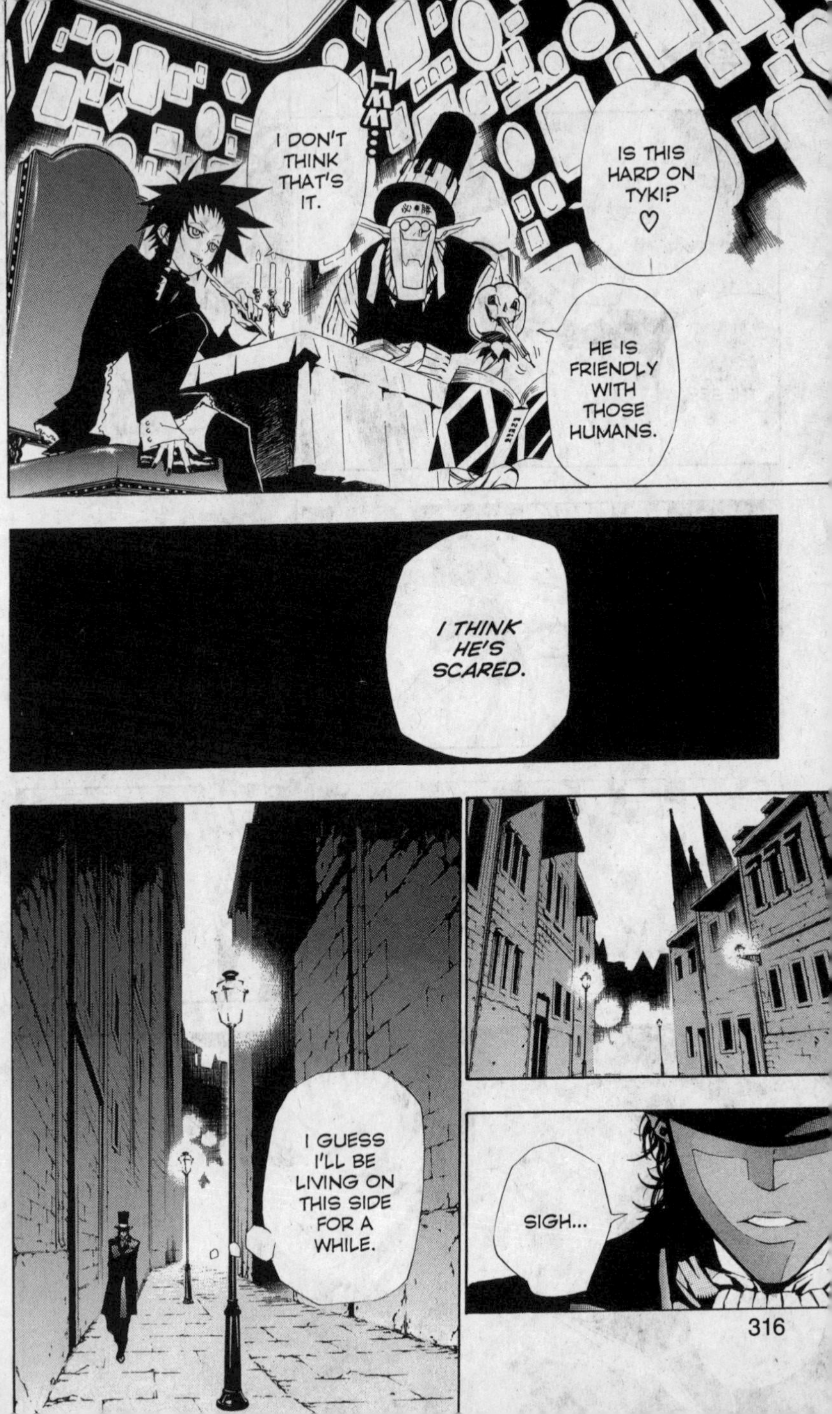
IS THIS HARD ON TYKI? ♡
HE IS FRIENDLY WITH THOSE HUMANS.
HMM...
I DON'T THINK THAT'S IT.
I THINK HE'S SCARED.
SIGH...
I GUESS I'LL BE LIVING ON THIS SIDE FOR A WHILE.

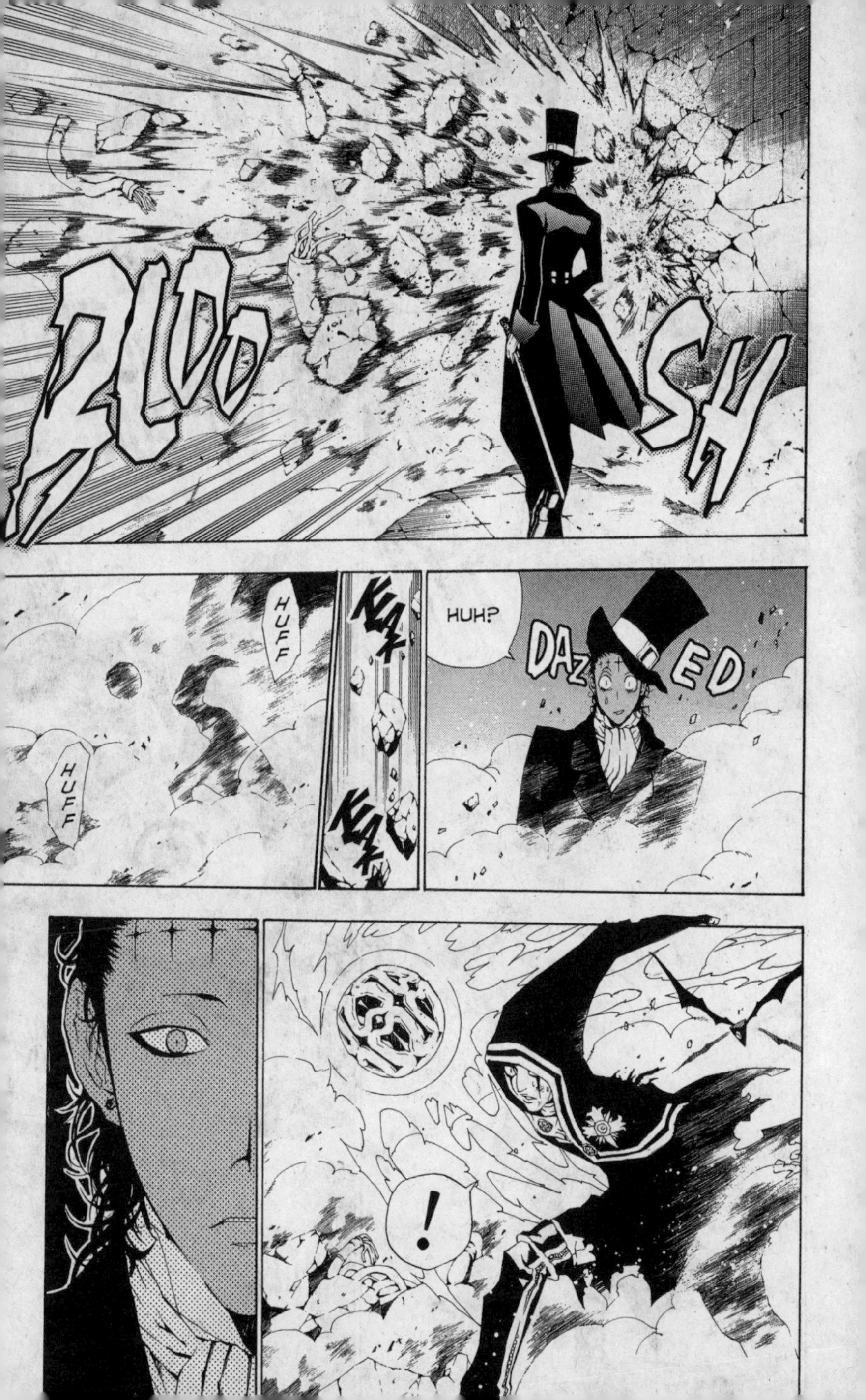
ZUOOSH
HUH?
DAZED
KLAK KLAK
HUFF HUFF
!

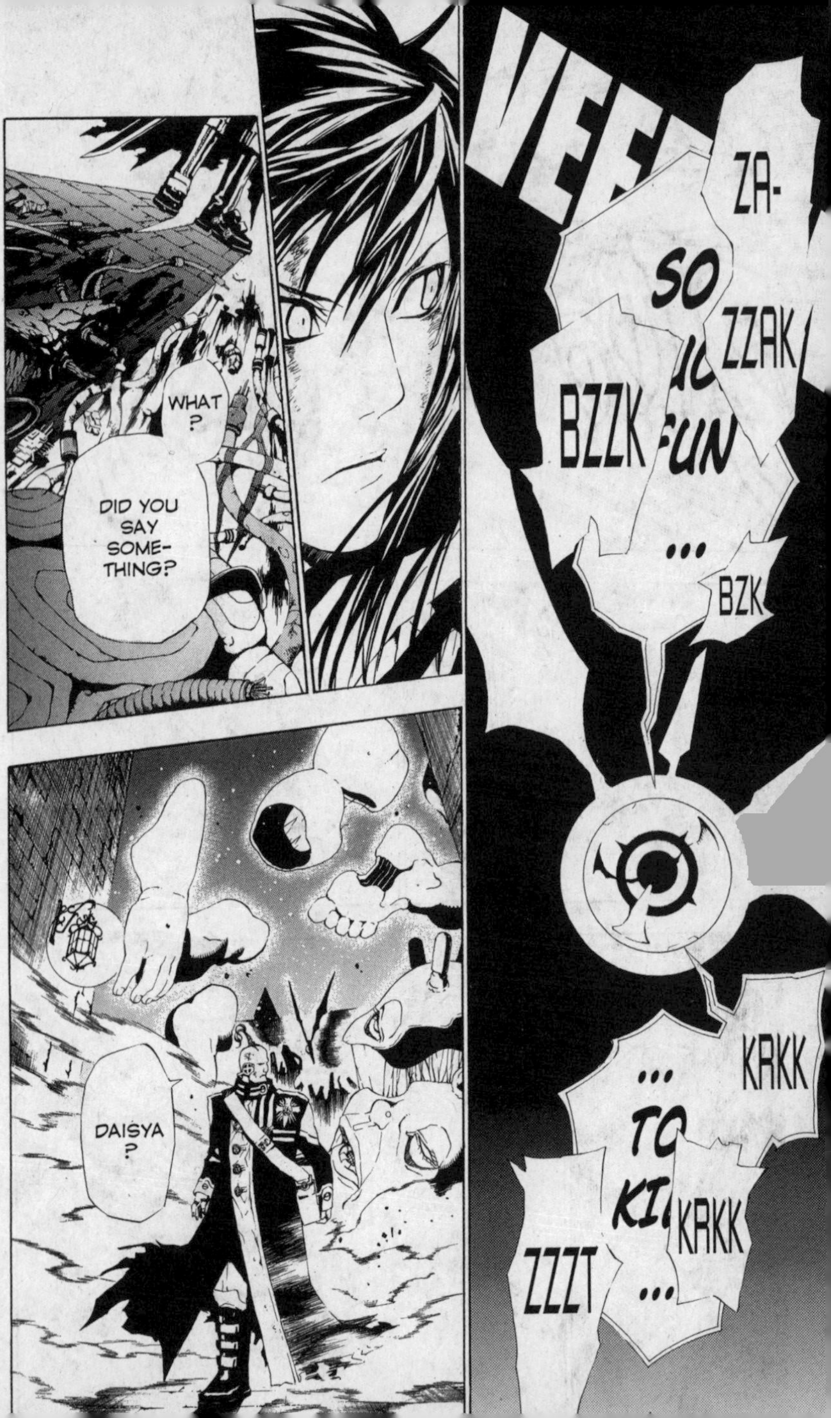

VEEE
ZA-ZZAK
SO UC FUN ...
BZZK
BZK
KRKK
... TO KI ...
KRKK
ZZZT
WHAT?
DID YOU SAY SOMETHING?
DAISYA?

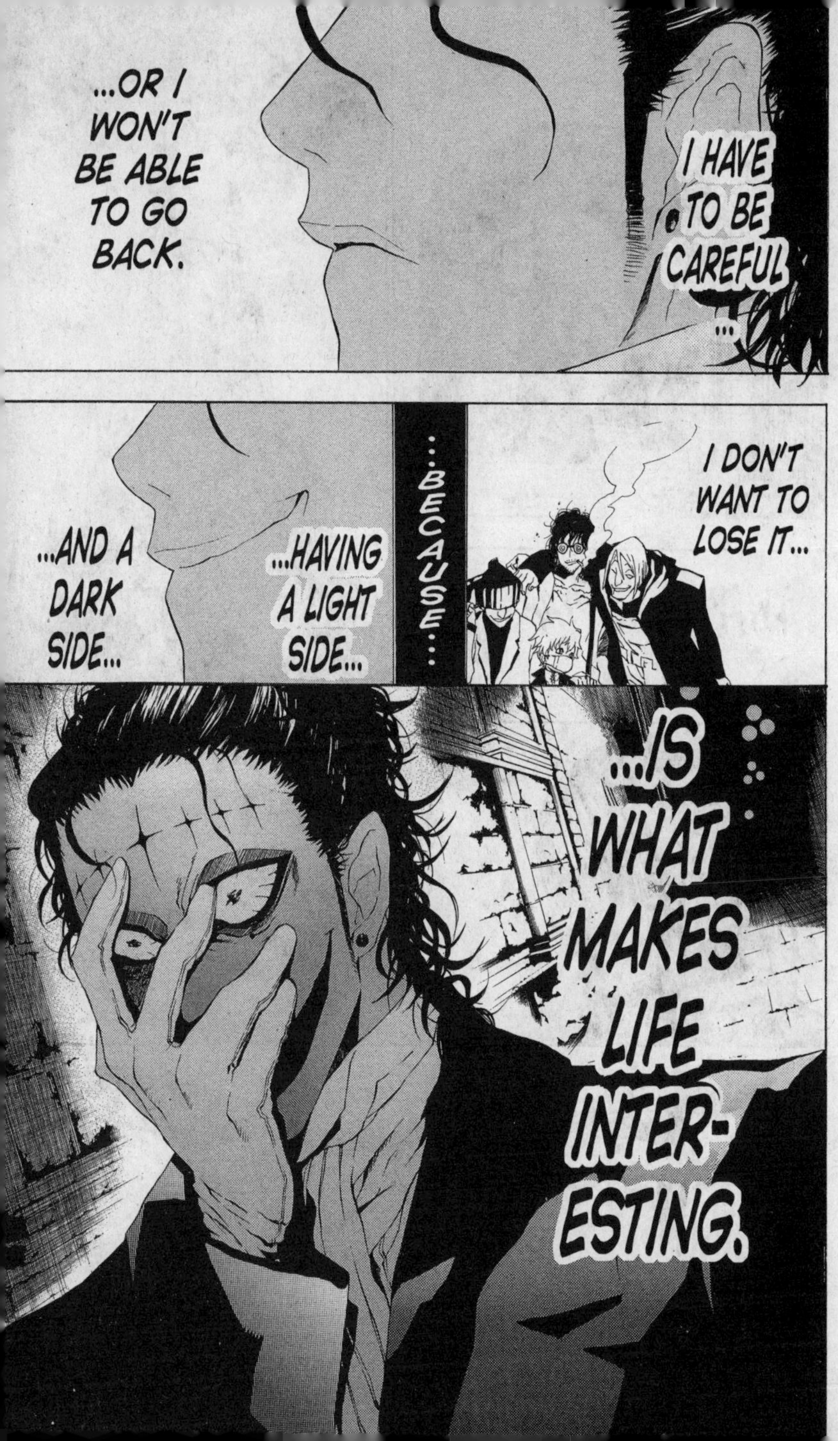
I HAVE TO BE CAREFUL...
...OR I WON'T BE ABLE TO GO BACK.
I DON'T WANT TO LOSE IT...
...BECAUSE...
...HAVING A LIGHT SIDE...
...AND A DARK SIDE...
...IS WHAT MAKES LIFE INTER-ESTING.

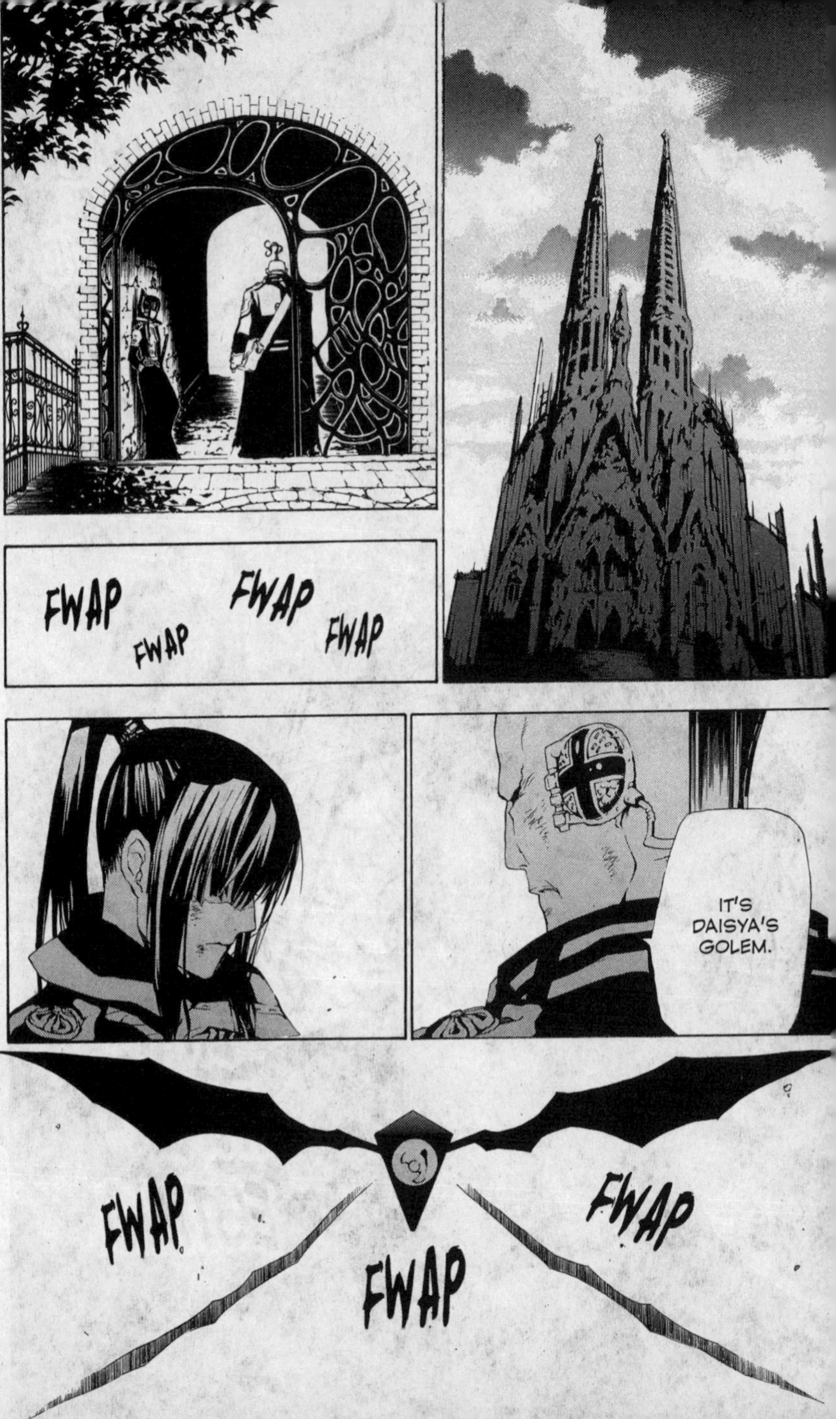
FWAP
FWAP
FWAP
FWAP
IT'S DAISYA'S GOLEM.
FWAP
FWAP
FWAP

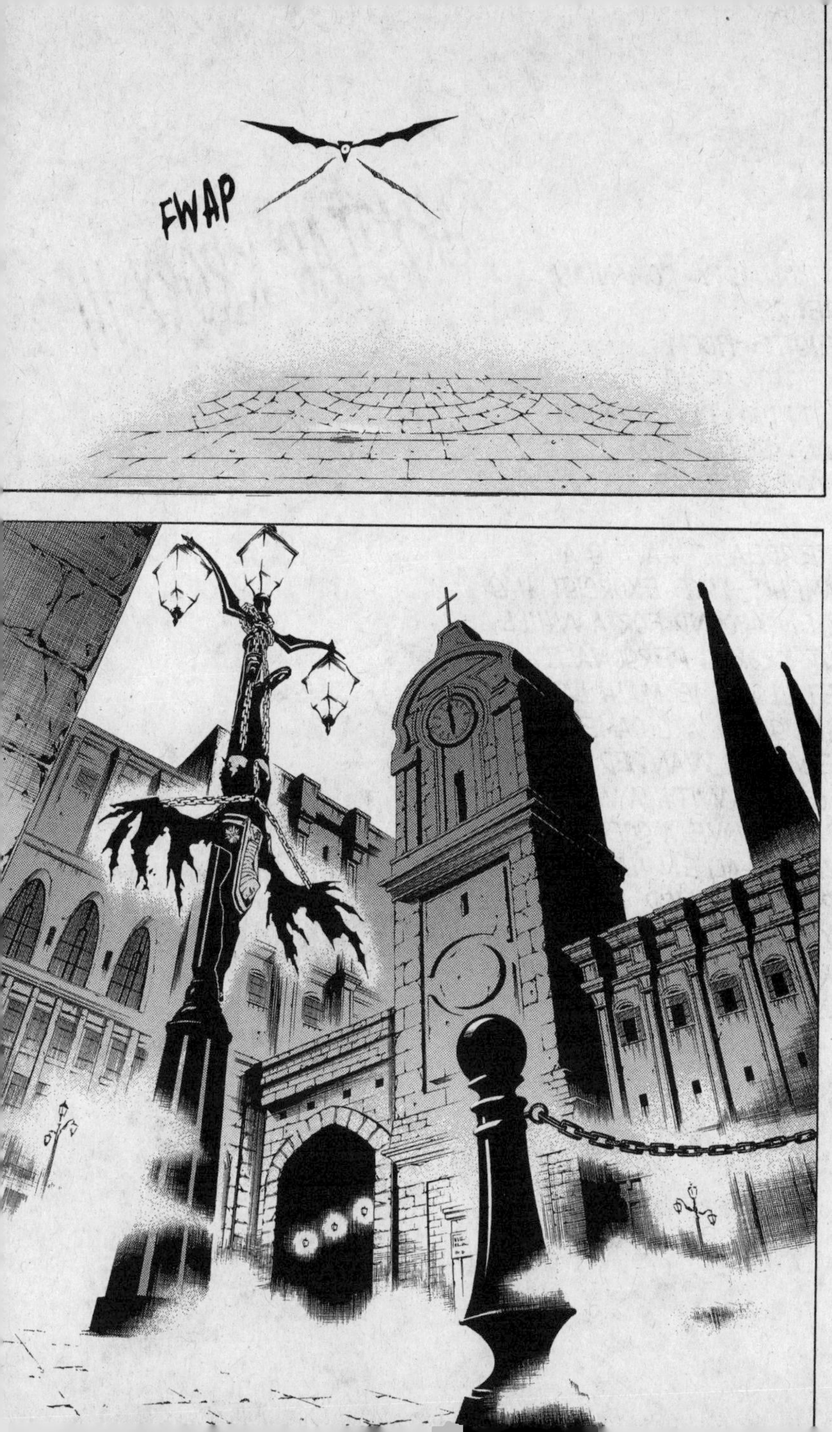
FWAP

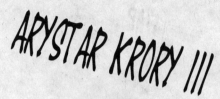

ARYSTAR KRORY III

NATIONALITY: ROMANIAN
AGE: 28
HEIGHT: 190CM
WEIGHT: 77KG
BIRTHDAY: DECEMBER 1
SIGN: SAGITTARIUS
BLOOD TYPE: AB

THE IDEA OF HAVING A VAMPIRE-LIKE EXORCIST HAS BEEN AROUND FOR A WHILE, BUT KRORY'S PERSONALITY AND DETAILS CAME MUCH LATER. THIS STORY ARC CAME ABOUT BECAUSE I WANTED TO DRAW A CASTLE WITH A VAMPIRE IN IT AND HAVE A SCENE WHERE ALLEN HAS TO DIG UP A GRAVEYARD. (HMM?) BY THE WAY, THE MODEL FOR KRORY WAS ACTOR/SINGER YUSUKE SANTAMARIA.

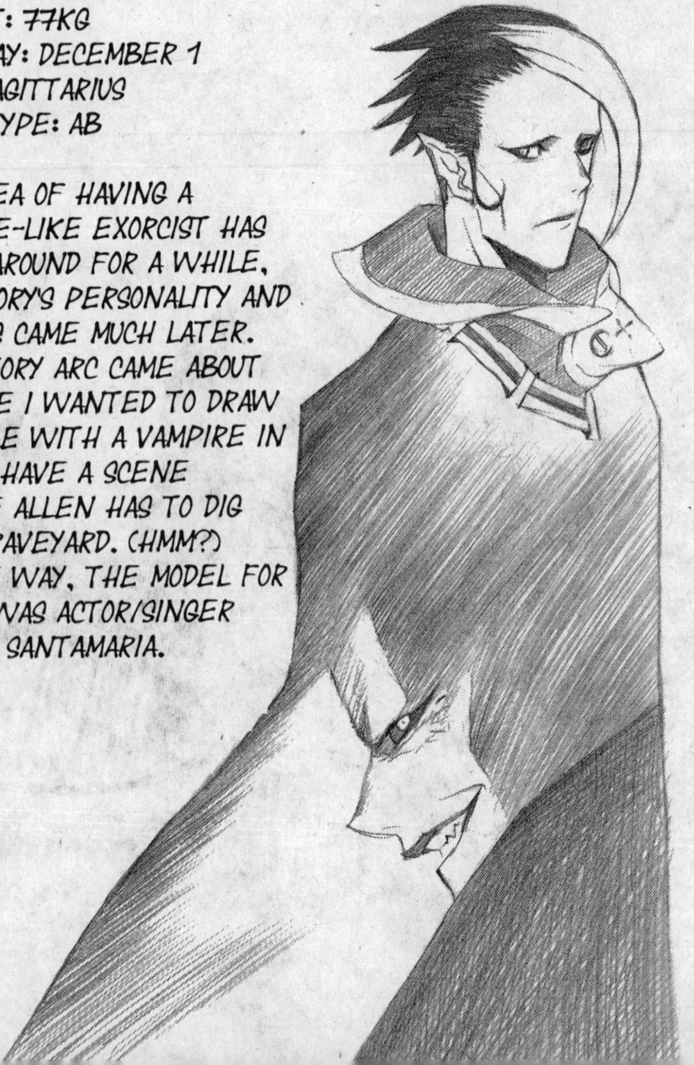

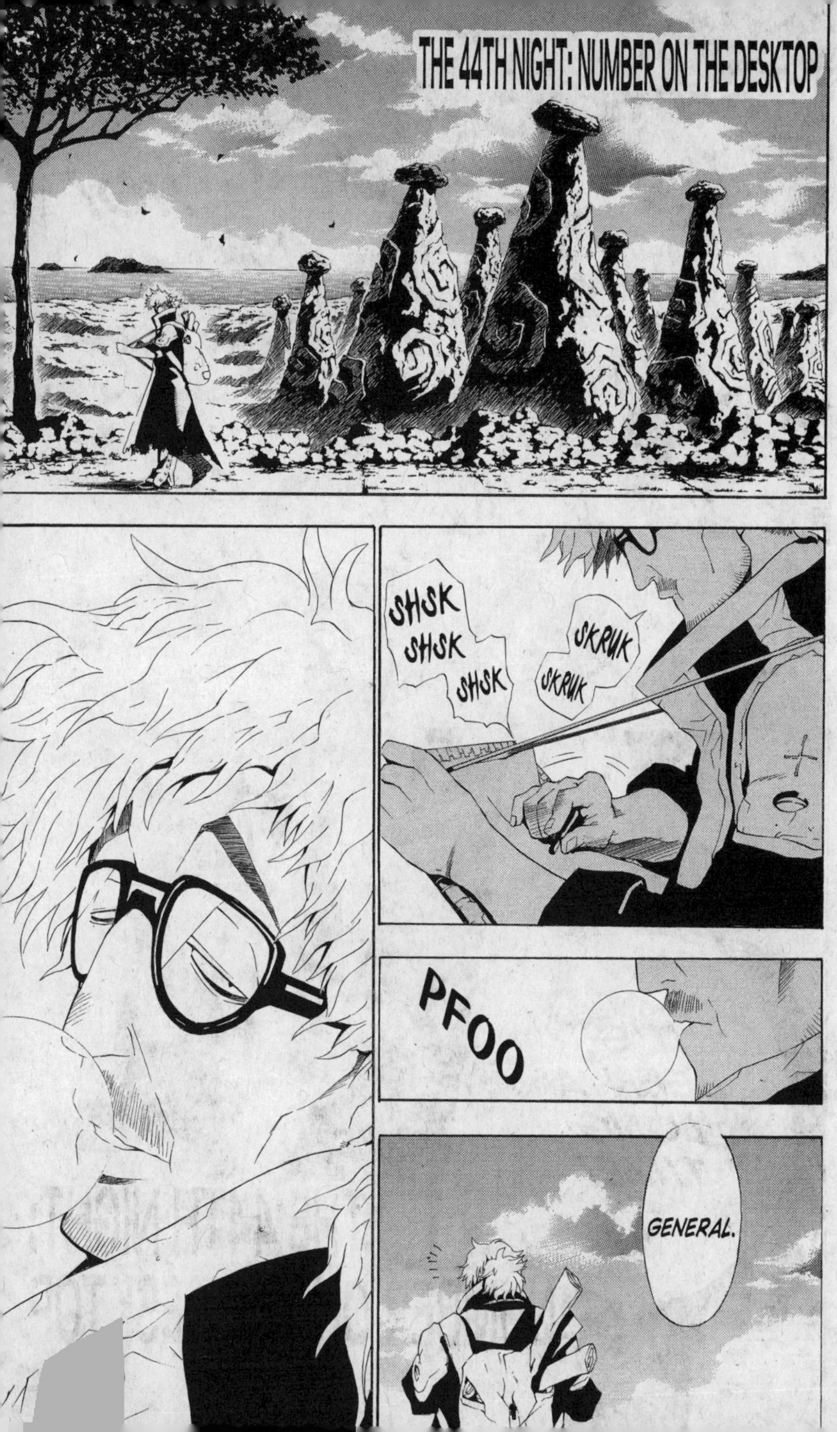
THE 44TH NIGHT: NUMBER ON THE DESKTOP
SKRUK SKRUK
SHSK SHSK SHSK
PFOO
GENERAL.

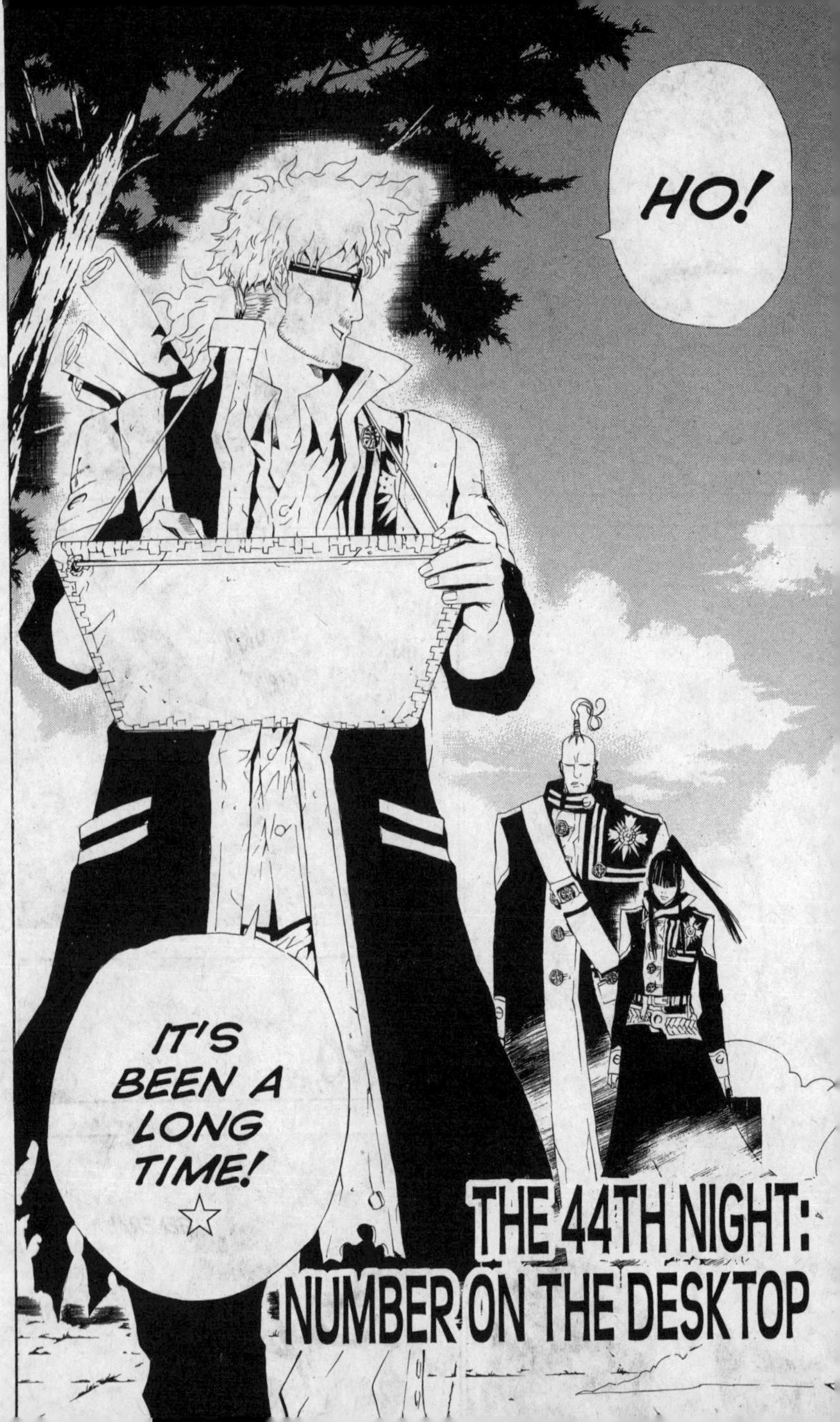
HO!
IT'S BEEN A LONG TIME! ☆
THE 44TH NIGHT: NUMBER ON THE DESKTOP

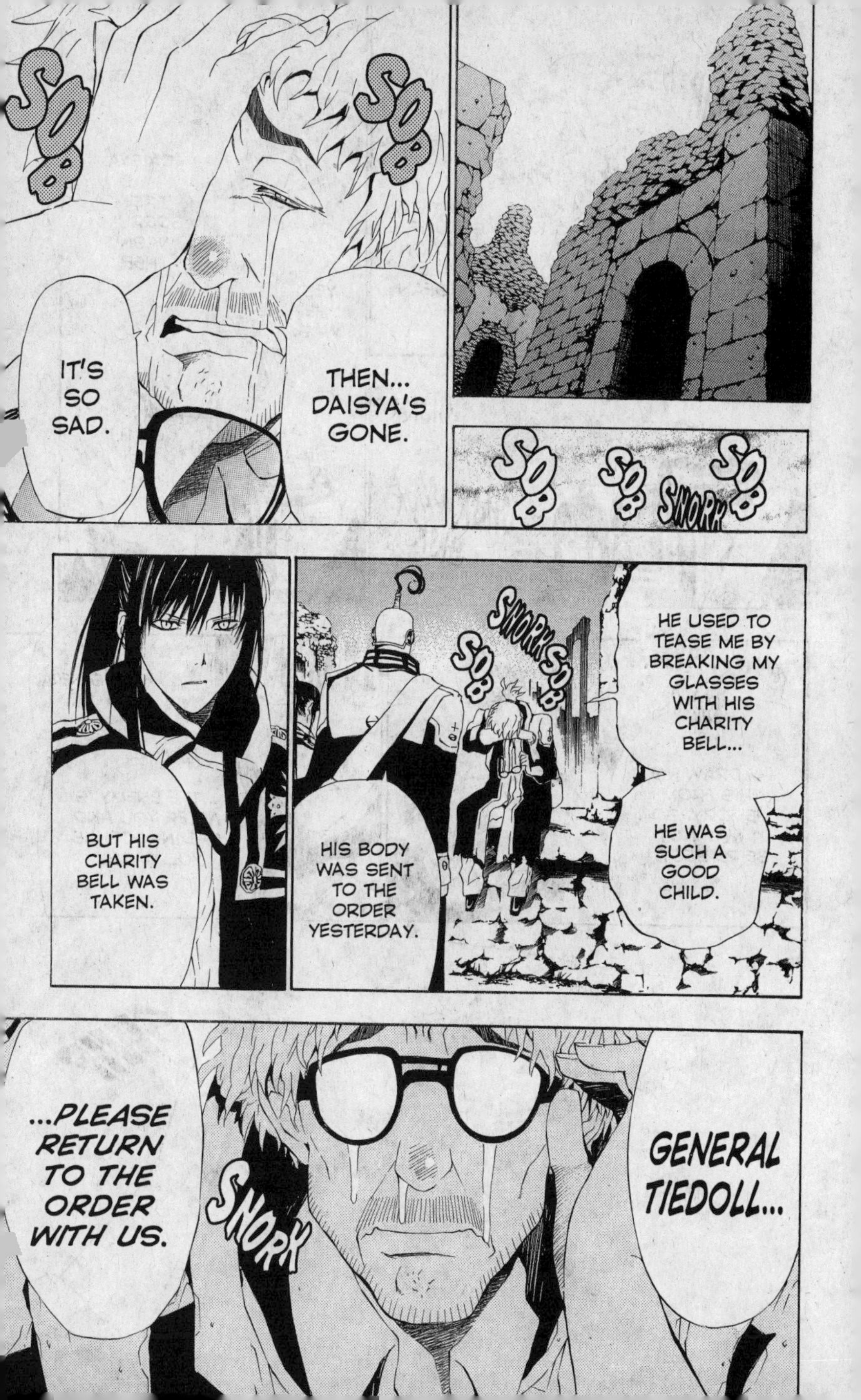
SOB SOB SNORK SOB
SOB
SOB
THEN... DAISYA'S GONE.
IT'S SO SAD.
SNORK SOB
SOB
HE USED TO TEASE ME BY BREAKING MY GLASSES WITH HIS CHARITY BELL...
HE WAS SUCH A GOOD CHILD.
HIS BODY WAS SENT TO THE ORDER YESTERDAY.
BUT HIS CHARITY BELL WAS TAKEN.
GENERAL TIEDOLL...
SNORK
...PLEASE RETURN TO THE ORDER WITH US.

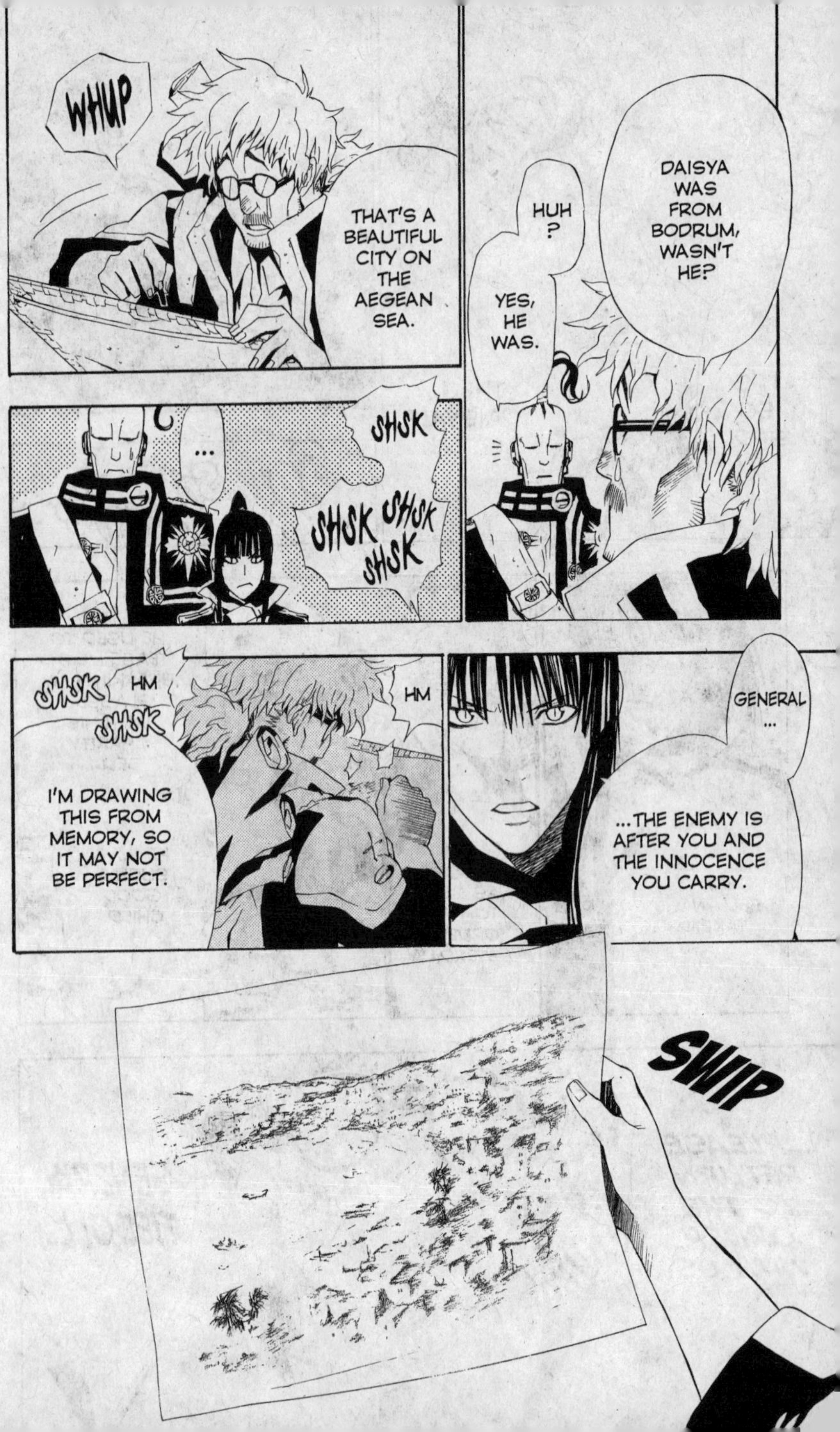
DAISYA WAS FROM BODRUM, WASN'T HE?
HUH?
YES, HE WAS.
THAT'S A BEAUTIFUL CITY ON THE AEGEAN SEA.
WHUP
SHSK
SHSK SHSK SHSK
...
GENERAL...
...THE ENEMY IS AFTER YOU AND THE INNOCENCE YOU CARRY.
HM
HM
SHSK
SHSK
I'M DRAWING THIS FROM MEMORY, SO IT MAY NOT BE PERFECT.
SWIP

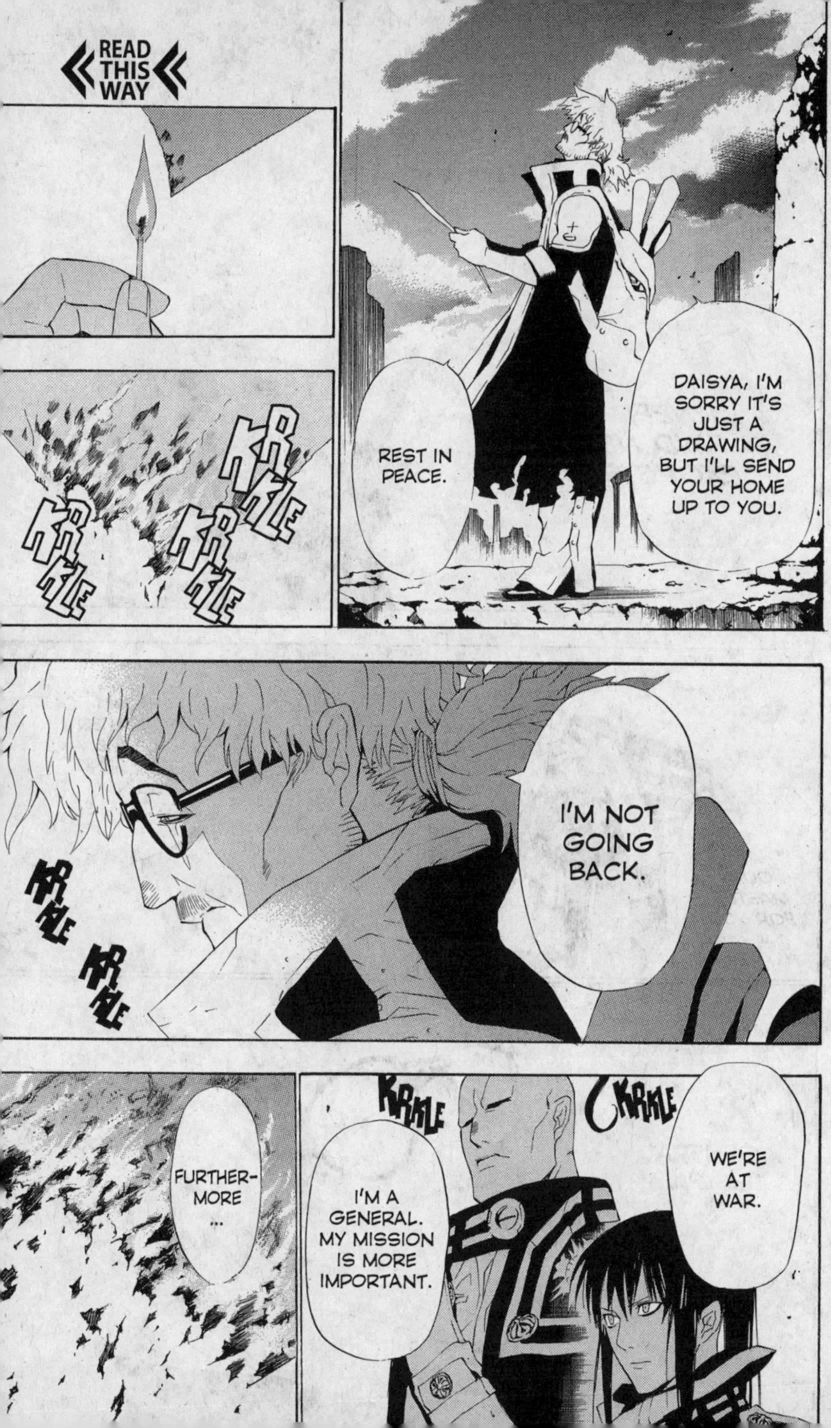
READ THIS WAY
DAISYA, I'M SORRY IT'S JUST A DRAWING, BUT I'LL SEND YOUR HOME UP TO YOU.
REST IN PEACE.
KRKLE
KRKLE
KRKLE
I'M NOT GOING BACK.
KRKLE
KRKLE
WE'RE AT WAR.
CKRKLE
KRKLE
I'M A GENERAL. MY MISSION IS MORE IMPORTANT.
FURTHER-MORE ...

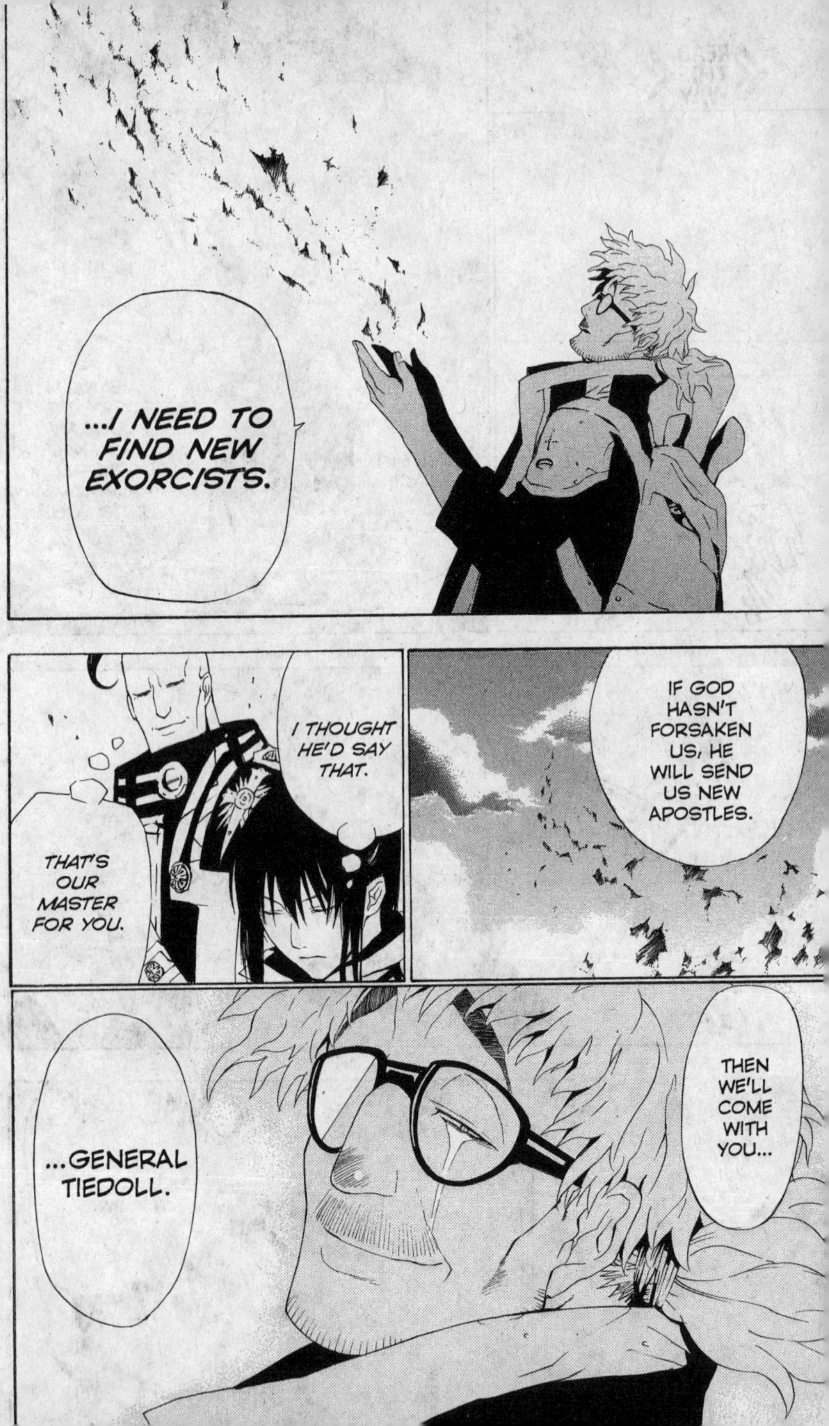
...I NEED TO FIND NEW EXORCISTS.
IF GOD HASN'T FORSAKEN US, HE WILL SEND US NEW APOSTLES.
I THOUGHT HE'D SAY THAT.
THAT'S OUR MASTER FOR YOU.
THEN WE'LL COME WITH YOU...
...GENERAL TIEDOLL.

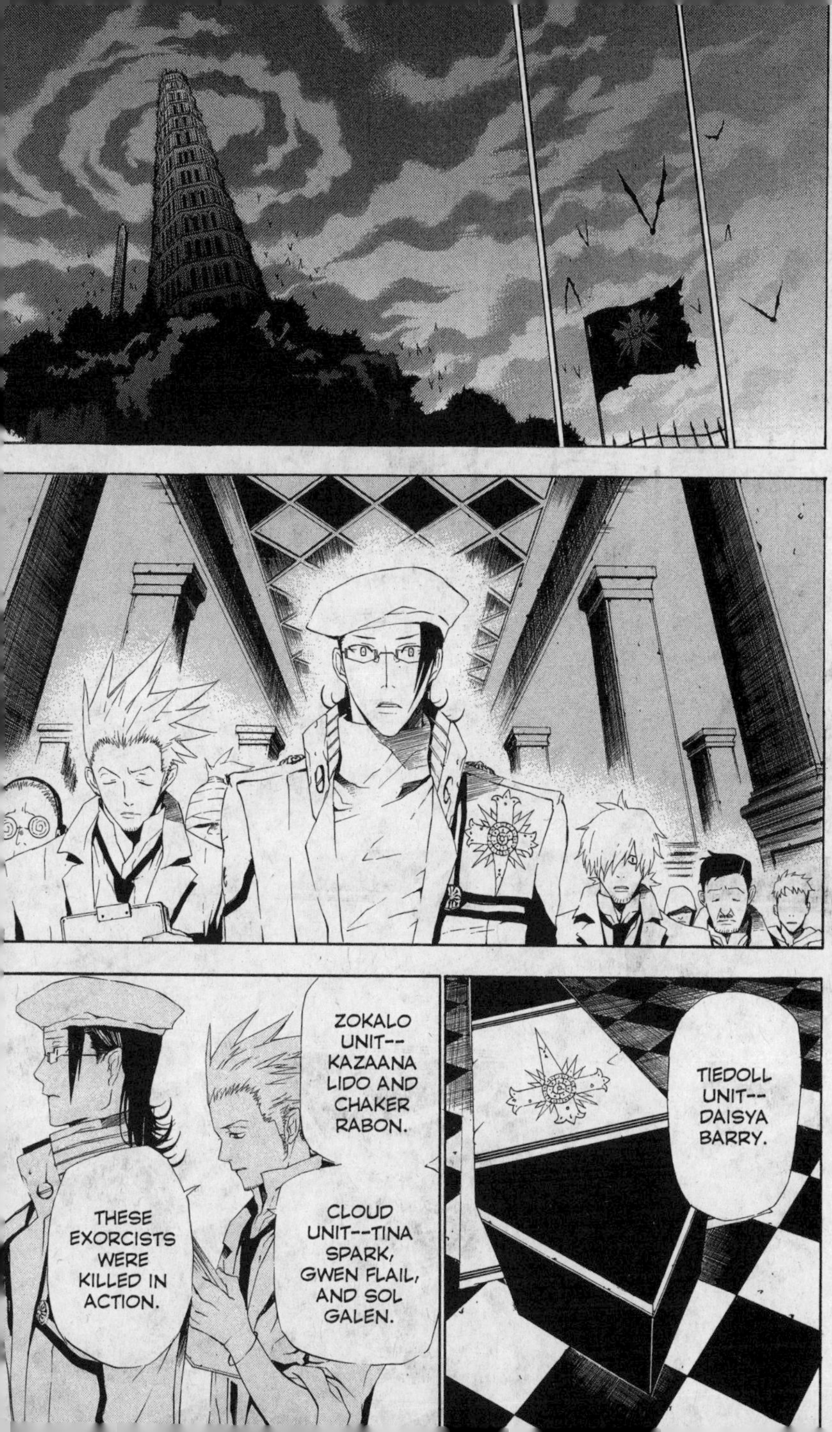
TIEDOLL UNIT--DAISYA BARRY.
ZOKALO UNIT--KAZAANA LIDO AND CHAKER RABON.
CLOUD UNIT--TINA SPARK, GWEN FLAIL, AND SOL GALEN.
THESE EXORCISTS WERE KILLED IN ACTION.

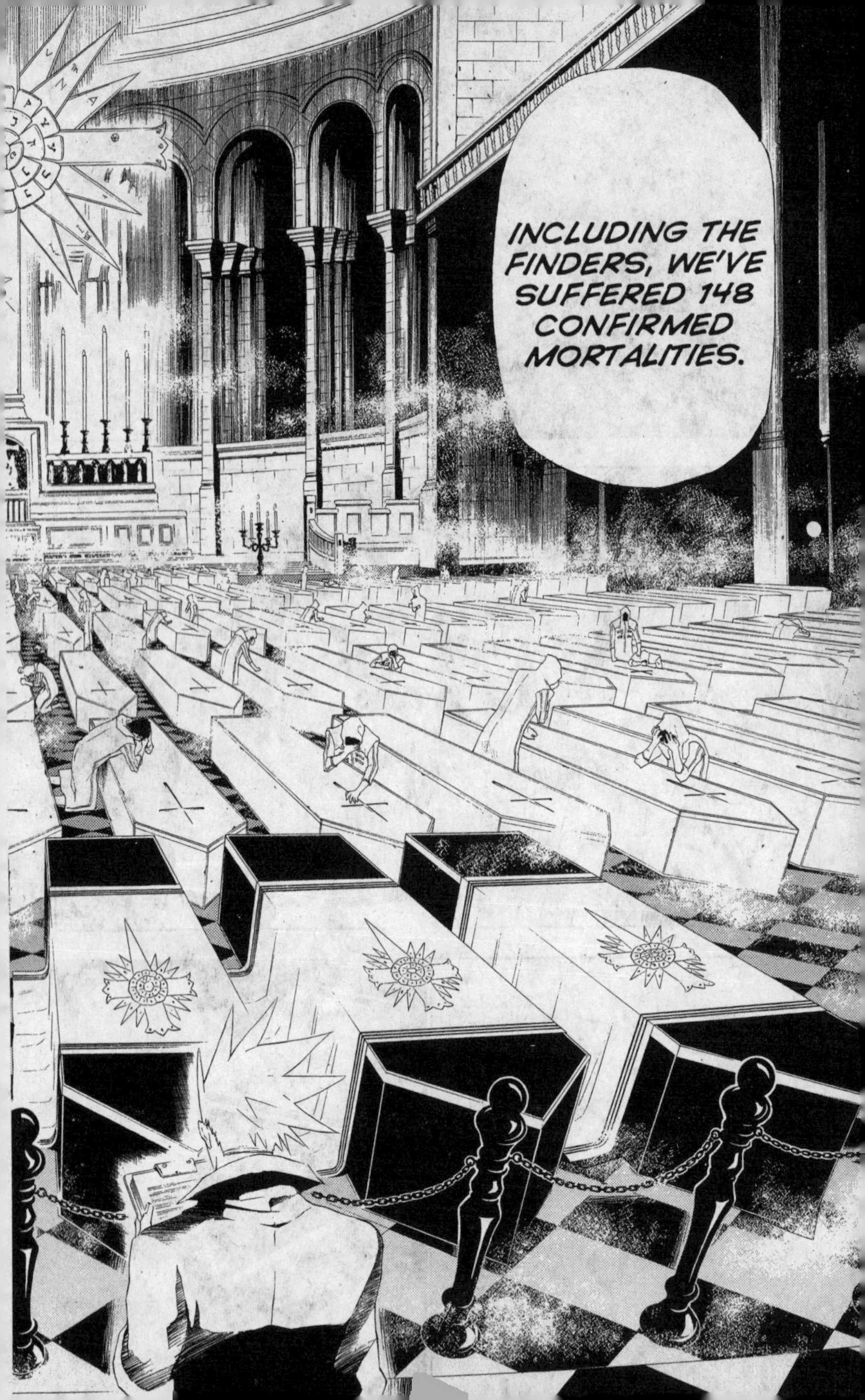
INCLUDING THE FINDERS, WE'VE SUFFERED 148 CONFIRMED MORTALITIES.

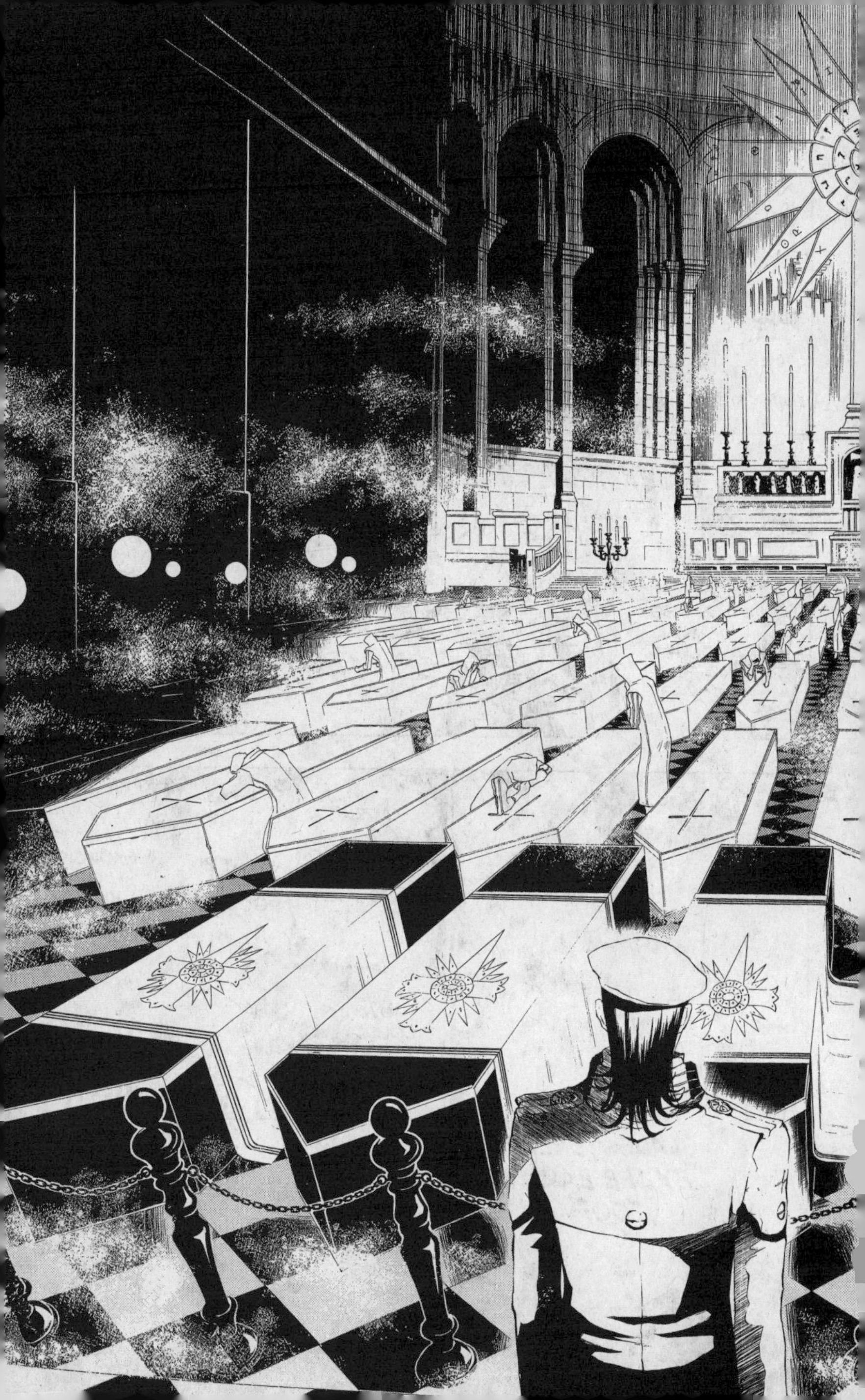

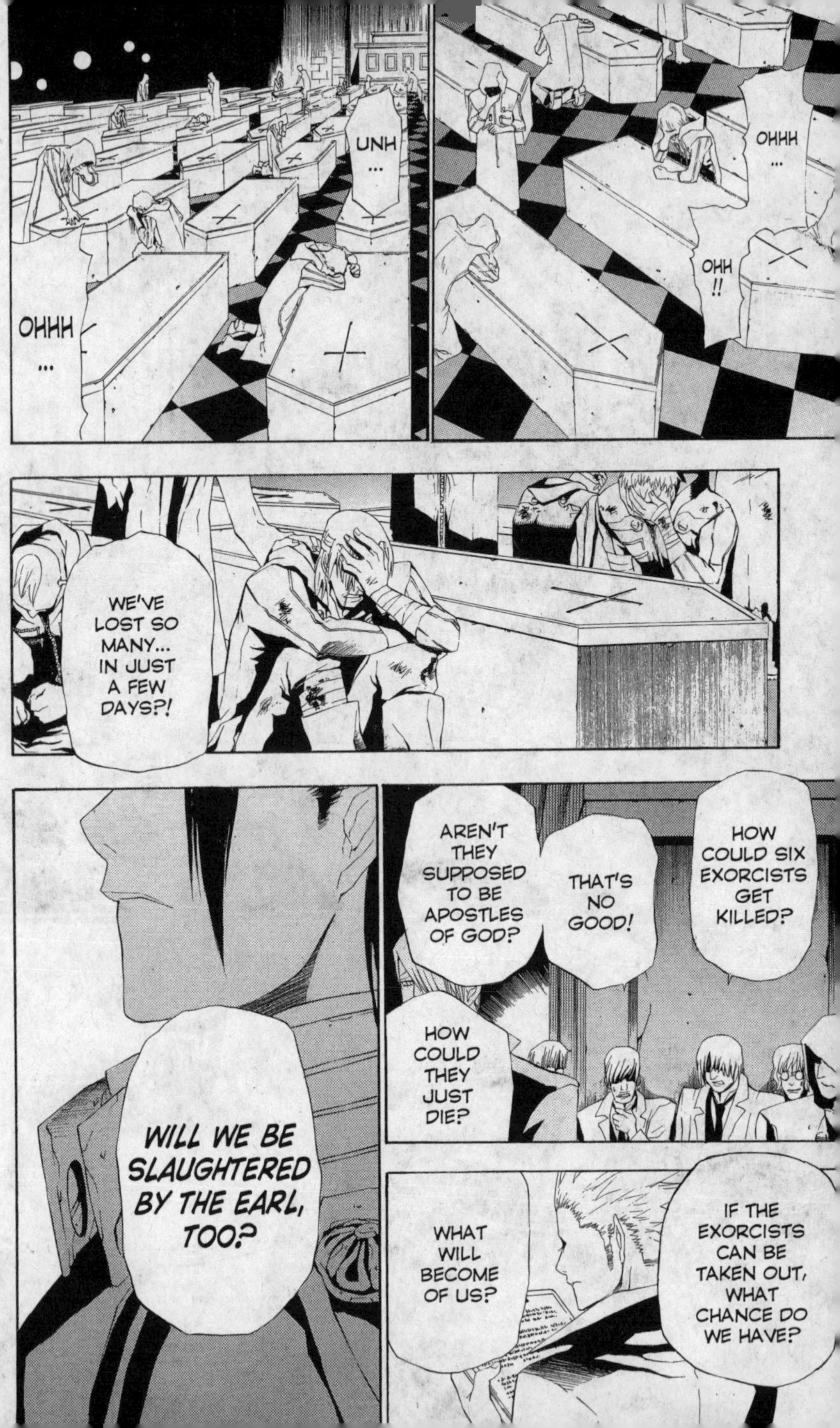
OHHH ...
OHH !!
UNH ...
OHHH ...
WE'VE LOST SO MANY... IN JUST A FEW DAYS?!
HOW COULD SIX EXORCISTS GET KILLED?
THAT'S NO GOOD!
AREN'T THEY SUPPOSED TO BE APOSTLES OF GOD?
HOW COULD THEY JUST DIE?
IF THE EXORCISTS CAN BE TAKEN OUT, WHAT CHANCE DO WE HAVE?
WHAT WILL BECOME OF US?
WILL WE BE SLAUGHTERED BY THE EARL, TOO?

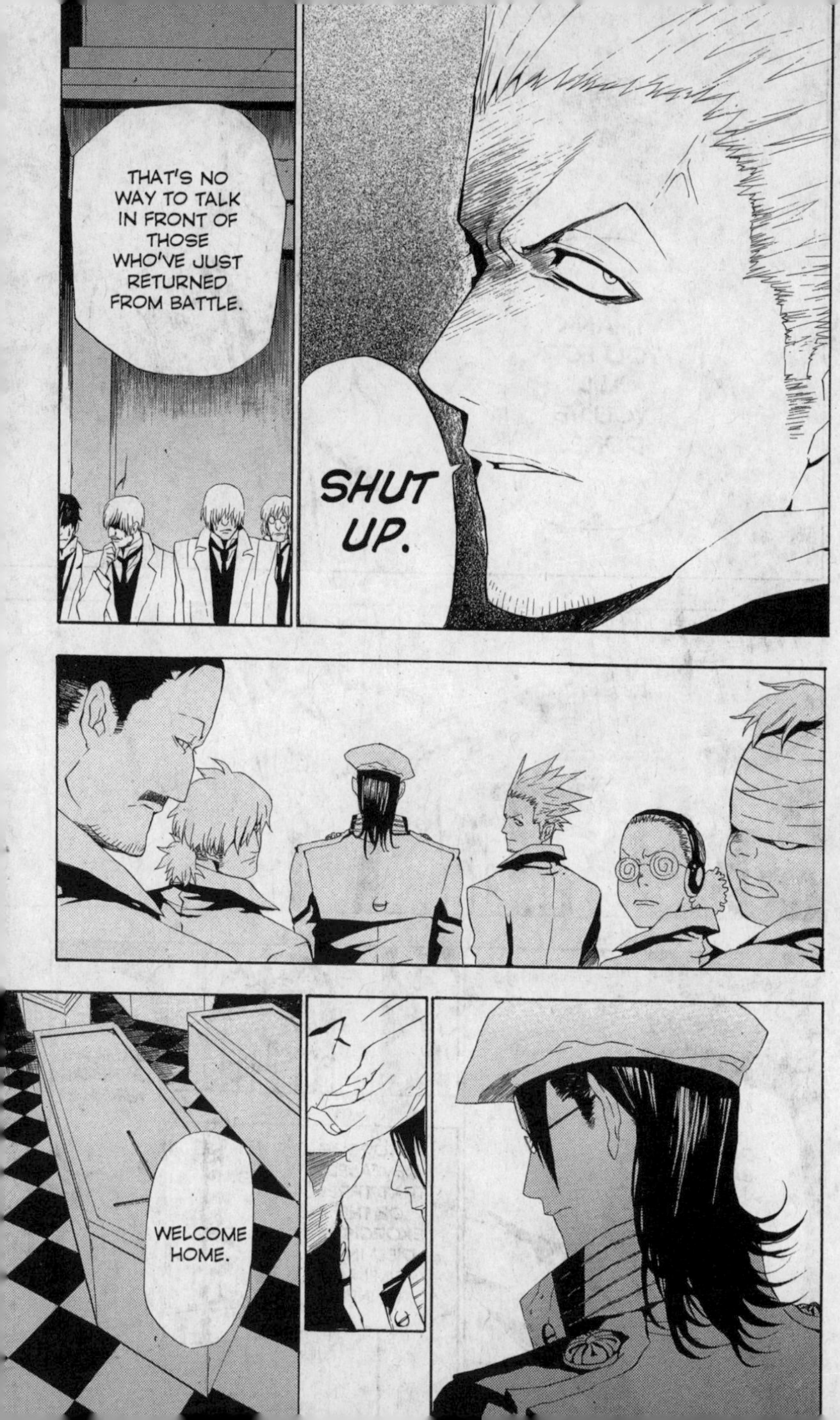
SHUT UP.
THAT'S NO WAY TO TALK IN FRONT OF THOSE WHO'VE JUST RETURNED FROM BATTLE.
WELCOME HOME.

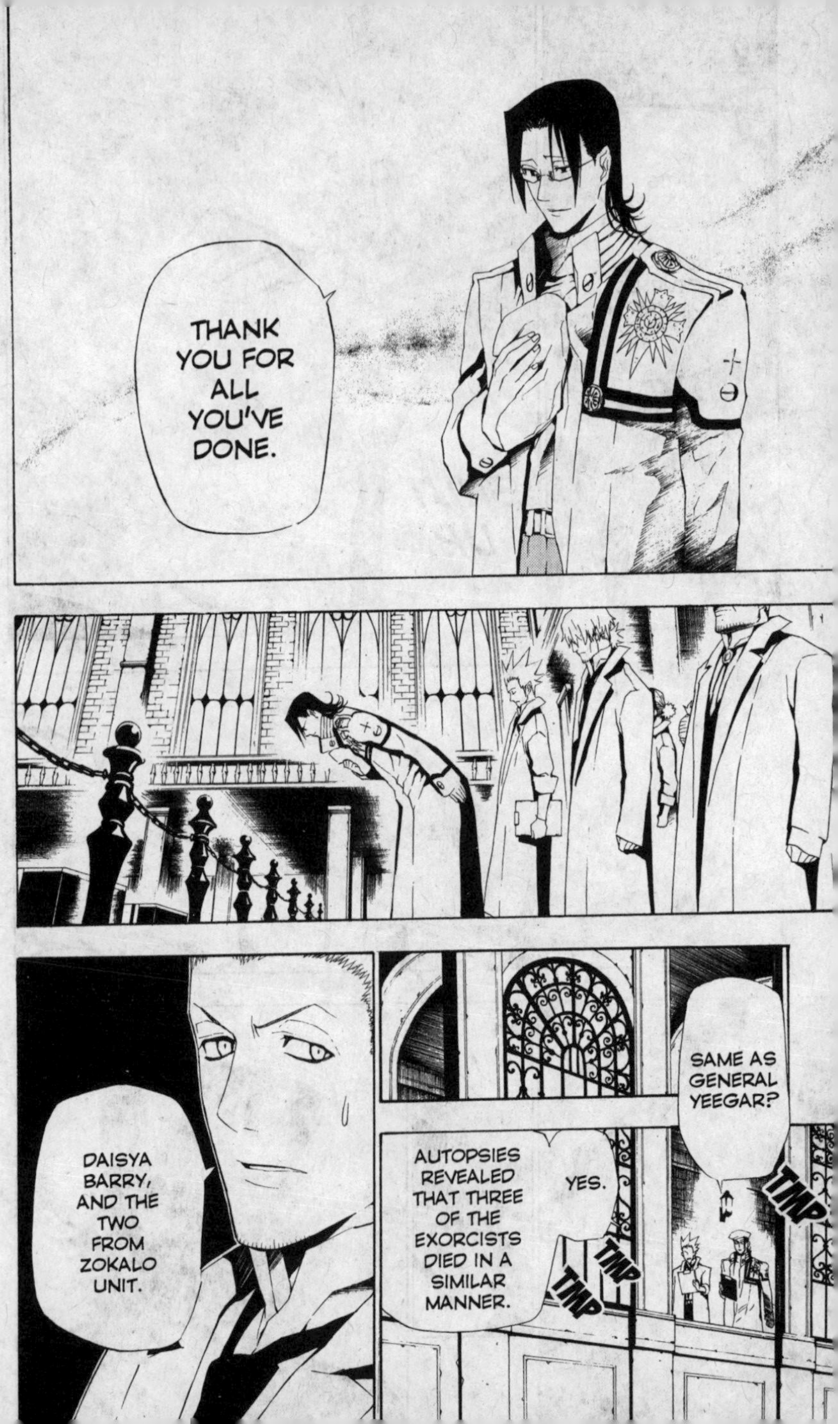
THANK YOU FOR ALL YOU'VE DONE.
SAME AS GENERAL YEEGAR?
TMP
YES.
AUTOPSIES REVEALED THAT THREE OF THE EXORCISTS DIED IN A SIMILAR MANNER.
TMP
TMP
DAISYA BARRY, AND THE TWO FROM ZOKALO UNIT.

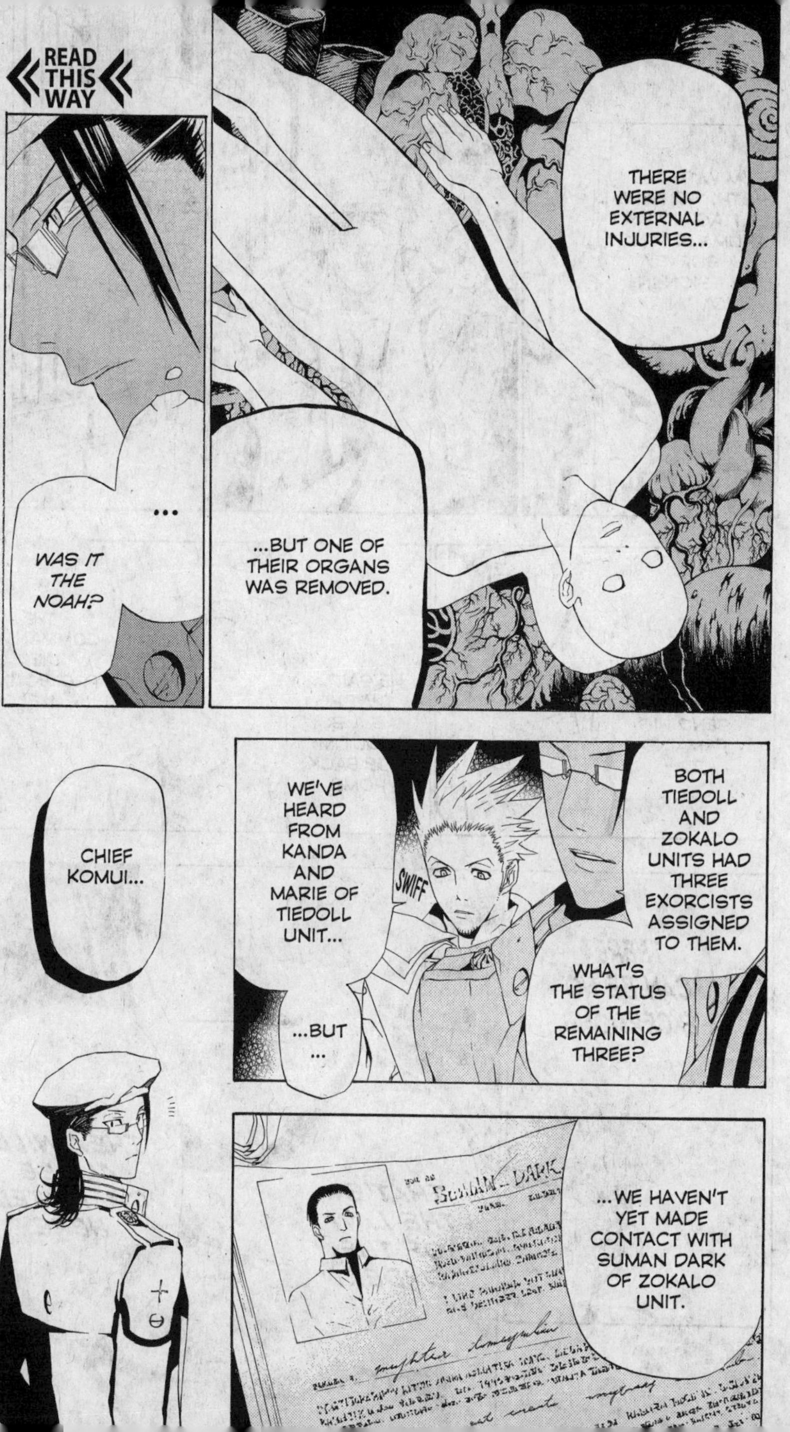
READ THIS WAY
THERE WERE NO EXTERNAL INJURIES...
...BUT ONE OF THEIR ORGANS WAS REMOVED.
...
WAS IT THE NOAH?
BOTH TIEDOLL AND ZOKALO UNITS HAD THREE EXORCISTS ASSIGNED TO THEM.
WHAT'S THE STATUS OF THE REMAINING THREE?
SWIFF
WE'VE HEARD FROM KANDA AND MARIE OF TIEDOLL UNIT...
...BUT ...
CHIEF KOMUI...
...WE HAVEN'T YET MADE CONTACT WITH SUMAN DARK OF ZOKALO UNIT.

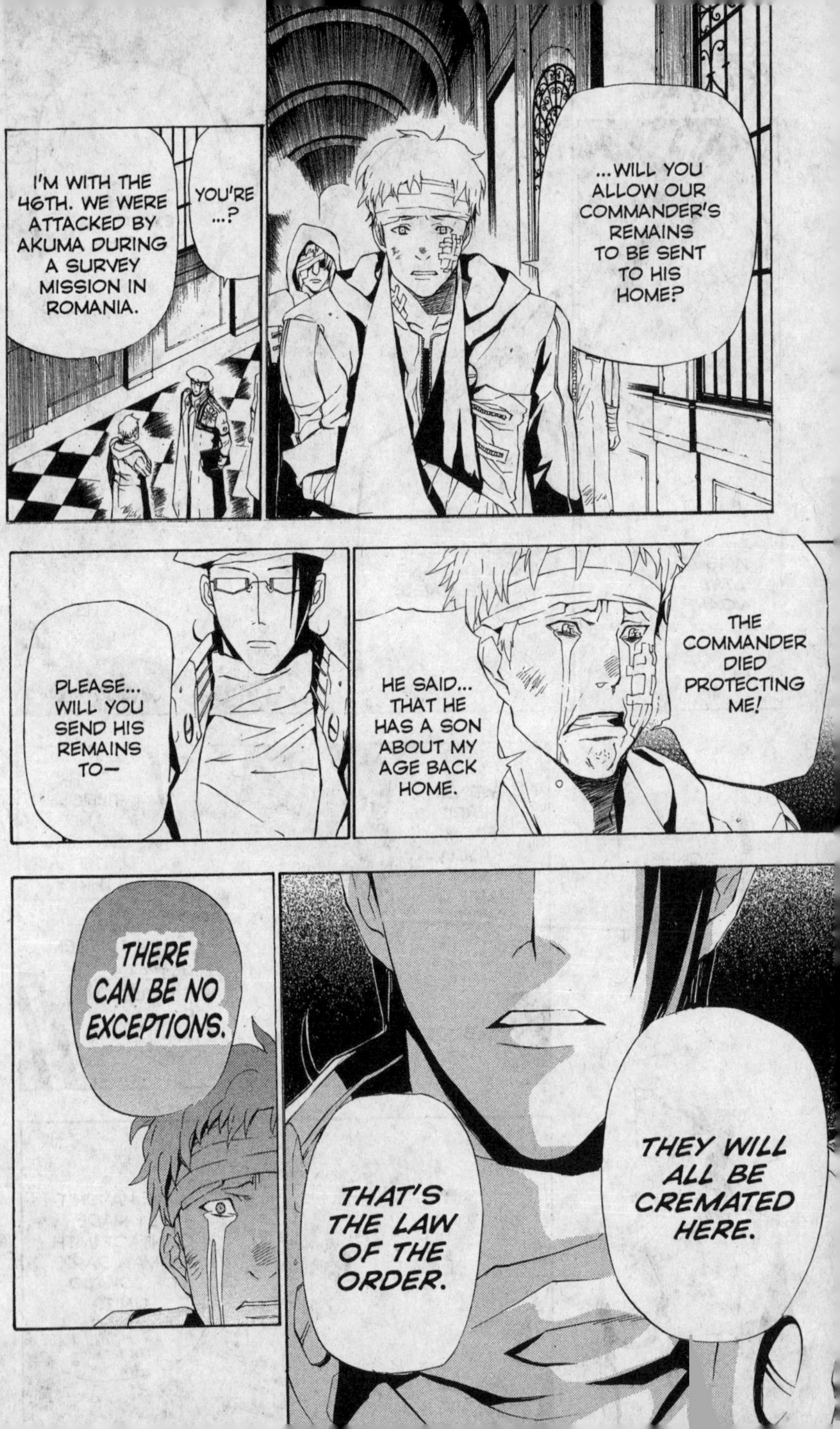
...WILL YOU ALLOW OUR COMMANDER'S REMAINS TO BE SENT TO HIS HOME?
YOU'RE ...?
I'M WITH THE 46TH. WE WERE ATTACKED BY AKUMA DURING A SURVEY MISSION IN ROMANIA.
THE COMMANDER DIED PROTECTING ME!
HE SAID... THAT HE HAS A SON ABOUT MY AGE BACK HOME.
PLEASE... WILL YOU SEND HIS REMAINS TO—
THEY WILL ALL BE CREMATED HERE.
THAT'S THE LAW OF THE ORDER.
THERE CAN BE NO EXCEPTIONS.

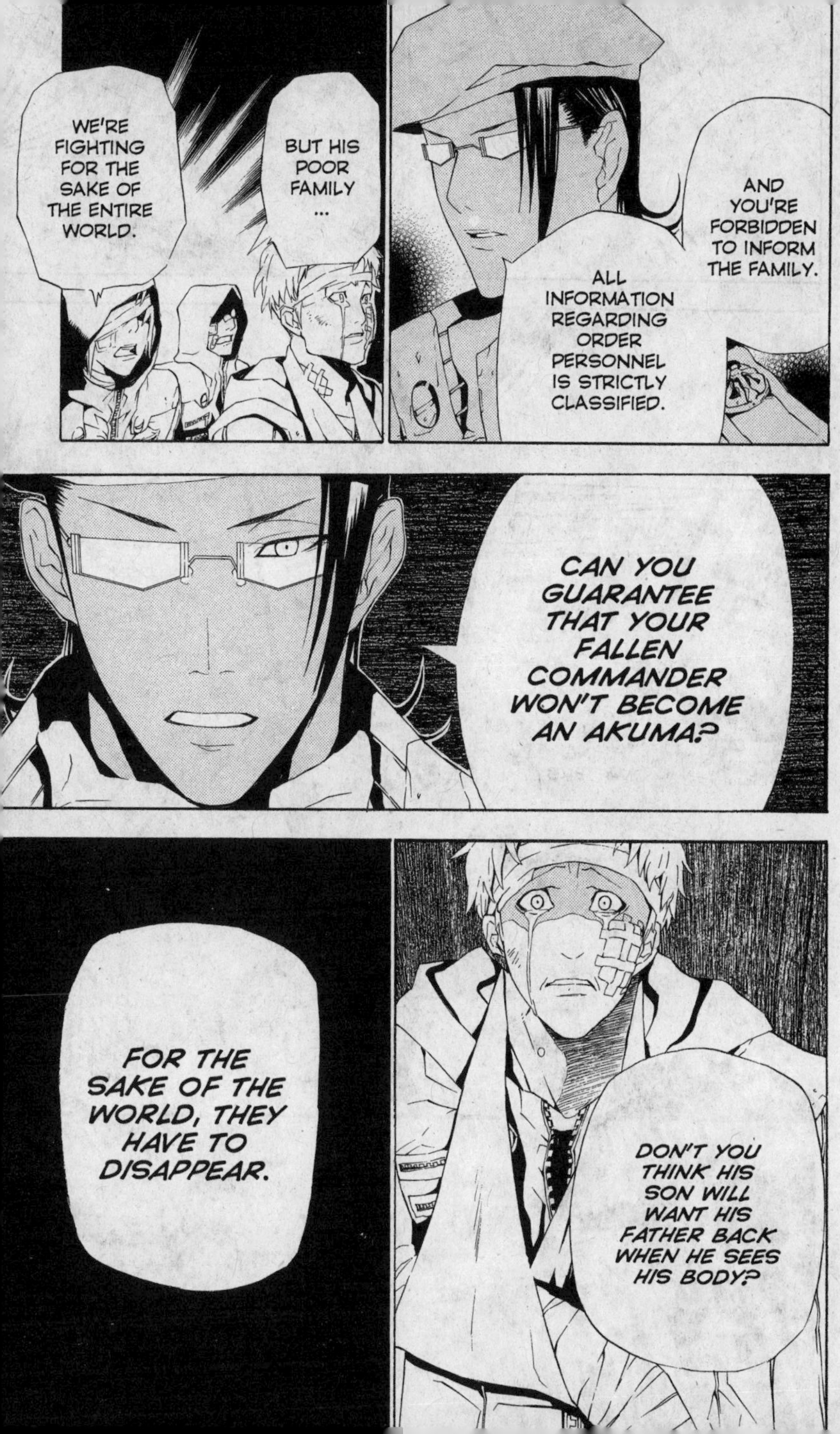
AND YOU'RE FORBIDDEN TO INFORM THE FAMILY.
ALL INFORMATION REGARDING ORDER PERSONNEL IS STRICTLY CLASSIFIED.
BUT HIS POOR FAMILY ...
WE'RE FIGHTING FOR THE SAKE OF THE ENTIRE WORLD.
CAN YOU GUARANTEE THAT YOUR FALLEN COMMANDER WON'T BECOME AN AKUMA?
DON'T YOU THINK HIS SON WILL WANT HIS FATHER BACK WHEN HE SEES HIS BODY?
FOR THE SAKE OF THE WORLD, THEY HAVE TO DISAPPEAR.

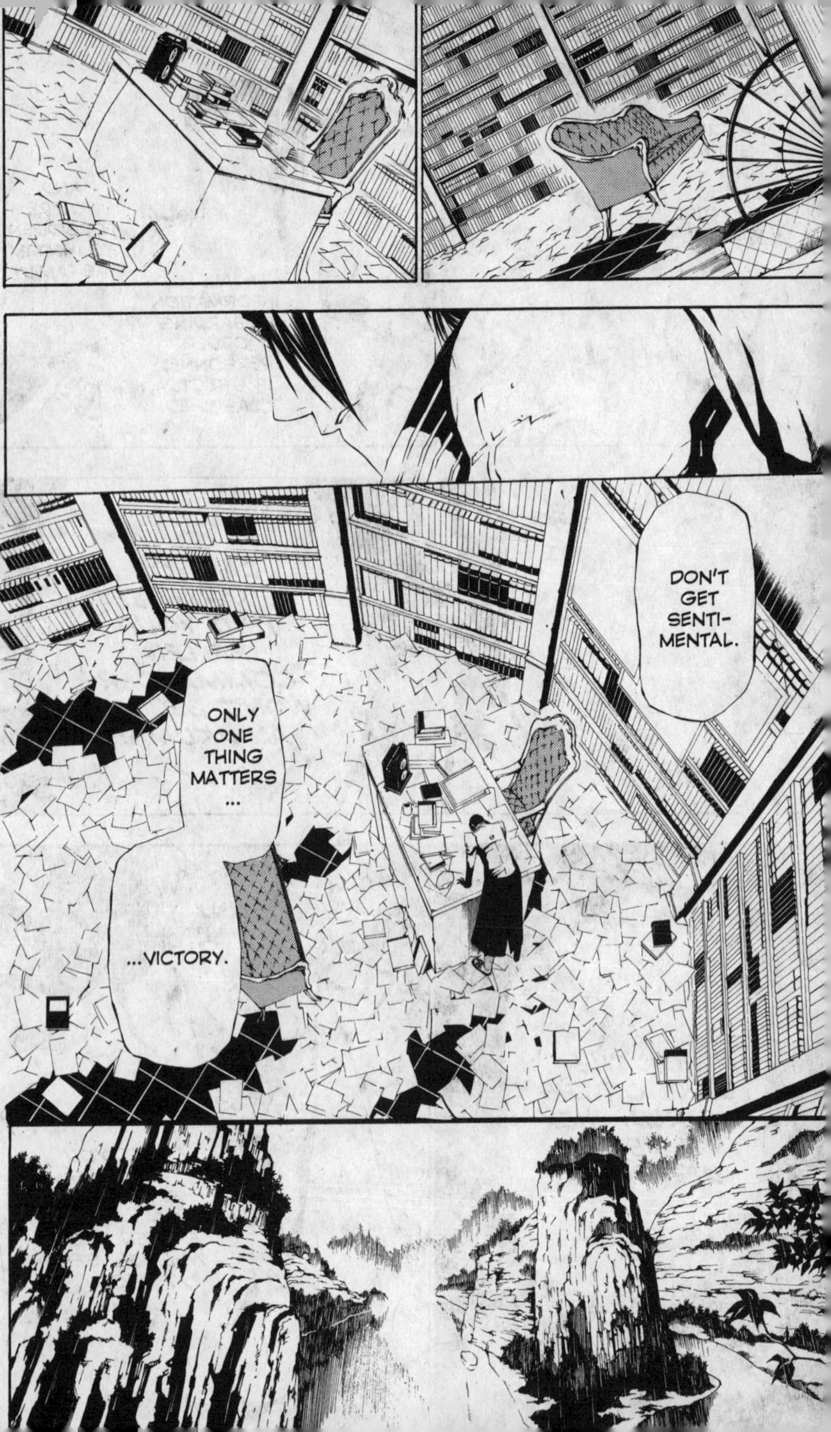
DON'T GET SENTI-MENTAL.
ONLY ONE THING MATTERS ...
...VICTORY.

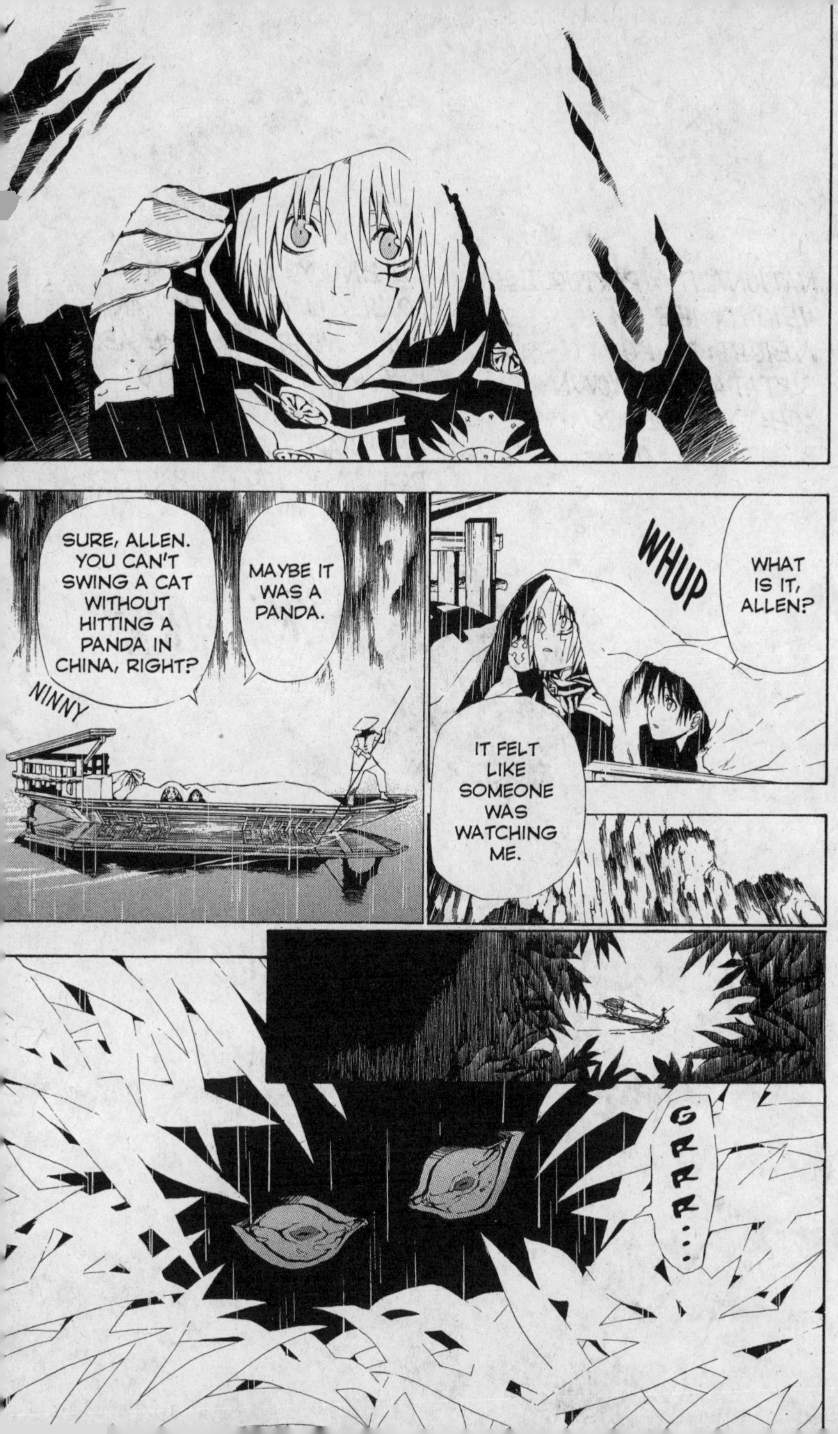
WHUP
WHAT IS IT, ALLEN?
IT FELT LIKE SOMEONE WAS WATCHING ME.
MAYBE IT WAS A PANDA.
SURE, ALLEN. YOU CAN'T SWING A CAT WITHOUT HITTING A PANDA IN CHINA, RIGHT?
NINNY
GRRR...

NATIONALITY: PORTUGUESE
HEIGHT: 188 CM
WEIGHT: 70 KG
BIRTHDAY: UNKNOWN
AGE: PROBABLY 26
BLOOD TYPE: O

HE ENJOYS LEADING A
DOUBLE LIFE AS A HUMAN
AND A NOAH. HE CAME ABOUT
BECAUSE I WANTED TO
DRAW A HANDSOME GUY LIKE
BECKHAM. I REALLY ENJOY
DRAWING THIS CHARACTER.

TYKI MIKK

NOAH

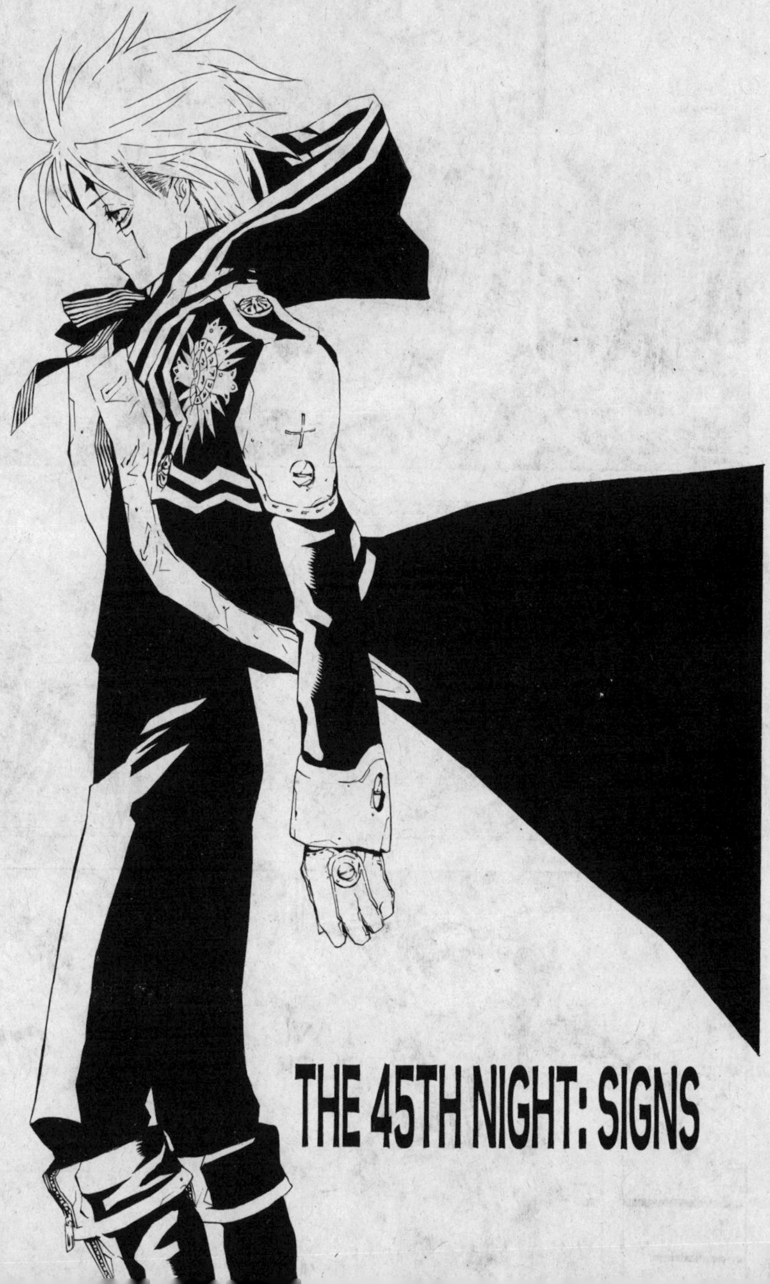

THE 45TH NIGHT: SIGNS

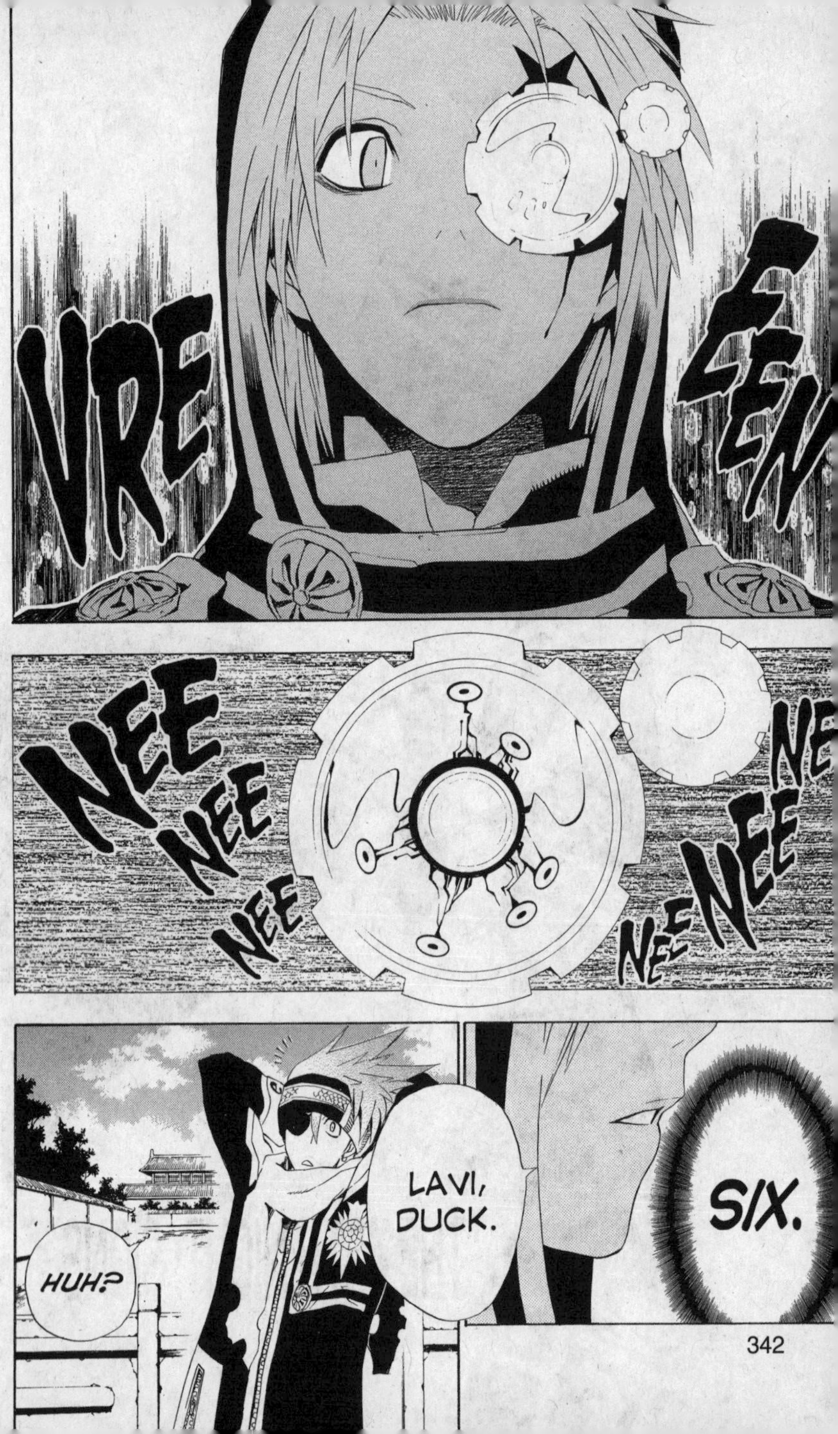
VRE
EEN
NEE
NEE
NEE
NEE
NEE
NE
SIX.
LAVI, DUCK.
HUH?

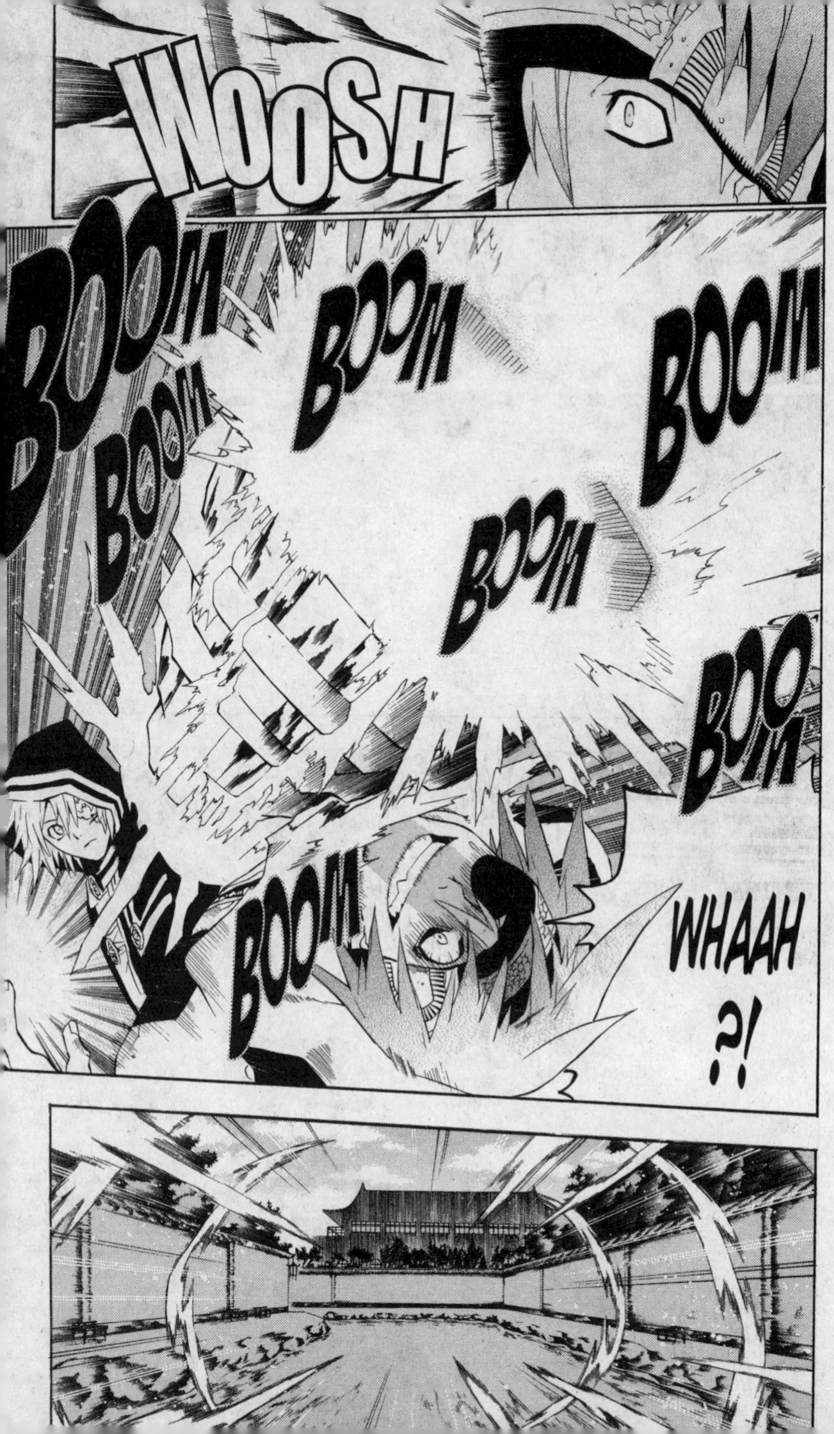
WOOSH
BOOM
BOOM
BOOM
BOOM
BOOM
BOOM
WHAAH ?!
BOOM

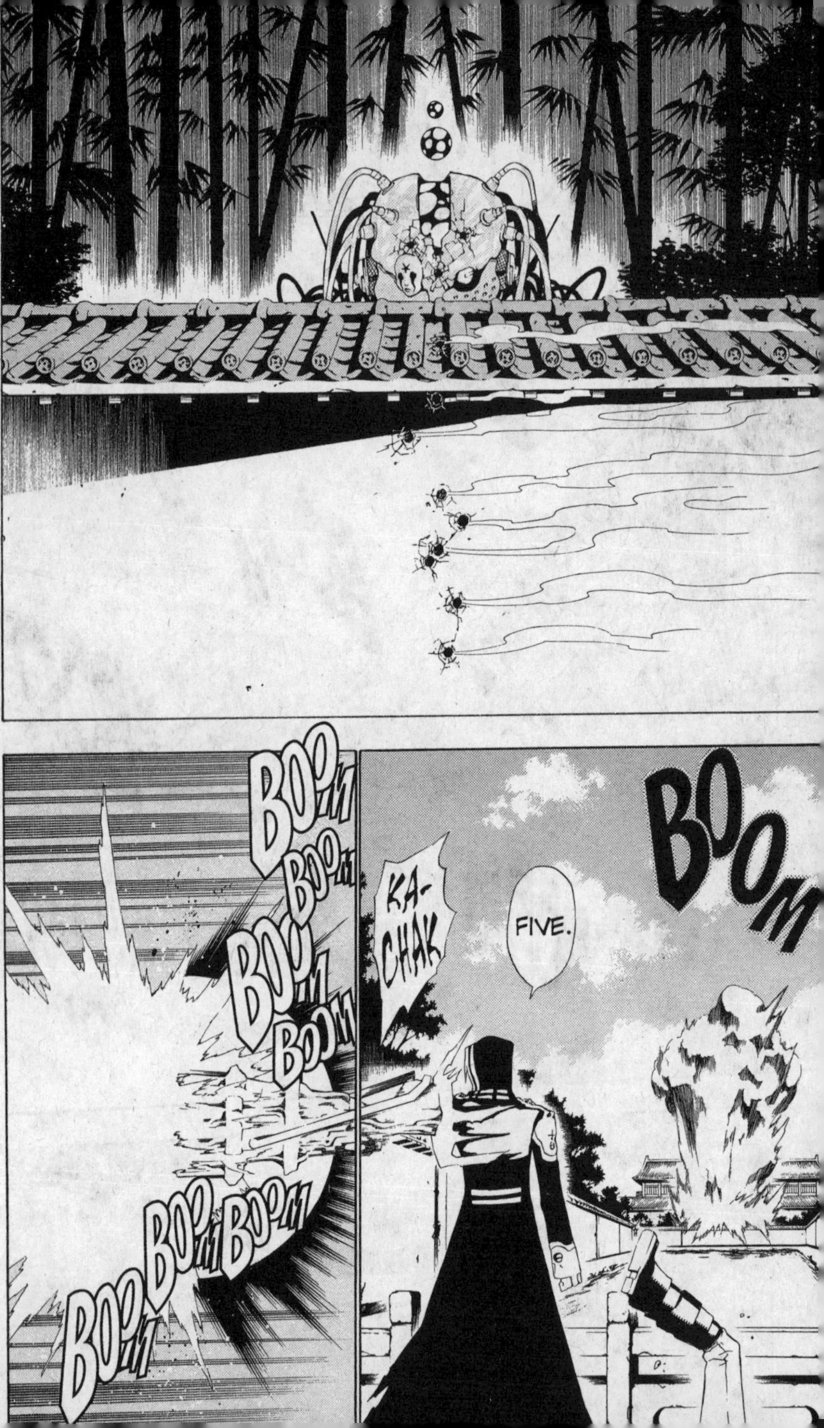
BOOM
FIVE.
KA-CHAK
BOOM
BOOM
BOOM
BOOM
BOOM
BOOM
BOOM

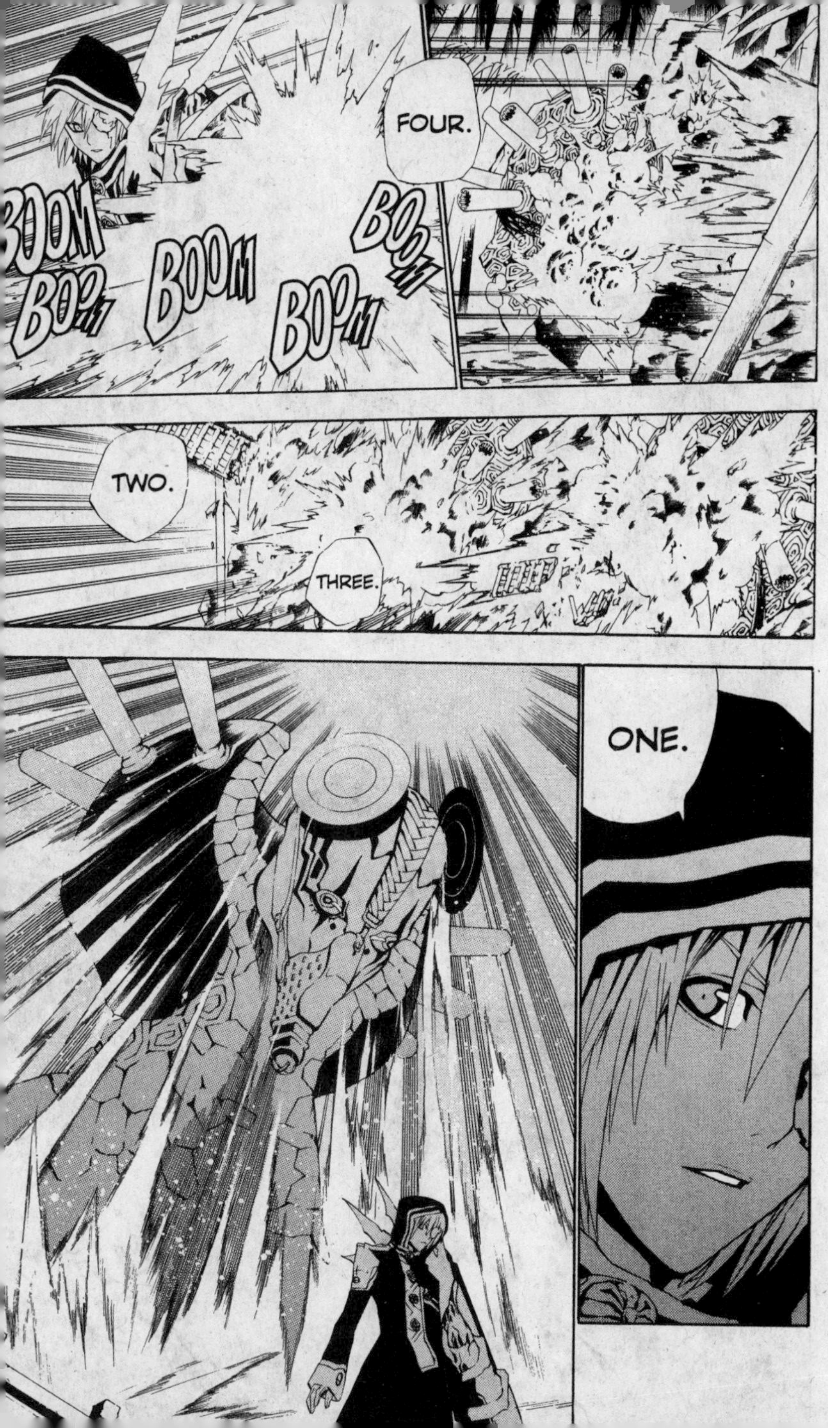
FOUR.
BOOM
BOOM
BOOM
BOOM
BOOM
THREE.
TWO.
ONE.

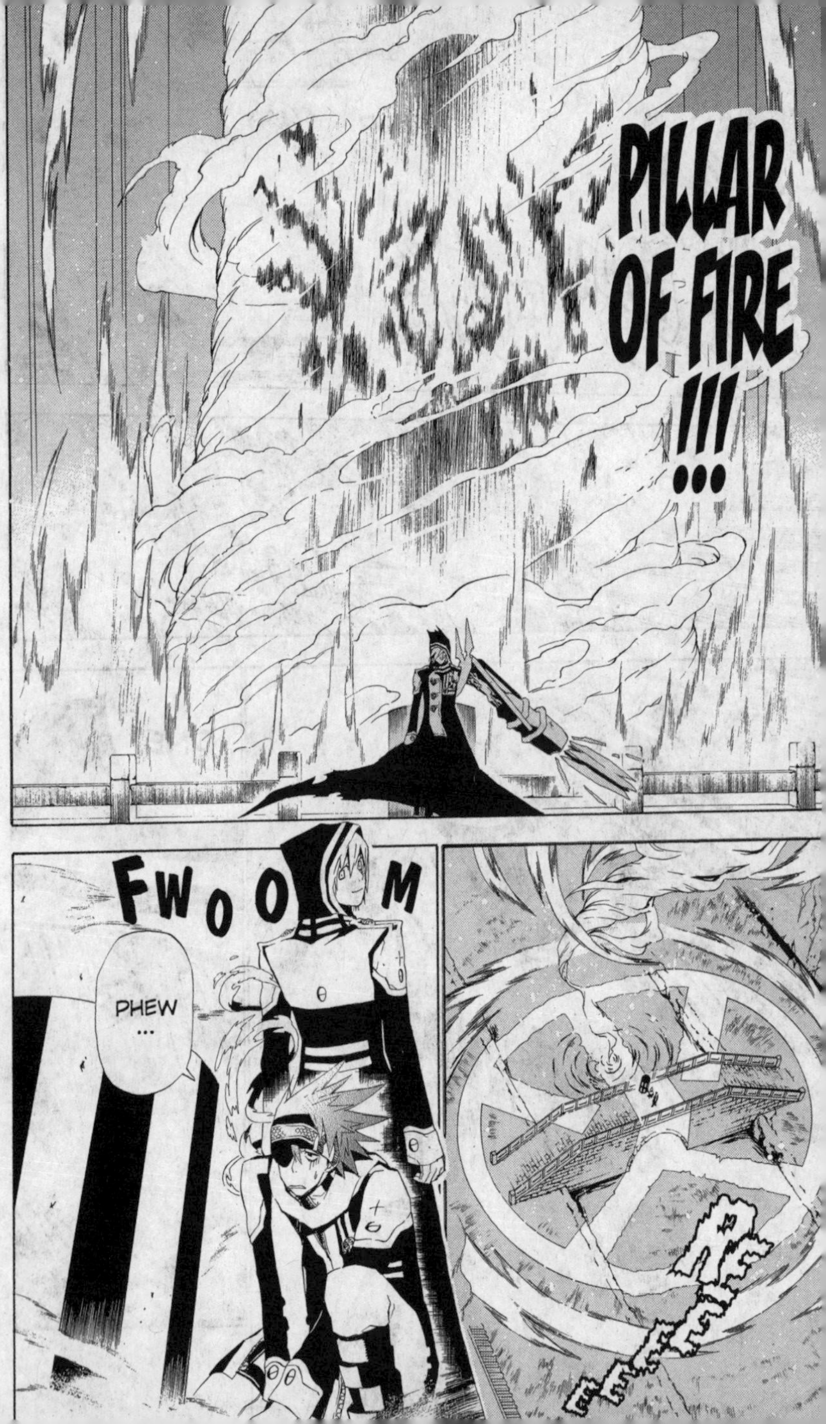
PILLAR OF FIRE !!! ...
FWOOM
PHEW ...

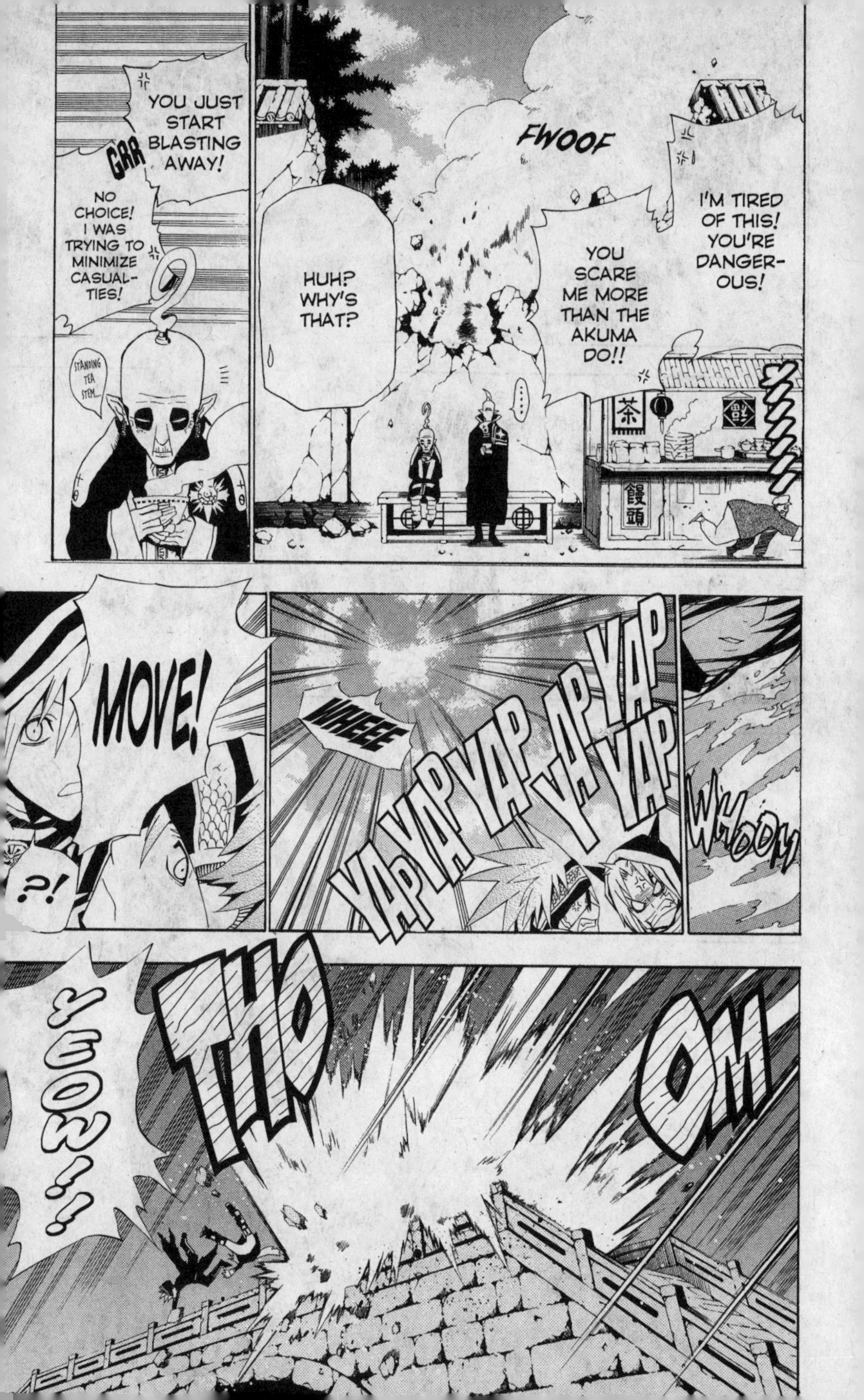
I'M TIRED OF THIS! YOU'RE DANGEROUS!
YOU SCARE ME MORE THAN THE AKUMA DO!!
FWOOF
HUH? WHY'S THAT?
...
YOU JUST START BLASTING AWAY!
GRR
NO CHOICE! I WAS TRYING TO MINIMIZE CASUALTIES!
STANDING TEA STEM...
WHOOM
WHEEE
YAP YAP YAP YAP YAP YAP YAP YAP
MOVE!
?!
THOOM
YEOW!!

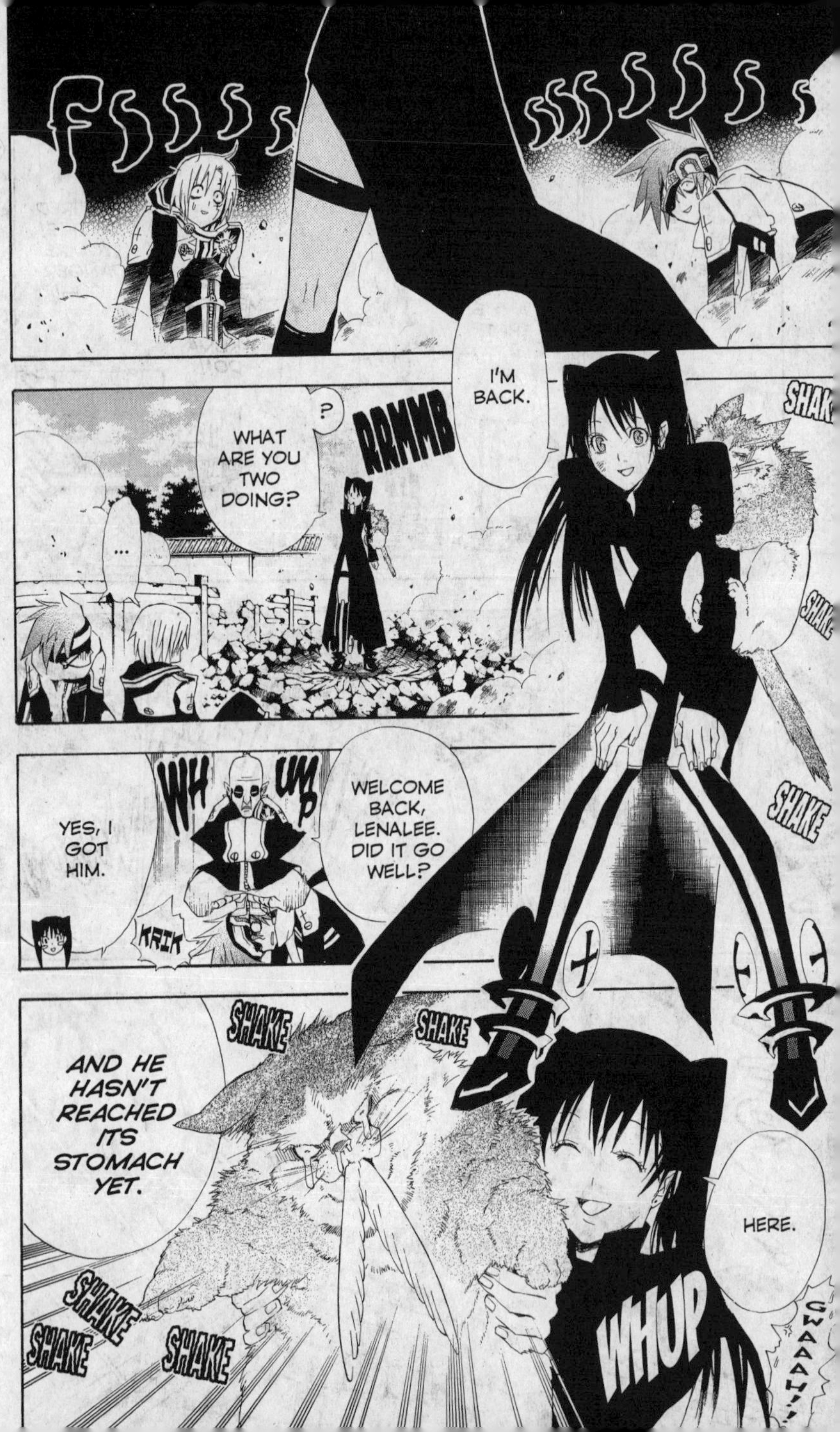
sssssss s
Fssss
I'M BACK.
SHAKE
SHAKE
SHAKE
?
RRMMB
WHAT ARE YOU TWO DOING?
...
WELCOME BACK, LENALEE. DID IT GO WELL?
WHUMP
YES, I GOT HIM.
KRIK
HERE.
GWAAAAH!!
WHUP
SHAKE
SHAKE
AND HE HASN'T REACHED ITS STOMACH YET.
SHAKE
SHAKE
SHAKE

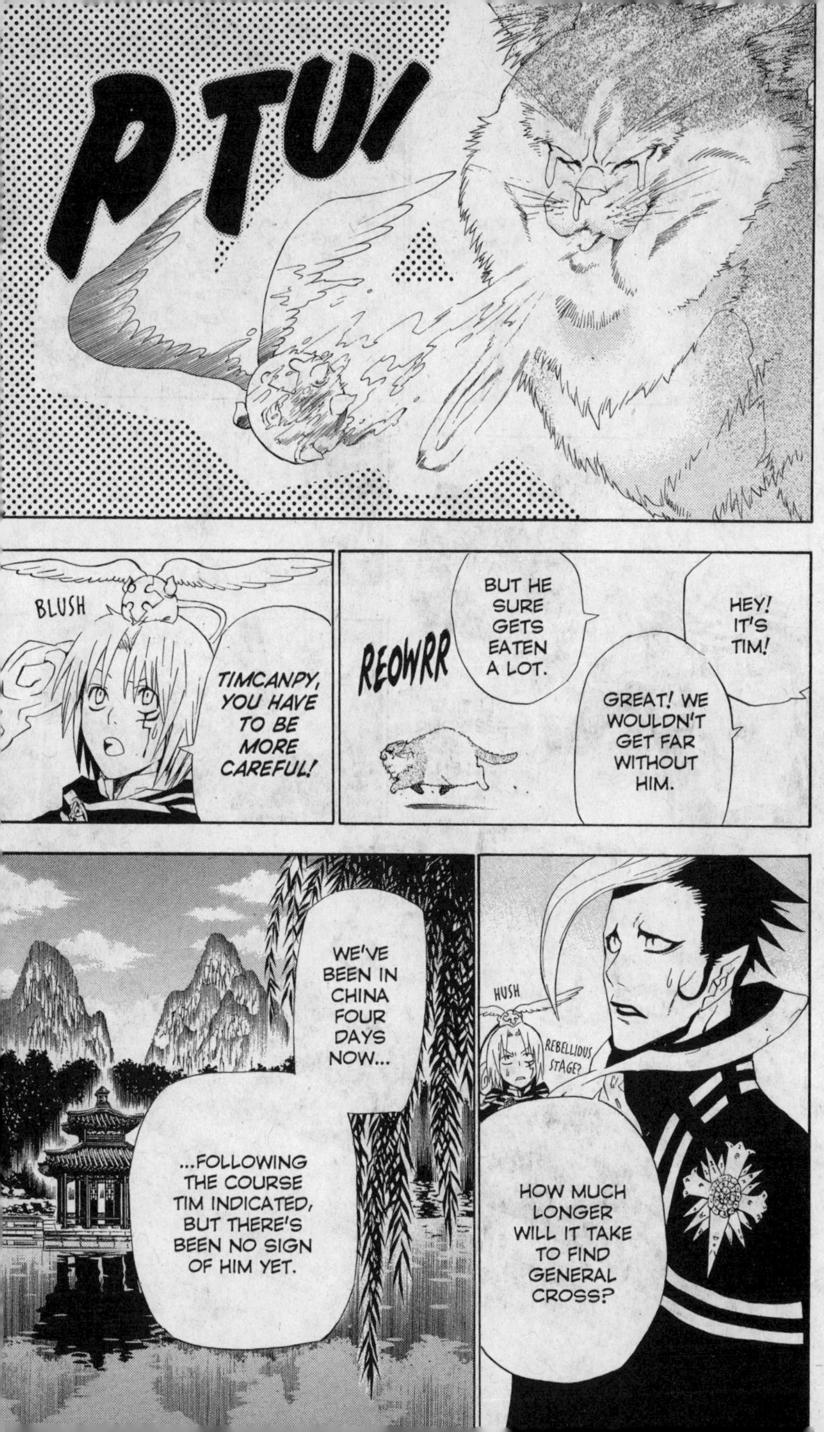
PTUI
HEY! IT'S TIM!
GREAT! WE WOULDN'T GET FAR WITHOUT HIM.
BUT HE SURE GETS EATEN A LOT.
REOWRR
BLUSH
TIMCANPY, YOU HAVE TO BE MORE CAREFUL!
HUSH
REBELLIOUS STAGE?
HOW MUCH LONGER WILL IT TAKE TO FIND GENERAL CROSS?
WE'VE BEEN IN CHINA FOUR DAYS NOW...
...FOLLOWING THE COURSE TIM INDICATED, BUT THERE'S BEEN NO SIGN OF HIM YET.

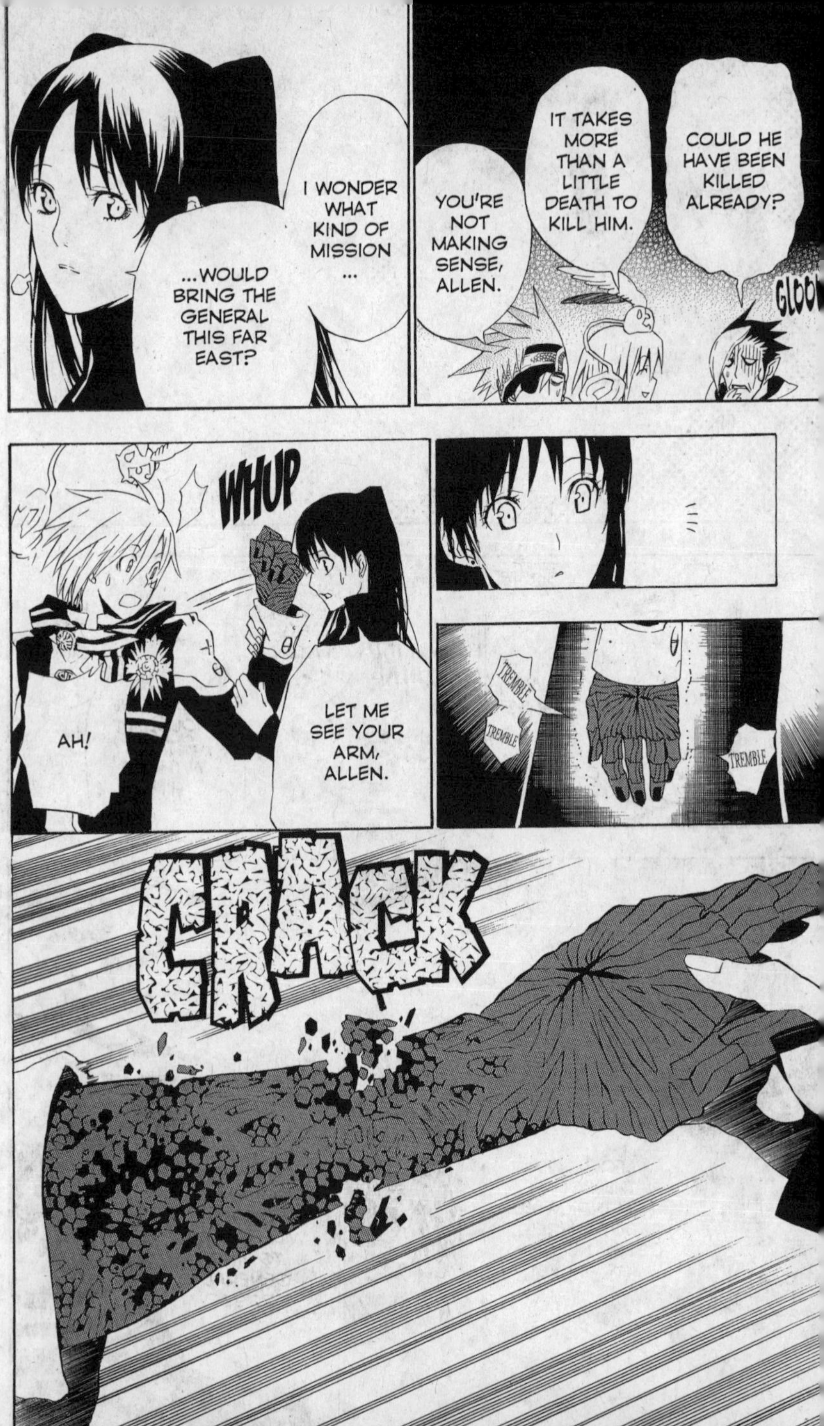
COULD HE HAVE BEEN KILLED ALREADY?
GLOO
IT TAKES MORE THAN A LITTLE DEATH TO KILL HIM.
YOU'RE NOT MAKING SENSE, ALLEN.
I WONDER WHAT KIND OF MISSION ...
...WOULD BRING THE GENERAL THIS FAR EAST?
TREMBLE
TREMBLE
TREMBLE
WHUP
LET ME SEE YOUR ARM, ALLEN.
AH!
CRACK

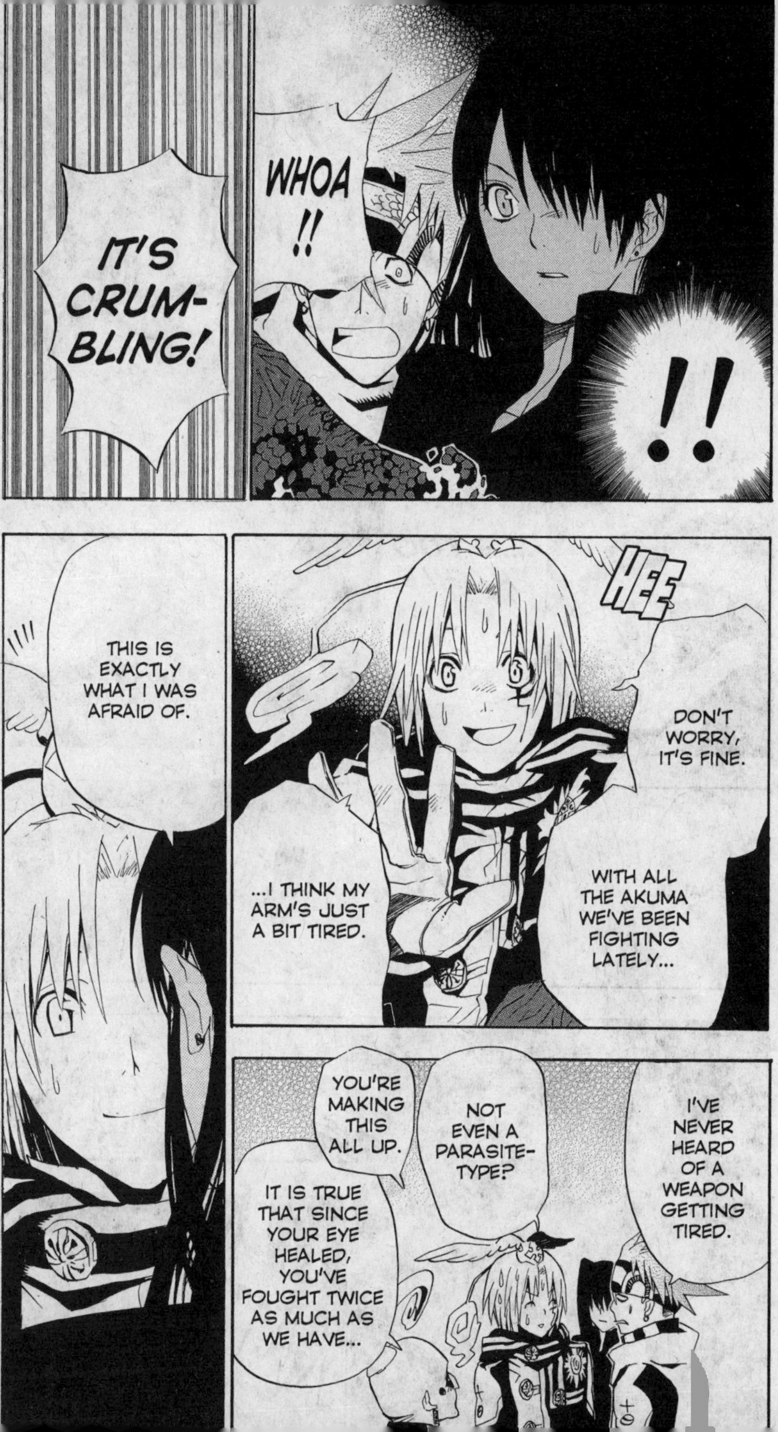
WHOA !!
!!
IT'S CRUMBLING!
HEE
DON'T WORRY, IT'S FINE.
WITH ALL THE AKUMA WE'VE BEEN FIGHTING LATELY...
...I THINK MY ARM'S JUST A BIT TIRED.
I'VE NEVER HEARD OF A WEAPON GETTING TIRED.
NOT EVEN A PARASITE-TYPE?
YOU'RE MAKING THIS ALL UP.
IT IS TRUE THAT SINCE YOUR EYE HEALED, YOU'VE FOUGHT TWICE AS MUCH AS WE HAVE...
THIS IS EXACTLY WHAT I WAS AFRAID OF.

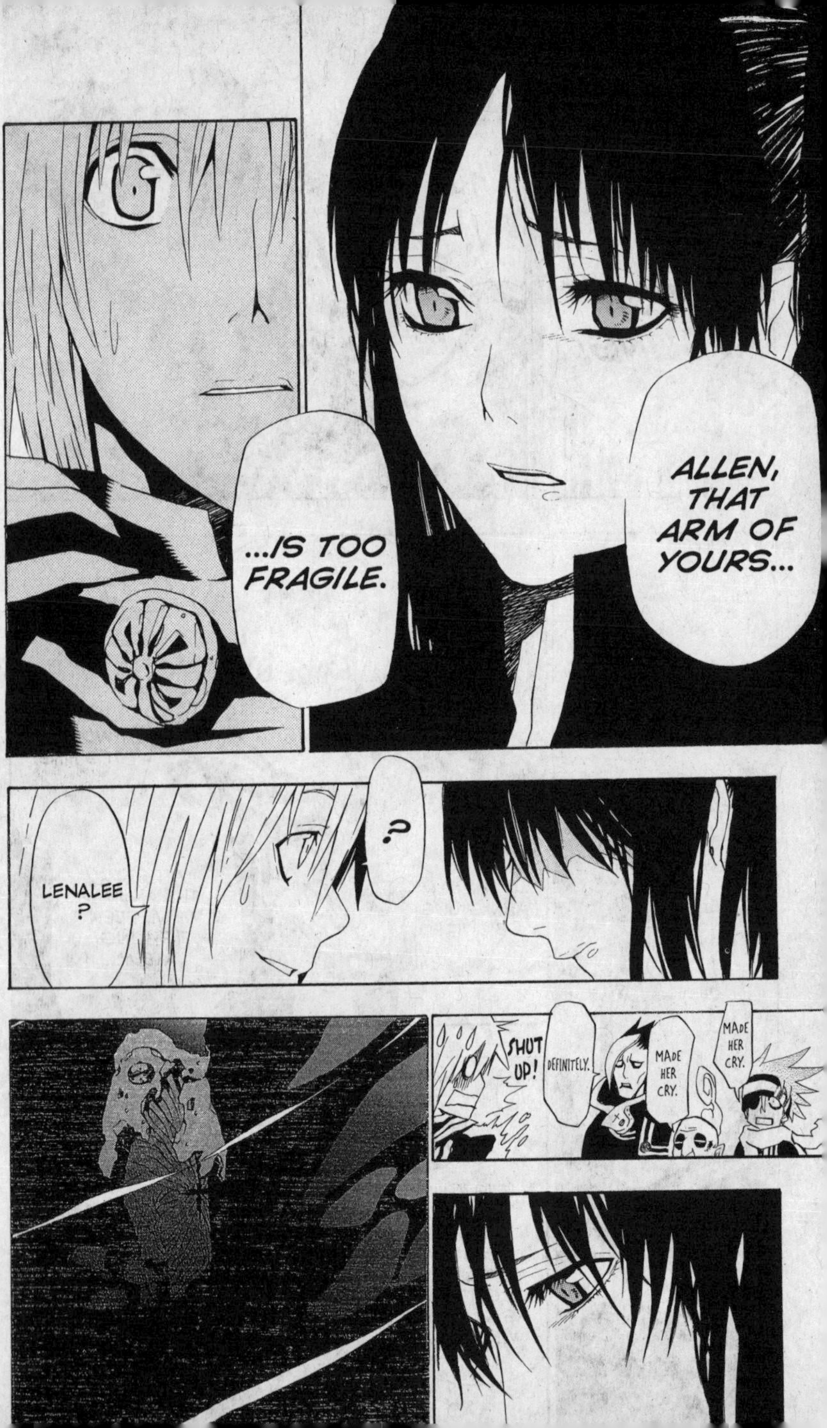
ALLEN, THAT ARM OF YOURS...
...IS TOO FRAGILE.
?
LENALEE ?
MADE HER CRY.
MADE HER CRY.
DEFINITELY.
SHUT UP!

B-BMP

WAAAH!!

PL OOSH

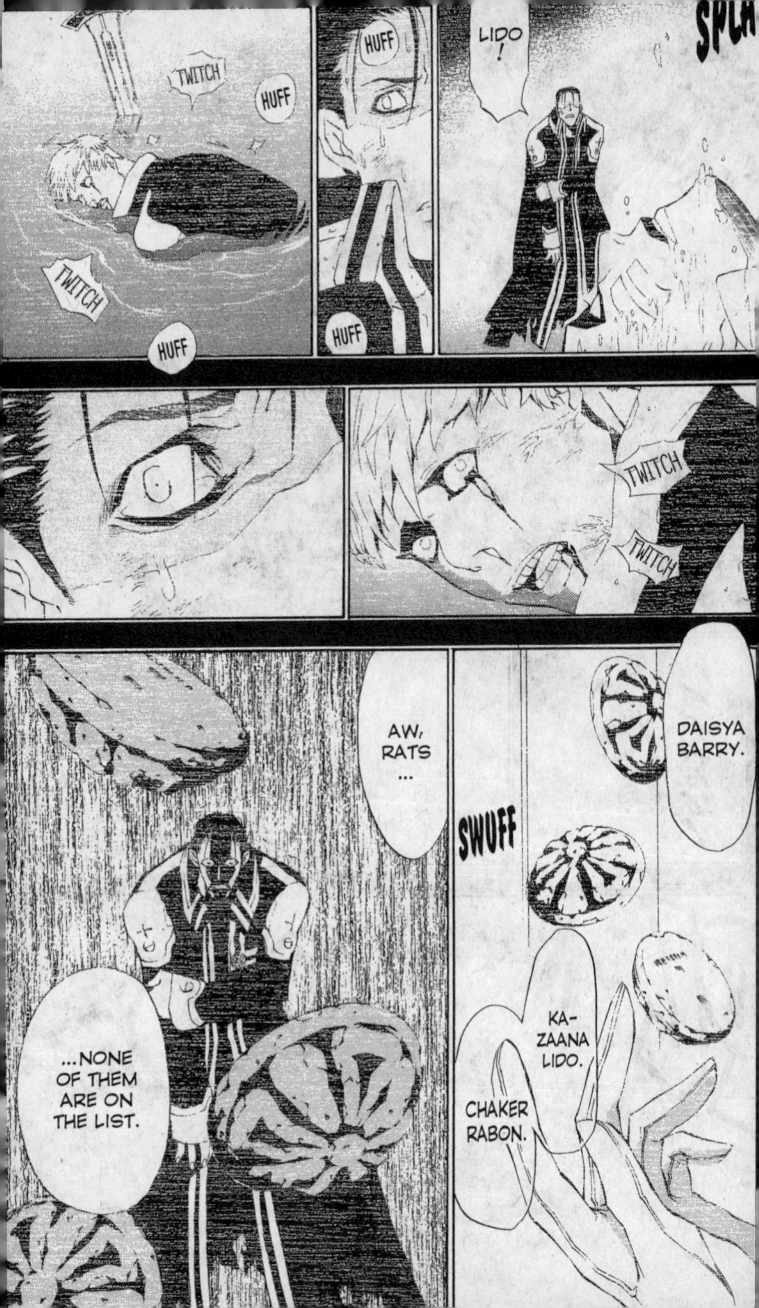
SPLA
LIDO!
HUFF
HUFF
TWITCH
HUFF
TWITCH
HUFF
TWITCH
TWITCH
DAISYA BARRY.
SWUFF
KA-ZAANA LIDO.
CHAKER RABON.
AW, RATS...
...NONE OF THEM ARE ON THE LIST.

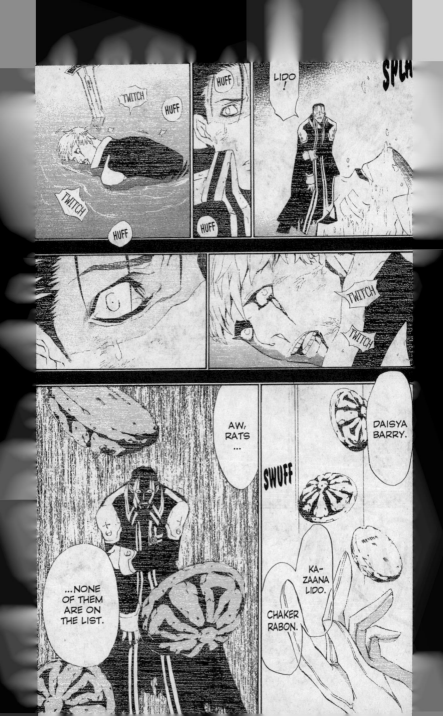

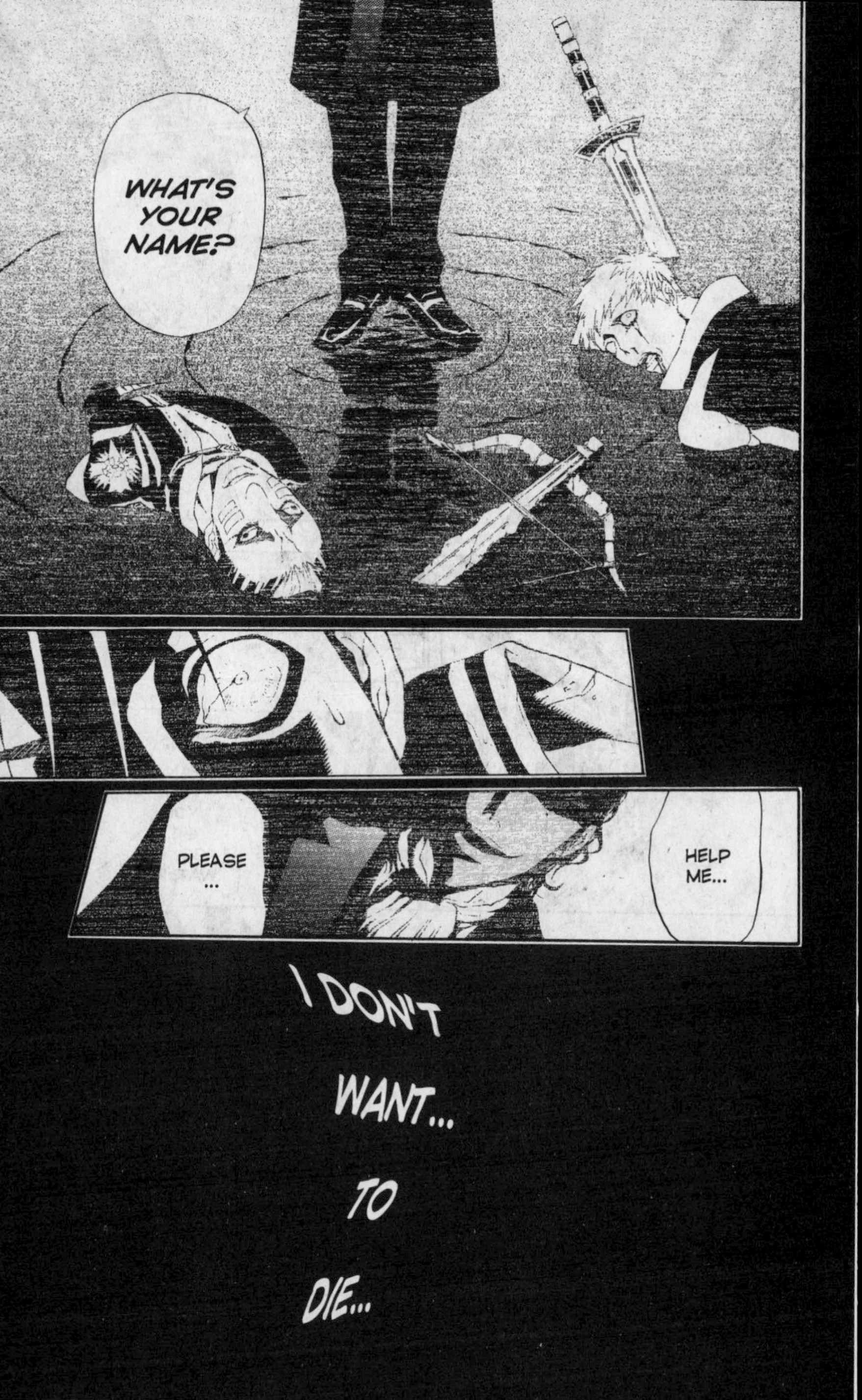
WHAT'S YOUR NAME?
HELP ME...
PLEASE ...
I DON'T
WANT...
TO
DIE...

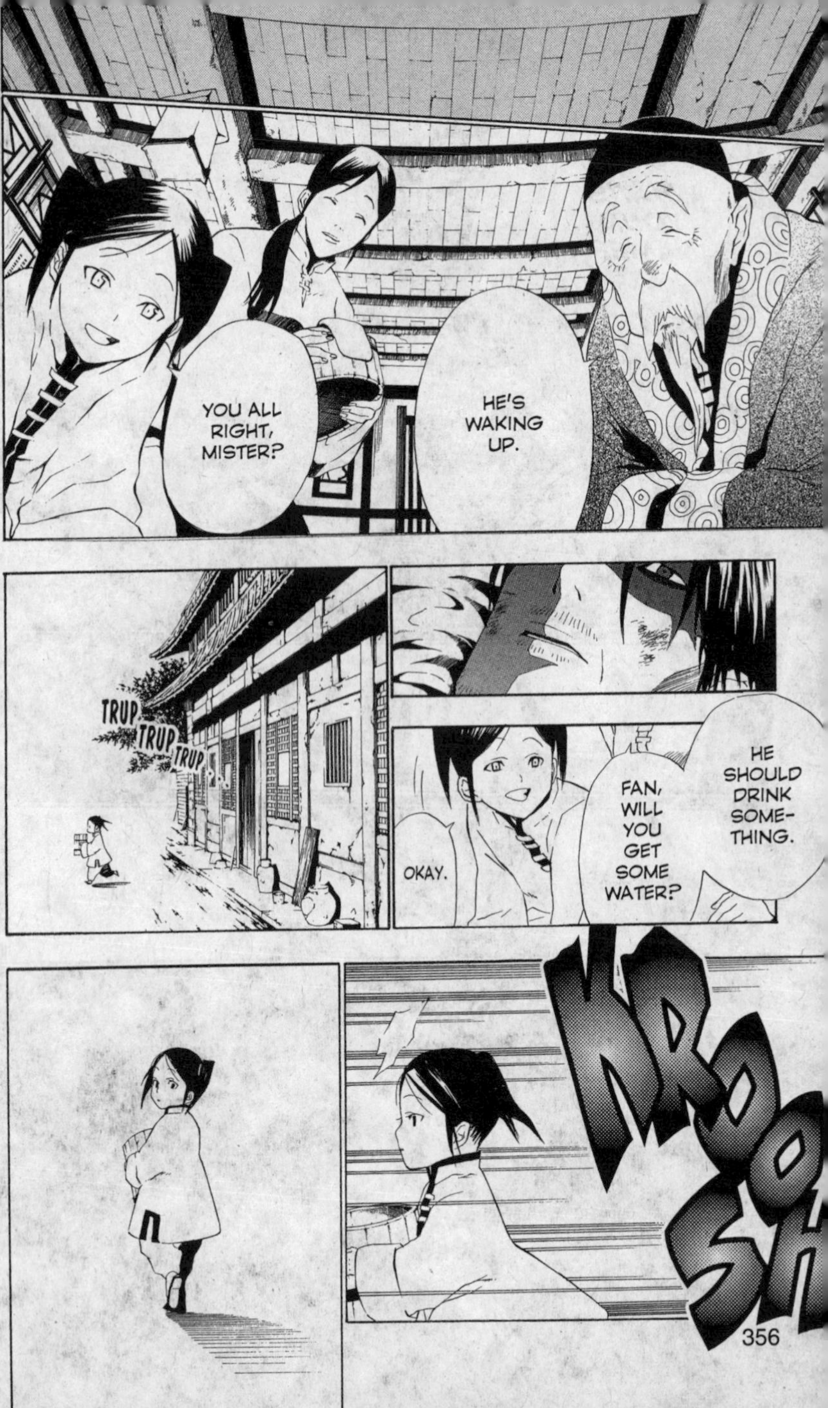
HE'S WAKING UP.
YOU ALL RIGHT, MISTER?
HE SHOULD DRINK SOMETHING.
FAN, WILL YOU GET SOME WATER?
OKAY.
TRUP TRUP TRUP
VROOSH

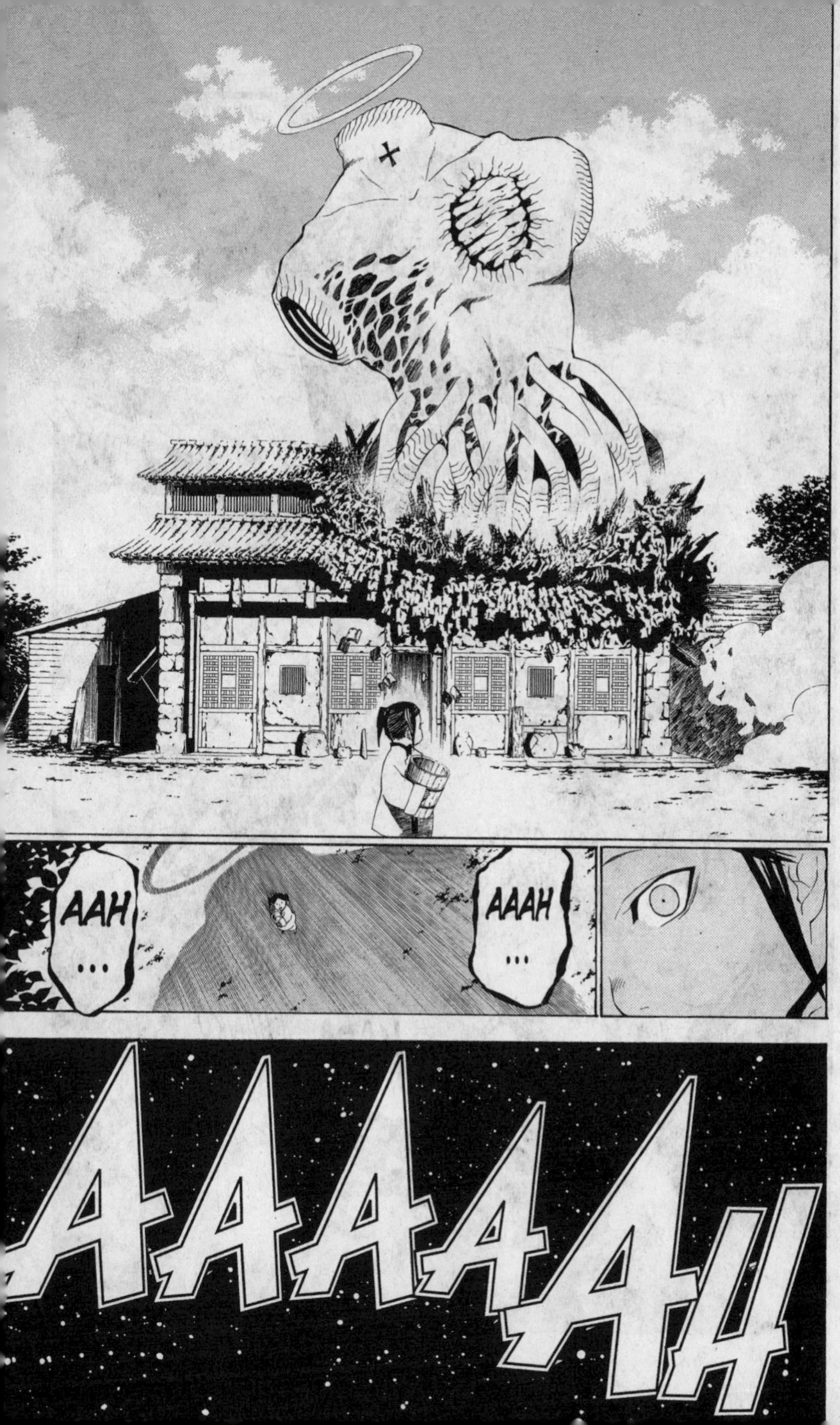
AAAH ...
AAH ...
AAAAAH

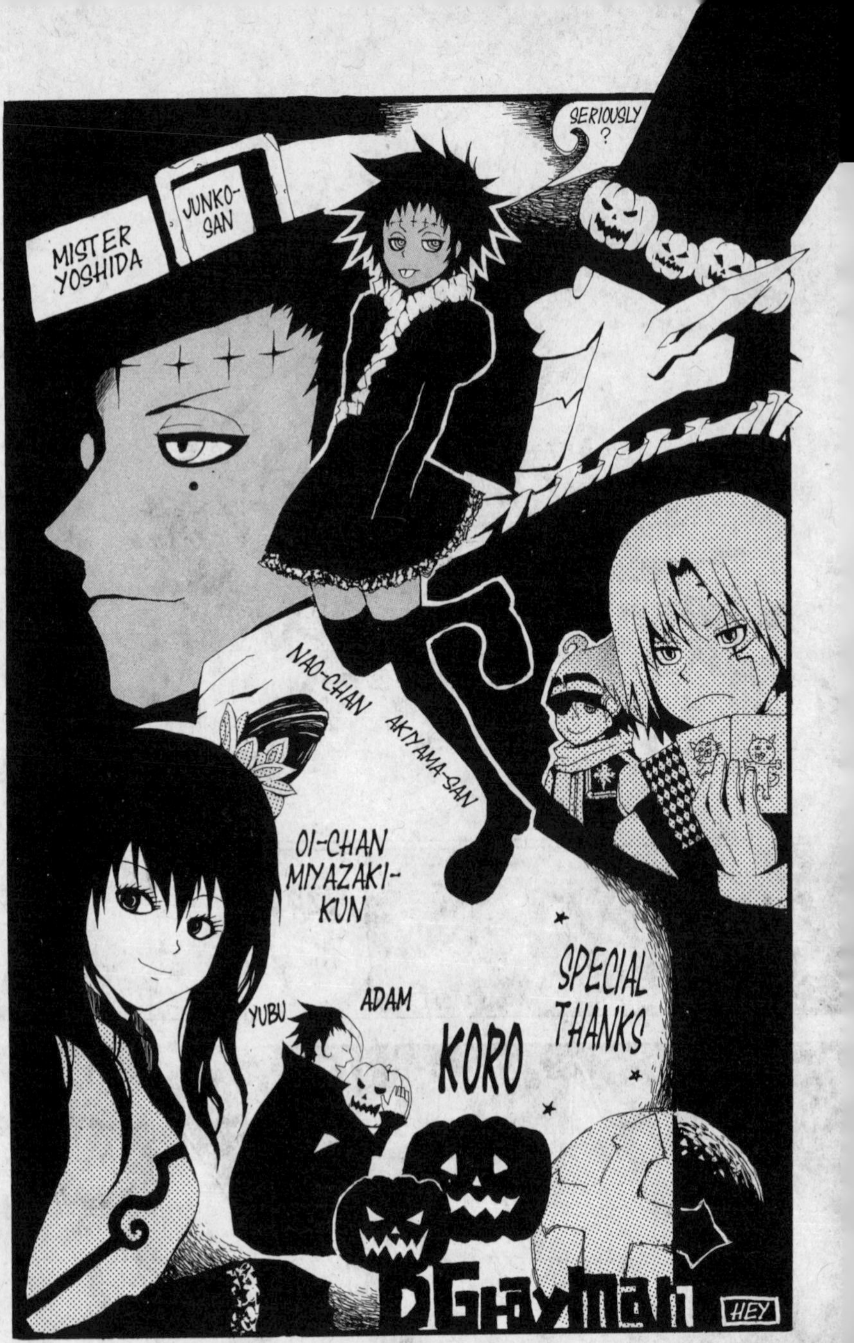
SERIOUSLY?
JUNKO-SAN
MISTER YOSHIDA
NAO-CHAN
AKIYAMA-SAN
OI-CHAN
MIYAZAKI-KUN
SPECIAL THANKS
ADAM
YUBU
KORO
D.Grayman
HEY

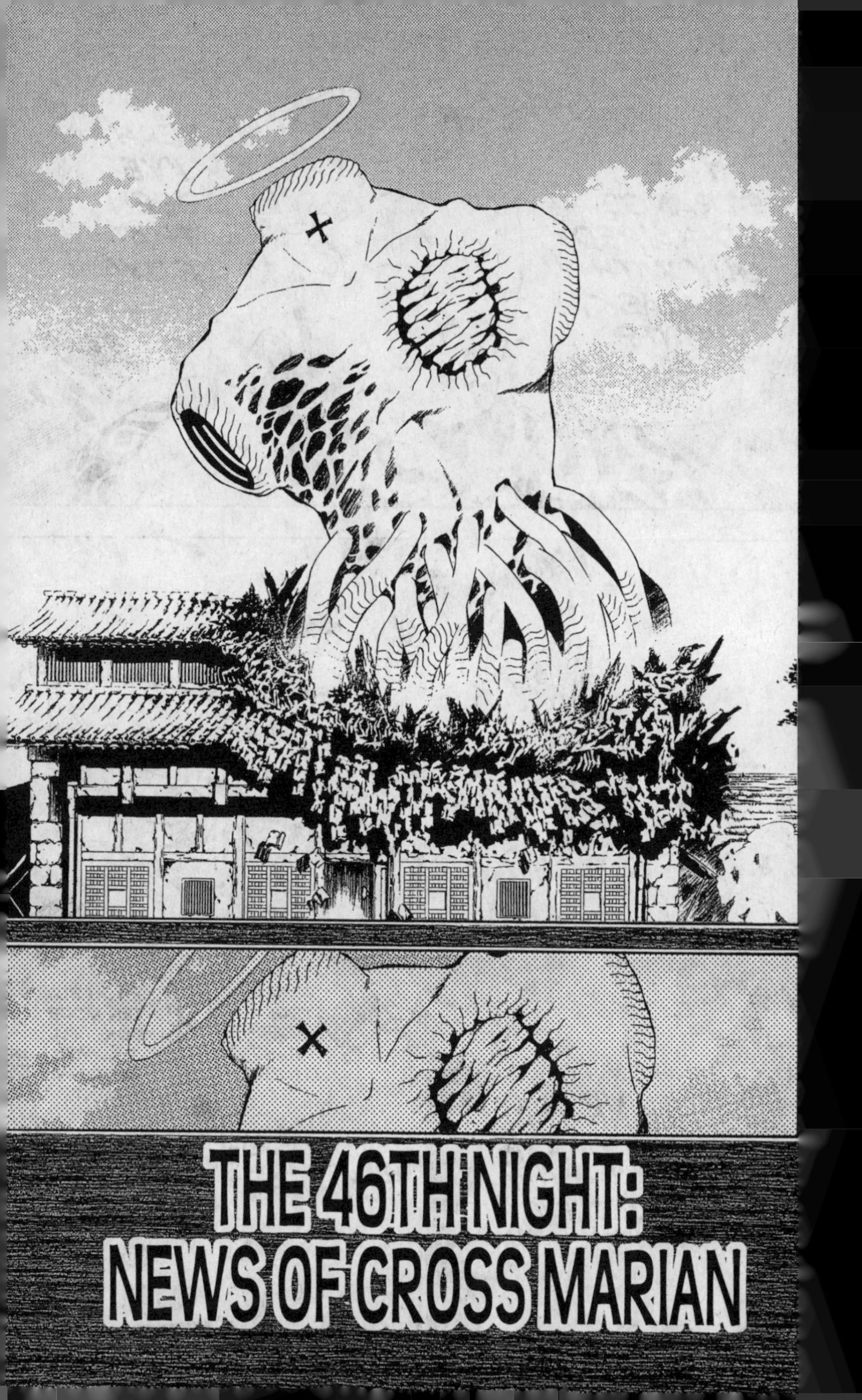

THE 46TH NIGHT: NEWS OF CROSS MARIAN

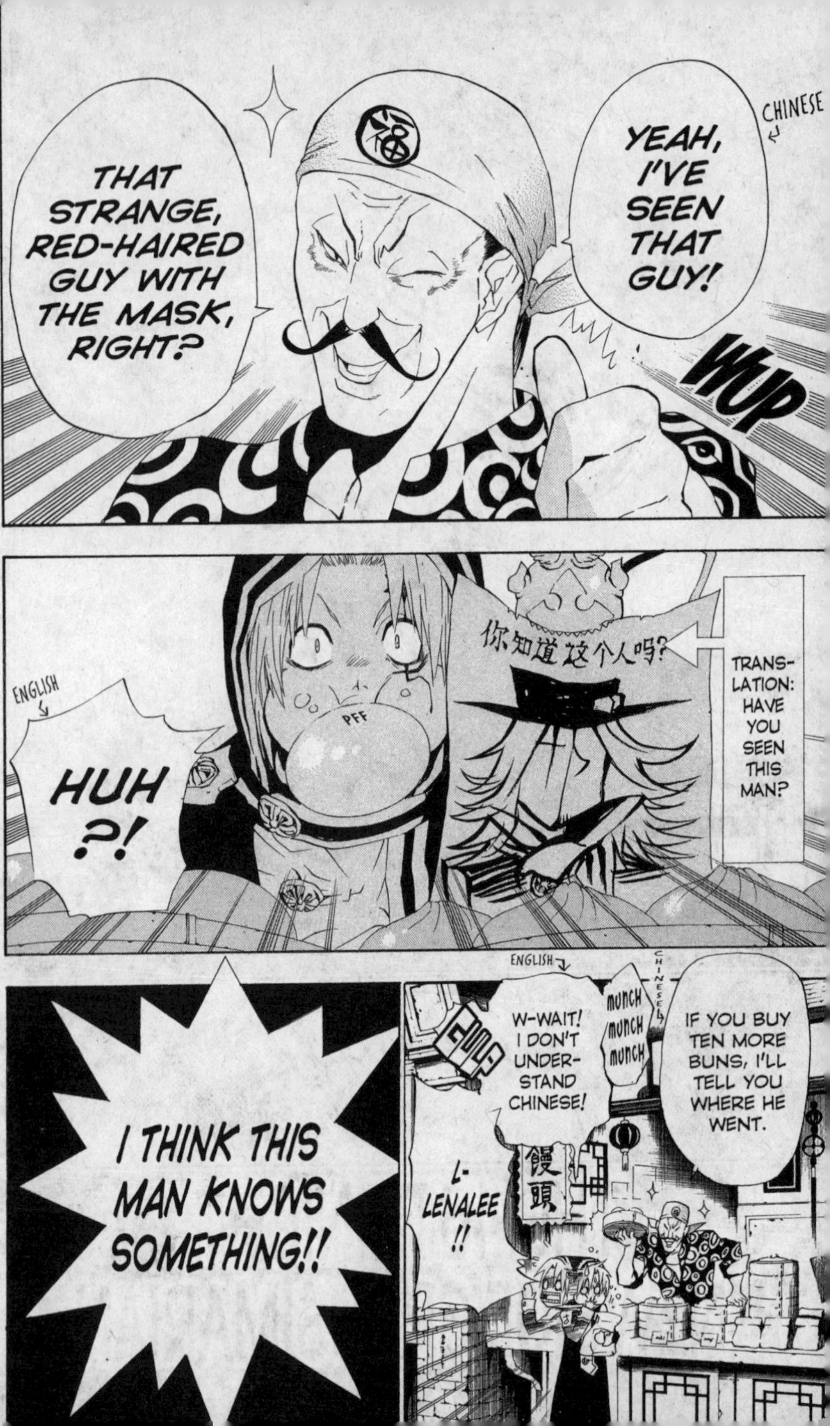
CHINESE
YEAH, I'VE SEEN THAT GUY!
THAT STRANGE, RED-HAIRED GUY WITH THE MASK, RIGHT?
WUP
TRANSLATION: HAVE YOU SEEN THIS MAN?
你知道这个人吗?
PFF
ENGLISH
HUH ?!
CHINESE
IF YOU BUY TEN MORE BUNS, I'LL TELL YOU WHERE HE WENT.
MUNCH MUNCH MUNCH
ENGLISH
W-WAIT! I DON'T UNDER-STAND CHINESE!
GULP
饅頭
L-LENALEE !!
I THINK THIS MAN KNOWS SOMETHING!!

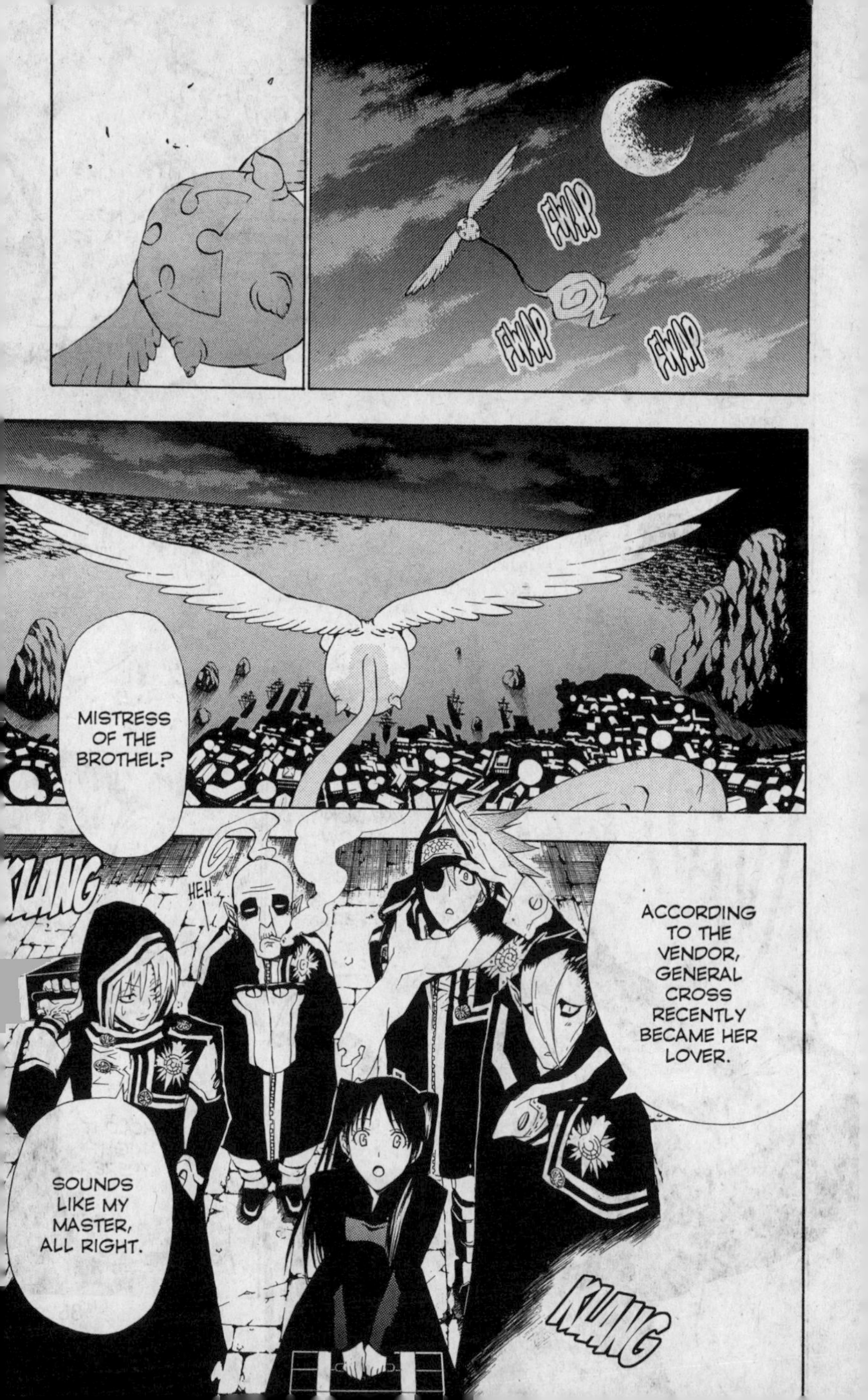
FWAP
FWAP
FWAP
MISTRESS OF THE BROTHEL?
ACCORDING TO THE VENDOR, GENERAL CROSS RECENTLY BECAME HER LOVER.
HEH
KLANG
SOUNDS LIKE MY MASTER, ALL RIGHT.
KLANG

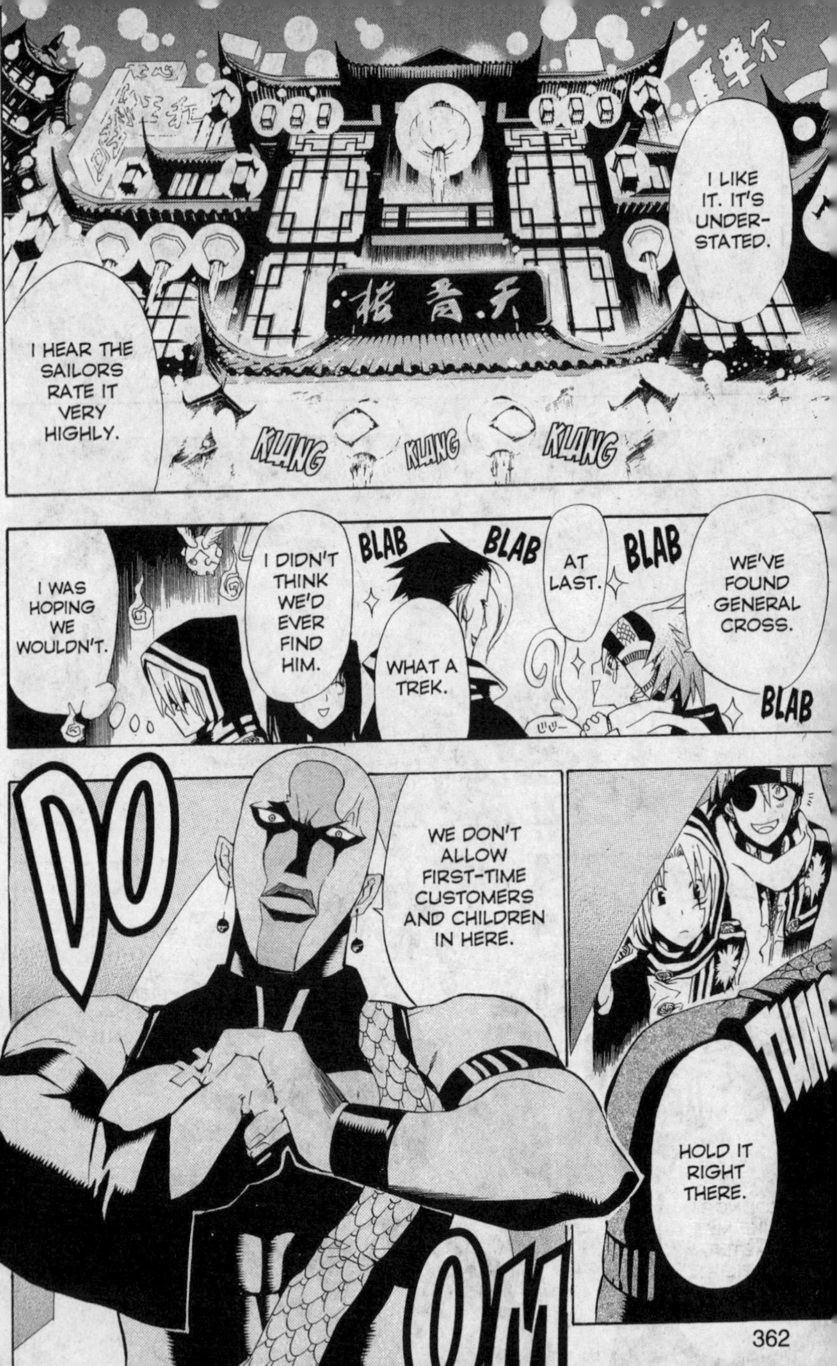
I LIKE IT. IT'S UNDER-STATED.
I HEAR THE SAILORS RATE IT VERY HIGHLY.
KLANG
KLANG
KLANG
BLAB
WE'VE FOUND GENERAL CROSS.
BLAB
AT LAST.
BLAB
BLAB
WHAT A TREK.
I DIDN'T THINK WE'D EVER FIND HIM.
I WAS HOPING WE WOULDN'T.
TUM
HOLD IT RIGHT THERE.
WE DON'T ALLOW FIRST-TIME CUSTOMERS AND CHILDREN IN HERE.
DO
OM

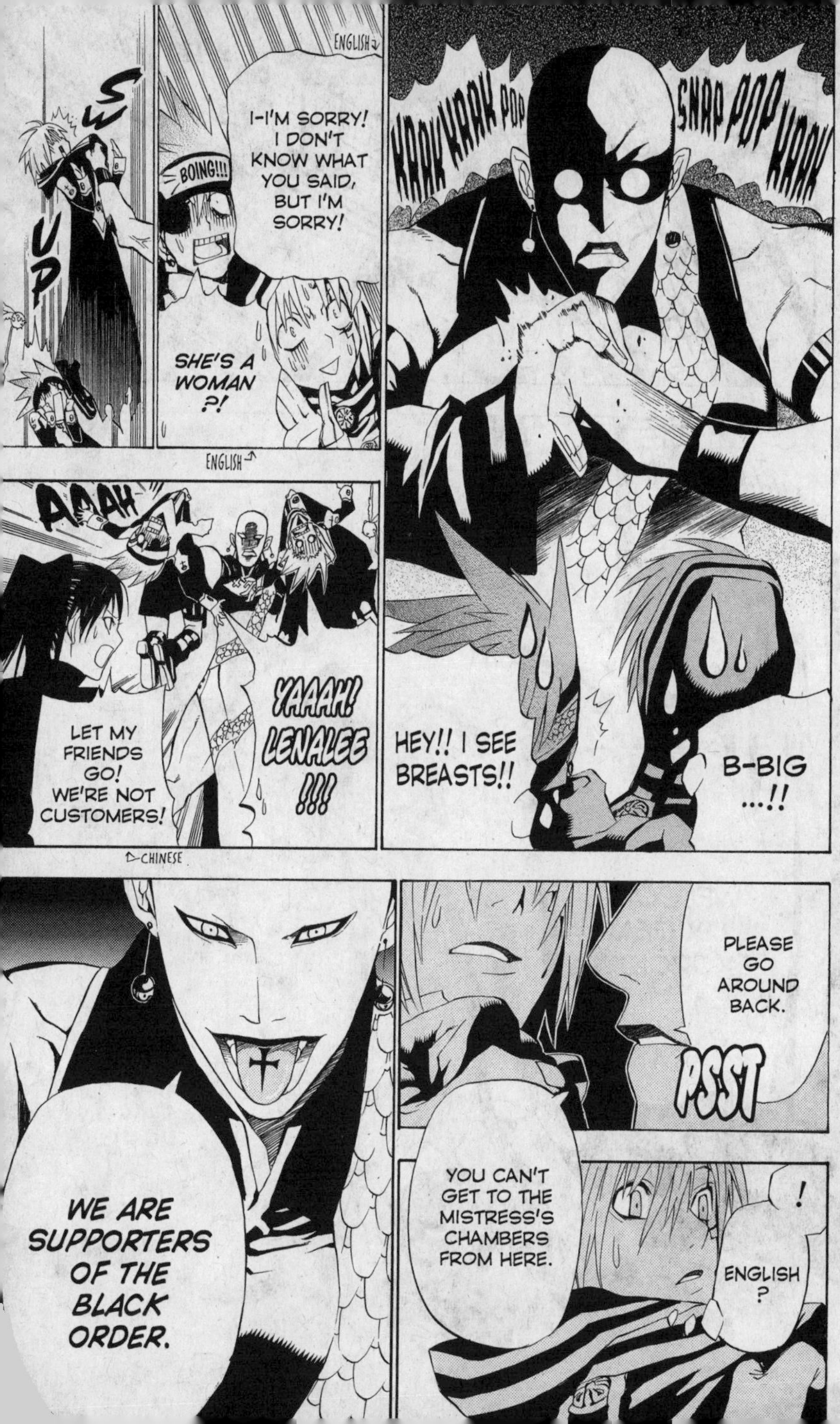

SNAP POP KRAK
KRAK KRAK POP
B-BIG ...!!
HEY!! I SEE BREASTS!!
ENGLISH
I-I'M SORRY! I DON'T KNOW WHAT YOU SAID, BUT I'M SORRY!
BOING!!!
SHE'S A WOMAN ?!
ENGLISH
SWUP
YAAAH! LENALEE !!!
AAAH
LET MY FRIENDS GO! WE'RE NOT CUSTOMERS!
CHINESE
PLEASE GO AROUND BACK.
PSST
!
ENGLISH ?
YOU CAN'T GET TO THE MISTRESS'S CHAMBERS FROM HERE.
WE ARE SUPPORTERS OF THE BLACK ORDER.

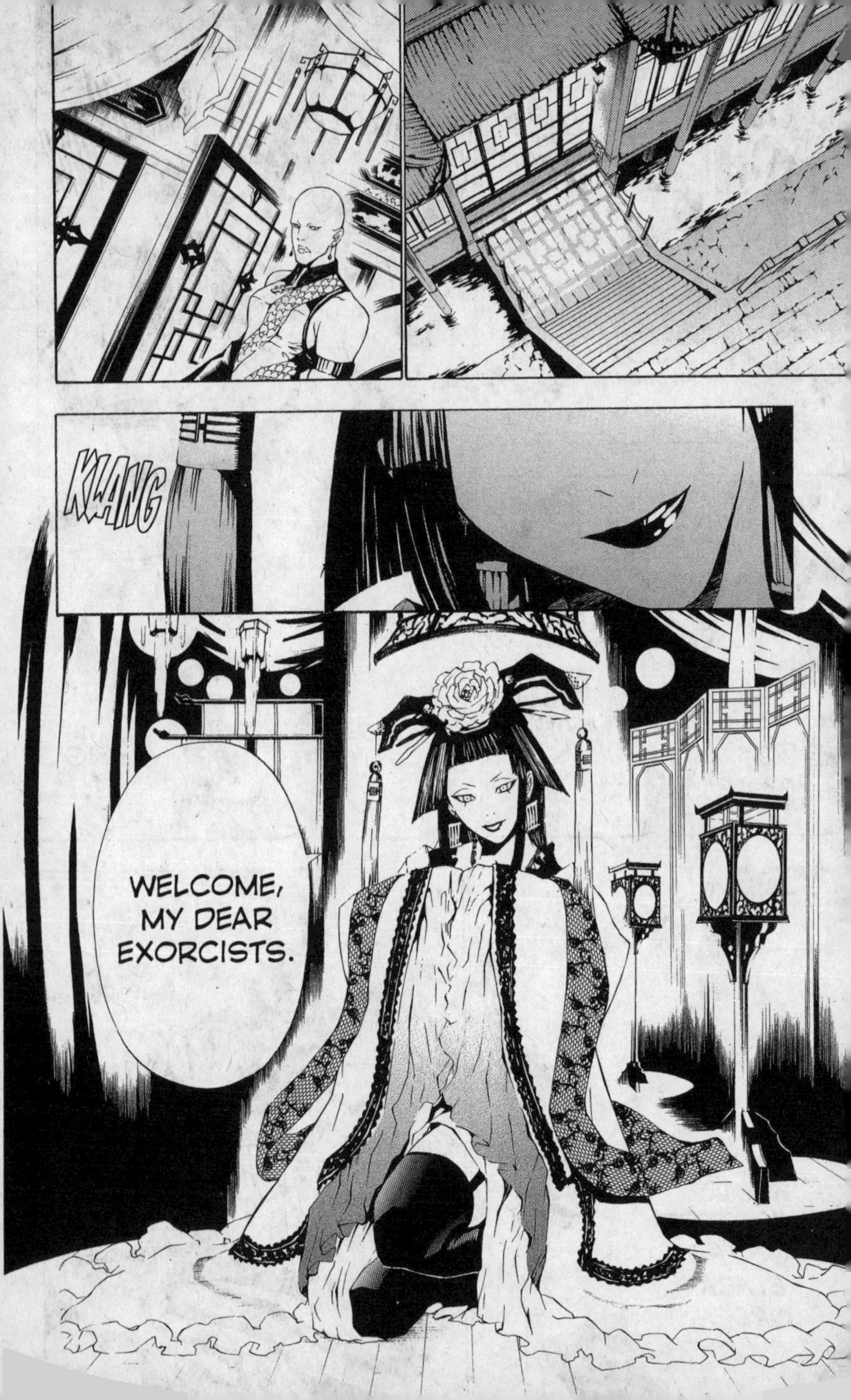
KWANG
WELCOME, MY DEAR EXORCISTS.

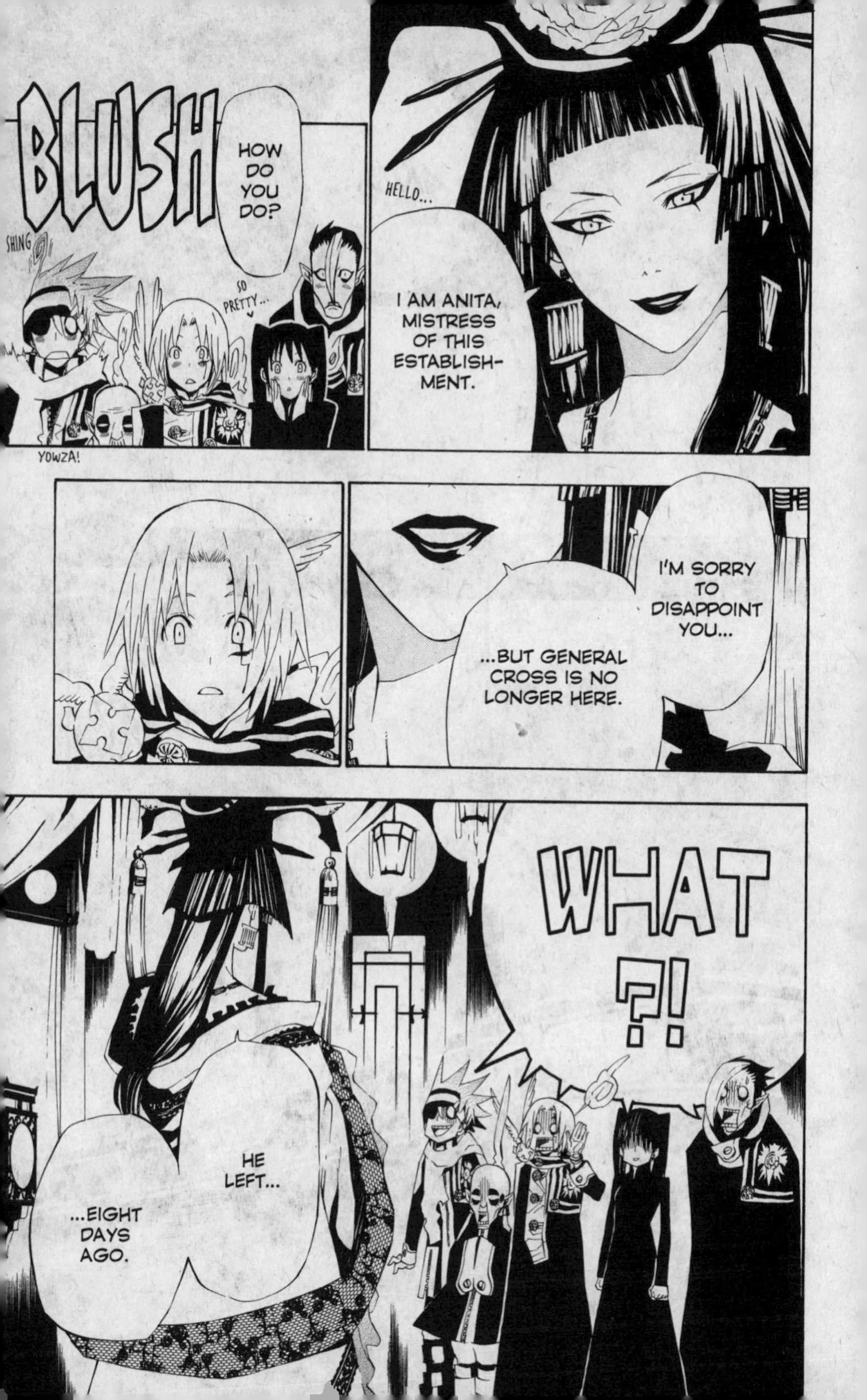
HELLO...
I AM ANITA, MISTRESS OF THIS ESTABLISHMENT.
HOW DO YOU DO?
BLUSH
SO PRETTY...
SHING
YOWZA!
I'M SORRY TO DISAPPOINT YOU...
...BUT GENERAL CROSS IS NO LONGER HERE.
WHAT ?!
HE LEFT...
...EIGHT DAYS AGO.

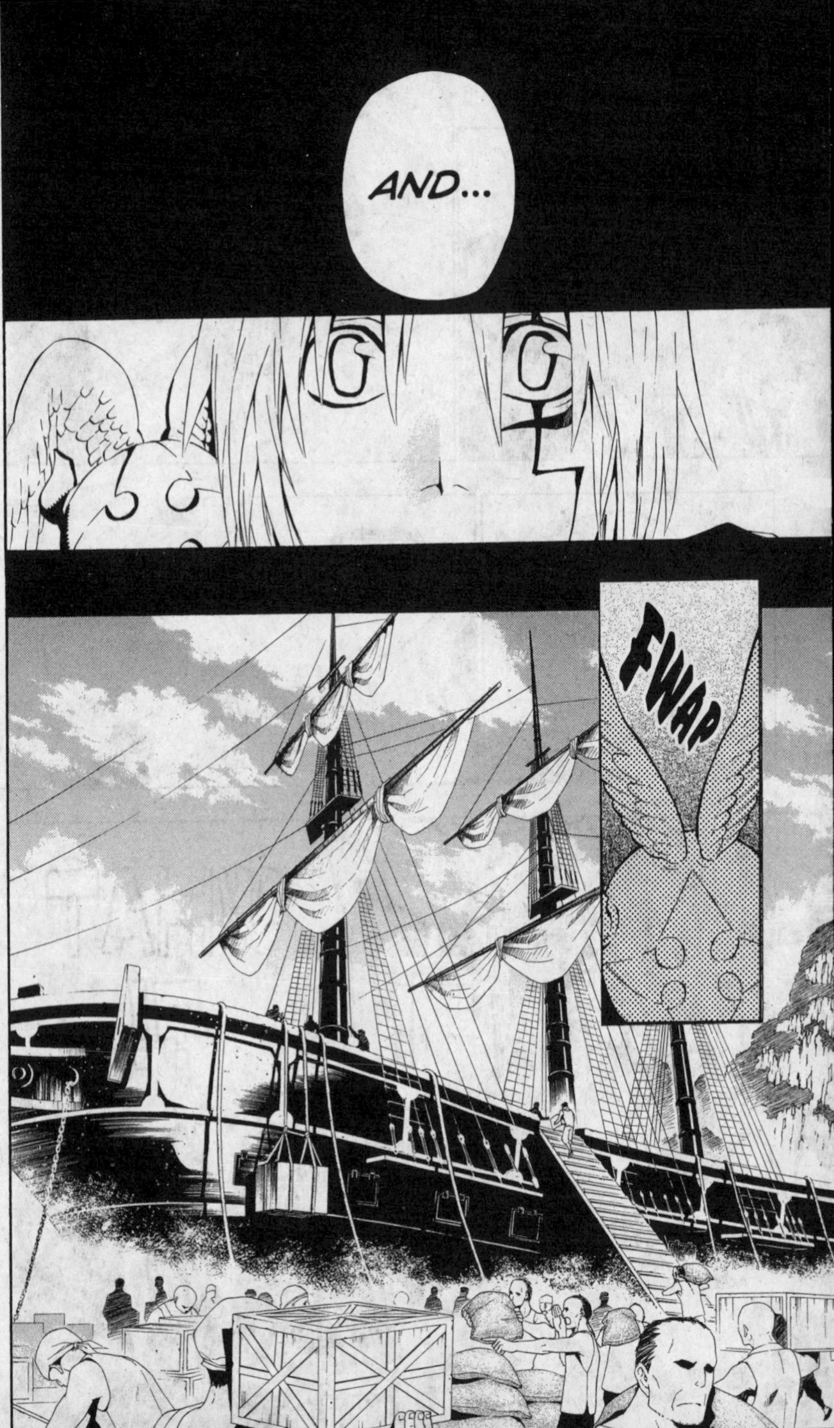
AND...
FWAP

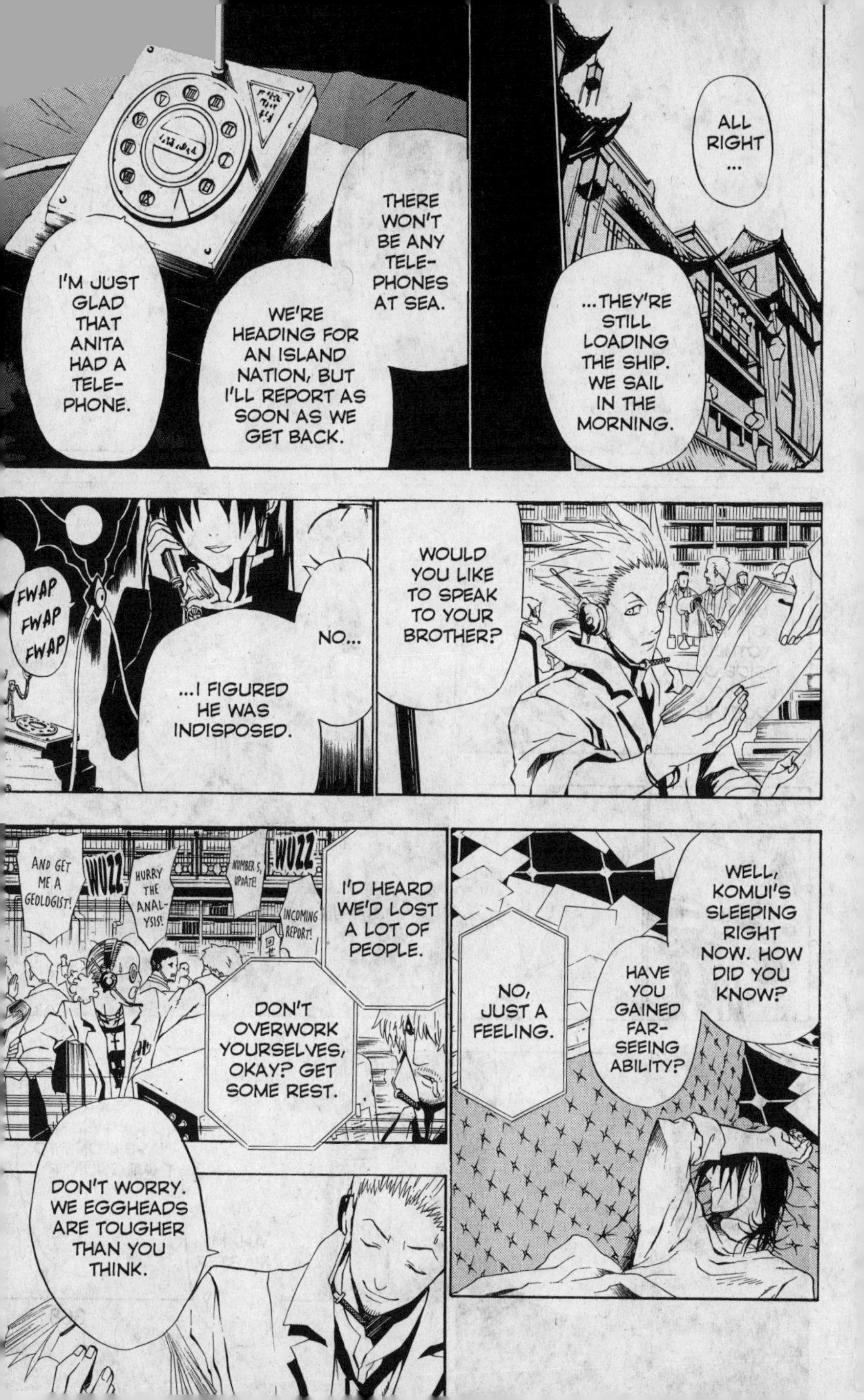
ALL RIGHT ...
...THEY'RE STILL LOADING THE SHIP. WE SAIL IN THE MORNING.
THERE WON'T BE ANY TELE-PHONES AT SEA.
WE'RE HEADING FOR AN ISLAND NATION, BUT I'LL REPORT AS SOON AS WE GET BACK.
I'M JUST GLAD THAT ANITA HAD A TELE-PHONE.
WOULD YOU LIKE TO SPEAK TO YOUR BROTHER?
NO...
FWAP FWAP FWAP
...I FIGURED HE WAS INDISPOSED.
WELL, KOMUI'S SLEEPING RIGHT NOW. HOW DID YOU KNOW?
HAVE YOU GAINED FAR-SEEING ABILITY?
NO, JUST A FEELING.
I'D HEARD WE'D LOST A LOT OF PEOPLE.
WUZZ
NUMBER 5, UPDATE!
INCOMING REPORT!
HURRY THE ANAL-YSIS!
WUZZ
AND GET ME A GEOLOGIST!
DON'T OVERWORK YOURSELVES, OKAY? GET SOME REST.
DON'T WORRY. WE EGGHEADS ARE TOUGHER THAN YOU THINK.

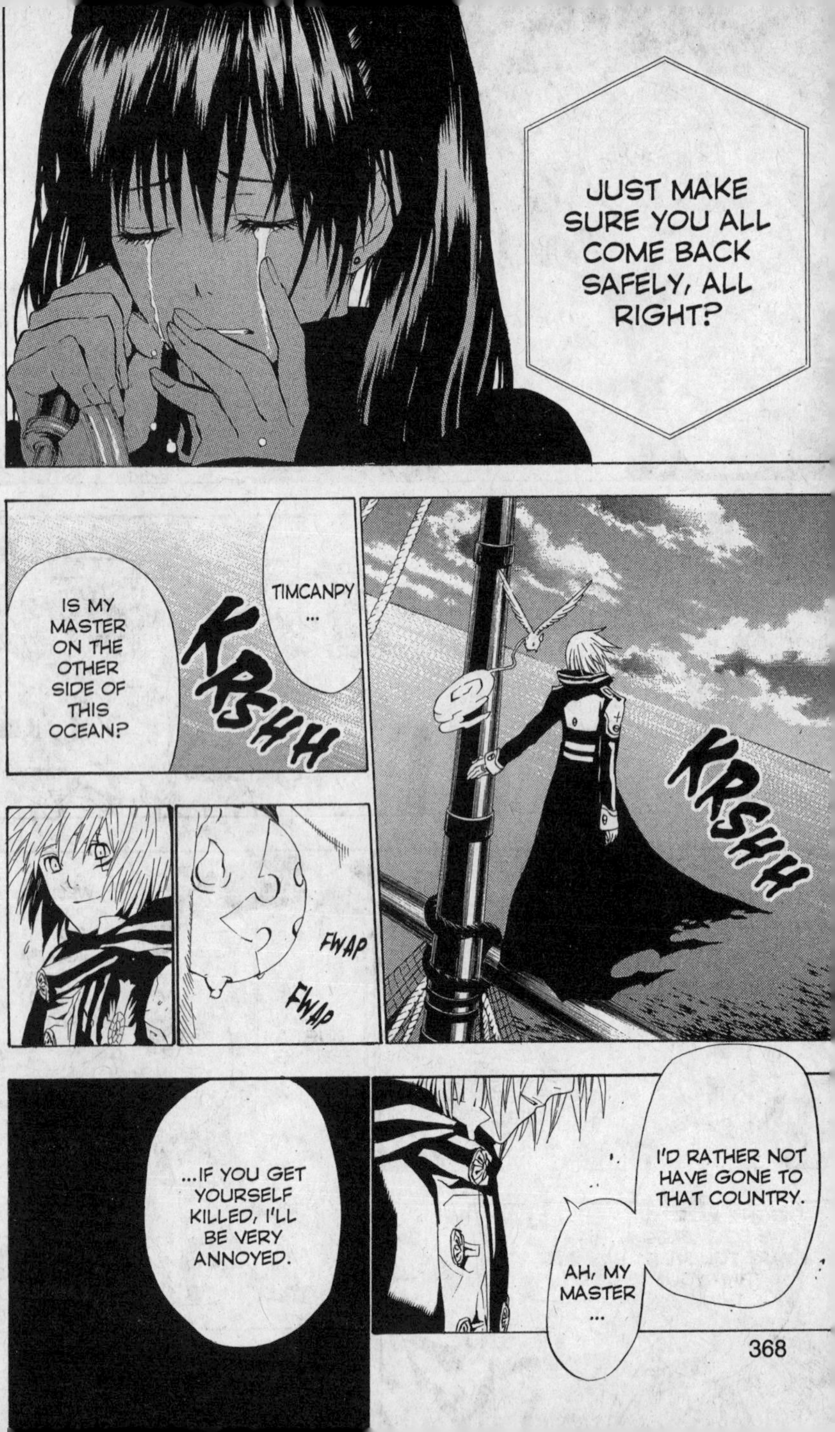
JUST MAKE SURE YOU ALL COME BACK SAFELY, ALL RIGHT?
KRSHH
TIMCANPY ...
IS MY MASTER ON THE OTHER SIDE OF THIS OCEAN?
KRSHH
FWAP
FWAP
I'D RATHER NOT HAVE GONE TO THAT COUNTRY.
AH, MY MASTER ...
...IF YOU GET YOURSELF KILLED, I'LL BE VERY ANNOYED.

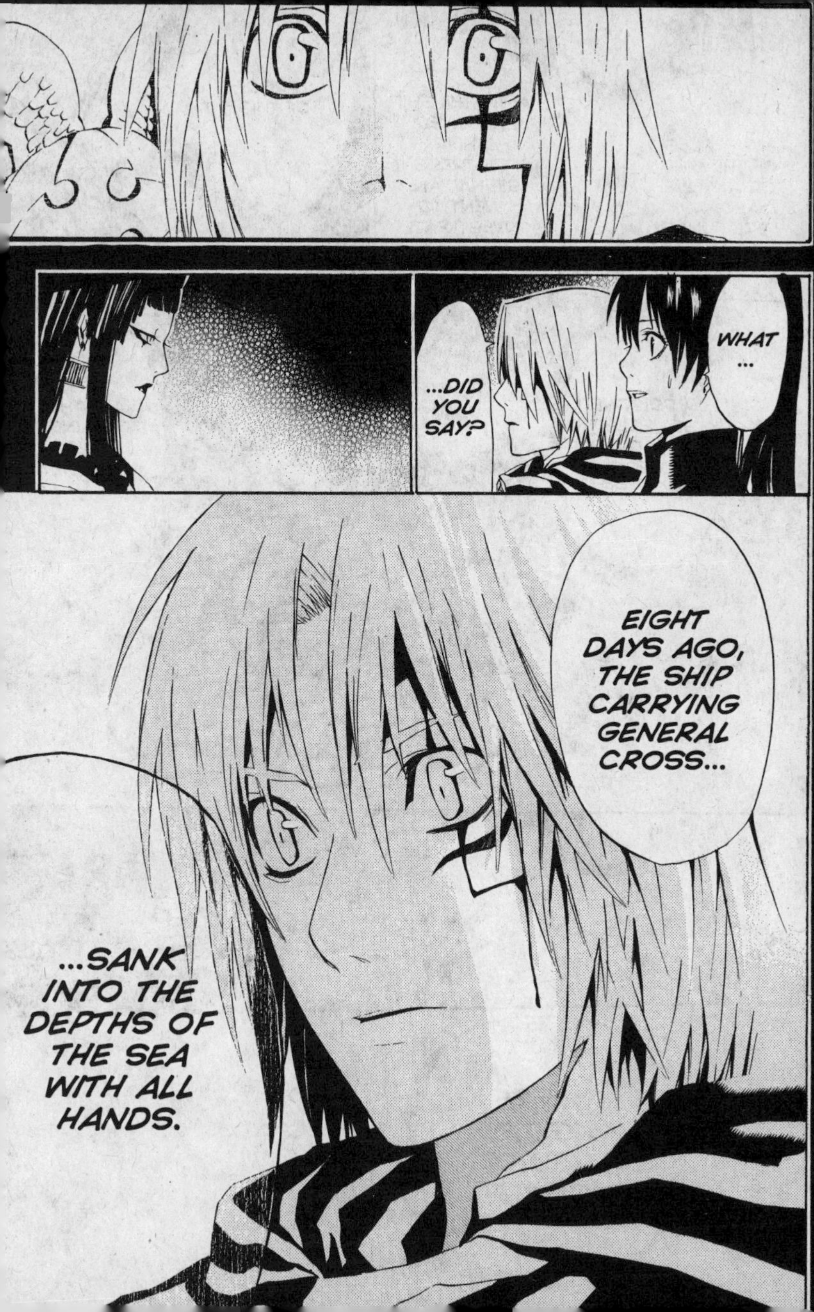
WHAT ...
...DID YOU SAY?
EIGHT DAYS AGO, THE SHIP CARRYING GENERAL CROSS...
...SANK INTO THE DEPTHS OF THE SEA WITH ALL HANDS.

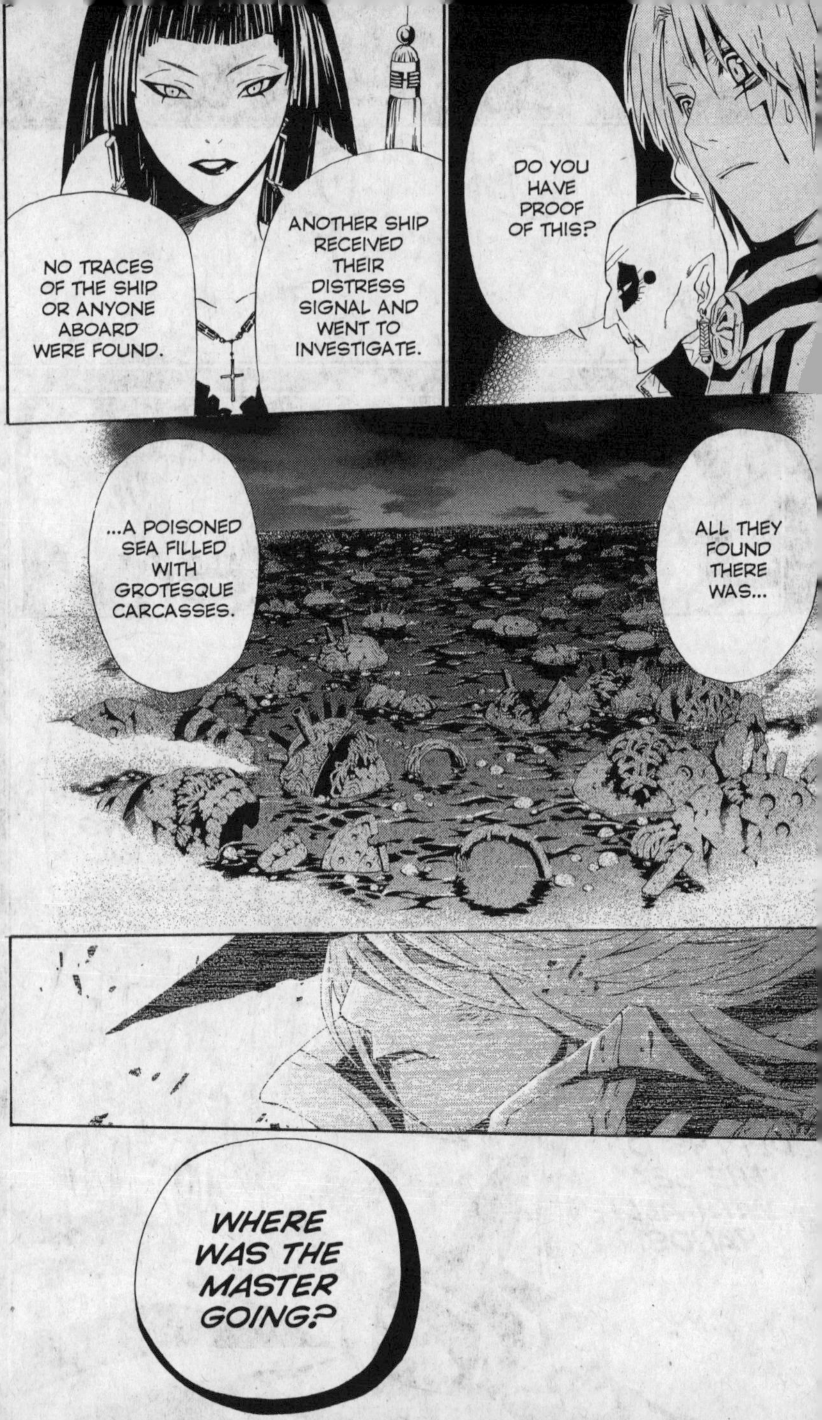
DO YOU HAVE PROOF OF THIS?
ANOTHER SHIP RECEIVED THEIR DISTRESS SIGNAL AND WENT TO INVESTIGATE.
NO TRACES OF THE SHIP OR ANYONE ABOARD WERE FOUND.
ALL THEY FOUND THERE WAS...
...A POISONED SEA FILLED WITH GROTESQUE CARCASSES.
WHERE WAS THE MASTER GOING?

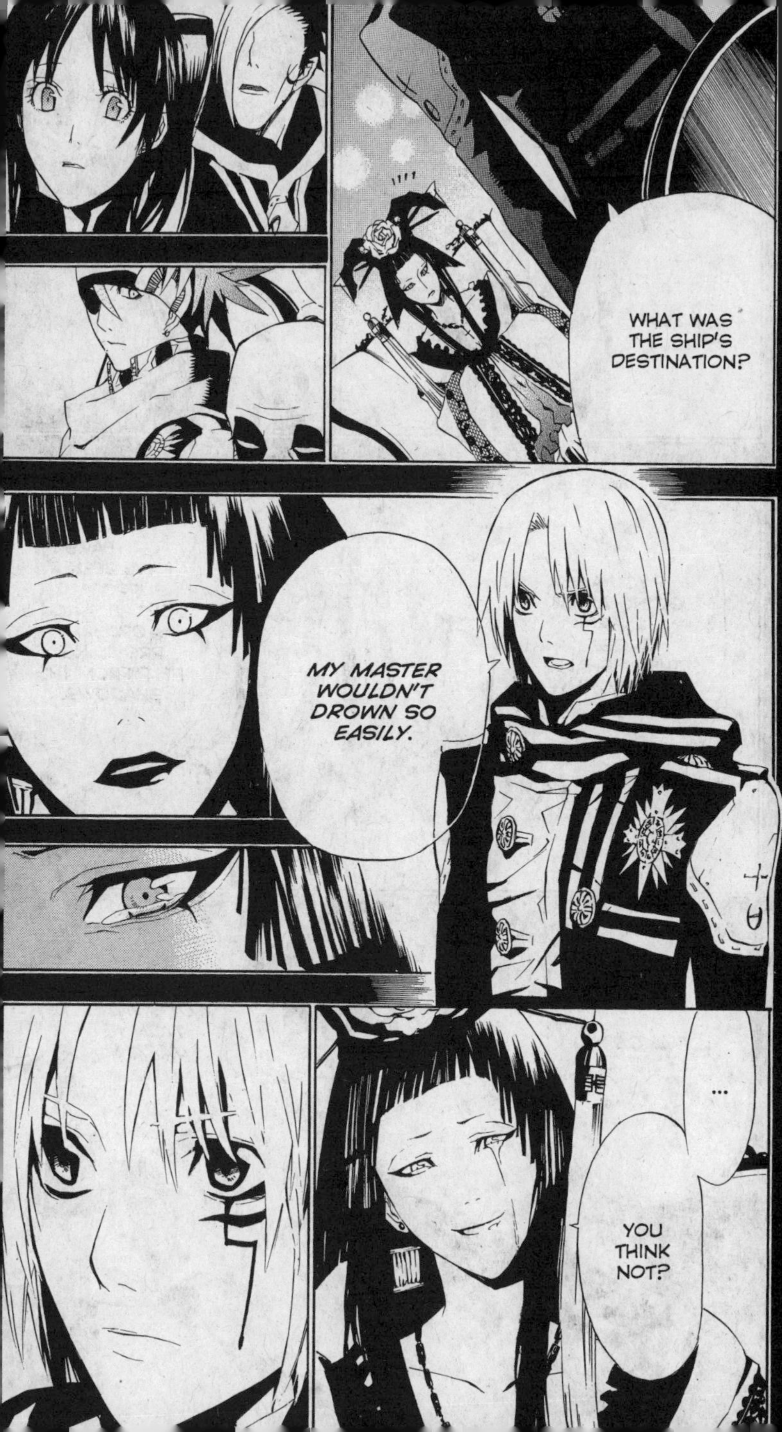
WHAT WAS THE SHIP'S DESTINATION?
MY MASTER WOULDN'T DROWN SO EASILY.
...
YOU THINK NOT?

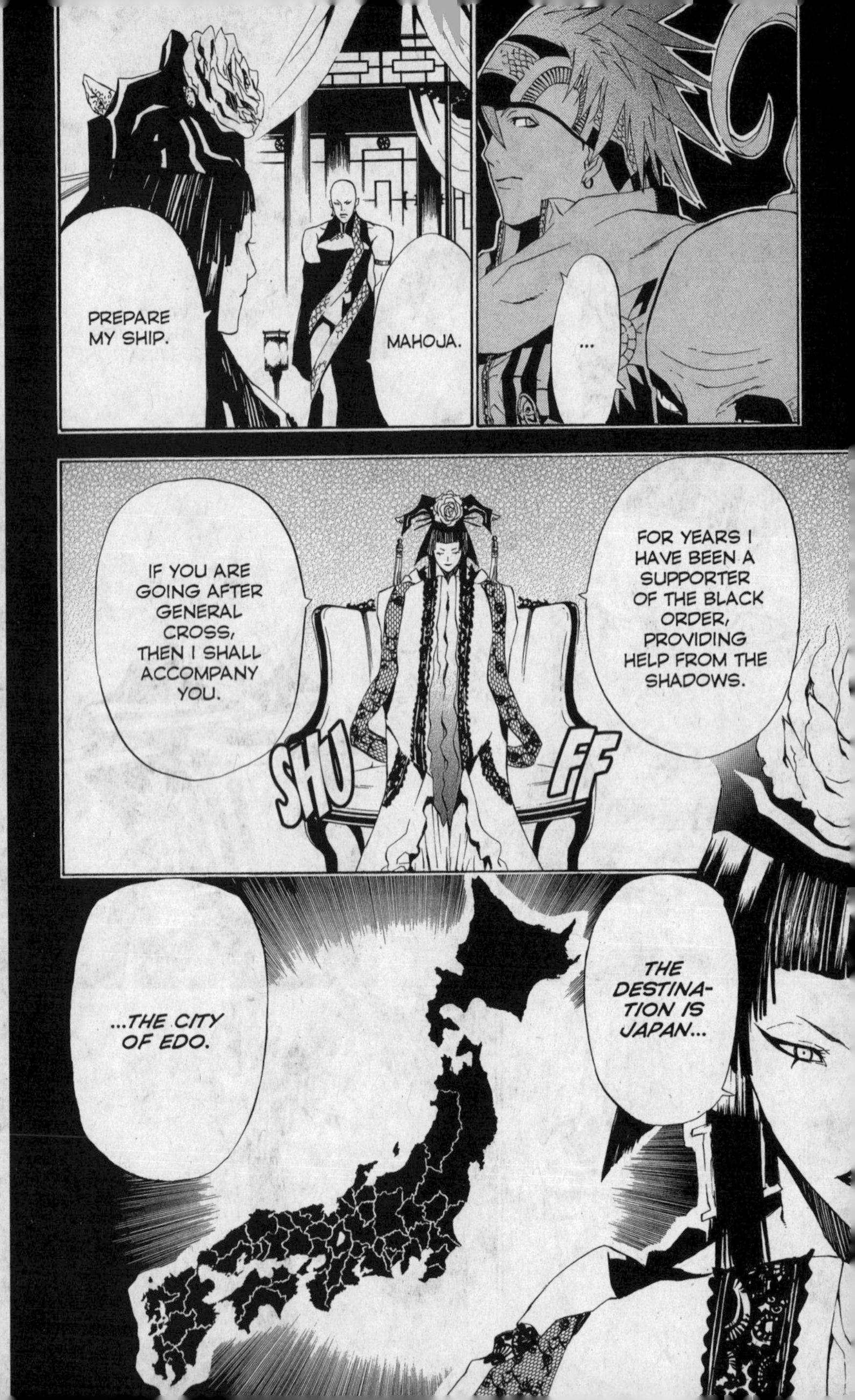
...
MAHOJA.
PREPARE MY SHIP.
FOR YEARS I HAVE BEEN A SUPPORTER OF THE BLACK ORDER, PROVIDING HELP FROM THE SHADOWS.
IF YOU ARE GOING AFTER GENERAL CROSS, THEN I SHALL ACCOMPANY YOU.
SHUFF
THE DESTINATION IS JAPAN...
...THE CITY OF EDO.

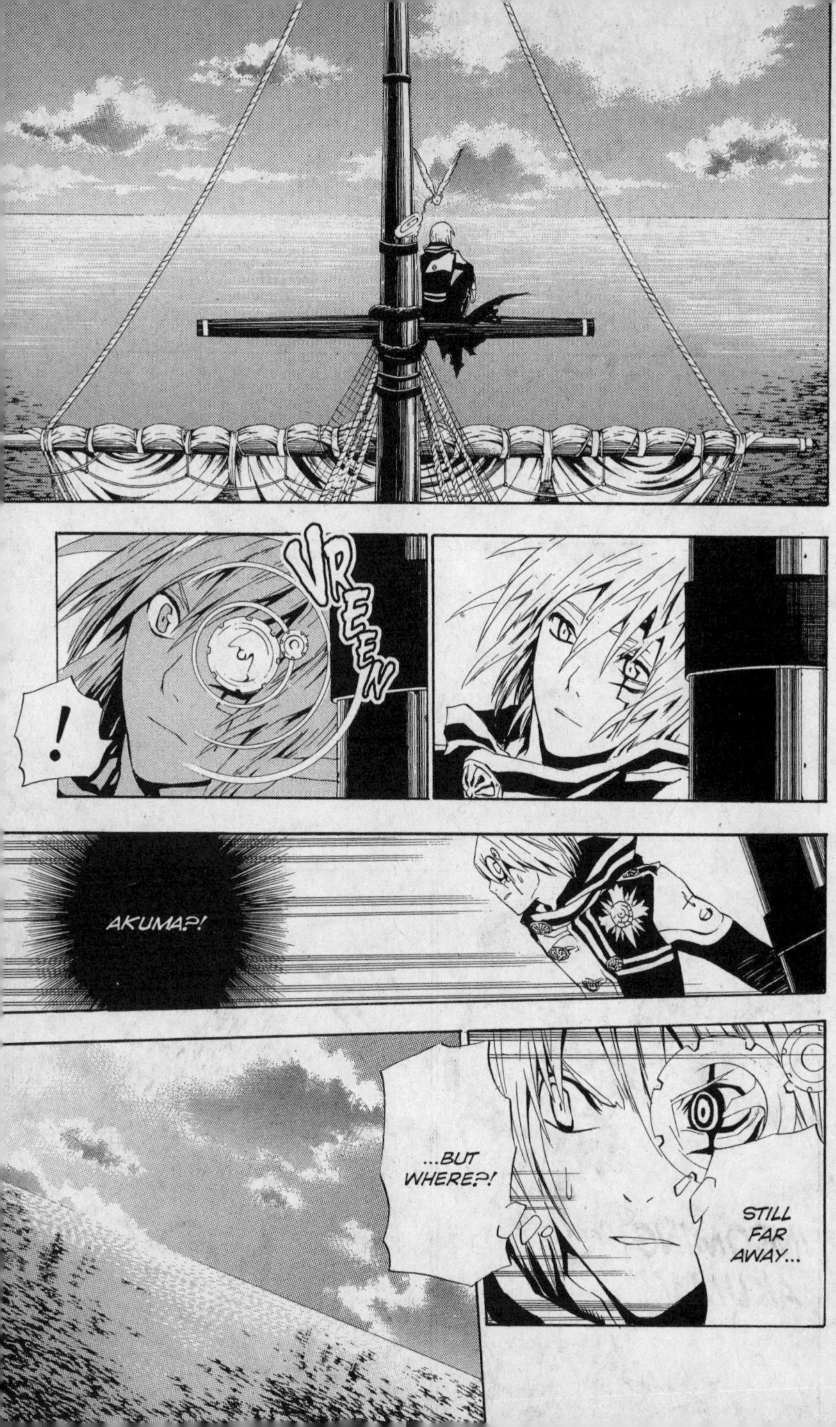
VREEN
!
AKUMA?!
STILL FAR AWAY...
...BUT WHERE?!

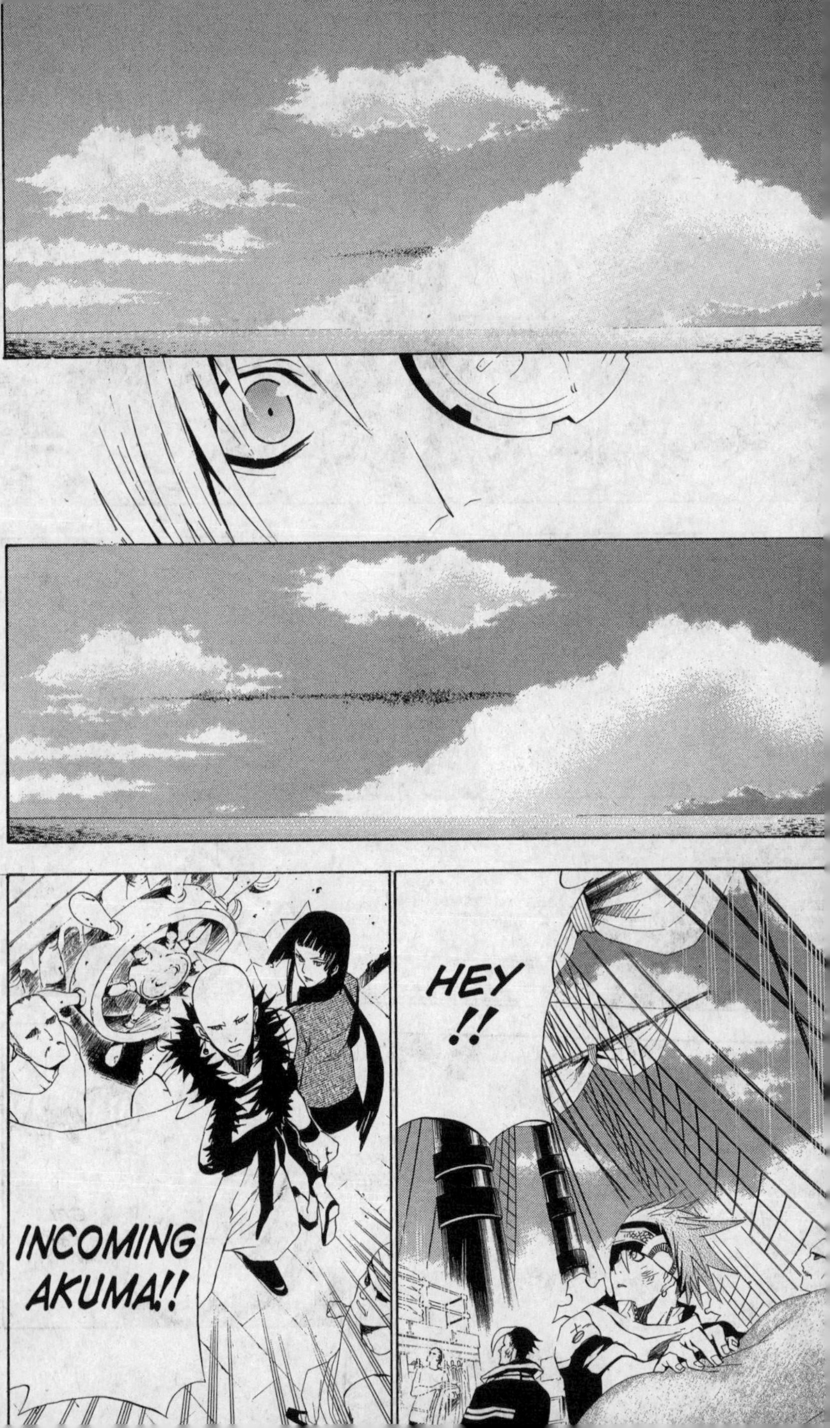
HEY !!
INCOMING AKUMA!!

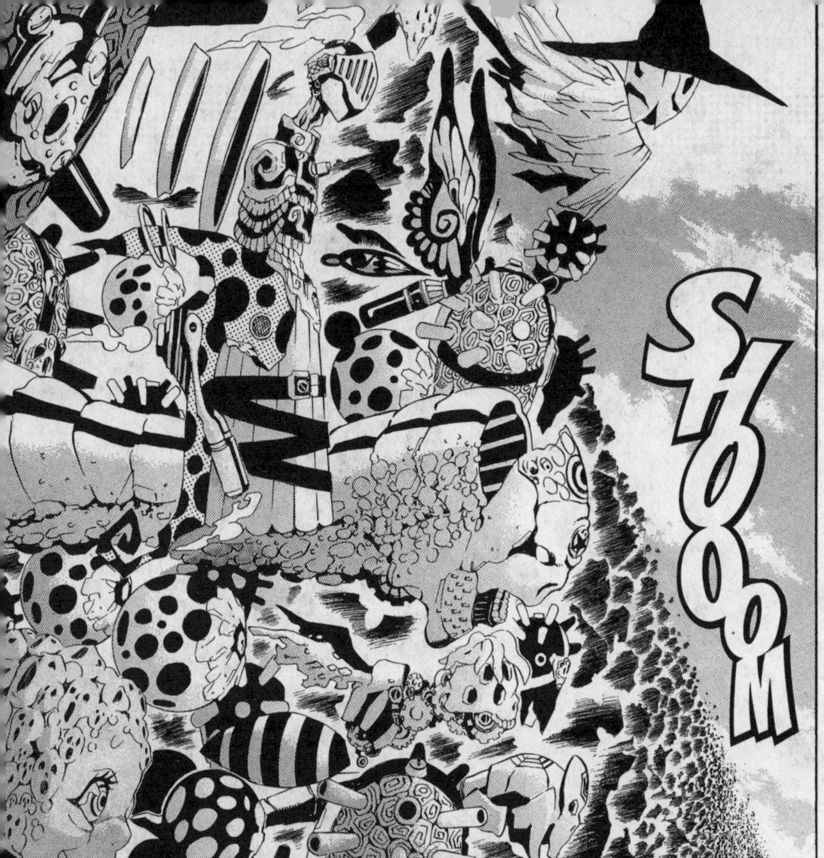
SHOOOOM
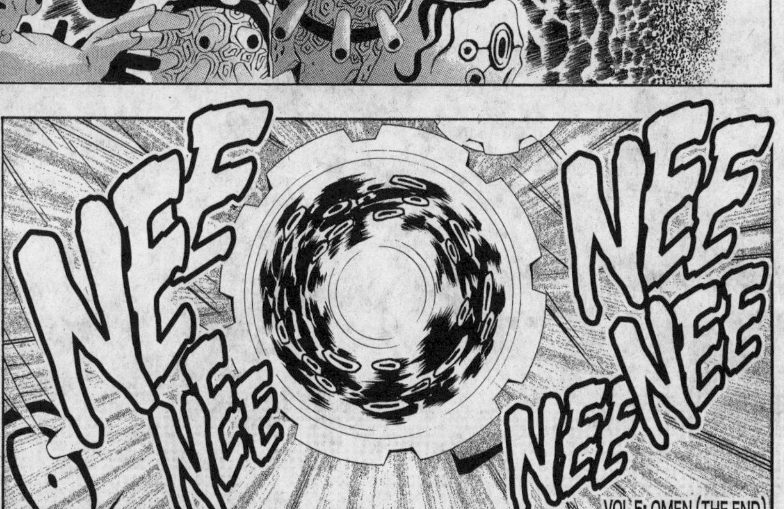
NEE
NEE
NEE
NEE
NEE
NEE
VOL 5: OMEN (THE END)

IN THE NEXT VOLUME...

A horde of Akuma close in on Allen, but they bypass him and head straight for another Exorcist, Suman Dark! His long tragic story and the secret of his unique "Innocence" is revealed, but in the process Suman's life is threatened. Allen tries his best to save his comrade, but his efforts put him in grave danger!

Available August 2007!

SHONEN JUMP ADVANCED MANGA EDITION

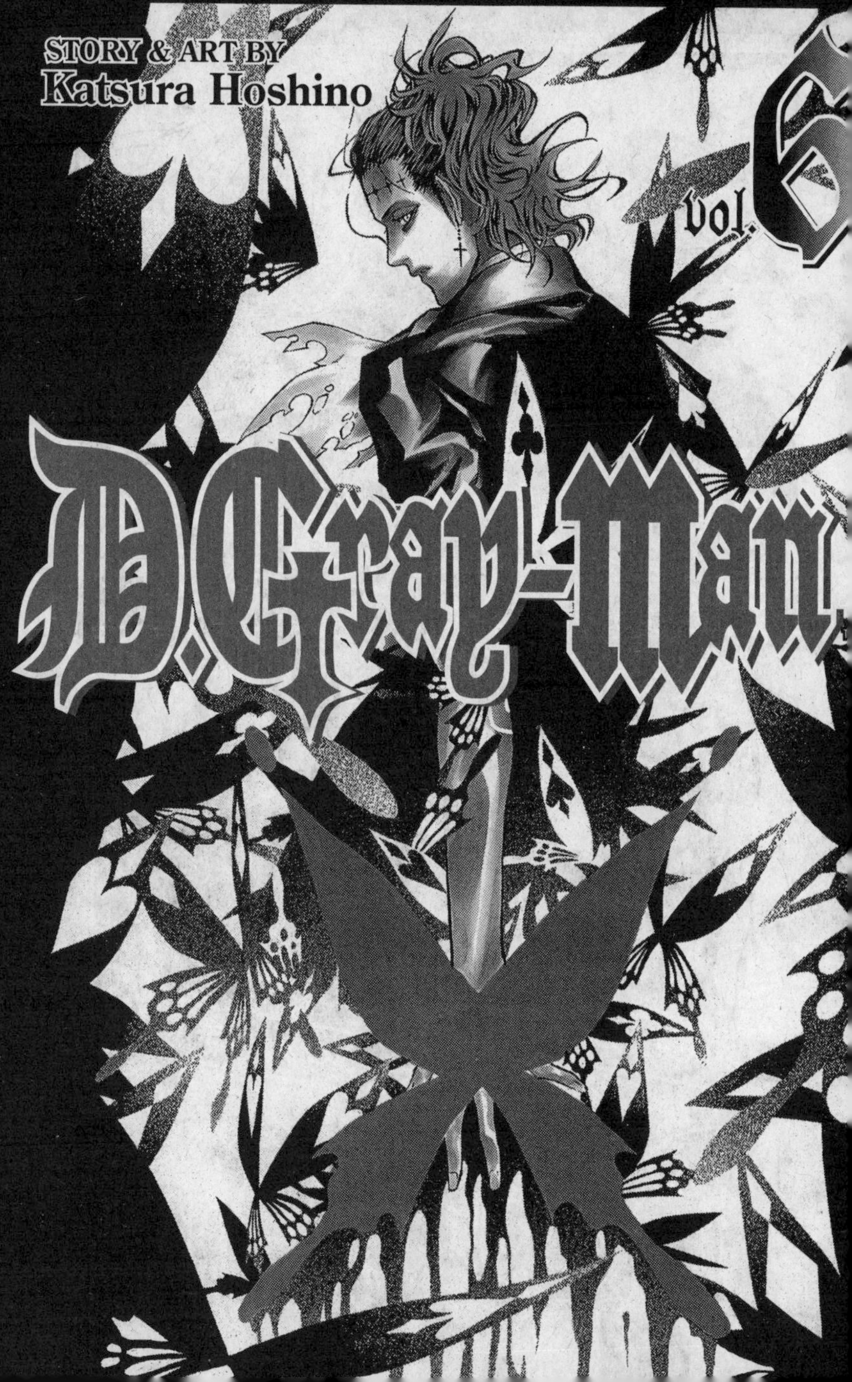

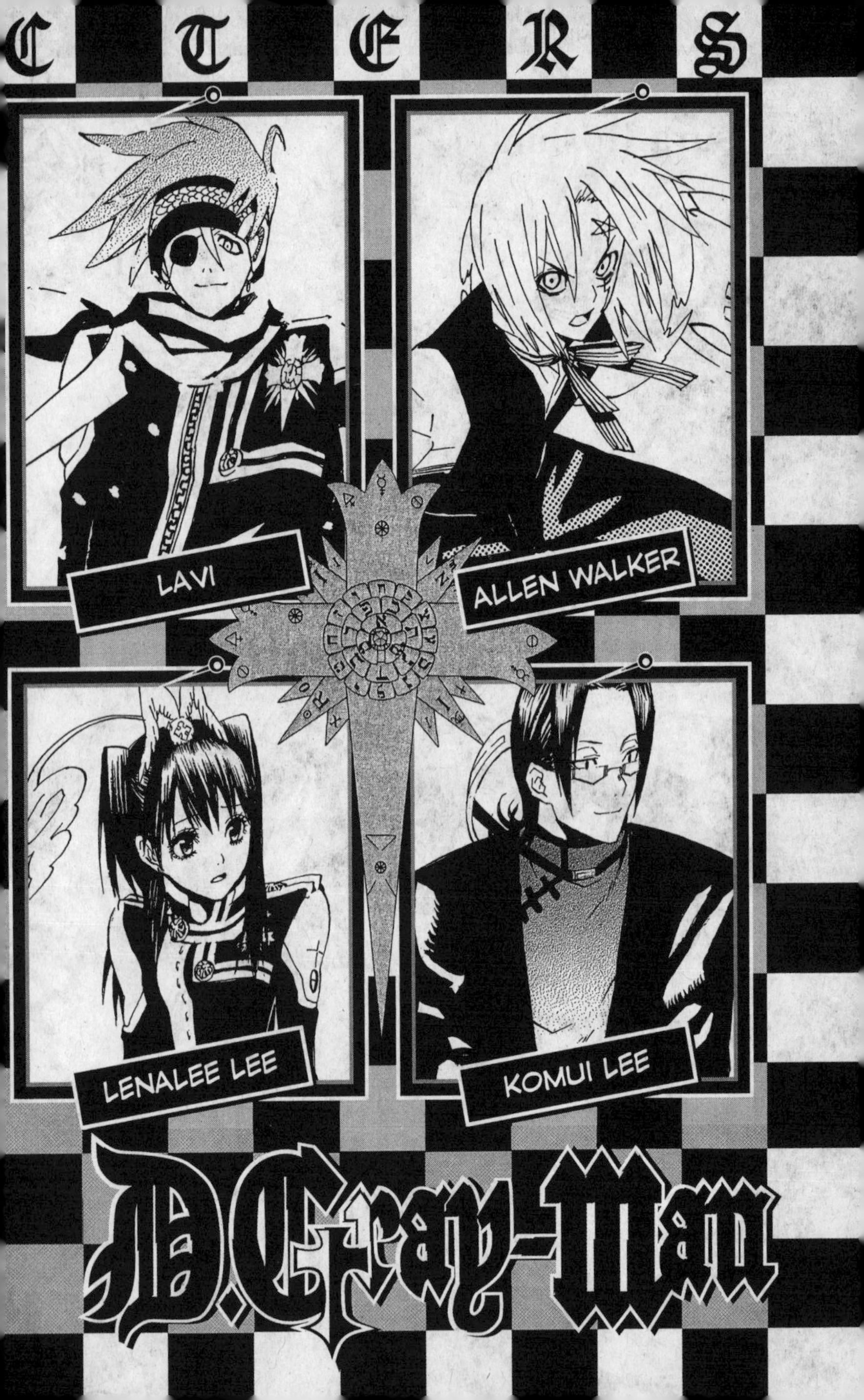
C T E R S
LAVI
ALLEN WALKER
LENALEE LEE
KOMUI LEE
D.Gray-man

CHARA

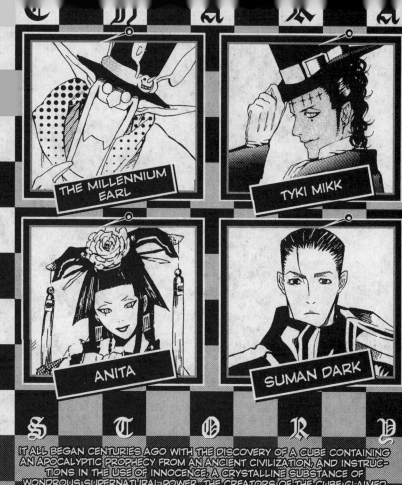

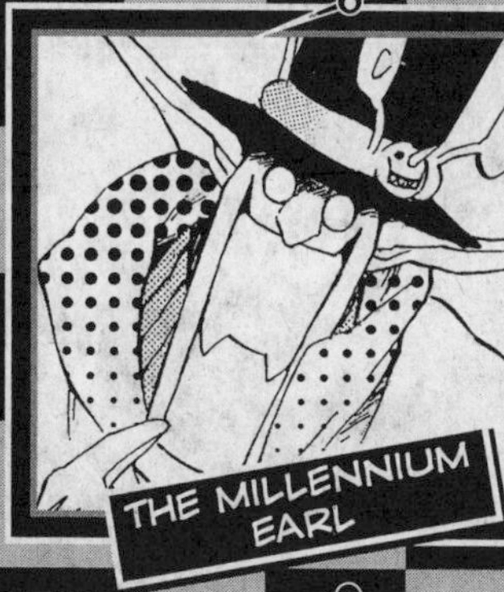
THE MILLENNIUM EARL

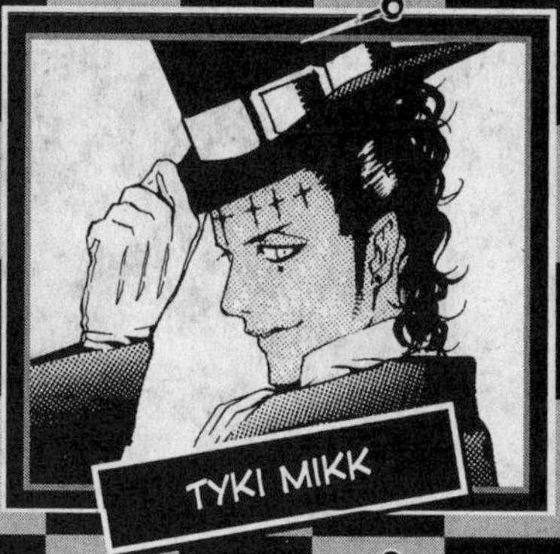
TYKI MIKK

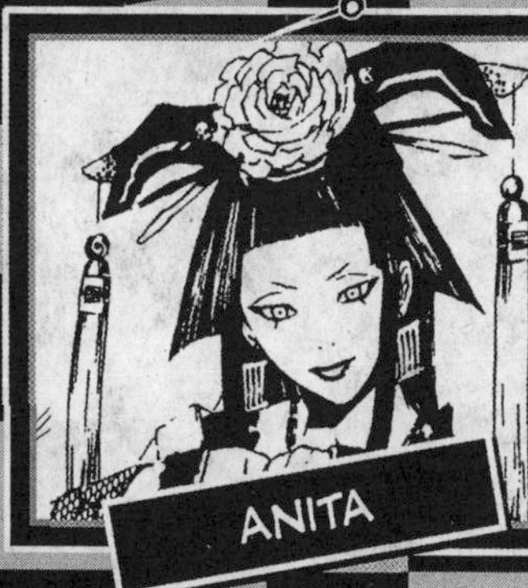
ANITA

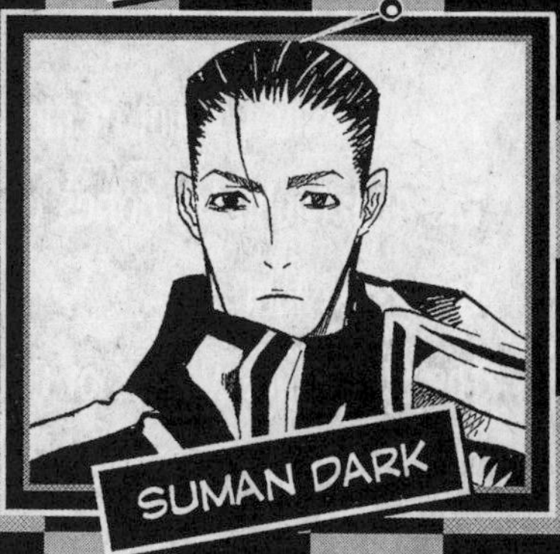
SUMAN DARK

STORY

IT ALL BEGAN CENTURIES AGO WITH THE DISCOVERY OF A CUBE CONTAINING AN APOCALYPTIC PROPHECY FROM AN ANCIENT CIVILIZATION, AND INSTRUCTIONS IN THE USE OF INNOCENCE, A CRYSTALLINE SUBSTANCE OF WONDROUS SUPERNATURAL POWER. THE CREATORS OF THE CUBE CLAIMED TO HAVE DEFEATED AN EVIL KNOWN AS THE MILLENNIUM EARL USING THE INNOCENCE. NEVERTHELESS, THE WORLD WAS DESTROYED BY THE GREAT FLOOD OF THE OLD TESTAMENT. NOW TO AVERT A SECOND END OF THE WORLD, A GROUP OF EXORCISTS WIELDING WEAPONS MADE OF INNOCENCE MUST BATTLE THE MILLENNIUM EARL AND HIS TERRIBLE MINIONS, THE AKUMA.

FORCES OF THE MILLENNIUM EARL LAUNCH A MASSIVE ATTACK AGAINST THE BLACK ORDER IN AN ATTEMPT TO OBTAIN THE HEART, AN INNOCENCE OF FANTASTIC POWER. MORE THAN A HUNDRED EXORCISTS PERISH IN THE ONSLAUGHT. BUT THERE IS LITTLE TIME TO MOURN AS ALLEN AND HIS COMPANIONS PREPARE TO SAIL FOR JAPAN IN PURSUIT OF GENERAL CROSS. BUT EVEN AS THEY SET OUT, A VAST SWARM OF AKUMA DARKENS THE SKIES...

D.GRAY-MAN
Vol. 6

CONTENTS

The 47th Night: Point of the Attack — 381

The 48th Night: Memories of the Dark — 399

The 49th Night: Sin — 417

The 50th Night: Voices of Comrades — 435

The 51st Night: Lost Sheep — 453

The 52nd Night: Beginning of the Night of the End — 471

The 53rd Night: The Last Words of Suman Dark — 491

The 54th Night: Rend Allen's Heart — 509

The 55th Night: Delete — 527

The 56th Night: Nightmare — 545

THE 47TH NIGHT: POINT OF THE ATTACK

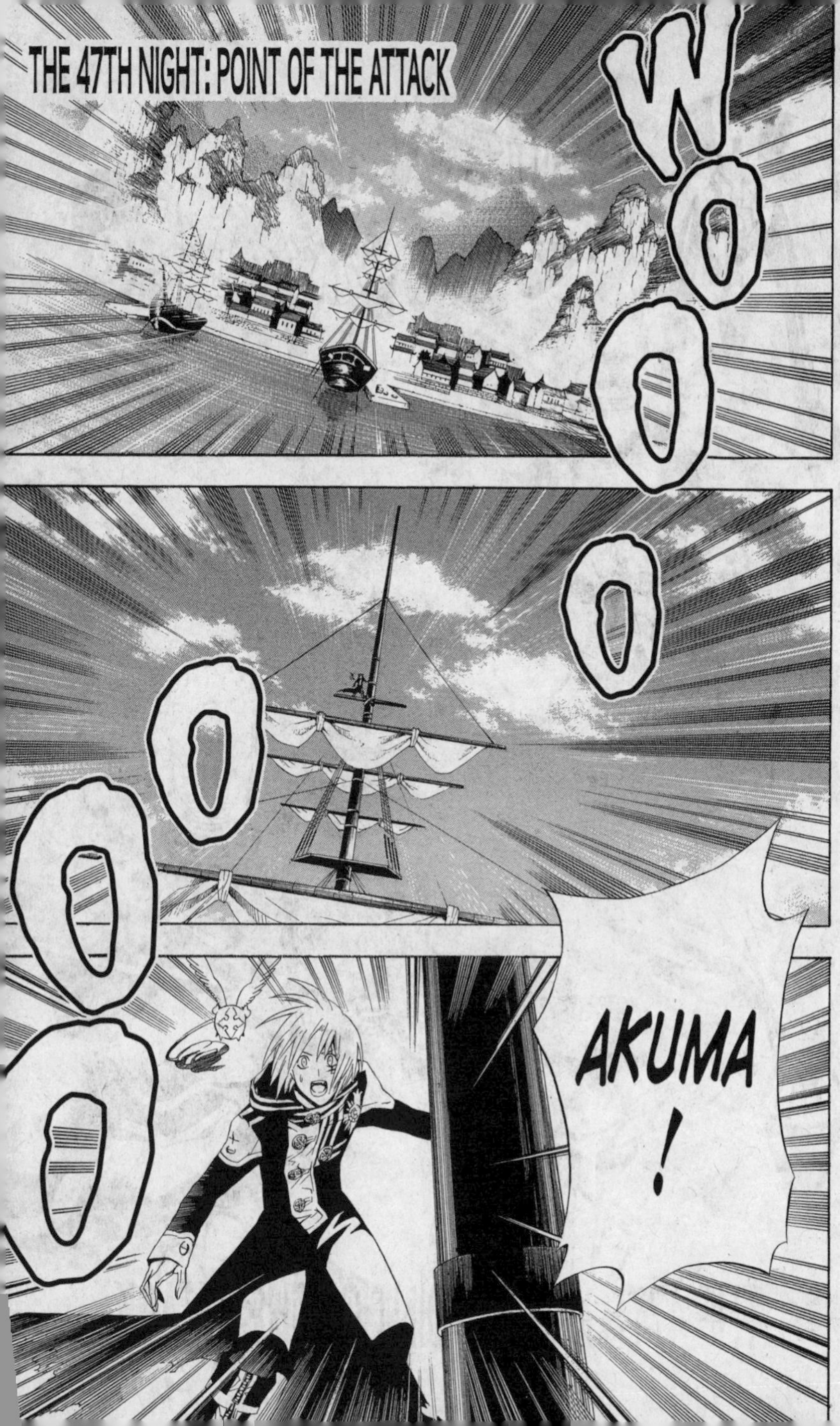
WOOOOOO
AKUMA!

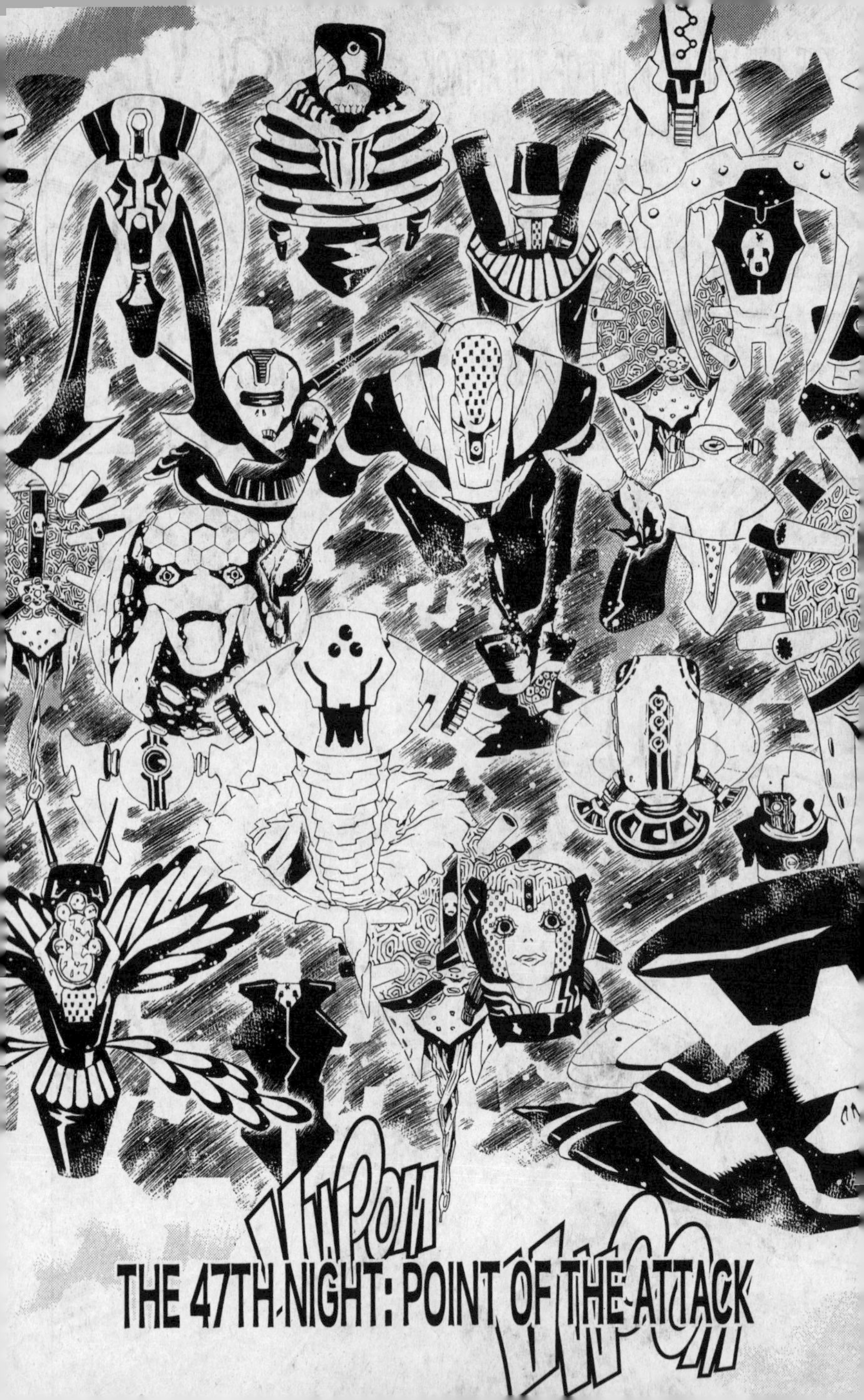

THE 47TH NIGHT: POINT OF THE ATTACK

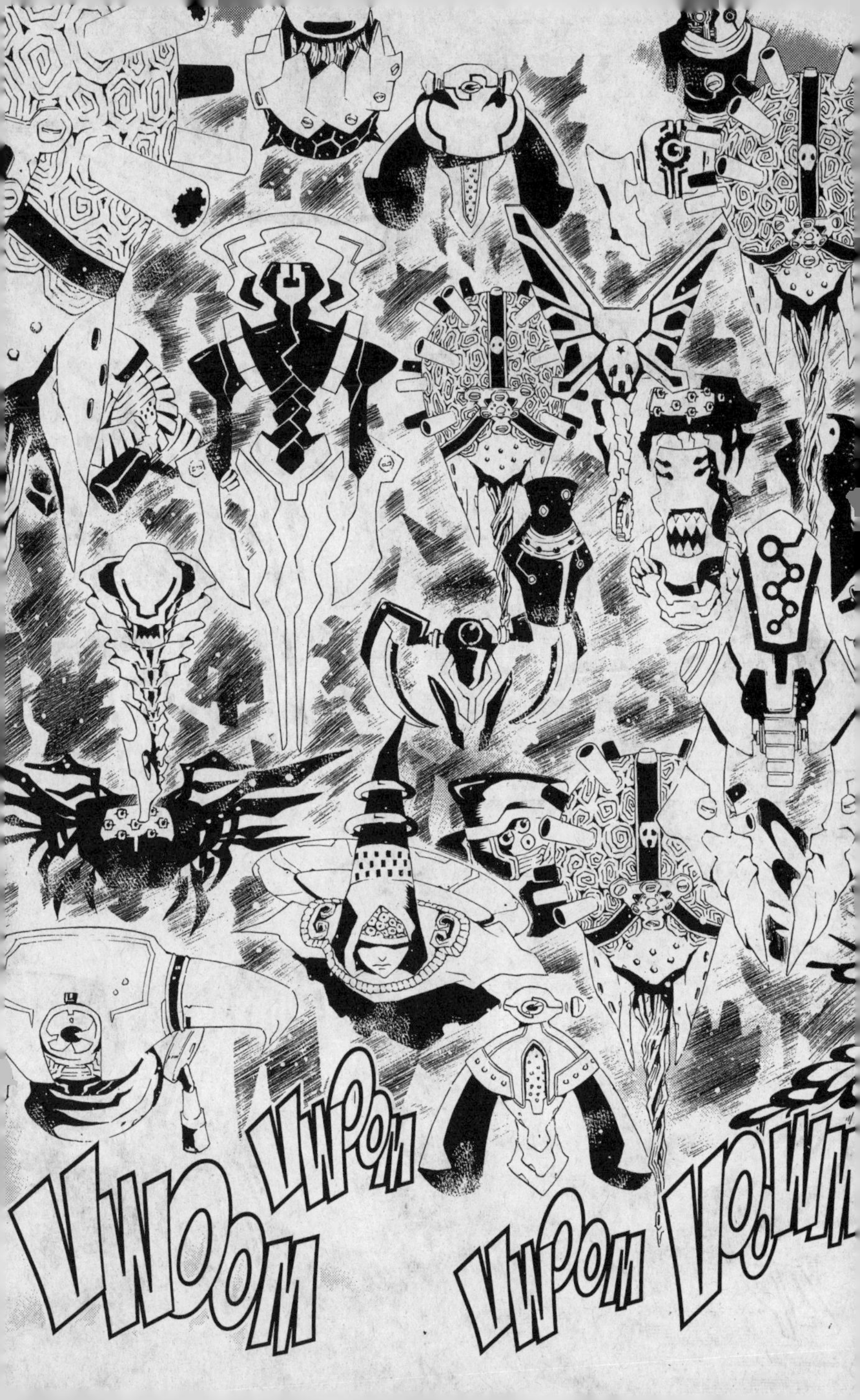
VWOOM
VWOOM
VWOOM

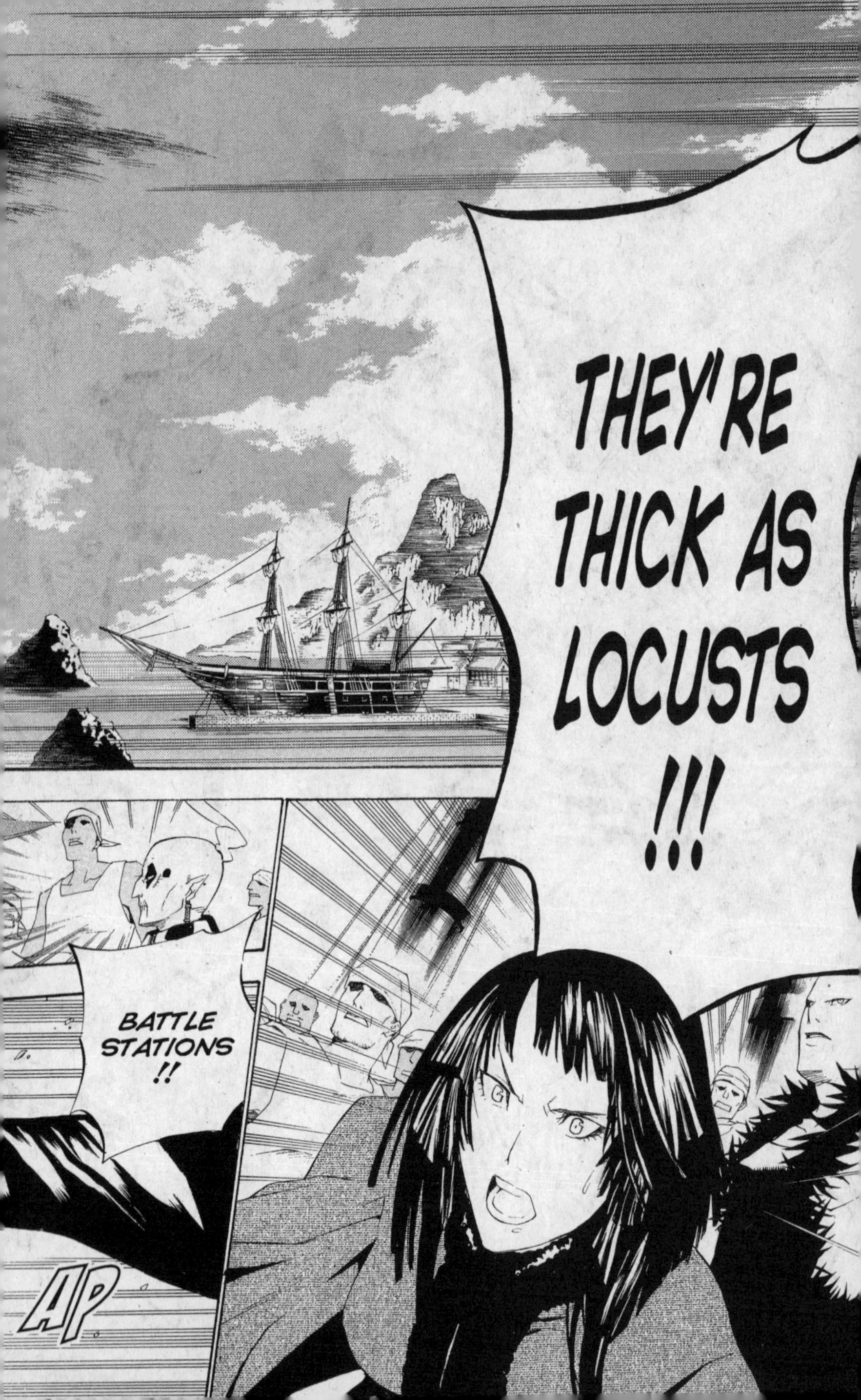
THEY'RE THICK AS LOCUSTS !!!
BATTLE STATIONS !!
AP

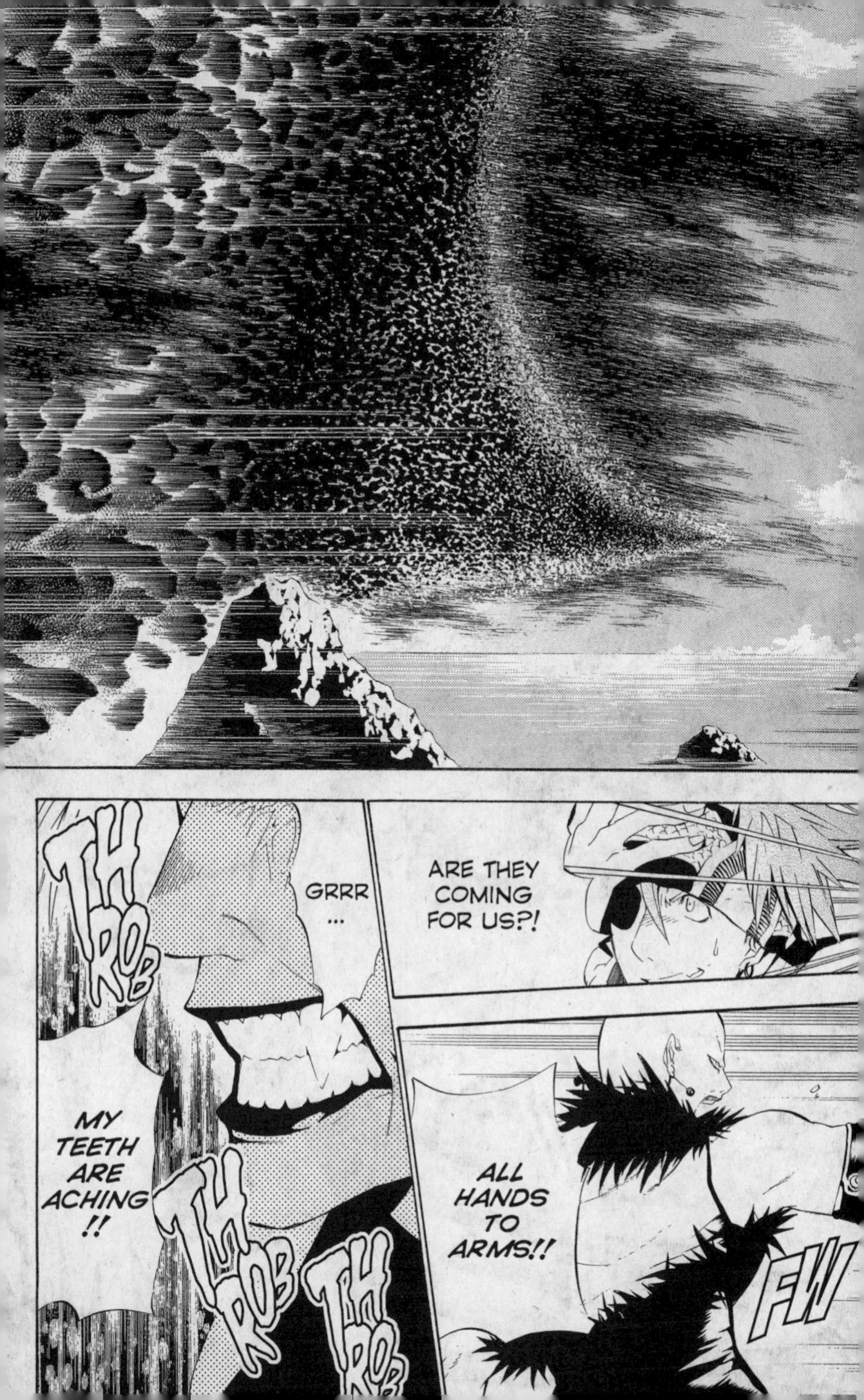
ARE THEY COMING FOR US?!
ALL HANDS TO ARMS!!
FW
THROB
GRRR ...
MY TEETH ARE ACHING!!
THROB
THROB

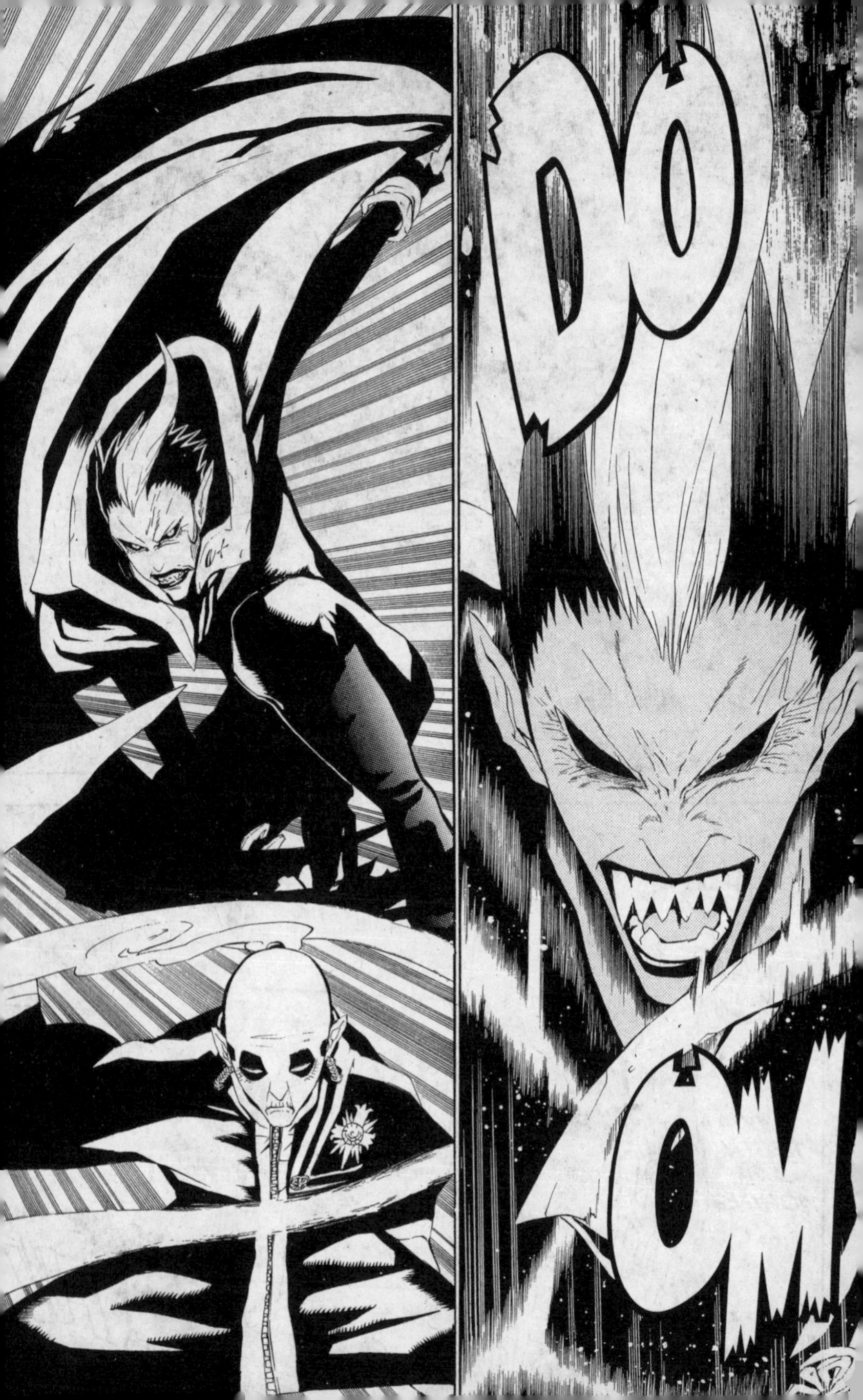
DOOM!

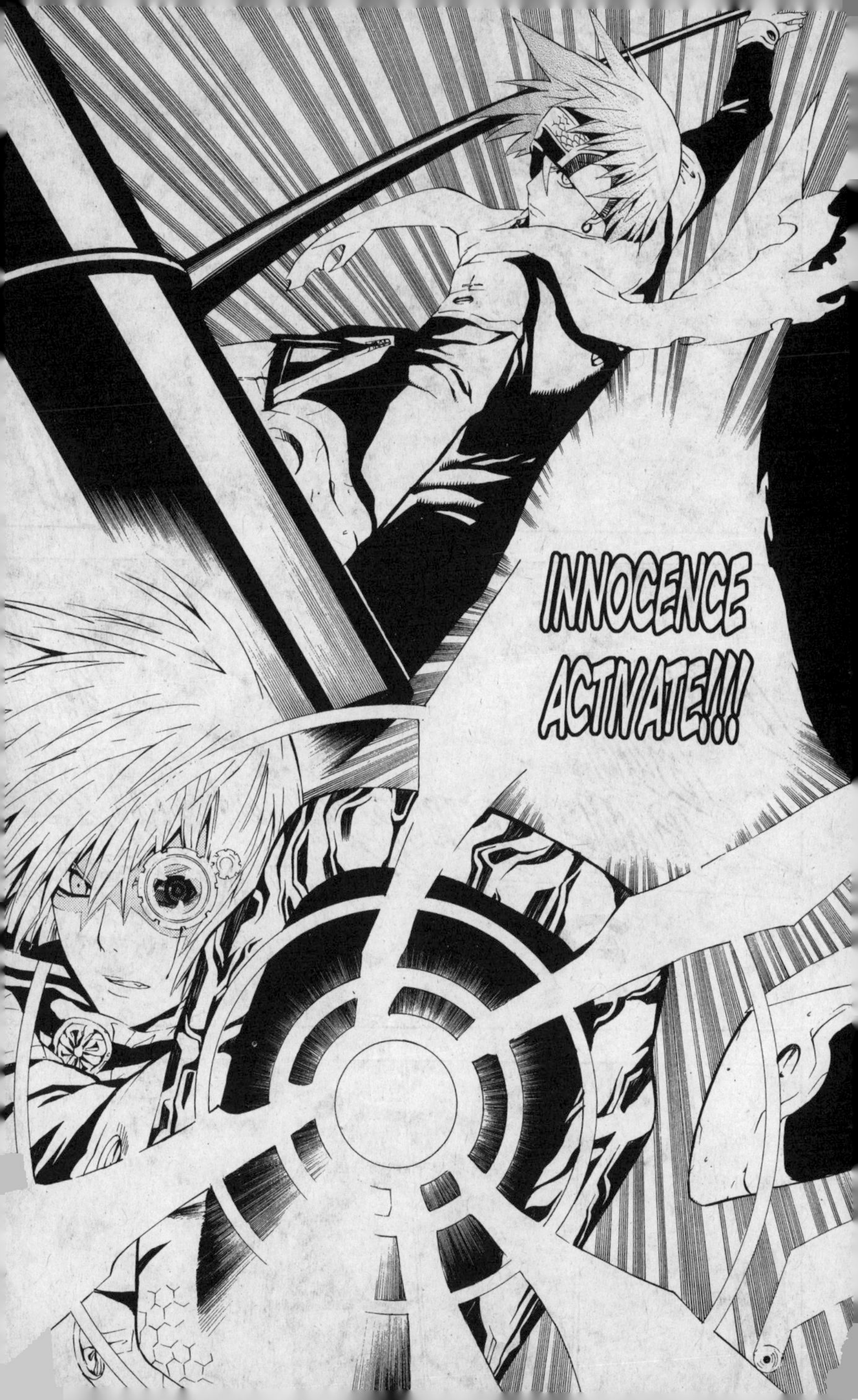
INNOCENCE ACTIVATE!!!

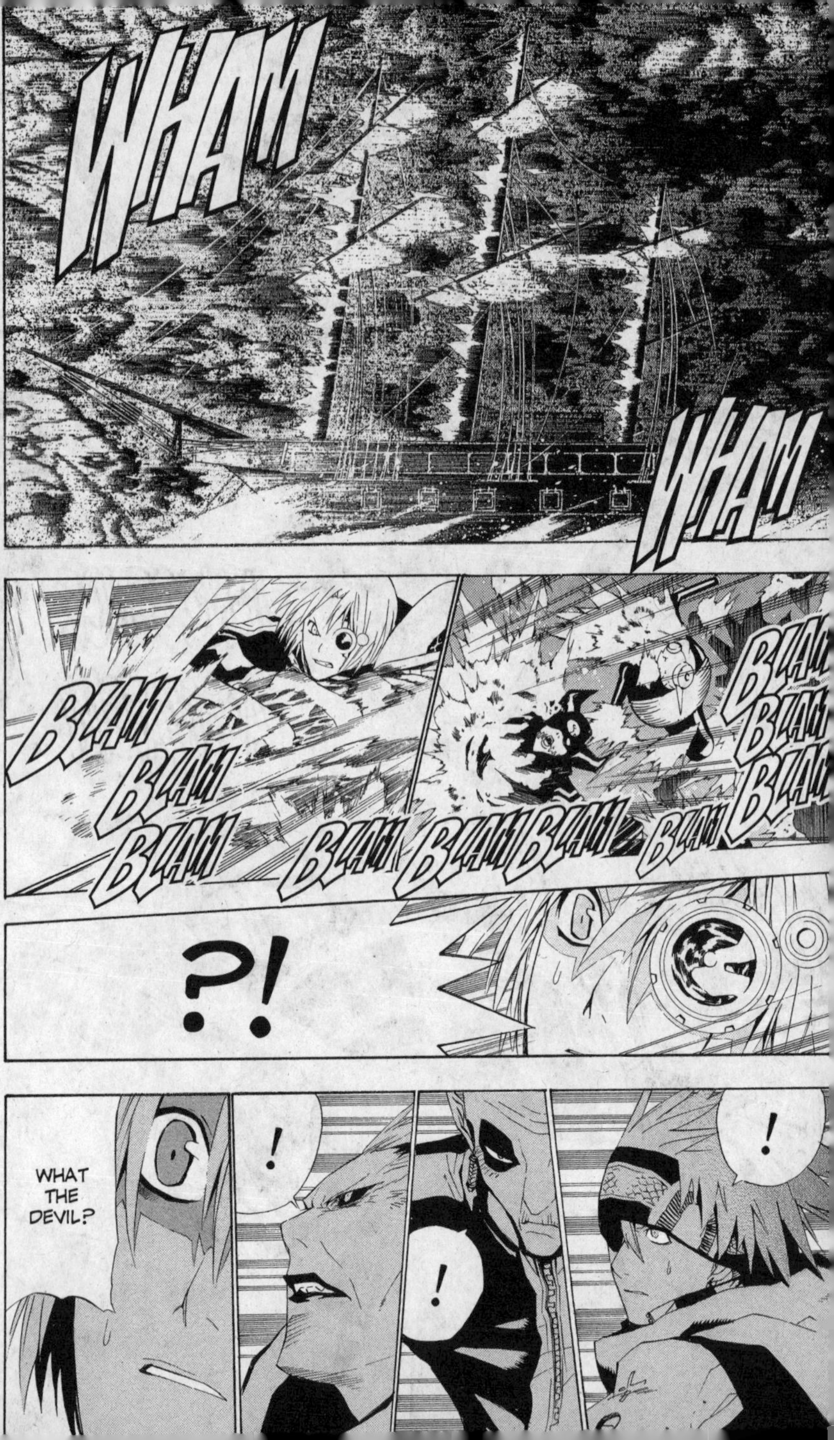
WHAM
WHAM
BLAM BLAM BLAM
BLAM BLAM BLAM
BLAM
BLAM
BLAM BLAM BLAM
?!
!
!
!
WHAT THE DEVIL?

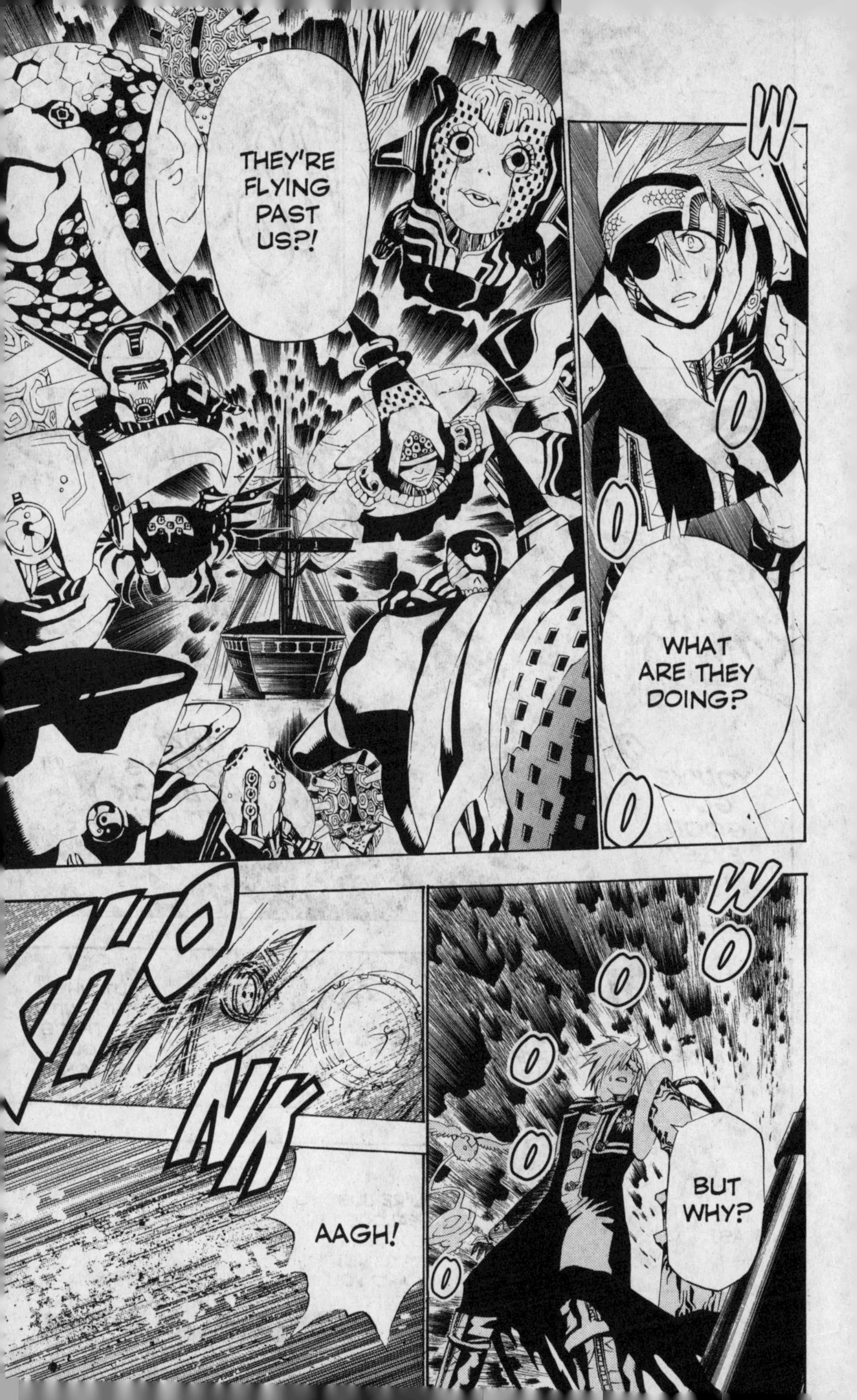
WOOO
WHAT ARE THEY DOING?
THEY'RE FLYING PAST US?!
WOOOOO
BUT WHY?
CHUNK
AAGH!

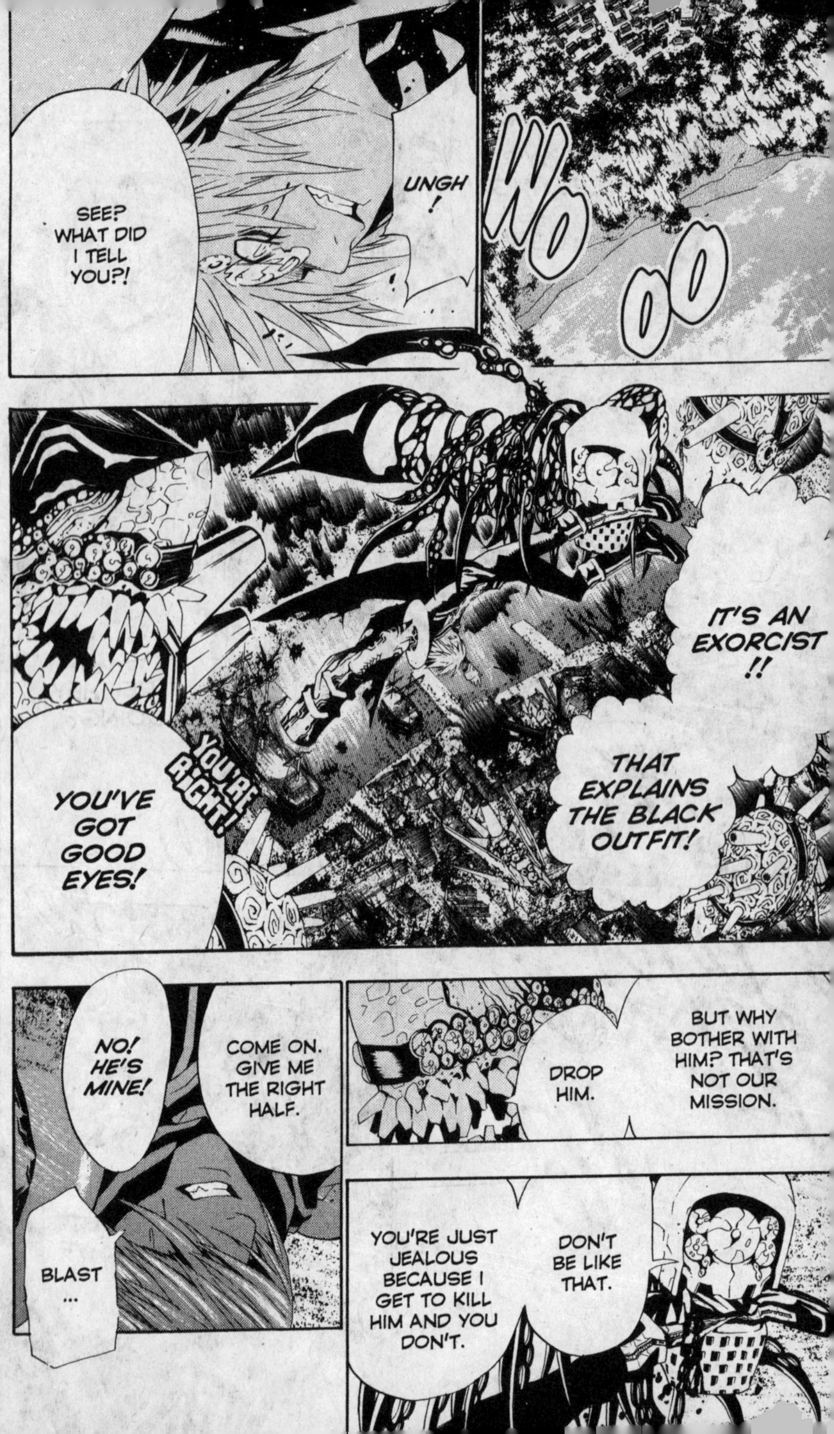
WOOO
UNGH!
SEE? WHAT DID I TELL YOU?!
IT'S AN EXORCIST!!
THAT EXPLAINS THE BLACK OUTFIT!
YOU'RE RIGHT!
YOU'VE GOT GOOD EYES!
BUT WHY BOTHER WITH HIM? THAT'S NOT OUR MISSION.
DROP HIM.
DON'T BE LIKE THAT.
YOU'RE JUST JEALOUS BECAUSE I GET TO KILL HIM AND YOU DON'T.
COME ON. GIVE ME THE RIGHT HALF.
NO! HE'S MINE!
BLAST...

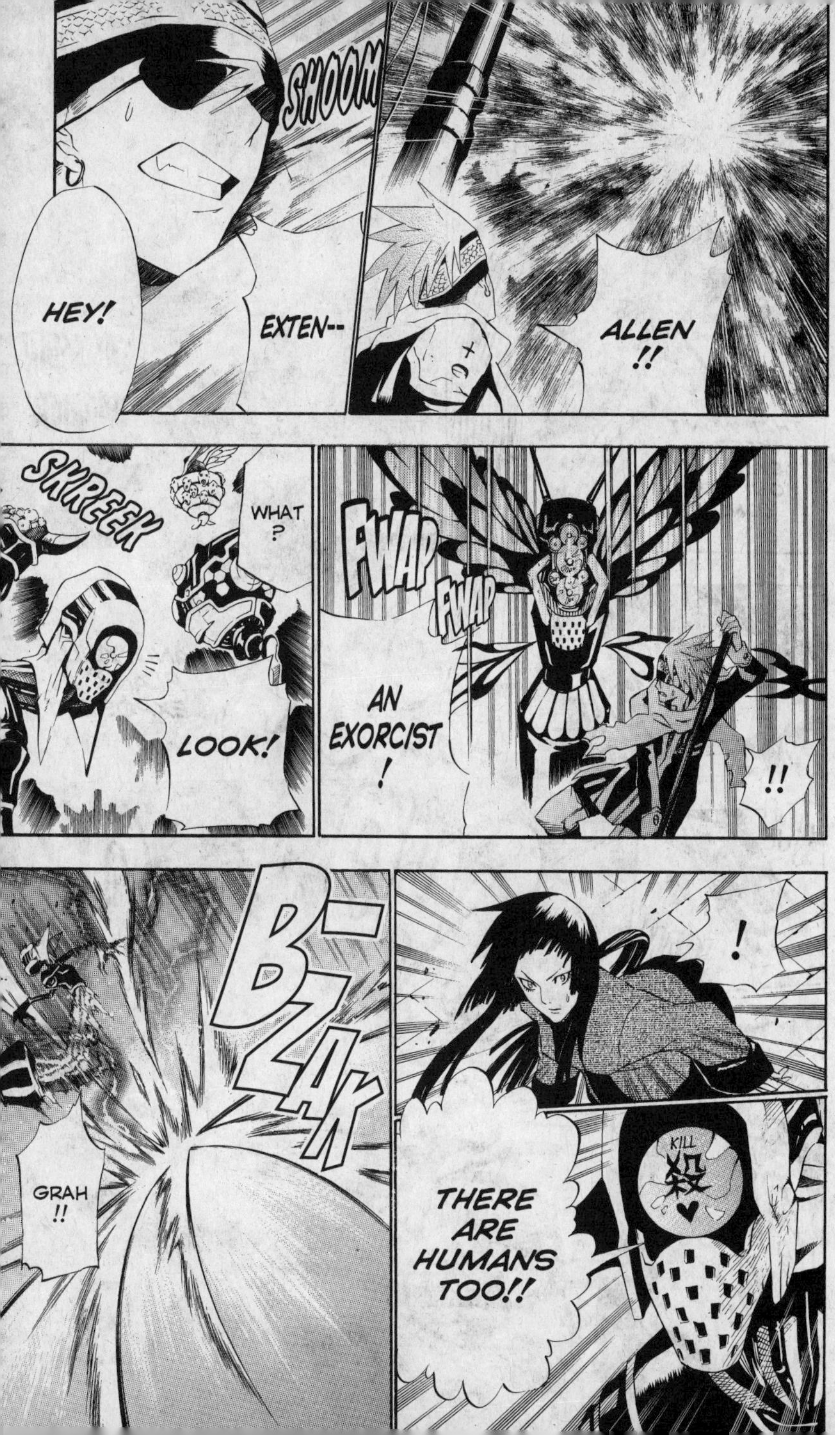
ALLEN !!
SHOOM
EXTEN--
HEY!
FWAP
FWAP
!!
AN EXORCIST !
WHAT ?
SKREEEK
LOOK!
!
KILL
THERE ARE HUMANS TOO!!
B-ZAK
GRAH !!

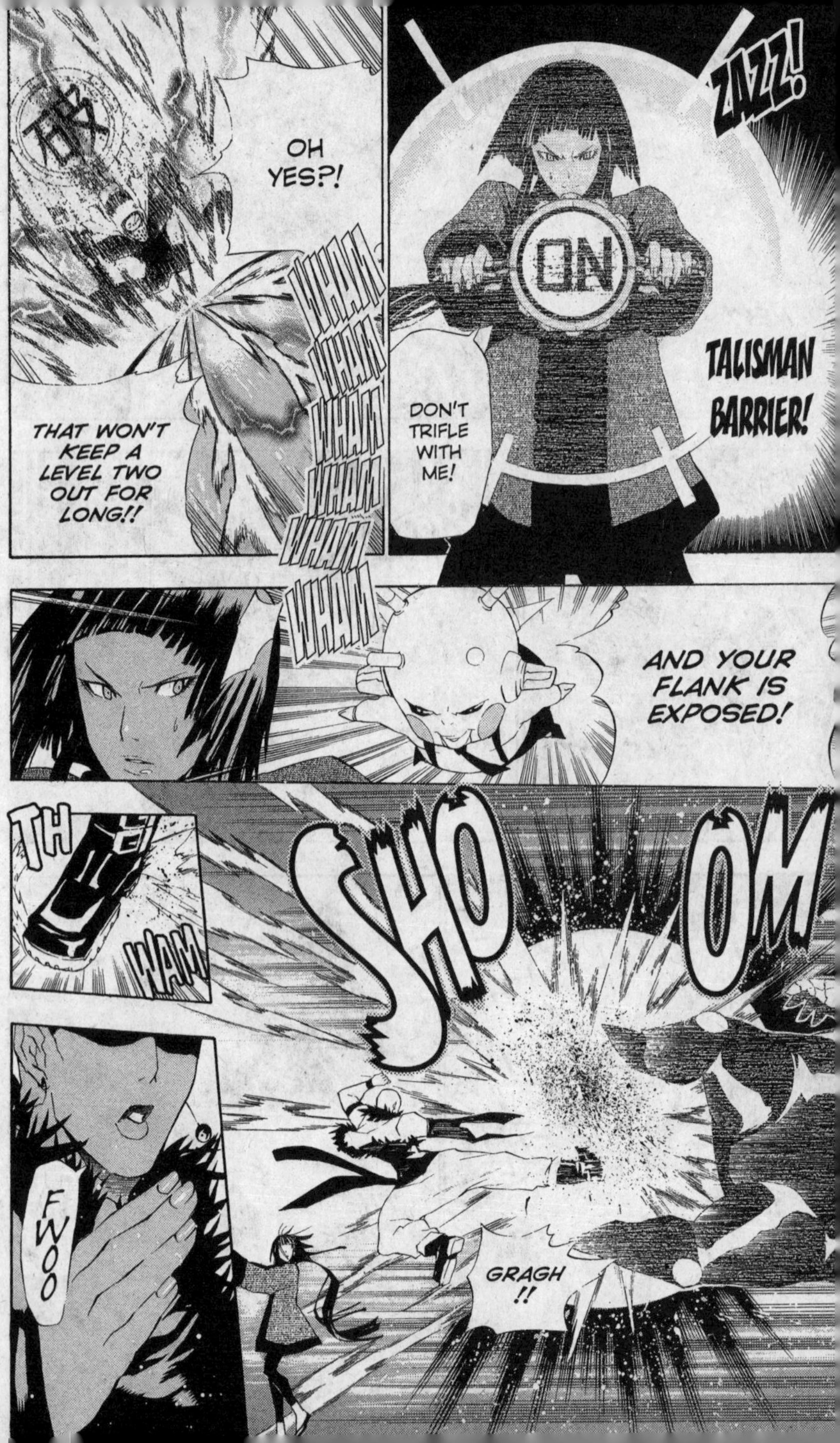
ZAZZ!
ON
TALISMAN BARRIER!
OH YES?!
DON'T TRIFLE WITH ME!
THAT WON'T KEEP A LEVEL TWO OUT FOR LONG!!
WHAM WHAM WHAM WHAM WHAM WHAM
AND YOUR FLANK IS EXPOSED!
SHOOM
TH WAM
GRAGH !!
FWOO

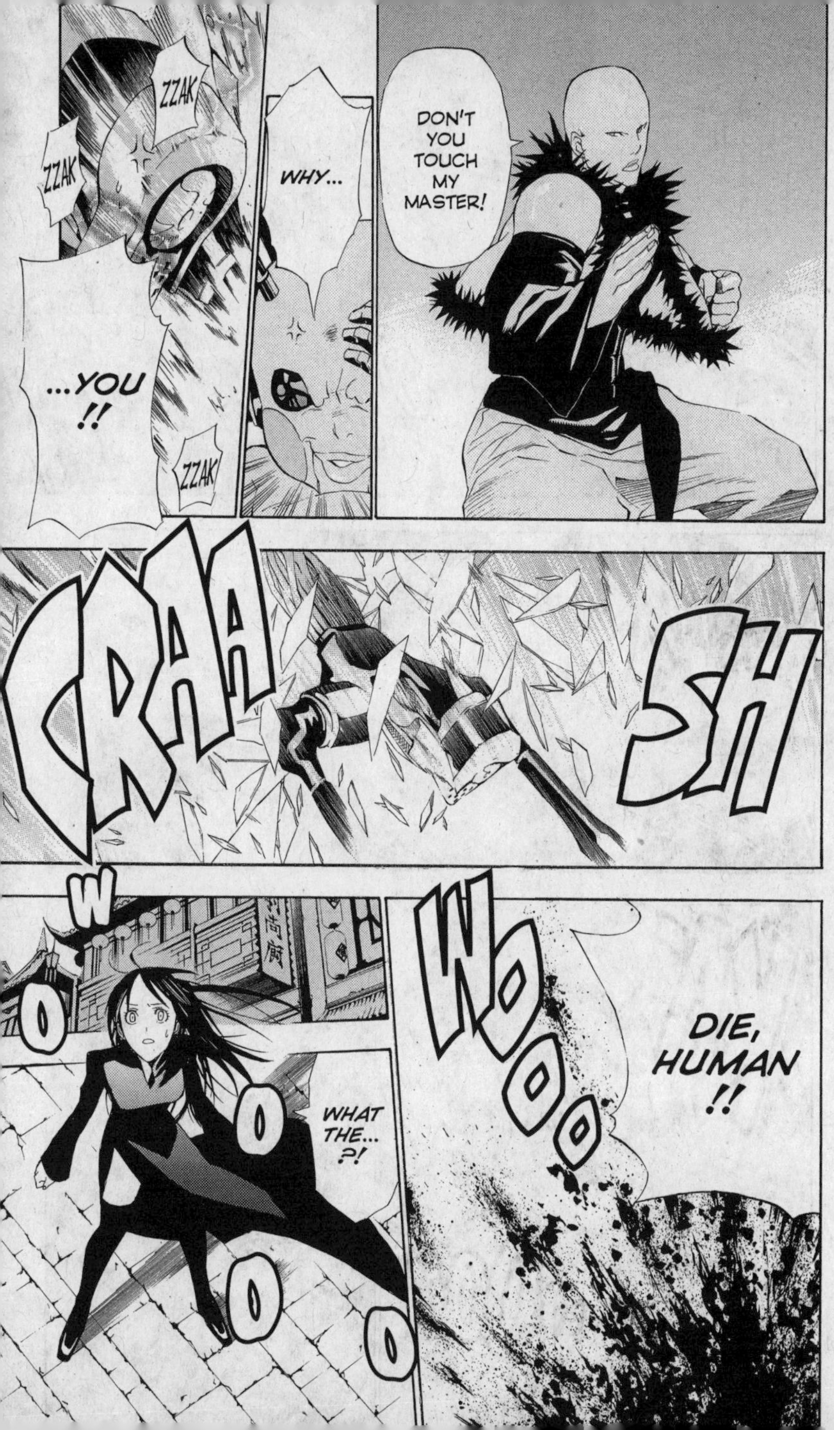
DON'T YOU TOUCH MY MASTER!
WHY...
ZZAK
ZZAK
...YOU !!
ZZAK
CRAASH
WOOOO
DIE, HUMAN !!
WOOOOO
WHAT THE... ?!

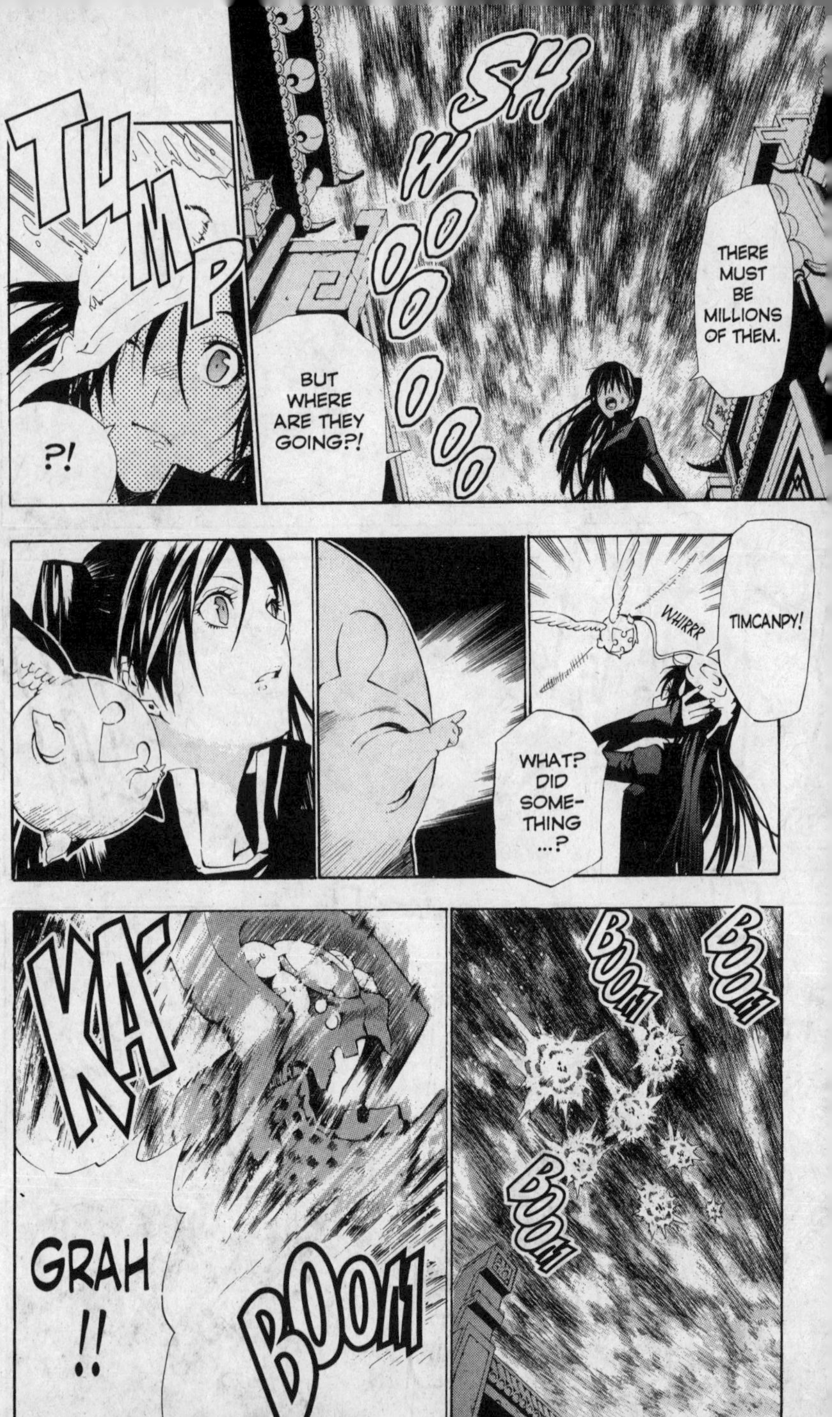
THERE MUST BE MILLIONS OF THEM.
SHWOOOOOOOO
BUT WHERE ARE THEY GOING?!
TUMP
?!
TIMCANPY!
WHIRRR
WHAT? DID SOMETHING ...?
BOOM
BOOM
BOOM
KA-
BOOM
GRAH !!

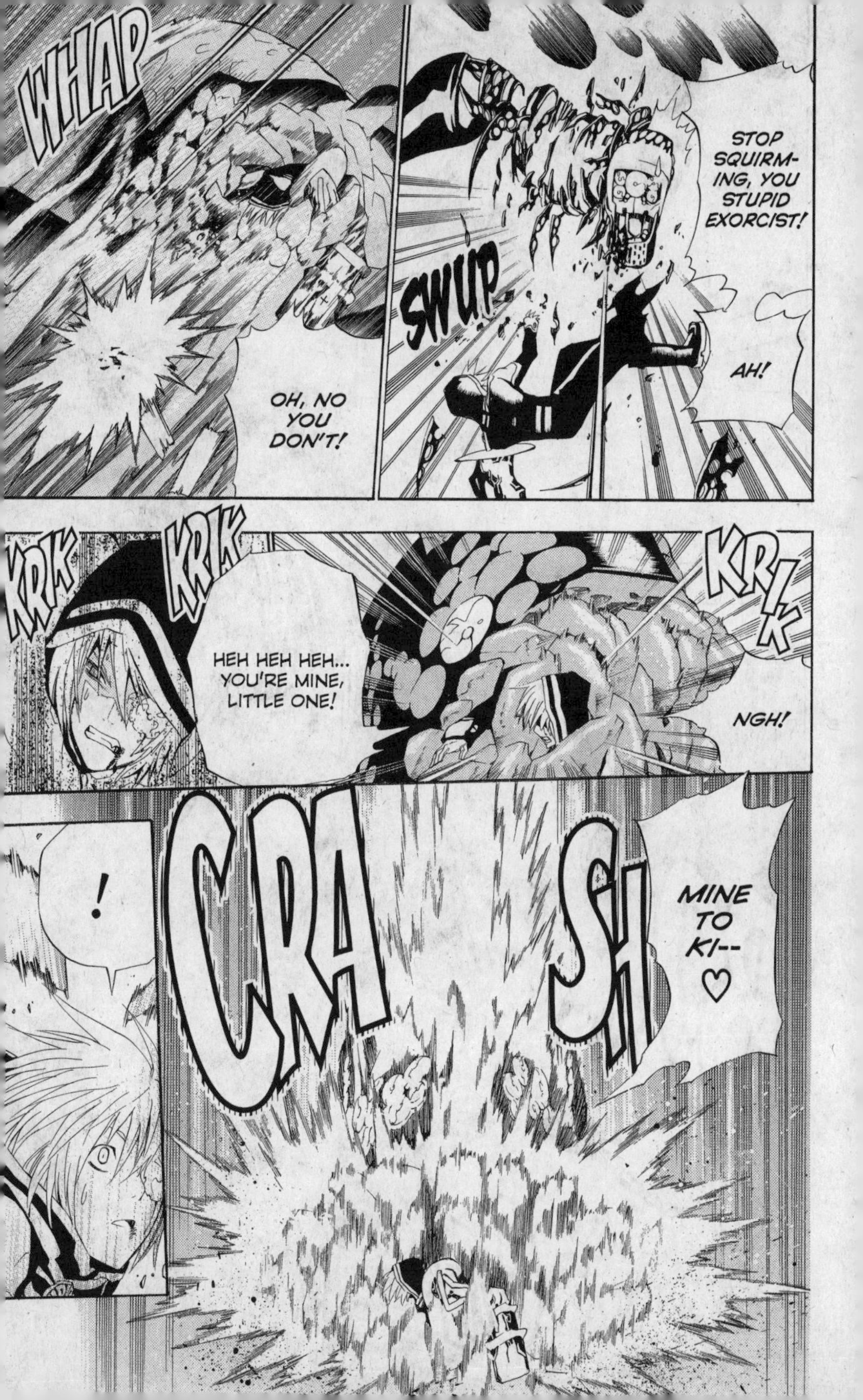

STOP SQUIRMING, YOU STUPID EXORCIST!
SWUP
AH!
WHAP
OH, NO YOU DON'T!
KRIK
NGH!
KRIK
KRIK
HEH HEH HEH... YOU'RE MINE, LITTLE ONE!
MINE TO KI-- ♥
CRASH
!

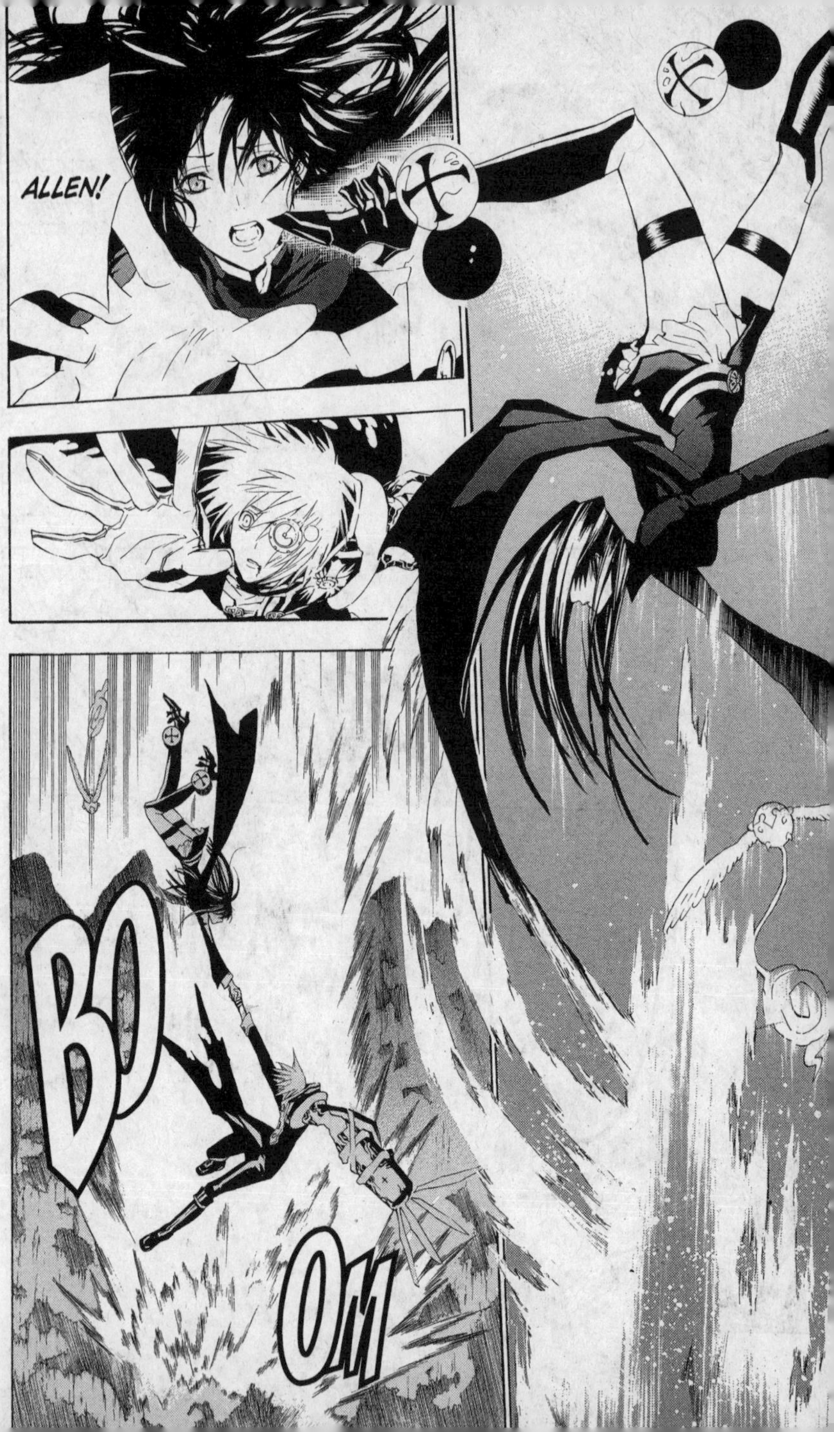
ALLEN!
BOOM

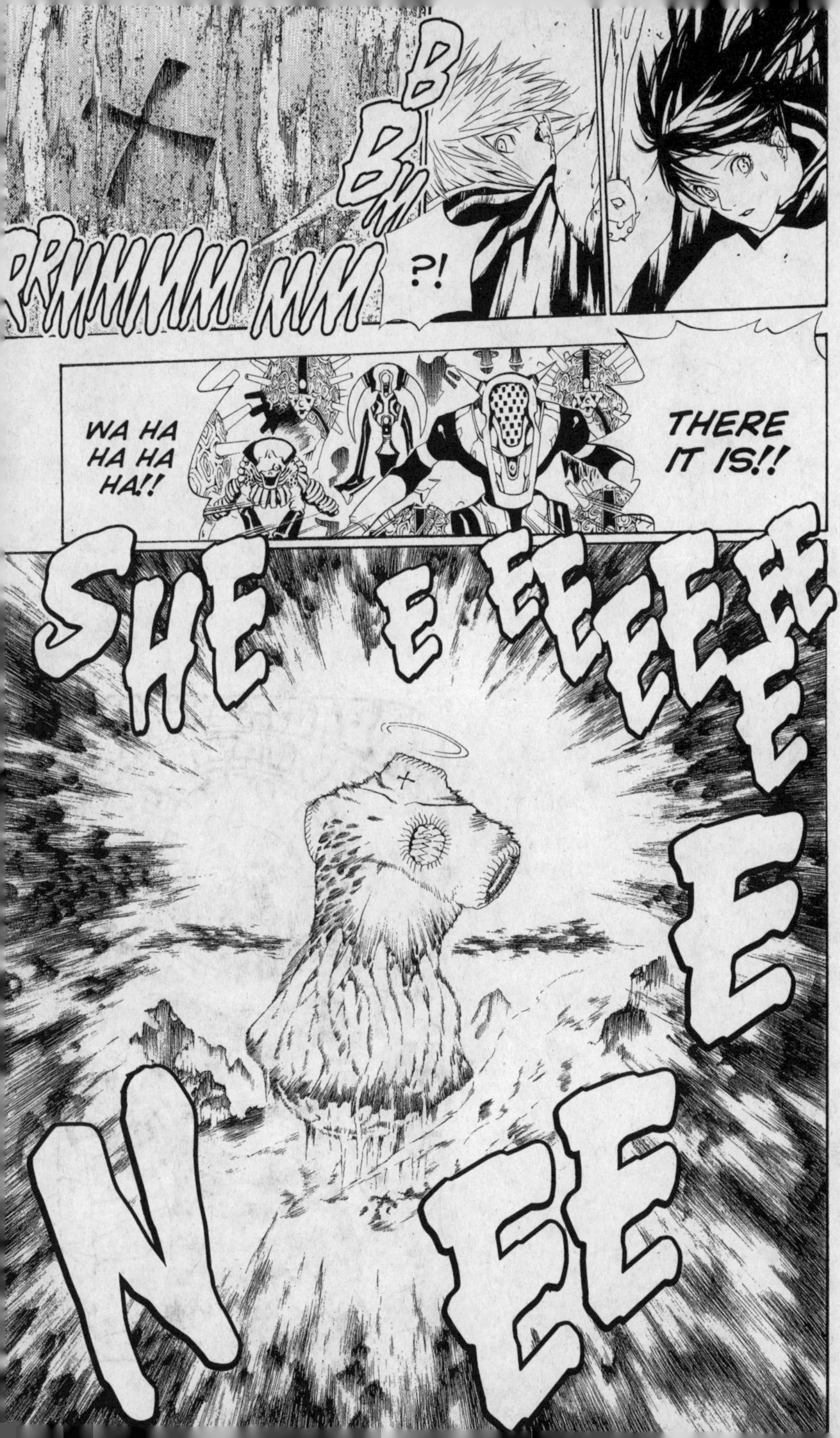
?!
THERE IT IS!!
WA HA HA HA HA!!
SHEEEEEEEEE
NEE

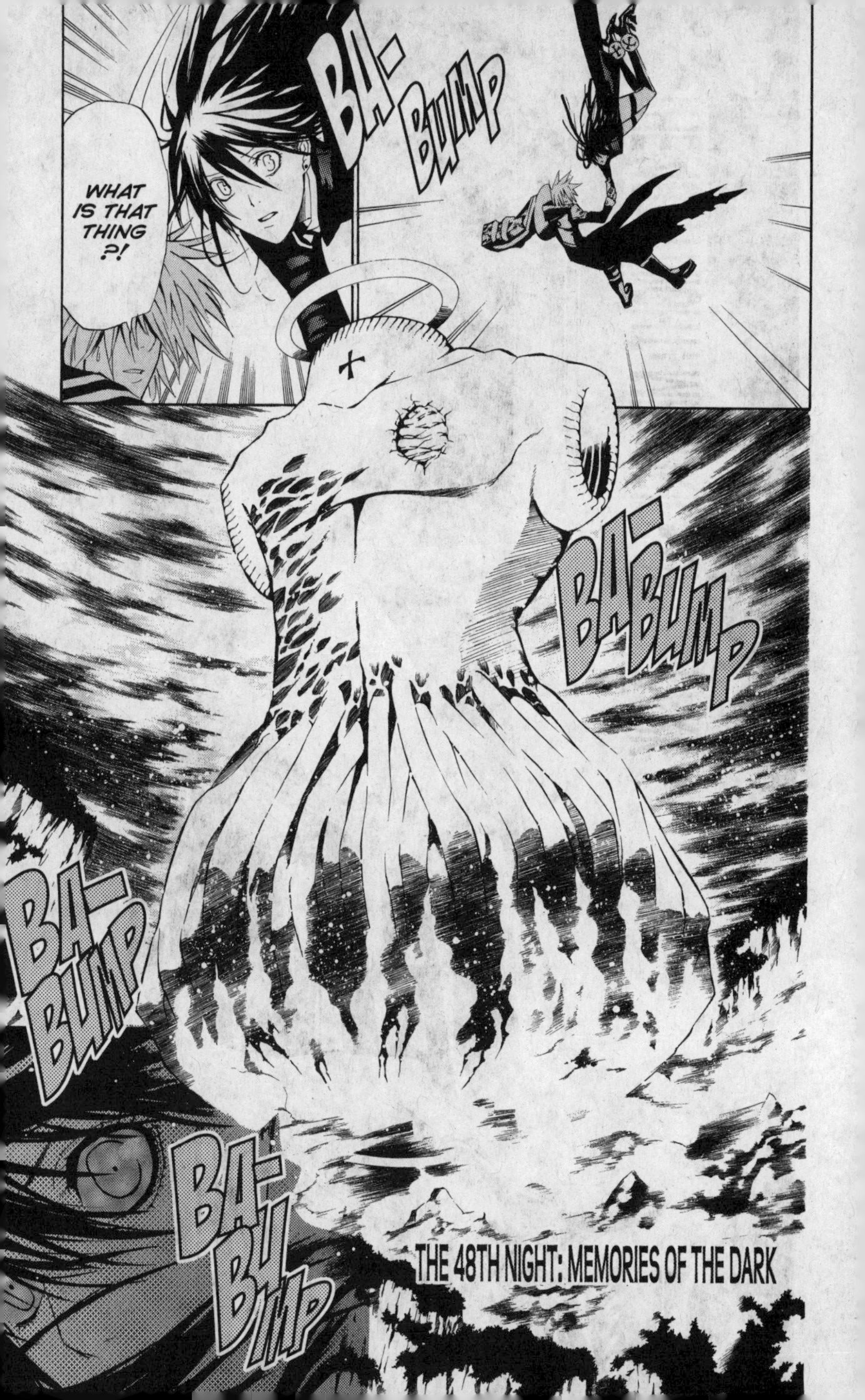
BA-BUMP
WHAT IS THAT THING?!
BA-BUMP
BA-BUMP
BA-BU-BUMP
THE 48TH NIGHT: MEMORIES OF THE DARK

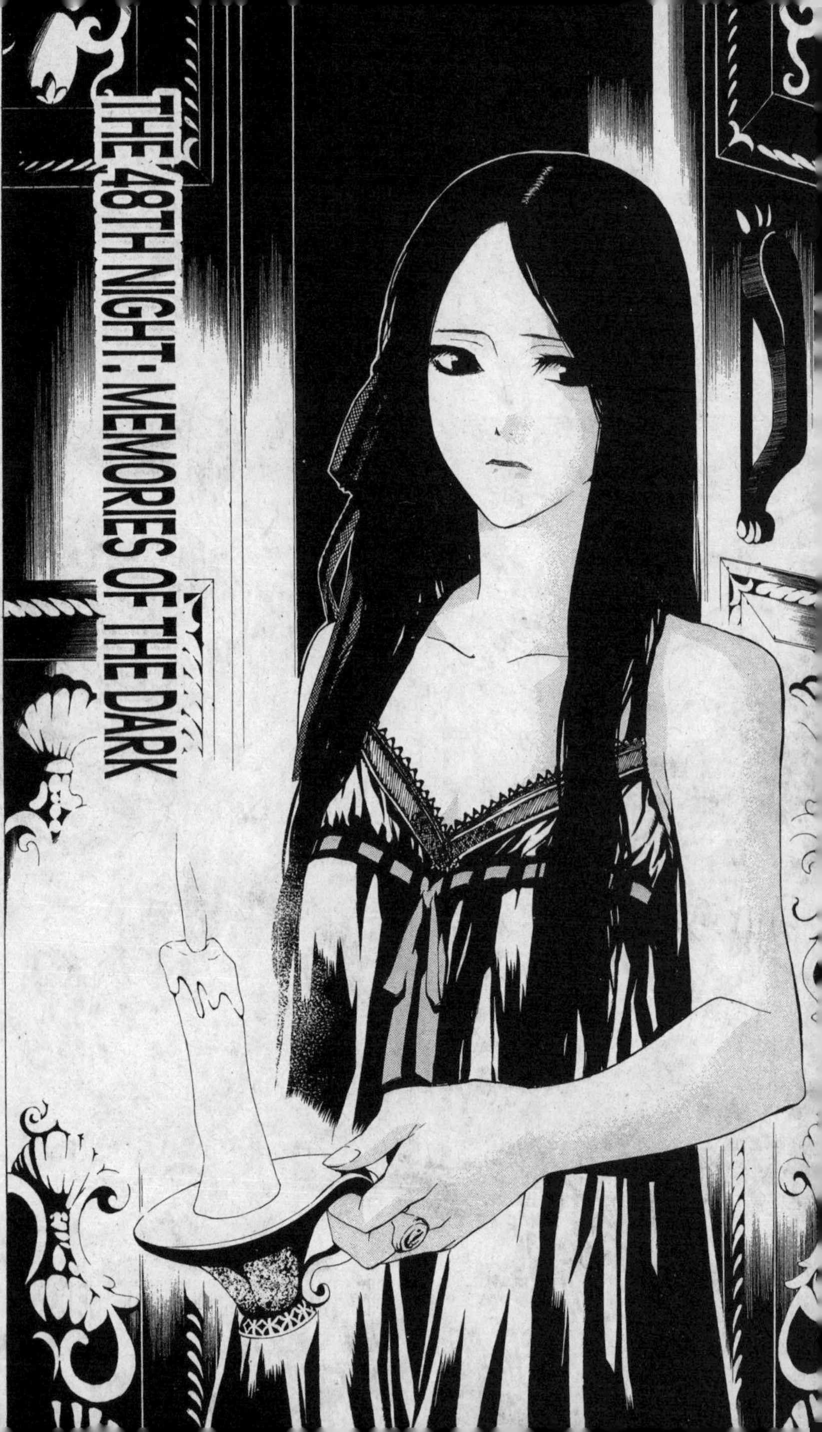
THE 48TH NIGHT: MEMORIES OF THE DARK

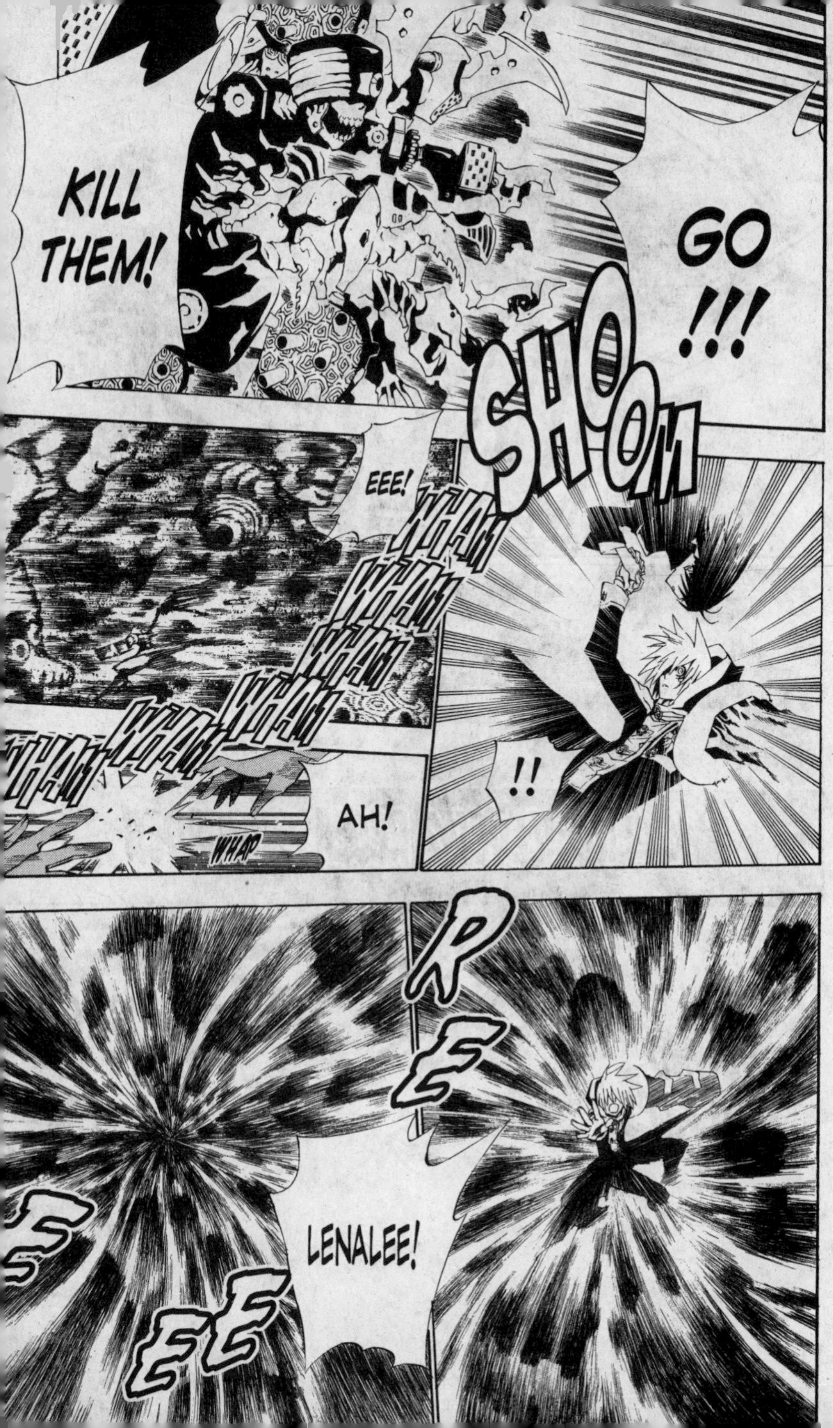
GO!!!
SHOOM
KILL THEM!
!!
EEE!
WHAM WHAM WHAM WHAM WHAM WHAM WHAM
AH!
WHAP
REEEE
LENALEE!

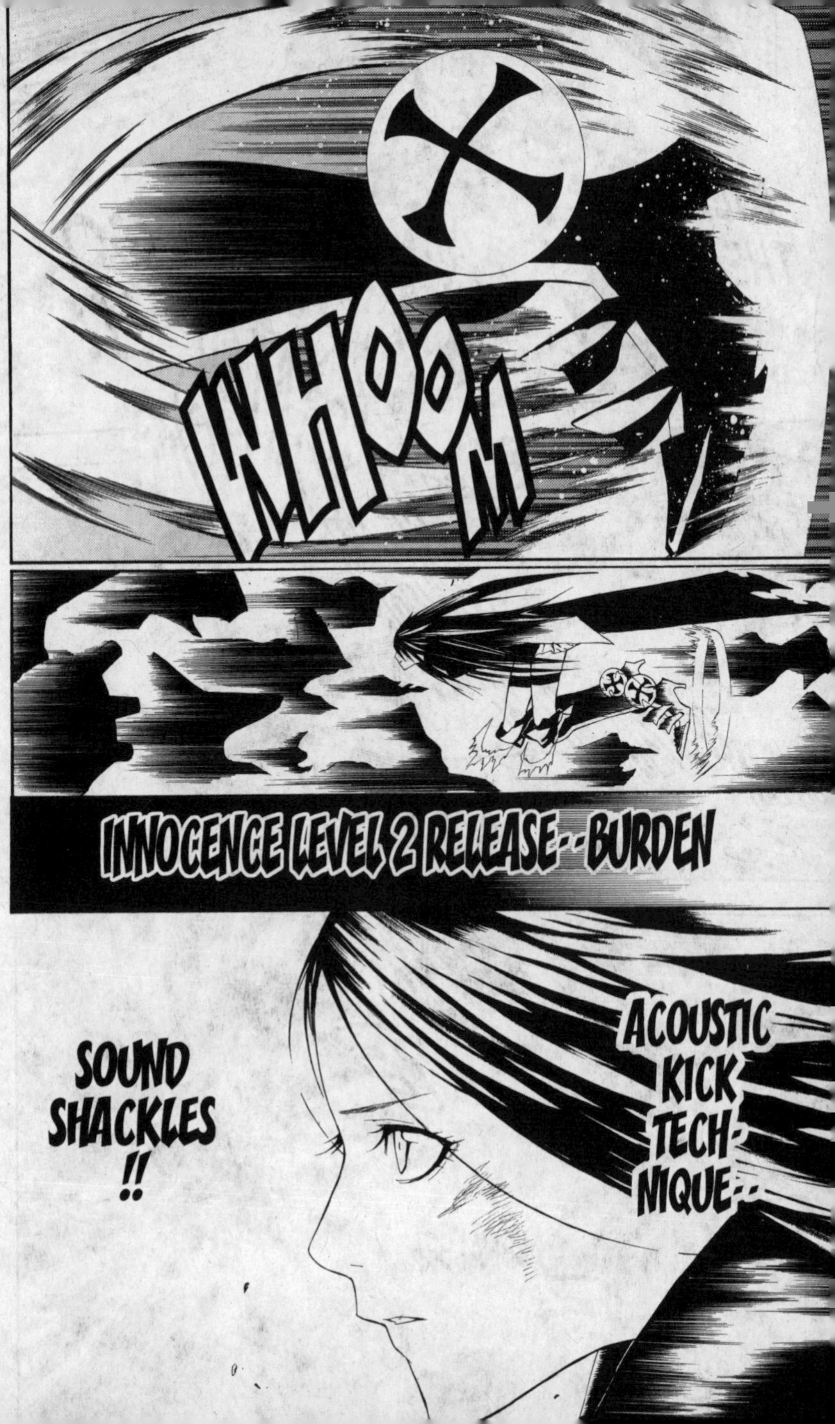
WHOOM
INNOCENCE LEVEL 2 RELEASE--BURDEN
ACOUSTIC KICK TECH-NIQUE--
SOUND SHACKLES !!

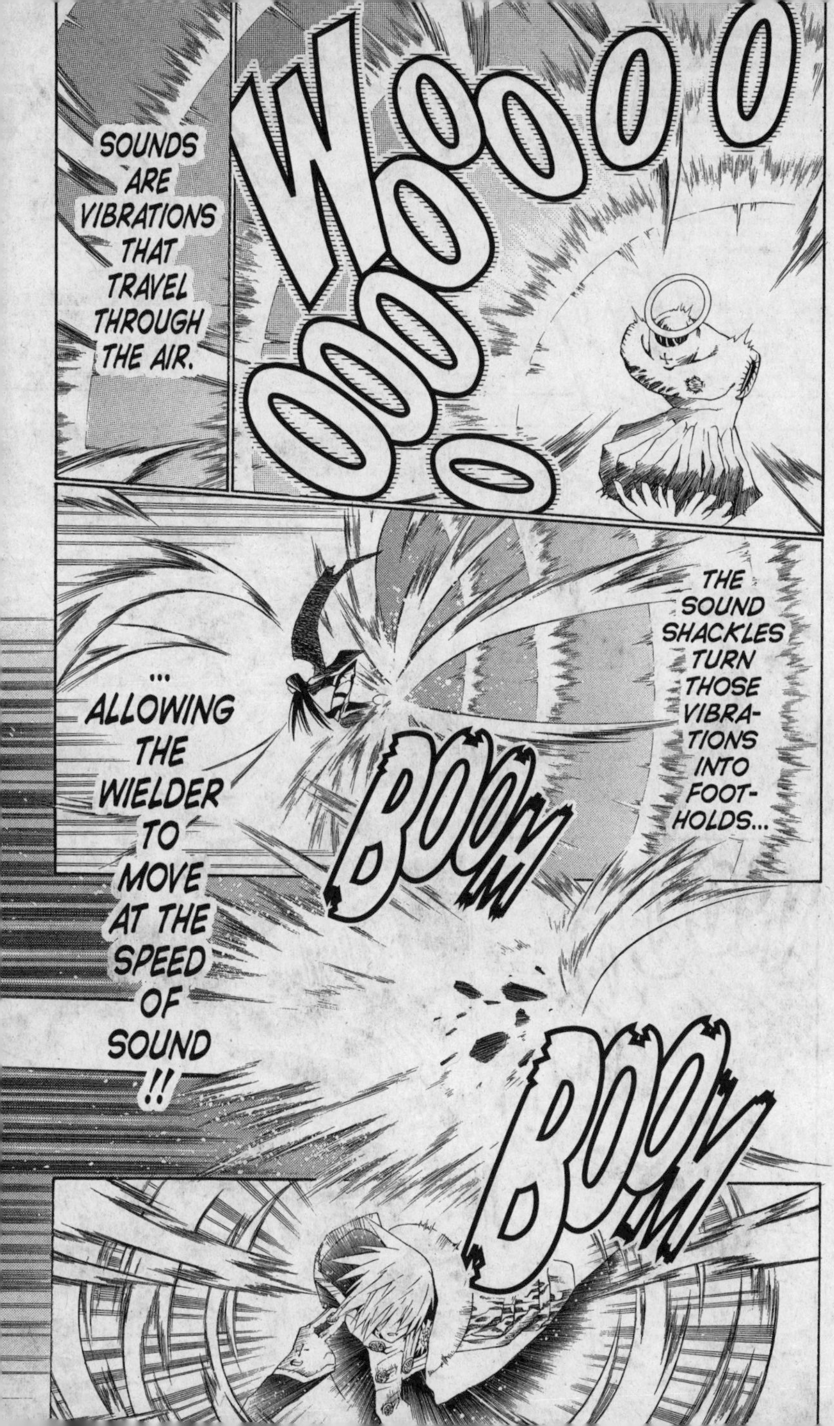

WOOOOOOOOOO
SOUNDS ARE VIBRATIONS THAT TRAVEL THROUGH THE AIR.
THE SOUND SHACKLES TURN THOSE VIBRA-TIONS INTO FOOT-HOLDS...
... ALLOWING THE WIELDER TO MOVE AT THE SPEED OF SOUND !!
BOOM
BOOM

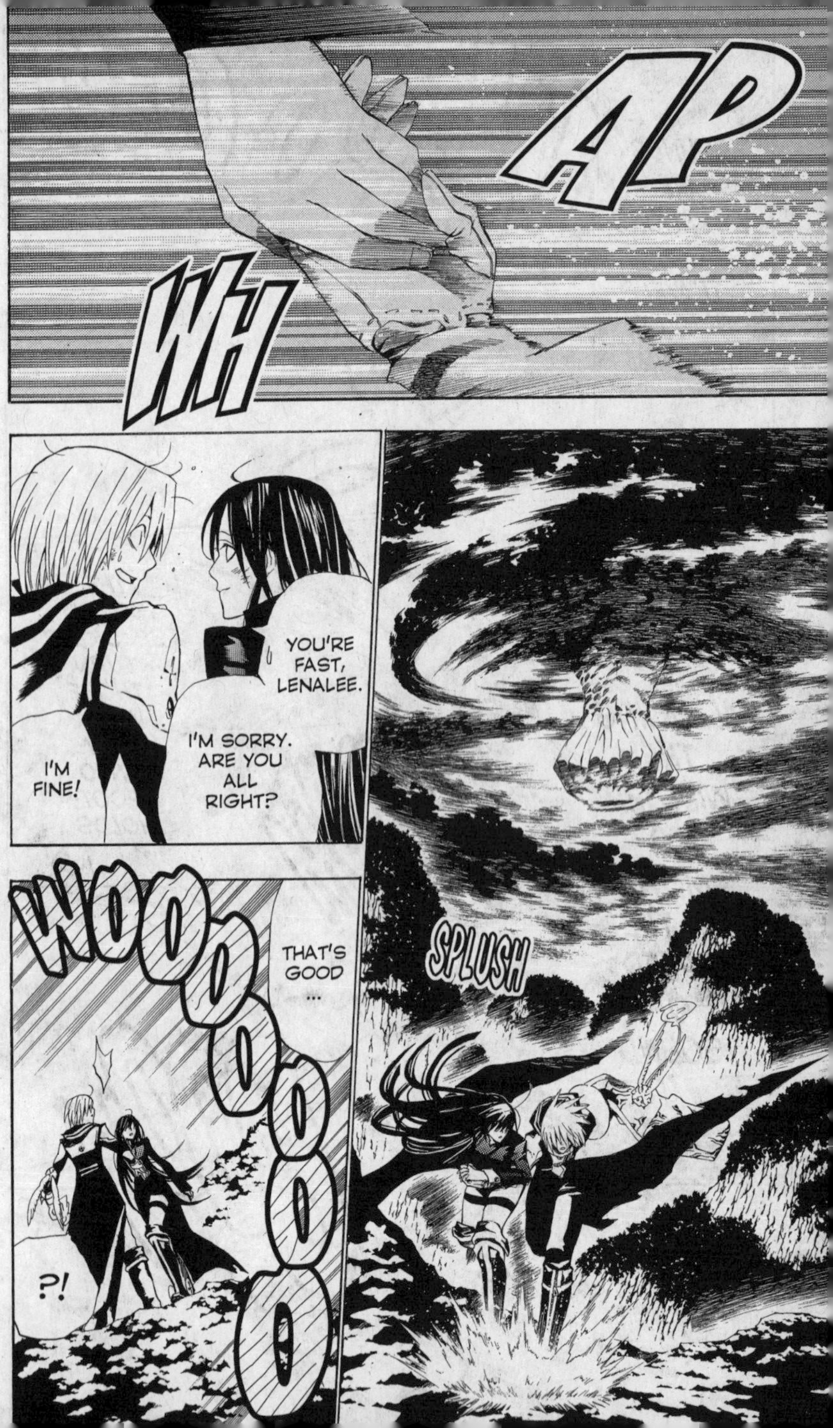
WHAP
SPLUSH
YOU'RE FAST, LENALEE.
I'M SORRY. ARE YOU ALL RIGHT?
I'M FINE!
WOOOOOOOOOO
THAT'S GOOD ...
?!

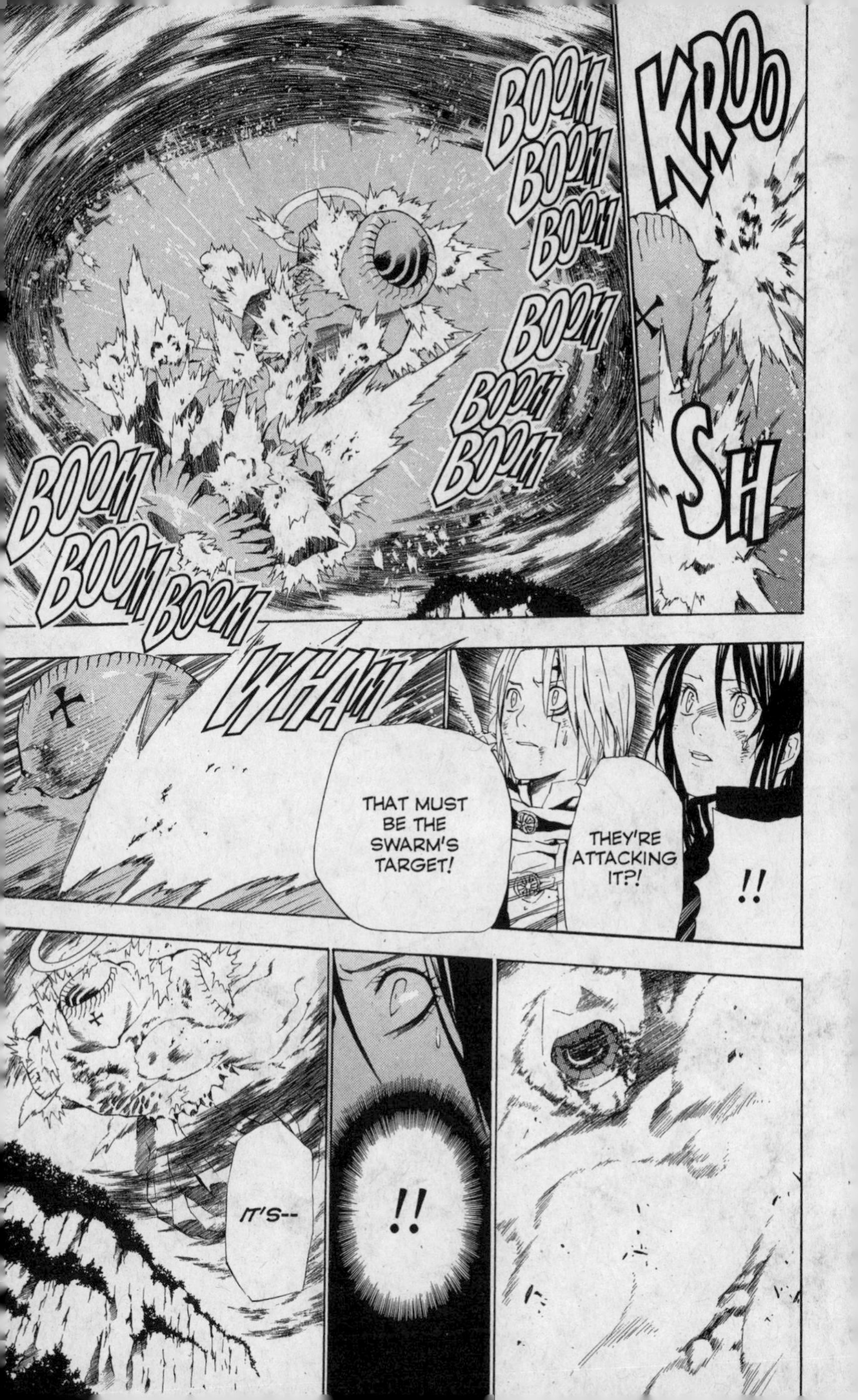
KROO
SH
BOOM
BOOM
BOOM
BOOM
BOOM
BOOM
BOOM
BOOM
BOOM
WHAM
!!
THEY'RE ATTACKING IT?!
THAT MUST BE THE SWARM'S TARGET!
!!
IT'S--

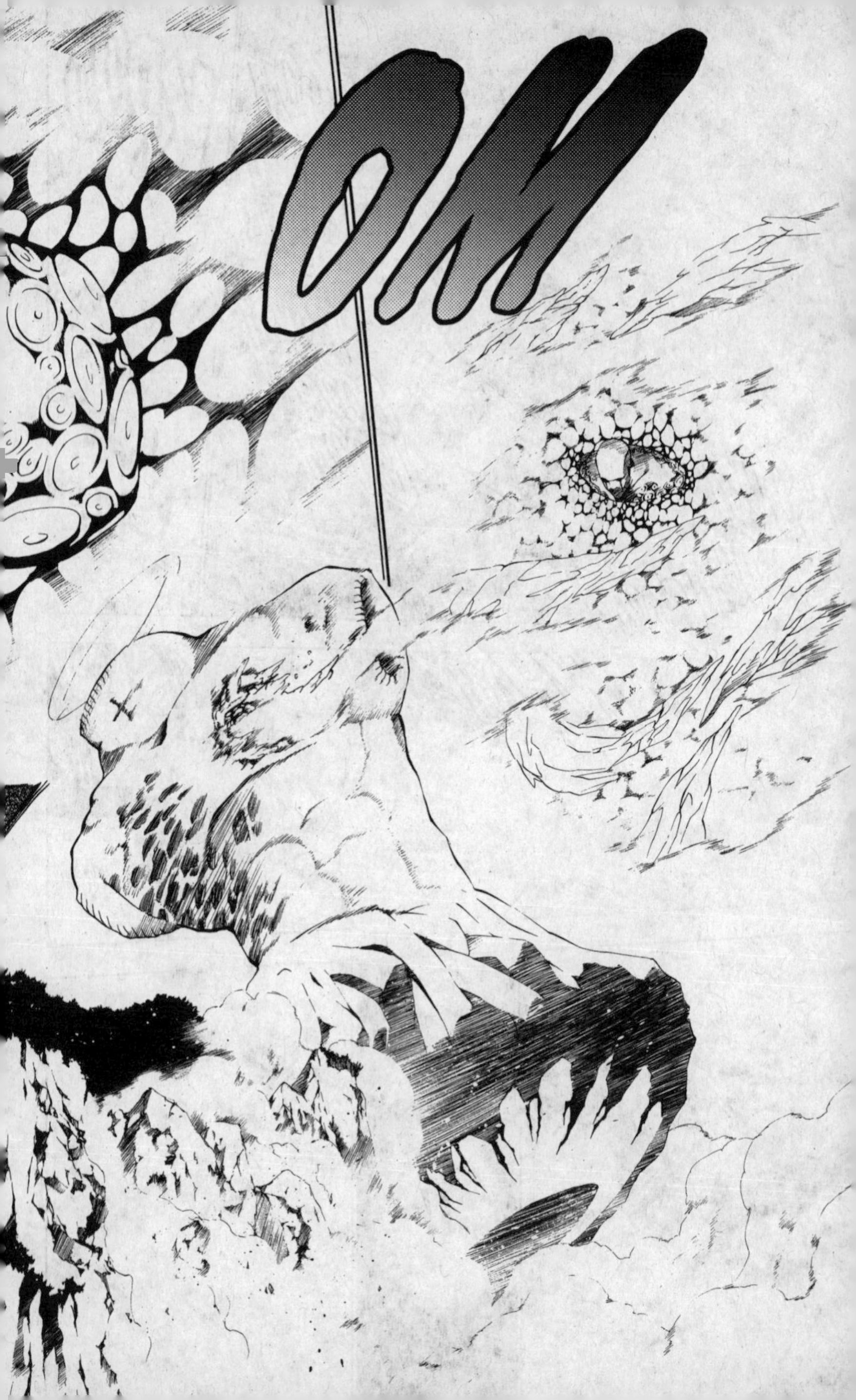
OM

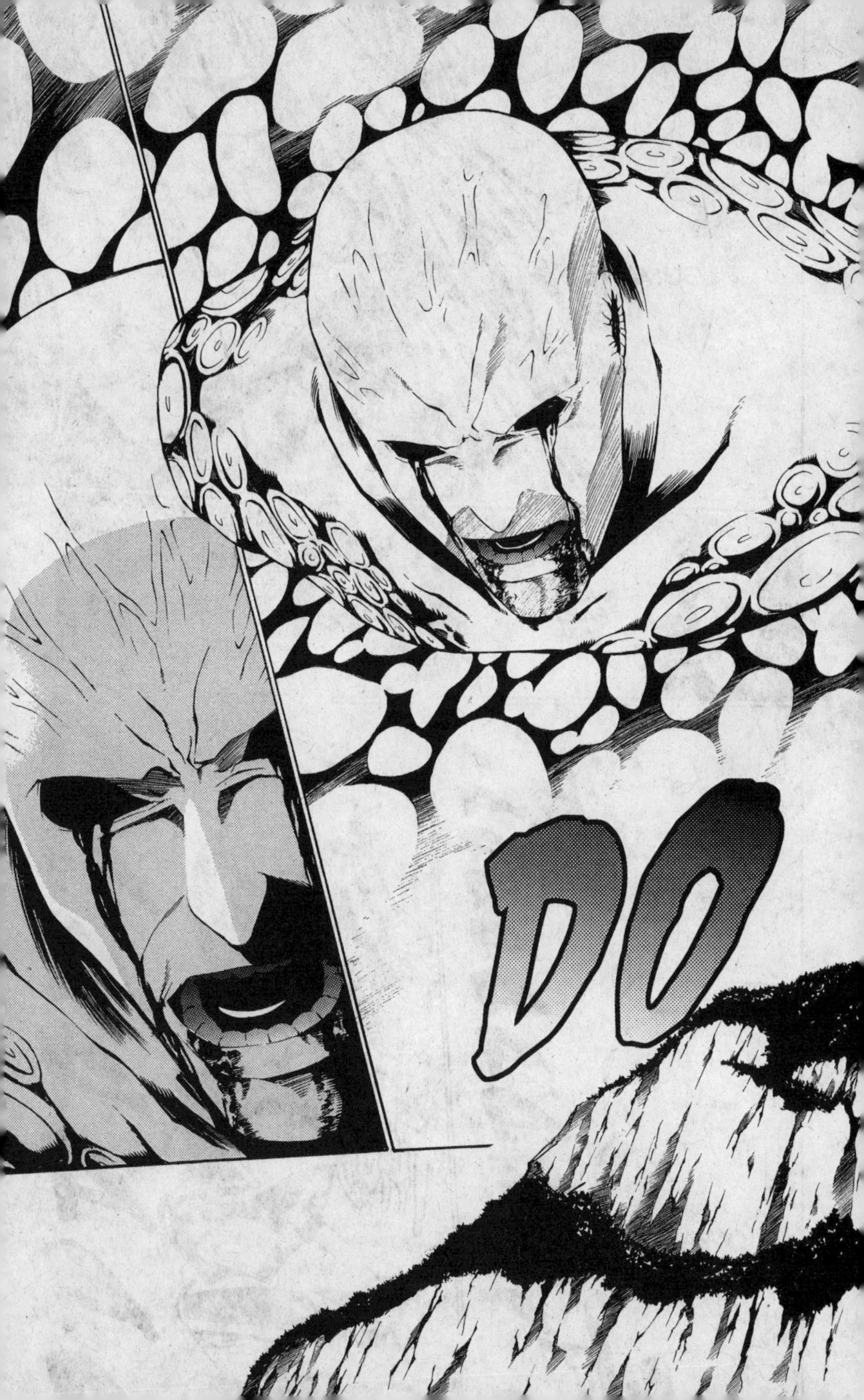
DO

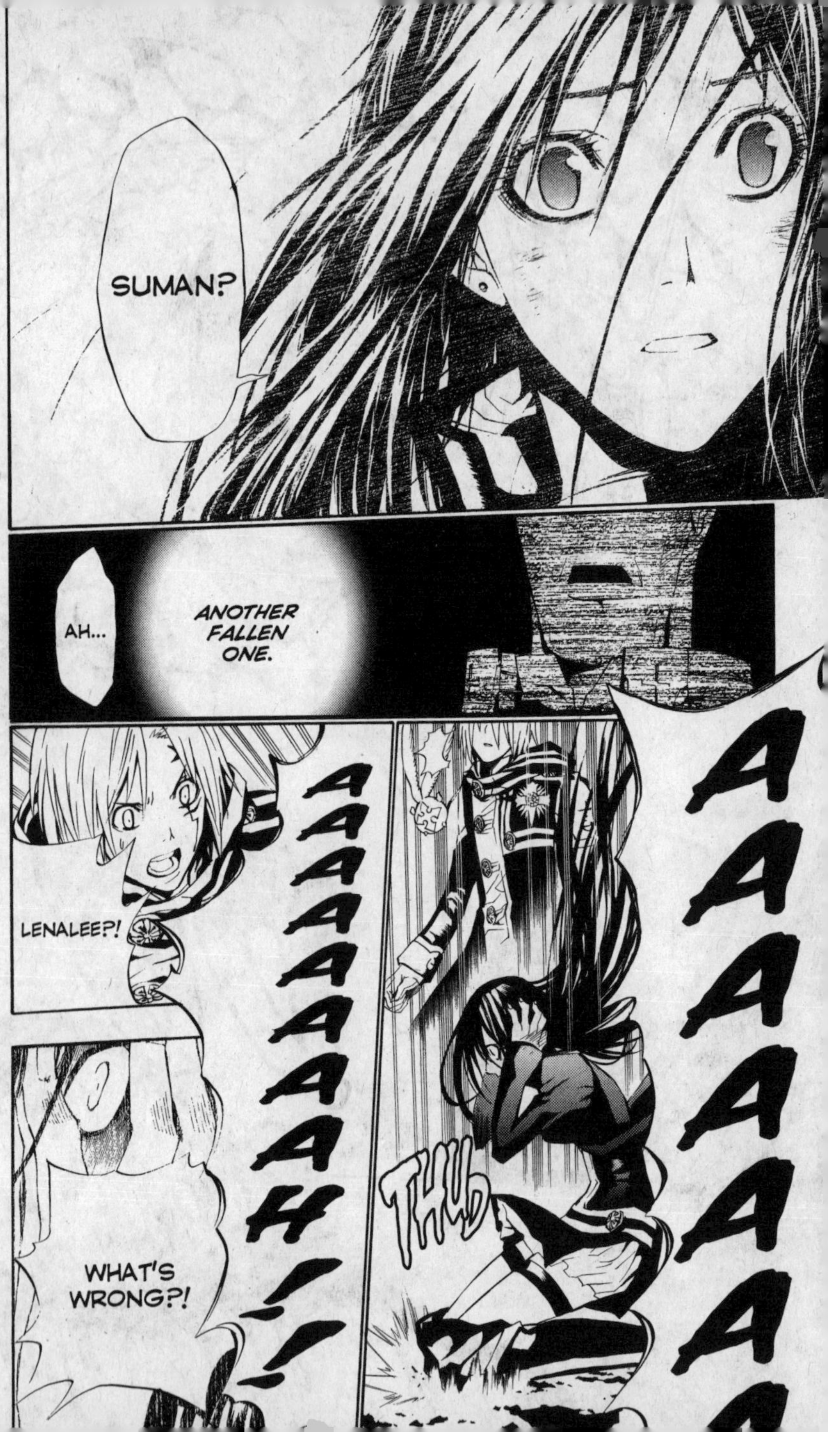
SUMAN?
ANOTHER FALLEN ONE.
AH...
AAAAAAAAAA
AAAAAAAAAAH!!!
THUD
LENALEE?!
WHAT'S WRONG?!

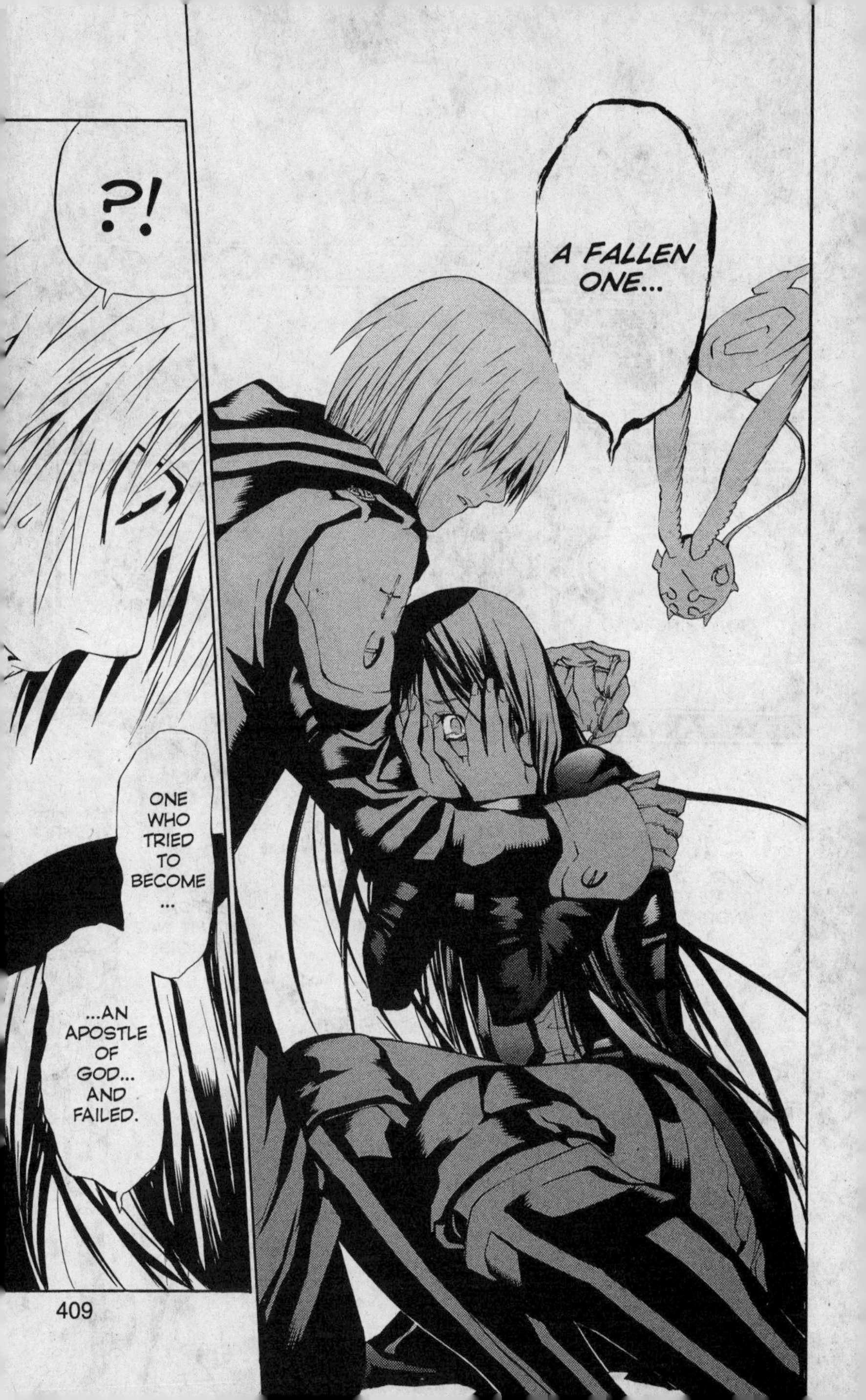
A FALLEN ONE...
?!
ONE WHO TRIED TO BECOME ...
...AN APOSTLE OF GOD... AND FAILED.

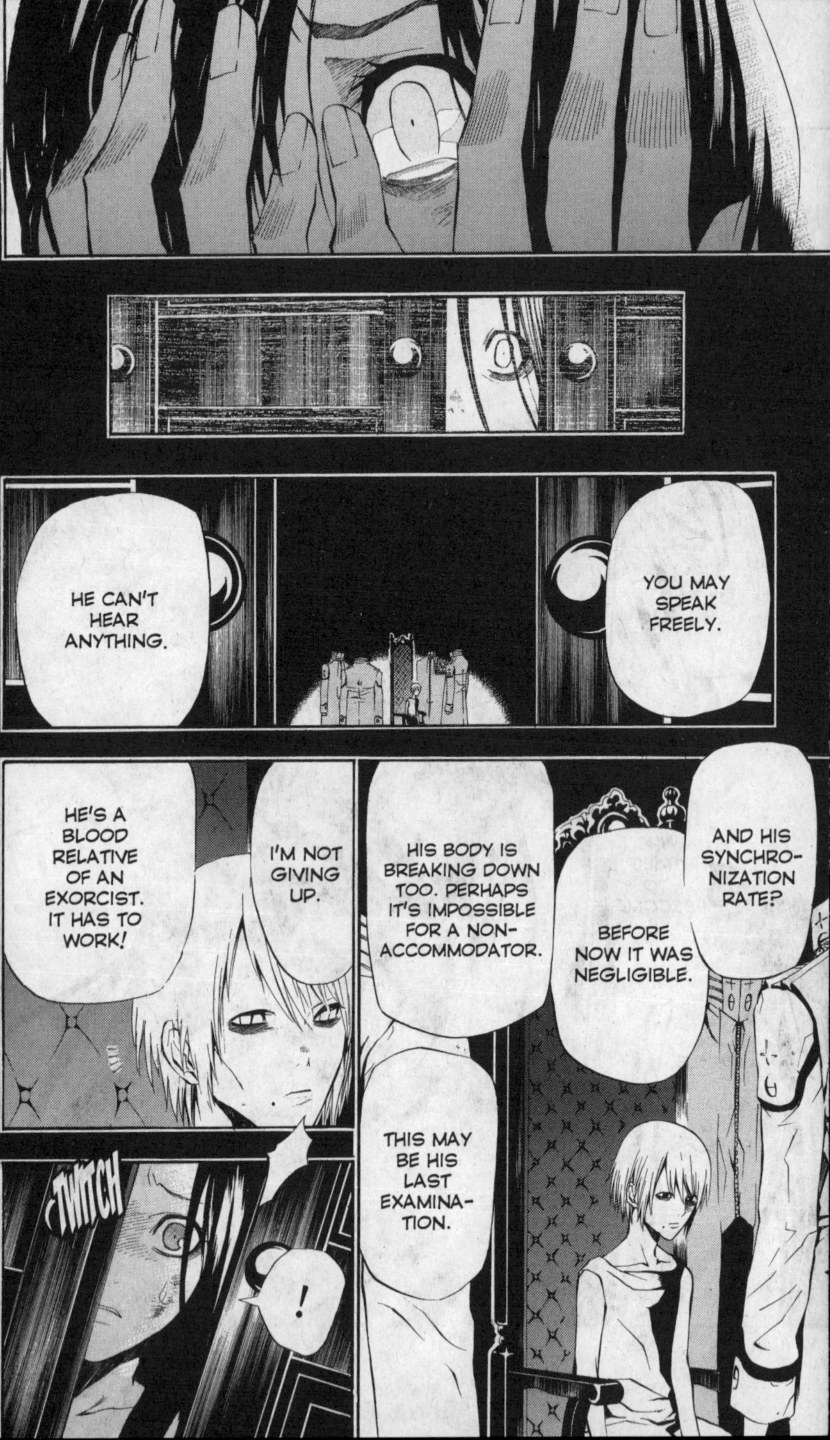
YOU MAY SPEAK FREELY.
HE CAN'T HEAR ANYTHING.
AND HIS SYNCHRONIZATION RATE?
BEFORE NOW IT WAS NEGLIGIBLE.
HIS BODY IS BREAKING DOWN TOO. PERHAPS IT'S IMPOSSIBLE FOR A NON-ACCOMMODATOR.
THIS MAY BE HIS LAST EXAMINATION.
I'M NOT GIVING UP.
HE'S A BLOOD RELATIVE OF AN EXORCIST. IT HAS TO WORK!
TWITCH
!

KLAK

IT'S TIME. LET'S BEGIN.

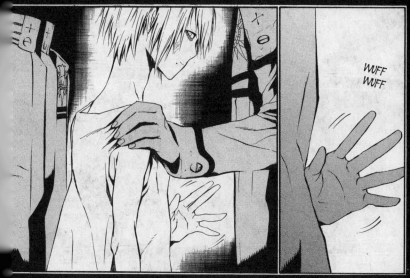

WUFF WUFF

...IMPLANT AN INNOCENCE IN HIM.

HEVLASKA...

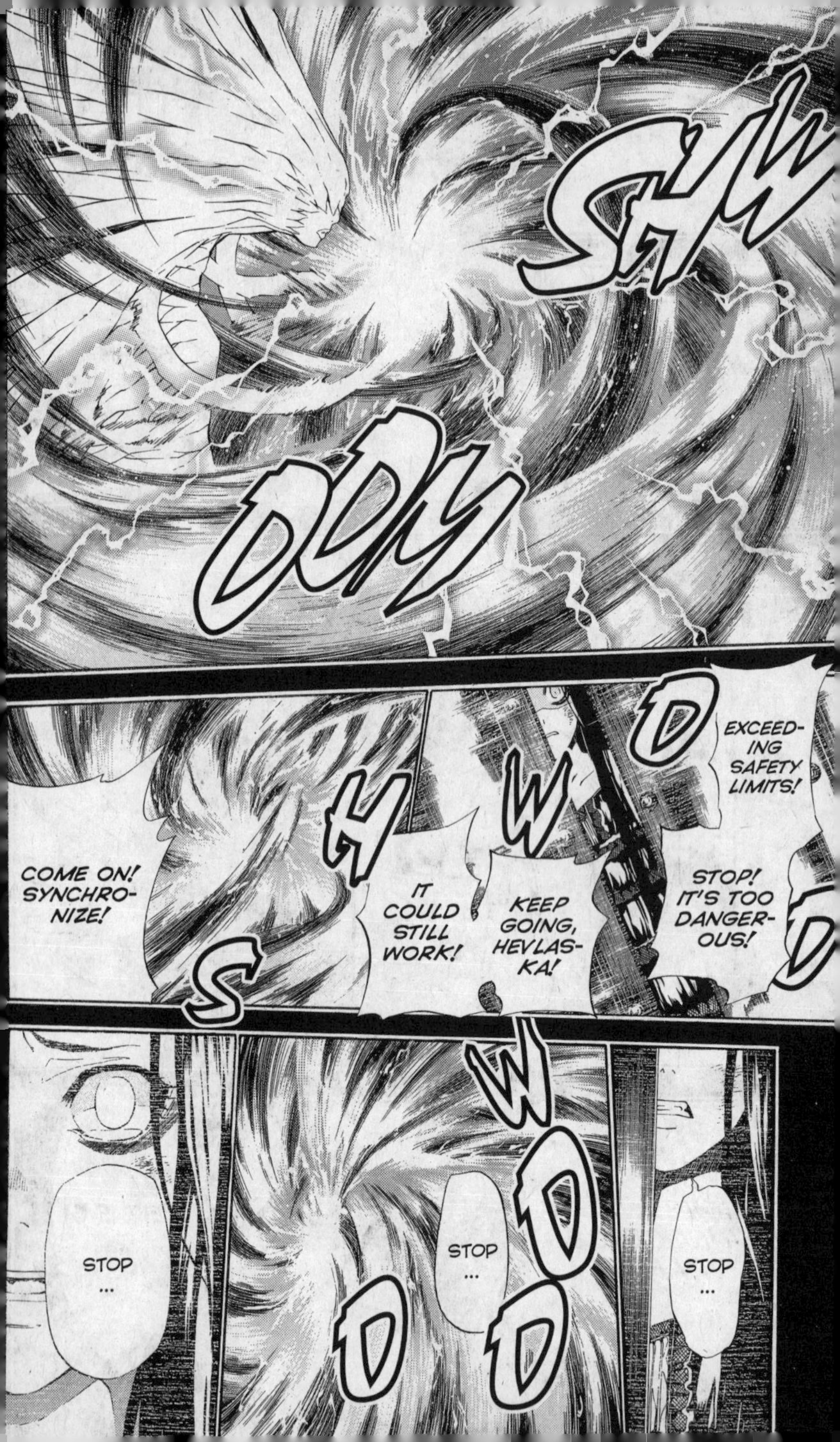

SHU
EXCEEDING SAFETY LIMITS!
STOP! IT'S TOO DANGEROUS!
KEEP GOING, HEVLASKA!
IT COULD STILL WORK!
COME ON! SYNCHRONIZE!
STOP ...
STOP ...
STOP ...

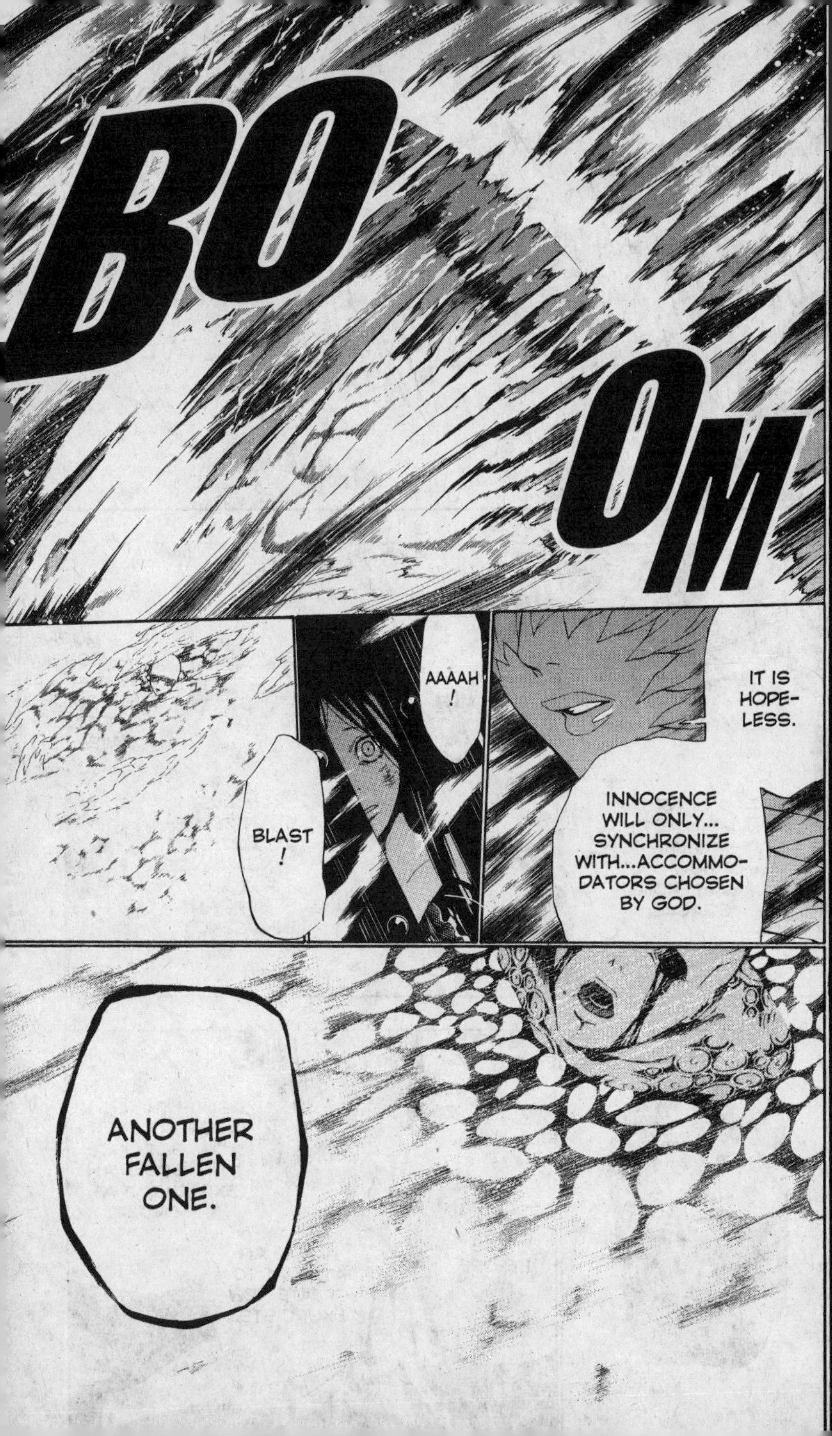
BOOM
IT IS HOPELESS.
INNOCENCE WILL ONLY... SYNCHRONIZE WITH...ACCOMMODATORS CHOSEN BY GOD.
AAAAH!
BLAST!
ANOTHER FALLEN ONE.

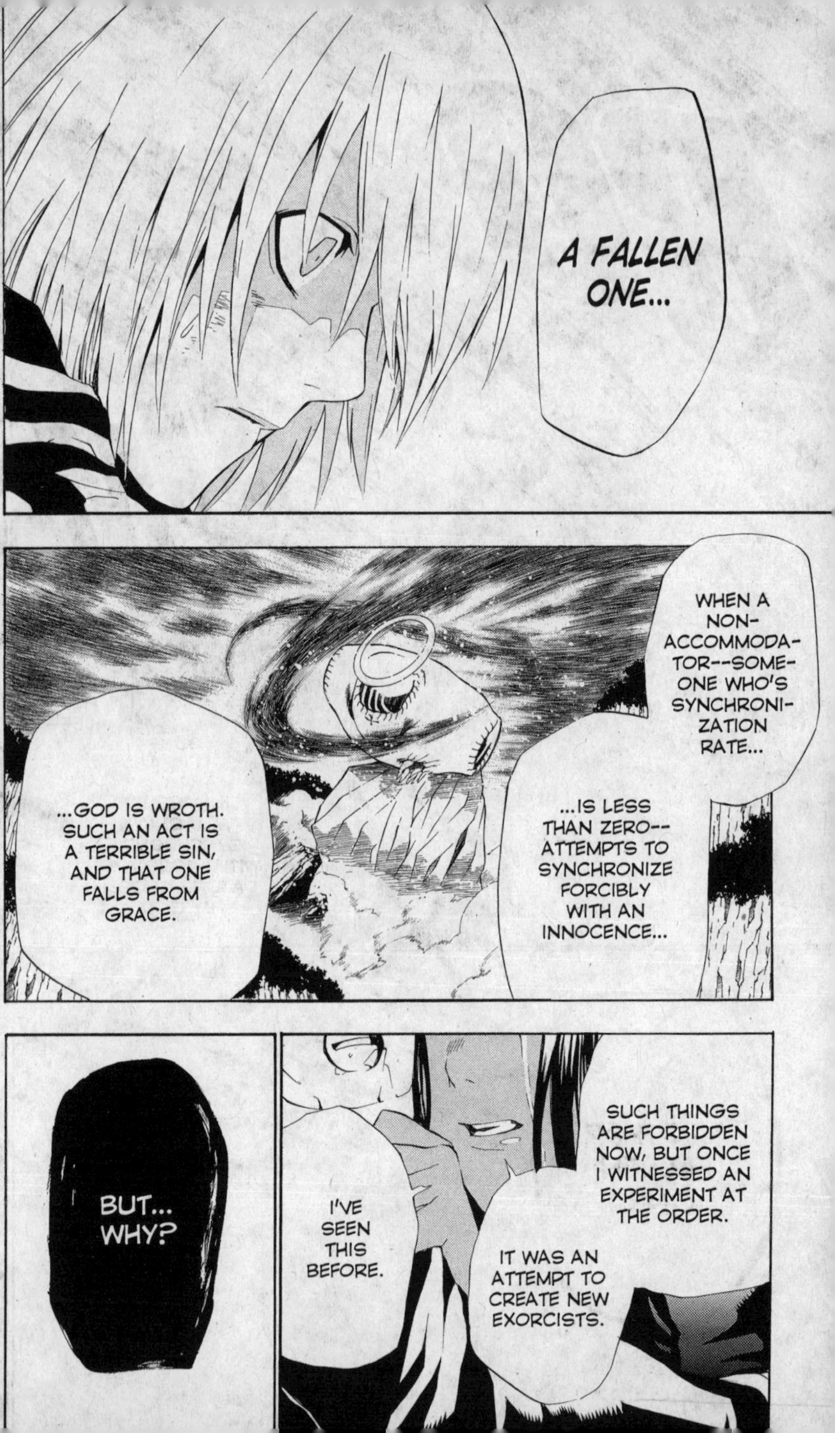
A FALLEN ONE...
WHEN A NON-ACCOMMODATOR--SOMEONE WHO'S SYNCHRONIZATION RATE...
...IS LESS THAN ZERO--ATTEMPTS TO SYNCHRONIZE FORCIBLY WITH AN INNOCENCE...
...GOD IS WROTH. SUCH AN ACT IS A TERRIBLE SIN, AND THAT ONE FALLS FROM GRACE.
SUCH THINGS ARE FORBIDDEN NOW, BUT ONCE I WITNESSED AN EXPERIMENT AT THE ORDER.
I'VE SEEN THIS BEFORE.
IT WAS AN ATTEMPT TO CREATE NEW EXORCISTS.
BUT... WHY?

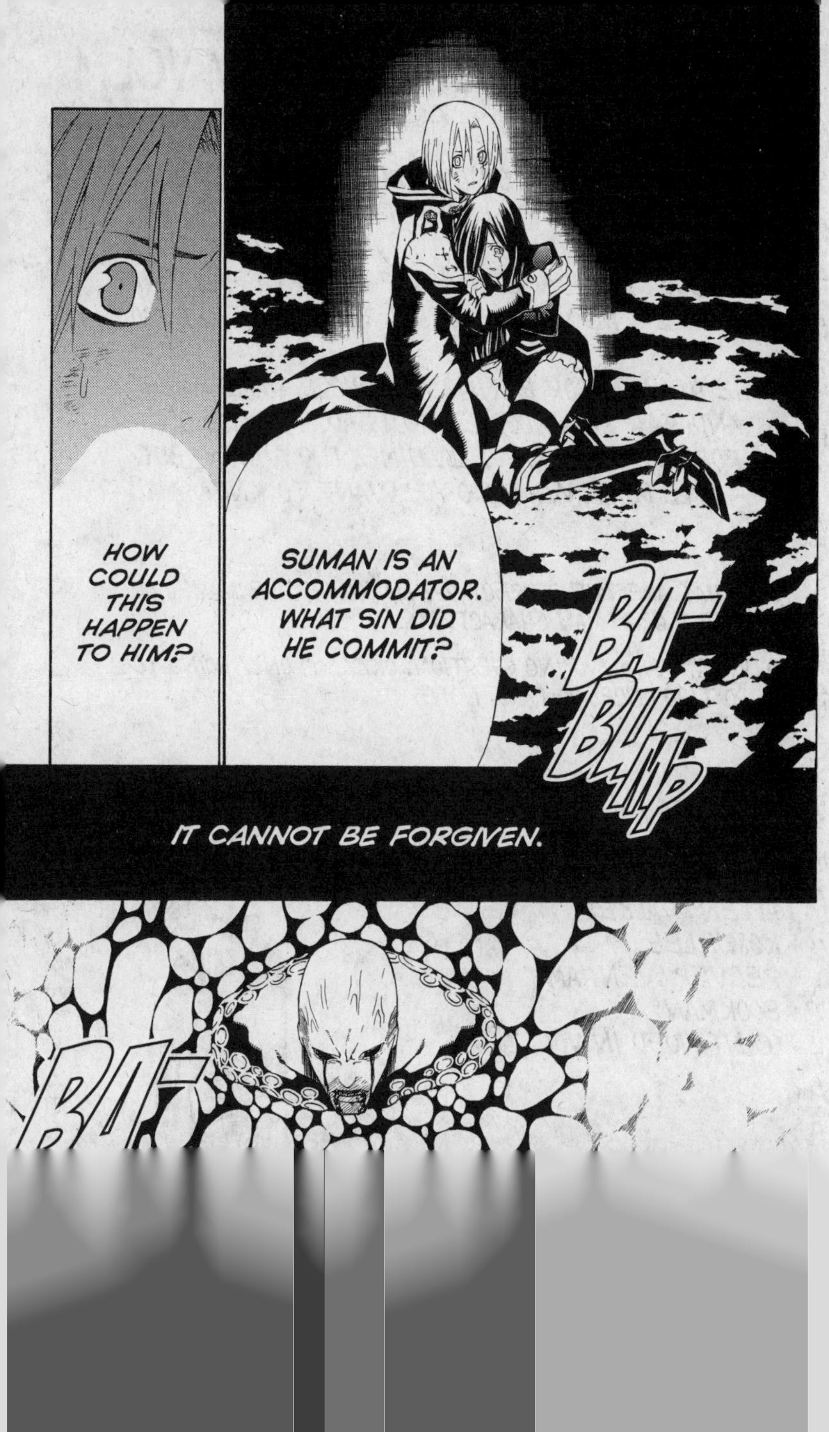
SUMAN IS AN ACCOMMODATOR. WHAT SIN DID HE COMMIT?
BA-BUMP
HOW COULD THIS HAPPEN TO HIM?
IT CANNOT BE FORGIVEN.
BA-

KOMUI'S DISCUSSION ROOM VOL. 1

HEY, WHAT AM I DOING HERE? YOU WANT ME TO ANSWER QUESTIONS FROM THE READERS? WHY ME? WHAT HAPPENED TO THAT HOSHINO GUY? A BELLYACHE? HOW LONG IS HE GOING TO MILK THAT EXCUSE? HE'S BEEN SAYING THAT SINCE VOL. 4!

HE SHOULD STOP EATING ALL THOSE HAMBURGERS AND EAT SOBA NOODLES INSTEAD. THEY'RE GOOD FOR YOU. REALLY. WELL, FINE, IT'S A PAIN, BUT I'LL DO IT. WHAT DO YOU WANT TO KNOW?

Q. WHAT ARE THE CORRECT SPELLINGS OF THE NAMES OF THE D.GRAY-MAN CHARACTERS?

A. WHAT AN ANNOYING QUESTION. OKAY, I'M ONLY GOING TO DO THIS ONCE, SO TAKE NOTE.

YU KANDA
LENALEE LEE
LAVI
ALLEN WALKER
KOMUI LEE
REEVER WENHAM
BOOKMAN
(CONTINUED IN VOL. 2)

THE 49TH NIGHT: SIN

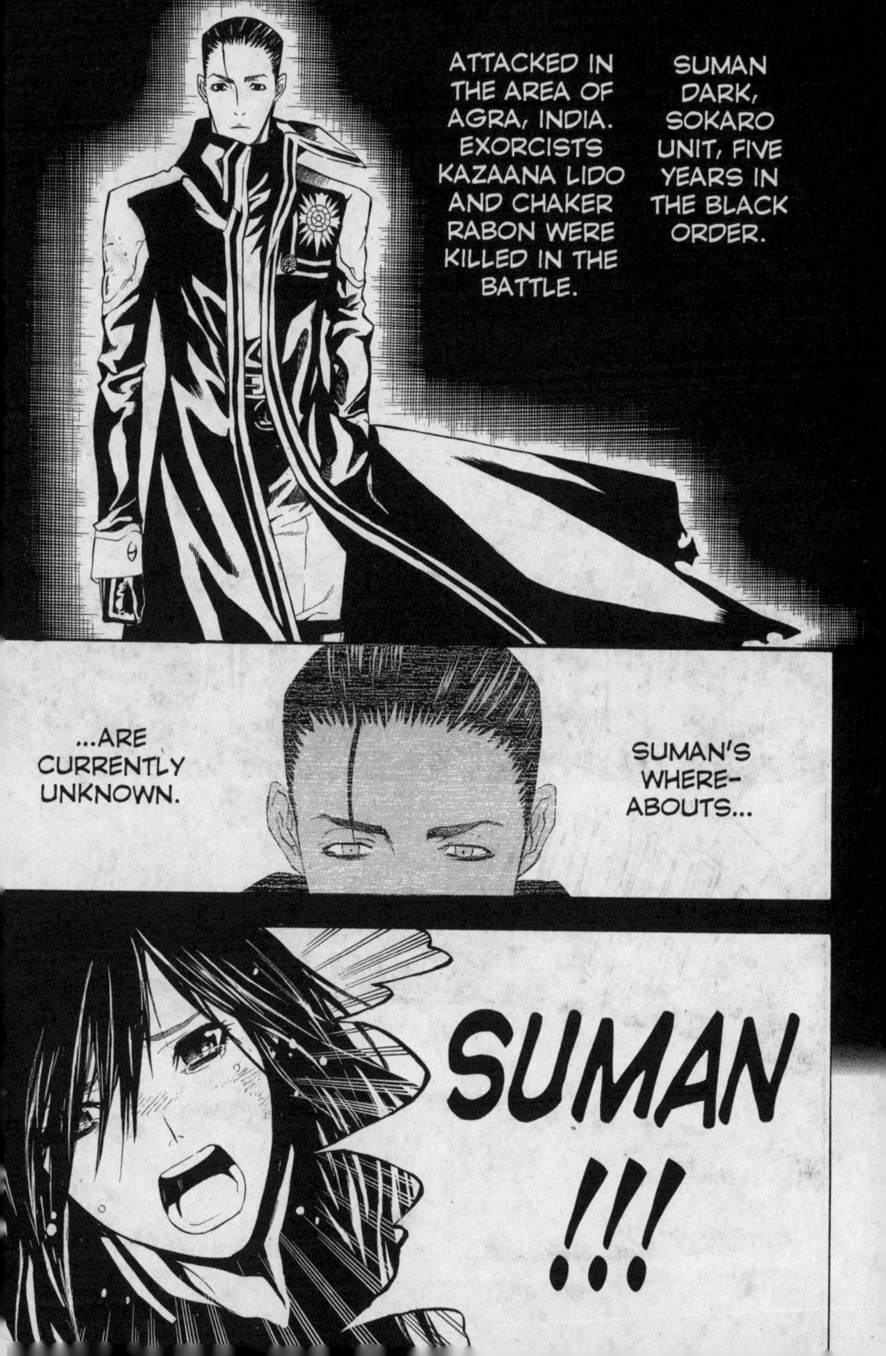
SUMAN DARK, SOKARO UNIT, FIVE YEARS IN THE BLACK ORDER.
ATTACKED IN THE AREA OF AGRA, INDIA. EXORCISTS KAZAANA LIDO AND CHAKER RABON WERE KILLED IN THE BATTLE.
SUMAN'S WHERE-ABOUTS...
...ARE CURRENTLY UNKNOWN.
SUMAN !!!

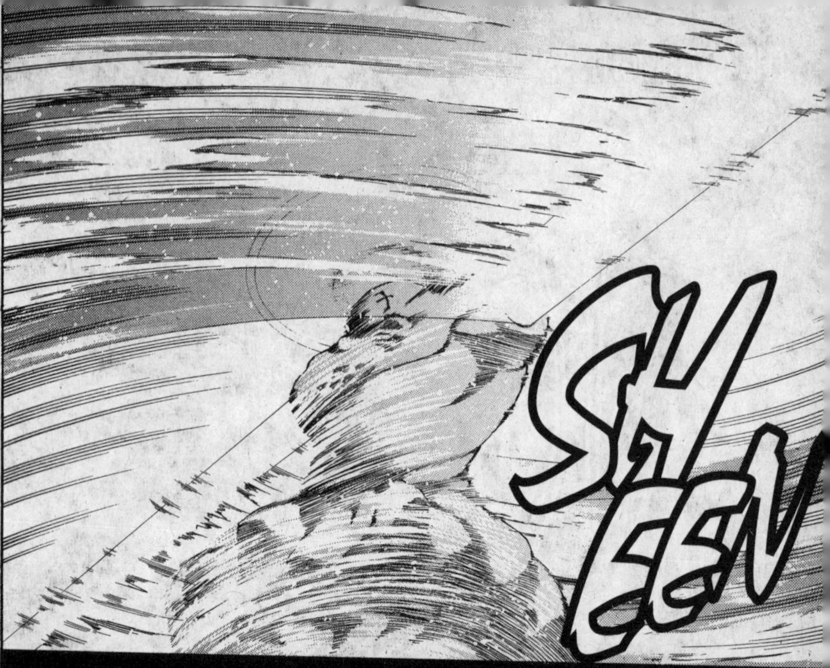
SHEEN

THE 49TH NIGHT: SIN

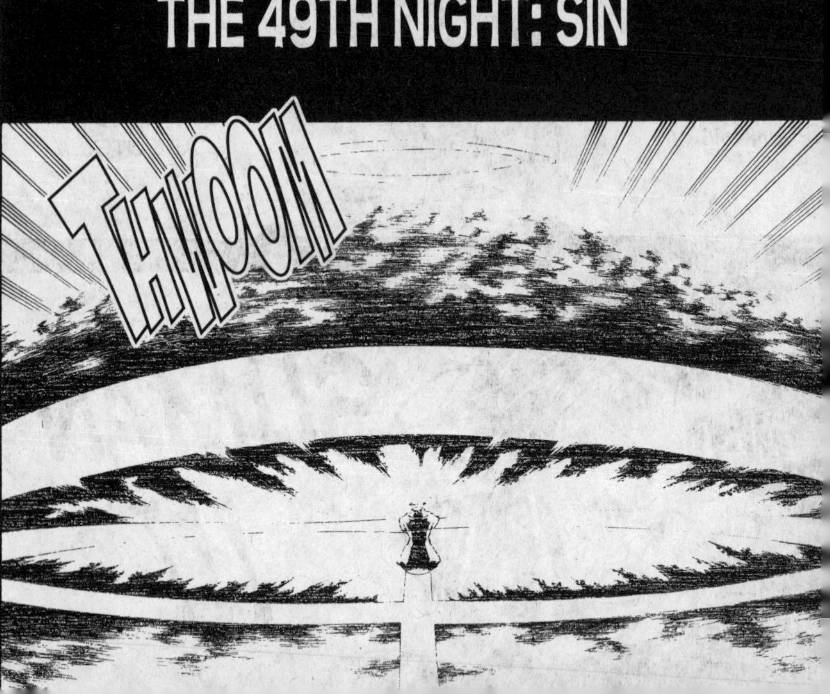
THWOOM

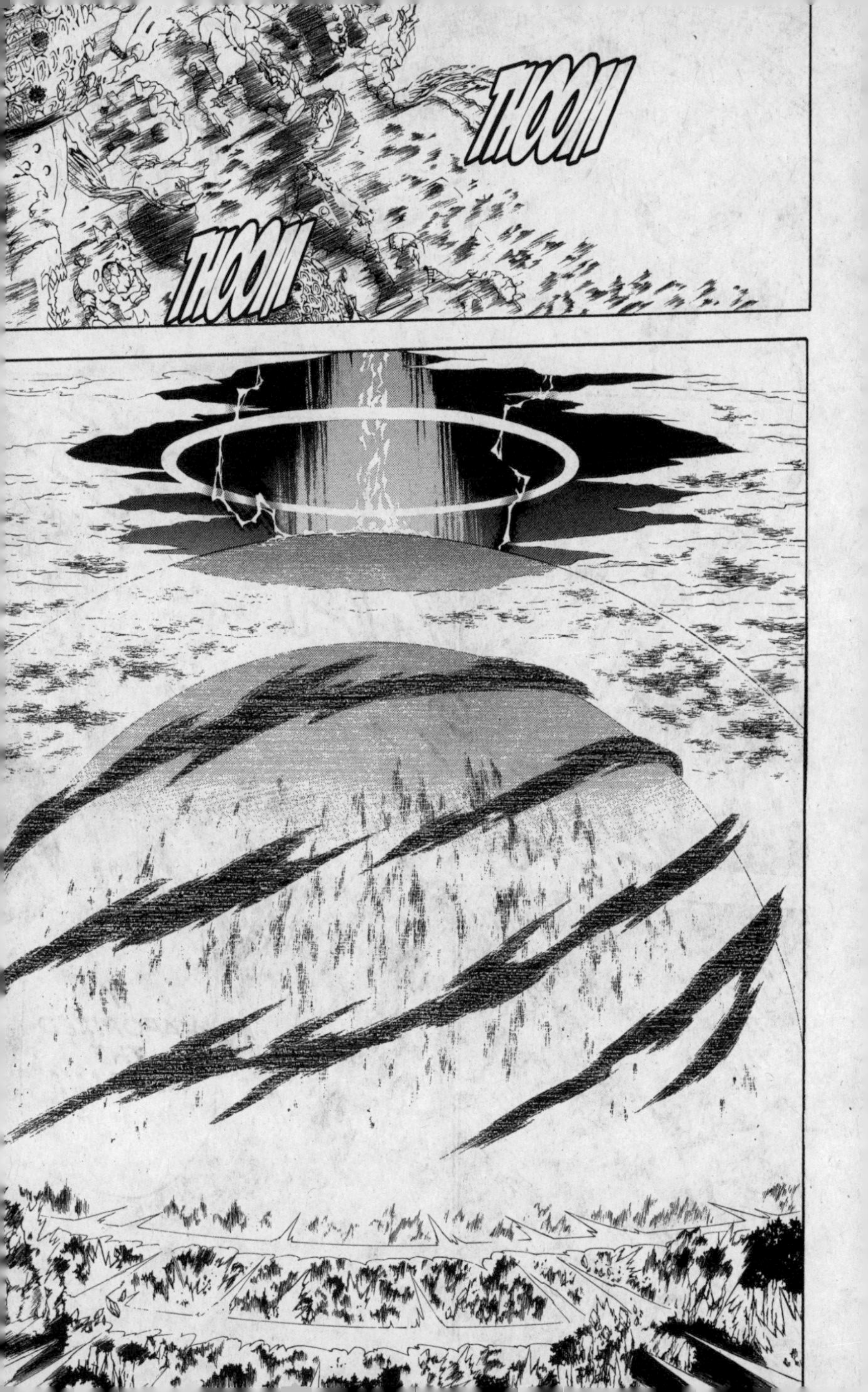
THOOM
THOOM

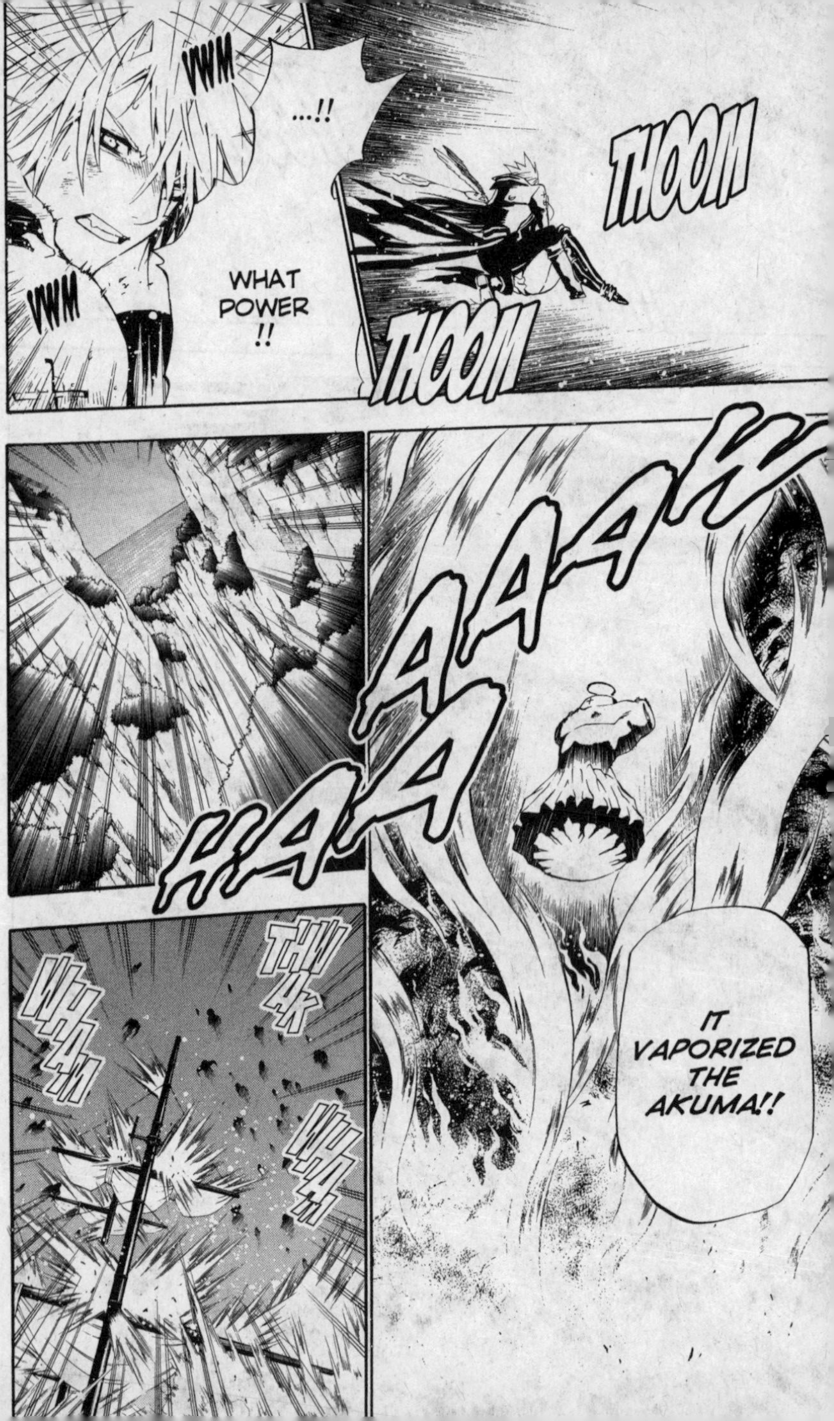
THOOM
THOOM
VWM
...!!
WHAT POWER !!
VWM
HAAAAAA
IT VAPORIZED THE AKUMA!!
THWAK
WHAM
WHAM

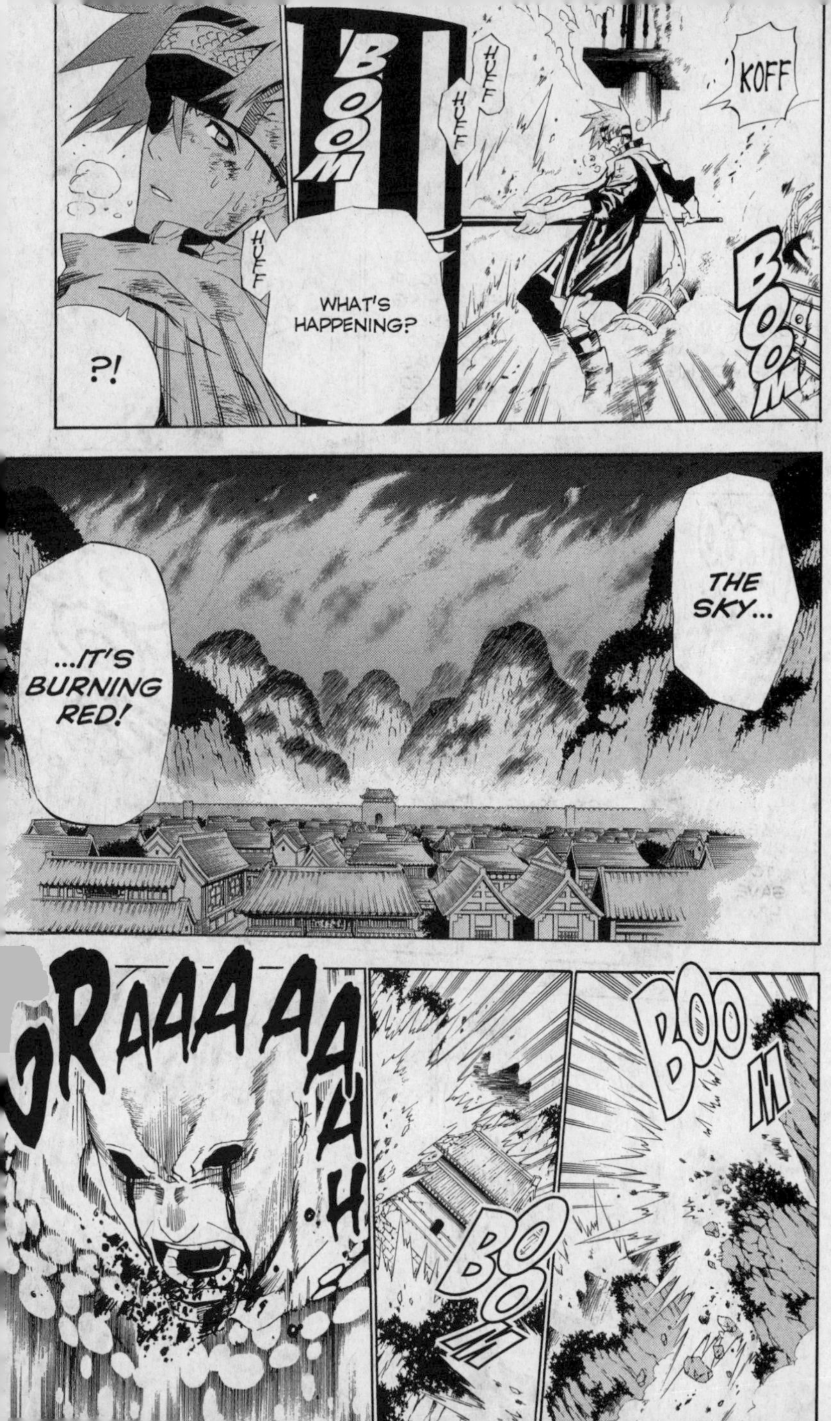
KOFF
BOOM
HUFF HUFF
BOOM
HUFF
WHAT'S HAPPENING?
?!
THE SKY...
...IT'S BURNING RED!
BOOM
BOOM
GRAAAAAAAH

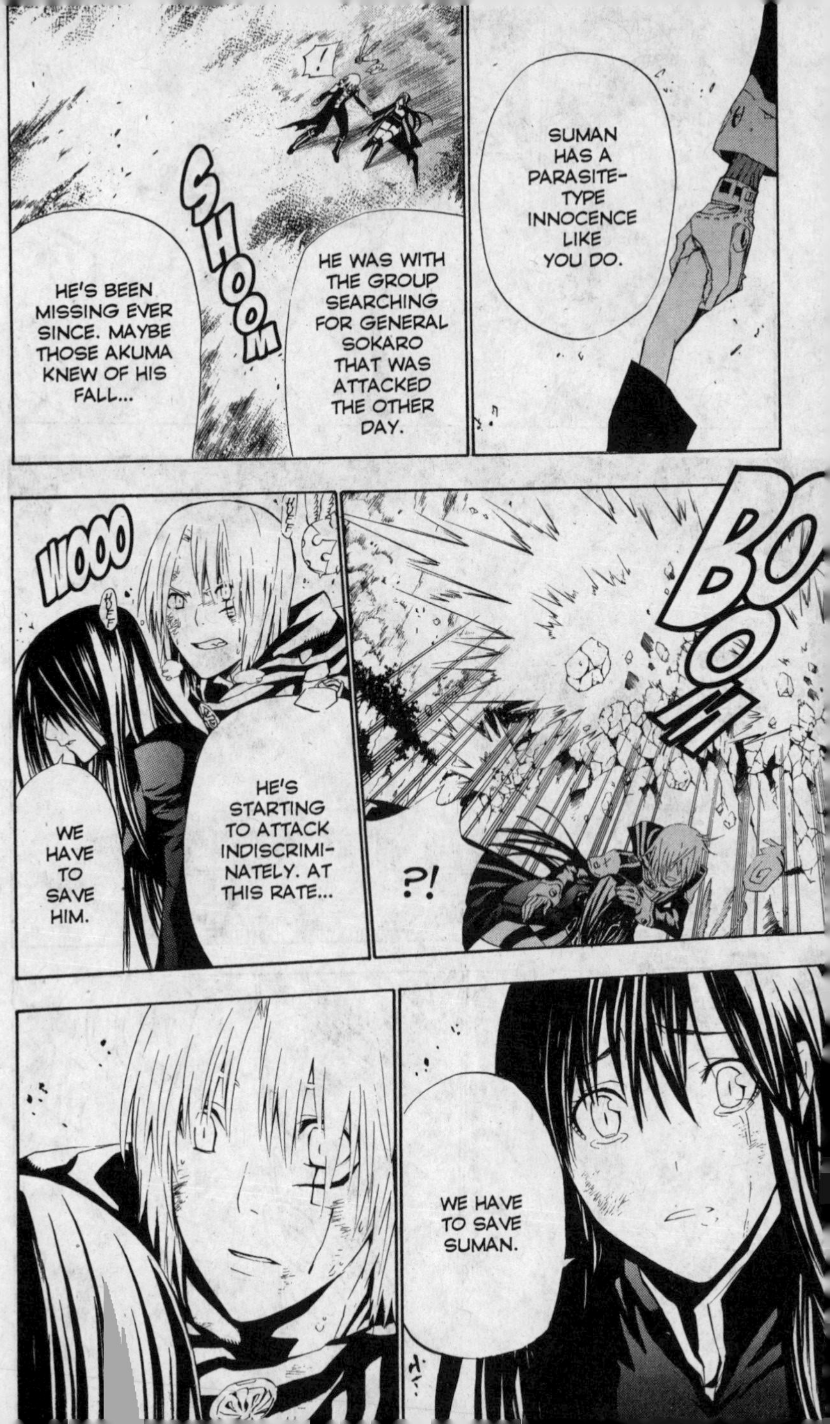
SUMAN HAS A PARASITE-TYPE INNOCENCE LIKE YOU DO.
!
HE WAS WITH THE GROUP SEARCHING FOR GENERAL SOKARO THAT WAS ATTACKED THE OTHER DAY.
SHOOOM
HE'S BEEN MISSING EVER SINCE. MAYBE THOSE AKUMA KNEW OF HIS FALL...
BOOOM
?!
WOOO
HE'S STARTING TO ATTACK INDISCRIMI-NATELY. AT THIS RATE...
WE HAVE TO SAVE HIM.
WE HAVE TO SAVE SUMAN.

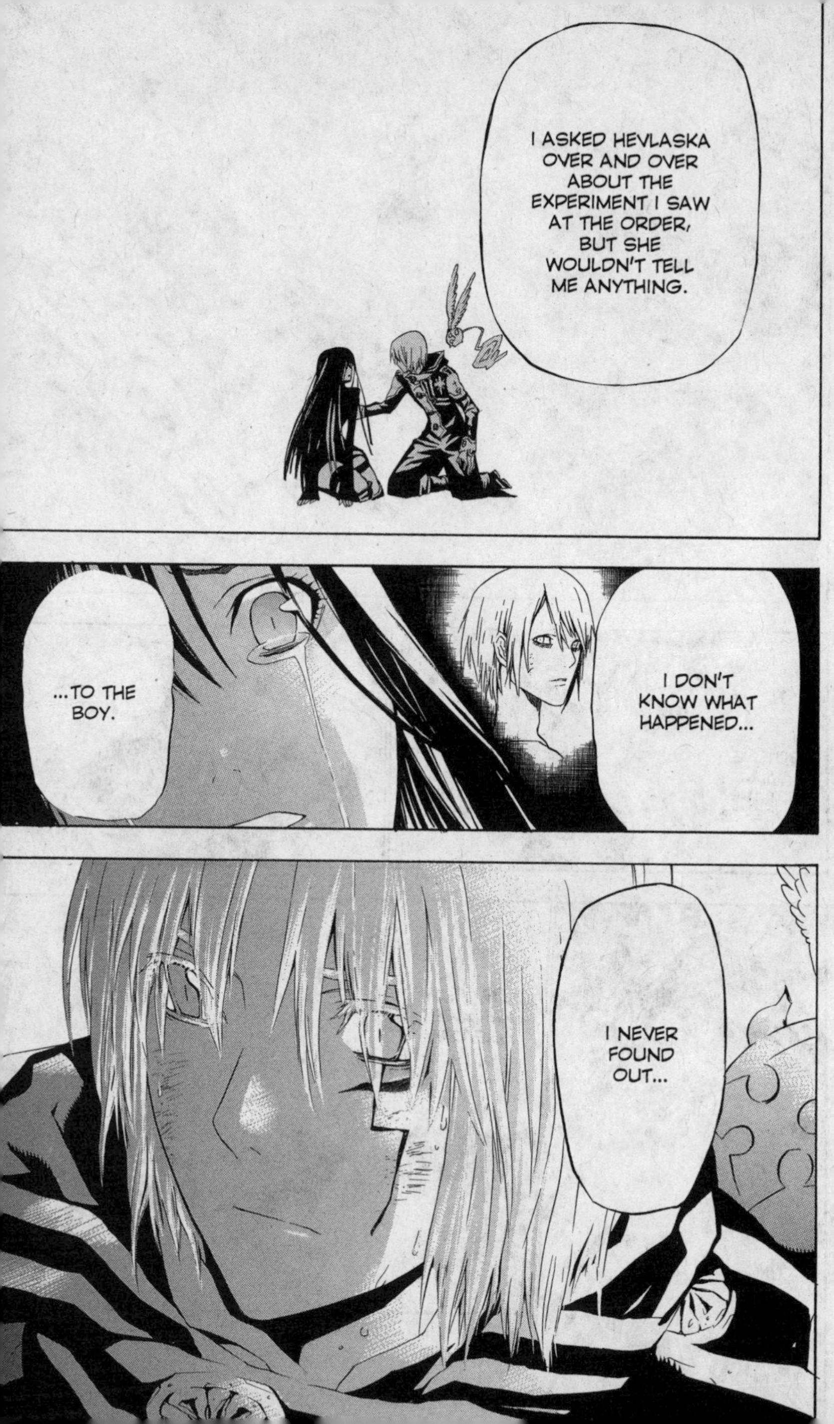
I ASKED HEVLASKA OVER AND OVER ABOUT THE EXPERIMENT I SAW AT THE ORDER, BUT SHE WOULDN'T TELL ME ANYTHING.
I DON'T KNOW WHAT HAPPENED...
...TO THE BOY.
I NEVER FOUND OUT...

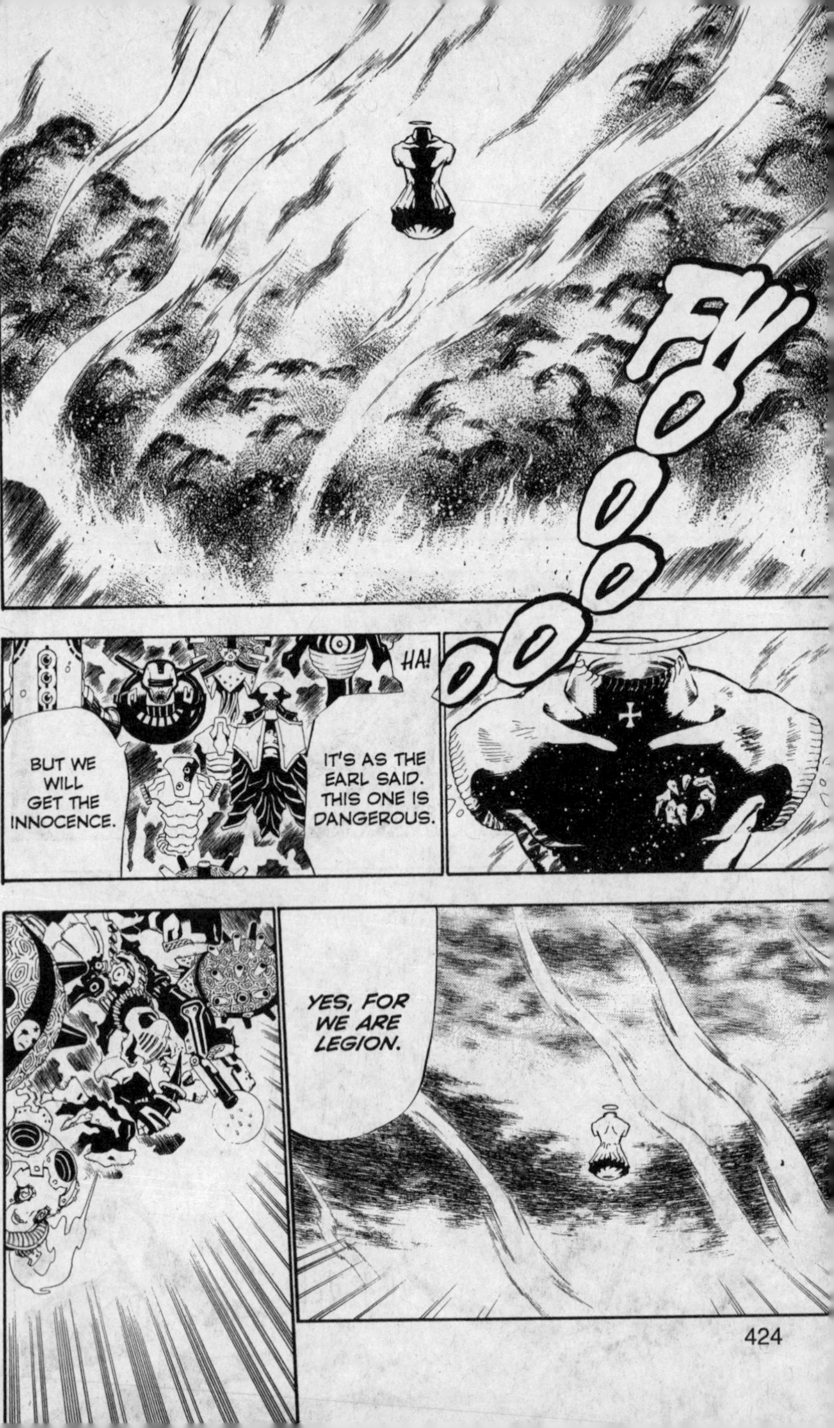
FWOOOOOOO
HA!
IT'S AS THE EARL SAID. THIS ONE IS DANGEROUS.
BUT WE WILL GET THE INNOCENCE.
YES, FOR WE ARE LEGION.

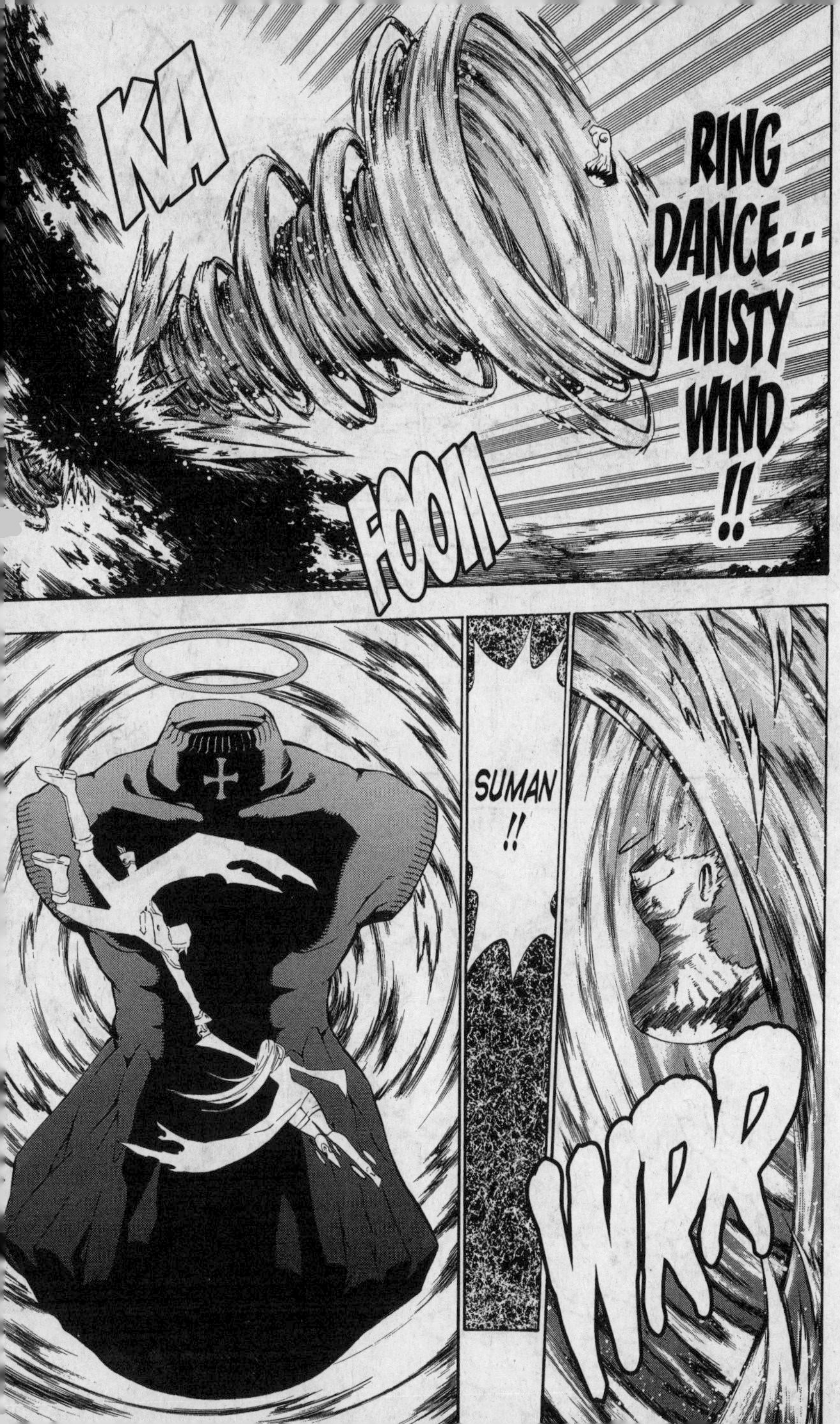
RING DANCE... MISTY WIND!!
KA
FOOM
WRAP
SUMAN!!

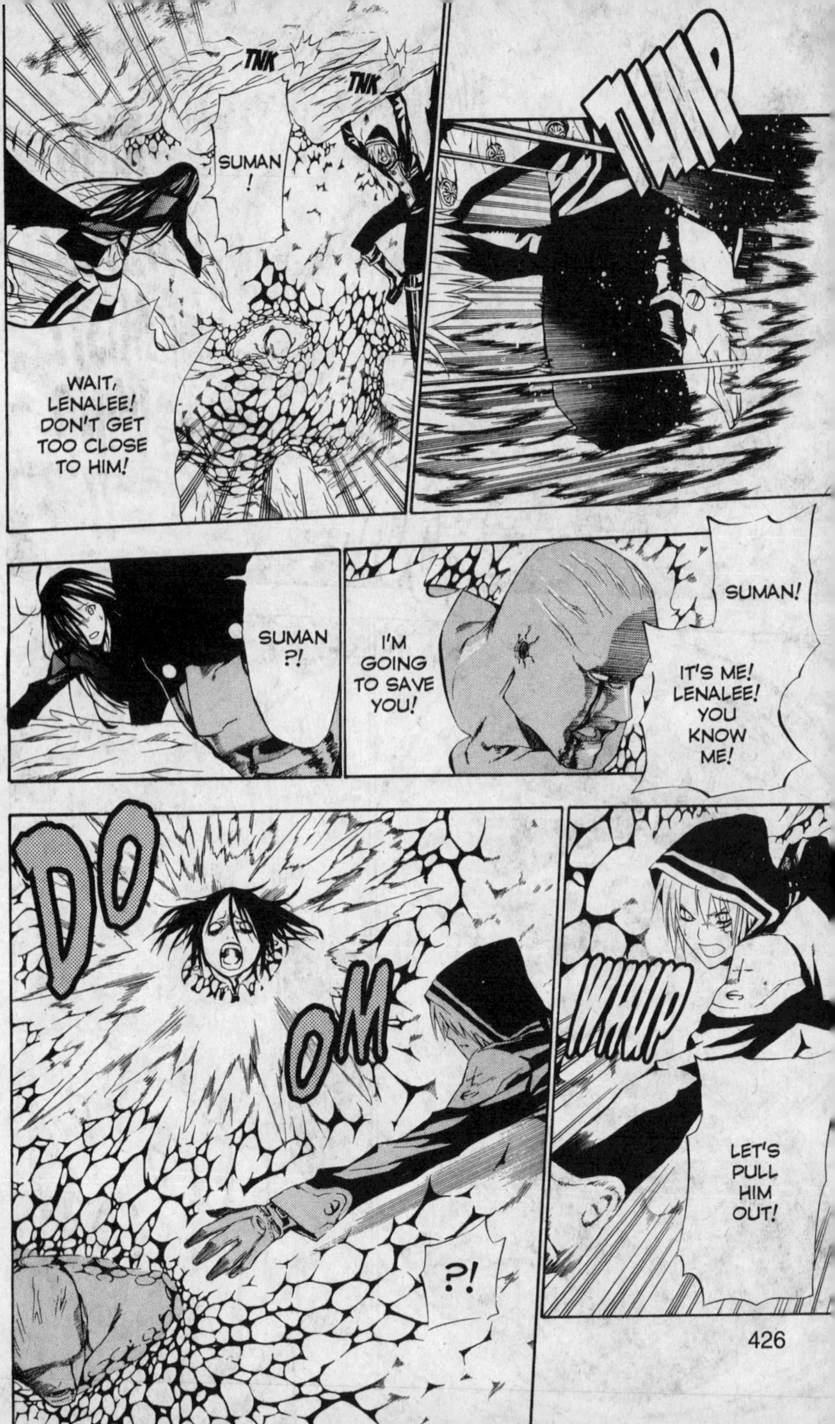

THMP
TNK
TNK
SUMAN!
WAIT, LENALEE! DON'T GET TOO CLOSE TO HIM!
SUMAN!
IT'S ME! LENALEE! YOU KNOW ME!
I'M GOING TO SAVE YOU!
SUMAN?!
WHUP
LET'S PULL HIM OUT!
DOOM
?!

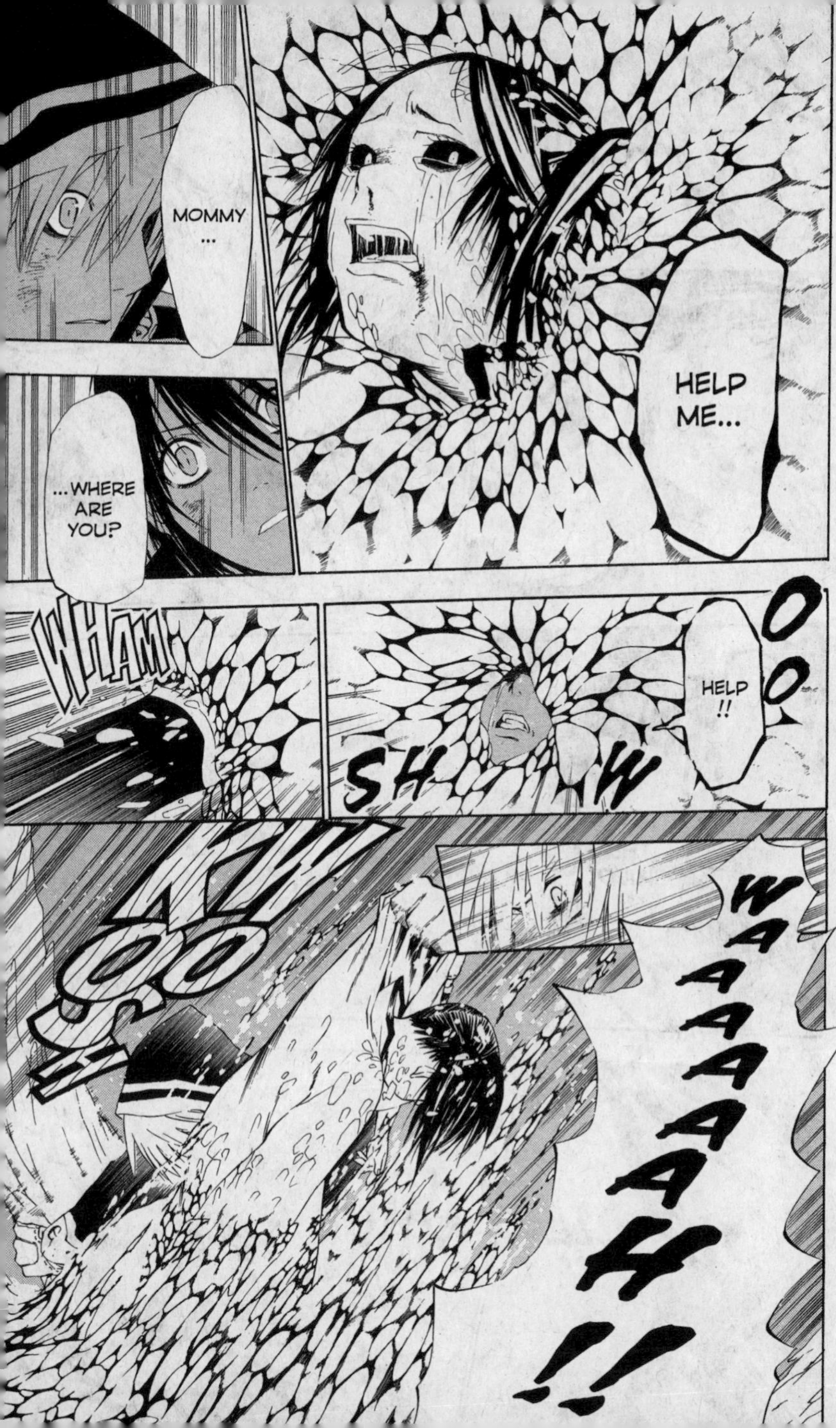
HELP ME...
MOMMY ...
...WHERE ARE YOU?
HELP !!
OO
SH
W
WHAM
WAAAAAAAH!!

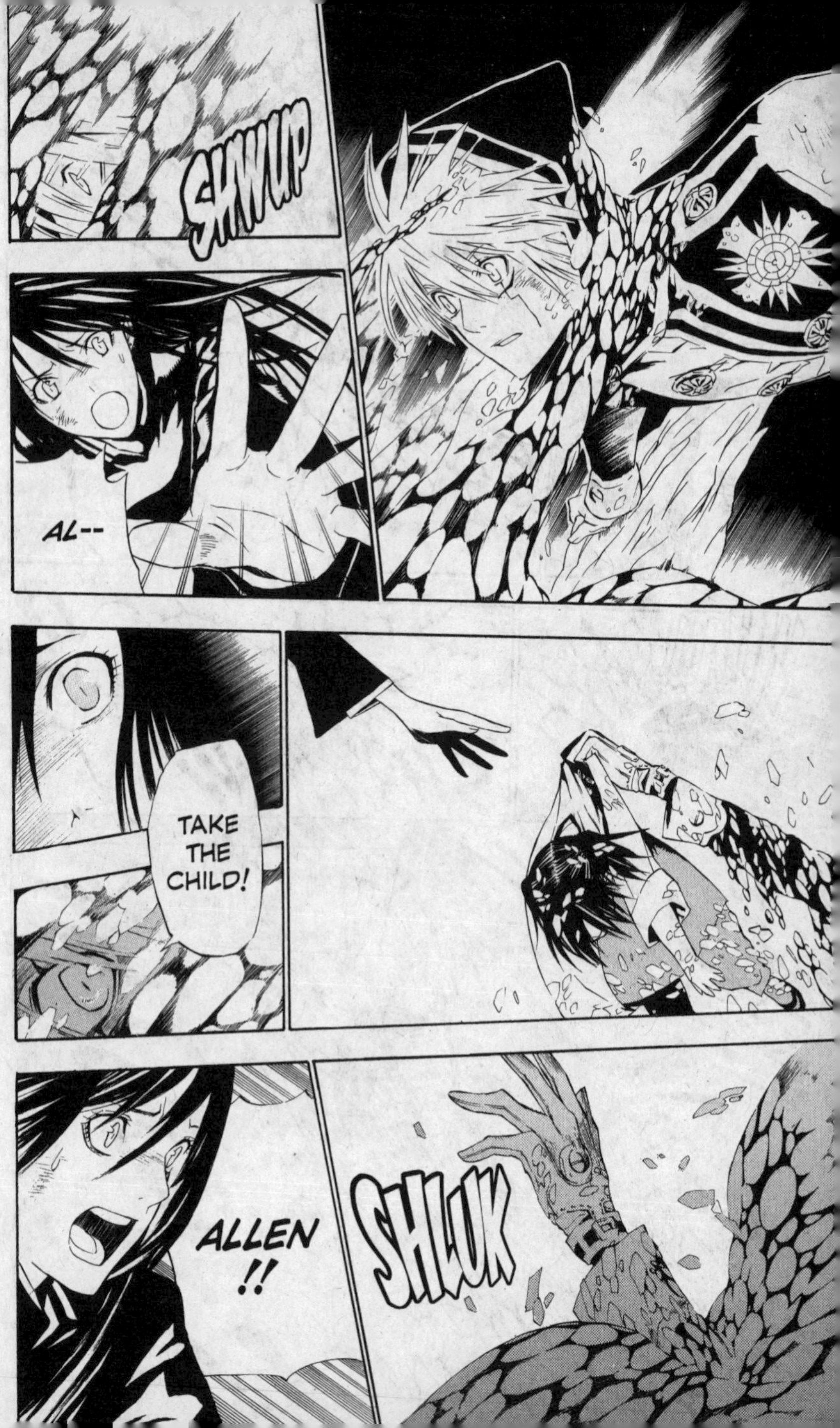
SHWUP
AL--
TAKE THE CHILD!
SHLUK
ALLEN !!

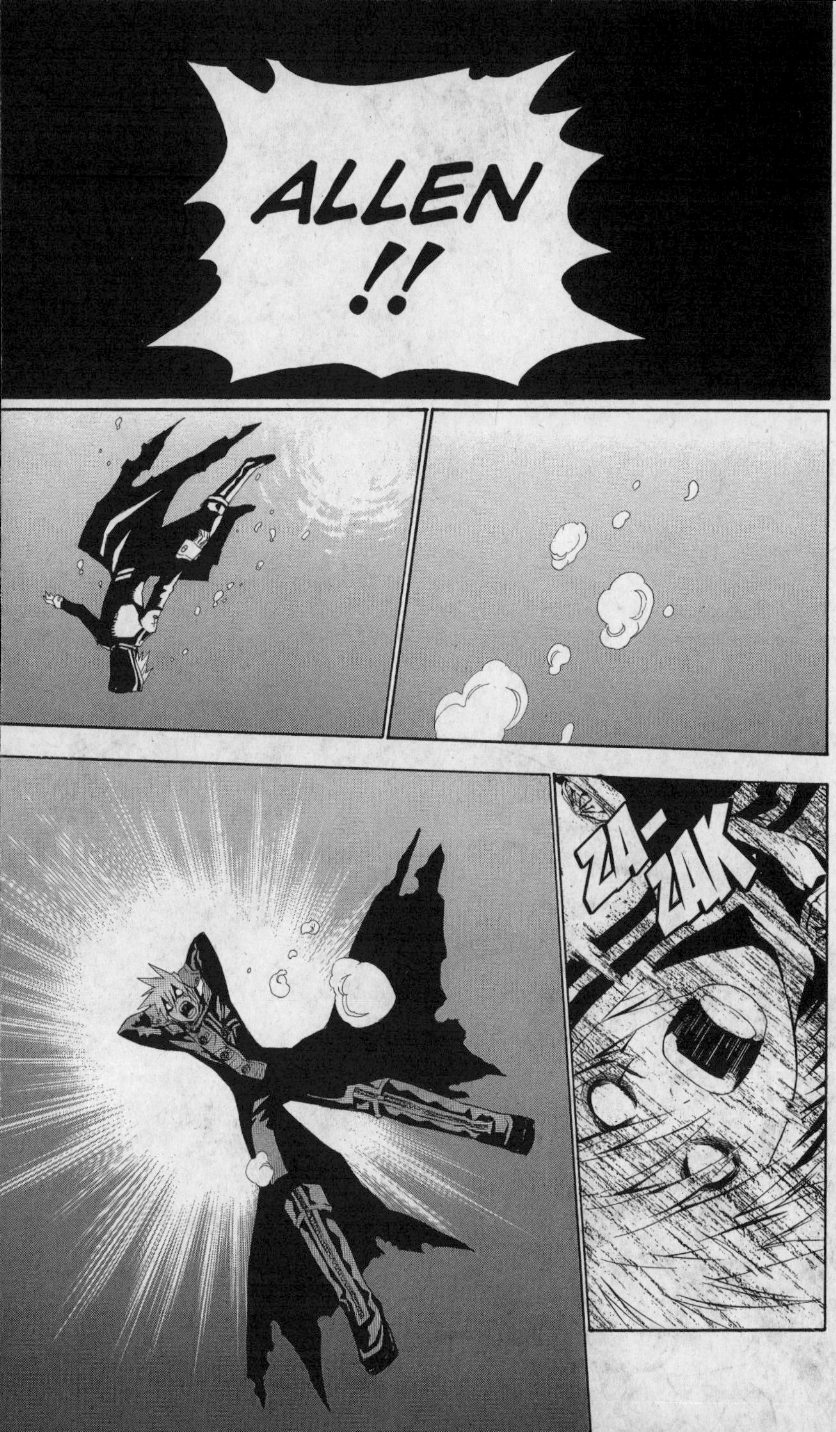
ALLEN !!
ZA-ZAK

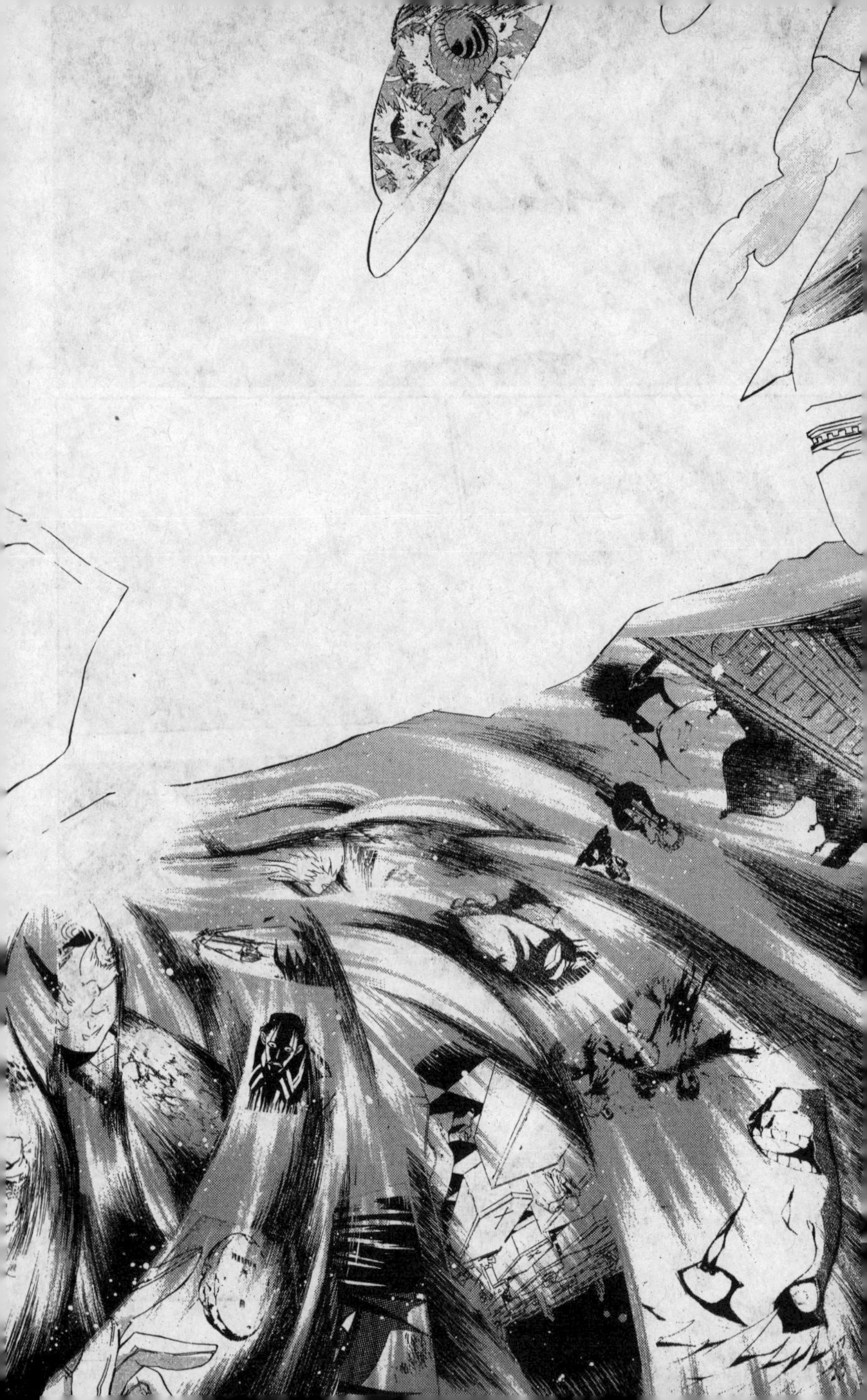

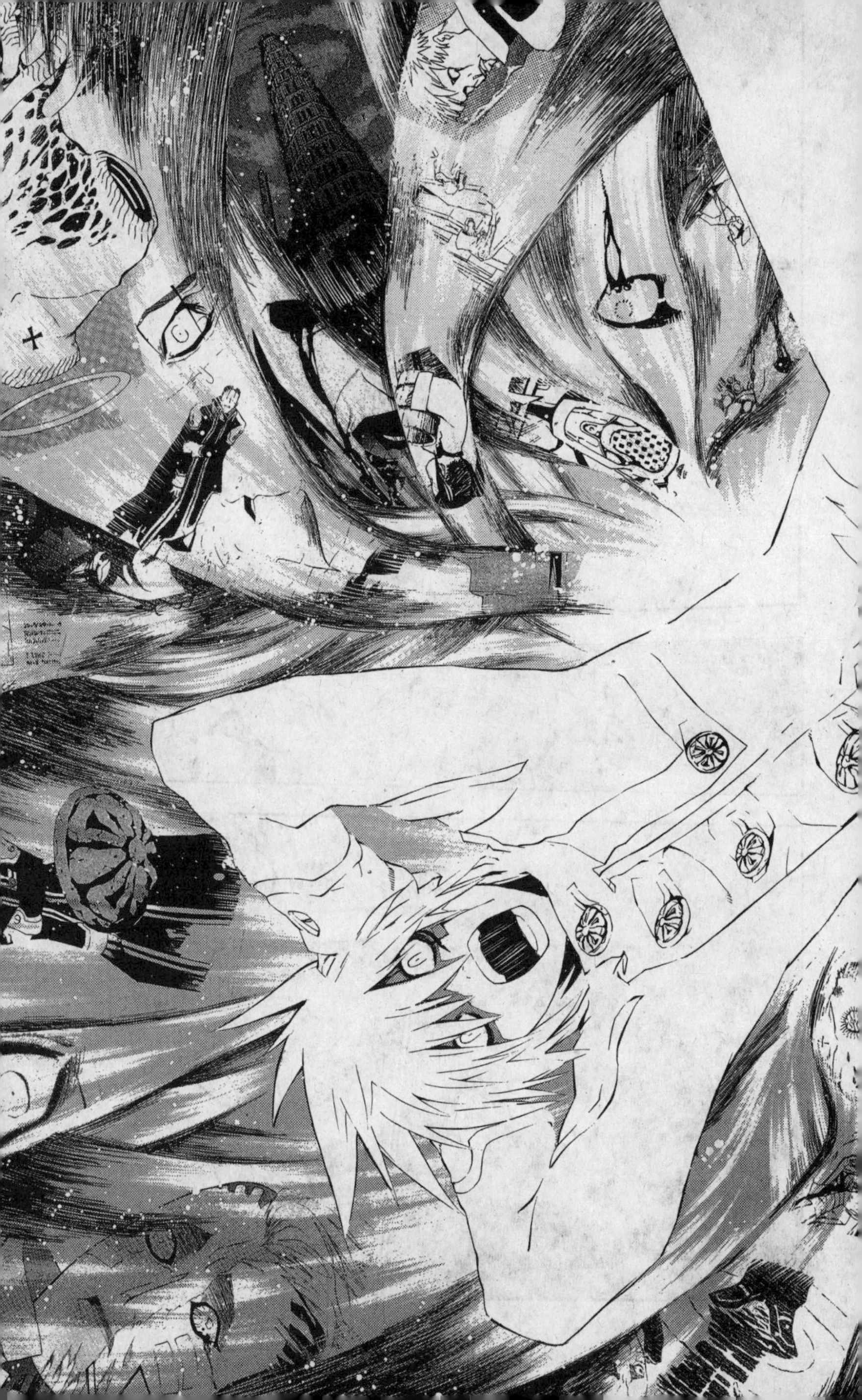

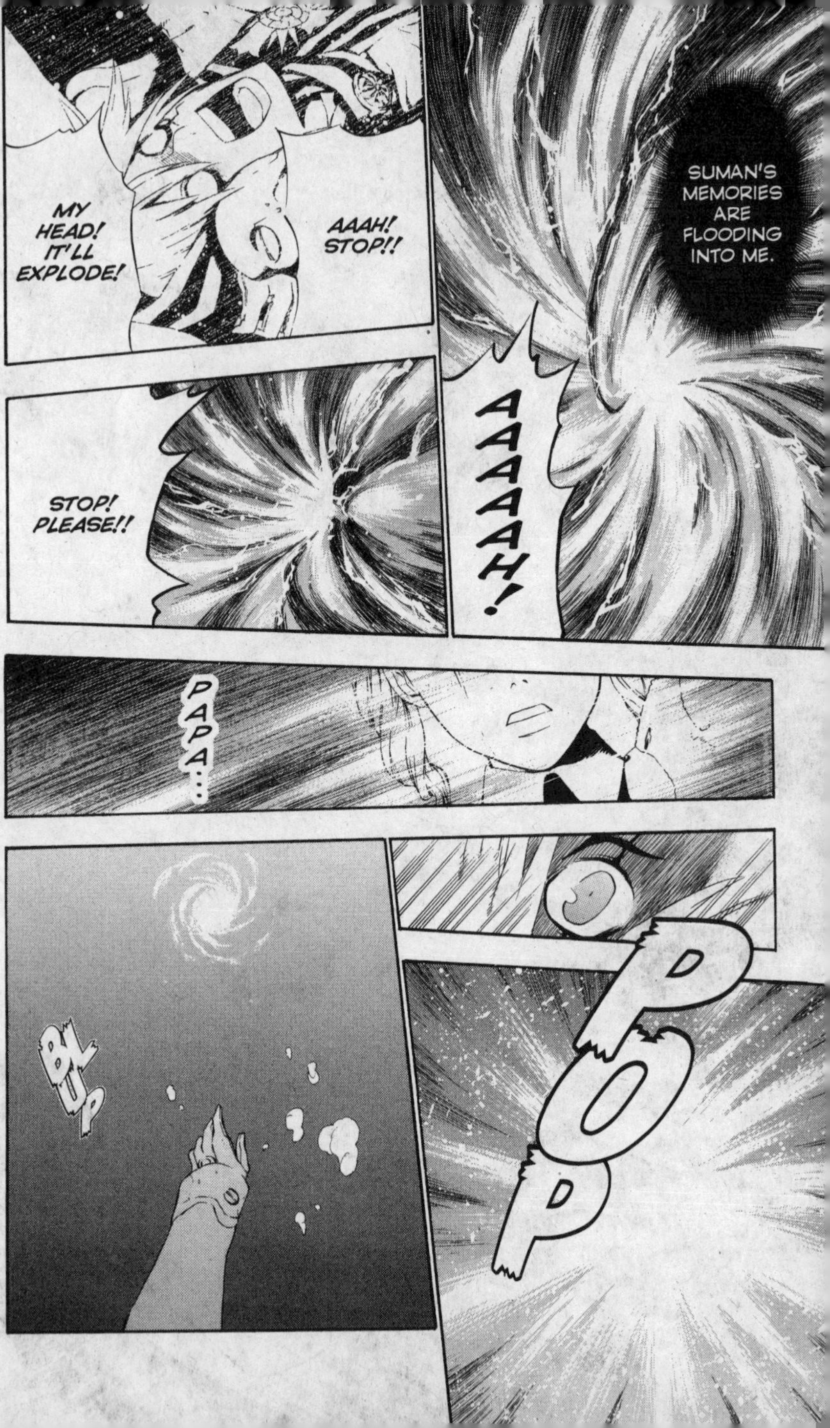
SUMAN'S MEMORIES ARE FLOODING INTO ME.
AAAAAAH!
AAAH! STOP!!
MY HEAD! IT'LL EXPLODE!
STOP! PLEASE!!
PAPA...
POP
BLUP

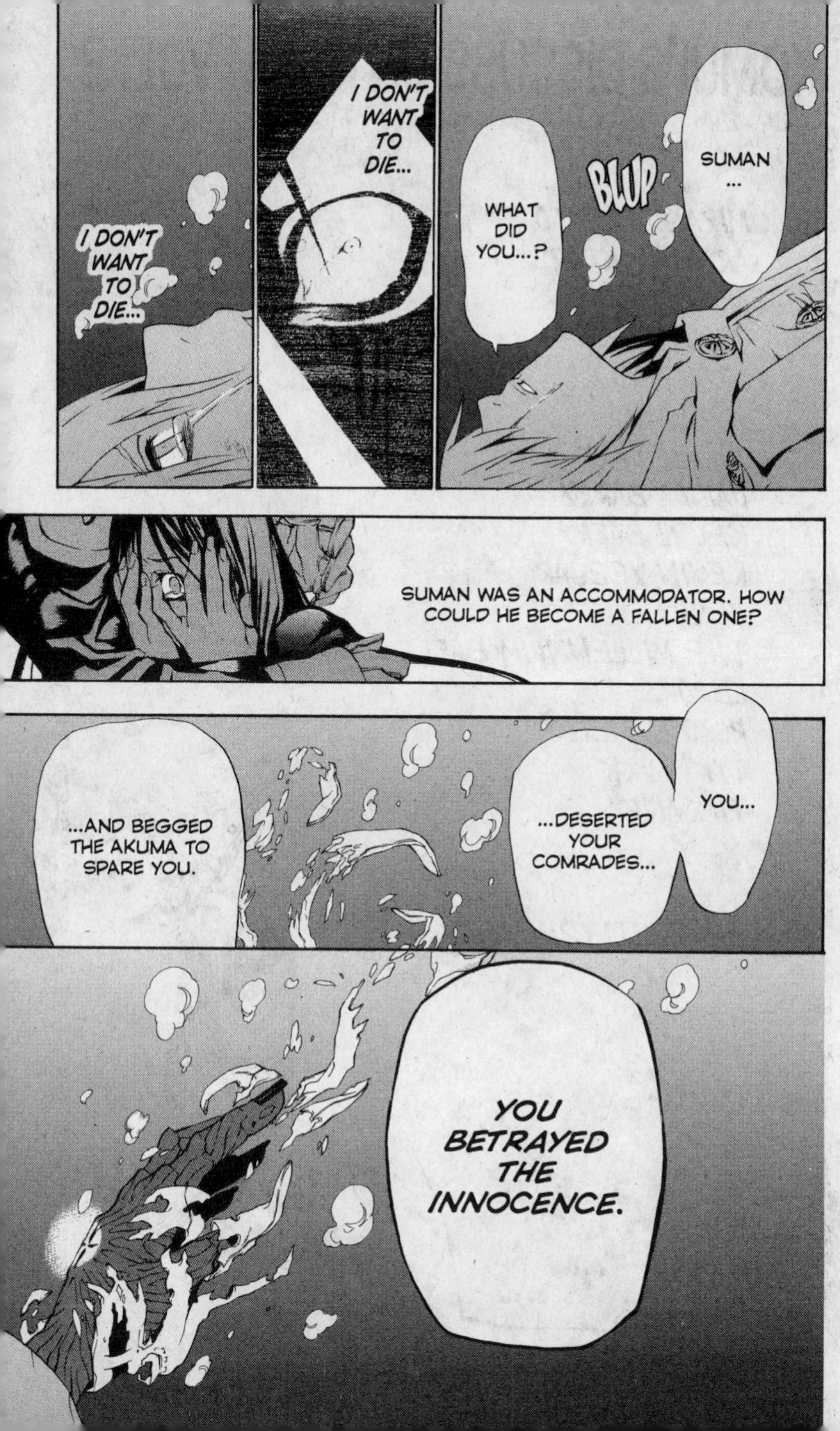
SUMAN ...
BLUP
WHAT DID YOU...?
I DON'T WANT TO DIE...
I DON'T WANT TO DIE...
SUMAN WAS AN ACCOMMODATOR. HOW COULD HE BECOME A FALLEN ONE?
YOU...
...DESERTED YOUR COMRADES...
...AND BEGGED THE AKUMA TO SPARE YOU.
YOU BETRAYED THE INNOCENCE.

KOMUI'S DISCUSSION ROOM VOL. 2

MIRANDA LOTTO
ARYSTAR KRORY
NOISE MARIE
CROSS MARIAN
FROI TIEDOLL
HEVLASKA
SUMAN DARK
DAISYA BARRY
KEVIN BARRY
KEVIN YEEGAR
JERRY
THE MILLENNIUM EARL
LERO
ROAD KAMELOT
TYKI MIKK
TIMCANPY

THAT'S IT! (PHEW)

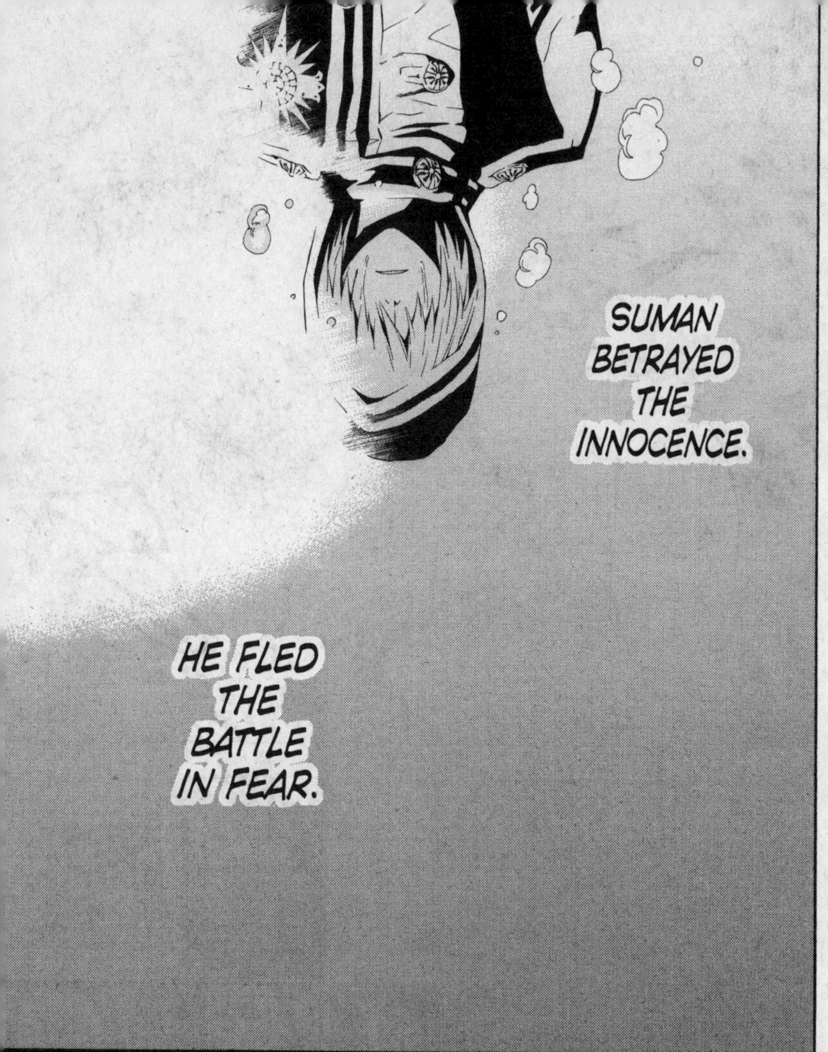
SUMAN BETRAYED THE INNOCENCE.
HE FLED THE BATTLE IN FEAR.

THE 50TH NIGHT: VOICES OF COMRADES

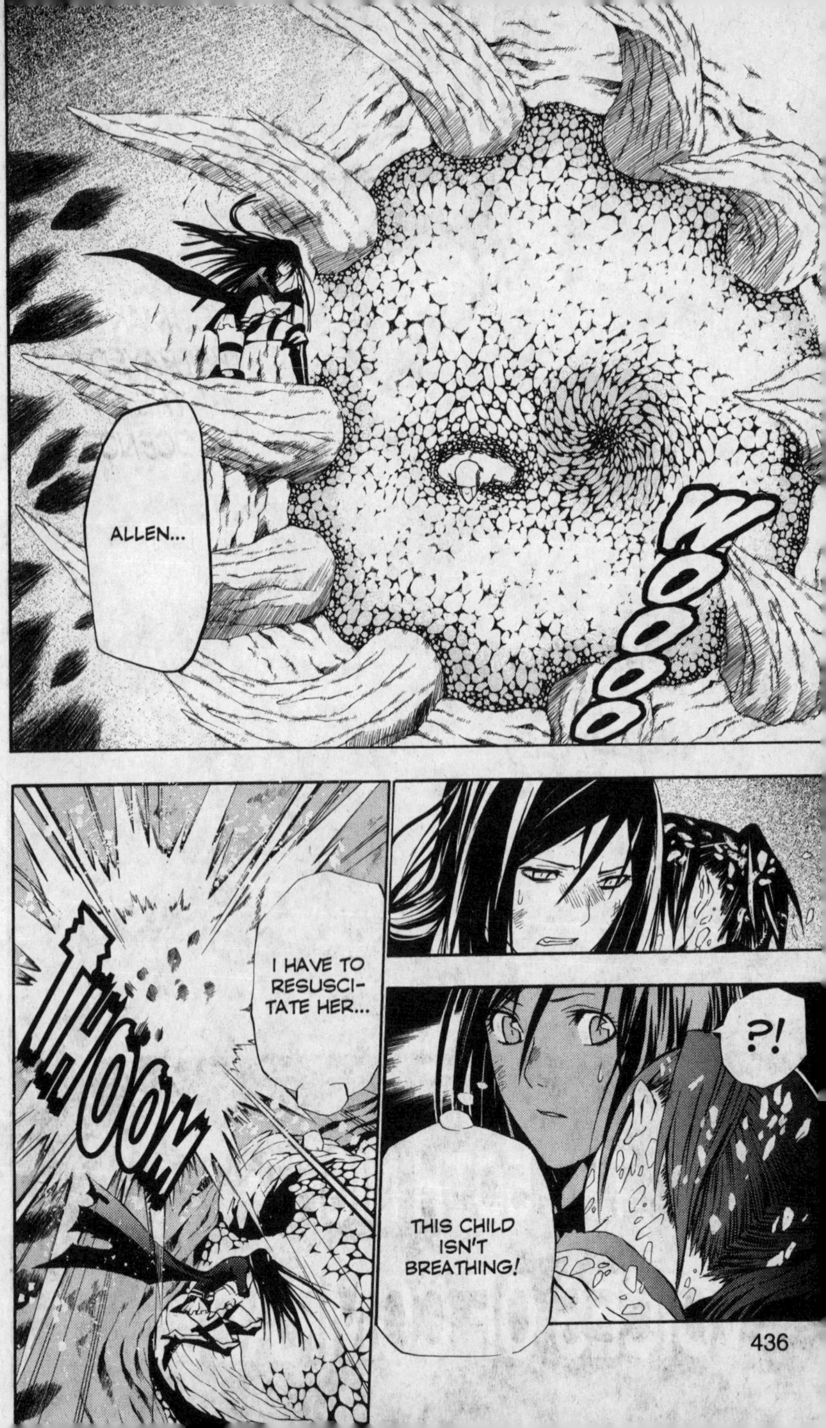
ALLEN...
WOOOOO
?!
THIS CHILD ISN'T BREATHING!
I HAVE TO RESUSCITATE HER...

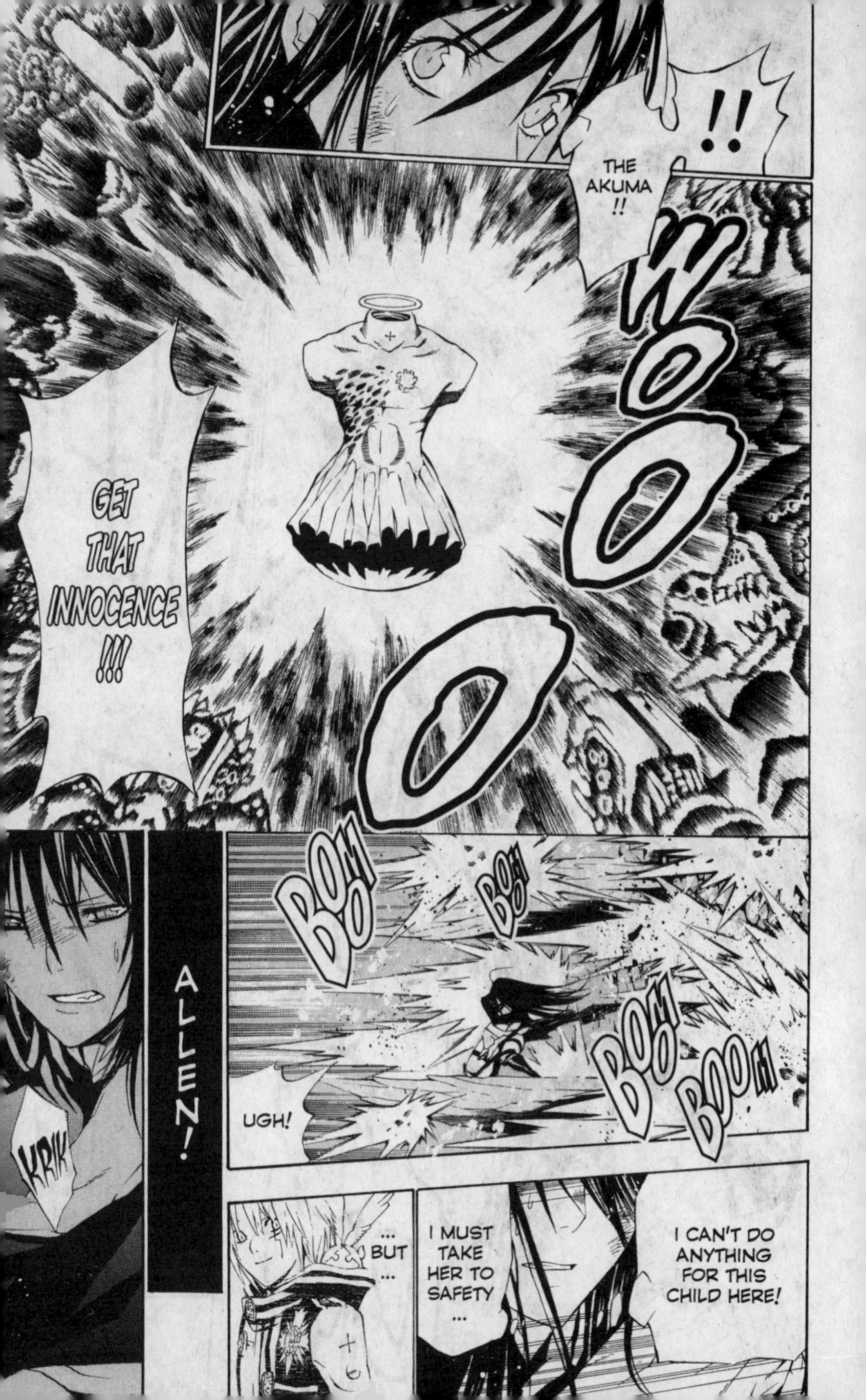
!!
THE AKUMA !!
WOOOOO
GET THAT INNOCENCE !!!
BOOM
BOOM
BOOM
BOOM
UGH!
I CAN'T DO ANYTHING FOR THIS CHILD HERE!
I MUST TAKE HER TO SAFETY ...
... BUT ...
ALLEN!
KRIK

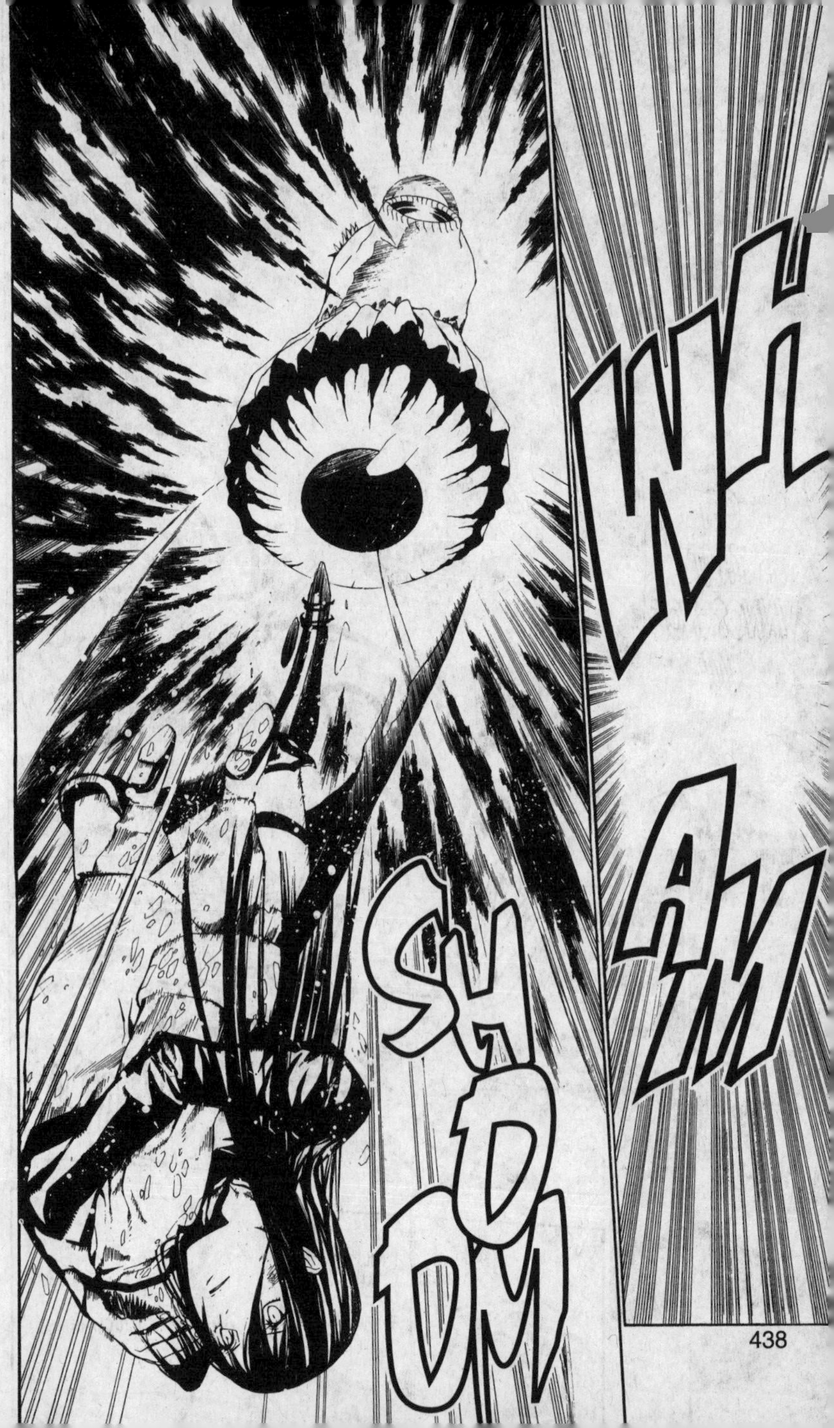
WHAM

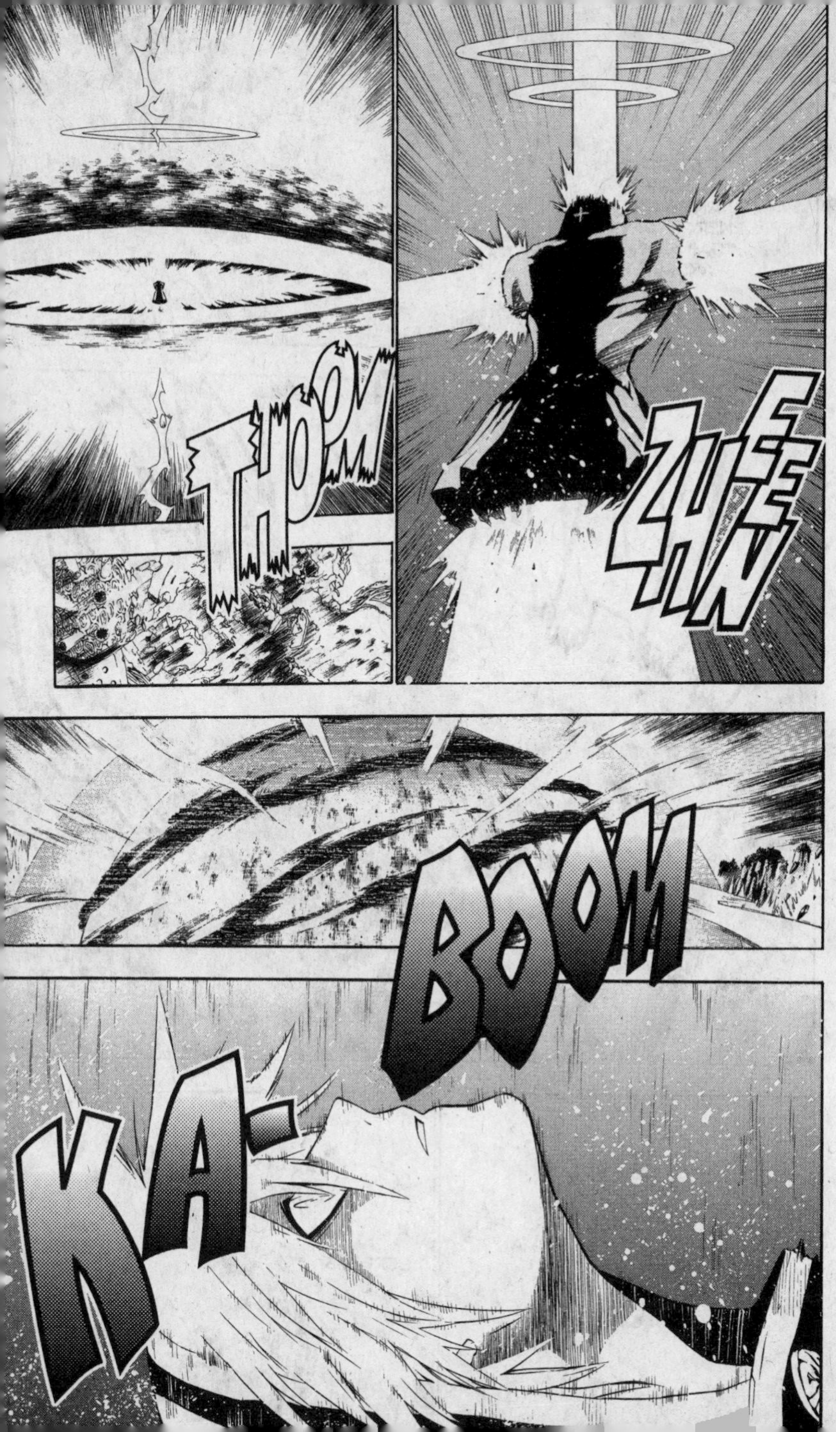
ZHEEEN
THOOM
BOOM
KA-

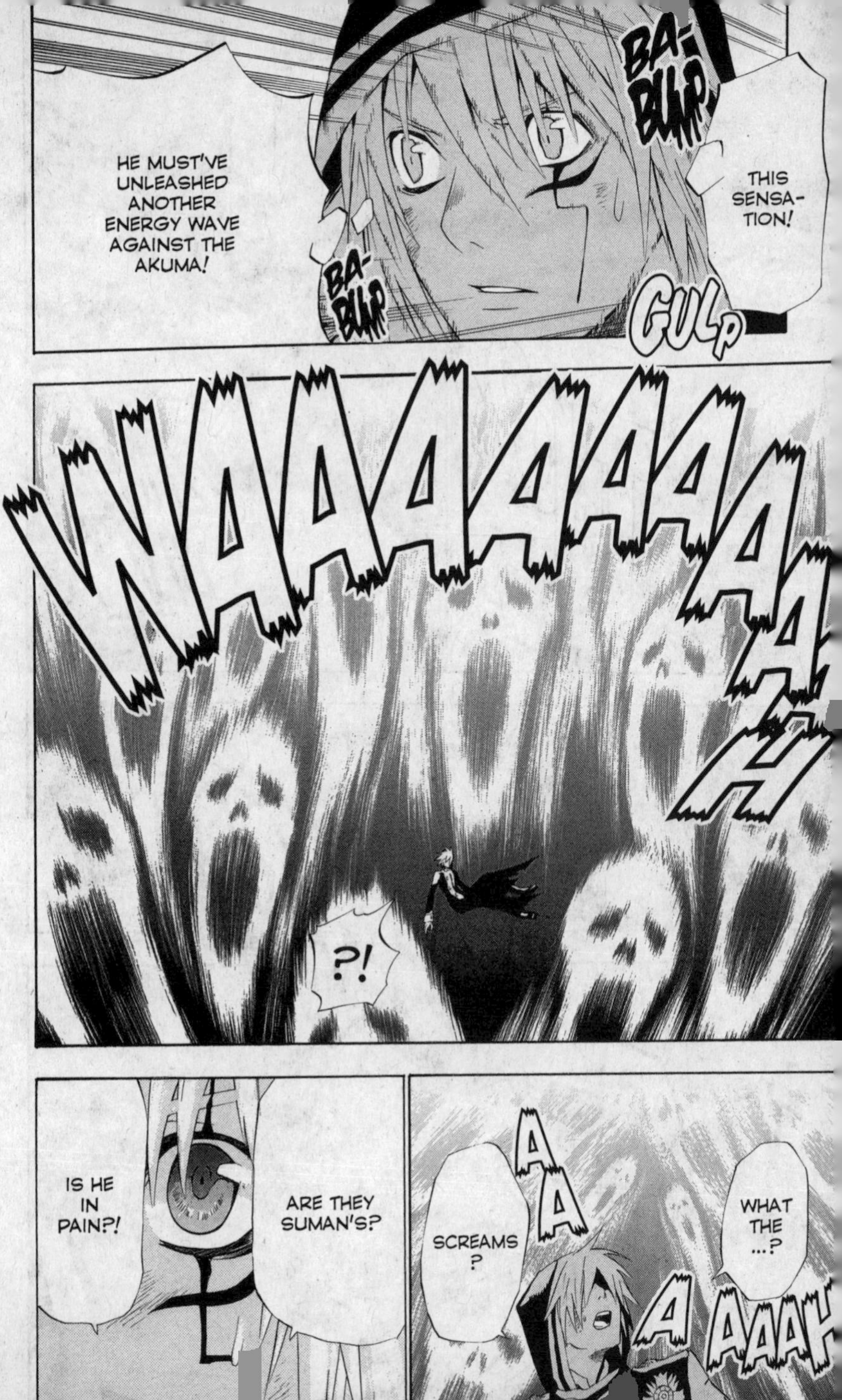
BA-BUMP
THIS SENSA-TION!
GULP
BA-BUMP
HE MUST'VE UNLEASHED ANOTHER ENERGY WAVE AGAINST THE AKUMA!
WAAAAAAAAAH
?!
WHAT THE ...?
AAA
SCREAMS?
AAAAH
ARE THEY SUMAN'S?
IS HE IN PAIN?!

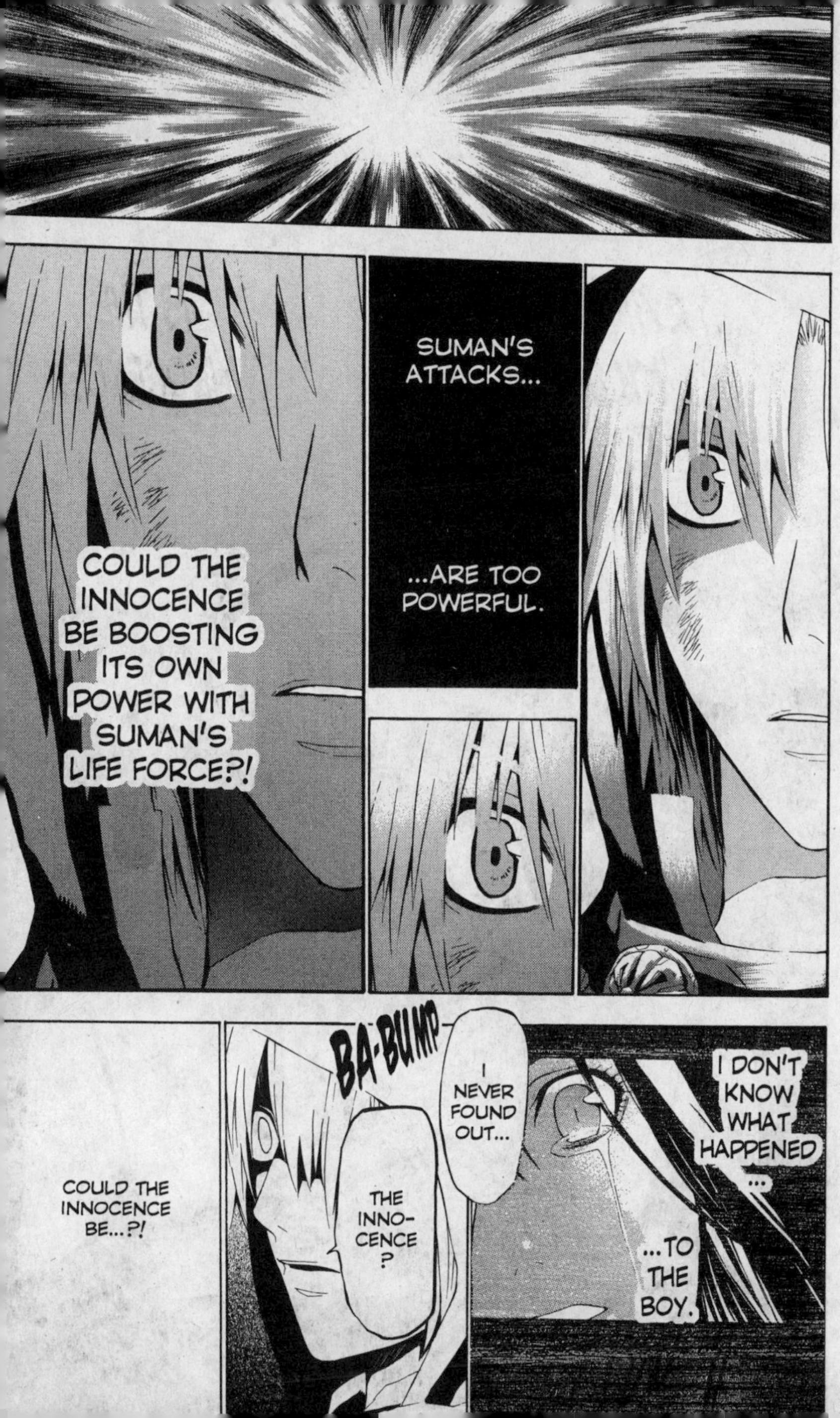
SUMAN'S ATTACKS...
...ARE TOO POWERFUL.
COULD THE INNOCENCE BE BOOSTING ITS OWN POWER WITH SUMAN'S LIFE FORCE?!
I DON'T KNOW WHAT HAPPENED...
...TO THE BOY.
BA-BUMP
I NEVER FOUND OUT...
THE INNO-CENCE?
COULD THE INNOCENCE BE...?!

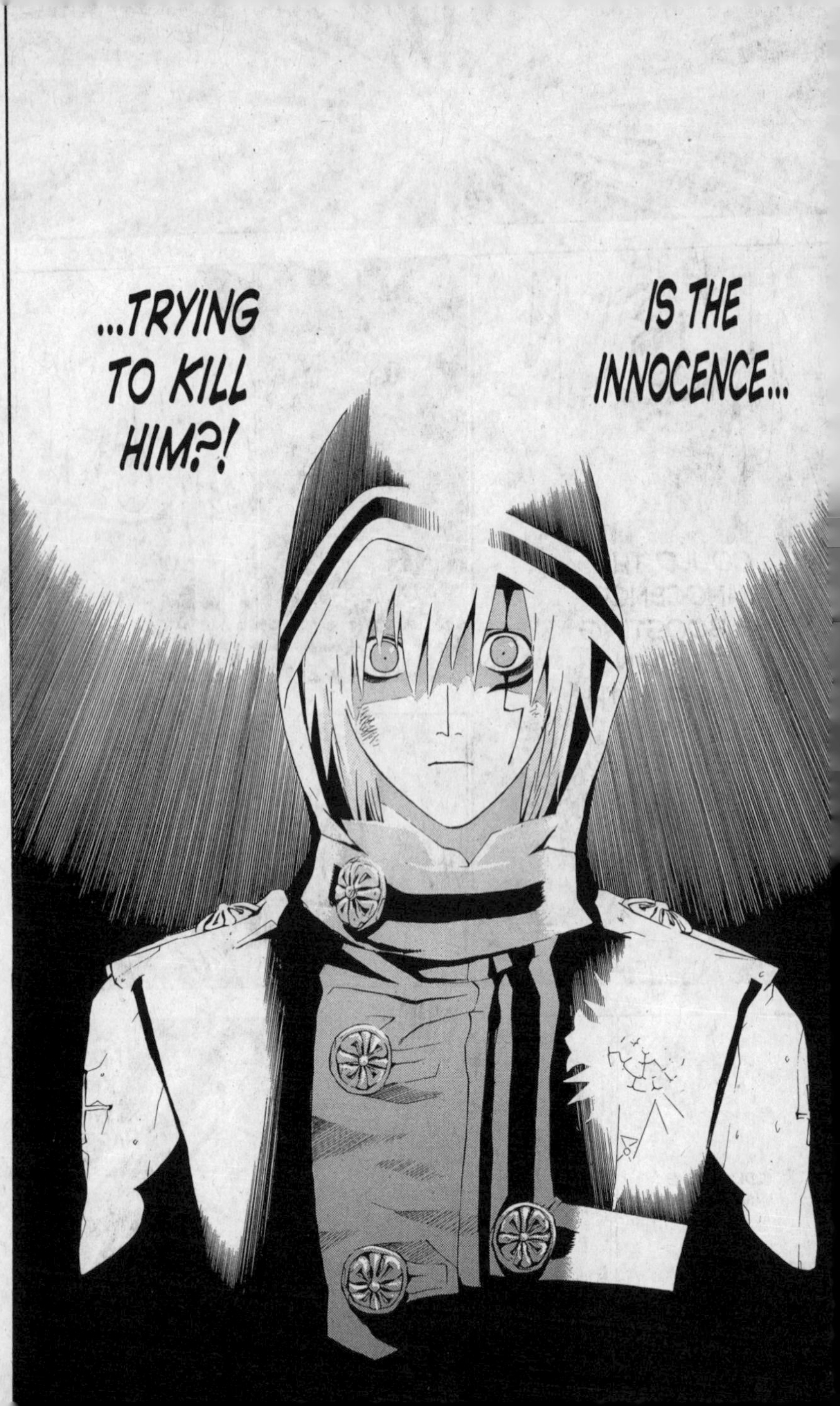
IS THE INNOCENCE...
...TRYING TO KILL HIM?!

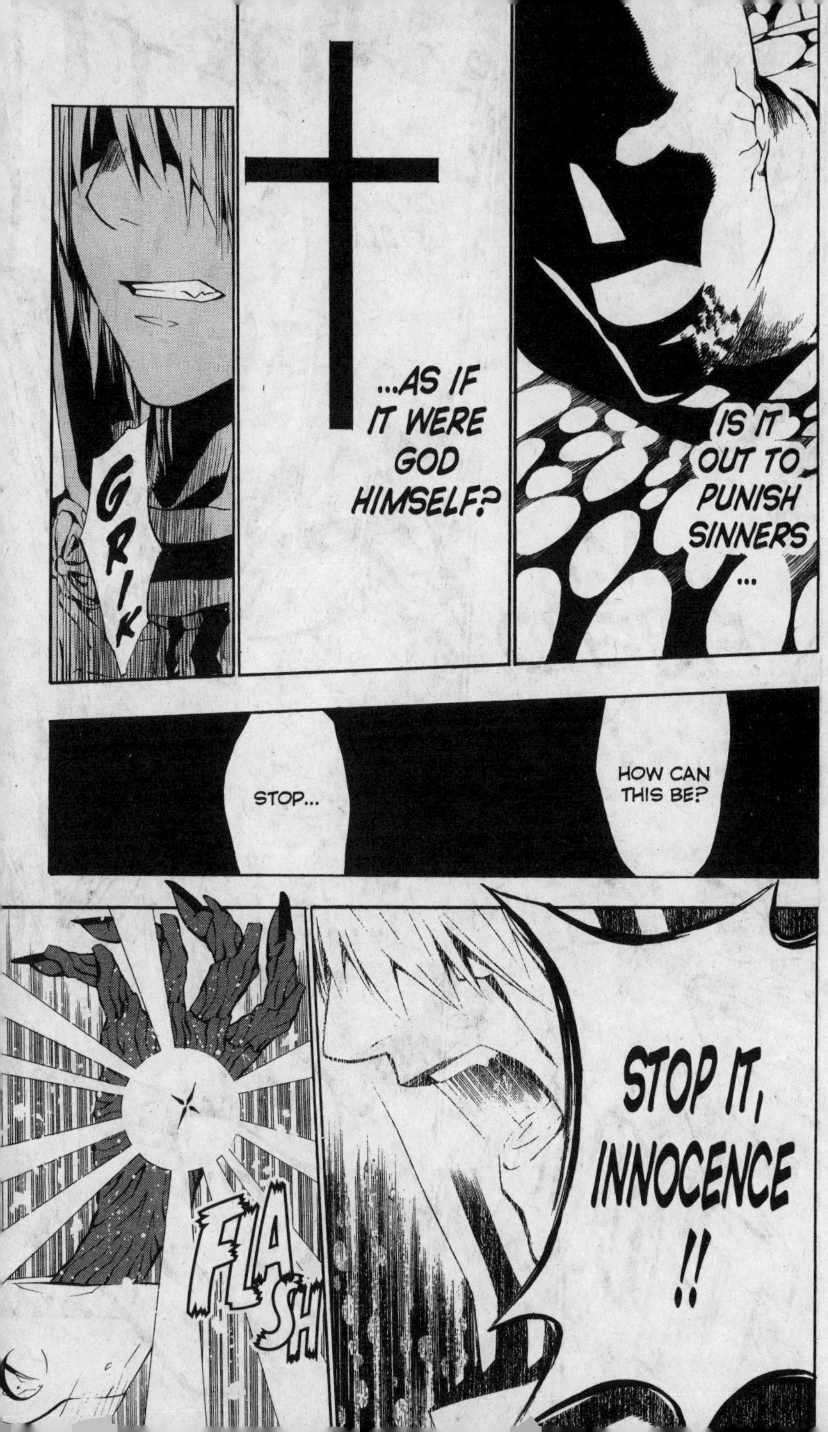
IS IT OUT TO PUNISH SINNERS ...
...AS IF IT WERE GOD HIMSELF?
GRIK
HOW CAN THIS BE?
STOP...
STOP IT, INNOCENCE !!
FLASH

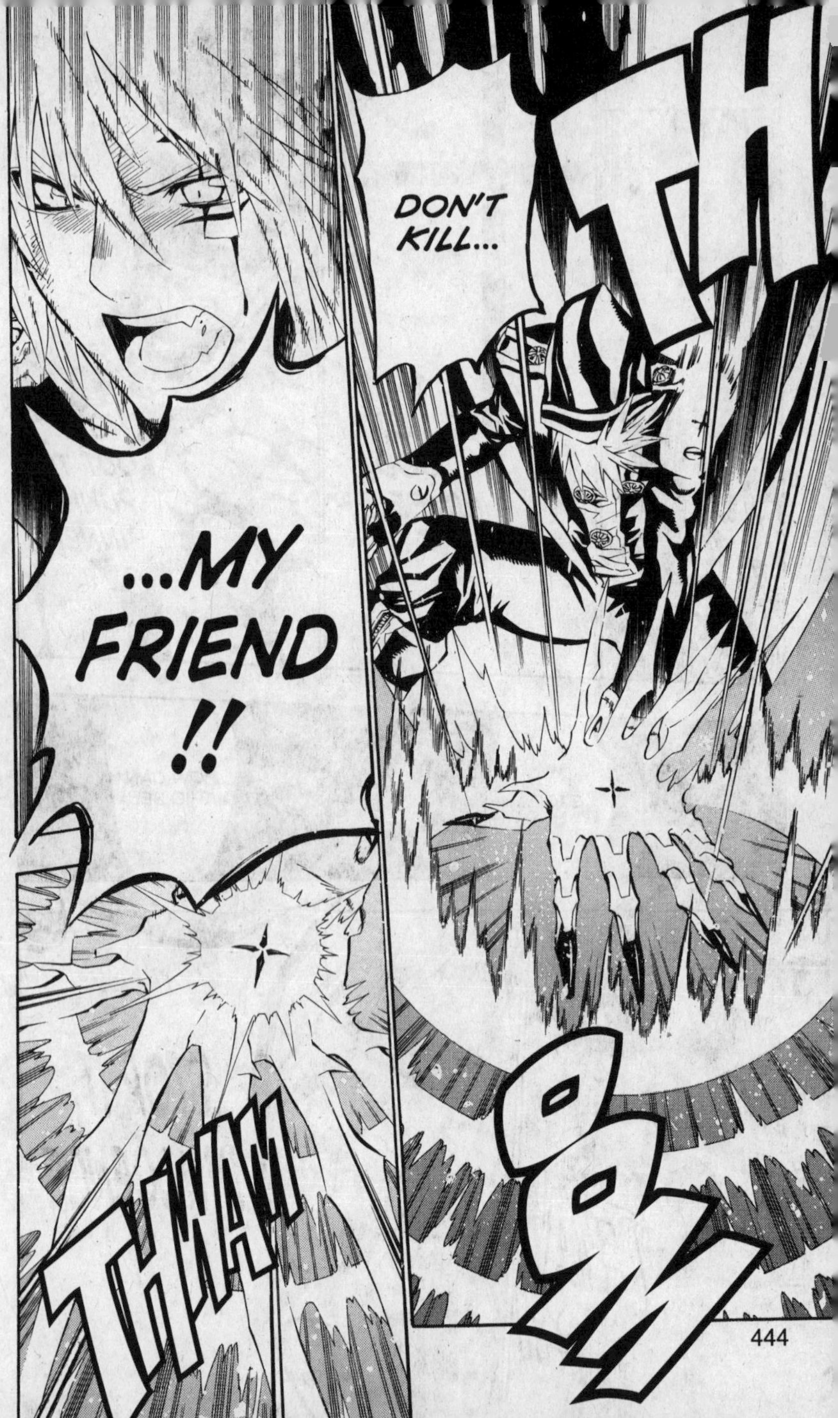
DON'T KILL...
...MY FRIEND !!

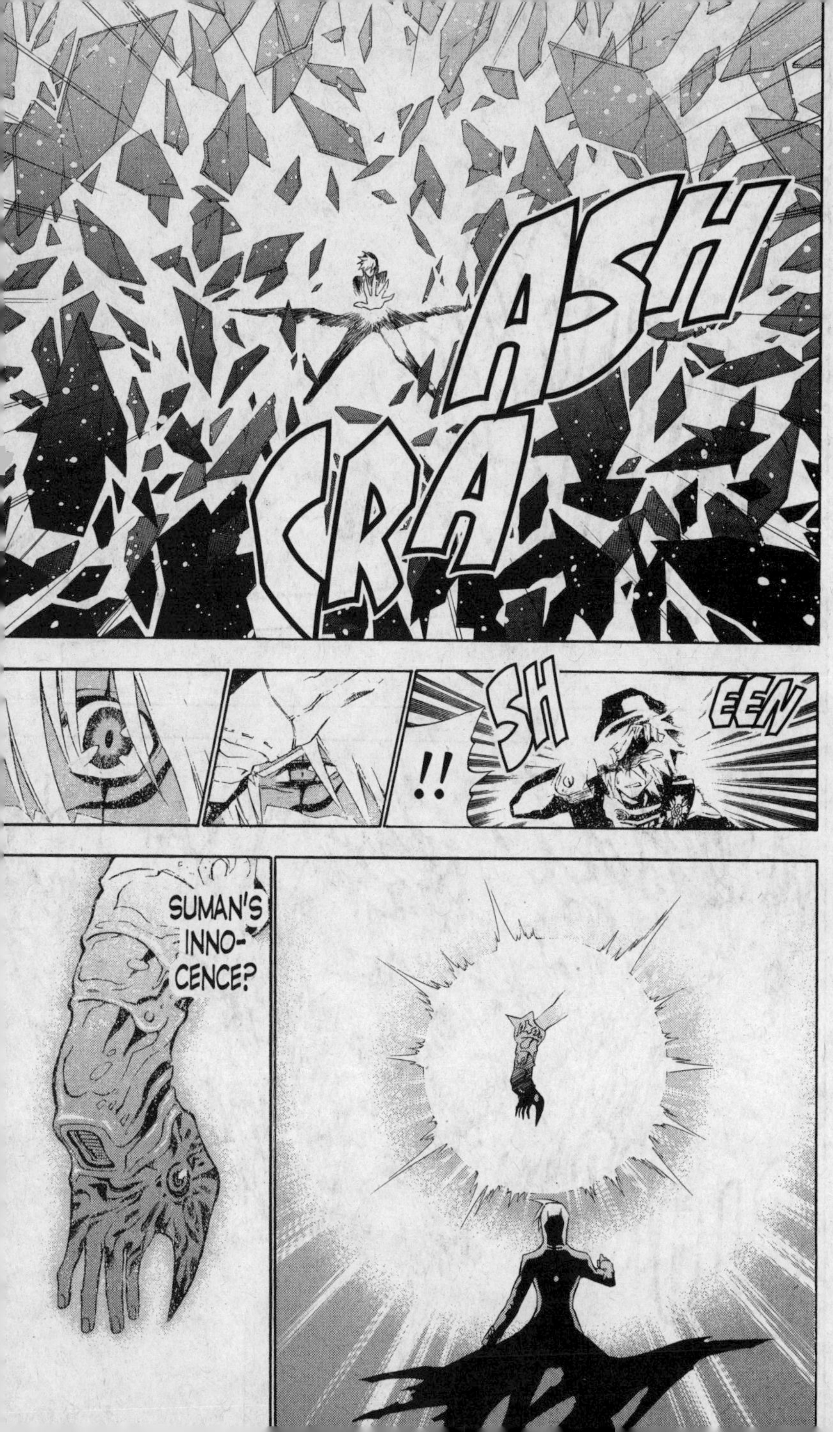
CRA
ASH
SH
EEN
!!
SUMAN'S INNO-CENCE?

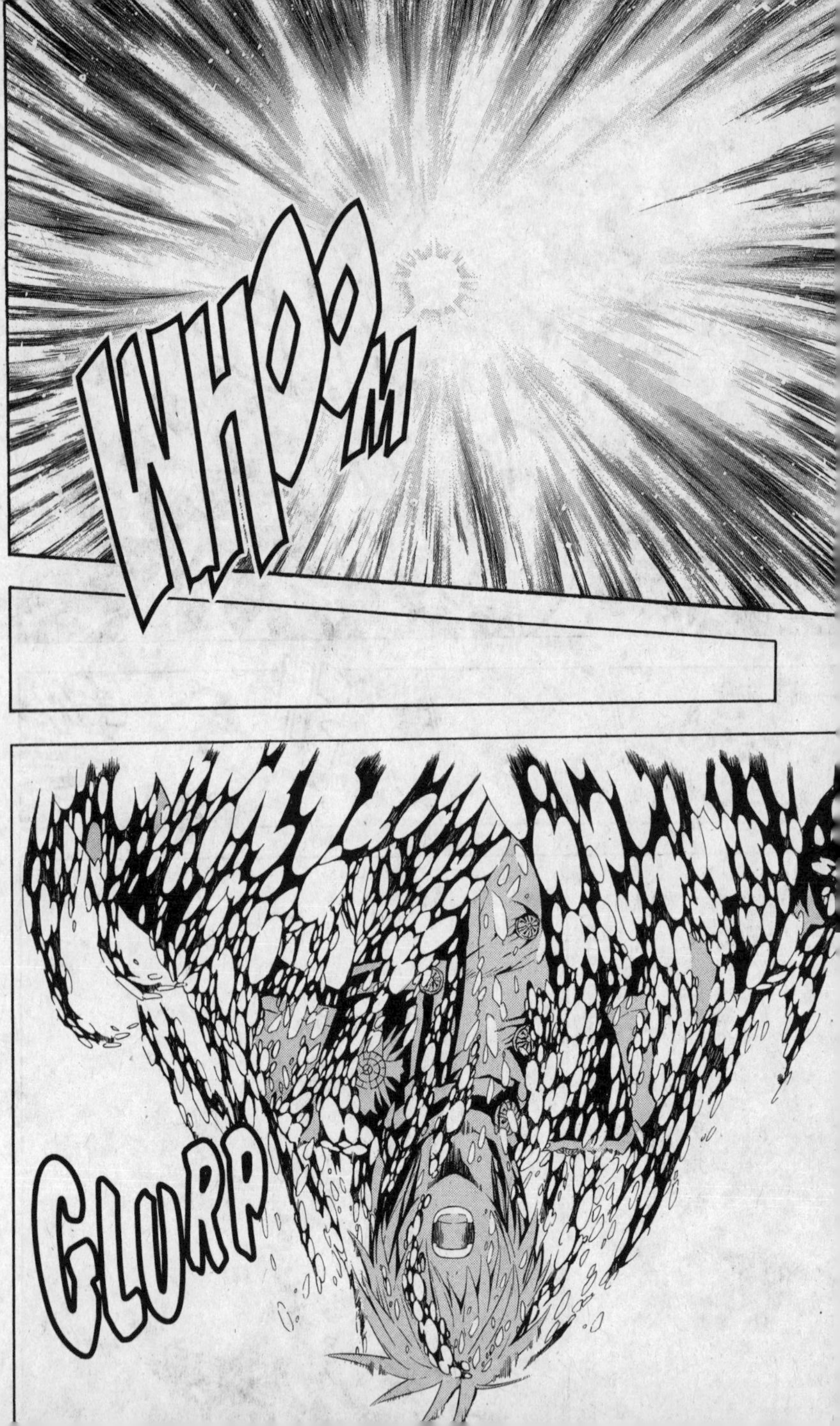
WHOOM
GLURP

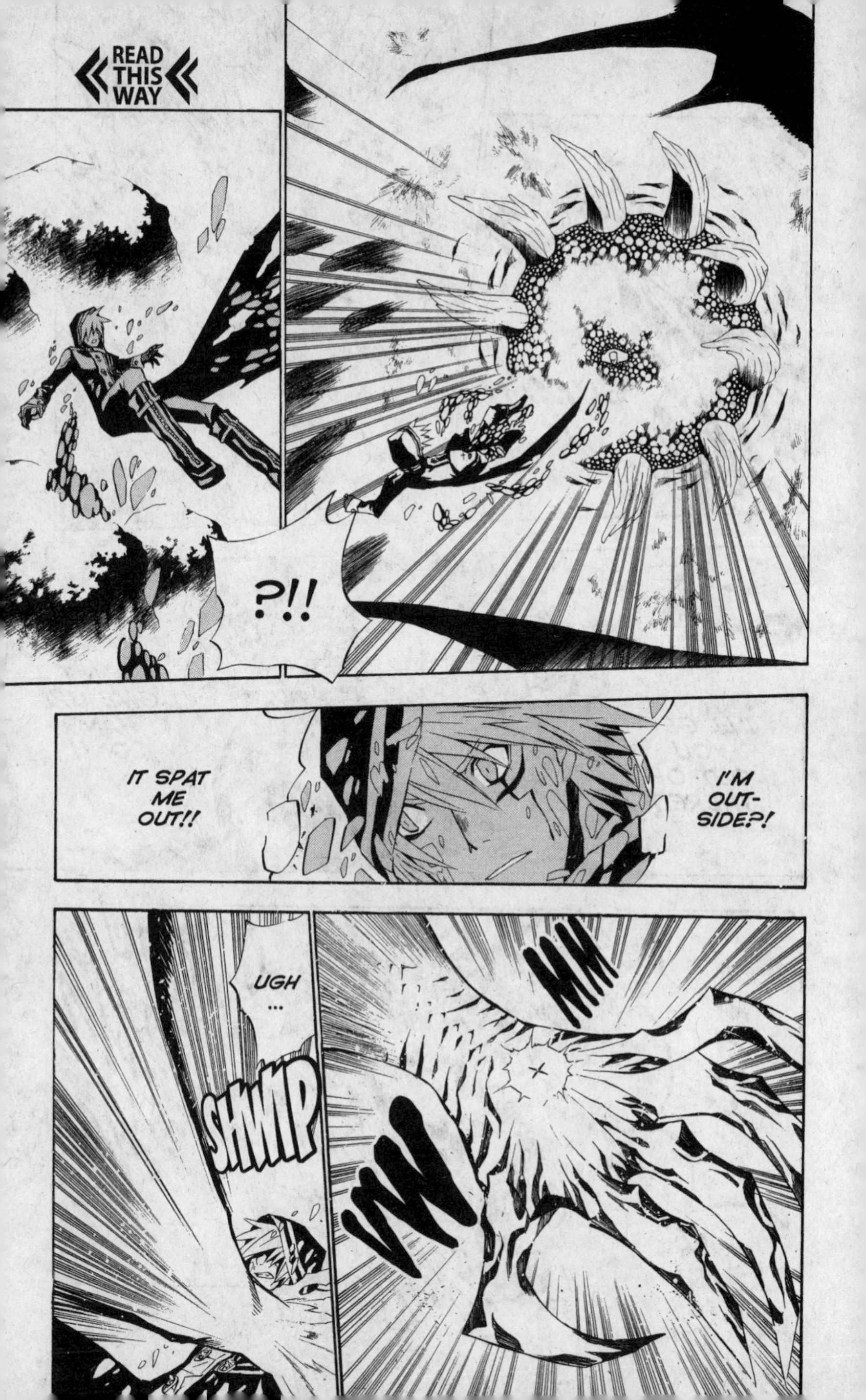
READ THIS WAY
?!!
I'M OUT-SIDE?!
IT SPAT ME OUT!!
MM
WW
UGH ...
SHWIP

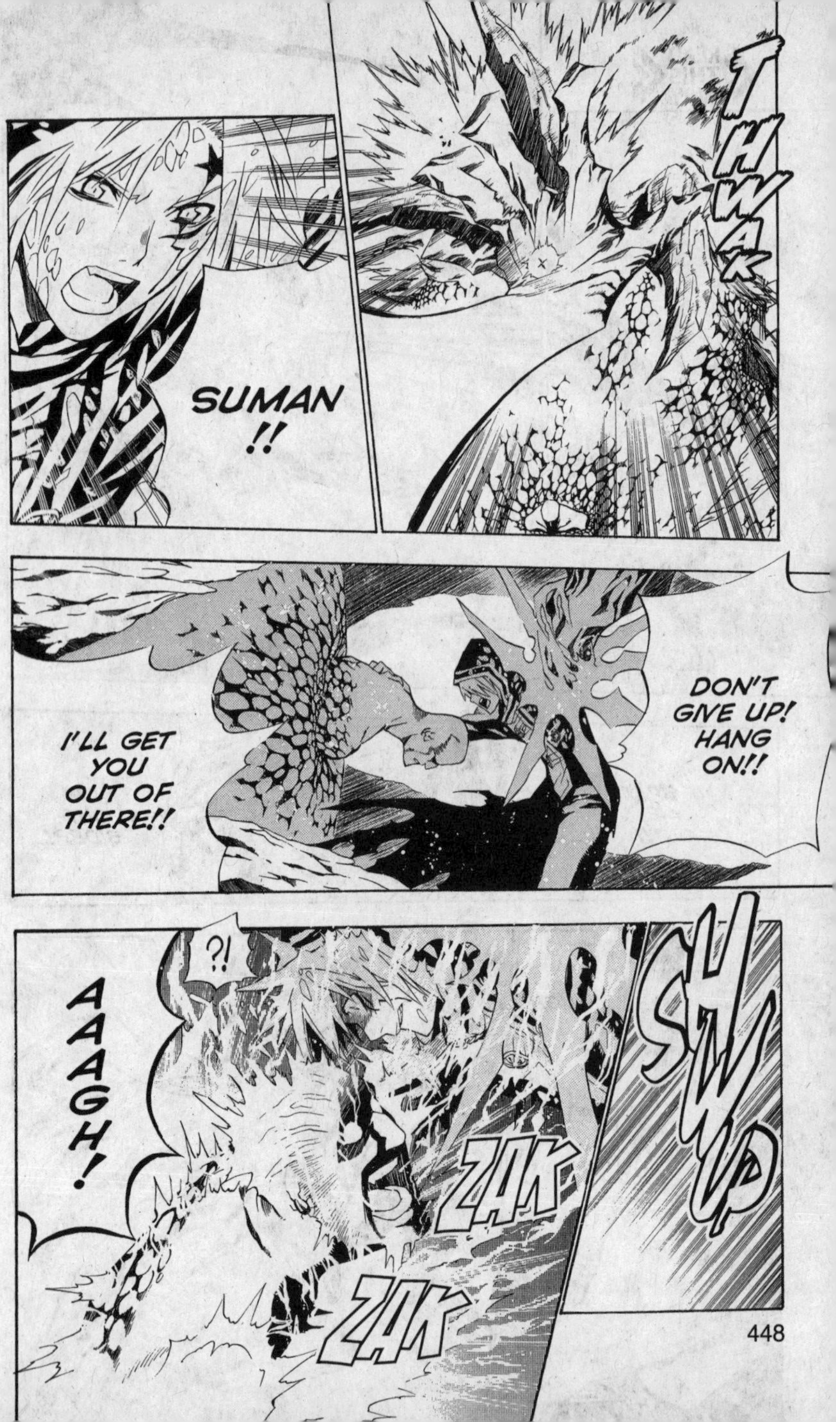
THWAK
SUMAN !!
DON'T GIVE UP! HANG ON!!
I'LL GET YOU OUT OF THERE!!
SHWUP
?!
AAAGH!
ZAK
ZAK

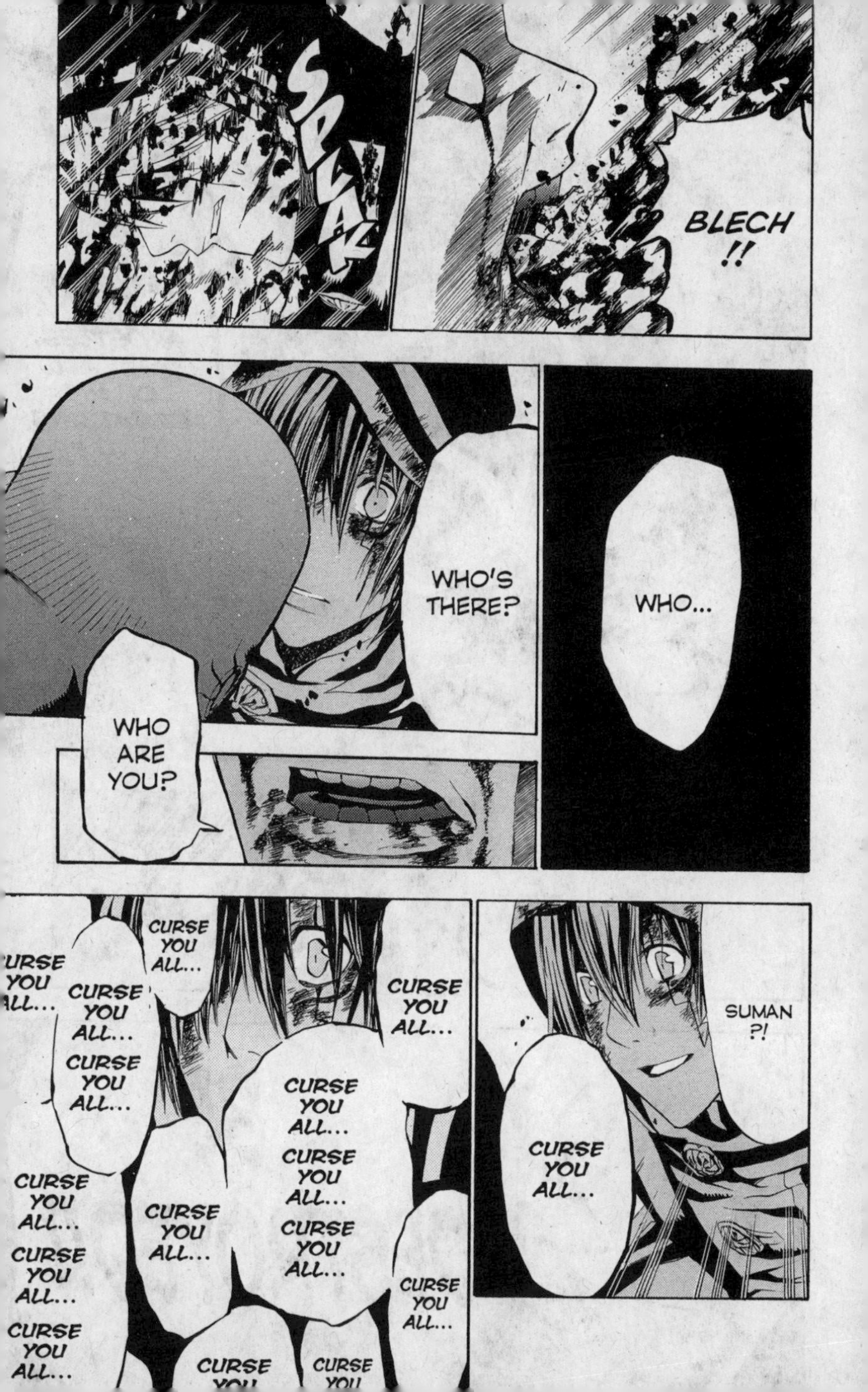
BLECH !!
SPLAK
WHO...
WHO'S THERE?
WHO ARE YOU?
SUMAN ?!
CURSE YOU ALL...
CURSE YOU ALL...
CURSE YOU ALL...
CURSE YOU ALL...
CURSE YOU ALL...
CURSE YOU ALL...
CURSE YOU ALL...
CURSE YOU ALL...
CURSE YOU ALL...
CURSE YOU ALL...
CURSE YOU ALL...
CURSE YOU ALL...
CURSE YOU ALL...
CURSE YOU ALL...
CURSE
CURSE

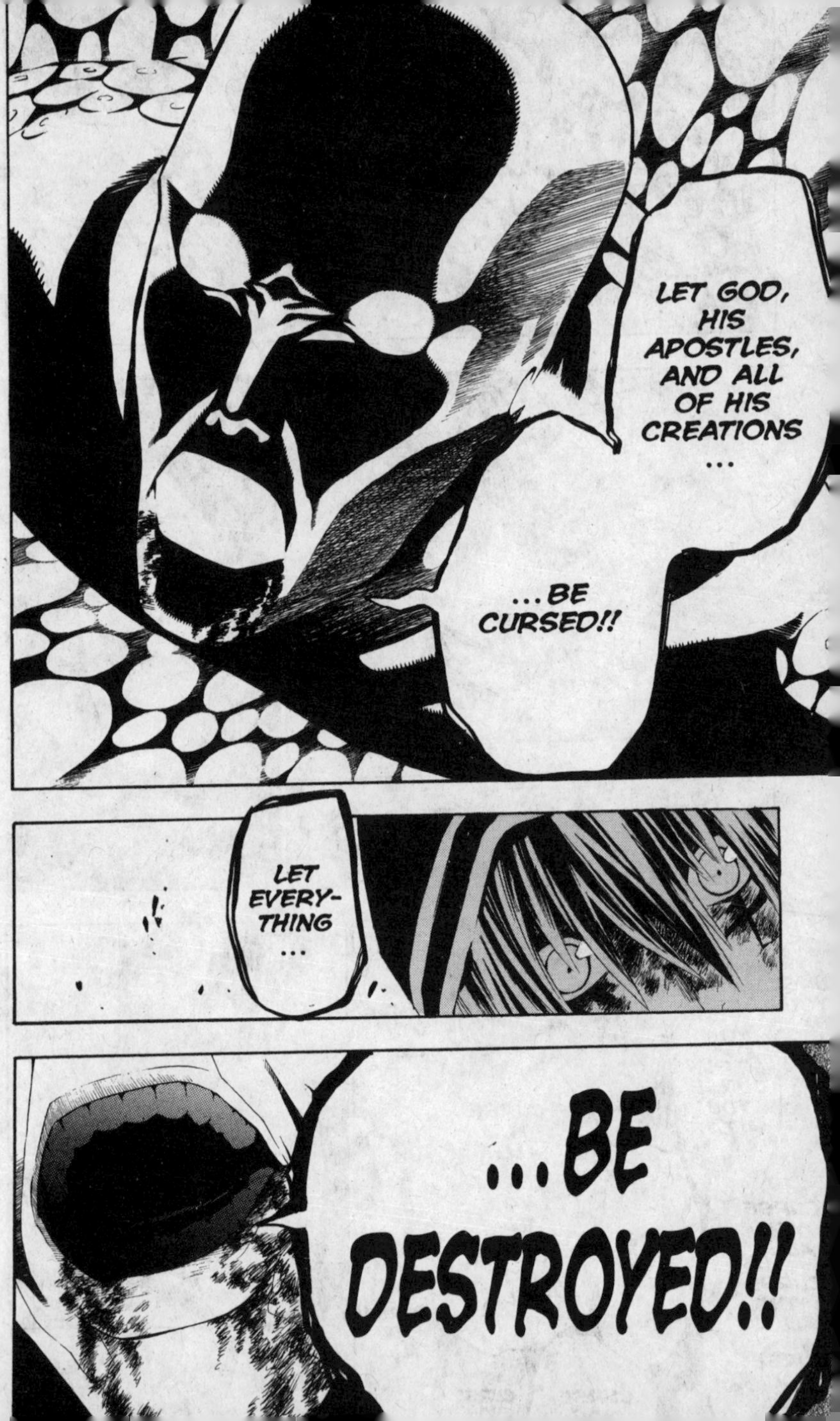
LET GOD, HIS APOSTLES, AND ALL OF HIS CREATIONS ...
...BE CURSED!!
LET EVERY- THING ...
...BE DESTROYED!!

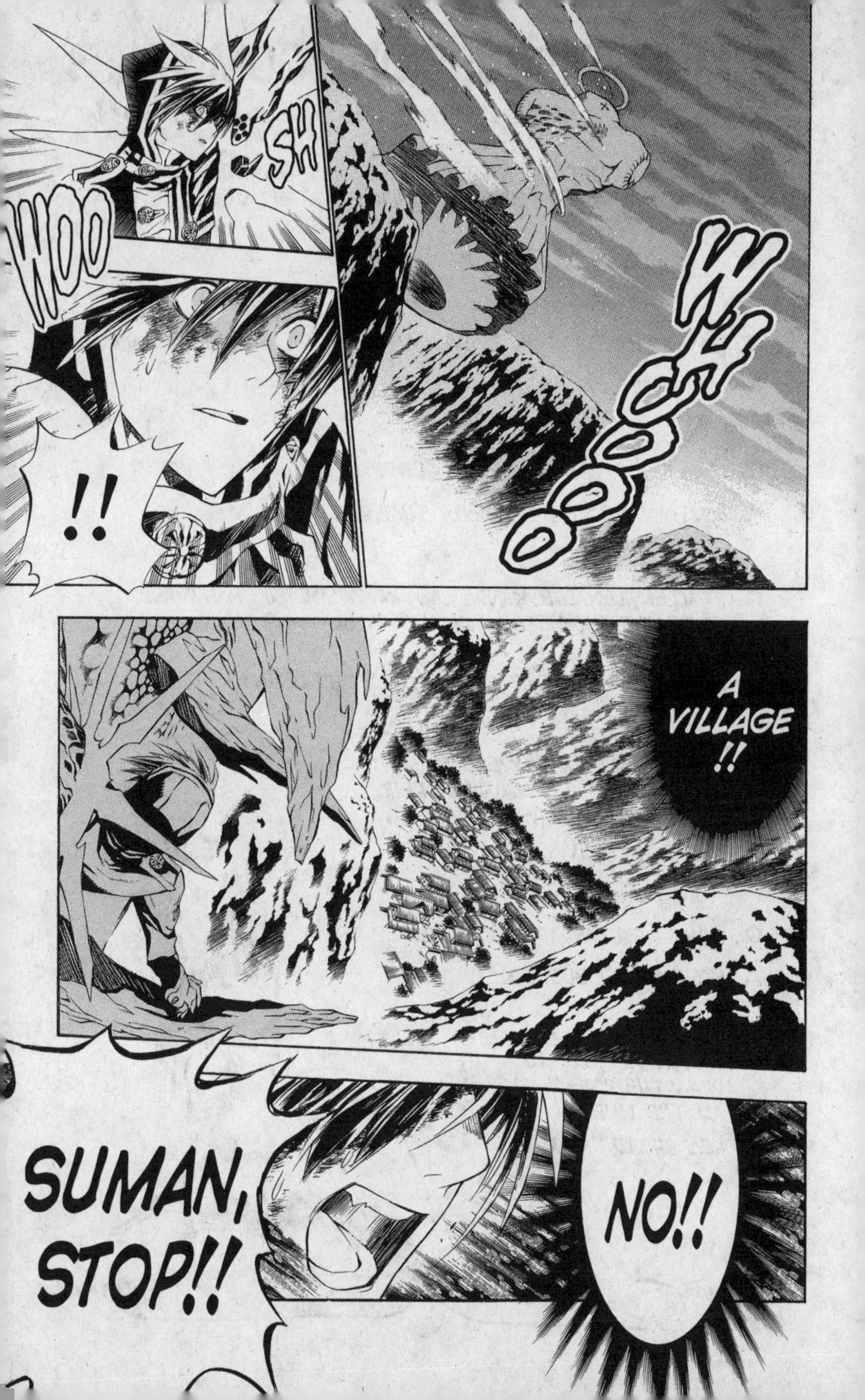
WHOOOOO
WOO
SH
!!
A VILLAGE !!
NO!!
SUMAN, STOP!!

KOMUI'S DISCUSSION ROOM VOL. 3

Q. DOES KANDA LIKE ANY NOODLES OTHER THAN SOBA (LIKE UDON AND SUCH)? DOES HE CONSIDER NOODLES THAT AREN'T SOBA AN ABOMINATION?

A. WHAT KIND OF STUPID QUESTION IS THAT?

Q. HOW MUCH SLEEP DOES REEVER WENHAM GET IN A TYPICAL DAY?

A. HOW SHOULD I KNOW?

Q. WHO DOES ALLEN FEAR MORE, GENERAL CROSS OR CHIEF KOMUI?

A. DON'T ASK ME QUESTIONS ABOUT THAT GUY.

Q. IF ALLEN, LENALEE, KANDA, LAVI, KRORY, AND BOOKMAN WERE TO RUN THE 100-METER DASH, WHO WOULD WIN?

A. ...(AFTER A MOMENT OF THOUGHT) PROBABLY LENALEE.

Q. IF ALLEN AND KANDA WERE TO FIGHT EACH OTHER FOR REAL (USING THEIR INNOCENCES), WHO WOULD WIN?

A. I'D CUT HIM IN TWO.

Q. WHAT DOES KANDA'S ROOM LOOK LIKE?

A. NONE OF YOUR BUSINESS.

Q. ISN'T IT DIFFICULT TO DRAW THE ROSE CROSS ALL THE TIME?

A. HOW SHOULD I KNOW?

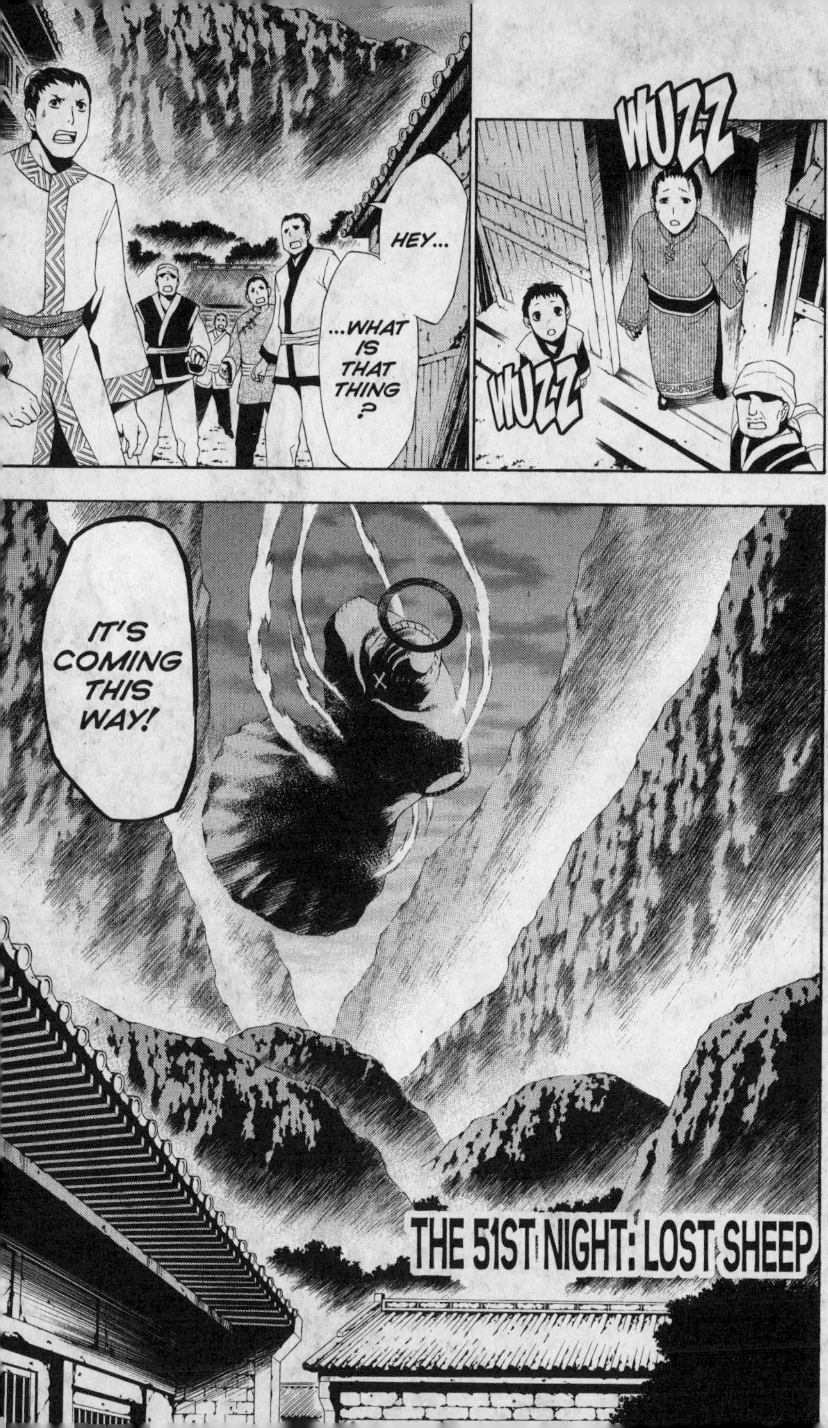
WUZZ
WUZZ
HEY...
...WHAT IS THAT THING?
IT'S COMING THIS WAY!
THE 51ST NIGHT: LOST SHEEP

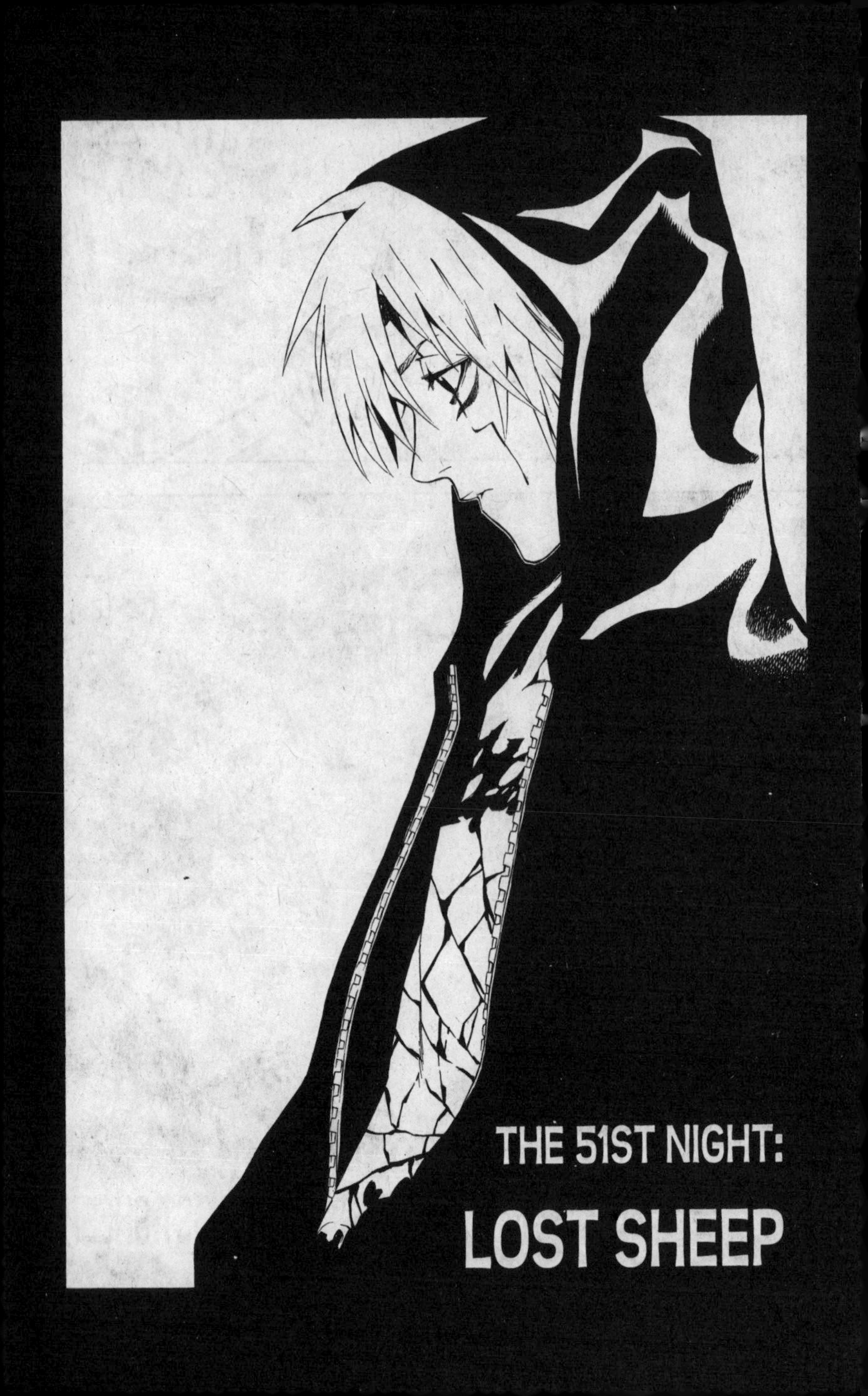
THE 51ST NIGHT:
LOST SHEEP

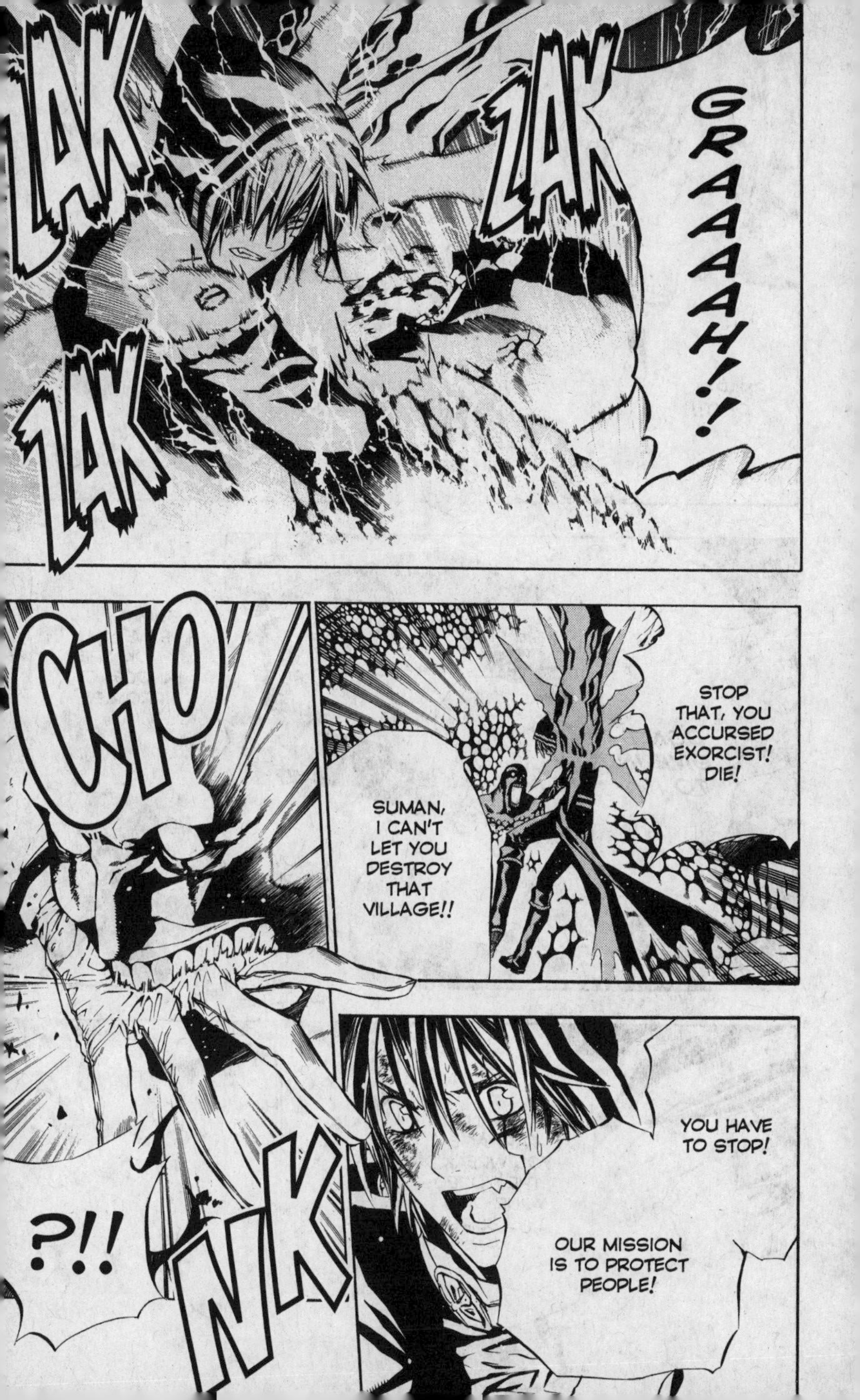
GRAAAAAH!!
ZAK
ZAK
ZAK
STOP THAT, YOU ACCURSED EXORCIST! DIE!
SUMAN, I CAN'T LET YOU DESTROY THAT VILLAGE!!
YOU HAVE TO STOP!
OUR MISSION IS TO PROTECT PEOPLE!
CHO
NK
?!!

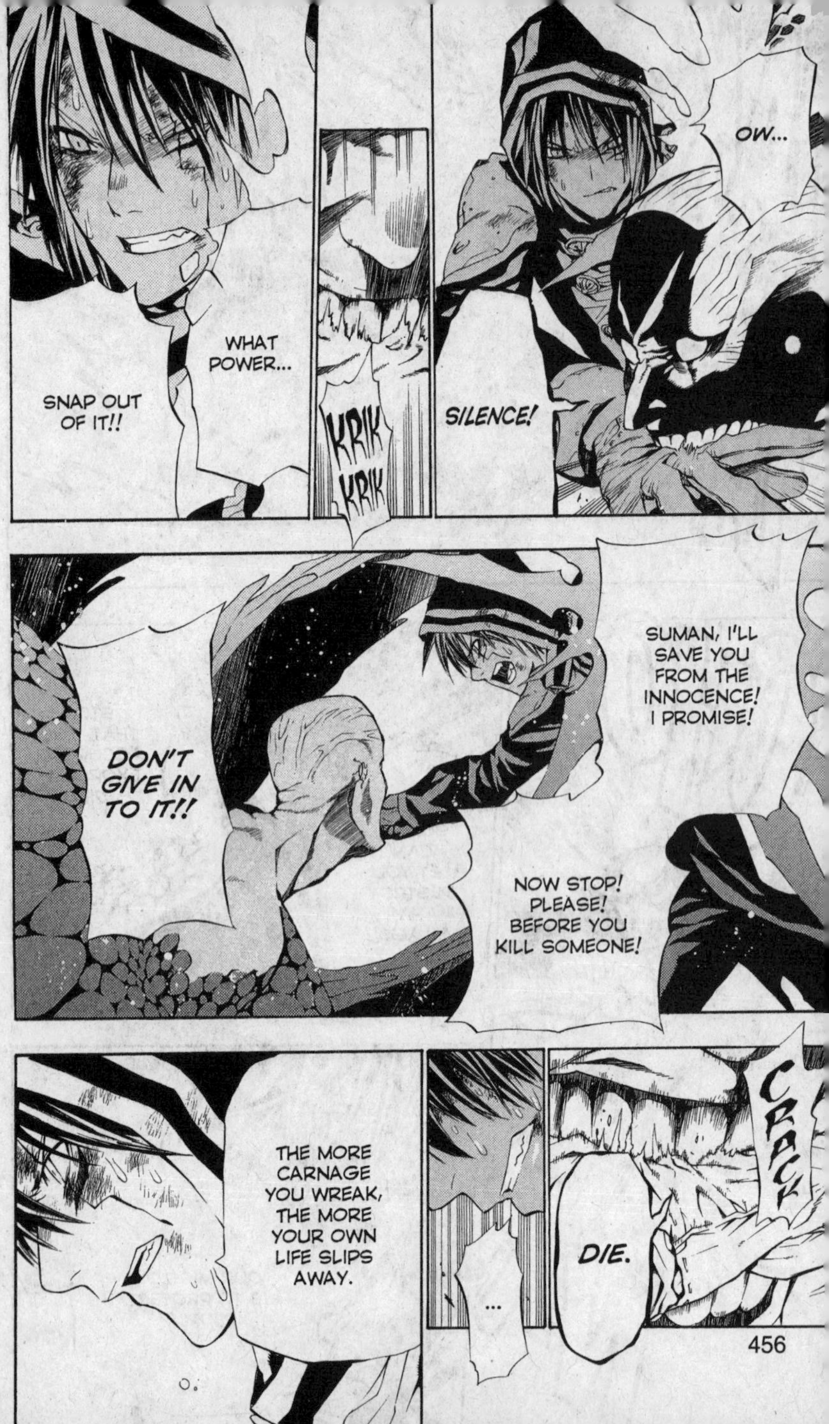
OW...
SILENCE!
KRIK KRIK
WHAT POWER...
SNAP OUT OF IT!!
SUMAN, I'LL SAVE YOU FROM THE INNOCENCE! I PROMISE!
NOW STOP! PLEASE! BEFORE YOU KILL SOMEONE!
DON'T GIVE IN TO IT!!
CRACK
DIE.
...
THE MORE CARNAGE YOU WREAK, THE MORE YOUR OWN LIFE SLIPS AWAY.

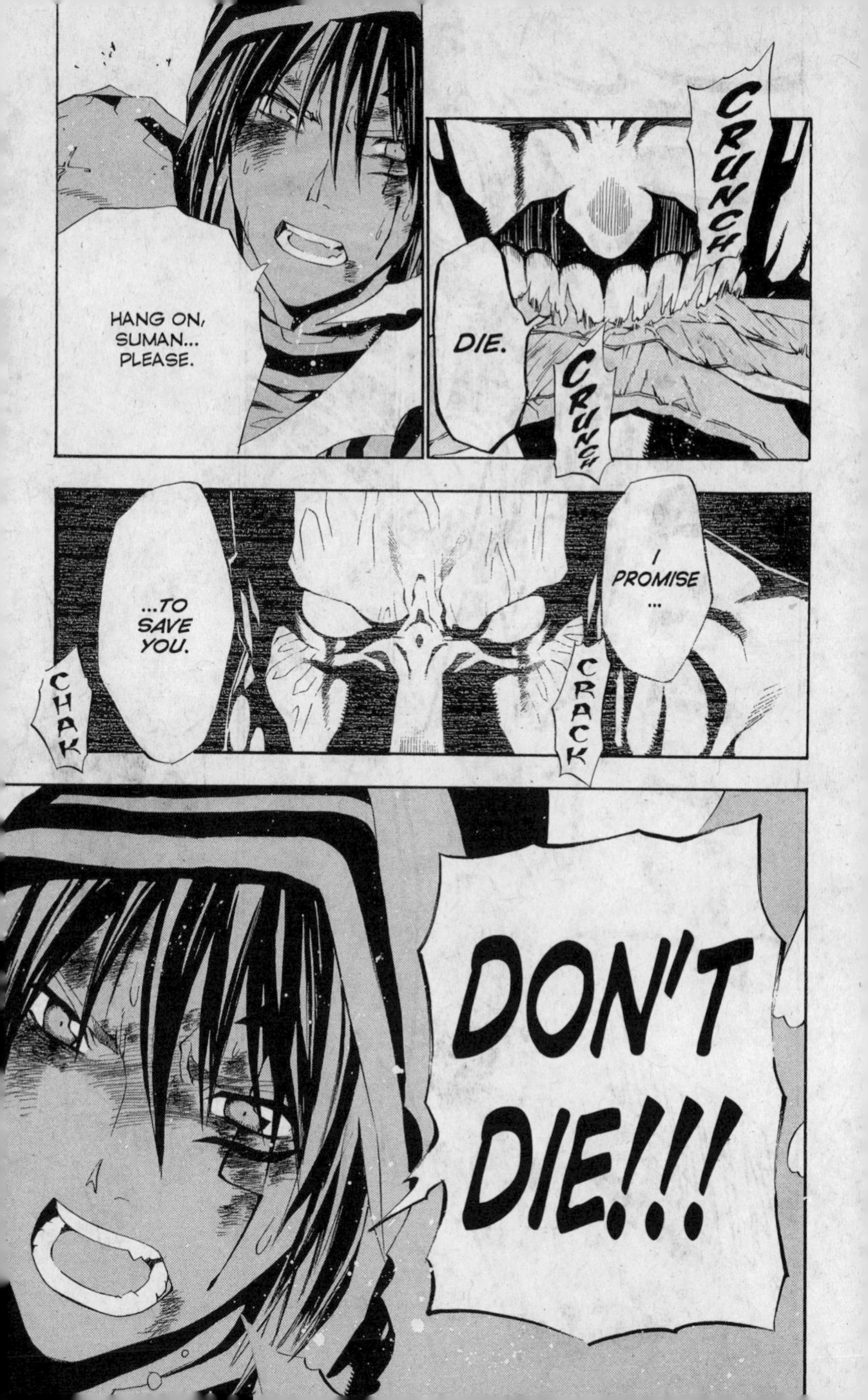
CRUNCH
DIE.
CRUNCH
HANG ON, SUMAN... PLEASE.
I PROMISE ...
CRACK
...TO SAVE YOU.
CHAK
DON'T DIE!!!

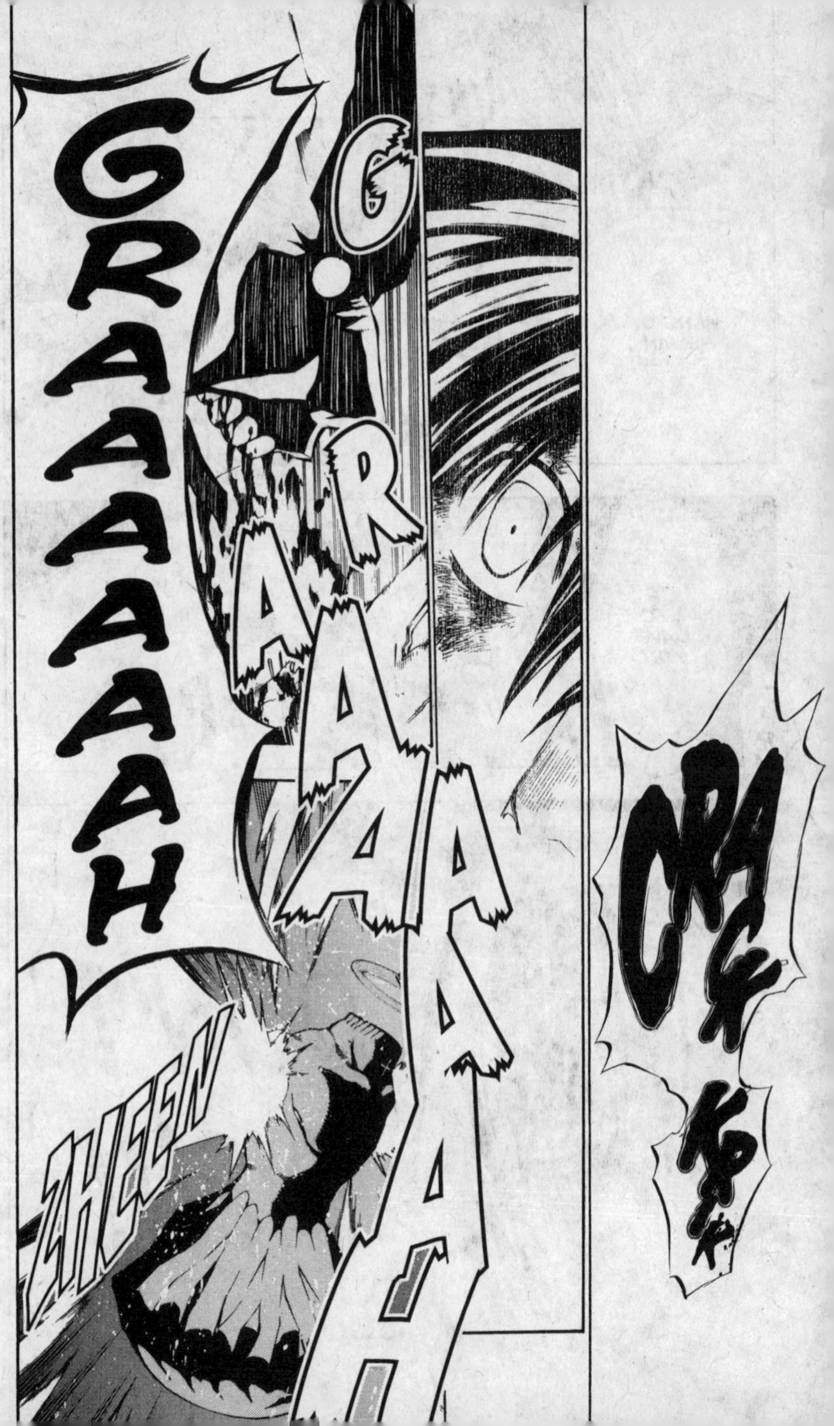
CRACK
GRAAAAAAH
GRAAAAAAH
SHEEN

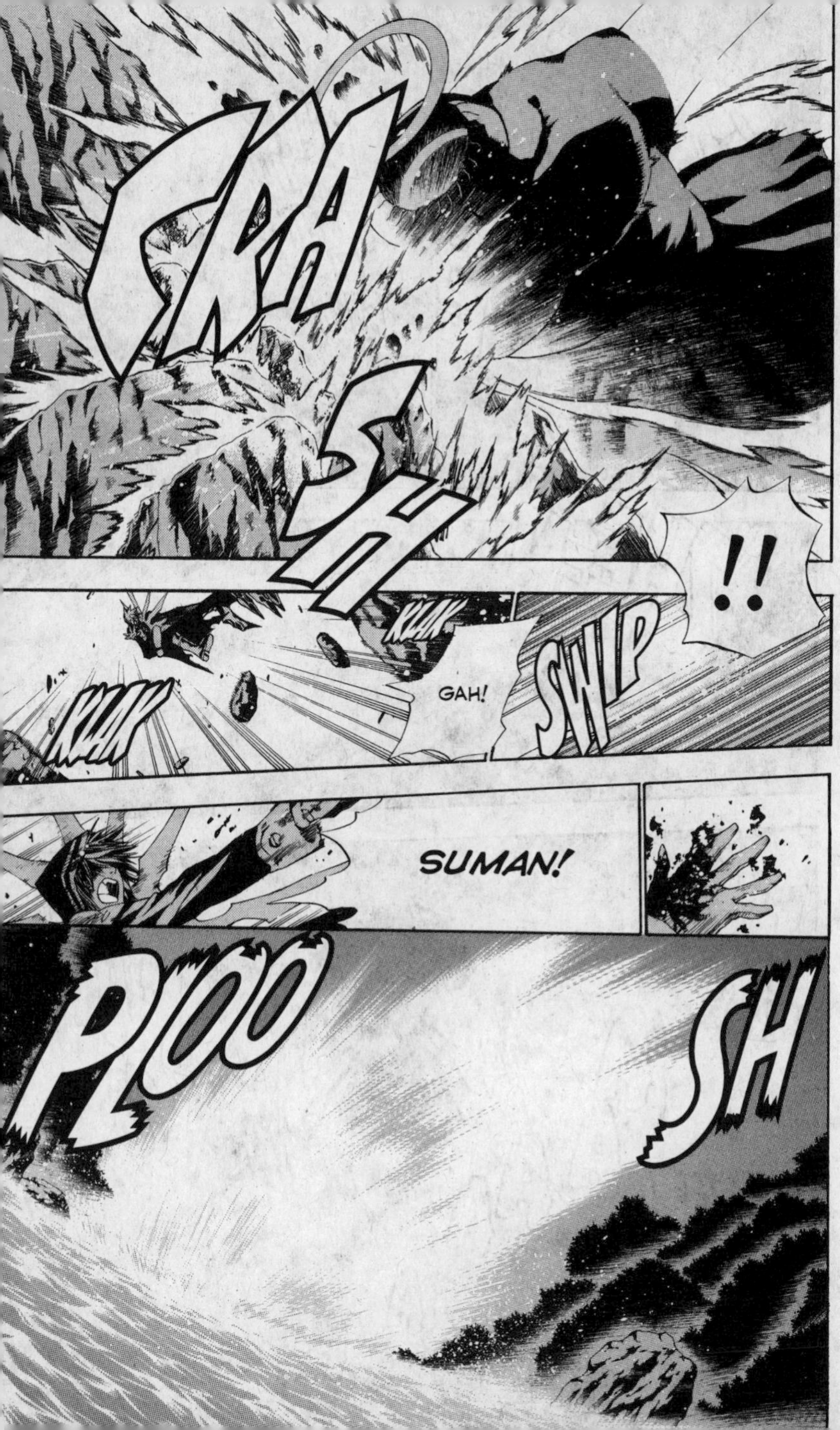
CRASH
!!
SWIP
GAH!
KLAK
KLAK
SUMAN!
PLOOSH

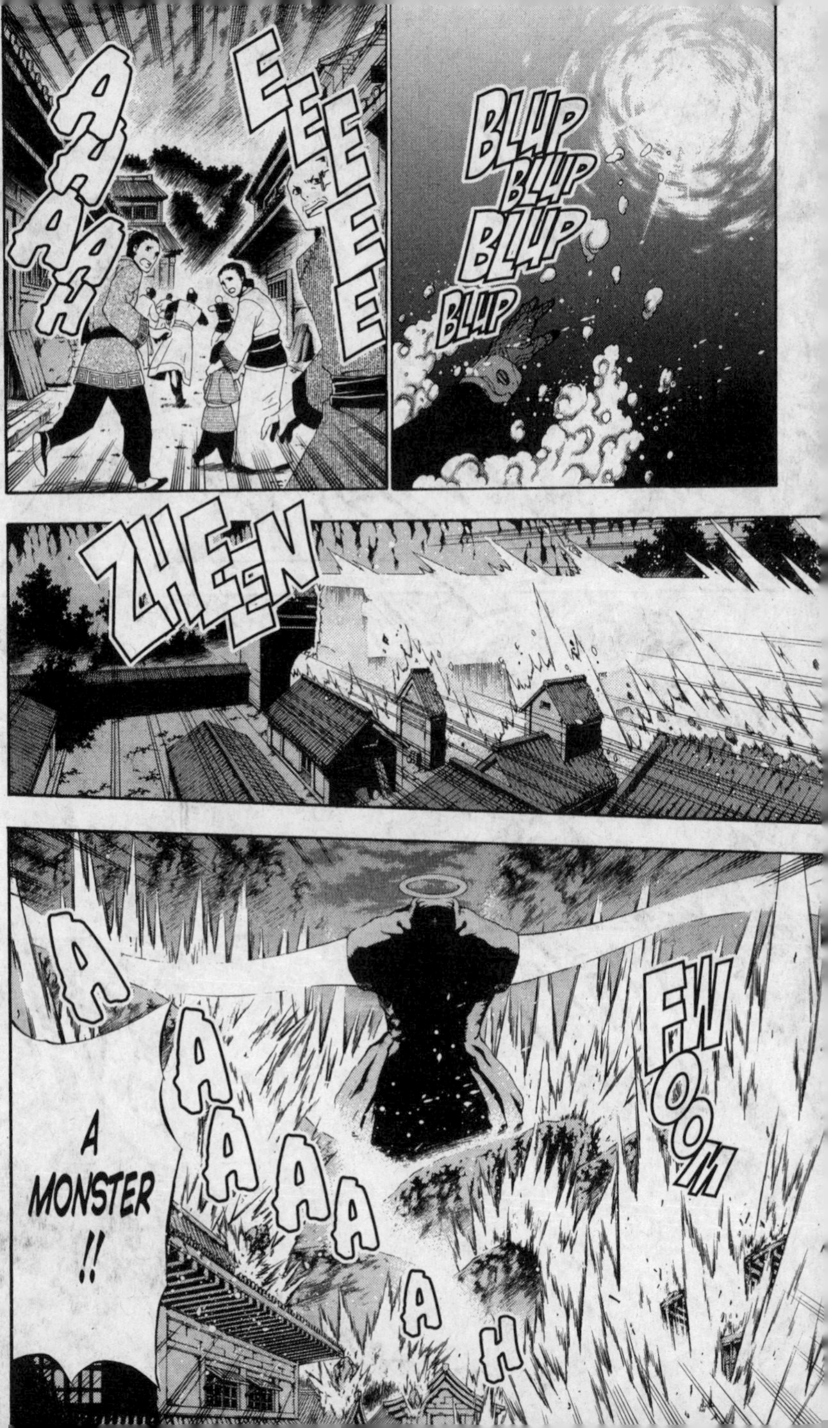
BLUP BLUP BLUP BLUP
EEEEEE
AAAAH
ZHEEEN
FWOOOM
AAAAAAAH
A MONSTER!!

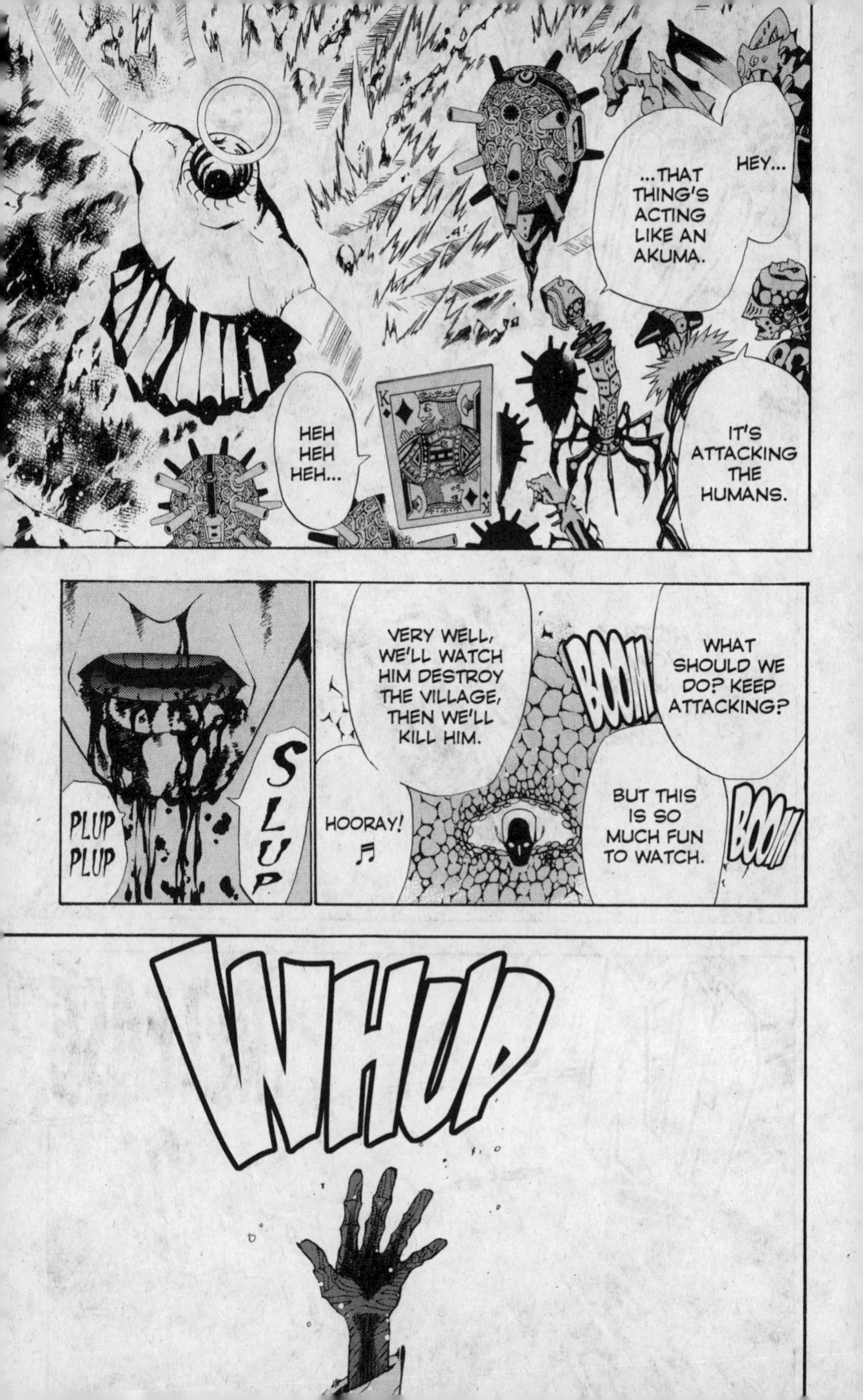
HEY...
...THAT THING'S ACTING LIKE AN AKUMA.
IT'S ATTACKING THE HUMANS.
HEH HEH HEH...
WHAT SHOULD WE DO? KEEP ATTACKING?
BOOM
VERY WELL, WE'LL WATCH HIM DESTROY THE VILLAGE, THEN WE'LL KILL HIM.
BUT THIS IS SO MUCH FUN TO WATCH.
BOOM
HOORAY! ♬
SLUP
PLUP PLUP
WHUD

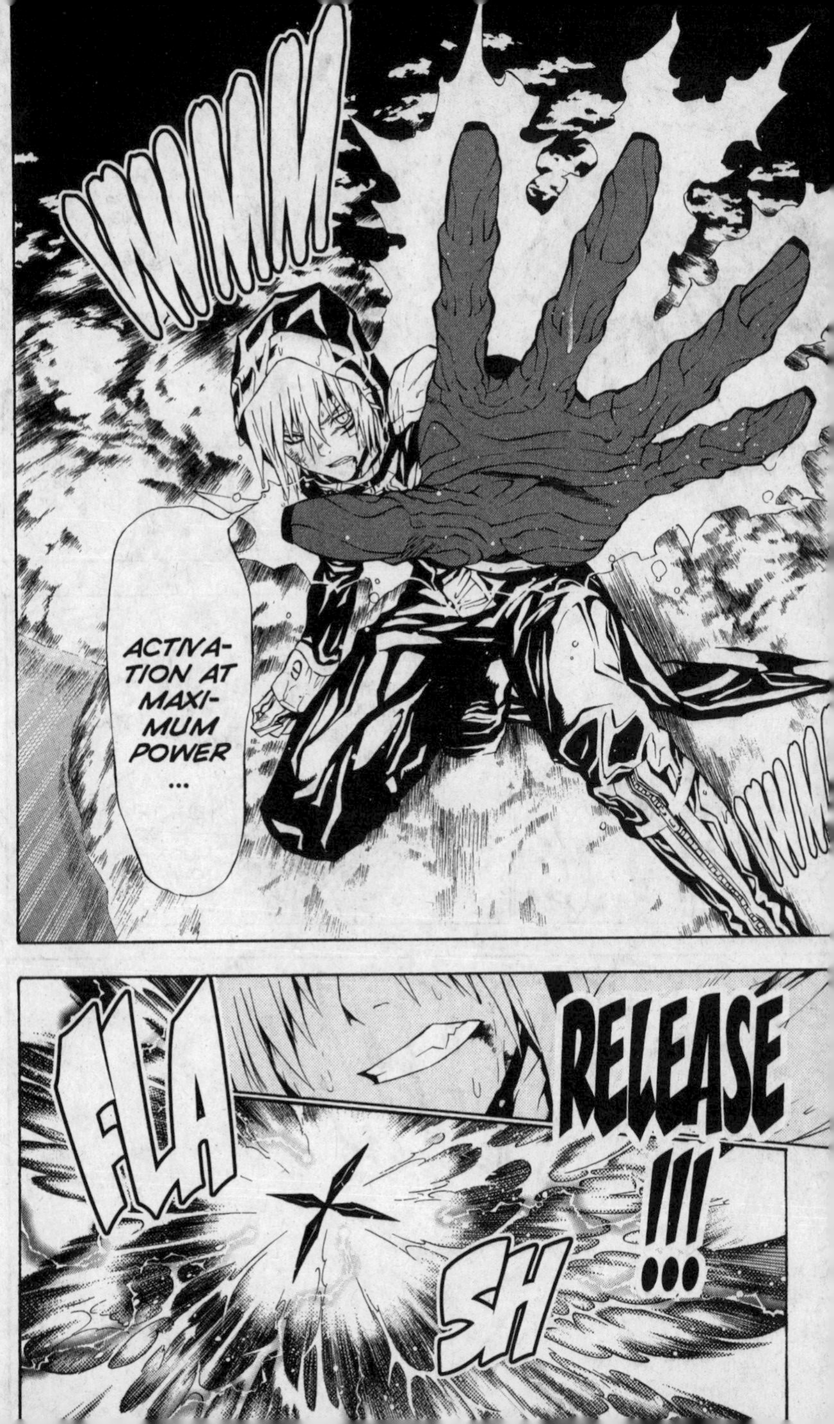
WMMMM
ACTIVATION AT MAXIMUM POWER ...
RELEASE !!!...
FLASH

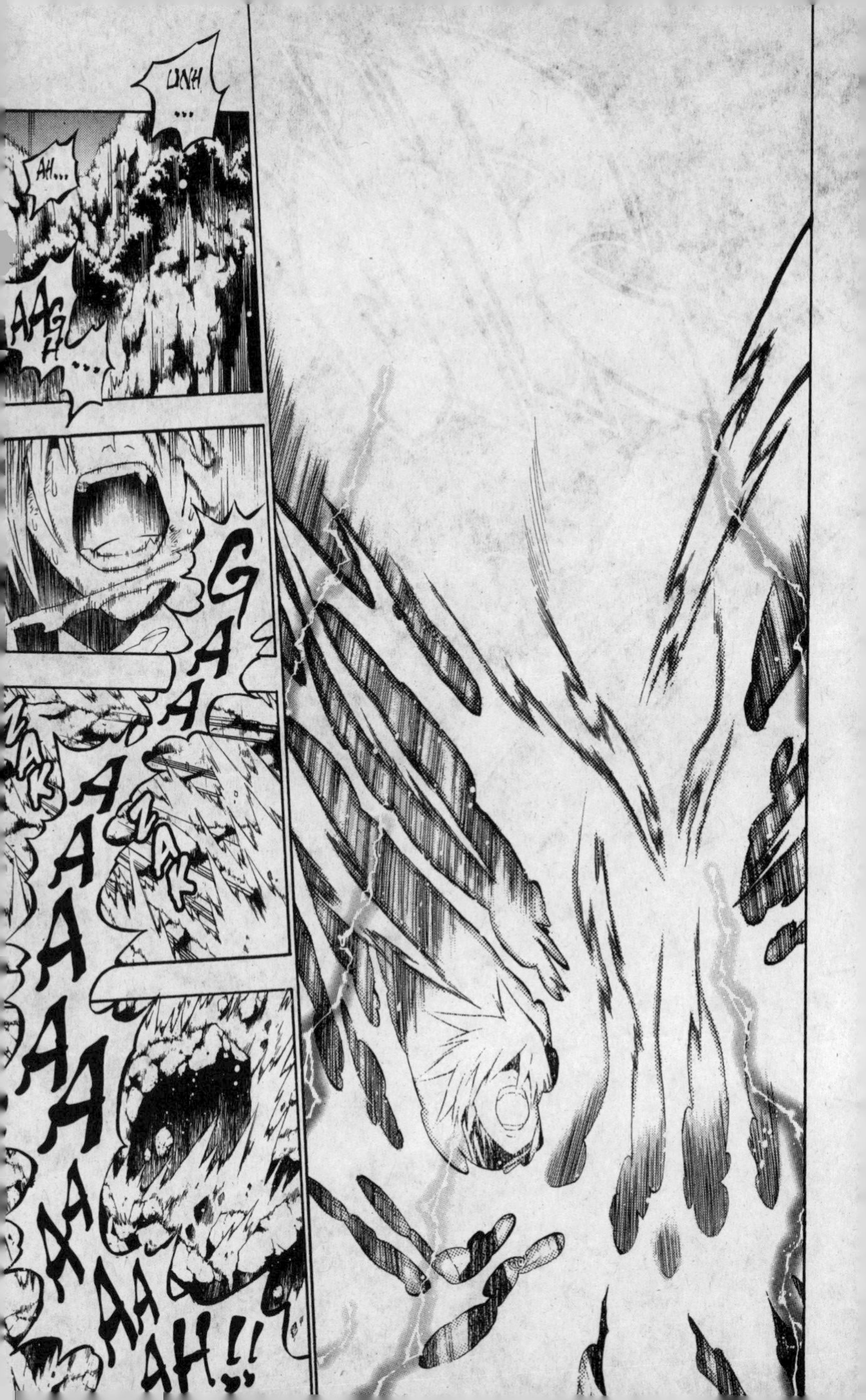
UNH ...
AH...
AAGH...
GAAAAAAAAAAAAAAH!!
NAK
NAK

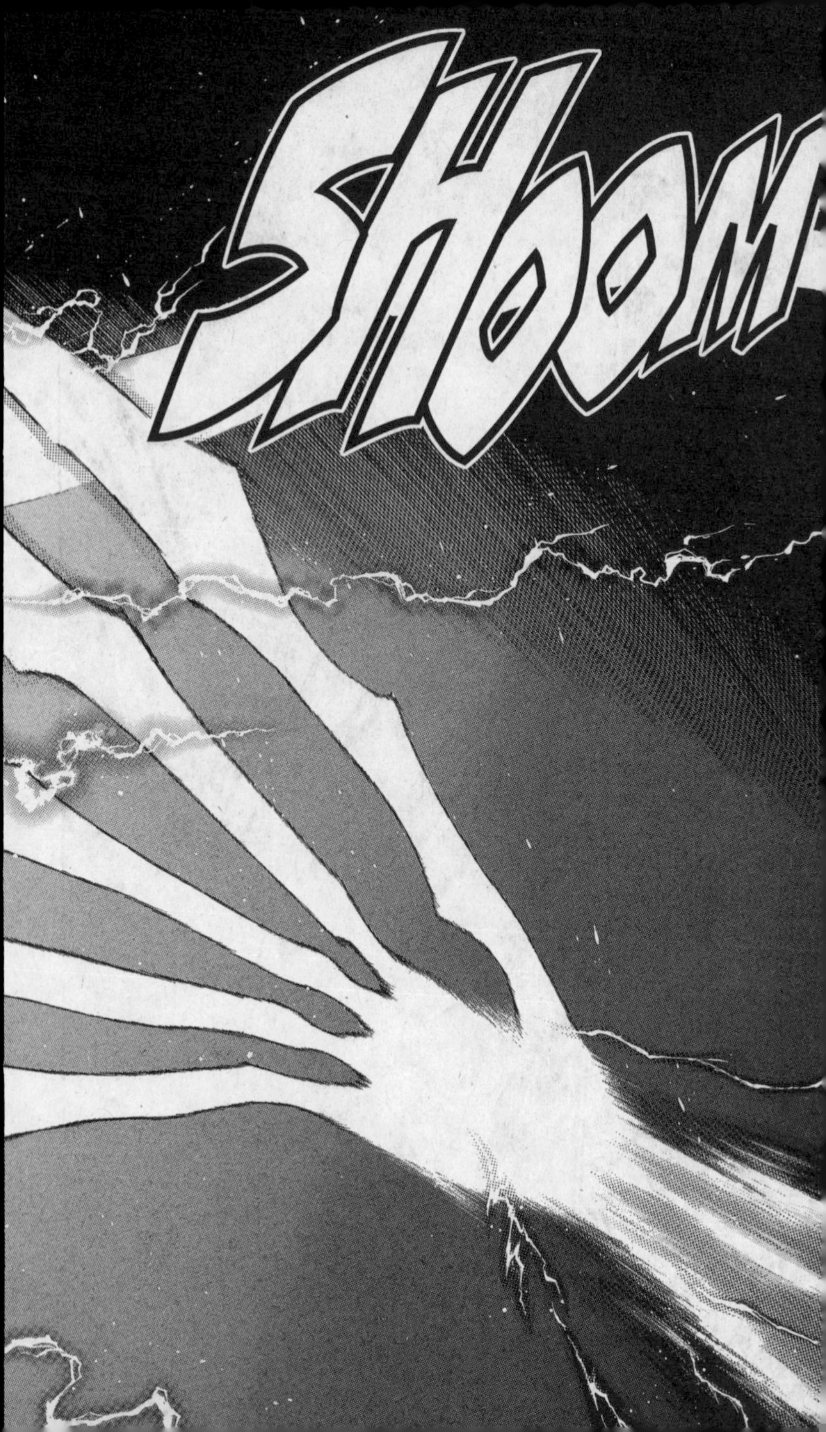
SHOOM

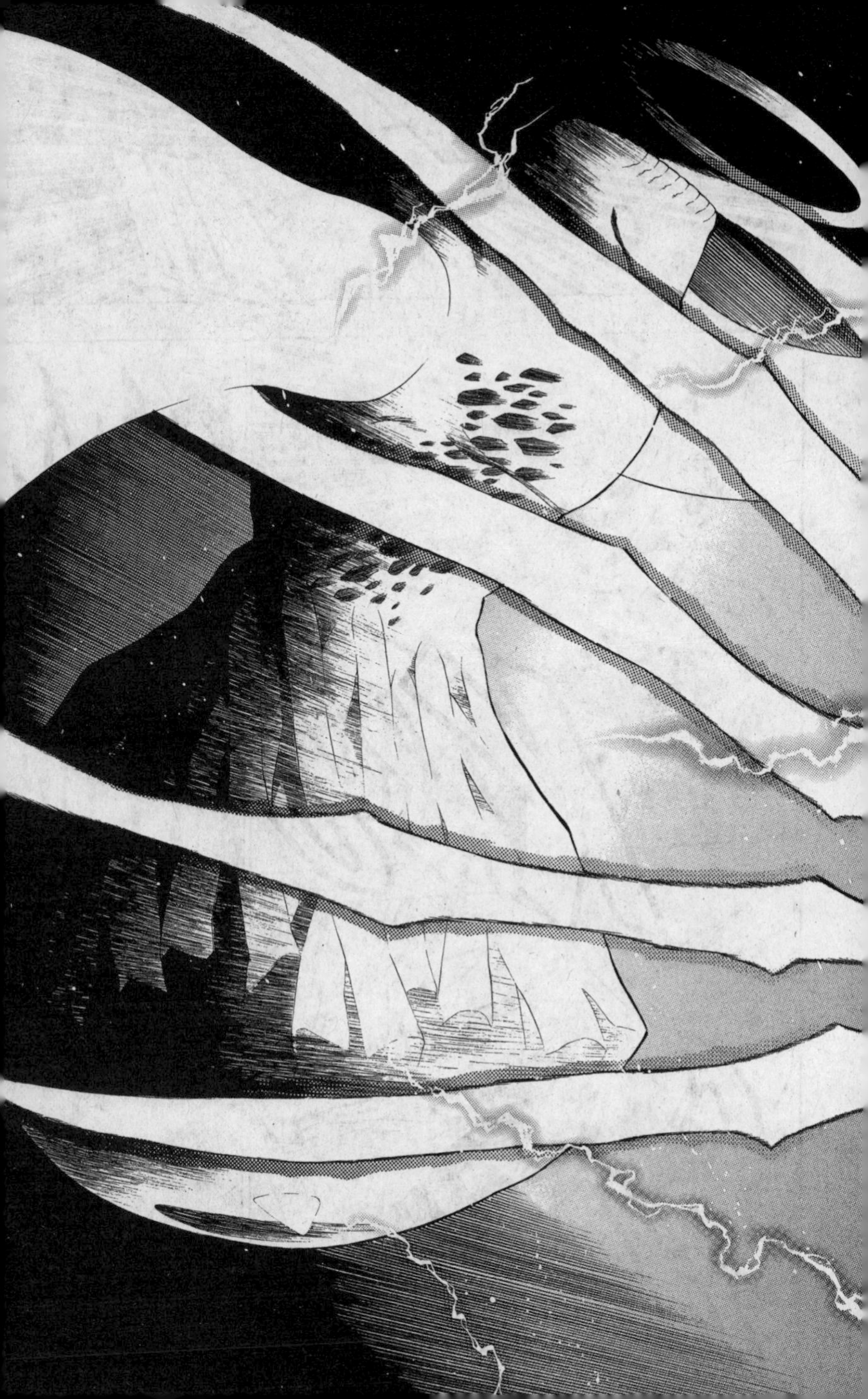

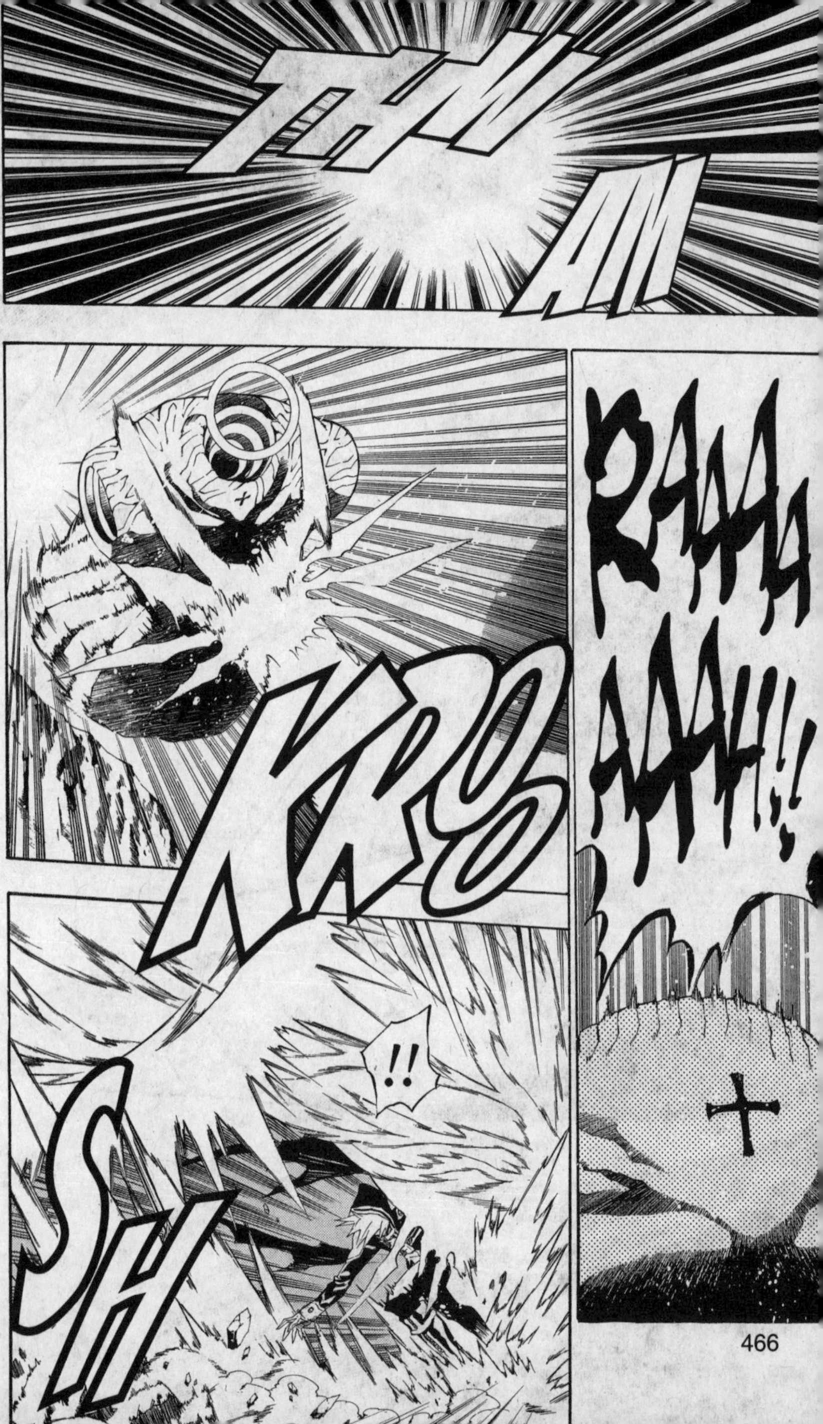
RAAAAAAAH!!
!!
SH

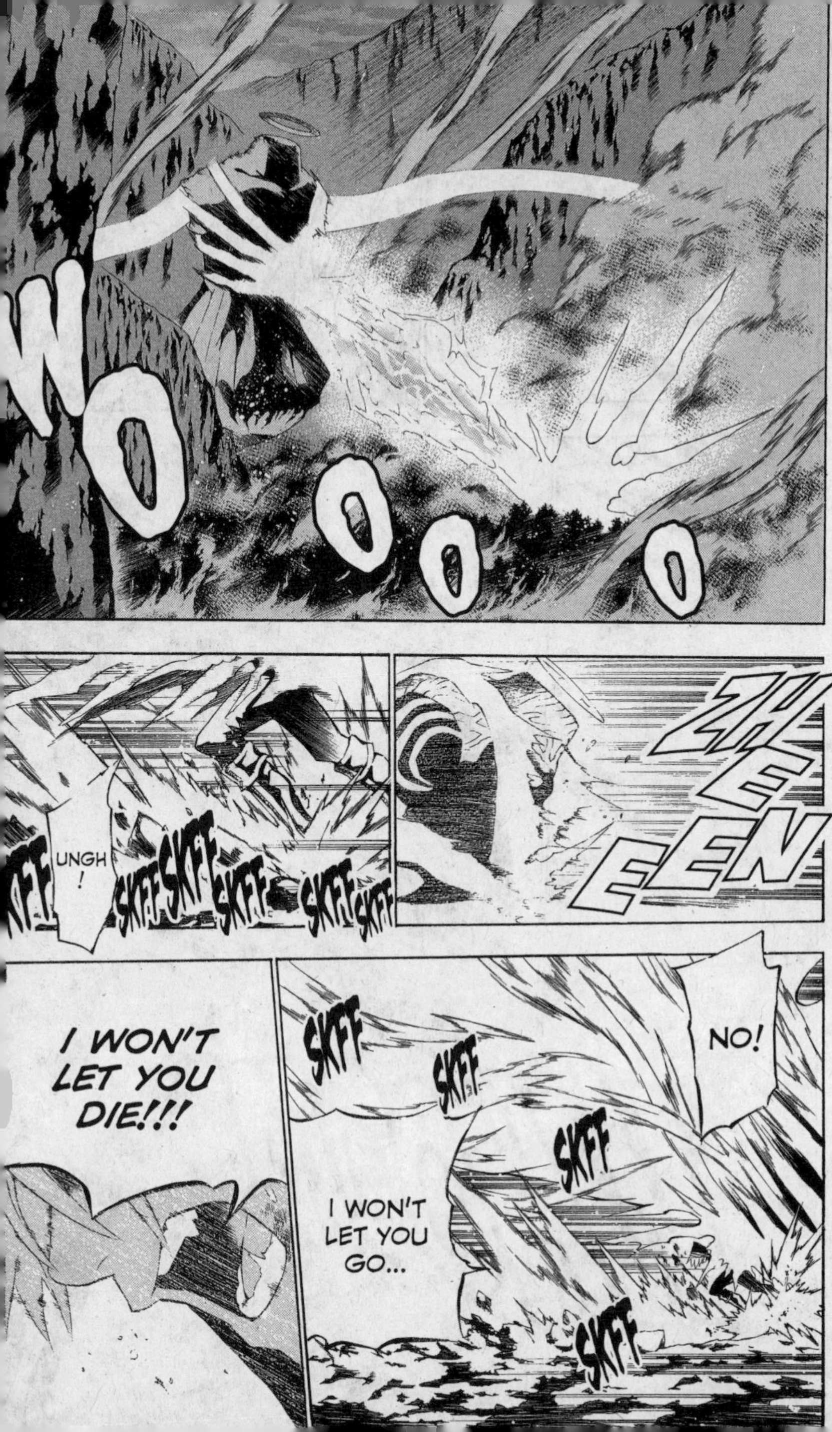
WOOOO
ZHEEEN
SKFF
SKFF
SKFF
SKFF
SKFF
UNGH!
SKFF
NO!
SKFF
SKFF
SKFF
I WON'T LET YOU GO...
SKFF
I WON'T LET YOU DIE!!!

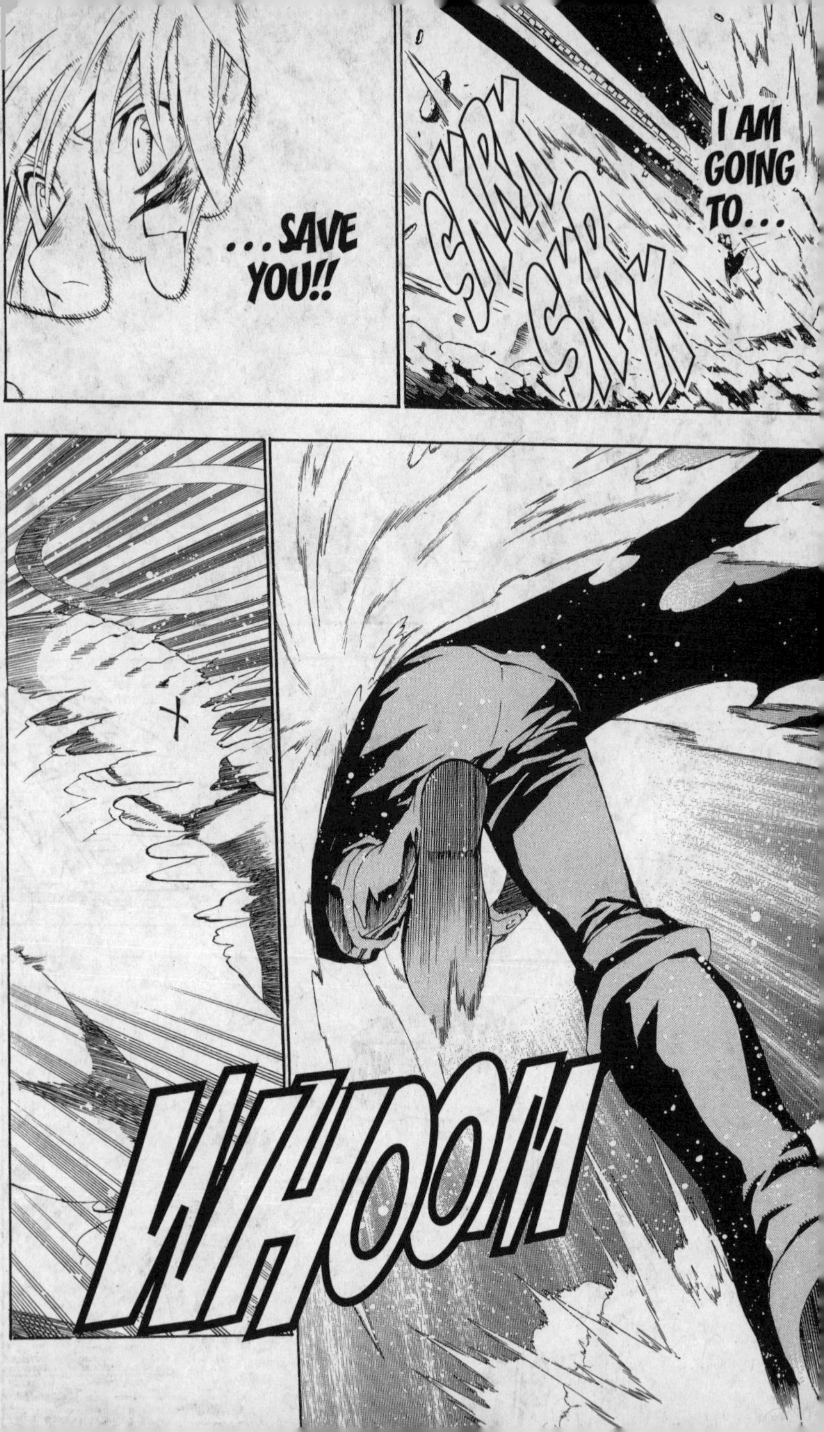
I AM GOING TO...
...SAVE YOU!!
WHOOM

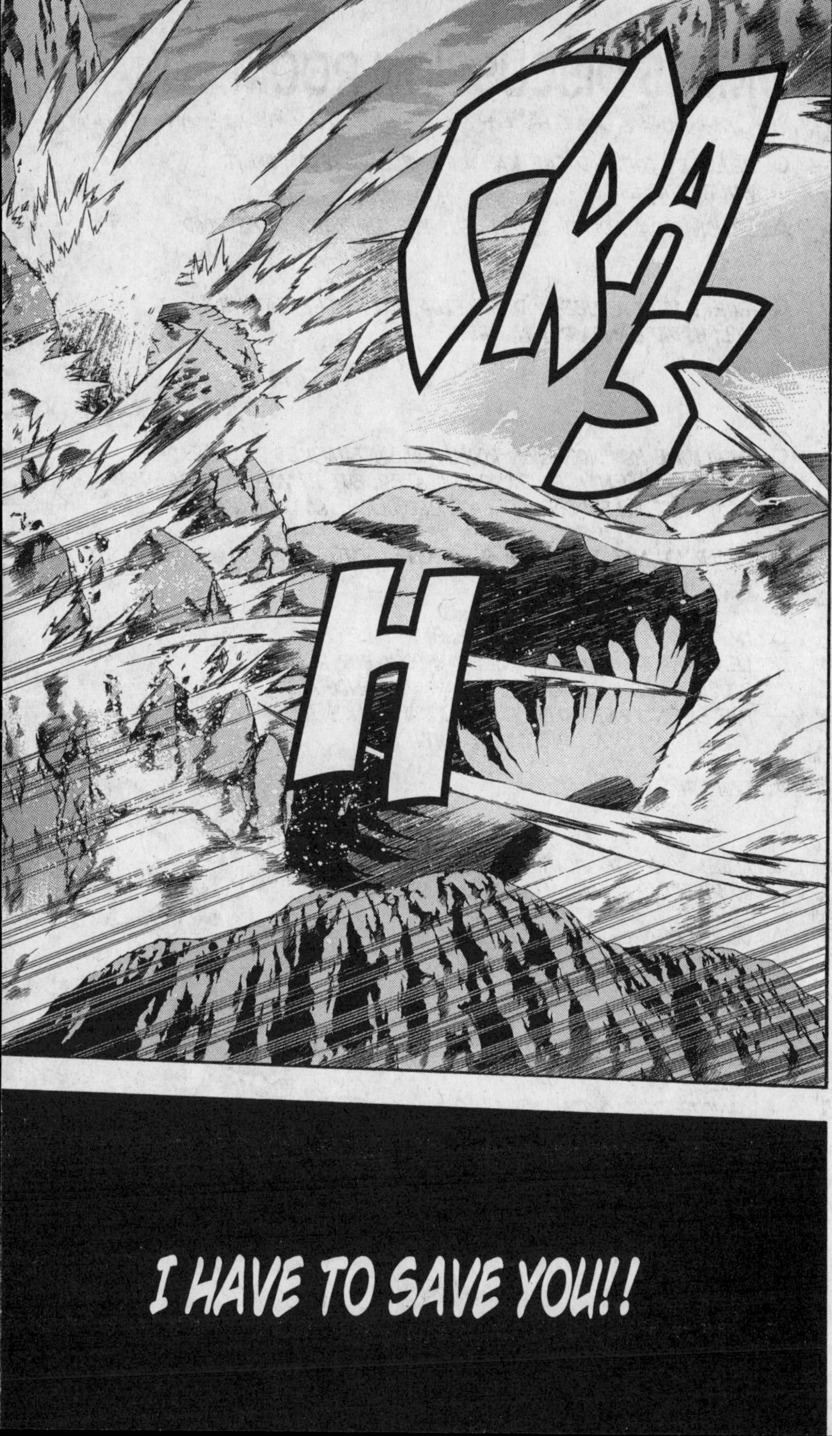
CRASH
I HAVE TO SAVE YOU!!

KOMUI'S DISCUSSION ROOM VOL. 4

Q. REEVER'S CUP HAD THE KANJI FOR BUBBLE/FOAM ON IT. WHAT WAS IN IT?

A. LEMON SODA. I DON'T GET IT, BUT IT'S SUPPOSED TO BE GOOD.

Q. THERE WAS A RUBBER DUCKY FLOATING IN THE BATH IN VOL. 4. DID KANDA PUT IT THERE?

A. GRR...

Q. IN VOLUME 4'S "DISCUSSION ROOM," ALLEN THANKED THE READER FOR THE VALENTINE'S DAY CHOCOLATES, BUT IN VOLUME 5 REEVER SAYS THAT ALLEN DOESN'T LIKE CHOCOLATE. SO WHICH IS IT?

A. I TOLD YOU NOT TO ASK ME QUESTIONS ABOUT THAT GUY!

Q. I'M SERIOUSLY IN LOVE WITH ALLEN!!! I'M EVEN LEARNING TO COOK SO THAT I CAN COOK FOR HIM! I BOUGHT A BOOK ON MAKING MITARASHI DANGO AND I'VE BEEN PRACTICING! IF I LEARN TO MAKE THEM WELL, WILL HE GO OUT WITH ME?

A. TWITCH

Q. ALLEN IS A BOY, RIGHT? BUT HE'S SO PRETTY!! I LOVE ALLEN!

A. DO YOU PEOPLE WANT TO DIE?!!! (GRRR...)

DUE TO KANDA DRAWING HIS SWORD, THIS INSTALLMENT OF THE DISCUSSION ROOM IS NOW OVER. (HOSHINO)

THE 52ND NIGHT: BEGINNING OF THE NIGHT OF THE END

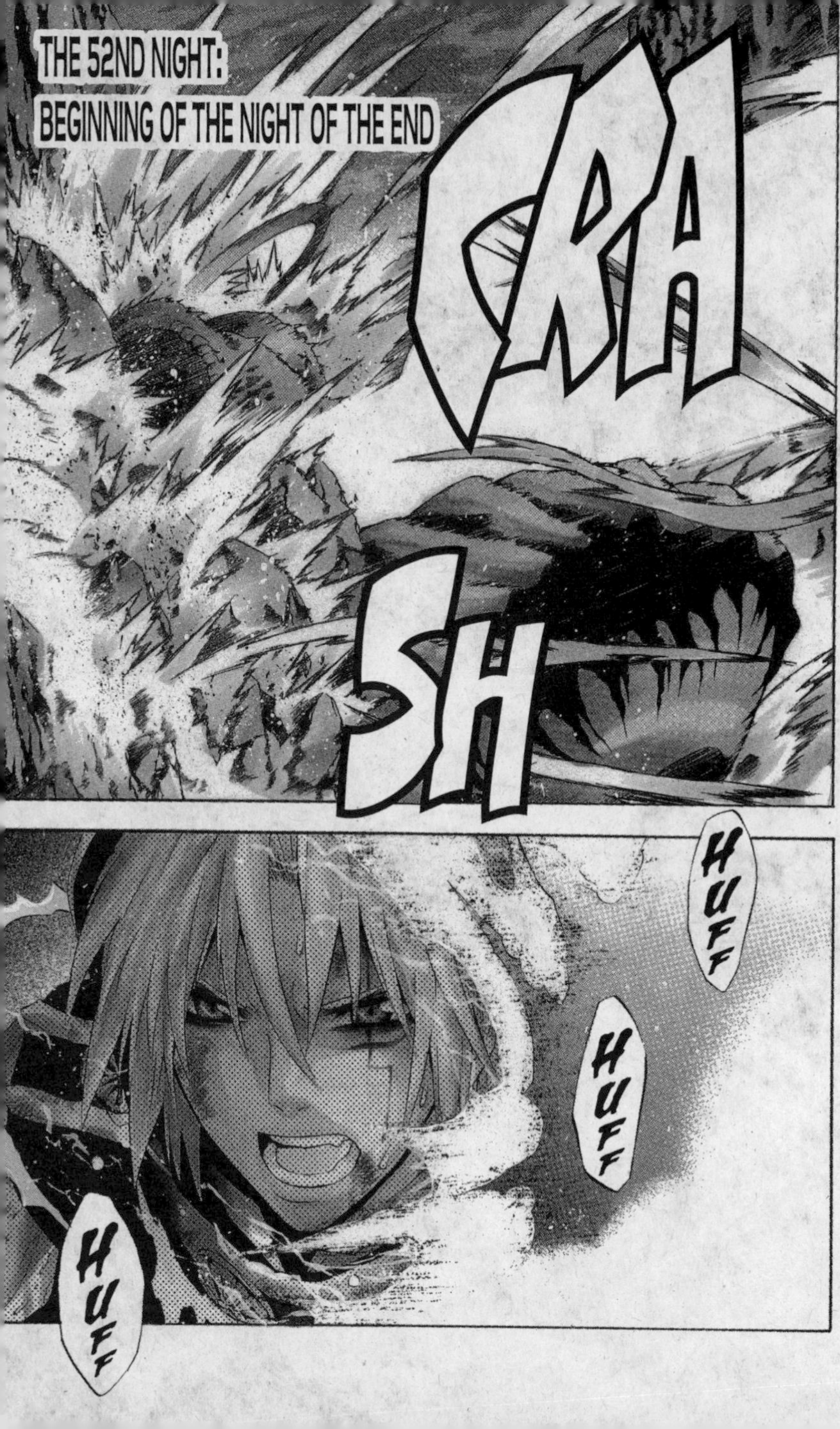
CRA
SH
HUFF
HUFF
HUFF

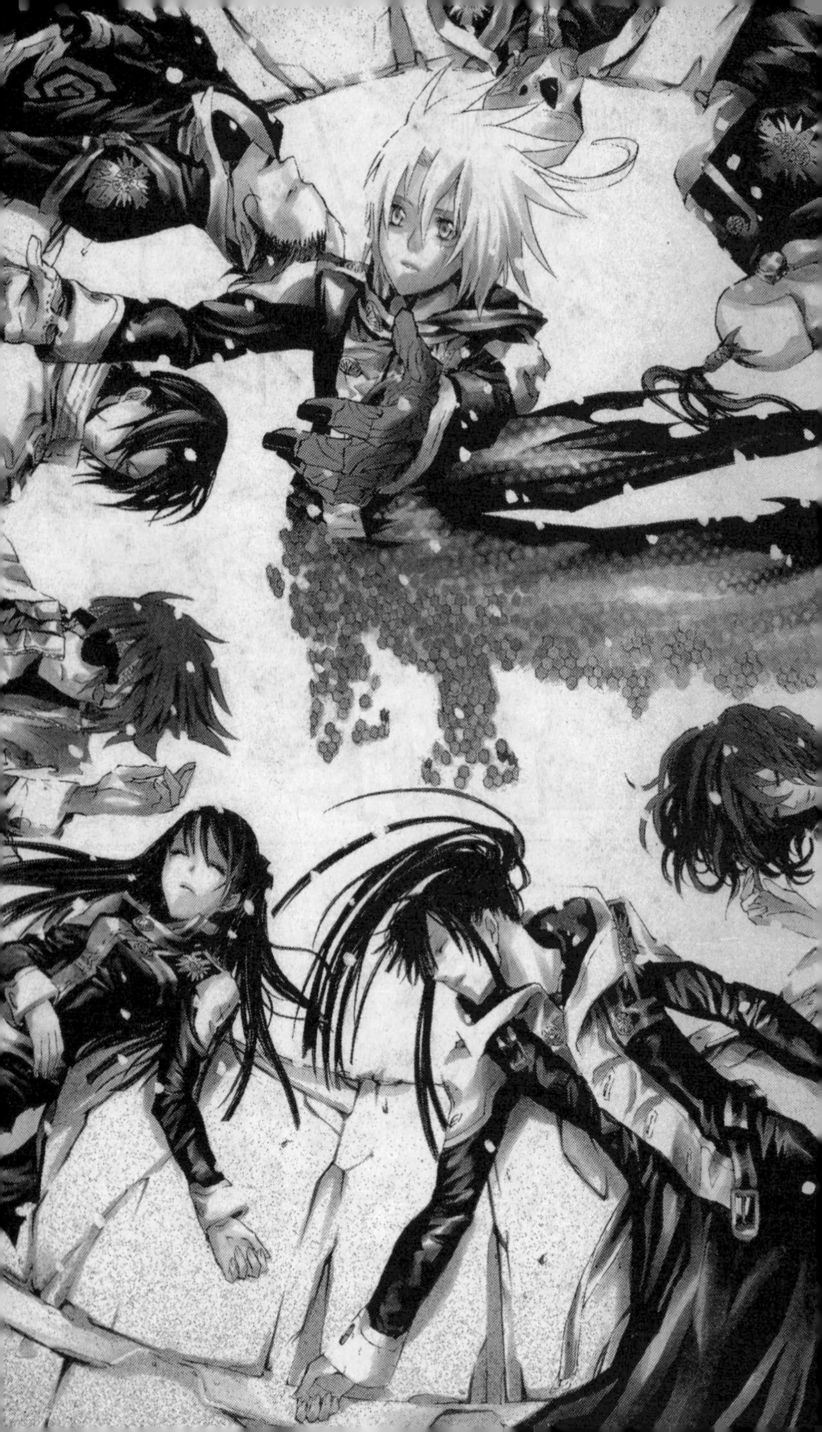

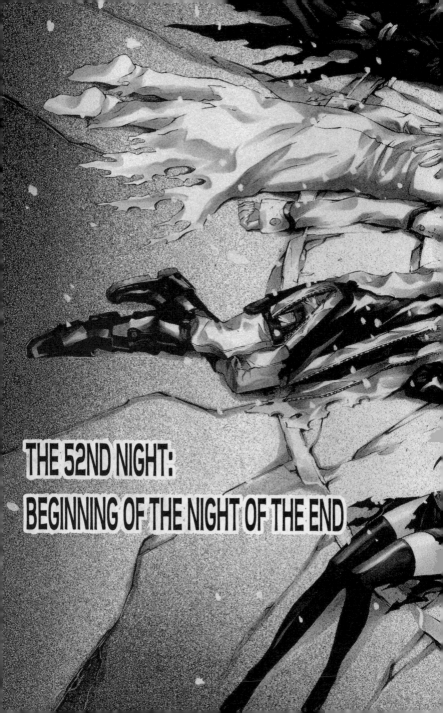

THE 52ND NIGHT:

BEGINNING OF THE NIGHT OF THE END

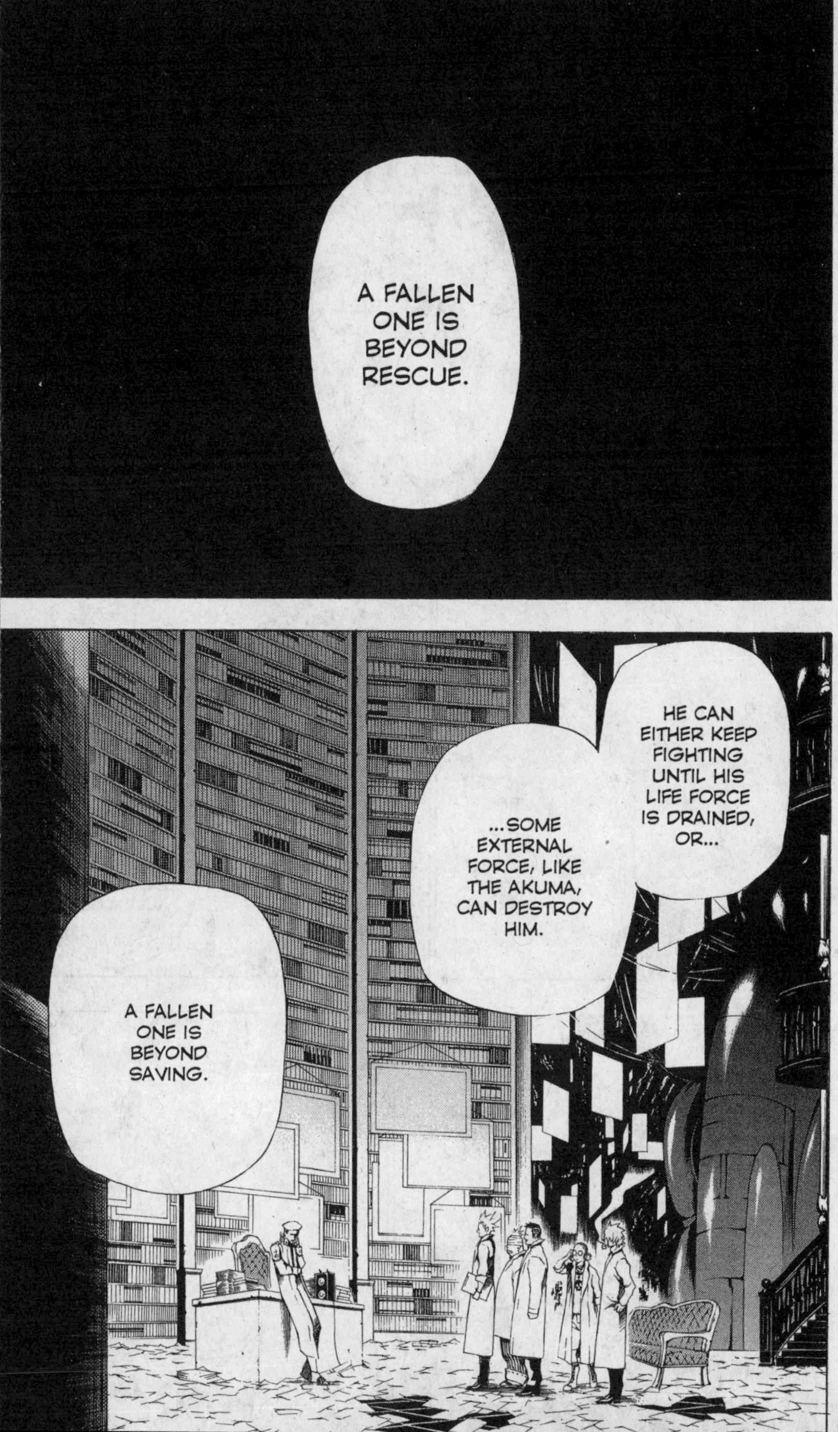
A FALLEN ONE IS BEYOND RESCUE.
HE CAN EITHER KEEP FIGHTING UNTIL HIS LIFE FORCE IS DRAINED, OR...
...SOME EXTERNAL FORCE, LIKE THE AKUMA, CAN DESTROY HIM.
A FALLEN ONE IS BEYOND SAVING.

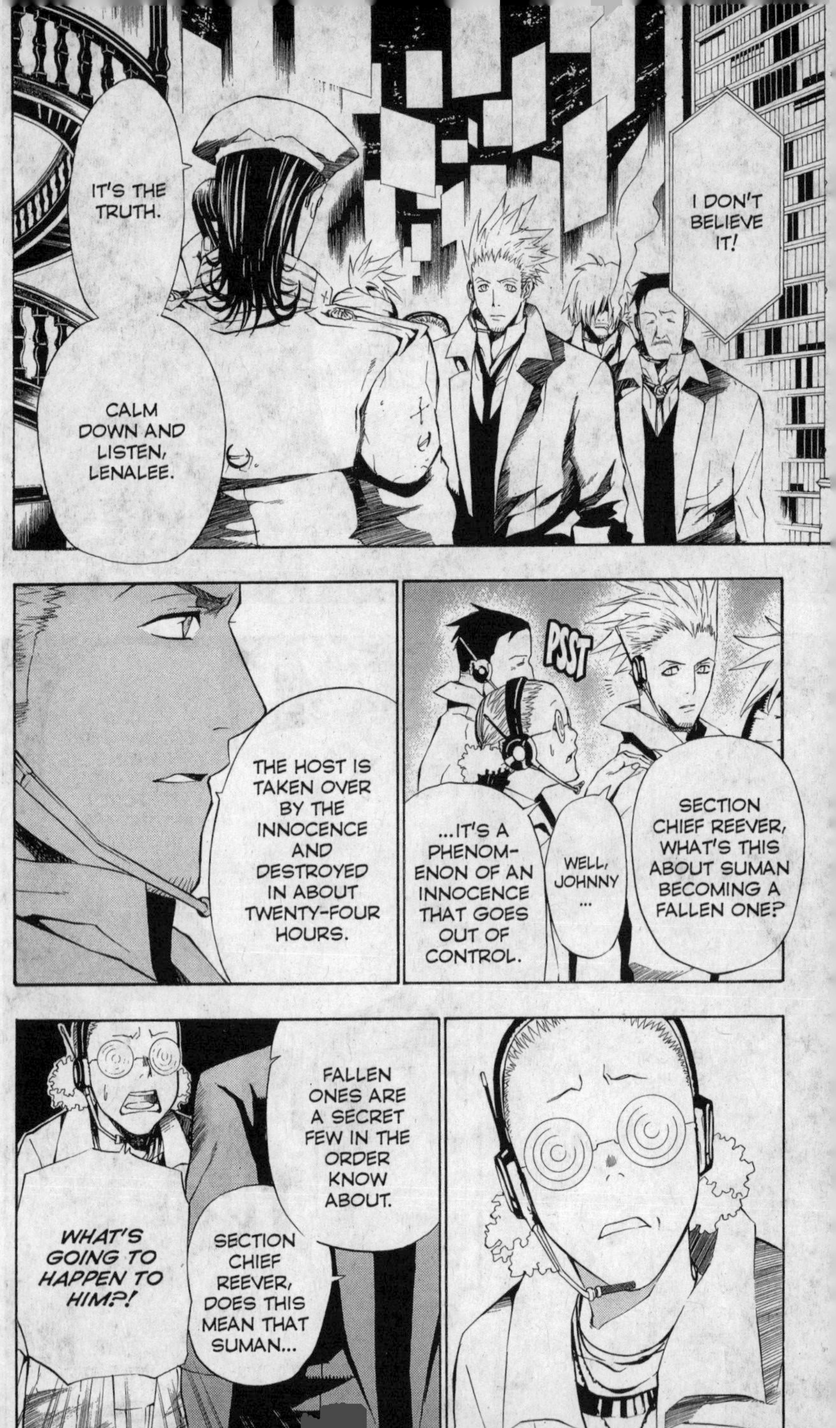
I DON'T BELIEVE IT!
IT'S THE TRUTH.
CALM DOWN AND LISTEN, LENALEE.
PSST
SECTION CHIEF REEVER, WHAT'S THIS ABOUT SUMAN BECOMING A FALLEN ONE?
WELL, JOHNNY ...
...IT'S A PHENOMENON OF AN INNOCENCE THAT GOES OUT OF CONTROL.
THE HOST IS TAKEN OVER BY THE INNOCENCE AND DESTROYED IN ABOUT TWENTY-FOUR HOURS.
FALLEN ONES ARE A SECRET FEW IN THE ORDER KNOW ABOUT.
SECTION CHIEF REEVER, DOES THIS MEAN THAT SUMAN...
WHAT'S GOING TO HAPPEN TO HIM?!

READ THIS WAY

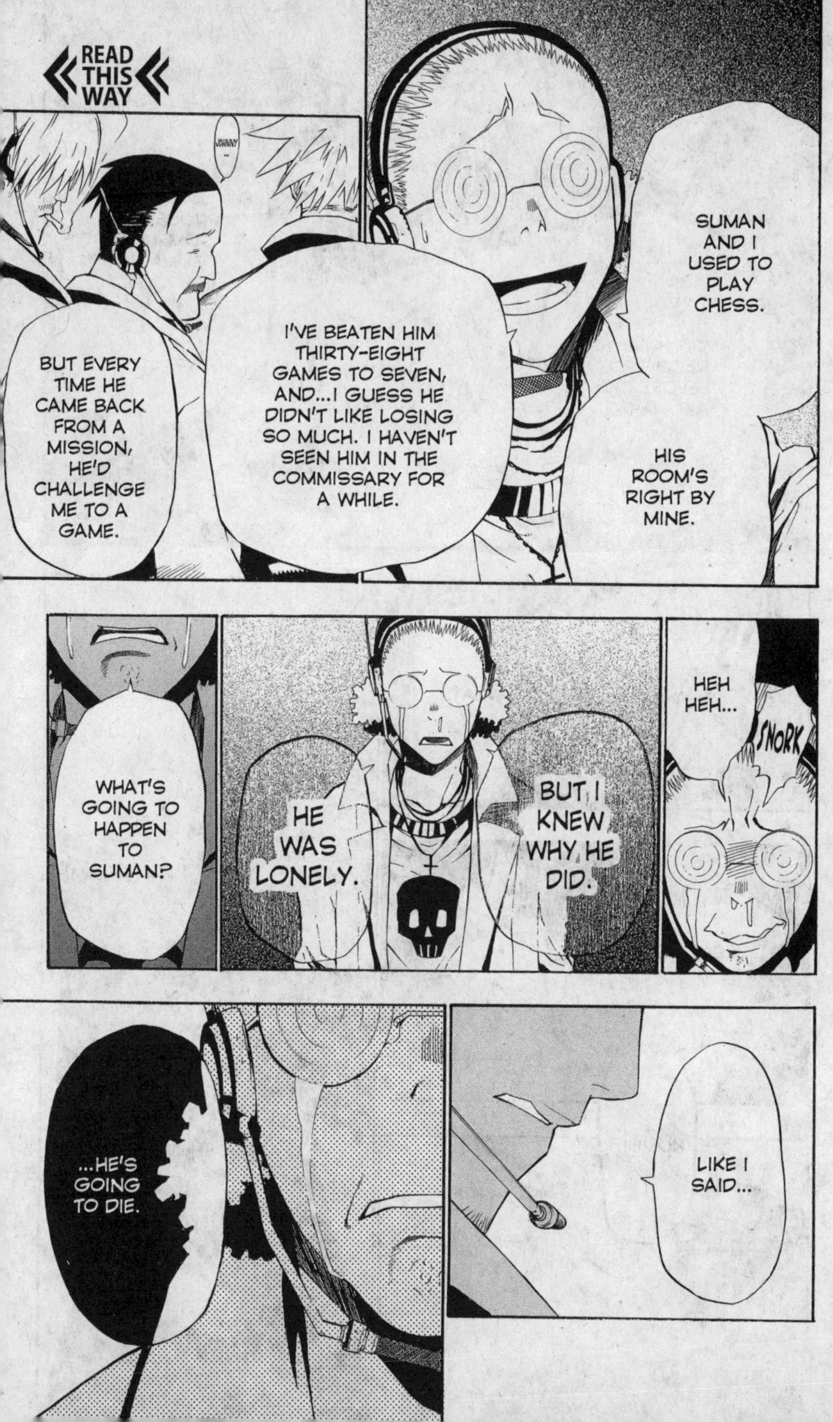

SUMAN AND I USED TO PLAY CHESS.
HIS ROOM'S RIGHT BY MINE.
I'VE BEATEN HIM THIRTY-EIGHT GAMES TO SEVEN, AND...I GUESS HE DIDN'T LIKE LOSING SO MUCH. I HAVEN'T SEEN HIM IN THE COMMISSARY FOR A WHILE.
JOHNNY...
BUT EVERY TIME HE CAME BACK FROM A MISSION, HE'D CHALLENGE ME TO A GAME.
HEH HEH...
SNORK
BUT I KNEW WHY HE DID.
HE WAS LONELY.
WHAT'S GOING TO HAPPEN TO SUMAN?
LIKE I SAID...
...HE'S GOING TO DIE.

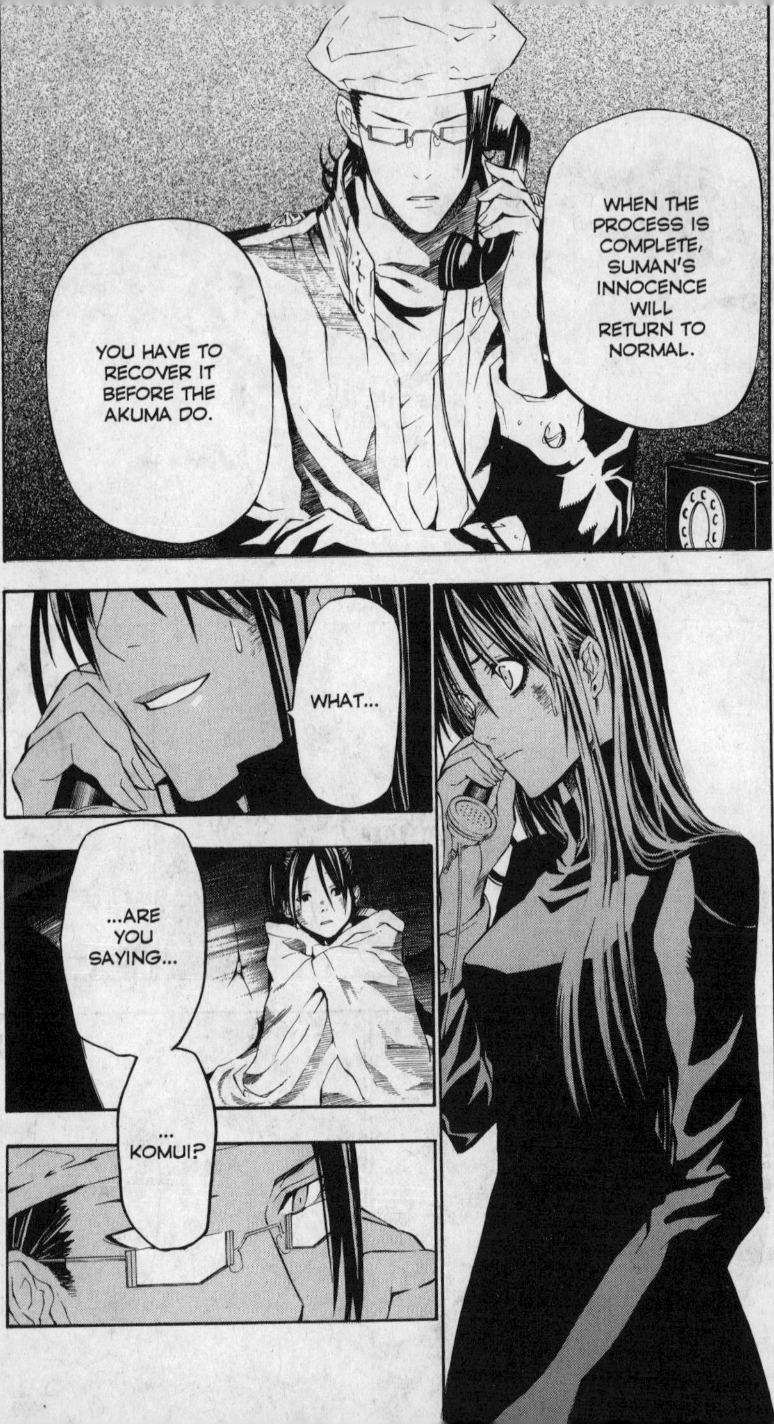
WHEN THE PROCESS IS COMPLETE, SUMAN'S INNOCENCE WILL RETURN TO NORMAL.
YOU HAVE TO RECOVER IT BEFORE THE AKUMA DO.
WHAT...
...ARE YOU SAYING...
... KOMUI?

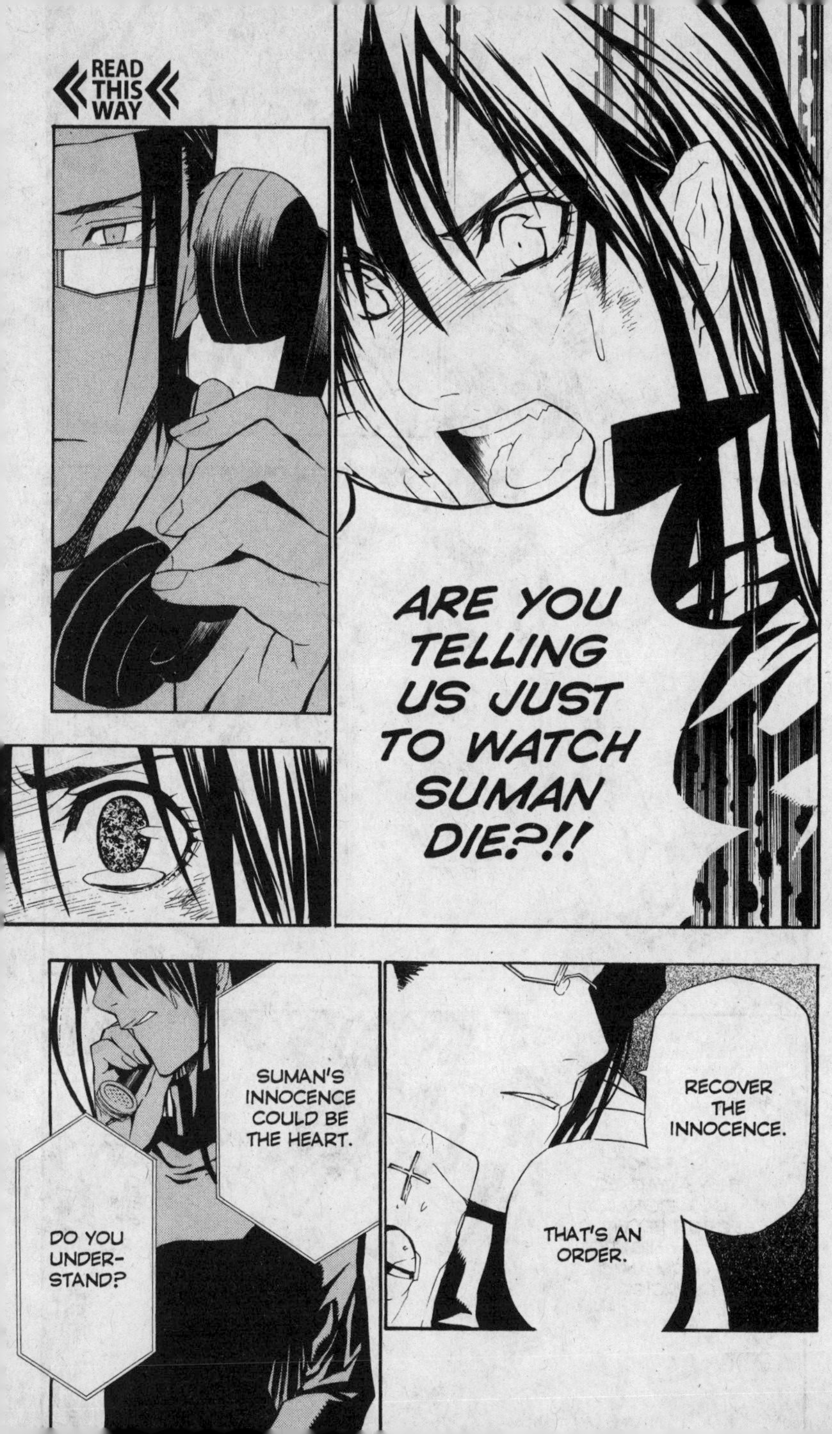
READ THIS WAY
ARE YOU TELLING US JUST TO WATCH SUMAN DIE?!!
RECOVER THE INNOCENCE.
THAT'S AN ORDER.
SUMAN'S INNOCENCE COULD BE THE HEART.
DO YOU UNDER-STAND?

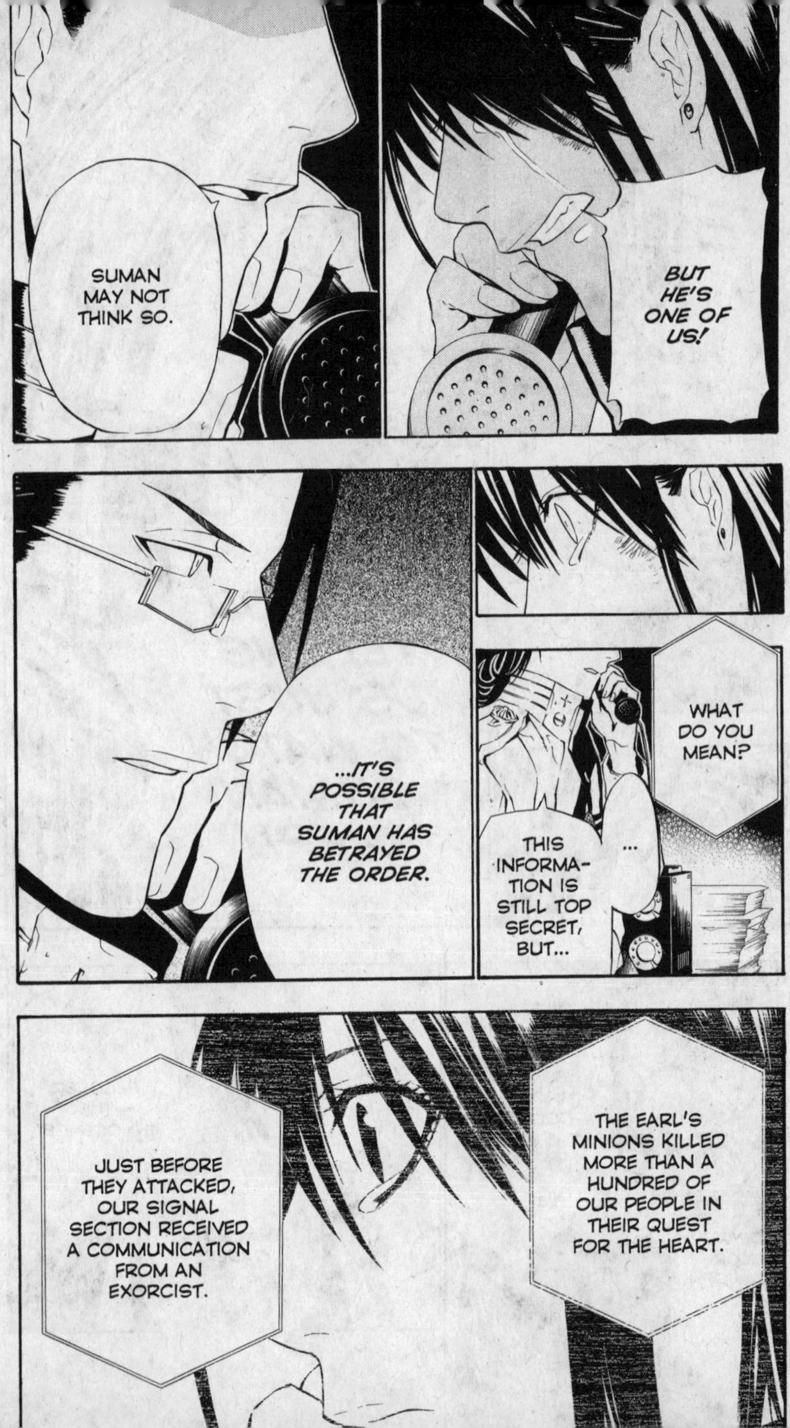
BUT HE'S ONE OF US!
SUMAN MAY NOT THINK SO.
WHAT DO YOU MEAN?
...
THIS INFORMATION IS STILL TOP SECRET, BUT...
...IT'S POSSIBLE THAT SUMAN HAS BETRAYED THE ORDER.
THE EARL'S MINIONS KILLED MORE THAN A HUNDRED OF OUR PEOPLE IN THEIR QUEST FOR THE HEART.
JUST BEFORE THEY ATTACKED, OUR SIGNAL SECTION RECEIVED A COMMUNICATION FROM AN EXORCIST.

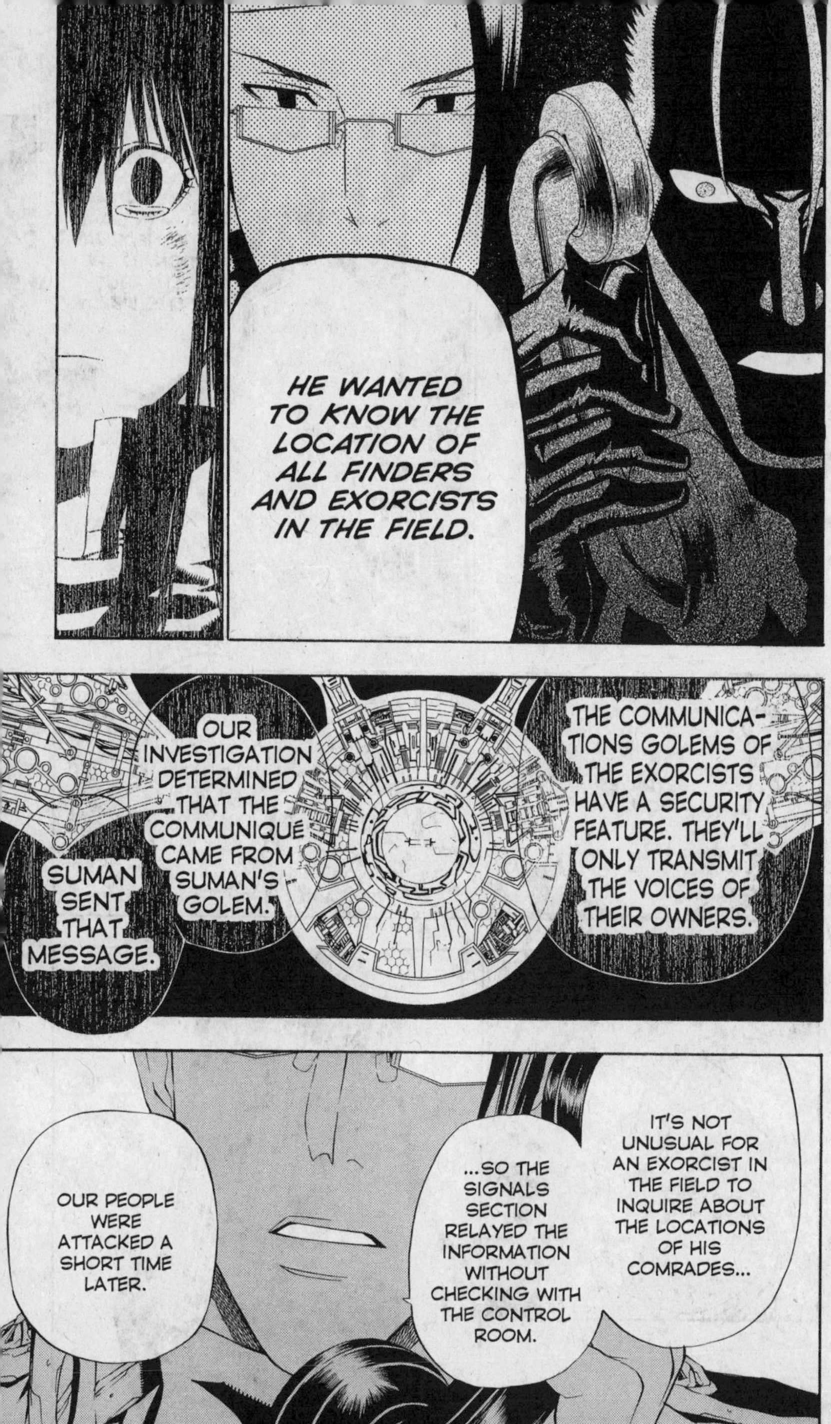
HE WANTED TO KNOW THE LOCATION OF ALL FINDERS AND EXORCISTS IN THE FIELD.
THE COMMUNICATIONS GOLEMS OF THE EXORCISTS HAVE A SECURITY FEATURE. THEY'LL ONLY TRANSMIT THE VOICES OF THEIR OWNERS.
OUR INVESTIGATION DETERMINED THAT THE COMMUNIQUÉ CAME FROM SUMAN'S GOLEM.
SUMAN SENT THAT MESSAGE.
IT'S NOT UNUSUAL FOR AN EXORCIST IN THE FIELD TO INQUIRE ABOUT THE LOCATIONS OF HIS COMRADES...
...SO THE SIGNALS SECTION RELAYED THE INFORMATION WITHOUT CHECKING WITH THE CONTROL ROOM.
OUR PEOPLE WERE ATTACKED A SHORT TIME LATER.

OF COURSE, WE'RE NOT CERTAIN THAT SUMAN GAVE THE INFORMATION TO THE ENEMY, BUT IT SEEMS LIKELY.

AND NOW HE'S A FALLEN ONE.

THAT WOULD SUGGEST THAT HE SOLD US OUT TO SAVE HIS OWN LIFE.

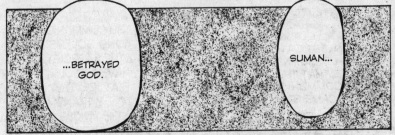

...BETRAYED GOD.

SUMAN...

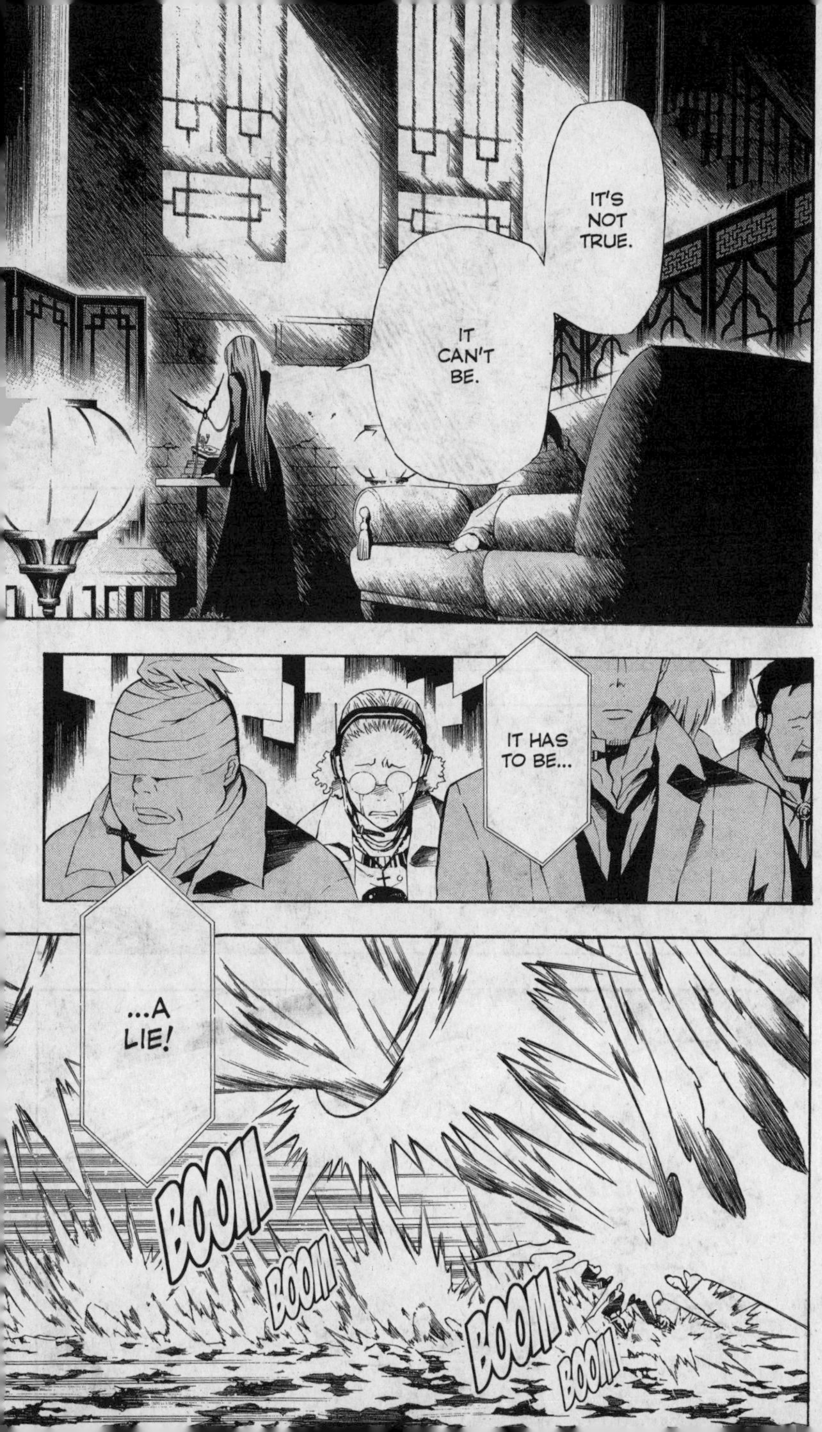
IT'S NOT TRUE.
IT CAN'T BE.
IT HAS TO BE...
...A LIE!
BOOM
BOOM
BOOM
BOOM

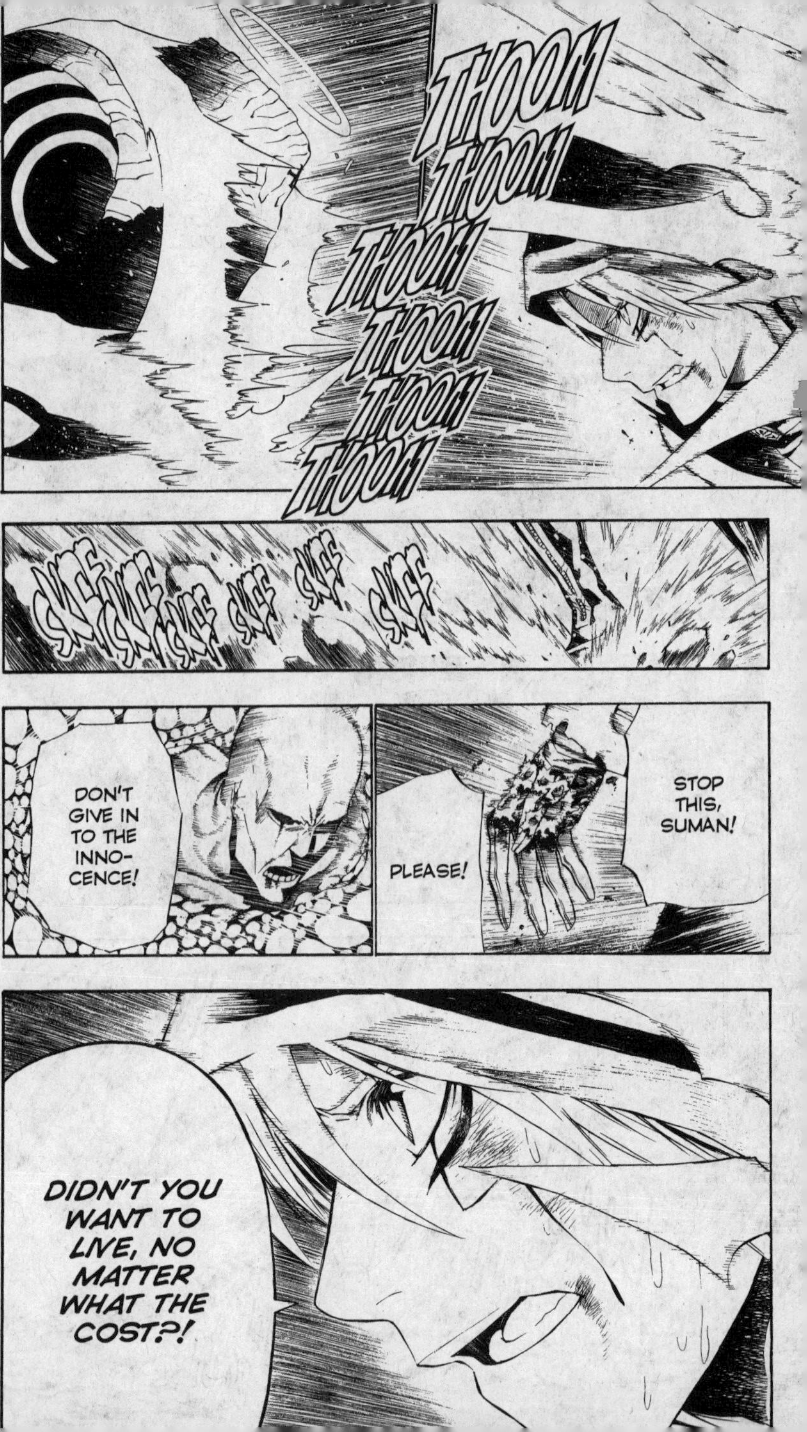
THOOM THOOM THOOM THOOM THOOM THOOM
SKFF SKFF SKFF SKFF SKFF SKFF
STOP THIS, SUMAN!
PLEASE!
DON'T GIVE IN TO THE INNO-CENCE!
DIDN'T YOU WANT TO LIVE, NO MATTER WHAT THE COST?!

READ THIS WAY

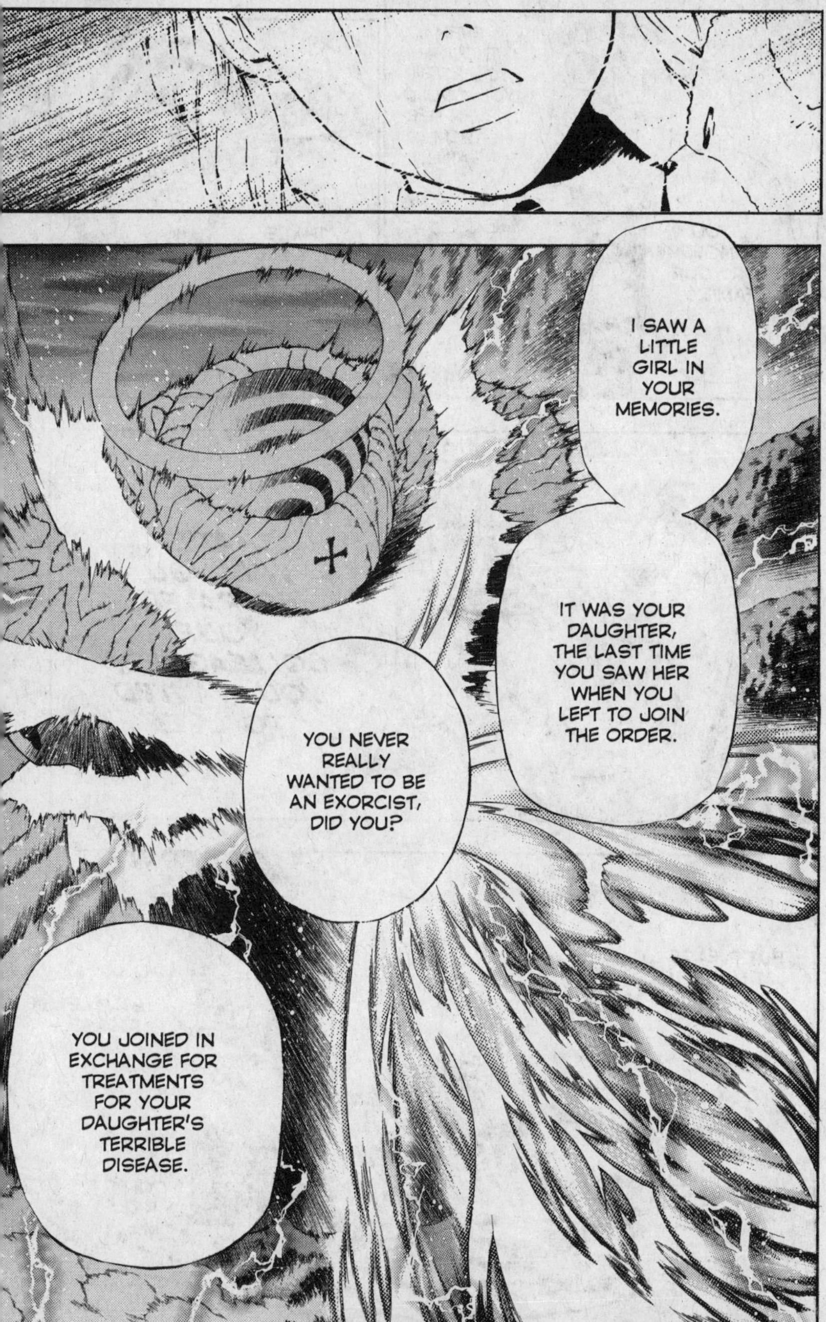
I SAW A LITTLE GIRL IN YOUR MEMORIES.
IT WAS YOUR DAUGHTER, THE LAST TIME YOU SAW HER WHEN YOU LEFT TO JOIN THE ORDER.
YOU NEVER REALLY WANTED TO BE AN EXORCIST, DID YOU?
YOU JOINED IN EXCHANGE FOR TREATMENTS FOR YOUR DAUGHTER'S TERRIBLE DISEASE.

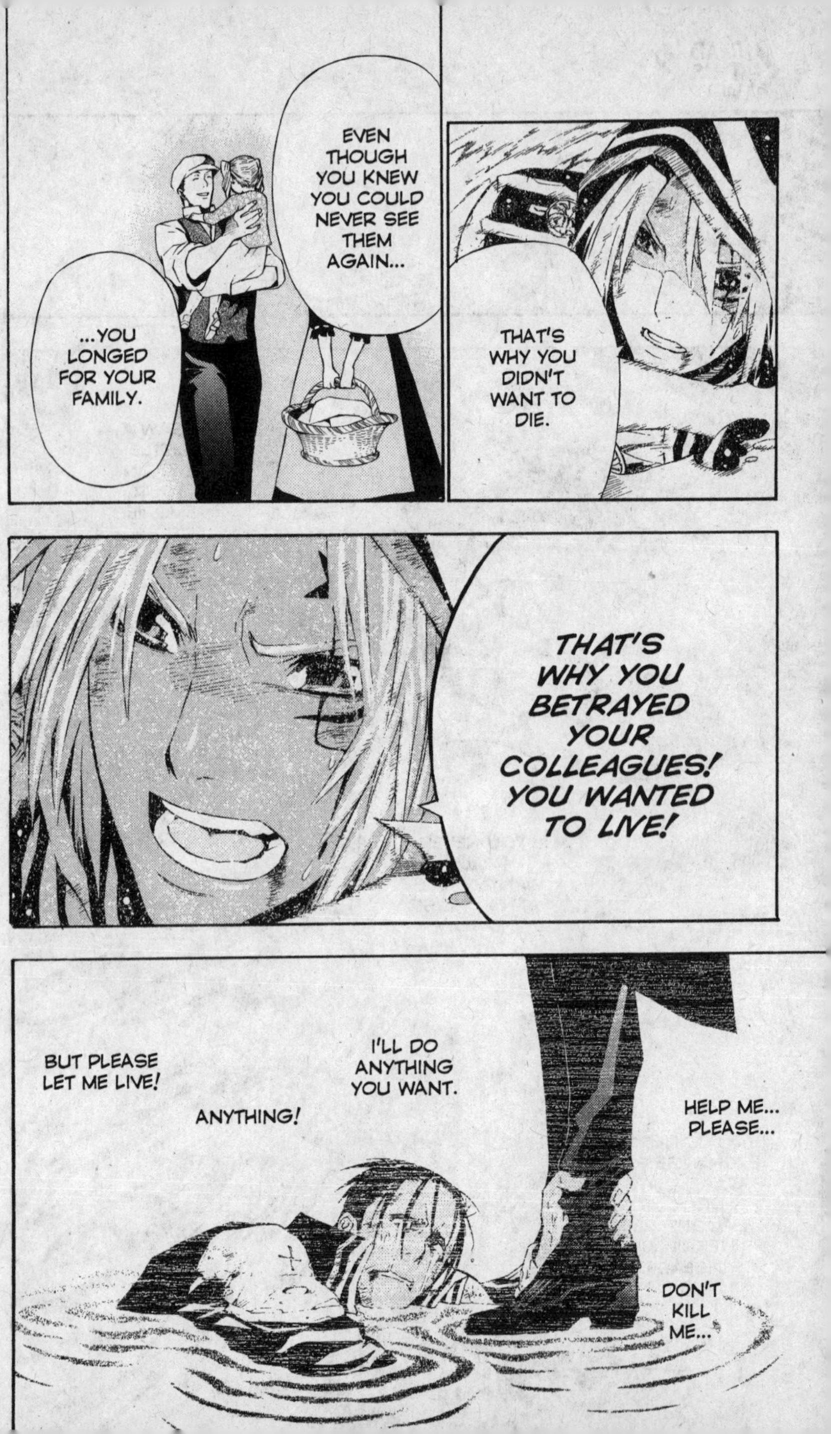
EVEN THOUGH YOU KNEW YOU COULD NEVER SEE THEM AGAIN...
...YOU LONGED FOR YOUR FAMILY.
THAT'S WHY YOU DIDN'T WANT TO DIE.
THAT'S WHY YOU BETRAYED YOUR COLLEAGUES! YOU WANTED TO LIVE!
HELP ME... PLEASE...
I'LL DO ANYTHING YOU WANT.
BUT PLEASE LET ME LIVE!
ANYTHING!
DON'T KILL ME...

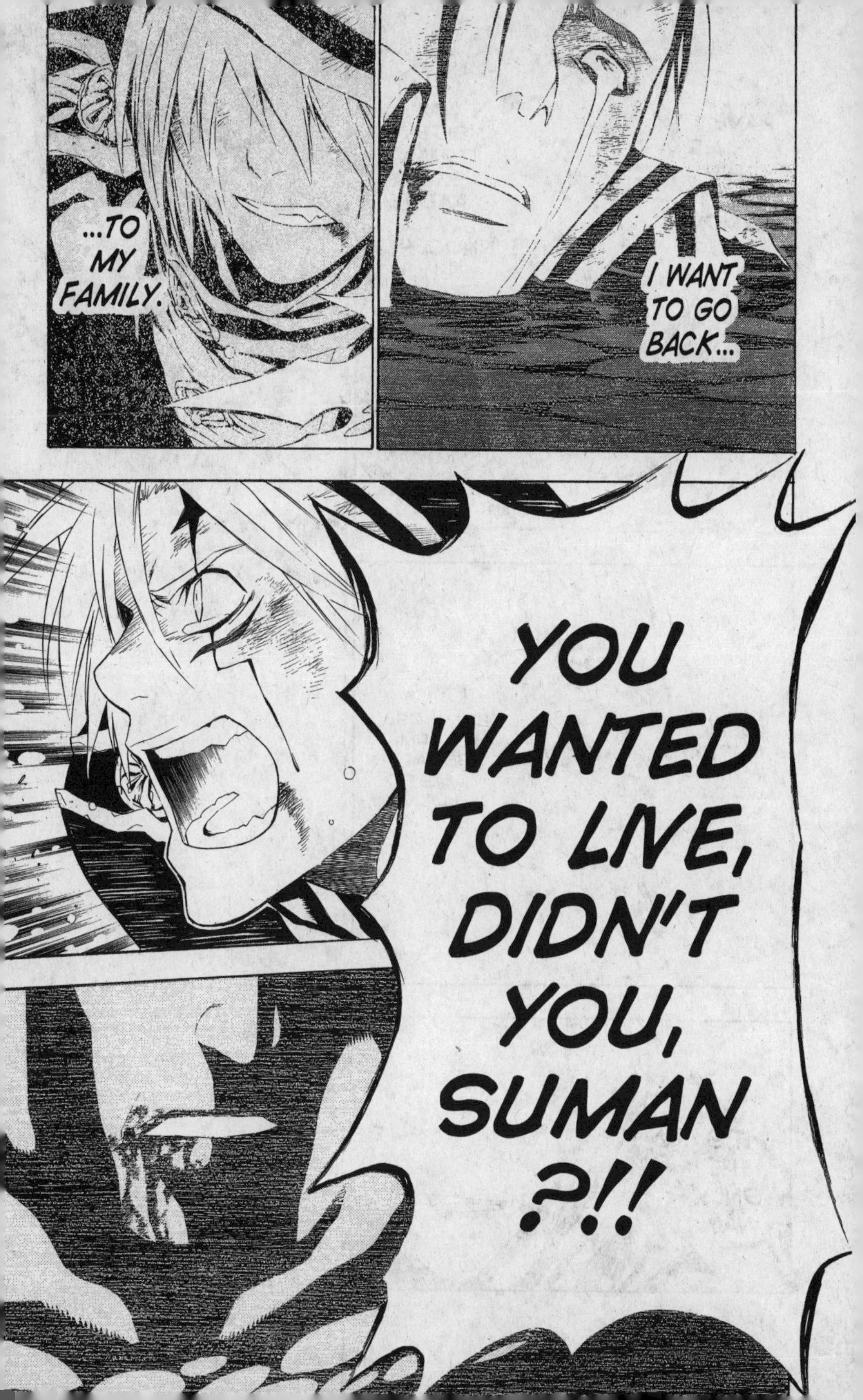
I WANT TO GO BACK...
...TO MY FAMILY.
YOU WANTED TO LIVE, DIDN'T YOU, SUMAN ?!!

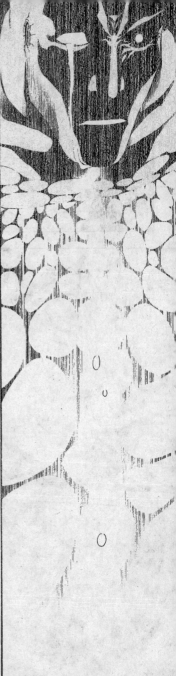

WHEN I WAS INSIDE OF SUMAN, I SAW A PARASITE-TYPE INNOCENCE IN HIS RIGHT ARM.

I'LL HAVE TO SEVER HIS ARM TO REMOVE IT.

HE'LL LOSE HIS ARM, BUT AT LEAST HE'LL LIVE.

I HAVE TO BELIEVE THAT HE WANTS TO LIVE THAT BADLY.

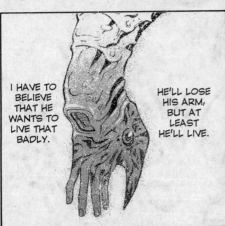

IT'S THE ONLY WAY.

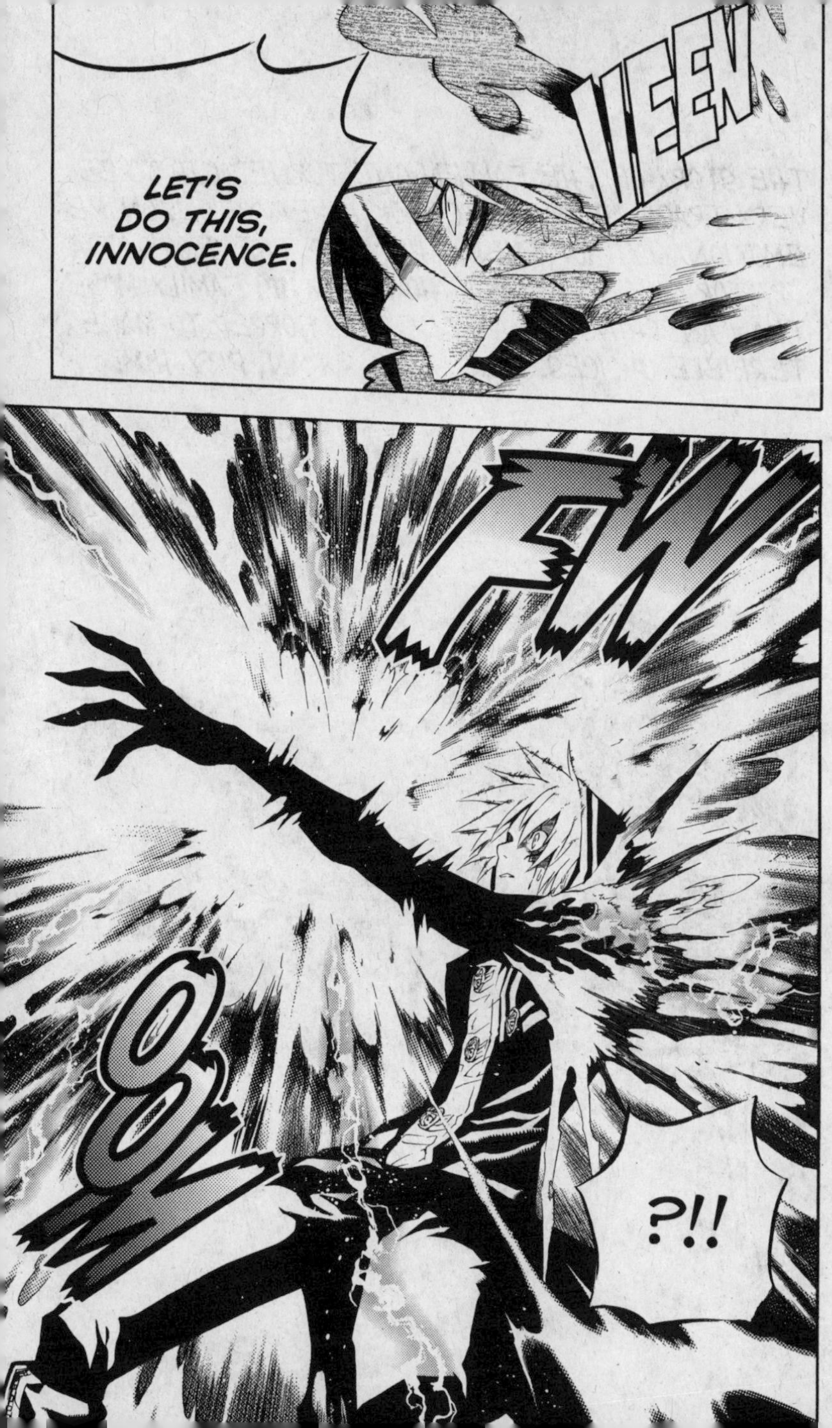
LET'S DO THIS, INNOCENCE.
VEEN
FW
OOM
?!!

THE STORY OF THE FALLEN ONE TURNED OUT TO BE
VERY TRAGIC. DRAWING IT TOOK A HEAVY TOLL ON ME
EMOTIONALLY. HOWEVER, THIS ISN'T THE STORY OF A
TRAITOR, BUT OF A MAN WHO LOVED HIS FAMILY MORE
THAN ANYTHING, A MAN WHO WAS FORCED TO MAKE
TERRIBLE CHOICES. DON'T HATE SUMAN, PITY HIM.

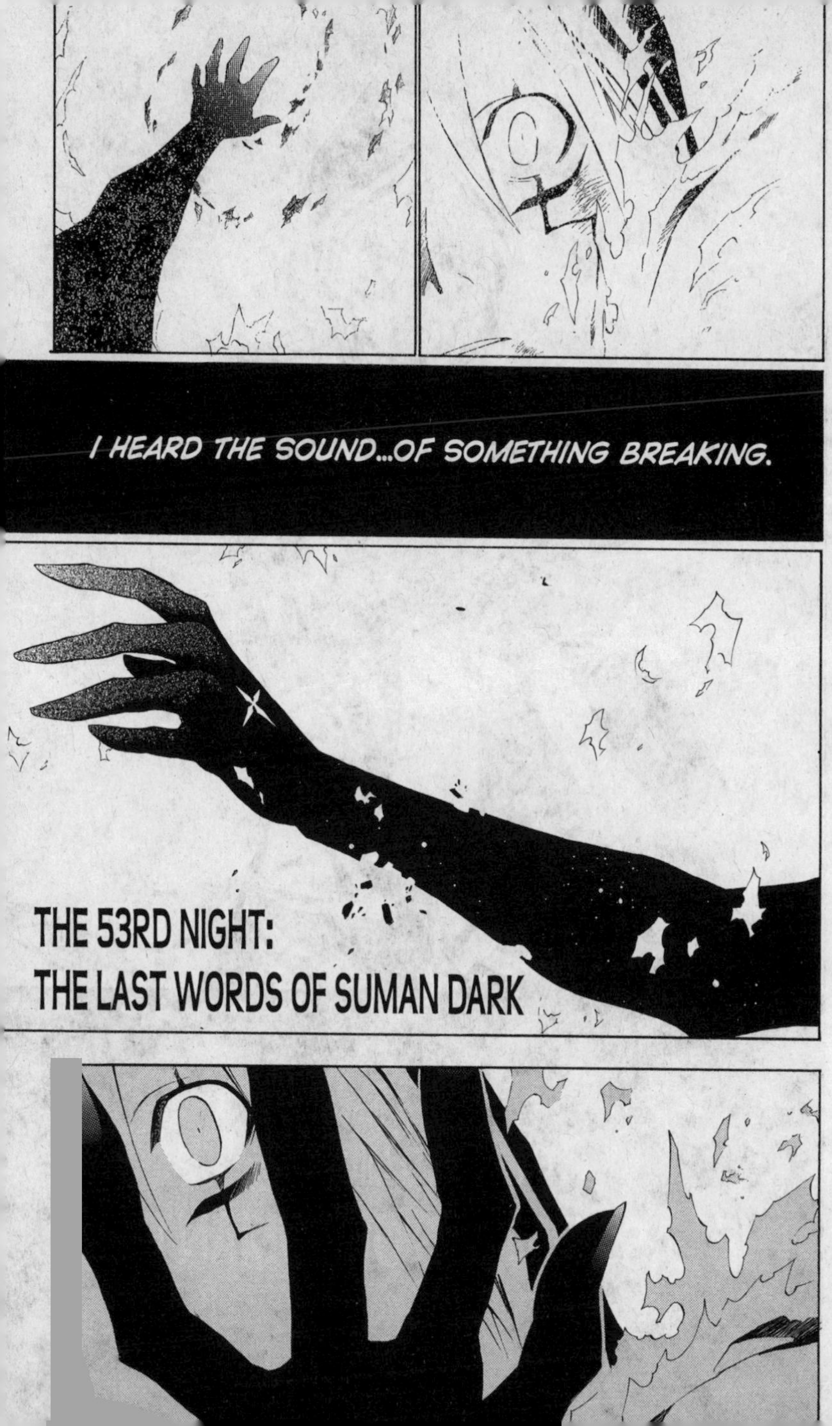
I HEARD THE SOUND...OF SOMETHING BREAKING.
THE 53RD NIGHT:
THE LAST WORDS OF SUMAN DARK

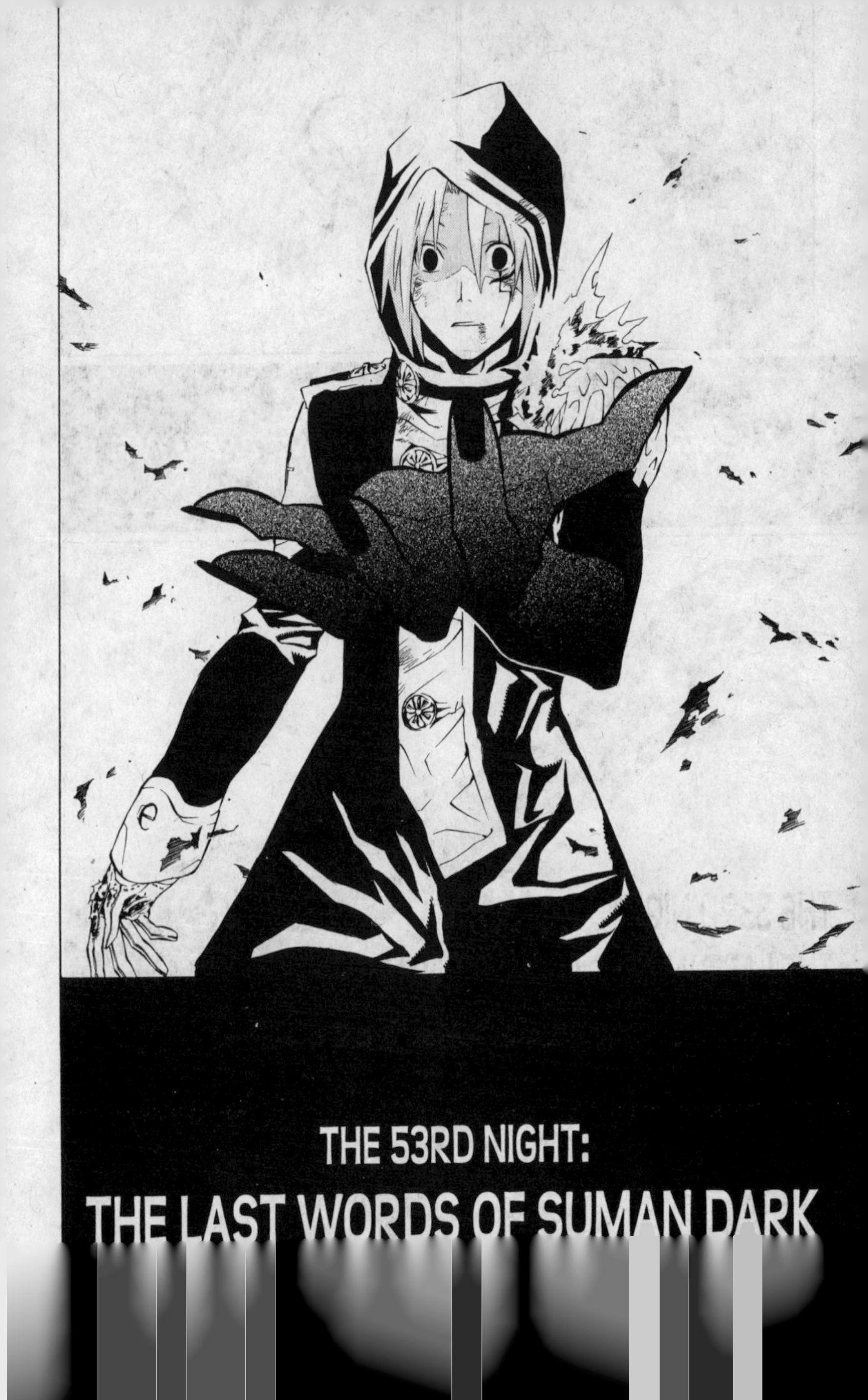

THE 53RD NIGHT:
THE LAST WORDS OF SUMAN DARK

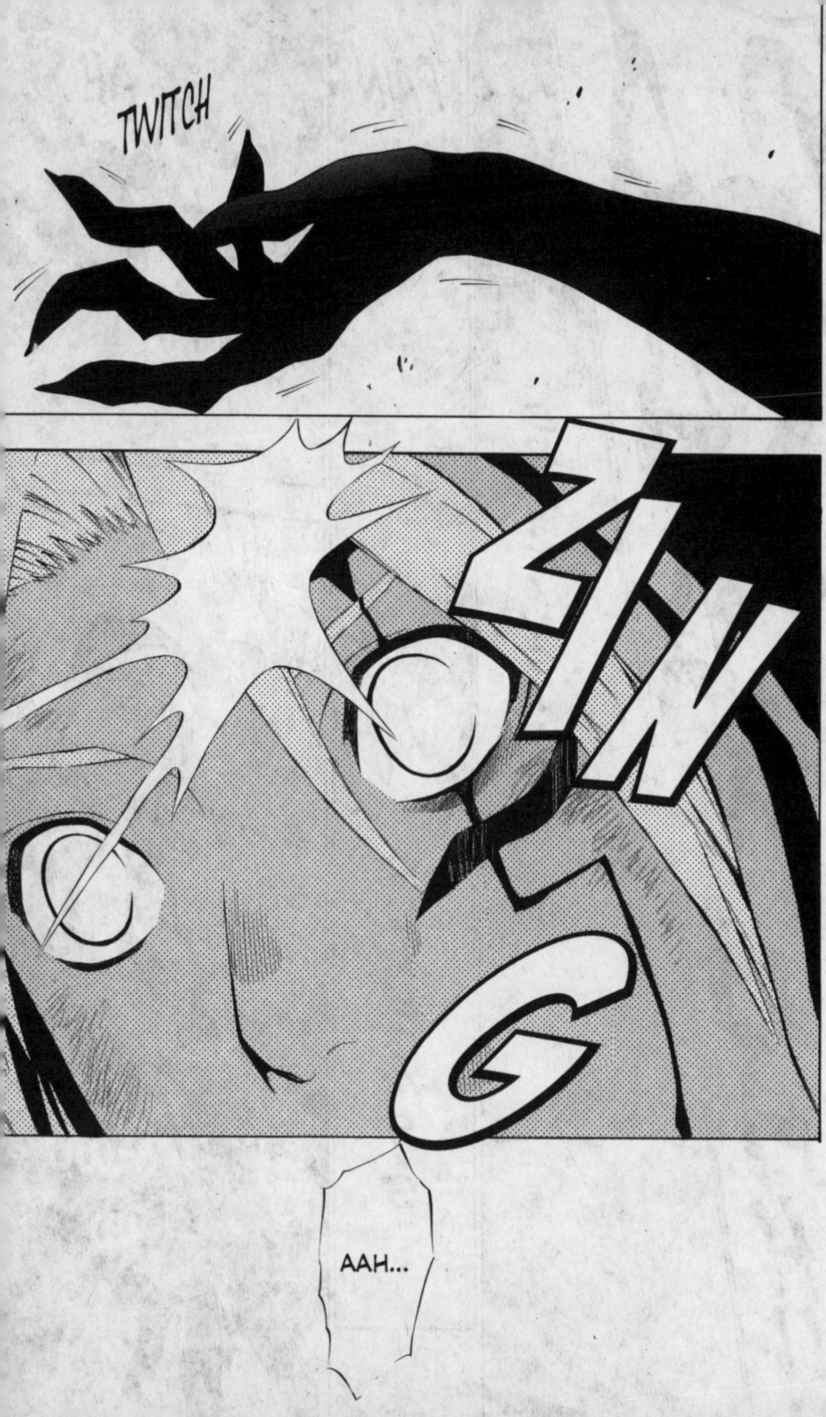
TWITCH
ZING
AAH...

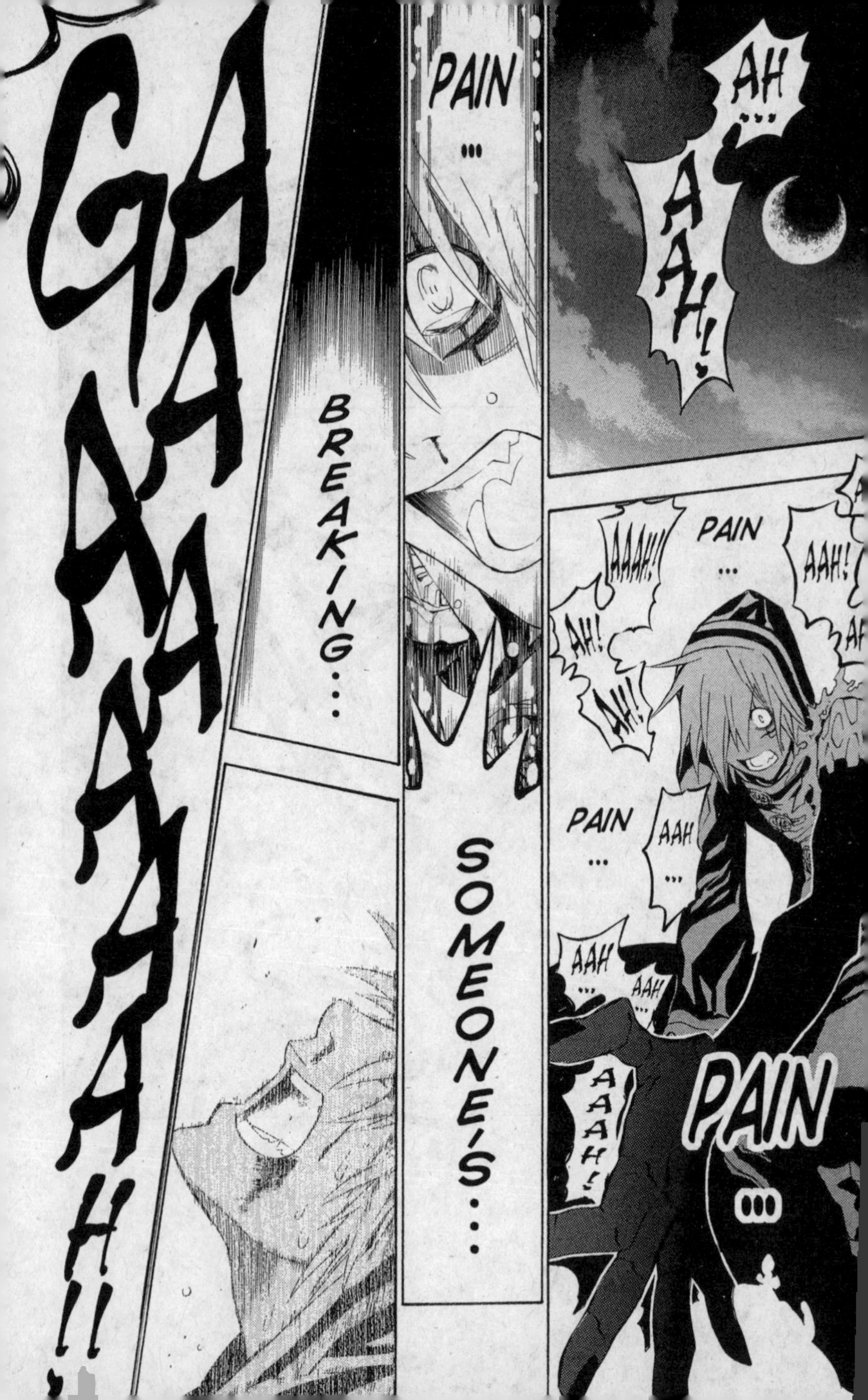
AH... AAH!
PAIN ...
AAAH!!
AAH!
AH!
AH!!
PAIN ...
AAH ...
AAH ...
AAH ...
AAAH!
PAIN ...
PAIN ...
SOMEONE'S ...
BREAKING ...
GAAAAAAAH!!

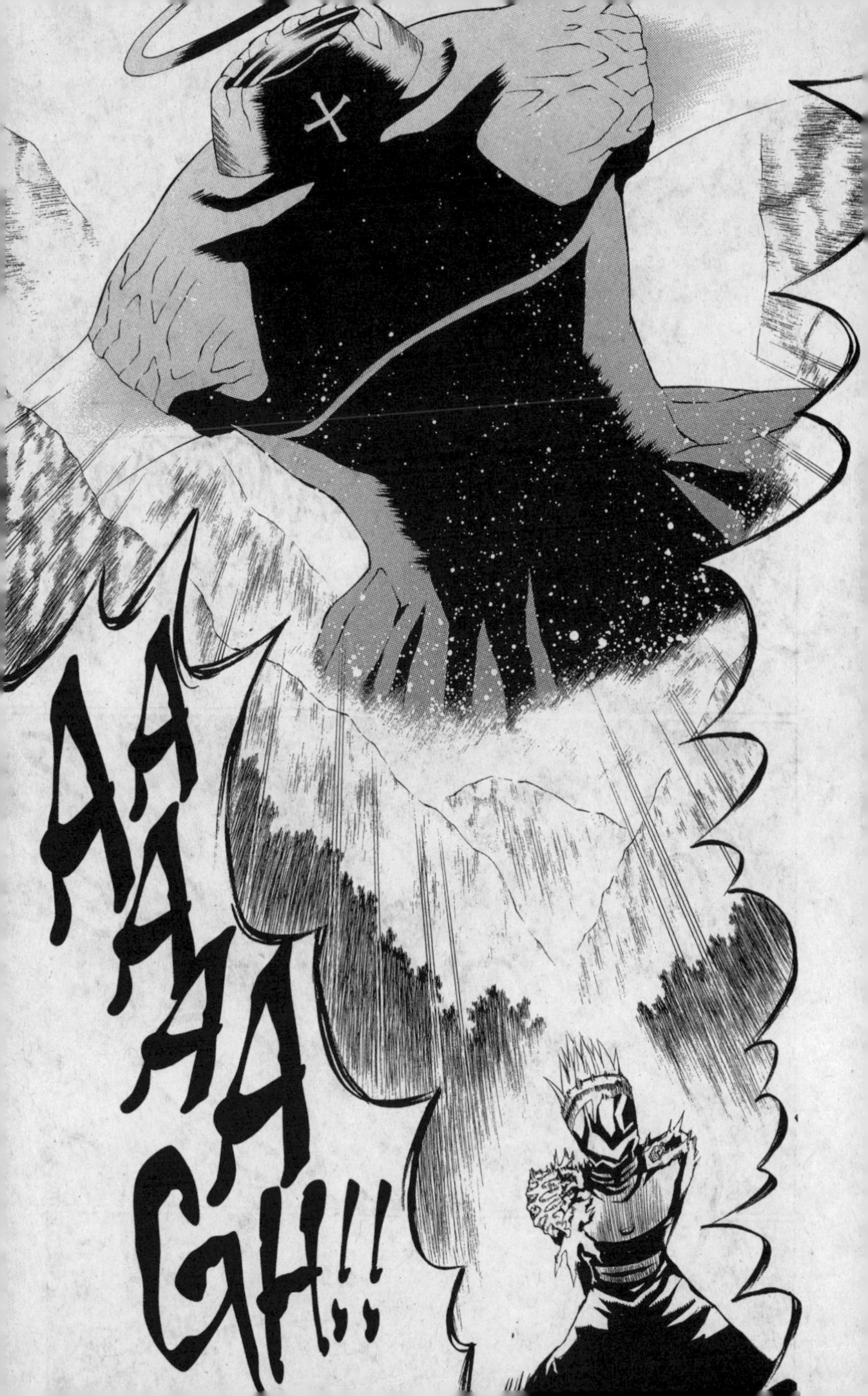
AAAAAGH!!

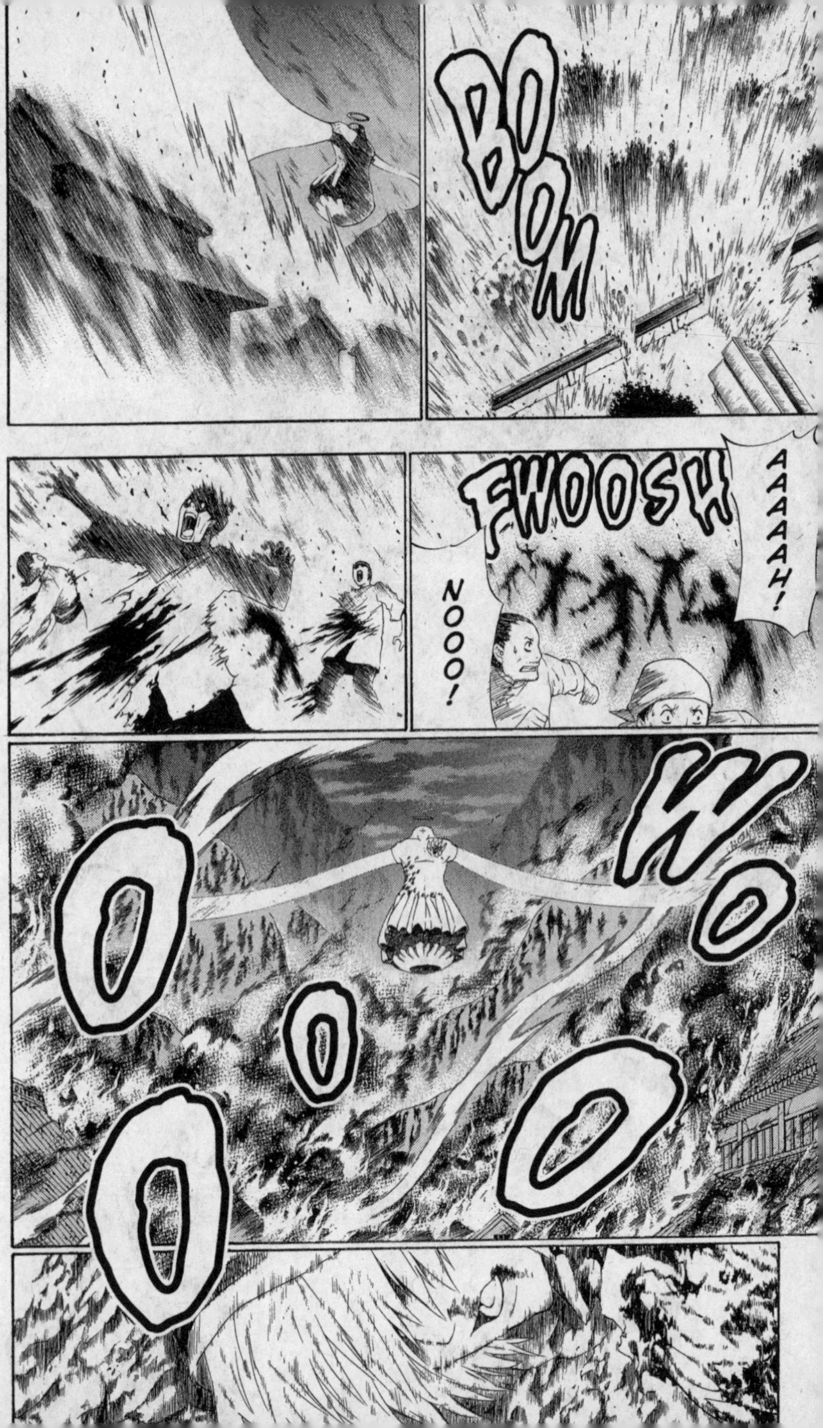
BOOM
AAAAAH!
FWOOSH
NOOO!
WOOOOO

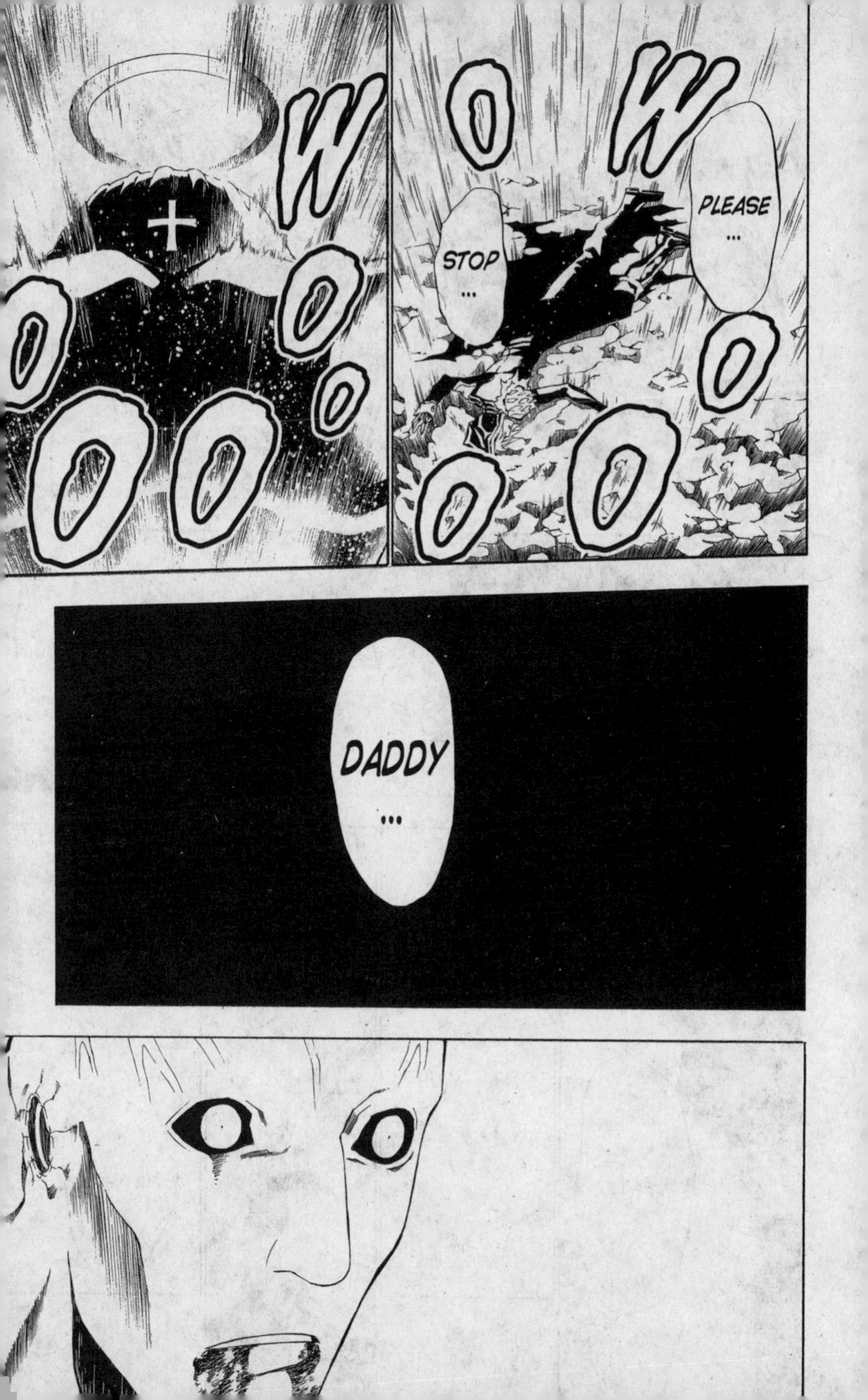
PLEASE ...
STOP ...
WOOOOOO WOOOO
DADDY ...

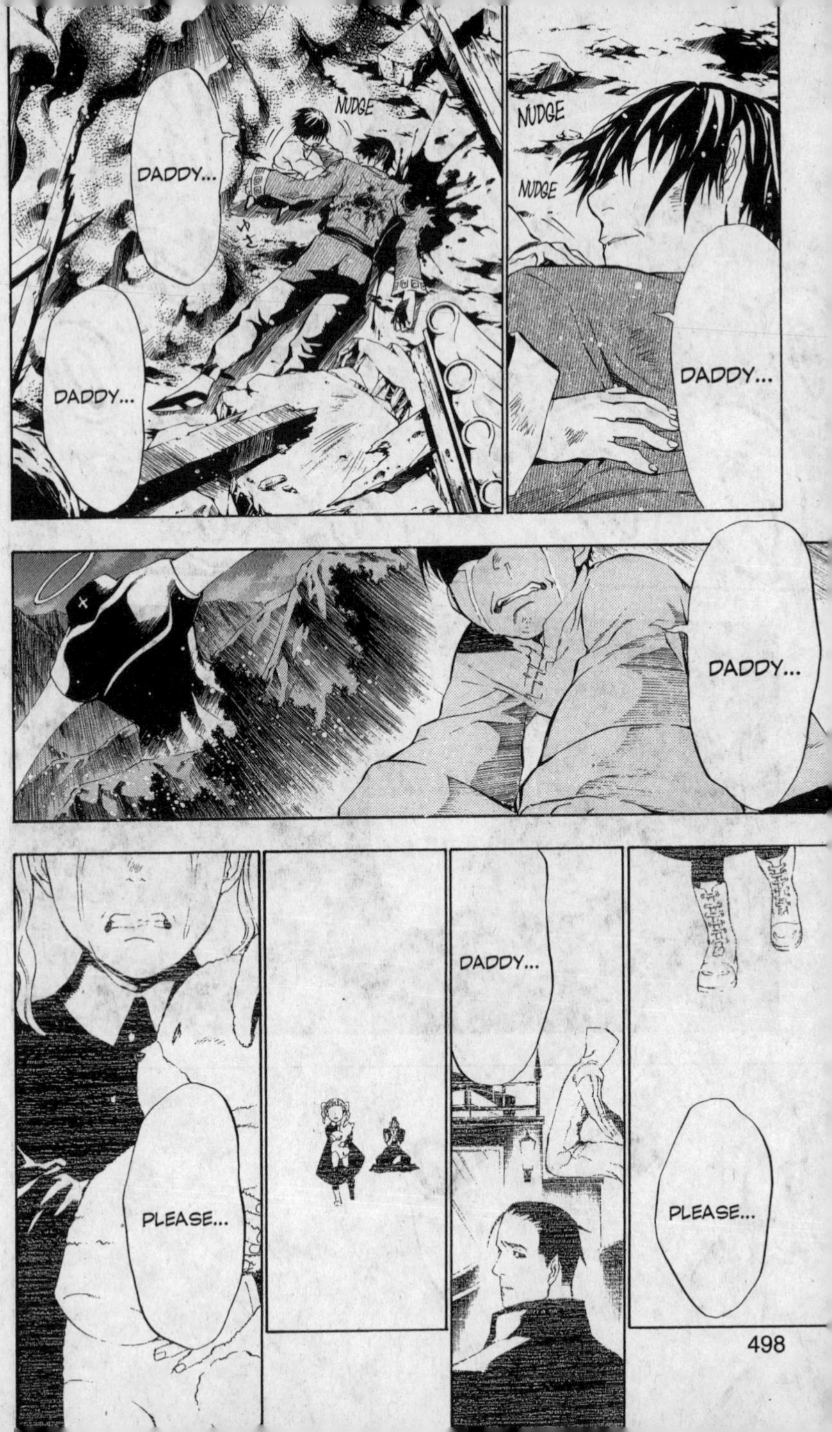
NUDGE
NUDGE
DADDY...
NUDGE
DADDY...
DADDY...
DADDY...
PLEASE...
DADDY...
PLEASE...

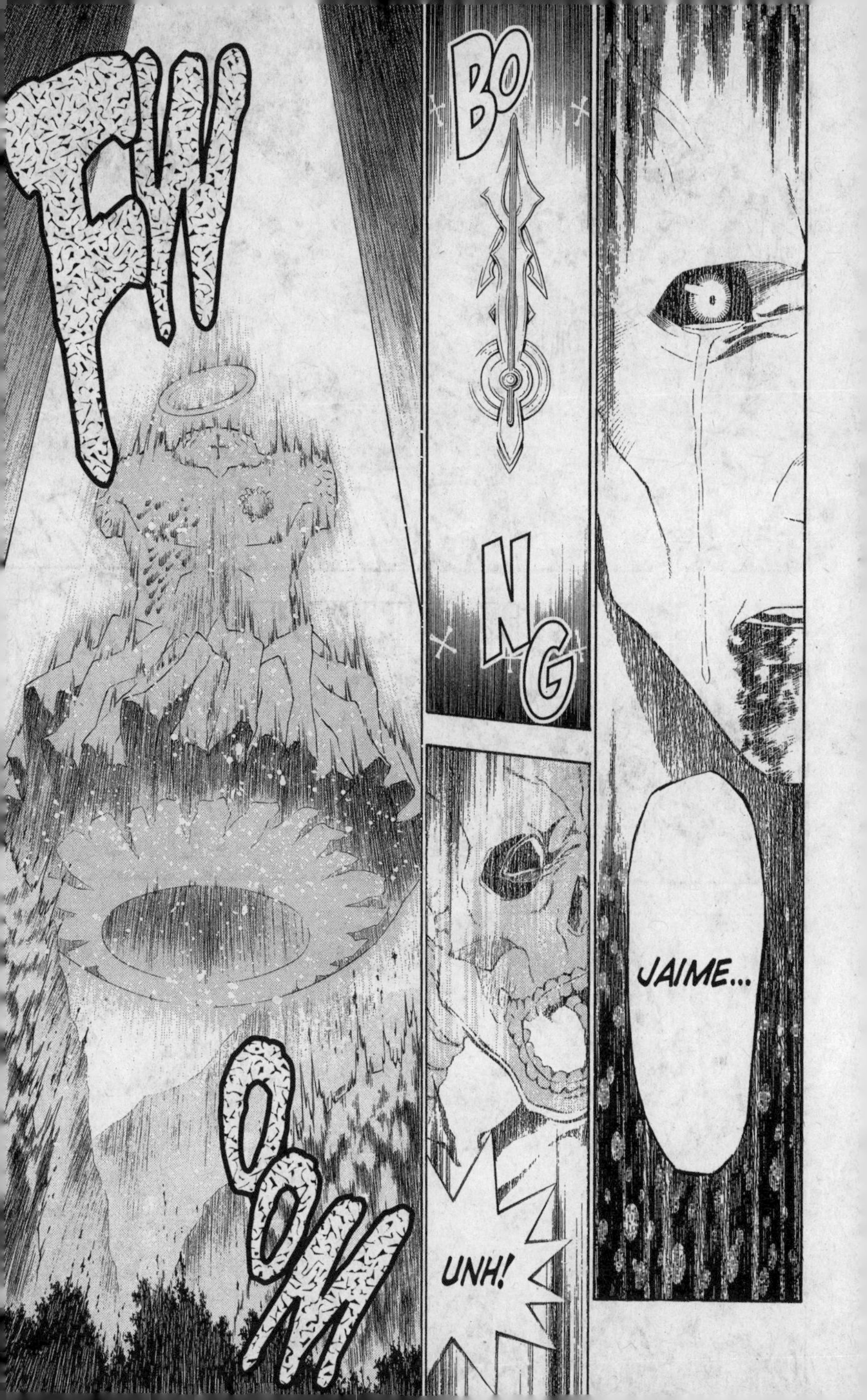
JAIME...
BONG
UNH!
CHW
OOM

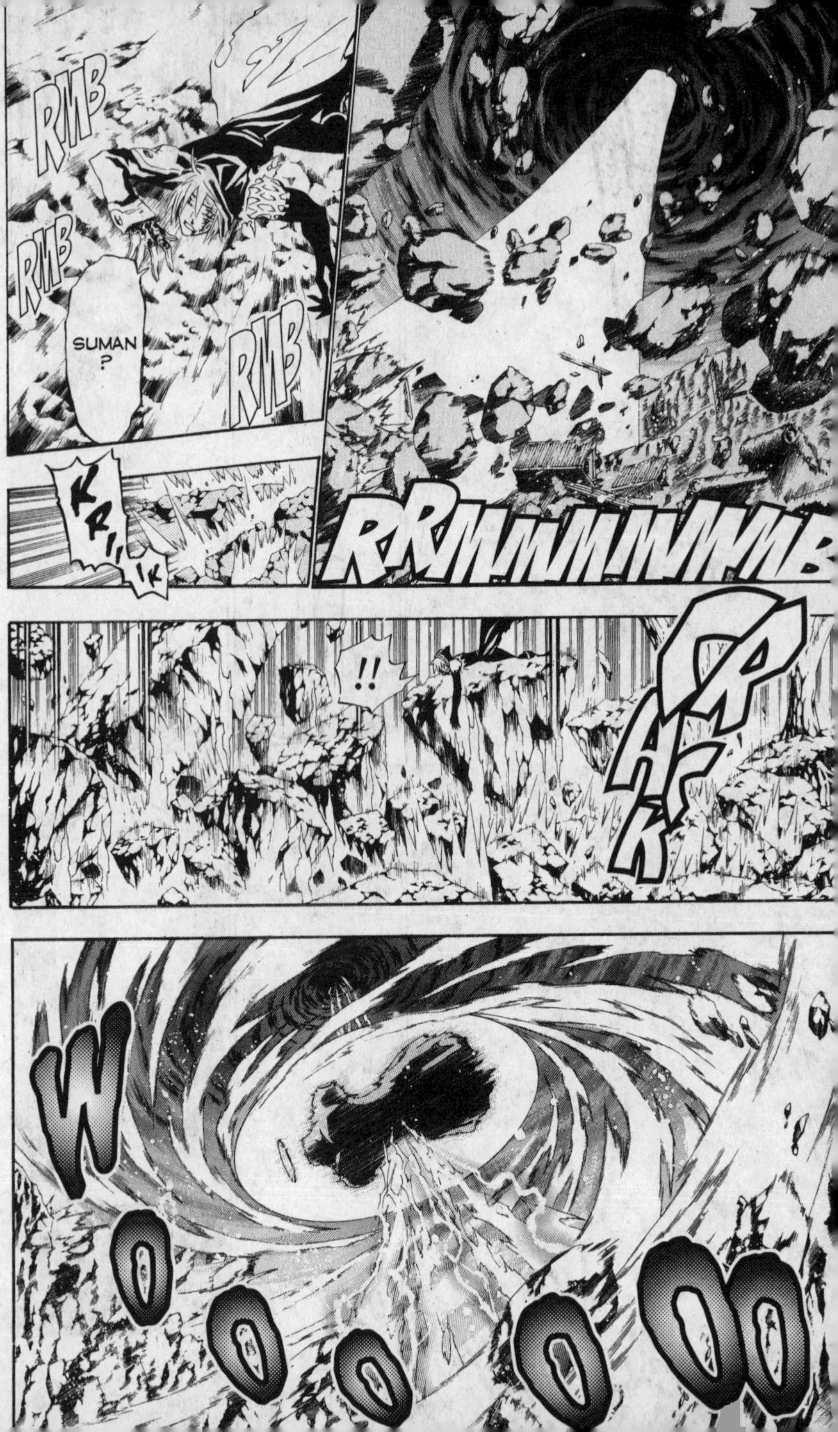
RRMMMMMMMB
RMB
RMB
SUMAN?
RMB
KRIIK
CRACK
!!
WOOOOOOO

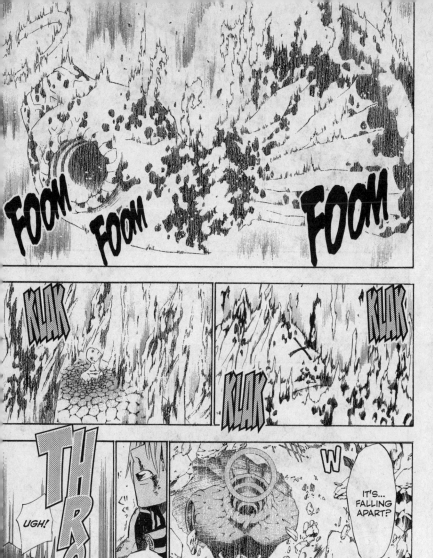

FOOM FOOM FOOM

KUAK KUAK KUAK

THROB

UGH!

IS SUMAN ...

WHY?

W

IT'S... FALLING APART?

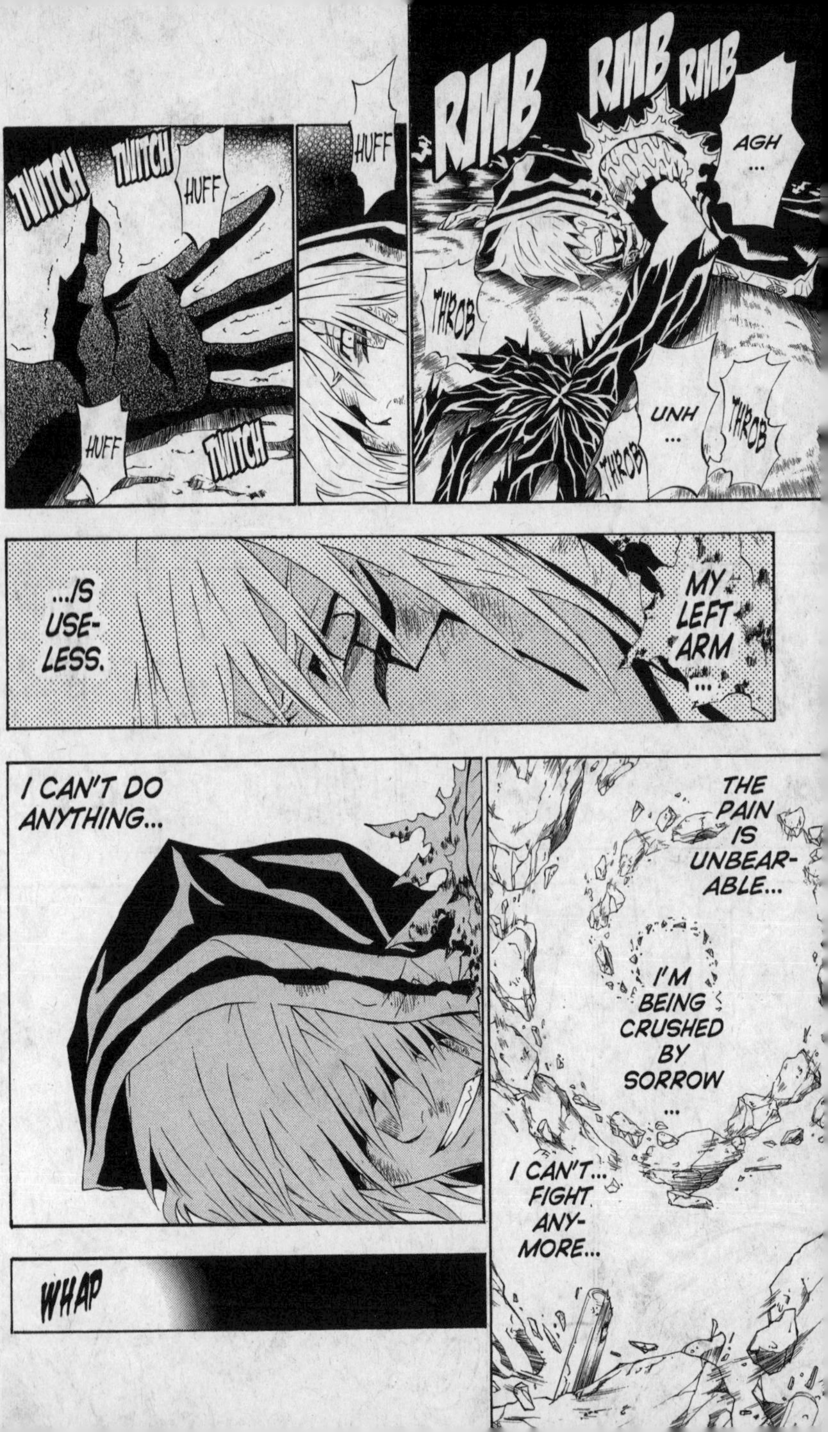
RMB RMB RMB
AGH...
THROB
UNH...
THROB
THROB
HUFF
TWITCH
TWITCH
HUFF
HUFF
TWITCH
MY LEFT ARM...
...IS USELESS.
THE PAIN IS UNBEARABLE...
I'M BEING CRUSHED BY SORROW...
I CAN'T... FIGHT ANYMORE...
I CAN'T DO ANYTHING...
WHAP

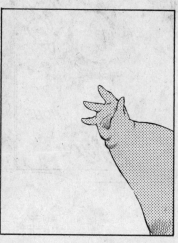

WHAP

--CANDY...

TIM--

WHAT ARE YOU...

WHUP

PLURT

BLEEDING

YOWWW!!!

CHONK

WHOOM

503

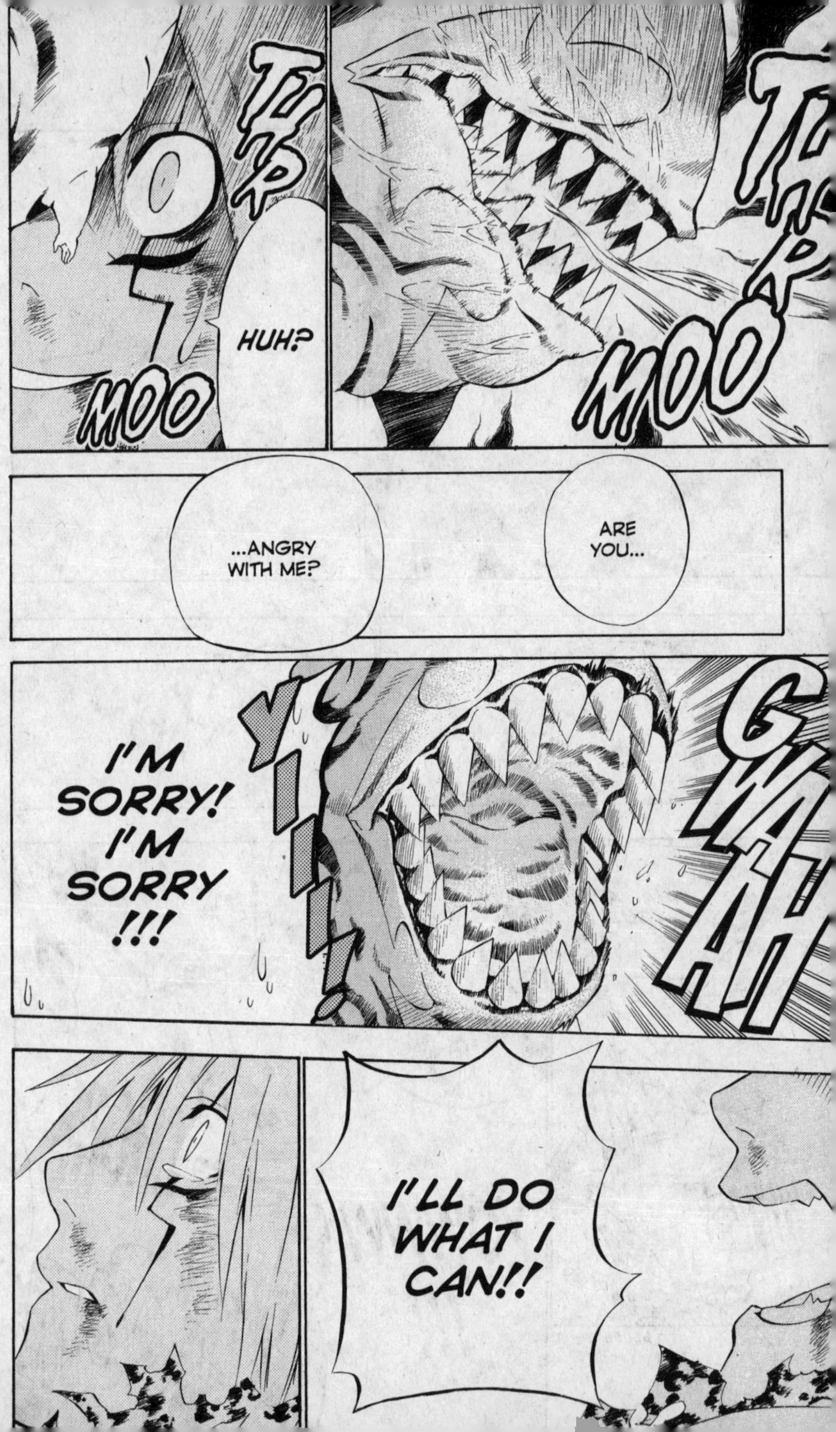
MOO
MOO
HUH?
ARE YOU...
...ANGRY WITH ME?
GWAAH
I'M SORRY! I'M SORRY!!!
I'LL DO WHAT I CAN!!

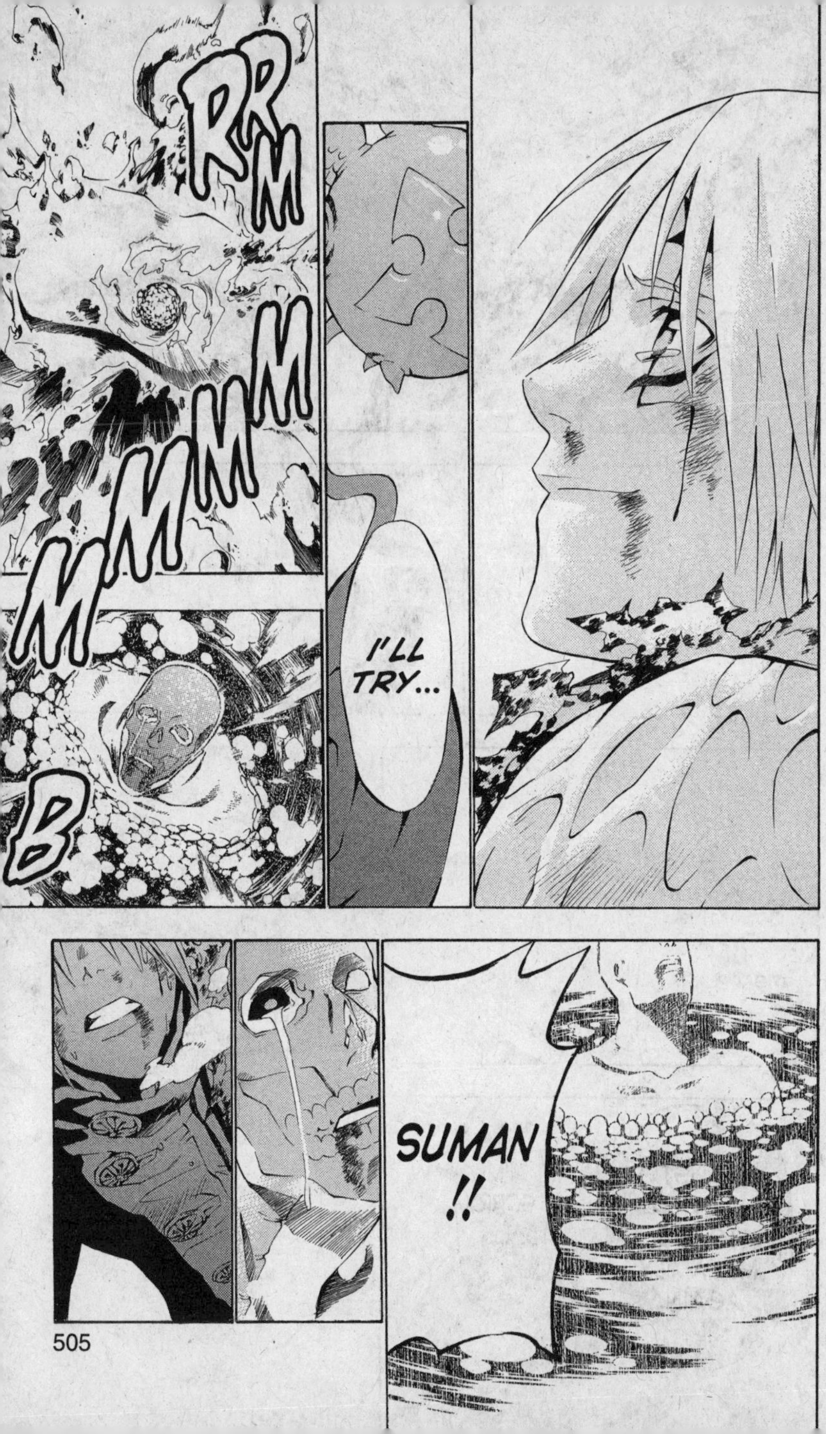
I'LL TRY...
RRMMMMMMB
SUMAN !!

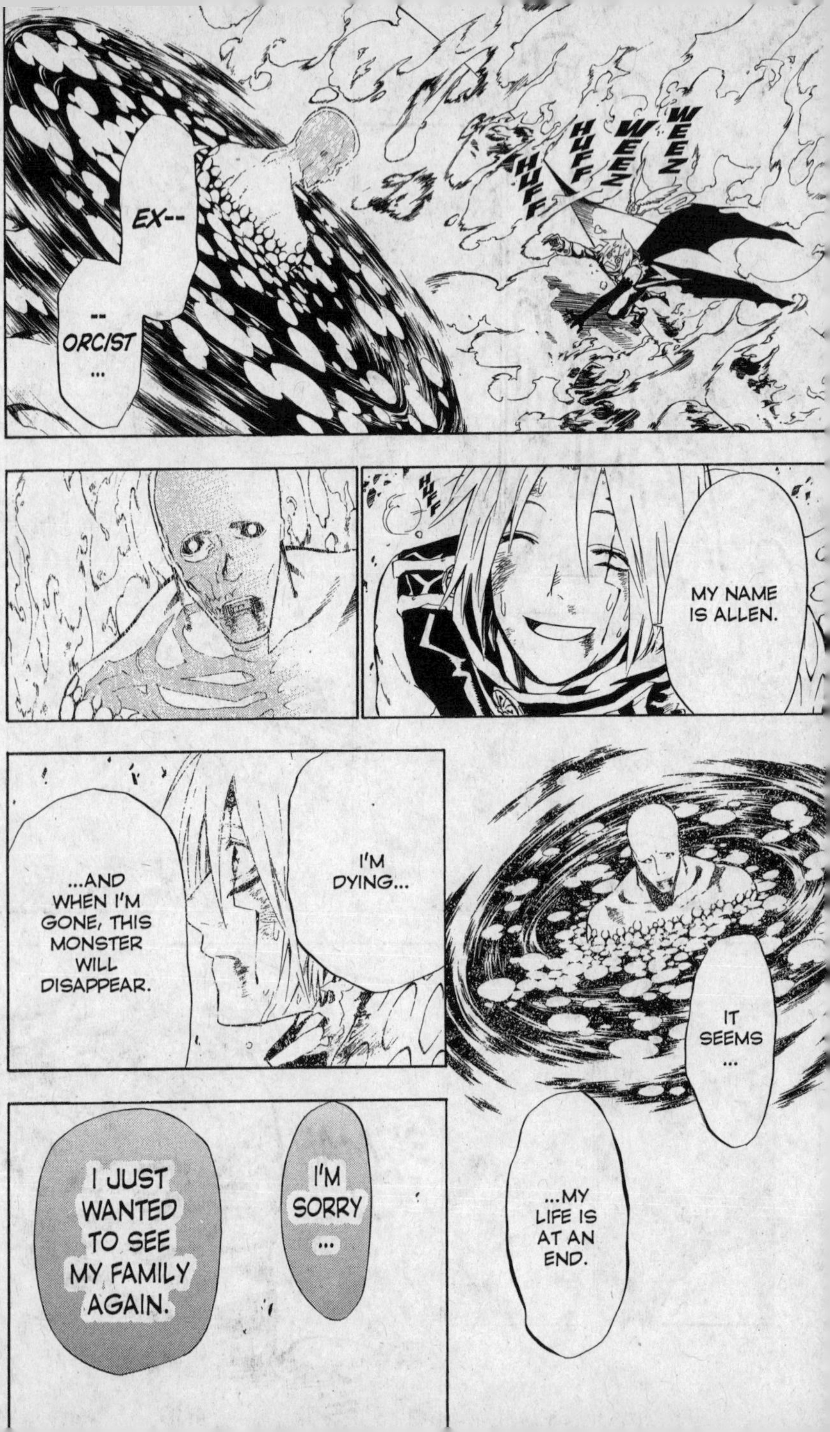
WEEZ
WEEZ
HUFF
HUFF
EX--
--ORCIST ...
HUFF
MY NAME IS ALLEN.
IT SEEMS ...
...MY LIFE IS AT AN END.
I'M DYING...
...AND WHEN I'M GONE, THIS MONSTER WILL DISAPPEAR.
I'M SORRY ...
I JUST WANTED TO SEE MY FAMILY AGAIN.

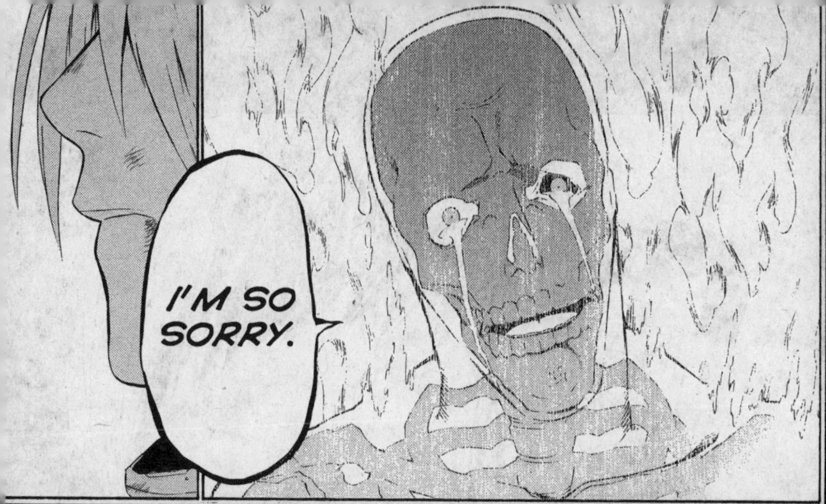
I'M SO SORRY.

I HEARD THE SOUND OF SOMETHING BREAKING.

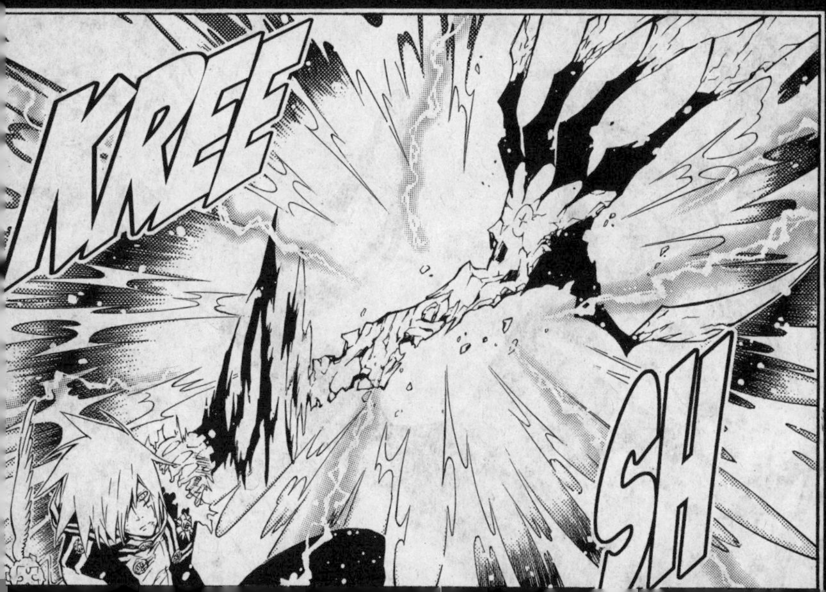
KREE
SH

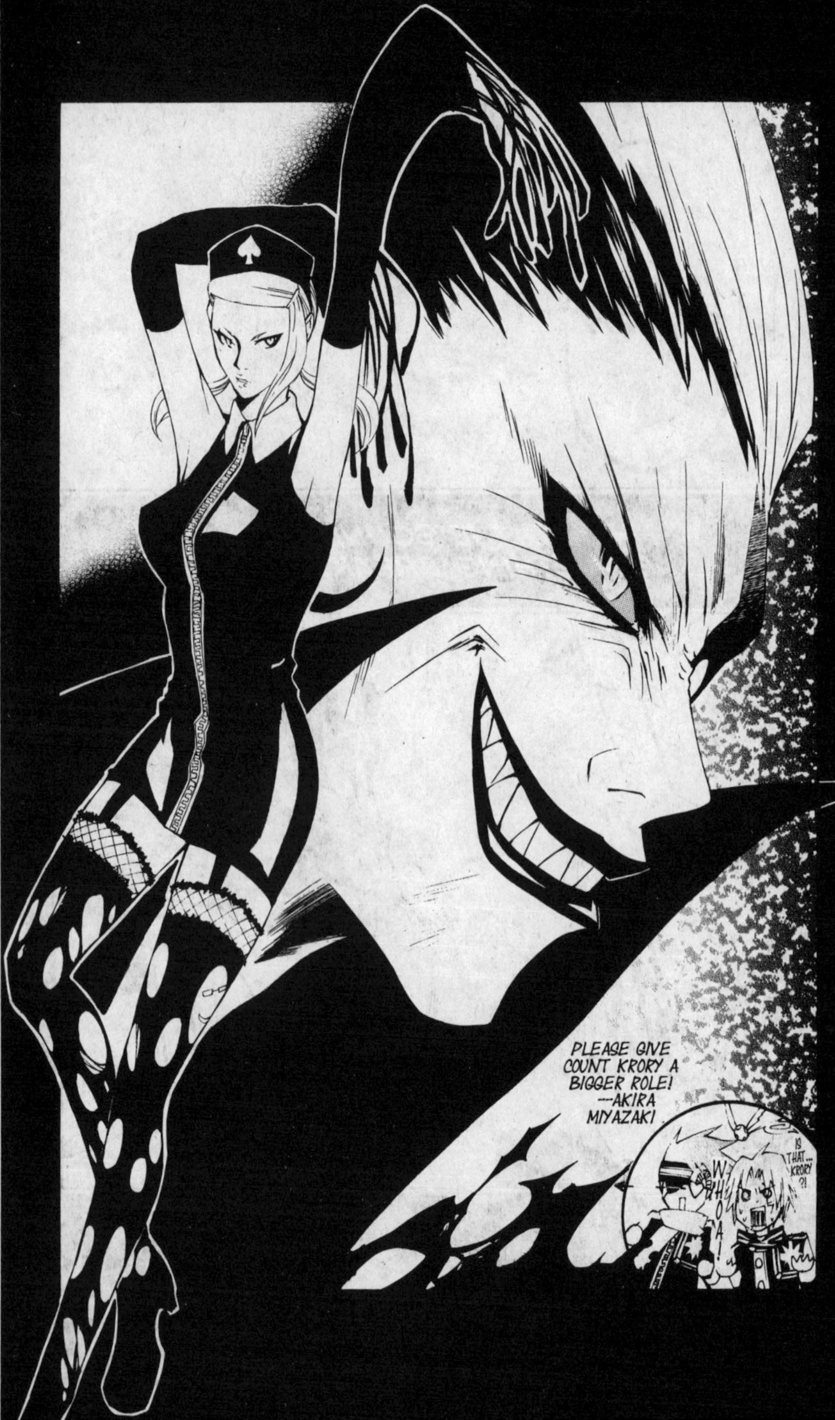
PLEASE GIVE COUNT KRORY A BIGGER ROLE! ---AKIRA MIYAZAKI
IS THAT... KRORY ?!
WHOA!

THE 54TH NIGHT: REND ALLEN'S HEART

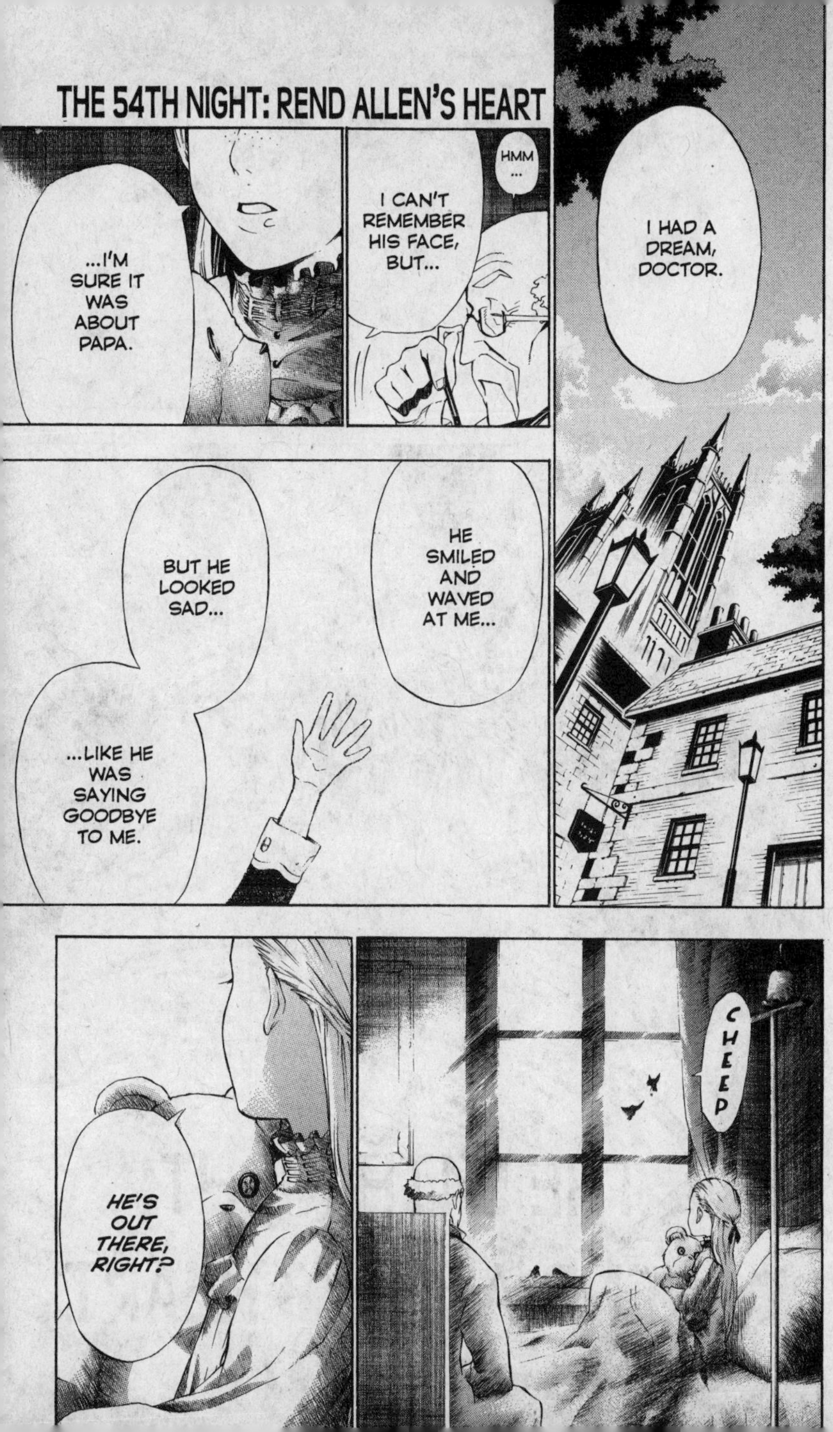
I HAD A DREAM, DOCTOR.
HMM...
I CAN'T REMEMBER HIS FACE, BUT...
...I'M SURE IT WAS ABOUT PAPA.
HE SMILED AND WAVED AT ME...
BUT HE LOOKED SAD...
...LIKE HE WAS SAYING GOODBYE TO ME.
CHEEP
HE'S OUT THERE, RIGHT?

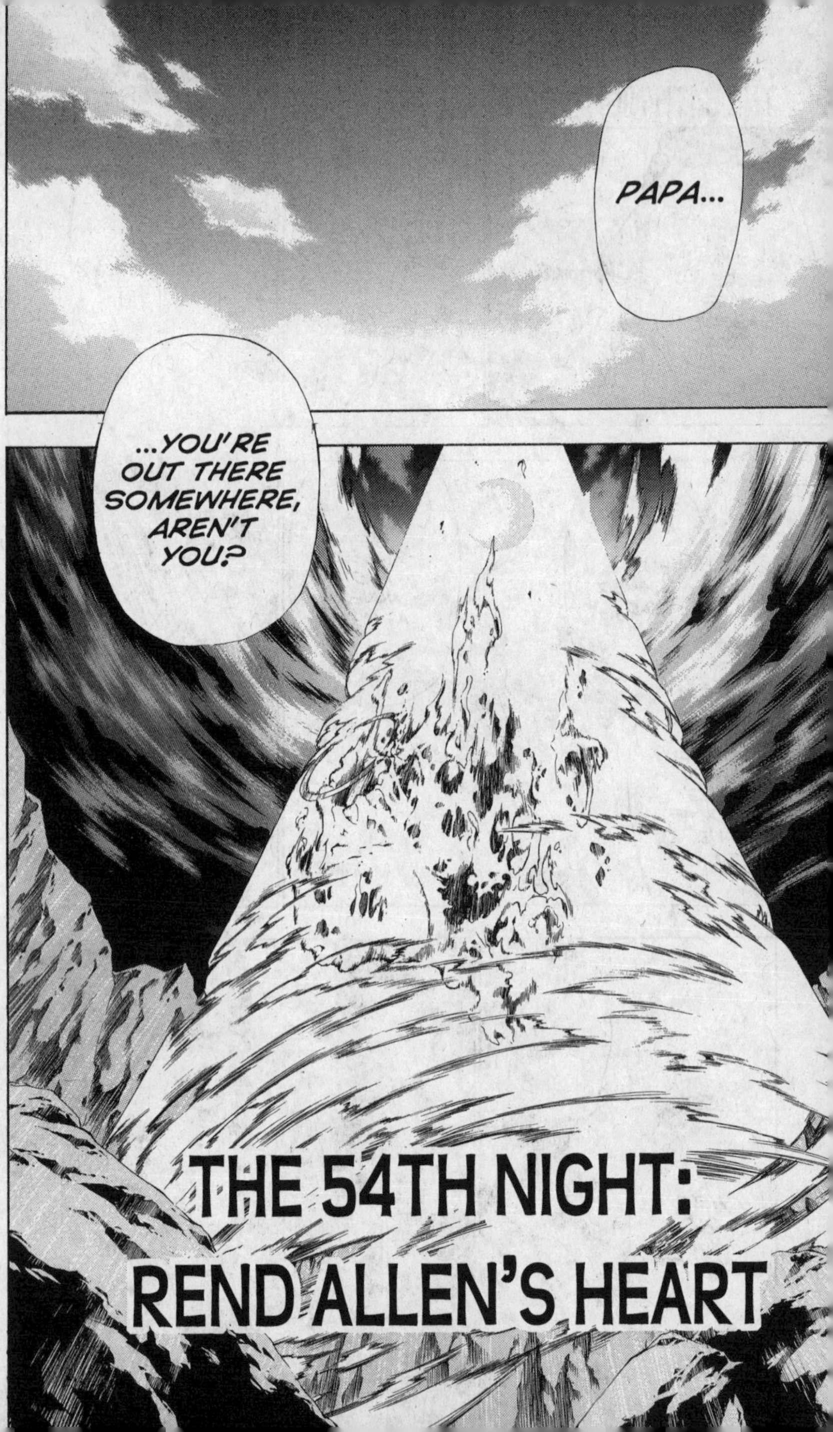
PAPA...
...YOU'RE OUT THERE SOMEWHERE, AREN'T YOU?
THE 54TH NIGHT: REND ALLEN'S HEART

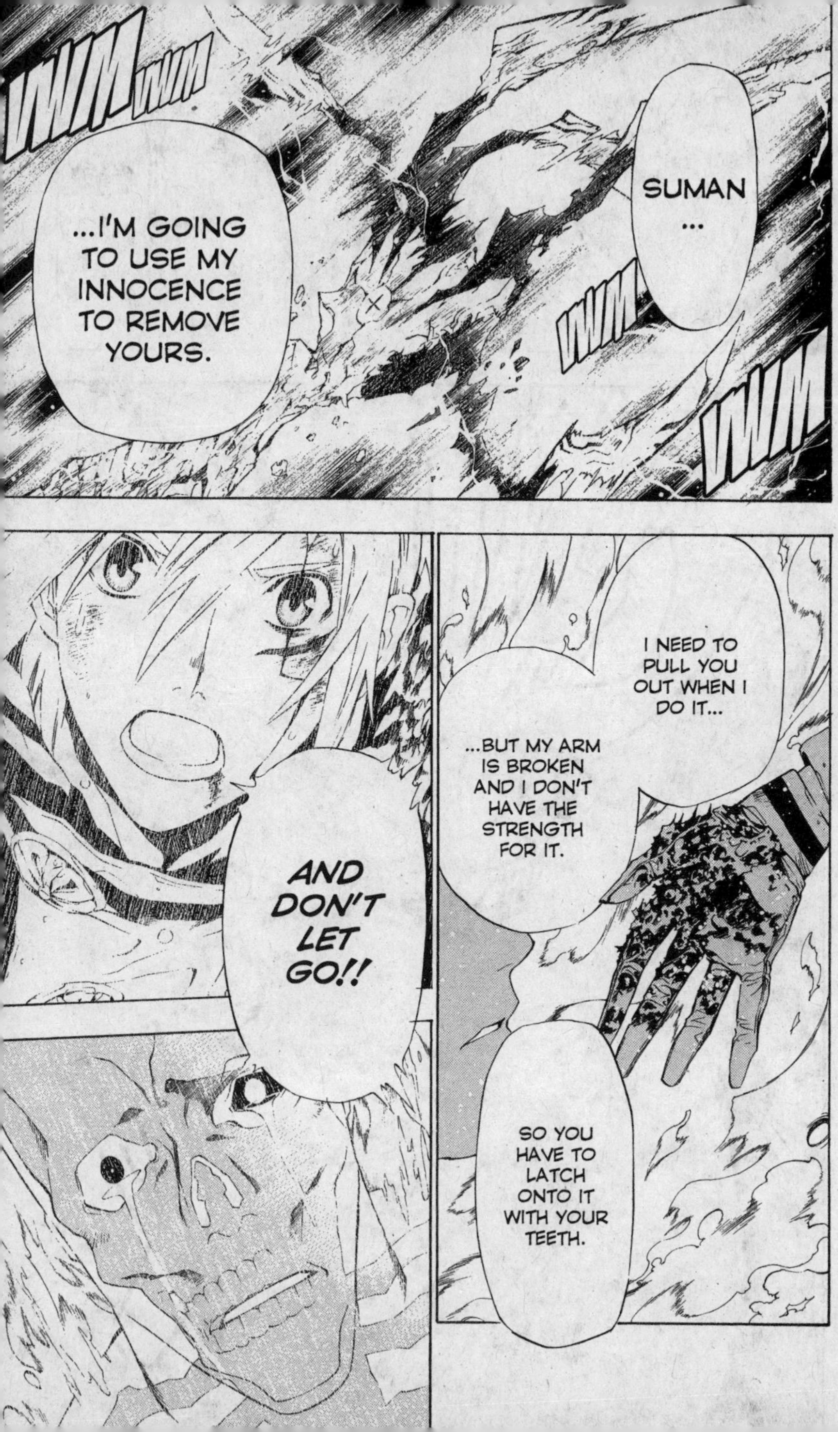
SUMAN ...
VWM
VWM
VWM VWM
...I'M GOING TO USE MY INNOCENCE TO REMOVE YOURS.
I NEED TO PULL YOU OUT WHEN I DO IT...
...BUT MY ARM IS BROKEN AND I DON'T HAVE THE STRENGTH FOR IT.
SO YOU HAVE TO LATCH ONTO IT WITH YOUR TEETH.
AND DON'T LET GO!!

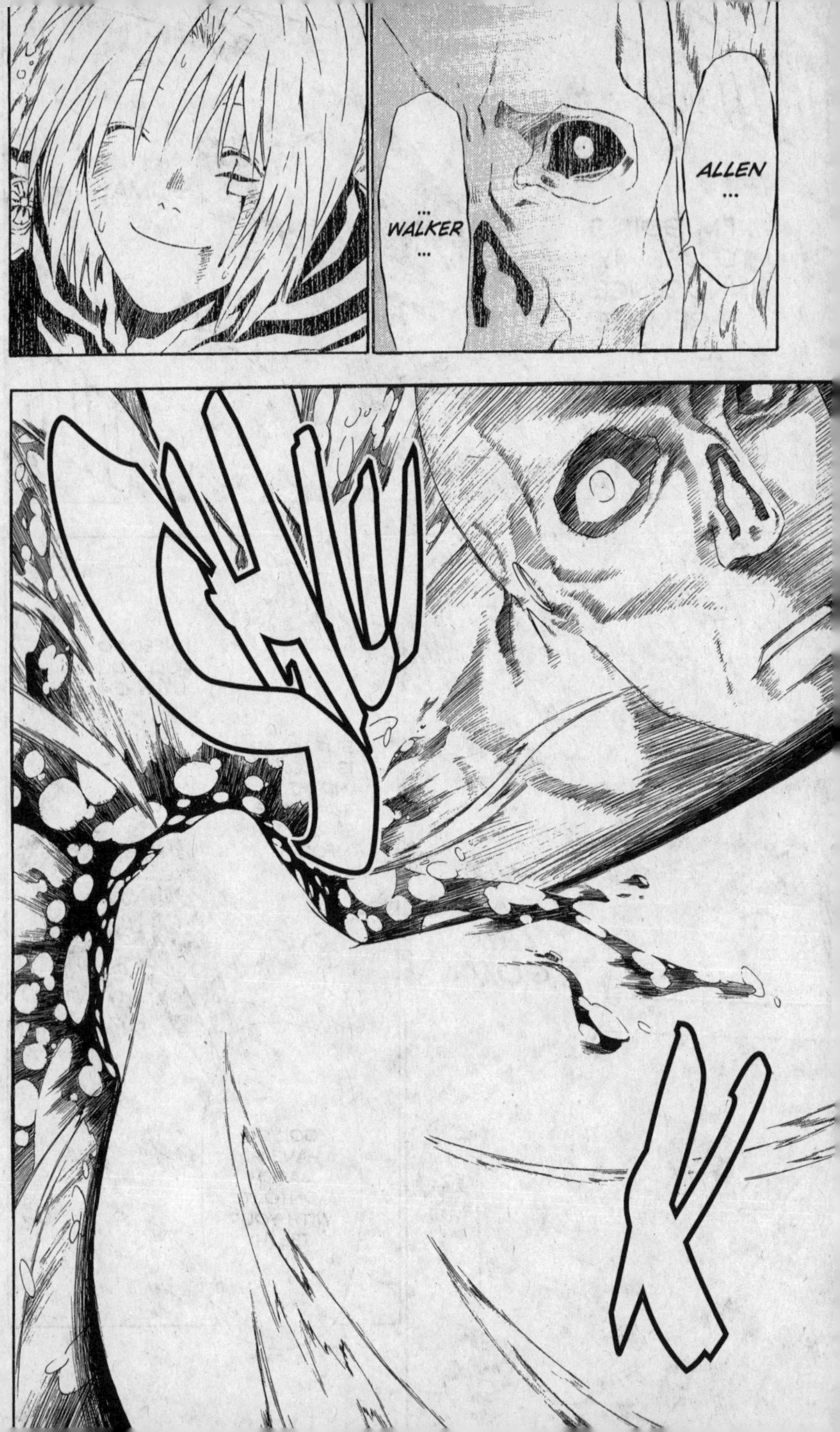
ALLEN ...
... WALKER ...

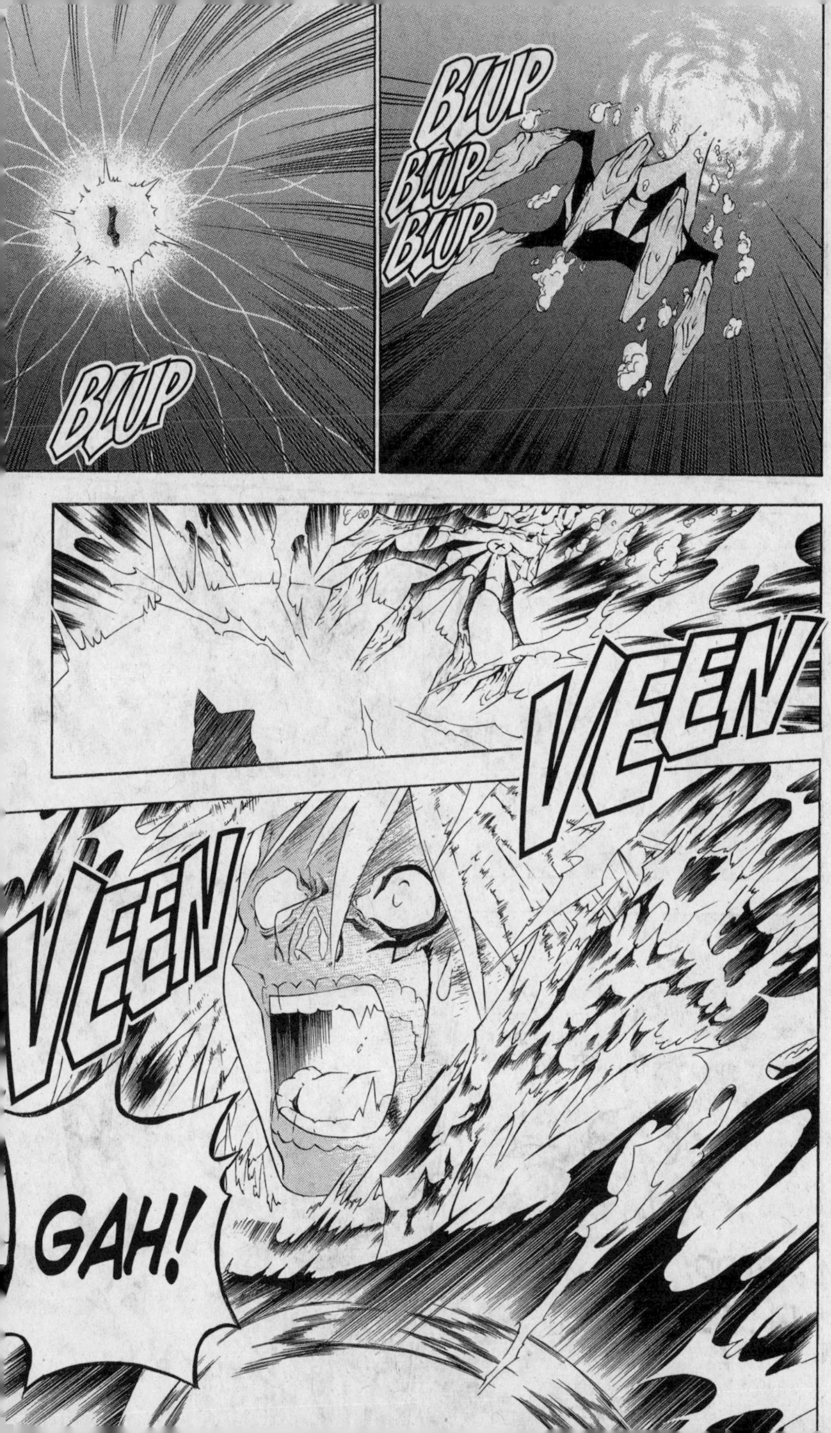
BLUP
BLUP
BLUP
BLUP
VEEN
VEEN
GAH!

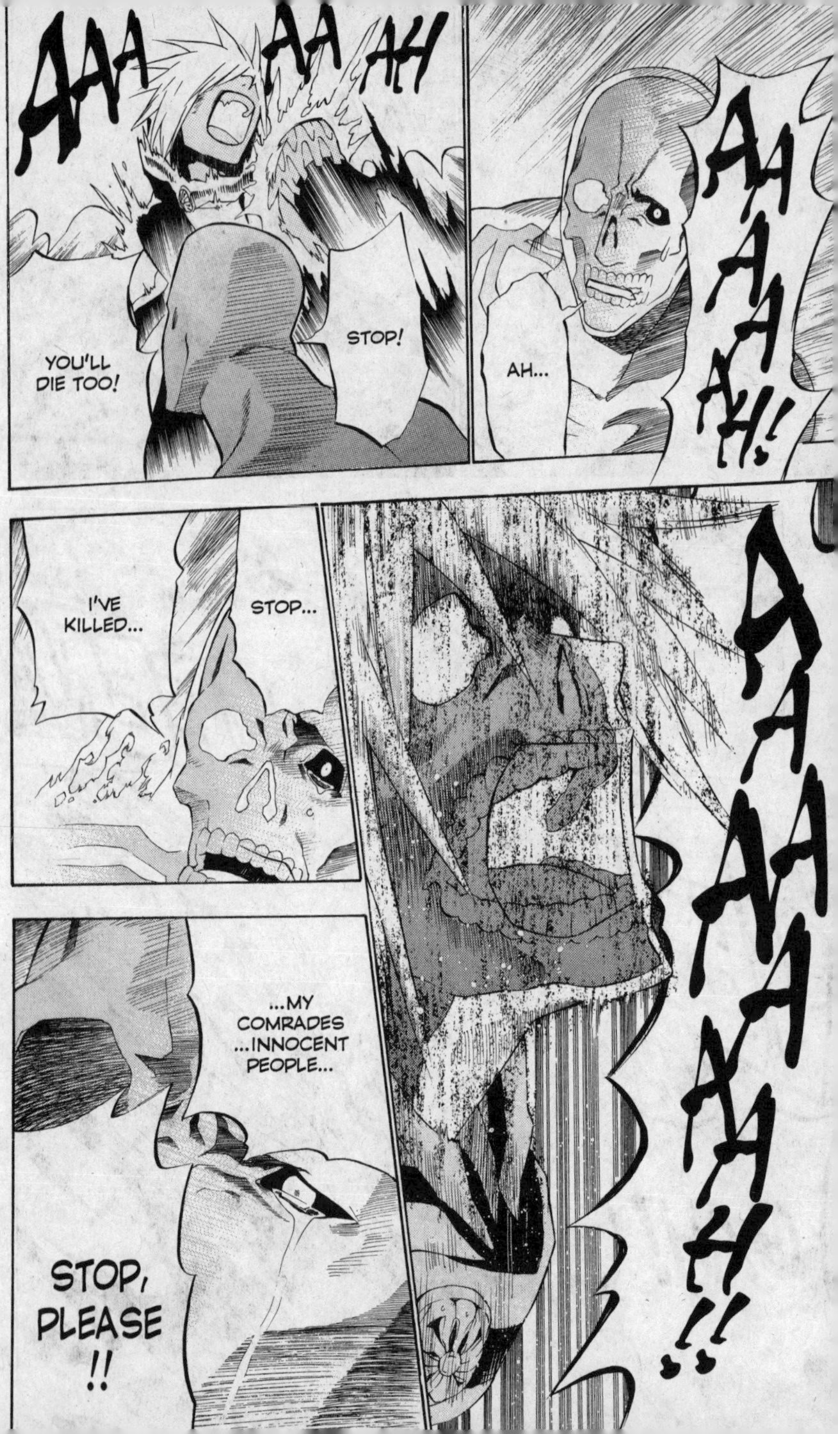
AAAAAH!
AH...
AAA AA AH
STOP!
YOU'LL DIE TOO!
AAAAAAAH!!
STOP...
I'VE KILLED...
...MY COMRADES ...INNOCENT PEOPLE...
STOP, PLEASE !!

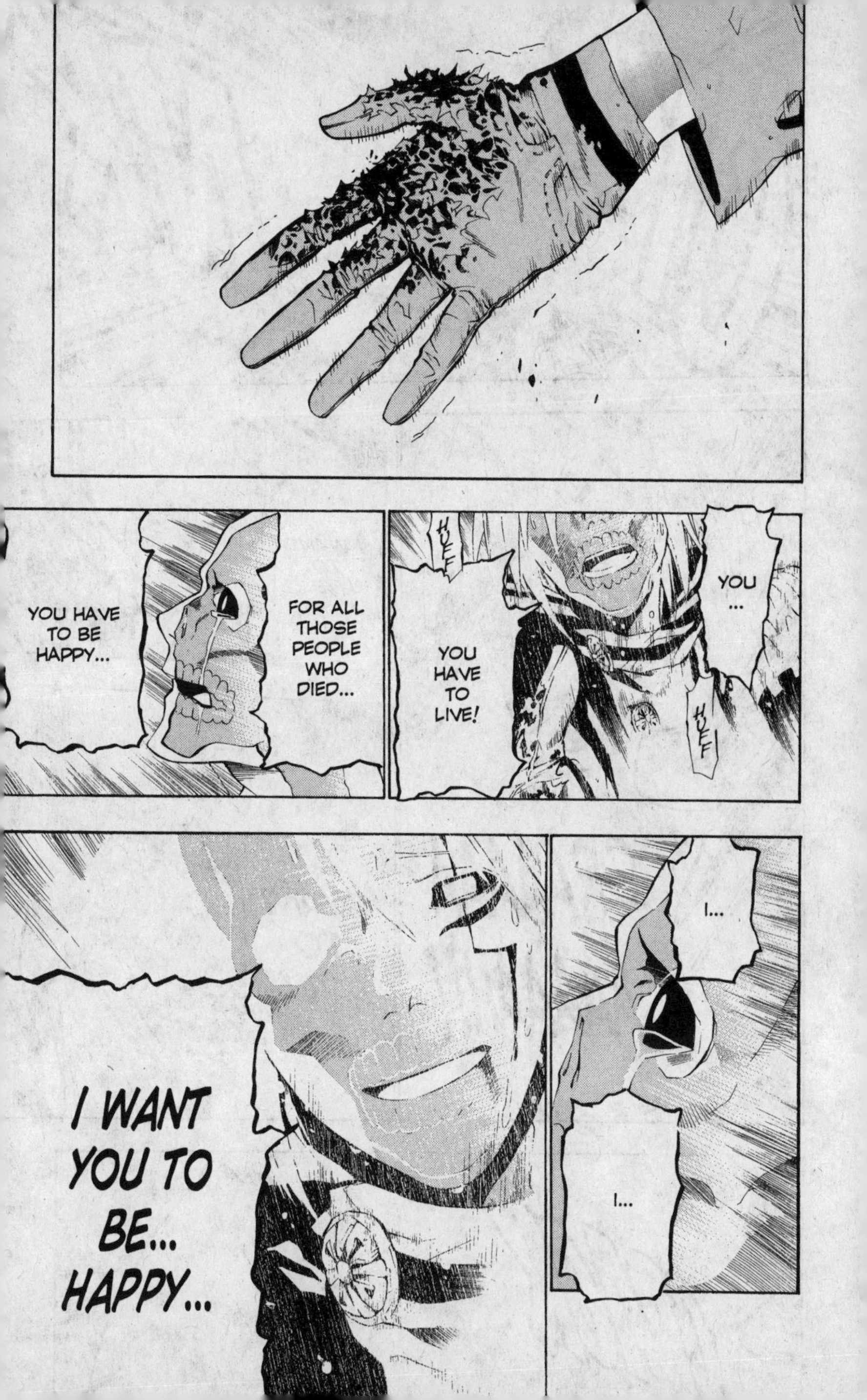
YOU ...
HUFF
YOU HAVE TO LIVE!
HUFF
FOR ALL THOSE PEOPLE WHO DIED...
YOU HAVE TO BE HAPPY...
I...
I...
I WANT YOU TO BE... HAPPY...

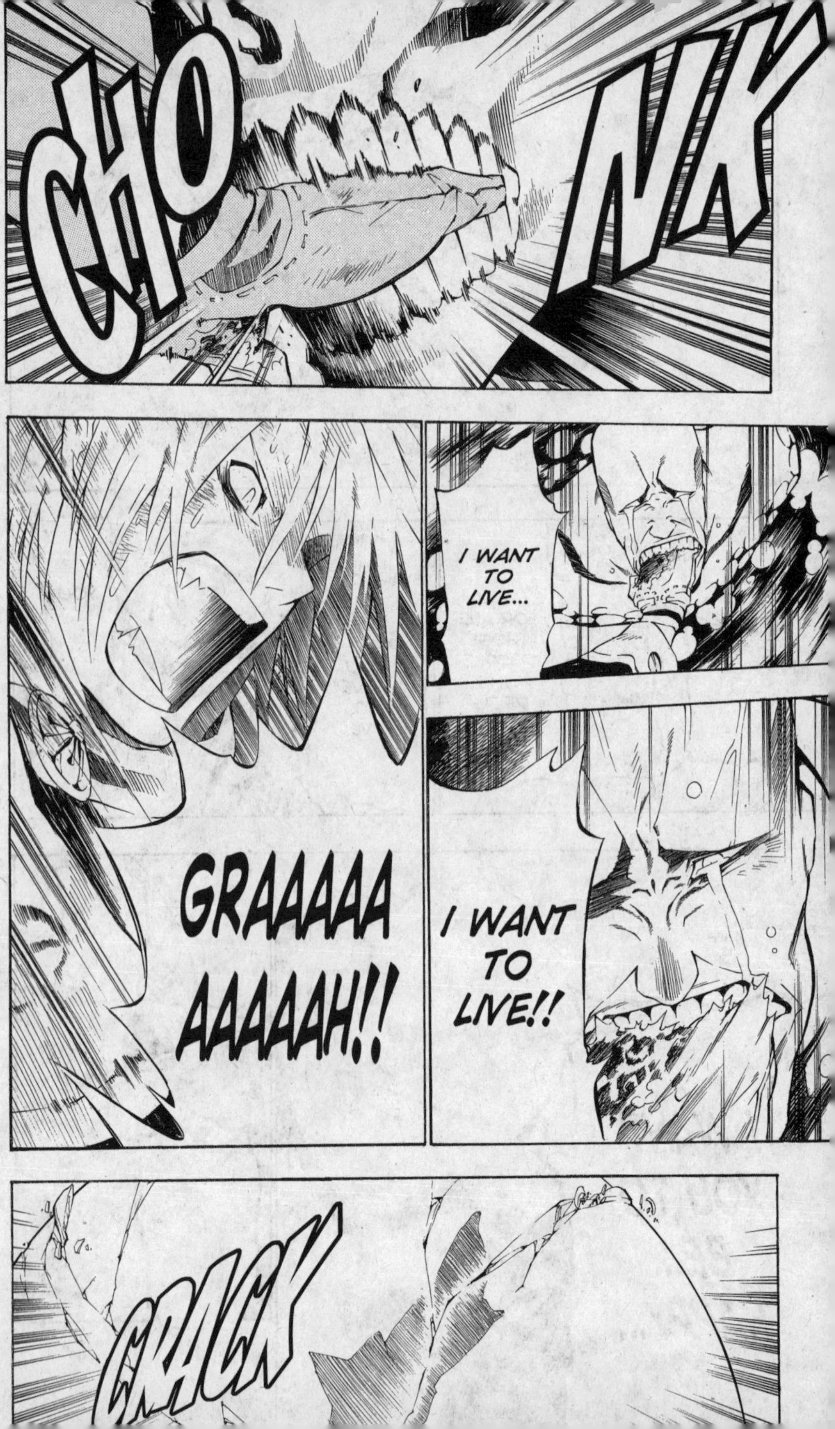
CHOMNK
I WANT TO LIVE...
I WANT TO LIVE!!
GRAAAAAAAAAAAH!!
CRACK

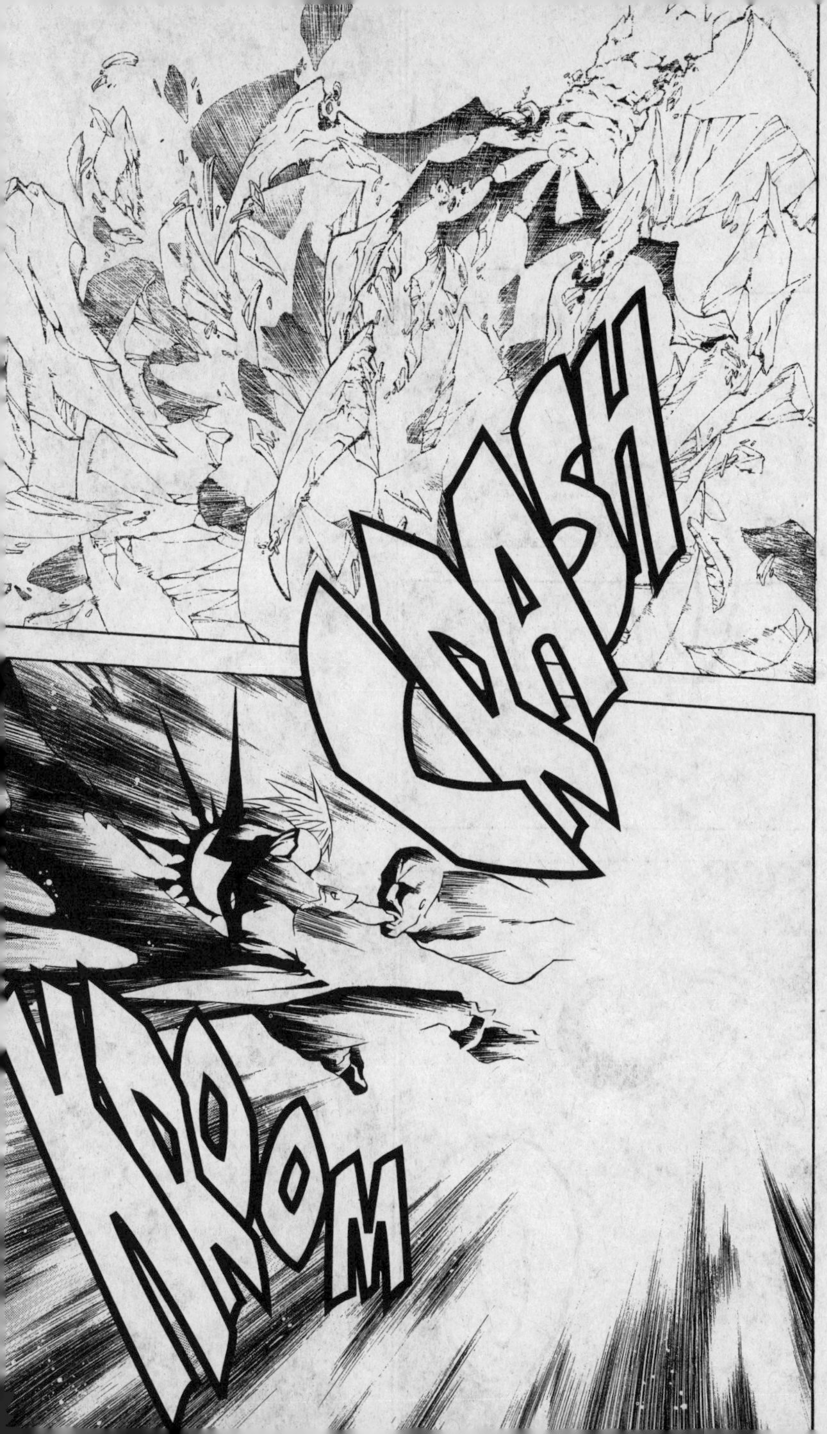
CRASH
VROOM

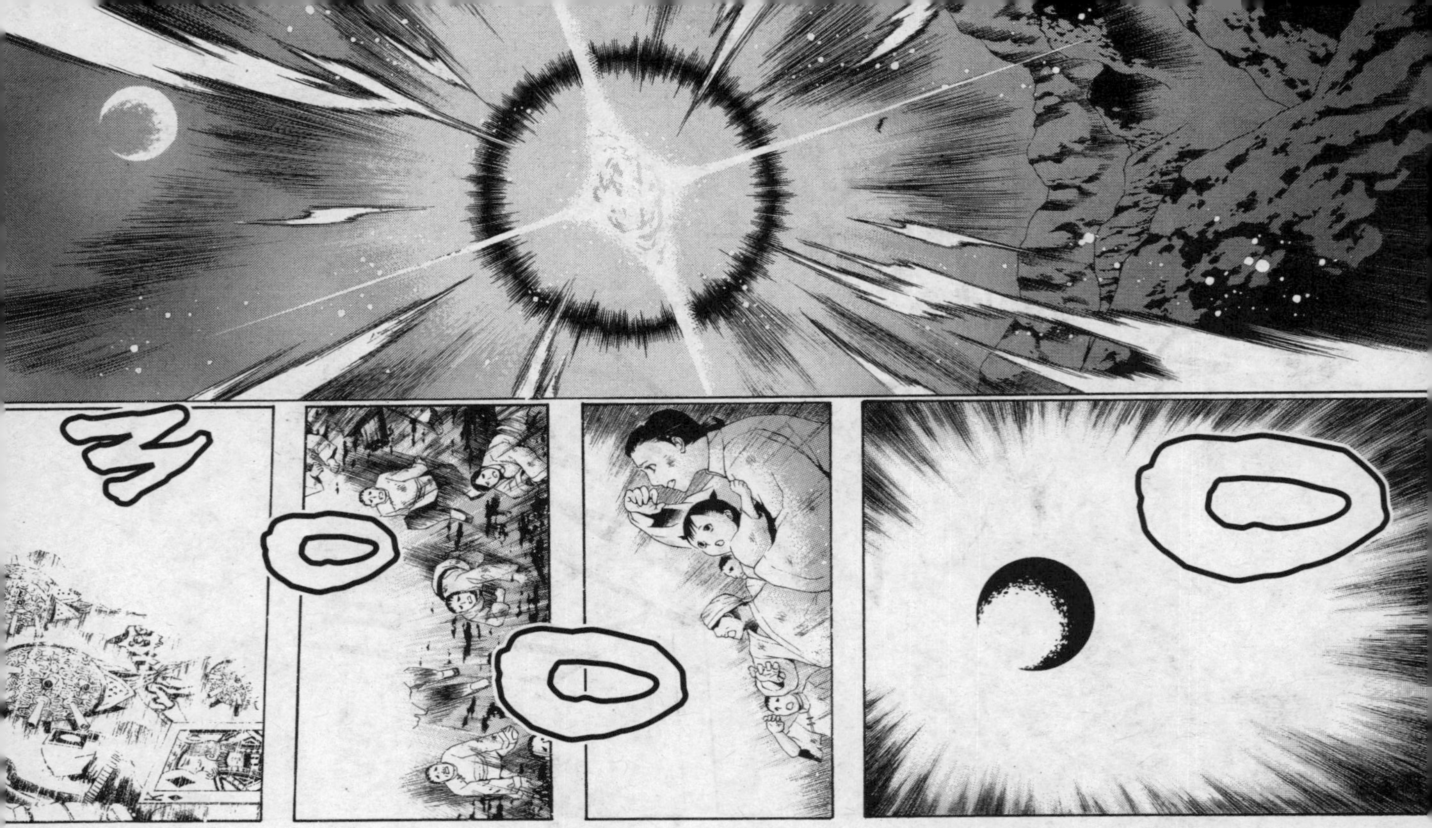
WOOO

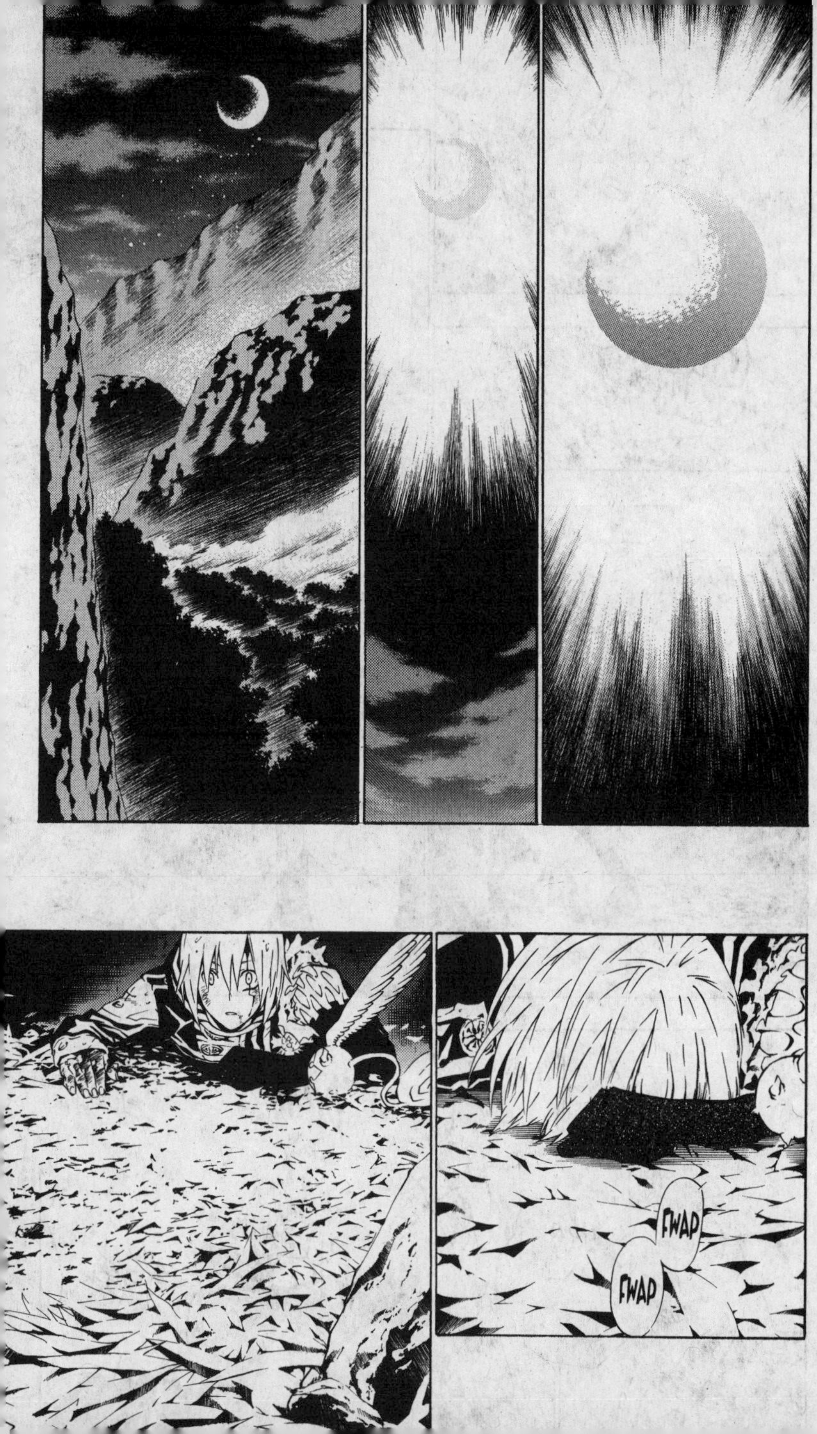
FWAP
FWAP

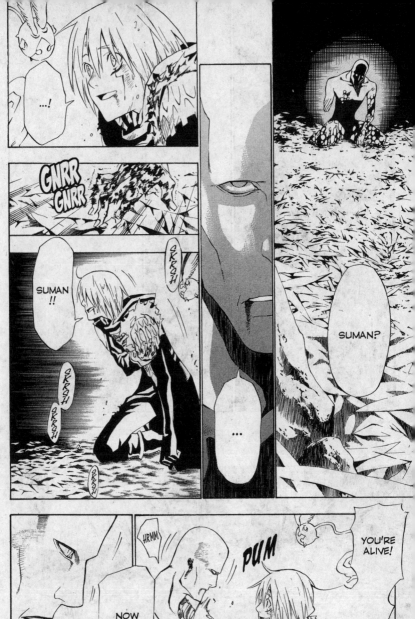

...!

GNRR
GNRR

SUMAN !!

SKROSH

...

SKROSH

SKROSH

SKROSH

SUMAN?

HRMM

PUM

WOB

WOB

NOW YOU CAN...

YOU'RE ALIVE!

THANK GOD FOR THAT!

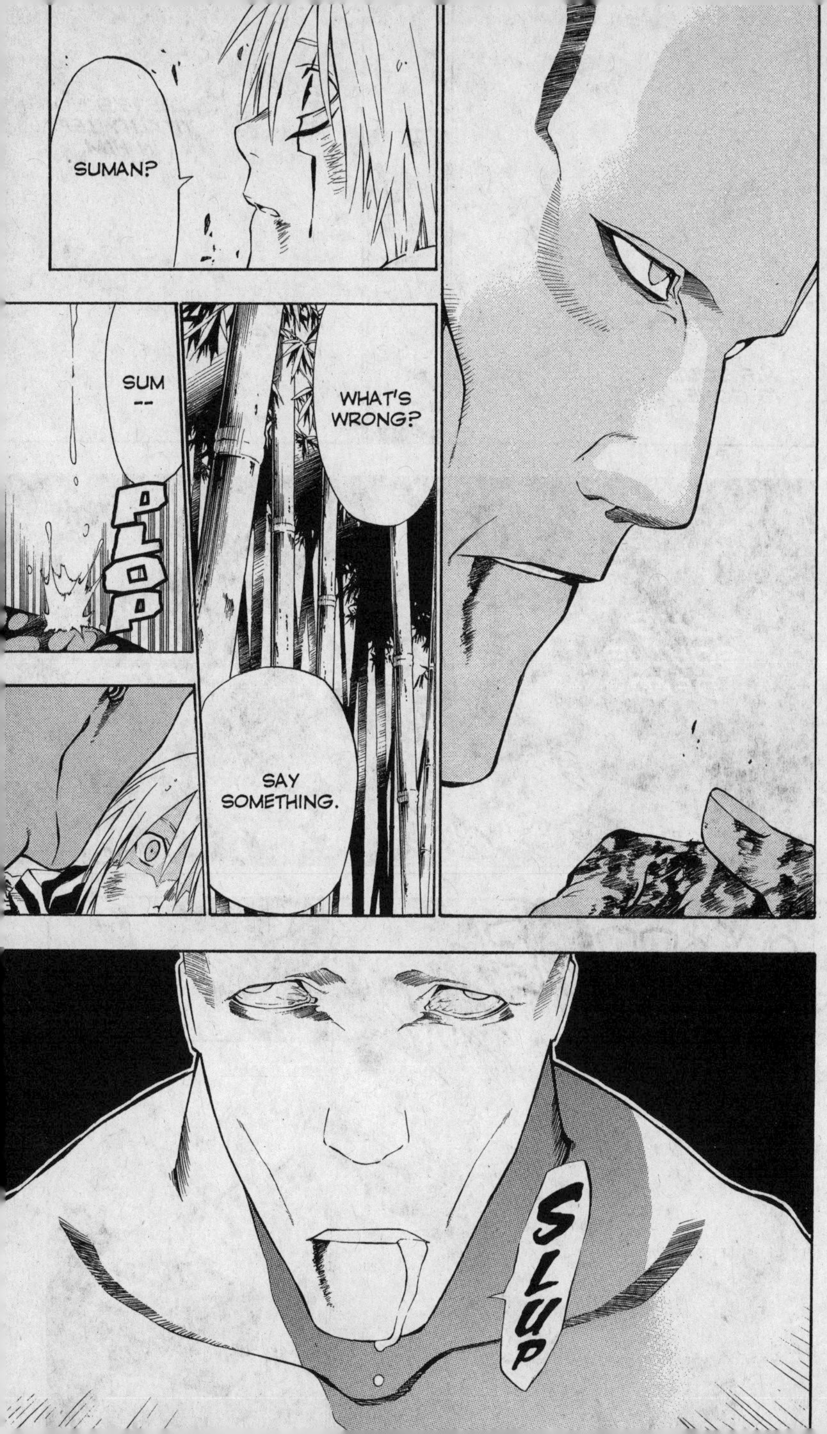
SUMAN?
WHAT'S WRONG?
SAY SOMETHING.
SUM --
PLOP
SLUP

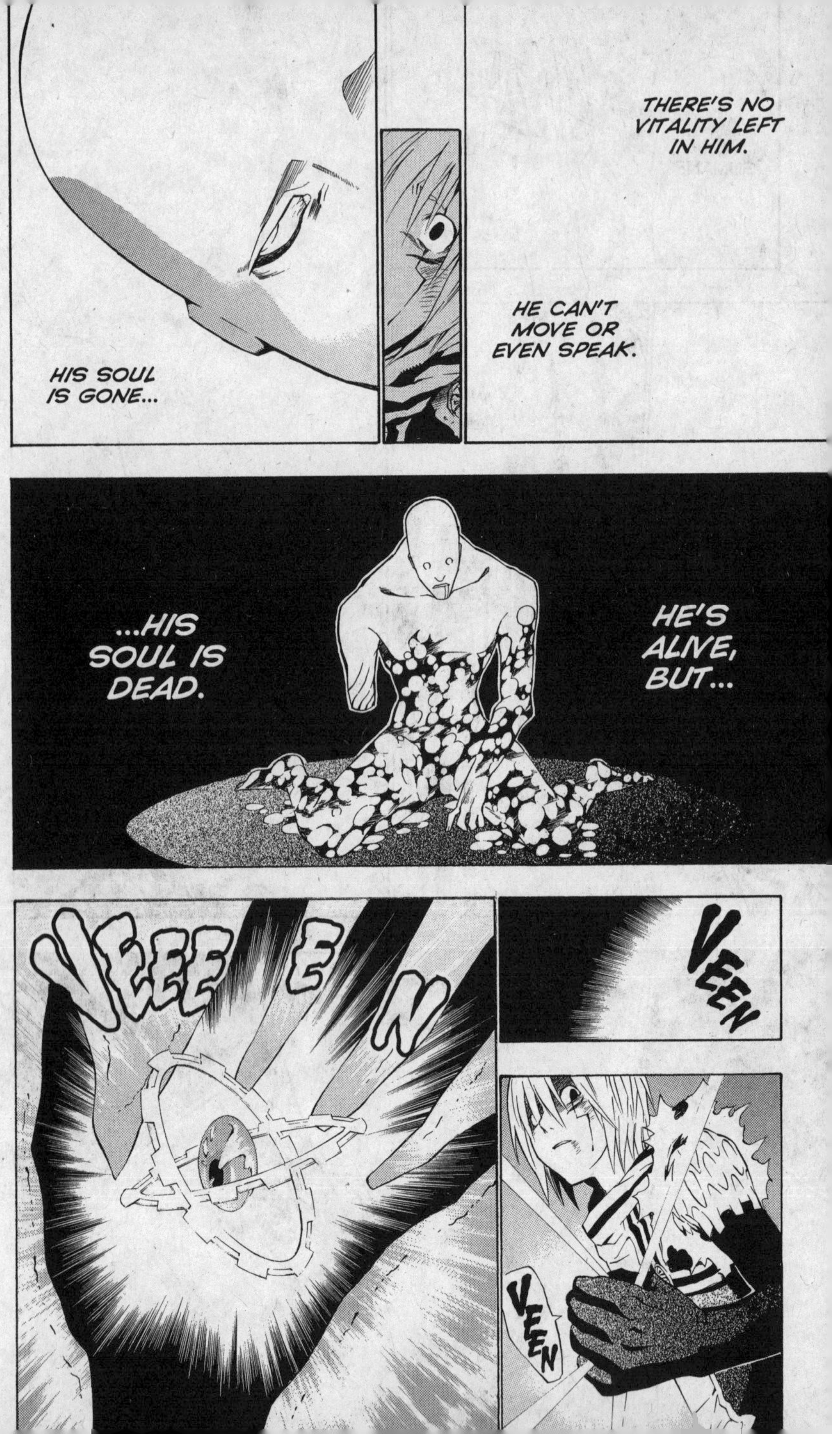
THERE'S NO VITALITY LEFT IN HIM.
HE CAN'T MOVE OR EVEN SPEAK.
HIS SOUL IS GONE...
HE'S ALIVE, BUT...
...HIS SOUL IS DEAD.
VEEN
VEEN
VEEEEN

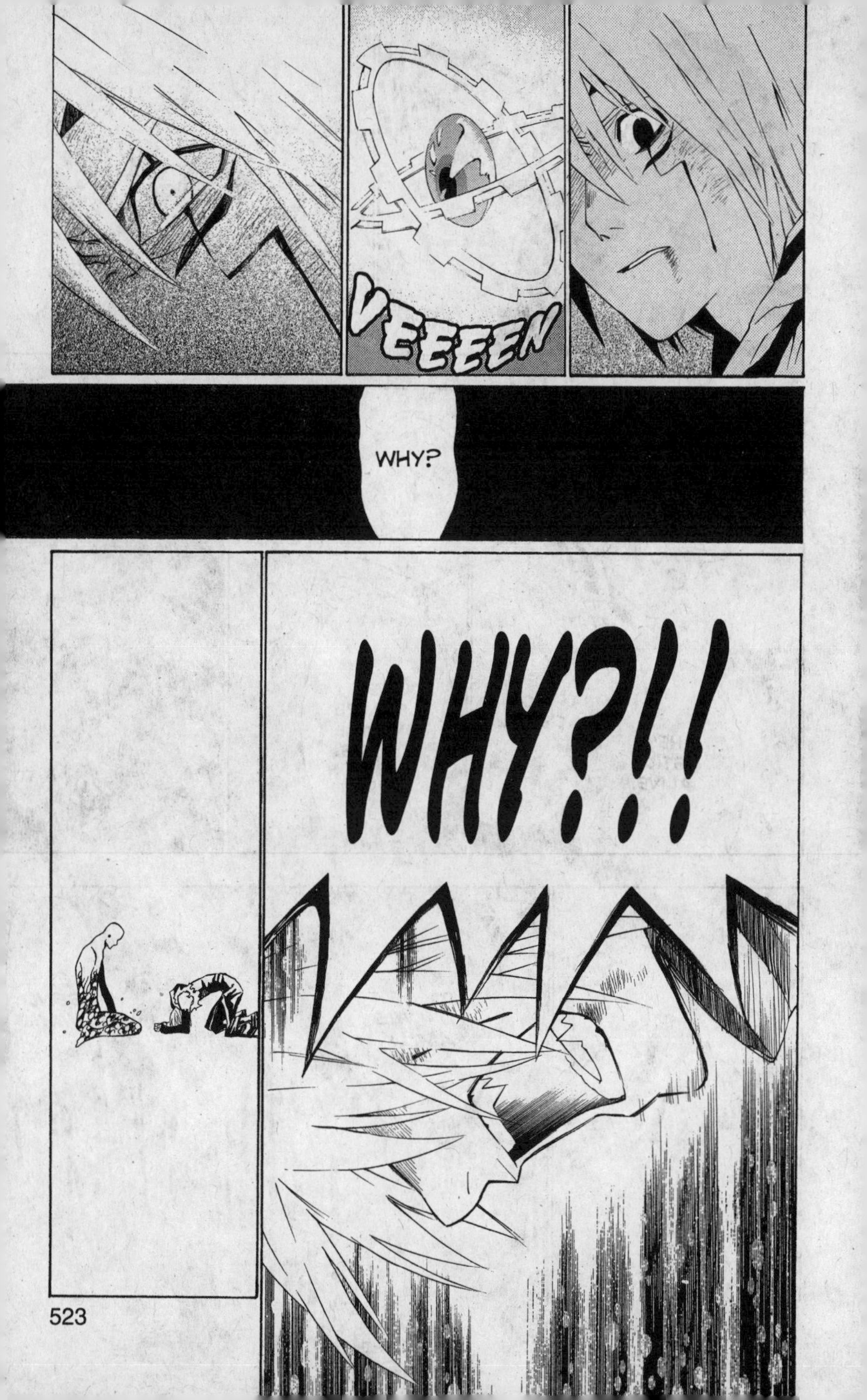
VEEEEN
WHY?
WHY?!!

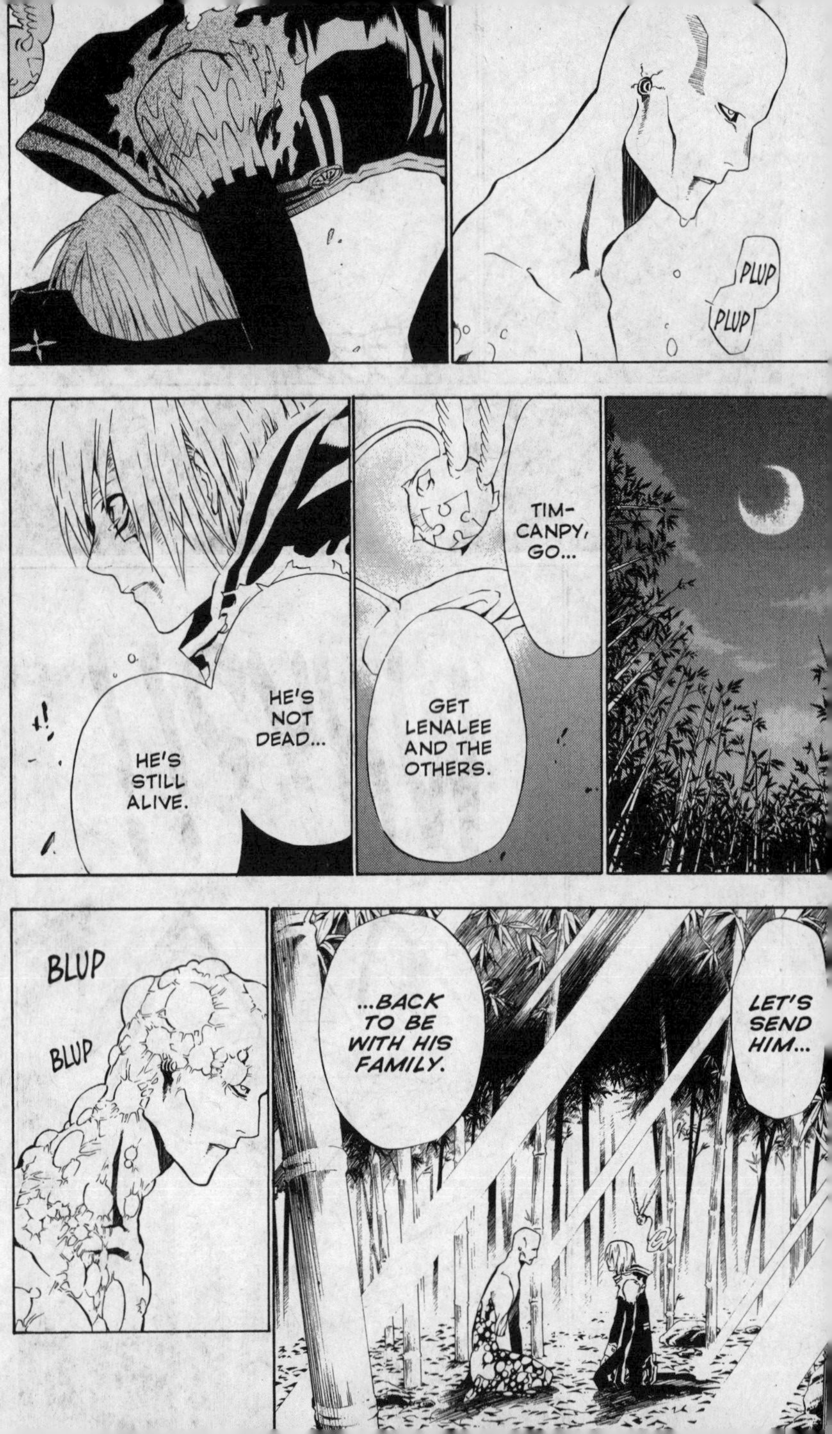
PLUP
PLUP
TIM-CANPY, GO...
GET LENALEE AND THE OTHERS.
HE'S NOT DEAD...
HE'S STILL ALIVE.
LET'S SEND HIM...
...BACK TO BE WITH HIS FAMILY.
BLUP
BLUP

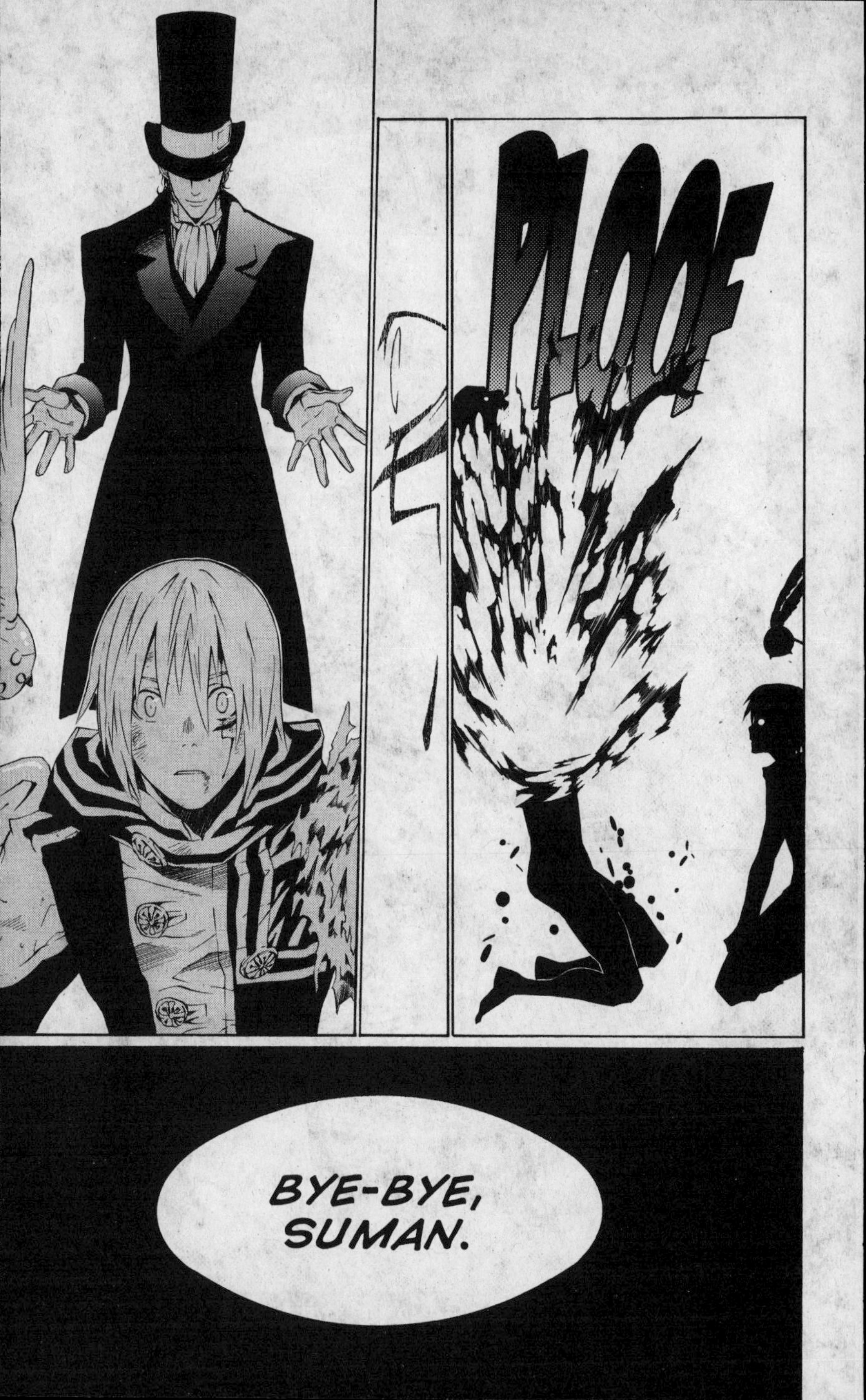
PLOOF
BYE-BYE, SUMAN.

I THINK WE CAN PLAY A GAME WITHOUT YOU CHEATING WITH THESE CARDS.♡

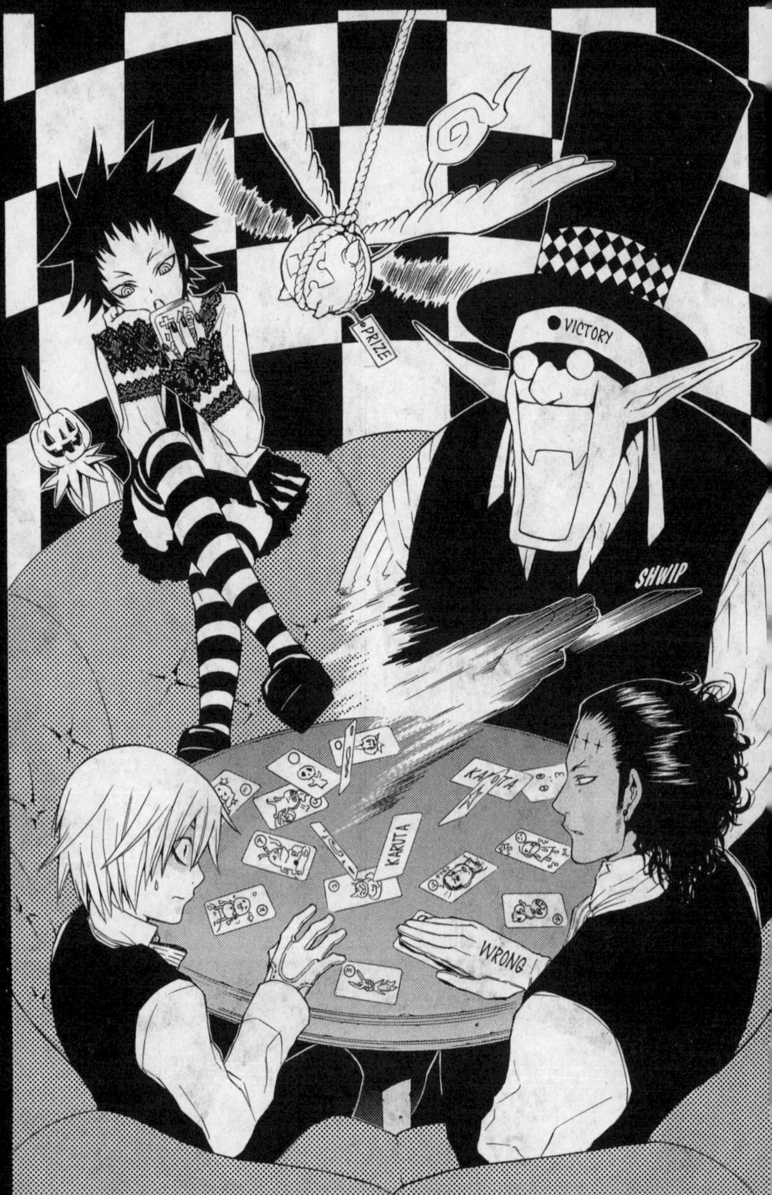
PRIZE
VICTORY
SHWIP
KARUTA
WRONG

THE 55TH NIGHT: DELETE

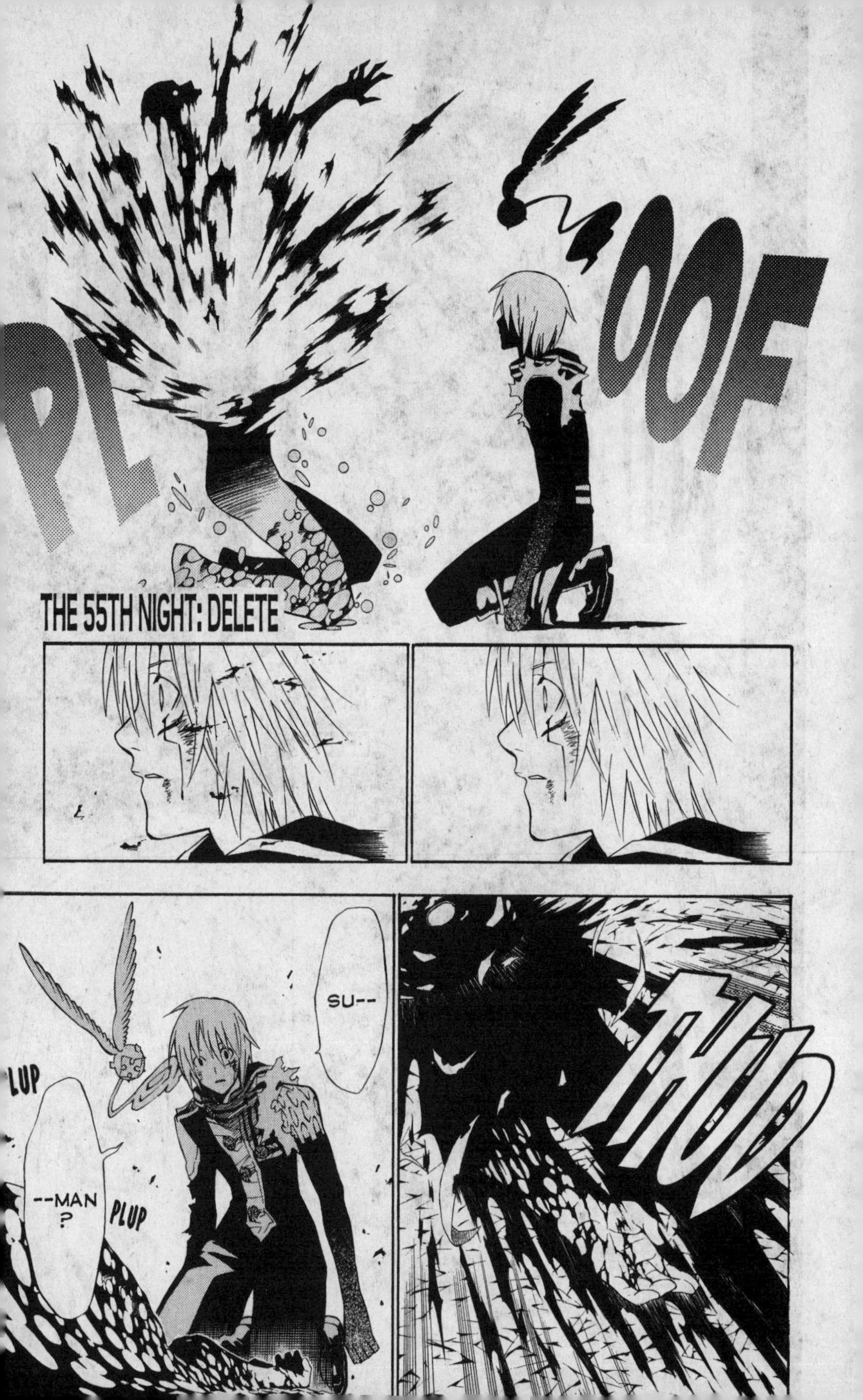
OOF
PL
THUD
SU--
PLUP
--MAN ?
PLUP

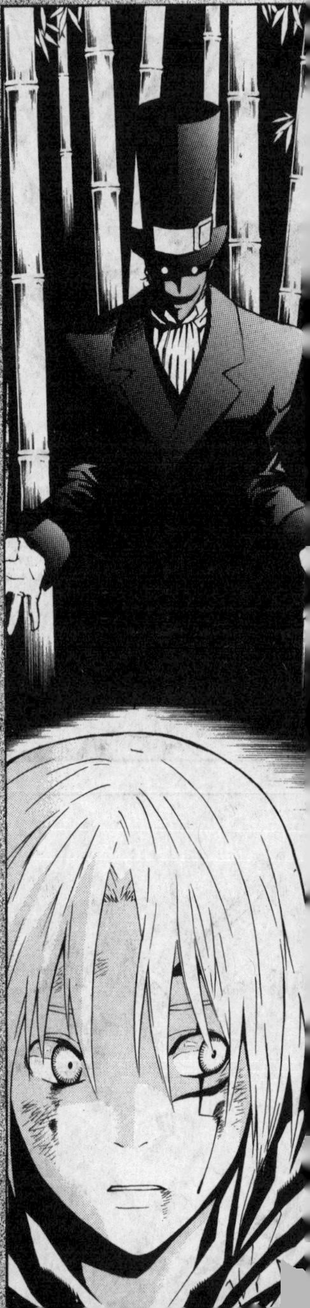

THE 55TH NIGHT: DELETE

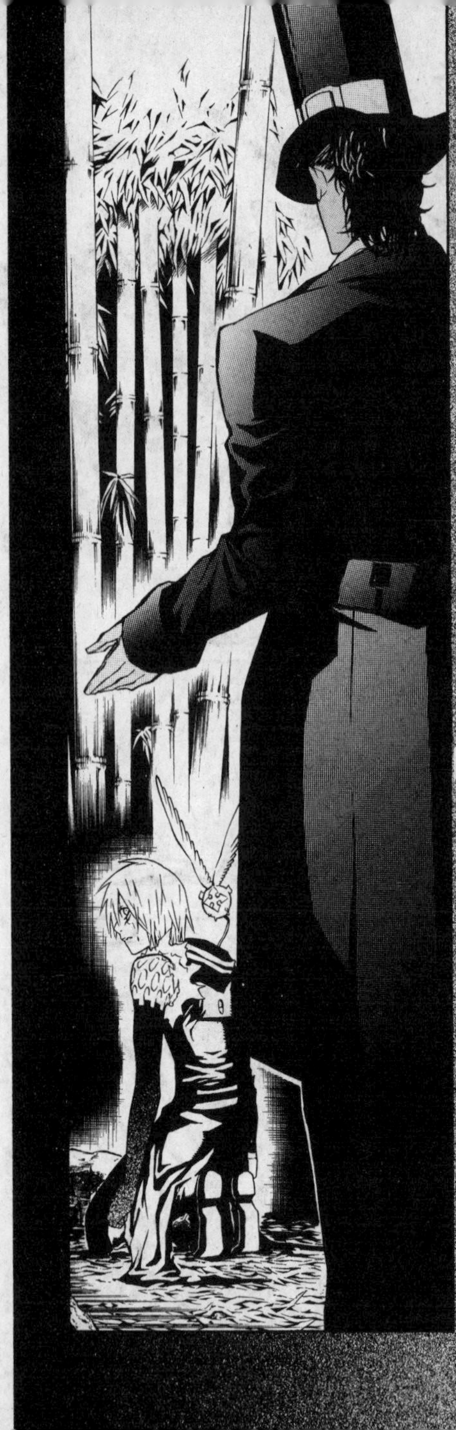

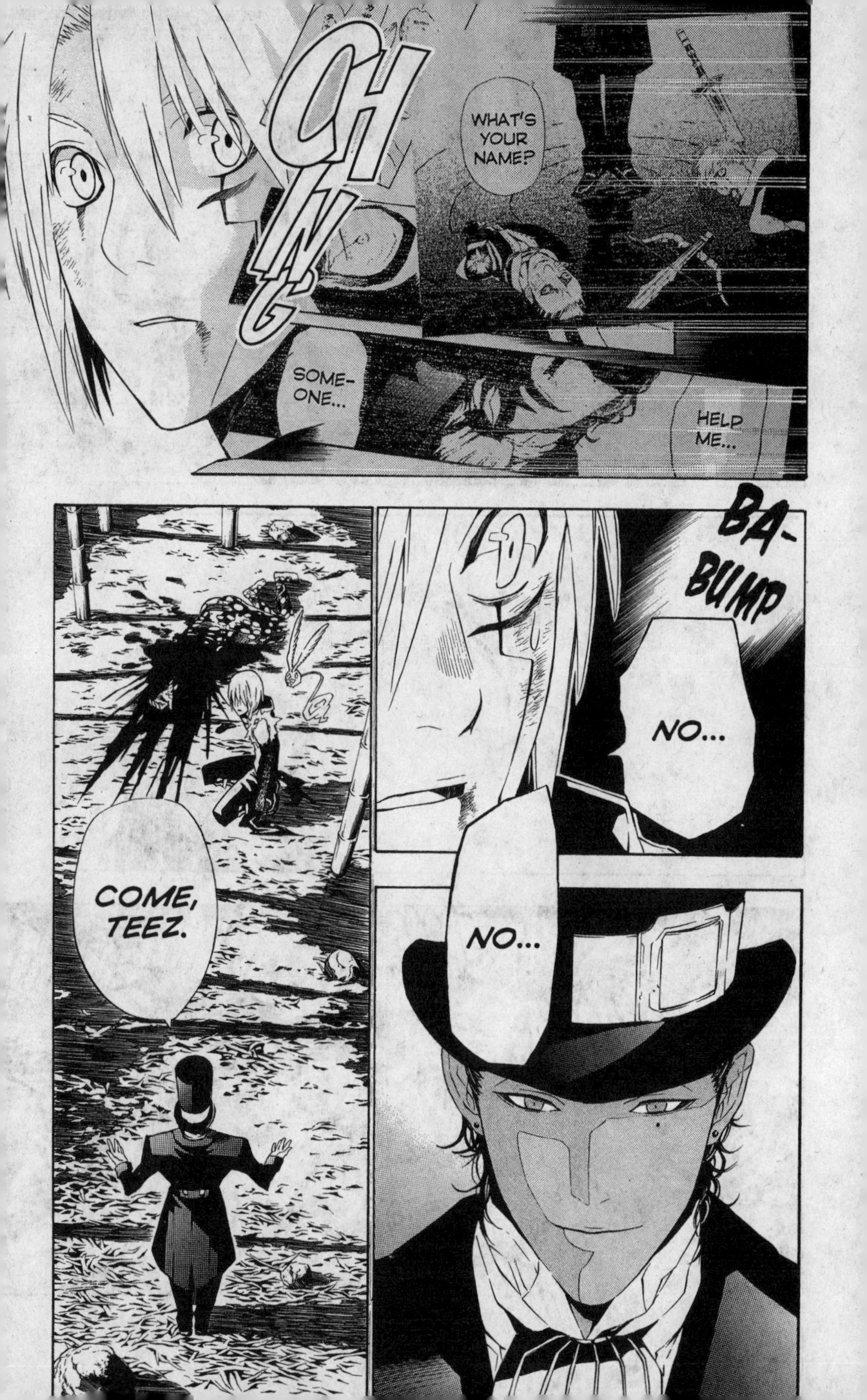
WHAT'S YOUR NAME?
CHING
HELP ME...
SOME-ONE...
BA-BUMP
NO...
NO...
COME, TEEZ.

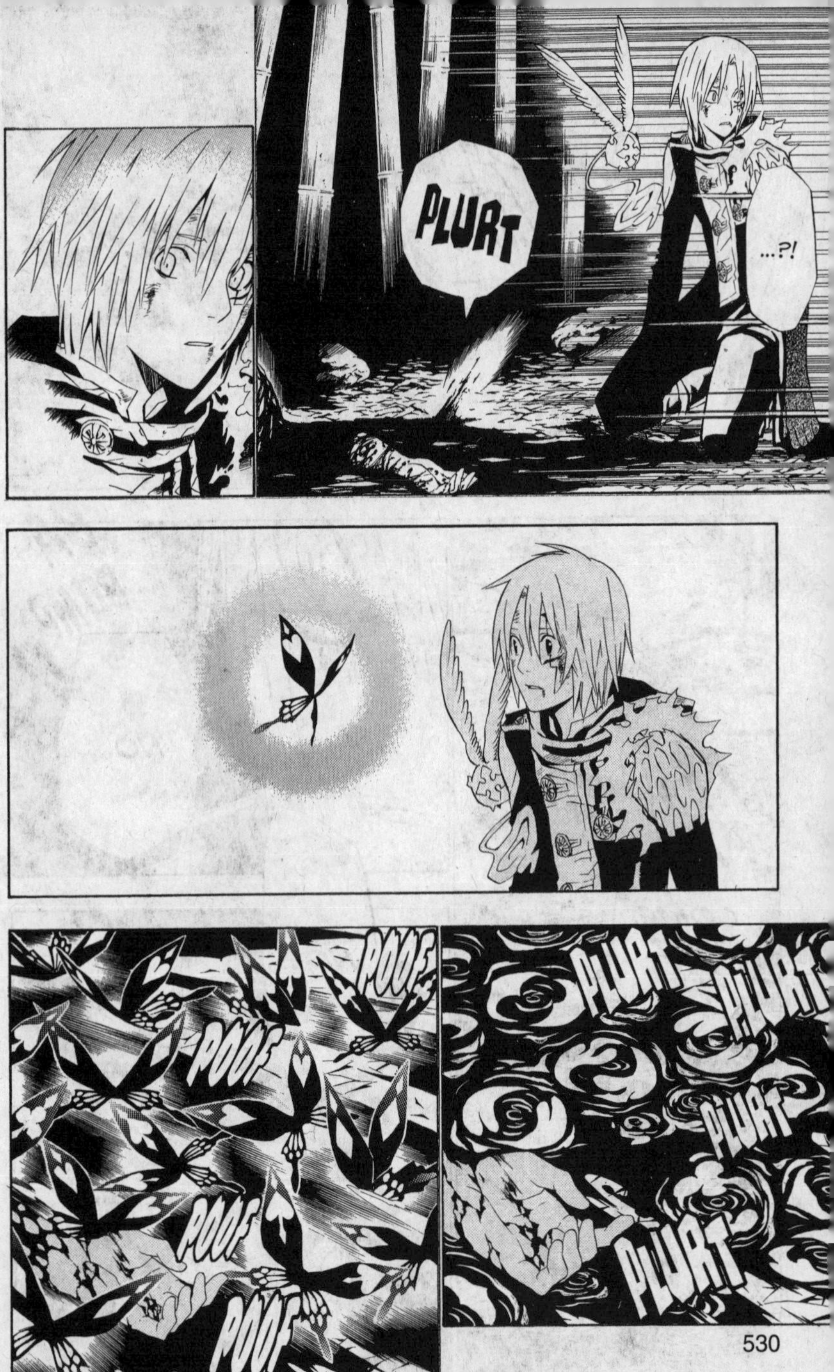
...?!
PLURT
PLURT
PLURT
PLURT
PLURT
POOF
POOF
POOF
POOF

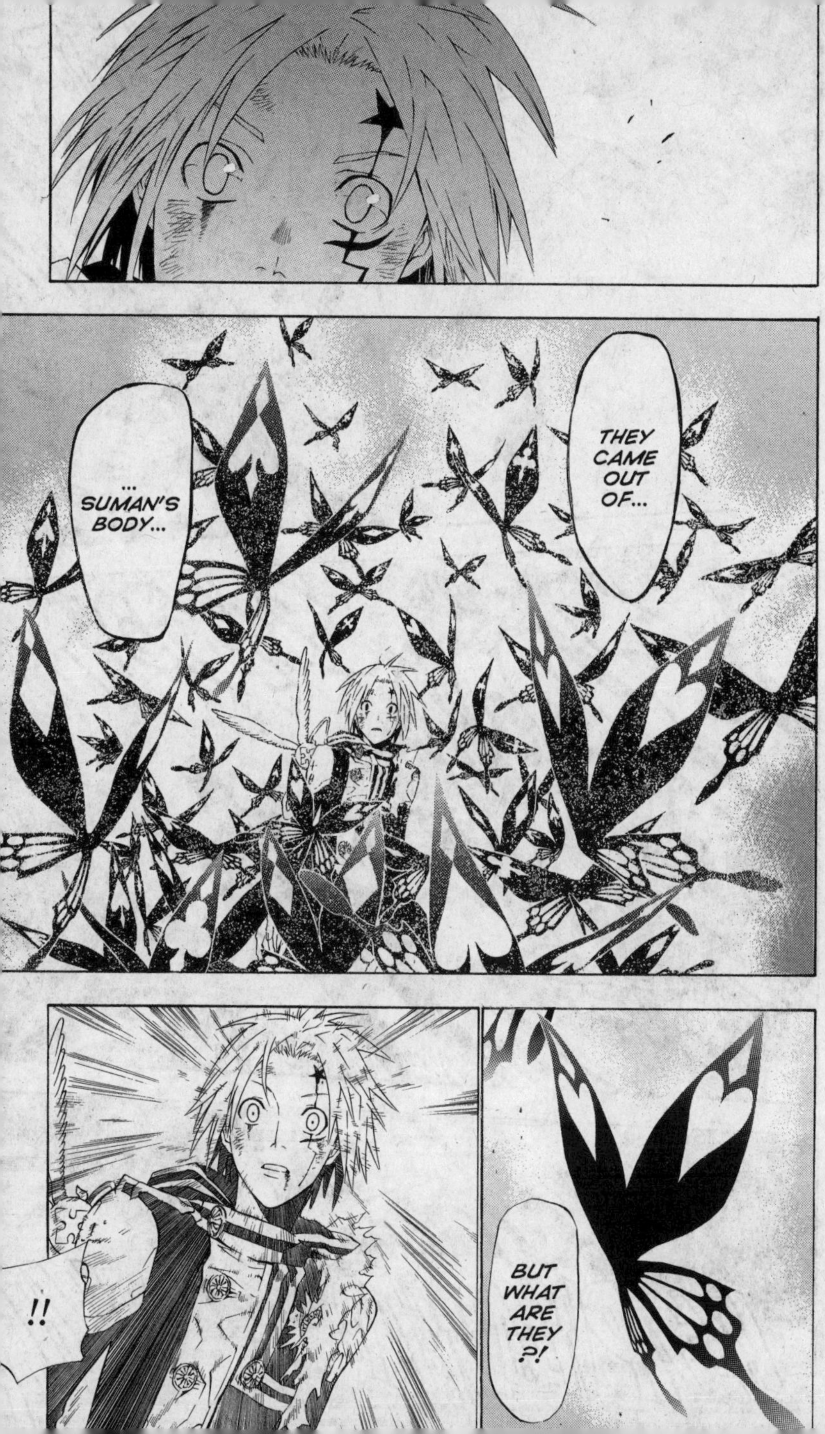
THEY CAME OUT OF...
... SUMAN'S BODY...
BUT WHAT ARE THEY ?!
!!

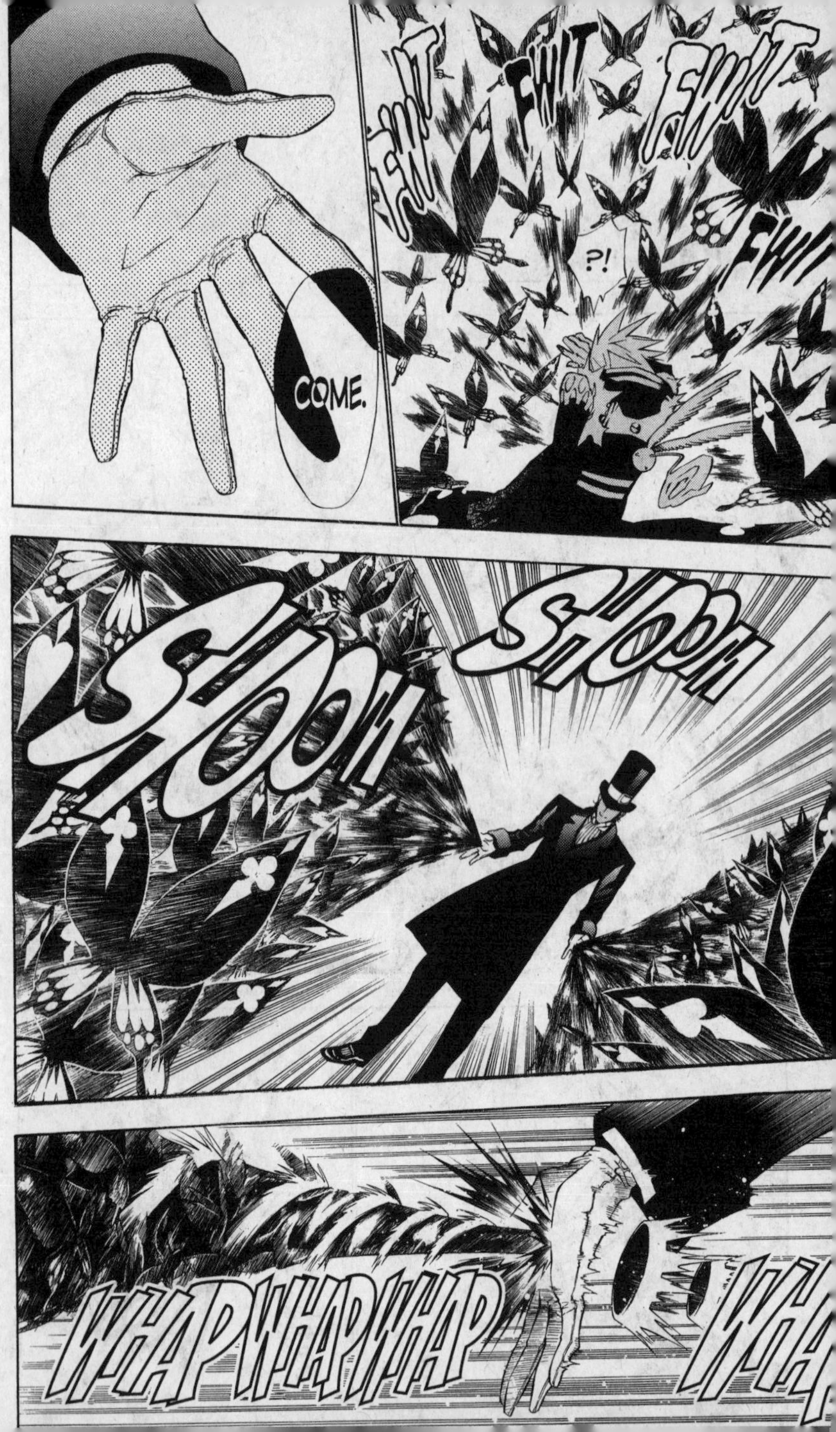
FWIT
FWIT
FWIT
FWIT
FWIT
?!
COME.
SHOOM
SHOOM
WHAPWHAPWHAP
WHA

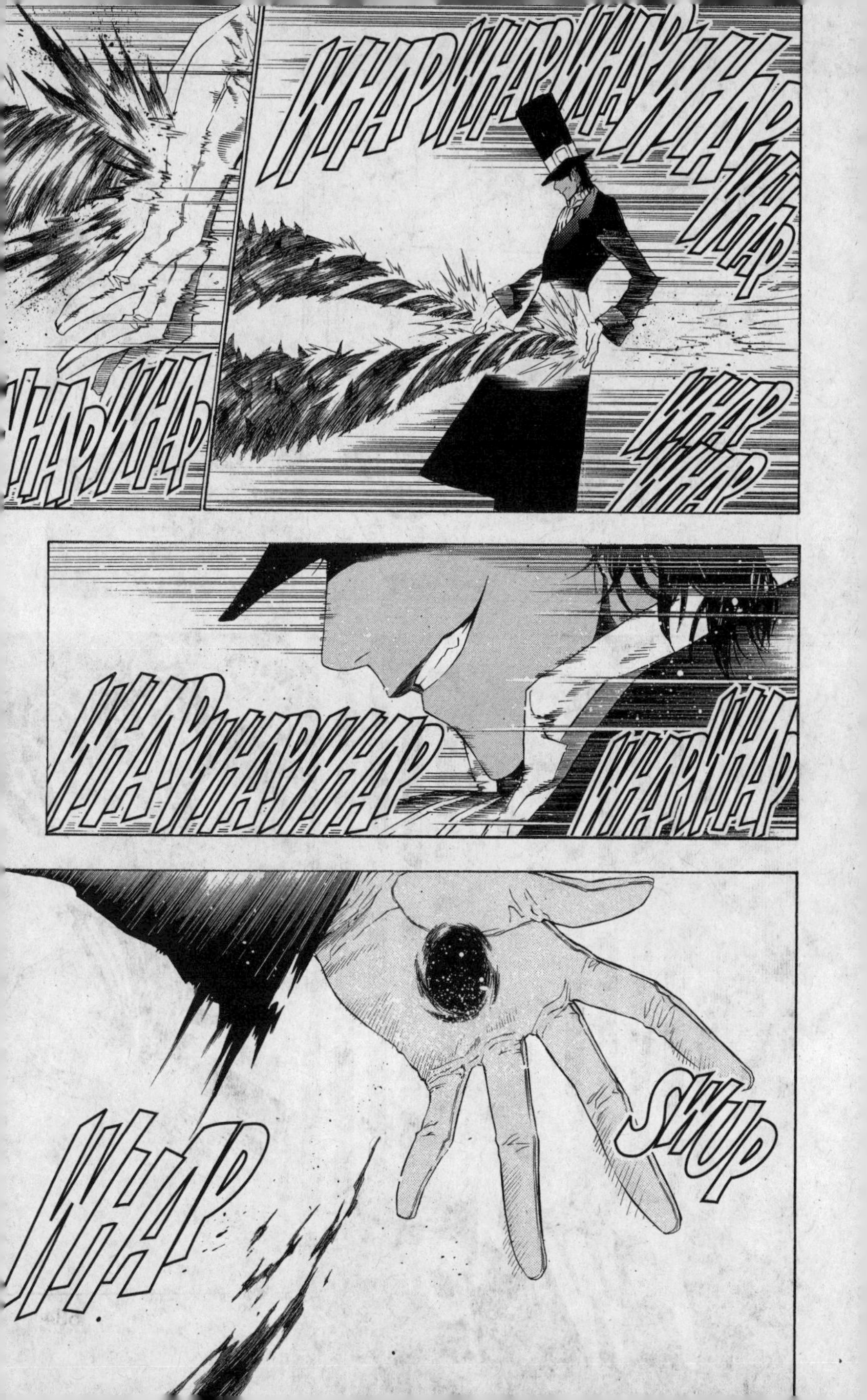
WHAP WHAP WHAP WHAP WHAP WHAP
WHAP WHAP
WHAP WHAP
WHAP WHAP
WHAP WHAP
WHAP WHAP WHAP
SHUP
WHAP

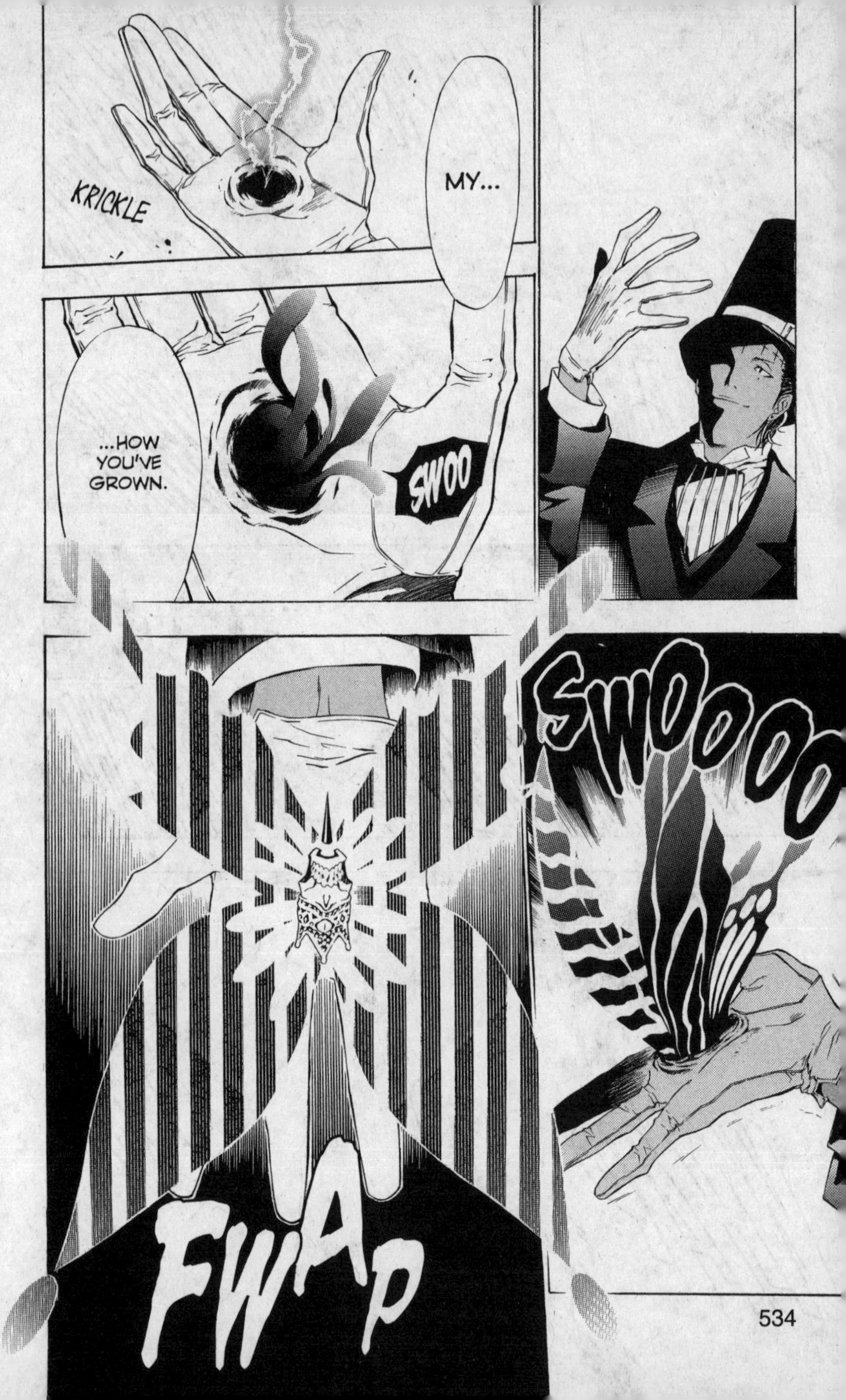
MY...
KRICKLE
...HOW YOU'VE GROWN.
SWOO
SWOOOOO
FWAP

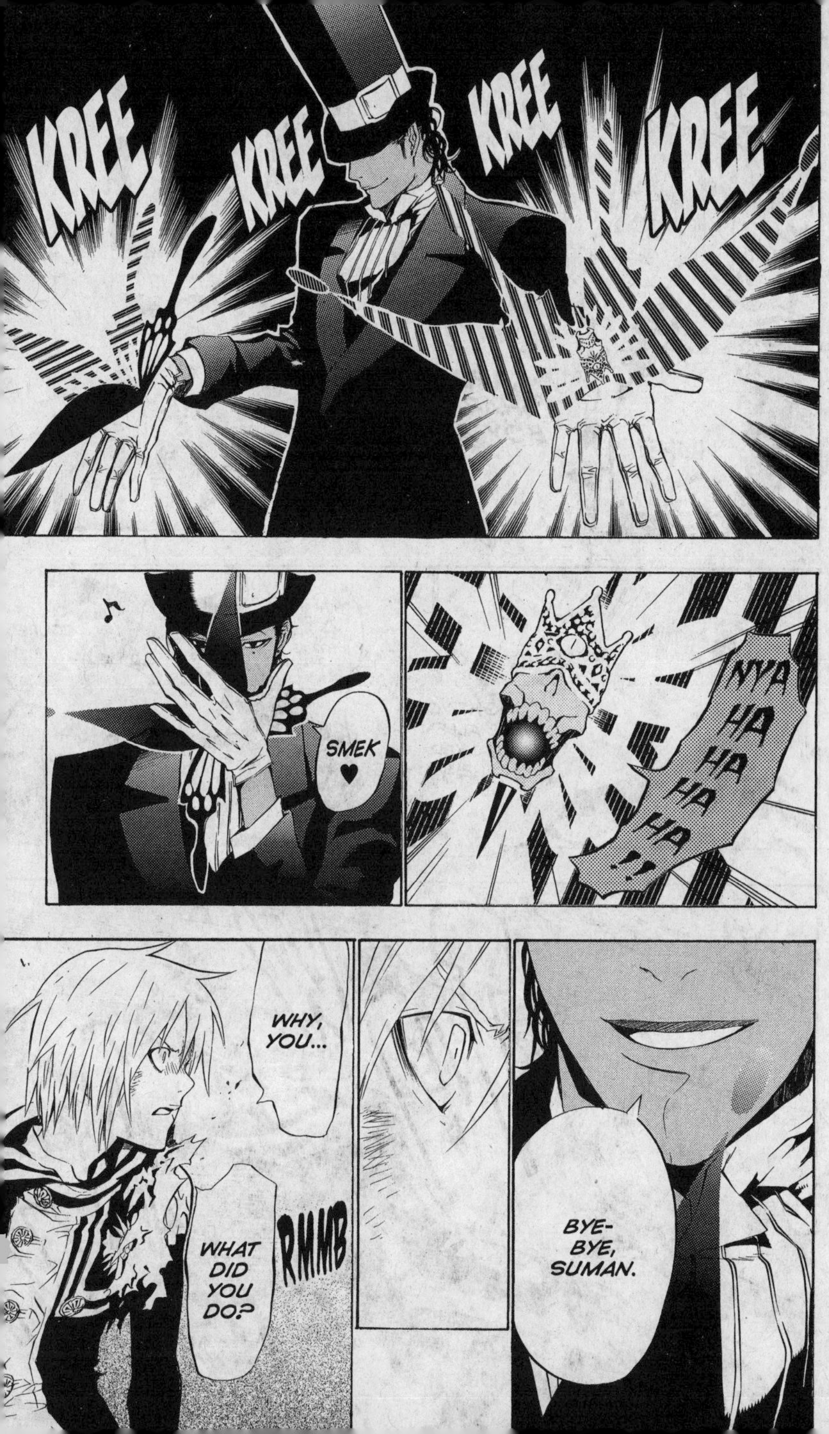
KREE
KREE
KREE
KREE
NYA HA HA HA HA!!
SMEK ♥
BYE-BYE, SUMAN.
WHY, YOU...
RMMB
WHAT DID YOU DO?

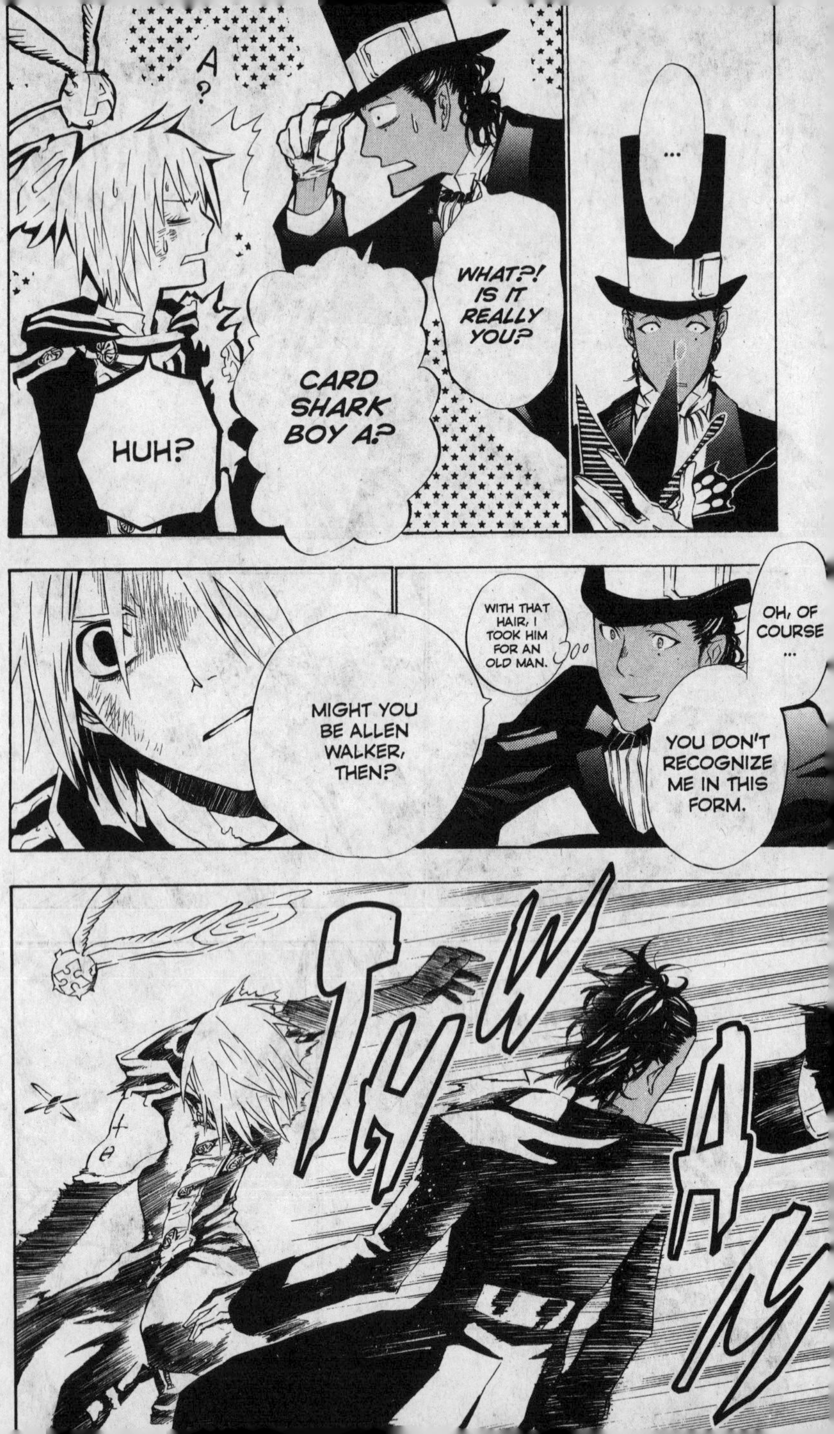
...
WHAT?! IS IT REALLY YOU?
CARD SHARK BOY A?
A?
HUH?
OH, OF COURSE ...
YOU DON'T RECOGNIZE ME IN THIS FORM.
WITH THAT HAIR, I TOOK HIM FOR AN OLD MAN.
MIGHT YOU BE ALLEN WALKER, THEN?
THWAM

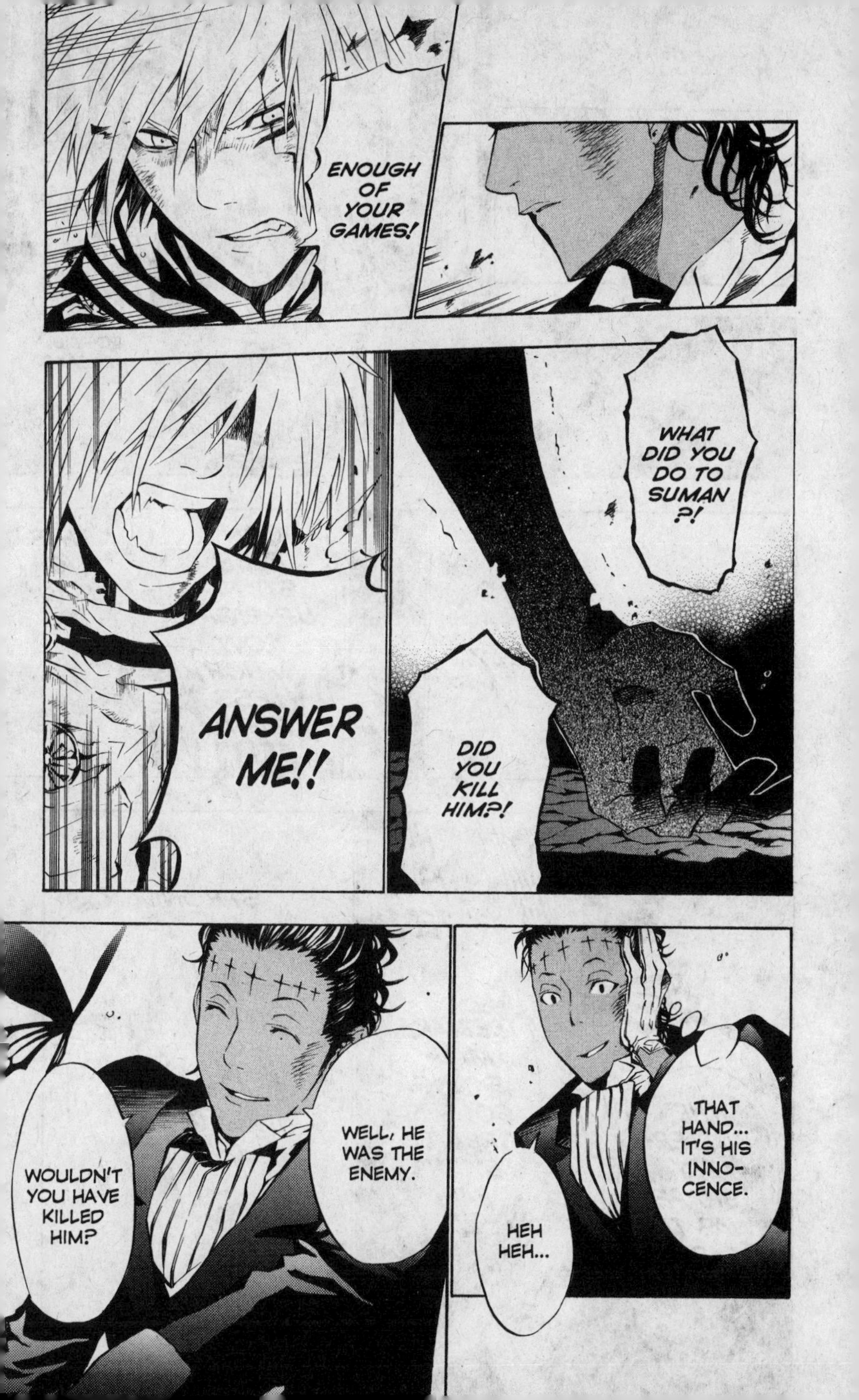
ENOUGH OF YOUR GAMES!
WHAT DID YOU DO TO SUMAN ?!
DID YOU KILL HIM?!
ANSWER ME!!
THAT HAND... IT'S HIS INNO-CENCE.
HEH HEH...
WELL, HE WAS THE ENEMY.
WOULDN'T YOU HAVE KILLED HIM?

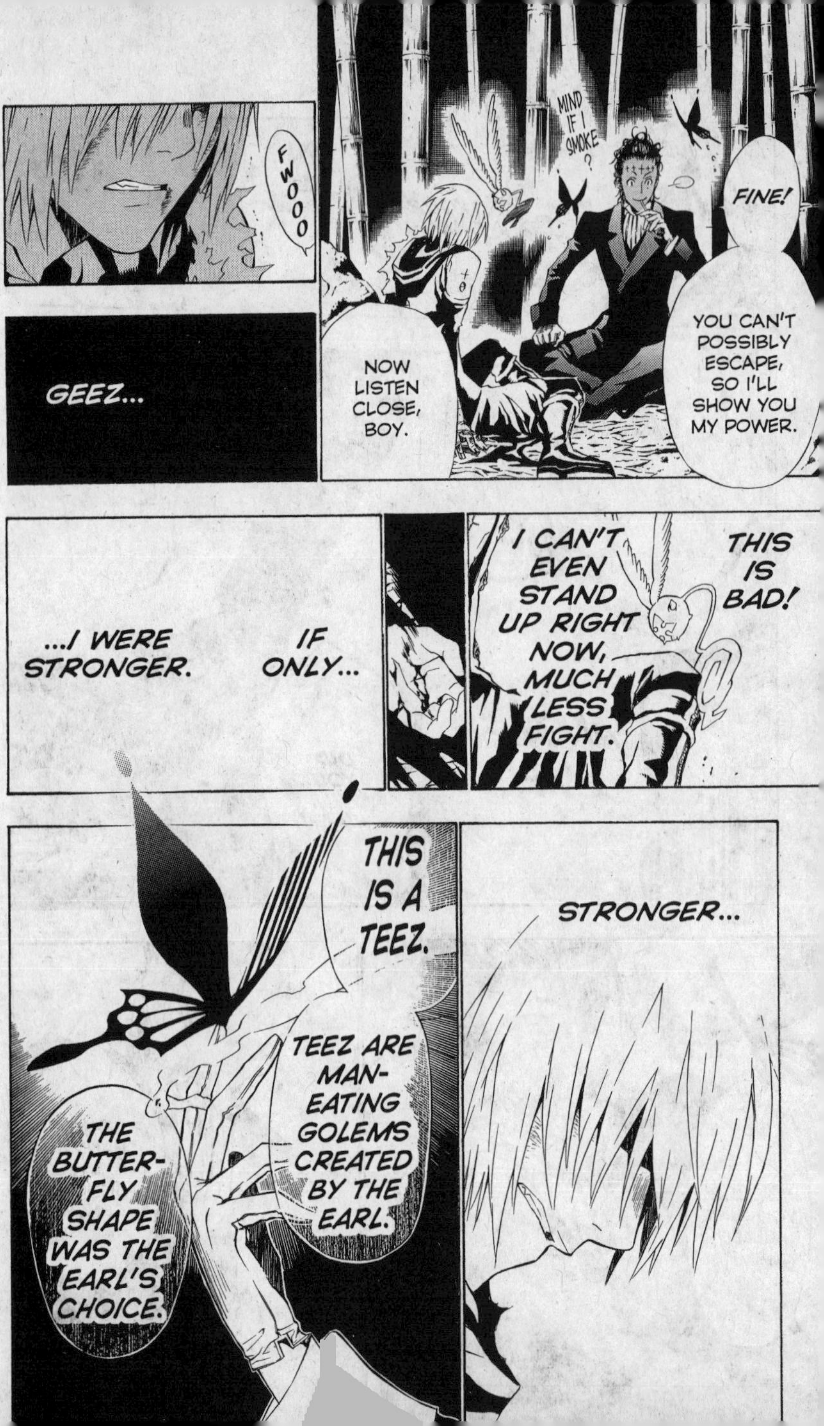
MIND IF I SMOKE?
FINE!
YOU CAN'T POSSIBLY ESCAPE, SO I'LL SHOW YOU MY POWER.
NOW LISTEN CLOSE, BOY.
FWOOO
GEEZ...
THIS IS BAD!
I CAN'T EVEN STAND UP RIGHT NOW, MUCH LESS FIGHT.
IF ONLY...
...I WERE STRONGER.
STRONGER...
THIS IS A TEEZ.
TEEZ ARE MAN-EATING GOLEMS CREATED BY THE EARL.
THE BUTTER-FLY SHAPE WAS THE EARL'S CHOICE.

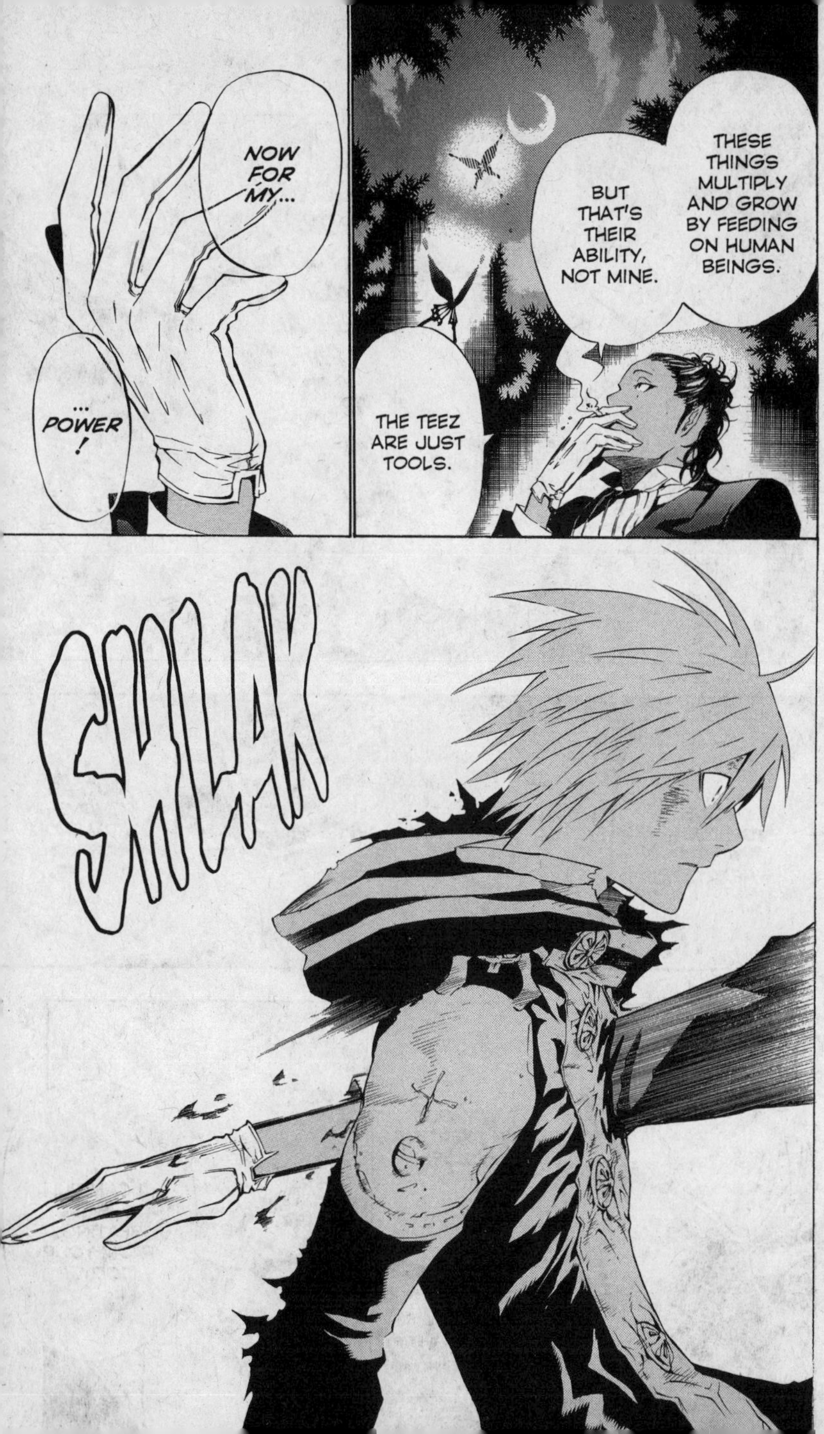
THESE THINGS MULTIPLY AND GROW BY FEEDING ON HUMAN BEINGS.
BUT THAT'S THEIR ABILITY, NOT MINE.
THE TEEZ ARE JUST TOOLS.
NOW FOR MY...
...POWER!
SHLAK

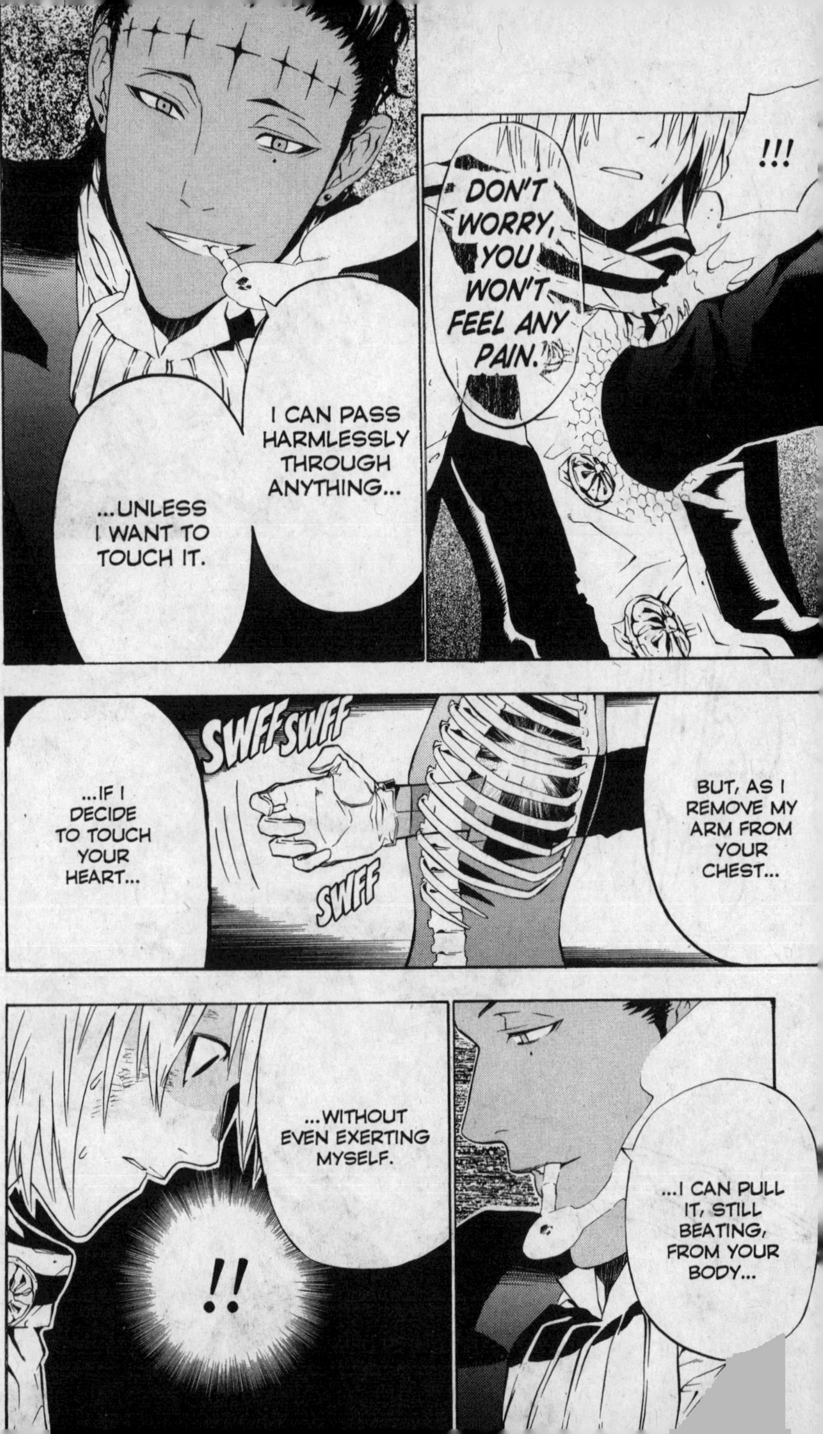
!!!
DON'T WORRY, YOU WON'T FEEL ANY PAIN.
I CAN PASS HARMLESSLY THROUGH ANYTHING...
...UNLESS I WANT TO TOUCH IT.
BUT, AS I REMOVE MY ARM FROM YOUR CHEST...
SWFF SWFF
SWFF
...IF I DECIDE TO TOUCH YOUR HEART...
...I CAN PULL IT, STILL BEATING, FROM YOUR BODY...
...WITHOUT EVEN EXERTING MYSELF.
!!

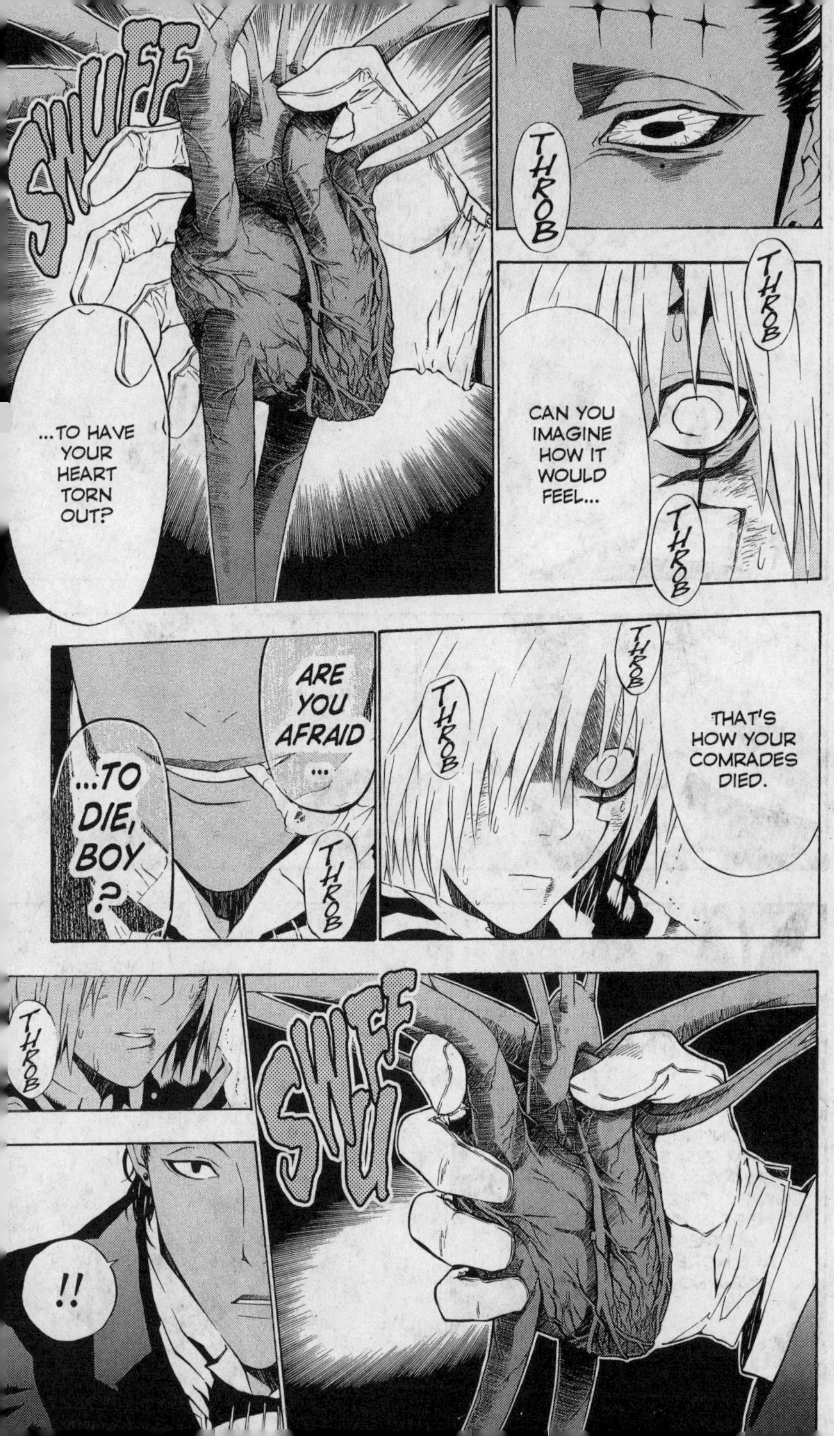
THROB
CAN YOU IMAGINE HOW IT WOULD FEEL...
THROB
THROB
SNUFF
...TO HAVE YOUR HEART TORN OUT?
THROB
THAT'S HOW YOUR COMRADES DIED.
THROB
ARE YOU AFRAID ...
...TO DIE, BOY?
THROB
SNUFF
THROB
!!

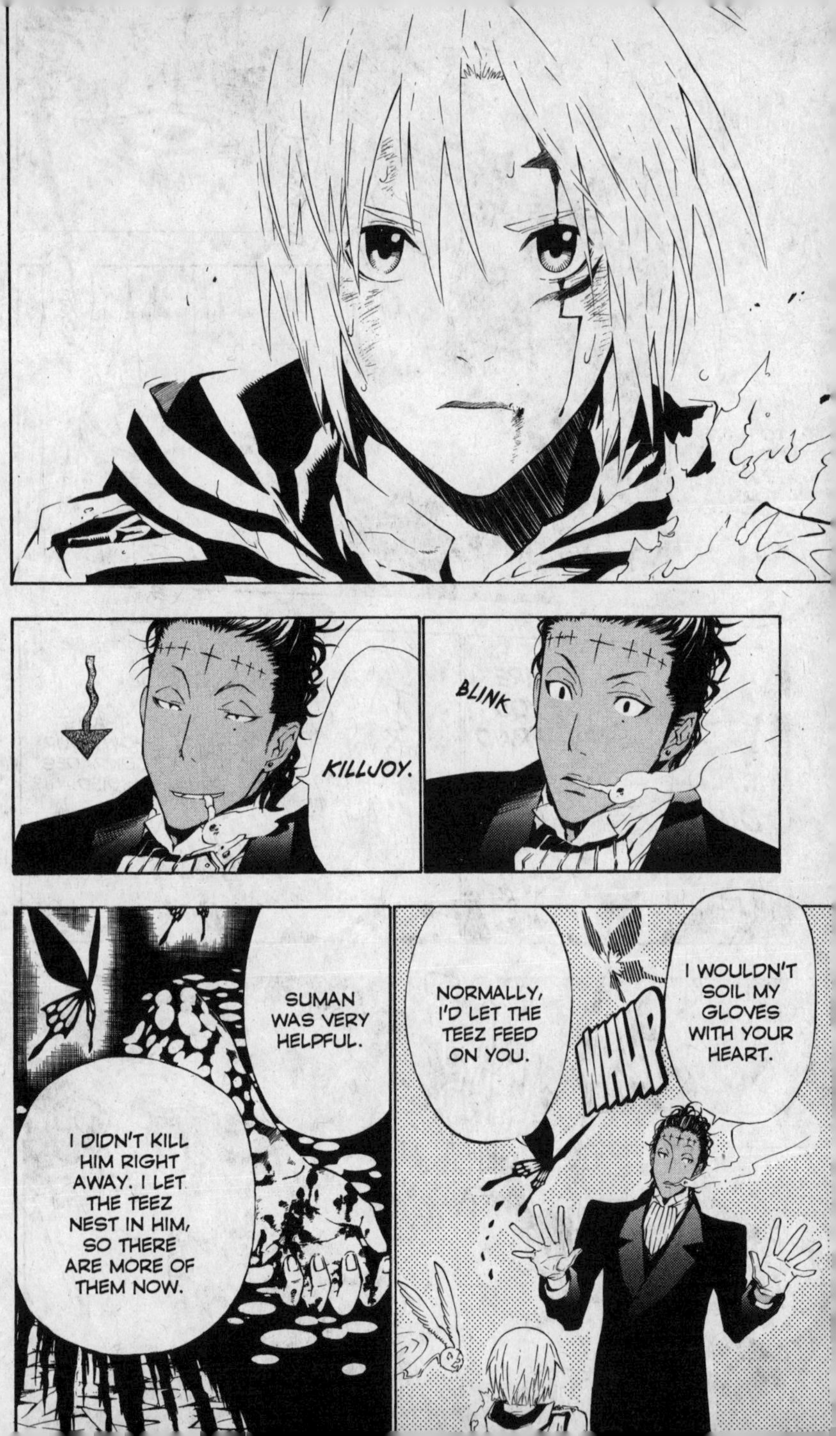
BLINK
KILLJOY.
I WOULDN'T SOIL MY GLOVES WITH YOUR HEART.
WHUP
NORMALLY, I'D LET THE TEEZ FEED ON YOU.
SUMAN WAS VERY HELPFUL.
I DIDN'T KILL HIM RIGHT AWAY. I LET THE TEEZ NEST IN HIM, SO THERE ARE MORE OF THEM NOW.

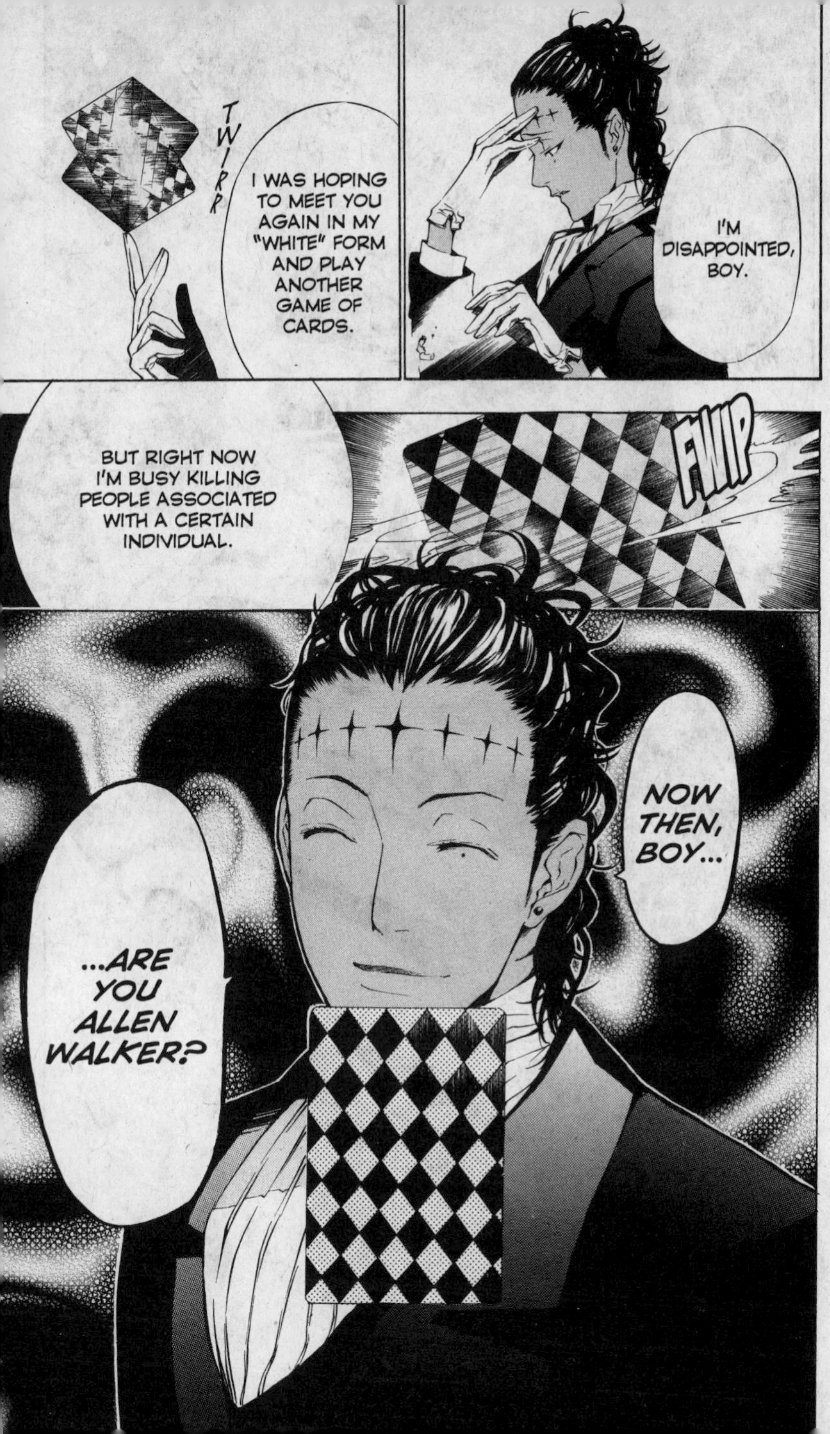
I'M DISAPPOINTED, BOY.
TWIRR
I WAS HOPING TO MEET YOU AGAIN IN MY "WHITE" FORM AND PLAY ANOTHER GAME OF CARDS.
FWIP
BUT RIGHT NOW I'M BUSY KILLING PEOPLE ASSOCIATED WITH A CERTAIN INDIVIDUAL.
NOW THEN, BOY...
...ARE YOU ALLEN WALKER?

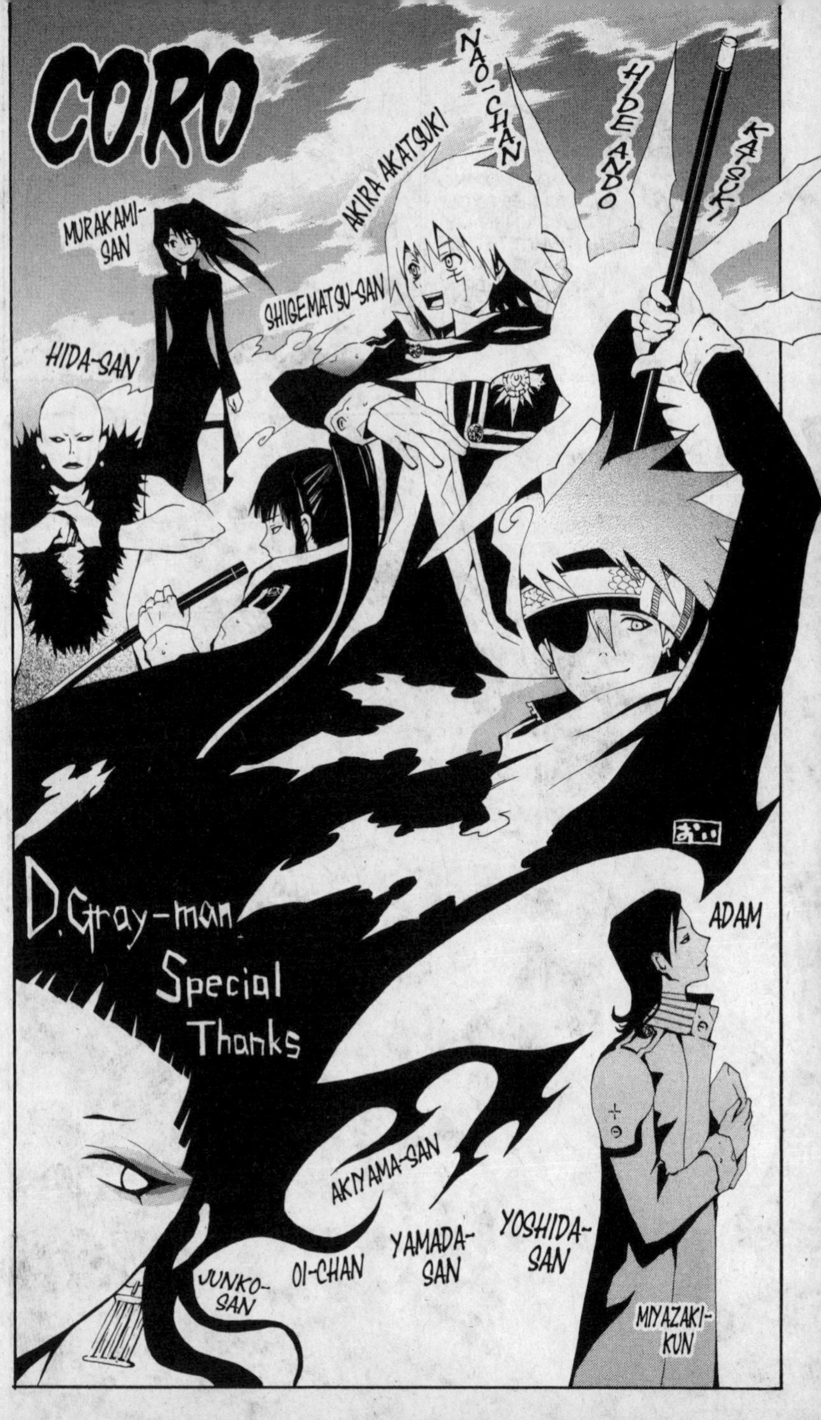
CORO
KATSUKI
HIDE ANDO
NAO-CHAN
AKIRA AKATSUKI
MURAKAMI-SAN
SHIGEMATSU-SAN
HIDA-SAN
ADAM
D.Gray-man Special Thanks
AKIYAMA-SAN
YOSHIDA-SAN
YAMADA-SAN
OI-CHAN
MIYAZAKI-KUN
JUNKO-SAN

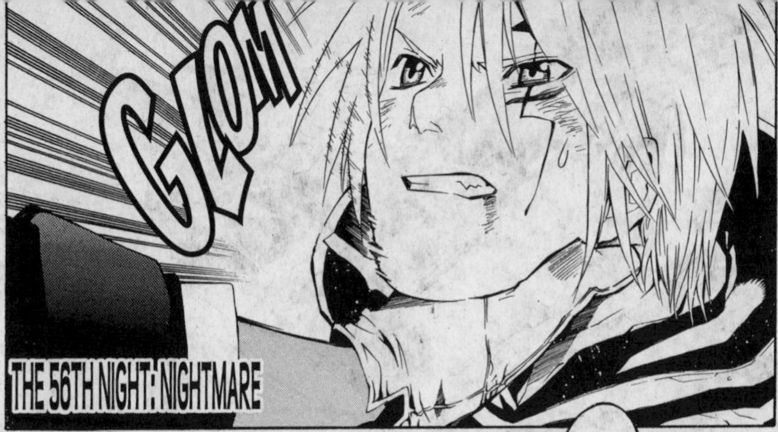
GLOM
THE 56TH NIGHT: NIGHTMARE

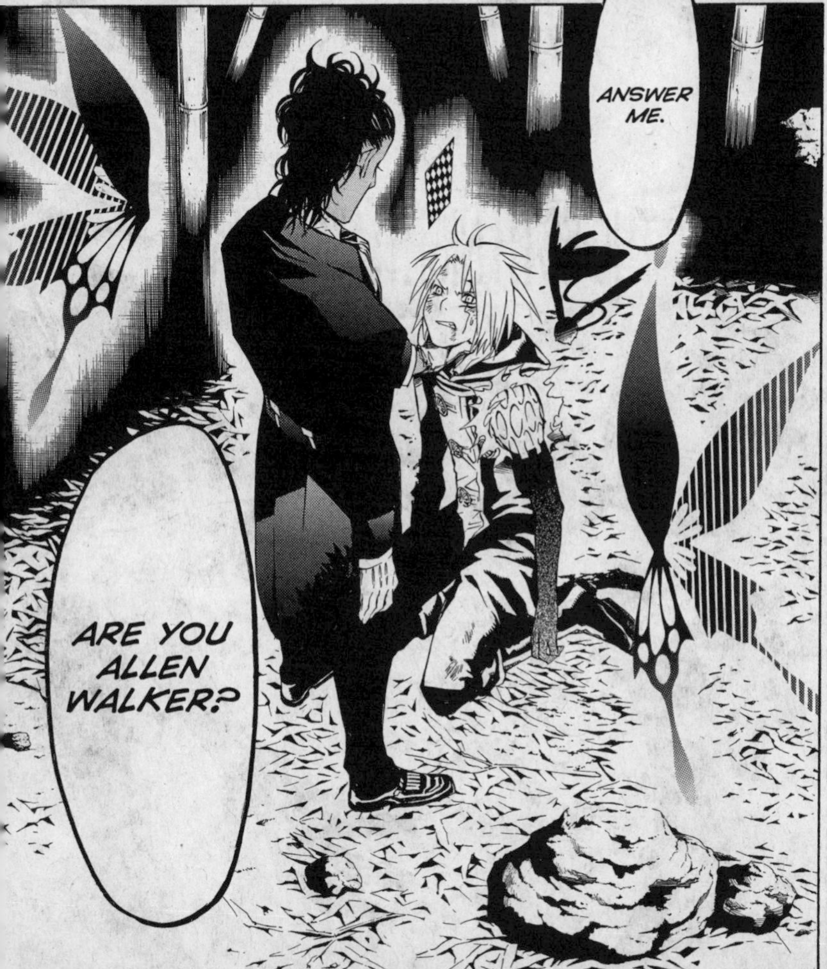
ANSWER ME.
ARE YOU ALLEN WALKER?

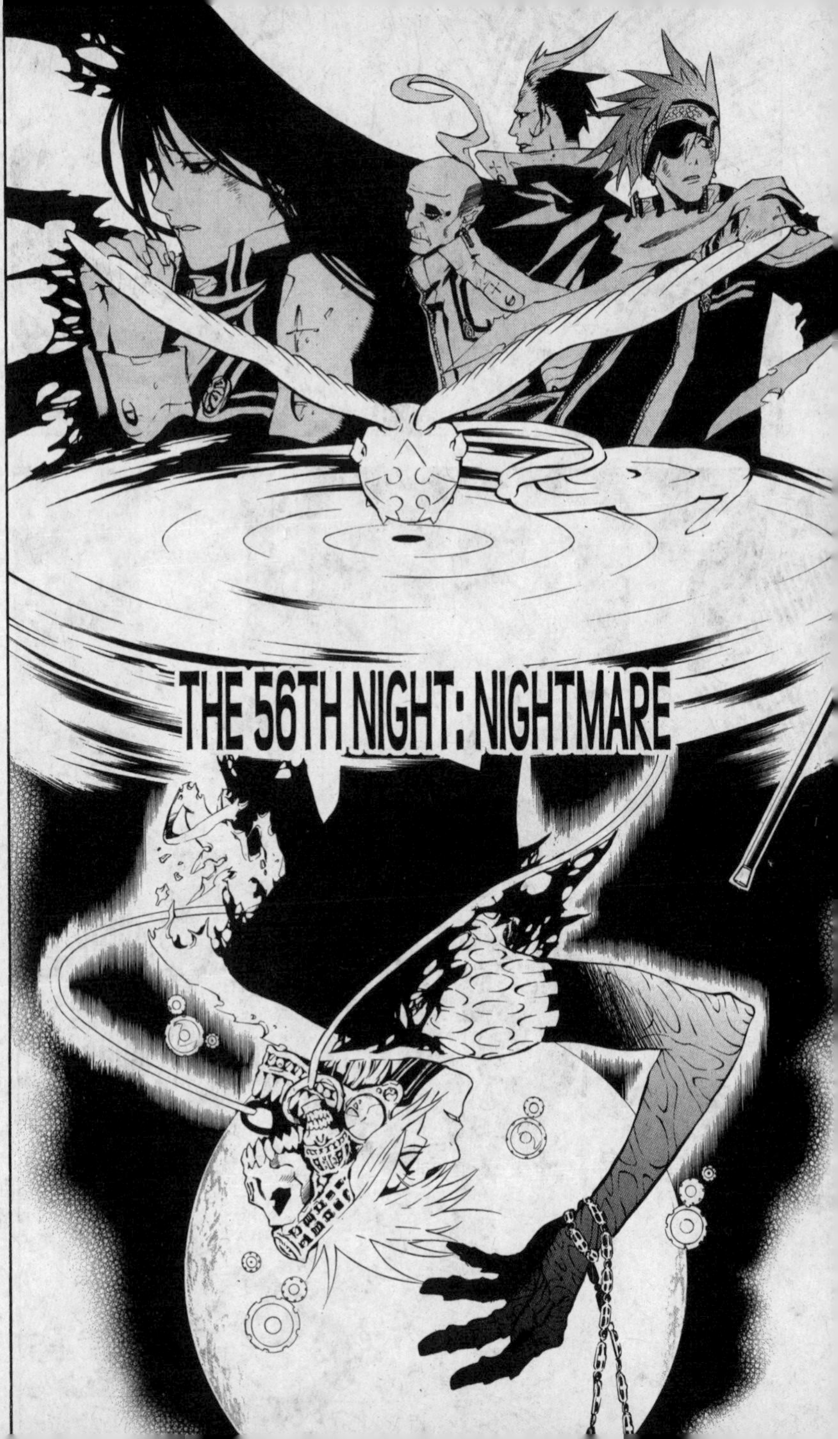
THE 56TH NIGHT: NIGHTMARE

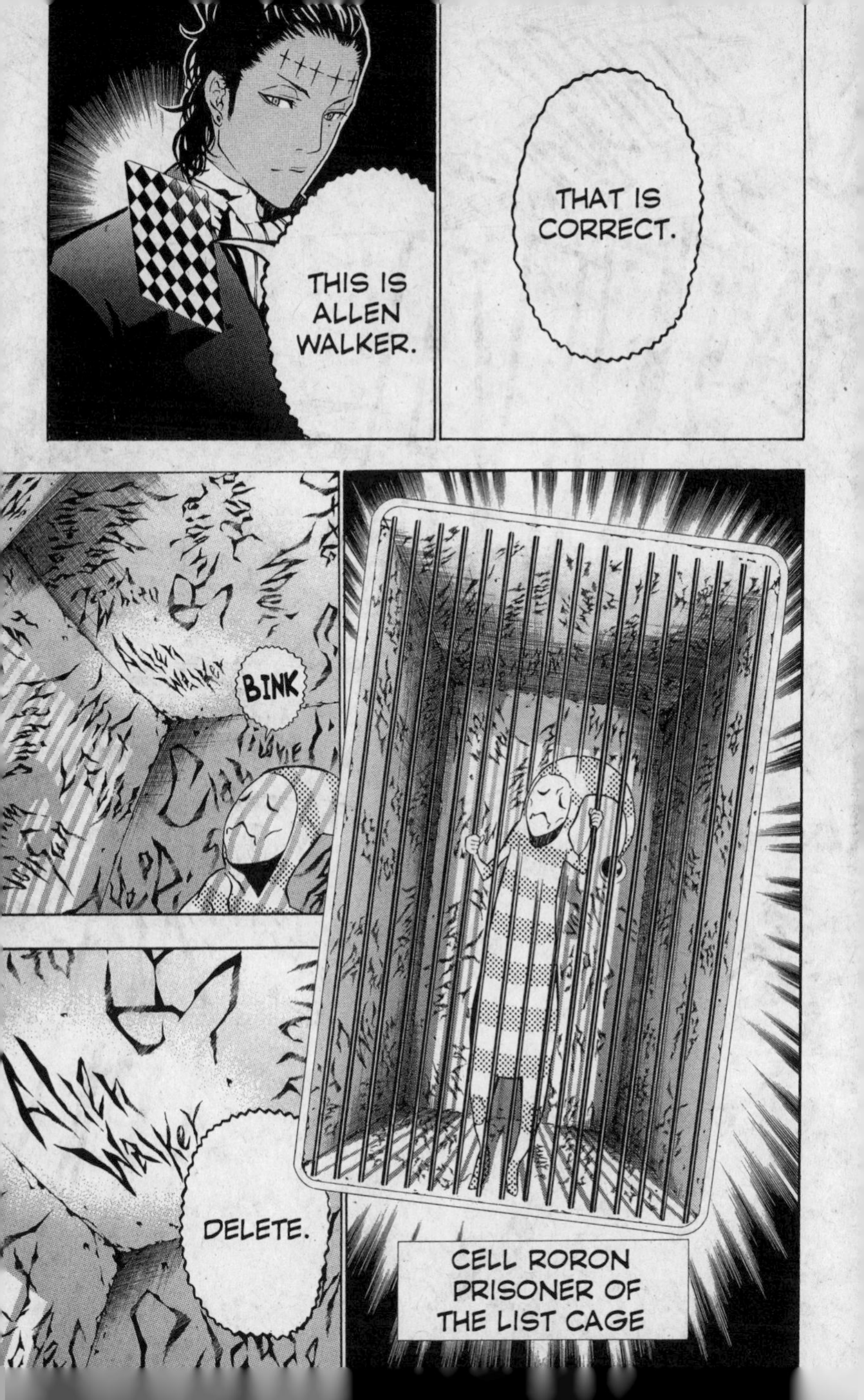
THAT IS CORRECT.
THIS IS ALLEN WALKER.
CELL RORON PRISONER OF THE LIST CAGE
BINK
Allen Walker
DELETE.

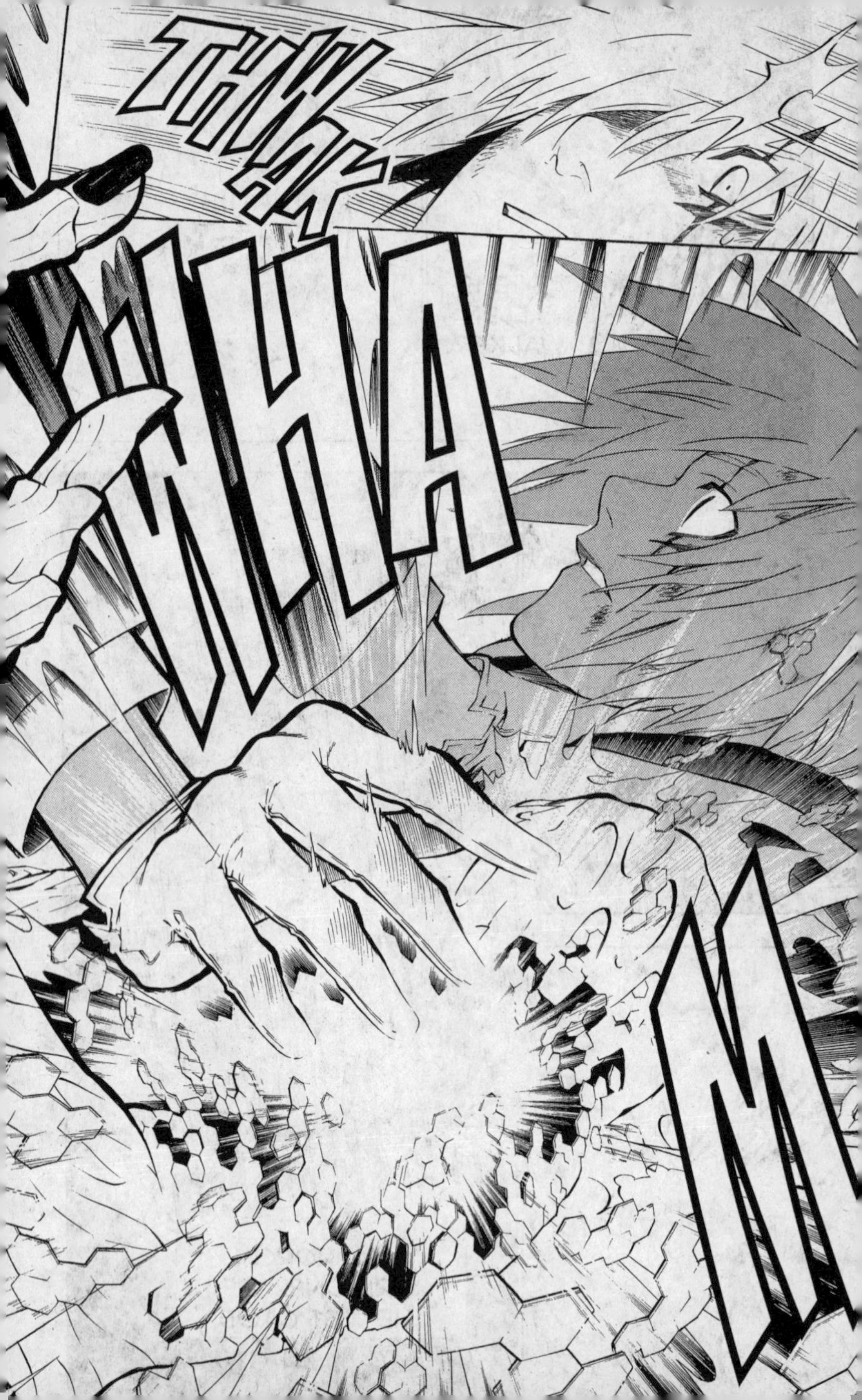
THWAK
WHAM

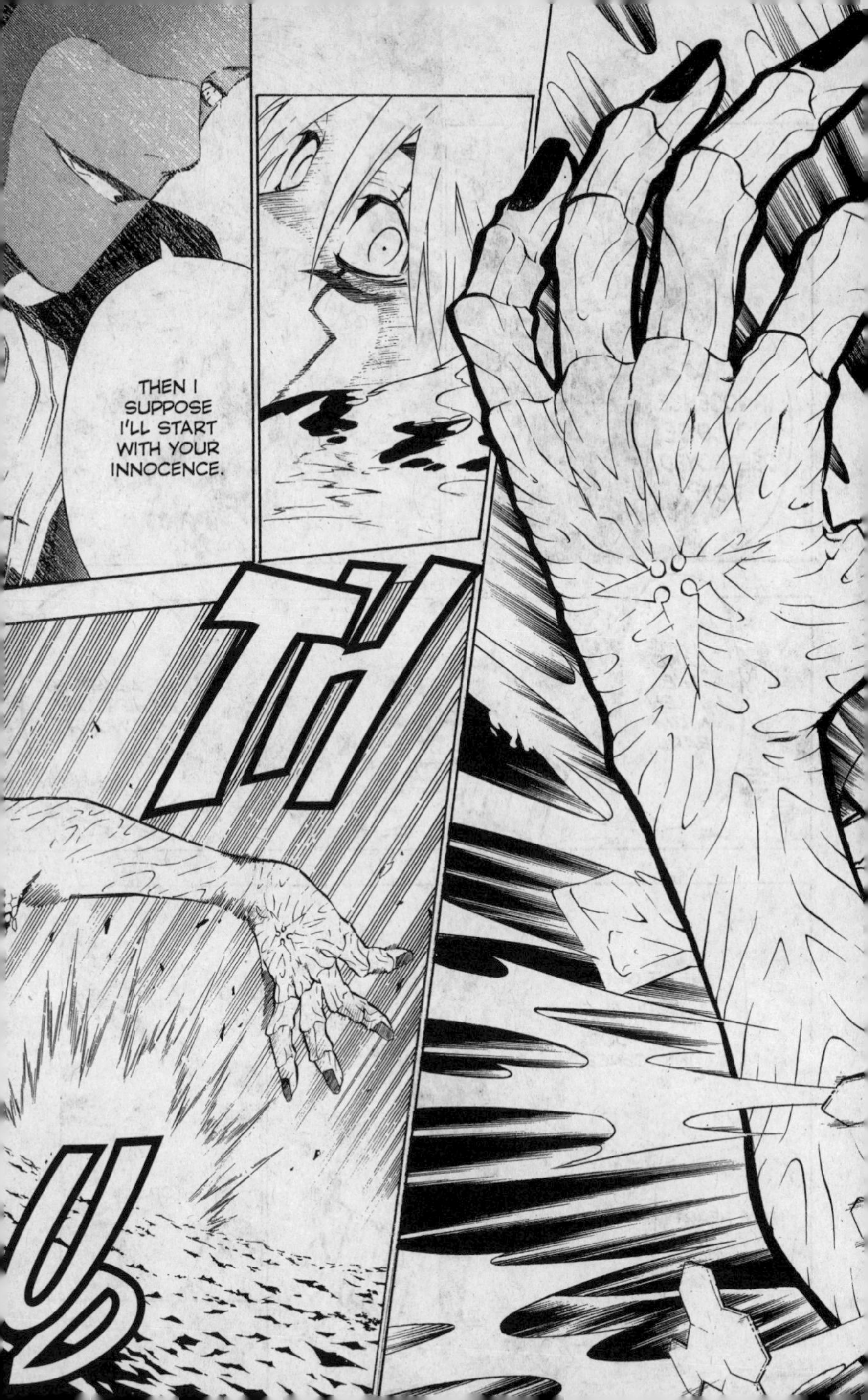
THEN I SUPPOSE I'LL START WITH YOUR INNOCENCE.

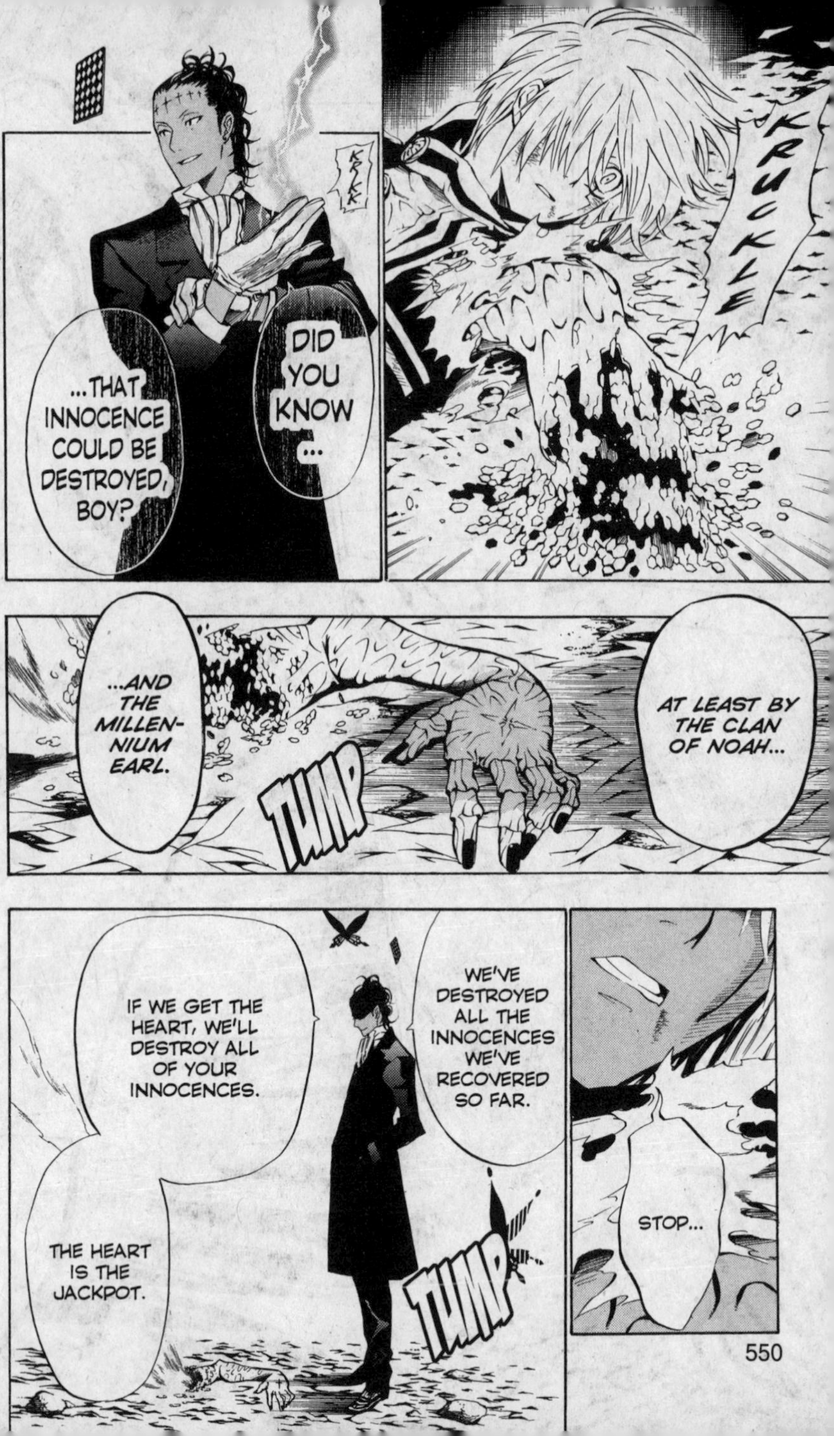
KRUCKLE
KRIKK
DID YOU KNOW...
...THAT INNOCENCE COULD BE DESTROYED, BOY?
AT LEAST BY THE CLAN OF NOAH...
...AND THE MILLEN-NIUM EARL.
TUMP
STOP...
WE'VE DESTROYED ALL THE INNOCENCES WE'VE RECOVERED SO FAR.
IF WE GET THE HEART, WE'LL DESTROY ALL OF YOUR INNOCENCES.
TUMP
THE HEART IS THE JACKPOT.

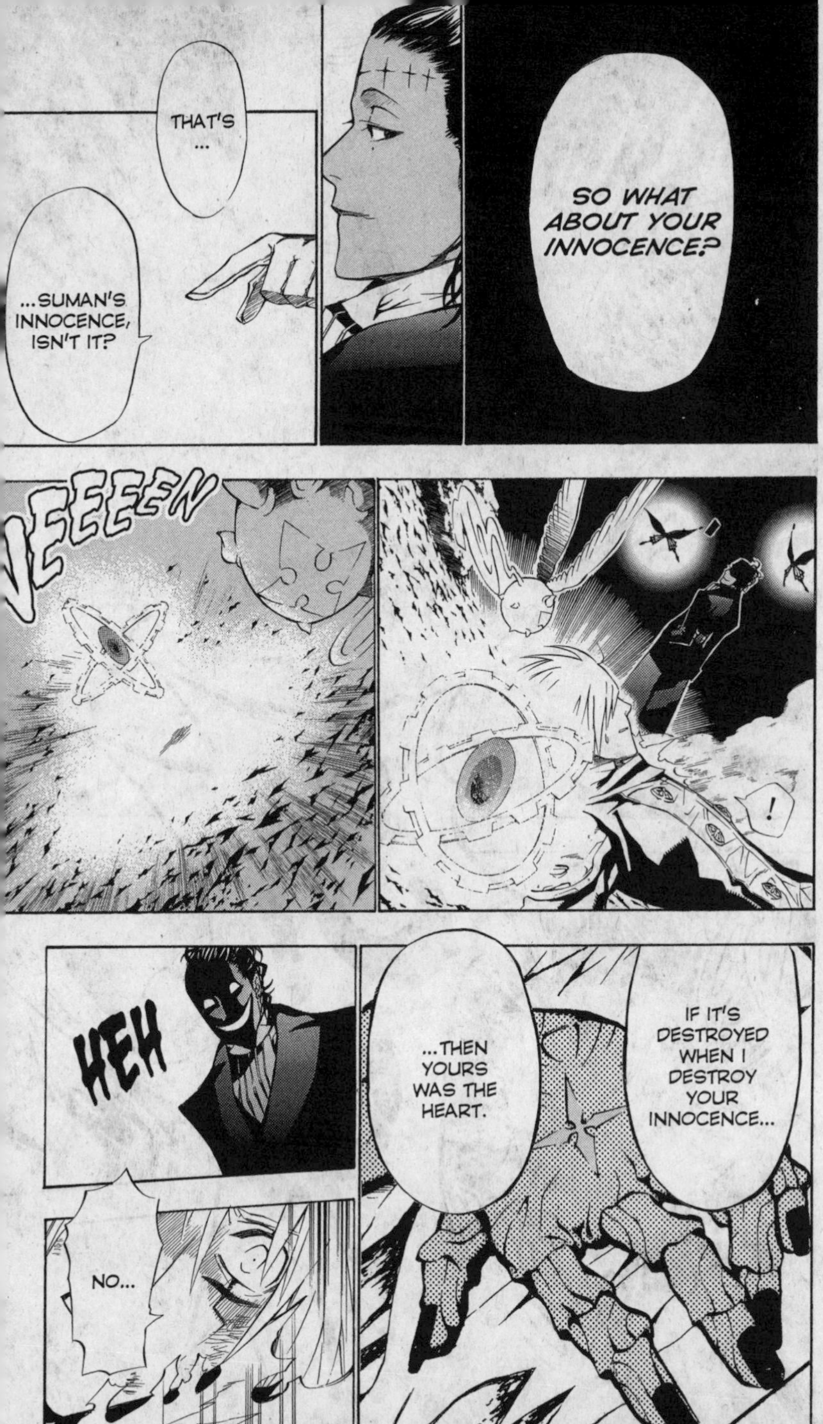
SO WHAT ABOUT YOUR INNOCENCE?
THAT'S ...
...SUMAN'S INNOCENCE, ISN'T IT?
!
VEEEEEN
IF IT'S DESTROYED WHEN I DESTROY YOUR INNOCENCE...
...THEN YOURS WAS THE HEART.
HEH
NO...

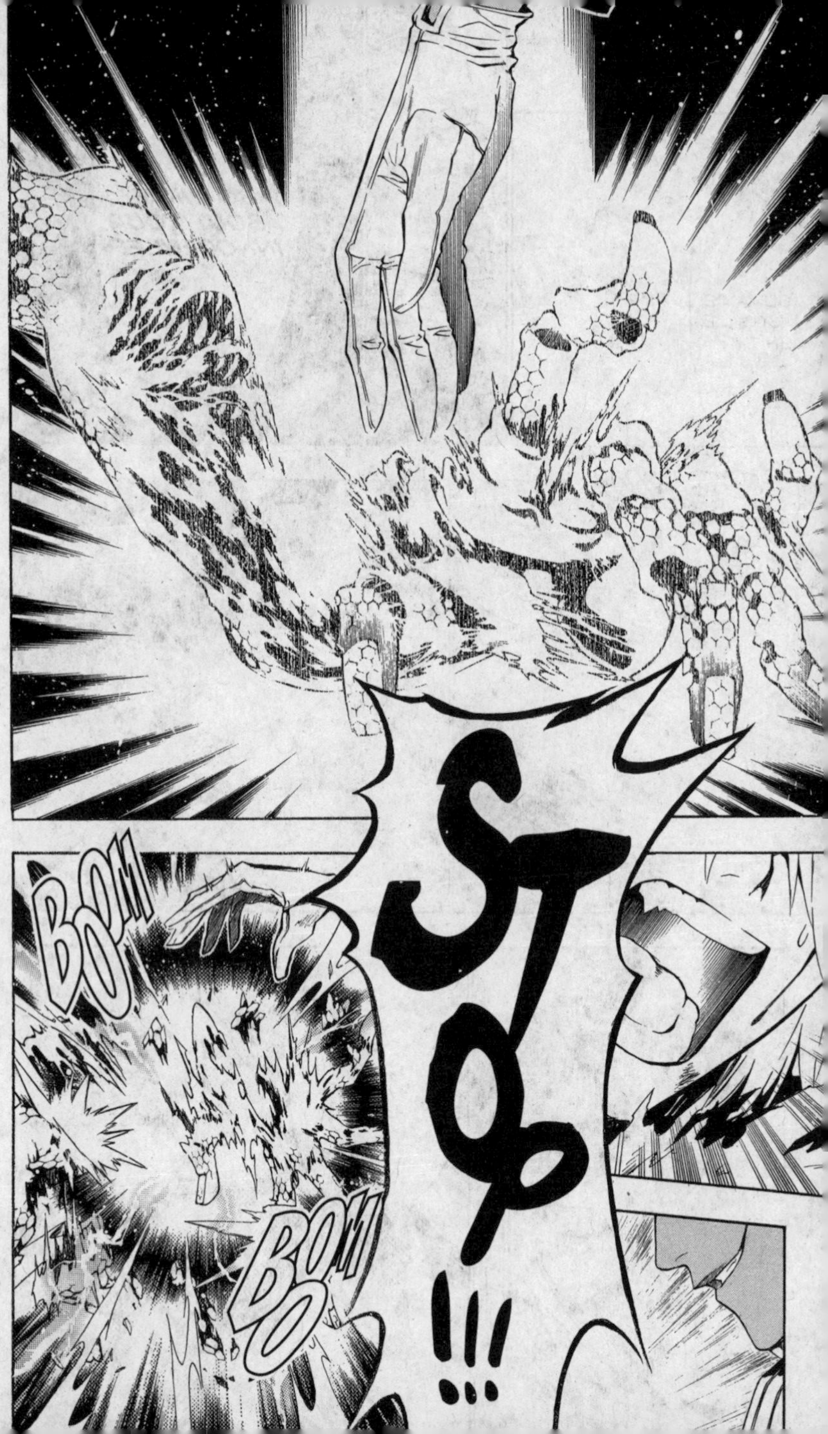
STOP!!!
BOOM
BOOM

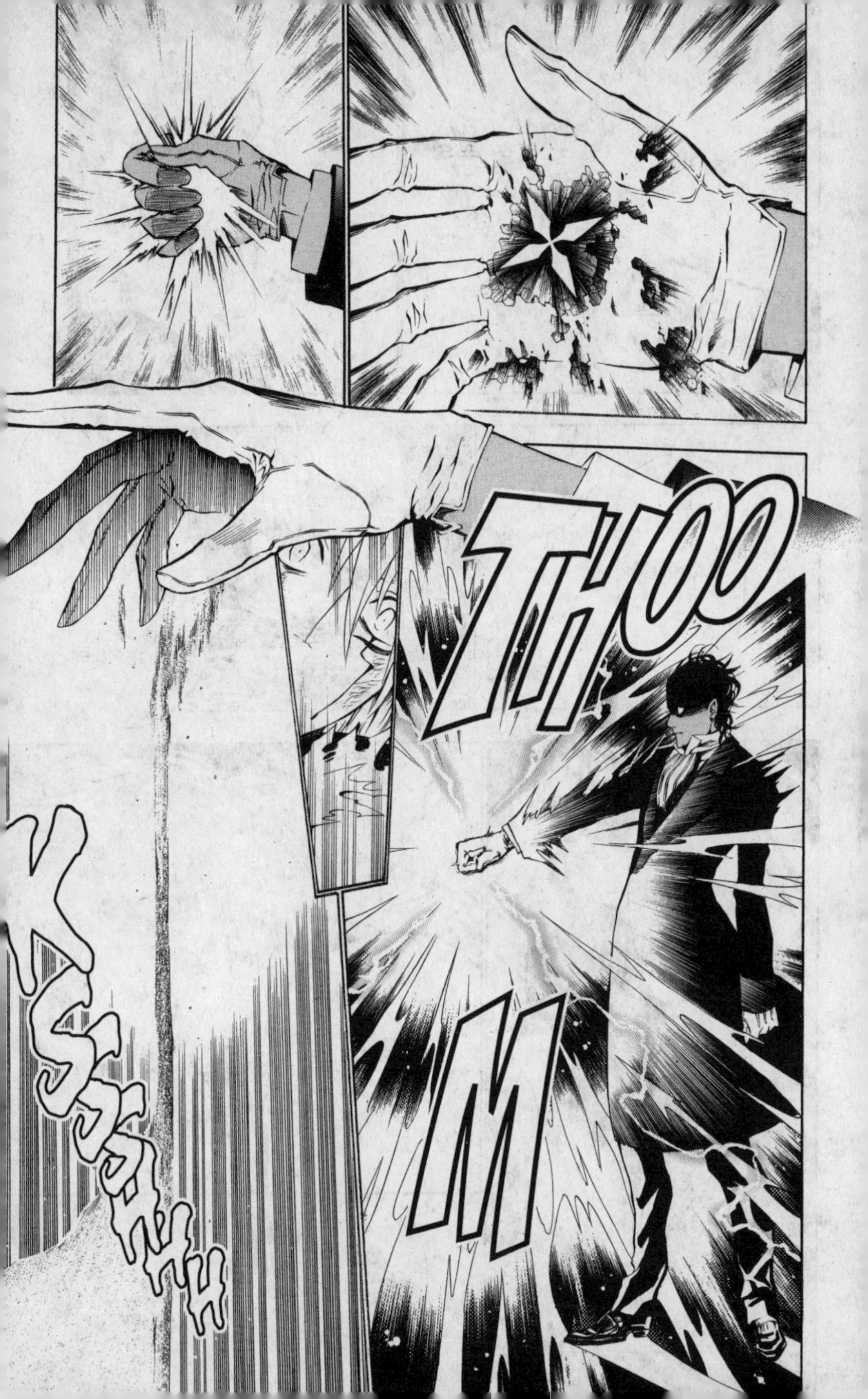
THOOM
KSSSHH

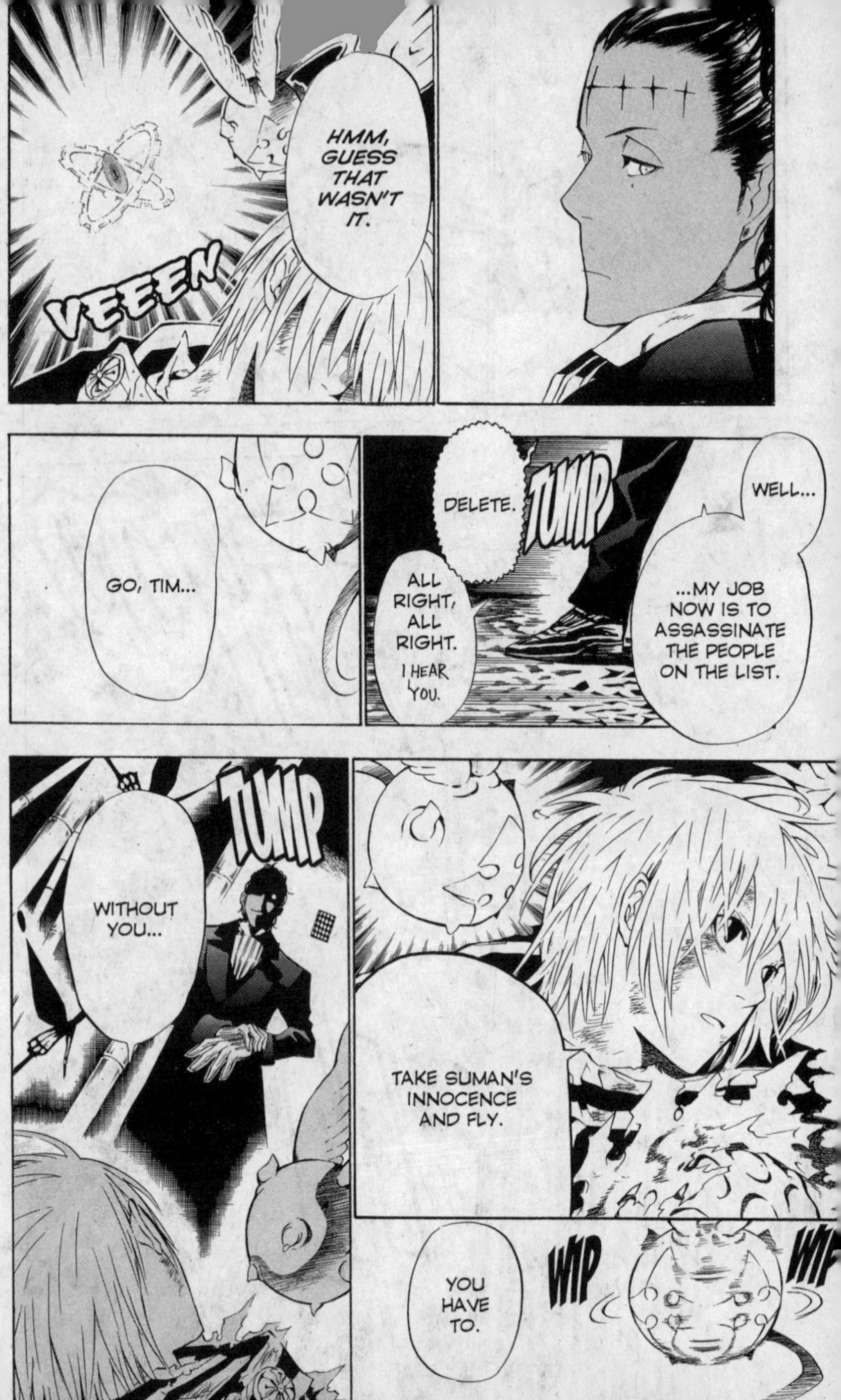
HMM, GUESS THAT WASN'T IT.
VEEEN
WELL...
...MY JOB NOW IS TO ASSASSINATE THE PEOPLE ON THE LIST.
TUMP
DELETE.
ALL RIGHT, ALL RIGHT. I HEAR YOU.
GO, TIM...
TAKE SUMAN'S INNOCENCE AND FLY.
WIP
WIP
YOU HAVE TO.
TUMP
WITHOUT YOU...

...WILL NEVER FIND MY MASTER.

...THE OTHERS...

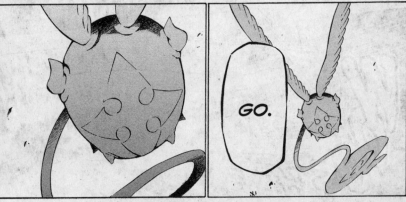

GO.

OH!

CHONK

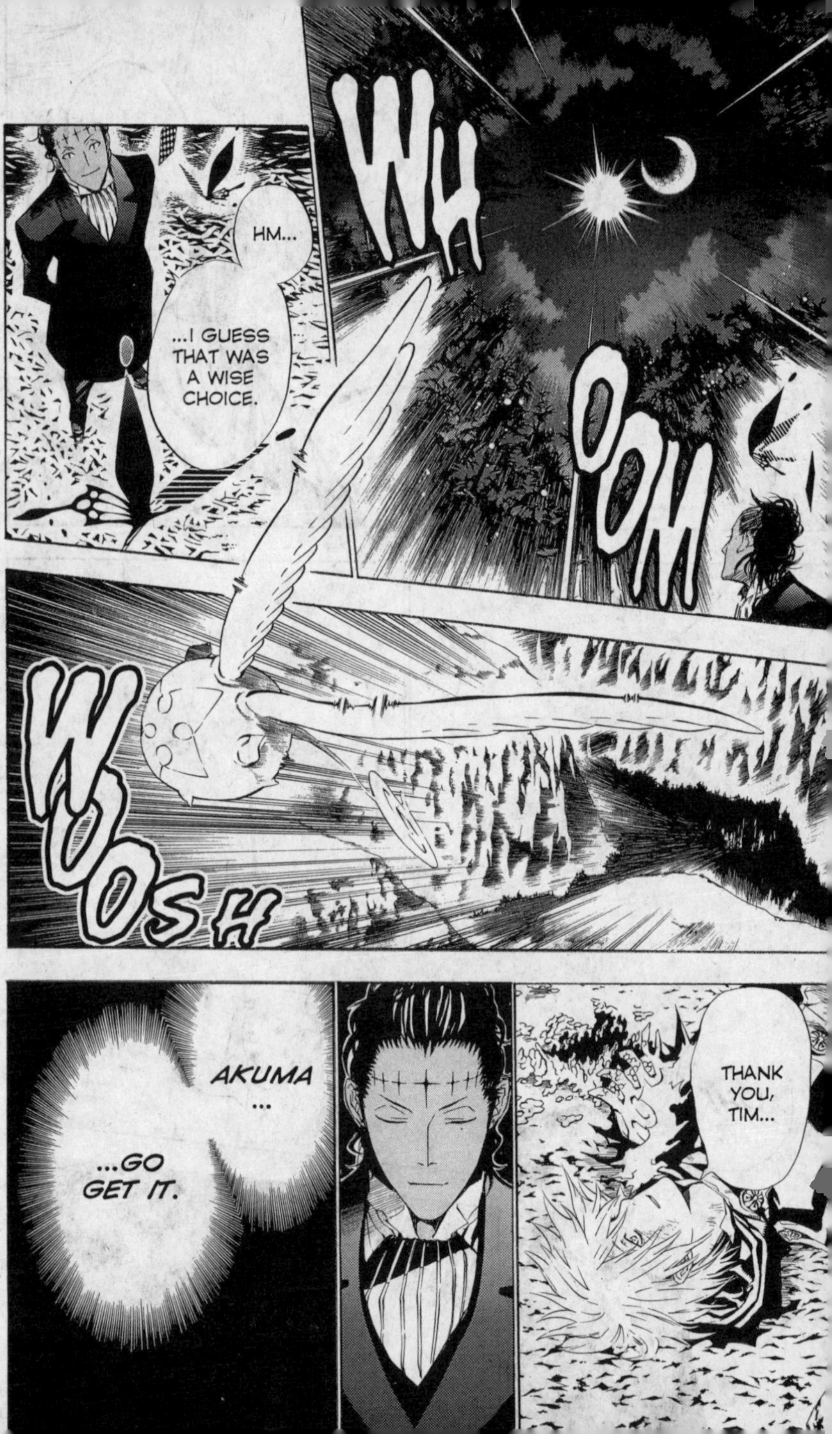
WHOOM
HM...
...I GUESS THAT WAS A WISE CHOICE.
WHOOSH
THANK YOU, TIM...
AKUMA...
...GO GET IT.

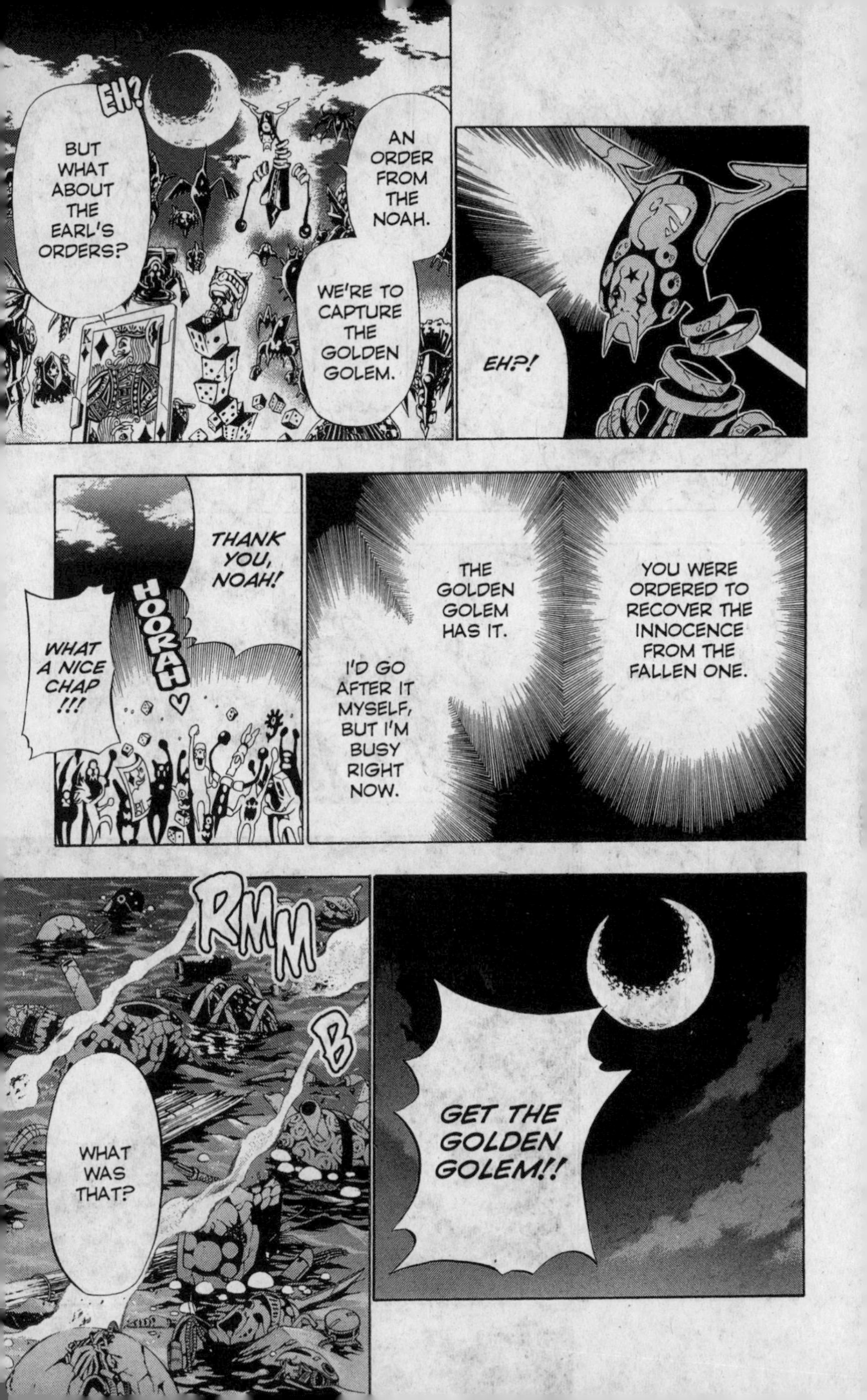
EH?!
AN ORDER FROM THE NOAH.
WE'RE TO CAPTURE THE GOLDEN GOLEM.
EH?
BUT WHAT ABOUT THE EARL'S ORDERS?
YOU WERE ORDERED TO RECOVER THE INNOCENCE FROM THE FALLEN ONE.
THE GOLDEN GOLEM HAS IT.
I'D GO AFTER IT MYSELF, BUT I'M BUSY RIGHT NOW.
THANK YOU, NOAH!
HOORAH ♥
WHAT A NICE CHAP!!!
GET THE GOLDEN GOLEM!!
RMMB
WHAT WAS THAT?

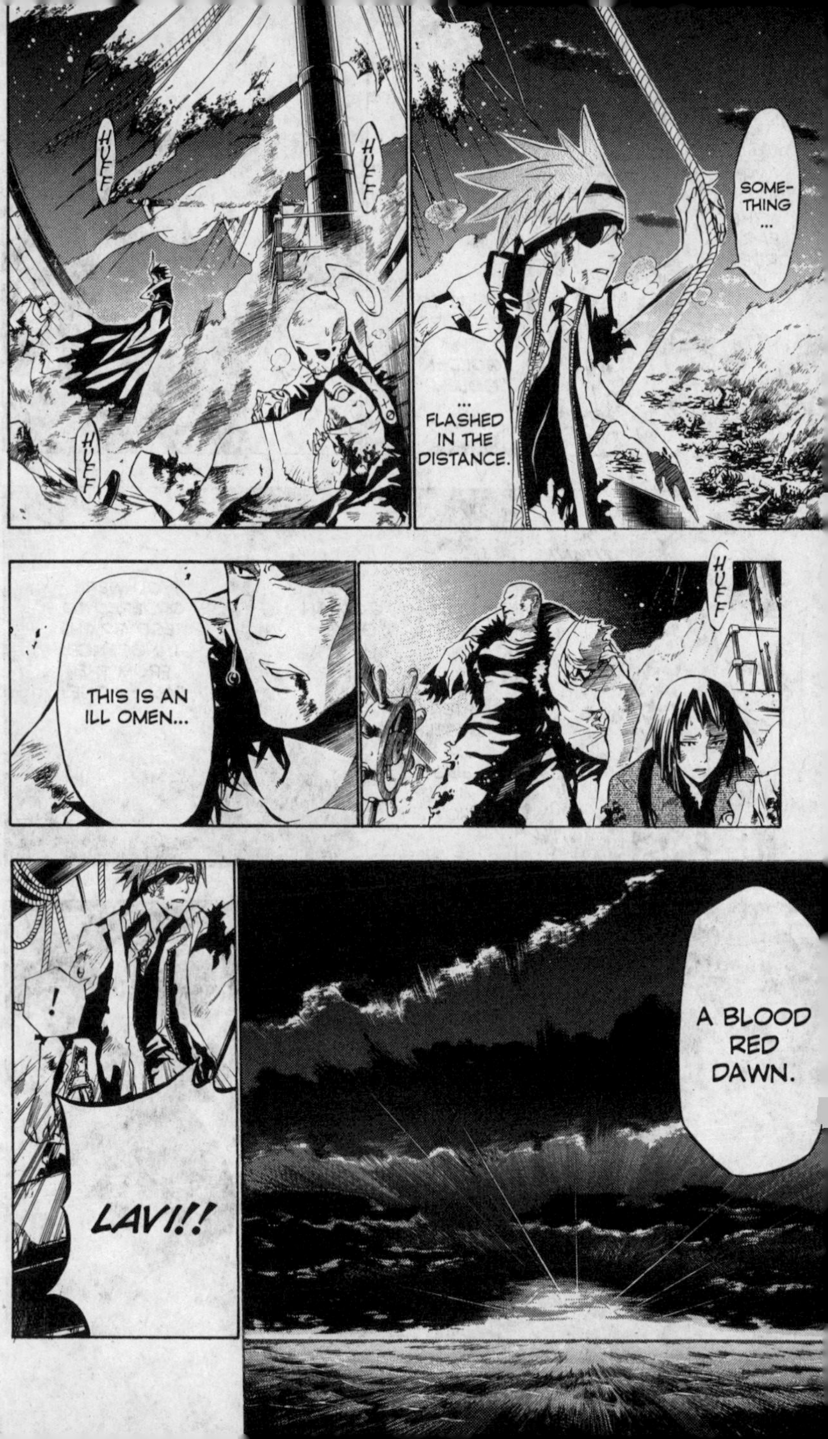
SOME-THING ...
... FLASHED IN THE DISTANCE.
HUFF
HUFF
HUFF
HUFF
THIS IS AN ILL OMEN...
A BLOOD RED DAWN.
!
LAVI!!

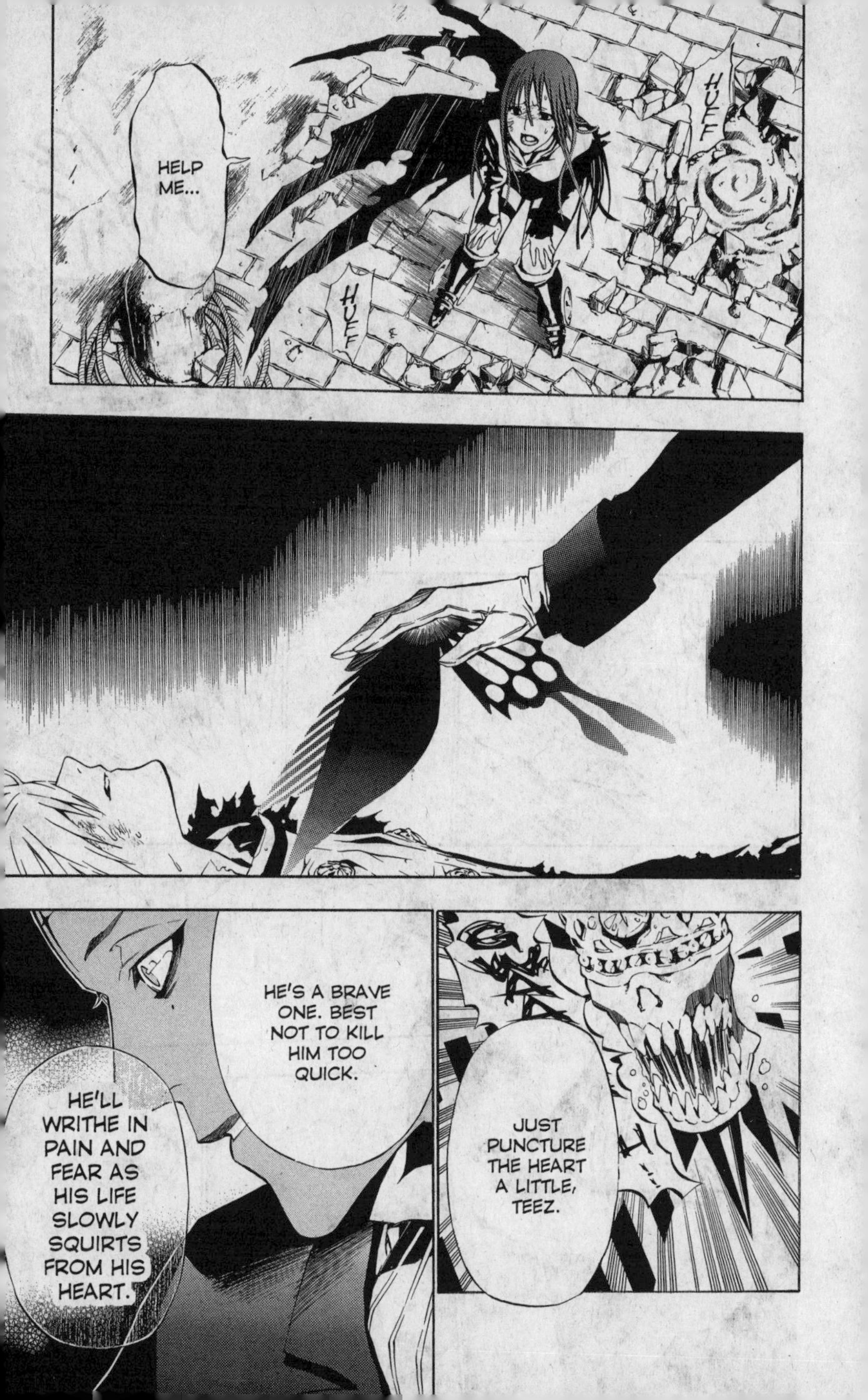
HUFF
HELP ME...
HUFF
JUST PUNCTURE THE HEART A LITTLE, TEEZ.
HE'S A BRAVE ONE. BEST NOT TO KILL HIM TOO QUICK.
HE'LL WRITHE IN PAIN AND FEAR AS HIS LIFE SLOWLY SQUIRTS FROM HIS HEART.

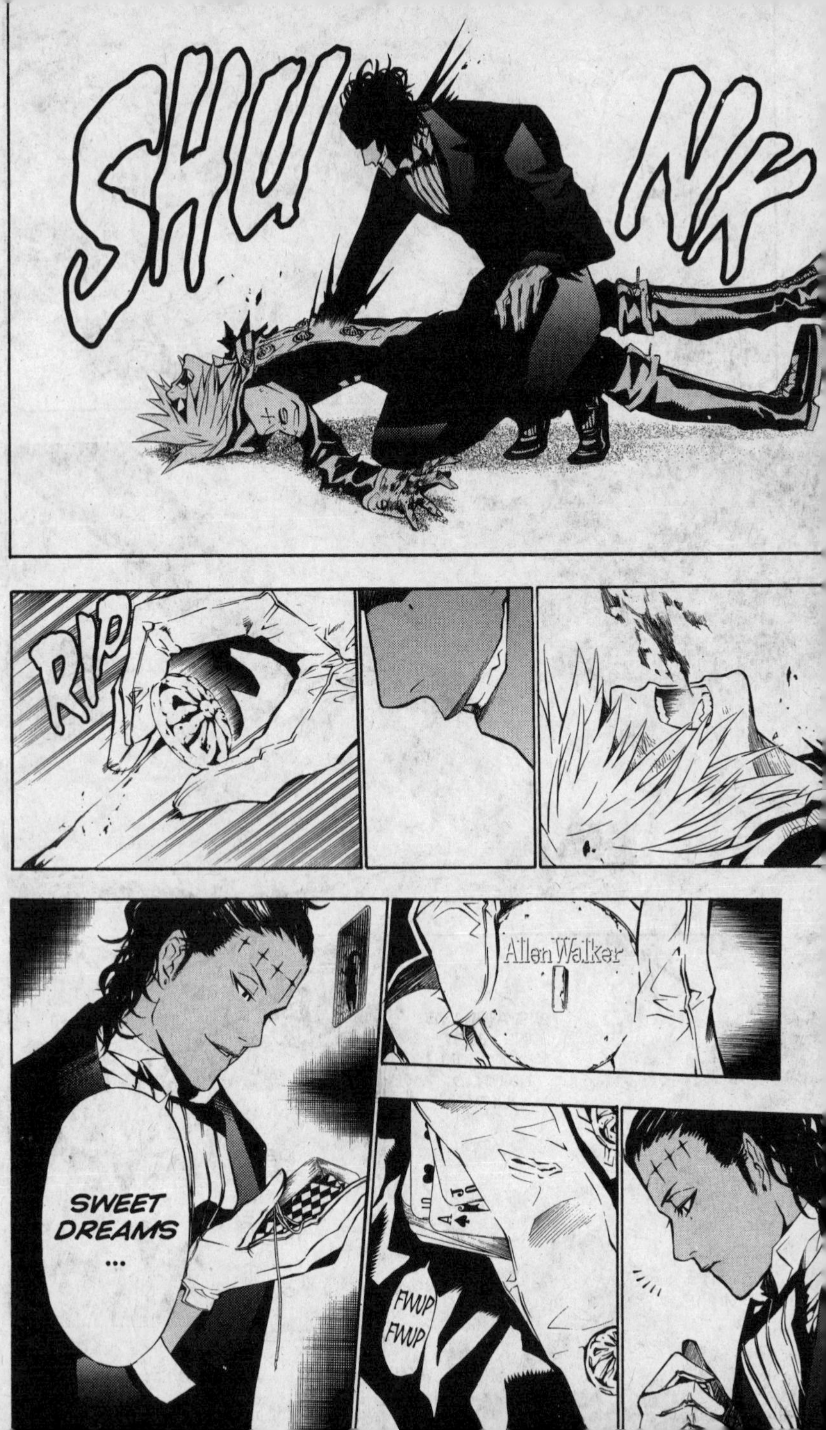
SHUNK
RIP
Allen Walker
FWUP FWUP
SWEET DREAMS ...

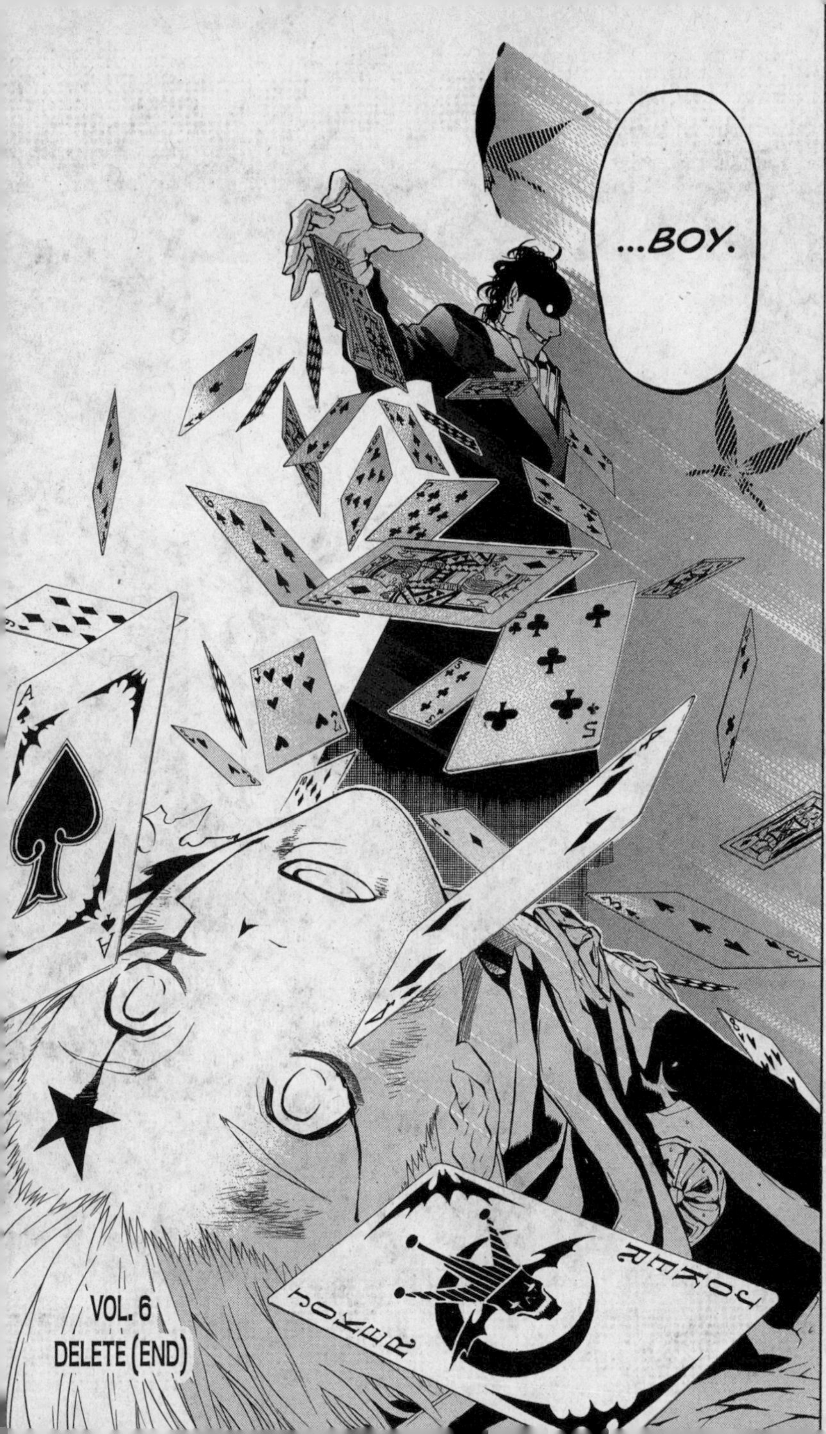
...BOY.
JOKER
JOKER
VOL. 6
DELETE (END)

IN THE NEXT VOLUME...

Allen has disappeared after his latest
with Tyki Mikk. Lavi and Lenalee try to
have to be satisfied with saving Timca
pursuing horde of akuma. Eventually th
their mission with Allen's replacement
Miranda Lotto. As for Allen, he has to
deal with the staggering loss of his In

Now!

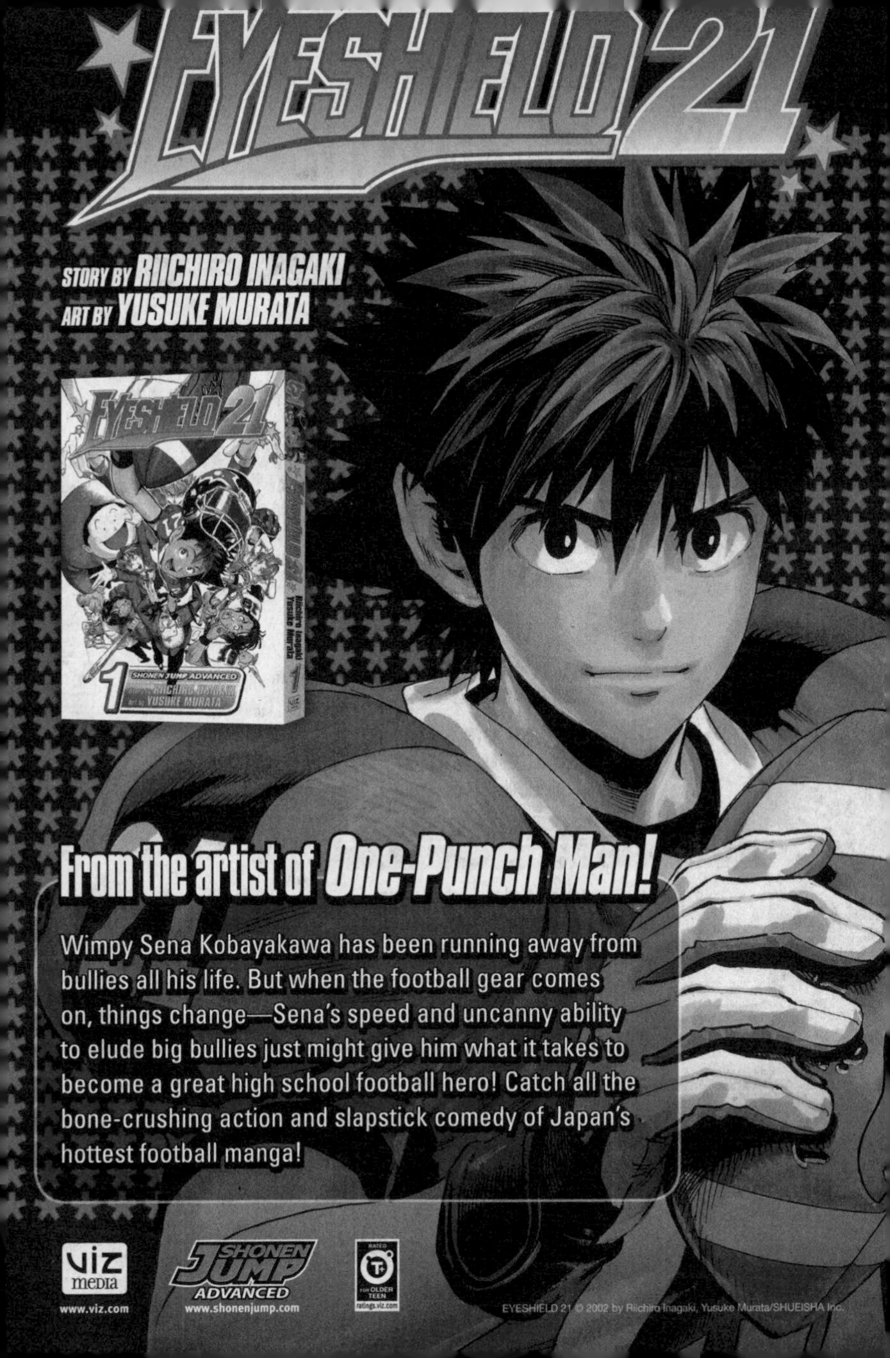
EYESHIELD 21
STORY BY RIICHIRO INAGAKI
ART BY YUSUKE MURATA
From the artist of One-Punch Man!
Wimpy Sena Kobayakawa has been running away from bullies all his life. But when the football gear comes on, things change—Sena's speed and uncanny ability to elude big bullies just might give him what it takes to become a great high school football hero! Catch all the bone-crushing action and slapstick comedy of Japan's hottest football manga!
viz media
www.viz.com
SHONEN JUMP ADVANCED
www.shonenjump.com
RATED T+ FOR OLDER TEEN
ratings.viz.com
EYESHIELD 21 © 2002 by Riichiro Inagaki, Yusuke Murata/SHUEISHA Inc.

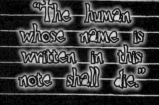

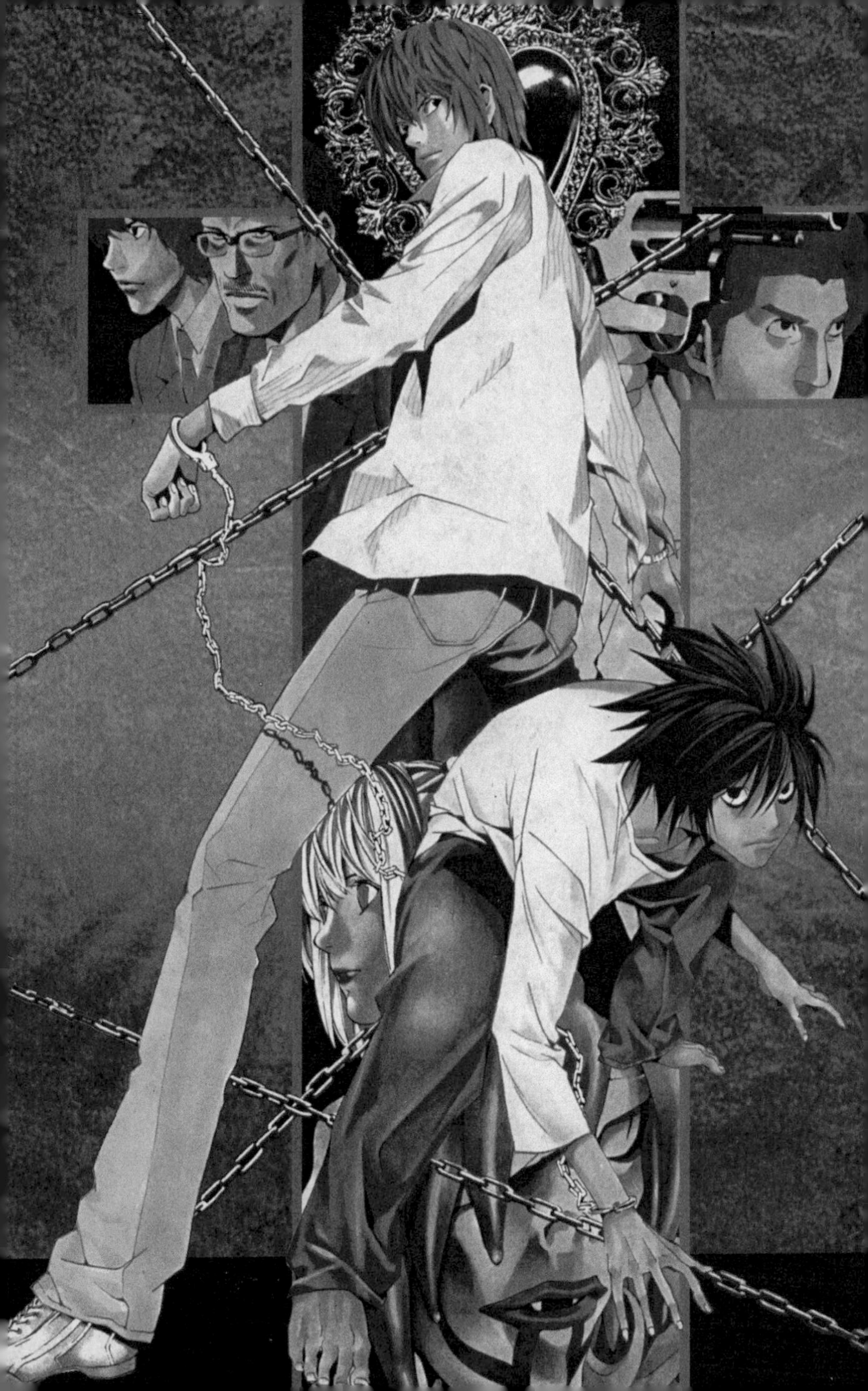

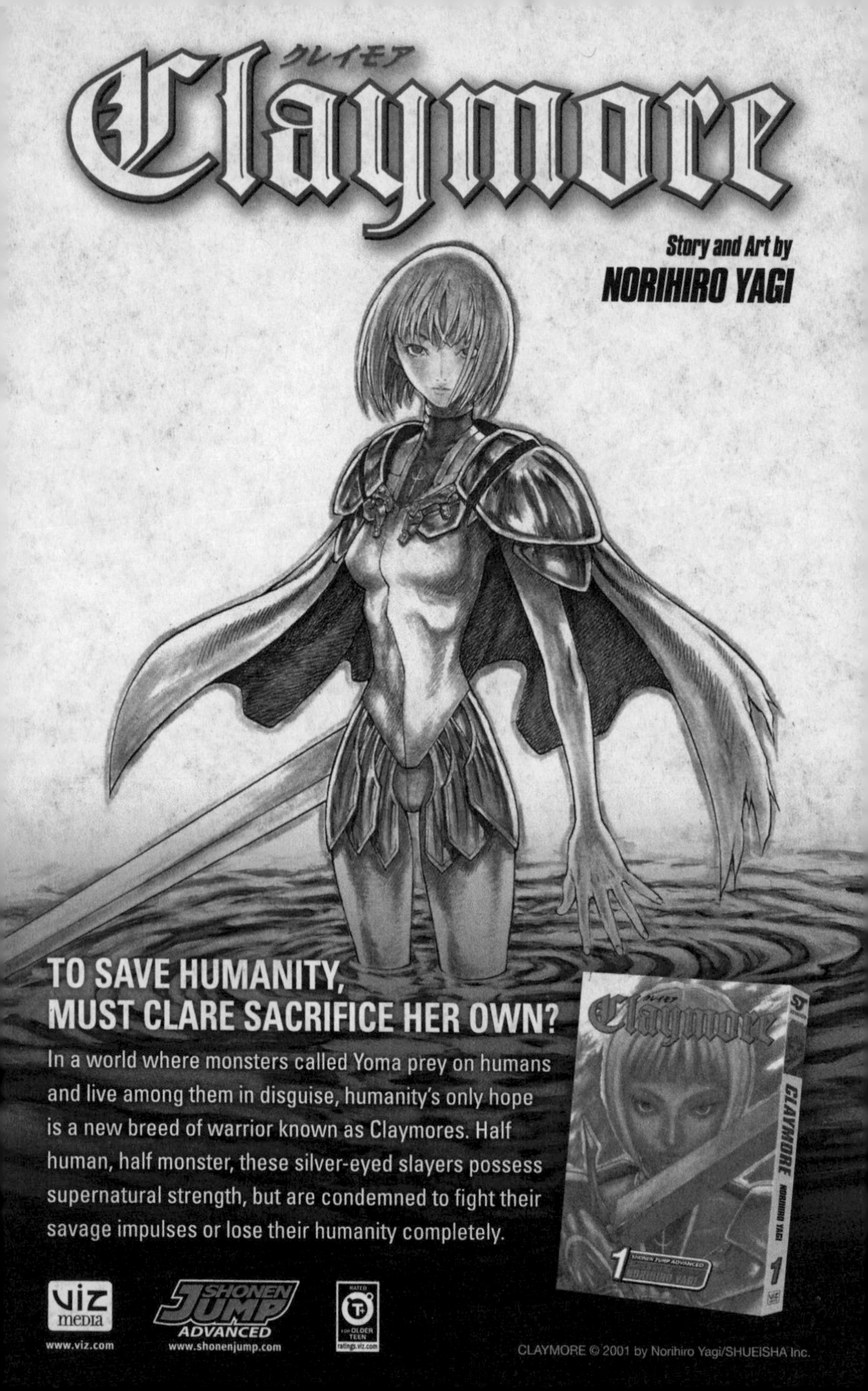

Claymore
クレイモア
Story and Art by
NORIHIRO YAGI
TO SAVE HUMANITY,
MUST CLARE SACRIFICE HER OWN?
In a world where monsters called Yoma prey on humans and live among them in disguise, humanity's only hope is a new breed of warrior known as Claymores. Half human, half monster, these silver-eyed slayers possess supernatural strength, but are condemned to fight their savage impulses or lose their humanity completely.
CLAYMORE
NORIHIRO YAGI
1
viz media
www.viz.com
SHONEN JUMP ADVANCED
www.shonenjump.com
RATED T+ FOR OLDER TEEN
ratings.viz.com
CLAYMORE © 2001 by Norihiro Yagi/SHUEISHA Inc.

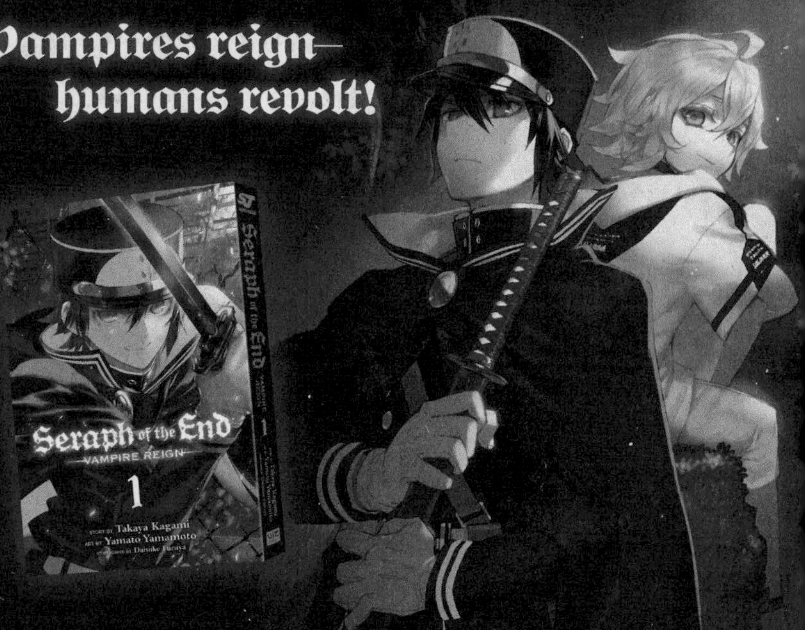

Seraph of the End
VAMPIRE REIGN
1
STORY BY Takaya Kagami
ART BY Yamato Yamamoto

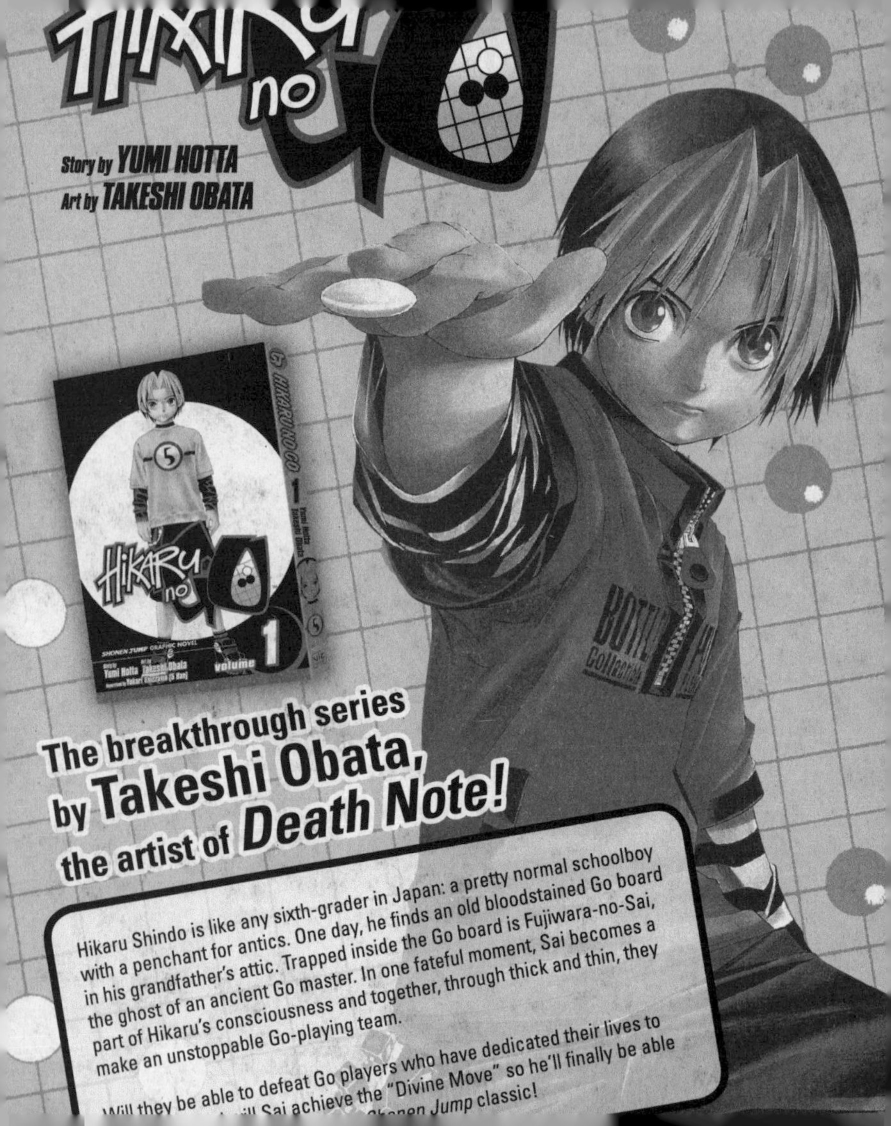

Hikaru no Go
Story by YUMI HOTTA
Art by TAKESHI OBATA
The breakthrough series by Takeshi Obata, the artist of Death Note!
Hikaru Shindo is like any sixth-grader in Japan: a pretty normal schoolboy with a penchant for antics. One day, he finds an old bloodstained Go board in his grandfather's attic. Trapped inside the Go board is Fujiwara-no-Sai, the ghost of an ancient Go master. In one fateful moment, Sai becomes a part of Hikaru's consciousness and together, through thick and thin, they make an unstoppable Go-playing team.
Will they be able to defeat Go players who have dedicated their lives to
will Sai achieve the "Divine Move" so he'll finally be able
Shonen Jump classic!

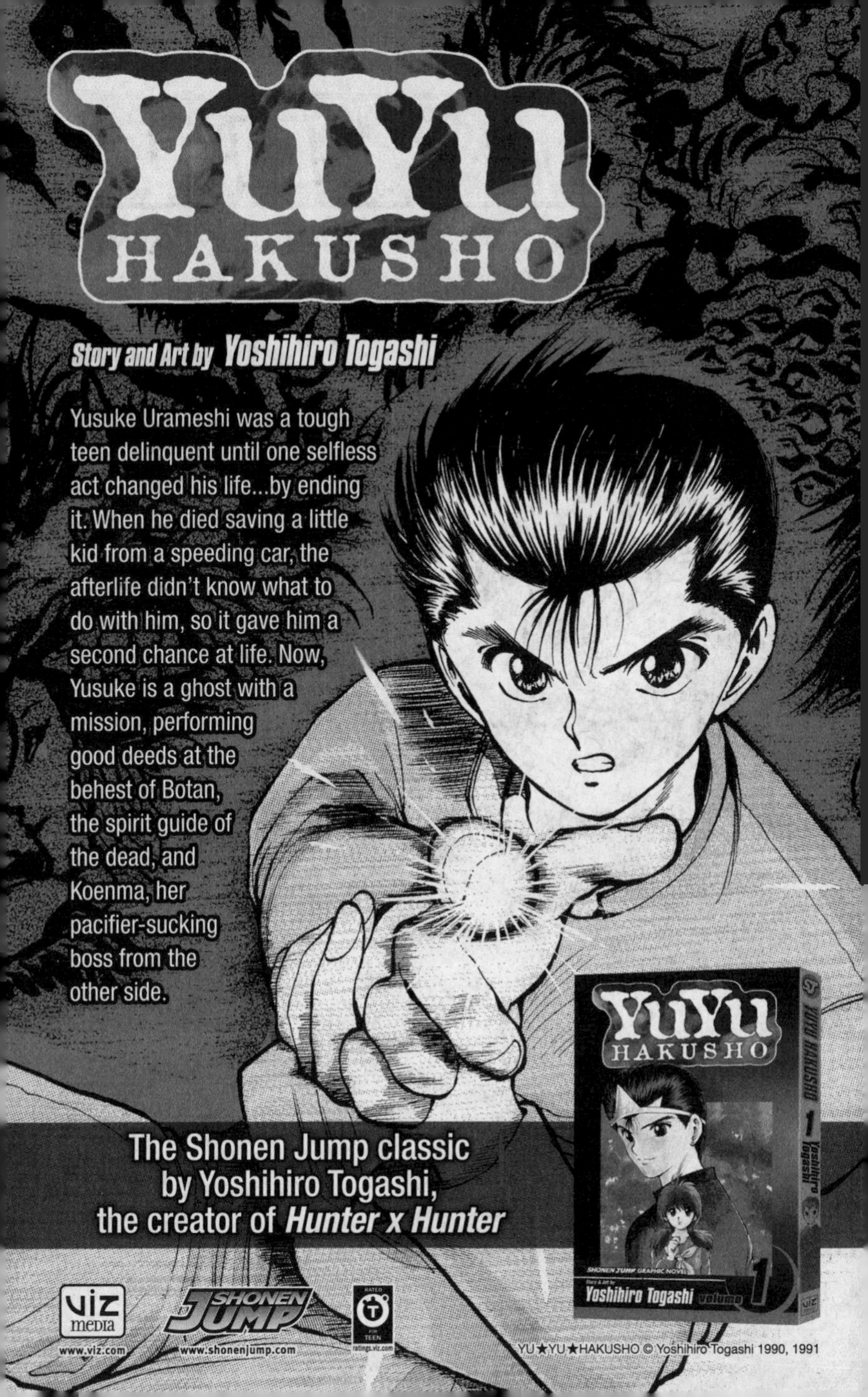
YuYu HAKUSHO
Story and Art by Yoshihiro Togashi
Yusuke Urameshi was a tough teen delinquent until one selfless act changed his life...by ending it. When he died saving a little kid from a speeding car, the afterlife didn't know what to do with him, so it gave him a second chance at life. Now, Yusuke is a ghost with a mission, performing good deeds at the behest of Botan, the spirit guide of the dead, and Koenma, her pacifier-sucking boss from the other side.
YuYu HAKUSHO
Yoshihiro Togashi volume 1
The Shonen Jump classic by Yoshihiro Togashi, the creator of Hunter x Hunter
viz media
www.viz.com
SHONEN JUMP
www.shonenjump.com
RATED T FOR TEEN
ratings.viz.com
YU★YU★HAKUSHO © Yoshihiro Togashi 1990, 1991

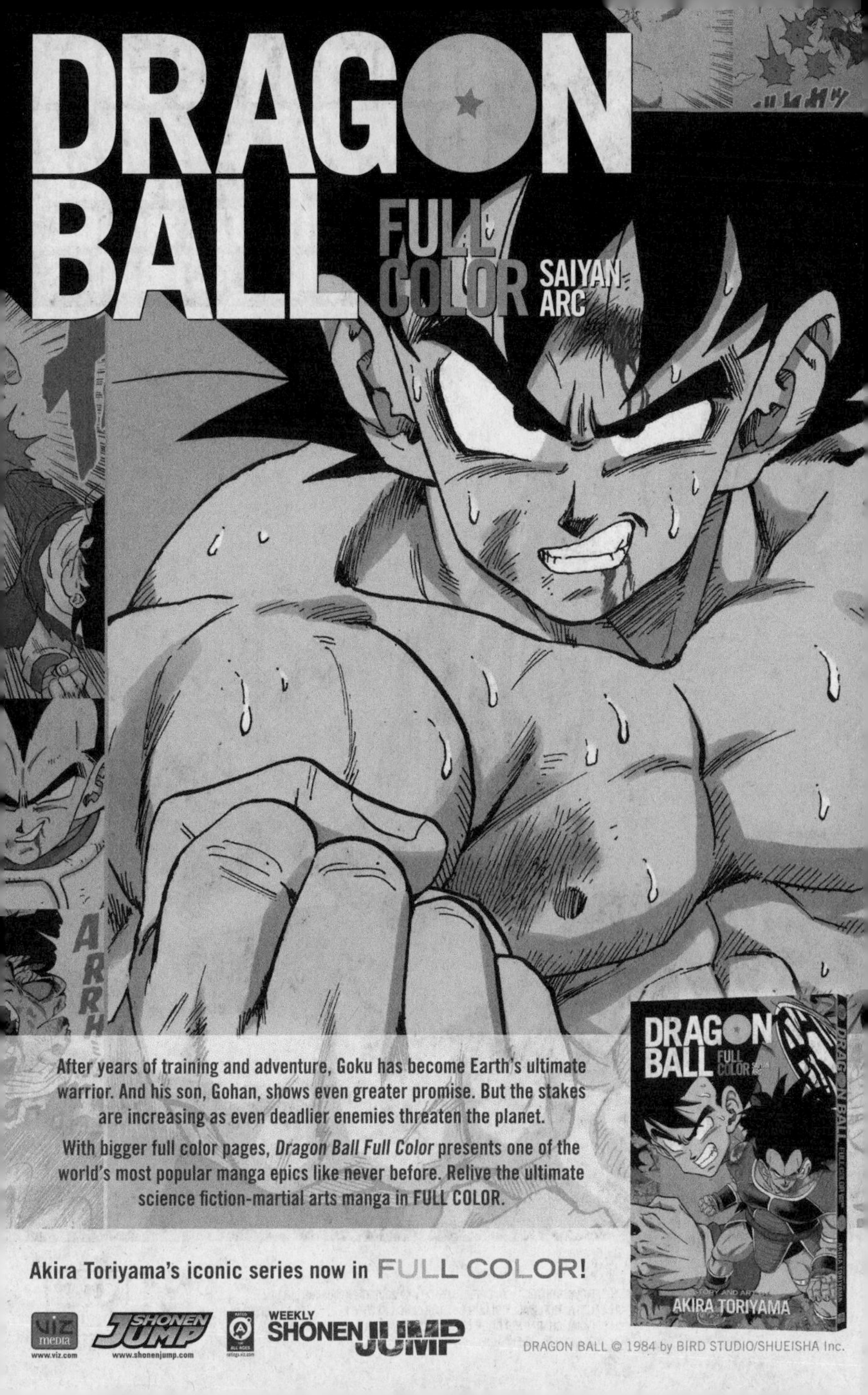
DRAGON BALL
FULL COLOR
SAIYAN ARC
ARRH
After years of training and adventure, Goku has become Earth's ultimate warrior. And his son, Gohan, shows even greater promise. But the stakes are increasing as even deadlier enemies threaten the planet.
With bigger full color pages, *Dragon Ball Full Color* presents one of the world's most popular manga epics like never before. Relive the ultimate science fiction-martial arts manga in FULL COLOR.
DRAGON BALL FULL COLOR
STORY AND ART BY
AKIRA TORIYAMA
Akira Toriyama's iconic series now in FULL COLOR!
VIZ media
www.viz.com
SHONEN JUMP
www.shonenjump.com
RATED A FOR ALL AGES
ratings.viz.com
WEEKLY SHONEN JUMP
DRAGON BALL © 1984 by BIRD STUDIO/SHUEISHA Inc.

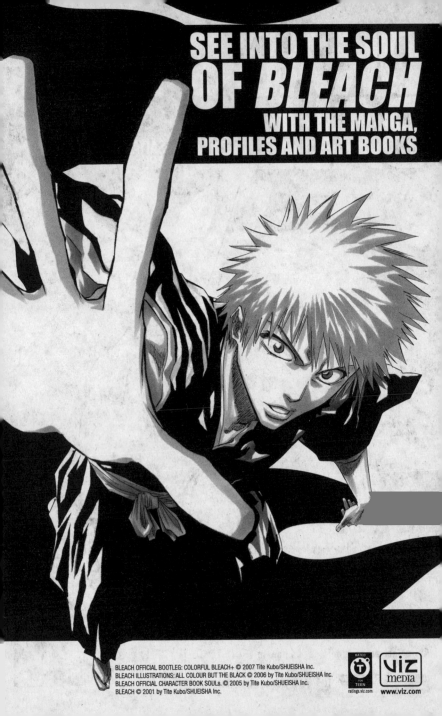